3-9-76

Selling Real Estate By Mortgage-Equity Analysis

Selling Real Estate by Mortgage-Equity Analysis

Tools and Techniques for Marketing Investment Properties

Irvin E. Johnson

Lexington Books
D.C. Heath and Company
Lexington, Massachusetts
Toronto   London

Library of Congress Cataloging in Publication Data

Johnson, Irvin E
    Selling real estate by mortgage-equity analysis.

    Includes index.
    1. Real property—Valuation. 2. Interest and usury—Tables, etc.
I. Title.
HD1387.J654   658.89'3333'3   74-15543
ISBN 0-669-95588-4

Published simultaneously in Canada

Printed in the United States of America

International Standard Book Number: 0-669-95588-4

Library of Congress Catalog Card Number: 75-15543

1897805

To my wife
Florence
(My best investment: a two-dollar marriage license
. . . interest compounded daily)

Contents

In the First Place . . .

Out of the Ivory Tower and into the Workshop

A popular do-it-yourself book on home repairs begins with the suggestion, "First, buy a box of band-aids."

Perhaps a number of books on investment properties should advise, "First, take a refresher course in advanced algebra and calculus." Not so here! This writer has been dedicated to his on going crusade to "uncomplicate the complicated"—to bring the mortgage-equity technique, compound interest tables, and other tools of valuation and real estate investment analysis down out of the ivory tower into the workshop where they belong. Forget the algebra—and the band-aids!

While the text is directed primarily to real estate brokers and marketing personnel, it should also prove of benefit to investors, lenders, builders, developers, analysts, appraisers, assessors, counsellors, accountants, attorneys, property managers, students, instructors—to any one concerned with valuation and analysis of investment properties.

Selling Real Estate by Mortgage-Equity Analysis explores two types of real estate investments:

1. Income-producing properties.
2. Nonproducing properties purchased for appreciation.

The textbook is a specialized one. It obviously does not attempt to cover every phase of dealing with investment properties. Its prime purpose is to provide effective tools and techniques, with some guidance in their practical application. Tables of precomputed mortgage-equity Overall Rates and compound interest factors are utilized and explained in easy-to-follow illustrated patterned procedures.

The writer assumes that the student has a working knowledge of the basic aspects of investment properties, that he is acquainted with the three "approaches" to value (cost, market or comparative sales, and income), that he is somewhat familiar with the traditional capitalization techniques, and that he can prepare a realistic operating statement of income and expenses.

Any one with the elementary background in real estate as noted can comprehend and apply any of the procedures in the text, if he can do six things: (1) add, (2) subtract, (3) multiply, (4) divide, (5) put a decimal point where it belongs, and (6) *follow instructions*!

Simple Procedures, Sophisticated Results—
A Demonstration

The mortgage-equity technique is unique in that it gives full consideration
to the down-to-earth realities of the contemporary real estate market:
financing; relatively low down payment and high yield on equity; a limited
term of ownership before selling, refinancing, or exchanging the property;
and possible appreciation or depreciation in market value within the anticipated holding period.

The key to mortgage-equity is the Overall Rate (OAR) which has six
significant components built in: (1) the holding period, (2) rate of yield on
equity (on down payment). (3) loan ratio, (4) loan interest rate, (5) loan
term and (6) appreciation/depreciation.

Here is a preliminary problem, demonstrating that the instant
mortgage-equity technique works, how it works, how fast and simply it
works:

Assume you are testing the owner's asking price for a small apartment
house. The property is listed at $675,000. You need data from the
mortgage market and from the local real estate investment market. In
checking with local lending institutions you find that financing can be
arranged on the subject property for 80% of value at 9½% interest on a
loan to be amortized in 25 years. You determine that the typical investor
in this area at this point in time and dealing with this type of property
anticipates a holding period of 10 years and expects a yield of 15% on his
equity. An economic study of the neighborhood and the community
indicates a probability of 10% appreciation in the market value of the
apartment house within the next 10 years. Questions to be answered in
testing the asking price are:

1. What amount of net annual income must the property produce in
   order to justify a price of $675,000, based on the problem data and
   projections?
2. How does calculated required income compare with income being
   produced by the property?

You turn to the OAR Tables to find an Overall Rate that matches six
points in the problem: (1) 10-year holding period, (2) 15% equity yield
rate, (3) 80% loan ratio, (4) 9½% loan interest rate, (5) 25-year loan
term, and (6) 10% appreciation. From page 338 select the appropriate
OAR, .102515, and use it as a multiplier to calculate required income:

Income = Rate × Value
       = .102515 × $675,000
       = $69,200 (rounded)

This calculation tells you that the property must generate at least $69,200 net annual income to support a value of $675,000 and return 15% yield on equity.

Next, you compare this calculation with a carefully reconstructed operating statement of income and expenses. Assume you find the property can be expected to produce net annual income of only $58,000. Another question must now be answered: What is a feasible offering price? You find the answer by using the same Overall Rate, .102515. Now, however, you apply it as a divisor:

$$\text{Value} = \text{Income} \div \text{Rate}$$
$$= \$58,000 \div .102515$$
$$= \$565,770 \text{ (rounded)}$$

The indication to your client is that the property is overpriced. Based on income the property is producing, the investor can pay no more than $565,770, if he is to realize an equity yield of 15%. On the other hand, presume the reconstructed operating statement shows net annual income of $72,000. The indication now is that the list price of $675,000 is reasonable, and that there is a possibility of realizing a little more than 15% yield on equity. By proper analysis the broker/salesman can put the client into a "good deal" and keep him out of a bad one.

In making the calculations required in the problem, you found that "easy does it." You select the Overall Rate. There is no need to compute the rate . . . no call for algebra, complex equations, or confusing symbols. And therein lies one of the principal differences between the *instant* mortgage-equity technique and any other version of it.

New Routes to Old Objectives

Most of the books that probe and measure the time value of money have been written by mathematicians for mathematicians. *Selling Real Estate by Mortgage-Equity Analysis* has been prepared by a real estate broker for real estate brokers and other nonmathematicians. It is designed to express rather than impress and is more practical than profound.

Mortgage-equity is frequently equated with Ellwood. The appraisal profession owes a great debt of gratitude to the late L.W. (Pete) Ellwood for his pioneering in this area and for his scholarly work built around the Ellwood Tables.

Our version of mortgage-equity provides a new (and, we believe, easier and more direct) route to old objectives. Totally precomputed Overall Rates and patterned procedures in our *instant mortgage-equity technique* are based on extended discounted cash flow concepts and on the definition that value is the present worth of future net benefits. The future net benefits, generated by income-producing property, typically consist of cash flow over a period of years (the difference between net income and loan payments) and a single lump sum payment at the end of a limited period of ownership (difference between resale value and unpaid loan balance). While our approach differs in procedure from the Ellwood method, the results are identical.

Selling Real Estate by Mortgage-Equity Analysis, as the title implies, is directed specifically to practising members of the real estate profession. This volume is an outgrowth and an extension of the writer's appraisal textbooks completed in 1972: *Mini-Math For Appraisers*, published by the International Association of Assessing Officers, Chicago, Illinois; and *The Instant Mortgage-Equity Technique*, published by Lexington Books, D.C. Heath and Company, Lexington, Massachusetts. The wide circulation of both books, subsequent reprintings, and the scores of workshops and seminars presented by request since publication indicated that the simplified, streamlined version of mortgage-equity was filling a real need among professional appraisers. John D. Hewitt in his review of *The Instant Mortgage-Equity Technique* termed it "a breakthrough in simplifying a very difficult concept."

The mortgage-equity technique, one of the most meaningful approaches to real estate valuation and investment analysis, need not be confined within professional appraisal circles. It can be used, is being used, and should be used by real estate sales personnel. Relatively few brokers and salesmen understand and are able to use the Ellwood method. Streamlined instant mortgage-equity, presented in the text especially for the real estate profession, clarifies and simplifies the techique for both novice and expert. This book was written to fill a need. We believe it will.

The book is not intended to convert a real estate broker into a professional appraiser. Is objective is to provide specialized assistance in every phase of initiating and consummating a sales transaction:

1. Analyzing income property.
2. Listing investment property at a realistic, justifiable price.
3. Making a clear, comprehensive written presentation to a client.
4. Building knowledgeable bases for investment decision-making,
5. Making the sale.
6. Obtaining the acceptance of a reasonable offer.
7. Financing the sale.
8. Keeping a client out of a "bad deal" and putting him into a good one.

What's in a Name?

Only to avoid monotony in the textbook have you, the reader, been called by a variety of titles: broker, salesman, sales person (if you prefer), analyst, counsellor, student, et cetera. Whoever you may be, the book has been written for *you*.

Here's a Preview

The sequence of presentation in this book treats the mortgage-equity theory first. Chapters 1 and 2 show what mortgage-equity *is*, what it *does*, and how it can be *applied*. Chapter 3 outlines procedural practice in illustrated pattern format. It covers two types of investments: (1) income-producing properties, and (2) nonproducing properties purchased for appreciation. Chapter 3 also contains a section of special mortgage-equity worksheets.

A case study of income property valuation and investment analysis is given in Chapter 4. Three types of tables appear in Chapter 5: (1) Compound Interest Tables of present worth and amortization, (2) Supplemental Tables of Loan Balances and Loan Constants, and (3) OAR Tables of precomputed mortgage-equity Overall Rates. The Appendix contains a few additional procedures, programs, and illustrations. A final section of Problems with Answers and Suggested Solutions completes the text.

Here are a few suggestions for programming your study:

— Make your own initial survey of the entire book to see what it contains and where.
— Go through Chapters 1 and 2 in order.
— Study the introduction to the Patterned Procedures in Chapter 3 and scan the Ready Reference Roster, noting the range and scope of the procedures.
— Move on to Chapter 4 and work through the Case Study, relating it to the pertinent procedures in Chapter 3 and to the three types of tables in Chapter 5.
— Make a survey of the tables in Chapter 5 and note sequential arrangement.
— Go back to Chapter 3 and study the first section under Rate. Practice so that you can locate readily any Overall Rate in the OAR Tables to match a given set of variables.
— Refer next to The Basic Five, Chapter 3. Study and master these five fundamental procedures. (These alone would make your study of mortgage-equity a constructive experience, but do go on from there.)

— Study other Patterned Procedures in Chapter 3 according to the priorities of your interests.
— Survey the Appendix and relate supplemental material to relevant sections of Chapter 3.
— Tackle the Problems and do a bit of drill and self-testing.
— Mark and tab-index the book in any way that will assist you. Emphasis should not be on the memorization of formulas or procedures but on knowing how and where to find what you need when you need it.
— Whenever Factors and Overall Rates are used in the text, verify by locating them in the tables.
— Make the actual calculations shown in the examples, and check for accuracy.
— Use an electronic calculator, if available, for ease, speed, and accuracy in computation.
— If calculation is a "by hand" operation, rounding Factors and Overall Rates in to three significant decimal places will simplify your arithmetic.
— Make some trial runs, solving your own problems of valuation and investment analysis by following the appropriate methods outlined and illustrated in Chapter 3. Check the results against those arrived at by other methods you have customarily used. Now, you may be ready to apply the *instant mortgage-equity technique* in your sales program with care, skill, and good judgment.

This book has been prepared as a tool, to be used with confidence, speed, and efficiency. Chapter 3, outlining the Mortgage-Equity Patterned Procedures and Chapter 5 containing the Compound Interest, Supplemental, and OAR Tables, have been designed for quick reference and constitute the actual working parts of the book. Pages in these two areas of the text will, through continued reference and use by the analyst, experience the greatest degree of physical depreciation. However, we foresee no probability of accelerated functional obsolescence.

Check and Double Check

While every attempt has been made to ensure accuracy in the text and tables, we cannot claim nor guarantee complete freedom from fault. Variance in "rounding" factors and rates in numerous steps of computation might account for slight differences between our calculations and yours. However, the realities of the real estate market allow a reasonable range of tolerance in "rounding" any indicator of value. If you discover a significant mistake, kindly do two things:

a. Let us know.
b. Consider that such an error has added the human touch to *Selling Real Estate by Mortgage-Equity Analysis*.

Where Credit is Due

I wish to give special credit to C. Henry Lasley of St. Petersburg, Florida, who has been of particular guidance and encouragement throughout the project of fashioning a contemporary appraisal technique into a handbook for real estate personnel. Others who have assisted in bringing this work to the attention of professional real estate organizations include Albert N. Justice, 1975 President of the Institute of Real Estate Management; N. Arthur Hamilton; and Jean C. Felts.

Favorable book reviews of our previous texts (*Mini-Math For Appraisers* and *The Instant Mortgage-Equity Technique*), which appeared in various appraisal journals, furnished stimulus to the writing of the present volume. My special thanks to the reviewers: Charles B. Akerson, John Carl Brogdon, Gene Dilmore, Robert P. Flood, John D. Hewitt, and Bernard W. Saler.

My deep appreciation to those whose work has been utilized in various parts of the text: Clifford R. Johnson of Clifford R. Johnson and Associates, Inc., Minneapolis, for the diagrams depicting the "View of an Investment;" Richard Laquess, Appraiser, Ventura, California, for the form "OAR From the Market;" William N. Kinnard, Jr., University of Connecticut, for examples of operating statements (before and after reconstruction) and for quotations from his textbook *Income Property Valuation* (Lexington Books, D.C. Heath and Company, 1971); Sheldon A. Leveston, Sheldon A. Leveston Associates, Inc., Avon, Connecticut, for a set of income-expense statements; and to Jonathan E. Moyer, First Financial Service, Valpraiso, Indiana, for items to be displayed in a written presentation for a client.

For valuable services rendered, I wish to give credit to Seiji Thomas Masuda, for suggestions on new procedures; and to William E. Steinlicht for assistance in proofreading and checking computations.

My special thanks to a special category—my former instructors in the art of appraisal: Daryl R. Brown, Ventura County Assessor's Office; Berton E. Black, Ventura College; and Hugh L. McCormick, UCLA Extension. Also, special thanks to Charles Burnham, my associate instructor at Ventura College, for his continuing assistance.

"I am a part of all that I have met." So goes a line from Tennyson's "Ulysses." In compiling a list of those I have met whose particular interest in my work has been both stimulating and gratifying, I hardly know where to begin—or end. Here are some (appraisers, brokers, loan officers, government officials, investors, etc.) who have assisted greatly along the line: William W. Abelmann, Al Alcouloumre, Charles E. Austin, Edward B. Babcock, Preston Bank, Curtis T. Bliss, Grant E. Bricker, Howard R. Brower, Lloyd S. Brunk, Michael Y. Cannon, Martin W. Carlson, Noland B. Cavey, Jack A. Clark, Robert F. Davies, Richard J. Dennis, Oliver J. English, Darwin K. Eshelman, Charles H. Fleming, Jack C. Flynn, Robert Fournier, Oscar R. Giesecke, Jacques Gosselin, Gale B. Graham, K.E. "Froggy" Graham, Gordon E. Grober, John H. Hiatt, Frederick M. Javer, Walter C. Hunter, Ernest C. Johnson, Robert H. Johnson, James W. Law, Jean Guy Martel, John B. McLaughlin, Fred M. McPheeters, Robert H. McSwain, David Oyer, Martin Oyer, William Oyer, Mike and Marion Patton, A.E. Reisman, Jr., W. Calvin Reynolds, Ralph J. Sanford, Alan N. Sayford, Audrey and Cyril Schill, Albert A. Skarupa, J. Mikel Smith Gerard D. Snover, David J. Stagg, Raymond Steinhardt, Robert P. Strell, and Richard B. Sullivan. My sincere apologies if I omitted your name—it must have been an oversight.

My appreciation also goes to the many students who have attended my classes at Ventura College and Pasadena City College, And thanks to the thousands who since 1972 have participated in workshops and seminars I have conducted throughout the United States and in Canada, under the national and/or local sponsorship of these professional appraisal organizations; American Institute of Real Estate Appraisers, American Society of Appraisers, Corporation of Chartered Appraisers of Quebec, International Association of Assessing Officers, National Association of Independent Fee Appraisers, Society of Governmental Appraisers, and the Society of Real Estate Appraisers. Many practical, constructive, new procedures have been developed in response to specific questions and problems that have come in from those who attended these sessions. My thanks to the problem-posers—they have contributed to the growth of this book.

It's All Yours!

Selling Real Estate by Mortgage-Equity Analysis is easier than you think. It's also easier *if* you think. No, *go to it*!

Irvin E. Johnson
Ventura, California
July 15, 1975

**Selling Real Estate By
Mortgage-Equity Analysis**

1

Mortgage-Equity Talks The Investor's Language

The mortgage-equity technique of real estate valuation and investment analysis talks the investor's language. It answers his most significant questions . . . tells him what he wants to know.

An investor in the current marketplace focuses on three major matters:

1. *What he puts into an investment.* Typically, this amounts to a minimum cash down payment, the balance of the purchase price being financed on a maximum loan.
2. *What he gets out of the investment.* Normally, he receives two future benefits from an investment in income-producing property: *cash flow* over a period of years (the difference between net operating income and loan payments), and a *single cash lump sum payment* at the end of a term of ownership (the difference between resale value and the unpaid loan balance).
3. *The yield rate on the dollar amount he invests.* This relates what he puts in to what he gets out in terms of a rate of yield on equity. If he goes into a million dollar deal with two hundred thousand dollars down, he isn't interested in the rate of yield on a million—he didn't invest a million. He *is* concerned about the yield on two hundred thousand—his actual cash investment. It's *yield on equity* on his original down payment that is meaningful to him, not yield on total property value.

The mortgage-equity technique, applied by the broker/analyst, zeroes in on that topical trio. Mortgage-equity, and only mortgage-equity, gives full consideration to all of the economic facts and factors involved in today's high leverage real estate equity investment market.

Basic Concepts

A summary of some of the concepts on which the mortgage-equity technique of property valuation and investment analysis is based is presented in the context of the investor's motivation, actions, and objectives.

- Income property is usually purchased on a relatively "low" down

1

payment and "high" loan. It would be quite an understatement to say that today's real estate market is not totally a cash market.

- The investor using a high degree of leverage has two purposes in mind: (1) hopefully, to maximize his projected gains; and (2) as a safety measure, to minimize unexpected but possible losses.

- The investor plans to hold the property for a limited time only. Since deductible payments on interest decline period by period and nondeductible payments on principal increase accordingly, a turnover point is reached, in spite of allowable depreciation. Income tax considerations seldom allow a lengthy term of ownership. Few investors project a holding period of more than 12 years or less than 7 years before selling, refinancing, or exchanging the property. A holding period of 10 years is typical.

- Within the holding period either appreciation, stability, or depreciation in market value is anticipated. Only those three things can happen, and one of them is bound to occur.

- Investor's equity at the time of purchase is his down payment, his initial cash investment.

- Investor's equity at the end of the holding period (or at any point in time) is resale value less loan balance.

- Two factors contribute to growth of the equity within the limited period of ownership: (1) debt reduction or loan amortization, and (2) possible appreciation in market value.

- Even though a piece of property may depreciate in value within the holding period, the investor's equity may increase because of loan amortization.

- The income stream generated by the property and received by the investor consists of two segments: (1) an annuity, and (2) a reversion. The annuity is cash flow received periodically during the holding period: net annual income less loan payments. The reversion is a single lump sum payment receivable at the end of the holding period: resale value less loan balance. The total income stream represents both a return on capital (yield) and a recovery of the original equity (the capital investment).

- A portion of the yield is received periodically as it is earned. This cash flow (the difference between net annual income and loan payments) is compoundable by reinvestment.

- The balance of the yield is deferred yield, received or receivable at the end of the holding period. It is locked in and is being compounded.

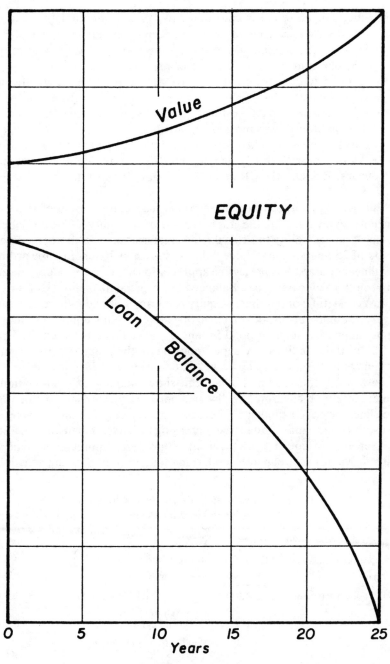

Profile of an Equity

- Since current yield is considered as being compoundable, and deferred yield is calculated as having been compounded, the analyst is dealing with compound interest all the way, giving full and proper consideration to the time-value of money.
- Yield on equity (the initial cash investment) is of greater significance to the investor than yield on total purchase price. Research by the writer indicates that investors typically require a yield of from 12% to 20% on equity, variances being attributable to such factors as risk and loan ratio. A yield rate of 14% or 15% seems quite representative. (At 14% or 15%, compounded annually, money doubles in about 5 years. Refer to the "Rule of 72," pages 40 and 116.)

Further explanations and illustrations may clarify some of the basic concepts reviewed. Note the graph "Profile of an Equity." The line labeled "Loan Balance" plots the curvilinear amortization of a mortgage over a period of 25 years. The "Value" line is shown as extending upward in a curvilinear course, thus projecting appreciation in property value. The area between the Value and Loan Balance lines represents the investor's Equity. In Year 0 (time of purchase) Equity is the amount of down payment, the buyer's actual out-of-pocket cash investment. The dollar measure of Equity at any subsequent point in time is the distance between the Value and Loan Balance lines. By superimposing on the graph other straight or curvilinear lines representing Value, extending from Year 0 in either a level or downward course, the student can show stability or depreciation in value. Note by measuring the distance between the Value and Loan Balance lines that even though a parcel of property may decline in value, the investor's equity may actually be increasing because of loan amortization.

Concepts of equity growth, whether property appreciates or depreciates in value, are related to dollar amounts in the following schedules:

Equity Growth—5% Depreciation in Value
(Ten-Year Holding Period)

Year 0		Year 10	
Purchase Price	$1,000,000	Resale Value	$ 950,000
Mortgage	800,000	Less Loan Balance	650,000
Equity (Down Payment	$ 200,000	Equity at End of Holding Period	$ 300,000
		Less Return of Capital (Down Payment)	200,000
		Equity Growth (Through Debt Reduction)	$ 100,000

Equity Growth—20% Appreciation in Value
(Ten-Year Holding Period)

Year 0		Year 10	
Purchase Price	$1,000,000	Resale Value	$1,200,000
Mortgage	800,000	Less Loan Balance	650,000
Equity (Down Payment)	$ 200,000	Equity at End of Holding Period	$ 550,000
		Less Return of Capital (Down Payment)	200,000
		Equity Growth (Through Debt Reduction and Appreciation)	$ 350,000

Presume an investor purchases property for $1,000,000, paying $200,000 down and financing the balance on possibly a 25-year loan at 8½% interest. Assume that at the end of a 10-year holding period market value of the property has dropped to $950,000 and loan balance unpaid is calculated to be $650,000. Has the investor actually "lost" $50,000 on the investment? Even though the property has depreciated by $50,000 the investor's equity has grown by $100,000; for at the time of purchase his equity was $200,000 (the down payment), and at the end of the 10-year holding period it amounts to $300,000 (resale value of $950,000 less loan balance of $650,000). Equity growth has resulted solely from debt reduction.

On the other hand, presume that the property appreciates 20% within the 10-year holding period, value increasing to $1,200,000. Now the investor's equity is $550,000 ($1,200,000 less loan balance of $650,000). After returning the purchaser's original equity or down payment of $200,000, there is a remainder of $350,000 ($550,000 less $200,000). The increase in equity has been generated by two means: appreciation, $200,000; debt reduction, $150,000. (Since this is income-producing property, the investor would presumably also receive periodic cash flow. However, up to this point only equity growth has been discussed and illustrated.)

The Essence of Mortgage-Equity

The mortgage-equity technique, as applied to the valuation of income properties, can be defined briefly as a method of converting an income stream into an indicator of value by dividing a composite Overall Rate into net annual (operating) income. Other uses of the Overall Rate (OAR) in investment analysis are explained and illustrated in subsequent sections.

The special OAR has built into it six significant components that relate to the basic concepts of mortgage-equity. Three of the variables concern *financing*: (1) the *loan ratio* (dollar amount of the mortgage as a percent of value), (2) the *term* of the loan in years, and (3) the loan *interest rate*. The other three include: (1) the *holding period*, which is a limited term of ownership before selling, refinancing, or exchanging the property; (2) the *equity yield rate* (yield to maturity, which encompasses both current yield and deferred yield); and (3) estimate of *appreciation or depreciation* in property value within the duration of the expected holding period. Selection of a precomputed rate from the OAR Tables eliminates the necessity of calculating the rate for application in valuation or investment analysis.

A short definition provides a foundation for the mathematics of the mortgage-equity technique: *Value is the present worth of future net benefits*.

Analysis of a bond can illustrate this definitive equation. For example: Face amount of an industrial bond is $10,000. Interest at 7% is paid annually. Bond matures in 10 years, at which time the principal amount will be paid off. The investor who buys the bond for $10,000 has acquired, in appraisal terms, *future benefits* consisting of *two segments*:

— An annuity or income stream of annual interest payments for the next 10 years. (.07 × $10,000 = $700.)
— A reversion or single income payment of $10,000 to be received at the end of 10 years.

We will go back to the definition of value, express it as an equation, expand it, and apply it to show that the value or present worth of the future net benefits generated by the bond is precisely $10,000, at a yield rate of 7%. As a simple equation, the definition states:

Value = The present worth of future net benefits.

By substitution in the bond illustration:

Value = The present worth of $700 each year for 10 years plus the present worth of $10,000 to be received at the end of 10 years.

A computation of the present worth of the annual interest payment (the annuity) calls for the use of the Present Worth of 1 Per Period factor (PW 1/P, the annuity factor or Inwood Coefficient), at 7% (the interest rate on the bond) for 10 years. The present worth of the $10,000 single payment (the reversion) to be received at the end of 10 years can be calculated by using the Present Worth of 1 factor (PW 1 or Reversionary Factor) at 7% for 10 years.

The equation can be expressed more concisely in this way:

Value = (Annuity × PW 1/P) + (Reversion × PW 1)

From the Compound Interest Tables we select two factors:

PW 1/P, 7%, 10 years: 7.023582
PW 1, 7%, 10 years: .508349

In the equation above, use the factors selected, $700 for the annuity, and $10,000 for the reversion. By substitution:

Value = ($700 × 7.023582) + ($10,000 × .508349)
      = $4,917 + $5,083
      = $10,000

This calculation proves that the value of the $10,000 bond, at a yield rate of 7%, is actually $10,000. Or, perhaps it should be said that the present worth of the income stream (future net benefits), consisting of an annuity of $700 paid each year for 10 years and a reversion of $10,000 at the end of 10 years, is precisely $10,000. The investor receives a yield of 7% on his investment, plus a return of capital.

Analysis of real estate investments as well as bonds and other types of investments reveals the same basic financial structure: the annuity-reversion pattern . . . an income stream over a period of years and a single terminal payment or value. However, before making a switch from bonds to real estate, we will go back to the preceding illustration and pose a second problem in valuation.

Assume the owner decides to sell the bond, which still has 10 years to run to maturity. He finds that the bond is saleable to another investor, only if it is discounted to yield 12%. The problem is to calculate the present worth of the bond, at a yield rate of 12% (or more exactly, the present worth of the income stream generated by the terms of the bond). The same equation is used:

Value = (Annuity × PW 1/P) + (Reversion × PW 1)

The dollar amount of the annuity has not changed; it remains at $700 a year for 10 years. The reversion stays at $10,000, to be paid at the end of 10 years. However, the purchaser will not pay $10,000 for the bond. He wants 12% yield, not 7%. To calculate present worth (discounted value) at 12%, select two compound interest factors:

PW 1/P, 12%, 10 years: 5.650223
PW 1, 12%, 10 years: .321973

By substitution:

Value = ($700 × 5.650223) + ($10,000 × .321973)
     = $3,955 + $3,220
     = $7,175

This calculation shows that the investor who requires a yield rate of 12% can feasibly pay $7,175 for the bond. If he does so, he will earn a true 12% on his investment of $7,175 (not on $10,000), and he will receive a return of his capital.

The second problem and solution illustrate, in addition to the annuity and reversion pattern, *three types of yield* that pertain to the mortgage-equity concept of real estate valuation and investment analysis: (1) *current* yield, (2) *deferred* yield, and (3) yield *to maturity*.

— If the investor pays $7,175 for the bond and receives $700 interest annually, the *rate of current yield* can be found by the equation:

Rate = Income ÷ Value
     = $700 ÷ $7,175
     = .09756, or 9.756%

— *Deferred yield* is locked in until the maturity of the bond (time of reversion). The investor purchases the bond for $7,175, yet he receives $10,000 at the end of 10 years. From this payment he makes a full capital recovery. There is left over an amount of $2,825, which can be classified only as deferred yield ($10,000 less $7,175). These deferred dollars were earned by the investment of $7,175, as were the annual payments (current yield) of $700. However, they were not received nor were they receivable until the time of reversion. Analysis of the bond at a yield rate of 7% shows current yield only—no deferred yield.
— *Current yield* of 9.756% is exceeded by *yield to maturity*, which is 12%; for *yield to maturity includes both current yield and deferred yield*. "Proof" of 12% yield to maturity can be read from the prior calculation which discounted the income stream to a present worth of $7,175.

The accompanying summary of calculations made in the bond problems may help to fortify some basic concepts.

Value of the Income Stream,
Current Yield, Deferred Yield, Yield to Maturity
(Bond Illustration)

Face amount of bond is $10,000. Interest at 7% is paid annually. Bond matures in 10 years, at which time principal amount will be paid off.

Problem:
What income stream is generated by the terms of the bond?

Solution:
  Annuity: .07 × $10,000 = $700 per year
  Reversion: $10,000 at the end of 10 years

Problem:
Value the bond at a yield rate of 7%.

Solution:
  Annuity: $700 × 7.023582   = $ 4,917   (PW 1/P, 7%, 10 years)
  Reversion: $10,000 × .508349 =   5,083   (PW 1, 7%, 10 years)
  Value at 7% Yield: $10,000

Problem:
Discount the bond to yield 12% and analyze yield.

Solution:
  Annuity: $700 × 5.650223   = $3,955   (PW 1/P, 12%, 10 years)
  Reversion: $10,000 × .321973 =   3,220   (PW 1, 12%, 10 years)
  Discounted Value: $7,175
  Rate of Current Yield: $700 ÷ $7,175 = .09756, or 9.756%
  Amount of Deferred Yield: $10,000 − $7,175 = $2,825
  Yield to Maturity (Proven Above): 12%

It is an easy shift from bonds to the valuation and analysis of a real estate investment. Differences between the two types of investments are apparent: risk, rate, liquidity, growth, and leverage. However, in this section of the study we are concerned only with the areas common to both. These points of relativity include:

— Definition: Value is the present worth of future net benefits.
— Delineation of future net benefits (pattern of the income stream):
     An annuity.
     A reversion.

— Basic equation of *value*:

Value = (Annuity × PW 1/P) + (Reversion × PW 1)

— Types of *yield*:
Current yield.
Deferred yield
Yield to maturity.

Definition and equation of value from the bond problem will be used to explain and illustrate the structure of mortgage-equity and what makes it tick.

Village Square: Valuation and Investment Analysis

Village Square is a small, attractive community shopping center built five years ago in a growing area. The property is offered for sale. Your task as a broker/counsellor is to value the property and prepare an investment analysis for a client. Income from short- and long-term leases has been carefully analyzed, and a realistic operating statement has been constructed. Net annual income is calculated to be $180,000 and is not expected to decline during the next 10 years.

You find that the property can be financed by a local lending institution for 75% of market value on a 25-year loan at 9½% interest. Required cash down payment is 25% of value. The prospective purchaser expects to hold the property as an investment for 10 years before selling, refinancing, or exchanging it. He estimates that the shopping center should appreciate 20% in market value during the holding period. An anticipated equity yield rate of 16% is one of the investor's prime requirements.

Your task is to calculate an indication of value by the mortgage-equity technique and to prepare an investment analysis of Village Square. Your solutions follow.

Computation of Value Estimate
Mortgage-Equity Technique

Data Required:	
Holding Period:	10 years
Equity Yield Rate:	16%
Mortgage Specifications:	
Loan Ratio:	75%
Interest Rate:	9½%
Term:	25 years

Computation of Value Estimate
Mortgage-Equity Technique
(cont.)

Appreciation/Depreciation:	20%
Net Annual Income:	$180,000
Valuation:	
Overall Rate:	.103508

Value = Income ÷ Rate

= $180,000 ÷ .103508

= $1,738,996

Investment Analysis and Proof of Computations
Fifteen-Point Summary of Calculations

1. Over-all Rate Selected from OAR Tables or Computed   .103508

2. **Property Value** — $180,000 (INCOME) ÷ .103508 (OAR) = $1,738,996

3. **Original Equity** (Down Payment) — .25 (Equity Ratio) x $1,738,996 (Value) = 434,749

4. **Amount of Loan** (Original Principal) — .75 (Loan Ratio) x 1,738,996 (Value) = 1,304,247

5. **Debt Service** (Yearly Payments) — .104844 (Loan Constant) x 1,304,247 (Principal) = 136,742

6. **Cash Flow** (Annuity) — 180,000 (Net Income) − 136,742 (Debt Service) = 43,258

7. **Debt Coverage Ratio** — 180,000 (Net Income) ÷ 136,742 (Debt Service) = 1.31635

8. **Rate of Current Yield On Equity** — 43,258 (Cash Flow) ÷ 434,749 (Orig. Equity) = .0995

9. **Loan Balance** (End Holding Period) — .836694 (% Unpaid) x 1,304,247 (Principal) = 1,091,256

10. **Resale Value as % of Original Value** — 100 (Orig. Val. as %) + − 20 (% Appr/Dep) = 120%

11. **Resale Value as a Dollar Amount** — 120% (Resale Val. as %) x 1,738,996 (Original Value) = 2,086,795

12. **Reversion, Net** (Terminal Equity) — 2,086,795 (Resale Value) − 1,091,256 (Loan Balance) = 995,539

13. **Deferred Yield** (Amount) — 995,539 (Reversion Net) − 434,749 (Down Payment) = 560,790

Investment Analysis and Proof of Computations
Fifteen-Point Summary of Calculations
(cont.)

14. Terminal Equity Ratio $\underline{\quad 995,539 \quad}$ $\div$ $\underline{\quad 2,086,795 \quad}$ = $\underline{\quad .477066 \quad}$
     (Reversion Net)   (Resale Value)

15. Proof of Yield on Equity
    Equity Yield Rate: $\underline{\quad 16 \quad}$ Term in Years: $\underline{\quad 10 \quad}$
                      (Percent)   (Holding Period)
    Present Worth of 1 Per Period: $\underline{\quad 4.833227 \quad}$ Present Worth of 1: $\underline{\quad .226684 \quad}$
                                   (PW 1/P)   (PW 1)

    Equation of Proof
    Present Worth = ($\underline{\$43,258}$ x $\underline{4.833227}$) + ($\underline{\$995,539}$ x $\underline{.226684}$)
                     (Cash Flow)   (PW 1/P)   (Net Reversion)   (PW 1)
               = $\underline{\$209,076}$ + $\underline{\$225,673}$ = $\underline{\$434,749}$

Final Check Target Figure = $\underline{\quad \$434,749 \quad}$
                            (Down Payment, Orig. Equity)

    $\underline{\quad \$434,749 \quad}$ − $\underline{\quad \$434,749 \quad}$ = $\underline{\quad 0 \quad}$
         Target Figure   (Present Worth)   (Rounding Adjustment)

The valuation and analysis of Village Square illustrates many of the fundamentals of the mortgage-equity concept and technique, as can be noted in these observations:

Computation of Value Estimate listed six variables from the problem. You matched these points with components in the OAR Tables and selected the appropriate precomputed Overall Rate, .103508. You used the OAR as a divisor and valued the property at $1,738,996 (unrounded). The OAR chosen required neither calculation nor adjustment, the six variables having been built in. The validity of the Overall Rate was substantiated by the "Investment Analysis" form in which all elements fit together and are "proven" in Point 15.

Investment Analysis and Proof of Computations arrays the structure of the investment in detail. First, relate the analysis to the three points noted earlier as being of major concern to the investor:

1. What the buyer puts into the investment:

   Down payment: $434,749 (Line 3)

2. What he gets out of the investment:

   Annuity (cash flow): $43,258 a year for 10 years (Line 6) Net reversion (resale value less loan balance): $995,539 at the end of 10 years (Line 12)

3. Yield rate on the dollar amount he invests:

Equity yield rate to maturity: 16% (Item 15)

Now, follow through the Analysis, point by point:

1. OAR: .103508 (see OAR Tables, Chapter 5). Variables built in: 10-year holding period, 16% equity yield rate, 75% loan ratio, 9½% loan interest rate, 25-year loan term, 20% appreciation.
2. Value = Income ÷ Rate.
3. Original equity is the down payment, 25% of value.

Steps 4 and 5 will lead up to a calculation of cash flow (Annuity) in Step 6.

4. Principal amount of loan is 75% of value.
5. Loan constant, .104844, listed in the Supplemental Tables, matches loan terms specified. Payments made in the course of a year are calculated: $136,742. (One-twelfth is paid each month.)
6. Cash Flow = Net Income less Debt Service. This annuity of $43,258 is the first of the investor's future net benefits.
7. Debt coverage ratio calculated shows that net income is more than 130% of debt service, indicating an adequate safety margin for both lender and investor.
8. Rate of current yield on equity (cash on cash) is a little less than 10% (9.95%), yet yield to maturity is specified as being 16% (a point to be verified in Item 15).

Steps 9, 10, and 11 are required for a calculation of the net reversion in Line 12, the second of the investor's future net benefits.

9. At the end of a 10-year holding period, 83.6694% of the original principal remains unpaid. (See Supplemental Tables.)
10. Since 20% appreciation has been estimated, resale value would be 120% of purchase price. (Original value or purchase price is considered to be 100%. *Add* for appreciation; *subtract* for depreciation.)
11. Projected value at end of 10-year holding period is 120% of purchase price, or $2,086,795.
12. Net reversion, the second of the investor's future net benefits, is calculated by subtracting loan balance from resale value. Equity has grown from $434,749 to $995,539 in 10 years.
13. The net reversion ($995,539) is segregated into two parts: (1) a recapture of the capital investment or down payment of $434,749;

and (2) deferred yield, amounting to $560,790. Debt reduction contributed $212,991 to the equity buildup; and appreciation, $347,799.

14. Equity ratio at the end of the holding period is 47.7066% of resale value. This indicates a possibility of refinancing rather than selling.

15. The basic equation of value is used as "proof" of 16% yield to maturity:

$$\text{Value} = (\text{Annuity} \times \text{PW } 1/P) + (\text{Reversion} \times \text{PW } 1)$$

"Value" as used here represents the original equity or down payment, not total property value. Down payment of $434,749 is the "target figure." It is the present worth of the future net benefits at a yield rate of 16%:

The cash flow or net annuity of $43,258 a year for 10 years, plus the net reversion of $995,539 receivable at the end of 10 years.

Throughout the Analysis dollar amounts calculated are used unrounded so that a close check can be made. Item 15 serves as a check point, as well as proof of yield to maturity. If the calculation misses the "target figure" by a substantial margin, it indicates an error. Figures and calculations should be rechecked, beginning with the selection of the OAR.

Point 15 demonstrates that the future benefits of the annuity and the reversion have a present worth of $434,749 at a yield rate of 16%. Therefore, the investor is justified in paying $434,749 as a down payment on a total purchase price of $1,738,996. His investment decision is based on income analysis, loan data, and reasonable estimates and projections of holding period, appreciation, and equity yield.

Both counsellor and investor must be aware at all times that real estate is a *risk* investment, no matter how precise calculations may be. In the analysis of Village Square by mortgage-equity, yield to maturity of 16% is an *anticipated* rate, *not* a guaranteed rate.

Refer to blank worksheet forms in Chapter 3, and see examples and additional explanation in the Case Study in Chapter 4.

The Traditional and the Contemporary

We believe it is time to question some traditional concepts of the income approach. Are the residual techniques realistic in today's investment market? Is the straight line declining income method appropriate to the usual current valuation problem; or is it, for general use, becoming as outdated as

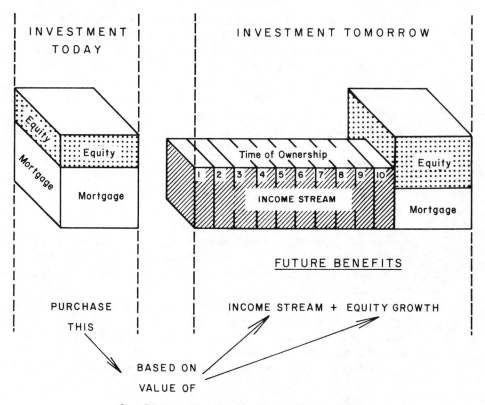

One Picture Tells it all: View of Investment

The message is clear. No comment is called for, other than to advise the broker/counsellor to "get the picture."

the buggy whip? Is it possible that analysts have been coming up with approximately the right valuations but by unrealistic procedures?

There are a few points of similarity between the mortgage-equity technique and the residual techniques of the income approach:

— The validity of each depends on a reasonably accurate projection and processing of income to the point at which it can be capitalized.
— Both the mortgage-equity technique and the residual techniques process income into an indicator of value.

However, there are more significant differences than similarities.

— The old "tried and true" residual techniques are all *summation* approaches: land value plus improvement value. Valuation by summation is not regarded as the best appraisal practice, if another technique can be used—for the value of the whole is not necessarily equal to the sum of its parts. A typical investor doesn't purchase land plus improvements plus personal property. He buys a total income-producing package. The mortgage-equity technique is allied with the *total property* or unit appraisal concept.

— Mortgage-equity makes no artificial, pointless segregation of income attributable to land and income attributable to improvements.

— Mortgage-equity does not assume that land is to be valued separately "as if vacant." If there is a building on the land, it isn't vacant. And if the improvement is a proper one, representing highest and best use, it has enhanced land value.

— It is not assumed that the subject property is "free and clear." If the purpose of the appraisal is to estimate *market value* (value to persons in general), the analyst assumes that the property is encumbered by new typical institutional financing, the purchaser paying cash to the loan. If the analyst is seeking *investment value* (value to a specific client) he will consider the special, nontypical terms that may be available.

— There is no estimate of remaining economic life called for, hence, subjective judgment of depreciation is minimized.

— Projection of the size and shape of the income stream extends through a relatively short term holding period of possibly 10 years—not 40 or 50.

— Recapture is provided for at the end of a realistically limited holding period, rather than being spread over twenty-five to fifty years.

— The mortgage-equity technique gives full consideration not only to current yield but also to deferred yield at the time of reversion—growth of equity resulting from both loan amortization and possible appreciation.

— The investor is concerned with what he puts into an investment and what he gets out of it. Mortgage-equity considers both.

— The mortgage-equity technique answers the investor's most meaningful question: "What is the yield on my equity, my actual cash investment?" The residual techniques all sidestep and ignore the issue.

— Calculation of value by mortgage-equity is a simple, one-step computation: income divided by overall rate.

The analyst may not wish to despense with the residual techniques. But neither should he ignore the mortgage-equity technique that speaks the investor's language and gives him the answers he seeks.

On Educating the Investor

The total real estate investment market, like ancient Gaul, can be divided into three parts. These areas are:

1. The investor interested primarily in equity growth, mainly through appreciation. Current income (cash flow or net spendable) doesn't interest or motivate him. He invests with or without leverage, in improved or unimproved property, and relies totally on deferred yield. (He is the type of individual who in the stock market buys "growth stock" that may be paying no cash dividends.)
2. The investor concerned with current yield (cash flow) only. He usually uses leverage but says, "Forget about equity growth, debt reduction, and appreciation." He considers the total loan payment (including the portion applicable to principal) as an "expense" because it decreases the dollar amount of cash flow. He looks no farther than "cash on cash", the annual rate of return on his invested capital (down payment).
3. The investor who wants both cash flow and equity growth. He is totally aware that deferred yield is generated by both debt reduction and appreciation in market value. He knows that deferred yield is additional money earned by his actual investment (his down payment) and that in a typical situation his true rate of yield to maturity exceeds substantially the rate of current yield.

See "Nonproducing Properties, Purchased for Appreciation" in Chapter 3 for procedures related specifically to the first class of investor listed. Emphasis should be placed on the effect of holding costs and holding periods on the rate of yield on equity. For example, the illustration given on pages 141 to 145 shows that if the subject property, purchased for $1,500,000, is held for 5 years and is resold for $2,500,000, the equity yield rate is about 11.67%. But if the holding period must be extended to 7 years before the property can be sold for $2,500,000, the true rate of yield on equity drops to about 4 3/4%. Accent must be on the *time-value of money*.

Class 2 needs educating. The broker/salesman can go along with the investor who contends that he is interested only in cash flow, but he should proceed from that point and show that there is more to an investment than current yield. For an illustration, refer to two procedures: "OAR, based on current yield requirements;" and "Depreciation, limits of, within which yield to maturity and current yield correspond," both in Chapter 3. In this example an Overall Rate is derived by an adjusted band-of-investment method, based on financing data and on the investor's requirement of a current yield rate of 10%. Income capitalized by the calculated rate indicates a value of $625,000. Further analysis by the mortgage-equity technique shows that if the property appreciates 20% within a 10-year holding period, yield to maturity would be 18%; at 0% appreciation, yield to maturity is nearly 16%; and at 20% depreciation, yield to maturity is measured at about 13%. A simple calculation indicates that the property would have to depreciate a totally unreasonable 36% within a 10-year holding period if yield to maturity were held at 10%, corresponding to the rate of current yield. Proper education on the point of yield to maturity typically exceeding current yield should benefit the client—and the broker/salesman.

The greater portion of this book has been related to Class 3, which represents the typical real estate investor.

Mortgage-equity talks straight. The investor understands, listens, and profits.

2

Tools and Techniques— Mortgage-Equity Applied

Valuation and analysis of real estate is an art. It is also a craft. The analyst, as a craftsman, requires specialized tools of the trade. Few craftsmen in any line have either the time or the skill to fashion their own tools; yet they may be very proficient in using them.

This text has been designed as a tool—or, more correctly, a kit of many tools. Each Overall Rate is a separate tool with a specific application— ready-made—ready to use. There is no call to slave over a hot calculator at a desk piled high with equations, symbols, formulas, and factors to manufacture your own mortgage-equity tools . . . Overall Rates, that is.

Further, the text supplies "Patterned Procedures" . . . "blueprints" to follow in illustrated how-to-do-it format.

Mortgage-Equity: A Multi-Purpose Technique

Mortgage-equity is neither a single-purpose nor an all-purpose tool. It can and does serve analyst and investor in a variety of ways. Here are a few:

1. Appraisal for market value.
2. Appraisal for investment value.
3. Establishing a band of value for purchase price negotiations.
4. Projecting a possible range of yield on equity as a basis for decision-making.
5. Investment analysis of present or prospective holdings, with the focus on equity yield rate.
6. Check on other indicators of value.

The analyst/counsellor recognizes the difference between a feasibility study and an appraisal for market value. A feasibility study to calculate *investment value* for a particular client considers such points as possible unorthodox high-leverage financing with two or more mortgages, the investor's individual objectives, and his income tax position, et cetera. His key question concerning the value of the property is not "What is it worth?" Rather, it is "What is it worth *to me*?"

An appraisal for market value assumes the property to be encumbered by a new maximum conventional loan at current interest rates. It is also assumed that the buyer pays cash to the new loan; thus, market price is automatically adjusted to a cash equivalent. *Market value* is considered to be *value to persons in general*, without being related to unusual financing or to particular income tax brackets.

"When market rentals, typical mortgage financing terms, and market-derived equity yield rates are employed in mortgage-equity analysis, the present worth estimate is market value. When contract rentals, specific mortgage financing terms, and an equity yield rate required by a specific investor are employed in mortgage-equity analysis, the present worth estimate is either investment value for a specific potential investor, or value in use for a specific owner." So writes William N. Kinnard, Jr., in *Income Property Valuation.* *

Bands of value and ranges of yield rates are as significant as specific points. The band may set upper and lower limits of value, within which there may be a meeting of minds by purchaser and seller or it may project a range of indicated yield on equity, based on such assumptions as possible 20% depreciation or 20% appreciation within a holding period. Besides telling the analyst the market value or investment value of the property and a possible rate of yield on equity, the use of this technique may also point out properties that are not economic units. It may help the investor to avoid mistakes and may set up criteria that will minimize losses as well as maximize and retain gains.

Variations on a Theme

The analyst, using the mortgage-equity technique, should not be overwhelmed by the realization that there is an almost infinite number of possible combinations of the six variable components in an Overall Rate. However, he should understand the impact of each type of variable on *value* and on the *rate of yield on equity*.

We will illustrate the effect on *value* by altering each of the following variables (making, however, only one change at a time): holding period, equity yield rate, loan ratio, loan term, loan interest rate, and appreciation.

Given:
  Holding period: 10 years
  Equity yield rate: 14%
  Loan ratio: 75%
  Loan term: 20 years
  Loan interest rate: 9%
  Appreciation: 0%

*Copyright 1971, Lexington Books, D.C. Heath and Company.

Net annual income: $120,000
OAR: .104738
Indicated value: $120,000 ÷ .104738 = $1,145,716

Note the change in OAR and consequently in value by altering each variable, making only one modification at a time, with all other data remaining constant:

Holding period: 5 years
   OAR: .103162
   Value: $120,000 ÷ .103162 = $1,163,219
Equity yield rate: 12%
   OAR: .098592
   Value: $120,000 ÷ .098592 = $1,217,137
Loan ratio: 60%
   OAR: .111790
   Value: $120,000 ÷ .111790 = $1,073,441
Loan term: 30 years
   OAR: .103316
   Value: $120,000 ÷ .103316 = $1,161,485
Interest rate: 10%
   OAR: .111389
   Value: $120,000 ÷ .111389 = $1,077,306
Appreciation: 20%
   OAR: .094395
   Value: $120,000 ÷ .094395 = $1,271,254

Note that all six variables affect value. Changes in holding period and loan term appear less critical than the other four components of the OAR, when only one variable is altered. A shift of two or more variables simultaneously will compound the differences in value conclusions and in equity yield rates.

Going back to the preceding illustration, we will consider as constants net income of $120,000, OAR of .104738, and consequently value of $1,145,176 (unrounded). Note the effect on *equity yield rate*, as we change the more critical variables in the given data:

Loan ratio: An increase from 75% to 90% Raises equity yield rate to about 18.4%.
Interest rate: Raising from 9% to 11% Lowers equity yield rate to about 9.5%.
Appreciation: Projection of 30% appreciation Increases equity yield rate to about 18.2%

(For procedures to calculate rate of yield on equity, see pages 81 to 92.)

Variations in Overall Rate components affect matters other than value and equity yield rate to maturity: size of the down payment, amount of cash flow, net reversion, debt coverage ratio, current yield, and deferred yield.

Variables in the mortgage-equity technique concern the investor and the counsellor. The analyst will weigh possibilities as well as probabilities in delineating bands of value and ranges of equity yield for investment decision-making.

Mortgage-Equity Applied

As any real estate broker or salesman knows, his work doesn't begin and end with showing a piece of property and drawing up a deposit receipt. Four major sales functions are involved in a typical transaction:
1. Listing the property at fair market value.
2. Presenting the property to a client and obtaining his offer to purchase.
3. Securing the seller's acceptance of the prospective buyer's offer, or negotiating an agreement between buyer and seller.
4. Arranging suitable financing for the buyer.
(A fifth might be added: Managing the property for the investor after the sale is consummated.)

Mortgage-equity can assist in each step. The following outline, listing a few of the patterned procedures and examples related to each area may serve as a study and a working guide to the broker/analyst.

Phase 1: Listing the Property

A good sale begins with a good listing. The real estate broker or salesman may not be a professional appraiser, but he appraises whenever he expresses an opinion of value in listing property. The analyst doesn't appraise property but property rights. He doesn't estimate the value of bricks, mortar, and land, but the value to the investor of the future net benefits (the anticipated income stream generated by the real estate or attributable to it.)

Price and terms specified in a listing may not correspond to the actual price and terms of the sale when it is finally completed, but they should be close enough in reality to induce an investor to make a firm offer.

The following steps in listing income property are suggested, and reference is made to relevant sections of the text:

1. Make a preliminary survey of the property and the area, and prepare an operating statement or reconstruct the owner's statement of income and expenses.

— Procedure, "The Operating Statement," pages 50 to 52.
— Examples, "Operating Statements Before and After Reconstruction," pages 478 to 482.
2. From the market gather data concerning the six variables in a mortgage-equity Overall Rate (data applicable to the subject property): holding period, equity yield rate, financing data, projections of appreciation/depreciation.
3. Select or calculate a mortgage-equity Overall Rate.
— Procedures using precomputed OAR's, pages 64 to 72.
— Procedures using Compound Interest Tables, pages 72 to 76.
— Procedure deriving an Overall Rate from the market, pages 77 to 78.
4. If analysis of the income stream as shown in Step 1 indicates that its characteristics are other than those of an ordinary annuity, convert it to an ordinary annuity equivalent.
— Procedures, "Processing the Income Stream to an Ordinary Annuity Equivalent," pages 52 to 61.
5. Calculate indicated market value by capitalizing income delineated in Step 1 (or Step 4 if applicable).
— Procedure, "Valuation by the mortgage-equity technique," pages 97 to 106.
6. Relate the results of Step 5 to other indicators of value (preferably, comparative sales); correlate. The value conclusion may be the figure that the analyst must endeavor to "sell" the seller.
7. (Alternate) If the owner has specified a list price, check it, using the OAR from Step 3 and Income from Step 1 (or Step 4 if applicable).
— Procedure, "Income required to meet equity yield demands," pages 61 to 64.
— Illustration, "Introduction." If income required, as shown by calculation, is significantly above (or below) income produced, go back to Steps 5 and 6, compute an estimate of value, and work with the owner to bring his list price in line with realities.

Phase 2: Presenting and Selling the Property

The next step in marketing income property is selling an idea—selling the prospective buyer on the concept of investing in real estate. This may be an infrequent exercise on the part of the broker, for most of his clients have probably already bought the idea that *The Right Investment Is Worth A Lifetime of Toil*.

A member of a sales organization should not be timid about venturing into the marketing of income property. Many find it *easier* to deal with an experienced client who has money to invest than with a typical, inexperienced prospective home-buyer who has financing problems. Another aspect also tends to make it less difficult. The physical characteristics of the income property do not have to satisfy the personal preferences of the investor in every respect—it's the income produced by the property that is of prime interest to him. The broker doesn't sell land and buildings—he sells an income stream, an annuity, growth, and a high equity yield rate—he sells an idea.

Suggested sales steps follow, with textbook references noted:

1. Prepare for and present to the client a written analysis of the offering. Such a brochure might contain items from this book that many professional appraisers include in their narrative appraisals:
   a. Three matters of major concern to the contemporary investor, page 1.
   b. Basic concepts of mortgage-equity. A number might be selected from pages 1 to 4.
   c. Charts with dollar amounts entered:
      — "Profile of an Equity," page 3.
      — "View of Investment," page 15.
      — "Analysis of Yield to Maturity," page 168.
   d. Fifteen-point "Investment Analysis and Proof of Computations," or a portion of it:
      — Worksheet form, pages 150, 151.
      — Explanations and illustrations, pages 11 to 14, and 155 to 161.
   The presentation might be compared to a "performance report" written by an automotive engineer/analyst: efficiency, safety, maintenance, economic life, resale value, etc.
2. Escort the client on an inspection tour of the property.
3. If the client requests an after-income tax analysis, determine his tax bracket and prepare one.
   — Illustration and explanation of "After Income Tax Analysis and Yield on Equity," pages 171 to 176.
4. Write up the deposit receipt, using the listed price and terms, or the client's offer.
5. If the client offers price and/or terms that differ from the listing, prepare other calculations and analyses, based on his requirements. Here are a few possibilities, with related procedures listed.
   a. Frequently, such an offer includes a provision that maximum financing be obtained on a first mortgage, and that the seller carry a portion of the remainder on a second. If so, the investor will pose one of two questions:
      — "What can I offer for the property, based on my desired rate of

yield on equity?'' To answer Question 1: Procedure, "OAR, multiple financing," pages 74 to 76.

— "If I purchase the property on these multiple-financing terms and at the list price, what rate of yield can I anticipate?" Question 2: Procedure, "Yield to Maturity—Rate, if secondary (junior or multiple) financing," pages 84 to 85.

b. If there is an existing, favorable, assumable loan on the property, the investor's question may be, "What can I offer the seller for his equity, assume the existing loan instead of refinancing, and realize the rate of yield I want on my equity investment?"

— Procedure, "Investment value when loan ratio is unknown," pages 100 to 103.

— If the offer involves also assuming a second mortgage, procedure, "Investment value when loan ratios are unknown (multiple financing)," pages 104 to 106.

c. If the offer is based on requirements that differ from the six components of the OAR by which the property was valued at the time of listing, select or calculate an OAR as in Step 3 of Phase 1 and capitalize income by the new OAR.

— Procedure, "Valuation by the mortgage-equity technique," pages 98 to 99.

d. The offer may specify a lower purchase price but no change in terms. Now, the investor's question is, "If I pay this offered price, what would be the expected yield on equity?"

— Procedures, "Yield to Maturity—Rate, if single mortgage financing," pages 81 to 84.

The "market" for investment properties is made by the *decisions* investors make. You have the offer—now, present it.

Phase 3: Presenting the Offer; Negotiating an Agreement

The seller makes it easy when he simply asks, "Where do I sign?"

The transaction may not, however, go that smoothly. This phase frequently brings out counter offers and counter-counter offers, leading to a final "meeting of the minds." A value range within which to negotiate is frequently bounded by the list price at the upper end and the prospective purchaser's first offer at the lower end. When the actual sales price is resolved, it will doubtlessly be the highest price the buyer is willing to pay and the lowest price the seller is willing to accept. In the final analysis it is the *buyers* who by their actions in the market place set prices—and values.

During the negotiating phases alternate computations of investment value, calculations of equity yield rate, and a final reconstructed 15-point investment analysis may be called for. Procedures used in Phase 2 apply here.

If the seller weighs the advisability of carrying a second mortgage the broker/analyst might calculate for the owner the amount that could be accumulated over the term of the loan, if all loan payments received are reinvested or deposited in a savings account. For the proper procedure and a specific illustration of this point, see "Amount to which a uniform series of uniform deposits will grow at compound interest," pages 114 to 115.

The broker should not overlook the opportunity to discuss the seller's own future financial program and possibly move him up into a larger investment.

Once the final deposit receipt bears signatures of both buyer and seller, the broker steps into the final phase of the sale.

Phase 4: Financing the Sale

The signed agreement to purchase may be contingent upon the buyer's arranging suitable financing. When the broker first analyzed the property by the mortgage-equity technique in the listing process, he probably obtained financing data of a somewhat general nature from a local lending institution. Now he moves into specifics in securing a firm loan commitment for his client.

Copies of four documents should be presented to the loan officer: (1) the deposit receipt; (2) the detailed listing form; (3) the reconstructed operating statement; and (4) the 15-point "Investment Analysis." Line 7 of the analysis form, "Debt Coverage Ratio," will be of special significance to the lender. Also, it would be beneficial to show that the Overall Capitalization Rate was derived directly from the market, or that the precomputed mortgage-equity OAR was based purely on market-derived data.

The lender will rely on his own staff appraiser. However, the expertise shown by the broker in his clear, thorough presentation, should assist greatly in "selling" the lender.

Now that the sale is financed, papers recorded, and funds disbursed, the broker is ready to enter into a management contract with the new owner . . . and, looking ahead, move him up into a bigger investment at the end of his holding period.

Glad You Asked . . .

A number of "what if" or "how about" questions might be raised—and answered—concerning valuation and investment analysis by the mortgage-equity technique:

— To what types of property is valuation by the mortgage-equity technique applicable? Answer: Basically, it has a broad application to nearly every common type of income-producing property: apartments, commercial buildings, mobile home parks, shopping centers, industrial parks, office buildings, et cetera. There are a few exceptions. Heavy industrial properties, typically owned and occupied by the manufacturer, can in most cases be valued most appropriately by the cost approach; for there are few if any market sales, and economic rents are difficult to establish. Mortgage-equity is of doubtful applicability in the appraisal of residential properties that are not generally considered to be economic units— properties of possibly less than 10 or 15 units. The market approach is recommended in the valuation of smaller properties, including duplexes. Although mortgage-equity may not be a prime technique in the *appraisal* of smaller income properties, it can be applied in *analyzing* them. Commonly, rate of equity yield on the smaller units will be comparatively and surprisingly low, if an operating statement includes such frequently omitted items as professional management, hired maintenance, and reserves for replacements. If no value is assigned to the owner's time in managing and maintaining his property, he may be building up "sweat equity" to meet his own individual objectives.

— How is mortgage-equity related to the market? Answer: Yield rates and Overall Rates can be derived from analysis of market sales. Economic rents are determined in the market. Financing data is obtained from the mortgage market. Holding periods can be found by observing the actions and reactions of investors in the real estate market. Projections of possible value changes are based on economic trends in the market. Mortgage-equity recognizes the realities of the market and is inseparable from the market.

— How about mortgage-equity, appreciation, and inflation? Answer: A projection of possible appreciation, if any, is made as a percent, and is translated into dollars, not purchasing power. Increase in the dollar-value of real estate is attributable to the operation of the law of supply and demand, as well as to inflation. One of the prime reasons for investing in real estate is to provide a hedge against inflation. If an investor actually believes the property under consideration will decline in dollar value over a relatively short term of ownership, will he invest in it at all? In general, in dealing with economically feasible income property, well-located, wouldn't it be more realistic to project a modest degree of appreciation than stability or depreciation over a typical 10-year holding period? In a growing area land values continue to escalate because of increasing demand and decreasing supply. The dollar amount of actual physical depreciation of buildings—well-designed, constructed, located, and maintained—has been largely offset by rising construction costs. The analyst and the investor must not discount the possibility of a decline in value. Whatever the forecast, it should be based on a careful analysis of the subject property and an economic study of the area in which it is located. Particular attention should be given to trends.

— What about variable interest rates? Answer: Generally, appraisers using the mortgage-equity technique attempt to estimate a "stabilized" rate, which may be less than or greater than the current rate. Any error in projecting a stablized rate is minimized by the relatively short holding period for which the estimate is made. Guidelines are furnished by the terms of the mortgage that specify the maximum variation permitted within a given time frame. A loan may be set up on a schedule that increases the interest rate but does not increase the loan amortization payment. It does, however, extend the term of the loan. Cash flow (after debt service) is not reduced under such an arrangement. The extension of the loan term does cause a reduction in the amount of net reversion at the end of the holding period, because of a higher remaining unpaid principal balance. However, its effect on yield rate is minimized because the reversion takes a rather heavy discount to present worth.

— Is a real estate investment that produces a negative cash flow feasible under any circumstance? Answer: There are several situations in which negative cash flow is warranted:

1. If nonproducing property (particularly, unimproved land) shows a positive growth potential, an investor would be justified in purchasing it for appreciation. All yield is deferred, and required holding costs result in not only negative cash flow but also in negative income. (Refer to pages 141 to 145.)
2. If the investor elects to pay off the loan at an accelerated pace to meet some personal objective, the negative cash flow is a matter of his choice. It does not indicate that the investment is an uneconomic one.
3. If the income-producing property is purchased with 100% financing—no down payment—net income may be insufficient to cover loan amortization payments. The investor builds an equity by installments as he makes out-of-pocket expenditures to offset the negative cash flow. (See pages 71 to 72, and pages 476 to 478.)
4. Frequently income property shows an initial negative income or

negative cash flow after construction and during an incubation or buildup period.

— Must the loan constant always be less than the Overall Rate, in the interests of both lender and borrower? Answer: No. In many feasible transactions the loan constant *exceeds* the Overall Rate. The truly significant relationship is found by comparing the *product* of the loan constant and the loan ratio to the Overall Rate. If that product is less than the Overall Rate, there will be a positive cash flow. (See page 95.)

— What are the advantages, if any, of deferred yield? Answer: Three might be enumerated:

1. The prospects of deferred yield make feasible, under certain circumstances, investments in low-producing or nonproducing properties.
2. Deferred yield is typically a substantial part of the bundle taxed as long term capital gains. Current yield is normally either partially or totally subject to tax as ordinary income, at the regular rate.
3. Deferred yield, in contrast to current yield, poses less of a problem in immediate reinvestment of funds. A large single lump sum, receivable in possibly 10 years, might be reinvested with greater ease than small amounts received periodically.

— If appraisal for market value assumes new typical conventional financing, what adjustment should a lender make for a favored client in valuing the property and analyzing the investment by the mortgage-equity technique? Answer: It would be advisable to use normal terms in appraising the property, then make an adjustment in loan terms. For example, if a loan ratio of 70% is typical for the subject property, select the Overall Rate with a 70% loan ratio in valuing it. Then, possibly the special client can be favored by an 80% loan—80% of market value, not of a distorted or inflated value. The investor will be using a greater degree of leverage and will be in a position to realize a higher than normal rate of yield on equity. Or, the lender might stick to the 70% loan ratio but cut the interest rate or extend the loan term, thus making concessions to his favored client without distorting market value.

— How about the fact that equity increases with each loan payment on principal? Answer: Equity growth is "locked in" until the time of reversion (resale, refinancing, or exchange). Therefore, it should be considered as *deferred yield*. Amounts applied to principal are not additional out-of-pocket investments, but additional earnings from the income-producing property. *Yield to maturity* is computed on the original equity—the initial investment or down payment—and recognizes both current and deferred yield.

— How do income taxes affect yield on equity? Answer: The best explanation may be an illustration. See the analysis in Chapter 4 of the Sunset Point Apartments case study. Mortgage-equity appraisal for market value is made without a calculation of "typical" tax brackets or levies. Indicated yield on equity is the rate of yield *before* income taxes. Cash flow in the 15-point investment analysis is computed *before* income taxes. In analyzing sales and deriving Overall Rates from the market, it is reasonable to assume that the market has adjusted for income tax considerations. On any type of investment, other than tax-free municipal bonds, after-tax yield is obviously less than before-tax yield. This is one of the economic facts of life. While *appraisal* by mortgage-equity indicates yield *before* income taxes, *special analysis* by mortgage-equity can calculate yield *after* taxes.

Real estate as an investment offers several specific tax advantages over most other types of investments: particularly, allowable depreciation and long-term capital gains. For tax purposes there is no relationship between permissible depreciation and actual depreciation or appreciation in market value. Accelerated depreciation, which may be taken on certain types of property, may provide totally tax-sheltered income in the initial years of a holding period. Further, it may convert a portion of current yield to deferred yield, taxable at the time of resale at half the rate on ordinary income. The taxpayer has the advantage of the use of this money—his deferred income taxes—until resale of the property. The time value of money is working for him. On the other hand, if the investor takes straight line instead of accelerated depreciation he may be able to extend the holding period.

In many cases too much emphasis is placed on the "tax shelter" aspect of a real estate investment. We do not concur with the thought that seeking a tax shelter should be either the sole or the prime motivation for entering into a transaction. We support the premise that a real estate investment should make economic sense on its own merits and that income tax advantages will merely provide additional "fringe benefits."

Cautions, Precautions, and Suggestions

A few miscellaneous "do's and don't's" may be in order to serve as reminders:

- Don't disregard the "market." Market value is determined not only by market *sales* but also by factors that influence and shape the market, providing a basis for decision-making.

- Don't put your client into over-priced property with the expectation that he will be bailed out of a bad deal by (1) inflation, (2) the benefits of a "tax shelter", or (3) resale to another uninformed misguided buyer.
- Do avoid these pitfalls:
  — Overestimating income.
  — Underestimating expenses.
  — Taking an owner's operating statement without question or re-construction.
  — Relying on arithmetic rather than the market . . . and good judgment.
- Do relate *risk* to *rate*. The higher the risk, the higher the rate by way of compensation. Consequently, the lower the indicated property value.
- Do use timesaving precomputed Overall Rates and Patterned Procedures. When you can cut down on mechanics and mathematics you have more time to do your "field work"—to gather data from the market, analyze it, evaluate it, exercise good judgment in coming up with valid value conclusions.
- From your work in the market do build up a file of Overall Rates, equity yield rates (current and to maturity), expense ratios, debt coverage ratios, financing terms, et cetera, for different types of property in different areas. (Pay particular attention to points of *comparability* in gathering the information, and to the *date* of compilation.)
- Do encourage cooperating brokers in the Multiple Listing Service to use the same comprehensive "Investment Analysis" forms.
- Don't overlook the possibility of using the elementary, detailed, simplified explanations in this textbook in your sales training program and in educating an unsophisticated client.
- Do apply mortgage-equity concepts, tools, and techniques to your own personal investment program.
- Do engage in a planned educational program of lifelong learning to continue in the development of your professional skills.

Let's Talk Terms

The following glossary defines, explains, and/or illustrates valuation terms in the context of the instant mortgage-equity technique. (It is suggested that this section be *studied* as an integral part of the basic text, rather than being utilized merely as a reference lexicon.)

Adjusted sales price. Nominal sales price, from which may be deducted the value of excess land or the value of personal property, when using the sale as a comparable in deriving an Overall Rate or equity yield rate from the market. Other allowances may be called for: e.g., computing the cash equivalent of mortgages or other noncash items involved in the transaction, to adjust sales price for terms.

Amortization. Return of a capital investment over a period of time. Also, paying off a debt by periodic instalments, principal and interest included.

Annuity. A level terminal income stream or its equivalent. An *ordinary annuity* is one in which equal payments are received or assumed to be received at the *end* of each period. An *annuity in advance* calls for payments at the *beginning* of each period. When rent is received monthly in advance, the analyst may, in most cases, consider it to constitute an *ordinary annuity*. Since certain major expenses, such as property taxes, are paid on an annual or semiannual basis, insurance is paid annually or once in three years, and maintenance costs are not spread evenly over the year, net income is more realistically calculated as a yearly rather than a monthly sum. A net-net-net lease, rental being prepaid period by period, clearly constitutes an annuity in advance and should be so treated.

Variations of the income stream include a graduated step-up or step-down annuity, a deferred annuity, an increasing or decreasing annuity, or a totally irregular income stream. Net annual income to be processed by the mortgage-equity technique is the *ordinary annuity* or the ordinary annuity equivalent. Methods are given in the procedural section, Chapter 3, for converting any class or shape of income stream to an ordinary annuity equivalent for purposes of capitalization. Net annual income before loan payments can be termed the investor's *gross annuity*; and net income after debt service as the *net annuity* (cash flow).

Appraisal. An estimate or opinion of value, arrived at and substantiated by knowledgeable collection and processing of all pertinent data.

Appreciation. Increase in market value. It is measured in dollars, not in purchasing power, and may be offset in varying degrees by inflation.

Approaches to value. The three traditional approaches: cost of replacement or reproduction, market or comparative sales, and income. Theoretically, the cost approach usually sets the upper limit of value; and the income approach, the lower limit. Correlation of value indicators is considered to be a matter of judgment in arriving at a value conclusion, a point within the indicated range.

Balloon payment. A single lump sum payment, usually in the amount of unpaid principal balance owing at a time specified in a note, secured by a mortgage or trust deed. (Don't believe the wag who says a balloon payment is a perfect example of inflation.)

Capitalization. Any mathematical procedure which converts an income stream to a capital sum or value.

Cash equivalent. The cash value of noncash items, given as consideration in the purchase of property. If a purchaser pays cash down to a loan made at current interest rates by a lending institution, the cash equivalent of the mortgage or trust deed is its face value, and the cash equivalent of the sale is the full sales price. In a common type of situation, a portion of the sales price is a "purchase money mortgage" carried by the seller. Whether a "first" or a "second," the cash equivalent of such a mortgage is its value, discounted to a yield rate that would make it saleable on the open market to another investor. The computation of cash equivalent is one step in the market approach in adjusting sales price for terms. It is also important in the mortgage-equity technique of the income approach in order to derive current, realistic Overall Rates from the market.

Cash flow. The term as used in procedures and the investment analysis form in this text refers to net annual income after loan payments but before income taxes. Positive cash flow, in most cases, is current yield on equity. (The terms "cash throw-off" and "equity dividend," as used in a number of textbooks, equate with *cash flow* and *current yield* in this book.) If loan payments exceed net annual income a negative cash flow or expenditure results. While this is generally not a feasible situation (particularly, with income-producing properties), it may be warranted under certain circumstances, all yield being deferred until the time of reversion. See examples listed under "Glad you asked . . ." earlier in this chapter.

Compound interest and annuity tables. Six "standard" tables of factors that are used as multipliers or divisors in calculating future or present worth of a single lump sum amount or of a series of periodic payments. Compound interest (the time value of money) is built into each factor. Names of the factors vary. The following is representative and recommended. Principal use is also given: Future Worth of 1 (growth of a single sum or value at compound interest). Future Worth of 1 Per Period (growth of a level series of deposits or investments at compound interest). Sinking Fund (amount to be deposited periodically, which will grow to a stated future sum). Present Worth of 1 (present worth of a single future income payment or value—a reversion). Present Worth of 1 Per Period (present worth of a level series of future income payments—an annuity). Periodic Repayment (periodic payment required to amortize a capital sum, interest and return of principal included). This book provides a limited number of factors from the last three tables named. A comprehensive, easy-to-understand survey of the derivations, interrelationships, and functions of the compound interest tables, appears in the author's textbook *Mini-Math For Appraisers*, published in 1972 by the International Association of Assessing Officers, Chicago, Illinois. The book also explains and illustrates how to use three tables to do the work of six.

Contract rent. Rent agreed upon by owner and tenant or lessor and lessee. It is rent actually stipulated, and may be greater than, less than, or equal to economic rent.

Current yield. Cash flow, after debt service (loan payments) and before income taxes. (The terms "equity dividend" and "cash throw-off to equity," which are used in some textbooks, are synonymous with *current yield* and *cash flow*.) Within the framework of mortgage-equity, the total net periodic income stream can be considered current yield on equity, if the amount of net reversion equals or exceeds the original equity or down payment. However, in the event the net reversion is less than the original equity, a portion of cash flow is attributable to a partial recovery of capital, thereby decreasing current yield on the capital investment. In a typical situation in which the net reversion exceeds the original equity, all of the cash flow can be considered current yield. Recapture of capital investment occurs at the end of the holding period. The net reversion may also include deferred yield after providing a return of the capital invested. In such a case, yield to maturity (which includes both current and deferred yield) will exceed the current yield rate. Current yield is considered to be *compoundable* by reinvestment.

Debt coverage ratio. Net annual income divided by annual debt service. For example, if net annual income is $140,000 and debt service is $100,000, the debt coverage ratio is $140,000 divided by $100,000, or 1.40. It is a measure of safety from the lender's point of view. (Refer to procedure, page 80. Also, see explanation of Item 7, "Investment Analysis" form, pages 13, 158, and 162.)

Debt service. Total loan payments made in one year.

Deferred yield. Yield generated by loan amortization and/or property appreciation. It is locked in until the time of reversion, and is thus *compounded*. As a dollar amount, it is calculated: (1) in the case of income-producing properties, by subtracting the original equity or down payment from the net reversion; and (2) in the case of nonproducing properties purchased for appreciation, by subtracting down payment, loan payments, and other holding costs from the net reversion. 1897805

Depreciation. Loss in market value for any reason. It is not to be equated with allowable depreciation used in income tax calculations.

Economic rent. The rent the property would bring if offered for rent or lease on the current market. It may correspond to contract rent or deviate from it.

Effective gross income. Estimated annual gross income, less a percentage allowance for vacancies and collection losses, plus service and miscellaneous income.

Equity. Original equity is the down payment. Equity at the end of the holding period or at any point in time is the difference between market value and loan balance.

Equity ratio: Original equity ratio is the down payment divided by the sales price. It is also 100% less the loan ratio. It is the complement of the loan ratio. For example: If sales price is $100,000 and down payment is $30,000, equity ratio is $30,000 divided by $100,000 or 30% (.30). If loan ratio is 80%, equity ratio is 100% less 80%, or 20% (.20). Terminal equity ratio may be computed in two ways: (1) It is net reversion divided by resale price or value at end of holding period. For example: At the end of a 15-year holding period, resale price is $1,000,000, and loan balance is $300,000. Net reversion is $1,000,000 less $300,000, or $700,000. Equity ratio is $700,000 divided by $1,000,000, or 70% (.70). (2) Another concept relates terminal equity or net reversion to original value. For example, property purchased for $600,000 has appreciated in a 10-year holding period to $800,000. Original loan of $400,000 has been reduced to $300,000. Terminal equity or net reversion is $800,000 less $300,000, or $500,000. Original equity ratio was $200,000 divided by $600,000 or 33%. Terminal equity ratio, as related to original value, is $500,000 divided by $600,000, or 83%. Related to resale value, it is $500,000 divided by $800,000, or 62.5%. The practical significance of an increased equity ratio is the possibility of refinancing rather than selling at the end of a given holding period.

Equity yield rate. Percent of yield to maturity on original equity or down payment. It is calculated on a combination of current yield and deferred yield. The rate of yield on equity is one of the investor's most significant considerations in decision-making. The instant mortgage-equity technique calculates the rate of yield on equity when value is known or computes an estimate of value when a rate of yield on equity is stipulated. Equity yield rate should always be calculated and expressed as an annual rate, compounded.

Expenses. Allowable expenses in an operating statement, classified as fixed, operating, and reserves for replacements. Loan payments, depreciation, and income taxes are to be excluded.

Expense ratio. Allowable expenses divided by effective gross income. The analyst should compare the reconstructed operating statement prepared for the subject property with the "norm" for the type of property in the area at a given point in time. (See suggested references, page 483.)

Factors. As used in the context of this book, factors are percents, expressed as decimals, and appear in the compound interest and annuity tables. Factors are used as multipliers or divisors to compute present or future worth of dollar values. Factors also serve as "target figures" in solving for rate or time. Multiplying or dividing by a compound interest factor either computes and adds compound interest to present worth, or it calculates and subtracts compound interest from future worth. Calculation of compound interest (the time value of money) is built into the factors. (Refer to the entry under "Compound interest and annuity tables" in this glossary.)

Feasibility study. An appraisal and analysis for investment value or value in use, in contrast to an appraisal for market value. Its purpose is a determination of value to a specific individual, rather than to persons in general. Such a study considers the client's income tax position, his personal objectives, specially tailored terms, et cetera. It frequently determines, by means of the mortgage-equity technique, ranges of value for bargaining, or ranges of potential yield on equity as the basis for decision-making.

Gross income. An estimate of gross annual income, before deductions for vacancies and collection losses or allowable expenses.

Gross rent multiplier (GRM). Sales price or value divided by gross annual income. For example, it sales price is $325,000 and gross annual income is

$50,000, the GRM is 6.5 ($325,000 ÷ $50,000.) It is a "rule of thumb" used by many investors, who set their own individual standard or derive it from the market.

Holding period. A limited term of ownership between time of purchase and resale, exchange, or refinancing of the property. It is often determined by income tax considerations. In the case of a relatively substantial loan ratio, the holding period is normally about 10 years. While this text lists precomputed Overall Rates for holding periods of 5, 10, and 15 years, interpolation by simple proportion can be made to any intermediate point in time.

Income approach. Valuation of property, based on its income-producing capabilities.

Income stream. The size, shape, and duration of net annual income generated by a property determine the measurable flow of income produced. Mortgage-equity considers the income stream to consist of two segments: (1) a level, terminal ordinary annuity or its calculated equivalent: and (2) a single terminal lump sum payment (net reversion). An estimate of value is made by dividing net annual income by the composite mortgage-equity Overall Rate.

Interest rate. A stipulated rate agreed upon by borrower and lender, or a fixed rate on a savings account. It is not to be confused with a yield rate, which is an investor's anticipated rate of return.

Investment value. Worth to an individual, considering his income tax position, special objectives, nontypical financing, et cetera. It may differ from market value, which is considered to be value to persons in general.

Inwood coefficient. The annuity factor, or Present Worth of 1 Per Period.

Lease. An agreement in writing between owner (the lessor) and tenant (the lessee), conveying to the lessee the right to the occupancy and use of property under specified terms for a stipulated period of time.

Leased fee. The lessor's interest, consisting of the rights to receive rents from the lessee and the reversionary rights of repossession of the property upon termination of the lease.

Leasehold interest. The lessee's interest, produced and measured by: (1) The excess of economic rent over contract rent, or (2) If improvements are erected by the lessee, the difference between economic rent of the total property and contract rent paid on the ground lease.

Leverage. Advantageous use of borrowed funds so as to produce a relatively high rate of yield on a comparatively low-equity investment.

Loan constant. The amount paid annually on a loan (principal and interest included) as a percent of original principal. See Supplemental Tables of Loan Constants, page 212. Also, refer to procedures, page 118.

Loan ratio. Original principal amount of a loan as a percent of value. For example, if property is purchased for $500,000 and is financed by a bank loan for $300,000, the loan ratio is 60% or .60 ($300,000 ÷ $500,000).

Loan term. Length of a loan in years.

Market value. Value to persons in general; the most probable selling price. (If the objective of valuation by mortgage-equity is to estimate market value, the analyst assumes that the property is encumbered by new typical institutional financing and that the buyer pays cash to the loan.)

Mortgage (or trust deed). Legal document making property security for the repayment of a loan, terms of which are stipulated in a promissory note.

Mortgage-equity technique. A method of converting an income stream into an indicator of value by dividing an Overall Rate into net annual income. In computing the Overall Rate, full consideration is given to loan and equity ratios, loan terms, holding period, projected appreciation or depreciation, and anticipated yield on equity. The *instant mortgage-equity technique* provides totally precomputed Overall Rates, specially designed forms, and a wide range of patterned procedures for quick calculations in income property valuation and investment analysis.

Net annual income. Annual income after allowable expenses but before debt service, income taxes, and recapture. (The term is equivalent to "Net Operating Income" or "NOI.") Net annual income is the income to be capitalized by an appropriate technique.

Net Income Multiplier. The reciprocal of the Overall Rate. Identical answers are found by multiplying net annual income by the Net Income Multiplier (NIM) or by dividing it by the Overall Rate. To illustrate: In the case study, Chapter 4, Sunset Point Apartments is valued by an Overall Rate of .106137: $240,000 ÷ .106137 = $2,261,228. The Net Income Multiplier is calculated to be 9.421785, and $240,000 × 9.421785 = $2,261,228. (Refer to the entry "Reciprocal" in the glossary.)

Overall Rate. Net annual income divided by value. It is the reciprocal of the Net Income Multiplier. The composite mortgage-equity Overall Rate has six variables built into it: the holding period, the anticipated equity yield rate, loan ratio, loan interest rate, loan term, and projected appreciation or depreciation. In different procedures of the instant mortgage-equity technique, the Overall Rate (OAR) is used as a divisor, a multiplier, and a "target figure" to perform a variety of functions. (Refer to "The Basic Five," page 46.)

Periodic Repayment (PR). The PR factor is the loan amortization factor, also known as the Partial Payment factor. At any given rate of interest, for any stipulated period of time, the PR factor multiplied by the original principal amount of a loan computes the level periodic payment (principal and interest included) to amortize a loan. Calculation of interest on a declining principal balance is built into the factor. The PR factor is the reciprocal of the Present Worth of 1 Per Period factor. It is also the Sinking Fund factor plus the interest rate.

Present worth. As an amount, present worth of an income stream or single income payment due in the future is future worth less compound interest. It is the original capital amount or value that will generate the future income stream or sum at an anticipated yield rate within a specified period of time. The present worth factors, applied as multipliers in a "discounting" process, automatically compute and subtract compound interest from the payment or payments receivable in the future so that original principal remains. Thus is the time value of money measured.

Present Worth of 1 (PW 1). The PW 1 factor, sometimes called the reversionary factor, multiplied by a single future income payment or value (a reversion), deducts compound interest from future worth and calculates "discounted" present worth. The PW 1 factor is a percent, expressed as a decimal, "1" representing one dollar.

Present Worth of 1 Per Period (PW 1/P). This is the Inwood Coefficient or annuity factor. The PW 1/P multiplied by one payment of a level terminal series of income payments computes the present worth of the future income stream at a given yield or interest rate. The mortgage-equity concept considers the investor's total income stream of future net benefits to be both an annuity (annual cash flow) and a reversion (resale value less loan balance The two present worth factors are used in the basic equation: Value = (Annuity × PW 1/P) + (Reversion × PW 1).

Recapture. A return of capital. In the residual techniques of the income approach, the allocated value of improvements (usually buildings) is calculated to be returned to or recaptured by the investor in annual increments over the estimated remaining economic life of the wasting assets. Allowance for recapture (also termed amortization) is built into the capitalization rate or is provided for in the annuity factor. The mortgage-equity technique usually provides for total recapture at the end of the holding period (time of sale, exchange, or refinancing). No allowance is made for periodic recapture. If, however, the net reversion is less than the original equity or down payment, it must be presumed that such a deficiency has been recovered periodically from cash flow, in which case yield to maturity would be less than current yield.

Reciprocal. The reciprocal of any number can be found by dividing it into 1. The product of two reciprocal numbers is always 1. Identical results are achieved by multiplying by a number or by dividing by the reciprocal of the number. Thus, one factor can substitute for another, or do the work of two. In the compound interest and annuity tables there are three sets of reciprocal factors: Future Worth of 1 and Present Worth of 1; Future Worth of 1 Per Period and Sinking Fund; Present Worth of 1 Per Period and Periodic Repayment. Example of reciprocal numbers: 5 and .2. ($1 \div 5 = .2$) Note that $8 \times 5 = 40$, and $8 \div .2 = 40$.

Reversion. A single future terminal sum or value to be received by the investor. In the case of a lease, the owner receives a reversion of the property upon expiration of the lease. In mortgage-equity concept, the *gross* reversion at the end of a holding period is the resale value. The *net* reversion is resale value less the loan balance. In this book unless otherwise specified, the term "reversion" refers to the *net* reversion. The excess of net reversion (terminal equity) over down payment (original equity) indicates equity growth (deferred yield) through appreciation in value and/or loan reduction by periodic amortization.

"Rule of 72." Divide any yield or interest rate into 72 to determine the approximate time required to double an investment at the given rate, compounded annually. The quotient gives the answer to the nearest year (not the exact month). For example, money at 8% compounded annually will double in 9 years ($72 \div 8 = 9$). Currently, most investors appear to be seeking *yield on equity* investments in real estate from 12% to 18%. A magic number seems to be 14%, an investment doubling at that rate in about 5

years. The range from 12% to 18% provides for doubling in from 4 to 6 years. In deriving or selecting Overall Rates for computations of indicated market value, the analyst will frequently work within this band.

Secondary (junior) financing. Loans secured by a mortgage or trust deed, which are subordinate to a first mortgage or trust deed. Included in this category are seconds, thirds, et cetera. In an appraisal for investment value to an individual, the analyst may show the feasibility of possibly paying a higher price in view of particularly favorable secondary financing. Procedures are given in this text for making adjustments in computing the mortgage-equity Overall Rate or calculating rate of yield on equity in a transaction that involves multiple financing.

Value. A definition most applicable to any technique of the income approach: Value is the present worth of future net benefits. Value is not necessarily equal to either *cost* or *price*. The analyst must differentiate between market value and investment value. In the mortgage-equity concept, pertinent equations of value are: Value = Income ÷ Rate, and Value of the Equity = Present Worth of the Cash Flow + Present Worth of the Net Reversion.

Yield rate. An *anticipated* rate of yield on an investment. It is not to be confused with a fixed interest rate on a loan or on a savings account. Yield rate in the mortgage-equity technique is yield on equity, not on total property value.

Yield to maturity. Yield on equity, calculated on both cash flow and net reversion. It includes current yield and deferred yield.

Now, Take Ten

Selling Real Estate by Mortgage-Equity Analysis is designed to assist the broker/counsellor in his quest for value and in his marketing program. Here is a list of suggestions, applicable to the solution of a typical problem in valuation and investment analysis:

1. Gather, evaluate, organize, and outline the pertinent data: net annual income as an ordinary annuity equivalent; loan terms; investor's projections of holding period, appreciation or depreciation, and rate of the yield on equity.
2. Spell out the specific question or questions to be answered. What are the unknowns? Is the purpose of the appraisal to estimate

market value to persons in general or investment value to a specific client?

3. If you are dealing with a lengthy, complex problem, break it up into a number of smaller, component problems.
4. Arrange the individual segments of the total problem in logical sequence.
5. Consult the "Patterned Procedures" to find the applicable method for each separate part of the problem and for the whole problem.
6. Study the suggested solution of a similar problem.
7. Select, list, and label the proper rates and factors from the Compound Interest, Supplemental, and OAR Tables.
8. Follow the applicable procedures, step by step, relating rates and factors to the data given, in order to find the unknown you are seeking.
9. Check and prove your calculations.
10. Look again at the problem and your solution. Ask yourself, "Is it a reasonable answer?"

3 Patterned Procedures

By design, methods of valuation and investment analysis in the instant mortgage-equity technique avoid complicated equations and special symbols. Instead, the steps in calculation by simple arithmetic are spelled out in proper sequence. The format for each type of computation includes three parts:

1. The procedure.
2. An illustrative problem.
3. A sample solution.

In many cases a fourth section is added: proof. Procedures could be expressed in equation form, but that phase will be left to the analyst as an optional but unnecessary do-it-yourself project.

The following sequence in studying a procedure is suggested. First, read the sample problem; then go back to the procedure itself and relate each step to the calculations in the suggested solution. Check the computations made and check each factor and rate used against those in the tables.

The number of mortgage-equity procedures may seem formidable (there are about seventy), and some of the multistep methods may appear complex. However, the basic uses of the technique are short, simple, and direct.

In making the more difficult calculations and detailed analyses, don't attempt to memorize the methods—just turn to the "Ready Reference Roster"to find the patterned procedure you need when you need it. The roster can serve as a guide and a reminder.

Procedures are arrayed under five general headings: Income, Rate, Value, Miscellaneous, and Nonproducing Properties. The arrangement may be to a great extent arbitrary and artificial. A few broad labels were selected primarily for purposes of organization. Specific procedures have been grouped under classifications to which they relate directly. The categories are closely interrelated and overlapping. For example, many of the procedures shown under "Rate" could have been listed under "Value"; for a prime function of an Overall Rate is a calculation of a value indicator.

43

Meet I-R-V

I-R-V (Income, Rate, and Value) constitute a triad basic to mortgage-equity calculations in the patterned procedures which follow. A simple diagram, which might serve as a memory-jogger, demonstrates meaningful relationships.

I-R-V

If you will equate the short, horizontal line in the triangle with a division sign, the vertical line with a multiplication sign, and block out the one unknown, you have the equation for it; that is:

$$I = R \times V$$
$$R = I \div V$$
$$V = I \div R$$

(Don't listen to the critic who says the author inserted the device as his monogram or coat-of-arms, just because his friends call him "Irv.")

By way of illustration, the same figures will be used in the three equations:

If property Value is known to be $200,000 and capitalization Rate is .105:

> Income = Rate × Value
> = .105 × $200,000
> = $21,000

If Value is known ($200,000) and Income is given ($21,000):

> Rate = Income ÷ Value
> = $21,000 ÷ $200,000
> = .105

If Income is known ($21,000) and capitalization Rate is given (.105):

> Value = Income ÷ Rate
> = $21,000 ÷ .105
> = $200,000

In the mortgage-equity technique, the Overall Rate (OAR) is used for Rate (R).

The IRV equation of value leads to another, the VIF equation, in which "F" represents a factor:

$$V = I \times F$$

To illustrate, we will value a lease that runs for 15 years and pays $12,000 a year net, using a yield rate of 10%. The Present Worth of 1 Per Period (PW 1/P) at 10% for 15 years is 7.606080.

> Value = Income × Factor
> = $12,000 × 7.606080
> = $91,273

By expansion of the VIF equation, comes the formula with many applications in mortgage-equity:

> Value = (Net Annuity × PW 1/P) + (Net Reversion × PW 1)

"I" for Income is segregated into the net annuity or cash flow (net annual income less debt service), and the net reversion (resale value less loan balance). "V" represents value of the equity, not total property value. The equation is a mathematical statement of the definition: Value is the present worth of future net benefits. For an illustration refer to the valuation and analysis of Village Square, in Chapter 1. Note particularly Item 15 of the "Investment Analysis."

Value of the Equity = (Net Annuity × PW 1/P) + (Net Reversion × PW 1)
= ($43,258 × 4.833227) + ($995,539 × .226684)
= $209,076 + $225,673
= $434,749 (corresponding precisely to the amount of down payment)

The Basic Five

As a guide to the beginner in the mortgage-equity technique, the writer suggests an initial study program that uses the preceding equations and covers five fundamental procedures only:

1. *Testing value or list price* by calculating *required income* (pages 61 to 64). The student uses a precomputed OAR as a *multiplier* in the simple procedure: Income = Rate × Value.
2. Finding *rate of yield on equity* by calculating an OAR and matching it in the OAR Tables (pages 81 and 82). The Overall Rate is used as a *target figure*: Rate = Income ÷ Value.
3. Determining the *percent of appreciation* required to produce a given rate of yield on equity by calculating an Overall Rate and matching it in the OAR Tables (pages 106 and 107). Here, too, the OAR is used as a *target figure*: Rate = Income ÷ Value.
4. Calculating an estimate of *market value* or *investment value* by selecting an OAR from the tables and using it as a *divisor*: Value = Income ÷ Rate (pages 98 to 100).
5. Preparing a 15-point *investment analysis* (pages 150 and 151, and 155 to 161).

Use Your Tools

Selling Real Estate by Mortgage-Equity Analysis should be considered as a tool rather than a mere textbook. The cutting edges of the tool consist of the "Tables" and the "Patterned Procedures."

Match your problem or segment of a problem with a related procedure listed in the "Ready Reference Roster," then follow the pattern. Simple methods can produce sophisticated results.

Ready Reference Roster

INCOME

RATE

Overall Rates In Valuation

Equity Yield Rates in Investment Analysis

VALUE

MISCELLANEOUS PROCEDURES

Mortgage-Equity Procedures Outlined and Illustrated

INCOME

"Net Operating Income (NOI) is the basic building block in income capitalization analysis. It is the *I* in virtually every variant form of income capitalization seeking property value as the final result. . . . It is a modified or 'stabilized' cash flow forecast of what the property is capable of generating for its ownership, before deducting mortgage debt service if cash flow to the investor is needed, and before deducting any charge for capital recovery if the total return *on* the investment in the property is required." So writes William N. Kinnard, Jr. in his widely accepted textbook *Income Property Valuation.**

Selling Real Estate by Mortgage-Equity Analysis is a *specialized* book of procedures and tables related to valuation and analysis by the *instant mortgage-equity* technique. Therefore, the writer will make no attempt to expand the book into a comprehensive text on appraisal in general, on all methods and techniques of the income approach in particular, or even on detailed aspects of gathering and processing income and expense data. It is presumed that the reader has sufficient background in prior study and experience to prepare realistic operating statements of income and expenses for properties being analyzed. For specific assistance in this area, note the list of suggested references at the end of the book.

The Operating Statement

Here is a review in outline form of steps to be followed in processing income to the point at which it can be capitalized:

Income Property Valuation, by William N. Kinnard, Jr., copyright 1971 by D.C. Heath and Company.

Gross Annual Income

− Vacancy and Collection Losses

= Rental Collections

+ Service and Other Income

= Effective Gross Income

− Allowable Expenses:

Fixed

Operating

Reserves

= Net Annual Income

The old saw, "Watch out for that top step—it's a humdinger" is probably pertinent here. However, it must be followed by the admonition, "Watch out for *the bottom line*." It is most critical in the valuation of income-producing properties. A few "do's and dont's" may serve as relevent reminders:

— Do reconstruct the owner's operating statement. (Examples are given on pages 478 to 482.)
— Don't include these items as expenses: loan payments (exclude both principal and interest), depreciation, income taxes, or capital expenditures.
— Do include a management fee, even though the property is being managed by the owner.
— Do include reserves for replacement of rapidly depreciating items, such as appliances.
— Don't duplicate reserve allowances by including the same replacement items under operating expenses.
— Do make sufficient allowance for utility costs, which may be increasing at an accelerated rate.
— Do include an allowance for vacancies and collection losses. (If the owner boasts of 100% occupancy and says he never has a vacancy, chances are the rents are too low.)
— Do compare the expense ratio for the subject property with typical expense ratios as given in various trade publications. (See references, page 483.) If, for example, the analyst calculates an expense ratio of 28% for the subject property and the industry as a whole indicates an expense ratio of 45%, he should look for a significant omission or underestimation.
— Don't prepare the income-expense statement on the basis of present management, unless it appears to be typically good management.

Correct inequities that may be attributable to either inferior or superior management.

— Do study the leases and tenancy agreements. Determine responsibilities of both owner and tenant.

— Do analyze quality, quantity, shape, and durability of the income stream for the duration of the holding period.

— Don't base the reconstructed operating statement entirely on past history of the property. Project into the future, remembering that value is the present worth of *future* net benefits.

Processing the Income Stream to an Ordinary Annuity Equivalent

If the shape of the projected income stream does not appear to be a true annuity but shows some irregularity or special characteristic, don't "average" it. Averages disregard the time value of money. (Averages can be both deceiving and dangerous, as in the case of the government statistician who, it is reported, drowned, wading across a river with an average depth of two feet.) Instead of averaging the income stream, convert it to a level ordinary annuity equivalent by utilizing the following patterned procedures.

Annuity in advance:

In the case of an annuity in advance, as the name implies, payment is received at the *beginning* of each period, in contrast to the *ordinary annuity*, in which payment is received or assumed to be received at the *end* of the period. A typical annuity in advance involves a combination of a net-net-net lease, a stable tenant with a high credit rating, and medium to long term tenancy.

Month-to-month rental on such income properties as apartments should, in most circumstances, be classed as an ordinary annuity, even though paid in advance, assuming the income stream is expected to remain relatively level during a projected holding period. Maintenance costs may be irregular over the months, taxes are paid once or twice a year, and the owner cannot determine actual net income until the end of the year.

Present worth of an annuity in advance exceeds present worth of an ordinary annuity, although the dollar amount of both income streams may be identical. For example, assume terms of an annuity in advance call for payments of $20,000 net a year for ten years. The first payment, received at the *beginning* of the first year, cannot be discounted for there has been no passage of time, during which yield is generated. Each of the succeeding nine annual payments is made one year in advance. The lessor has the earning power of prepaid rent. Consideration of the time value of money indicates a higher present worth for an annuity in advance than for an ordinary annuity in which payments are received at the *end* of each period.

In valuation by mortgage-equity, the analyst should convert an annuity in advance to an ordinary annuity equivalent before capitalizing income.

- *Procedure:*
  1. a. Add 1.0 to the PW 1/P factor for the next-to-the-final period.
     b. Multiply the periodic income payment by the adjusted factor computed in *a*. The product is the present worth of the income stream.
     c. Multiply *b* by the PR factor for the full term. The product is the level ordinary annuity equivalent of the annuity in advance.
  2. (Alternate)
     a. Multiply the PW 1/P factor for the final period by 1.0 plus the interest or yield rate $(1 + i)$.
     b. Multiply the periodic income payment by the adjusted factor computed in *a*. The product is the present worth of the income stream.
     c. Multiply *b* by the PR factor for the full term. The product is the level ordinary annuity equivalent of the annuity in advance.

Problem:
A net-net-net lease specifies annual rental payments of $50,000 to be made at the beginning of each year for 15 years. At a yield rate of 12%, calculate the ordinary annuity equivalent.

Solution (Procedure 1):
a. 6.628168 + 1.0 = 7.628168   (PW 1/P, 12%, 14 years)
b. $50,000 × 7.628168 = $381,408
c. $381,408 × .146824 = $56,000   (PR, 12%, 15 years)

Solution (Procedure 2):
a. 6.810864 × 1.12 = 7.628168   (PW 1/P, 12%, 15 years)
b. $50,000 × 7.628168 = $381,408
c. $381,408 × .146824 = $56,000   (PR, 12%, 15 years)

Proof:
$56,000 × 6.810864 = $381,408   (PW 1/P, 12%, 15 years)
The present worth of an ordinary annuity of $56,000 a year for 15 years is $381,408, at a yield rate of 12%. This is identical to the present worth of the annuity in advance as calculated in *b*.

Note: The ordinary annuity equivalent of $56,000 is the adjusted net annual income figure that would be capitalized by mortgage-equity at a yield rate of 12%, assuming a 15-year holding period.

Decreasing income:

The following procedure can be used to calculate the present worth and the ordinary annuity equivalent of an income stream that the analyst estimates will decline each year by a uniform dollar amount over a stipulated period of time.

- *Procedure:*
    a. Multiply the amount of decline per period by the total number of periods.
    b. Subtract the product in *a* from the income received the first period (year).
    c. Multiply *b* by the PW 1/P factor.
    d. Subtract the PW 1/P factor from the number of periods.
    e. Multiply *d* by the amount of decline per period.
    f. Divide *e* by the yield rate.
    g. Add *c* and *f*. The sum is the present worth of the income stream.
    h. Multiply *g* by the PR factor. The product is the level ordinary annuity equivalent.

Problem:
Current net annual income of $60,000, generated by a 20-year-old apartment house, is expected to decline (straight line) at a rate of 3% or $1,800 per year for each of the next ten years. At a yield rate of 16%, compute the present worth of the income stream and calculate the level ordinary annuity equivalent.

Solution:
    a. $1,800 × 10 = $18,000
    b. $60,000 − $18,000 = $42,000
    c. $42,000 × 4.833227 = $202,996   (PW 1/P, 16%, 10 years)
    d. 10 − 4.833227 = 5.166773   (PW 1/P, 16%, 10 years)
    e. $1,800 × 5.166773 = $9,300
    f. $9,300 ÷ .16 = $58,125
    g. $202,996 + $58,125 = $261,121
    h. $261,121 × .206901 = $54,026   (PR, 16%, 10 years)

Proof:
      $54,026 × 4.833227 = $261,120   (PW 1/P, 16%, 10 years)

An ordinary annuity of $54,026 per year for 10 years has the same present worth (at a yield rate of 16%) as the declining income stream. (Adjust $1 for rounding.)

Deferred annuity:

During a fill-up or incubation period after construction of a project is completed, income may be sufficient to meet operating expenses only. Yield is deferred. Conversion to an ordinary annuity equivalent, with no delay, must be made before valuation by mortgage-equity.

- *Procedure*:
  1. a. Subtract the PW 1/P factor for the period immediately preceding the start of the annuity from the PW 1/P factor for the final period of the annuity.
     b. Multiply the periodic income payment by the adjusted factor computed in *a*. The product is the present worth of the deferred annuity.
     c. Multiply *b* by the PR factor for the full term. The product is the level ordinary annuity equivalent of the deferred annuity.
  2. (Alternate)
     a. Multiply the PW 1/P factor, selected as though there were no deferred start, by the PW 1 factor for the period immediately preceding the start of the annuity.
     b. Multiply the periodic income payment by the adjusted factor computed in *a*. The product is the present worth of the deferred annuity.
     c. Multiply *b* by the PR factor for the full term. The product is the level ordinary annuity equivalent of the deferred annuity.

Problem:
Income from a mobile home park, just completed, is expected for the next three years, to meet operating expenses only, after which stabilized net annual income is estimated to be $80,000 a year. Assume a holding period of 12 years and a yield rate of 14%. Calculate the level ordinary annuity equivalent of the deferred annuity.

Solution (Procedure 1):
(Obviously, the analyst is dealing with a nine-year annuity and a three-year deferred start):
Net annual income, years 1-3: $0
Net annual income, years 4-12: $80,000.)
a. 5.660292 − 2.321632 = 3.33866   (PW 1/P, 14%, 12 years
                                           − 3 years)

b. $80,000 × 3.33866 = $267,093
c. $267,093 × .176669 = $47,187   (PR, 14%, 12 years)

Solution (Procedure 2):
   a. 4.946372 × .674972 = 3.33866   (PW 1/P, 14%, 9 years ×
                                             PW 1, 14%, 3 years)

   b. $80,000 × 3.33866 = $267,093
   c. $267,093 × .176669 = $47,187   (PR, 14%, 12 years)

Proof:
      $47,187 × 5.660292 = $267,092   (PW 1/P, 14%, 12 years)
      It is apparent that the calculated hypothetical income stream of
      $47,187 a year for 12 years (no deferred start) has the same present
      worth at a 14% yield rate as the actual projected income stream of
      $80,000 a year for 9 years with a 3 year deferment. (Adjust $1 for
      rounding.)

Graduated annuity:

The income stream may consist of a series of step-up or step-down segments, each spanning a period of years. This is a common pattern observed
in commercial property leases. The initial level portion is valued as a
regular annuity. Each subsequent segment should be treated as an annuity
with a deferred start. The sum of the separate valuations is the present
worth of the total income stream. The level ordinary annuity equivalent is
calculated by applying the PR factor at the yield rate for the full term.

• *Procedure:*
   a. Multiply the periodic payment in the first level series of payments by
      the PW 1/P factor for the final period in the first series.
   b. Subtract the factor used in *a* from the PW 1/P factor for the final
      period in the next level series of payments.
      Use the same method in adjusting PW 1/P factors for each additional
      series of payments.
   c. Multiply the adjusted factor(s) from *b* by the periodic payment(s).
   d. Add the products calculated in *a* and *c*. The sum is the present worth
      of the total income stream.
   e. Multiply *d* by the PR factor for the total term. The product is the level
      ordinary annuity equivalent.

Problem:
A net-net-net lease on a retail store building calls for rental payments of
$40,000 a year for the first 6 years of a 20-year lease, $50,000 each of the
next 9 years, and $60,000 per year for the final 5 years. At a yield rate of

10%, calculate (1) the present worth of the lease, and (2) the level ordinary annuity equivalent.

Solution:
Note that the income stream can be broken down into three segments:
>Years 1 through 6: an ordinary annuity of $40,000 per year for 6 years.
>Years 7 through 15: an annuity of $50,000 per year for 9 years, with a 6-year deferred start.
>Years 16 through 20: an annuity of $60,000 per year for 5 years, with a 15-year deferred start.

The analyst may find it advantageous to select and list initially all compound interest factors required in the problem:
>PW 1/P, 10%, 6 years: 4.355261
>PW 1/P, 10%, 15 years: 7.606080
>PW 1/P, 10%, 20 years: 8.513564
>PR, 10%, 20 years: .117460

a. $40,000 × 4.355261 = $174,210   (PW 1/P, 10%, 6 years)
b. Adjusted factors:
>7.606080 − 4.355261 = 3.250819   (PW 1/P, 10%, 15 years − 6 years)
>8.513564 − 7.606080 = .907484   (PW 1/P, 10%, 20 years − 15 years)

c. $50,000 × 3.250819 = $162,541
>60,000 × .907484 =   54,449
d. Present worth:

Years 1-6:	$174,210
Years 7-15:	162,541
Years 16-20:	54,449
	$391,200

e. $391,200 × .117460 = $45,950   (PR, 10%, 20 years)
(The income stream has now been processed to the point at which it can be capitalized.)

Proof:
>$45,950 × 8.513564 = $391,198   (PW 1/P, 10%, 20 years)
>Present worth of the hypothetical level annuity equivalent is within $2 of the calculated present worth of the actual graduated annuity (step *d*).

Increasing income:

This procedure applies to an income stream which increases annually by a specified uniform dollar amount.

● *Procedure:*
   a. Multiply the amount of periodic increase by the total number of periods.
   b. Add the product in *a* to the income received the first period (year).
   c. Multiply *b* by the PW 1/P factor.
   d. Subtract the PW 1/P factor from the number of periods.
   e. Multiply *d* by the amount of increase per period.
   f. Divide *e* by the yield rate.
   g. Subtract *f* from *c*. The difference is the present worth of the income stream.
   h. Multiply *g* by the PR factor. The product is the level ordinary annuity equivalent.

Problem:
Net annual income of $300,000 from a new shopping center is expected to increase $50,000 a year for the next 8 years, at which time it is projected to level off at $650,000 per year. Compute the level ordinary annuity equivalent of the first eight years' income; use a 12% yield rate. (Consider income for Year 1 to be $300,000, not $350,000.)

Solution:
   a. $50,000 × 8 = $400,000
   b. $300,000 + $400,000 = $700,000
   c. $700,000 × 4.967640 = $3,477,348   (PW 1/P, 12%, 8 years)
   d. 8.0 − 4.967640 = 3.03236   (PW 1/P, 12%, 8 years)
   e. $50,000 × 3.03236 = $151,618
   f. $151,618 ÷ .12 = $1,263,483
   g. $3,477,348 − $1,263,483 = $2,213,865
   h. $2,213,865 × .201303 = $445,658   (PR, 12%, 8 years)

Proof:
   $445,658 × 4.967640 = $2,213,869   (PW 1/P, 12%, 8 years)
   The level ordinary annuity equivalent, $445,658, has the same present worth (at a yield rate of 12%) as the increasing income stream. (Compare with Step *g* and adjust $4 for rounding.)

Additional proof:

Year	Income	×	PW 1 Factor	=	Present Worth
1	$300,000	×	.892857	=	$267,857
2	350,000	×	.797194	=	279,018
3	400,000	×	.711780	=	284,712
4	450,000	×	.635518	=	285,983

5	500,000	×	.567427	=	283,714
6	550,000	×	.506631	=	278,647
7	600,000	×	.452349	=	271,409
8	650,000	×	.403883	=	262,524
					$2,213,864

Irregular income:

Net annual income may increase and/or decrease year by year with no degree of uniformity. In such a case present worth of the income stream is calculated by use of Present Worth Of 1 (PW 1) factors only. The level ordinary annuity equivalent can be computed by applying the Periodic Repayment (PR) factor.

- *Procedure:*
  a. Multiply each annual income payment by PW 1.
  b. Add the products calculated in *a*.
  c. Multiply the sum from *b* by the PR factor for the full term.

Problem:
Net annual income from residential rental property is expected to increase over the next three years, then decline the following two years because of anticipated major expenses. Projections for the five-year period are:
  Year 1: $40,000
  Year 2: 45,000
  Year 3: 47,000
  Year 4: 42,000
  Year 5: 39,000
At a yield rate of 15%, calculate (1) present worth of the income stream, and (2) the level ordinary annuity equivalent.

Solution:
  a. $40,000 × .869565 = $ 34,783   (PW 1, 15%, 1 year)
     45,000 × .756144 =   34,026   (PW 1, 15%, 2 years)
     47,000 × .657516 =   30,903   (PW 1, 15%, 3 years)
     42,000 × .571753 =   24,014   (PW 1, 15%, 4 years)
     39,000 × .497177 =   19,390   (PW 1, 15%, 5 years)
  b. Present worth: $143,116
  c. $143,116 × .298316 = $42,694   (PR, 15%, 5 years)

Proof:
     $42,694 × 3.352155 = $143,117   (PW 1/P, 15%, 5 years)

Present worth of the level ordinary annuity equivalent ($42,694) is within $1 of the present worth of the irregular income stream.

Negative income during buildup period:

Initially expenses may exceed income upon completion of such properties as office buildings, apartments, et cetera. Following an incubation period, net annual income moves out of the red into the black as occupancy builds up. A procedure follows for calculating both present worth and level ordinary annuity equivalent of the negative-positive income stream.

● *Procedure:*
    a. Calculate the present worth of the negative portion of the income stream.
    b. Calculate the present worth of the positive portion of the income stream.
    c. Subtract *a* from *b*. The difference is present worth of the total stream.
    d. Multiply *c* by the PR factor at the yield rate for the full term. The product is the level ordinary annuity equivalent.

Problem:
Income from an office building nearing completion is projected for the next 10 years as follows:

Year 1:	⟨$100,000⟩	(loss – negative income)
2:	⟨50,000⟩	(loss – negative income)
3:	100,000	
4:	250,000	
5:	375,000	
6-10:	550,000 per year	

At a yield rate of 14% calculate (1) the present worth of the income stream, and (2) the level ordinary annuity equvalent.

Solution:
Analysis indicates that income for years 1 through 5, both negative and positive, will be classified as irregular. Income for years 6 through 10 is identified as a 5-year annuity, deferred for 5 years. Present worth of the negative income should be subtracted from the present worth of the positive income to calculate present worth of the total income stream as a base for computing the level ordinary annuity equivalent.

  a. ⟨$100,000⟩ × .877193 = ⟨$87,719⟩   (PW 1, 14%, 1 year)
      ⟨50,000⟩ × .769468 = ⟨38,473⟩   (PW 1, 14%, 2 years)
                    ⟨$126,192⟩

b.

\$100,000	×	.674972	= \$67,497	(PW 1, 14%, 3 years)
250,000	×	.592080	= 148,020	(PW 1, 14%, 4 years)
375,000	×	.519369	= 194,763	(PW 1, 14%, 5 years)
550,000	×	1.783055	= 980,669	(PW 1/P, 14%, 10 years − 5 years)

$$\$1,390,949$$

c. \$1,390,949 − \$126,192 = \$1,264,757

d. \$1,264,757 × .191714 = \$242,472   (PR, 14%, 10 years)

Proof:

$242,472 × 5.216116 = \$1,264,762   (PW 1/P, 14%, 10 years)
Present worth of the level ordinary annuity equivalent is within \$5 of the present worth of the actual income stream (Step *c*).

Testing Value by Income Analysis

Income required to meet equity yield rate demands:

Arithmetic in this calculation is so simple that the analyst may possibly overlook the practical, meaningful applications of the procedure. The first of the I-R-V equations is used:

Income = Rate × Value

Income to be calculated is the net annual income the property must produce in order to justify a given value and return the rate of yield on equity desired by the investor. *Rate* in this context is the mortgage-equity OAR (Overall Rate) which has built into it six significant variables: limited holding period; specified equity yield rate; financing data—loan ratio, term, and interest rate; projected appreciation/depreciation. *Value* is given. Typically, value is a list price which is being tested. To the analyst, the procedure is more than an exercise in multiplication. His task involves three phases:

1. Computation of income required, considering the investor's expected equity yield rate (I = R × V).
2. Comparison with a realistically reconstructed operating statement of income and expenses.
3. Calculation of a justifiable offering price for the property, if income required is not being produced by the subject property (V = I ÷ R).

In Phase 1 the OAR is used as a multiplier, and in Phase 3 the same OAR will be employed as a divisor. Careful analysis should assist in supplying answers:

— Under normal management, can the property be expected to produce sufficient net income to justify the asking price and return the desired yield on equity?
— If not, what purchase price can feasibly be offered?
— If the property is purchased at the list price but net income is less than the calculated requirement, will the equity yield rate be affected adversely? To what extent?

The technique illustrated is designed to provide guidance and assistance to the broker/salesman in listing property at a fair price, in making a knowledgeable presentation to a prospective buyer, and in obtaining the acceptance of a reasonable offer which may be less than the asking price. It may also aid in arranging financing.

• *Procedure:*
Multiply value by the mortgage-equity OAR (Overall Rate).

Problem:
An investor is studying the feasibility of purchasing a commercial building listed at $4,500,000. Financing is available for 70% of value at 9% interest, on a loan to be amortized by monthly payments in 25 years. The investor anticipates stability in market value during a ten-year holding period, and desires a yield of 14% on equity.
  a. What amount of net annual (operating) income is required to meet equity yield demands?
  b. Based on a reconstructed operating statement which shows the property can be expected to generate $425,000 net income annually, calculate a reasonable offering price.

Solution:
  a. OAR: .106244
     Income required: $4,500,000 × .106244 = $478,098, say $478,000
  b. Value = Income ÷ Rate
           = $425,000 ÷ .106244
           = $4,000,226, say $4,000,000

Notes:
— Unless the subject property produces $478,000 or more in net annual income, a purchase price of $4,500,000 is not justified, if equity yield requirements are to be met.

— If the reconstructed operating statement shows an expectation of $425,000 net annual income, an offering price of $4,000,000 would be feasible.

— If the property is purchased for $4,500,000 and net income is only $425,000, the Overall Rate is lowered to .094444 ($425,000 ÷ $4,500,000); and rate of yield on equity drops to about 10.456%. (See procedure on pages 81 to 82 for calculating equity yield rate.)

— Assume that the reconstructed operating statement shows that the property can be expected to generate net annual income of $500,000. The indication now is that it appears to be a good investment, with the possibility of a yield rate somewhat in excess of 14%.

— The *reconstructed* operating statement of income and expenses, as distinguished from the owner's pro forma statement, shows economic rent; makes a proper vacancy and collection loss allowance; assumes typical management; includes all allowable expenses (fixed, operating, and reserves); and excludes such items as income taxes, loan payments, and depreciation. Total expense ratio for the subject property will be measured against the typical expense ratio for comparable properties in the area or in comparable areas.

— For purposes of comparative analysis, consider three possibilities:

	#1	#2	#3
Net Income	$478,098	$425,000	$425,000
OAR	.106244	.106244	.094444
Purchase Price	$4,500,000	$4,000,226	$4,500,000
Debt Service	$317,218	$281,987	$317,218
Cash Flow	$160,880	$143,013	$107,782
Rate of Current Yield on Equity	11.9%	11.9%	7.98%
Resale Value	$4,500,000	$4,000,226	$4,500,000
Equity Yield Rate (to Maturity)	14%	14%	10.456%

In the analysis above, holding period, financing terms, and appreciation/depreciation remain as given in the problem. Cases 1 and 2 appear favorable, in the light of the prospective purchaser's expectations. Case 3 is of questionable feasibility.

SPECIAL NOTE: The one-step procedure given can be used in establishing net-net-net rent in a sale-leaseback transaction. For example: A triple A-1 national corporation purchases a site for $1,500,000 on which it erects a building costing $5,000,000. After completion the property is offered to a real estate investor for $6,500,000 on a 30-year leaseback arrangement. The property can be financed for 75% of value on a 25-year loan at 9½%

interest. Assume the prospective purchaser projects a 15-year holding period, 0% appreciation, and a yield rate of 12%. What monthly rent would be required to produce an equity yield rate (to maturity) of 12%? To solve the problem:

Select the proper OAR: .102098. Multiply Rate by Value: .102098 × $6,500,000 = $663,637. Monthly rental: $663,737 ÷ 12 = $55,303.

RATE

Procedures follow for selecting, calculating, deriving, and adjusting two types of rates essential to the mortgage-equity technique:

1. Overall Rate.
2. Equity yield rate.

When value is unknown, income can be capitalized by the Overall Rate. Other applications of the Overall Rate (OAR) are also explained and illustrated. When value is known, the analyst may be seeking the equity yield rate: *yield to maturity* or the rate of *current yield*. Equity yield rate and Overall Rate are interrelated, for yield to maturity is one of the six components of the mortgage-equity OAR.

Overall Rates in Valuation

Precomputed OAR's

Convenient, timesaving OAR Tables of totally precomputed mortgage-equity Overall Rates furnish the key to the streamlined *instant mortgage-equity technique*. Each OAR has built into it six variables: (1) holding period, (2) equity yield rate, (3) loan ratio, (4) interest rate, (5) term, and (6) appreciation/depreciation.

If the function of the appraisal is to estimate *market value* (value to persons in general) the variables must be extracted from the market itself. Financing data is obtained from the mortgage market (local lending institutions). Actions and reactions of knowledgeable investors establish a typical holding period and determine equity yield requirements. A study of economic trends in the area in which the subject property is located provides a base for projections of appreciation or depreciation. If all six variables are market-derived, it can then be said that the mortgage-equity OAR has come from the market—not from textbook, tables, or computer.

When the analyst prepares a feasibility study to determine *investment value* for a client, the variables he uses will be based on the individual investor's special requirements, nontypical financing available to him, et cetera.

The OAR (or R) is used in three basic ways in valuation and investment analysis by the mortgage-equity technique:

1. As a *multiplier* to calculate income required to generate a specified rate of yield on equity, when testing a list price or given value. $(I = R \times V)$.
2. As a *target figure* in computing:
   a. Rate of yield on equity.
   b. Percent of appreciation required to produce a given equity yield. $(R = I \div V)$
3. As a *divisor* in estimating either *market value* or *investment value*. $(V = I \div R)$

The patterned procedures in the text explore, expand, adapt, and apply this trilogy of fundamental methods in problem solving.

Subsequent portions of this section of the book explain and illustrate:

1. *Selection* of an appropriate Overall Rate from the OAR Tables.
2. *Interpolation* (by simple proportion) within the tables to adjust for differing variables.
3. *Extension* by extrapolation in going outside the range of the tables.

Selection of an OAR from the Tables:

- *Procedure:*
  a. Match three variables from the problem with three in the upper left hand corner of a page of Overall Rates: (1) holding period, (2) equity yield rate, (3) loan ratio. (These three variables identify the proper page.)
  b. Proceed down the left vertical column to the appropriate loan term in years.
  c. Move to the right across the page to the relevant loan interest rate column.
  d. Select the OAR from the line that matches the percent of appreciation/depreciation projected. (Application of a straight edge will assist in adhering to the correct horizontal line).

Problem:
Find the precomputed OAR's for the following sets of variables:

	1	2	3	4
Holding Period:	10 yrs.	5 yrs.	15 yrs.	10 yrs.
Equity Yield Rate:	14%	10%	12%	20%
Loan Ratio:	80%	60%	75%	70%
Loan Term:	20 yrs.	15 yrs.	40 yrs.	30 yrs.
Loan Interest Rate:	9½%	10%	8%	8½%
Appreciation/Depreciation:	+10%	0%	−10%	+20%

Solution:

	OAR	Page
1	.100744	332
2	.099010	232
3	.093266	409
4	.113811	354

Notes:
— It is suggested that the student take time to observe the range, scope, and sequence of variables for ease and accuracy in selecting OAR's from the Tables.
— Rates for a 5-year holding period appear only in the first third of the OAR Tables, followed by 10-year holding period in the middle third, then 15-year holding period in the remainder.
— In each of the three holding period sections note an upward progression of equity yield rates and loan ratios, from 4% equity yield rate and 60% loan ratio up to 50% equity yield rate and 90% loan ratio.
— Equity yield rate, loan ratio, and appreciation/depreciation are given as *decimals*; e.g., a loan ratio of 80% is expressed as ".800." Note that an equity yield rate of ".040" is 4%, not 40%.
— Do not confuse loan "interest rate" with "equity yield rate."
— On every page of the OAR Tables appears a nine-point scale of appreciation/depreciation for each loan term and loan interest rate. Stability (no change in property value during the holding period) is indicated by the "0.00" entry. Figures *below* this line represent depreciation, from −10% down to −40%. Entries *above* the "0.00" line indicate appreciation from 10% up to 40%. A plus sign is understood for appreciation, although it is not given in the printout.
— Convenience afforded by the tables should be matched by care in selecting the OAR. It might be well to follow the motto of an old world cabinet maker, a master craftsman: "Measure twice—saw once." To avoid errors, check and double-check the OAR selected before applying it as a multiplier, target figure, or divisor.
— The following form can serve as a check list of data to be gathered by

the analyst. The Overall Rate selected or calculated must have the six significant components built in. As an example, data from the first set of variables in the problem have been entered.

**Data Required
In the Computation or Selection of
Mortgage-Equity Overall Rate**

Holding Period:	10 years
Equity Yield Rate:	14%
Mortgage Specifications:	
Loan Ratio:	80%
Interest Rate:	9½%
Term:	20 years
Appreciation/Depreciation:	+10%
Overall Rate:	.100744

Interpolation in the OAR Tables:

The OAR Tables can be expanded almost indefinitely, interpolating by simple proportion. Results are usually accurate to about four decimal places. Calculations are thus approximate, not precise to six places, because the progression of compound interest is curvilinear rather than straight line. Rounding the OAR to four places is close enough for most calculations, considering that the value conclusion will also be rounded to a reasonable figure. A few guidelines in interpolation may be of assistance:

— Determine by observation the variable for which interpolation is required, and whether interpolation will be made to a midpoint or to other than a midpoint.
— Interpolate within as narrow a range as possible, for greater accuracy. For example, in dealing with a holding period of 12 years, interpolate between OAR's for 10 and 15 years, not 5 and 15 years.
— Check to see that the OAR calculated by interpolation is *within* the range of the OAR's that establish the upper and lower limits. If the Rate is *outside* the range, locate an error in procedure.
— By observation, verify that the OAR determined by interpolation is closer to the limit to which it should most nearly correspond (if interpolation is not made to a midpoint). To illustrate: If interpolation is made for Appreciation of 18%, see that the OAR calculated is closer to the OAR for 20% than for 10% Appreciation.

— In a given situation interpolation can be related to any of the six variables that differ from the precomputed OAR's: holding period; equity yield rate; loan ratio, term, interest rate; and appreciation/depreciation.

— When several variables differ, the analyst may dispense with interpolation and calculate a mortgage-equity Overall Rate from the Compound Interest Tables (see procedure, page 73.) It is possible, however, to make multiple interpolation with a surprising degree of accuracy. An example of triple interpolation appears on pages 472 and 473.

● *Procedure:*
1. If Overall Rate to be calculated lies at a point midway between two given OAR's:
   a. Add the two OAR's that bracket the unknown subject OAR.
   b. Divide *a* by 2. The quotient is the OAR sought.

Problem:
Calculate by interpolation the OAR for which the following variables are given: 10-year holding period, 16% equity yield rate, 75% loan ratio, 25-year loan term, 9¾% loan interest rate, 10% appreciation.

Solution:
   a. OAR at 10% loan interest rate: .111662
      OAR at 9½% loan interest rate: .108198
                                            .219860
   b. .21986 ÷ 2 = .10993
   The rationale is that since 9¾% is midway between 9½% and 10%, the OAR will also be at midpoint.

2. If Overall Rate to be calculated lies at a point other than midway between the closest given OAR's:
   a. Find the difference between the upper and lower limits that determine the range within which to interpolate.
   b. Calculate the difference between the nonmatching variable in the problem and the lower limit of the range.
   c. Divide *b* by *a*.
   d. Locate the OAR's for the limits established in *a* and compute the difference (distance) between them.
   e. Multiply *c* by *d*.
   f. Add *e* to the OAR for the lower limit of the range.
   The sum is the OAR sought.

Problem:

Given:

      Holding period: 7 years

      Equity yield rate: 14%

      Financing data: 80% loan ratio, 20 year term, 81/2% interest

      Appreciation: 0%

Solution:

    a. 10 years − 5 years = 5 years

    b. 7 years − 5 years = 2 years

    c. 2 ÷ 5 = .4, or 40%

    d. OAR for 10 year holding period: .098897

       OAR for 5 year holding period: − .096942

                                            .001955

    e. .4 × .001955 = .000782

    f. .096942 + .000782 = .097724

Note: As 7 is 40% of the distance between 5 and 10 it is assumed that the OAR for a 7-year holding period will also be 40% of the difference between or distance between the OAR's for 5-year and 10-year holding periods. The OAR to be calculated will be either 40% of the way up from the 5-year OAR toward the 10, or 60% of the way down from the 10 toward the 5. *Simple proportion* are the significant words in this procedure.

Extension of the OAR Tables:

The OAR Tables can be extended beyond their existing range by *extrapolation*. If the analyst *interpolates* to calculate an Overall Rate, he stays within the bounds of the OAR Tables. If he *extrapolates*, he goes outside the range. Procedures are outlined and illustrated for three extensions of the OAR Tables, to adjust for:

    1. A 40-year loan term (Holding period of 5 or 10 years).

    2. A loan ratio of 50%.

    3. A loan ratio of 100% (no down payment).

Calculation by extrapolation is approximate, not precise. However, it is usually accurate to 3 or 4 decimal places—close enough for most practical work. The writer suggests that when an OAR computed by extrapolation is rounded, it should be rounded *up*. A check on relative accuracy appears in each procedure that follows.

- *Procedure:*
  1. For a 40-year loan term:
     a. Subtract the OAR for a 30-year loan term from the OAR for a 25-year loan term.
     b. Subtract the difference found in *a* from the OAR for a 30-year loan term. Difference is the OAR for a 40-year loan term.

Problem:

Calculate by extrapolation a mortgage-equity OAR based on these variables:

Holding period: 10 years

Equity yield rate: 15%

Financing:

Loan ratio: 90%

Loan term: 40 years, monthly payments to amortize

Interest rate: 9%

Appreciation: 0%

Solution:

a. OAR, 25-year loan term: .097982
   OAR, 30-year loan term: − .097214
   _____
                             .000768

b. OAR, 30-year loan term: .097214
                             − .000768
   _____
   OAR, 40-year loan term: .096446

Notes:
— Precomputed OAR's for 40-year loan term and a 15-year holding period, are given in the OAR Tables.
— A word of caution: Do not extrapolate to a 40-year loan term by extending the difference between 20 and 30 years. Because of the curvilinear progression of compound interest, the difference in the OAR between a 30- and a 40-year loan term is almost identical to the difference between a 25- and a 30-year loan term.
— Check on relative accuracy: By precise calculation, using the procedure given on page 73, the 40-year OAR is .096475. By way of comparison, in capitalizing net annual income of $120,000 by the extrapolated OAR of .096446, indicated value is $1,244,220. Using the same illustration, capitalized value by the precise rate of .096475 is $1,243,845. The slight difference of $375 would be eliminated in "rounding" to a significant value conclusion.

2. For a 50% loan ratio:
   a. Subtract the OAR for a 70% loan ratio from the OAR for a 60% loan ratio.
   b. Add the difference calculated in *a* to the OAR for the 60% loan ratio. The sum is the OAR for a 50% loan ratio.

Problem:
Calculate by extrapolation a mortgage-equity OAR based on these data:
   Holding period: 10 years
   Equity yield rate: 14%
   Financing:
      Loan ratio: 50%
      Loan term: 20 years, monthly payments to amortize
      Interest rate: 9%
   Appreciation: 20%

Solution:
   a. OAR, 60% loan ratio: .101447
      OAR, 70% loan ratio: − .096746
                               .004701
   b. OAR, 60% loan ratio: .101447
                             + .004701
      OAR, 50% loan ratio: .106148, round to .10615

Note: By precise calculation (see procedure, page 73) the OAR for a 50% loan ratio, based on variables given, is .1061716, compared to the extrapolated rate of .10615. Capitalization of $100,000 net annual income by the two OAR's would show an insignificant difference of $192 in calculated value.

3. For a 100% loan ratio:
   a. Subtract the OAR for a 90% loan ratio from the OAR for an 80% loan ratio.
   b. Subtract the difference calculated in *a* from the OAR for a 90% loan ratio. The difference is the OAR for a loan ratio of 100%.

Problem:
Owner of commercial property agrees to sell with no down payment required. The full purchase price will be carried by the seller at 9% interest, monthly payments to amortize in 20 years. By extrapolation, calculate a mortgage-equity Overall Rate, based on the financing data given (including 100% loan ratio) and on these projections: 25% equity yield rate, 10-year

holding period, and 0% appreciation. Net annual income is estimated to be $7,940. Capitalize income by the OAR calculated.

Solution:
  a. OAR, 80% loan ratio: .129403
     OAR, 90% loan ratio: − .114328
                               .015075
  b. OAR, 90% loan ratio: .114328
                              − .015075

     OAR, 100% loan ratio: .099253,   round to .09926
     Indicated value: $7,940 ÷ .09926 = $80,000 (rounded)

Notes:
  — Precise calculation gives an OAR of .099294 in this problem. Slight difference in calculated value using this rate instead of the extrapolated rate would be negligible.
  — Refer to pages 476 to 478 for a complete 15-point investment analysis of the subject property. The analysis shows annual debt service of $8,637, which results in a negative cash flow of $697 per year ($8,637 − $7,940). The purchaser goes into the transaction with no down payment and builds up an equity by making out-of-pocket expenditures to compensate for the difference between loan payments and net income.

OAR's Calculated from the Compound Interest Tables

The three procedures that follow in this section, by which a mortgage-equity Overall Rate can be calculated from the Compound Interest Tables, are based on the equation:

  Value of the Equity = [(Net Annual Income
                         − Debt Service) × PW 1/P]
           + [(Resale Value − Loan Balance) × PW 1]

Abbreviated, the equation is:

  V = (Net Annuity × PW 1/P) + (Net Reversion × PW 1)

These equations are simply an expansion of the definition: Value is the present worth of future net benefits.
  Probably in most problems of valuation and analysis by the mortgage-

equity technique Overall Rates can be selected from the OAR Tables. No calculation, adjustment, interpolation, nor extension may be required. However, in special situations involving several variables that differ from the precomputed tables, the analyst may go the longer route and calculate a precise Overall Rate by the procedures outlined and illustrated.

The first procedure was followed in programming by Fortran the EDP printout of OAR Tables in the text. This pattern can be used by the analyst in building mortgage-equity into a desk-top programmable calculator. The next procedure relates to property financed by more than one loan. The last procedure should be employed in calculating an OAR when the loan term is shorter than the holding period.

OAR, one loan only:

● *Procedure:*

Steps in Computation	Factor Selection		
	Rate	Term	Period
a. Multiply Loan Ratio by Loan Constant.	Interest	Total Loan Term	Monthly
b. Multiply *a* by adjusted PW 1/P.	Interest	Total Loan Term Less Holding Period	Monthly ÷ 12
c. Express projected resale value as a percent of purchase price and subtract *b*.			
d. Multiply *a* by PW 1/P.	Equity Yield	Holding Period	Annual
e. Multiply *c* by PW 1.	Equity Yield	Holding Period	Annual
f. Subtract *e* from *d*.			
g. Add Equity Ratio to *f*.			
h. Divide *g* by PW 1/P. (Quotient is the Overall Rate.)	Equity Yield	Holding Period	Annual

Problem:
Given:
Loan specifications:
Loan ratio: 72%
Interest rate: 9½%
Term: 23 years
Holding period: 9 years
Anticipated depreciation: 12%
Equity yield rate: 13%
Calculate the mortgage-equity Overall Rate.

Solution:

   a. Loan Constant: $12 \times .00893 = .10716$ (PR, 8½%, 276 months)
      $.72 \times .10716 = .0771552$
   b. $92.732722 \div 12 = 7.7277268$ (PW 1/P, 9½%, 168 months)
      $.0771552 \times 7.7277268 = .5962343$
   c. $1.0 - .12 = .88$
      $.88 - .5962343 = .2837657$
   d. $.0771552 \times 5.131655 = .395934$ (PW 1/P, 13%, 9 years)
   e. $.2837657 \times .332885 = .094461345$ (PW 1, 13%, 9 years)
   f. $.395934 - .094461345 = .301472655$
   g. $.28 + .301472655 = .581472655$
   h. $.581472655 \div 5.131655 = .113311$ (PW 1/P, 13%, 9 years)

Note: A play-by-play running commentary related to both procedure and illustrative problem follows, by way of further explanation:

   a. The loan constant can be calculated by multiplying the monthly PR factor by 12. PR factor at 9½% for 276 months or 23 years is .00893. Supplemental Tables of Loan Constants in the text are not used because the loan term does not correspond to the precomputed loan constants.
   b. PW 1/P factor is selected at the loan interest rate for the number of loan periods remaining unpaid at the end of the holding period. (loan term is 276 months; holding period, 9 years or 108 months: $276 - 108 = 168$). PW 1/P at 9½% for 168 months is adjusted by dividing it by 12.
   c. Purchase price or value is expressed as 100%, 1.0 being the decimal equivalent. A specified percent of appreciation should be added; or the indicated depreciation, subtracted: $1.0 - .12 = .88$. This calculation says that if 12% depreciation is projected, resale value will be 88% of purchase price. (If 12% *appreciation* were anticipated, the calculation would be $1.0 + .12$, or 1.12.)
  d., e. PW 1/P and PW 1 factors are selected from the *Annual* Compound Interest Tables at the equity yield rate for the term of the holding period.
   f. Equity ratio equals 100% less loan ratio. Here it is $1.0 - .72$, or .28 expressed as a decimal.
   h. OAR, as calculated, has built into it the six significant variables from the problem.

OAR, multiple financing:

- *Procedure:*

Steps in Computation	Factor Selection		
	Rate	Term	Period
a. Multiply each Loan Ratio by its corresponding Loan Constant.	Interest	Total Loan Term	Monthly
b. Multiply each product in *a* by its corresponding adjusted PW 1/P.	Interest	Total Loan Term Less Holding Period	Monthly ÷ 12
c. Express projected resale value as a percent of purchase price and subtract the sum of the products calculated in *b*.			
d. Multiply the sum of the products calculated in *a* by PW 1/P.	Equity Yield	Holding Period	Annual
e. Multiply *c* by PW 1.	Equity Yield	Holding Period	Annual
f. Subtract *e* from *d*.			
g. Add Equity Ratio to *f*.			
h. Divide *g* by PW 1/P. (Quotient is the Overall Rate.)	Equity Yield	Holding Period	Annual

Problem:

A commercial building can be financed partially by a first mortgage for 60% of value at 9% interest, monthly payments to amortize in 25 years. The seller will carry a second mortgage for 25% of value at 8½% interest for 15 years, monthly payments to amortize. Assume 10% appreciation during a 10-year holding period. Net annual income is $96,000. The prospective purchaser anticipates an equity yield rate of 20%. Based on the problem data, compute the mortgage-equity Overall Rate and the indicated property value.

Solution:

a. 1st: .60 × .100704 = .0604224
   2nd: .25 × .118169 = .02954225
b. 1st: 98.593409 ÷ 12 = 8.2161174   (PW 1/P, 9%, 180 months)
   .0604224 × 8.2161174 = .4964375
   2nd: 48.741183 ÷ 12 = 4.06176525   (PW 1/P, 8½%, 60 months)
   .02954225 × 4.06176525 = .1199937
c. .4964375 + .1199937 = .6164312
   1.1 − .6164312 = .4835688
d. .0604224 + .02954225 = .08996465
   .08996465 × 4.192472 = .37717428   (PW 1/P, 20%, 10 years)
e. .4835688 × .161506 = .07809926   (PW 1, 20%, 10 years)

f. .37717428 − .07809926 = .299075

g. .15 + .299075 = .449075

h. .449075 ÷ 4.192472 = .1071146   (PW 1/P, 20%, 10 years)

Indicated Value: $96,000 ÷ .1071146 = $896,236 (unrounded)

OAR, holding period exceeding loan term:

- *Procedure:*

(The preceding procedures relate to problems in which loan term(s) equal or exceed the holding period. Use this procedure to calculate the OAR if loan term is shorter than the holding period.)

  a. Multiply loan ratio by loan constant.
  b. Express resale value projected as a percent of purchase price.
  c. Multiply *a* by the PW 1/P annual factor at the equity yield rate for the term of the loan.
  d. Multiply *b* by the annual PW 1 factor at the equity yield rate for the term of the holding period.
  e. Subtract *d* from *c*.
  f. Add equity ratio to *e*.
  g. Divide *f* by the annual PW 1/P factor at the equity yield rate for the term of the holding period. Quotient is the OAR.

Problem:

Income property can be financed for 60% of value at 9% interest, monthly payments to amortize in 8 years. Calculate a mortgage-equity Overall Rate, based on the loan data given and on the prospective purchaser's projections of a 12-year holding period, 14% equity yield rate, and 10% depreciation in property value within the holding period. Capitalize net annual income of $100,000 by the OAR.

Solution:

  a. Loan Constant: 12 × .01465 = .1758   (PR, 9%, 96 months)

  .60 × .1758 = .10548

  b. 1.0 − .10 = .90

  c. .10548 × 4.638864 = .489307   (PW 1/P, 14%, 8 years)

  d. .90 × .207559 = .186803   (PW 1, 14%, 12 years)

  e. .489307 − .186803 = .302504

  f. .40 + .302504 = .702504

  g. .702504 ÷ 5.660292 = .1241109   (PW 1/P, 14%, 12 years)

  Indicated Value: $100,000 ÷ .1241109 = $805,731 (unrounded)

OAR's from the Market

An Overall Rate can be derived from the market (which is the supreme source) by careful analysis of sales prices, rents, vacancies, and expenses, gathered from recent sales of comparable properties in the area. The Overall Rate for each property is found by dividing net annual income by the adjusted sales price (Rate = Income ÷ Value). Many raw sales prices require no adjustment and are good indicators of value. Some, however, must be adjusted for unusual terms and conditions, excess land included in the sale, et cetera.

Overall Rates, calculated separately for each sale, will vary, thus establishing a range of rates. If the sales are truly comparable, the range will probably be a rather narrow one. The analyst must exercise judgment in deciding on a reasonable point within the range. When this is done he has an Overall Rate derived from the market, by which to value the subject property.

An Overall Rate extracted from the market can be converted to an equity yield rate (yield to maturity), as shown on pages 91 and 92. It can then be said that the equity yield rate has also been derived from the market. Rate of current yield on equity may also be drawn from the market (refer to procedure, pages 96 and 97).

- *Procedure:*
    a. Analyze sales, rents, and expenses of comparable properties.
    b. Calculate the Overall Rate for each comparable.
       (Rate = ÷ Value.)
    c. Determine a reasonable point *within* the range of rates found in *b* to arrive at a market-derived Overall Rate.
    d. Value the subject property by the Overall Rate from *c*.
       (Value = Income ÷ Rate.)

Problem:
Your approach to valuing the Loma Vista Apartments is to capitalize income by an Overall Rate derived from the market. The property is located in a stable multifamily neighborhood. You find four similar properties in the general area that have sold recently. Each is comparable to the subject property in age, quality of construction, type, condition, and location. Size varies from 50 to 70 rental units. Sales have been verified and sales prices adjusted if required. Data has been gathered on rents, vacancies, and expenses. Operating statements have been carefully reconstructed. You have processed net annual income produced by the subject property to be a level ordinary annuity equivalent of $74,400. The following

solution displays your work in deriving an Overall Rate from comparables in the market and in valuing Loma Vista Apartments by capitalizing income.

a.

OAR From Market

Sale Number	I	II	III	IV
Date of Sale	3/10/75	7/1/75	4/25/75	8/17/75
Location	Brookside	College Heights	Palisades	Glenview
Adjusted Sales Price	925,000	650,000	840,000	780,000
Gross Income	168,000	122,700	155,000	147,600
Effective Gross @ 5% Vacancy Factor	159,600	116,565	147,250	140,220
Expenses or Exp. Ratio	63,900	49,065	61,250	59,000
Net Income	95,700	67,500	86,000	81,220
General Comparability	Good	Good	Fair	Good
OAR	.10346	.10385	.10238	.10413

b. OAR, Sale I: $95,700 ÷ $925,000 = .10346
OAR, Sale II: 67,500 ÷ 650,000 = .10385
OAR, Sale III: 86,000 ÷ 840,000 = .10238
OAR, Sale IV: 81,220 ÷ 780,000 = .10413

c. OAR's range from .10238 to .10413. Sale III appears to be less comparable to the subject property than are Sales I, II, and IV. The range can be narrowed to .10346 to .10413. As a matter of appraisal judgment, you decide that the market has dictated an Overall Rate of .1038.

d. Indicated value of Loma Vista Apartments:
$74,400 ÷ .1038 = $716,763, say $716,760

Special Capitalization Rates

Procedures are given for computing capitalization rates based on two special considerations:

1. *Current yield requirements.* An investor may demand a specified rate of cash flow (cash on cash) regardless of equity buildup or deferred yield.

2. *Debt coverage ratio requirements.* The lender may stipulate a precise ratio to provide a minimum safety margin.

Overall capitalization rates can be calculated to meet both conditions, as shown in the subsequent patterned procedures. The first is shaped by financing terms and after debt service cash flow. The second is based solely on financing terms and ratio of net income to debt service. Neither rate computed can be classed by strict interpretation as a mortgage-equity Overall Rate. However, they are related to mortgage-equity, and in some cases may coincide with or approximate a mortgage-equity OAR. Both procedures can be utilized by the real estate broker/analyst in working with and educating a prospective purchaser, and in negotiating suitable financing terms with a lender.

It must be emphasized that the patterned procedures in the text provide specialized *tools* in valuation and investment analysis—tools to be applied with discretion and skill. They should not be regarded as constituting easy answers.

OAR, based on current yield (cash flow) requirements:

● *Procedure:*
   a. Multiply loan ratio by loan constant.
   b. Multiply equity ratio by desired current yield rate.
   c. Add *a* and *b*.

Problem:
The Uppin Arms apartment house can be financed at 9% for a term of 15 years, monthly payments to amortize. Loan commitment is based on 70% of value. Net annual income is calculated to be a level ordinary annuity equivalent of $72,000. The prospective investor's prime consideration is a required current yield on equity of 10%, after debt service. Calculate an overall capitalization rate and indicated property value.

Solution:
   a. $.70 \times .121712 = .0852$
   b. $.30 \times .10 \quad\;\; = \underline{.03}$
   c. Rate: $\qquad\qquad .1152$
      Indicated Value: $\$72,000 \div .1152 = \$625,000$

Proof:
   Principal amount of loan: $70 \times \$625,000 = \$437,500$
   Debt Service: $.121712 \times \$437,500 = \$53,250$ (rounded)

Cash flow: $72,000 − $53,250 = $18,750
Equity (down payment): .30 × $625,000 = $187,500
Rate of current yield on equity: $18,750 ÷ $187,500 = 10%

Notes:
— The preceding procedure relates particularly to the investor who says, "I am interested in current yield only (cash on cash). Forget about equity buildup, debt reduction, and appreciation." The analyst can go along with him in valuing the property by an adjusted band-of-investment capitalization rate, calculated by weighted average, as illustrated. However, he should then proceed to show the client that in a representative transaction, there is more to be gained than merely current yield.
— In the illustrative problem, if Uppin Arms were held for 10 years, the rate of yield to maturity would normally exceed the 10% rate of current yield by a significant figure:
  • If 20% appreciation were projected and realized, yield to maturity would be 18%.
  • At 0% appreciation, yield to maturity would be nearly 16%.
  • At 20% depreciation, yield to maturity would be about 13%.
  (See procedure on calculating rate of yield on equity, pages 81 to 84.)
— The property would have to suffer depreciation of nearly 36% within a 10-year holding period, wiping out all equity buildup, if yield to maturity were only 10% (corresponding to the rate of current yield). (Refer to procedure, pages 110 and 111.)
— Such an analysis as shown here could assist in educating the client and might prove to be an effective sales tool, a possible "clincher."

OAR, based on debt coverage ratio requirements:

• *Procedure:*
  a. Multiply loan ratio by loan constant.
  b. Multiply *a* by debt coverage ratio.

Problem:
A bank will make the following loan commitment on a commercial building offered for sale: loan ratio, 70%; interest rate, 10%; and term, 25 years, monthly payments to amortize. The lender stipulates a debt coverage ratio of 1.3. (Net annual income must be 130% of annual debt service.) The analyst has calculated net annual income produced by the property to be $58,000. Based on the given data and requirements, determine (1) the Overall Capitalization Rate, and (2) the indicated property value.

Solution:
  a. .70 × .109044 = .0763308
  b. 1.3 × .0763308 = .09923
    Capitalization Rate: .09923
    Indicated Value: $58,000 ÷ .09923 = $584,500

Proof:
    Principal amount of loan: .70 × $584,500 = $409,150
    Debt service: .109044 × $409,150 = $44,615
    Debt coverage ratio: $58,000 ÷ $44,615 = 1.3, or 130%

Equity Yield Rates in Investment Analysis

Yield to Maturity

The mortgage-equity technique could well be justified if it served no other function than to be utilized in investment analysis. In the problems and procedures that follow the unknown is not *value*—it is *rate of yield on equity* at a given value. (Yield to maturity includes both *current* yield and *deferred* yield.)

Rate, if single mortgage financing:

• *Procedure:*
1. Using OAR Tables:
  a. Compute Overall Rate by dividing property value by net annual income (Rate = Income ÷ Value).
  b. Find equity yield rate in the OAR Tables by estimate, search, and interpolation. (Use Overall Rate calculated in *a* as a "target figure" and match it with a precomputed OAR.)

Problem:
A mini-warehouse can be purchased for $300,000 on a down payment of $75,000; balance of $225,000 to be financed at an interest rate of 11% for a term of 15 years, monthly payments to amortize. Net annual income is estimated to be $37,650. The investor anticipates stability in market value during a holding period of 10 years. Based on the data and assumptions given, calculate the rate of yield to maturity which could be generated by the investment.

Solution:
  a. Overall Rate: $37,650 ÷ $300,000 = .1255

b. From the OAR Tables:
OAR at 16% Equity Yield Rate: .125506
Answer: 16% Equity Yield Rate.

Notes:
— In the problem data five of the six OAR variables are given: 10 year
holding period, 75% loan ratio ($225,000 ÷ $300,000), 15 year loan
term, 11% mortgage interest rate, 0% appreciation. The single
unknown is the *equity yield rate*.
— The OAR calculated in *a* is .1255. The precedure now calls for finding
this rate, or one close to it, in the OAR Tables.
— To begin this matching exercise, use the five variables given and
estimate the sixth—the equity yield rate being sought.
— Assume that in solving this problem you first try an equity yield rate
of 15%. You turn to the OAR Tables and find an OAR of .122165, all
given variables tied in. By comparison to the target figure of .1255,
you note the difference and determine that 15% is too low. Now you
try 18% and find the OAR to be .132076. Too high! You have thus
bracketed the yield rate. It is more than 15%, less than 18%. You try
16%. You find the OAR: .125506. It is so close to the calculated OAR
of .1255 that interpolation is not required. You have "zeroed in" on
the target figure and have found the answer.

2. Using Compound Interest Tables:

This method provides a longer, alternate route, which does not utilize the
OAR Tables, in answering the investor's prime question: "What is the rate
of yield I can reasonably anticipate in this investment?"

a. Compute Overall Rate by dividing net annual income by property
value. (Rate = Income ÷ Value).
b. Multiply loan ratio by loan constant.
c. Subtract *b* from the Overall Rate.
d. Multiply the loan ratio by the percent of loan unpaid at the end of the
holding period.
e. Subtract *d* from estimated value at end of holding period expressed as
a percent of purchase price.
f. Make the following considerations:
   c computes the *net annuity* as a percent of purchase price.
   e gives the *net reversion* as a percent of purchase price.
   Equity ratio is the "*target figure*," or value.
Use the following equation in dual "cut and try" calculations to
bracket the equity yield rate:
   Value = (Net Annuity × PW 1/P) + (Net Reversion × PW 1)

Select PW 1/P and PW 1 factors at estimated equity yield rates for the term of the holding period. Zero in on equity yield rate by interpolation.

Problem:

Commercial property producing net annual income of $65,000 is listed at a firm price of $550,000. Financing can be obtained on a first mortgage for 60% of value at 10% interest, monthly payments to amortize in 20 years. The seller requires a down payment of cash to the loan. Assume a 10-year holding period and 10% depreciation. Calculate the rate of yield to maturity on equity, based on the data and projections given.

Solution:
  a. OAR: $65,000 ÷ $550,000 = .118182
  b. .60 × .115803 = .0694818
  c. .118182 − .0694818 = .0487002
  d. .60 × .730243 = .4381458
  e. .90 − .4381458 = .4618542
  f. "Target figure" is the Equity Ratio: .40
     Net Annuity (*c*): .0487002
     Net Reversion (*e*): .4618542
     Try 14%:
     .0487002 × 5.216116 =   .2540259   (PW 1/P, 14%, 10 years)
     .4618542 ×   .269744 =   .1245824   (PW 1, 14%, 10 years)
                            ─────────
                             .3786083
     Try 13%:
     .0487002 × 5.426243 =   .2642591   (PW 1/P, 13%, 10 years)
     .4618542 × .294588 =   .1360567
                            ─────────
                             .4003158

Answer: Slightly over 13% Equity Yield Rate. Calculation at 13% is so close to the "target figure" of .40 that interpolation is not required.

Notes:
  — The preceding procedures, utilizing either the OAR Tables or the Compound Interest Tables, can be employed to convert an Overall Rate derived from the market to an equity yield rate. Financing data and projections of holding period and value change should also be extracted from the market.
  — To translate net annuity (cash flow) from *c* to dollars:
     .0487 × $550,000 = $26,785
     Cash flow is 4.87% of property value. Refer to procedure, page 95.
  — To calculate net reversion from *e* in terms of dollars:
     .4618542 × $550,000 = $254,020

— Compare equity yield of 13% with equity yield on the same investment, when a second mortgage provides a greater degree of leverage. (See next section.)

Rate, if secondary (junior or multiple) financing:

• *Procedure:*
   a. Compute Overall Rate by dividing net annual income by property value (Rate = Income ÷ Value).
   b. Multiply each loan ratio by its corresponding loan constant.
   c. Add the products calculated in *b*.
   d. Subtract *c* from *a*.
   e. Multiply each loan ratio by the corresponding percent of loan unpaid at the end of the holding period.
   f. Add the products calculated in *e*.
   g. Subtract *f* from estimated value at end of holding period, expressed as a percent of purchase price.
   h. Make the following considerations:
       d computes the *net annuity* as a percent of purchase price.
       g gives the *net reversion* as a percent of purchase price.
       Equity ratio is the "target figure," or value.
   Use the following equation in dual "cut and try" calculations to bracket the equity yield rate:
       Value = (Net Annuity × PW 1/P) + (Net Reversion × PW 1)
   Select PW 1/P and PW 1 factors at estimated equity yield rates for the term of the holding period. Zero in on equity yield rate by interpolation.

Problem:
Commercial property valued at $550,000 produces net annual income of $65,000. (This is the same property as in the problem on page 83. Note that financing now includes a second mortgage.) It is offered to a prospective purchaser on these terms:
   Down payment: 10% of purchase price
   First mortgage: 60% loan ratio, 10% interest rate, monthly payments to amortize in 20 years
   Second mortgage: 30% loan ratio, 8½% interest rate, monthly payments to amortize in 15 years
Assume a 10-year holding period and 10% depreciation. Calculate the equity yield rate.

Solution:
   a. OAR: $65,000 ÷ $550,000 = .118182

b. 1st mortgage: .60 × .115803 = .0694818
   2nd mortgage: .30 × .118169 = .0354507

c. .1049325

d. .118182 − .1049325 = .0132495

e. 1st mortgage: .60 × .730243 = .4381458
   2nd mortgage: .30 × .479974 = .1439922

f. .5821380

g. .90 − .582138 = .317862

h. "Target figure" is the Equity Ratio: .10
   Net Annuity (*d*): .0132495
   Net Reversion (*g*): .317862
   Try 25%:
   .0132495 × 3.570503 = .0473074   (PW 1/P, 25%, 10 years)
   .317862 × .107374 = .0341301   (PW 1, 25%, 10 years)
   .0814375
   Try 20%:
   .0132495 × 4.192472 = .0555482   (PW 1/P, 20%, 10 years)
   .317862 × .161506 = .0513366   (PW 1, 20% 10 years)
   .1068848

Interpolate to "target figure": .10
Answer: Slightly over 21% Equity Yield Rate. Interpolation by simple proportion shows 21.35%. Further refinement gives 21.17%. However, such precision is not required for decision-making in real estate investments. *Value* can best be expressed as a *range* rather than an exact *point;* and a *yield rate* is a calculated *anticipated* rate.

Proof:

The most comprehensive verification of the calculated rate of yield on equity is a 15-point analysis, which follows.

Investment Analysis and Proof of Computations
Fifteen-Point Summary of Calculations

1.	Over-all Rate Selected from OAR Tables or Computed			.118182
2.	Property Value	$65,000 (INCOME)	÷ .118182 (OAR)	= $550,000
3.	Original Equity (Down Payment)	.10 (Equity Ratio)	x $550,000 (Value)	= 55,000
4.	Amount of Loan (Original Principal)	1st: .60 2nd: .30 (Loan Ratio)	X 550,000 x 550,000 (Value)	= 330,000 = 165,000

Investment Analysis and Proof of Computations
Fifteen-Point Summary of Calculations
(cont.)

5.	**Debt Service** (Yearly Payments)	1st: .115803 2nd: .118169 (Loan Constant)	X x	330,000 165,000 (Principal)	= =	38,215 19,498 ‾‾57,713
6.	**Cash Flow** (Annuity)	65,000 (Net Income)	−	57,713 (Debt Service)	=	7,287
7.	**Debt Coverage Ratio**	65,000 (Net Income)	÷	57,713 (Debt Service)	=	1.126263
8.	**Rate of Current Yield On Equity**	7,287 (Cash Flow)	÷	55,000 (Orig. Equity)	=	.13249
9.	**Loan Balance** (End Holding Period)	1st: .730243 2nd: .479974 (% Unpaid)	X x	330,000 165,000 (Principal)	= =	240,980 79,196 ‾‾320,176
10.	**Resale Value as % of Original Value**	100 (Orig. Val. as %)	+ −	− 10 (% Appr/Dep)	=	90%
11.	**Resale Value as a Dollar Amount**	90% (Resale Val. as %)	x	550,000 (Original Value)	=	495,000
12.	**Reversion, Net** (Terminal Equity)	495,000 (Resale Value)	−	320,176 (Loan Balance)	=	174,824
13.	**Deferred Yield** (Amount)	174,824 (Reversion Net)	−	55,000 (Down Payment)	=	119,824
14.	**Terminal Equity Ratio**	174,824 (Reversion Net)	÷	495,000 (Resale Value)	=	.3518

15. **Proof of Yield on Equity**
Equity Yield Rate: 21.17 (Percent) Term in Years: 10 (Holding Period)
Present Worth of 1 Per Period: 4.031312 (PW 1/P) Present Worth of 1: .146571 (PW 1)

Equation of Proof
Present Worth = ($7,287 (Cash Flow) x 4.031312 (PW 1/P)) + ($174,824 (Net Reversion) x .146571 (PW 1))
= $29,376 + $25,624 = $55,000

Final Check Target Figure = $55,000 (Down Payment, Orig. Equity)

$55,000 (Target Figure) − $55,000 (Present Worth) = 0 (Rounding Adjustment)

Notes:
— Relate the preceding problem to page 83. The property is the same in each. However, change in financing has dropped the down payment required to "swing the deal" from $220,000 to $55,000. Additional

leverage provided by the second mortgage has made a dramatic difference, raising the equity yield rate from a respectable 13% to an enviable 21%. Careful analysis by the counsellor will provide the client with an informed base for decision-making. If the investor has a choice of terms, he will doubtless take the "high road."

— *d* of the Solution gives the net annuity (cash flow) as a percent of property value: .0132495. Translated into dollars, this shows: .0132495 × $550,000 = $7,287. The figure corresponds to Item 6 in the 15-point analysis.

— *g* of the Solution calculates net reversion (resale value less loan balance) to be .317862 times property value. In dollars, this is: .317862 × $550,000 = $174,824. It is identical to the calculation in Step 12 of the analysis.

— If property value should remain constant or increase during the holding period, yield on equity will obviously be greater than 21%; for analysis has been based on a projection of 10% depreciation.

Rate, if negative cash flow:

The following procedure can be used to calculate rate of yield on equity when net annual income (after operating expenses) is less than debt service. Motivation for investing under these circumstances is the anticipation of high rate of appreciation because of upgraded changing use patterns, rezoning, and redevelopment prospects. Such an investment produces *no current yield*. All yield is *deferred* until the time of resale. The purchaser makes not only an initial cash investment (his down payment) but also a series of additional investments during the period of ownership. Out-of-pocket expenditures are required to offset the dollar amount of negative cash flow.

• *Procedure:*
  a. Calculate annual debt service.
  b. Subtract net annual income from *a*.
  c. Compute loan balance at end of holding period.
  d. Subtract *c* from estimated resale value at end of holding period.
  e. Make these considerations:
     b computes the *negative* net annuity.
     d gives the *positive* net reversion.
     Down payment or original equity is the "target figure" or value. Use the following equation in dual "cut and try" calculations to bracket the equity yield rate:
     Value = (Net Reversion × PW 1) − (Negative Net Annuity × PW 1/P)
Select PW 1/P and PW 1 factors at estimated equity yield rates for the term of the holding period. Zero in on equity yield rate by interpolation.

Problem:

Land in a transitional area is improved with a 30-year old fourplex. The area has been rezoned commercial, and should be ripe for redevelopment in five years. Net annual income from the four units is $3,500. The property is sold for $70,000. Seller accepts a down payment of $10,000 and carries $60,000 on a first trust deed at 9%, with monthly payments of $600 for five years, unpaid balance of $48,686 due at the end of five years. It is estimated that the land alone will have a value of $110,000 net in five years. Salvage value of the building will, it is anticipated, pay the cost of demolition and removal. The purchaser expects to resell at the end of a five-year holding period. Based on the data and projections given, what is the rate of yield on equity?

Solution:

a. Annual debt service: $12 \times \$600 = \$7,200$
b. Negative cash flow: $\$7,200 - \$3,500 = \$3,700$
c. Loan balance at end of 5 years: $48,686 (given)
d. Net reversion: $\$110,000 - \$48,686 = \$61,314$
e. "Target figure" is the down payment or original equity: $10,000.
   Try 25%:

$61,314 × .327680	=	$20,091	(PW 1, 25%, 5 years)
$3,700 × 2.689280	= −	9,950	(PW 1/P, 25%, 5 years)
		$10,141	

   Try 30%:

$61,314 × .269329	=	$16,514	(PW 1, 30%, 5 years)
$3,700 × 2.435570	= −	9,012	(PW 1/P, 30%, 5 years)
		$ 7,502	

Answer: About 25¼% yield to maturity (by interpolation).

Notes:
— At a yield rate of 25.25% an investment of $10,000 (the down payment) would grow to $30,824 in 5 years:
   $\$10,000 \div .324423 = \$30,824$ (PW 1, 25.25%, 5 years)
At the same rate a series of annual investments of $3,700 (the negative yearly cash flow) would accumulate a total of $30,514:
   $\$3,700 \div .121254 = \$30,514$ (PR − i, 25.25%, 5 years)
Combined, the single initial investment and the 5 additional annual investments grow to $61,338 ($30,824 + $30,514), within $24 of the calculated net reversion of $61,314. (Slight difference is due to interpolation and rounding.)

— Net reversion includes:
Capital recapture:

Down payment:	$10,000
Annual payments (5 @ $3,700):	18,500
	$28,500
Deferred yield:	32,814
Total:	$61,314

— Refer to page 476 for an example of a 15-point investment analysis involving a negative cash flow.

Rate, if 100% equity (no mortgage):

A logical question would be, "If property is purchased for cash, isn't it true that the equity yield rate and the Overall Rate coincide?" The answer is yes, if there is neither appreciation nor depreciation during a period of ownership and if income remains constant. However, if either appreciation or depreciation is projected and income is stable during a limited period of ownership, rate of yield on 100% equity is either greater than or less than the Overall Rate at which the property was purchased. If the property *appreciates,* deferred yield is produced. Net reversion at time of resale will return capital and unlock deferred yield. If the property *depreciates,* a portion of net annual income must be applied to partial capital recapture for the net reversion (resale value) will not be sufficient in itself to provide total capital recovery.

● *Procedure:*
   a. Estimate resale value at end of a specified period of ownership.
   b. Make the following considerations:
      Net annual income is the *net annuity.*
      Resale value is the *net reversion.*
      Purchase price is value, the "target figure."
   Use the following equation in dual "cut and try" calculations to bracket the yield rate:
      Value = (Net Annuity × PW 1/P) + (Net Reversion × PW 1)
   Select PW 1/P and PW 1 factors at estimated equity yield rates for the term of the holding period. By interpolation, zero in on yield rate on 100% equity.

Problem:
An apartment house producing net annual income of $94,500 is purchased for $900,000 cash, at an Overall Rate of 10.5%. Assume a holding period of

10 years and stabilized income. Compute the rate of yield on equity, based on (a) appreciation of 30%, and (b) depreciation of 25%.

Solution a:
 a. Resale value: 1.30 × $900,000 = $1,170,000.
 b. Value: $900,000 (purchase price, "target figure")
 Net Annuity: $94,500
 Net Reversion: $1,170,000
 Try 13%:
 $94,500 × 5.426243 = $512,780 (PW 1/P, 13%, 10 years)
 $1,170,000 × .294588 = 344,668 (PW 1, 13%, 10 years)
 $857,448

 Try 12%:
 $94,500 × 5.650223 = $533,946 (PW 1/P, 12%, 10 years)
 $1,170,000 × .321973 = 376,708 (PW 1, 12%, 10 years)
 $910,654

 Answer: About 12.2% Equity Yield Rate (by interpolation).

Solution b:
 a. Resale value: .75 × $900,000 = $675,000
 b. Value: $900,000 (purchase price, "target figure")
 Net Annuity: $94,500
 Net Reversion: $675,000
 Try 9%:
 $94,500 × 6.417658 = $606,469 (PW 1/P, 9%, 10 years)
 $675,000 × .422411 = 285,127 (PW 1, 9%, 10 years)
 $891,596

 Try 8½%:
 $94,500 × 6.561348 = $620,047 (PW 1/P, 8½%, 10 years)
 $675,000 × .442285 = 298,542 (PW 1, 8½%, 10 years)
 $918,589

 Answer: About 8.8% Equity Yield Rate (by interpolation).

Note: Compare yield rates calculated with equity yield rates, if property were financed on these terms at the time of purchase: down payment: 20%; loan ratio: 80%; loan interest rate: 9½%; and loan term: 25 years, monthly payments to amortize. All other problem data remain unchanged.
 — If 30% appreciation, equity yield rate would be slightly in excess of 19%. (Refer to procedure, pages 81 to 84.)
 — If 25% depreciation, equity yield rate is barely above 6%.

Rate, derived from the market:

Procedure in this section is basically the same as the one headed "Rate, if single mortgage financing." However, in that prior problem the Overall Rate was calculated from known value and income of the subject property only. In the following procedure the Overall Rate has been derived from the market (see pages 77 to 78) and is to be converted to an equity yield rate. When such a routine is followed, it can then be asserted that the equity yield rate itself is market-derived.

- *Procedure:*
  a. Derive an Overall Rate from an analysis of rents and sales of comparable properties (R = I ÷ V).
  b. Determine from the market in a specific area and for the particular type of property being valued and/or analyzed:
     1. Typical holding period.
     2. Financing data: loan ratio, term, and interest rate.
     3. Projections of appreciation/depreciation, based on an economic study of the area.

     Array the five known mortgage-equity variables.
  c. Find equity yield rate in the OAR Tables by estimate, search, and interpolation. Use Overall Rate from *a* as a "target figure" and match it with a precomputed OAR.

Problem:
Use data from the problem and solution under the procedure "Overall Rate derived from the market." To summarize the valuation of Loma Vista Apartments:

   Net annual income: $74,400
   OAR from the market: .1038
   Value: $716,760

The analyst determines from local lending institutions that property of this type, age, and condition in the area can be financed for 75% of value at 9% interest for a term of 25 years. He further finds that the typical local investor anticipates a holding period of 10 years before selling, refinancing, or exchanging the property. The economic outlook in the area indicates quite stable values (0% appreciation). Based on these data and projections, convert the Overall Rate of .1038 to an equity yield rate (yield to maturity). Calculate the equity yield rate if property should depreciate 10% within the holding period.

Solution:
  a. Overall Rate from the market: .1038
  b. Holding period: 10 years   Loan term: 25 years
     Equity yield rate: ?   Loan interest rate: 9%
     Loan ratio: 75%   Appreciation: 0%
  c. From the OAR Tables:
     Assume 0% Appreciation:
     OAR at 14% Equity Yield Rate: .103833
     Compare to Overall Rate from the market (*a*): .1038
     Interpolation is not required.
     Answer: About 14% yield to maturity.
     Assume 10% Depreciation:
     OAR at 12% Equity Yield Rate: .103849
     Compare to Overall Rate from the market (*a*): .1038
     Interpolation is not required.
     Answer: About 12% yield to maturity.

Note: A convenient form is given on page 150 for displaying both valuation by an Overall Rate derived from the market, and *analysis* which converts the OAR to an equity yield rate. Here it is, completed for the Loma Vista Apartments.

Equity Yield Rate and Property Value from OAR

Holding Period:	10 years	
Mortgage Specifications:		
Loan Ratio:	75%	
Interest Rate:	9%	
Term:	25 years	
OAR:	.1038	
Appreciation/Depreciation:	a. 0%	b. −10%
Equity Yield Rate:*	a. 14%	b. 12%
Net Annual Income:	$74,400	
Indicated Value: $74,400 ÷ .1038 = $716,760		
(Income) (OAR)		

*Calculated from OAR Tables or Compound Interest Tables. (See alternate procedures.)

Current Yield

Current yield as a percent of original equity:

The relationship of "cash on cash," commonly referred to by investors, can be expressed as a rate of current yield on equity. A simple procedure will calculate the rate, which can readily be converted to a dollar amount.

- *Procedure:*
  - a. Multiply loan ratio by loan constant.
  - b. Subtract *a* from the Overall Rate.
  - c. Divide *b* by the equity ratio.

Problem 1:
Given:

      Holding period: 10 years
      Equity yield rate: 15%
      Mortgage specifications:
          Loan ratio: 75%
          Interest rate: 9%
          Term: 25 years
      Appreciation: 10%

Calculate annual cash flow (current yield) as a percent of original equity (down payment).

Solution:
  a. $.75 \times .100704 = .075528$
  b. $.101727 - .075528 = .026199$
  c. $.026199 \div .25 = .104796$

Problem 2:
Apply solution given in Problem 1 to property producing net annual income of $48,000. What is the dollar amount of annual cash flow (current yield)?

Solution:
    Property value: $48,000 \div .101727 = $471,851$
    Equity (down payment): $.25 \times $471,851 = $117,963$
    Cash flow (current yield): $117,963 \times .104796 = $12,362$

Proof:
    The 15-point analysis which follows will verify the rate of current yield on equity: .104796.

Investment Analysis and Proof of Computations
Fifteen-Point Summary of Calculations

1.	Over-all Rate Selected from OAR Tables or Computed		.101727
2.	Property Value	$48,000 (INCOME) ÷ .101727 (OAR)	= $471,851

Investment Analysis and Proof of Computations
Fifteen-Point Summary of Calculations
(cont.)

3. **Original Equity** (Down Payment)

   .25 (Equity Ratio) x $471,851 (Value) = 117,963

4. **Amount of Loan** (Original Principal)

   .75 (Loan Ratio) x 471,851 (Value) = 353,888

5. **Debt Service** (Yearly Payments)

   .100704 (Loan Constant) x 353,888 (Principal) = 35,638

6. **Cash Flow** (Annuity)

   48,000 (Net Income) − 35,638 (Debt Service) = 12,362

7. **Debt Coverage Ratio**

   48,000 (Net Income) ÷ 35,638 (Debt Service) = 1.346877

8. **Rate of Current Yield On Equity**

   12,362 (Cash Flow) ÷ 117,963 (Orig. Equity) = .104796

9. **Loan Balance** (End Holding Period)

   .827392 (% Unpaid) x 353,888 (Principal) = 292,804

10. **Resale Value as % of Original Value**

    100 (Orig. Val. as %) ± 10 (% Appr/Dep) = 110%

11. **Resale Value as a Dollar Amount**

    110% (Resale Val. as %) x 471,851 (Original Value) = 519,036

12. **Reversion, Net** (Terminal Equity)

    519,036 (Resale Value) − 292,804 (Loan Balance) = 226,232

13. **Deferred Yield** (Amount)

    226,232 (Reversion Net) − 117,963 (Down Payment) = 108,269

14. **Terminal Equity Ratio**

    226,232 (Reversion Net) ÷ 519,036 (Resale Value) = .43587

15. **Proof of Yield on Equity**

    Equity Yield Rate: 15 (Percent)   Term in Years: 10 (Holding Period)

    Present Worth of 1 Per Period: 5.018769 (PW 1/P)   Present Worth of 1: .247185 (PW 1)

    Equation of Proof

    Present Worth = ($12,362 (Cash Flow) x 5.018769 (PW 1/P)) + ($226,232 (Net Reversion) x .247185 (PW 1))

    = $62,042 + $55,921 = $117,963

    Final Check   Target Figure = $117,963 (Down Payment, Orig. Equity)

    $117,963 (Target Figure) − $117,963 (Present Worth) = 0 (Rounding Adjustment)

Notes:
- — Regardless of dollar amounts, the rate of current yield on equity is 10.4796%, based on the given variables built into the OAR.
- — Whenever equity buildup occurs (through debt reduction and possible appreciation) yield to maturity will exceed the rate of current yield—in this problem, 10.4796% current yield compared to 15% yield to maturity.
- — Rate of current yield is not dependent on a specified holding period—yield to maturity is.

Current yield as a percent of property value:

● *Procedure:*
   a. Multiply loan ratio by loan constant.
   b. Subtract *a* from the Overall Rate.

Problem:
Use data from preceding problem "Current yield as a percent of original equity." Calculate the rate of current yield as a percent of property value.

Solution:
   a. .75 × .100704 = .075528
   b. .101727 − .075528 = .026199

Proof:
   Value as calculated in the prior problem is $471,851. Cash flow (current yield): $471,851 × .026199 = $12,362. Calculation by this method corresponds to Item 6 in the preceding 15-point analysis.

Notes:
- — Steps in the procedure above are identical to Steps *a* and *b* in the preceding method for calculating "Current yield as a percent of original equity."
- — If the product of the loan ratio and the loan constant (*a*) is *less* than the Overall Rate (*b*) there will be a *positive* cash flow. If the product of the loan ratio and the loan constant is *greater* than the Overall Rate, a *negative* cash flow will result. The procedure outlined can be used as a direct route in a given situation to determine whether there will be a positive or a negative cash flow. The percentage calculated, whether plus or minus, can then be converted readily to a dollar amount.

Current equity yield rate, derived from the market:

• *Procedure:*
   a. Derive an Overall Rate from analysis of rents and sales of comparable properties (R = I ÷ V).
   b. Determine typical financing terms for the subject property.
   c. Multiply loan ratio by loan constant.
   d. Subtract *c* from *a*.
   e. Divide *d* by the equity ratio. Quotient is the rate of current yield on equity.

Problem:
Use data from the problem and the solutions given under the procedures "Overall Rate derived from the market" and "Rate of equity yield to maturity, derived from the market." To summarize valuation and analysis of Loma Vista Apartments:
   Net annual income: $74,400
   Value: $716,760
   OAR from market: .1038
   Holding period: 10 years
   Equity yield to maturity (by conversion of OAR): 14%
   Financing specifications:

   Loan ratio: 75%
   Term: 25 years
   Interest rate: 9%
Convert the Overall Rate to a rate of current yield on equity and calculate the dollar amount of current yield (cash flow).

Solution:
   a. OAR from market: .1038
   b. Loan ratio, 75%; term, 25 years; interest rate, 9%
   c. .75 × .100704 = .075528
   d. .1038 − .075528 = .028272
   e. .028272 ÷ .25 = .113088
      Down payment: .25 × $716,760 = $179,190
      Calculate cash flow: .113088 × $179,190 = $20,264

Proof:
      Principal amount of loan: .75 × $716,760 = $537,570
      Debt service: .100704 × $537,570 = $54,136
      Cash flow: $74,400 − $54,136 = $20,264
      Rate of current yield on equity: $20,264 ÷ $179,190 = .113087
      Difference of .000001 is due to rounding to the nearest dollar.

Notes:
— A summary of the valuation and analysis of Loma Vista Apartments shows the following rates, all derived from the market:
Overall Rate: 10.38%
Equity yield rate (to maturity): 14%
Rate of current yield on equity: 11.3088%
When the analyst goes this route he has justified all three rates, which have come from the market itself. Tables in the textbook have served as procedural tools, not as prime sources.
— Rates extracted from the market do not possess the quality of universal applicability. Rather, they should be interpreted as being related to a particular type of comparable properties in a specified area at a given point in time.

VALUE

In the appraisal or valuation process the analyst must determine initially the type of value sought: (1) market value, or (2) investment value. Market value is considered to be value to persons in general. If the purpose of the appraisal is to find an indication of market value by the mortgage-equity technique, the appraiser assumes that the property is encumbered by new, typical, institutional financing and that the buyer pays cash to the loan. Equity yield rate and holding period estimates are based on general requirements in the market.

If, however, the analyst seeks investment value, he is in effect making a feasibility study; for investment value is value to a specific client, rather than to persons in general. Valuation is based on the nontypical financing available to the client, on the investor's special objectives, and on his particular equity yield requirements.

Market value and investment value may or may not equate. An investor's unusually high yield requirements may tend to lower investment value for him. On the other hand, a high degree of leverage provided by favorable multiple financing may afford the investor a higher rate of yield than on normal financing, even at a higher purchase price.

Both market and investment value can often be expressed best as a range rather than a specific point. Such a range can be established by changing any of the six variables built into a mortgage-equity Overall Rate; for example, differing projections for the same property on appreciation/depreciation, equity yield rates, financing terms, or holding periods. The same short equation is used in seeking either market value or investment value:

98

Value = Income ÷ Rate

Procedures on *rate* and on *value* are interrelated. Problems in the section dealing with "Overall Rates in Valuation" serve a dual purpose. Besides illustrating the selection, derivation, and calculation of a mortgage-equity rate, they serve as examples of using the rate to determine value.

The broker/analyst, recognizing each type of value, may use the mortgage-equity technique effectively in answering the prime questions of both of his principals:

— The owner in listing his property who wants to know, "What is it worth?"
— The prospective buyer who asks, "What is it worth *to me*?"

Of such questions and answers are decisions—and deals—made.

Market Value

Valuation by the mortgage-equity technique:

• *Procedure:*
Divide net annual income by the Overall Rate.

Problem 1:
Briarwood Estates, a four-star mobile home park, is offered for sale three years after completion. It is well located, efficiently managed and maintained, and shows a negligible vacancy factor. Net annual income from space rentals and related services is estimated to be $150,000. The park can be financed for 75% of market value at 9% interest, monthly payments to amortize in 20 years. Land values in the area have generally doubled in the last 10 years. You are valuing Briarwood Estates for a prospective purchaser. A typical investor in this area at this point in time and dealing with this type of property, projects a holding period of 10 years, anticipates 20% appreciation within that time, and expects a yield of 16% on his equity. By the mortgage-equity technique, calculate an indicator of value.

Solution:
Array six variables from the problem. Each variable will be built into the appropriate precomputed Overall Rate to be selected from the OAR Tables:
Holding period: 10 years
Equity yield rate: 16%
Loan ratio: 75%

Loan interest rate: 9%
Loan term: 20 years
Appreciation: 20%
OAR: .101403
Indicated Value: $150,000 ÷ .101403 = $1,479,246 (unrounded)

Problem 2:
The counsellor's task is the computation of a band of value for decision-making and within which to negotiate a purchase price. Net annual income from the property under consideration is estimated to be $70,000. Financing can be obtained for 80% of market value at 10% interest for a term of 25 years, monthly payments to amortize. The investor expects to hold the property for 10 years and anticipates a yield to maturity of 14% on his equity. A survey of economic trends and conditions within the area indicates a fair probability of appreciation of 10% within the next 10 years. However, there are a few unfavorable influences that show the possibility of a decline in value of up to 10%. Establish a value range, based on two differing projections: (a) appreciation of 10%, and (b) depreciation of 10%.

Solution:
  a. $70,000 ÷ .103677 = $675,174
  b. $70,000 ÷ .114020 = $613,927

Note: The form which follows has been completed for Problem 2, based on 10% Appreciation, illustrating the use of the worksheet "Computation of Value Estimate—Mortgage-Equity Technique."

Computation of Value Estimate
Mortgage-Equity Technique

Data Required:	
Holding Period:	10 years
Equity Yield Rate:	14%
Mortgage Specifications:	
Loan Ratio:	80%
Interest Rate:	10%
Term:	25 years
Appreciation/Depreciation:	+10%
Net Annual Income:	$70,000
Valuation:	
Overall Rate:	.103677
Value = Income ÷ Rate	
= $70,000 ÷ .103677	
= $675,174	

Investment Value

Calculations to determine investment value as distinguished from market value are commonly based on nonconventional terms—multiple mortgages, one hundred percent financing, et cetera. Several cases of this type have been explored, explained, and illustrated in the section on "Rates—Overall Rates in Valuation." No purpose would be served in repeating them; however, it is suggested that the student relate them specifically to the area of investment value.

Variations to accommodate a client's individual requirements may consider points other than financing. Whatever the nontypical specifications may be, the analyst should be guided by them is selecting a mortgage-equity Overall Rate by which to calculate investment value. The same basic equation applies to both market value and investment value:

Value = Income ÷ Rate

A procedure follows for calculating investment value when the loan ratio is unknown. A precomputed Overall Rate cannot be used, for a selection cannot be made from the OAR Tables unless the loan ratio is specified. There are two situations in which a loan ratio is unknown:

1. *Loan assumption*, if an existing mortgage is written at a favorable interest rate, and if it can be assumed by the purchaser. It may be advantageous to the buyer to go this route rather than taking out a new loan at higher current interest rates. The investor's key question then is, "In order to realize the rate of yield I expect on my equity, what can I offer the seller for *his equity*, provided I assume the existing loan on the property?"
2. *New financing*, if a loan commitment is made in terms of a dollar amount, without relating it to value. For example, a banker may say, "We will lend $700,000 on this project." If he does not indicate that $700,000 is a specified percent of value, loan ratio is unknown.

The first circumstance is the more common. It is illustrated in the following procedure, which enables the counsellor to calculate a feasible offering price. The broker or salesman may find the next patterned procedure to be a most practical one in the marketing of investment properties.

Investment value, when loan ratio is unknown:

• *Procedure:*
   a. Calculate annual cash flow, after debt service.

b. Compute loan balance at end of projected holding period.
c. Multiply annual cash flow from *a* by PW 1/P.
d. Add the product from *c* to the principal amount of the loan assumed.
e. Multiply loan balance at end of holding period by PW 1.
f. Subtract *e* from *d*.
g. Express value at end of holding period as a decimal percent of original value and multiply by PW 1.
h. Subtract the product from *g* from 1.0.
i. Divide *f* by *h*. The quotient is indicated investment value.
Note: Present worth factors in *c, e,* and *g* are selected at equity yield rates for the term of the holding period.

Problem:
An apartment house is encumbered by a loan made 5 years ago at 7½% interest, monthly payments to amortize in 25 years. The unpaid principal balance is now $625,000. According to the terms of the mortgage, it can be assumed. Interest rates on the same type of property in this area are currently at 10%. A prospective buyer wishes to take advantage of the low interest rate and assume the existing loan. He projects 10% depreciation during a holding period of 10 years and anticipates a yield of 15% on equity. Net annual income, processed to a calculated level ordinary annuity equivalent, is $90,000. Based on the data and assumptions given, calculate a feasible offering price for the seller's equity.

Solution:
(To avoid complications, disregard the initial 5 years of the 25-year loan term. It does not matter what the amount of the loan was when taken out originally. Balance is now $625,000. Look at it as though it were a new loan at 7½%, running for the next 20 years.)
a. Debt service: .096671 × $625,000 = $60,419
   Cash flow: $90,000 − $60,419 = $29,581
b. Loan balance: .678670 × $625,000 = $424,169
c. $29,581 × 5.018769 = $148,460   (PW 1/P, 15%, 10 years)
d. $625,000 + $148,460 = $773,460
e. $424,169 × .247185 = $104,848   (PW 1, 15%, 10 years)
f. $773,460 − $104,848 = $668,612
g. .90 × .247185 = .2224665   (PW 1, 15%, 10 years)
h. 1.0 − .2224665 = .7775335
i. $668,612 ÷ .7775335 = $859,914
   Investment Value: $859,914, round to $859,900
   Feasible offer for equity: $859,900 − $625,000 = $234,900

Proof:
See the following 15-point analysis.

Investment Analysis and Proof of Computations
Fifteen-Point Summary of Calculations

1. Over-all Rate Selected from OAR Tables or Computed   .10466163

2. Property Value $90,000 (INCOME) ÷ .10466163 (OAR) = $859,914

3. Original Equity (Down Payment)   .273183 (Equity Ratio) x $859,914 (Value) = 234,914

4. Amount of Loan (Original Principal)   .726817 (Loan Ratio) x 859,914 (Value) = 625,000

5. Debt Service (Yearly Payments)   .096671 (Loan Constant) x 625,000 (Principal) = 60,419

6. Cash Flow (Annuity)   90,000 (Net Income) − 60,419 (Debt Service) = 29,581

7. Debt Coverage Ratio   90,000 (Net Income) ÷ 60,419 (Debt Service) = 1.4896

8. Rate of Current Yield On Equity   29,581 (Cash Flow) ÷ 234,914 (Orig. Equity) = .12592

9. Loan Balance (End Holding Period)   .678670 (% Unpaid) x 625,000 (Principal) = 424,169

10. Resale Value as % of Original Value   100 (Orig. Val. as %) $\pm$ − 10 (% Appr/Dep) = 90%

11. Resale Value as a Dollar Amount   90% (Resale Val. as %) x 859,914 (Original Value) = 773,923

12. Reversion, Net (Terminal Equity)   773,923 (Resale Value) − 424,169 (Loan Balance) = 349,754

13. Deferred Yield (Amount)   349,754 (Reversion Net) − 234,914 (Down Payment) = 114,840

14. Terminal Equity Ratio   349,754 (Reversion Net) ÷ 773,923 (Resale Value) = .451924

15. Proof of Yield on Equity

    Equity Yield Rate: 15 (Percent)   Term in Years: 10 (Holding Period)

    Present Worth of 1 Per Period: 5.018769 (PW 1/P)   Present Worth of 1: .247185 (PW 1)

    Equation of Proof

    Present Worth = ($29,581 (Cash Flow) x 5.018769 (PW 1/P)) + ($349,754 (Net Reversion) x .247185 (PW 1))

    = $148,460 + $86,454 = $234,914

    Final Check   Target Figure = $234,914 (Down Payment, Orig. Equity)

    $234,914 (Target Figure) − $234,914 (Present Worth) = 0 (Rounding Adjustment)

Notes:
- Now it can be told—loan ratio is nearly 73%, as calculated *after* the problem was solved.
- The analyst can "back into" some items in the 15-point analysis:

    Items 1 and 2: OAR = $90,000 ÷ $859,914, or .10466163

    Item 3: Equity ratio = $234,914 ÷ $859,914, or .273183

    Item 4: Loan ratio = $625,000 ÷ $859,914, or .726817
- In Step *g* of the Procedure and Solution, consider purchase price as being 100%, or, expressed as a decimal, 1.0. Add for appreciation—subtract for depreciation. In this problem, if 10% appreciation were projected, 1.10 would be used. Since 10% depreciation is anticipated, estimated resale value will be 90% of purchase price.
- Procedure as outlined for the computation of investment value actually gives the steps in arithmetic which would be followed in solving this equation:

    Value of Equity = [(Net Income − Debt Service) × PW 1/P]
    + [(Resale Value − Loan Balance)
    × PW 1]
- Calculation of the original amount of the loan when it was initiated 5 years ago is not essential to solving the problem. However, it can be determined easily by alternate methods:

    1. Monthly loan payment: $60,419 ÷ 12 = $5,035 (rounded)
    $5,035 × 135.319613 = $681,334 (PW 1/P, 7½%, 300 months)
    2. $625,000 ÷ .917326 = $681,328 (Supplemental Tables)
    Difference of $6 in the two calculations of the original principal amount of the loan is due to rounding factors and rounding amounts to the nearest dollar.
- A common question is, "Hasn't the loan constant changed from what it was when the loan was taken out 5 years ago?" Yes, it has changed, as have the principal amount and the loan term. But the payment to amortize and the interest rate have *not* changed. Principal has been reduced in the prior 5-year period from approximately $681,330 to $625,000; term has been shortened from 25 years to 20 years; but debt service remains constant at $5,035 a month—$60,419 in one year.

    Loan Constant, 7½%, 25 years: .088679

    Loan Constant, 7½%, 20 years: .096671

    Annual Debt Service, 25 year loan term: $681,330 × .088679 = $60,419

    Annual Debt Service, 20 year loan term: $625,000 × .096671 = $60,419

To summarize a point: At an interest rate of 7½%, annual debt service of $60,419 will amortize a loan of $681,330 in 25 years, or $625,000 in 20 years.

Investment value when loan ratios are unknown (multiple financing):

Additional preliminary steps are required in a procedure to calculate investment value, when two or more existing loans are to be assumed.

- *Procedure:*
  - a. Calculate annual debt service and principal balance unpaid at end of holding period for each loan.
  - b. Calculate the following for all loans combined:
    1. Principal amount.
    2. Annual debt service.
    3. Loan balance at end of holding period.
  - c. Follow each step in the preceding procedure "Investment value when loan ratio is unknown."

Problem:

A warehouse under lease to a triple A tenant is producing net annual income of $42,000. The property is encumbered by two assumable loans:
  1st Mortgage:
  Current principal balance: $224,000
  Interest rate: 6½%
  Remaining loan term: 19 years (228 months)
  Monthly payments to amortize: $1,713.37
  2nd Mortgage:
  Current principal balance: $87,000
  Interest rate: 9%
  Remaining loan term: 14 years (168 months)
  Monthly payments to amortize: $912.54
A prospective purchaser wishes to acquire the property without refinancing and plans to pay cash to the existing loans. He projects a holding period of 10 years, during which time he expects the property to remain stable in value. The investor anticipates a yield to maturity of 20% on equity. Based on the data and projections given, calculate a feasible price the client can offer, and prepare an investment analysis.

Solution:

- a. 1st Mortgage:
  Loan constant: .007649 × 12 = .091788   (PR, 6½%, 228 months)
  Annual debt service: .091788 × $224,000 = $20,561
  Principal balance at end of 10 years:
    Percent unpaid: .007649 × 81.602576 = .624178
      (PR, 6½%, 228 months, times PW 1/P, 6½%, 108 months—the loan term remaining after 10 years)
    Amount unpaid: .624178 × $224,000 = $139,816

2nd Mortgage:

Loan constant: $.010489 \times 12 = .125868$ (PR, 9%, 168 months)

Annual debt service: $.125868 \times \$87,000 = \$10,951$

Principal balance at end of 10 years:

Percent unpaid: $.010489 \times 40.184782 = .421498$

(PR, 9%, 168 months, times PW 1/P, 9%, 48 months—the loan term remaining after 10 years)

Amount unpaid: $.421498 \times \$87,000 = \$36,670$

b. 1. Total principal amount assumed: $\$224,000 + \$87,000 = \$311,000$
2. Total annual debt service: $\$20,561 + \$10,951 = \$31,512$
3. Combined loan balances, end of 10 years: $\$139,816 + \$36,670 = \$176,486$

c. 1. Cash flow: $\$42,000 - \$31,512 = \$10,488$
2. Combined loan balances: $\$176,486$
3. $\$10,488 \times 4.192472 = \$43,971$ (PW 1/P, 20%, 10 years)
4. $\$311,000 + \$43,971 = \$354,971$
5. $\$176,486 \times .161506 = \$28,504$ (PW 1, 20%, 10 years)
6. $\$354,971 - \$28,504 = \$326,467$
7. $1.0 \times .161506 = .161506$ (PW 1, 20%, 10 years)
8. $1.0 - .161506 = .838494$
9. $\$326,467 \div .838494 = \$389,350$

Feasible offering price:

For property: $\$389,350$

For seller's equity: $\$389,350 - \$311,000 = \$78,350$

Investment Analysis and Proof of Computations
Fifteen-Point Summary of Calculations

1.	Over-all Rate Selected from OAR Tables or Computed					.107872
2.	Property Value	$42,000 (INCOME)	÷	.107872 (OAR)	=	$389,350
3.	Original Equity (Down Payment)	.201233 (Equity Ratio)	x	$389,350 (Value)	=	78,350
4.	Amount of Loan (Original Principal)	1st: .575318	x	389,350	=	224,000
		2nd: .223449 (Loan Ratio)	x	389,350 (Value)	=	87,000
						311,000
5.	Debt Service (Yearly Payments)	1st: .091788	x	224,000	=	20,561
		2nd: .125868 (Loan Constant)	x	87,000 (Principal)	=	10,951
						31,512
6.	Cash Flow (Annuity)	42,000 (Net Income)	–	31,512 (Debt Service)	=	10,488
7.	Debt Coverage Ratio	42,000 (Net Income)	÷	31,512 (Debt Service)	=	1.332826

Investment Analysis and Proof of Computations
Fifteen-Point Summary of Calculations
(cont.)

8. Rate of Current Yield On Equity

$$\frac{10,488}{\text{(Cash Flow)}} \div \frac{78,350}{\text{(Orig. Equity)}} = \underline{.13386}$$

9. Loan Balance
(End Holding Period)

1st: $\frac{.624718}{\text{(% Unpaid)}}$ x $\frac{224,000}{}$ = 139,816

2nd: $\frac{.421498}{\text{(% Unpaid)}}$ x $\frac{87,000}{\text{(Principal)}}$ = 36,670

176,486

10. Resale Value as % of Original Value

$$\frac{100}{\text{(Orig. Val. as %)}} \pm \frac{0}{\text{(% Appr/Dep)}} = \underline{100\%}$$

11. Resale Value as a Dollar Amount

$$\frac{100\%}{\text{(Resale Val. as %)}} \times \frac{389,350}{\text{(Original Value)}} = \underline{389,350}$$

12. Reversion, Net (Terminal Equity)

$$\frac{389,350}{\text{(Resale Value)}} - \frac{176,486}{\text{(Loan Balance)}} = \underline{212,864}$$

13. Deferred Yield (Amount)

$$\frac{212,864}{\text{(Reversion Net)}} - \frac{78,350}{\text{(Down Payment)}} = \underline{134,514}$$

14. Terminal Equity Ratio

$$\frac{212,864}{\text{(Reversion Net)}} \div \frac{389,350}{\text{(Resale Value)}} = \underline{.546716}$$

15. Proof of Yield on Equity

Equity Yield Rate: $\underline{20}$ (Percent)   Term in Years: $\underline{10}$ (Holding Period)

Present Worth of 1 Per Period: $\underline{4.192472}$ (PW 1/P)   Present Worth of 1: $\underline{.161506}$ (PW 1)

Equation of Proof

Present Worth = ($\underline{\$10,488}$ (Cash Flow) x $\underline{4.192472}$ (PW 1/P)) + ($\underline{\$212,864}$ (Net Reversion) x $\underline{.161506}$ (PW 1))

= $\underline{\$43,971}$ + $\underline{\$34,379}$ = $\underline{\$78,350}$

Final Check   Target Figure = $\underline{\$78,350}$ (Down Payment, Orig. Equity)

$$\frac{\$78,350}{\text{Target Figure}} - \frac{\$78,350}{\text{(Present Worth)}} = \frac{0}{\text{(Rounding Adjustment)}}$$

MISCELLANEOUS PROCEDURES

Appreciation

Appreciation required to generate a specified rate of yield on equity:

By what percent must the subject property appreciate within a given holding period to produce a specified rate of yield on equity? This is the question answered by the following procedures.

- *Procedure:*

1. Using OAR Tables:
   a. Compute Overall Rate by dividing net annual income by property value.
   b. Array the five known mortgage-equity variables.
   c. Find the percent of appreciation by search and interpolation in the OAR Tables.

Problem:

The Town and Country regional shopping center has been sold to a syndicate for $8,500,000. Down payment in cash amounted to 25% of purchase price, the remaining 75% being financed on a 25-year loan at 8% interest. Net annual income is calculated to be $848,500. The investors anticipate a holding period of 10 years. What percent of appreciation would be required in order to produce a yield on equity of 18%

Solution:

   a. Overall Rate: $848,500 ÷ $8,500,000 = .099824
   b. Mortgage-equity variables:

Holding period: 10 years	Loan term: 25 years
Equity yield rate: 18%	Loan interest rate: 8%
Loan ratio: 75%	Appreciation: ?

   c. OAR at 20% Appreciation: .099827
      Precomputed OAR at 20% appreciation is so close to the calculated OAR of .099827 that interpolation is not required.

Notes:

— The procedure is a simple one, for three of the known variables in *b* will identify the relevant page in the OAR Tables: holding period, equity yield rate, and loan ratio.
— After the loan term and interest rate are also matched, the search narrows down to a list of nine Overall Rates, ranging from 40% appreciation to 40% depreciation. Interpolation will be required, if a reasonably close facsimile of the calculated OAR does not appear in the tables.

2. Using Compound Interest Tables:
The longer alternate method is of particular assistance when known variables in the problem do not match those in the OAR Tables. For purposes of illustration, the preceding problem is solved by the alternate

procedure, and is followed by one to which the preceding *procedure* would not be applicable.

a. Multiply loan ratio by loan constant.
b. Subtract the product from *a* from the Overall Rate.
c. Multiply *b* by PW 1/P
d. Multiply loan ratio by percent of loan unpaid at end of holding period.
e. Multiply *d* by PW 1.
f. Add equity ratio to *e*.
g. Subtract *c* from *f*.
h. Divide *g* by PW 1.
i. Subtract 1.0 from *h*. The difference is the plus or minus percent of appreciation/depreciation.
Note: Select PW 1 and PW 1/P factors in this procedure at the equity yield rate for the term of the holding period.

Problem 1:
Use data in the preceding problem and calculate the required percent of appreciation.

Solution:
a. $.75 \times .092618 = .0694635$
b. $.099824 - .0694635 = .0303605$
c. $.0303605 \times 4.494086 = .1364427$ (PW 1/P, 18%, 10 years)
d. $.75 \times .807633 = .60572475$
e. $.60572475 \times .191064 = .1157322$ (PW 1, 18%, 10 years)
f. $.25 + .1157322 = .3657322$
g. $.3657322 - .1364427 = .2292895$
h. $.2292895 \div .191064 = 1.2000665$ (PW 1, 18%, 10 years)
i. $1.2000665 - 1.0 = .2000665$, round to .20 or 20% appreciation

Proof:
Down payment: $.25 \times \$8,500,000 = \$2,125,000$
Loan: $.75 \times \$8,500,000 = \$6,375,000$
Debt service: $.092618 \times \$6,375,000 = \$590,440$
Cash flow: $\$848,500 - \$590,440 = \$258,060$
Resale value: $1.2000665 \times \$8,500,000 = \$10,200,565$
Loan balance, end of 10 years: $.807633 \times \$6,375,000 = \$5,148,660$
Net reversion: $\$10,200,565 - \$5,148,660 = \$5,051,905$
Present worth of cash flow (net annuity) and net reversion:
    $\$258,060 \times 4.494086 = \$1,159,744$ (PW 1/P, 18%,
                                                 10 years)

$$\$5{,}051{,}905 \times .191064 \quad = \quad 965{,}237 \qquad \text{(PW 1, 18\%,}$$
$$\text{10 years)}$$

$$\begin{array}{r} \$2{,}124{,}981 \\ \hline \end{array}$$

Adjust for rounding: $\underline{\qquad 19}$

$$\$2{,}125{,}000$$

"Target figure" is the down payment: $2,125,000.

Notes:
— Relative accuracy of the first procedure (the shorter method using the OAR Tables) is shown by the precise calculation using the Compound Interest Tables and following the last procedure.
— Adjustment of a mere $19 for rounding in the Proof is totally insignificant when analyzing an 8.5 million dollar investment.

Problem 2:
Given:
       Net annual income: $80,000
       Property value: $800,000
       Holding period: 7 years
       Equity yield rate: 14%
       Financing specifications:
             Loan ratio: 65%
             Loan term: 18 years
             Loan interest rate: 9%
Calculate the percent of appreciation required to produce an equity yield rate of 14%.

Solution:
     a. Loan Constant: $12 \times .009364 = .112368$ (PR, 9%, 216 months)
         $.65 \times .112368 = .0730392$
     b. OAR: $\$80{,}000 \div \$800{,}000 = .10$
         $.10 - .0730392 = .0269608$
     c. $.0269608 \times 4.288305 = .115616$ (PW 1/P, 14%, 7 years)
     d. Percent of Loan Unpaid, end of 7 years:
           $.009364 \times 83.606420 = .782891$ [(PR, 9%, 216 months)
           $.65 \times .782891 = .50887915$ $\times$ (PW 1/P, 9%, 132 months)]
     e. $.50887915 \times .399637 = .203367$ (PW 1, 14%, 7 years)
     f. $.35 + .203367 = .553367$
     g. $.553367 - .115616 = .437751$
     h. $.437751 \div .399637 = 1.0953715$ (PW 1, 14%, 7 years)
     i. $1.0953715 - 1.0 = .0953715$ or 9.53715%

Proof:

Down Payment: .35 × $800,000 = $280,000
Loan: .65 × $800,000 = $520,000
Debt Service: .112368 × $520,000 = $58,431
Cash Flow: $80,000 − $58,431 = $21,569
Resale Value: 1.0953715 × $800,000 = $876,297
Loan Balance, end of 7 years: .782891 × $520,000 = $407,103
Net Reversion: $876,297 − $407,103 = $469,194
Present Worth of Cash Flow (Net Annuity) and Net Reversion:

$21,569 × 4.288305 = $92,494   (PW 1/P, 14%, 7 years)
$469,194 × .399637 = $187,507   (PW 1, 14%, 7 years)

$280,001

Adjust for rounding: −   1

$280,000

"Target figure" is the down payment: $280,000.

Depreciation

Depreciation, limits of, within which yield to maturity and current yield correspond:

This procedure is directed to the client who needs to learn that there is more to a typical investment in income-producing property than current yield—"cash on cash." Deferred yield, built up through debt reduction and possible appreciation, should not be disregarded. Yield to maturity, which includes both current and deferred yield, normally *exceeds* the rate of current yield.

The illustrative problem is the same as given on page 79 under the procedure headed: "Overall Capitalization Rate, based on current yield (cash flow) requirements."

Multiply percent of debt reduction during holding period by the loan ratio.

Problem:

The Uppin Arms apartment house is valued at $625,000, applying an OAR of .1152 to net annual income of $72,000. Financing data includes the following: loan ratio, 70%; interest rate, 9%; and loan term, 15 years. A holding period of 10 years is anticipated. The prospective purchaser requires a current yield on equity of 10%. By what percent could the property depreciate in value within the holding period, if yield to maturity will also be 10%?

Solution:
.511394 × .70 = .3579758, round to .36 or 36% depreciation, if yield to maturity is only 10% (corresponding to current yield rate of 10%)

Proof:
Down Payment: .30 × $625,000 = $187,500
Loan: .70 × $625,000 = $437,500
Loan Balance, end of 10 years: .488606 × $437,500 = $213,765
Required Resale Value:

Return of Capital (Down Payment):	$187,500
Loan Balance (assumed or paid off):	$213,765
Total:	$401,265

Amount of Depreciation: $625,000 − $401,265 = $223,735
Percent of Depreciation: $223,735 ÷ $625,000 = .357976, round to *36%*

Notes:
— Refer to page 79 to place the problem in context.
— Uppin Arms apartments would depreciate 36% in 10 years, if 10% yield is *all* the investor realizes. Equity buildup through debt reduction would be wiped out completely. Required resale value includes only a recapture of the down payment made at the time of purchase, and the loan balance to be assumed by a new buyer or paid off.
— It is unreasonable to assume that any investor would purchase the property for $625,000 if he believes it would be worth only about $400,000 after 10 years.
— The preceding procedure, appropriately applied, can serve as an effective sales tool.

Extension of the Compound Interest Tables

Procedures outlined expand the range of the prepared tables by extending them to a greater number of time periods or to a monthly term that does not correspond to an annual interval.

In this book three types of compound interest factors are used: Present Worth of 1, Present Worth of 1 Per Period, and Periodic Repayment. By making a simple adjustment and by utilizing factors as divisors as well as multipliers, the analyst can employ three tables to do the work of six. PW 1 factors can be extended directly. PW 1/P and PR factors are extended indirectly, as detailed in the procedures.

112

Present Worth of 1:

● *Procedure:*

Multiply PW 1 factors for any two or more time periods whose sum equals the number of the period for which a factor is sought.

Problem:

By extension, compute the monthly PW 1 factor at 9% nominal annual rate for 8 years 4 months.

Solution:

From the Compound Interest Tables, select the following factors:
PW 1, 9%, 4 months: .970554
PW 1, 9%, 96 months: .488062
Multiplying: .970554 × .488062 = .473691

Present Worth of 1 Per Period:

● *Procedure:*

a. Compute the corresponding PW 1 factor by extension.
b. Subtract factor in *a* from 1.0.
c. Divide *b* by the effective interest rate.
Note: PW 1/P = (1.0 − PW 1) ÷ i

Problem:

Calculate the annual PW 1/P factor at 6% for 75 years.

Solution:

a. .097222 × .130105 = .0126491   (PW 1, 6%, 40 years and 35 years)
b. 1.0 − .0126491 = .9873509
c. .9873509 ÷ .06 = 16.455848

Periodic Repayment:

● *Procedure:*

a. Compute the corresponding PW 1 factor by extension.
b. Subtract factor in *a* from 1.0.
c. Divide the effective interest rate by *b*.
Note: PR = i ÷ (1.0 − PW 1)

Problem:

Calculate the annual PR factor at 6% for 75 years.

Solution:
- a. $.097222 \times .130105 = .0126491$ (PW 1, 6%, 40 years and 35 years)
- b. $1.0 - .0126491 = .9873509$
- c. $.06 \div .9873509 = .060769$

Notes:
- — In *a* the PW 1 factors for any two or more periods adding up to 75 could have been used, such as PW 1 factors for years 37 and 38; or 20, 40, and 15.
- — Steps *a* and *b* are the same in calculating both PW 1/P and PR. In *c* the same figures are used in each, but division is reversed. (PW 1/P and PR are reciprocals.)

Growth of Money at Compound Interest

Growth of a Series of Periodic Deposits

Procedure:
1. Amount of periodic deposit required, which will grow to a specified future sum:

This procedure in effect determines the deposit to be made in a sinking fund. Known elements include: (1) amount to be accumulated (a future goal set); (2) frequency of deposit; (3) interest rate to be received; and (4) the specified time during which deposits are to be made. The single unknown is the amount of periodic deposit required.

Multiply the specified future sum by (PR − i).

Problem:
An investor wished to accumulate $15,000 in 8 years by placing monthly deposits in an account paying 5% nominal annual rate, interest to be compounded monthly. Determine the amount of monthly deposit required.

Solution:
PR factor at 5% for 96 months: .012660
Effective monthly interest rate: .00417
PR − i: $.012660 − .00417 = .00849$
$15,000 \times .00849 = \$127.35$

Notes:
- — The periodic repayment factor minus the interest rate (PR − i) *is* the sinking fund factor.

— Monthly deposits of $127.35 will grow to $15,000 in 8 years at a nominal annual interest rate of 5% (.417% effective monthly rate), interest compounded monthly.

2. Amount to which a series of uniform deposits will grow at compound interest:

Divide the periodic deposit by (PR − i).

Problem 1:
A deposit of $200 is made at the end of each month for 10 years in an account paying a nominal annual rate of 6%, interest to be compounded monthly. To what sum would the deposits grow in 10 years?

Solution:
    PR factor at 6% for 120 months: .011102
    Effective monthly interest rate: .005
    PR − i: .011102 − .005 = .006102
    $200 ÷ .006102 = $32,776

Problem 2:
A client's offer to purchase an apartment house is contingent upon the seller's agreeing to carry $40,000 of the purchase price on a second mortgage. Terms as written up on the deposit receipt specify an interest rate of 9% and a loan term of 8 years, with monthly payments to amortize. Before presenting the offer to the seller, the broker calculates the monthly payment required on the second mortgage. He also computes the sum to which these loan amortization payments would grow, if the seller places each payment received in a 6% savings account, and lets the deposits compound monthly for 8 years, at which time the second mortgage is paid in full. If the seller accepts the offer and carries the second mortgage, what amount could be accumulated in his savings account in 8 years?

Solution:
    Monthly payment to amortize $40,000 at 9% in 8 years:
        $40,000 × .014650 = $586   (PR, 9% 96 months)
    Monthly deposit for 8 years in a 6% savings account: $586

    Growth of 96 monthly deposits of $586 at a nominal annual rate of 6%, interest compounded monthly:
        PR factor at 6% for 96 months: .013141
        Effective monthly interest rate:.005
        PR − i: .013141 − .005 = .008141
        $586 ÷ .008141 = $71,981

Notes:
- — If the seller does not need the $40,000 in cash at the time of sale, the possible future sum of nearly $72,000 may look good to him.
- — Such a simple analysis as shown here might assist in securing the seller's signature of acceptance.

Growth of a Single Deposit or Investment

Procedure:
1. Amount of single deposit or investment required when future worth is given:
Future worth is known or is estimated. The unknown to be calculated is present worth.

Multiply future worth by PW 1.

Problem:
Land lying in the direction of urban growth has an estimated value of $12,000 an acre 7 years hence, when it is anticipated that residential development is due. Interim rental of the parcel is sufficient to pay ad valorem property taxes only. The purchaser plans to pay cash for the land and expects a yield of 12% on his investment. What price per acre can he feasibly offer?

Solution:
$12,000 × .452349 = $5,428   (PW 1, 12%, 7 years)

Note: Resale of the land in 7 years at $12,000 per acre would return the capital investment of $5,428 per acre, plus 12% yield compounded annually. In other words, $5,428 invested at 12% would grow to $12,000 in 7 years . . . which leads into the next procedure.

2. Amount to which a single deposit or investment will grow:
Present worth is known—future worth is to be calculated.

Divide amount of deposit or investment by PW 1.

Problem:
Don Shure has purchased land for cash, paying $3,600 an acre. He anticipates appreciation at the rate of 14% a year for the next 12 years. Calculate the expected sales price (future worth) at the end of the 12-year holding period.

Solution:
    $3,600 ÷ .207559 = $17,344   (PW 1, 14%, 12 years)

Note: If expectations were not to be realized and property simply doubled in value in 12 years, the rate would be cut to about 6% . . . which leads into the next procedure.

3. Time required to double a sum at any interest or yield rate, compounded:

• *Procedure 1 ("Rule of 72"):*
    Divide 72 by the interest or yield rate.

Problem:
In how many years will an investment double in value at 18% yield?

Solution:
    72 ÷ 18 = 4 years

Notes:
    — The "Rule of 72" is accurate to the nearest year; it does not determine the month.
    — A precise calculation shows that money will double in 70 years at 1%. Why not a "Rule of 70?" For a very practical reason: more figures can be divided evenly into 72 than into 70. This deviation does not distort calculation to the nearest year.
    — Conversely, the "Rule of 72" can be used to determine the yield rate required to double an investment in a given period of time: Divide 72 by the number of years. For example, to find the rate needed to double money in 8 years: 72 ÷ 8 = 9%.

• *Procedure 2 (Present Worth of 1 Table):*
    In the PW 1 tables at the specified yield rate, find the entry of a factor which is approximately .50. (The number of the period opposite the .50 factor indicates the year in which money will double at the given rate.)

Problem:
In how many years will money double at a rate of 15% compounded annually?

Solution:
    PW 1 factor at 15% for 5 years: .497177

Mortgage and Trust Deed Analysis

Expertise in mortgage analysis will benefit the counsellor in his under-
standing and utilization of the mortgage-equity technique. Supplemental
Tables in the textbook array precomputed loan constants, loan balances,
and debt reduction in five-year intervals to facilitate computations. The
analyst should, however, be able to make these calculations (and a number
of related ones) at any interest rate for any period of time. So far as
possible, he should calculate rather than interpolate.

Determination of cash flow and net reversion, which are basic ingre-
dients of the mortgage-equity technique, cannot be made without analyzing
the given terms of the mortgage or trust deed; nor can a sales price be
adjusted for terms without a proper conversion of nonconventional
financing instruments (particularly purchase-money mortgages carried by
the seller) to a cash equivalent.

Balloon payment, calculation of:

- *Procedure:*
  a. Multiply the periodic loan payment by PW 1/P for the final period of
     the payment schedule.
  b. Subtract the product computed in *a* from the original principal
     amount.
  c. Divide the difference found in *b* by PW 1 for the final period.

Problem:
A purchase-money mortgage for $450,000 is carried by the seller. Terms of
the loan call for an interest rate of 9½%, monthly payments of $4,000 for 12
years, and unpaid principal balance due and payable at the end of 12 years.
Compute the balloon payment.

Solution:

    a. $4,000 × 85.735849 = $342,943   (PW 1/P, 9½%, 144 months)
    b. $450,000 − $342,943 = $107,057
    c. $107,057 ÷ .321258 = $333,243   (PW 1, 9½%, 144 months)

Proof:

    Value = (Annuity × PW 1/P) + (Reversion × PW 1)

        = ($4,000 × 85.735849) + ($333,243 × .321258)

        = $342,943 + $107,057

        = $450,000

From the lender's point of view the periodic loan payment he receives constitutes an annuity, and the balloon payment, a reversion.

Loan constant:

The loan constant is the amount paid annually on a loan (principal and interest included) as a percent of original principal, debt service to remain constant until the loan is fully amortized.

- *Procedure:*
    a. Annual PR factor as a percent (if annual payment is specified), or
    b. Monthly PR factor multiplied by 12 (if monthly payments are called for), or
    c. Payment(s) made in one year divided by original principal, or
    d. Any stipulated percent in excess of the annual interest rate.

Illustrations:
    a. On a 9½% loan for 15 years with annual payments, the PR factor is .127744. Therefore, the loan constant is .127744, or 12.7744%.
    b. If a loan is made at 10% with monthly payments for 14 years, the loan constant is the PR factor of .0110802 × 12, or .132984 (13.2984%).
    c. On a loan of $75,000, annual payments of $7,000 until paid, the loan constant is $7,000 ÷ $75,000, or .0933 (9.33%).
    d. An 8% loan might be set up with a loan constant of 9.5% to amortize. On a loan of $100,000 annual payments would be $9,500, including principal and interest.

Payment, periodic, to amortize a loan:

- *Procedure:*
    Multiply the principal amount by the PR factor.

Problem:
Compute the monthly payment to amortize a loan of $375,000 at 8½% in 29 years.

Solution:
   $375,000 × .007748 = $2,905.50   (PR, 9½%, 348 months)

Payment, periodic, to amortize a specified percent of principal in a stipulated period of time:

- *Procedure:*
    a. Subtract the effective interest rate from the PR factor.

b. Multiply *a* by the percent to be amortized.
c. Add the effective interest rate to the product computed in *b*.
d. Multiply the original principal amount by the adjusted PR factor as determined by *c*.

Problem:
A loan on a commercial building is made on the following terms:
  Principal amount: $800,000
  Interest rate: 9%
  Term: 15 years
  Payment schedule: Monthly payments to amortize 60% of the principal amount by maturity. Balance of 40% due as a balloon payment at the end of 15 years.
Compute the monthly payment required.

Solution:
  a. Nominal annual interest rate: .09
     Effective monthly interest rate: .0075
     .010143 − .0075 = .002643   (PR, 9%, 180 months)
  b. .60 × .002643 = .0015858
  c. .0015858 + .0075 = .0090858
  d. $800,000 × .0090858 = $7,268.64
     Monthly payment of $7,268.64 will keep all interest current and reduce the principal amount by $480,000, leaving $320,000 due as a balloon payment at the end of 15 years.

Present worth of a mortgage discounted to a yield rate higher or lower than the loan interest rate:

● *Procedure:*
  a. Determine current yield rate as indicated by the mortgage market.
  b. Multiply the periodic loan payment by PW 1/P.
  c. Multiply the balloon payment (if any) by PW 1.
  d. Add *b* and *c*.

Problem:
A mortgage for $450,000 at 9½% runs for 12 years. Payment schedule specifies monthly payments of $4,000 for 144 months and a balloon payment of $333,243 at the end of 144 months. The lender wishes to "cash out" and offers the mortgage for sale. Assume that the private money market indicates the mortgage would be saleable if discounted to yield 15%. Calculate the discounted value.

Solution:

   a. Yield rate given: 15%
   b. $4,000 × 66.627722   = $266,511   (PW 1/P, 15%, 144 months)
   c. $333,243 × .167153   = <u>$55,703</u>   (PW 1, 15%, 144 months)
   d. Discounted value: $322,214

Notes:
   — Problem is the same as given under the procedure "Balloon payment, calculation of."
   — The income stream generated by the terms of the mortgage is discounted precisely to a true yield rate. This is in contrast to the "broad brush" approach of discounting the principal amount of the mortgage by a given percent.
   — Discounting to a yield rate rather than taking a percent "off the top" is recommended. This procedure automatically considers and adjusts for all variable factors in the mortgage note: principal amount, stated interest rate, term of the loan, periodic payment, balloon payment, and the higher yield rate that the purchaser of the mortgage or trust deed requires.
   — The procedure outlined and illustrated in this section can be used by the analyst in calculating the "cash equivalent" of nonconventional purchase-money mortgages carried by the seller. Adjusting sales price for terms by such a computation is an essential step in deriving an Overall Rate from the market.

Principal amount of loan when other terms are known:

● *Procedure:*
   Multiply the periodic loan payment by PW 1/P.

Problem:
Monthly payments of $540.26 will amortize a loan at 8% interest in 25 years. What is the principal amount of the loan?

Solution:
   $540.26 × 129.564523 = $69,998.50, round to $70,000

                                  (PW 1/P, 8%, 300 months)

Note: As a sidelight, note that this procedure can be used to calculate the amount of loan a home buyer is able to handle, within the limitations of a specified monthly payment. For example, assume he can pay $300 a month on principal and interest. A loan can be arranged at 9½%, monthly payments to amortize in 30 years. What is the maximum loan he should consider? Here is the calculation:

$300 × 118.926681 = $35,678   (PW 1/P, 9½%, 360 months)

He should stay within about $35,500

Principal balance unpaid, amount of, at any time on an amortized loan:

- *Procedure:*
  Multiply the periodic loan payment by PW 1/P for the number of periods remaining unpaid in the full amortization schedule.

Problem:
On a 25-year loan of $150,000 at 8½%, monthly payments of $1,270.80, what is the principal balance remaining unpaid after 10 years?

Solution:
$1,207.80 × 101.549693 = $122,652   (PW 1/P, 8½%, 180 months)

Principal balance unpaid, percent of, at any time on an amortized loan:

- *Procedure:*
  Multiply the PR factor for the full loan term by the PW 1/P factor for the number of periods remaining unpaid.

Problem:
Calculate the percent of loan unpaid at the end of 12 years on a 9% loan with monthly payments to amortize in 18 years.

Solution:
PR, 9%, 216 months: .009364
PW 1/P, 9%, 72 months: 55.476849
.009364 × 55.476849 = .519485 or 51.9485%

Note: This procedure was used to calculate "Loan Balances" for the Supplemental Tables.

Principal paid off, amount of, at any time on an amortized loan:

- *Procedure:*
  a. Multiply the periodic loan payment by PW 1/P for the number of periods remaining unpaid.
  b. Subtract *a* from the original principal amount.

Problem:
Monthly payments to amortize a loan of $80,000 at 8½% in 15 years amount to $787.76. What amount has been applied to principal by the end of 7 years?

Solution:
   a. $787.76 × 69.482425 = 54,735   (PW 1/P, 8½%, 96 months)
   b. $80,000 − $54,735 = $25,265

Principal paid off, percent of, at any time on an amortized loan:

● *Procedure:*
   a. Multiply the PR factor for the full loan term by PW 1/P for the number of periods remaining unpaid.
   b. Subtract *a* from 1.0.

Problem:
Use data from the prior problem and calculate the percent by which principal has been reduced in 7 years.

Solution:
   a. .009847 × 69.482425 = .6841934   (PR, 8½%, 180 months)
                                        × (PW 1/P, 8½%, 96 months)
   b. 1.0 − .6841934 = .3158066 or 31.58066%

Note: This procedure was used to calculate "Debt Reduction" for the Supplemental Tables.

Rate of interest on an amortized loan:

● *Procedure:*
   a. Divide periodic loan payment by original principal.
   b. Locate quotient from *a* in the PR tables.
   c. Interpolate, if necessary.

Problem:
Monthly payments to amortize a loan of $320,000 in 20 years are $2,577.92. What is the rate of interest?

Solution:
   a. $2,577.92 ÷ $320,000 = .008056
   b. By search in the PR tables: 7½% interest rate. PR factor at 7½% for 240 months is .008056, corresponding precisely to the quotient in *a*.

Note: Step *b* involves a *horizontal* search, for loan term is known. First, estimate an interest rate, turn to the PR tables, then compare the pre-computed PR factor with the one calculated in *a*, which is the "target figure." If the two factors do not match, go forward to a higher rate or back to a lower one. Stay on the proper horizontal time line throughout the search. If the figure calculated in *a* falls between two rates, interpolate by simple proportion.

Rate of interest (true rate) on a loan with "points" paid by the borrower:

- *Procedure:*
    a. Subtract initial "point" charge in dollars from principal amount of loan.
    b. Divide periodic loan payment by the remainder calculated in *a*.
    c. Locate the quotient from *b* in the PR tables.
    d. Interpolate, if necessary.

Problem:
A borrower pays 4 "points" on a loan of $150,000 at 9%, monthly payments to amortize in 20 years. Calculate the true interest rate.

Solution:
    a. Point charge: .04 × $150,000 = $6,000
       Net loan proceeds: $150,000 − $6,000 = $144,000
    b. Monthly payment: $150,000 × .008997 = $1,349.55
                                            (PR, 9%, 240 months)

       $1,349.55 ÷ $144,000 = .009371875
    c. PR, 9½%, 240 months: .009321
       PR, 10%, 240 months: .009650
    d. "Target figure" of .009371875 from *b* is bracketed between 9½% and 10%. Observation indicates the true rate is closer to 9½% than to 10%. By interpolation: true interest rate, about 9.5773%

Note: As the actual interest rate is *increased* the loan ratio is in effect being *decreased*.

Time required to amortize a loan:

- *Procedure:*
    a. Divide the periodic loan payment by original principal.
    b. Locate the quotient from *a* in the PR tables.

124

Problem:
A loan of $45,000 at 8% calls for monthly payments of $416.21 until paid.
What is the term of the loan?

Solution:
  a. $416.21 ÷ $45,000 = .009249 (target figure)
  b. PR factor at 8% for 192 months (16 years): .009249. Loan will be fully
     amortized in 16 years.

Note: The search is a quick, vertical one, for interest rate is known.

**Time when, in an amortized loan schedule, a specified percent of loan
payment applies to principal:**

• *Procedure:*
  a. Add 1 to the loan term in months or years.
  b. Find the month or year in which the PW 1 factor is equal to or
     approximates the stipulated percent applied to principal.
  c. Subtract the number of the month or year in *b* from the sum deter-
     mined in *a*.

Problem:
Income property can be financed at 8½% interest on a 25-year loan to be
amortized by equal annual payments. The prospective buyer estimates a
turnover point would be reached when 25% of the annual payment to
amortize applies to principal. Based on this premise, what is the length of
the projected holding period?

Solution:
  a. 25 + 1 = 26
  b. PW 1 at 8½% for year 17 is .249859 (approximately .25)
  c. 26 − 17 = 9 years
     In year 9 about 25% of the total loan payment applies to principal
     (nondeductible for income tax purposes) and 75% to interest (de-
     ductible).

Notes:
  — Prior to year 9 *less* than 25% of each payment applies to principal and
    more than 75% applies to interest. After year 9 the converse is true.
  — The PW 1 factors can be used in reverse order as a "read out" of the
    percent of total loan payment applied to principal each succeeding
    period. For example, in the illustration given, 13.0094% of the
    payment made in year 1 applies to principal; 14.1152% in year 2; and
    so on, up the table to year 25, when 92.1659% applies to principal.

This method is a practical one in preparing a complete loan amortization schedule. The total periodic loan payment, as a constant, is multiplied by the PW 1 factors in reverse order. The products indicate the amount applied to principal from each payment in the schedule.

— The same procedure can be used to find the point in time when any given percent of the total periodic payment applies to principal. For example, to determine in the preceding problem when approximately 40% applies to principal: $(25 + 1) - 11 =$ year 15. The analyst can also follow these guidelines in coming up with an answer to a question frequently asked by a borrower, particularly a homebuyer, "When do we reach the point when we are paying as much on principal as we are on interest?"

— The method outlined can be used in a monthly amortization schedule. However, to identify the specific month rather than the year only, the analyst should utilize a complete monthly tabulation of PW 1 factors, such as in the recommended "Financial Compound Interest and Annuity Tables," Financial Publishing Company, Boston, Massachusetts. To illustrate in the problem given, assume monthly payments, rather than annual, to amortize in 300 months. Calculation of the exact month in which 25% of the loan payment applies to principal is as follows:

    a. $300 + 1 = 301$
    b. PW 1 factor for month 196 is .250715
    c. $301 - 196 = 105$
       When payment is made in month 105 (8 years, 9 months) slightly more than 25% applies to principal.

— The basic rationale for this procedure is that the scheduled payments to amortize a loan can be considered as a series of consecutive investments, all payments reverting to the borrower at the end of the loan term, when the property can be declared "free and clear." In the case of the 25-year loan with annual payments stipulated, payment number 1 is tied up for 25 years; payment 2, for 24 years; payment 3, for 23 years; and so on. PW 1 factors, applied to the payments, automatically compute and deduct interest on a declining principal balance, the remainder of each payment (present worth) being the amount applied to principal.

"Mortgaging Out"

Market value required for investor to "mortgage out":

An investor may choose to refinance instead of selling at the end of a

126

feasible holding period. A plausible objective would be to obtain a new conventional loan in an amount sufficient to (1) pay off the existing mortgage balance, and (2) provide an additional amount of cash equal to the down payment made at the time of purchase. Equity buildup through debt reduction and appreciation provides the base for refinancing.

Total capital recapture through refinancing enables the investor to "mortgage out" and retain ownership of the property. He can initiate a new holding period for the present property and make an additional investment with dollars which were previously locked in.

Maximum loan ratio at the time of refinancing may be equal to, greater than, or less than the loan ratio at the time of purchase. Whatever the new loan ratio may be, application of the following procedure should determine the minimum dollar amount of market value required at the end of a specified holding period, if the investor "mortgages out."

- *Procedure:*
  1. **Required market value as a dollar amount:**
     a. Calculate loan balance at end of initial holding period (time of refinancing).
     b. Add original equity (down payment) to *a*.
     c. Divide *b* by estimated new loan ratio (at time of refinancing).

Problem:
Assume the purchaser of Sunset Point Apartments holds the property for 10 years, at which time he expects to "mortgage out" by refinancing. The new loan must be large enough to pay off the balance owing on the existing loan and provide an additional amount equal to the down payment made when the investor purchased Sunset Point. Sales price was $2,261,228, and property was financed for $1,695,921 (75% of value) on a 20-year loan at 9½% interest. Buyer paid a cash down payment of $565,307. On the assumption that the property can be refinanced for 75% of value at the end of 10 years, calculate required market value which would enable the investor to "mortgage out."

Solution:
    a. Loan balance: .720362 × $1,695,921 = $1,221,677
    b. $1,221,677 + $565,307 = $1,786,984
    c. $1,786,984 ÷ .75 = $2,382,645
Proof:
    Amount of new loan: .75 × $2,382,645 = $1,786,984
    Less old loan balance: −   1,221,677

    Return of capital investment
      (down payment) $565,307

Notes:
- — Based on a loan ratio of 75% and a market value of $2,382,645 at the time of refinancing, the investor's equity is calculated to be $595,661 *after* a recapture of his down payment of $565,307 the original equity. The equity remaining in the investment represents deferred yield, built up by debt reduction and appreciation. These deferred-yield dollars stay locked in for the duration of the second holding period.
- — Assume new loan ratio is lower than the original 75% loan ratio. See the effect in raising the required market value, if the investor "mortgages out" completely at 70% loan ratio:
    $$\$1,786,984 \div .70 = \$2,552,834$$
  at 65% loan ratio:
    $$\$1,786,984 \div .65 = \$2,749,206$$
- — Conversely, a possible increase in loan ratio would lower the required market value as a base for refinancing in order to "mortgage out" at 80% loan ratio:
    $$\$1,786,984 \div .80 = \$2,233,730$$

2. Required market value as a percent of purchase price:
   a. Multiply original loan ratio by the percent of principal unpaid at end of initial holding period (time of refinancing).
   b. Add original equity ratio to *a*.
   c. Divide *b* by estimated new loan ratio (at time of refinancing).

Problem:
Use data from prior problem:
   Initial holding period: 10 years
   Equity ratio: 25%
   Loan ratio: 75%
   Loan term: 20 years
   Loan interest rate: 9½%
   Assumed loan ratio at time of refinancing: 75%
Calculate required market value as a percent of purchase price, to enable the investor to "mortgage out."

Solution:
   a. $.75 \times .720362 = .5402715$
   b. $.25 + .5402715 = .7902715$
   c. $.7902715 \div .75 = 1.0536953$ or 105.36953%

Proof:
   Required market value: $\$2,261,228 \times 1.0536953 = \$2,382,645$
   Calculation corresponds to answer in the previous solution.

Notes:
   — If property appreciates 5.37% or more within the next 10 years, the investor can "mortgage out", assuming Sunset Point can be refinanced for 75% of market value.
   — A greater percentage of appreciation and/or a higher loan ratio would provide not only a total return of invested capital (down payment) but also a partial capture of deferred yield. For example, presume Sunset Point appreciates 10% during the initial 10-year holding period and can be refinanced for 75% of value:
   Increased market value: 1.10 × $2,261,228 = $2,487,351
   New loan: .75 × $2,487,351 = $1,865,513
   Net proceeds from refinancing:
   $1,865,513
   − 1,221,677   (old loan balance)
   $643,836
   Partial capture of deferred yield:
   $643,836
   − 565,307   (down payment)
   $78,529
   — If Sunset Point is refinanced after the initial holding period for 75% of value (market value at time of refinancing) the investor can reestablish an advantageous leverage position. Equity ratio will have increased in 10 years from 25% to over 50% and by taking out a new loan the owner may reduce his equity once more to possibly 25%.
   — Refinancing might place the investor in a more favorable income tax position so that he can extend the initial 10-year holding period.
   — Negotiating a new loan *may* be feasible, even at a higher interest rate.
   — There are no stock answers as to the advisability of selling versus "mortgaging out" by refinancing. Informed decision-making will rely on careful analysis of the alternatives.

Net Annuity (Cash Flow)

The term "Cash Flow" as used in this book refers to net annual income after loan payments (debt service) but before income taxes. Positive cash flow is, in a typical situation, current yield on equity. If loan payments exceed net annual income, a negative cash flow or out-of-pocket expenditure results. While a favorable positive cash flow is a requirement of many investors, there are special circumstances under which a negative cash flow (or even negative income) may be feasible: (1) 100% financing; (2) nonproducing property purchased for appreciation; and (3) election by an investor to shorten a normal loan term and accelerate debt reduction. The Supplemental Tables of "Loan Constants" will expedite calculation of cash flow in mortgage-equity analysis.

Cash flow, annual amount of:

- *Procedure:*
    a. Multiply original principal amount of the loan by the loan constant.
    b. Subtract *a* from net annual income.

Problem 1:
Property purchased for $600,000 produces net annual income of $68,000. It is financed for 80% of value on a 25-year loan at 10% interest. Calculate annual cash flow.

Solution:
    a. Principal amount of loan: .80 × $600,000 = $480,000
       Debt service: .109044 × $480,000 = $52,341
    b. Cash flow: $68,000 − $52,341 = $15,659

Problem 2:
Assume a loan term of 10 years, with all other data in Problem 1 remaining unchanged. Determine the effect on cash flow.

Solution:
    a. Debt service: .158581 × $480,000 = $76,119
    b. Negative cash flow: $68,000 − $76,119 = −$8,119

Note: Refer to pages 92 to 95 to calculate cash flow as a percent of (1) equity, or (2) property value.

Cash flow, present worth of:

Net annual income, properly processed to a level ordinary annuity equivalent, is the *gross annuity*. Cash flow (which is net annual income less loan payments) constitutes to the investor a *net annuity*. Present worth is calculated by the annuity factor. Cash flow is the first of the investor's "future net benefits" as shown in the 15-point analysis form.

- *Procedure:*
    Multiply cash flow by PW 1/P at the specified yield rate for the term of the holding period.

Problem:
Property in preceding problem produces annual cash flow of $15,659. Calculate present worth at a yield rate of 14% for a period of 10 years.

Solution:
$15,659 × 5.216116 = $81,679   (PW 1/P, 14%, 10 years)

Note: The Present Worth of 1 Per Period factor, as a multiplier, automatically calculates and subtracts compound interest from the future income stream and thus "discounts" it to present worth.

Net Reversion

A reversion is a single future income payment or value to be received by the investor. In the mortgage-equity concept, the *gross reversion* is the resale value of the property at the end of a limited holding period. The *net reversion* is resale value less loan balance. The net reversion includes (1) capital recapture and (2) deferred yield. Capital recapture provides a return of the down payment, the actual dollar investment. Deferred yield, built up by debt reduction and possible appreciation, is locked in until the time of reversion. Relate the following procedures to the "Investment Analysis and Proof of Computations—Fifteen-Point Summary of Calculations."

Net reversion, dollar amount of:

- *Procedure:*
    a. Calculate estimated resale value at end of holding period.
    b. Compute loan balance at end of holding period.
    c. Subtract *b* from *a*.

Problem:
Given:
        Property value: $750,000
        Holding period: 10 years
        Appreciation: 20%
        Financing:
                Loan ratio: 70%
                Loan term: 30 years
                Loan interest rate: 8½%
Calculate the net reversion at the end of the holding period.

Solution:
  a. Resale value: 1.20 × \$750,000 = \$900,000
  b. Principal amount of loan: .70 × \$750,000 = \$525,000
    Loan balance, end of 10 years: .886025 × \$525,000 = \$465,163
  c. Net reversion: \$900,000 − \$465,163 = \$434,837

Notes:
— Down payment: .30 × \$750,000 = \$225,000
— Net reversion of \$434,837 includes:

Recapture of capital:	\$225,000
Deferred yield:	
Debt reduction: .113975 × \$525,000 =	59,837
Appreciation: .20 × \$750,000 =	150,000
	\$434,837

Net reversion, present worth of:

The net reversion is the second portion of the investor's "future net benefits." This single lump sum payment is the terminal segment of the total income stream, as shown in the mortgage-equity 15-point analysis.

• *Procedure:*
Multiply net reversion by PW 1 at the specified yield rate for the term of the holding period.

Problem:
Net reversion computed in the preceding problem amounts to \$434,837 at the end of a 10-year holding period. Calculate its present worth at a yield rate of 16%.

Solution:
  \$434,837 × .226684 = \$98,571   (PW 1, 16%, 10 years)

Notes:
— A deposit of \$98,571 in a hypothetical account paying 16% compounded annually would grow to \$434,837 in 10 years.
— Item 15 of the "Investment Analysis and Proof of Computations" ties together present worth of both cash flow (net annuity) and net reversion in a basic equation:
    Value of Equity = (Cash Flow × PW 1/P) + (Net Reversion × PW 1)
The down payment (original equity) is the "target figure." To reiterate and emphasize: Value is the present worth of future net benefits.

Net reversion as a percent of purchase price (value):

- *Procedure:*
  a. Express estimated resale value as a percent of purchase price.
  b. Multiply loan ratio by percent of loan unpaid at end of holding period.
  c. Subtract Step *b* from Step *a*. (Difference is net reversion as a percent of purchase price. To calculate dollar amount of net reversion, multiple Step *c* by purchase price.)

Problem:

Given:

        Net annual income: $96,000
        Holding period: 10 years
        Equity yield rate: 14%
        Appreciation: 20%
        Loan ratio: 75%
        Loan term: 20 years
        Loan interest rate: 9%

Calculate the net reversion at the end of the holding period as a percent of purchase price and determine the dollar amount of net reversion.

Solution:

    a. $1.0 + .20 = 1.20$
    b. $.75 \times .710259 = .53269425$
    c. $1.20 - .53269425 = .66730575$
    Dollar amount of net reversion:
        Value (purchase price): $96,000 \div .094395 = \$1,017,003$
        Net reversion: $.66730575 \times \$1,017,003 = \$678,652$

Proof:

    See 15-point investment analysis. Note Item 12: Net Reversion, $678,653 (adjust $1 for rounding)

Investment Analysis and Proof of Computations
Fifteen-Point Summary of Calculations

1.	Over-all Rate Selected from OAR Tables or Computed				.094395
2.	Property Value	$96,000 (INCOME)	÷	.094395 (OAR)	= $1,017,003
3.	Original Equity (Down Payment)	.25 (Equity Ratio)	x	$1,017,003 (Value)	= 254,251
4.	Amount of Loan (Original Principal)	.75 (Loan Ratio)	x	1,017,003 (Value)	= 762,752
5.	Debt Service (Yearly Payments)	.107967 (Loan Constant)	x	762,752 (Principal)	= 82,352

Investment Analysis and Proof of Computations
Fifteen-Point Summary of Calculations
(cont.)

6. Cash Flow
(Annuity)

$$\underset{\text{(Net Income)}}{96,000} - \underset{\text{(Debt Service)}}{82,352} = 13,648$$

7. Debt Coverage Ratio

$$\underset{\text{(Net Income)}}{96,000} \div \underset{\text{(Debt Service)}}{82,352} = 1.165728$$

8. Rate of Current Yield On Equity

$$\underset{\text{(Cash Flow)}}{13,648} \div \underset{\text{(Orig. Equity)}}{254,251} = .05368$$

9. Loan Balance
(End Holding Period)

$$\underset{\text{(\% Unpaid)}}{.710259} \times \underset{\text{(Principal)}}{762,752} = 541,751$$

10. Resale Value as % of Original Value

$$\underset{\text{(Orig. Val. as \%)}}{100} \overset{+}{\underset{-}{}} \underset{\text{(\% Appr/Dep)}}{20} = 120\%$$

11. Resale Value as a Dollar Amount

$$\underset{\text{(Resale Val. as \%)}}{120\%} \times \underset{\text{(Original Value)}}{1,017,003} = 1,220,404$$

12. Reversion, Net
(Terminal Equity)

$$\underset{\text{(Resale Value)}}{1,220,404} - \underset{\text{(Loan Balance)}}{541,751} = 678,653$$

13. Deferred Yield
(Amount)

$$\underset{\text{(Reversion Net)}}{678,653} - \underset{\text{(Down Payment)}}{254,251} = 424,402$$

14. Terminal Equity Ratio

$$\underset{\text{(Reversion Net)}}{678,653} \div \underset{\text{(Resale Value)}}{1,220,404} = .55609$$

15. Proof of Yield on Equity

Equity Yield Rate: ___14___ (Percent)   Term in Years: ___10___ (Holding Period)

Present Worth of 1 Per Period: __5.216116__ (PW 1/P)   Present Worth of 1: __.269744__ (PW 1)

Equation of Proof

Present Worth = ($\underset{\text{(Cash Flow)}}{\$13,648}$ × $\underset{\text{(PW 1/P)}}{5.216116}$) + ($\underset{\text{(Net Reversion)}}{\$678,653}$ × $\underset{\text{(PW 1)}}{.269744}$)

= __$71,190__ + __$183,063__ = __$254,253__

Final Check Target Figure = __$254,251__

(Down Payment, Orig. Equity)

$$\underset{\text{Target Figure}}{\$254,251} - \underset{\text{(Present Worth)}}{\$254,253} = \underset{\text{(Rounding Adjustment)}}{-\$2}$$

Resale Value Required

Resale value required to produce a specified yield on equity:

- *Procedure:*
  a. Multiply cash flow by PW 1/P at equity yield rate for term of holding period.

b. Subtract *a* from the down payment (original equity).
c. Divide *b* by PW 1 at equity yield rate for term of holding period.
d. Add *c* to loan balance at end of holding period.

Problem:
Property valued at $900,000 can be financed for 75% of value on a loan at 9½% interest to be amortized in 25 years by monthly payments. Net annual income is $96,000. The prospective purchaser plans to hold the property for 10 years and expects a yield to maturity of 16%. What resale value would be required to generate equity yield of 16%?

Solution:
a. Amount of loan: .75 × $900,000 = $675,000
Debt service: .104844 × $675,000 = $70,770
Cash flow: $96,000 − $70,770 = $25,230
$25,230 × 4.833227 = $121,942 (PW 1/P, 16%, 10 years)
b. Down payment: .25 × $900,000= $225,000
$225,000 − $121,942 = $103,058
c. $103,058 ÷ .226684 = $454,633 (PW 1, 16%, 10 years)
d. Loan balance, end of 10 years: .836694 × $675,000 = $564,768
$454,633 + $564,768 = $1,019,401

Proof:
Down Payment: $225,000
Cash Flow: $25,230
Net Reversion: $1,019,401 − $564,768 = $454,633
Present Worth of Cash Flow (Net Annuity) and Net Reversion:
$25,230 × 4.833227 = $121,942 (PW 1/P, 16%, 10 years)
$454,633 × .226684 = $103,058 (PW 1, 16%, 10 years)
$225,000
Target figure (down payment): $225,000

NONPRODUCING PROPERTY, PURCHASED FOR APPRECIATION

Nonproducing property, acquired for appreciation, necessitates two types of investments: (1) a down payment, or total purchase price in cash; and (2) holding costs, consisting of property taxes and possibly loan payments. It also calls for a special type of investor—one who is not motivated by a desire for immediate cash flow. All yield is *deferred* yield. There is no income, no *current* yield. Analysis of this type of investment relates to the definition: Value is the present worth of future net benefits. Future net benefits in this context consist of a net cash reversion only, received at the end of a given period of ownership (holding period). The net reversion may be measured by subtracting loan balance at the time of resale from resale value. Present worth of the net reversion is diminished by the present worth of the holding costs, or negative income.

Investors in nonproducing real estate are motivated by two objectives: (1) future resale at a profit, or (2) future development of the property. In either case, appreciation in market value is anticipated. Such expectations should be fortified and justified by economic and feasibility studies.

Examples of this type of investment may be placed in two categories: (1) raw land, which is nonagricultural and/or nonproducing; and (2) improved properties, with a conversion or redevelopment potential, such as old depots, fire stations, vacated factories, et cetera. (To illustrate the latter class, San Francisco provides classic examples in the colorful, popular Ghirardelli Square and The Cannery.) If property is improved, annual holding costs should include insurance.

The appraiser/broker applies compound interest factors, not mortgage-equity Overall Rates, in the analysis of nonproducing investment real estate. There is no income to capitalize. However, the analyst is dealing typically with a mortgage and an equity, a projected holding period, and an estimated resale value. To the investor in vacant land, rate of yield on equity is of as great concern as it is to the owner of income-producing property.

The following procedural section outlines three basic methods concerning the calculation of:

1. *Investment value* (offering price), based on a specified equity yield rate and a projected holding period.
2. *Rate of yield on equity,* when purchase price is given and resale value and holding period are estimated.
3. *Resale value required* to generate a specified yield rate, purchase price and holding period given.

"Time value" of money is built into the procedures.

Analyses which follow the patterned procedures outlined and illustrated answer a number of significant questions:

1. Based on an anticipated resale value, projected holding period, and specified equity yield rate, what is a feasible offering price for the subject property?
2. At a given purchase price, known financing, anticipated holding period, calculated holding costs, and estimated resale value, what is the rate of yield on equity? How would an extended holding period affect the yield rate?

3. When purchase price and holding period are given, what resale value will be required in order to generate a stipulated yield rate for the investor?

Careful analysis provides answers that could put the client into a feasible investment and should help to keep him from making a costly financial blunder.

Investment Value, Based on Specified Equity Yield Rate

- *Procedure:*
    a. Calculate net cash reversion at end of holding period.
    b. Multiply *a* by PW1.
    c. Calculate annual holding costs.
    d. Multiply *c* by PW 1/P.
    e. Subtract *d* from *b*.
    f. Add *e* to the original amount of the loan, if any. The sum is the feasible offering price.

Problem 1:
An investor is studying the feasibility of purchasing a bare parcel of land, located in the direction of the city's growth. He anticipates that it will be ripe for development in five years, and he estimates its value at that time to be $500,000 net, after sales commission and closing costs. The seller will carry a loan of $150,000 at 7 percent interest. Terms call for annual payments of interest only for 10 years, the entire principal amount due and payable at the end of 10 years. Property taxes amount to $3,000 a year. The prospective purchaser expects a yield of 12% on his investment. He plans to hold the property for 5 years and resell at a price of $500,000 net. What can he offer for the property now?

Solution:
  a. Resale value: $500,000
       Less Loan Balance: −   150,000
       Net Cash Reversion: $350,000
  b. $350,000 × .567427 = $198,600   (PW 1, 12%, 5 years)
  c. Holding Costs:
       Interest on loan: .07 × $150,000 = $10,500
       Property taxes: 3,000
                             $13,500
  d. $13,500 × 3.604776 = $48,665   (PW 1/P, 12%, 5 years)

137

e. $198,600 − $48,665 = $149,935
f. $149,935 + $150,000 = $299,935

Notes:
— Value of the equity (down payment) is the present worth of future net benefits. These benefits consist of a net cash reversion of $350,000 at the end of the holding periods.
— PW 1 and PW 1/P factors are selected at the equity yield rate (12%) for the term of the holding period (5 years).
— Present worth of the total net cash reversion (b) is diminished by the present worth of the holding costs or negative income (d and e).
— In effect, the purchaser makes an initial investment of $149,935 (the down payment) plus a series of additional annual investments of $13,500 each year for 5 years (holding costs).
— "Proof" related to the time value of money can be given by noting that $149,935 invested at 12% compounded annually would grow to $264,237 in 5 years, and $13,500 invested at the end of each year for 5 years would accumulate $85,763 at 12% compounded annually. Adding, $264,237 plus $85,763 equals $350,000, the amount of net cash reversion calculated to be received at the end of 5 years. Here is the arithmetic:

$149,935 ÷ .567427 = $264,237   (PW 1, 12%, 5 years)
  13,500 ÷ .157410 =   85,763   (PR − i, 12%, 5 years)
                     $350,000

(Refer to pages 114 and 115, which outline the procedures for calculating the growth at compound interest of a single deposit or investment and the growth of a series of deposits or investments.)

Problem 2:
Assume that loan terms in Problem 1 specify annual payments to amortize in 10 years. All other data remain unchanged. Recalculate a feasible offering price.

Solution:
a. Annual loan payment: $150,000 × .142378 = $21,357
                                           (PR, 7%, 10 years)
   Loan balance, end of 5 years:
     $21,357 × 4.100197 = $87,568   (PW 1/P, 7%, 5 years)
   Resale value: $500,000
   Less loan balance: −   87,568
   Net cash reversion: $412,432
b. $412,432 × .567427 = $234,025   (PW 1/P, 12%, 5 years)

138

c. Holding costs:
    Loan payments: $21,357
    Property taxes: 3,000
                    $24,357

d. $24,357 \times 3.604776 = \$87,802$ (PW 1/P, 12%, 5 years)

e. $234,025 - \$87,802 = \$146,223$

f. $146,223 + \$150,000 = \$296,223$

Proof:

    $146,223 \div .567427 = \$257,695$ (PW 1, 12%, 5 years)

      $24,357 \div .157410 = 154,736$ (PR − i, 12%, 5 years)

                        $412,431

                +   1   (Adjust $1 for rounding)

                        $412,432

Notes:
— This solution indicates a slightly lower offering price because annual holding costs are increased. Net reversion is $412,432, up $62,432 from Problem 1 because of partial loan amortization. In both solutions a true 12% yield plus capital recapture is calculated. The second case offers two advantages to the buyer: a lower purchase price and a higher net reversion. However, annual holding costs, which involve additional out-of-pocket expenditures, are up by $10,857.
— The increased holding cost may be a disadvantage to the buyer in that it is mandatory additional cash investment. On the other hand, the extra dollars expended are earning 12%.
— At the end of the projected holding period the investor may elect to sell the property instead of developing it himself or extending his holding period. If he sells at that time, the financing terms in Problem 1 might offer some inducement to the subsequent purchaser. Provided the loan is assumable, the new buyer could have the advantage of financing $150,000 of the purchase price at a favorable interest rate of 7%.
— The seller's advantage in Problem 1 is a higher sales price. In Problem 2 capital recapture is accelerated, which may be an advantage to the seller if he reinvests funds received from loan amortization at a yield rate in excess of 7%. (Initially he may have agreed to carry the loan at a relatively low interest rate of 7% in order to effect the sale of the property.)
— Financing *does* affect investment value, as shown by changing loan payment terms only, interest rate remaining in both cases at 7%. In both Problems 1 and 2, if the interest rate were increased above 7%,

holding costs would be greater, and obviously offering price would be less, predicated on a desired 12% yield.

Problem 3:

Assume that the subject property in Problem 1 will be purchased for cash. No loan is involved. Other data remains unchanged: 12% yield, 5-year holding period, annual payment of $3,000 property taxes, and estimated resale value of $500,000. What purchase price can the investor offer?

Solution:
 a. Net reversion: $500,000
 b. $500,000 × .567427 = $283,714   (PW 1, 12%, 5 years)
 c. Annual holding costs: $3,000
 d. $3,000 × 3.604776 = $10,814   (PW 1/P, 12%, 5 years)
 e. $283,714 − $10,814 = $272,900

Proof:

$272,900 ÷ .567427 =	$480,943	(PW 1, 12%, 5 years)
3,000 ÷ .157410 =	19,059	(PR − i, 12%, 5 years)
	$500,002	
−	2	(Adjust $2 for rounding)
	$500,000	

Note: A single investment of $272,900 grows to $480,943 in 5 years, at 12% compounded annually. A series of deposits or investments of $3,000 at the end of each year for 5 years would amount to $19,059 at the end of 5 years, at 12% compounded annually. Total: $500,002. Since no loan exists, net cash reversion at the end of the 5-year holding period is the resale value of $500,000, which is within $2 of the future worth calculated, verifying 12% yield.

Problem 4:

Assume that terms in Problem 1 call for the seller to carry a loan for $250,000, all other data remaining unchanged. Calculate a feasible offering price, based on a projected resale value of $500,000 at the end of 5 years and an anticipated yield rate of 12%.

Solution:
 a. Resale value: $500,000
    Less loan balance: −   250,000
    Net cash reversion: $250,000
 b. $250,000 × .567427 = $141,857   (PW 1, 12%, 5 years)

c. Holding costs:
   Interest on loan: .07 × $250,000 = $17,500
   Property taxes: 3,000
                                        $20,500

d. $20,500 × 3.604776 = $73,898   (PW 1/P, 12%, 5 years)
e. $141,857 − $73,898 = $67,959
f. $67,959 + $250,000 = $317,959

Proof:

$67,960 ÷ .567427 = $119,769   (PW 1, 12%, 5 years)
 20,500 ÷ .157410 = 130,233   (PR − i, 12%, 5 years)
                      $250,002
           −   2   (Adjust $2 for rounding)
                      $250,000

Problem 5:
Assume the seller agrees to carry a loan of $300,000, other terms in Problem 1 remaining unchanged. Calculate a feasible offering price.

Solution:
a. Resale value: $500,000
   Less loan balance: −   300,000
   Net cash reversion: $200,000
b. $200,000 × .567427 = $113,485   (PW 1, 12%, 5 years)
c. Holding costs:
   Interest on loan: .07 × $300,000 = $21,000
   Property taxes: 3,000
                                       $24,000
d. $24,000 × 3.604776 = $86,515   (PW 1/P, 12%, 5 years)
e. $113,485 − $86,515 = $26,970
f. $26,970 + $300,000 = $326,970

Proof:

$26,970 ÷ .567427 = $ 47,530   (PW 1, 12%, 5 years)
 24,000 ÷ .157410 = 152,468   (PR − i, 12%, 5 years)
                      $199,998
           +   2   (Adjust $2 for rounding)
                      $200,000

Comparative Summary
Problem Number

	1	2	3	4	5
Equity Yield Rate	12%	12%	12%	12%	12%
Holding Period in Years	5	5	5	5	5
Resale Value, End of 5 Years	$500,000	$500,000	$500,000	$500,000	$500,000
Principal Amount of Loan	$150,000	$150,000	0	$250,000	$300,000
Loan Balance, End of 5 Years	$150,000	$87,568	0	$250,000	$300,000
Down Payment	$149,935	$146,223	$272,900	$67,959	$26,970
Holding Costs, Annual	$13,500	$24,357	$3,000	$20,500	$24,000
Total Dollars Invested (Down Payment Plus Holding Costs)	$217,435	$268,008	$287,900	$170,459	$146,970
Net Cash Reversion	$350,000	$412,432	$500,000	$250,000	$200,000
Feasible Offering Price	$299,935	$296,223	$272,900	$317,959	$326,970

Notes:
— Equity yield rate, holding period, and resale value are identical in each of the five preceding cases. These factors are the constants. Variables consist of terms and offering price.
— The more favorable the terms, the higher the feasible offering price for the property.
— Band of investment value, as affected by terms, ranges from $272,900 to $326,970.
— In practice, purchase prices and down payments would be rounded to a reasonable figure. Precise calculations are given here for purposes of illustrating procedures and checking in the "proof."
— Consideration of advantages and disadvantages in the various options, by both buyer and seller, may provide the basis for negotiation and the consummation of a transaction satisfactory to all parties.

Rate of Yield on Equity

Known elements are: purchase price, terms, holding costs, projected holding period(s), and estimated resale value. There is either no income or income which is insufficient to meet holding costs or to justify the purchase price. Property is purchased for appreciation, and yield is deferred until the time of resale. The unknown is the rate of yield on equity. Estimate of the holding period is particularly critical in its effect on the equity yield rate, as shown in the following example.

- *Procedure:*
    a. Calculate annual holding costs.
    b. Subtract loan balance at end of holding period from anticipated resale value. Difference is the dollar measure of equity or net cash reversion at the end of the holding period. Consider it as the *future worth* of the down payment and the holding costs.
    c. Substitute in the equation:
       Future Worth = (Down Payment ÷ PW 1)
                  + [Annual Holding Costs ÷ (PR − i)]
       Future Worth from *b* becomes the "target figure" in the equation. PW 1 (Present Worth of 1) and PR (Periodic Repayment) factors are selected for the term of the holding period and at *estimated* yield rates. Choice of two or more rates may "bracket" the true rate to be calculated in a cut-and-try procedure, using the equation two or more times.
    d. Compare the Future Worth or final equity from *b* with Future Worth values from *c,* in which estimated rates are used. Interpolate by simple proportion to find the indicated yield rate.

Problem:

A syndicate, formed to purchase a parcel of nonproducing acreage, zoned commercial, offers participating interests to small investors. Property is located adjacent to an Interstate Freeway, a few miles from the site of a proposed supersonic international airport. The syndicators expect to hold the property for a period of 5 years in anticipation of appreciation, then resell at a substantial profit. Terms of the planned purchase are as follows:

Sales price: $1,500,000
Down payment: $500,000
First mortgage, carried by seller:
  Principal: $1,000,000
  Interest rate: 7%
  Payment schedule:
    Annual interest payments of $70,000 for 12 years.
    Principal amount of $1,000,000 due as a balloon payment at the
      end of 12 years.
Annual property taxes are estimated at $30,000. An individual client invests $10,000 and acquires a 2% interest in the project. (His contribution of

$10,000 is 2% of the total down payment of $500,000.) The investor's prorata share of the yearly "call" or holding costs of interest and taxes is 2% of $100,000 or $2,000. Compute the yield rate if the land is held for 5 years and is sold at that time for $2,500,000 net. How would the yield rate be affected if the holding period were extended to 7 years, all other data remaining unchanged?

Solution:
  a. Annual holding costs: $2,000
  b. Total equity at time of resale: $2,500,000 − 1,000,000 = $1,500,000
     2% interest: .02 × $1,500,000 = $30,000
  c. If holding period is 5 years, try 12% and 10%:
     Try 12% (use PW 1 and PR factors at 12% for 5 years):
       Future Worth = ($10,000 ÷ .567427)
                    + [$2,000 ÷ (.27741 − .12)]
                    = $17,623 + ($2,000 ÷ .15741)
                    = $17,623 + $12,706
                    = $30,329
     Try 10% (use PW 1 and PR factors at 10% for 5 years):
       Future Worth = ($10,000 ÷ .620921)
                    + [$2,000 ÷ (.263797 − .10)]
                    = $16,105 + ($2,000 ÷ .163797)
                    = $16,105 + $12,210
                    = $28,315
  d. "Target figure" from *b* is the individual investor's equity of $30,000 at the time of resale. This figure has been "bracketed" between $30,329 at 12% yield and future worth of $28,315 at 10% yield. Interpolating by simple proportion: equity yield rate, about 11.673%.
  c. If Holding Period is 7 years, try 5% and 4½%:
     Try 5% (use PW 1 and PR factors at 5% for 7 years):
       Future Worth = ($10,000 ÷ .710681)
                    + [$2,000 ÷ (.17282 − .05)]
                    = $14,071 + ($2,000 ÷ .12282)
                    = $14,071 + $16,284
                    = $30,355
     Try 4½% (use PW 1 and PR factors at 4½% for 7 years):
       Future Worth = ($10,000 ÷ .734828)
                    + [$2,000 ÷ (.169701 − .045)]
                    = $13,609 + ($2,000 ÷ .124701)
                    = $13,609 + $16,038
                    = $29,647
  d. "Target figure" is $30,000, from *b*. By interpolation: equity yield rate, about 4¾%.

Notes:
— The example above illustrates vividly the time value of money and points up the impact on yield rate if the holding period must be extended without a compensating increase in market value. Obviously, this case analysis indicates that the investment offered should be rejected, if an economic study shows a fair possiblity of a holding period in excess of 5 years before the property can be marketed for $2,500,000 net.
— Extension of the holding period by two years cuts the equity yield rate from a respectable 11.673% to a marginal 4.75%. Additional extension would drop yield to a vanishing point, and could possibly result in a loss of capital investment. A holding period less than 5 years would increase the yield rate above 11.673%, assuming a resale value of $2,500,000 or more, net.
— If the analyst has access to and is using the six standard compound interest and annuity tables, he can substitute the following equation for the one given in c of the Procedure:

Future Worth = (Down Payment × Future Worth of 1)
+ (Annual Holding Cost
× Future Worth of 1 Per Period)

Results will be identical. (In this text, for purposes of brevity, three tables are used to do the work of six. This is possible because of the fact that there are three sets of reciprocals in the six standard tables, and also because the difference between the Periodic Repayment (loan amortization) Table and the Sinking Fund Table is the interest rate (i) only. Factors can do double duty, when used as both multipliers and divisors, or when adjusted.)
— In the illustration above, the individual investor makes an initial investment of $10,000 (his prorata share of the down payment) and a series of additional annual investments of $2,000 (holding costs) for a period of 5 or 7 years. All yield is deferred. The anticipated net cash reversion of $30,000 at the time of resale includes both capital recapture and yield on the investment.
— A single investment of $10,000 would grow to $17,368 in 5 years, at a rate of 11.673% compounded annually. Periodic deposits or investments of $2,000 made at the end of each year for 5 years would accumulate $12,623 at 11.673% compounded annually. Combined sums amount to $29,991, within $9 of the net cash reversion of $30,000. (A slight adjustment of $9 is made because of rounding and interpolation to a rate of 11.673%.)

$10,000 ÷ .575783 = $17,368   (PW 1, 11.673%, 5 years)
$2,000 ÷ .158436 = <u>12,623</u>   (PR − i, 11.673%, 5 years)
$29,991

(See procedures, pages 114 and 115, for calculating the growth at compound interest of a single deposit or investment, and the growth of a series of deposits or investments. Also refer to procedures for interpolation, pages 67 to 69, and to procedures for calculating PW 1 and PR factors, pages 469 to 472.

— Similarly, a single initial investment of $10,000, in an account paying 4.75% compounded annually, would amount to $13,838 in 7 years. And periodic deposits of $2,000 made at the end of each year for 7 years would accumulate to $16,161.
Total: $13,838 + $16,161 = $29,999 (within $1 of the "target figure" of $30,000.)

$$\$10,000 \div .722640 = \$13,838 \quad \text{(PW 1, 4¾\%, 7 years)}$$
$$\$2,000 \div .123757 = \underline{\$16,161} \quad \text{(PR} - \text{i, 4¾\%, 7 years)}$$
$$\$29,999$$

— Prior computations, showing the growth of money at compound interest, illustrate yield and capital recapture in the land syndication problem and show the relative accuracy of the yield rates calculated: 11.673% for a 5-year holding period, and 4.75% for a 7-year holding period.

— The illustration given analyzes the individual investor's fractional interest in the syndicate. However, yield rates calculated are identical to those that would be computed for the investment as a whole.

— Analysis relating to two or more possible holding periods, as demonstrated here, could provide an enlightened basis for investment decision-making.

Resale Value Required, in Order to Generate a Specified Yield Rate

Known factors include: purchase price, financing, projected holding period, and anticipated equity yield rate. The single unknown is the net resale value (after sales commission and closing costs) required in order to return all capital invested (down payment and holding costs), pay off the loan balance, and produce the desired rate of yield on the dollars invested.

• *Procedure:*
   a. Divide down payment by PW 1.
   b. Divide annual holding costs by (PR − i).
   c. Add *a* and *b* to the loan balance at the end of the holding period.

Problem 1:

Unimproved nonproducing property is offered for sale on the following terms:

    Purchase price: $438,000

    Down payment: $44,000

    Mortgage, carried by the seller:

        Principal amount: $394,000

        Interest rate: 6%

        Payment schedule:

        Annual payments of interest only for 10 years.

        Principal due and payable in full at the end of 10 years.

Ad valorem property taxes amount to $11,000 annually. If the buyer projects a holding period of 5 years before disposing of the property, and if he anticipates a yield of 20% on equity, what resale value would be required?

Solution:

    a. $44,000 ÷ .401878 = $109,486   (PW 1, 20%, 5 years)

    b. Annual interest payments: .06 × $394,000 = $23,640

Annual property taxes:	$11,000
Total annual holding costs:	$34,640 (negative cash flow)

        $34,640 ÷ .13438 = $257,776   (PR − i, 20%, 5 years)

    c. $109,486 + 257,776 + 394,000 = $761,262

Proof:

        Value of equity or down payment = (Net Reversion × PW 1)

                                              − (Negative Cash Flow × PW 1/P)

    Net reversion: $761,262 − $394,000 = $367,262

    Negative cash flow or annual holding cost: $34,640

    Factors at 20% for 5 years: PW 1, .401878; PW 1/P, 2.990612

    Substituting in the equation:

        Down Payment or Equity = ($367,262 × .401878)

                                  − ($34,640 × 2.990612)

                            = $147,595 − $103,595

                            = $44,000

Notes:

    — In this type of transaction the purchaser makes an initial investment (down payment). Annual holding costs should be considered a series of additional investments.

    — In the illustrative problem the down payment or original equity of

$44,000 would grow to $109,486 in 5 years at 20% compounded annually (*a*). A series of annual investments of $34,640 would grow in 5 years to $257,776 (*b*). Combined, the total is $367,262. Resale price must include this amount plus the unamortized loan balance of $394,000 ($367,262 + $394,000 = $761,262).

— In *a* of the Procedure the Future Worth of 1 factor could be used as a multiplier instead of employing the Present Worth of 1 factor (PW 1) as a divisor. In *b* the analyst can multiply by the Future Worth of 1 Per Period rather than dividing by the Periodic Repayment factor minus the interest rate (PR − i). Results would correspond.

— Resale value of $761,262 includes:

Mortgage payoff or assumption by new purchaser: $394,000
Return of capital investment:

Down payment:	$ 44,000
Holding costs: 5 × $34,640 =	173,200
	$611,200

Difference between $761,262 and $611,200, is deferred yield at 20% compounded annually, amounting to $150,062.

— Property must appreciate $323,262 or 73.8% within 5 years if the investor earns an anticipated 20% yield on equity. Required appreciation would be at the rate of 11.69% compounded annually.

— As a basis for decision-making on the part of the prospective investor and to determine the feasibility of purchasing the property at a given price, such an analysis as outlined here should be related to an economic study of the area. A realistic answer should be found to the question: "Is it reasonable to anticipate that the property will appreciate within the holding period to the calculated resale price required? If not, would a possibly lower rate of yield constitute an acceptable basis for consummating a capital investment?"

Problem 2:
Data and projections remain the same as in Problem 1, except that loan terms specify annual payments to amortize $394,000 at 6% interest in 15 years. Calculate the resale value required at the end of 5 years to produce a yield on equity of 20%.

Solution:
a. $44,000 ÷ .401878 = $109,486   (PW 1, 20%, 5 years)
b. Annual loan payments:

.102963 × $394,000 =	$40,567	(PR, 6%, 15 years)
Annual property taxes:	$11,000	
Total annual holding costs:	$51,567	

$51,567 ÷ .13438 = $383,740   (PR − i, 20%, 5 years)

   c. Loan balance at end of 5 years:
        .102963 × 7.360087 = .757817   (PR, 6%,15 years)
                                        × (PW 1/P, 6%, 10 yrs.)
        .757817 × $394,000 = $298,580
        $109,486 + 383,740 + 298,580 = $791,806

Proof:
   Net reversion: $791,806 − $298,580 = $493,226
   Down Payment or Equity = ($493,226 × .401878)
                            − ($51,567 × 2.990612)
                          = $198,217 − $154,217
                          = $44,000

Notes:
   — Refer to page 121 for the procedure to calculate the principal balance
     unpaid at any point in time in an amortized loan schedule.
   — Required resale value is higher in Problem 2 than in Problem 1
     because the annual holding cost or negative cash flow amounts to
     $51,567, in contrast to $34,640. More capital outlay is required in
     Problem 2—more dollars are "tied up" until the time of reversion
     (resale). There is no basis for anticipating the possibility of a higher
     resale value in the second case. Terms and conditions of Problem 1
     are more advantageous to the buyer.
   — Procedures outlined and illustrated above can be utilized in a similar
     situation in which some income is produced—exceeded, however,
     by holding costs, with a resulting negative cash flow.

Mortgage-Equity Worksheets

The following suggested forms may serve as guidlines in (1) gathering and
processing data, (2) valuation, and (3) investment analysis:
   — "Data Required in the Computation or Selection of Mortgage-Equity
     Overall Rate,"
     See example of completed form: page 67.
   — "Computation of Value Estimate."
     Example: pages 10 and 11.
   — "OAR From Market."
     Example: page 78.
   — "Equity Yield Rate and Property Value from OAR."
     Example: page 92.
   — "Investment Analysis and Proof of Computations—Fifteen-Point
     Summary of Calculations."
     Examples: pages 11 to 14, 155 to 162, 474 to 477.

Date Required
In the Computation or Selection of
Mortgage-Equity Overall Rate

Holding Period: _____
Equity Yield Rate: _____
Mortgage Specifications: _____
  Loan Ratio: _____
  Interest Rate: _____
  Term: _____
Appreciation/Depreciation: _____
Overall Rate: _____

Computation of Value Estimate
Mortgage-Equity Technique

Data Required: _____
Holding Period: _____
Equity Yield Rate: _____
Mortgage Specifications: _____
  Loan Ratio: _____
  Interest Rate: _____
  Term: _____
Appreciation/Depreciation: _____
Net Annual Income: _____
Valuation: _____
  Overall Rate: _____
  Value = Income ÷ Rate
    = _____ ÷ _____
    = _____

OAR From Market

Sale Number	I	II	III	IV
Date of Sale				
Location				
Adjusted Sales Price				
Gross Income				
Effective Gross @ %				
Vacancy Factor				
Expenses or Expense Ratio				
Net Income				
General Comparability				
Overall Rate (OAR)				

Equity Yield Rate and Property Value from OAR

Holding Period: _____

Mortgage Specifications:

    Loan Ratio: _____

    Interest Rate: _____

    Term: _____

OAR: _____

Appreciation/Depreciation: a. _____   b. _____

Equity Yield Rate:*   a. _____   b. _____

Net Annual Income: _____

Indicated Value: _____ ÷ _____ = _____

             (Income)   (OAR)

*Calculated from OAR Tables or Compound Interest Tables. (See alternate procedures.)

Investment Analysis and Proof of Computations
Fifteen-Point Summary of Calculations

1. Over-all Rate Selected from OAR Tables or Computed   _____

2. Property Value   _____ ÷ _____ = _____
                      (INCOME)   (OAR)

3. Original Equity   _____ x _____ = _____
   (Down Payment)   (Equity Ratio)   (Value)

4. Amount of Loan   _____ x _____ = _____
   (Original Principal)   (Loan Ratio)   (Value)

5. Debt Service   _____ x _____ = _____
   (Yearly Payments)   (Loan Constant)   (Principal)

6. Cash Flow   _____ − _____ = _____
   (Annuity)   (Net Income)   (Debt Service)

7. Debt Coverage Ratio   _____ ÷ _____ = _____
              (Net Income)   (Debt Service)

8. Rate of Current Yield On Equity   _____ ÷ _____ = _____
              (Cash Flow)   (Orig. Equity)

9. Loan Balance   _____ x _____ = _____
   (End Holding Period)   (% Unpaid)   (Principal)

10. Resale Value as % of Original Value   100   +   _____ = _____
              (Orig. Val. as %)   −   (% Appr/Dep)

11. Resale Value as a Dollar Amount   _____ x _____ = _____
             (Resale Val. as %)   (Original Value)

Investment Analysis and Proof of Computations
Fifteen-Point Summary of Calculations
(cont.)

12. Reversion, Net
    (Terminal Equity)   _____ — _____ = _____
                           (Resale Value)   (Loan Balance)

13. Deferred Yield
    (Amount)   _____ — _____ = _____
                           (Reversion Net)   (Down Payment)

14. Terminal Equity Ratio   _____ ÷ _____ = _____
                              (Reversion Net)   (Resale Value)

15. Proof of Yield on Equity
    Equity Yield Rate: _____ Term in Years: _____
                          (Percent)   (Holding Period)
    Present Worth of 1 Per Period: _____ Present Worth of 1: _____
                                        (PW 1/P)   (PW 1)

    Equation of Proof
    Present Worth = (_____ x _____) + (_____ x _____)
                         (Cash Flow)   (PW 1/P)   (Net Reversion)   (PW 1)
                  = _____ + _____ = _____

    Final Check   Target Figure = _____
                                   (Down Payment, Orig. Equity)

    _____ — _____ = _____
      Target Figure   (Present Worth)   (Rounding Adjustment)

4

Case Study:
Sunset Point Apartments

Sunset Point Apartments, nearing completion, is offered for sale by the owner-builder. Attractive architectural design of the building harmonizes with other adjacent developments. Demand for small, middle-class rental units in the area exceeds current supply. Location is in reasonably close proximity to a regional shopping center, recently constructed office buildings, rapid transit, recreational facilities, and a new branch university campus.

The complex contains 150 furnished units: 70 studios, and 80 one-bedroom apartments. Monthly rental schedule is set at $225 for the studio apartments and $275 for the one-bedroom units. All utilities except telephone are included. A carport is provided without additional charge.

You have listed the property for $2,350,000. The builder indicates he will consider a reasonable offer, if it does not entail his carrying a second mortgage.

A summary of an operating statement you have prepared shows the following:

Gross Annual Income:
    70 units at $225 = $15,750
    80 units at $275 =   22,000
                         $37,750

$37,750 × 12 =	$453,000
Less Vacancy and Collection Losses	
(at 4½%)	−20,385
	$432,615
Plus Service Income (laundry, vending machines)	4,200
Effective Gross Income:	$436,815
Less Expenses at 45% (fixed, operating, and reserves)	−196,567
Net Operating (Annual) Income (NOI):	$240,248 round to $240,000

You are working with a prospective buyer who has cash to invest. You determine from local lending institutions that the property upon completion will support a 20-year loan for 75% of value at 9½% interest, monthly payments to amortize. The investor estimates a holding period of 10 years before resale, refinancing, or exchange. Based on the economic outlook for the area, scarcity of comparable building sites, and inflationary trends, he believes that anticipation of 10% appreciation (net to the investor) would be conservative and realistic. The client expects a yield of 15% on his equity before income taxes.

Three major tasks are involved in preparing a comprehensive analysis for the investor:

1. Valuation by the mortgage-equity technique. (Such a calculated value will be the price the client can feasibly pay, based on the data and projections given. It may also be the "reasonable offer" the contractor-seller will accept, since no secondary financing is required.)
2. Before income tax 15-point investment analysis and proof of equity yield calculation.
3. After income tax analysis and computation of after-tax yield on equity.

Suggested solutions and analyses with added explanatory comments follow.

Computation of Value Estimate
Mortgage-Equity Technique

Data Required:	
Holding Period:	10 years
Equity Yield Rate:	15%
Mortgage Specifications:	
Loan Ratio:	75%
Interest Rate:	9½%
Term:	20 years
Appreciation/Depreciation:	+10%
Valuation:	
Overall Rate:	.106137
Value = Income ÷ Rate	
= $240,000 ÷ .106137	
= $2,261,228	

Offering price would be rounded to possibly $2,250,000. However, for purposes of analysis and "proof" of the accuracy of all calculations, the precise, unrounded calculation is used. The analysis that follows, based on the data and projections given, verifies the validity of the mortgage-equity Overall Rate (OAR), exposes the major financial aspects of the investment over the ten-year holding period, and substantiates 15% equity yield to maturity.

Investment Analysis and Proof of Computations
Fifteen-Point Summary of Calculations

1.	Over-all Rate Selected from OAR Tables or Computed					.106137
2.	Property Value	$240,000 (INCOME)	÷	.106137 (OAR)	=	$2,261,228
3.	Original Equity (Down Payment)	.25 (Equity Ratio)	x	$2,261,228 (Value)	=	565,307
4.	Amount of Loan (Original Principal)	.75 (Loan Ratio)	x	2,261,228 (Value)	=	1,695,921
5.	Debt Service (Yearly Payments)	.111856 (Loan Constant)	x	1,695,921 (Principal)	=	189,699
6.	Cash Flow (Annuity)	240,000 (Net Income)	−	189,699 (Debt Service)	=	50,301
7.	Debt Coverage Ratio	240,000 (Net Income)	÷	189,699 (Debt Service)	=	1.265162
8.	Rate of Current Yield On Equity	50,301 (Cash Flow)	÷	565,307 (Orig. Equity)	=	.08898
9.	Loan Balance (End Holding Period)	.720362 (% Unpaid)	x	1,695,921 (Principal)	=	1,221,677
10.	Resale Value as % of Original Value	100 (Orig. Val. as %)	+−	10 (% Appr/Dep)	=	110%
11.	Resale Value as a Dollar Amount	110% (Resale Val. as %)	x	2,261,228 (Original Value)	=	2,487,351
12.	Reversion, Net (Terminal Equity)	2,487,351 (Resale Value)	−	1,221,677 (Loan Balance)	=	1,265,674
13.	Deferred Yield (Amount)	1,265,674 (Reversion Net)	−	565,307 (Down Payment)	=	700,367
14.	Terminal Equity Ratio	1,265,674 (Reversion Net)	÷	2,487,351 (Resale Value)	=	.508844

Investment Analysis and Proof of Computations
Fifteen-Point Summary of Calculations
(cont.)

```
15.  Proof of Yield on Equity
     Equity Yield Rate: _____15%_____ Term in Years: _____10_____
                          (Percent)                      (Holding Period)
     Present Worth of 1 Per Period: 5.018769   Present Worth of 1:_____.247185_____
                                     (PW 1/P)                          (PW 1)

     Equation of Proof
     Present Worth = $50,301  x  5.018769   ) + ($1,265,674 x  .247185    )
                     (Cash Flow)   (PW 1/P)      (Net Reversion)   (PW 1)
                   = $252,449  +  $312,856   =      $565,305
Final Check  Target Figure = _____$565,307_____
                              (Down Payment, Orig. Equity)

         $565,307    —    $565,305    =         $2
       Target Figure      (Present Worth)    (Rounding Adjustment)
```

Let's Analyze the Analysis

It is axiomatic that three factors are of primary significance to the investor. By way of emphasis we repeat that he is concerned with: (1) What he puts into an investment (his down payment); (2) What he gets out of the investment (future benefits consisting of cash flow over a period of years, and a net reversion); and (3) The relationship between what he puts in and what he gets out in terms of a yield rate on the dollars invested, with full consideration given to the time value of money.

Looking at the valuation problem in the case study and its fifteen-point analysis, we note:

1. What the buyer puts into the investment:
   $565,307 down payment (Line 3).
2. What he gets out of the investment:
   $50,301 cash flow annually for 10 years (Line 6);
   $1,265,674 net cash reversion at the end of 10 years (Line 12).
3. Proof of 15% yield to maturity on equity (Item 15).

The completed form arrays and displays major financial aspects of the investment in a concise, uncluttered manner for buyer, seller, broker, and lender. This analysis in effect puts on exhibit *the anatomy of an investment*. Follow through, point by point:

1. OAR of .106137 has six variables from the problem built into it: holding period; equity yield rate; loan ratio, term, and interest rate; and appreciation/depreciation.

2. The net annual income of $240,000 has been properly processed from gross income to the point at which it can be capitalized. Allowances have been made for vacancy and collection losses; incidental income from supplemental services has been added; and allowable expenses (fixed, operating, and reserves) have been deducted. The result is net annual operating income (NOI) before loan payments, "recapture", and income taxes. (If the shape of the projected income stream is assumed to be other than level, it must be converted to a level ordinary annuity equivalent before capitalization. See relevant procedures, pages 52 to 61.) Value of $2,261,228, on which subsequent steps are based, is used unrounded for purposes of precise analysis only, in consideration of hitting or coming reasonably close to the "target figure" in Point 15.

3. The original equity is the down payment. Equity ratio and loan ratio add up to 100% of value. Loan ratio of 75% is given; therefore, equity ratio is 25% (100% − 75%). Line 3 calculates in dollars what the investor puts into the transaction: a down payment of $565,307. Equity ratio is down payment divided by purchase price. The following three steps lead up to a computation of the first of the investor's future net benefits—annual cash flow produced by the property.

4. The loan ratio is 100% less the equity ratio or it can be calculated by dividing the dollar amount of the loan by property value. By multiplying purchase price by loan ratio of 75%, the original amount of the loan is determined to be $1,695,921 (unrounded).

5. The loan constant is the percent of the original principal amount of the loan which is paid in the course of each year to amortize the loan over the full loan term (principal and interest included). From the Supplement Tables the analyst selects a loan constant of .111856 (9½%, 20 years, monthly payment frequency). Multiplication calculates annual debt service to be $189,699. (The borrower pays one-twelfth of this amount or $15,808.25 each month. However, for purposes of this analysis, annual debt service, not monthly payment, is the significant figure.)

6. The analyst calculates annual cash flow by subtracting debt service (loan payments) from net annual income. Annual cash flow of $50,301 constitutes a net annuity for the estimated holding period. This net income stream is the first of the investor's future net benefits to be received. Cash flow is current yield on the investment (on the initial equity or down payment). Since these dollars earned are received "cash in hand" they are compoundable by reinvestment.

7. Line 7 lists the same figures as Line 6. However, here they are related by division rather than subtraction. The quotient of the net annual income divided by the annual debt service is the debt coverage ratio, a calculation of significance to the lender. In the case study it is 1.265, rounded. This indicates that net annual income is 126.5% of annual debt service, and thus provides a safety margin. The lender's position is that income must be more than sufficient to cover loan payments. An excess provides a reasonable amount of cash flow to the investor and furnishes a "cushion". Many lenders have as a rule of thumb a requirement that net annual income must be a minimum of 1.2 to 1.3 times debt service. On a relatively high risk investment, such as an individually operated motel, the lender may require a higher debt coverage ratio, possibly 1.5 or more. (Procedure for calculating an Overall Rate, based on debt coverage ratio and financing terms, is outlined on page 80.)

8. The dollar amount of current yield is the cash flow: net annual income less debt service. The rate of current yield on equity is calculated by dividing cash flow by the original equity (down payment). Investors refer to this relationship as "cash on cash." Current yield rate may be relatively low, compared to the desired or required yield on equity. In this example the rate of current yield is slightly less than 9% (.08898), while yield to maturity is indicated as being 15%. (This latter point has yet to be proven, in Item 15 of the analysis.) Yield to maturity exceeds the rate of current yield generated by income-producing property in a typical situation; for yield to maturity includes not only current yield (cash on cash) but also deferred yield, built up by debt reduction and possible appreciation in market value. In order to compute the dollar amount of the investor's second future cash benefit (the net reversion), the analyst estimates resale value and calculates loan balance at the end of the holding period as shown in Steps 9, 10, 11, and 12.

9. Supplemental Tables provide precomputed loan balances unpaid at the end of a projected holding period, as a percent of original principal. Note that at the end of 10 years the unpaid principal balance on a 20-year loan written at 9½% interest is 72.0362% of the original principal. By multiplication, loan balance is calculated to be $1,221,677.

10. Original value is considered to be 100%, to which a percent of appreciation can be added or from which a percent of depreciation can be subtracted. In the case study, 10% appreciation within the 10-year holding period is estimated. Resale value would thus be 110% of purchase price. (If 10% depreciation had been projected, resale value would be 90% of purchase price.) Estimates of ap-

preciation or depreciation should be based on an economic study of the area. The analyst seeks and finds answers to a number of probing questions: Is the subject property in a growing, stable, or declining area? Is it in the direction of urban expansion? What is the economic history of the area? Has a trend been established? Is it probable that the trend will continue? Resale value is estimated in terms of current dollars, not future purchasing power of the dollar. Appreciation in terms of money will be the product of both inflation and the operation of the law of supply and demand. It is suggested that the analyst in preparing a 15-point summary, project appreciation/depreciation in Item 10 and 11 as a percent of increase or decline in market value which is net to the seller. The gross estimate of resale value should include an allowance of possibly 5% to 10% for sales commission and closing costs. In the case study an estimate of 20% gross increase in market value was made. A deduction of 10% for all sales expenses leaves 10% net increase, as indicated in the analysis. Property is being valued as of today, not ten years from now. Today's estimate of value is, however, based on certain projections that extend to the end of the holding period. The broker is marketing futures, the purchaser invests in futures, and the lender makes commitments on future expectations. Value is the present worth of future net benefits. One of the most significant sections of an appraisal is the briefest: the date on the appraisal, the date the value conclusion was reached. As time passes and changing value influences are at work, reappraisals may be in order.

11. If the subject property appreciates in a dollar amount which is 10% net to the seller, estimated resale value at the end of a 10-year holding period is 110% of purchase price, or $2,487,351. (Value conclusion, as arrived at by the instant mortgage—equity technique, is, however, $2,261,228. The property is being valued as of today; it is not being appraised ten years in advance.)

12. Reversion as generally used in appraisal literature equates with total resale or terminal value. However, in the mortgage-equity procedures in this text we refer to a net reversion as being the seller's calculated and presumed net proceeds or terminal equity—estimated resale value less loan balance at the end of the holding period. In the analysis, Line 12 gives the second of the investor's future net benefits: a net reversion of $1,265,674 at the end of the 10-year holding period. If the property were sold at that time for $2,487,351 and the new purchaser paid cash to the existing loan or refinanced the property, the net cash proceeds to the seller would be $1,265,674.

13. The net reversion on an economically sound investment consists of two elements: (1) a return to the investor of his original equity or down payment, and (2) equity growth through loan amortization (debt reduction) and possibly appreciation as well. Capital recapture in the mortgage-equity concept occurs realistically in a single lump sum at the end of a limited holding period; it is not spread over estimated "remaining economic life" of the improvements, as calculated by the residual techniques of the income approach. The amount by which the net reversion exceeds the original equity constitutes deferred yield on equity. In Line 13 of the analysis the net reversion of $1,265,674 is segregated into two sums. First, the investor makes a capital recapture of his cash investment, his down payment of $565,307. The remainder of $700,367 deferred yield is attributable to two sources: (1) debt reduction or loan amortization of $474,244 ($1,695,921 original principal less $1,221,677 loan balance) and (2) net appreciation of $226,123 ($2,487,351 net resale value less $2,261,228 purchase price, or 10% of $2,261,228). Deferred yield of $700,367 is earned by the down payment of $565,307. However, these dollars are locked in until the end of the holding period. They are not received nor are they receivable until the time of reversion. Yield to maturity includes not only the annual cash flow or net annuity of $50,301 but also the deferred dollars, a sum of $700,367 after capital recapture. The knowledgeable investor realizes that income-producing property which makes economic sense produces more than current "cash on cash." He does not overlook deferred dollars.

14. The terminal equity ratio relates net reversion to resale value. Note that while the equity ratio was only 25% when the property was purchased, it is over 50% at the time of reversion. The indication is that the investor is now in a favorable position to refinance the property, rather than reselling, and begin a new holding period. If he exercises this option, he can free some of the locked-in deferred yield dollars for additional investment and reestablish a favorable leverage position through a larger loan. It may be advisable for him to go this route, even though refinancing arrangements call for a higher interest rate.

15. The last section of the analysis form relates what the investor puts into the transaction (Line 3) to what he gets out of it (Lines 6 and 12). The equation of proof is a mathematical translation of the definition: Value is the present worth of future net benefits. Value in this context is the value of the original equity, the down payment—not total property value. Future net benefits include the cash flow or net annuity from Line 6 and the net reversion from

Line 12. Annual Present Worth of 1 and Present Worth of 1 Per Period factors are selected at the equity yield rate for the term of the holding period. Theoretically, in the case study the down payment of $565,307 is the present worth of an annuity of $50,301 a year for 10 years, plus the present worth of a single lump sum payment of $1,265,674, at a yield or discount rate of 15%. Note that the calculation of $565,305 (present worth) is within $2 of the "target figure." Line 15 provides a check point. In the problem above it verifies and substantiates a number of items: the Overall Rate, by which the property was valued; the proper selection of loan constant, loan balance, and compound interest factors; and the accuracy of the calculations in analyzing the investment. It also substantiates the rate of yield (to maturity) on equity, assuming the reliability of data and projections. If the analyst misses the "target figure" by a substantial margin, he should retrace his steps to locate an error. (Variance of possibly $50 to a few hundred dollars, depending on total value involved, may be due to rounding only. It does not necessarily indicate an error.) Real estate is at best a risk investment, no matter how thoroughly analyzed. A prime function of the mortgage-equity technique is to assist in providing a reasonable basis for decision-making. Line 15 should not be interpreted as *guaranteeing* a yield of 15%. It does show that this possibility exists. The element of risk should at all times be recognized; it must not be ignored. It may be minimized but it cannot be eliminated.

Tie Them Together

Further study points up a number of interrelationships between various sections of the "Investment Analysis and Proof of Computations." Here are a few to be noted in the case study:

1. *Cash Flow*
   a. From the OAR (Line 1) subtract the product of the loan ratio and the loan constant (Lines 4 and 5). The difference is cash flow as a percent of property value. For example, in the current problem:
   $$.106137 - (.75 \times .111856) = .106137 - .083892$$
   $$= .022245$$
   Cash flow (after debt service) is calculated to be 2.2245% of property value. A check, using dollar amounts, follows:
   $$.022245 \times \$2,261,228 = \$50,301$$
   This computation is identical to the figure arrived at in Line 6 of the analysis. When the product of the loan ratio and the loan constant is

less than the Overall Rate, there will be a *positive cash flow*. (Refer to the procedure on page 95.) If the product *equals* the OAR, there will be *no cash flow*. If the product *exceeds* the OAR a *negative cash flow* results. Note that the loan constant of .111856 is greater than the OAR of .106137, yet there is a positive cash flow. The rule of thumb stating that the Overall Rate must exceed the loan constant in every case is quite unrealistic. The significant relationship is the product of the loan ratio and the loan constant compared to the Overall Rate.

b. A corollary to the preceding calculation determines cash flow as a percent of down payment: i.e., the rate of current yield on equity:

Divide cash flow as a percent of value by the equity ratio.

.022245 ÷ .25 = .08898

Identical figure appears in Step 8 of the analysis. Procedures used in outlining these interrelationships can be employed to determine readily in a given situation whether or not there will be a positive cash flow generated. These methods will also determine the amount of cash flow and the rate of current yield on equity.

2. *Debt Coverage Ratio and Overall Rate (OAR)*

Multiply debt coverage ratio (Line 7) by loan constant (Line 5) by loan ratio (Line 4). The product should equal the OAR:

1.265162 × .111856 × .75 = .106137 (See Line 1.)

This procedure, outlined on page 80, can be utilized to develop an Overall Rate based on the lender's debt coverage ratio requirements and financing terms. For example, in the case study, if the lender requires a debt coverage ratio of 1.3, financing terms remaining as given, the Overall Rate could be computed thus:

1.3 × .111856 × .75 = .1090596

Calculated property value would be lowered accordingly.

3. *Net Reversion*

Net Reversion, as a percent of purchase price, can be determined in this way:

From resale value as a percent of purchase price (Line 10) subtract the product of the loan ratio (Line 4) and the loan balance as a percent of original principal (Line 9):

1.1 − (.75 × .720362) = 1.1 − .5402715
= .5597285

Net reversion required under the case study problem data is 55.97285% of purchase price:

.5597285 × $2,261,228 = $1,265,674

The figure calculated coincides with Line 12. Utilization of the procedure illustrated will determine quickly the dollar amount of net reversion in a given situation, without intermediate steps or the completion of a full 15-point analysis.

More Proof

To convince the skeptic, we go another route and take a different approach to demonstrate 15% yield on equity, plus a return of capital. The following schedule shows the buildup of equity from $565,307 to $1,265,674. The table has been prepared for illustrative purposes only, to help clarify the concepts of current yield, deferred yield, and yield to maturity. It is *not* the type of analysis an accountant would prepare for his client.

Note the five columns arrayed. Year 0 should be interpreted as being the beginning of Year 1, the time of acquisition. Other figures in the time schedule (Column 1) refer to the end of each year. The term yield heads columns 2, 3, and 4: yield at 15%, calculated annually on the increasing unrecovered capital balance; yield received annually (cash flow); and yield deferred, earned at 15% but not received (Column 2 minus Column 3). Column 5 begins with the down payment in Year 0 and increases annually by the dollar amount of yield deferred. Final figure for Year 10 corresponds (with a slight adjustment for rounding) to the net reversion, which includes, in a single lump sum payment to be received, a recapture of the down payment and a payoff of all yield deferred.

Current yield, as was calculated in the 15-point analysis, is 8.9% (rounded), considerably less than 15% equity yield on which valuation and analysis are based. Only through a consideration of deferred yield can 15% yield to maturity be generated. Yield *earned* annually exceeds cash flow— that is, yield *received* annually.

Look at it this way. The investor anticipates 15% yield on his actual out-of-pocket cash investment of $565,307 (his down payment). Fifteen percent yield, if received by the end of the first year of ownership, would amount to $84,796. However, actual cash flow (current yield) is only $50,30l, which the investor receives. The result is a shortage of $34,495 ($84,796 − $50,301). This deficit is then added to the outstanding capital investment of $565,307. The total unrecovered capital amount at the beginning of the second year of ownership is now $599,802 ($565,307 + $34,495). Expected yield for Year 2 is 15% of $599,802, or $89,870. Again, $50,301 yield is received; $39,669 is deferred and added to the prior capital balance of $599,802, for an increased outstanding capital sum of $639,471. Note in the following completed schedule that this routine continues, unrecovered capital building up to $1,265,685 by the end of the ten-year holding period. (A slight adjustment is made for rounding.) According to projections and computations, the investor's net reversion should amount to $1,265,674 (Line 12 of the analysis). His original capital investment of $565,307 will then have been returned (Line 13) and the deferred yield received (Line 13) will have brought the total yield to maturity up to a full 15%.

Please observe that the total of Column 2, yield earned at 15%, is $1,203,388. This is precisely the sum of Columns 3 and 4: yield received annually and yield deferred ($503,010 + $700,378). Note that yield deferred (Column 4) is within $11 of the calculation of $700,367 in Line 13 of the analysis summary. Deferred yield of $700,378 in Column 4, plus $565,307 capital outstanding in Year 0 (Column 5), amounts to $1,265,685, as in Year 10, Column 5. (Again, adjust $11 for rounding.)

Proof of 15% Yield to Maturity on Equity

Original Equity (Down Payment): $565,307
Net Annuity (Annual Cash Flow for 10 Years): $50,301
Net Cash Reversion at End of 10 Years: $1,265,674

Year	Earned at 15%	Yield Received	Deferred	Capital Outstanding (Unrecovered)
0	—	—	—	$565,307
1	$84,796	$50,301	$34,495	599,802
2	89,970	50,301	39,669	639,471
3	95,921	50,301	45,620	685,091
4	102,764	50,301	52,463	737,554
5	110,633	50,301	60,332	797,886
6	119,683	50,301	69,382	867,268
7	130,090	50,301	79,789	947,057
8	142,059	50,301	91,758	1,038,815
9	155,822	50,301	105,521	1,144,336
10	171,650	50,301	121,349	1,265,685
	$1,203,388	$503,010	$700,378	

Adjustment for rounding: − 11

$1,265,674

Less Net Reversion: − 1,265,674

0

A parallel reference to a hypothetical loan situation may adjust the focus slightly in clarifying the concept of deferred yield, capital buildup, and total recapture. Presume a loan is arranged on very unusual terms. Principal amount borrowed is $565,307 for 10 years at 15% interest on the following repayment schedule:

— Annual payments of a portion of the interest each year for 10 years;

precisely, the payment is $50,301 annually, which is 8.898% of the principal amount.
— Each year the difference between interest charged at 15% and interest actually paid according to schedule is added to the prior unpaid principal amount.
— At the end of 10 years the entire outstanding balance (original principal plus accrued unpaid interest) is due and payable in a single lump sum: $1,265,674.

In the case study problem, in which valuation and investment analysis employ the mortgage-equity technique, the investment generates a true 15% yield for the full 10-year term. Current yield or cash flow of $50,301 received annually is compoundable by reinvestment, for it is cash in hand. Yield which is deferred annually is not compoundable until the time of reversion, for it is locked in until the end of the holding period. However, deferred yield is compounded, as shown in the preceding schedule of proof. To summarize the point: current yield is *compoundable* yield; deferred yield is *compounded* yield.

Same Picture from a Different Angle

The concept of yield and capital recapture is of such significance the writer takes an additional approach for purposes of illustration and clarification. To the knowledgeable analyst this section may seem repetitious. However, even the expert may find a fresh perspective to be of assistance in working with a client or in a real estate training program.

By reference to Item 15 of the "Investment Analysis and Proof of Computations," note these points:

— The present worth of the net annuity or cash flow of $50,301 a year for 10 years is $252,449, at a yield rate of 15%.
— The present worth of the net reversion receivable at the end of 10 years (resale value less loan balance) is $312,856, at a yield rate of 15%.
— Combined, the present worth of both net annuity and net reversion is $565,305, which is within $2 of the calculated down payment or actual cash investment made at the time of purchase.

For purposes of illustration, stretch both imagination and credibility a bit, journey into "Never-Never Land" and presume that the investor's friendly home town bank pays 15% compounded annually on savings accounts. Assume the investor deposits $565,305, an amount equal to the down payment on Sunset Point Apartments. The total deposit is segregated into two accounts, each paying 15% compounded annually:

— In Account #1 he deposits $252,449. He arranges to withdraw the entire sum (together with interest earned) in 10 equal installments at the end of each year for the next 10 years. In effect, he has set up an annuity which will pay him $50,301 a year for 10 years. (Periodic Repayment factor at 15% for 10 years is .199252; and $252,449 × .199252 = $50,301.)

— In Account #2 he deposits $312,856 to be left untouched for 10 years, at which time it will be withdrawn in a single lump sum. (Present Worth of 1 factor at 15% for 10 years is .247185; and $312,856 ÷ .247185 = $1,265,676, the future worth of the deposit.)

Note in the two following schedules a true 15% yield or interest rate and a total capital recapture, whether related to the savings accounts or to the real estate investment. In the case of the annuity account the annual payment of $50,301 per year for 10 years includes interest earned and received annually on a declining principal balance. There is no capital outstanding at the end of 10 years. Calculations of the second account show that all yield on the deposit of $312,856 is deferred. Interest at 15% is compounded annually on an increasing base. By the end of year 10 a total of $1,265,676 has been accumulated and can be withdrawn intact. (The term "interest" rather than "yield" is used here, as the schedule illustrates specifically the progression of the two hypothetical savings accounts.)

Account #1—Annuity

Year	Payment Received Annually	15% Interest Earned	Capital Recapture	Outstanding Capital Balance
0	—	—	—	$252,449
1	$50,301	$37,867	$12,434	240,015
2	50,301	36,002	14,299	225,716
3	50,301	33,857	16,444	209,272
4	50,301	31,391	18,910	190,362
5	50,301	28,554	21,747	168,615
6	50,301	25,292	25,009	143,606
7	50,301	21,541	28,760	114,846
8	50,301	17,227	33,074	81,772
9	50,301	12,266	38,035	43,737
10	50,301	6,561	43,740	−3
		Adjust $3 for rounding:		0

Account #2—Reversion

Year	15% Interest Earned	Capital Sum Accumulated
0	—	$312,856
1	$46,928	359,784
2	53,968	413,752
3	62,063	475,815
4	71,372	547,187
5	82,078	629,265
6	94,390	723,655
7	108,548	832,203
8	124,830	957,033
9	143,555	1,100,588
10	165,088	1,265,676

Comparisons between the mythical savings accounts and the realistic investment in Sunset Point Apartments are obvious. Interest or yield and recapture follow parallel lines. Time value of money is measured precisely. However, the fact must be kept in mind that real estate is both a growth and a risk investment, in contrast to a guaranteed, fixed-dollar investment.

Take Another Look

The following diagram depicts graphically the financial structure of Sunset Point Apartments as an investment. (It should not be interpreted as representing two high-rise buildings connected by a picket fence!) In order to avoid the hazard of unrounded numbers cluttering the thought process, the writer has taken the liberty of rounding figures without distorting them.

At the time of purchase the financial structure consists of two blocks: Equity and Mortgage. Initial value of $2,261,000 is segregated into a down payment of $565,250 and a loan of $1,695,750. All future benefits accruing to the investor over the subsequent 10-year holding period are generated by the dollars invested at the time of purchase, combined with the leverage power utilized.

Annual cash flow over the entire holding period amounts to $50,300 per year and constitutes a 10-year annuity.

Analysis indicates that the financial structure at the end of ten years has grown to a value of $2,487,000. The mortgage block has shrunk from $1,695,750 to $1,221,500 by debt reduction, making way for an added block of $474,250 loan amortization. Down payment or original equity of $565,250 is intact and constitutes total capital recapture in a single lump sum. On top is an added block, ten percent appreciation, amounting to $226,000.

Initially the equity consists of a single element: the down payment. At the end of the holding period three segments make up the terminal equity or net reversion: loan amortization, return of down payment, and appreciation in value. Thus the equity has grown from $565,250 to $1,265,500.

Invested capital of $565,250 has produced current yield of $50,300 per year for ten years at a rate of slightly less than 9% ($50,300 ÷ $565,250). It has also created deferred yield of $700,250 ($474,250 Loan Amortization + $226,000 Appreciation). Yield to maturity, which includes both current and deferred yield, proves to be a full 15% as shown by use of the compound interest factors.

Value of the original equity or down payment of $565,250 is equal to the present worth of the net annuity or cash flow plus the present worth of the net reversion at a true yield rate of 15%.

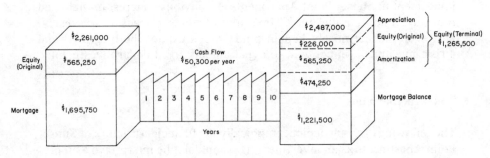

SUNSET POINT APARTMENTS
Analysis of 15% Yield to Maturity

Sunset Point Apartments: Analysis of 15% Yield to Maturity

Invested Capital: $565,250
Future Net Benefits:
    Annuity: $50,300 a year for 10 years
    Reversion: $1,265,500 at the end of 10 years
Present Worth of Future Net Benefits at 15% Yield Rate:
$$\$50,300 \times 5.02 \quad = \quad \$252,500$$
$$\$1,265,500 \times \ .2472 = \quad \underline{312,750}$$
$$\$565,250$$

Analysis of the Total Net Income Stream

Net annual income of $240,000 after allowable expenses can be shown diverted into three separate channels: (1) cash flow, (2) mortgage reduction or loan amortization, and (3) interest on the mortgage. Cash flow remains constant at $50,300 per year. Combined payment of mortgage reduction and interest on the loan stays level at $189,700 per year. However, as debt reduction increases period by period, interest payments decrease accordingly, interest being calculated each period on a declining principal balance. The progression of debt reduction is curvilinear, not straight line. Declining interest payments follow the same pattern. The analysis chart has been drawn out of proportion in order to emphasize curvilinear relationships.

Net Income	$240,000	$240,000	$240,000	$240,000	$240,000	$240,000	$240,000	$240,000	$240,000	$240,000
Cash Flow	$50,300	$50,300	$50,300	$50,300	$50,300	$50,300	$50,300	$50,300	$50,300	$50,300
Mortgage Reduction	$29,860	$32,830	$36,085	$39,670	$43,605	$47,930	$52,690	$57,920	$63,665	$69,990
Interest on Mortgage	$159,840	$156,870	$153,615	$150,030	$146,095	$141,770	$137,010	$131,780	$126,035	$119,710
Year	1	2	3	4	5	6	7	8	9	10

Analysis of the Total Net Income Stream

When Variables Vary

Bands of investment value and ranges of equity yield rate can be established by the analyst when financing data and/or projections are changed. Following are a few examples.

Assume the estimates of appreciation/depreciation only are altered, with all other data in the Case Study remaining unchanged.

— At 20% appreciation:
  Value = $240,000 ÷ .101212
  = $2,371,260
— At 0% appreciation:
  Value = $240,000 ÷ .111062
  = $2,160,955
— At 10% depreciation:
  Value = $240,000 ÷ .115987
  = $2,069,197

Assume that the seller agrees to carry a second mortgage for 15% of value at 8½% interest, monthly payments to amortize in 15 years. Terms of the first mortgage for 75% of value remain unchanged. Purchaser pays 10% down. Note how *financing terms affect investment value:*

— At 15% equity yield rate, as in the Case Study specifications:
  Value = $240,000 ÷ .097521
    = $2,461,008
— At *18%* equity yield rate:
  Value = $240,000 ÷ .103133
    = $2,327,092

Assume property is purchased at list price of $2,350,000. Note possible changes in equity yield rate:

— Financing terms and other problem data remain unchanged, except equity yield rate, Overall Rate, and value:
  Equity yield rate: About 13.75%
(Calculate by procedures, pages 81 to 84.)
— Seller carries a second mortgage for 15% of value at 8½% interest, monthly payments to amortize in 15 years; buyer pays 10% down; terms of the first mortgage and other problem data except Equity Yield Rate, Overall Rate, and Value remain unchanged:
  Equity yield rate: About 17.45%
(Calculate by procedures, pages 84 to 87.)

Assume property is purchased at list price of $2,350,000, other terms, data, and conditions except estimate of appreciation unchanged. What percent of appreciation would be required to generate a true 15% yield on equity, as specified in the Case Study?

— Required appreciation: About 18.14%
(Refer to procedures, pages 106 to 110.)

Ranges of value as illustrated relate more to investment value, value to an individual client, than to market value, which is value to persons in general. Appraisal for market value by the mortgage-equity technique is based on conventional institutional financing and on an assumption that the buyer pays cash to the loan. A calculation of investment value, on the other hand, gives full consideration to secondary and other special financing which may be available to a specific investor. Investment value often exceeds market value because of the advantages offered by a greater degree of leverage. Note that in the basic Case Study analysis, Sunset Point Apartments is encumbered by a single conventional loan, value is indicated to be $2,261,228, and equity yield rate is 15%. If additional leverage is provided by a second mortgage, a higher equity yield rate of 18% would be possible even at a higher purchase price of $2,327,092, as shown in this supplemental analysis.

Bands of value and ranges of equity yield rate, realistically established, serve two purposes: they can provide a base for (1) decision-making, and (2) purchase price negotiation.

In the after income tax study that follows, calculated value of $2,261,228, conventional financing, and 15% before tax equity yield are assumed, as shown in the 15-point "Investment Analysis and Proof of Computations."

After Income Tax Analysis and Yield on Equity

After tax analysis assumes the following segregation or allocation of value to improvements and to land:

Improvements:	$1,861,228
Land:	400,000
Total Value:	$2,261,228

Economic life of improvements is estimated (for income tax purposes) to be 33 1/3 years. Salvage value is presumed to be an amount sufficient to cover costs of demolition and removal.

If the investor elects to use accelerated depreciation of 150% declining balance, rate per year is 4.5% (100% ÷ 33 1/3 = 3%, and 1.5 × 3% = 4.5%). You determine that the investor is currently in the 50% tax bracket. Subject to changes in the economic status of the investor and tax legislation, the top tax levy on capital gains is projected as of the end of the holding period: 25% on the first $50,000 and 35% thereafter.

Based on these assumptions, the following suggested analysis is given.

	Year				
	1	2	3	4	5
1. Net Annual Income	240,000	240,000	240,000	240,000	240,000
2. Loan Payments	189,699	189,699	189,699	189,699	189,699
3. Before Tax Cash Flow	50,301	50,301	50,301	50,301	50,301
4. Loan Amortization	29,919	32,828	36,084	39,666	43,604
5. Interest on Loan	159,780	156,871	153,615	150,033	146,095
6. Depreciation*	83,755	79,986	76,387	72,950	69,667

172

7. Total Allowable Deductions	243,535	236,857	230,002	222,983	215,762
8. Taxable Income	⟨3,535⟩	3,143	9,998	17,017	24,238
9. Income Taxes (50%)	⟨1,768⟩	1,572	4,999	8,509	12,119
10. After Tax Cash Flow	52,069	48,729	45,302	41,792	38,182
11. Undepreciated Balance	1,777,473	1,697,487	1,621,100	1,548,150	1,478,483
12. Loan Balance	1,666,002	1,633,174	1,597,090	1,557,424	1,513,820
13. % Principal Unpaid	.982358	.963001	.941724	.918335	.892624
14. % Paid Off in Year	.017642	.019357	.021277	.023389	.025711
15. Cumulative % Principal Paid Off	.017642	.036999	.058276	.081665	.107376

*Depreciation is calculated at the rate of 4.5% per year on a declining balance, starting with a base of $1,861,228 improvement value the first year.

	Year				
	6	7	8	9	10
1. Net Annual Income	240,000	240,000	240,000	240,000	240,000
2. Loan Payments	189,699	189,699	189,699	189,699	189,699
3. Before Tax Cash Flow	50,301	50,301	50,301	50,301	50,301
4. Loan Amortization	47,930	52,689	57,916	63,665	69,943
5. Interest on Loan	141,769	137,010	131,783	126,034	119,756
6. Depreciation	66,532	63,538	60,679	57,948	55,340
7. Total Allowable Deductions	208,301	200,548	192,462	183,982	175,096
8. Taxable Income	31,699	39,452	47,538	56,018	64,904
9. Income Taxes (50%)	15,850	19,726	23,769	28,009	32,452
10. After Tax Cash Flow	34,451	30,575	26,532	22,292	17,849
11. Undepreciated Balance	1,411,951	1,348,413	1,287,734	1,229,786	1,174,446
12. Loan Balance	1,465,890	1,413,201	1,355,285	1,291,620	1,221,677
13. % Principal Unpaid	.864362	.833294	.799144	.761604	.720362
14. % Paid Off in Year	.028262	.031068	.034150	.037540	.041242
15. Cumulative % Principal Paid Off	.135638	.166706	.200856	.238396	.279638

Notes:

1. *Net annual income*   Net annual income after allowable expenses but before loan payments, depreciation for income tax purposes, and before income taxes.
2. *Loan payments*   Loan constant multiplied by the original principal amount of the loan.
3. *Before tax cash flow*   Net annual income less loan payments (Line 1 minus Line 2).

4. *Loan amortization* Debt reduction in the course of any one year can be calculated by multiplying Line 14 by the original amount of the loan; e.g., loan amortization in Year 3 = .021277 × $1,695,921, or $36,084.
5. *Interest on loan* Line 2 minus Line 4.
6. *Depreciation* Based on 150% accellerated depreciation on a declining balance and an estimated depreciable life of 33 1/3 years, annual depreciation rate is 1.5 × (1.0 ÷ 33 1/3), or .045 (4½%). Initial undepreciated balance is $1,861,228 building value.
7. *Total allowable deductions* Line 5 plus Line 6.
8. *Taxable income* Line 1 minus Line 7.
9. *Income taxes* Line 8 multiplied by tax rate. (In the case study a tax rate of 50% is assumed.)
10. *After tax cash flow* Line 3 minus Line 9.
11. *Undepreciated balance* Prior year's undepreciated balance minus Line 6.
12. *Loan balance* Line 13 multiplied by the original amount of the loan.
13. *% principal unpaid* Multiply the Periodic Repayment factor (PR) at the loan interest rate for the full loan term by the Present Worth of 1 Per Period factor (PW 1/P) for the number of periods remaining unpaid: e.g., unpaid balance at end of Year 1: .009321 × 105.391883 = .982358 (PR, 9½%, 240 months) × (PW 1/P, 9½%, 228 months).
14. *% paid off in year* From Line 13 subtract % principal unpaid at end of year from % principal unpaid at end of prior year; e.g., principal paid off in Year 4: .941724 − .918335 = .023389.
15. *Cumulative % principal paid off* Cumulative sum of percentages in Line 14.

Three of the fifteen elements in the after-tax analysis are projected as remaining *constant:*

1. Net Annual Income.
2. Loan Payments.
3. Before Tax Cash Flow.

Seven of the factors *decrease:*

5. Interest on Loan.
6. Depreciation.
7. Total Allowable Deductions.
10. After Tax Cash Flow.
11. Undepreciated Balance.

12. Loan Balance.
13. % Principal Unpaid.

The other five segments *increase;*

4. Loan Amortization.
8. Taxable Income.
9. Income Taxes.
14. % Paid Off in Year (Principal).
15. Cumulative % Principal Paid Off.

Note that deductible payments of interest decrease from $159,780 in Year 1 to $119,756 in Year 10. Nondeductible payments on principal increase from $29,919 to $69,943. At the same time allowable deductible depreciation decreases from $83,755 to $55,340. Taxable income increases from a "sheltered" low of −$3,535 to a high of $64,904; income taxes escalate from −$1,768 to $32,452; after tax cash flow tumbles from $52,069 in Year 1 to $17,849 in Year 10.

A decision as to the length of a feasible holding period relates to weighing the items that decrease against those that increase. A turnover point is usually reached in about 10 years, 7 to 12 years being a reasonable range. Because of income tax considerations, the typical investor will resell, refinance, or exchange the property at the end of a limited holding period.

Capital Gains Tax Computation:

Undepreciated balance, end of 10 years:	
Improvements:	$1,174,446
Land:	400,000
	$1,574,446
Capital gains:	
Resale value:	$2,487,351
Less undepreciated balance:	1,574,446
	$ 912,905
Capital gains tax (long term):	
$50,000 × .25 =	$ 12,500
$862,905 × .35 =	302,017
	$ 314,517

Net Reversion Calculation:

Before capital gains tax:

Resale value:	$2,487,351
Less loan balance:	$1,221,677
	$1,265,674

After capital gains tax and "recapture"
of excess depreciation:

Net reversion before tax:	$1,265,674
Less capital gains tax:	$ 314,517
	$ 951,157
Less "recapture" of excess depreciation:*	$ 51,366
	$ 899,791

*See IRS regulations on "recapture" of excess of accelerated depreciation over straight line depreciation.

Present Worth of After-Tax Cash Flow
At 15% (Equity Yield Rate)

Year	After-Tax Cash Flow		PW 1		Present Worth
1	$52,069	×	.869565	=	$45,277
2	48,729	×	.756144	=	36,846
3	45,302	×	.657516	=	29,787
4	41,792	×	.571753	=	23,895
5	38,182	×	.497177	=	18,983
6	34,450	×	.432328	=	14,894
7	30,575	×	.375937	=	11,494
8	26,532	×	.326902	=	8,673
9	22,292	×	.284262	=	6,337
10	17,849	×	.247185	=	4,412
					$200,598

Level Annuity Equivalent of After-Tax Cash Flow

Computation:
$200,598 × .199252 = $39,970   (PR, 15%, 10 years)

Proof:

$39,970 × 5.018769 = $200,600   (PW 1/P, 15%, 10 years)
(Adjust $2 for rounding. A level annuity of $39,970 a year for 10 years has the same present worth as the declining after-tax cash flow, at a yield rate of 15%. An annual sum of $39,970 *is* the level annuity equivalent.)

Rate of Yield on Equity, After Tax

Annuity equivalent, after tax: $39,970
Reversion, net, after tax: $899,791
Original equity (down payment): $565,307
Equation:
   Value of Original Equity = (Annuity × PW 1/P) + (Reversion × PW 1)
Computation:
   At 11%:
   $39,970 × 5.889232 = $235,393   (PW 1/P, 11%, 10 years)
   $899,791 × .352184 = $316,892   (PW 1, 11%, 10 years)
                        ――――――――
                        $552,185

   At 10.5%:
   $39,970 × 6.014773 = $240,410   (PW 1/P, 10½%, 10 years)
   $899,791 × .368449 = $331,527   (PW 1, 10½%, 10 years)
                        ――――――――
                        $571,937

"Target figure" is $565,307. Computations above bracket the yield rate between 10½% and 11%. By interpolation: equity yield rate after taxes: About 10.67%.

Steps that Lead to the SOLD Sign

Thorough analysis by mortgage-equity can assist in every phase of marketing the Sunset Point Apartments:

1. Listing the property initially at a saleable, justifiable figure.
2. Making a comprehensive investment analysis for a prospective buyer as the basis for obtaining a reasonable offer to purchase, price and terms considered.
3. Selling the seller on accepting the offer.
4. Assisting in arranging suitable financing, through an incisive analysis prepared for the lender.

The best sign of a successful sales person is probably the SOLD sign.

Steps leading up to the consummation of a transaction, however, are not necessarily labeled SELL, SELL, SELL! Initially the route should be marked *analyze, analyze, analyze*. Only by thorough analysis can the true professional fulfill his obligation to keep his client out of a "bad deal" and put him into a good one in the dynamic world of real estate investments—a world of calculated risks and anticipated rewards.

Ending the Endless

So, there you have it—*SELLING REAL ESTATE by MORTGAGE-EQUITY ANALYSIS*. The professional practitioner will find the mathematics and concepts of mortgage-equity valuation and analysis to be a rewarding, continuing, and challenging study. For while there is a last letter in the alphabet and the last word is sometimes spoken, there is no last number. Now, it's up to you to "turn the tables." They are your tools.

5 Tables

Compound Interest and Annuity Tables

Monthly Tables:
    Compounding Periods and Interest Rates:
        1 to 360 Months: 3% to 30%
Annual Tables:
    Compounding Periods and Interest Rates:
        1 to 45 Years: 3% to 30%
        1 to 20 Years: 35% to 100%

Abbreviation	*Represents*
PW 1	Present Worth Of 1 (Reversion)
PW 1/P	Present Worth Of 1 Per Period (Annuity; (Inwood Coefficient)
PR	Periodic Repayment (Partial Payment; Amortization)

Notes: The three types of compound interest factors not given in these tables can be calculated from the PW 1 and PR factors as follows:

Future Worth (Amount) Of $1 = 1.0 \div$ PW 1
Future Worth (Amount) Of 1 Per Period $= 1.0 \div (PR - i)$
Sinking Fund $= PR - i$

("1" represents one dollar, and "i" is the interest rate.)

The PW 1 and PR factors given can do double or triple duty in these ways:
    — Dividing by the Present Worth Of 1 factor produces the same answer as multiplying by the Future Worth of 1 factor.
    — Subtract the interest rate from the Periodic Repayment factor and divide by it to make the same computation as multiplying by the Future Worth Of 1 Per Period factor.
    — Subtract the interest rate from the Periodic Repayment factor to calculate the corresponding Sinking Fund factor; multiply by it.

179

The following cross-references should be checked:
— Principal uses of the Compound Interest and Annuity Tables, pages 33 and 34.
— Extension of the tables, pages 112 and 113.
— Interpolation within the tables, pages 67 to 69.
— Programs for computing factors with a mini-calculator, pages 469 to 472.

MONTHLY COMPOUND INTEREST TABLES

3.0 PERCENT NOMINAL ANNUAL RATE   3.5 PERCENT NOMINAL ANNUAL RATE

.250 PERCENT EFFECTIVE MONTHLY RATE   .292 PERCENT EFFECTIVE MONTHLY RATE

MONTHS	PW 1	PW 1/P	PR		PW 1	PW 1/P	PR	MONTHS
1	.997506	.997506	1.002500		.997092	.997092	1.002917	1
2	.995019	1.992525	.501876		.994192	1.991284	.502189	2
3	.992537	2.985062	.335001		.991301	2.982585	.335280	3
4	.990062	3.975124	.251564		.988418	3.971003	.251826	4
5	.987593	4.962718	.201502		.985543	4.956546	.201753	5
6	.985130	5.947848	.168128		.982677	5.939223	.168372	6
7	.982674	6.930522	.144289		.979819	6.919043	.144529	7
8	.980223	7.910745	.126410		.976970	7.896013	.126646	8
9	.977779	8.888524	.112505		.974129	8.870141	.112738	9
10	.975340	9.863864	.101380		.971296	9.841437	.101611	10
11	.972908	10.836772	.092278		.968471	10.809908	.092508	11
12	.970482	11.807254	.084694		.965655	11.775563	.084922	12

YEARS

	PW 1	PW 1/P	PR	YRS	PW 1	PW 1/P	PR	
12	.970482	11.807254	.084694	1	.965655	11.775563	.084922	12
24	.941835	23.265980	.042981	2	.932489	23.146690	.043203	24
36	.914034	34.386465	.029081	3	.900462	34.127270	.029302	36
48	.887053	45.178695	.022134	4	.869535	44.730719	.022356	48
60	.860869	55.652358	.017969	5	.839671	54.969988	.018192	60
72	.835458	65.816858	.015194	6	.810832	64.857585	.015418	72
84	.810797	75.681321	.013213	7	.782984	74.405589	.013440	84
96	.786863	85.254603	.011730	8	.756092	83.625663	.011958	96
108	.763637	94.545300	.010577	9	.730124	92.529069	.010807	108
120	.741096	103.561753	.009656	10	.705047	101.126685	.009889	120
132	.719220	112.312057	.008904	11	.680832	109.429013	.009138	132
144	.697990	120.804069	.008278	12	.657449	117.446193	.008515	144
156	.677386	129.045412	.007749	13	.634868	125.188021	.007988	156
168	.657391	137.043486	.007297	14	.613063	132.663952	.007538	168
180	.637986	144.805471	.006906	15	.592008	139.883120	.007149	180
192	.619154	152.338338	.006564	16	.571675	146.854342	.006809	192
204	.600878	159.648848	.006264	17	.552040	153.586135	.006511	204
216	.583141	166.743566	.005997	18	.533080	160.086722	.006247	216
228	.565928	173.628861	.005759	19	.514772	166.364044	.006011	228
240	.549223	180.310914	.005546	20	.497092	172.425768	.005800	240
252	.533011	186.795726	.005353	21	.480019	178.279301	.005609	252
264	.517277	193.089119	.005179	22	.463532	183.931791	.005437	264
276	.502008	199.196742	.005020	23	.447612	189.390145	.005280	276
288	.487190	205.124080	.004875	24	.432239	194.661029	.005137	288
300	.472809	210.876453	.004742	25	.417393	199.750883	.005006	300
312	.458852	216.459028	.004620	26	.403058	204.665923	.004886	312
324	.445308	221.876815	.004507	27	.389215	209.412155	.004775	324
336	.432163	227.134679	.004403	28	.375847	213.995375	.004673	336
348	.419407	232.237341	.004306	29	.362938	218.421183	.004578	348
360	.407027	237.189382	.004216	30	.350473	222.694985	.004490	360

MONTHLY COMPOUND INTEREST TABLES

4.0 PERCENT NOMINAL ANNUAL RATE				4.5 PERCENT NOMINAL ANNUAL RATE			
.333 PERCENT EFFECTIVE MONTHLY RATE				.375 PERCENT EFFECTIVE MONTHLY RATE			
MONTHS	PW 1	PW 1/P	PR	PW 1	PW 1/P	PR	MONTHS
1	.996678	.996678	1.003333	.996264	.996264	1.003750	1
2	.993367	1.990044	.502501	.992542	1.988806	.502814	2
3	.990066	2.980111	.335558	.988834	2.977640	.335836	3
4	.986777	3.966888	.252087	.985140	3.962779	.252348	4
5	.983499	4.950386	.202004	.981459	4.944239	.202256	5
6	.980231	5.930618	.168617	.977792	5.922031	.168861	6
7	.976975	6.907592	.144768	.974139	6.896170	.145008	7
8	.973729	7.881321	.126882	.970500	7.866670	.127119	8
9	.970494	8.851815	.112971	.966874	8.833544	.113205	9
10	.967270	9.819085	.101842	.963262	9.796806	.102074	10
11	.964056	10.783141	.092737	.959663	10.756470	.092967	11
12	.960853	11.743994	.085150	.956078	11.712548	.085379	12

YEARS

12	.960853	11.743994	.085150	1	.956078	11.712548	.085379	12
24	.923239	23.028251	.043425	2	.914085	22.910656	.043648	24
36	.887097	33.870766	.029524	3	.873937	33.616921	.029747	36
48	.852371	44.288834	.022579	4	.835551	43.852944	.022803	48
60	.819003	54.299069	.018417	5	.798852	53.639380	.018643	60
72	.786942	63.917437	.015645	6	.763765	62.995976	.015874	72
84	.756136	73.159278	.013669	7	.730219	71.941611	.013900	84
96	.726536	82.039332	.012189	8	.698146	80.494336	.012423	96
108	.698094	90.571761	.011041	9	.667482	88.671407	.011278	108
120	.670766	98.770175	.010125	10	.638165	96.489324	.010364	120
132	.644508	106.647648	.009377	11	.610136	103.963862	.009619	132
144	.619278	114.216744	.008755	12	.583337	111.110104	.009000	144
156	.595035	121.489536	.008231	13	.557716	117.942467	.008479	156
168	.571741	128.477623	.007783	14	.533220	124.474740	.008034	168
180	.549360	135.192149	.007397	15	.509800	130.720101	.007650	180
192	.527854	141.643824	.007060	16	.487408	136.691153	.007316	192
204	.507190	147.842937	.006764	17	.466000	142.399945	.007022	204
216	.487335	153.799376	.006502	18	.445533	147.857994	.006763	216
228	.468258	159.522640	.006269	19	.425964	153.076315	.006533	228
240	.449927	165.021858	.006060	20	.407255	158.065437	.006326	240
252	.432314	170.305800	.005872	21	.389367	162.835426	.006141	252
264	.415390	175.382893	.005702	22	.372265	167.395907	.005974	264
276	.399129	180.261235	.005548	23	.355915	171.756083	.005822	276
288	.383505	184.948607	.005407	24	.340282	175.924751	.005684	288
300	.368492	189.452483	.005278	25	.325336	179.910322	.005558	300
312	.354067	193.780048	.005160	26	.311047	183.720839	.005443	312
324	.340206	197.938203	.005052	27	.297385	187.363990	.005337	324
336	.326888	201.933580	.004952	28	.284323	190.847126	.005240	336
348	.314091	205.772552	.004860	29	.271835	194.177276	.005150	348
360	.301796	209.461240	.004774	30	.259896	197.361159	.005067	360

MONTHLY COMPOUND INTEREST TABLES

5.0 PERCENT NOMINAL ANNUAL RATE

.417 PERCENT EFFECTIVE MONTHLY RATE

5.5 PERCENT NOMINAL ANNUAL RATE

.458 PERCENT EFFECTIVE MONTHLY RATE

MONTHS	PW 1	PW 1/P	PR	PW 1	PW 1/P	PR	MONTHS
1	.995851	.995851	1.004167	.995438	.995438	1.004583	1
2	.991718	1.987569	.503127	.990896	1.986334	.503440	2
3	.987603	2.975173	.336115	.986375	2.972709	.336394	3
4	.983506	3.958678	.252610	.981875	3.954583	.252871	4
5	.979425	4.938103	.202507	.977395	4.931979	.202758	5
6	.975361	5.913463	.169106	.972936	5.904914	.169350	6
7	.971313	6.884777	.145248	.968497	6.873411	.145488	7
8	.967283	7.852060	.127355	.964078	7.837489	.127592	8
9	.963269	8.815329	.113439	.959680	8.797169	.113673	9
10	.959272	9.774602	.102306	.955301	9.752470	.102538	10
11	.955292	10.729894	.093198	.950943	10.703413	.093428	11
12	.951328	11.681222	.085607	.946604	11.650017	.085837	12

YEARS

MONTHS	PW 1	PW 1/P	PR	YEARS	PW 1	PW 1/P	PR	MONTHS
12	.951328	11.681222	.085607	1	.946604	11.650017	.085837	12
24	.905025	22.793898	.043871	2	.896059	22.677971	.044096	24
36	.860976	33.365701	.029971	3	.848213	33.117077	.030196	36
48	.819071	43.422956	.023029	4	.802922	42.998777	.023256	48
60	.779205	52.990706	.018871	5	.760050	52.352835	.019101	60
72	.741280	62.092777	.016105	6	.719466	61.207425	.016338	72
84	.705201	70.751835	.014134	7	.681049	69.589216	.014370	84
96	.670877	78.989441	.012660	8	.644684	77.523453	.012899	96
108	.638225	86.826108	.011517	9	.610261	85.034035	.011760	108
120	.607161	94.281350	.010607	10	.577675	92.143582	.010853	120
132	.577609	101.373733	.009864	11	.546830	98.873509	.010114	132
144	.549496	108.120917	.009249	12	.517631	105.244084	.009502	144
156	.522751	114.539704	.008731	13	.489992	111.274498	.008987	156
168	.497308	120.646077	.008289	14	.463828	116.982911	.008548	168
180	.473103	126.455243	.007908	15	.439062	122.386519	.008171	180
192	.450076	131.981666	.007577	16	.415618	127.501597	.007843	192
204	.428170	137.239108	.007287	17	.393425	132.343550	.007556	204
216	.407331	142.240661	.007030	18	.372418	136.926962	.007303	216
228	.387505	146.998780	.006803	19	.352532	141.265639	.007079	228
240	.368645	151.525313	.006600	20	.333709	145.372649	.006879	240
252	.350702	155.831532	.006417	21	.315890	149.260361	.006700	252
264	.333633	159.928159	.006253	22	.299023	152.940485	.006538	264
276	.317394	163.825396	.006104	23	.283056	156.424105	.006393	276
288	.301946	167.532948	.005969	24	.267942	159.721715	.006261	288
300	.287250	171.060047	.005846	25	.253635	162.843245	.006141	300
312	.273269	174.415476	.005733	26	.240092	165.798099	.006031	312
324	.259968	177.607590	.005630	27	.227272	168.595175	.005931	324
336	.247315	180.644338	.005536	28	.215137	171.242899	.005840	336
348	.235278	183.533283	.005449	29	.203649	173.749245	.005755	348
360	.223827	186.281617	.005368	30	.192775	176.121763	.005678	360

MONTHLY COMPOUND INTEREST TABLES

6.0 PERCENT NOMINAL ANNUAL RATE				6.5 PERCENT NOMINAL ANNUAL RATE			
.500 PERCENT EFFECTIVE MONTHLY RATE				.542 PERCENT EFFECTIVE MONTHLY RATE			
MONTHS	PW 1	PW 1/P	PR	PW 1	PW 1/P	PR	MONTHS
1	.995025	.995025	1.005000	.994613	.994613	1.005417	1
2	.990075	1.985099	.503753	.989254	1.983867	.504066	2
3	.985149	2.970248	.336672	.983924	2.967791	.336951	3
4	.980248	3.950496	.253133	.978624	3.946415	.253395	4
5	.975371	4.925866	.203010	.973351	4.919766	.203262	5
6	.970518	5.896384	.169595	.968107	5.887873	.169841	6
7	.965690	6.862074	.145729	.962892	6.850765	.145969	7
8	.960885	7.822959	.127829	.957704	7.808469	.128066	8
9	.956105	8.779064	.113907	.952545	8.761014	.114142	9
10	.951348	9.730412	.102771	.947413	9.708426	.103003	10
11	.946615	10.677027	.093659	.942309	10.650735	.093890	11
12	.941905	11.618932	.086066	.937232	11.587967	.086296	12

YEARS

MONTHS	PW 1	PW 1/P	PR	YEARS	PW 1	PW 1/P	PR	MONTHS
12	.941905	11.618932	.086066	1	.937232	11.587967	.086296	12
24	.887186	22.562866	.044321	2	.878404	22.448578	.044546	24
36	.835645	32.871016	.030422	3	.823268	32.627489	.030649	36
48	.787098	42.580318	.023485	4	.771593	42.167488	.023715	48
60	.741372	51.725561	.019333	5	.723161	51.108680	.019566	60
72	.698302	60.339514	.016573	6	.677770	59.488649	.016810	72
84	.657735	68.453042	.014609	7	.635227	67.342623	.014849	84
96	.619524	76.095218	.013141	8	.595355	74.703617	.013386	96
108	.583533	83.293424	.012006	9	.557986	81.602576	.012255	108
120	.549633	90.073453	.011102	10	.522962	88.068500	.011355	120
132	.517702	96.459599	.010367	11	.490137	94.128569	.010624	132
144	.487626	102.474743	.009759	12	.459372	99.808260	.010019	144
156	.459298	108.140440	.009247	13	.430538	105.131446	.009512	156
168	.432615	113.476990	.008812	14	.403514	110.120506	.009081	168
180	.407482	118.503515	.008439	15	.378186	114.796412	.008711	180
192	.383810	123.238025	.008114	16	.354448	119.178820	.008391	192
204	.361513	127.697486	.007831	17	.332200	123.286152	.008111	204
216	.340511	131.897876	.007582	18	.311348	127.135675	.007866	216
228	.320729	135.854246	.007361	19	.291806	130.743570	.007649	228
240	.302096	139.580772	.007164	20	.273490	134.125004	.007456	240
252	.284546	143.090806	.006989	21	.256323	137.294192	.007284	252
264	.268015	146.396927	.006831	22	.240234	140.264456	.007129	264
276	.252445	149.510979	.006688	23	.225155	143.048282	.006991	276
288	.237779	152.444121	.006560	24	.211023	145.657372	.006865	288
300	.223966	155.206864	.006443	25	.197777	148.102695	.006752	300
312	.210954	157.809106	.006337	26	.185363	150.394529	.006649	312
324	.198699	160.260172	.006240	27	.173728	152.542509	.006556	324
336	.187156	162.568844	.006151	28	.162823	154.555664	.006470	336
348	.176283	164.743394	.006070	29	.152603	156.442457	.006392	348
360	.166042	166.791614	.005996	30	.143025	158.210820	.006321	360

MONTHLY COMPOUND INTEREST TABLES

7.0 PERCENT NOMINAL ANNUAL RATE   7.5 PERCENT NOMINAL ANNUAL RATE

.583 PERCENT EFFECTIVE MONTHLY RATE   .625 PERCENT EFFECTIVE MONTHLY RATE

MONTHS	PW 1	PW 1/P	PR		PW 1	PW 1/P	PR	MONTHS
1	.994200	.994200	1.005833		.993789	.993789	1.006250	1
2	.988435	1.982635	.504379		.987616	1.981405	.504692	2
3	.982702	2.965337	.337230		.981482	2.962887	.337509	3
4	.977003	3.942340	.253656		.975386	3.938273	.253918	4
5	.971337	4.913677	.203514		.969327	4.907600	.203766	5
6	.965704	5.879381	.170086		.963307	5.870907	.170331	6
7	.960103	6.839484	.146210		.957324	6.828231	.146451	7
8	.954535	7.794019	.128304		.951377	7.779608	.128541	8
9	.948999	8.743018	.114377		.945468	8.725076	.114612	9
10	.943495	9.686513	.103236		.939596	9.664672	.103470	10
11	.938024	10.624537	.094122		.933760	10.598432	.094354	11
12	.932583	11.557120	.086527		.927960	11.526392	.086757	12

YEARS

	PW 1	PW 1/P	PR	YR	PW 1	PW 1/P	PR	
12	.932583	11.557120	.086527	1	.927960	11.526392	.086757	12
24	.869712	22.335099	.044773	2	.861110	22.222423	.045000	24
36	.811079	32.386464	.030877	3	.799076	32.147913	.031106	36
48	.756399	41.760201	.023946	4	.741510	41.358371	.024179	48
60	.705405	50.501994	.019801	5	.688092	49.905308	.020038	60
72	.657849	58.654444	.017049	6	.638522	57.836524	.017290	72
84	.613499	66.257285	.015093	7	.592523	65.196376	.015338	84
96	.572139	73.347569	.013634	8	.549837	72.026024	.013884	96
108	.533568	79.959850	.012506	9	.510227	78.363665	.012761	108
120	.497596	86.126354	.011611	10	.473470	84.244743	.011870	120
132	.464050	91.877134	.010884	11	.439362	89.702148	.011148	132
144	.432765	97.240216	.010284	12	.407710	94.766401	.010552	144
156	.403590	102.241738	.009781	13	.378339	99.465827	.010054	156
168	.376381	106.906074	.009354	14	.351083	103.826706	.009631	168
180	.351007	111.255958	.008988	15	.325791	107.873427	.009270	180
192	.327343	115.312587	.008672	16	.302321	111.628623	.008958	192
204	.305275	119.095732	.008397	17	.280542	115.113294	.008687	204
216	.284694	122.623831	.008155	18	.260332	118.346930	.008450	216
228	.265501	125.914077	.007942	19	.241577	121.347615	.008241	228
240	.247602	128.982506	.007753	20	.224174	124.132131	.008056	240
252	.230910	131.844073	.007585	21	.208025	126.716051	.007892	252
264	.215342	134.512723	.007434	22	.193039	129.113825	.007745	264
276	.200825	137.001461	.007299	23	.179132	131.338863	.007614	276
288	.187286	139.322418	.007178	24	.166227	133.403610	.007496	288
300	.174660	141.486903	.007068	25	.154252	135.319613	.007390	300
312	.162885	143.505467	.006968	26	.143140	137.097587	.007294	312
324	.151904	145.387946	.006878	27	.132828	138.747475	.007207	324
336	.141663	147.143515	.006796	28	.123259	140.278506	.007129	336
348	.132112	148.780729	.006721	29	.114380	141.699242	.007057	348
360	.123206	150.307568	.006653	30	.106140	143.017627	.006992	360

MONTHLY COMPOUND INTEREST TABLES

8.0 PERCENT NOMINAL ANNUAL RATE   8.5 PERCENT NOMINAL ANNUAL RATE

.667 PERCENT EFFECTIVE MONTHLY RATE   .708 PERCENT EFFECTIVE MONTHLY RATE

MONTHS	PW 1	PW 1/P	PR	PW 1	PW 1/P	PR	MONTHS
1	.993377	.993377	1.006667	.992966	.992966	1.007083	1
2	.986799	1.980176	.505006	.985982	1.978949	.505319	2
3	.980264	2.960440	.337788	.979048	2.957996	.338067	3
4	.973772	3.934212	.254181	.972161	3.930158	.254443	4
5	.967323	4.901535	.204018	.965324	4.895482	.204270	5
6	.960917	5.862452	.170577	.958534	5.854016	.170823	6
7	.954553	6.817005	.146692	.951792	6.805808	.146933	7
8	.948232	7.765237	.128779	.945098	7.750906	.129017	8
9	.941952	8.707189	.114848	.938450	8.689356	.115083	9
10	.935714	9.642903	.103703	.931850	9.621206	.103937	10
11	.929517	10.572420	.094586	.925296	10.546501	.094818	11
12	.923361	11.495782	.086988	.918788	11.465289	.087220	12

YEARS

MONTHS	PW 1	PW 1/P	PR	YEARS	PW 1	PW 1/P	PR	MONTHS
12	.923361	11.495782	.086988	1	.918788	11.465289	.087220	12
24	.852596	22.110544	.045227	2	.844171	21.999453	.045456	24
36	.787255	31.911806	.031336	3	.775613	31.678112	.031568	36
48	.726921	40.961913	.024413	4	.712624	40.570744	.024648	48
60	.671210	49.318433	.020276	5	.654750	48.741183	.020517	60
72	.619770	57.034522	.017533	6	.601576	56.248080	.017778	72
84	.572272	64.159261	.015586	7	.552721	63.145324	.015836	84
96	.528414	70.737970	.014137	8	.507833	69.482425	.014392	96
108	.487917	76.812497	.013019	9	.466590	75.304875	.013279	108
120	.450523	82.421481	.012133	10	.428698	80.654470	.012399	120
132	.415996	87.600600	.011415	11	.393882	85.569611	.011686	132
144	.384115	92.382800	.010825	12	.361894	90.085581	.011101	144
156	.354677	96.798498	.010331	13	.332504	94.234798	.010612	156
168	.327495	100.875784	.009913	14	.305500	98.047046	.010199	168
180	.302396	104.640592	.009557	15	.280690	101.549693	.009847	180
192	.279221	108.116871	.009249	16	.257894	104.767881	.009545	192
204	.257822	111.326733	.008983	17	.236950	107.724713	.009283	204
216	.238063	114.290596	.008750	18	.217707	110.441412	.009055	216
228	.219818	117.027313	.008545	19	.200026	112.937482	.008854	228
240	.202971	119.554292	.008364	20	.183782	115.230840	.008678	240
252	.187416	121.887606	.008204	21	.168856	117.337948	.008522	252
264	.173053	124.042099	.008062	22	.155143	119.273933	.008384	264
276	.159790	126.031475	.007935	23	.142543	121.052692	.008261	276
288	.147544	127.868388	.007821	24	.130967	122.686994	.008151	288
300	.136237	129.564523	.007718	25	.120331	124.188570	.008052	300
312	.125796	131.130668	.007626	26	.110559	125.568199	.007964	312
324	.116155	132.576786	.007543	27	.101580	126.835785	.007884	324
336	.107253	133.912076	.007468	28	.093330	128.000428	.007812	336
348	.099033	135.145031	.007399	29	.085751	129.070487	.007748	348
360	.091443	136.283494	.007338	30	.078787	130.053643	.007689	360

MONTHLY COMPOUND INTEREST TABLES

9.0 PERCENT NOMINAL ANNUAL RATE	9.5 PERCENT NOMINAL ANNUAL RATE
.750 PERCENT EFFECTIVE MONTHLY RATE	.792 PERCENT EFFECTIVE MONTHLY RATE

MONTHS	PW 1	PW 1/P	PR	PW 1	PW 1/P	PR	MONTHS
1	.992556	.992556	1.007500	.992146	.992146	1.007917	1
2	.985167	1.977723	.505632	.984353	1.976498	.505945	2
3	.977833	2.955556	.338346	.976621	2.953119	.338625	3
4	.970554	3.926110	.254705	.968950	3.922070	.254967	4
5	.963329	4.889440	.204522	.961340	4.883409	.204775	5
6	.956158	5.845598	.171069	.953789	5.837198	.171315	6
7	.949040	6.794638	.147175	.946297	6.783496	.147417	7
8	.941975	7.736613	.129256	.938865	7.722360	.129494	8
9	.934963	8.671576	.115319	.931490	8.653851	.115555	9
10	.928003	9.599580	.104171	.924174	9.578024	.104406	10
11	.921095	10.520675	.095051	.916915	10.494940	.095284	11
12	.914238	11.434913	.087451	.909713	11.404E53	.087684	12

YEARS

MONTHS	PW 1	PW 1/P	PR		PW 1	PW 1/P	PR	MONTHS
12	.914238	11.434913	.087451	1	.909713	11.404E53	.087684	12
24	.835831	21.889146	.045685	2	.827578	21.779615	.045914	24
36	.764149	31.446805	.031800	3	.752859	31.217856	.032033	36
48	.698614	40.184782	.024885	4	.684885	39.803947	.025123	48
60	.638700	48.173374	.020758	5	.623049	47.614827	.021002	60
72	.583924	55.476849	.018026	6	.566796	54.720488	.018275	72
84	.533845	62.153965	.016089	7	.515622	61.184601	.016344	84
96	.488062	68.258439	.014650	8	.469068	67.065090	.014911	96
108	.446205	73.839382	.013543	9	.426717	72.414648	.013809	108
120	.407937	78.941693	.012668	10	.388190	77.281211	.012940	120
132	.372952	83.606420	.011961	11	.353142	81.708388	.012239	132
144	.340967	87.871092	.011380	12	.321258	85.735849	.011664	144
156	.311725	91.770018	.010897	13	.292253	89.399684	.011186	156
168	.284991	95.334564	.010489	14	.265866	92.732722	.010784	168
180	.260549	98.593409	.010143	15	.241862	95.764831	.010442	180
192	.238204	101.572769	.009845	16	.220025	98.523180	.010150	192
204	.217775	104.296613	.009588	17	.200159	101.032487	.009898	204
216	.199099	106.786856	.009364	18	.182088	103.315236	.009679	216
228	.182024	109.063531	.009169	19	.165648	105.391883	.009488	228
240	.166413	111.144954	.008997	20	.150692	107.281037	.009321	240
252	.152141	113.047870	.008846	21	.137086	108.999624	.009174	252
264	.139093	114.787589	.008712	22	.124709	110.563046	.009045	264
276	.127164	116.378106	.008593	23	.113450	111.985311	.008930	276
288	.116258	117.832218	.008487	24	.103207	113.279165	.008828	288
300	.106288	119.161622	.008392	25	.093888	114.456200	.008737	300
312	.097172	120.377014	.008307	26	.085412	115.526965	.008656	312
324	.088839	121.488172	.008231	27	.077700	116.501054	.008584	324
336	.081220	122.504035	.008163	28	.070685	117.387195	.008519	336
348	.074254	123.432776	.008102	29	.064303	118.193330	.008461	348
360	.067886	124.281866	.008046	30	.058497	118.926681	.008409	360

MONTHLY COMPOUND INTEREST TABLES

10.0 PERCENT NOMINAL ANNUAL RATE   10.5 PERCENT NOMINAL ANNUAL RATE

.833 PERCENT EFFECTIVE MONTHLY RATE   .875 PERCENT EFFECTIVE MONTHLY RATE

MONTHS	PW 1	PW 1/P	PR	PW 1	PW 1/P	PR	MONTHS
1	.991736	.991736	1.008333	.991326	.991326	1.008750	1
2	.983539	1.975275	.506259	.982727	1.974053	.506572	2
3	.975411	2.950686	.338904	.974203	2.948256	.339184	3
4	.967350	3.918036	.255230	.965752	3.914008	.255493	4
5	.959355	4.877391	.205028	.957375	4.871384	.205280	5
6	.951427	5.828817	.171561	.949071	5.820455	.171808	6
7	.943563	6.772381	.147659	.940839	6.761293	.147901	7
8	.935765	7.708146	.129733	.932678	7.693971	.129972	8
9	.928032	8.636178	.115792	.924588	8.618559	.116029	9
10	.920362	9.556540	.104640	.916568	9.535126	.104875	10
11	.912756	10.469296	.095517	.908617	10.443743	.095751	11
12	.905212	11.374508	.087916	.900736	11.344479	.088149	12

YEARS

MONTHS	PW 1	PW 1/P	PR	YEARS	PW 1	PW 1/P	PR	MONTHS
12	.905212	11.374508	.087916	1	.900736	11.344479	.088149	12
24	.819410	21.670855	.046145	2	.811325	21.562858	.046376	24
36	.741740	30.991236	.032267	3	.730789	30.766918	.032502	36
48	.671432	39.428160	.025363	4	.658248	39.057344	.025603	48
60	.607789	47.065369	.021247	5	.592908	46.524827	.021494	60
72	.550178	53.978665	.018526	6	.534053	53.251057	.018779	72
84	.498028	60.236667	.016601	7	.481041	59.309613	.016861	84
96	.450821	65.901488	.015174	8	.433291	64.766771	.015440	96
108	.408089	71.029355	.014079	9	.390280	69.682229	.014351	108
120	.369407	75.671163	.013215	10	.351540	74.109758	.013493	120
132	.334392	79.872986	.012520	11	.316644	78.097792	.012804	132
144	.302696	83.676528	.011951	12	.285213	81.689957	.012241	144
156	.274004	87.119542	.011478	13	.256901	84.925549	.011775	156
168	.248032	90.236201	.011082	14	.231400	87.839962	.011384	168
180	.224521	93.057439	.010746	15	.208431	90.465078	.011054	180
192	.203240	95.611259	.010459	16	.187741	92.829614	.010772	192
204	.183975	97.923008	.010212	17	.169105	94.959437	.010531	204
216	.166536	100.015633	.009998	18	.152319	96.877844	.010322	216
228	.150751	101.909902	.009813	19	.137199	98.605822	.010141	228
240	.136462	103.624619	.009650	20	.123568	100.162274	.009984	240
252	.123527	105.176801	.009508	21	.111313	101.564226	.009846	252
264	.111818	106.581856	.009382	22	.100264	102.827014	.009725	264
276	.101219	107.853730	.009272	23	.090311	103.964453	.009619	276
288	.091625	109.005045	.009174	24	.081346	104.988985	.009525	288
300	.082940	110.047230	.009087	25	.073272	105.911817	.009442	300
312	.075078	110.990629	.009010	26	.065998	106.743045	.009368	312
324	.067962	111.844605	.008941	27	.059447	107.491762	.009303	324
336	.061520	112.617635	.008880	28	.053546	108.166158	.009245	336
348	.055688	113.317392	.008825	29	.048231	108.773611	.009193	348
360	.050410	113.950820	.008776	30	.043443	109.320766	.009147	360

MONTHLY COMPOUND INTEREST TABLES

11.0 PERCENT NOMINAL ANNUAL RATE

.917 PERCENT EFFECTIVE MONTHLY RATE

12.0 PERCENT NOMINAL ANNUAL RATE

1.000 PERCENT EFFECTIVE MONTHLY RATE

MONTHS	PW 1	PW 1/P	PR	PW 1	PW 1/P	PR	MONTHS
1	.990917	.990917	1.009167	.990099	.990099	1.010000	1
2	.981916	1.972832	.506885	.980296	1.970395	.507512	2
3	.972997	2.945829	.339463	.970590	2.940985	.340022	3
4	.964158	3.909987	.255755	.960980	3.901966	.256281	4
5	.955401	4.865388	.205533	.951466	4.853431	.206040	5
6	.946722	5.812110	.172055	.942045	5.795476	.172548	6
7	.938123	6.750233	.148143	.932718	6.728195	.148628	7
8	.929602	7.679835	.130211	.923483	7.651678	.130690	8
9	.921158	8.600992	.116266	.914340	8.566018	.116740	9
10	.912790	9.513783	.105111	.905287	9.471305	.105582	10
11	.904499	10.418282	.095985	.896324	10.367628	.096454	11
12	.896283	11.314565	.088382	.887449	11.255077	.088849	12

YEARS

MONTHS	PW 1	PW 1/P	PR	YR	PW 1	PW 1/P	PR	MONTHS
12	.896283	11.314565	.088382	1	.887449	11.255077	.088849	12
24	.803323	21.455619	.046608	2	.787566	21.243387	.047073	24
36	.720005	30.544874	.032739	3	.698925	30.107505	.033214	36
48	.645329	38.691421	.025846	4	.620260	37.973959	.026334	48
60	.578397	45.993034	.021742	5	.550450	44.955038	.022244	60
72	.518408	52.537346	.019034	6	.488496	51.150391	.019550	72
84	.464640	58.402903	.017122	7	.433515	56.648453	.017653	84
96	.416449	63.660103	.015708	8	.384723	61.527703	.016253	96
108	.373256	68.372043	.014626	9	.341422	65.857790	.015184	108
120	.334543	72.595275	.013775	10	.302995	69.700522	.014347	120
132	.299846	76.380487	.013092	11	.268892	73.110752	.013678	132
144	.268747	79.773109	.012536	12	.238628	76.137157	.013134	144
156	.240873	82.813859	.012075	13	.211771	78.822939	.012687	156
168	.215890	85.539231	.011691	14	.187936	81.206434	.012314	168
180	.193499	87.981937	.011366	15	.166783	83.321664	.012002	180
192	.173430	90.171293	.011090	16	.148012	85.198824	.011737	192
204	.155442	92.133576	.010854	17	.131353	86.864707	.011512	204
216	.139320	93.892337	.010650	18	.116569	88.343095	.011320	216
228	.124870	95.468685	.010475	19	.103449	89.655089	.011154	228
240	.111919	96.881539	.010322	20	.091806	90.819416	.011011	240
252	.100311	98.147856	.010189	21	.081473	91.852698	.010887	252
264	.089907	99.282835	.010072	22	.072303	92.769683	.010779	264
276	.080582	100.300098	.009970	23	.064165	93.583461	.010686	276
288	.072225	101.211853	.009880	24	.056944	94.305647	.010604	288
300	.064734	102.029044	.009801	25	.050534	94.946551	.010532	300
312	.058020	102.761478	.009731	26	.044847	95.515321	.010470	312
324	.052002	103.417947	.009670	27	.039799	96.020075	.010414	324
336	.046609	104.006328	.009615	28	.035320	96.468019	.010366	336
348	.041775	104.533685	.009566	29	.031345	96.865546	.010324	348
360	.037442	105.006346	.009523	30	.027817	97.218331	.010286	360

MONTHLY COMPOUND INTEREST TABLES

13.0 PERCENT NOMINAL ANNUAL RATE	14.0 PERCENT NOMINAL ANNUAL RATE
1.083 PERCENT EFFECTIVE MONTHLY RATE	1.167 PERCENT EFFECTIVE MONTHLY RATE

MONTHS	PW 1	PW 1/P	PR	PW 1	PW 1/P	PR	MONTHS
1	.989283	.989283	1.010833	.988468	.988468	1.011667	1
2	.978680	1.967963	.508140	.977069	1.965537	.508767	2
3	.968192	2.936155	.340581	.965801	2.931338	.341141	3
4	.957815	3.893970	.256807	.954663	3.886001	.257334	4
5	.947550	4.841520	.206547	.943654	4.829655	.207054	5
6	.937395	5.778915	.173043	.932772	5.762427	.173538	6
7	.927349	6.706264	.149114	.922015	6.684442	.149601	7
8	.917410	7.623674	.131170	.911382	7.595824	.131651	8
9	.907578	8.531253	.117216	.900872	8.496696	.117693	9
10	.897851	9.429104	.106055	.890483	9.387178	.106528	10
11	.888229	10.317333	.096924	.880214	10.267392	.097396	11
12	.878710	11.196042	.089317	.870063	11.137455	.089787	12

YEARS

MONTHS	PW 1	PW 1/P	PR	YEARS	PW 1	PW 1/P	PR	MONTHS
12	.878710	11.196042	.089317	1	.870063	11.137455	.089787	12
24	.772130	21.034112	.047542	2	.757010	20.827743	.048013	24
36	.678478	29.678917	.033694	3	.658646	29.258904	.034178	36
48	.596185	37.275190	.026827	4	.573064	36.594546	.027326	48
60	.523874	43.950107	.022753	5	.498601	42.977016	.023268	60
72	.460333	49.815421	.020074	6	.433815	48.530168	.020606	72
84	.404499	54.969328	.018192	7	.377446	53.361760	.018740	84
96	.355437	59.498115	.016807	8	.328402	57.565549	.017372	96
108	.312326	63.477604	.015754	9	.285730	61.223111	.016334	108
120	.274444	66.974419	.014931	10	.248603	64.405420	.015527	120
132	.241156	70.047103	.014276	11	.216301	67.174230	.014887	132
144	.211906	72.747100	.013746	12	.188195	69.583269	.014371	144
156	.186204	75.119613	.013312	13	.163742	71.679284	.013951	156
168	.163619	77.204363	.012953	14	.142466	73.502950	.013605	168
180	.143774	79.036253	.012652	15	.123954	75.089654	.013317	180
192	.126336	80.645952	.012400	16	.107848	76.470187	.013077	192
204	.111012	82.060410	.012186	17	.093834	77.671337	.012875	204
216	.097548	83.303307	.012004	18	.081642	78.716413	.012704	216
228	.085716	84.395453	.011849	19	.071034	79.625696	.012559	228
240	.075319	85.355132	.011716	20	.061804	80.416829	.012435	240
252	.066184	86.198412	.011601	21	.053773	81.105164	.012330	252
264	.058156	86.939409	.011502	22	.046786	81.704060	.012239	264
276	.051103	87.590531	.011417	23	.040707	82.225136	.012162	276
288	.044904	88.162677	.011343	24	.035417	82.678506	.012095	288
300	.039458	88.665428	.011278	25	.030815	83.072966	.012038	300
312	.034672	89.107200	.011222	26	.026811	83.416171	.011988	312
324	.030467	89.495389	.011174	27	.023328	83.714781	.011945	324
336	.026771	89.836495	.011131	28	.020296	83.974591	.011908	336
348	.023524	90.136227	.011094	29	.017659	84.200641	.011876	348
360	.020671	90.399605	.011062	30	.015365	84.397320	.011849	360

MONTHLY COMPOUND INTEREST TABLES

15.0 PERCENT NOMINAL ANNUAL RATE   16.0 PERCENT NOMINAL ANNUAL RATE

1.250 PERCENT EFFECTIVE MONTHLY RATE   1.333 PERCENT EFFECTIVE MONTHLY RATE

MONTHS	PW 1	PW 1/P	PR	PW 1	PW 1/P	PR	MONTHS
1	.987654	.987654	1.012500	.986842	.986842	1.013333	1
2	.975461	1.963115	.509394	.973857	1.960699	.510022	2
3	.963418	2.926534	.341701	.961043	2.921743	.342261	3
4	.951524	3.878058	.257861	.948398	3.870141	.258389	4
5	.939777	4.817835	.207562	.935919	4.806060	.208071	5
6	.928175	5.746010	.174034	.923604	5.729665	.174530	6
7	.916716	6.662726	.150089	.911452	6.641116	.150577	7
8	.905398	7.568124	.132133	.899459	7.540575	.132616	8
9	.894221	8.462345	.118171	.887624	8.428199	.118649	9
10	.883181	9.345526	.107003	.875945	9.304144	.107479	10
11	.872277	10.217803	.097868	.864419	10.168563	.098342	11
12	.861509	11.079312	.090258	.853045	11.021609	.090731	12

YEARS

MONTHS	PW 1	PW 1/P	PR	YEARS	PW 1	PW 1/P	PR	MONTHS
12	.861509	11.079312	.090258	1	.853045	11.021609	.090731	12
24	.742197	20.624235	.048487	2	.727686	20.423539	.048963	24
36	.639409	28.847267	.034665	3	.620749	28.443811	.035157	36
48	.550856	35.931481	.027831	4	.529527	35.285465	.028340	48
60	.474568	42.034592	.023790	5	.451711	41.121706	.024318	60
72	.408844	47.292474	.021145	6	.385330	46.100283	.021692	72
84	.352223	51.822185	.019297	7	.328704	50.347235	.019862	84
96	.303443	55.724570	.017945	8	.280399	53.970077	.018529	96
108	.261419	59.086509	.016924	9	.239193	57.060524	.017525	108
120	.225214	61.982847	.016133	10	.204042	59.696816	.016751	120
132	.194024	64.478068	.015509	11	.174057	61.945692	.016143	132
144	.167153	66.627722	.015009	12	.148479	63.864085	.015658	144
156	.144004	68.479668	.014603	13	.126659	65.500561	.015267	156
168	.124061	70.075134	.014270	14	.108046	66.896549	.014948	168
180	.106879	71.449643	.013996	15	.092168	68.087390	.014687	180
192	.092078	72.633794	.013768	16	.078624	69.103231	.014471	192
204	.079326	73.653950	.013577	17	.067069	69.969789	.014292	204
216	.068340	74.532823	.013417	18	.057213	70.709003	.014142	216
228	.058875	75.289980	.013282	19	.048806	71.339585	.014017	228
240	.050722	75.942278	.013168	20	.041633	71.877501	.013913	240
252	.043697	76.504237	.013071	21	.035515	72.336367	.013824	252
264	.037645	76.988370	.012989	22	.030296	72.727801	.013750	264
276	.032432	77.405455	.012919	23	.025844	73.061711	.013687	276
288	.027940	77.764777	.012859	24	.022046	73.346552	.013634	288
300	.024071	78.074336	.012808	25	.018806	73.589534	.013589	300
312	.020737	78.341024	.012765	26	.016043	73.796809	.013551	312
324	.017865	78.570778	.012727	27	.013685	73.973623	.013518	324
336	.015391	78.768713	.012695	28	.011674	74.124454	.013491	336
348	.013260	78.939236	.012668	29	.009958	74.253120	.013467	348
360	.011423	79.086142	.012644	30	.008495	74.362878	.013448	360

MONTHLY COMPOUND INTEREST TABLES

18.0 PERCENT NOMINAL ANNUAL RATE   20.0 PERCENT NOMINAL ANNUAL RATE

1.500 PERCENT EFFECTIVE MONTHLY RATE   1.667 PERCENT EFFECTIVE MONTHLY RATE

MONTHS	PW 1	PW 1/P	PR	PW 1	PW 1/P	PR	MONTHS
1	.985222	.985222	1.015000	.983607	.983607	1.016667	1
2	.970662	1.955883	.511278	.967482	1.951088	.512534	2
3	.956317	2.912200	.343383	.951622	2.902710	.344506	3
4	.942184	3.854385	.259445	.936021	3.838731	.260503	4
5	.928260	4.782645	.209089	.920677	4.759408	.210110	5
6	.914542	5.697187	.175525	.905583	5.664991	.176523	6
7	.901027	6.598214	.151556	.890738	6.555729	.152538	7
8	.887711	7.485925	.133584	.876136	7.431865	.134556	8
9	.874592	8.360517	.119610	.861773	8.293637	.120574	9
10	.861667	9.222185	.108434	.847645	9.141283	.109394	10
11	.848933	10.071118	.099294	.833749	9.975032	.100250	11
12	.836387	10.907505	.091680	.820081	10.795113	.092635	12

YEARS

MONTHS	PW 1	PW 1/P	PR	YEARS	PW 1	PW 1/P	PR	MONTHS
12	.836387	10.907505	.091680	1	.820081	10.795113	.092635	12
24	.699544	20.030405	.049924	2	.672534	19.647986	.050896	24
36	.585090	27.660684	.036152	3	.551532	26.908062	.037164	36
48	.489362	34.042554	.029375	4	.452301	32.861916	.030430	48
60	.409296	39.380269	.025393	5	.370924	37.744561	.026494	60
72	.342330	43.844667	.022808	6	.304188	41.748727	.023953	72
84	.286321	47.578633	.021018	7	.249459	45.032470	.022206	84
96	.239475	50.701675	.019723	8	.204577	47.725406	.020953	96
108	.200294	53.313749	.018757	9	.167769	49.933833	.020027	108
120	.167523	55.498454	.018019	10	.137585	51.744924	.019326	120
132	.140114	57.325714	.017444	11	.112831	53.230165	.018786	132
144	.117190	58.854011	.016991	12	.092530	54.448184	.018366	144
156	.098016	60.132260	.016630	13	.075882	55.447059	.018035	156
168	.081979	61.201371	.016340	14	.062230	56.266217	.017773	168
180	.068567	62.095562	.016104	15	.051033	56.937994	.017563	180
192	.057348	62.843452	.015913	16	.041852	57.488906	.017395	192
204	.047965	63.468978	.015756	17	.034322	57.940698	.017259	204
216	.040118	63.992160	.015627	18	.028147	58.311205	.017149	216
228	.033554	64.429743	.015521	19	.023082	58.615050	.017060	228
240	.028064	64.795732	.015433	20	.018930	58.864229	.016988	240
252	.023472	65.101841	.015361	21	.015524	59.068575	.016929	252
264	.019632	65.357866	.015300	22	.012731	59.236156	.016882	264
276	.016420	65.572002	.015250	23	.010440	59.373585	.016843	276
288	.013733	65.751103	.015209	24	.008562	59.486289	.016811	288
300	.011486	65.900901	.015174	25	.007021	59.578715	.016785	300
312	.009607	66.026190	.015146	26	.005758	59.654512	.016763	312
324	.008035	66.130980	.015122	27	.004722	59.716672	.016744	324
336	.006721	66.218625	.015101	28	.003873	59.767648	.016731	336
348	.005621	66.291930	.015085	29	.003176	59.809452	.016720	348
360	.004701	66.353242	.015071	30	.002604	59.843735	.016710	360

MONTHLY COMPOUND INTEREST TABLES

25.0 PERCENT NOMINAL ANNUAL RATE		30.0 PERCENT NOMINAL ANNUAL RATE		
2.083 PERCENT EFFECTIVE MONTHLY RATE		2.500 PERCENT EFFECTIVE MONTHLY RATE		

MONTHS	PW 1	PW 1/P	PR	PW 1	PW 1/P	PR	MONTHS
1	.979592	.979592	1.020833	.975610	.975610	1.025000	1
2	.959600	1.939192	.515679	.951814	1.927424	.518827	2
3	.940016	2.879208	.347318	.928599	2.856024	.350137	3
4	.920832	3.800041	.263155	.905951	3.761974	.265818	4
5	.902040	4.702081	.212672	.883854	4.645828	.215247	5
6	.883631	5.585712	.179028	.862297	5.508125	.181550	6
7	.865598	6.451310	.155007	.841265	6.349391	.157495	7
8	.847932	7.299242	.137001	.820747	7.170137	.139467	8
9	.830628	8.129870	.123003	.800728	7.970866	.125457	9
10	.813676	8.943546	.111812	.781198	8.752064	.114259	10
11	.797070	9.740616	.102663	.762145	9.514209	.105106	11
12	.780804	10.521420	.095044	.743556	10.257765	.097487	12

YEARS

MONTHS	PW 1	PW 1/P	PR		PW 1	PW 1/P	PR	MONTHS
12	.780804	10.521420	.095044	1	.743556	10.257765	.097487	12
24	.609654	18.736585	.053372	2	.552875	17.884986	.055913	24
36	.476021	25.151016	.039760	3	.411094	23.556251	.042452	36
48	.371679	30.159427	.033157	4	.305671	27.773154	.036006	48
60	.290208	34.070014	.029351	5	.227284	30.908656	.032353	60
72	.226596	37.123415	.026937	6	.168998	33.240078	.030084	72
84	.176927	39.507522	.025312	7	.125659	34.973620	.028593	84
96	.138145	41.369041	.024173	8	.093435	36.262606	.027577	96
108	.107864	42.822522	.023352	9	.069474	37.221039	.026867	108
120	.084221	43.957406	.022749	10	.051658	37.933687	.026362	120
132	.065760	44.843528	.022300	11	.038410	38.463581	.025999	132
144	.051346	45.535414	.021961	12	.028560	38.857586	.025735	144
156	.040091	46.075642	.021703	13	.021236	39.150552	.025542	156
168	.031303	46.497454	.021507	14	.015790	39.368388	.025401	168
180	.024442	46.826807	.021355	15	.011741	39.530361	.025297	180
192	.019084	47.083966	.021239	16	.008730	39.650797	.025220	192
204	.014901	47.284757	.021148	17	.006491	39.740348	.025163	204
216	.011635	47.441536	.021079	18	.004827	39.806934	.025121	216
228	.009084	47.563949	.021024	19	.003589	39.856445	.025090	228
240	.007093	47.659530	.020982	20	.002669	39.893259	.025067	240
252	.005538	47.734160	.020949	21	.001984	39.920632	.025050	252
264	.004324	47.792431	.020924	22	.001475	39.940985	.025037	264
276	.003376	47.837929	.020904	23	.001097	39.956119	.025027	276
288	.002636	47.873455	.020888	24	.000816	39.967372	.025020	288
300	.002058	47.901193	.020876	25	.000607	39.975739	.025015	300
312	.001607	47.922851	.020867	26	.000451	39.981961	.025011	312
324	.001255	47.939762	.020860	27	.000335	39.986587	.025008	324
336	.000980	47.952966	.020854	28	.000249	39.990027	.025006	336
348	.000765	47.963275	.020849	29	.000185	39.992584	.025005	348
360	.000597	47.971325	.020846	30	.000138	39.994486	.025003	360

ANNUAL COMPOUND INTEREST TABLES

	3.0 PERCENT			3.5 PERCENT			
PERIOD	PW 1	PW 1/P	PR	PW 1	PW 1/P	PR	PERIOD
1	.970874	.970874	1.030000	.966184	.966184	1.035000	1
2	.942596	1.913470	.522611	.933511	1.899694	.526400	2
3	.915142	2.828611	.353530	.901943	2.801637	.356934	3
4	.888487	3.717098	.269027	.871442	3.673079	.272251	4
5	.862609	4.579707	.218355	.841973	4.515052	.221481	5
6	.837484	5.417191	.184598	.813501	5.328553	.187668	6
7	.813092	6.230283	.160506	.785991	6.114544	.163544	7
8	.789409	7.019692	.142456	.759412	6.873956	.145477	8
9	.766417	7.786109	.128434	.733731	7.607687	.131446	9
10	.744094	8.530203	.117231	.708919	8.316605	.120241	10
11	.722421	9.252624	.108077	.684946	9.001551	.111092	11
12	.701380	9.954004	.100462	.661783	9.663334	.103484	12
13	.680951	10.634955	.094030	.639404	10.302738	.097062	13
14	.661118	11.296073	.088526	.617782	10.920520	.091571	14
15	.641862	11.937935	.083767	.596891	11.517411	.086825	15
16	.623167	12.561102	.079611	.576706	12.094117	.082685	16
17	.605016	13.166118	.075953	.557204	12.651321	.079043	17
18	.587395	13.753513	.072709	.538361	13.189682	.075817	18
19	.570286	14.323799	.069814	.520156	13.709837	.072940	19
20	.553676	14.877475	.067216	.502566	14.212403	.070361	20
21	.537549	15.415024	.064872	.485571	14.697974	.068037	21
22	.521893	15.936917	.062747	.469151	15.167125	.065932	22
23	.506692	16.443608	.060814	.453286	15.620410	.064019	23
24	.491934	16.935542	.059047	.437957	16.058368	.062273	24
25	.477606	17.413148	.057428	.423147	16.481515	.060674	25
26	.463695	17.876842	.055938	.408838	16.890352	.059205	26
27	.450189	18.327031	.054564	.395012	17.285365	.057852	27
28	.437077	18.764108	.053293	.381654	17.667019	.056603	28
29	.424346	19.188455	.052115	.368748	18.035767	.055445	29
30	.411987	19.600441	.051019	.356278	18.392045	.054371	30
31	.399987	20.000428	.049999	.344230	18.736276	.053372	31
32	.388337	20.388766	.049047	.332590	19.068865	.052442	32
33	.377026	20.765792	.048156	.321343	19.390208	.051572	33
34	.366045	21.131837	.047322	.310476	19.700684	.050760	34
35	.355383	21.487220	.046539	.299977	20.000661	.049998	35
36	.345032	21.832252	.045804	.289833	20.290494	.049284	36
37	.334983	22.167235	.045112	.280032	20.570525	.048613	37
38	.325226	22.492462	.044459	.270562	20.841087	.047982	38
39	.315754	22.808215	.043844	.261413	21.102500	.047388	39
40	.306557	23.114772	.043262	.252572	21.355072	.046827	40
41	.297628	23.412400	.042712	.244031	21.599104	.046298	41
42	.288959	23.701359	.042192	.235779	21.834883	.045798	42
43	.280543	23.981902	.041698	.227806	22.062689	.045325	43
44	.272372	24.254274	.041230	.220102	22.282791	.044878	44
45	.264439	24.518713	.040785	.212659	22.495450	.044453	45

195

ANNUAL COMPOUND INTEREST TABLES

4.0 PERCENT   4.5 PERCENT

PERIOD	PW 1	PW 1/P	PR	PW 1	PW 1/P	PR	PERIOD
1	.961538	.961538	1.040000	.956938	.956938	1.045000	1
2	.924556	1.886095	.530196	.915730	1.872668	.533998	2
3	.888996	2.775091	.360349	.876297	2.748964	.363773	3
4	.854804	3.629895	.275490	.838561	3.587526	.278744	4
5	.821927	4.451822	.224627	.802451	4.389977	.227792	5
6	.790315	5.242137	.190762	.767896	5.157872	.193878	6
7	.759918	6.002055	.166610	.734828	5.892701	.169701	7
8	.730690	6.732745	.148528	.703185	6.595886	.151610	8
9	.702587	7.435332	.134493	.672904	7.268790	.137574	9
10	.675564	8.110896	.123291	.643928	7.912718	.126379	10
11	.649581	8.760477	.114149	.616199	8.528917	.117248	11
12	.624597	9.385074	.106552	.589664	9.118581	.109666	12
13	.600574	9.985648	.100144	.564272	9.682852	.103275	13
14	.577475	10.563123	.094669	.539973	10.222825	.097820	14
15	.555265	11.118387	.089941	.516720	10.739546	.093114	15
16	.533908	11.652296	.085820	.494469	11.234015	.089015	16
17	.513373	12.165669	.082199	.473176	11.707191	.085418	17
18	.493628	12.659297	.078993	.452800	12.159992	.082237	18
19	.474642	13.133939	.076139	.433302	12.593294	.079407	19
20	.456387	13.590326	.073582	.414643	13.007936	.076876	20
21	.438834	14.029160	.071280	.396787	13.404724	.074601	21
22	.421955	14.451115	.069199	.379701	13.784425	.072546	22
23	.405726	14.856842	.067309	.363350	14.147775	.070682	23
24	.390121	15.246963	.065587	.347703	14.495478	.068987	24
25	.375117	15.622080	.064012	.332731	14.828209	.067439	25
26	.360689	15.982769	.062567	.318402	15.146611	.066021	26
27	.346817	16.329586	.061239	.304691	15.451303	.064719	27
28	.333477	16.663063	.060013	.291571	15.742874	.063521	28
29	.320651	16.983715	.058880	.279015	16.021889	.062415	29
30	.308319	17.292033	.057830	.267000	16.288889	.061392	30
31	.296460	17.588494	.056855	.255502	16.544391	.060443	31
32	.285058	17.873551	.055949	.244500	16.788891	.059563	32
33	.274094	18.147646	.055104	.233971	17.022862	.058745	33
34	.263552	18.411198	.054315	.223896	17.246758	.057982	34
35	.253415	18.664613	.053577	.214254	17.461012	.057270	35
36	.243669	18.908282	.052887	.205028	17.666041	.056606	36
37	.234297	19.142579	.052240	.196199	17.862240	.055984	37
38	.225285	19.367864	.051632	.187750	18.049990	.055402	38
39	.216621	19.584485	.051061	.179665	18.229656	.054856	39
40	.208289	19.792774	.050523	.171929	18.401584	.054343	40
41	.200278	19.993052	.050017	.164525	18.566109	.053862	41
42	.192575	20.185627	.049540	.157440	18.723550	.053409	42
43	.185168	20.370795	.049090	.150661	18.874210	.052982	43
44	.178046	20.548841	.048665	.144173	19.018383	.052581	44
45	.171198	20.720040	.048262	.137964	19.156347	.052202	45

ANNUAL COMPOUND INTEREST TABLES

	5.0 PERCENT				5.5 PERCENT		
PERIOD	PW 1	PW 1/P	PR	PW 1	PW 1/P	PR	PERIOD
1	.952381	.952381	1.050000	.947867	.947867	1.055000	1
2	.907029	1.859410	.537805	.898452	1.846320	.541618	2
3	.863838	2.723248	.367209	.851614	2.697933	.370654	3
4	.822702	3.545951	.282012	.807217	3.505150	.285294	4
5	.783526	4.329477	.230975	.765134	4.270284	.234176	5
6	.746215	5.075692	.197017	.725246	4.995530	.200179	6
7	.710681	5.786373	.172820	.687437	5.682967	.175964	7
8	.676839	6.463213	.154722	.651599	6.334566	.157864	8
9	.644609	7.107822	.140690	.617629	6.952195	.143839	9
10	.613913	7.721735	.129505	.585431	7.537626	.132668	10
11	.584679	8.306414	.120389	.554911	8.092536	.123571	11
12	.556837	8.863252	.112825	.525982	8.618518	.116029	12
13	.530321	9.393573	.106456	.498561	9.117079	.109684	13
14	.505068	9.898641	.101024	.472569	9.589648	.104279	14
15	.481017	10.379658	.096342	.447933	10.037581	.099626	15
16	.458112	10.837770	.092270	.424581	10.462162	.095583	16
17	.436297	11.274066	.088699	.402447	10.864609	.092042	17
18	.415521	11.689587	.085546	.381466	11.246074	.088920	18
19	.395734	12.085321	.082745	.361579	11.607654	.086150	19
20	.376889	12.462210	.080243	.342729	11.950382	.083679	20
21	.358942	12.821153	.077996	.324862	12.275244	.081465	21
22	.341850	13.163003	.075971	.307926	12.583170	.079471	22
23	.325571	13.488574	.074137	.291873	12.875042	.077670	23
24	.310068	13.798642	.072471	.276657	13.151699	.076036	24
25	.295303	14.093945	.070952	.262234	13.413933	.074549	25
26	.281241	14.375185	.069564	.248563	13.662495	.073193	26
27	.267848	14.643034	.068292	.235605	13.898100	.071952	27
28	.255094	14.898127	.067123	.223322	14.121422	.070814	28
29	.242946	15.141074	.066046	.211679	14.333101	.069769	29
30	.231377	15.372451	.065051	.200644	14.533745	.068805	30
31	.220359	15.592811	.064132	.190184	14.723929	.067917	31
32	.209866	15.802677	.063280	.180269	14.904198	.067095	32
33	.199873	16.002549	.062490	.170871	15.075069	.066335	33
34	.190355	16.192904	.061755	.161963	15.237033	.065630	34
35	.181290	16.374194	.061072	.153520	15.390552	.064975	35
36	.172657	16.546852	.060434	.145516	15.536068	.064366	36
37	.164436	16.711287	.059840	.137930	15.673999	.063800	37
38	.156605	16.867893	.059284	.130739	15.804738	.063272	38
39	.149148	17.017041	.058765	.123924	15.928662	.062780	39
40	.142046	17.159086	.058278	.117463	16.046125	.062320	40
41	.135282	17.294368	.057822	.111339	16.157464	.061891	41
42	.128840	17.423208	.057395	.105535	16.262999	.061489	42
43	.122704	17.545912	.056993	.100033	16.363032	.061113	43
44	.116861	17.662773	.056616	.094818	16.457851	.060761	44
45	.111297	17.774070	.056262	.089875	16.547726	.060431	45

197

ANNUAL COMPOUND INTEREST TABLES

6.0 PERCENT · · · · · · · · · · · · · · · · · · 6.5 PERCENT

PERIOD	PW 1	PW 1/P	PR	PW 1	PW 1/P	PR	PERIOD
1	.943396	.943396	1.060000	.938967	.938967	1.065000	1
2	.889996	1.833393	.545437	.881659	1.820626	.549262	2
3	.839619	2.673012	.374110	.827849	2.648476	.377576	3
4	.792094	3.465106	.288591	.777323	3.425799	.291903	4
5	.747258	4.212364	.237396	.729881	4.155679	.240635	5
6	.704961	4.917324	.203363	.685334	4.841014	.206568	6
7	.665057	5.582381	.179135	.643506	5.484520	.182331	7
8	.627412	6.209794	.161036	.604231	6.088751	.164237	8
9	.591898	6.801692	.147022	.567353	6.656104	.150238	9
10	.558395	7.360087	.135868	.532726	7.188830	.139105	10
11	.526788	7.886875	.126793	.500212	7.689042	.130055	11
12	.496969	8.383844	.119277	.469683	8.158725	.122568	12
13	.468839	8.852683	.112960	.441017	8.599742	.116283	13
14	.442301	9.294984	.107585	.414100	9.013842	.110940	14
15	.417265	9.712249	.102963	.388827	9.402669	.106353	15
16	.393646	10.105895	.098952	.365095	9.767764	.102378	16
17	.371364	10.477260	.095445	.342813	10.110577	.098906	17
18	.350344	10.827603	.092357	.321890	10.432466	.095855	18
19	.330513	11.158116	.089621	.302244	10.734710	.093156	19
20	.311805	11.469921	.087185	.283797	11.018507	.090756	20
21	.294155	11.764077	.085005	.266476	11.284983	.088613	21
22	.277505	12.041582	.083046	.250212	11.535196	.086691	22
23	.261797	12.303379	.081278	.234941	11.770137	.084961	23
24	.246979	12.550358	.079679	.220602	11.990739	.083398	24
25	.232999	12.783356	.078227	.207138	12.197877	.081981	25
26	.219810	13.003166	.076904	.194496	12.392373	.080695	26
27	.207368	13.210534	.075697	.182625	12.574998	.079523	27
28	.195630	13.406164	.074593	.171479	12.746477	.078453	28
29	.184557	13.590721	.073580	.161013	12.907490	.077474	29
30	.174110	13.764831	.072649	.151186	13.058676	.076577	30
31	.164255	13.929086	.071792	.141959	13.200635	.075754	31
32	.154957	14.084043	.071002	.133295	13.333929	.074997	32
33	.146186	14.230230	.070273	.125159	13.459088	.074299	33
34	.137912	14.368141	.069598	.117520	13.576609	.073656	34
35	.130105	14.498246	.068974	.110348	13.686957	.073062	35
36	.122741	14.620987	.068395	.103613	13.790570	.072513	36
37	.115793	14.736780	.067857	.097289	13.887859	.072005	37
38	.109239	14.846019	.067358	.091351	13.979210	.071535	38
39	.103056	14.949075	.066894	.085776	14.064986	.071099	39
40	.097222	15.046297	.066462	.080541	14.145527	.070694	40
41	.091719	15.138016	.066059	.075625	14.221152	.070318	41
42	.086527	15.224543	.065683	.071010	14.292161	.069968	42
43	.081630	15.306173	.065333	.066676	14.358837	.069644	43
44	.077009	15.383182	.065006	.062606	14.421443	.069341	44
45	.072650	15.455832	.064700	.058785	14.480228	.069060	45

ANNUAL COMPOUND INTEREST TABLES

	7.0 PERCENT				7.5 PERCENT		
PERIOD	PW 1	PW 1/P	PR	PW 1	PW 1/P	PR	PERIOD
1	.934579	.934579	1.070000	.930233	.930233	1.075000	1
2	.873439	1.808018	.553092	.865333	1.795565	.556928	2
3	.816298	2.624316	.381052	.804961	2.600526	.384538	3
4	.762895	3.387211	.295228	.748801	3.349326	.298568	4
5	.712986	4.100197	.243891	.696559	4.045885	.247165	5
6	.666342	4.766540	.209796	.647962	4.693846	.213045	6
7	.622750	5.389289	.185553	.602755	5.296601	.188800	7
8	.582009	5.971299	.167468	.560702	5.857304	.170727	8
9	.543934	6.515232	.153486	.521583	6.378887	.156767	9
10	.508349	7.023582	.142378	.485194	6.864081	.145686	10
11	.475093	7.498674	.133357	.451343	7.315424	.136697	11
12	.444012	7.942686	.125902	.419854	7.735278	.129278	12
13	.414964	8.357651	.119651	.390562	8.125840	.123064	13
14	.387817	8.745468	.114345	.363313	8.489154	.117797	14
15	.362446	9.107914	.109795	.337966	8.827120	.113287	15
16	.338735	9.446649	.105858	.314387	9.141507	.109391	16
17	.316574	9.763223	.102425	.292453	9.433960	.106000	17
18	.295864	10.059087	.099413	.272049	9.706009	.103029	18
19	.276508	10.335595	.096753	.253069	9.959078	.100411	19
20	.258419	10.594014	.094393	.235413	10.194491	.098092	20
21	.241513	10.835527	.092289	.218989	10.413480	.096029	21
22	.225713	11.061240	.090406	.203711	10.617191	.094187	22
23	.210947	11.272187	.088714	.189498	10.806689	.092535	23
24	.197147	11.469334	.087189	.176277	10.982967	.091050	24
25	.184249	11.653583	.085811	.163979	11.146946	.089711	25
26	.172195	11.825779	.084561	.152539	11.299485	.088500	26
27	.160930	11.986709	.083426	.141896	11.441381	.087402	27
28	.150402	12.137111	.082392	.131997	11.573378	.086405	28
29	.140563	12.277674	.081449	.122788	11.696165	.085498	29
30	.131367	12.409041	.080586	.114221	11.810386	.084671	30
31	.122773	12.531814	.079797	.106252	11.916638	.083916	31
32	.114741	12.646555	.079073	.098839	12.015478	.083226	32
33	.107235	12.753790	.078408	.091943	12.107421	.082594	33
34	.100219	12.854009	.077797	.085529	12.192950	.082015	34
35	.093663	12.947672	.077234	.079562	12.272511	.081483	35
36	.087535	13.035208	.076715	.074011	12.346522	.080994	36
37	.081809	13.117017	.076237	.068847	12.415370	.080545	37
38	.076457	13.193473	.075795	.064044	12.479414	.080132	38
39	.071455	13.264928	.075387	.059576	12.538989	.079751	39
40	.066780	13.331709	.075009	.055419	12.594409	.079400	40
41	.062412	13.394120	.074660	.051553	12.645962	.079077	41
42	.058329	13.452449	.074336	.047956	12.693918	.078778	42
43	.054513	13.506962	.074036	.044610	12.738528	.078502	43
44	.050946	13.557908	.073758	.041498	12.780026	.078247	44
45	.047613	13.605522	.073500	.038603	12.818629	.078011	45

ANNUAL COMPOUND INTEREST TABLES

	8.0 PERCENT				8.5 PERCENT		
PERIOD	PW 1	PW 1/P	PR	PW 1	PW 1/P	PR	PERIOD
1	.925926	.925926	1.080000	.921659	.921659	1.085000	1
2	.857339	1.783265	.560769	.849455	1.771114	.564616	2
3	.793832	2.577097	.388034	.782908	2.554022	.391539	3
4	.735030	3.312127	.301921	.721574	3.275597	.305288	4
5	.680583	3.992710	.250456	.665045	3.940642	.253766	5
6	.630170	4.622880	.216315	.612945	4.553587	.219607	6
7	.583490	5.206370	.192072	.564926	5.118514	.195369	7
8	.540269	5.746639	.174015	.520669	5.639183	.177331	8
9	.500249	6.246888	.160080	.479880	6.119063	.163424	9
10	.463193	6.710081	.149029	.442285	6.561348	.152408	10
11	.428883	7.138964	.140076	.407636	6.968984	.143493	11
12	.397114	7.536078	.132695	.375702	7.344686	.136153	12
13	.367698	7.903776	.126522	.346269	7.690955	.130023	13
14	.340461	8.244237	.121297	.319142	8.010097	.124842	14
15	.315242	8.559479	.116830	.294140	8.304237	.120420	15
16	.291890	8.851369	.112977	.271097	8.575333	.116614	16
17	.270269	9.121638	.109629	.249859	8.825192	.113312	17
18	.250249	9.371887	.106702	.230285	9.055476	.110430	18
19	.231712	9.603599	.104128	.212244	9.267720	.107901	19
20	.214548	9.818147	.101852	.195616	9.463337	.105671	20
21	.198656	10.016803	.099832	.180292	9.643628	.103695	21
22	.183941	10.200744	.098032	.166167	9.809796	.101939	22
23	.170315	10.371059	.096422	.153150	9.962945	.100372	23
24	.157699	10.528758	.094978	.141152	10.104097	.098970	24
25	.146018	10.674776	.093679	.130094	10.234191	.097712	25
26	.135202	10.809978	.092507	.119902	10.354093	.096580	26
27	.125187	10.935165	.091448	.110509	10.464602	.095560	27
28	.115914	11.051078	.090489	.101851	10.566453	.094639	28
29	.107328	11.158406	.089619	.093872	10.660326	.093806	29
30	.099377	11.257783	.088827	.086518	10.746844	.093051	30
31	.092016	11.349799	.088107	.079740	10.826584	.092365	31
32	.085200	11.434999	.087451	.073493	10.900078	.091742	32
33	.078889	11.513888	.086852	.067736	10.967813	.091176	33
34	.073045	11.586934	.086304	.062429	11.030243	.090660	34
35	.067635	11.654568	.085803	.057539	11.087781	.090189	35
36	.062625	11.717193	.085345	.053031	11.140812	.089760	36
37	.057986	11.775179	.084924	.048876	11.189689	.089368	37
38	.053690	11.828869	.084539	.045047	11.234736	.089010	38
39	.049713	11.878582	.084185	.041518	11.276255	.088682	39
40	.046031	11.924613	.083860	.038266	11.314520	.088382	40
41	.042621	11.967235	.083561	.035268	11.349788	.088107	41
42	.039464	12.006699	.083287	.032505	11.382293	.087856	42
43	.036541	12.043240	.083034	.029959	11.412252	.087625	43
44	.033834	12.077074	.082802	.027612	11.439864	.087414	44
45	.031328	12.108402	.082587	.025448	11.465312	.087220	45

ANNUAL COMPOUND INTEREST TABLES

	9.0 PERCENT			9.5 PERCENT			
PERIOD	PW 1	PW 1/P	PR	PW 1	PW 1/P	PR	PERIOD
1	.917431	.917431	1.090000	.913242	.913242	1.095000	1
2	.841680	1.759111	.568469	.834011	1.747253	.572327	2
3	.772183	2.531295	.395055	.761654	2.508907	.398580	3
4	.708425	3.239720	.308669	.695574	3.204481	.312063	4
5	.649931	3.889651	.257092	.635228	3.839709	.260436	5
6	.596267	4.485919	.222920	.580117	4.419825	.226253	6
7	.547034	5.032953	.198691	.529787	4.949612	.202036	7
8	.501866	5.534819	.180674	.483824	5.433436	.184046	8
9	.460428	5.995247	.166799	.441848	5.875284	.170205	9
10	.422411	6.417658	.155820	.403514	6.278798	.159266	10
11	.387533	6.805191	.146947	.368506	6.647304	.150437	11
12	.355535	7.160725	.139651	.336535	6.983839	.143188	12
13	.326179	7.486904	.133567	.307338	7.291178	.137152	13
14	.299246	7.786150	.128433	.280674	7.571852	.132068	14
15	.274538	8.060688	.124059	.256323	7.828175	.127744	15
16	.251870	8.312558	.120300	.234085	8.062260	.124035	16
17	.231073	8.543631	.117046	.213777	8.276037	.120831	17
18	.211994	8.755625	.114212	.195230	8.471266	.118046	18
19	.194490	8.950115	.111730	.178292	8.649558	.115613	19
20	.178431	9.128546	.109546	.162824	8.812382	.113477	20
21	.163698	9.292244	.107617	.148697	8.961080	.111594	21
22	.150182	9.442425	.105905	.135797	9.096876	.109928	22
23	.137781	9.580207	.104382	.124015	9.220892	.108449	23
24	.126405	9.706612	.103023	.113256	9.334148	.107134	24
25	.115968	9.822588	.101806	.103430	9.437578	.105959	25
26	.106393	9.928972	.100715	.094457	9.532034	.104909	26
27	.097608	10.026580	.099735	.086262	9.618296	.103969	27
28	.089548	10.116128	.098852	.078778	9.697074	.103124	28
29	.082155	10.198283	.098056	.071943	9.769018	.102364	29
30	.075371	10.273654	.097336	.065702	9.834719	.101681	30
31	.069148	10.342802	.096686	.060002	9.894721	.101064	31
32	.063438	10.406240	.096096	.054796	9.949517	.100507	32
33	.058200	10.464441	.095562	.050042	9.999559	.100004	33
34	.053395	10.517835	.095077	.045700	10.045259	.099549	34
35	.048986	10.566821	.094636	.041736	10.086995	.099138	35
36	.044941	10.611763	.094235	.038115	10.125109	.098764	36
37	.041231	10.652993	.093870	.034808	10.159917	.098426	37
38	.037826	10.690820	.093538	.031788	10.191705	.098119	38
39	.034703	10.725523	.093236	.029030	10.220735	.097840	39
40	.031838	10.757360	.092960	.026512	10.247247	.097587	40
41	.029209	10.786569	.092708	.024211	10.271458	.097357	41
42	.026797	10.813366	.092478	.022111	10.293569	.097148	42
43	.024584	10.837950	.092268	.020193	10.313762	.096958	43
44	.022555	10.860505	.092077	.018441	10.332203	.096785	44
45	.020692	10.881197	.091902	.016841	10.349043	.096627	45

ANNUAL COMPOUND INTEREST TABLES

	10.0 PERCENT			10.5 PERCENT			
PERIOD	PW 1	PW 1/P	PR	PW 1	PW 1/P	PR	PERIOD
1	.909091	.909091	1.100000	.904977	.904977	1.105000	1
2	.826446	1.735537	.576190	.818984	1.723961	.580059	2
3	.751315	2.486852	.402115	.741162	2.465123	.405659	3
4	.683013	3.169865	.315471	.670735	3.135858	.318892	4
5	.620921	3.790787	.263797	.607000	3.742858	.267175	5
6	.564474	4.355261	.229607	.549321	4.292179	.232982	6
7	.513158	4.868419	.205405	.497123	4.789303	.208799	7
8	.466507	5.334926	.187444	.449885	5.239188	.190869	8
9	.424098	5.759024	.173641	.407136	5.646324	.177106	9
10	.385543	6.144567	.162745	.368449	6.014773	.166257	10
11	.350494	6.495061	.153963	.333438	6.348211	.157525	11
12	.318631	6.813692	.146763	.301754	6.649964	.150377	12
13	.289664	7.103356	.140779	.273080	6.923045	.144445	13
14	.263331	7.366687	.135746	.247132	7.170176	.139467	14
15	.239392	7.606080	.131474	.223648	7.393825	.135248	15
16	.217629	7.823709	.127817	.202397	7.596221	.131644	16
17	.197845	8.021553	.124664	.183164	7.779386	.128545	17
18	.179859	8.201412	.121930	.165760	7.945146	.125863	18
19	.163508	8.364920	.119547	.150009	8.095154	.123531	19
20	.148644	8.513564	.117460	.135755	8.230909	.121493	20
21	.135131	8.648694	.115624	.122855	8.353764	.119707	21
22	.122846	8.771540	.114005	.111181	8.464945	.118134	22
23	.111678	8.883218	.112572	.100616	8.565561	.116747	23
24	.101526	8.984744	.111300	.091055	8.656616	.115519	24
25	.092296	9.077040	.110168	.082403	8.739019	.114429	25
26	.083905	9.160945	.109159	.074573	8.813592	.113461	26
27	.076278	9.237223	.108258	.067487	8.881079	.112599	27
28	.069343	9.306567	.107451	.061074	8.942153	.111830	28
29	.063039	9.369606	.106728	.055271	8.997423	.111143	29
30	.057309	9.426914	.106079	.050019	9.047442	.110528	30
31	.052099	9.479013	.105496	.045266	9.092707	.109978	31
32	.047362	9.526376	.104972	.040964	9.133672	.109485	32
33	.043057	9.569432	.104499	.037072	9.170744	.109042	33
34	.039143	9.608575	.104074	.033549	9.204293	.108645	34
35	.035584	9.644159	.103690	.030361	9.234654	.108288	35
36	.032349	9.676508	.103343	.027476	9.262131	.107967	36
37	.029408	9.705917	.103030	.024865	9.286996	.107677	37
38	.026735	9.732651	.102747	.022503	9.309499	.107417	38
39	.024304	9.756956	.102491	.020364	9.329863	.107183	39
40	.022095	9.779051	.102259	.018429	9.348292	.106971	40
41	.020086	9.799137	.102050	.016678	9.364970	.106781	41
42	.018260	9.817397	.101860	.015093	9.380064	.106609	42
43	.016600	9.833998	.101688	.013659	9.393723	.106454	43
44	.015091	9.849089	.101532	.012361	9.406084	.106314	44
45	.013719	9.862808	.101391	.011187	9.417271	.106188	45

ANNUAL COMPOUND INTEREST TABLES

11.0 PERCENT				12.0 PERCENT			
PERIOD	PW 1	PW 1/P	PR	PW 1	PW 1/P	PR	PERIOD
1	.900901	.900901	1.110000	.892857	.892857	1.120000	1
2	.811622	1.712523	.583934	.797194	1.690051	.591698	2
3	.731191	2.443715	.409213	.711780	2.401831	.416349	3
4	.658731	3.102446	.322326	.635518	3.037349	.329234	4
5	.593451	3.695897	.270570	.567427	3.604776	.277410	5
6	.534641	4.230538	.236377	.506631	4.111407	.243226	6
7	.481658	4.712196	.212215	.452349	4.563757	.219118	7
8	.433926	5.146123	.194321	.403883	4.967640	.201303	8
9	.390925	5.537048	.180602	.360610	5.328250	.187679	9
10	.352184	5.889232	.169801	.321973	5.650223	.176984	10
11	.317283	6.206515	.161121	.287476	5.937699	.168415	11
12	.285841	6.492356	.154027	.256675	6.194374	.161437	12
13	.257514	6.749870	.148151	.229174	6.423548	.155677	13
14	.231995	6.981865	.143228	.204620	6.628168	.150871	14
15	.209004	7.190870	.139065	.182696	6.810864	.146824	15
16	.188292	7.379162	.135517	.163122	6.973986	.143390	16
17	.169633	7.548794	.132471	.145644	7.119630	.140457	17
18	.152822	7.701617	.129843	.130040	7.249670	.137937	18
19	.137678	7.839294	.127563	.116107	7.365777	.135763	19
20	.124034	7.963328	.125576	.103667	7.469444	.133879	20
21	.111742	8.075070	.123838	.092560	7.562003	.132240	21
22	.100669	8.175739	.122313	.082643	7.644646	.130811	22
23	.090693	8.266432	.120971	.073788	7.718434	.129560	23
24	.081705	8.348137	.119787	.065882	7.784316	.128463	24
25	.073608	8.421745	.118740	.058823	7.843139	.127500	25
26	.066314	8.488058	.117813	.052521	7.895660	.126652	26
27	.059742	8.547800	.116989	.046894	7.942554	.125904	27
28	.053822	8.601622	.116257	.041869	7.984423	.125244	28
29	.048488	8.650110	.115605	.037383	8.021806	.124660	29
30	.043683	8.693793	.115025	.033378	8.055184	.124144	30
31	.039354	8.733146	.114506	.029802	8.084986	.123686	31
32	.035454	8.768600	.114043	.026609	8.111594	.123280	32
33	.031940	8.800541	.113629	.023758	8.135352	.122920	33
34	.028775	8.829316	.113259	.021212	8.156564	.122601	34
35	.025924	8.855240	.112927	.018940	8.175504	.122317	35
36	.023355	8.878594	.112630	.016910	8.192414	.122064	36
37	.021040	8.899635	.112364	.015098	8.207513	.121840	37
38	.018955	8.918590	.112125	.013481	8.220993	.121640	38
39	.017077	8.935666	.111911	.012036	8.233030	.121462	39
40	.015384	8.951051	.111719	.010747	8.243777	.121304	40
41	.013860	8.964911	.111546	.009595	8.253372	.121163	41
42	.012486	8.977397	.111391	.008567	8.261939	.121037	42
43	.011249	8.988646	.111251	.007649	8.269589	.120925	43
44	.010134	8.998780	.111126	.006830	8.276418	.120825	44
45	.009130	9.007910	.111014	.006098	8.282516	.120736	45

ANNUAL COMPOUND INTEREST TABLES

	13.0 PERCENT			14.0 PERCENT			
PERIOD	PW 1	PW 1/P	PR	PW 1	PW 1/P	PR	PERIOD
1	.884956	.884956	1.130000	.877193	.877193	1.140000	1
2	.783147	1.668102	.559484	.769468	1.646661	.607290	2
3	.693050	2.361153	.423522	.674972	2.321632	.430731	3
4	.613319	2.974471	.336194	.592080	2.913712	.343205	4
5	.542760	3.517231	.284315	.519369	3.433081	.291284	5
6	.480319	3.997550	.250153	.455587	3.888668	.257157	6
7	.425061	4.422610	.226111	.399637	4.288305	.233192	7
8	.376160	4.798770	.208387	.350559	4.638864	.215570	8
9	.332885	5.131655	.194869	.307508	4.946372	.202168	9
10	.294588	5.426243	.184290	.269744	5.216116	.191714	10
11	.260698	5.686941	.175841	.236617	5.452733	.183394	11
12	.230706	5.917647	.168986	.207559	5.660292	.176669	12
13	.204165	6.121812	.163350	.182069	5.842362	.171164	13
14	.180677	6.302488	.158667	.159710	6.002072	.166609	14
15	.159891	6.462379	.154742	.140096	6.142168	.162809	15
16	.141496	6.603875	.151426	.122892	6.265060	.159615	16
17	.125218	6.729093	.148608	.107800	6.372859	.156915	17
18	.110812	6.839905	.146201	.094561	6.467420	.154621	18
19	.098064	6.937969	.144134	.082948	6.550369	.152663	19
20	.086782	7.024752	.142354	.072762	6.623131	.150986	20
21	.076798	7.101550	.140814	.063826	6.686957	.149545	21
22	.067963	7.169513	.139479	.055988	6.742944	.148303	22
23	.060144	7.229658	.138319	.049112	6.792056	.147231	23
24	.053225	7.282883	.137308	.043081	6.835137	.146303	24
25	.047102	7.329985	.136426	.037790	6.872927	.145498	25
26	.041683	7.371668	.135655	.033149	6.906077	.144800	26
27	.036888	7.408556	.134979	.029078	6.935155	.144193	27
28	.032644	7.441200	.134387	.025507	6.960662	.143664	28
29	.028889	7.470088	.133867	.022375	6.983037	.143204	29
30	.025565	7.495653	.133411	.019627	7.002664	.142803	30
31	.022624	7.518277	.133009	.017217	7.019881	.142453	31
32	.020021	7.538299	.132656	.015102	7.034983	.142147	32
33	.017718	7.556016	.132345	.013248	7.048231	.141880	33
34	.015680	7.571696	.132071	.011621	7.059852	.141646	34
35	.013876	7.585572	.131829	.010194	7.070045	.141442	35
36	.012279	7.597851	.131616	.008942	7.078987	.141263	36
37	.010867	7.608718	.131428	.007844	7.086831	.141107	37
38	.009617	7.618334	.131262	.006880	7.093711	.140970	38
39	.008510	7.626844	.131116	.006035	7.099747	.140850	39
40	.007531	7.634376	.130986	.005294	7.105041	.140745	40
41	.006665	7.641040	.130872	.004644	7.109685	.140653	41
42	.005898	7.646938	.130771	.004074	7.113759	.140573	42
43	.005219	7.652158	.130682	.003573	7.117332	.140502	43
44	.004619	7.656777	.130603	.003135	7.120467	.140440	44
45	.004088	7.660864	.130534	.002750	7.123217	.140386	45

ANNUAL COMPOUND INTEREST TABLES

	15.0 PERCENT			16.0 PERCENT			
PERIOD	PW 1	PW 1/P	PR	PW 1	PW 1/P	PR	PERIOD
1	.869565	.869565	1.150000	.862069	.862069	1.160000	1
2	.756144	1.625709	.615116	.743163	1.605232	.622963	2
3	.657516	2.283225	.437977	.640658	2.245890	.445258	3
4	.571753	2.854978	.350265	.552291	2.798181	.357375	4
5	.497177	3.352155	.298316	.476113	3.274294	.305409	5
6	.432328	3.784483	.264237	.410442	3.684736	.271390	6
7	.375937	4.160420	.240360	.353830	4.038565	.247613	7
8	.326902	4.487322	.222850	.305025	4.343591	.230224	8
9	.284262	4.771584	.209574	.262953	4.606544	.217082	9
10	.247185	5.018769	.199252	.226684	4.833227	.206901	10
11	.214943	5.233712	.191069	.195417	5.028644	.198861	11
12	.186907	5.420619	.184481	.168463	5.197107	.192415	12
13	.162528	5.583147	.179110	.145227	5.342334	.187184	13
14	.141329	5.724476	.174688	.125195	5.467529	.182898	14
15	.122894	5.847370	.171017	.107927	5.575456	.179358	15
16	.106865	5.954235	.167948	.093041	5.668497	.176414	16
17	.092926	6.047161	.165367	.080207	5.748704	.173952	17
18	.080805	6.127966	.163186	.069144	5.817848	.171885	18
19	.070265	6.198231	.161336	.059607	5.877455	.170142	19
20	.061100	6.259331	.159761	.051385	5.928841	.168667	20
21	.053131	6.312462	.158417	.044298	5.973139	.167416	21
22	.046201	6.358663	.157266	.038188	6.011326	.166353	22
23	.040174	6.398837	.156278	.032920	6.044247	.165447	23
24	.034934	6.433771	.155430	.028380	6.072627	.164673	24
25	.030378	6.464149	.154699	.024465	6.097092	.164013	25
26	.026415	6.490564	.154070	.021091	6.118183	.163447	26
27	.022970	6.513534	.153526	.018182	6.136364	.162963	27
28	.019974	6.533508	.153057	.015674	6.152038	.162548	28
29	.017369	6.550877	.152651	.013512	6.165550	.162192	29
30	.015103	6.565980	.152300	.011648	6.177198	.161886	30
31	.013133	6.579113	.151996	.010042	6.187240	.161623	31
32	.011420	6.590533	.151733	.008657	6.195897	.161397	32
33	.009931	6.600463	.151505	.007463	6.203359	.161203	33
34	.008635	6.609099	.151307	.006433	6.209792	.161036	34
35	.007509	6.616607	.151135	.005546	6.215338	.160892	35
36	.006529	6.623137	.150986	.004781	6.220119	.160769	36
37	.005678	6.628815	.150857	.004121	6.224241	.160662	37
38	.004937	6.633752	.150744	.003553	6.227794	.160571	38
39	.004293	6.638045	.150647	.003063	6.230857	.160492	39
40	.003733	6.641778	.150562	.002640	6.233497	.160424	40
41	.003246	6.645025	.150489	.002276	6.235773	.160365	41
42	.002823	6.647848	.150425	.001962	6.237736	.160315	42
43	.002455	6.650302	.150369	.001692	6.239427	.160271	43
44	.002134	6.652437	.150321	.001458	6.240886	.160234	44
45	.001856	6.654293	.150279	.001257	6.242143	.160201	45

205

ANNUAL COMPOUND INTEREST TABLES

18.0 PERCENT   20.0 PERCENT

PERIOD	PW 1	PW 1/P	PR	PW 1	PW 1/P	PR	PERIOD
1	.847458	.847458	1.180000	.833333	.833333	1.200000	1
2	.718184	1.565642	.638716	.694444	1.527778	.654545	2
3	.608631	2.174273	.459924	.578704	2.106481	.474725	3
4	.515789	2.690062	.371739	.482253	2.588735	.386289	4
5	.437109	3.127171	.319778	.401878	2.990612	.334380	5
6	.370432	3.497603	.285910	.334898	3.325510	.300706	6
7	.313925	3.811528	.262362	.279082	3.604592	.277424	7
8	.266038	4.077566	.245244	.232568	3.837160	.260609	8
9	.225456	4.303022	.232395	.193807	4.030967	.248079	9
10	.191064	4.494086	.222515	.161506	4.192472	.238523	10
11	.161919	4.656005	.214776	.134588	4.327060	.231104	11
12	.137220	4.793225	.208628	.112157	4.439217	.225265	12
13	.116288	4.909513	.203686	.093464	4.532681	.220620	13
14	.098549	5.008062	.199678	.077887	4.610567	.216893	14
15	.083516	5.091578	.196403	.064905	4.675473	.213882	15
16	.070776	5.162354	.193710	.054088	4.729561	.211436	16
17	.059980	5.222334	.191485	.045073	4.774634	.209440	17
18	.050830	5.273164	.189639	.037561	4.812195	.207805	18
19	.043077	5.316241	.188103	.031301	4.843496	.206462	19
20	.036506	5.352746	.186820	.026084	4.869580	.205357	20
21	.030937	5.383683	.185746	.021737	4.891316	.204444	21
22	.026218	5.409901	.184846	.018114	4.909430	.203690	22
23	.022218	5.432120	.184090	.015095	4.924525	.203065	23
24	.018829	5.450949	.183454	.012579	4.937104	.202548	24
25	.015957	5.466906	.182919	.010483	4.947587	.202119	25
26	.013523	5.480429	.182467	.008735	4.956323	.201762	26
27	.011460	5.491889	.182087	.007280	4.963602	.201467	27
28	.009712	5.501601	.181765	.006066	4.969668	.201221	28
29	.008230	5.509831	.181494	.005055	4.974724	.201016	29
30	.006975	5.516806	.181264	.004213	4.978936	.200846	30
31	.005911	5.522717	.181070	.003511	4.982447	.200705	31
32	.005009	5.527726	.180906	.002926	4.985372	.200587	32
33	.004245	5.531971	.180767	.002438	4.987810	.200489	33
34	.003598	5.535569	.180650	.002032	4.989842	.200407	34
35	.003049	5.538618	.180550	.001693	4.991535	.200339	35
36	.002584	5.541201	.180466	.001411	4.992946	.200283	36
37	.002190	5.543391	.180395	.001176	4.994122	.200235	37
38	.001856	5.545247	.180335	.000980	4.995101	.200196	38
39	.001573	5.546819	.180284	.000816	4.995918	.200163	39
40	.001333	5.548152	.180240	.000680	4.996598	.200136	40
41	.001129	5.549281	.180204	.000567	4.997165	.200113	41
42	.000957	5.550238	.180172	.000472	4.997638	.200095	42
43	.000811	5.551049	.180146	.000394	4.998031	.200079	43
44	.000687	5.551737	.180124	.000328	4.998359	.200066	44
45	.000583	5.552319	.180105	.000273	4.998633	.200055	45

ANNUAL COMPOUND INTEREST TABLES

	25.0 PERCENT			30.0 PERCENT			
PERIOD	PW 1	PW 1/P	PR	PW 1	PW 1/P	PR	PERIOD
1	.800000	.800000	1.250000	.769231	.769231	1.300000	1
2	.640000	1.440000	.694444	.591716	1.360947	.734783	2
3	.512000	1.952000	.512295	.455166	1.816113	.550627	3
4	.409600	2.361600	.423442	.350128	2.166241	.461629	4
5	.327680	2.689280	.371847	.269329	2.435570	.410582	5
6	.262144	2.951424	.338819	.207176	2.642746	.378394	6
7	.209715	3.161139	.316342	.159366	2.802112	.356874	7
8	.167772	3.328911	.300399	.122589	2.924702	.341915	8
9	.134218	3.463129	.288756	.094300	3.019001	.331235	9
10	.107374	3.570503	.280073	.072538	3.091539	.323463	10
11	.085899	3.656403	.273493	.055799	3.147338	.317729	11
12	.068719	3.725122	.268448	.042922	3.190260	.313454	12
13	.054976	3.780098	.264543	.033017	3.223277	.310243	13
14	.043980	3.824078	.261501	.025398	3.248675	.307818	14
15	.035184	3.859263	.259117	.019537	3.268211	.305978	15
16	.028147	3.887410	.257241	.015028	3.283239	.304577	16
17	.022518	3.909928	.255759	.011560	3.294800	.303509	17
18	.018014	3.927942	.254586	.008892	3.303692	.302692	18
19	.014412	3.942354	.253656	.006840	3.310532	.302066	19
20	.011529	3.953883	.252916	.005262	3.315794	.301587	20
21	.009223	3.963107	.252327	.004048	3.319842	.301219	21
22	.007379	3.970485	.251858	.003113	3.322955	.300937	22
23	.005903	3.976388	.251485	.002395	3.325350	.300720	23
24	.004722	3.981111	.251186	.001842	3.327192	.300554	24
25	.003778	3.984888	.250948	.001417	3.328609	.300426	25
26	.003022	3.987911	.250758	.001090	3.329700	.300327	26
27	.002418	3.990329	.250606	.000839	3.330538	.300252	27
28	.001934	3.992263	.250485	.000645	3.331183	.300194	28
29	.001547	3.993810	.250387	.000496	3.331679	.300149	29
30	.001238	3.995048	.250310	.000382	3.332061	.300115	30
31	.000990	3.996039	.250248	.000294	3.332355	.300088	31
32	.000792	3.996831	.250198	.000226	3.332581	.300068	32
33	.000634	3.997465	.250159	.000174	3.332754	.300052	33
34	.000507	3.997972	.250127	.000134	3.332888	.300040	34
35	.000406	3.998377	.250101	.000103	3.332991	.300031	35
36	.000325	3.998702	.250081	.000079	3.333070	.300024	36
37	.000260	3.998962	.250065	.000061	3.333131	.300018	37
38	.000208	3.999169	.250052	.000047	3.333177	.300014	38
39	.000166	3.999335	.250042	.000036	3.333213	.300011	39
40	.000133	3.999468	.250033	.000028	3.333241	.300008	40
41	.000106	3.999575	.250027	.000021	3.333262	.300006	41
42	.000085	3.999660	.250021	.000016	3.333279	.300005	42
43	.000068	3.999728	.250017	.000013	3.333291	.300004	43
44	.000054	3.999782	.250014	.000010	3.333301	.300003	44
45	.000044	3.999826	.250011	.000007	3.333308	.300002	45

ANNUAL COMPOUND INTEREST TABLES

35.0 PERCENT

PERIOD	PW 1	PW 1/P	PR
1	.740741	.740741	1.350000
2	.548697	1.289438	.775532
3	.406442	1.695880	.589664
4	.301068	1.996948	.500764
5	.223014	2.219961	.450458
6	.165195	2.385157	.419260
7	.122367	2.507523	.398800
8	.090642	2.598165	.384887
9	.067142	2.665308	.375191
10	.049735	2.715043	.368318
11	.036841	2.751884	.363387
12	.027289	2.779173	.359819
13	.020214	2.799387	.357221
14	.014974	2.814361	.355320
15	.011092	2.825453	.353926
16	.008216	2.833669	.352899
17	.006086	2.839755	.352143
18	.004508	2.844263	.351585
19	.003339	2.847602	.351173
20	.002474	2.850076	.350868

40.0 PERCENT

PW 1	PW 1/P	PR	PERIOD
.714286	.714286	1.400000	1
.510204	1.224490	.816667	2
.364431	1.588921	.629358	3
.260308	1.849229	.540766	4
.185934	2.035164	.491361	5
.132810	2.167974	.461260	6
.094865	2.262839	.441923	7
.067760	2.330599	.429074	8
.048400	2.378999	.420345	9
.034572	2.413571	.414324	10
.024694	2.438265	.410128	11
.017639	2.455904	.407182	12
.012599	2.468503	.405104	13
.008999	2.477502	.403632	14
.006428	2.483930	.402588	15
.004591	2.488521	.401845	16
.003280	2.491801	.401316	17
.002343	2.494144	.400939	18
.001673	2.495817	.400670	19
.001195	2.497012	.400479	20

50.0 PERCENT

PERIOD	PW 1	PW 1/P	PR
1	.666667	.666667	1.500000
2	.444444	1.111111	.900000
3	.296296	1.407407	.710526
4	.197531	1.604938	.623077
5	.131687	1.736626	.575829
6	.087791	1.824417	.548120
7	.058528	1.882945	.531083
8	.039018	1.921963	.520301
9	.026012	1.947975	.513354
10	.017342	1.965317	.508824
11	.011561	1.976878	.505848
12	.007707	1.984585	.503884
13	.005138	1.989724	.502582
14	.003425	1.993149	.501719
15	.002284	1.995433	.501144
16	.001522	1.996955	.500762
17	.001015	1.997970	.500508
18	.000677	1.998647	.500339
19	.000451	1.999098	.500226
20	.000301	1.999399	.500150

60.0 PERCENT

PW 1	PW 1/P	PR	PERIOD
.625000	.625000	1.600000	1
.390625	1.015625	.984615	2
.244141	1.259766	.793798	3
.152588	1.412354	.708038	4
.095367	1.507721	.663253	5
.059605	1.567326	.638030	6
.037253	1.604578	.623217	7
.023283	1.627862	.614303	8
.014552	1.642413	.608860	9
.009095	1.651508	.605507	10
.005684	1.657193	.603430	11
.003553	1.660745	.602139	12
.002220	1.662966	.601335	13
.001388	1.664354	.600834	14
.000867	1.665221	.600521	15
.000542	1.665763	.600325	16
.000339	1.666102	.600203	17
.000212	1.666314	.600127	18
.000132	1.666446	.600079	19
.000083	1.666529	.600050	20

ANNUAL COMPOUND INTEREST TABLES

75.0 PERCENT   80.0 PERCENT

PERIOD	PW 1	PW 1/P	PR	PW 1	PW 1/P	PR	PERIOD
1	.571429	.571429	1.750000	.555556	.555556	1.800000	1
2	.326531	.897959	1.113636	.308642	.864198	1.157143	2
3	.186589	1.084548	.922043	.171468	1.035665	.965563	3
4	.106622	1.191170	.839510	.095260	1.130925	.884232	4
5	.060927	1.252097	.798660	.052922	1.183847	.844704	5
6	.034815	1.286913	.777053	.029401	1.213249	.824233	6
7	.019895	1.306807	.765224	.016334	1.229583	.813284	7
8	.011368	1.318176	.758624	.009074	1.238657	.807326	8
9	.006496	1.324672	.754904	.005041	1.243698	.804054	9
10	.003712	1.328384	.752794	.002801	1.246499	.802247	10
11	.002121	1.330505	.751594	.001556	1.248055	.801247	11
12	.001212	1.331717	.750910	.000864	1.248919	.800692	12
13	.000693	1.332410	.750520	.000480	1.249400	.800384	13
14	.000396	1.332806	.750297	.000267	1.249667	.800213	14
15	.000226	1.333032	.750170	.000148	1.249815	.800119	15
16	.000129	1.333161	.750097	.000082	1.249897	.800066	16
17	.000074	1.333235	.750055	.000046	1.249943	.800037	17
18	.000042	1.333277	.750032	.000025	1.249968	.800020	18
19	.000024	1.333301	.750018	.000014	1.249982	.800011	19
20	.000014	1.333315	.750010	.000008	1.249990	.800006	20

90.0 PERCENT   100.0 PERCENT

PERIOD	PW 1	PW 1/P	PR	PW 1	PW 1/P	PR	PERIOD
1	.526316	.526316	1.900000	.500000	.500000	2.000000	1
2	.277008	.803324	1.244828	.250000	.750000	1.333333	2
3	.145794	.949118	1.053610	.125000	.875000	1.142857	3
4	.076734	1.025852	.974800	.062500	.937500	1.066667	4
5	.040386	1.066238	.937877	.031250	.968750	1.032258	5
6	.021256	1.087494	.919546	.015625	.984375	1.015873	6
7	.011187	1.098681	.910182	.007813	.992188	1.007874	7
8	.005888	1.104569	.905331	.003906	.996094	1.003922	8
9	.003099	1.107668	.902798	.001953	.998047	1.001957	9
10	.001631	1.109299	.901470	.000977	.999023	1.000978	10
11	.000858	1.110157	.900773	.000488	.999512	1.000489	11
12	.000452	1.110609	.900407	.000244	.999756	1.000244	12
13	.000238	1.110847	.900214	.000122	.999878	1.000122	13
14	.000125	1.110972	.900113	.000061	.999939	1.000061	14
15	.000066	1.111038	.900059	.000031	.999969	1.000031	15
16	.000035	1.111073	.900031	.000015	.999985	1.000015	16
17	.000018	1.111091	.900016	.000008	.999992	1.000008	17
18	.000010	1.111100	.900009	.000004	.999996	1.000004	18
19	.000005	1.111105	.900005	.000002	.999998	1.000002	19
20	.000003	1.111108	.900002	.000001	.999999	1.000001	20

Supplemental Tables

Loan Balance and Debt Reduction at End of 5 Years
as a Percent of Original Principal*

	Interest Rate						
Loan Term	5%	6%	7%	7½%	8%	8½%	9%
10 Years							
Balance	.562049	.574260	.586371	.592385	.598369	.604321	.610240
Reduction	.437951	.425740	.413629	.407615	.401631	.395679	.389760
15 Years							
Balance	.745571	.760091	.774128	.780959	.787663	.794236	.800679
Reduction	.254429	.239909	.225872	.219041	.212337	.205764	.199321
20 Years							
Balance	.834549	.848996	.862566	.869021	.875256	.881272	.887070
Reduction	.165451	.151004	.137434	.130979	.124744	.118728	.112930
25 Years							
Balance	.885802	.899321	.911622	.917326	.922739	.927870	.932724
Reduction	.114198	.100679	.088378	.082674	.077261	.072130	.067276
30 Years							
Balance	.918287	.930544	.941316	.946174	.950699	.954903	.958801
Reduction	.081713	.069456	.058684	.053826	.049301	.045097	.041199

	Interest Rate						
Loan Term	9½%	10%	10½%	11%	12%	13%	14%
10 Years							
Balance	.616124	.621972	.627783	.633555	.644974	.656222	.667288
Reduction	.383876	.378028	.372217	.366445	.355026	.343778	.332712
15 Years							
Balance	.806989	.813166	.819208	.825113	.836523	.847388	.857713
Reduction	.193011	.186834	.180792	.174887	.163477	.152612	.142287
20 Years							
Balance	.892654	.898024	.903185	.908136	.917443	.925967	.933755
Reduction	.107346	.101976	.096815	.091864	.082557	.074033	.066245
25 Years							
Balance	.937311	.941637	.945714	.949551	.956532	.962665	.968026
Reduction	.062689	.058363	.054286	.050449	.043468	.037335	.031974
30 Years							
Balance	.962410	.965743	.968818	.971649	.976633	.980817	.984308
Reduction	.037590	.034257	.031182	.028351	.023367	.019183	.015692

*Loan Balance and Debt Reduction calculations are based on *monthly* payment frequency.

Loan Balance and Debt Reduction at End of 10 Years
as a Percent of Original Principal

	Interest Rate						
Loan Term	5%	6%	7%	7½%	8%	8½%	9%
15 Years							
Balance	.419047	.436490	.453926	.462628	.471313	.479974	.488606
Reduction	.580953	.563510	.546074	.537372	.528687	.520026	.511394
20 Years							
Balance	.622215	.645314	.667737	.678670	.689406	.699938	.710259
Reduction	.377785	.354686	.332263	.321330	.310594	.300062	.289741
25 Years							
Balance	.739245	.763520	.786334	.797174	.807633	.817706	.827392
Reduction	.260755	.236480	.213666	.202826	.192367	.182294	.172608
30 Years							
Balance	.813421	.836857	.858121	.867950	.877248	.886025	.894297
Reduction	.186579	.163143	.141879	.132050	.122752	.113975	.105703

	Interest Rate						
Loan Term	9½%	10%	10½%	11%	12%	13%	14%
15 Years							
Balance	.497206	.505767	.514285	.522753	.539536	.556075	.572341
Reduction	.502794	.494233	.485715	.477247	.460464	.443925	.427659
20 Years							
Balance	.720362	.730243	.739897	.749316	.767463	.784653	.800894
Reduction	.279638	.269757	.260103	.250684	.232537	.215347	.199106
25 Years							
Balance	.836694	.845613	.854155	.862324	.877564	.891398	.903899
Reduction	.163306	.154387	.145845	.137676	.122436	.108602	.096101
30 Years							
Balance	.902077	.909380	.916224	.922627	.934180	.944198	.952836
Reduction	.097923	.090620	.083776	.077373	.065820	.055802	.047164

Loan Balance and Debt Reduction at End of 15 Years
as a Percent of Original Principal

	Interest Rate						
Loan Term	5%	6%	7%	7½%	8%	8½%	9%
20 Years							
Balance	.349715	.370578	.391541	.402034	.412519	.422987	.433428
Reduction	.650285	.629422	.608459	.597966	.587481	.577013	.566572
25 Years							
Balance	.551159	.580345	.608723	.622560	.636142	.649452	.662476
Reduction	.448841	.419655	.391277	.377440	.363858	.350548	.337524
30 Years							
Balance	.678839	.710488	.740189	.754267	.767816	.780829	.793305
Reduction	.321161	.289512	.259811	.245733	.232184	.219171	.206695

	Interest Rate						
Loan Term	9½%	10%	10½%	11%	12%	13%	14%
20 Years							
Balance	.443833	.454191	.464495	.474732	.494994	.514907	.534427
Reduction	.556167	.545809	.535505	.525268	.505006	.485093	.465573
25 Years							
Balance	.675204	.687624	.699731	.711516	.734103	.755360	.775286
Reduction	.324796	.312376	.300269	.288484	.265897	.244640	.224714
30 Years							
Balance	.805243	.816646	.827520	.837873	.857057	.874298	.889715
Reduction	.194757	.183354	.172480	.162127	.142943	.125702	.110285

Loan Constant as an Annual Percent of Original Principal*

				Interest Rate			
Loan Term	5%	6%	7%	7½%	8%	8½%	9%
10 Years	.127279	.133225	.139330	.142442	.145593	.148783	.152011
15 Years	.094895	.101263	.107859	.111241	.114678	.118169	.121712
20 Years	.079195	.085972	.093036	.096671	.100373	.104139	.107967
25 Years	.070151	.077316	.084814	.088679	.092618	.096627	.100704
30 Years	.064419	.071946	.079836	.083906	.088052	.092270	.096555

				Interest Rate			
Loan Term	9½%	10%	10½%	11%	12%	13%	14%
10 Years	.155277	.158581	.161922	.165300	.172165	.179173	.186319
15 Years	.125307	.128953	.132648	.136391	.144020	.151829	.159808
20 Years	.111856	.115803	.119806	.123862	.132130	.140588	.149222
25 Years	.104844	.109044	.113302	.117613	.126387	.135340	.144451
30 Years	.100903	.105309	.109769	.114278	.123434	.132744	.142184

*Loan Constant calculations are based on monthly payment frequency.

Notes:
— Loan balance and debt reduction, at each interval, add up to 100% (1.0).
— To calculate loan balance at any point in time, see procedure, page 121.
— To compute a Loan Constant, refer to procedure, page 118.
— The Supplemental Tables have been designed to save time in investment analysis' particularly in utilizing the 15-point form, as shown on pages 150 and 151.

OAR Tables
(Precomputed Mortgage-Equity
Overall Rates)

Holding Periods: 5, 10, and 15 years
Equity Yield Rates: 4, 6, 8, 10, 12, 14, 15, 16, 18, 20, 25, 30, 40, and 50%
Loan Ratios: 60, 66.7, 70, 75, 80, and 90%
Loan Term:
    For 5 and 10 year holding periods: 10, 15, 20, 25, and 30 years
    For 15 year holding period: 15, 20, 25, 30, and 40 years
Loan Interest Rates: 5, 6, 7, 7 1/2, 8, 8 1/2, 9, 9 1/2, 10, 11, 12, 13, and 14%
Appreciation/Depreciation: 40, 30, 20, 10, 0, −10, −20, −30, and −40%

Notes:
— To expedite locating an OAR in problem solving, the analyst should
match the six variables in his problem with those from the OAR
Tables by following the order listed above. The first three variables
identify the page on which the relevant OAR is located: holding
period, equity yield rate, and loan ratio.
— The precomputed mortgage-equity OAR can be used in four basic
ways:
    1. As a *divisor* to calculate indicated value (Value = Income ÷ Rate).
See pages 98 and 99.
    2. As a *multiplier* to compute income required to justify a given value
(Income = Rate × Value). Refer to pages 61 and 62.
    3. As a *target figure* (Rate = Income ÷ Value) to determine:
      a. Rate of yield on equity, pages 81 and 82, or
      b. Percent of appreciation required to generate a specified rate of
yield on equity. See procedure, page 107.
— Equity yield rate in the tables is expressed as a decimal. Note, for
example, that a rate of .040 is 4%, not 40%.
— In certain problems, several variables may differ from those built into
the precomputed OAR's. If multiple interpolation is not advisable,
the analyst may follow the procedure on page 73 and make a precise
calculation of the OAR from the compound interest factors. This
procedure was used in programming the EDP run of OAR Tables in
this text. The same procedure may be followed in building
mortgage-equity into a desk top programable calculator.
— For procedures on interpolation within the OAR Tables, see pages
67 to 69.
— To extend the OAR Tables, refer to procedures on extrapolation,
pages 69 to 72.
— For an example of multiple interpolation, see pages 472 and 473.

5.0 YEAR HOLDING PERIOD
.040 EQUITY YIELD RATE
.600 LOAN RATIO

INTEREST RATE

TERM YEARS	APPR DEP	5.0	6.0	7.0	7.5	8.0	8.5	9.0	9.5	10.0	11.0	12.0	13.0	14.0
10	.40	-.029998	-.025078	-.020073	-.017540	-.014986	-.012413	-.009820	-.007209	-.004579	.000736	.006120	.011570	.017084
	.30	-.011536	-.006615	-.001610	.000923	.003477	.006050	.008642	.011254	.013884	.019198	.024583	.030033	.035547
	.20	.006927	.011847	.016852	.019386	.021939	.024512	.027105	.029716	.032347	.037661	.043045	.048496	.054010
	.10	.025390	.030310	.035315	.037848	.040402	.042975	.045568	.048179	.050809	.056124	.061508	.066959	.072472
	0.00	.043853	.048773	.053778	.056311	.058865	.061438	.064030	.066642	.069272	.074586	.079971	.085421	.090935
	-.10	.062315	.067236	.072241	.074774	.077327	.079901	.082493	.085105	.087735	.093049	.098433	.103884	.109398
	-.20	.080778	.085698	.090703	.093237	.095790	.098363	.100956	.103567	.106197	.111512	.116896	.122347	.127861
	-.30	.099241	.104161	.109166	.111699	.114253	.116826	.119419	.122030	.124660	.129975	.135359	.140809	.146323
	-.40	.117703	.122624	.127629	.130162	.132715	.135289	.137881	.140493	.143123	.148437	.153821	.159272	.164786
15	.40	-.029098	-.023669	-.018156	-.015370	-.012566	-.009743	-.006904	-.004048	-.001176	.004611	.010452	.016341	.022273
	.30	-.010636	-.005207	.000306	.003092	.005897	.008719	.011559	.014415	.017287	.023074	.028915	.034804	.040735
	.20	.007827	.013256	.018769	.021555	.024360	.027182	.030022	.032878	.035749	.041537	.047377	.053266	.059198
	.10	.026290	.031719	.037232	.040018	.042822	.045645	.048484	.051340	.054212	.059999	.065840	.071729	.077661
	0.00	.044752	.050181	.055694	.058480	.061285	.064108	.066947	.069803	.072675	.078462	.084303	.090192	.096123
	-.10	.063215	.068644	.074157	.076943	.079748	.082570	.085410	.088266	.091138	.096925	.102765	.108654	.114586
	-.20	.081678	.087107	.092620	.095406	.098210	.101033	.103873	.106729	.109600	.115387	.121228	.127117	.133049
	-.30	.100141	.105570	.111083	.113868	.116673	.119496	.122335	.125191	.128063	.133850	.139691	.145580	.151512
	-.40	.118603	.124032	.129545	.132331	.135136	.137958	.140798	.143654	.146526	.152313	.158154	.164043	.169974
20	.40	-.028662	-.022995	-.017254	-.014358	-.011446	-.008520	-.005580	-.002629	.000334	.006291	.012282	.018302	.024344
	.30	-.010199	-.004533	.001209	.004105	.007017	.009943	.012882	.015834	.018797	.024753	.030745	.036764	.042807
	.20	.008263	.013930	.019672	.022568	.025480	.028406	.031345	.034297	.037260	.043216	.049207	.055227	.061270
	.10	.026726	.032393	.038134	.041031	.043942	.046868	.049808	.052759	.055722	.061679	.067670	.073690	.079732
	0.00	.045189	.050855	.056597	.059493	.062405	.065331	.068270	.071222	.074185	.080142	.086133	.092153	.098195
	-.10	.063651	.069318	.075060	.077956	.080868	.083794	.086733	.089685	.092648	.098604	.104596	.110615	.116658
	-.20	.082114	.087781	.093523	.096419	.099330	.102256	.105196	.108147	.111111	.117067	.123058	.129078	.135121
	-.30	.100577	.106244	.111985	.114881	.117793	.120719	.123658	.126610	.129573	.135530	.141521	.147541	.153583
	-.40	.119040	.124706	.130448	.133344	.136256	.139182	.142121	.145073	.148036	.153992	.159984	.166003	.172046
25	.40	-.028411	-.022614	-.016753	-.013802	-.010839	-.007865	-.004881	-.001889	.001110	.007128	.013166	.019217	.025278
	.30	-.009948	-.004151	.001710	.004661	.007624	.010598	.013581	.016574	.019573	.025591	.031629	.037680	.043741
	.20	.008514	.014311	.020172	.023124	.026087	.029061	.032044	.035036	.038036	.044054	.050091	.056143	.062203
	.10	.026977	.032774	.038635	.041586	.044549	.047523	.050507	.053499	.056499	.062517	.068554	.074606	.080666
	0.00	.045440	.051237	.057098	.060049	.063012	.065986	.068970	.071962	.074961	.080979	.087017	.093068	.099129
	-.10	.063903	.069700	.075561	.078512	.081475	.084449	.087432	.090424	.093424	.099442	.105480	.111531	.117592
	-.20	.082365	.088162	.094023	.096974	.099938	.102911	.105895	.108887	.111887	.117905	.123942	.129994	.136054
	-.30	.100828	.106625	.112486	.115437	.118400	.121374	.124358	.127350	.130349	.136367	.142405	.148456	.154517
	-.40	.119291	.125088	.130949	.133900	.136863	.139837	.142820	.145813	.148812	.154830	.160868	.166919	.172980
30	.40	-.028252	-.022377	-.016450	-.013470	-.010481	-.007485	-.004485	-.001473	.001539	.007576	.013621	.019670	.025722
	.30	-.009789	-.003915	.002013	.004993	.007982	.010978	.013981	.016989	.020002	.026038	.032083	.038133	.044184
	.20	.008674	.014548	.020476	.023455	.026444	.029441	.032444	.035452	.038465	.044501	.050546	.056596	.062647
	.10	.027137	.033011	.038938	.041918	.044907	.047903	.050906	.053915	.056928	.062964	.069009	.075059	.081110
	0.00	.045599	.051474	.057401	.060381	.063370	.066366	.069369	.072377	.075390	.081426	.087472	.093521	.099573
	-.10	.064062	.069936	.075864	.078844	.081832	.084829	.087832	.090840	.093853	.099889	.105934	.111984	.118035
	-.20	.082525	.088399	.094326	.097306	.100295	.103291	.106294	.109303	.112316	.118352	.124397	.130447	.136498
	-.30	.100987	.106862	.112789	.115769	.118758	.121754	.124757	.127766	.130778	.136815	.142860	.148909	.154961
	-.40	.119450	.125324	.131252	.134232	.137220	.140217	.143220	.146228	.149241	.155277	.161322	.167372	.173424

5.0 YEAR HOLDING PERIOD
.040 EQUITY YIELD RATE
.667 LOAN RATIO

INTEREST RATE

TERM YEARS	APPR DEP	14.0	13.0	12.0	11.0	10.0	9.5	9.0	8.5	8.0	7.5	7.0	6.0	5.0
10	.40	.022744	.016618	.010561	.004579	-.001326	-.004249	-.007150	-.010031	-.012890	-.015727	-.018542	-.024103	-.029570
	.30	.041207	.035080	.029024	.023042	.017137	.014214	.011312	.008432	.005573	.002775	-.000079	-.005640	-.011107
	.20	.059670	.053543	.047487	.041504	.035599	.032677	.029775	.026895	.024035	.021198	.018383	.012822	.007355
	.10	.078132	.072006	.065949	.059967	.054062	.051140	.048238	.045357	.042498	.039661	.036846	.031285	.025818
	0.00	.096595	.090468	.084412	.078429	.072525	.069602	.066701	.063820	.060960	.058124	.055309	.049748	.044281
	-.10	.115058	.108931	.102875	.096892	.090987	.088065	.085163	.082283	.079424	.076586	.073771	.068210	.062743
	-.20	.133521	.127394	.121337	.115355	.109450	.106528	.103626	.100745	.097886	.095049	.092234	.086673	.081206
	-.30	.151983	.145857	.139800	.133818	.127913	.124990	.122089	.119208	.116349	.113512	.110697	.105136	.099669
	-.40	.170446	.164319	.158263	.152280	.146375	.143453	.140551	.137671	.134812	.131974	.129160	.123599	.118131
15	.40	.028509	.021918	.015375	.008885	.002455	-.000736	-.003909	-.007065	-.010201	-.013317	-.016413	-.022538	-.028570
	.30	.046972	.040381	.033837	.027348	.020917	.017727	.014553	.011398	.008262	.005146	.002050	-.004075	-.010108
	.20	.065434	.058843	.052300	.045810	.039380	.036189	.033016	.029861	.026725	.023608	.020513	.014387	.008355
	.10	.083897	.077306	.070763	.064273	.057843	.054652	.051479	.048324	.045187	.042071	.038976	.032850	.026818
	0.00	.102360	.095769	.089226	.082736	.076306	.073115	.069941	.066786	.063650	.060534	.057438	.051313	.045281
	-.10	.120822	.114232	.107688	.101198	.094768	.091578	.088404	.085249	.082113	.078997	.075901	.069776	.063743
	-.20	.139285	.132694	.126151	.119661	.113231	.110040	.106867	.103712	.100576	.097459	.094364	.088238	.082206
	-.30	.157748	.151157	.144614	.138124	.131694	.128503	.125330	.122174	.119038	.115922	.112826	.106701	.100669
	-.40	.176211	.169620	.163076	.156587	.150156	.146966	.143792	.140637	.137501	.134385	.131289	.125164	.119131
20	.40	.030811	.024097	.017408	.010751	.004133	.000840	-.002439	-.005705	-.008956	-.012191	-.015410	-.021789	-.028086
	.30	.049273	.042560	.035871	.029214	.022595	.019303	.016024	.012758	.009506	.006272	.003053	-.003327	-.009623
	.20	.067736	.061022	.054334	.047677	.041058	.037766	.034486	.031220	.027969	.024734	.021516	.015136	.008840
	.10	.086199	.079485	.072796	.066139	.059521	.056229	.052949	.049683	.046432	.043197	.039979	.033599	.027303
	0.00	.104662	.097948	.091259	.084602	.077984	.074691	.071412	.068146	.064894	.061659	.058441	.052062	.045765
	-.10	.123124	.116410	.109722	.103065	.096446	.093154	.089874	.086608	.083357	.080122	.076904	.070524	.064228
	-.20	.141587	.134873	.128184	.121527	.114909	.111617	.108337	.105071	.101820	.098585	.095367	.088987	.082691
	-.30	.160050	.153336	.146647	.139990	.133372	.130079	.126800	.123534	.120283	.117048	.113829	.107450	.101153
	-.40	.178512	.171799	.165110	.158453	.151834	.148542	.145263	.141997	.138745	.135510	.132292	.125912	.119616
25	.40	.031848	.025114	.018390	.011682	.004995	.001662	-.001662	-.004977	-.008282	-.011574	-.014853	-.021365	-.027806
	.30	.050311	.043577	.036853	.030145	.023458	.020125	.016800	.013485	.010181	.006889	.003610	-.002903	-.009344
	.20	.068774	.062040	.055316	.048607	.041921	.038588	.035263	.031948	.028644	.025351	.022072	.015560	.009119
	.10	.087236	.080502	.073779	.067070	.060383	.057050	.053726	.050411	.047106	.043814	.040535	.034023	.027582
	0.00	.105699	.098965	.092241	.085533	.078846	.075513	.072189	.068874	.065569	.062277	.058998	.052485	.046045
	-.10	.124162	.117428	.110704	.103996	.097309	.093976	.090651	.087336	.084032	.080739	.077460	.070948	.064507
	-.20	.142625	.135891	.129167	.122458	.115771	.112439	.109114	.105799	.102494	.099202	.095923	.089411	.082970
	-.30	.161087	.154353	.147629	.140921	.134234	.130901	.127577	.124262	.120957	.117665	.114386	.107874	.101433
	-.40	.179550	.172816	.166092	.159384	.152697	.149364	.146039	.142724	.139420	.136128	.132849	.126336	.119895
30	.40	.032341	.025618	.018896	.012179	.005472	.002124	-.001218	-.004555	-.007884	-.011205	-.014516	-.021102	-.027629
	.30	.050804	.044080	.037358	.030641	.023935	.020587	.017244	.013908	.010578	.007257	.003946	-.002640	-.009167
	.20	.069267	.062543	.055821	.049104	.042397	.039050	.035707	.032370	.029041	.025720	.022409	.015823	.009296
	.10	.087729	.081006	.074284	.067567	.060860	.057512	.054170	.050833	.047504	.044183	.040872	.034286	.027759
	0.00	.106192	.099468	.092746	.086030	.079323	.075975	.072632	.069296	.065966	.062645	.059335	.052748	.046222
	-.10	.124655	.117931	.111209	.104492	.097785	.094438	.091095	.087758	.084429	.081108	.077797	.071211	.064684
	-.20	.143117	.136394	.129672	.122955	.116248	.112900	.109558	.106221	.102892	.099571	.096260	.089674	.083147
	-.30	.161580	.154857	.148135	.141418	.134711	.131363	.128020	.124684	.121355	.118034	.114723	.108137	.101610
	-.40	.180043	.173319	.166597	.159880	.153174	.149826	.146483	.143147	.139817	.136496	.133185	.126599	.120072

INTEREST RATE

5.0 YEAR HOLDING PERIOD
.040 EQUITY YIELD RATE
.700 LOAN RATIO

TERM YEARS	APPR DEP	5.0	6.0	7.0	7.5	8.0	8.5	9.0	9.5	10.0	11.0	12.0	13.0	14.0
10	.40	-.029356	-.023616	-.017777	-.014821	-.011842	-.008840	-.005815	-.002769	.000300	.006500	.012782	.019141	.025574
	.30	-.010893	-.005153	.000686	.003642	.006621	.009623	.012647	.015694	.018763	.024963	.031244	.037603	.044036
	.20	.007569	.013310	.019149	.022104	.025083	.028085	.031110	.034157	.037225	.043425	.049707	.056066	.062499
	.10	.026032	.031772	.037611	.040567	.043546	.046548	.049573	.052620	.055688	.061888	.068170	.074529	.080962
	0.00	.044495	.050235	.056074	.059030	.062009	.065011	.068035	.071082	.074151	.080351	.086632	.092992	.099425
	-.10	.062957	.068698	.074537	.077492	.080471	.083474	.086498	.089545	.092613	.098814	.105095	.111454	.117887
	-.20	.081420	.087160	.093000	.095955	.098934	.101936	.104961	.108008	.111076	.117276	.123558	.129917	.136350
	-.30	.099883	.105623	.111462	.114418	.117397	.120399	.123424	.126470	.129539	.135739	.142021	.148380	.154813
	-.40	.118345	.124086	.129925	.132881	.135860	.138862	.141886	.144933	.148002	.154202	.160483	.166842	.173275
15	.40	-.028306	-.021972	-.015541	-.012290	-.009018	-.005725	-.002412	.000920	.004270	.011021	.017836	.024706	.031626
	.30	-.009844	-.003510	.002922	.006172	.009444	.012737	.016050	.019382	.022732	.029484	.036298	.043169	.050089
	.20	.008619	.014953	.021385	.024635	.027907	.031200	.034513	.037845	.041195	.047947	.054761	.061632	.068551
	.10	.027082	.033416	.039847	.043098	.046370	.049663	.052976	.056308	.059658	.066410	.073224	.080094	.087015
	0.00	.045545	.051878	.058310	.061560	.064833	.068125	.071438	.074770	.078121	.084872	.091687	.098557	.105477
	-.10	.064007	.070341	.076773	.080023	.083295	.086588	.089901	.093233	.096583	.103335	.110149	.117020	.123940
	-.20	.082470	.088804	.095236	.098486	.101758	.105051	.108364	.111696	.115046	.121798	.128612	.135482	.142403
	-.30	.100933	.107267	.113698	.116949	.120221	.123514	.126827	.130159	.133509	.140260	.147075	.153945	.160865
	-.40	.119395	.125729	.132161	.135411	.138683	.141976	.145289	.148621	.151971	.158723	.165537	.172408	.179328
20	.40	-.027797	-.021186	-.014488	-.011109	-.007712	-.004298	-.000869	.002575	.006032	.012981	.019971	.026994	.034044
	.30	-.009335	-.002724	.003975	.007354	.010751	.014165	.017594	.021038	.024494	.031444	.038434	.045457	.052506
	.20	.009128	.015739	.022438	.025817	.029214	.032627	.036057	.039500	.042957	.049906	.056896	.063919	.070969
	.10	.027591	.034202	.040901	.044280	.047676	.051090	.054519	.057963	.061420	.068369	.075359	.082382	.089432
	0.00	.046053	.052665	.059363	.062742	.066139	.069553	.072982	.076426	.079883	.086832	.093822	.100845	.107894
	-.10	.064516	.071127	.077826	.081205	.084602	.088016	.091445	.094888	.098345	.105295	.112284	.119307	.126357
	-.20	.082979	.089590	.096289	.099668	.103065	.106478	.109908	.113351	.116808	.123757	.130747	.137770	.144820
	-.30	.101442	.108053	.114751	.118130	.121527	.124941	.128370	.131814	.135271	.142220	.149210	.156233	.163283
	-.40	.119904	.126515	.133214	.136593	.139990	.143404	.146833	.150277	.153733	.160683	.167673	.174696	.181745
25	.40	-.027504	-.020741	-.013903	-.010460	-.007003	-.003534	-.000053	.003438	.006937	.013958	.021002	.028062	.035133
	.30	-.009041	-.002278	.004559	.008002	.011459	.014929	.018410	.021901	.025400	.032421	.039465	.046525	.053596
	.20	.009421	.016184	.023022	.026465	.029922	.033392	.036872	.040363	.043863	.050884	.057928	.064988	.072058
	.10	.027884	.034647	.041485	.044928	.048385	.051854	.055335	.058826	.062325	.069347	.076390	.083450	.090521
	0.00	.046347	.053110	.059948	.063390	.066847	.070317	.073798	.077289	.080788	.087809	.094853	.101913	.108984
	-.10	.064809	.071572	.078410	.081853	.085310	.088780	.092261	.095751	.099251	.106272	.113316	.120376	.127446
	-.20	.083272	.090035	.096873	.100316	.103773	.107242	.110723	.114214	.117714	.124735	.131778	.138838	.145909
	-.30	.101735	.108498	.115336	.118779	.122236	.125705	.129186	.132677	.136176	.143197	.150241	.157301	.164372
	-.40	.120198	.126960	.133798	.137241	.140698	.144168	.147649	.151139	.154639	.161660	.168704	.175764	.182835
30	.40	-.027318	-.020465	-.013550	-.010073	-.006586	-.003090	.000413	.003923	.007438	.014480	.021533	.028591	.035650
	.30	-.008856	-.002002	.004913	.008390	.011876	.015372	.018876	.022386	.025901	.032943	.039995	.047053	.054113
	.20	.009607	.016460	.023376	.026852	.030339	.033835	.037338	.040848	.044363	.051405	.058458	.065516	.072576
	.10	.028070	.034923	.041838	.045315	.048802	.052298	.055801	.059311	.062826	.069868	.076921	.083979	.091039
	0.00	.046533	.053386	.060301	.063777	.067265	.070760	.074264	.077774	.081289	.088331	.095383	.102442	.109501
	-.10	.064995	.071848	.078764	.082240	.085727	.089223	.092727	.096236	.099751	.106793	.113846	.120904	.127964
	-.20	.083458	.090311	.097227	.100703	.104190	.107686	.111189	.114699	.118214	.125256	.132309	.139367	.146427
	-.30	.101921	.108774	.115689	.119166	.122653	.126149	.129652	.133162	.136677	.143719	.150772	.157830	.164889
	-.40	.120383	.127237	.134152	.137628	.141115	.144611	.148115	.151624	.155140	.162182	.169234	.176292	.183352

5.0 YEAR HOLDING PERIOD
.040 EQUITY YIELD RATE
.750 LOAN RATIO

INTEREST RATE

TERM YEARS	APPR DEP	5.0	6.0	7.0	7.5	8.0	8.5	9.0	9.5	10.0	11.0	12.0	13.0	14.0
10	.40	-.029035	-.022885	-.016629	-.013462	-.010270	-.007054	-.003813	-.000548	.002739	.009382	.016112	.022926	.029818
	.30	-.010572	-.004422	.001834	.005001	.008193	.011409	.014650	.017914	.021202	.027845	.034575	.041389	.048281
	.20	.007890	.014041	.020297	.023464	.026655	.029872	.033113	.036377	.039665	.046308	.053038	.059851	.066744
	.10	.026353	.032503	.038760	.041926	.045118	.048335	.051575	.054840	.058127	.064770	.071501	.078314	.085206
	0.00	.044816	.050966	.057222	.060389	.063583	.066797	.070038	.073302	.076590	.083233	.089963	.096777	.103669
	-.10	.063278	.069429	.075685	.078852	.082044	.085260	.088501	.091765	.095053	.101696	.108426	.115239	.122132
	-.20	.081741	.087891	.094148	.097314	.100506	.103723	.106963	.110228	.113515	.120159	.126889	.133702	.140595
	-.30	.100204	.106354	.112610	.115777	.118969	.122185	.125426	.128691	.131978	.138621	.145351	.152165	.159057
	-.40	.118667	.124817	.131073	.134240	.137432	.140648	.143889	.147153	.150441	.157084	.163814	.170627	.177520
15	.40	-.027910	-.021124	-.014233	-.010750	-.007245	-.003716	-.000167	.003403	.006993	.014227	.021528	.028889	.036303
	.30	-.009448	-.002661	.004230	.007712	.011218	.014746	.018296	.021866	.025455	.032689	.039990	.047352	.054766
	.20	.009015	.015801	.022693	.026175	.029681	.033209	.036759	.040329	.043918	.051152	.058453	.065814	.073229
	.10	.027478	.034264	.041155	.044638	.048144	.051672	.055221	.058791	.062381	.069615	.076916	.084277	.091692
	0.00	.045941	.052727	.059618	.063100	.066606	.070134	.073684	.077254	.080844	.088077	.095378	.102740	.110154
	-.10	.064403	.071190	.078081	.081563	.085069	.088597	.092147	.095717	.099306	.106540	.113841	.121202	.128617
	-.20	.082866	.089652	.096543	.100026	.103532	.107060	.110609	.114179	.117769	.125003	.132304	.139665	.147080
	-.30	.101329	.108115	.115006	.118489	.121994	.125523	.129072	.132642	.136232	.143466	.150767	.158128	.165542
	-.40	.119791	.126578	.133469	.136951	.140457	.143985	.147535	.151105	.154694	.161928	.169229	.176590	.184005
20	.40	-.027365	-.020282	-.013104	-.009484	-.005845	-.002187	.001487	.005177	.008881	.016326	.023815	.031340	.038893
	.30	-.008902	-.001819	.005358	.008979	.012618	.016276	.019950	.023639	.027343	.034789	.042278	.049803	.057356
	.20	.009560	.015644	.023821	.027441	.031081	.034738	.038413	.042102	.045806	.053252	.060741	.068265	.075819
	.10	.028023	.035107	.042284	.045904	.049544	.053201	.056875	.060565	.064269	.071714	.079203	.086728	.094281
	0.00	.046486	.053583	.060746	.064366	.068006	.071664	.075338	.079028	.082731	.090177	.097666	.105191	.112744
	-.10	.064949	.072032	.079209	.082829	.086469	.090126	.093801	.097490	.101194	.108640	.116129	.123654	.131207
	-.20	.083411	.090495	.097672	.101292	.104932	.108589	.112263	.115953	.119657	.127102	.134592	.142116	.149669
	-.30	.101874	.108957	.116135	.119755	.123394	.127052	.130726	.134416	.138119	.145565	.153054	.160579	.168132
	-.40	.120337	.127420	.134597	.138218	.141857	.145515	.149189	.152878	.156582	.164028	.171517	.179042	.186595
25	.40	-.027051	-.019805	-.012479	-.008790	-.005086	-.001368	.002361	.006101	.009851	.017373	.024920	.032485	.040060
	.30	-.008588	-.001342	.005984	.009673	.013377	.017094	.020824	.024564	.028313	.035836	.043383	.050947	.058523
	.20	.009875	.017121	.024447	.028136	.031840	.035557	.039287	.043027	.046776	.054299	.061846	.069410	.076986
	.10	.028337	.035583	.042910	.046599	.050302	.054020	.057749	.061489	.065239	.072761	.080308	.087873	.095448
	0.00	.046800	.054046	.061372	.065061	.068765	.072483	.076212	.079952	.083702	.091224	.098771	.106335	.113911
	-.10	.065263	.072509	.079835	.083524	.087228	.090945	.094675	.098415	.102164	.109687	.117234	.124798	.132374
	-.20	.083725	.090971	.098298	.101987	.105691	.109408	.113137	.116878	.120627	.128150	.135697	.143261	.150837
	-.30	.102188	.109434	.116760	.120449	.124153	.127871	.131600	.135340	.139090	.146612	.154159	.161724	.169299
	-.40	.120651	.127897	.135223	.138912	.142616	.146333	.150063	.153803	.157552	.165075	.172622	.180186	.187762
30	.40	-.026852	-.019509	-.012100	-.008375	-.004639	-.000893	.002860	.006621	.010387	.017932	.025489	.033051	.040615
	.30	-.008389	-.001046	.006363	.010088	.013824	.017569	.021323	.025084	.028850	.036395	.043951	.051513	.059077
	.20	.010074	.017416	.024826	.028551	.032287	.036032	.039786	.043546	.047312	.054858	.062414	.069976	.077540
	.10	.028536	.035879	.043289	.047013	.050749	.054495	.058249	.062009	.065775	.073320	.080877	.088439	.096003
	0.00	.046999	.054342	.061751	.065476	.069212	.072958	.076711	.080472	.084238	.091783	.099339	.106902	.114466
	-.10	.065462	.072805	.080214	.083939	.087675	.091420	.095174	.098934	.102701	.110246	.117802	.125364	.132928
	-.20	.083925	.091267	.098677	.102401	.106137	.109883	.113637	.117397	.121163	.128708	.136265	.143827	.151391
	-.30	.102387	.109730	.117139	.120864	.124600	.128346	.132099	.135860	.139626	.147171	.154728	.162290	.169854
	-.40	.120850	.128193	.135602	.139327	.143063	.146808	.150562	.154323	.158089	.165634	.173190	.180752	.188316

5.0 YEAR HOLDING PERIOD
.040 EQUITY YIELD RATE
.800 LOAN RATIO

INTEREST RATE

TERM YEARS	APPR DEP	5.0	6.0	7.0	7.5	8.0	8.5	9.0	9.5	10.0	11.0	12.0	13.0	14.0
10	.40	-.028714	-.022154	-.015480	-.012103	-.008698	-.005267	-.001810	.001672	.005179	.012264	.019443	.026711	.034063
	.30	-.010251	-.003691	.002982	.006360	.009765	.013196	.016652	.020134	.023641	.030727	.037906	.045174	.052526
	.20	.008211	.014772	.021445	.024823	.028227	.031658	.035115	.038597	.042104	.049190	.056369	.063636	.070988
	.10	.026674	.033235	.039908	.043286	.046690	.050121	.053578	.057060	.060567	.067653	.074831	.082099	.089451
	0.00	.045137	.051697	.058370	.061748	.065153	.068584	.072041	.075523	.079029	.086115	.093294	.100562	.107914
	-.10	.063599	.070160	.076833	.080211	.083616	.087047	.090503	.093985	.097492	.104578	.111757	.119024	.126376
	-.20	.082062	.088623	.095296	.098674	.102078	.105509	.108966	.112448	.115955	.123041	.130220	.137487	.144839
	-.30	.100525	.107085	.113759	.117136	.120541	.123972	.127429	.130911	.134418	.141503	.148682	.155950	.163302
	-.40	.118988	.125548	.132221	.135599	.139004	.142435	.145891	.149373	.152880	.159966	.167145	.174413	.181765
15	.40	-.027514	-.020276	-.012925	-.009210	-.005471	-.001707	.002079	.005887	.009716	.017432	.025220	.033071	.040980
	.30	-.009052	-.001813	.005538	.009252	.012992	.016755	.020541	.024349	.028178	.035894	.043682	.051534	.059443
	.20	.009411	.016650	.024000	.027715	.031455	.035218	.039004	.042812	.046641	.054357	.062145	.069997	.077906
	.10	.027874	.035113	.042463	.046178	.049917	.053681	.057467	.061275	.065104	.072820	.080608	.088460	.096369
	0.00	.046337	.053575	.060926	.064640	.068380	.072143	.075930	.079738	.083566	.091283	.099070	.106922	.114831
	-.10	.064799	.072038	.079389	.083103	.086843	.090606	.094392	.098200	.102029	.109745	.117533	.125385	.133294
	-.20	.083262	.090501	.097851	.101566	.105305	.109069	.112855	.116663	.120492	.128208	.135996	.143848	.151757
	-.30	.101725	.108963	.116314	.120029	.123768	.127532	.131318	.135126	.138955	.146671	.154458	.162310	.170219
	-.40	.120187	.127426	.134777	.138491	.142231	.145994	.149780	.153588	.157417	.165133	.172921	.180773	.188682
20	.40	-.026933	-.019377	-.011721	-.007860	-.003978	-.000076	.003843	.007779	.011729	.019671	.027660	.035686	.043743
	.30	-.008470	-.000914	.006741	.010603	.014485	.018387	.022306	.026241	.030192	.038134	.046122	.054149	.062205
	.20	.009993	.017548	.025204	.029066	.032948	.036849	.040768	.044704	.048655	.056597	.064585	.072611	.080668
	.10	.028456	.036011	.043667	.047528	.051411	.055312	.059231	.063167	.067117	.075059	.083048	.091074	.099131
	0.00	.046918	.054474	.062130	.065991	.069873	.073775	.077694	.081629	.085580	.093522	.101511	.109537	.117594
	-.10	.065381	.072937	.080592	.084454	.088336	.092237	.096157	.100092	.104043	.111985	.119973	.128000	.136056
	-.20	.083844	.091399	.099055	.102917	.106799	.110700	.114619	.118555	.122506	.130448	.138436	.146462	.154519
	-.30	.102306	.109862	.117518	.121379	.125261	.129163	.133082	.137018	.140968	.148910	.156899	.164925	.172982
	-.40	.120769	.128325	.135980	.139842	.143724	.147626	.151545	.155480	.159431	.167373	.175361	.183388	.191444
25	.40	-.026597	-.018868	-.011054	-.007119	-.003168	.000797	.004775	.008765	.012764	.020788	.028838	.036907	.044988
	.30	-.008135	-.000406	.007409	.011343	.015295	.019260	.023238	.027227	.031227	.039251	.047301	.055370	.063450
	.20	.010328	.018057	.025872	.029807	.033757	.037723	.041701	.045690	.049690	.057714	.065764	.073832	.081913
	.10	.028791	.036520	.044334	.048269	.052220	.056185	.060163	.064153	.068152	.076176	.084227	.092295	.100376
	0.00	.047253	.054982	.062797	.066732	.070683	.074648	.078626	.082616	.086615	.094639	.102689	.110758	.118839
	-.10	.065716	.073445	.081260	.085195	.089146	.093111	.097089	.101078	.105078	.113102	.121152	.129221	.137301
	-.20	.084179	.091908	.099723	.103657	.107608	.111573	.115552	.119541	.123540	.131565	.139615	.147683	.155764
	-.30	.102642	.110371	.118185	.122120	.126071	.130036	.134014	.138004	.142003	.150027	.158077	.166146	.174227
	-.40	.121104	.128833	.136648	.140583	.144534	.148499	.152477	.156466	.160466	.168490	.176540	.184609	.192689
30	.40	-.026385	-.018553	-.010650	-.006676	-.002691	.001304	.005308	.009319	.013336	.021384	.029444	.037511	.045579
	.30	-.007922	-.000090	.007813	.011786	.015771	.019767	.023771	.027782	.031799	.039847	.047907	.055974	.064042
	.20	.010540	.018373	.026276	.030249	.034234	.038229	.042233	.046244	.050262	.058310	.066370	.074436	.082505
	.10	.029003	.036835	.044739	.048712	.052697	.056692	.060696	.064707	.068724	.076772	.084833	.092899	.100967
	0.00	.047466	.055298	.063201	.067174	.071159	.075155	.079159	.083170	.087187	.095235	.103295	.111362	.119430
	-.10	.065928	.073761	.081664	.085637	.089622	.093617	.097621	.101633	.105650	.113698	.121758	.129824	.137893
	-.20	.084391	.092223	.100127	.104100	.108085	.112080	.116084	.120095	.124113	.132161	.140221	.148287	.156355
	-.30	.102854	.110686	.118589	.122563	.126548	.130543	.134547	.138558	.142575	.150623	.158683	.166750	.174818
	-.40	.121317	.129149	.137052	.141025	.145010	.149006	.153010	.157021	.161038	.169086	.177146	.185213	.193281

5.0 YEAR HOLDING PERIOD
.040 EQUITY YIELD RATE
.900 LOAN RATIO

INTEREST RATE

TERM YEARS	APPR DEP	5.0	6.0	7.0	7.5	8.0	8.5	9.0	9.5	10.0	11.0	12.0	13.0	14.0
10	.40	-.028072	-.020692	-.013184	-.009384	-.005554	-.001694	.002195	.006112	.010057	.018029	.026105	.034281	.042552
	.30	-.009609	-.002229	.005279	.009079	.012909	.016769	.020657	.024575	.028520	.036492	.044568	.052744	.061015
	.20	.008853	.016234	.023741	.027541	.031372	.035231	.039120	.043037	.046983	.054954	.063031	.071207	.079478
	.10	.027316	.034697	.042204	.046004	.049834	.053694	.057583	.061500	.065445	.073417	.081493	.089669	.097940
	0.00	.045779	.053159	.060667	.064467	.068297	.072157	.076046	.079963	.083908	.091880	.099956	.108132	.116403
	-.10	.064242	.071622	.079129	.082929	.086760	.090619	.094508	.098426	.102371	.110342	.118419	.126595	.134866
	-.20	.082704	.090085	.097592	.101392	.105222	.109082	.112971	.116888	.120833	.128805	.136881	.145057	.153328
	-.30	.101167	.108547	.116055	.119855	.123685	.127545	.131434	.135351	.139296	.147268	.155344	.163520	.171791
	-.40	.119630	.127010	.134518	.138318	.142148	.146008	.149896	.153814	.157759	.165731	.173807	.181983	.190254
15	.40	-.026722	-.018579	-.010309	-.006130	-.001923	.002310	.006570	.010854	.015161	.023842	.032603	.041437	.050334
	.30	-.008259	-.000116	.008153	.012332	.016539	.020773	.025033	.029317	.033624	.042305	.051066	.059899	.068797
	.20	.010203	.018347	.026616	.030795	.035002	.039236	.043495	.047779	.052087	.060767	.069529	.078362	.087260
	.10	.028666	.036810	.045079	.049258	.053465	.057699	.061958	.066242	.070550	.079230	.087991	.096825	.105722
	0.00	.047129	.055272	.063542	.067721	.071928	.076161	.080421	.084705	.089012	.097693	.106454	.115288	.124185
	-.10	.065591	.073735	.082004	.086183	.090390	.094624	.098883	.103168	.107475	.116156	.124917	.133750	.142648
	-.20	.084054	.092198	.100467	.104646	.108853	.113087	.117346	.121630	.125938	.134618	.143380	.152213	.161111
	-.30	.102517	.110660	.118930	.123109	.127316	.131549	.135809	.140093	.144400	.153081	.161842	.170676	.179573
	-.40	.120979	.129123	.137392	.141571	.145778	.150012	.154272	.158556	.162863	.171544	.180305	.189138	.198036
20	.40	-.026068	-.017568	-.008955	-.004611	-.000243	.004146	.008555	.012982	.017427	.026362	.035348	.044378	.053442
	.30	-.007605	.000895	.009508	.013852	.018219	.022608	.027017	.031445	.035889	.044824	.053811	.062841	.071905
	.20	.010858	.019358	.027970	.032315	.036682	.041071	.045480	.049908	.054352	.063287	.072274	.081304	.090367
	.10	.029320	.037820	.046433	.050777	.055145	.059534	.063943	.068370	.072815	.081750	.090737	.099766	.108830
	0.00	.047783	.056283	.064896	.069240	.073607	.077997	.082406	.086833	.091278	.100212	.109199	.118229	.127293
	-.10	.066246	.074746	.083358	.087703	.092070	.096459	.100868	.105296	.109740	.118675	.127662	.136692	.145755
	-.20	.084709	.093208	.101821	.106165	.110533	.114922	.119331	.123758	.128203	.137138	.146125	.155154	.164218
	-.30	.103171	.111671	.120284	.124628	.128996	.133385	.137794	.142221	.146666	.155601	.164587	.173617	.182681
	-.40	.121634	.130134	.138747	.143091	.147458	.151847	.156256	.160684	.165128	.174063	.183050	.192080	.201144
25	.40	-.025691	-.016996	-.008204	-.003777	.000667	.005128	.009604	.014092	.018591	.027618	.036675	.045752	.054842
	.30	-.007228	.001467	.010259	.014685	.019130	.023591	.028066	.032554	.037054	.046081	.055137	.064214	.073305
	.20	.011235	.019930	.028721	.033148	.037593	.042054	.046529	.051017	.055517	.064544	.073600	.082677	.091768
	.10	.029697	.038393	.047184	.051611	.056055	.060516	.064992	.069480	.073979	.083006	.092063	.101140	.110230
	0.00	.048160	.056855	.065647	.070073	.074518	.078979	.083454	.087943	.092442	.101469	.110525	.119603	.128693
	-.10	.066623	.075318	.084110	.088536	.092981	.097442	.101917	.106405	.110905	.119932	.128988	.138065	.147156
	-.20	.085085	.093781	.102572	.106999	.111444	.115904	.120380	.124868	.129367	.138395	.147451	.156528	.165619
	-.30	.103548	.112243	.121035	.125462	.129906	.134367	.138843	.143331	.147830	.156857	.165914	.174991	.184081
	-.40	.122011	.130706	.139498	.143924	.148369	.152830	.157305	.161793	.166293	.175320	.184376	.193453	.202544
30	.40	-.025452	-.016641	-.007749	-.003280	.001204	.005698	.010203	.014715	.019235	.028289	.037356	.046431	.055508
	.30	-.006989	.001822	.010713	.015183	.019666	.024161	.028665	.033178	.037697	.046751	.055819	.064894	.073971
	.20	.011474	.020285	.029176	.033646	.038129	.042624	.047128	.051641	.056160	.065214	.074282	.083357	.092433
	.10	.029936	.038748	.047639	.052109	.056592	.061086	.065591	.070103	.074623	.083677	.092745	.101819	.110896
	0.00	.048399	.057210	.066101	.070571	.075054	.079549	.084053	.088566	.093085	.102140	.111207	.120282	.129359
	-.10	.066862	.075673	.084564	.089034	.093517	.098012	.102516	.107029	.111548	.120602	.129670	.138745	.147821
	-.20	.085324	.094136	.103027	.107497	.111980	.116475	.120979	.125492	.130011	.139065	.148133	.157207	.166284
	-.30	.103787	.112598	.121490	.125959	.130443	.134937	.139442	.143954	.148474	.157528	.166595	.175670	.184747
	-.40	.122250	.131061	.139952	.144422	.148905	.153400	.157904	.162417	.166936	.175990	.185058	.194133	.203210

5.0 YEAR HOLDING PERIOD
.060 EQUITY YIELD RATE
.600 LOAN RATIO

INTEREST RATE

TERM YEARS	APPR DEP	5.0	6.0	7.0	7.5	8.0	8.5	9.0	9.5	10.0	11.0	12.0	13.0	14.0
10	.40	-.017206	-.012339	-.007386	-.004879	-.002351	.000196	.002763	.005349	.007954	.013218	.018552	.023954	.029420
	.30	.000534	.005401	.010353	.012861	.015388	.017936	.020502	.023088	.025693	.030958	.036292	.041694	.047160
	.20	.018273	.023141	.028093	.030600	.033128	.035675	.038242	.040828	.043433	.048697	.054032	.059433	.064899
	.10	.036013	.040880	.045833	.048340	.050867	.053415	.055982	.058568	.061172	.066437	.071771	.077173	.082639
	0.00	.053753	.058620	.063572	.066080	.068607	.071154	.073721	.076307	.078912	.084176	.089511	.094913	.100379
	-.10	.071492	.076360	.081312	.083819	.086347	.088894	.091461	.094047	.096652	.101916	.107251	.112652	.118118
	-.20	.089232	.094099	.099052	.101559	.104086	.106634	.109201	.111787	.114391	.119656	.124990	.130392	.135858
	-.30	.106971	.111839	.116791	.119299	.121826	.124373	.126940	.129526	.132131	.137395	.142730	.148132	.153598
	-.40	.124711	.129578	.134531	.137038	.139566	.142113	.144680	.147266	.149871	.155135	.160469	.165871	.171337
15	.40	-.017102	-.011736	-.006284	-.003528	-.000752	.002042	.004853	.007682	.010527	.016262	.022053	.027895	.033782
	.30	.000637	.006003	.011455	.014212	.016987	.019781	.022593	.025422	.028266	.034002	.039793	.045635	.051522
	.20	.018377	.023743	.029195	.031951	.034727	.037521	.040332	.043161	.046006	.051741	.057533	.063375	.069261
	.10	.036117	.041483	.046935	.049691	.052467	.055261	.058072	.060901	.063746	.069481	.075272	.081114	.087001
	0.00	.053856	.059222	.064674	.067431	.070206	.073000	.075812	.078641	.081485	.087221	.093012	.098854	.104741
	-.10	.071596	.076962	.082414	.085170	.087946	.090740	.093551	.096380	.099225	.104960	.110752	.116593	.122480
	-.20	.089336	.094702	.100154	.102910	.105685	.108480	.111291	.114120	.116965	.122700	.128491	.134333	.140220
	-.30	.107075	.112441	.117893	.120650	.123425	.126219	.129031	.131859	.134704	.140440	.146231	.152073	.157960
	-.40	.124815	.130181	.135633	.138389	.141165	.143959	.146770	.149599	.152444	.158179	.163971	.169812	.175699
20	.40	-.017052	-.011448	-.005765	-.002897	-.000012	.002888	.005802	.008729	.011669	.017582	.023532	.029515	.035524
	.30	.000688	.006292	.011974	.014843	.017727	.020627	.023541	.026469	.029409	.035321	.041272	.047255	.053264
	.20	.018427	.024031	.029714	.032582	.035467	.038367	.041281	.044208	.047148	.053061	.059012	.064995	.071003
	.10	.036167	.041771	.047454	.050322	.053207	.056106	.059021	.061948	.064888	.070800	.076751	.082734	.088743
	0.00	.053907	.059510	.065193	.068062	.070946	.073846	.076760	.079688	.082627	.088540	.094491	.100474	.106483
	-.10	.071646	.077250	.082933	.085801	.088686	.091586	.094500	.097427	.100367	.106280	.112231	.118213	.124222
	-.20	.089386	.094990	.100673	.103541	.106425	.109325	.112240	.115167	.118107	.124019	.129970	.135953	.141962
	-.30	.107125	.112729	.118412	.121281	.124165	.127065	.129979	.132907	.135846	.141759	.147710	.153693	.159701
	-.40	.124865	.130469	.136152	.139020	.141905	.144805	.147719	.150646	.153586	.159499	.165450	.171432	.177441
25	.40	-.017023	-.011285	-.005477	-.002551	.000389	.003340	.006303	.009275	.012256	.018240	.024247	.030272	.036309
	.30	.000717	.006455	.012262	.015189	.018128	.021080	.024043	.027015	.029996	.035979	.041987	.048011	.054049
	.20	.018456	.024194	.030002	.032928	.035868	.038819	.041782	.044754	.047735	.053719	.059726	.065751	.071788
	.10	.036196	.041934	.047742	.050668	.053608	.056559	.059522	.062494	.065475	.071459	.077466	.083491	.089528
	0.00	.053935	.059674	.065481	.068408	.071347	.074299	.077261	.080234	.083214	.089198	.095206	.101230	.107268
	-.10	.071675	.077413	.083221	.086147	.089087	.092038	.095001	.097973	.100954	.106938	.112945	.118970	.125007
	-.20	.089415	.095153	.100960	.103887	.106827	.109778	.112741	.115713	.118694	.124677	.130685	.136710	.142747
	-.30	.107154	.112893	.118700	.121627	.124566	.127518	.130480	.133453	.136433	.142417	.148424	.154449	.160487
	-.40	.124894	.130632	.136440	.139366	.142306	.145258	.148220	.151192	.154173	.160157	.166164	.172189	.178226
30	.40	-.017005	-.011184	-.005303	-.002344	.000625	.003603	.006589	.009582	.012580	.018591	.024614	.030646	.036682
	.30	.000735	.006556	.012437	.015395	.018365	.021343	.024329	.027322	.030320	.036330	.042354	.048386	.054422
	.20	.018475	.024296	.030176	.033135	.036104	.039082	.042068	.045061	.048060	.054070	.060094	.066125	.072161
	.10	.036214	.042035	.047916	.050875	.053844	.056822	.059808	.062801	.065799	.071810	.077833	.083865	.089901
	0.00	.053954	.059775	.065656	.068614	.071584	.074562	.077548	.080540	.083539	.089549	.095573	.101605	.107641
	-.10	.071693	.077514	.083395	.086354	.089323	.092301	.095287	.098280	.101279	.107289	.113313	.119344	.125380
	-.20	.089433	.095254	.101135	.104094	.107063	.110041	.113027	.116020	.119018	.125029	.131052	.137084	.143120
	-.30	.107173	.112994	.118874	.121833	.124802	.127781	.130767	.133759	.136758	.142768	.148792	.154823	.160859
	-.40	.124912	.130733	.136614	.139573	.142542	.145520	.148506	.151499	.154497	.160508	.166531	.172563	.178599

5.0 YEAR HOLDING PERIOD
.060 EQUITY YIELD RATE
.667 LOAN RATIO

INTEREST RATE

TERM YEARS	APPR DEP	5.0	6.0	7.0	7.5	8.0	8.5	9.0	9.5	10.0	11.0	12.0	13.0	14.0
10	.40	-.017900	-.012492	-.006989	-.004203	-.001395	.001435	.004287	.007161	.010055	.015904	.021831	.027834	.033907
	.30	-.000161	.005248	.010750	.013536	.016345	.019175	.022027	.024900	.027795	.033644	.039571	.045573	.051647
	.20	.017579	.022987	.028490	.031276	.034084	.036915	.039767	.042640	.045534	.051383	.057311	.063313	.069386
	.10	.035319	.040727	.046230	.049016	.051824	.054654	.057506	.060380	.063274	.069123	.075050	.081053	.087126
	0.00	.053058	.058467	.063969	.066755	.069563	.072394	.075246	.078119	.081014	.086863	.092790	.098792	.104866
	-.10	.070798	.076206	.081709	.084495	.087303	.090134	.092986	.095859	.098753	.104602	.110530	.116532	.122605
	-.20	.088538	.093946	.099449	.102234	.105043	.107873	.110725	.113599	.116493	.122342	.128269	.134271	.140345
	-.30	.106277	.111685	.117188	.119974	.122782	.125613	.128465	.131338	.134232	.140082	.146009	.152011	.158084
	-.40	.124017	.129425	.134928	.137714	.140522	.143352	.146205	.149078	.151972	.157821	.163749	.169751	.175824
15	.40	-.017785	-.011823	-.005765	-.002702	.000382	.003486	.006610	.009753	.012914	.019287	.025722	.032213	.038754
	.30	-.000045	.005917	.011975	.015037	.018121	.021226	.024350	.027493	.030654	.037026	.043461	.049952	.056493
	.20	.017694	.023657	.029714	.032777	.035861	.038965	.042090	.045233	.048393	.054766	.061201	.067692	.074233
	.10	.035434	.041396	.047454	.050517	.053601	.056705	.059829	.062972	.066133	.072506	.078941	.085431	.091973
	0.00	.053174	.059136	.065194	.068256	.071340	.074445	.077569	.080712	.083873	.090245	.096680	.103171	.109712
	-.10	.070913	.076876	.082933	.085996	.089080	.092184	.095309	.098451	.101612	.107985	.114420	.120911	.127452
	-.20	.088653	.094615	.100673	.103736	.106820	.109924	.113048	.116191	.119352	.125725	.132159	.138650	.145191
	-.30	.106393	.112355	.118413	.121475	.124559	.127664	.130788	.133931	.137092	.143464	.149899	.156390	.162931
	-.40	.124132	.130094	.136152	.139215	.142299	.145403	.148527	.151670	.154831	.161204	.167639	.174130	.180671
20	.40	-.017729	-.011502	-.005188	-.002001	.001204	.004426	.007664	.010917	.014183	.020753	.027365	.034013	.040689
	.30	.000011	.006237	.012552	.015738	.018944	.022166	.025404	.028656	.031923	.038492	.045105	.051752	.058429
	.20	.017750	.023977	.030291	.033478	.036683	.039905	.043143	.046396	.049663	.056232	.062844	.069492	.076168
	.10	.035490	.041716	.048031	.051218	.054423	.057645	.060883	.064136	.067402	.073972	.080584	.087231	.093908
	0.00	.053229	.059456	.065770	.068957	.072162	.075385	.078623	.081875	.085142	.091711	.098324	.104971	.111648
	-.10	.070969	.077196	.083510	.086697	.089902	.093124	.096362	.099615	.102881	.109451	.116063	.122711	.129387
	-.20	.088709	.094935	.101250	.104437	.107642	.110864	.114102	.117355	.120621	.127191	.133803	.140450	.147127
	-.30	.106448	.112675	.118989	.122176	.125381	.128604	.131842	.135094	.138361	.144930	.151542	.158190	.164866
	-.40	.124188	.130415	.136729	.139916	.143121	.146343	.149581	.152834	.156100	.162670	.169282	.175930	.182606
25	.40	-.017697	-.011321	-.004868	-.001617	.001650	.004929	.008221	.011523	.014835	.021484	.028159	.034853	.041561
	.30	.000043	.006419	.012871	.016123	.019389	.022669	.025961	.029263	.032575	.039224	.045898	.052593	.059301
	.20	.017782	.024158	.030611	.033863	.037129	.040409	.043700	.047003	.050315	.056963	.063638	.070332	.077041
	.10	.035522	.041898	.048351	.051602	.054869	.058148	.061440	.064742	.068054	.074703	.081378	.088072	.094780
	0.00	.053262	.059638	.066090	.069342	.072608	.075888	.079180	.082482	.085794	.092443	.099117	.105812	.112520
	-.10	.071001	.077377	.083830	.087082	.090348	.093627	.096919	.100222	.103534	.110182	.116857	.123551	.130259
	-.20	.088741	.095117	.101570	.104821	.108087	.111367	.114659	.117961	.121273	.127922	.134597	.141291	.147999
	-.30	.106481	.112856	.119309	.122561	.125827	.129107	.132398	.135701	.139013	.145662	.152336	.159031	.165739
	-.40	.124220	.130596	.137049	.140300	.143567	.146846	.150138	.153441	.156753	.163401	.170076	.176770	.183478
30	.40	-.017677	-.011209	-.004675	-.001387	.001912	.005221	.008539	.011864	.015196	.021874	.028567	.035269	.041976
	.30	.000063	.006531	.013065	.016353	.019652	.022961	.026279	.029604	.032936	.039614	.046307	.053009	.059715
	.20	.017803	.024271	.030805	.034092	.037391	.040700	.044018	.047344	.050675	.057354	.064046	.070748	.077455
	.10	.035542	.042010	.048544	.051832	.055131	.058440	.061758	.065083	.068415	.075093	.081786	.088488	.095195
	0.00	.053282	.059750	.066284	.069572	.072871	.076180	.079498	.082823	.086155	.092833	.099526	.106227	.112934
	-.10	.071022	.077489	.084024	.087311	.090610	.093919	.097237	.100563	.103894	.110572	.117265	.123967	.130674
	-.20	.088761	.095229	.101763	.105051	.108350	.111659	.114977	.118302	.121634	.128312	.135005	.141707	.148413
	-.30	.106501	.112969	.119503	.122790	.126090	.129399	.132717	.136042	.139373	.146052	.152745	.159446	.166153
	-.40	.124241	.130708	.137243	.140530	.143829	.147138	.150456	.153781	.157113	.163791	.170484	.177186	.183893

5.0 YEAR HOLDING PERIOD
.060 EQUITY YIELD RATE
.700 LOAN RATIO

INTEREST RATE

TERM 10 YEARS

APPR DEP	5.0	6.0	7.0	7.5	8.0	8.5	9.0	9.5	10.0	11.0	12.0	13.0	14.0
.40	-.018247	-.012569	-.006791	-.003866	-.000917	.002055	.005050	.008067	.011106	.017247	.023469	.029773	.036150
.30	-.000508	.005171	.010949	.013874	.016823	.019795	.022789	.025806	.028845	.034982	.041210	.047513	.053890
.20	.017232	.022911	.028688	.031614	.034562	.037534	.040529	.043546	.046585	.052726	.058950	.065252	.071629
.10	.034972	.040650	.046428	.049353	.052302	.055274	.058269	.061286	.064324	.070466	.076690	.082992	.089369
0.00	.052711	.058390	.064168	.067093	.070042	.073014	.076008	.079025	.082064	.088206	.094429	.100732	.107109
-.10	.070451	.076130	.081907	.084833	.087781	.090753	.093748	.096765	.099804	.105945	.112169	.118471	.124848
-.20	.088191	.093869	.099647	.102572	.105521	.108493	.111488	.114505	.117543	.123685	.129909	.136211	.142588
-.30	.105930	.111609	.117387	.120312	.123261	.126232	.129227	.132244	.135283	.141425	.147648	.153950	.160327
-.40	.123670	.129348	.135126	.138051	.141000	.143972	.146967	.149984	.153023	.159164	.165388	.171690	.178067

TERM 15 YEARS

APPR DEP	5.0	6.0	7.0	7.5	8.0	8.5	9.0	9.5	10.0	11.0	12.0	13.0	14.0
.40	-.018126	-.011866	-.005505	-.002289	.000949	.004208	.007489	.010789	.014108	.020799	.027555	.034371	.041239
.30	-.000387	.005874	.012234	.015450	.018688	.021948	.025228	.028528	.031847	.038539	.045295	.052111	.058979
.20	.017353	.023613	.029974	.033190	.036428	.039688	.042968	.046268	.049587	.056278	.063035	.069850	.076718
.10	.035093	.041353	.047714	.050929	.054168	.057427	.060708	.064008	.067327	.074018	.080774	.087590	.094458
0.00	.052832	.059093	.065453	.068669	.071907	.075167	.078447	.081747	.085066	.091757	.098514	.105329	.112198
-.10	.070572	.076832	.083193	.086409	.089647	.092907	.096187	.099487	.102806	.109497	.116254	.123069	.129937
-.20	.088312	.094572	.100933	.104148	.107387	.110646	.113927	.117227	.120546	.127237	.133993	.140809	.147677
-.30	.106051	.112312	.118672	.121888	.125126	.128386	.131666	.134966	.138285	.144976	.151733	.158548	.165416
-.40	.123791	.130051	.136412	.139628	.142866	.146125	.149406	.152706	.156025	.162716	.169473	.176288	.183156

TERM 20 YEARS

APPR DEP	5.0	6.0	7.0	7.5	8.0	8.5	9.0	9.5	10.0	11.0	12.0	13.0	14.0
.40	-.018068	-.011530	-.004900	-.001553	.001812	.005195	.008595	.012010	.015440	.022338	.029281	.036261	.043271
.30	-.000328	.006210	.012840	.016186	.019552	.022935	.026335	.029750	.033180	.040078	.047021	.054001	.061011
.20	.017412	.023950	.030580	.033926	.037291	.040675	.044074	.047490	.050919	.057818	.064760	.071740	.078750
.10	.035151	.041689	.048319	.051666	.055031	.058414	.061814	.065229	.068659	.075557	.082500	.089480	.096490
0.00	.052891	.059429	.066059	.069405	.072771	.076154	.079554	.082969	.086399	.093297	.100240	.107219	.114230
-.10	.070631	.077169	.083799	.087145	.090510	.093893	.097293	.100709	.104138	.111036	.117979	.124959	.131969
-.20	.088370	.094908	.101538	.104884	.108250	.111633	.115033	.118448	.121878	.128776	.135719	.142699	.149709
-.30	.106110	.112648	.119278	.122624	.125989	.129373	.132773	.136188	.139618	.146516	.153458	.160438	.167449
-.40	.123850	.130387	.137017	.140364	.143729	.147112	.150512	.153928	.157357	.164255	.171198	.178178	.185188

TERM 25 YEARS

APPR DEP	5.0	6.0	7.0	7.5	8.0	8.5	9.0	9.5	10.0	11.0	12.0	13.0	14.0
.40	-.018034	-.011339	-.004564	-.001150	.002280	.005724	.009180	.012647	.016125	.023106	.030115	.037143	.044187
.30	-.000294	.006401	.013176	.016590	.020020	.023463	.026919	.030387	.033865	.040846	.047854	.054883	.061927
.20	.017445	.024140	.030916	.034330	.037759	.041203	.044659	.048127	.051604	.058585	.065594	.072623	.079666
.10	.035185	.041880	.048655	.052069	.055499	.058943	.062399	.065866	.069344	.076325	.083333	.090362	.097406
0.00	.052925	.059619	.066395	.069809	.073239	.076682	.080138	.083606	.087084	.094065	.101073	.108102	.115146
-.10	.070664	.077359	.084134	.087549	.090978	.094422	.097878	.101346	.104823	.111804	.118813	.125842	.132885
-.20	.088404	.095099	.101874	.105288	.108718	.112161	.115618	.119085	.122563	.129544	.136552	.143581	.150625
-.30	.106144	.112838	.119614	.123028	.126457	.129901	.133357	.136825	.140302	.147283	.154292	.161321	.168364
-.40	.123883	.130578	.137353	.140768	.144197	.147641	.151097	.154564	.158042	.165023	.172032	.179061	.186104

TERM 30 YEARS

APPR DEP	5.0	6.0	7.0	7.5	8.0	8.5	9.0	9.5	10.0	11.0	12.0	13.0	14.0
.40	-.018012	-.011221	-.004360	-.000908	.002556	.006030	.009514	.013005	.016503	.023516	.030543	.037580	.044622
.30	-.000273	.006518	.013379	.016831	.020295	.023770	.027253	.030745	.034243	.041255	.048283	.055320	.062362
.20	.017467	.024258	.031119	.034571	.038035	.041509	.044993	.048485	.051983	.058995	.066022	.073059	.080101
.10	.035207	.041998	.048859	.052310	.055774	.059249	.062733	.066224	.069722	.076735	.083762	.090799	.097841
0.00	.052946	.059737	.066598	.070050	.073514	.076989	.080472	.083964	.087462	.094474	.101502	.108539	.115581
-.10	.070686	.077477	.084338	.087790	.091254	.094728	.098212	.101704	.105202	.112214	.119241	.126278	.133320
-.20	.088425	.095217	.102077	.105529	.108993	.112468	.115952	.119443	.122941	.129954	.136981	.144018	.151060
-.30	.106165	.112956	.119817	.123269	.126733	.130208	.133691	.137183	.140681	.147693	.154721	.161758	.168800
-.40	.123905	.130696	.137557	.141009	.144473	.147947	.151431	.154922	.158421	.165433	.172460	.179497	.186539

5.0 YEAR HOLDING PERIOD
.060 EQUITY YIELD RATE
.750 LOAN RATIO

INTEREST RATE

TERM YEARS	APPR DEP	5.0	6.0	7.0	7.5	8.0	8.5	9.0	9.5	10.0	11.0	12.0	13.0	14.0
10	.40	-.018768	-.012684	-.006493	-.003359	-.000200	.002985	.006193	.009426	.012682	.019262	.025930	.032682	.039515
	.30	-.001128	.005056	.011246	.014381	.017540	.020724	.023933	.027165	.030422	.037001	.043670	.050422	.057255
	.20	.016711	.022796	.028986	.032120	.035280	.038464	.041672	.044905	.048161	.054741	.061409	.068162	.074994
	.10	.034451	.040535	.046726	.049860	.053019	.056203	.059412	.062645	.065900	.072481	.079149	.085901	.092734
	0.00	.052191	.058275	.064465	.067599	.070759	.073943	.077152	.080384	.083640	.090220	.096889	.103641	.110473
	-.10	.069930	.076015	.082205	.085339	.088499	.091683	.094891	.098124	.101380	.107960	.114628	.121381	.128213
	-.20	.087670	.093754	.099945	.103079	.106238	.109422	.112631	.115863	.119119	.125700	.132368	.139120	.145953
	-.30	.105410	.111494	.117684	.120818	.123978	.127162	.130371	.133603	.136859	.143439	.150108	.156860	.163692
	-.40	.123149	.129233	.135424	.138558	.141717	.144902	.148110	.151343	.154599	.161179	.167847	.174600	.181432
15	.40	-.018638	-.011931	-.005116	-.001670	.001799	.005292	.008806	.012342	.015898	.023067	.030306	.037609	.044967
	.30	-.000899	.005809	.012624	.016069	.019539	.023031	.026546	.030082	.033638	.040807	.048046	.055348	.062707
	.20	.016841	.023549	.030364	.033809	.037278	.040771	.044286	.047821	.051377	.058547	.065786	.073088	.080447
	.10	.034581	.041288	.048103	.051549	.055018	.058511	.062025	.065561	.069117	.076286	.083525	.090828	.098186
	0.00	.052320	.059028	.065843	.069288	.072758	.076250	.079765	.083301	.086857	.094026	.101265	.108567	.115926
	-.10	.070060	.076768	.083583	.087028	.090497	.093990	.097505	.101040	.104596	.111765	.119005	.126307	.133666
	-.20	.087800	.094507	.101322	.104768	.108237	.111730	.115244	.118780	.122336	.129505	.136744	.144047	.151405
	-.30	.105539	.112247	.119062	.122507	.125977	.129469	.132984	.136520	.140076	.147245	.154484	.161786	.169145
	-.40	.123279	.129986	.136801	.140247	.143716	.147209	.150723	.154259	.157815	.164984	.172224	.179526	.186884
20	.40	-.018575	-.011570	-.004467	-.000882	.002724	.006349	.009992	.013651	.017326	.024717	.032155	.039634	.047145
	.30	-.000836	.006169	.013273	.016838	.020464	.024084	.027731	.031391	.035065	.042456	.049895	.057373	.064884
	.20	.016904	.023909	.031012	.034598	.038203	.041828	.045471	.049130	.052805	.060196	.067635	.075113	.082624
	.10	.034644	.041648	.048752	.052337	.055943	.059568	.063211	.066870	.070545	.077936	.085374	.092853	.100364
	0.00	.052383	.059388	.066492	.070077	.073683	.077308	.080950	.084610	.088284	.095675	.103114	.110592	.118103
	-.10	.070123	.077128	.084231	.087817	.091422	.095047	.098690	.102349	.106024	.113415	.120853	.128332	.135843
	-.20	.087862	.094867	.101971	.105556	.109162	.112787	.116430	.120089	.123764	.131154	.138593	.146072	.153582
	-.30	.105602	.112607	.119711	.123296	.126902	.130527	.134169	.137829	.141503	.148894	.156333	.163811	.171322
	-.40	.123342	.130347	.137450	.141036	.144641	.148266	.151909	.155568	.159243	.166634	.174072	.181551	.189062
25	.40	-.018539	-.011367	-.004107	-.000449	.003226	.006915	.010618	.014334	.018060	.025539	.033048	.040579	.048126
	.30	-.000800	.006373	.013633	.017291	.020965	.024655	.028358	.032073	.035799	.043279	.050788	.058319	.065866
	.20	.016940	.024113	.031372	.035030	.038705	.042394	.046098	.049813	.053539	.061018	.068528	.076059	.083605
	.10	.034680	.041852	.049112	.052770	.056445	.060134	.063837	.067552	.071278	.078758	.086267	.093798	.101345
	0.00	.052419	.059592	.066852	.070510	.074184	.077874	.081577	.085292	.089018	.096498	.104007	.111538	.119085
	-.10	.070159	.077332	.084591	.088249	.091924	.095613	.099316	.103032	.106758	.114237	.121747	.129278	.136824
	-.20	.087899	.095071	.102331	.105989	.109664	.113353	.117056	.120771	.124497	.131977	.139486	.147017	.154564
	-.30	.105638	.112811	.120071	.123729	.127403	.131093	.134796	.138511	.142237	.149717	.157226	.164757	.172303
	-.40	.123378	.130551	.137810	.141468	.145143	.148832	.152535	.156251	.159977	.167456	.174965	.182496	.190043
30	.40	-.018516	-.011240	-.003889	-.000191	.003521	.007244	.010976	.014717	.018465	.025978	.033508	.041047	.048592
	.30	-.000777	.006500	.013851	.017549	.021260	.024983	.028716	.032457	.036205	.043718	.051247	.058787	.066332
	.20	.016963	.024239	.031590	.035289	.039000	.042723	.046455	.050196	.053944	.061457	.068987	.076526	.084071
	.10	.034703	.041979	.049330	.053028	.056740	.060462	.064195	.067936	.071684	.079197	.086726	.094266	.101811
	0.00	.052442	.059719	.067069	.070768	.074479	.078202	.081935	.085676	.089424	.096937	.104466	.112006	.119551
	-.10	.070182	.077458	.084809	.088508	.092219	.095942	.099674	.103415	.107163	.114676	.122206	.129745	.137290
	-.20	.087922	.095198	.102549	.106247	.109959	.113681	.117414	.121155	.124903	.132416	.139945	.147485	.155030
	-.30	.105661	.112937	.120288	.123987	.127698	.131421	.135154	.138895	.142643	.150156	.157685	.165225	.172770
	-.40	.123401	.130677	.138028	.141727	.145438	.149161	.152893	.156634	.160382	.167895	.175425	.182964	.190509

5.0 YEAR HOLDING PERIOD
.060 EQUITY YIELD RATE
.800 LOAN RATIO

INTEREST RATE

TERM YEARS	APPR DEP	5.0	6.0	7.0	7.5	8.0	8.5	9.0	9.5	10.0	11.0	12.0	13.0	14.0
10	.40	-.019288	-.012799	-.006195	-.002852	.000518	.003914	.007337	.010785	.014258	.021277	.028389	.035592	.042880
	.30	-.001549	.004941	.011544	.014887	.018257	.021654	.025076	.028524	.031997	.039016	.046129	.053331	.060619
	.20	.016191	.022284	.029284	.032627	.035997	.039393	.042816	.046264	.049737	.056756	.063869	.071071	.078359
	.10	.033930	.040420	.047023	.050366	.053736	.057133	.060555	.064003	.067476	.074495	.081608	.088811	.096099
	0.00	.051670	.058160	.064763	.068106	.071476	.074873	.078295	.081743	.085216	.092235	.099348	.106550	.113838
	-.10	.069410	.075899	.082503	.085846	.089216	.092612	.096035	.099483	.102956	.109975	.117088	.124290	.131578
	-.20	.087149	.093639	.100242	.103585	.106955	.110352	.113774	.117222	.120695	.127714	.134827	.142030	.149318
	-.30	.104889	.111379	.117982	.121325	.124695	.128092	.131514	.134962	.138435	.145454	.152567	.159769	.167057
	-.40	.122629	.129118	.135722	.139065	.142435	.145831	.149254	.152702	.156175	.163194	.170306	.177509	.184797
15	.40	-.019150	-.011996	-.004726	-.001051	.002650	.006375	.010124	.013896	.017689	.025336	.033057	.040847	.048696
	.30	-.001411	.005743	.013013	.016689	.020389	.024115	.027864	.031635	.035428	.043075	.050797	.058586	.066435
	.20	.016329	.023484	.030753	.034428	.038129	.041854	.045603	.049375	.053168	.060815	.068537	.076326	.084175
	.10	.034069	.041223	.048493	.052168	.055869	.059594	.063343	.067114	.070908	.078555	.086276	.094065	.101915
	0.00	.051808	.058963	.066232	.069908	.073608	.077334	.081083	.084854	.088647	.096294	.104016	.111805	.119655
	-.10	.069548	.076703	.083972	.087647	.091348	.095073	.098822	.102594	.106387	.114034	.121756	.129545	.137394
	-.20	.087288	.094442	.101712	.105386	.109088	.112813	.116562	.120333	.124126	.131774	.139495	.147284	.155134
	-.30	.105027	.112182	.119451	.123126	.126827	.130553	.134301	.138073	.141866	.149513	.157235	.165024	.172873
	-.40	.122767	.129922	.137191	.140866	.144567	.148292	.152041	.155813	.159606	.167253	.174975	.182764	.190613
20	.40	-.019083	-.011611	-.004034	-.000210	.003636	.007503	.011389	.015292	.019211	.027095	.035029	.043007	.051018
	.30	-.001344	.006128	.013706	.017530	.021376	.025243	.029128	.033031	.036951	.044835	.052769	.060746	.068758
	.20	.016396	.023868	.031445	.035270	.039116	.042982	.046868	.050771	.054691	.062574	.070509	.078486	.086497
	.10	.034136	.041608	.049185	.053009	.056855	.060722	.064607	.068511	.072430	.080314	.088248	.096225	.104237
	0.00	.051875	.059347	.066924	.070749	.074595	.078461	.082347	.086250	.090170	.098053	.105988	.113965	.121977
	-.10	.069615	.077087	.084664	.088487	.092335	.096201	.100087	.103990	.107910	.115793	.123728	.131705	.139716
	-.20	.087355	.094827	.102404	.106228	.110074	.113941	.117826	.121730	.125649	.133533	.141467	.149444	.157456
	-.30	.105094	.112566	.120143	.123968	.127814	.131680	.135566	.139469	.143389	.151272	.159207	.167184	.175196
	-.40	.122834	.130306	.137883	.141707	.145553	.149420	.153306	.157209	.161129	.169012	.176947	.184924	.192935
25	.40	-.019045	-.011394	-.003650	.000252	.004171	.008107	.012057	.016020	.019994	.027972	.035982	.044015	.052065
	.30	-.001305	.006346	.014089	.017991	.021911	.025846	.029796	.033759	.037734	.045712	.053722	.061755	.069805
	.20	.016435	.024086	.031829	.035731	.039650	.043586	.047536	.051499	.055473	.063452	.071461	.079494	.087544
	.10	.034174	.041825	.049569	.053471	.057390	.061326	.065276	.069239	.073213	.081191	.089201	.097234	.105284
	0.00	.051914	.059565	.067308	.071210	.075130	.079065	.083015	.086978	.090953	.098931	.106941	.114974	.123023
	-.10	.069654	.077304	.085048	.088950	.092869	.096805	.100755	.104718	.108692	.116671	.124680	.132713	.140763
	-.20	.087393	.095044	.102788	.106690	.110609	.114545	.118495	.122457	.126432	.134410	.142420	.150453	.158503
	-.30	.105133	.112784	.120527	.124429	.128348	.132284	.136234	.140197	.144172	.152150	.160160	.168193	.176242
	-.40	.122873	.130523	.138267	.142169	.146088	.150024	.153974	.157937	.161911	.169890	.177899	.185932	.193982
30	.40	-.019020	-.011259	-.003418	.000527	.004486	.008457	.012438	.016429	.020427	.028441	.036472	.044514	.052562
	.30	-.001280	.006481	.014322	.018267	.022226	.026197	.030178	.034168	.038166	.046180	.054212	.062254	.070302
	.20	.016459	.024221	.032061	.036007	.039966	.043936	.047918	.051908	.055906	.063920	.071951	.079993	.088041
	.10	.034199	.041960	.049801	.053746	.057705	.061676	.065657	.069648	.073646	.081660	.089691	.097733	.105781
	0.00	.051938	.059700	.067541	.071486	.075445	.079416	.083397	.087387	.091385	.099399	.107431	.115473	.123521
	-.10	.069678	.077439	.085280	.089225	.093184	.097155	.101137	.105127	.109125	.117139	.125170	.133212	.141260
	-.20	.087418	.095179	.103020	.106965	.110924	.114895	.118876	.122867	.126865	.134878	.142910	.150952	.159000
	-.30	.105157	.112919	.120760	.124705	.128664	.132635	.136616	.140606	.144604	.152618	.160649	.168692	.176740
	-.40	.122897	.130658	.138499	.142444	.146403	.150374	.154356	.158346	.162344	.170358	.178389	.186431	.194479

5.0 YEAR HOLDING PERIOD
.060 EQUITY YIELD RATE
.900 LOAN RATIO

INTEREST RATE

TERM 10 YEARS

APPR DEP	5.0	6.0	7.0	7.5	8.0	8.5	9.0	9.5	10.0	11.0	12.0	13.0	14.0
.40	-.020330	-.013029	-.005600	-.001839	.001952	.005773	.009623	.013502	.017410	.025306	.033308	.041411	.049610
.30	-.002590	.004711	.012140	.015900	.019692	.023513	.027363	.031242	.035149	.043046	.051047	.059150	.067349
.20	.015150	.022450	.029879	.033640	.037431	.041252	.045103	.048981	.052889	.060785	.068787	.076890	.085089
.10	.032889	.040190	.047619	.051380	.055171	.058992	.062842	.066721	.070628	.078525	.086527	.094630	.102829
0.00	.050629	.057930	.065359	.069119	.072911	.076732	.080582	.084461	.088368	.096264	.104266	.112369	.120568
-.10	.068369	.075670	.083099	.086859	.090650	.094471	.098322	.102201	.106108	.114004	.122006	.130109	.138308
-.20	.086108	.093409	.100838	.104599	.108390	.112211	.116061	.119940	.123847	.131744	.139746	.147848	.156047
-.30	.103848	.111149	.118578	.122338	.126130	.129951	.133801	.137680	.141587	.149483	.157485	.165588	.173787
-.40	.121587	.128888	.136317	.140078	.143869	.147690	.151541	.155420	.159327	.167223	.175225	.183328	.191527

TERM 15 YEARS

APPR DEP	5.0	6.0	7.0	7.5	8.0	8.5	9.0	9.5	10.0	11.0	12.0	13.0	14.0
.40	-.020174	-.012125	-.003947	.000187	.004351	.008542	.012759	.017002	.021270	.029872	.038559	.047322	.056153
.30	-.002434	.005615	.013793	.017927	.022090	.026281	.030499	.034742	.039009	.047611	.056299	.065062	.073892
.20	.015305	.023354	.031532	.035667	.039830	.044021	.048239	.052482	.056749	.065351	.074039	.082801	.091632
.10	.033045	.041094	.049272	.053406	.057570	.061761	.065978	.070221	.074488	.083091	.091778	.100541	.109371
0.00	.050785	.058834	.067011	.071146	.075309	.079500	.083718	.087961	.092228	.100831	.109518	.118281	.127111
-.10	.068524	.076573	.084751	.088886	.093049	.097240	.101458	.105700	.109968	.118571	.127258	.136020	.144851
-.20	.086264	.094313	.102491	.106625	.110789	.114980	.119197	.123440	.127707	.136310	.144997	.153760	.162590
-.30	.104003	.112052	.120230	.124365	.128528	.132719	.136937	.141180	.145447	.154050	.162737	.171500	.180330
-.40	.121743	.129792	.137970	.142105	.146268	.150459	.154676	.158919	.163187	.171790	.180477	.189239	.198070

TERM 20 YEARS

APPR DEP	5.0	6.0	7.0	7.5	8.0	8.5	9.0	9.5	10.0	11.0	12.0	13.0	14.0
.40	-.020099	-.011693	-.003169	.001134	.005461	.009811	.014182	.018573	.022983	.031852	.040778	.049752	.058765
.30	-.002359	.006047	.014571	.018873	.023200	.027550	.031922	.036313	.040722	.049591	.058518	.067492	.076505
.20	.015381	.023786	.032311	.036613	.040940	.045290	.049661	.054052	.058462	.067331	.076257	.085231	.094245
.10	.033120	.041526	.050050	.054353	.058680	.063030	.067401	.071792	.076202	.085071	.093997	.102971	.111984
0.00	.050860	.059266	.067790	.072092	.076419	.080769	.085141	.089532	.093941	.102810	.111737	.120711	.129724
-.10	.068599	.077005	.085530	.089832	.094159	.098509	.102880	.107271	.111681	.120550	.129476	.138450	.147464
-.20	.086339	.094745	.103269	.107572	.111899	.116248	.120620	.125011	.129421	.138289	.147216	.156190	.165203
-.30	.104079	.112485	.121009	.125311	.129638	.133988	.138359	.142751	.147160	.156029	.164955	.173930	.182943
-.40	.121818	.130224	.138749	.143051	.147378	.151728	.156099	.160490	.164900	.173769	.182695	.191669	.200682

TERM 25 YEARS

APPR DEP	5.0	6.0	7.0	7.5	8.0	8.5	9.0	9.5	10.0	11.0	12.0	13.0	14.0
.40	-.020055	-.011448	-.002737	.001653	.006062	.010490	.014934	.019392	.023863	.032839	.041850	.050887	.059943
.30	-.002316	.006292	.015003	.019393	.023802	.028230	.032673	.037132	.041603	.050578	.059589	.068627	.077682
.20	.015424	.024031	.032743	.037132	.041542	.045969	.050413	.054871	.059342	.068318	.077329	.086366	.095422
.10	.033164	.041771	.050482	.054872	.059281	.063709	.068153	.072611	.077082	.086058	.095069	.104106	.113162
0.00	.050903	.059510	.068222	.072612	.077021	.081448	.085892	.090350	.094822	.103797	.112808	.121845	.130901
-.10	.068643	.077250	.085962	.090351	.094761	.099188	.103632	.108090	.112561	.121537	.130548	.139585	.148641
-.20	.086383	.094990	.103701	.108091	.112500	.116928	.121372	.125830	.130301	.139277	.148288	.157325	.166381
-.30	.104122	.112729	.121441	.125830	.130240	.134667	.139111	.143569	.148041	.157016	.166027	.175064	.184120
-.40	.121862	.130469	.139180	.143570	.147980	.152407	.156851	.161309	.165780	.174756	.183767	.192804	.201860

TERM 30 YEARS

APPR DEP	5.0	6.0	7.0	7.5	8.0	8.5	9.0	9.5	10.0	11.0	12.0	13.0	14.0
.40	-.020028	-.011296	-.002475	.001963	.006417	.010884	.015363	.019852	.024350	.033366	.042401	.051448	.060502
.30	-.002288	.006443	.015264	.019703	.024156	.028624	.033103	.037592	.042089	.051105	.060140	.069188	.078242
.20	.015451	.024183	.033004	.037442	.041896	.046363	.050842	.055331	.059829	.068845	.077880	.086927	.095982
.10	.033191	.041923	.050744	.055182	.059636	.064103	.068582	.073071	.077569	.086584	.095620	.104667	.113721
0.00	.050931	.059662	.068483	.072922	.077375	.081843	.086322	.090811	.095308	.104324	.113359	.122407	.131461
-.10	.068670	.077402	.086223	.090661	.095115	.099582	.104061	.108550	.113048	.122064	.131099	.140146	.149200
-.20	.086410	.095142	.103963	.108401	.112855	.117322	.121801	.126290	.130788	.139803	.148839	.157886	.166940
-.30	.104150	.112881	.121702	.126140	.130594	.135061	.139541	.144030	.148527	.157543	.166578	.175626	.184680
-.40	.121889	.130621	.139442	.143880	.148334	.152801	.157280	.161769	.166267	.175283	.184318	.193365	.202419

5.0 YEAR HOLDING PERIOD
.080 EQUITY YIELD RATE
.600 LOAN RATIO

INTEREST RATE

TERM YEARS	APPR DEP	5.0	6.0	7.0	7.5	8.0	8.5	9.0	9.5	10.0	11.0	12.0	13.0	14.0
10	.40	-.004606	.000210	.005112	.007594	.010097	.012619	.015162	.017723	.020304	.025520	.030807	.036162	.041582
	.30	.012439	.017256	.022158	.024640	.027143	.029665	.032208	.034769	.037350	.042566	.047853	.053208	.058628
	.20	.029485	.034301	.039203	.041686	.044188	.046711	.049253	.051814	.054395	.059611	.064898	.070253	.075673
	.10	.046531	.051347	.056249	.058731	.061234	.063756	.066299	.068860	.071441	.076657	.081944	.087299	.092719
	0.00	.063576	.068393	.073295	.075777	.078279	.080802	.083344	.085906	.088486	.093702	.098989	.104344	.109764
	-.10	.080622	.085438	.090340	.092823	.095325	.097848	.100390	.102951	.105532	.110748	.116035	.121390	.126810
	-.20	.097667	.102484	.107386	.109868	.112371	.114893	.117436	.119997	.122577	.127793	.133081	.138436	.143855
	-.30	.114713	.119530	.124432	.126914	.129416	.131939	.134481	.137043	.139623	.144839	.150126	.155481	.160901
	-.40	.131759	.136575	.141477	.143959	.146462	.148985	.151527	.154088	.156669	.161885	.167172	.172527	.177947
15	.40	-.005267	.000039	.005432	.008160	.010908	.013674	.016459	.019262	.022081	.027766	.033510	.039307	.045151
	.30	.011779	.017084	.022478	.025206	.027953	.030720	.033505	.036308	.039126	.044812	.050556	.056352	.062196
	.20	.028824	.034130	.039524	.042251	.044999	.047766	.050551	.053353	.056172	.061858	.067601	.073398	.079242
	.10	.045870	.051176	.056569	.059297	.062045	.064811	.067596	.070399	.073218	.078903	.084647	.090444	.096288
	0.00	.062916	.068221	.073615	.076343	.079090	.081857	.084642	.087444	.090263	.095949	.101693	.107489	.113333
	-.10	.079961	.085267	.090661	.093388	.096136	.098903	.101688	.104490	.107309	.112995	.118738	.124535	.130379
	-.20	.097007	.102313	.107706	.110434	.113182	.115948	.118733	.121536	.124355	.130040	.135784	.141581	.147424
	-.30	.114053	.119358	.124752	.127480	.130227	.132994	.135779	.138581	.141400	.147086	.152830	.158626	.164470
	-.40	.131098	.136404	.141797	.144525	.147273	.150040	.152824	.155627	.158446	.164131	.169875	.175672	.181516
20	.40	-.005587	-.000043	.005583	.008424	.011283	.014158	.017048	.019952	.022870	.028740	.034652	.040599	.046576
	.30	.011459	.017002	.022629	.025470	.028329	.031204	.034094	.036998	.039915	.045786	.051698	.057645	.063621
	.20	.028504	.034048	.039674	.042516	.045374	.048249	.051139	.054043	.056961	.062831	.068744	.074691	.080667
	.10	.045550	.051094	.056720	.059561	.062420	.065295	.068185	.071089	.074006	.079877	.085789	.091736	.097713
	0.00	.062595	.068139	.073766	.076607	.079466	.082340	.085231	.088135	.091052	.096923	.102835	.108782	.114758
	-.10	.079641	.085185	.090811	.093653	.096511	.099386	.102276	.105180	.108098	.113968	.119880	.125828	.131804
	-.20	.096687	.102231	.107857	.110698	.113557	.116432	.119322	.122226	.125143	.131014	.136926	.142873	.148850
	-.30	.113732	.119276	.124903	.127744	.130603	.133477	.136367	.139272	.142189	.148060	.153972	.159919	.165895
	-.40	.130778	.136322	.141948	.144790	.147648	.150523	.153413	.156317	.159235	.165105	.171017	.176965	.182941
25	.40	-.005772	-.000090	.005667	.008569	.011486	.014417	.017359	.020312	.023275	.029226	.035204	.041203	.047218
	.30	.011274	.016956	.022712	.025615	.028532	.031462	.034405	.037358	.040321	.046271	.052250	.058249	.064264
	.20	.028320	.034002	.039758	.042661	.045577	.048508	.051450	.054403	.057366	.063317	.069295	.075294	.081309
	.10	.045365	.051047	.056804	.059706	.062623	.065554	.068496	.071449	.074412	.080363	.086341	.092340	.098355
	0.00	.062411	.068093	.073849	.076752	.079669	.082599	.085542	.088495	.091458	.097408	.103386	.109386	.115401
	-.10	.079457	.085139	.090895	.093798	.096715	.099645	.102587	.105540	.108503	.114454	.120432	.126431	.132446
	-.20	.096502	.102184	.107941	.110843	.113760	.116691	.119633	.122586	.125549	.131500	.137478	.143477	.149492
	-.30	.113548	.119230	.124986	.127889	.130806	.133736	.136679	.139632	.142594	.148545	.154523	.160523	.166538
	-.40	.130594	.136275	.142032	.144935	.147852	.150782	.153724	.156677	.159640	.165591	.171569	.177568	.183583
30	.40	-.005888	-.000119	.005717	.008656	.011606	.014567	.017537	.020514	.023485	.029485	.035488	.041503	.047523
	.30	.011157	.016927	.022763	.025702	.028652	.031613	.034582	.037560	.040531	.046531	.052533	.058549	.064569
	.20	.028203	.033973	.039809	.042747	.045698	.048658	.051628	.054606	.057576	.063576	.069579	.075594	.081615
	.10	.045248	.051018	.056854	.059793	.062743	.065704	.068674	.071651	.074636	.080622	.086625	.092640	.098660
	0.00	.062294	.068064	.073900	.076838	.079789	.082749	.085719	.088697	.091682	.097667	.103670	.109685	.115706
	-.10	.079340	.085110	.090946	.093884	.096834	.099795	.102765	.105743	.108727	.114713	.120716	.126731	.132752
	-.20	.096385	.102155	.107991	.110930	.113880	.116841	.119811	.122788	.125773	.131759	.137761	.143776	.149797
	-.30	.113431	.119201	.125037	.127975	.130926	.133886	.136856	.139834	.142805	.148804	.154807	.160822	.166843
	-.40	.130477	.136247	.142083	.145021	.147971	.150932	.153902	.156880	.159850	.165850	.171853	.177867	.183888

5.0 YEAR HOLDING PERIOD
.080 EQUITY YIELD RATE
.667 LOAN RATIO

INTEREST RATE

TERM YEARS	APPR DEP	5.0	6.0	7.0	7.5	8.0	8.5	9.0	9.5	10.0	11.0	12.0	13.0	14.0
10	.40	-.006431	-.001080	.004367	.007125	.009906	.012709	.015533	.018379	.021247	.027042	.032917	.038867	.044889
	.30	.010614	.015966	.021413	.024171	.026951	.029754	.032579	.035425	.038292	.044088	.049962	.055912	.061935
	.20	.027660	.033012	.038458	.041216	.043997	.046800	.049625	.052471	.055338	.061133	.067008	.072958	.078980
	.10	.044706	.050057	.055504	.058262	.061043	.063846	.066670	.069516	.072383	.078179	.084054	.090004	.096026
	0.00	.061751	.067103	.072550	.075308	.078088	.080891	.083716	.086562	.089429	.095225	.101099	.107049	.113071
	-.10	.078797	.084149	.089595	.092353	.095134	.097937	.100762	.103608	.106475	.112270	.118145	.124095	.130117
	-.20	.095843	.101194	.106641	.109399	.112180	.114982	.117807	.120653	.123520	.129316	.135191	.141141	.147163
	-.30	.112888	.118240	.123687	.126445	.129225	.132028	.134853	.137699	.140566	.146362	.152236	.158186	.164208
	-.40	.129934	.135285	.140732	.143490	.146271	.149074	.151898	.154745	.157612	.163407	.169282	.175232	.181254
15	.40	-.007165	-.001270	.004723	.007754	.010807	.013881	.016975	.020089	.023221	.029538	.035921	.042361	.048854
	.30	.009880	.015776	.021768	.024799	.027852	.030926	.034021	.037134	.040267	.046584	.052966	.059407	.065900
	.20	.026926	.032821	.038814	.041845	.044898	.047972	.051066	.054180	.057312	.063630	.070012	.076453	.082946
	.10	.043972	.049867	.055860	.058891	.061944	.065018	.068112	.071226	.074358	.080675	.087057	.093498	.099991
	0.00	.061017	.066912	.072905	.075936	.078989	.082063	.085158	.088271	.091404	.097721	.104103	.110544	.117037
	-.10	.078063	.083958	.089951	.092982	.096035	.099109	.102203	.105317	.108449	.114767	.121149	.127589	.134083
	-.20	.095108	.101004	.106997	.110028	.113081	.116155	.119249	.122363	.125495	.131812	.138194	.144635	.151128
	-.30	.112154	.118049	.124042	.127073	.130126	.133200	.136295	.139408	.142541	.148858	.155240	.161681	.168174
	-.40	.129200	.135095	.141088	.144119	.147172	.150246	.153340	.156454	.159586	.165904	.172286	.178726	.185220
20	.40	-.007521	-.001361	.004890	.008047	.011224	.014418	.017629	.020856	.024098	.030620	.037190	.043798	.050438
	.30	.009525	.015684	.021936	.025093	.028269	.031464	.034675	.037902	.041143	.047666	.054235	.060843	.067483
	.20	.026570	.032730	.038982	.042139	.045315	.048509	.051720	.054947	.058189	.064712	.071281	.077889	.084529
	.10	.043616	.049776	.056027	.059184	.062361	.065555	.068766	.071993	.075235	.081757	.088326	.094935	.101575
	0.00	.060662	.066821	.073073	.076230	.079406	.082601	.085812	.089038	.092280	.098803	.105372	.111980	.118620
	-.10	.077707	.083867	.090119	.093276	.096452	.099646	.102857	.106084	.109326	.115849	.122418	.129026	.135666
	-.20	.094753	.100913	.107164	.110321	.113498	.116692	.119903	.123130	.126371	.132894	.139463	.146072	.152712
	-.30	.111798	.117958	.124210	.127367	.130543	.133737	.136949	.140176	.143317	.149940	.156509	.163117	.169758
	-.40	.128844	.135004	.141255	.144413	.147589	.150783	.153994	.157221	.160463	.166986	.173555	.180163	.186803
25	.40	-.007726	-.001413	.004983	.008208	.011450	.014706	.017975	.021256	.024548	.031160	.037803	.044468	.051152
	.30	.009320	.015633	.022029	.025254	.028495	.031751	.035020	.038302	.041594	.048206	.054848	.061514	.068197
	.20	.026365	.032678	.039075	.042300	.045541	.048797	.052066	.055347	.058639	.065251	.071894	.078560	.085243
	.10	.043411	.049724	.056120	.059345	.062587	.065843	.069112	.072393	.075685	.082297	.088939	.095605	.102289
	0.00	.060457	.066770	.073166	.076391	.079632	.082888	.086157	.089439	.092731	.099343	.105985	.112651	.119334
	-.10	.077502	.083815	.090211	.093437	.096678	.099934	.103203	.106484	.109776	.116388	.123031	.129697	.136380
	-.20	.094548	.100861	.107257	.110482	.113724	.116979	.120249	.123530	.126822	.133434	.140076	.146742	.153426
	-.30	.111594	.117907	.124303	.127528	.130769	.134025	.137294	.140576	.143868	.150480	.157122	.163788	.170471
	-.40	.128639	.134952	.141348	.144574	.147815	.151071	.154340	.157621	.160913	.167525	.174168	.180834	.187517
30	.40	-.007856	-.001445	.005040	.008305	.011583	.014872	.018172	.021481	.024797	.031448	.038118	.044800	.051491
	.30	.009190	.015601	.022085	.025350	.028628	.031918	.035218	.038526	.041843	.048494	.055163	.061846	.068536
	.20	.026235	.032646	.039131	.042396	.045674	.048964	.052264	.055572	.058888	.065539	.072209	.078892	.085582
	.10	.043281	.049692	.056176	.059442	.062720	.066009	.069309	.072618	.075934	.082585	.089255	.095937	.102628
	0.00	.060327	.066738	.073222	.076487	.079765	.083055	.086355	.089663	.092980	.099631	.106300	.112983	.119673
	-.10	.077372	.083783	.090268	.093533	.096811	.100101	.103400	.106709	.110025	.116676	.123346	.130028	.136719
	-.20	.094418	.100829	.107313	.110578	.113857	.117146	.120446	.123755	.127071	.133722	.140392	.147074	.153765
	-.30	.111464	.117875	.124359	.127624	.130902	.134192	.137492	.140800	.144117	.150768	.157437	.164120	.170810
	-.40	.128509	.134920	.141405	.144670	.147948	.151238	.154537	.157846	.161162	.167813	.174483	.181165	.187856

5.0 YEAR HOLDING PERIOD
.080 EQUITY YIELD RATE
.700 LOAN RATIO

INTEREST RATE

TERM YEARS	APPR DEP	5.0	6.0	7.0	7.5	8.0	8.5	9.0	9.5	10.0	11.0	12.0	13.0	14.0
10	.40	-.007344	-.001724	.003995	.006890	.009810	.012753	.015719	.018707	.021718	.027803	.033972	.040219	.046542
	.30	.009702	.015321	.021040	.023936	.026856	.029799	.032765	.035753	.038764	.044849	.051017	.057265	.063588
	.20	.026748	.032367	.038086	.040982	.043901	.046844	.049810	.052799	.055809	.061895	.068063	.074310	.080634
	.10	.043793	.049442	.055131	.058027	.060947	.063890	.066856	.069844	.072855	.078900	.085108	.091356	.097679
	0.00	.060839	.066458	.072177	.075073	.077993	.080936	.083902	.086890	.089901	.095986	.102154	.108402	.114725
	-.10	.077885	.083504	.089223	.092119	.095038	.097981	.100947	.103936	.106946	.113032	.119200	.125447	.131771
	-.20	.094930	.100549	.106268	.109164	.112084	.115027	.117993	.120981	.123992	.130077	.136245	.142493	.148816
	-.30	.111976	.117595	.123314	.126210	.129130	.132073	.135039	.138027	.141037	.147123	.153291	.159539	.165862
	-.40	.129021	.134641	.140360	.143256	.146175	.149118	.152084	.155073	.158083	.164168	.170337	.176584	.182907
15	.40	-.008114	-.001924	.004368	.007551	.010756	.013984	.017233	.020502	.023791	.030424	.037126	.043888	.050706
	.30	.008931	.015121	.021414	.024596	.027802	.031030	.034279	.037548	.040837	.047470	.054171	.060934	.067752
	.20	.025977	.032167	.038459	.041642	.044847	.048075	.051324	.054594	.057883	.064516	.071217	.077980	.084797
	.10	.043023	.049213	.055505	.058688	.061893	.065121	.068370	.071639	.074928	.081551	.088263	.095025	.101843
	0.00	.060068	.066258	.072550	.075733	.078939	.082167	.085416	.088685	.091974	.098607	.105308	.112071	.118889
	-.10	.077114	.083304	.089596	.092779	.095984	.099212	.102461	.105731	.109020	.115653	.122354	.129116	.135934
	-.20	.094160	.100349	.106642	.109824	.113030	.116258	.119507	.122776	.126065	.132698	.139399	.146162	.152980
	-.30	.111205	.117395	.123076	.126824	.130076	.133303	.136552	.139822	.143111	.149774	.156445	.163208	.170026
	-.40	.128251	.134441	.140733	.143916	.147121	.150349	.153598	.156868	.160156	.166790	.173491	.180253	.187071
20	.40	-.008488	-.002020	.004544	.007859	.011194	.014558	.017920	.021308	.024712	.031560	.038458	.045396	.052369
	.30	.008558	.015026	.021590	.024905	.028240	.031604	.034966	.038354	.041758	.048606	.055504	.062442	.069415
	.20	.025603	.032071	.038635	.041950	.045285	.048649	.052011	.055399	.058803	.065651	.072549	.079488	.086460
	.10	.042649	.049117	.055681	.058996	.062331	.065695	.069057	.072445	.075849	.082697	.089595	.096533	.103506
	0.00	.059695	.066162	.072727	.076041	.079377	.082731	.086102	.089491	.092894	.099743	.106641	.113579	.120551
	-.10	.076740	.083208	.089772	.093087	.096422	.099776	.103148	.106536	.109940	.116789	.123686	.130625	.137597
	-.20	.093786	.100254	.106818	.110133	.113468	.116822	.120194	.123582	.126985	.133834	.140732	.147670	.154643
	-.30	.110832	.117299	.123864	.127178	.130513	.133868	.137239	.140627	.144031	.150880	.157778	.164716	.171688
	-.40	.127877	.134345	.140909	.144224	.147559	.150913	.154285	.157673	.161077	.167926	.174823	.181762	.188734
25	.40	-.008703	-.002074	.004642	.008028	.011431	.014850	.018283	.021728	.025185	.032127	.039102	.046101	.053118
	.30	.008343	.014971	.021687	.025074	.028477	.031896	.035328	.038774	.042230	.049173	.056147	.063146	.070164
	.20	.025588	.032017	.038733	.042119	.045523	.048941	.052374	.055819	.059276	.066218	.073193	.080192	.087210
	.10	.042434	.049063	.055779	.059165	.062568	.065987	.069420	.072865	.076321	.083264	.090239	.097238	.104255
	0.00	.059480	.066108	.072824	.076211	.079613	.083033	.086465	.089910	.093367	.100310	.107284	.114283	.121301
	-.10	.076525	.083154	.089870	.093256	.096660	.100078	.103511	.106956	.110413	.117355	.124330	.131329	.138346
	-.20	.093571	.100200	.106915	.110302	.113705	.117124	.120556	.124002	.127458	.134401	.141376	.148375	.155392
	-.30	.110616	.117245	.123961	.127348	.130751	.134169	.137602	.141047	.144504	.151446	.158421	.165420	.172466
	-.40	.127662	.134291	.141007	.144393	.147796	.151215	.154648	.158093	.161550	.168492	.175467	.182466	.189483
30	.40	-.008839	-.002108	.004701	.008129	.011571	.015025	.018490	.021964	.025446	.032429	.039433	.046449	.053474
	.30	.008206	.014938	.021746	.025175	.028617	.032071	.035536	.039010	.042492	.049475	.056478	.063495	.070520
	.20	.025252	.031983	.038792	.042220	.045662	.049116	.052581	.056055	.059537	.066521	.073524	.080541	.087566
	.10	.042297	.049029	.055838	.059266	.062708	.066162	.069627	.073101	.076583	.083566	.090570	.097586	.104611
	0.00	.059343	.066075	.072883	.076312	.079754	.083208	.086672	.090147	.093629	.100612	.107615	.114632	.121657
	-.10	.076389	.083120	.089929	.093357	.096799	.100253	.103718	.107192	.110674	.117658	.124661	.131677	.138703
	-.20	.093434	.100166	.106975	.110403	.113845	.117299	.120764	.124238	.127720	.134703	.141707	.148723	.155769
	-.30	.110480	.117212	.124020	.127449	.130891	.134345	.137809	.141283	.144765	.151749	.158752	.165769	.172794
	-.40	.127526	.134257	.141066	.144494	.147936	.151390	.154855	.158329	.161811	.168795	.175798	.182814	.189839

5.0 YEAR HOLDING PERIOD
.080 EQUITY YIELD RATE
.750 LOAN RATIO

INTEREST RATE

TERM YEARS	APPR DEP	5.0	6.0	7.0	7.5	8.0	8.5	9.0	9.5	10.0	11.0	12.0	13.0	14.0
10	.40	-.008712	-.002692	.003436	.006539	.009667	.012820	.015998	.019200	.022425	.028945	.035554	.042248	.049023
	.30	.008333	.014354	.020481	.023584	.026712	.029866	.033043	.036245	.039471	.045991	.052600	.059293	.066068
	.20	.025379	.031400	.037527	.040630	.043758	.046911	.050089	.053291	.056516	.063036	.069645	.076339	.083114
	.10	.042425	.048445	.054573	.057675	.060804	.063957	.067135	.070337	.073562	.080082	.086691	.093385	.100160
	0.00	.059470	.065491	.071618	.074721	.077849	.081003	.084180	.087382	.090608	.097128	.103737	.110430	.117205
	-.10	.076516	.082536	.088664	.091767	.094895	.098048	.101226	.104428	.107653	.114173	.120782	.127476	.134251
	-.20	.093562	.099582	.105710	.108812	.111941	.115094	.118272	.121474	.124699	.131219	.137828	.144522	.151297
	-.30	.110607	.116628	.122755	.125858	.128986	.132140	.135317	.138519	.141745	.148265	.154873	.161567	.168342
	-.40	.127653	.133673	.139801	.142904	.146032	.149185	.152363	.155565	.158790	.165310	.171919	.178613	.185388
15	.40	-.009538	-.002906	.003836	.007246	.010680	.014139	.017620	.021123	.024647	.031754	.038933	.046179	.053484
	.30	.007508	.014140	.020882	.024291	.027726	.031184	.034665	.038168	.041692	.048799	.055979	.063225	.070530
	.20	.024553	.031185	.037927	.041337	.044772	.048230	.051711	.055214	.058738	.065845	.073025	.080270	.087575
	.10	.041599	.048231	.054973	.058383	.061817	.065276	.068757	.072260	.075784	.082890	.090070	.097316	.104621
	0.00	.058645	.065277	.072019	.075428	.078863	.082321	.085802	.089305	.092829	.099936	.107116	.114362	.121667
	-.10	.075690	.082322	.089064	.092474	.095909	.099367	.102848	.106351	.109875	.116982	.124162	.131407	.138712
	-.20	.092736	.099368	.106110	.109520	.112954	.116413	.119894	.123397	.126920	.134027	.141207	.148453	.155758
	-.30	.109782	.116414	.123155	.126565	.130000	.133459	.136939	.140442	.143966	.151073	.158253	.165499	.172803
	-.40	.126827	.133459	.140201	.143611	.147046	.150504	.153985	.157488	.161012	.168119	.175298	.182544	.189849
20	.40	-.009938	-.003008	.004024	.007576	.011149	.014743	.018356	.021986	.025633	.032971	.040361	.047795	.055265
	.30	.007107	.014037	.021070	.024622	.028195	.031789	.035401	.039031	.042678	.050016	.057407	.064841	.072311
	.20	.024153	.031083	.038116	.041667	.045241	.048834	.052447	.056077	.059724	.067062	.074452	.081886	.089357
	.10	.041199	.048128	.055161	.058713	.062286	.065880	.069493	.073123	.076770	.084108	.091498	.098932	.106402
	0.00	.058244	.065174	.072207	.075759	.079332	.082926	.086538	.090168	.093815	.101153	.108544	.115978	.123448
	-.10	.075290	.082220	.089253	.092804	.096378	.099971	.103584	.107214	.110861	.118199	.125589	.133023	.140494
	-.20	.092336	.099265	.106298	.109850	.113423	.117017	.120629	.124260	.127906	.135245	.142635	.150069	.157540
	-.30	.109381	.116311	.123344	.126896	.130469	.134063	.137675	.141305	.144952	.152290	.159680	.167115	.174585
	-.40	.126427	.133357	.140390	.143941	.147515	.151108	.154721	.158351	.161998	.169336	.176726	.184160	.191631
25	.40	-.010169	-.003067	.004129	.007757	.011404	.015067	.018744	.022436	.026139	.033578	.041051	.048550	.056068
	.30	.006877	.013979	.021175	.024803	.028449	.032112	.035790	.039481	.043185	.050623	.058096	.065595	.073114
	.20	.023922	.031025	.038220	.041849	.045495	.049158	.052836	.056527	.060231	.067669	.075142	.082641	.090160
	.10	.040968	.048070	.055266	.058894	.062541	.066204	.069881	.073573	.077276	.084715	.092187	.099687	.107205
	0.00	.058014	.065116	.072312	.075940	.079586	.083249	.086927	.090618	.094322	.101760	.109233	.116732	.124251
	-.10	.075059	.082162	.089357	.092986	.096632	.100295	.103973	.107664	.111368	.118806	.126279	.133778	.141297
	-.20	.092105	.099207	.106403	.110031	.113678	.117340	.121018	.124710	.128413	.135852	.143324	.150824	.158342
	-.30	.109151	.116253	.123449	.127077	.130723	.134386	.138064	.141755	.145459	.152897	.160370	.167869	.175388
	-.40	.126196	.133299	.140494	.144122	.147769	.151432	.155110	.158801	.162504	.169943	.177416	.184915	.192434
30	.40	-.010315	-.003103	.004192	.007866	.011553	.015254	.018967	.022689	.026419	.033902	.041405	.048923	.056450
	.30	.006731	.013943	.021238	.024911	.028599	.032300	.036012	.039734	.043465	.050947	.058451	.065969	.073495
	.20	.023776	.030989	.038284	.041957	.045645	.049346	.053058	.056780	.060511	.067993	.075496	.083014	.090541
	.10	.040822	.048034	.055329	.059002	.062690	.066391	.070103	.073826	.077556	.085039	.092542	.100060	.107587
	0.00	.057868	.065080	.072375	.076048	.079736	.083437	.087149	.090871	.094602	.102084	.109588	.117105	.124632
	-.10	.074913	.082126	.089421	.093094	.096782	.100483	.104195	.107917	.111648	.119130	.126633	.134151	.141678
	-.20	.091959	.099171	.106466	.110139	.113827	.117528	.121240	.124963	.128693	.136176	.143679	.151197	.158724
	-.30	.109005	.116217	.123512	.127185	.130873	.134574	.138286	.142008	.145739	.153221	.160725	.168242	.175769
	-.40	.126050	.133263	.140557	.144231	.147919	.151619	.155332	.159054	.162785	.170267	.177770	.185288	.192815

5.0 YEAR HOLDING PERIOD
.080 EQUITY YIELD RATE
.800 LOAN RATIO

INTEREST RATE

TERM YEARS	APPR DEP	5.0	6.0	7.0	7.5	8.0	8.5	9.0	9.5	10.0	11.0	12.0	13.0	14.0
10	.40	-.010081	-.003659	.002877	.006187	.009523	.012887	.016276	.019692	.023132	.030087	.037136	.044276	.051503
	.30	.006965	.013387	.019923	.023232	.026569	.029932	.033322	.036737	.040178	.047133	.054182	.061322	.068549
	.20	.024010	.030432	.036968	.040278	.043615	.046978	.050368	.053783	.057224	.064178	.071228	.078368	.085594
	.10	.041056	.047478	.054014	.057324	.060660	.064024	.067413	.070829	.074269	.081224	.088273	.095413	.102640
	0.00	.058102	.064524	.071060	.074369	.077706	.081069	.084459	.087874	.091315	.098270	.105319	.112459	.119686
	-.10	.075147	.081569	.088105	.091415	.094752	.098115	.101505	.104920	.108361	.115315	.122365	.129505	.136731
	-.20	.092193	.098615	.105151	.108460	.111797	.115161	.118550	.121966	.125406	.132361	.139410	.146550	.153777
	-.30	.109239	.115660	.122196	.125506	.128843	.132206	.135596	.139011	.142452	.149406	.156456	.163596	.170822
	-.40	.126284	.132706	.139242	.142552	.145889	.149252	.152642	.156057	.159497	.166452	.173502	.180642	.187868
15	.40	-.010962	-.003888	.003304	.006941	.010605	.014293	.018007	.021743	.025502	.033083	.040741	.048470	.056262
	.30	.006084	.013158	.020350	.023987	.027650	.031339	.035052	.038789	.042548	.050128	.057787	.065515	.073307
	.20	.023130	.030203	.037395	.041032	.044696	.048385	.052098	.055834	.059593	.067174	.074832	.082561	.090353
	.10	.040175	.047249	.054441	.058078	.061742	.065430	.069144	.072880	.076639	.084220	.091878	.099607	.107399
	0.00	.057221	.064295	.071486	.075124	.078787	.082476	.086189	.089926	.093684	.101265	.108924	.116652	.124444
	-.10	.074267	.081341	.088532	.092169	.095833	.099522	.103235	.106971	.110730	.118311	.125969	.133698	.141490
	-.20	.091312	.098386	.105578	.109215	.112878	.116567	.120280	.124017	.127776	.135356	.143015	.150744	.158536
	-.30	.108358	.115432	.122623	.126261	.129924	.133613	.137326	.141063	.144821	.152402	.160061	.167789	.175581
	-.40	.125404	.132478	.139669	.143306	.146970	.150659	.154372	.158108	.161867	.169448	.177106	.184835	.192627
20	.40	-.011389	-.003997	.003505	.007293	.011105	.014938	.018791	.022664	.026554	.034381	.042264	.050194	.058162
	.30	.005657	.013049	.020551	.024339	.028151	.031984	.035837	.039709	.043599	.051427	.059309	.067239	.075208
	.20	.022703	.030094	.037596	.041385	.045196	.049029	.052883	.056755	.060645	.068472	.076355	.084285	.092253
	.10	.039748	.047140	.054642	.058430	.062242	.066075	.069928	.073801	.077691	.085518	.093401	.101330	.109299
	0.00	.056794	.064186	.071688	.075476	.079287	.083121	.086974	.090846	.094736	.102563	.110446	.118376	.126345
	-.10	.073840	.081231	.088733	.092522	.096333	.100166	.104020	.107892	.111782	.119609	.127492	.135422	.143390
	-.20	.090885	.098277	.105779	.109567	.113379	.117212	.121065	.124938	.128827	.136655	.144538	.152467	.160436
	-.30	.107931	.115323	.122824	.126613	.130424	.134258	.138111	.141983	.145873	.153700	.161583	.169513	.177481
	-.40	.124977	.132368	.139870	.143659	.147470	.151303	.155157	.159029	.162919	.170746	.178629	.186559	.194527
25	.40	-.011635	-.004059	.003616	.007487	.011376	.015283	.019206	.023144	.027094	.035028	.042999	.050998	.059018
	.30	.005411	.012987	.020662	.024532	.028422	.032329	.036252	.040189	.044140	.052074	.060045	.068044	.076064
	.20	.022457	.030033	.037708	.041578	.045467	.049374	.053298	.057235	.061185	.069120	.077091	.085090	.093110
	.10	.039502	.047078	.054753	.058624	.062513	.066420	.070343	.074281	.078231	.086165	.094136	.102135	.110155
	0.00	.056548	.064124	.071799	.075669	.079559	.083466	.087389	.091326	.095277	.103211	.111182	.119181	.127201
	-.10	.073594	.081169	.088845	.092715	.096604	.100511	.104434	.108372	.112322	.120257	.128228	.136227	.144247
	-.20	.090639	.098215	.105890	.109761	.113650	.117557	.121480	.125418	.129368	.137302	.145273	.153272	.161292
	-.30	.107685	.115261	.122936	.126806	.130696	.134603	.138526	.142463	.146414	.154348	.162319	.170318	.178338
	-.40	.124731	.132306	.139982	.143852	.147741	.151648	.155571	.159509	.163459	.171394	.179365	.187364	.195384
30	.40	-.011790	-.004097	.003684	.007602	.011536	.015483	.019443	.023413	.027393	.035374	.043378	.051397	.059425
	.30	.005255	.012948	.020730	.024648	.028581	.032529	.036489	.040459	.044439	.052420	.060423	.068442	.076471
	.20	.022301	.029994	.037775	.041693	.045627	.049575	.053534	.057505	.061484	.069465	.077469	.085488	.093517
	.10	.039346	.047040	.054821	.058739	.062673	.066620	.070580	.074550	.078530	.086511	.094515	.102534	.110562
	0.00	.056392	.064085	.071867	.075785	.079718	.083666	.087626	.091596	.095575	.103557	.111560	.119579	.127608
	-.10	.073438	.081131	.088912	.092830	.096764	.100712	.104671	.108642	.112621	.120602	.128606	.136625	.144654
	-.20	.090483	.098177	.105958	.109876	.113810	.117757	.121717	.125687	.129667	.137648	.145652	.153670	.161699
	-.30	.107529	.115222	.123004	.126922	.130855	.134803	.138763	.142733	.146712	.154694	.162697	.170716	.178745
	-.40	.124575	.132268	.140049	.143967	.147901	.151849	.155808	.159779	.163758	.171739	.179743	.187762	.195790

5.0 YEAR HOLDING PERIOD
.080 EQUITY YIELD RATE
.900 LOAN RATIO

INTEREST RATE

TERM YEARS	APPR DEP	5.0	6.0	7.0	7.5	8.0	8.5	9.0	9.5	10.0	11.0	12.0	13.0	14.0
10	.40	-.012818	-.005594	.001759	.005483	.009237	.013021	.016834	.020676	.024547	.032371	.040301	.048334	.056464
	.30	.004227	.011452	.018805	.022528	.026282	.030066	.033879	.037722	.041592	.049416	.057347	.065379	.073510
	.20	.021273	.028498	.035851	.039574	.043328	.047112	.050925	.054767	.058638	.066462	.074393	.082425	.090555
	.10	.038319	.045543	.052896	.056620	.060374	.064157	.067971	.071813	.075684	.083508	.091438	.099471	.107601
	0.00	.055364	.062589	.069942	.073665	.077419	.081203	.085016	.088859	.092729	.100553	.108484	.116516	.124646
	-.10	.072410	.079635	.086988	.090711	.094465	.098249	.102062	.105904	.109775	.117599	.125529	.133562	.141692
	-.20	.089456	.096680	.104033	.107757	.111511	.115294	.119108	.122950	.126821	.134645	.142575	.150608	.158738
	-.30	.106501	.113726	.121079	.124802	.128556	.132340	.136153	.139996	.143866	.151690	.159621	.167653	.175783
	-.40	.123547	.130772	.138125	.141848	.145602	.149386	.153199	.157041	.160912	.168736	.176666	.184699	.192829
15	.40	-.013809	-.005851	.002240	.006332	.010453	.014603	.018780	.022984	.027212	.035741	.044356	.053051	.061817
	.30	.003237	.011195	.019285	.023377	.027499	.031649	.035826	.040029	.044258	.052786	.061402	.070097	.078863
	.20	.020282	.028241	.036331	.040423	.044544	.048694	.052872	.057075	.061304	.069832	.078448	.087143	.095909
	.10	.037328	.045286	.053377	.057468	.061590	.065740	.069917	.074121	.078349	.086878	.095493	.104188	.112954
	0.00	.054374	.062332	.070422	.074514	.078636	.082786	.086963	.091166	.095395	.103923	.112539	.121234	.130000
	-.10	.071419	.079378	.087468	.091560	.095681	.099831	.104008	.108212	.112441	.120969	.129585	.138280	.147045
	-.20	.088465	.096423	.104514	.108605	.112727	.116877	.121054	.125258	.129486	.138015	.146630	.155325	.164091
	-.30	.105510	.113469	.121559	.125651	.129773	.133922	.138100	.142303	.146532	.155060	.163676	.172371	.181137
	-.40	.122556	.130514	.138605	.142697	.146818	.150968	.155145	.159349	.163578	.172106	.180722	.189416	.198182
20	.40	-.014289	-.005974	.002466	.006728	.011016	.015328	.019663	.024020	.028396	.037201	.046070	.054991	.063955
	.30	.002757	.011072	.019512	.023774	.028061	.032374	.036709	.041065	.045441	.054247	.063115	.072036	.081001
	.20	.019802	.028118	.036557	.040819	.045107	.049419	.053755	.058111	.062487	.071293	.080161	.089082	.098046
	.10	.036848	.045163	.053603	.057865	.062153	.066465	.070800	.075156	.079533	.088338	.097207	.106127	.115092
	0.00	.053893	.062209	.070648	.074910	.079198	.083511	.087846	.092202	.096578	.105384	.114252	.123173	.132138
	-.10	.070939	.079255	.087694	.091956	.096244	.100556	.104891	.109248	.113624	.122430	.131298	.140219	.149183
	-.20	.087984	.096300	.104740	.109002	.113290	.117602	.121937	.126293	.130669	.139475	.148344	.157264	.166229
	-.30	.105030	.113346	.121785	.126047	.130335	.134648	.138983	.143339	.147715	.156521	.165389	.174310	.183275
	-.40	.122076	.130391	.138831	.143093	.147381	.151693	.156028	.160385	.164761	.173567	.182435	.191356	.200320
25	.40	-.014566	-.006043	.002591	.006945	.011321	.015716	.020130	.024559	.029004	.037930	.046897	.055896	.064919
	.30	.002480	.011002	.019637	.023991	.028367	.032762	.037175	.041605	.046049	.054975	.063943	.072942	.081964
	.20	.019525	.028048	.036683	.041037	.045412	.049808	.054221	.058651	.063095	.072021	.080988	.089987	.099010
	.10	.036571	.045094	.053728	.058082	.062458	.066853	.071267	.075696	.080141	.089067	.098034	.107033	.116055
	0.00	.053617	.062139	.070774	.075128	.079504	.083899	.088312	.092742	.097186	.106112	.115080	.124079	.133101
	-.10	.070662	.079185	.087820	.092173	.096549	.100945	.105358	.109788	.114232	.123158	.132125	.141124	.150147
	-.20	.087708	.096231	.104865	.109219	.113595	.117990	.122404	.126833	.131278	.140204	.149171	.158170	.167192
	-.30	.104753	.113276	.121911	.126265	.130640	.135036	.139449	.143879	.148323	.157249	.166217	.175216	.184238
	-.40	.121799	.130322	.138957	.143310	.147686	.152082	.156495	.160925	.165369	.174295	.183262	.192261	.201284
30	.40	-.014741	-.006086	.002667	.007075	.011501	.015942	.020396	.024863	.029340	.038319	.047323	.056344	.065376
	.30	.002304	.010959	.019713	.024121	.028546	.032987	.037442	.041909	.046385	.055364	.064368	.073390	.082422
	.20	.019350	.028005	.036759	.041166	.045592	.050033	.054488	.058954	.063431	.072410	.081414	.090435	.099468
	.10	.036395	.045050	.053804	.058212	.062638	.067079	.071533	.076000	.080477	.089456	.098460	.107481	.116513
	0.00	.053441	.062096	.070850	.075258	.079683	.084124	.088579	.093046	.097522	.106501	.115505	.124527	.133559
	-.10	.070487	.079142	.087896	.092303	.096729	.101170	.105625	.110091	.114568	.123547	.132551	.141572	.150604
	-.20	.087532	.096187	.104941	.109349	.113774	.118216	.122670	.127137	.131614	.140592	.149597	.158618	.167650
	-.30	.104578	.113233	.121987	.126395	.130820	.135261	.139716	.144182	.148659	.157638	.166642	.175664	.184696
	-.40	.121624	.130279	.139032	.143440	.147866	.152307	.156762	.161228	.165705	.174684	.183688	.192709	.201741

5.0 YEAR HOLDING PERIOD
.100 EQUITY YIELD RATE
.600 LOAN RATIO

INTEREST RATE

TERM YEARS	APPR DEP	5.0	6.0	7.0	7.5	8.0	8.5	9.0	9.5	10.0	11.0	12.0	13.0	14.0
10	.40	.007807	.012575	.017428	.019886	.022365	.024864	.027383	.029921	.032478	.037647	.042889	.048199	.053574
	.30	.024187	.028954	.033808	.036266	.038745	.041244	.043762	.046300	.048857	.054027	.059268	.064579	.069954
	.20	.040566	.045334	.050188	.052646	.055125	.057623	.060142	.062680	.065237	.070407	.075648	.080958	.086334
	.10	.056946	.061714	.066568	.069026	.071504	.074003	.076522	.079060	.081617	.086787	.092028	.097338	.102714
	0.00	.073326	.078094	.082947	.085405	.087884	.090383	.092902	.095440	.097997	.103166	.108408	.113718	.119093
	-.10	.089706	.094473	.099327	.101785	.104264	.106763	.109281	.111819	.114376	.119546	.124787	.130098	.135473
	-.20	.106085	.110853	.115707	.118165	.120644	.123142	.125661	.128199	.130756	.135926	.141167	.146477	.151853
	-.30	.122465	.127233	.132087	.134545	.137023	.139522	.142041	.144579	.147136	.152306	.157547	.162857	.168233
	-.40	.138845	.143613	.148466	.150924	.153403	.155902	.158421	.160959	.163516	.168685	.173927	.179237	.184612
15	.40	.006413	.011661	.016998	.019699	.022420	.025160	.027919	.030696	.033491	.039129	.044827	.050580	.056383
	.30	.022793	.028041	.033378	.036079	.038800	.041540	.044299	.047076	.049871	.055508	.061207	.066960	.072762
	.20	.039173	.044420	.049758	.052458	.055179	.057920	.060679	.063456	.066250	.071888	.077586	.083340	.089142
	.10	.055552	.060800	.066138	.068838	.071559	.074299	.077058	.079836	.082630	.088268	.093966	.099719	.105522
	0.00	.071932	.077180	.082517	.085218	.087939	.090679	.093438	.096215	.099010	.104648	.110346	.116099	.121902
	-.10	.088312	.093560	.098897	.101598	.104318	.107059	.109818	.112595	.115390	.121027	.126726	.132479	.138281
	-.20	.104692	.109939	.115277	.117977	.120698	.123439	.126198	.128975	.131769	.137407	.143105	.148859	.154661
	-.30	.121071	.126319	.131657	.134357	.137078	.139818	.142577	.145355	.148149	.153787	.159485	.165238	.171041
	-.40	.137451	.142699	.148036	.150737	.153458	.156198	.158957	.161734	.164529	.170167	.175865	.181618	.187421
20	.40	.005738	.011224	.016796	.019611	.022445	.025296	.028163	.031045	.033941	.039771	.045646	.051559	.057504
	.30	.022117	.027603	.033175	.035991	.038825	.041676	.044542	.047424	.050320	.056150	.062025	.067939	.073884
	.20	.038497	.043983	.049555	.052371	.055205	.058055	.060922	.063804	.066700	.072530	.078405	.084318	.090264
	.10	.054877	.060363	.065935	.068751	.071584	.074435	.077302	.080184	.083080	.088910	.094785	.100698	.106643
	0.00	.071257	.076743	.082315	.085130	.087964	.090815	.093682	.096564	.099460	.105290	.111165	.117078	.123023
	-.10	.087636	.093122	.098694	.101510	.104344	.107195	.110061	.112943	.115839	.121669	.127544	.133458	.139403
	-.20	.104016	.109502	.115074	.117890	.120724	.123574	.126441	.129323	.132219	.138049	.143924	.149837	.155783
	-.30	.120396	.125882	.131454	.134270	.137103	.139954	.142821	.145703	.148599	.154429	.160304	.166217	.172162
	-.40	.136775	.142262	.147834	.150649	.153483	.156334	.159201	.162083	.164979	.170809	.176684	.182597	.188542
25	.40	.005348	.010976	.016683	.019563	.022459	.025369	.028291	.031226	.034172	.040091	.046041	.052016	.058009
	.30	.021728	.027356	.033063	.035943	.038838	.041748	.044671	.047606	.050551	.056471	.062421	.068396	.074389
	.20	.038108	.043736	.049443	.052323	.055218	.058128	.061051	.063986	.066931	.072850	.078801	.084775	.090769
	.10	.054488	.060115	.065823	.068702	.071598	.074508	.077431	.080365	.083311	.089230	.095180	.101155	.107149
	0.00	.070867	.076495	.082202	.085082	.087978	.090888	.093810	.096745	.099691	.105610	.111560	.117535	.123528
	-.10	.087247	.092875	.098582	.101462	.104357	.107267	.110190	.113125	.116070	.121990	.127940	.133915	.139908
	-.20	.103627	.109255	.114962	.117842	.120737	.123647	.126570	.129505	.132450	.138369	.144320	.150294	.156288
	-.30	.120007	.125634	.131342	.134221	.137117	.140027	.142950	.145884	.148830	.154749	.160699	.166674	.172668
	-.40	.136386	.142014	.147721	.150601	.153497	.156407	.159329	.162264	.165210	.171129	.177079	.183054	.189047
30	.40	.005102	.010823	.016615	.019535	.022467	.025411	.028365	.031328	.034299	.040262	.046245	.052242	.058250
	.30	.021481	.027202	.032995	.035914	.038847	.041790	.044745	.047708	.050679	.056641	.062624	.068622	.074629
	.20	.037861	.043582	.049375	.052294	.055226	.058170	.061124	.064088	.067059	.073021	.079004	.085002	.091009
	.10	.054241	.059962	.065755	.068674	.071606	.074550	.077504	.080467	.083439	.089401	.095384	.101381	.107389
	0.00	.070621	.076342	.082134	.085054	.087986	.090930	.093884	.096847	.099818	.105781	.111764	.117761	.123769
	-.10	.087000	.092721	.098514	.101433	.104366	.107309	.110264	.113227	.116198	.122160	.128143	.134141	.140148
	-.20	.103380	.109101	.114894	.117813	.120745	.123689	.126643	.129607	.132578	.138540	.144523	.150521	.156528
	-.30	.119760	.125481	.131274	.134193	.137125	.140069	.143023	.145986	.148958	.154920	.160903	.166900	.172908
	-.40	.136140	.141861	.147653	.150573	.153505	.156449	.159403	.162366	.165337	.171300	.177283	.183280	.189288

5.0 YEAR HOLDING PERIOD
.100 EQUITY YIELD RATE
.667 LOAN RATIO

INTEREST RATE

TERM YEARS	APPR DEP	5.0	6.0	7.0	7.5	8.0	8.5	9.0	9.5	10.0	11.0	12.0	13.0	14.0
10	.40	.004843	.010141	.015533	.018265	.021019	.023795	.026594	.029414	.032255	.037999	.043823	.049723	.055696
	.30	.021223	.026522	.031913	.034645	.037399	.040175	.042974	.045794	.048635	.054379	.060203	.066103	.072076
	.20	.037603	.042900	.048293	.051024	.053778	.056555	.059353	.062173	.065014	.070759	.076582	.082483	.088456
	.10	.053982	.059280	.064673	.067404	.070158	.072935	.075733	.078553	.081394	.087138	.092962	.098862	.104835
	0.00	.070362	.075659	.081052	.083784	.086538	.089314	.092113	.094933	.097774	.103518	.109342	.115242	.121215
	-.10	.086742	.092039	.097432	.100164	.102918	.105694	.108493	.111313	.114154	.119898	.125722	.131622	.137595
	-.20	.103122	.108419	.113812	.116543	.119297	.122074	.124872	.127692	.130533	.136278	.142101	.148002	.153975
	-.30	.119501	.124799	.130192	.132923	.135677	.138454	.141252	.144072	.146913	.152657	.158481	.164381	.170354
	-.40	.135881	.141178	.146571	.149303	.152057	.154833	.157632	.160452	.163293	.169037	.174861	.180761	.186734
15	.40	.003294	.009125	.015056	.018056	.021080	.024124	.027190	.030276	.033381	.039645	.045976	.052369	.058816
	.30	.019674	.025505	.031435	.034436	.037459	.040504	.043570	.046656	.049761	.056025	.062356	.068749	.075196
	.20	.036054	.041885	.047815	.050816	.053839	.056884	.059950	.063035	.066140	.072405	.078736	.085128	.091576
	.10	.052434	.058264	.064195	.067196	.070219	.073264	.076329	.079415	.082520	.088784	.095116	.101508	.107956
	0.00	.068813	.074644	.080575	.083575	.086599	.089643	.092709	.095795	.098900	.105164	.111495	.117888	.124335
	-.10	.085193	.091024	.096954	.099955	.102978	.106023	.109089	.112175	.115280	.121544	.127875	.134268	.140715
	-.20	.101573	.107404	.113334	.116335	.119358	.122403	.125469	.128554	.131659	.137924	.144255	.150647	.157095
	-.30	.117953	.123783	.129714	.132715	.135738	.138783	.141848	.144934	.148039	.154303	.160635	.167027	.173475
	-.40	.134332	.140163	.146094	.149094	.152118	.155162	.158228	.161314	.164419	.170683	.177014	.183407	.189854
20	.40	.002544	.008639	.014831	.017959	.021108	.024275	.027461	.030663	.033881	.040358	.046886	.053456	.060062
	.30	.018923	.025019	.031210	.034487	.037487	.040655	.043840	.047043	.050260	.056738	.063266	.069836	.076442
	.20	.035303	.041399	.047590	.050719	.053867	.057035	.060220	.063422	.066640	.073118	.079646	.086216	.092822
	.10	.051683	.057779	.063970	.067098	.070247	.073414	.076600	.079802	.083020	.089498	.096025	.102596	.109202
	0.00	.068063	.074158	.080350	.083478	.086627	.089794	.092980	.096182	.099400	.105877	.112405	.118975	.125581
	-.10	.084442	.090538	.096729	.099858	.103006	.106174	.109359	.112562	.115779	.122257	.128785	.135355	.141961
	-.20	.100822	.106918	.113109	.116238	.119386	.122554	.125739	.128941	.132159	.138637	.145165	.151735	.158341
	-.30	.117202	.123298	.129489	.132617	.135766	.138933	.142119	.145321	.148539	.155017	.161544	.168115	.174721
	-.40	.133582	.139677	.145869	.148997	.152146	.155313	.158499	.161701	.164918	.171396	.177924	.184494	.191100
25	.40	.002111	.008364	.014706	.017906	.021123	.024356	.027604	.030865	.034137	.040714	.047326	.053964	.060624
	.30	.018491	.024744	.031086	.034285	.037503	.040736	.043983	.047244	.050517	.057094	.063705	.070344	.077004
	.20	.034871	.041124	.047465	.050665	.053882	.057115	.060363	.063624	.066897	.073474	.080085	.086724	.093383
	.10	.051250	.057504	.063845	.067045	.070262	.073495	.076743	.080004	.083277	.089853	.096465	.103104	.109763
	0.00	.067630	.073883	.080225	.083425	.086642	.089875	.093123	.096383	.099656	.106233	.112845	.119483	.126143
	-.10	.084010	.090263	.096605	.099804	.103022	.106255	.109502	.112763	.116036	.122613	.129224	.135863	.142523
	-.20	.100390	.106643	.112984	.116184	.119401	.122634	.125882	.129143	.132416	.138993	.145604	.152243	.158902
	-.30	.116769	.123023	.129364	.132564	.135781	.139014	.142262	.145523	.148796	.155372	.161984	.168623	.175282
	-.40	.133149	.139402	.145744	.148944	.152161	.155394	.158642	.161902	.165175	.171752	.178364	.185002	.191662
30	.40	.001837	.008194	.014630	.017874	.021132	.024403	.027685	.030978	.034279	.040904	.047552	.054216	.060891
	.30	.018217	.024573	.031010	.034253	.037512	.040783	.044065	.047358	.050659	.057284	.063931	.070595	.077270
	.20	.034597	.040953	.047390	.050633	.053891	.057162	.060445	.063739	.067039	.073664	.080311	.086975	.093650
	.10	.050976	.057333	.063769	.067013	.070271	.073542	.076825	.080117	.083419	.090043	.096691	.103355	.110030
	0.00	.067356	.073713	.080149	.083393	.086651	.089922	.093204	.096497	.099798	.106423	.113071	.119735	.126410
	-.10	.083736	.090092	.096529	.099772	.103031	.106302	.109584	.112877	.116178	.122803	.129450	.136114	.142789
	-.20	.100116	.106472	.112909	.116152	.119410	.122681	.125964	.129256	.132558	.139183	.145830	.152494	.159169
	-.30	.116495	.122852	.129288	.132532	.135790	.139061	.142344	.145636	.148938	.155562	.162210	.168874	.175549
	-.40	.132875	.139232	.145668	.148912	.152170	.155441	.158723	.162016	.165317	.171942	.178590	.185254	.191929

5.0 YEAR HOLDING PERIOD
.100 EQUITY YIELD RATE
.700 LOAN RATIO

INTEREST RATE

TERM YEARS	APPR DEP	5.0	6.0	7.0	7.5	8.0	8.5	9.0	9.5	10.0	11.0	12.0	13.0	14.0
10	.40	.003361	.008924	.014586	.017454	.020346	.023261	.026199	.029160	.032144	.038175	.044290	.050485	.056757
	.30	.019741	.025303	.030966	.033834	.036726	.039641	.042579	.045540	.048523	.054555	.060670	.066865	.073136
	.20	.036121	.041683	.047346	.050214	.053105	.056021	.058959	.061920	.064903	.070934	.077049	.083245	.089516
	.10	.052501	.058063	.063725	.066593	.069485	.072400	.075339	.078300	.081283	.087314	.093429	.099624	.105896
	0.00	.068880	.074443	.080105	.082973	.085865	.088780	.091718	.094679	.097663	.103694	.109809	.116004	.122276
	-.10	.085260	.090822	.096485	.099353	.102245	.105160	.108098	.111059	.114042	.120074	.126189	.132384	.138655
	-.20	.101640	.107202	.112865	.115733	.118624	.121540	.124478	.127439	.130422	.136453	.142568	.148764	.155035
	-.30	.118020	.123582	.129244	.132112	.135004	.137919	.140858	.143819	.146802	.152833	.158948	.165143	.171415
	-.40	.134399	.139962	.145624	.148492	.151384	.154299	.157237	.160198	.163182	.169213	.175328	.181523	.187795
15	.40	.001735	.007857	.014084	.017235	.020410	.023607	.026826	.030066	.033326	.039903	.046551	.053263	.060033
	.30	.018115	.024237	.030464	.033615	.036789	.039986	.043205	.046445	.049706	.056283	.062931	.069643	.076413
	.20	.034495	.040617	.046844	.049995	.053169	.056366	.059585	.062825	.066085	.072663	.079311	.086023	.092792
	.10	.050875	.056997	.063224	.066374	.069549	.072746	.075965	.079205	.082465	.089042	.095690	.102402	.109172
	0.00	.067254	.073376	.079603	.082754	.085929	.089126	.092345	.095585	.098845	.105422	.112070	.118782	.125552
	-.10	.083634	.089756	.095983	.099134	.102308	.105505	.108724	.111964	.115225	.121802	.128450	.135162	.141931
	-.20	.100014	.106136	.112363	.115514	.118688	.121885	.125104	.128344	.131604	.138182	.144830	.151542	.158311
	-.30	.116394	.122516	.128743	.131893	.135068	.138265	.141484	.144724	.147984	.154561	.161209	.167921	.174691
	-.40	.132773	.138895	.145122	.148273	.151448	.154645	.157864	.161104	.164364	.170941	.177589	.184301	.191071
20	.40	.000947	.007347	.013848	.017133	.020439	.023765	.027110	.030472	.033850	.040652	.047506	.054405	.061341
	.30	.017327	.023727	.030228	.033513	.036819	.040145	.043489	.046852	.050230	.057032	.063886	.070785	.077721
	.20	.033706	.040107	.046608	.049893	.053199	.056524	.059869	.063231	.066610	.073412	.080266	.087165	.094101
	.10	.050086	.056487	.062987	.066272	.069578	.072904	.076249	.079611	.082990	.089791	.096646	.103544	.110481
	0.00	.066466	.072866	.079367	.082652	.085958	.089284	.092629	.095991	.099369	.106171	.113025	.119924	.126860
	-.10	.082846	.089246	.095747	.099032	.102338	.105664	.109008	.112371	.115749	.122551	.129405	.136304	.143240
	-.20	.099225	.105626	.112127	.115412	.118718	.122043	.125388	.128750	.132129	.138931	.145785	.152684	.159620
	-.30	.115605	.122006	.128506	.131791	.135097	.138423	.141768	.145130	.148509	.155310	.162164	.169063	.176000
	-.40	.131985	.138385	.144886	.148171	.151477	.154803	.158148	.161510	.164888	.171690	.178544	.185443	.192379
25	.40	.000493	.007059	.013717	.017077	.020455	.023850	.027260	.030684	.034120	.041026	.047968	.054938	.061931
	.30	.016873	.023438	.030097	.033457	.036835	.040230	.043640	.047063	.050500	.057406	.064348	.071318	.078311
	.20	.033252	.039818	.046477	.049836	.053215	.056609	.060019	.063443	.066880	.073785	.080727	.087698	.094690
	.10	.049632	.056198	.062856	.066216	.069594	.072989	.076399	.079823	.083259	.090165	.097107	.104078	.111070
	0.00	.066012	.072578	.079236	.082596	.085974	.089369	.092779	.096203	.099639	.106545	.113487	.120457	.127450
	-.10	.082392	.088957	.095616	.098976	.102354	.105749	.109159	.112582	.116019	.122925	.129867	.136837	.143830
	-.20	.098771	.105337	.111996	.115355	.118733	.122128	.125538	.128962	.132399	.139304	.146246	.153217	.160209
	-.30	.115151	.121717	.128375	.131735	.135113	.138508	.141918	.145342	.148778	.155684	.162626	.169597	.176589
	-.40	.131531	.138097	.144755	.148115	.151493	.154888	.158298	.161722	.165158	.172064	.179006	.185976	.192969
30	.40	.000205	.006879	.013638	.017043	.020464	.023899	.027346	.030803	.034269	.041225	.048205	.055202	.062211
	.30	.016585	.023259	.030018	.033423	.036844	.040279	.043725	.047182	.050649	.057605	.064585	.071582	.078591
	.20	.032964	.039639	.046397	.049803	.053224	.056658	.060105	.063562	.067029	.073985	.080965	.087962	.094971
	.10	.049344	.056019	.062777	.066183	.069604	.073038	.076485	.079942	.083408	.090364	.097344	.104341	.111350
	0.00	.065724	.072398	.079157	.082562	.085983	.089418	.092865	.096322	.099788	.106744	.113724	.120721	.127730
	-.10	.082104	.088778	.095537	.098942	.102363	.105798	.109244	.112701	.116168	.123124	.130104	.137101	.144110
	-.20	.098483	.105158	.111916	.115322	.118743	.122177	.125624	.129081	.132548	.139504	.146484	.153481	.160490
	-.30	.114863	.121538	.128296	.131702	.135122	.138557	.142004	.145461	.148927	.155883	.162863	.169860	.176869
	-.40	.131243	.137917	.144676	.148081	.151502	.154937	.158384	.161841	.165307	.172263	.179243	.186240	.193249

5.0 YEAR HOLDING PERIOD
.100 EQUITY YIELD RATE
.750 LOAN RATIO

INTEREST RATE

TERM YEARS	APPR DEP	5.0	6.0	7.0	7.5	8.0	8.5	9.0	9.5	10.0	11.0	12.0	13.0	14.0
10	.40	.001138	.007098	.013165	.016238	.019336	.022460	.025608	.028780	.031977	.038439	.044991	.051628	.058348
	.30	.017518	.023478	.029545	.032618	.035716	.038839	.041988	.045160	.048356	.054819	.061370	.068008	.074728
	.20	.033898	.039858	.045925	.048997	.052096	.055219	.058367	.061540	.064736	.071198	.077750	.084388	.091107
	.10	.050278	.056237	.062304	.065377	.068475	.071599	.074747	.077920	.081116	.087578	.094130	.100767	.107487
	0.00	.066657	.072617	.078684	.081757	.084855	.087979	.091127	.094299	.097496	.103958	.110510	.117147	.123867
	-.10	.083037	.088997	.095064	.098137	.101235	.104358	.107507	.110679	.113875	.120338	.126889	.133527	.140247
	-.20	.099417	.105377	.111444	.114516	.117615	.120738	.123886	.127059	.130255	.136717	.143269	.149907	.156626
	-.30	.115797	.121756	.127823	.130896	.133994	.137118	.140266	.143439	.146635	.153097	.159649	.166286	.173006
	-.40	.132176	.138136	.144203	.147276	.150374	.153498	.156646	.159818	.163015	.169477	.176029	.182666	.189386
15	.40	-.000604	.005956	.012628	.016003	.019404	.022830	.026279	.029750	.033243	.040291	.047413	.054605	.061858
	.30	.015776	.022336	.029007	.032383	.035784	.039210	.042659	.046130	.049623	.056670	.063793	.070985	.078238
	.20	.032156	.038715	.045387	.048763	.052164	.055589	.059038	.062510	.066003	.073050	.080173	.087364	.094618
	.10	.048536	.055095	.061767	.065143	.068544	.071969	.075418	.078889	.082383	.089430	.096553	.103744	.110997
	0.00	.064915	.071475	.078147	.081522	.084923	.088349	.091798	.095269	.098762	.105810	.112932	.120124	.127377
	-.10	.081295	.087854	.094526	.097902	.101303	.104729	.108178	.111649	.115142	.122189	.129312	.136504	.143757
	-.20	.097675	.104234	.110906	.114282	.117683	.121108	.124557	.128029	.131522	.138569	.145692	.152883	.160137
	-.30	.114055	.120614	.127286	.130662	.134063	.137488	.140937	.144408	.147902	.154949	.162072	.169263	.176516
	-.40	.130434	.136994	.143666	.147041	.150442	.153868	.157317	.160788	.164281	.171329	.178451	.185643	.192896
20	.40	-.001448	.005409	.012374	.015894	.019436	.023000	.026583	.030186	.033805	.041093	.048437	.055828	.063260
	.30	.014931	.021789	.028754	.032274	.035816	.039379	.042963	.046565	.050185	.057473	.064817	.072208	.079640
	.20	.031311	.038169	.045134	.048653	.052196	.055759	.059343	.062945	.066565	.073853	.081196	.088588	.096019
	.10	.047691	.054548	.061514	.065033	.068575	.072139	.075722	.079325	.082945	.090232	.097576	.104968	.112399
	0.00	.064071	.070928	.077893	.081413	.084955	.088519	.092102	.095705	.099324	.106612	.113956	.121347	.128779
	-.10	.080450	.087308	.094273	.097793	.101335	.104898	.108482	.112084	.115704	.122992	.130336	.137727	.145159
	-.20	.096830	.103688	.110653	.114172	.117715	.121278	.124862	.128464	.132084	.139372	.146715	.154107	.161538
	-.30	.113210	.120067	.127033	.130552	.134094	.137658	.141241	.144844	.148464	.155751	.163095	.170487	.177918
	-.40	.129590	.136447	.143412	.146932	.150474	.154038	.157621	.161224	.164843	.172131	.179475	.186866	.194298
25	.40	-.001935	.005100	.012234	.015834	.019453	.023090	.026744	.030412	.034094	.041493	.048931	.056400	.063892
	.30	.014445	.021480	.028614	.032214	.035833	.039470	.043124	.046792	.050474	.057873	.065311	.072779	.080271
	.20	.030825	.037859	.044994	.048593	.052213	.055850	.059503	.063172	.066854	.074253	.081691	.089159	.096651
	.10	.047204	.054239	.061373	.064973	.068592	.072230	.075883	.079552	.083234	.090653	.098070	.105539	.113031
	0.00	.063584	.070619	.077753	.081353	.084972	.088609	.092263	.095931	.099613	.107012	.114450	.121919	.129411
	-.10	.079964	.086998	.094133	.097733	.101352	.104989	.108643	.112311	.115993	.123392	.130830	.138298	.145790
	-.20	.096344	.103378	.110512	.114112	.117732	.121369	.125022	.128691	.132373	.139772	.147210	.154678	.162170
	-.30	.112723	.119758	.126892	.130492	.134111	.137749	.141402	.145071	.148753	.156152	.163589	.171058	.178550
	-.40	.129103	.136138	.143272	.146872	.150491	.154128	.157782	.161450	.165132	.172531	.179969	.187438	.194930
30	.40	-.002243	.004908	.012149	.015798	.019463	.023143	.026836	.030540	.034254	.041707	.049185	.056682	.064192
	.30	.014136	.021288	.028529	.032178	.035843	.039523	.043216	.046920	.050634	.058087	.065565	.073062	.080571
	.20	.030516	.037667	.044908	.048557	.052223	.055903	.059595	.063299	.067014	.074466	.081945	.089442	.096951
	.10	.046896	.054047	.061288	.064937	.068602	.072282	.075975	.079679	.083393	.090846	.098325	.105822	.113331
	0.00	.063276	.070427	.077668	.081317	.084982	.088662	.092355	.096059	.099773	.107226	.114704	.122201	.129711
	-.10	.079655	.086807	.094048	.097697	.101362	.105042	.108735	.112439	.116153	.123606	.131084	.138581	.146090
	-.20	.096035	.103186	.110427	.114076	.117742	.121422	.125114	.128818	.132533	.139985	.147464	.154961	.162470
	-.30	.112415	.119566	.126807	.130456	.134121	.137801	.141494	.145198	.148912	.156365	.163844	.171341	.178850
	-.40	.128795	.135946	.143187	.146836	.150501	.154181	.157874	.161578	.165292	.172745	.180223	.187720	.195230

5.0 YEAR HOLDING PERIOD
.100 EQUITY YIELD RATE
.800 LOAN RATIO

INTEREST RATE

TERM YEARS	APPR DEP	5.0	6.0	7.0	7.5	8.0	8.5	9.0	9.5	10.0	11.0	12.0	13.0	14.0
10	.40	-.001084	.005273	.011744	.015022	.018327	.021658	.025016	.028400	.031810	.038703	.045691	.052771	.059939
	.30	.015295	.021652	.028124	.031401	.034706	.038038	.041396	.044780	.048189	.055082	.062071	.069151	.076319
	.20	.031675	.038032	.044504	.047781	.051086	.054418	.057776	.061160	.064569	.071462	.078451	.085531	.092698
	.10	.046055	.054412	.060883	.064161	.067466	.070798	.074156	.077540	.080949	.087842	.094830	.101911	.109078
	0.00	.064435	.070792	.077263	.080541	.083846	.087177	.090535	.093919	.097329	.104222	.111210	.118290	.125458
	-.10	.080814	.087171	.093643	.096920	.100225	.103557	.106915	.110299	.113708	.120601	.127590	.134670	.141838
	-.20	.097194	.103551	.110023	.113300	.116605	.119937	.123295	.126679	.130088	.136981	.143970	.151050	.158217
	-.30	.113574	.119931	.126402	.129680	.132985	.136317	.139675	.143059	.146468	.153361	.160349	.167430	.174597
	-.40	.129954	.136311	.142782	.146060	.149365	.152696	.156054	.159438	.162848	.169741	.176729	.183809	.190977
15	.40	-.002943	.004054	.011171	.014772	.018399	.022053	.025732	.029435	.033161	.040678	.048275	.055946	.063683
	.30	.013437	.020434	.027550	.031151	.034779	.038433	.042112	.045815	.049541	.057058	.064655	.072326	.080063
	.20	.029817	.036814	.043930	.047531	.051159	.054813	.058492	.062194	.065920	.073437	.081035	.088706	.096443
	.10	.046197	.053193	.060310	.063911	.067539	.071192	.074871	.078575	.082300	.089817	.097415	.105086	.112823
	0.00	.062576	.069573	.076690	.080291	.083918	.087572	.091251	.094954	.098680	.106197	.113794	.121465	.129202
	-.10	.078956	.085953	.093069	.096670	.100298	.103952	.107631	.111334	.115060	.122577	.130174	.137845	.145582
	-.20	.095336	.102333	.109449	.113050	.116678	.120332	.124010	.127713	.131439	.138956	.146554	.154225	.161962
	-.30	.111716	.118712	.125829	.129430	.133058	.136711	.140390	.144093	.147819	.155336	.162934	.170605	.178341
	-.40	.128095	.135092	.142209	.145810	.149437	.153091	.156770	.160473	.164199	.171716	.179313	.186984	.194721
20	.40	-.003844	.003471	.010901	.014655	.018433	.022234	.026057	.029899	.033760	.041534	.049367	.057251	.065178
	.30	.012536	.019851	.027280	.031034	.034813	.038614	.042436	.046279	.050140	.057914	.065747	.073631	.081558
	.20	.028916	.036231	.043660	.047414	.051193	.054994	.058816	.062659	.066520	.074293	.082127	.090011	.097938
	.10	.045296	.052610	.060040	.063794	.067572	.071373	.075196	.079038	.082900	.090673	.098506	.106391	.114318
	0.00	.061675	.068990	.076420	.080174	.083952	.087753	.091576	.095418	.099279	.107053	.114886	.122770	.130697
	-.10	.078055	.085370	.092799	.096553	.100332	.104133	.107955	.111798	.115659	.123433	.131266	.139150	.147077
	-.20	.094435	.101750	.109179	.112933	.116712	.120513	.124335	.128178	.132039	.139812	.147646	.155530	.163457
	-.30	.110815	.118129	.125559	.129313	.133091	.136892	.140715	.144557	.148419	.156192	.164025	.171910	.179837
	-.40	.127194	.134509	.141939	.145693	.149471	.153272	.157095	.160937	.164798	.172572	.180405	.188289	.196216
25	.40	-.004363	.003141	.010751	.014591	.018451	.022331	.026228	.030141	.034069	.041961	.049895	.057861	.065852
	.30	.012017	.019521	.027131	.030970	.034831	.038711	.042608	.046521	.050448	.058341	.066274	.074241	.082232
	.20	.028397	.035901	.043510	.047350	.051211	.055091	.058988	.062901	.066828	.074720	.082654	.090620	.098612
	.10	.044777	.052280	.059890	.063730	.067591	.071470	.075367	.079280	.083208	.091100	.099034	.107000	.114992
	0.00	.061156	.068660	.076270	.080110	.083970	.087850	.091747	.095660	.099588	.107480	.115414	.123380	.131371
	-.10	.077536	.085040	.092650	.096489	.100350	.104230	.108127	.112040	.115967	.123860	.131793	.139760	.147751
	-.20	.093916	.101420	.109029	.112869	.116730	.120610	.124507	.128420	.132347	.140239	.148173	.156139	.164131
	-.30	.110296	.117799	.125409	.129249	.133110	.136989	.140886	.144799	.148727	.156619	.164553	.172519	.180511
	-.40	.126675	.134179	.141789	.145629	.149489	.153369	.157266	.161179	.165107	.172999	.180933	.188899	.196890
30	.40	-.004692	.002936	.010660	.014552	.018462	.022387	.026326	.030277	.034239	.042189	.050166	.058162	.066172
	.30	.011688	.019316	.027040	.030932	.034842	.038767	.042706	.046657	.050619	.058568	.066545	.074542	.082552
	.20	.028068	.035696	.043420	.047312	.051222	.055147	.059086	.063037	.066998	.074948	.082925	.090922	.098932
	.10	.044448	.052076	.059799	.063692	.067601	.071526	.075465	.079417	.083378	.091328	.099305	.107302	.115312
	0.00	.060827	.068455	.076179	.080071	.083981	.087906	.091845	.095796	.099758	.107708	.115685	.123681	.131691
	-.10	.077207	.084835	.092559	.096451	.100361	.104286	.108225	.112176	.116138	.124087	.132064	.140061	.148071
	-.20	.093587	.101215	.108939	.112831	.116741	.120666	.124605	.128556	.132517	.140467	.148444	.156441	.164451
	-.30	.109967	.117595	.125318	.129211	.133120	.137045	.140984	.144936	.148897	.156847	.164824	.172821	.180831
	-.40	.126346	.133974	.141698	.145590	.149500	.153425	.157364	.161315	.165277	.173227	.181204	.189200	.197210

5.0 YEAR HOLDING PERIOD
.100 EQUITY YIELD RATE
.900 LOAN RATIO

INTEREST RATE

TERM YEARS	APPR DEP	5.0	6.0	7.0	7.5	8.0	8.5	9.0	9.5	10.0	11.0	12.0	13.0	14.0
10	.40	-.005530	.001621	.008902	.012589	.016307	.020055	.023833	.027640	.031476	.039230	.047093	.055058	.063121
	.30	.010850	.018001	.025282	.028969	.032687	.036435	.040213	.044020	.047856	.055610	.063472	.071437	.079501
	.20	.027229	.034381	.041661	.045349	.049067	.052815	.056593	.060400	.064235	.071990	.079852	.087817	.095881
	.10	.043609	.050761	.058041	.061728	.065446	.069195	.072973	.076780	.080615	.088370	.096232	.104197	.112260
	0.00	.059989	.067140	.074421	.078108	.081826	.085574	.089352	.093159	.096995	.104749	.112612	.120577	.128640
	-.10	.076369	.083520	.090801	.094488	.098206	.101954	.105732	.109539	.113375	.121129	.128991	.136956	.145020
	-.20	.092748	.099900	.107180	.110868	.114586	.118334	.122112	.125919	.129754	.137509	.145371	.153336	.161400
	-.30	.109128	.116280	.123560	.127247	.130965	.134714	.138492	.142299	.146134	.153889	.161751	.169716	.177779
	-.40	.125508	.132659	.139940	.143628	.147345	.151093	.154871	.158678	.162514	.170268	.178131	.186096	.194159
15	.40	-.007621	.000251	.008257	.012308	.016389	.020499	.024638	.028804	.032996	.041452	.050000	.058630	.067334
	.30	.008759	.016535	.024637	.028688	.032769	.036879	.041018	.045184	.049375	.057832	.066380	.075009	.083713
	.20	.025139	.033010	.041016	.045067	.049149	.053259	.057398	.061564	.065755	.074212	.082759	.091389	.100093
	.10	.041519	.049390	.057396	.061447	.065528	.069639	.073778	.077943	.082135	.090592	.099139	.107769	.116473
	0.00	.057898	.065770	.073776	.077827	.081908	.086018	.090157	.094323	.098515	.106971	.115519	.124149	.132853
	-.10	.074278	.082149	.090156	.094207	.098288	.102398	.106537	.110703	.114894	.123351	.131899	.140528	.149232
	-.20	.090658	.098529	.106535	.110586	.114668	.118778	.122917	.127083	.131274	.139731	.148278	.156908	.165612
	-.30	.107038	.114909	.122915	.126966	.131047	.135158	.139297	.143462	.147654	.156111	.164658	.173288	.181992
	-.40	.123417	.131289	.139295	.143346	.147427	.151538	.155676	.159842	.164034	.172490	.181038	.189668	.198372
20	.40	-.008634	-.000405	.007953	.012176	.016427	.020703	.025004	.029326	.033670	.042415	.051228	.060098	.069016
	.30	.007746	.015975	.024333	.028556	.032807	.037083	.041383	.045706	.050050	.058795	.067608	.076478	.085395
	.20	.024125	.032354	.040713	.044936	.049187	.053463	.057763	.062086	.066430	.075175	.083987	.092857	.101775
	.10	.040505	.048734	.057092	.061316	.065566	.069843	.074143	.078466	.082810	.091555	.100367	.109237	.118155
	0.00	.056885	.065114	.073472	.077695	.081946	.086222	.090523	.094845	.099189	.107934	.116747	.125617	.134535
	-.10	.073265	.081494	.089852	.094075	.098326	.102602	.106902	.111225	.115569	.124314	.133127	.141997	.150914
	-.20	.089644	.097873	.106232	.110455	.114706	.118982	.123282	.127605	.131949	.140694	.149506	.158376	.167294
	-.30	.106024	.114253	.122611	.126835	.131085	.135362	.139662	.143985	.148329	.157074	.165886	.174756	.183674
	-.40	.122404	.130633	.138991	.143214	.147465	.151741	.156042	.160364	.164708	.173453	.182266	.191136	.200054
25	.40	-.009218	-.000776	.007785	.012104	.016448	.020812	.025197	.029599	.034017	.042896	.051821	.060783	.069774
	.30	.007162	.015603	.024164	.028484	.032827	.037192	.041576	.045979	.050397	.059276	.068201	.077163	.086153
	.20	.023541	.031983	.040544	.044864	.049207	.053572	.057956	.062358	.066777	.075655	.084581	.093543	.102533
	.10	.039921	.048363	.056924	.061244	.065587	.069952	.074336	.078738	.083156	.092035	.100961	.109923	.118913
	0.00	.056301	.064743	.073304	.077623	.081967	.086331	.090716	.095118	.099536	.108415	.117340	.126302	.135293
	-.10	.072681	.081122	.089683	.094003	.098346	.102711	.107095	.111497	.115916	.124795	.133720	.142682	.151672
	-.20	.089060	.097502	.106063	.110383	.114726	.119091	.123475	.127877	.132296	.141174	.150100	.159062	.168052
	-.30	.105440	.113882	.122443	.126763	.131106	.135471	.139855	.144257	.148675	.157554	.166480	.175442	.184432
	-.40	.121820	.130262	.138823	.143142	.147486	.151850	.156235	.160637	.165055	.173934	.182859	.191821	.200812
30	.40	-.009588	-.001007	.007683	.012061	.016460	.020876	.025307	.029752	.034209	.043152	.052126	.061123	.070134
	.30	.006792	.015373	.024062	.028441	.032839	.037255	.041687	.046132	.050588	.059532	.068506	.077502	.086514
	.20	.023171	.031753	.040442	.044821	.049219	.053635	.058066	.062511	.066968	.075912	.084886	.093882	.102893
	.10	.039551	.048133	.056822	.061201	.065599	.070015	.074446	.078891	.083348	.092291	.101266	.110262	.119273
	0.00	.055931	.064512	.073202	.077580	.081979	.086395	.090826	.095271	.099728	.108671	.117645	.126642	.135653
	-.10	.072311	.080892	.089581	.093960	.098358	.102774	.107206	.111651	.116107	.125051	.134025	.143021	.152033
	-.20	.088690	.097272	.105961	.110340	.114738	.119154	.123585	.128030	.132487	.141431	.150405	.159401	.168412
	-.30	.105070	.113652	.122341	.126720	.131118	.135534	.139965	.144410	.148867	.157810	.166785	.175781	.184792
	-.40	.121450	.130031	.138721	.143099	.147498	.151914	.156345	.160790	.165247	.174190	.183164	.192161	.201172

5.0 YEAR HOLDING PERIOD
.120 EQUITY YIELD RATE
.600 LOAN RATIO

INTEREST RATE

TERM YEARS	APPR DEP	5.0	6.0	7.0	7.5	8.0	8.5	9.0	9.5	10.0	11.0	12.0	13.0	14.0
10	.40	.020041	.024761	.029569	.032004	.034460	.036936	.039431	.041947	.044481	.049607	.054804	.060071	.065405
	.30	.035782	.040502	.045310	.047745	.050201	.052677	.055172	.057688	.060222	.065348	.070545	.075812	.081146
	.20	.051523	.056243	.061051	.063486	.065942	.068418	.070913	.073429	.075963	.081089	.086286	.091553	.096887
	.10	.067264	.071984	.076792	.079227	.081682	.084158	.086654	.089170	.091704	.096830	.102027	.107294	.112628
	0.00	.083004	.087725	.092533	.094968	.097423	.099899	.102395	.104911	.107445	.112571	.117768	.123035	.128369
	-.10	.098745	.103466	.108274	.110709	.113164	.115640	.118136	.120652	.123186	.128312	.133509	.138776	.144110
	-.20	.114486	.119207	.124015	.126450	.128905	.131381	.133877	.136393	.138927	.144053	.149250	.154517	.159851
	-.30	.130227	.134948	.139755	.142191	.144646	.147122	.149618	.152134	.154668	.159794	.164991	.170258	.175592
	-.40	.145968	.150689	.155496	.157932	.160387	.162863	.165359	.167875	.170409	.175535	.180732	.185999	.191333
15	.40	.017943	.023135	.028419	.031094	.033789	.036504	.039238	.041991	.044762	.050354	.056009	.061720	.067483
	.30	.033684	.038876	.044160	.046834	.049530	.052245	.054979	.057732	.060503	.066095	.071749	.077461	.083224
	.20	.049425	.054617	.059901	.062575	.065271	.067986	.070720	.073473	.076244	.081836	.087490	.093202	.098965
	.10	.065166	.070358	.075642	.078316	.081012	.083727	.086461	.089214	.091985	.097577	.103231	.108943	.114706
	0.00	.080907	.086099	.091383	.094057	.096753	.099468	.102202	.104955	.107726	.113318	.118972	.124684	.130447
	-.10	.096648	.101840	.107124	.109798	.112494	.115209	.117943	.120696	.123467	.129059	.134713	.140425	.146188
	-.20	.112389	.117581	.122865	.125539	.128235	.130950	.133684	.136437	.139208	.144800	.150454	.156166	.161929
	-.30	.128130	.133322	.138606	.141280	.143975	.146691	.149425	.152178	.154949	.160541	.166195	.171907	.177670
	-.40	.143871	.149063	.154347	.157021	.159716	.162432	.165166	.167919	.170690	.176282	.181936	.187648	.193411
20	.40	.016927	.022357	.027878	.030668	.033478	.036306	.039151	.042011	.044886	.050678	.056517	.062398	.068313
	.30	.032668	.038098	.043619	.046409	.049219	.052047	.054892	.057752	.060627	.066419	.072258	.078139	.084054
	.20	.048409	.053839	.059360	.062150	.064960	.067788	.070633	.073493	.076368	.082160	.087999	.093880	.099795
	.10	.064150	.069580	.075101	.077891	.080701	.083529	.086374	.089234	.092109	.097901	.103740	.109621	.115536
	0.00	.079891	.085321	.090841	.093632	.096442	.099270	.102115	.104975	.107850	.113642	.119481	.125362	.131277
	-.10	.095632	.101062	.106582	.109373	.112183	.115011	.117856	.120716	.123591	.129383	.135222	.141103	.147018
	-.20	.111373	.116803	.122323	.125114	.127924	.130752	.133596	.136457	.139332	.145124	.150963	.156844	.162759
	-.30	.127114	.132544	.138064	.140855	.143665	.146493	.149337	.152198	.155073	.160865	.166703	.172585	.178500
	-.40	.142855	.148285	.153805	.156596	.159406	.162234	.165078	.167939	.170814	.176606	.182445	.188325	.194241
25	.40	.016341	.021917	.027577	.030435	.033310	.036200	.039104	.042022	.044950	.050839	.056763	.062714	.068687
	.30	.032082	.037658	.043318	.046176	.049051	.051941	.054845	.057763	.060691	.066580	.072504	.078455	.084428
	.20	.047823	.053399	.059059	.061917	.064792	.067682	.070586	.073503	.076432	.082321	.088245	.094196	.100169
	.10	.063564	.069140	.074800	.077658	.080533	.083423	.086327	.089244	.092173	.098062	.103986	.109937	.115910
	0.00	.079305	.084881	.090541	.093399	.096274	.099164	.102068	.104985	.107914	.113803	.119727	.125678	.131651
	-.10	.095046	.100622	.106282	.109140	.112015	.114905	.117809	.120726	.123655	.129544	.135468	.141419	.147392
	-.20	.110787	.116363	.122022	.124881	.127756	.130646	.133550	.136467	.139396	.145285	.151209	.157160	.163133
	-.30	.126528	.132104	.137764	.140622	.143497	.146387	.149291	.152208	.155137	.161026	.166950	.172901	.178874
	-.40	.142269	.147845	.153505	.156363	.159238	.162128	.165032	.167949	.170878	.176767	.182691	.188642	.194615
30	.40	.015970	.021644	.027395	.030296	.033211	.036139	.039078	.042027	.044986	.050926	.056889	.062871	.068865
	.30	.031711	.037385	.043136	.046037	.048952	.051880	.054819	.057768	.060727	.066666	.072630	.078612	.084606
	.20	.047452	.053126	.058877	.061778	.064693	.067621	.070560	.073509	.076468	.082407	.088371	.094353	.100347
	.10	.063193	.068867	.074618	.077519	.080434	.083362	.086301	.089250	.092209	.098148	.104112	.110094	.116088
	0.00	.078934	.084608	.090359	.093260	.096175	.099103	.102042	.104991	.107950	.113889	.119853	.125835	.131829
	-.10	.094675	.100349	.106100	.109001	.111916	.114843	.117783	.120732	.123691	.129630	.135594	.141576	.147570
	-.20	.110416	.116090	.121841	.124742	.127657	.130584	.133524	.136473	.139432	.145371	.151335	.157317	.163311
	-.30	.126157	.131831	.137582	.140483	.143398	.146325	.149265	.152214	.155173	.161112	.167076	.173057	.179052
	-.40	.141898	.147572	.153323	.156224	.159139	.162066	.165006	.167955	.170914	.176853	.182817	.188798	.194793

5.0 YEAR HOLDING PERIOD
.120 EQUITY YIELD RATE
.667 LOAN RATIO

INTEREST RATE

TERM YEARS	APPR DEP	5.0	6.0	7.0	7.5	8.0	8.5	9.0	9.5	10.0	11.0	12.0	13.0	14.0
10	.40	.015930	.021175	.026517	.029222	.031951	.034702	.037475	.040270	.043086	.048781	.054557	.060409	.066335
	.30	.031671	.036916	.042258	.044963	.047692	.050443	.053216	.056011	.058827	.064522	.070297	.076150	.082076
	.20	.047412	.052657	.057999	.060704	.063433	.066184	.068957	.071752	.074568	.080263	.086038	.091891	.097817
	.10	.063153	.068398	.073740	.076445	.079174	.081925	.084698	.087493	.090309	.096004	.101779	.107632	.113558
	0.00	.078894	.084139	.089480	.092186	.094915	.097666	.100439	.103234	.106050	.111745	.117520	.123373	.129299
	-.10	.094635	.099880	.105221	.107927	.110656	.113407	.116180	.118975	.121791	.127486	.133261	.139114	.145040
	-.20	.110376	.115621	.120962	.123668	.126397	.129148	.131921	.134716	.137532	.143227	.149002	.154855	.160780
	-.30	.126117	.131362	.136703	.139409	.142138	.144889	.147662	.150457	.153273	.158968	.164743	.170596	.176521
	-.40	.141858	.147103	.152444	.155150	.157879	.160630	.163403	.166198	.169014	.174709	.180484	.186337	.192262
15	.40	.013600	.019368	.025239	.028211	.031205	.034222	.037261	.040320	.043398	.049611	.055894	.062240	.068644
	.30	.029341	.035109	.040980	.043952	.046946	.049963	.053002	.056060	.059139	.065352	.071635	.077981	.084385
	.20	.045082	.050850	.056721	.059693	.062687	.065704	.068743	.071801	.074880	.081093	.087376	.093722	.100126
	.10	.060823	.066591	.072462	.075434	.078428	.081445	.084484	.087542	.090621	.096834	.103117	.109463	.115867
	0.00	.076564	.082332	.088203	.091175	.094169	.097186	.100225	.103283	.106362	.112575	.118858	.125204	.131608
	-.10	.092305	.098073	.103944	.106916	.109910	.112927	.115966	.119024	.122103	.128316	.134599	.140945	.147349
	-.20	.108045	.113814	.119685	.122657	.125651	.128668	.131706	.134765	.137844	.144057	.150340	.156686	.163090
	-.30	.123786	.129555	.135426	.138398	.141392	.144409	.147447	.150506	.153585	.159798	.166081	.172427	.178831
	-.40	.139527	.145296	.151167	.154139	.157133	.160150	.163188	.166247	.169326	.175539	.181822	.188168	.194572
20	.40	.012470	.018504	.024638	.027739	.030861	.034003	.037163	.040342	.043536	.049971	.056460	.062993	.069566
	.30	.028211	.034245	.040379	.043479	.046602	.049744	.052904	.056083	.059277	.065712	.072200	.078734	.085307
	.20	.043952	.049986	.056120	.059220	.062342	.065484	.068645	.071824	.075018	.081453	.087941	.094475	.101048
	.10	.059693	.065727	.071861	.074961	.078083	.081225	.084386	.087565	.090759	.097194	.103682	.110216	.116789
	0.00	.075434	.081468	.087601	.090702	.093824	.096966	.100127	.103306	.106500	.112935	.119423	.125957	.132530
	-.10	.091175	.097209	.103342	.106443	.109565	.112707	.115868	.119046	.122241	.128676	.135164	.141698	.148271
	-.20	.106916	.112950	.119083	.122184	.125306	.128448	.131609	.134787	.137982	.144417	.150905	.157439	.164012
	-.30	.122657	.128691	.134824	.137925	.141047	.144189	.147350	.150528	.153723	.160158	.166646	.173180	.179753
	-.40	.138398	.144432	.150565	.153666	.156788	.159930	.163091	.166269	.169464	.175899	.182387	.188921	.195494
25	.40	.011819	.018015	.024304	.027479	.030674	.033885	.037112	.040353	.043608	.050151	.056733	.063345	.069982
	.30	.027560	.033756	.040045	.043220	.046415	.049626	.052853	.056094	.059349	.065892	.072473	.079086	.085723
	.20	.043301	.049497	.055786	.058961	.062156	.065367	.068594	.071835	.075090	.081633	.088214	.094827	.101464
	.10	.059042	.065238	.071527	.074702	.077896	.081108	.084335	.087576	.090830	.097374	.103955	.110568	.117205
	0.00	.074783	.080979	.087268	.090443	.093637	.096849	.100076	.103317	.106571	.113115	.119696	.126309	.132946
	-.10	.090524	.096720	.103009	.106184	.109378	.112590	.115817	.119058	.122312	.128856	.135437	.142050	.148687
	-.20	.106265	.112461	.118750	.121925	.125119	.128331	.131558	.134799	.138053	.144597	.151178	.157791	.164428
	-.30	.122006	.128202	.134491	.137666	.140860	.144072	.147299	.150540	.153794	.160338	.166919	.173532	.180169
	-.40	.137747	.143943	.150232	.153407	.156601	.159813	.163040	.166281	.169535	.176079	.182660	.189273	.195910
30	.40	.011407	.017711	.024102	.027325	.030563	.033817	.037082	.040360	.043647	.050247	.056873	.063519	.070179
	.30	.027148	.033452	.039843	.043066	.046304	.049558	.052823	.056101	.059388	.065988	.072614	.079260	.085920
	.20	.042889	.049193	.055584	.058807	.062045	.065299	.068564	.071842	.075129	.081728	.088355	.095001	.101661
	.10	.058630	.064934	.071325	.074548	.077786	.081039	.084305	.087583	.090870	.097469	.104096	.110742	.117402
	0.00	.074371	.080675	.087066	.090289	.093527	.096780	.100046	.103324	.106611	.113210	.119837	.126463	.133143
	-.10	.090112	.096416	.102807	.106030	.109268	.112521	.115787	.119065	.122352	.128951	.135578	.142224	.148884
	-.20	.105853	.112157	.118548	.121771	.125009	.128262	.131528	.134805	.138093	.144692	.151319	.157965	.164605
	-.30	.121594	.127898	.134289	.137512	.140750	.144003	.147269	.150546	.153834	.160433	.167060	.173706	.180365
	-.40	.137334	.143639	.150030	.153252	.156491	.159744	.163010	.166287	.169575	.176174	.182801	.189447	.196107

5.0 YEAR HOLDING PERIOD
.120 EQUITY YIELD RATE
.700 LOAN RATIO

INTEREST RATE

TERM YEARS	APPR DEP	5.0	6.0	7.0	7.5	8.0	8.5	9.0	9.5	10.0	11.0	12.0	13.0	14.0
10	.40	.013875	.019382	.024991	.027832	.030697	.033585	.036497	.039432	.042389	.048369	.054433	.060577	.066800
	.30	.029616	.035123	.040732	.043573	.046438	.049326	.052238	.055173	.058130	.064110	.070174	.076318	.082541
	.20	.045357	.050864	.056473	.059314	.062179	.065067	.067979	.070914	.073871	.079851	.085914	.092059	.098281
	.10	.061098	.066605	.072214	.075055	.077920	.080808	.083720	.086655	.089612	.095592	.101655	.107800	.114022
	0.00	.076839	.082346	.087955	.090796	.093661	.096549	.099461	.102396	.105353	.111333	.117396	.123541	.129763
	-.10	.092580	.098087	.103696	.106537	.109402	.112290	.115202	.118137	.121094	.127073	.133137	.139282	.145504
	-.20	.108321	.113828	.119437	.122278	.125143	.128031	.130943	.133878	.136835	.142814	.148878	.155023	.161245
	-.30	.124061	.129569	.135178	.138019	.140884	.143772	.146684	.149619	.152576	.158555	.164619	.170764	.176986
	-.40	.139802	.145310	.150919	.153760	.156625	.159513	.162425	.165360	.168317	.174296	.180360	.186505	.192227
15	.40	.011428	.017485	.023650	.026770	.029914	.033082	.036272	.039484	.042716	.049204	.055837	.062501	.069224
	.30	.027169	.033226	.039391	.042511	.045655	.048823	.052013	.055225	.058457	.064981	.071578	.078242	.084965
	.20	.042910	.048967	.055132	.058252	.061396	.064564	.067754	.070966	.074198	.080722	.087319	.093983	.100706
	.10	.058651	.064708	.070872	.073993	.077137	.080305	.083495	.086707	.089939	.096463	.103060	.109724	.116447
	0.00	.074392	.080449	.086613	.089734	.092878	.096046	.099236	.102448	.105680	.112204	.118801	.125465	.132188
	-.10	.090133	.096190	.102354	.105475	.108619	.111787	.114977	.118189	.121421	.127945	.134542	.141206	.147929
	-.20	.105874	.111931	.118095	.121216	.124360	.127528	.130718	.133930	.137162	.143686	.150283	.156947	.163670
	-.30	.121615	.127672	.133836	.136957	.140101	.143269	.146459	.149671	.152903	.159427	.166024	.172687	.179411
	-.40	.137356	.143413	.149577	.152698	.155842	.159010	.162200	.165412	.168644	.175168	.181765	.188428	.195152
20	.40	.010242	.016578	.023018	.026274	.029552	.032851	.036170	.039507	.042862	.049618	.056431	.063291	.070193
	.30	.025983	.032319	.038759	.042015	.045293	.048592	.051911	.055248	.058603	.065359	.072172	.079032	.085934
	.20	.041724	.048060	.054500	.057756	.061034	.064333	.067652	.070989	.074344	.081100	.087913	.094773	.101675
	.10	.057465	.063801	.070241	.073497	.076775	.080074	.083393	.086730	.090084	.096841	.103654	.110514	.117416
	0.00	.073206	.079542	.085982	.089238	.092516	.095815	.099134	.102471	.105825	.112582	.119395	.126255	.133156
	-.10	.088947	.095283	.101723	.104979	.108257	.111556	.114875	.118212	.121565	.128323	.135136	.141996	.148897
	-.20	.104688	.111024	.117464	.120720	.123998	.127297	.130616	.133953	.137307	.144064	.150877	.157737	.164638
	-.30	.120429	.126765	.133205	.136461	.139739	.143038	.146357	.149694	.153048	.159805	.166617	.173478	.180379
	-.40	.136170	.142505	.148946	.152202	.155480	.158779	.162098	.165435	.168789	.175546	.182358	.189219	.196120
25	.40	.009559	.016064	.022667	.026002	.029356	.032727	.036116	.039519	.042936	.049807	.056717	.063660	.070629
	.30	.025300	.031805	.038408	.041743	.045097	.048468	.051857	.055260	.058677	.065548	.072458	.079401	.086370
	.20	.041040	.047546	.054149	.057484	.060838	.064209	.067598	.071001	.074418	.081288	.088199	.095142	.102111
	.10	.056781	.063287	.069890	.073225	.076578	.079950	.083339	.086742	.090159	.097029	.103940	.110883	.117852
	0.00	.072522	.079028	.085631	.088966	.092319	.095691	.099080	.102483	.105900	.112770	.119681	.126624	.133593
	-.10	.088263	.094769	.101372	.104707	.108060	.111432	.114821	.118224	.121641	.128511	.135422	.142365	.149334
	-.20	.104004	.110510	.117113	.120448	.123801	.127173	.130562	.133965	.137382	.144252	.151163	.158106	.165075
	-.30	.119745	.126251	.132854	.136189	.139542	.142914	.146303	.149706	.153123	.159993	.166904	.173847	.180816
	-.40	.135486	.141992	.148595	.151930	.155283	.158655	.162044	.165447	.168864	.175734	.182645	.189588	.196557
30	.40	.009125	.015745	.022455	.025839	.029240	.032656	.036085	.039526	.042977	.049907	.056865	.063843	.070836
	.30	.024867	.031486	.038196	.041580	.044981	.048397	.051826	.055267	.058718	.065648	.072606	.079584	.086577
	.20	.040607	.047227	.053937	.057321	.060722	.064138	.067567	.071008	.074459	.081389	.088347	.095325	.102318
	.10	.056348	.062968	.069678	.073062	.076463	.079879	.083308	.086749	.090200	.097130	.104088	.111066	.118059
	0.00	.072089	.078709	.085419	.088803	.092204	.095620	.099049	.102490	.105941	.112871	.119829	.126807	.133800
	-.10	.087830	.094450	.101160	.104544	.107945	.111361	.114790	.118231	.121682	.128612	.135570	.142548	.149541
	-.20	.103571	.110191	.116901	.120285	.123686	.127102	.130531	.133972	.137423	.144353	.151311	.158289	.165282
	-.30	.119312	.125932	.132642	.136026	.139427	.142843	.146272	.149713	.153164	.160094	.167052	.174030	.181023
	-.40	.135053	.141673	.148383	.151767	.155168	.158583	.162013	.165454	.168905	.175835	.182793	.189771	.196764

5.0 YEAR HOLDING PERIOD
.120 EQUITY YIELD RATE
.750 LOAN RATIO

INTEREST RATE

TERM YEARS	APPR DEP	5.0	6.0	7.0	7.5	8.0	8.5	9.0	9.5	10.0	11.0	12.0	13.0	14.0
10	.40	.010792	.016693	.022702	.025746	.028815	.031910	.035030	.038175	.041343	.047750	.054247	.060830	.067497
	.30	.026533	.032434	.038443	.041487	.044556	.047651	.050771	.053916	.057084	.063490	.069988	.076571	.083238
	.20	.042274	.048175	.054184	.057228	.060297	.063392	.066512	.069657	.072825	.079231	.085729	.092312	.098979
	.10	.058015	.063916	.069925	.072969	.076038	.079133	.082253	.085453	.088566	.094972	.101469	.108053	.114720
	0.00	.073756	.079657	.085666	.088710	.091779	.094874	.097994	.101138	.104407	.110713	.117210	.123794	.130461
	-.10	.089497	.095398	.101407	.104451	.107520	.110615	.113735	.116879	.120048	.126454	.132951	.139535	.146202
	-.20	.105238	.111139	.117148	.120192	.123261	.126356	.129476	.132620	.135789	.142195	.148692	.155276	.161943
	-.30	.120979	.126880	.132889	.135933	.139002	.142097	.145217	.148361	.151530	.157936	.164433	.171017	.177684
	-.40	.136720	.142621	.148630	.151674	.154743	.157838	.160958	.164102	.167271	.173677	.180174	.186758	.193425
15	.40	.008170	.014660	.021265	.024608	.027977	.031371	.034789	.038230	.041693	.048683	.055752	.062891	.070095
	.30	.023911	.030401	.037006	.040349	.043718	.047112	.050530	.053971	.057434	.064424	.071493	.078632	.085836
	.20	.039652	.046142	.052747	.056090	.059459	.062853	.066271	.069712	.073175	.080165	.087234	.094373	.101577
	.10	.055393	.061883	.068488	.071831	.075200	.078594	.082012	.085453	.088916	.095906	.102975	.110114	.117318
	0.00	.071134	.077624	.084229	.087572	.090941	.094335	.097753	.101194	.104657	.111647	.118716	.125855	.133059
	-.10	.086875	.093365	.099970	.103313	.106682	.110076	.113494	.116935	.120398	.127388	.134456	.141596	.148800
	-.20	.102616	.109106	.115711	.119054	.122423	.125817	.129235	.132676	.136139	.143129	.150197	.157337	.164541
	-.30	.118357	.124847	.131452	.134795	.138164	.141558	.144976	.148417	.151880	.158870	.165938	.173078	.180282
	-.40	.134098	.140588	.147193	.150536	.153905	.157299	.160717	.164158	.167621	.174611	.181679	.188819	.196023
20	.40	.006899	.013688	.020588	.024076	.027589	.031123	.034679	.038255	.041849	.049088	.056387	.063738	.071132
	.30	.022640	.029429	.036329	.039817	.043330	.046864	.050420	.053996	.057590	.064829	.072128	.079479	.086873
	.20	.038381	.045170	.052070	.055558	.059071	.062605	.066161	.069737	.073331	.080570	.087869	.095220	.102614
	.10	.054122	.060911	.067811	.071299	.074812	.078346	.081902	.085478	.089072	.096311	.103610	.110961	.118355
	0.00	.069863	.076652	.083552	.087040	.090553	.094087	.097643	.101219	.104813	.112052	.119351	.126702	.134096
	-.10	.085604	.092393	.099293	.102781	.106294	.109828	.113384	.116960	.120554	.127793	.135092	.142443	.149837
	-.20	.101345	.108134	.115034	.118522	.122035	.125569	.129125	.132701	.136295	.143534	.150833	.158184	.165578
	-.30	.117086	.123875	.130775	.134263	.137776	.141310	.144866	.148442	.152036	.159275	.166574	.173925	.181319
	-.40	.132827	.139616	.146516	.150004	.153517	.157051	.160607	.164183	.167777	.175016	.182315	.189666	.197060
25	.40	.006167	.013137	.020213	.023785	.027378	.030991	.034621	.038268	.041929	.049290	.056695	.064134	.071600
	.30	.021908	.028878	.035953	.039526	.043119	.046732	.050362	.054009	.057670	.065031	.072436	.079875	.087341
	.20	.037649	.044619	.051694	.055267	.058860	.062473	.066103	.069750	.073411	.080772	.088177	.095616	.103082
	.10	.053390	.060360	.067435	.071008	.074601	.078214	.081844	.085491	.089152	.096513	.103917	.111357	.118823
	0.00	.069131	.076101	.083176	.086749	.090342	.093955	.097585	.101232	.104893	.112254	.119658	.127098	.134564
	-.10	.084872	.091842	.098917	.102490	.106083	.109696	.113326	.116973	.120634	.127995	.135399	.142839	.150305
	-.20	.100613	.107583	.114658	.118231	.121824	.125437	.129067	.132714	.136375	.143736	.151140	.158579	.166046
	-.30	.116354	.123324	.130399	.133972	.137565	.141178	.144808	.148455	.152116	.159477	.166881	.174320	.181787
	-.40	.132095	.139065	.146140	.149713	.153306	.156919	.160549	.164196	.167857	.175218	.182622	.190061	.197528
30	.40	.005703	.012796	.019985	.023611	.027255	.030914	.034588	.038275	.041973	.049398	.056853	.064329	.071822
	.30	.021444	.028537	.035726	.039352	.042995	.046655	.050329	.054016	.057714	.065139	.072593	.080070	.087563
	.20	.037185	.044278	.051467	.055093	.058736	.062396	.066070	.069757	.073455	.080880	.088334	.095811	.103304
	.10	.052926	.060019	.067208	.070834	.074477	.078137	.081811	.085498	.089196	.096621	.104075	.111552	.119045
	0.00	.068667	.075760	.082949	.086575	.090218	.093878	.097552	.101239	.104937	.112362	.119816	.127293	.134786
	-.10	.084408	.091501	.098690	.102316	.105959	.109619	.113293	.116980	.120678	.128103	.135557	.143034	.150527
	-.20	.100149	.107242	.114431	.118057	.121700	.125360	.129034	.132721	.136419	.143844	.151298	.158775	.166268
	-.30	.115890	.122983	.130172	.133798	.137441	.141101	.144775	.148462	.152160	.159585	.167039	.174516	.182009
	-.40	.131631	.138724	.145913	.149539	.153182	.156842	.160516	.164203	.167901	.175326	.182780	.190257	.197750

242

5.0 YEAR HOLDING PERIOD
.120 EQUITY YIELD RATE
.800 LOAN RATIO

INTEREST RATE

TERM YEARS	APPR DEP	5.0	6.0	7.0	7.5	8.0	8.5	9.0	9.5	10.0	11.0	12.0	13.0	14.0
10	.40	.007709	.014003	.020413	.023660	.026934	.030235	.033563	.036917	.040297	.047130	.054061	.061083	.068194
	.30	.023450	.029740	.036154	.039401	.042675	.045976	.049304	.052658	.056038	.062817	.069802	.076824	.083935
	.20	.039191	.045485	.051895	.055142	.058416	.061717	.065045	.068399	.071779	.078612	.085543	.092565	.099676
	.10	.054932	.061226	.067636	.070883	.074157	.077458	.080786	.084140	.087520	.094353	.101284	.108306	.115417
	0.00	.070673	.076967	.083377	.086624	.089898	.093199	.096527	.099881	.103261	.110094	.117024	.124047	.131158
	-.10	.086414	.092708	.099118	.102365	.105639	.108940	.112268	.115622	.119001	.125835	.132765	.139788	.146899
	-.20	.102155	.108449	.114859	.118106	.121380	.124681	.128009	.131363	.134742	.141576	.148506	.155529	.162640
	-.30	.117896	.124190	.130600	.133847	.137121	.140422	.143750	.147104	.150483	.157317	.164247	.171270	.178381
	-.40	.133637	.139931	.146341	.149588	.152862	.156163	.159491	.162845	.166224	.173058	.179988	.187011	.194122
15	.40	.004913	.011835	.018880	.022446	.026040	.029660	.033306	.036976	.040671	.048127	.055666	.063281	.070965
	.30	.020654	.027576	.034621	.038187	.041781	.045401	.049047	.052717	.056412	.063868	.071407	.079022	.086706
	.20	.036395	.043317	.050362	.053928	.057521	.061142	.064788	.068458	.072153	.079610	.087148	.094763	.102447
	.10	.052136	.059058	.066103	.069669	.073262	.076883	.080529	.084199	.087894	.095350	.102889	.110504	.118188
	0.00	.067876	.074799	.081844	.085410	.089004	.092624	.096270	.099940	.103635	.111091	.118630	.126245	.133929
	-.10	.083617	.090540	.097585	.101151	.104744	.108365	.112011	.115681	.119375	.126831	.134371	.141986	.149670
	-.20	.099358	.106281	.113326	.116892	.120485	.124106	.127752	.131422	.135116	.142572	.150112	.157727	.165411
	-.30	.115099	.122022	.129067	.132633	.136226	.139847	.143492	.147163	.150857	.158313	.165853	.173468	.181152
	-.40	.130840	.137763	.144808	.148374	.151967	.155588	.159233	.162904	.166598	.174054	.181594	.189209	.196893
20	.40	.003557	.010798	.018158	.021879	.025626	.029396	.033189	.037003	.040837	.048558	.056344	.064485	.072072
	.30	.019298	.026539	.033899	.037620	.041367	.045137	.048930	.052744	.056578	.064299	.072085	.079926	.087813
	.20	.035039	.042280	.049640	.053361	.057108	.060878	.064671	.068485	.072319	.080040	.087826	.095667	.103554
	.10	.050780	.058021	.065381	.069102	.072849	.076619	.080412	.084226	.088060	.095781	.103567	.111408	.119295
	0.00	.066521	.073762	.081122	.084843	.088589	.092360	.096153	.099967	.103801	.111522	.119308	.127149	.135036
	-.10	.082262	.089503	.096863	.100584	.104330	.108101	.111894	.115708	.119541	.127263	.135049	.142890	.150777
	-.20	.098003	.105244	.112604	.116325	.120071	.123842	.127635	.131449	.135282	.143004	.150790	.158631	.166518
	-.30	.113744	.120985	.128345	.132066	.135812	.139583	.143376	.147190	.151023	.158745	.166531	.174372	.182259
	-.40	.129485	.136726	.144086	.147807	.151553	.155324	.159117	.162931	.166764	.174486	.182272	.190113	.198000
25	.40	.002776	.010211	.017758	.021568	.025401	.029255	.033127	.037017	.040922	.048774	.056672	.064607	.072571
	.30	.018517	.025952	.033499	.037309	.041142	.044996	.048868	.052758	.056663	.064515	.072413	.080348	.088312
	.20	.034258	.041693	.049240	.053050	.056883	.060737	.064609	.068499	.072404	.080256	.088154	.096089	.104053
	.10	.049999	.057434	.064981	.068791	.072624	.076478	.080350	.084240	.088145	.095997	.103895	.111830	.119794
	0.00	.065740	.073175	.080721	.084532	.088365	.092219	.096091	.099981	.103886	.111738	.119636	.127571	.135535
	-.10	.081481	.088916	.096462	.100273	.104106	.107960	.111832	.115722	.119627	.127479	.135377	.143312	.151276
	-.20	.097222	.104657	.112203	.116014	.119847	.123701	.127573	.131463	.135368	.143220	.151118	.159053	.167017
	-.30	.112963	.120398	.127944	.131755	.135588	.139442	.143314	.147203	.151109	.158961	.166859	.174794	.182758
	-.40	.128704	.136139	.143685	.147496	.151329	.155183	.159055	.162944	.166850	.174702	.182600	.190535	.198499
30	.40	.002281	.009846	.017515	.021383	.025269	.029173	.033092	.037024	.040969	.048889	.056840	.064816	.072808
	.30	.018022	.025587	.033256	.037124	.041010	.044914	.048833	.052765	.056710	.064633	.072581	.080557	.088549
	.20	.033763	.041328	.048997	.052865	.056751	.060655	.064574	.068506	.072451	.080371	.088322	.096297	.104290
	.10	.049504	.057069	.064738	.068606	.072492	.076396	.080315	.084247	.088192	.096112	.104063	.112038	.120031
	0.00	.065245	.072810	.080479	.084346	.088233	.092137	.096056	.099988	.103933	.111853	.119804	.127799	.135772
	-.10	.080986	.088551	.096220	.100087	.103974	.107878	.111797	.115729	.119674	.127594	.135545	.143520	.151513
	-.20	.096727	.104292	.111961	.115828	.119715	.123619	.127538	.131470	.135416	.143334	.151286	.159261	.167254
	-.30	.112468	.120033	.127702	.131569	.135456	.139360	.143279	.147211	.151156	.159075	.167002	.175002	.182995
	-.40	.128209	.135774	.143443	.147310	.151197	.155101	.159020	.162952	.166897	.174816	.182768	.190743	.198736

5.0 YEAR HOLDING PERIOD
.120 EQUITY YIELD RATE
.900 LOAN RATIO

INTEREST RATE

TERM YEARS	APPR DEP	5.0	6.0	7.0	7.5	8.0	8.5	9.0	9.5	10.0	11.0	12.0	13.0	14.0
10	.40	.001543	.008624	.015835	.019488	.023171	.026885	.030629	.034402	.038204	.045892	.053689	.061589	.069589
	.30	.017284	.024365	.031576	.035229	.038812	.042626	.046370	.050143	.053345	.061633	.069430	.077330	.085330
	.20	.033025	.040106	.047317	.050970	.054653	.058367	.062111	.065884	.069686	.077374	.085171	.093071	.101071
	.10	.048766	.055847	.063058	.066711	.070394	.074108	.077852	.081625	.085427	.093115	.100912	.108812	.116812
	0.00	.064507	.071588	.078799	.082452	.086135	.089849	.093593	.097366	.101168	.108856	.116653	.124553	.132553
	-.10	.080248	.087329	.094540	.098193	.101876	.105590	.109334	.113107	.116909	.124597	.132394	.140294	.148294
	-.20	.095989	.103070	.110281	.113934	.117617	.121331	.125075	.128848	.132650	.140338	.148135	.156035	.164035
	-.30	.111730	.118811	.126022	.129674	.133358	.137072	.140816	.144589	.148391	.156079	.163875	.171776	.179776
	-.40	.127471	.134552	.141763	.145415	.149099	.152813	.156557	.160330	.164132	.171820	.179616	.187517	.195517
15	.40	-.001603	.006185	.014111	.018122	.022165	.026238	.030339	.034469	.038625	.047013	.055495	.064062	.072707
	.30	.014138	.021926	.029852	.033863	.037906	.041979	.046080	.050210	.054366	.062754	.071236	.079803	.088448
	.20	.029879	.037667	.045593	.049606	.053647	.057720	.061821	.065951	.070107	.078495	.086977	.095544	.104189
	.10	.045620	.053408	.061333	.065345	.069388	.073461	.077562	.081692	.085848	.094236	.102718	.111285	.119930
	0.00	.061361	.069149	.077074	.081086	.085129	.089202	.093303	.097433	.101589	.109977	.118459	.127026	.135671
	-.10	.077102	.084890	.092815	.096827	.100870	.104943	.109044	.113174	.117330	.125718	.134200	.142767	.151412
	-.20	.092843	.100631	.108556	.112568	.116611	.120684	.124785	.128915	.133071	.141459	.149941	.158508	.167152
	-.30	.108584	.116372	.124297	.128309	.132352	.136425	.140526	.144656	.148812	.157200	.165682	.174249	.182893
	-.40	.124325	.132113	.140038	.144050	.148093	.152166	.156267	.160397	.164553	.172941	.181423	.189990	.198634
20	.40	-.003128	.005018	.013298	.017485	.021699	.025941	.030208	.034499	.038812	.047499	.056258	.065078	.073952
	.30	.012613	.020759	.029039	.033226	.037440	.041682	.045949	.050240	.054553	.063240	.071999	.080819	.089693
	.20	.028354	.036500	.044780	.048966	.053181	.057423	.061690	.065981	.070294	.078981	.087740	.096560	.105434
	.10	.044095	.052241	.060521	.064707	.068922	.073164	.077431	.081722	.086035	.094722	.103481	.112301	.121174
	0.00	.059836	.067982	.076262	.080448	.084663	.088905	.093172	.097463	.101776	.110463	.119222	.128042	.136915
	-.10	.075577	.083723	.092003	.096189	.100404	.104646	.108913	.113204	.117517	.126204	.134963	.143783	.152656
	-.20	.091318	.099464	.107744	.111930	.116145	.120387	.124654	.128945	.133258	.141945	.150704	.159524	.168397
	-.30	.107059	.115205	.123485	.127671	.131886	.136128	.140395	.144685	.148999	.157685	.166445	.175265	.184138
	-.40	.122800	.130946	.139226	.143412	.147627	.151869	.156136	.160426	.164739	.173426	.182185	.191006	.199879
25	.40	-.004006	.004358	.012848	.017135	.021447	.025782	.030138	.034514	.038908	.047741	.056626	.065553	.074513
	.30	.011735	.020099	.028589	.032876	.037188	.041523	.045879	.050255	.054649	.063482	.072367	.081294	.090254
	.20	.027475	.035840	.044330	.048617	.052929	.057264	.061620	.065996	.070390	.079223	.088108	.097035	.105995
	.10	.043216	.051580	.060071	.064358	.068670	.073005	.077361	.081737	.086131	.094964	.103849	.112776	.121736
	0.00	.058957	.067321	.075812	.080099	.084411	.088746	.093102	.097478	.101872	.110705	.119590	.128517	.137477
	-.10	.074698	.083062	.091553	.095840	.100153	.104487	.108843	.113219	.117613	.126446	.135331	.144258	.153218
	-.20	.090439	.098803	.107294	.111581	.115893	.120228	.124584	.128960	.133354	.142187	.151072	.159999	.168958
	-.30	.106180	.114544	.123035	.127322	.131634	.135969	.140325	.144701	.149094	.157928	.166813	.175740	.184699
	-.40	.121921	.130285	.138776	.143063	.147375	.151710	.156066	.160442	.164835	.173669	.182554	.191481	.200440
30	.40	-.004563	.003948	.012575	.016926	.021298	.025698	.030099	.034523	.038961	.047870	.056816	.065788	.074779
	.30	.011178	.019689	.028316	.032667	.037039	.041431	.045840	.050264	.054702	.063611	.072557	.081529	.090520
	.20	.026919	.035430	.044057	.048408	.052780	.057172	.061581	.066005	.070443	.079352	.088298	.097270	.106261
	.10	.042660	.051171	.059798	.064149	.068521	.072913	.077322	.081746	.086184	.095093	.104039	.113012	.122002
	0.00	.058401	.066912	.075539	.079890	.084262	.088654	.093063	.097487	.101925	.110834	.119780	.128752	.137743
	-.10	.074142	.082653	.091280	.095631	.100003	.104395	.108804	.113228	.117666	.126575	.135521	.144493	.153484
	-.20	.089883	.098394	.107021	.111372	.115744	.120136	.124545	.128969	.133407	.142316	.151262	.160234	.169225
	-.30	.105624	.114135	.122762	.127113	.131485	.135877	.140286	.144710	.149148	.158057	.167003	.175975	.184966
	-.40	.121364	.129876	.138503	.142854	.147226	.151618	.156027	.160451	.164889	.173798	.182744	.191716	.200707

5.0 YEAR HOLDING PERIOD
.140 EQUITY YIELD RATE
.600 LOAN RATIO

INTEREST RATE

TERM YEARS	APPR DEP	5.0	6.0	7.0	7.5	8.0	8.5	9.0	9.5	10.0	11.0	12.0	13.0	14.0
10	.40	.032101	.036777	.041540	.043953	.046386	.048840	.051315	.053808	.056321	.061404	.066560	.071786	.077078
	.30	.047229	.051905	.056668	.059081	.061515	.063969	.066443	.068937	.071450	.076533	.081688	.086914	.092207
	.20	.062358	.067034	.071796	.074209	.076643	.079097	.081571	.084065	.086578	.091661	.096817	.102042	.107335
	.10	.077486	.082162	.086925	.089338	.091771	.094225	.096700	.099193	.101707	.106789	.111945	.117171	.122463
	0.00	.092614	.097290	.102053	.104466	.106900	.109354	.111828	.114322	.116835	.121918	.127073	.132299	.137592
	-.10	.107743	.112419	.117181	.119594	.122028	.124482	.126956	.129450	.131963	.137046	.142202	.147427	.152720
	-.20	.122871	.127547	.132310	.134723	.137156	.139611	.142085	.144578	.147092	.152174	.157330	.162556	.167848
	-.30	.137999	.142675	.147438	.149851	.152285	.154739	.157213	.159707	.162220	.167303	.172458	.177684	.182977
	-.40	.153128	.157804	.162566	.164969	.167413	.169867	.172341	.174835	.177348	.182431	.187587	.192862	.198105
15	.40	.029329	.034468	.039700	.042349	.045020	.047711	.050421	.053151	.055899	.061447	.067060	.072731	.078457
	.30	.044458	.049596	.054828	.057477	.060148	.062839	.065550	.068280	.071028	.076576	.082188	.087860	.093585
	.20	.059586	.064724	.069956	.072606	.075276	.077967	.080678	.083408	.086156	.091704	.097317	.102988	.108713
	.10	.074714	.079853	.085085	.087734	.090405	.093096	.095806	.098536	.101284	.106832	.112445	.118117	.123842
	0.00	.089843	.094981	.100213	.102863	.105533	.108224	.110935	.113665	.116413	.121961	.127573	.133245	.138970
	-.10	.104971	.110109	.115342	.117991	.120661	.123352	.126063	.128793	.131541	.137089	.142702	.148373	.154098
	-.20	.120099	.125238	.130470	.133119	.135790	.138481	.141192	.143921	.146669	.152217	.157830	.163502	.169227
	-.30	.135228	.140366	.145598	.148248	.150918	.153609	.156320	.159050	.161798	.167346	.172958	.178630	.184355
	-.40	.150356	.155495	.160727	.163376	.166046	.168737	.171448	.174178	.176926	.182474	.188087	.193758	.199483
20	.40	.027985	.033363	.038833	.041600	.044387	.047193	.050016	.052856	.055712	.061466	.067271	.073120	.079007
	.30	.043114	.048491	.053962	.056729	.059516	.062321	.065145	.067985	.070840	.076594	.082399	.088249	.094135
	.20	.058242	.063620	.069090	.071857	.074450	.077450	.080273	.083113	.085969	.091723	.097528	.103377	.109264
	.10	.073370	.078748	.084218	.086985	.089772	.092578	.095401	.098241	.101097	.106851	.112656	.118505	.124392
	0.00	.088499	.093876	.099347	.102114	.104901	.107706	.110530	.113370	.116225	.121979	.127785	.133634	.139520
	-.10	.103627	.109005	.114475	.117242	.120029	.122835	.125658	.128498	.131354	.137108	.142913	.148762	.154649
	-.20	.118755	.124133	.129603	.132370	.135157	.137963	.140786	.143626	.146482	.152236	.158041	.163890	.169777
	-.30	.133884	.139261	.144732	.147499	.150286	.153091	.155915	.158755	.161610	.167364	.173170	.179019	.184906
	-.40	.149012	.154390	.159860	.162627	.165414	.168220	.171043	.173883	.176739	.182493	.188298	.194147	.200034
25	.40	.027211	.032738	.038353	.041190	.044044	.046916	.049802	.052702	.055615	.061475	.067373	.073302	.079255
	.30	.042340	.047866	.053481	.056318	.059173	.062044	.064930	.067831	.070744	.076604	.082501	.088430	.094383
	.20	.057468	.062994	.068609	.071446	.074301	.077172	.080059	.082959	.085872	.091732	.097630	.103559	.109512
	.10	.072596	.078123	.083738	.086575	.089429	.092301	.095187	.098088	.101001	.106860	.112758	.118687	.124640
	0.00	.087725	.093251	.098866	.101703	.104558	.107429	.110316	.113216	.116129	.121989	.127887	.133815	.139769
	-.10	.102853	.108379	.113994	.116831	.119686	.122557	.125444	.128344	.131257	.137117	.143015	.148944	.154897
	-.20	.117981	.123508	.129123	.131960	.134815	.137686	.140572	.143473	.146386	.152245	.158143	.164072	.170025
	-.30	.133110	.138636	.144251	.147088	.149943	.152814	.155701	.158601	.161514	.167374	.173272	.179201	.185154
	-.40	.148238	.153764	.159379	.162216	.165071	.167943	.170829	.173729	.176642	.182502	.188400	.194329	.200282
30	.40	.026721	.032350	.038062	.040944	.043843	.046755	.049680	.052616	.055562	.061480	.067426	.073392	.079373
	.30	.041849	.047478	.053191	.056073	.058971	.061883	.064808	.067744	.070691	.076609	.082554	.088520	.094501
	.20	.056977	.062606	.068318	.071201	.074099	.077012	.079937	.082873	.085819	.091737	.097682	.103648	.109630
	.10	.072106	.077735	.083447	.086329	.089228	.092140	.095065	.098001	.100947	.106865	.112811	.118777	.124758
	0.00	.087234	.092863	.098575	.101458	.104356	.107268	.110193	.113129	.116076	.121994	.127939	.133905	.139886
	-.10	.102362	.107991	.113703	.116586	.119484	.122397	.125322	.128258	.131204	.137122	.143067	.149033	.155015
	-.20	.117491	.123120	.128832	.131714	.134613	.137525	.140450	.143386	.146332	.152250	.158196	.164162	.170143
	-.30	.132619	.138248	.143960	.146843	.149741	.152653	.155578	.158514	.161461	.167379	.173324	.179290	.185271
	-.40	.147748	.153376	.159088	.161971	.164869	.167782	.170707	.173643	.176589	.182507	.188452	.194418	.200400

5.0 YEAR HOLDING PERIOD
.140 EQUITY YIELD RATE
.667 LOAN RATIO

INTEREST RATE

TERM YEARS	APPR DEP	5.0	6.0	7.0	7.5	8.0	8.5	9.0	9.5	10.0	11.0	12.0	13.0	14.0
10	.40	.026836	.032031	.037323	.040004	.042708	.045435	.048184	.050955	.053747	.059395	.065124	.070930	.076811
	.30	.041964	.047159	.052451	.055133	.057837	.060563	.063313	.066083	.068876	.074523	.080252	.086058	.091939
	.20	.057092	.062288	.067580	.070261	.072985	.075692	.078441	.081212	.084004	.089652	.095380	.101187	.107067
	.10	.072221	.077416	.082708	.085389	.088093	.090820	.093569	.096340	.099133	.104780	.110509	.116315	.122196
	0.00	.087349	.092545	.097836	.100518	.103222	.105949	.108698	.111469	.114261	.119908	.125637	.131443	.137324
	-.10	.102477	.107673	.112965	.115646	.118350	.121077	.123826	.126597	.129389	.135037	.140765	.146572	.152452
	-.20	.117606	.122801	.128093	.130774	.133478	.136205	.138954	.141725	.144518	.150165	.155894	.161700	.167581
	-.30	.132734	.137930	.143221	.145903	.148607	.151334	.154083	.156854	.159646	.165293	.171022	.176828	.182759
	-.40	.147862	.153058	.158350	.161031	.163735	.166462	.169211	.171982	.174774	.180422	.186150	.191957	.197837
15	.40	.023756	.029465	.035279	.038223	.041190	.044180	.047192	.050225	.053278	.059443	.065679	.071981	.078342
	.30	.038884	.044594	.050407	.053351	.056318	.059308	.062320	.065353	.068407	.074571	.080807	.087109	.093471
	.20	.054013	.059722	.065536	.068479	.071446	.074437	.077448	.080482	.083535	.089700	.095936	.102238	.108599
	.10	.069141	.074850	.080664	.083608	.086575	.089565	.092577	.095610	.098663	.104828	.111064	.117366	.123727
	0.00	.084269	.089979	.095792	.098736	.101703	.104693	.107705	.110738	.113792	.119956	.126192	.132494	.138856
	-.10	.099398	.105107	.110921	.113864	.116832	.119822	.122834	.125867	.128920	.135085	.141321	.147623	.153984
	-.20	.114526	.120235	.126049	.128993	.131960	.134950	.137962	.140995	.144048	.150213	.156449	.162751	.169112
	-.30	.129654	.135364	.141177	.144121	.147088	.150078	.153090	.156123	.159177	.165341	.171578	.177879	.184241
	-.40	.144783	.150492	.156306	.159249	.162217	.165207	.168219	.171252	.174305	.180470	.186706	.193008	.199369
20	.40	.022263	.028238	.034316	.037391	.040487	.043605	.046742	.049897	.053070	.059464	.065914	.072413	.078954
	.30	.037391	.043366	.049444	.052519	.055615	.058733	.061870	.065025	.068198	.074592	.081042	.087541	.094082
	.20	.052519	.058495	.064573	.067648	.070744	.073861	.076998	.080154	.083327	.089720	.096170	.102670	.109210
	.10	.067648	.073623	.079701	.082776	.085872	.088990	.092127	.095282	.098455	.104849	.111299	.117798	.124339
	0.00	.082776	.088751	.094829	.097904	.101001	.104118	.107255	.110411	.113583	.119977	.126427	.132926	.139467
	-.10	.097904	.103880	.109958	.113032	.116129	.119246	.122383	.125539	.128712	.135105	.141556	.148055	.154596
	-.20	.113033	.119008	.125086	.128161	.131257	.134375	.137512	.140667	.143840	.150234	.156684	.163183	.169724
	-.30	.128161	.134136	.140214	.143289	.146386	.149503	.152640	.155796	.158969	.165362	.171812	.178311	.184852
	-.40	.143290	.149265	.155343	.158514	.161514	.164631	.167768	.170924	.174097	.180490	.186941	.193440	.199981
25	.40	.021403	.027543	.033782	.036934	.040106	.043297	.046504	.049726	.052963	.059474	.066027	.072615	.079229
	.30	.036531	.042671	.048910	.052062	.055235	.058425	.061632	.064855	.068091	.074602	.081155	.087743	.094358
	.20	.051659	.057800	.064039	.067191	.070363	.073553	.076760	.079983	.083220	.089731	.096284	.102871	.109486
	.10	.066788	.072928	.079167	.082319	.085491	.088682	.091889	.095111	.098348	.104859	.111412	.118000	.124614
	0.00	.081916	.088056	.094295	.097448	.100620	.103810	.107017	.110240	.113476	.119987	.126541	.133128	.139743
	-.10	.097044	.103185	.109424	.112576	.115748	.118938	.122145	.125368	.128605	.135116	.141669	.148256	.154871
	-.20	.112173	.118313	.124552	.127704	.130877	.134067	.137274	.140496	.143733	.150244	.156797	.163385	.170000
	-.30	.127301	.133442	.139680	.142833	.146005	.149195	.152402	.155625	.158861	.165372	.171926	.178513	.185128
	-.40	.142429	.148570	.154809	.157961	.161133	.164323	.167531	.170753	.173990	.180501	.187054	.193641	.200256
30	.40	.020857	.027112	.033459	.036662	.039882	.043118	.046368	.049630	.052904	.059479	.066085	.072714	.079360
	.30	.035986	.042240	.048587	.051790	.055010	.058246	.061496	.064759	.068032	.074608	.081214	.087843	.094489
	.20	.051114	.057369	.063715	.066918	.070139	.073375	.076624	.079887	.083161	.089736	.096342	.102971	.109617
	.10	.066243	.072497	.078844	.082047	.085267	.088503	.091753	.095015	.098289	.104864	.111470	.118099	.124745
	0.00	.081371	.087625	.093972	.097175	.100395	.103631	.106881	.110144	.113417	.119993	.126599	.133228	.139874
	-.10	.096499	.102754	.109100	.112303	.115524	.118760	.122010	.125272	.128546	.135121	.141727	.148356	.155002
	-.20	.111628	.117882	.124229	.127432	.130652	.133888	.137138	.140400	.143674	.150250	.156856	.163485	.170130
	-.30	.126756	.133010	.139357	.142560	.145780	.149016	.152266	.155529	.158802	.165378	.171984	.178613	.185259
	-.40	.141884	.148139	.154485	.157688	.160909	.164145	.167395	.170657	.173931	.180506	.187112	.193741	.200387

5.0 YEAR HOLDING PERIOD
.140 EQUITY YIELD RATE
.700 LOAN RATIO RATE

INTEREST RATE

TERM YEARS	APPR DEP	5.0	6.0	7.0	7.5	8.0	8.5	9.0	9.5	10.0	11.0	12.0	13.0	14.0
10	.40	.024203	.029659	.035215	.038030	.040870	.043733	.046619	.049529	.052461	.058391	.064405	.070502	.076677
	.30	.039332	.044787	.050343	.053159	.055998	.058861	.061748	.064657	.067589	.073519	.079534	.085630	.091805
	.20	.054460	.059915	.065472	.068287	.071126	.073989	.077876	.079785	.082717	.088647	.094662	.100759	.106933
	.10	.069588	.075044	.080600	.083415	.086255	.089118	.092004	.094914	.097846	.103776	.109791	.115887	.122062
	0.00	.084717	.091172	.095728	.098544	.101383	.104246	.107133	.110042	.112974	.118904	.124919	.131015	.137190
	-.10	.099845	.105300	.110857	.113672	.116511	.119375	.122261	.125170	.128102	.134032	.140047	.146144	.152319
	-.20	.114973	.120429	.125985	.128800	.131640	.134503	.137389	.140299	.143231	.149161	.155176	.161272	.167447
	-.30	.130102	.135557	.141113	.143929	.146768	.149631	.152518	.155427	.158359	.164289	.170304	.176401	.182575
	-.40	.145230	.150685	.156242	.159057	.161896	.164760	.167646	.170556	.173487	.179417	.185432	.191529	.197704
15	.40	.020970	.026965	.033069	.036160	.039275	.042415	.045577	.048762	.051968	.058441	.064989	.071606	.078285
	.30	.036098	.042093	.048197	.051288	.054404	.057543	.060706	.063890	.067096	.073569	.080117	.086734	.093443
	.20	.051226	.057221	.063325	.066416	.069532	.072671	.075834	.079019	.082225	.088697	.095245	.101862	.108542
	.10	.066355	.072350	.078454	.081545	.084660	.087800	.090962	.094147	.097353	.103826	.110374	.116991	.123670
	0.00	.081483	.087478	.093582	.096673	.099789	.102928	.106091	.109275	.112481	.118954	.125502	.132119	.138798
	-.10	.096611	.102606	.108710	.111801	.114917	.118056	.121219	.124404	.127610	.130083	.140631	.147247	.153927
	-.20	.111740	.117735	.123839	.126930	.130045	.133185	.136347	.139532	.142738	.149211	.155759	.162376	.169055
	-.30	.126868	.132863	.138967	.142058	.145174	.148313	.151476	.154660	.157866	.164339	.170887	.177504	.184183
	-.40	.141996	.147991	.154095	.157186	.160302	.163441	.166604	.169739	.172995	.179468	.186016	.192632	.199312
20	.40	.019402	.025676	.032058	.035286	.038537	.041811	.045104	.048418	.051749	.058463	.065235	.072059	.078927
	.30	.034530	.040804	.047186	.050414	.053666	.056939	.060233	.063546	.066878	.073591	.080364	.087188	.094055
	.20	.049659	.055932	.062314	.065543	.068794	.072067	.075361	.078675	.082006	.088719	.095492	.102316	.109184
	.10	.064787	.071061	.077443	.080671	.083922	.087196	.090490	.093803	.097134	.103848	.110620	.117444	.124312
	0.00	.079915	.086189	.092571	.095799	.099051	.102324	.105618	.108931	.112263	.118976	.125749	.132573	.139441
	-.10	.095044	.101317	.107699	.110928	.114179	.117452	.120746	.124060	.127391	.134104	.140877	.147701	.154569
	-.20	.110172	.116446	.122828	.126056	.129307	.132581	.135875	.139188	.142519	.149233	.156005	.162829	.169697
	-.30	.125300	.131574	.137956	.141184	.144436	.147709	.151003	.154316	.157648	.164361	.171134	.177958	.184826
	-.40	.140429	.146703	.153085	.156313	.159564	.162837	.166131	.169445	.172776	.179489	.186262	.193086	.199954
25	.40	.018499	.024946	.031497	.034807	.038137	.041487	.044855	.048238	.051637	.058473	.065354	.072271	.079217
	.30	.033627	.040074	.046625	.049935	.053266	.056616	.059983	.063367	.066765	.073602	.080483	.087399	.094345
	.20	.048755	.055203	.061754	.065063	.068394	.071744	.075111	.078495	.081894	.088730	.095611	.102528	.109473
	.10	.063884	.070331	.076882	.080192	.083522	.086872	.090240	.093623	.097022	.103858	.110739	.117656	.124602
	0.00	.079012	.085460	.092010	.095320	.098651	.102001	.105368	.108752	.112150	.118987	.125868	.132784	.139730
	-.10	.094141	.100588	.107139	.110449	.113779	.117129	.120496	.123880	.127279	.134115	.140996	.147913	.154858
	-.20	.109269	.115716	.122267	.125577	.128907	.132257	.135625	.139009	.142407	.149243	.156124	.163041	.169987
	-.30	.124397	.130845	.137395	.140705	.144036	.147386	.150753	.154137	.157535	.164372	.171253	.178170	.185115
	-.40	.139526	.145973	.152524	.155834	.159164	.162514	.165882	.169265	.172664	.179500	.186381	.193298	.200243
30	.40	.017926	.024493	.031157	.034521	.037902	.041300	.044712	.048138	.051575	.058479	.065415	.072376	.079354
	.30	.033055	.039622	.046286	.049649	.053030	.056428	.059840	.063266	.066703	.073608	.080544	.087504	.094482
	.20	.048183	.054750	.061414	.064777	.068159	.071556	.074969	.078394	.081832	.088736	.095672	.102633	.109611
	.10	.063311	.069879	.076542	.079906	.083287	.086685	.090097	.093523	.096960	.103864	.110800	.117761	.124739
	0.00	.078440	.085007	.091671	.095034	.098415	.101813	.105225	.108651	.112088	.118993	.125929	.132889	.139867
	-.10	.093568	.100135	.106799	.110162	.113544	.116941	.120354	.123779	.127217	.134121	.141057	.148018	.154996
	-.20	.108696	.115264	.121928	.125291	.128672	.132070	.135482	.138908	.142345	.149249	.156186	.163146	.170124
	-.30	.123825	.130392	.137056	.140419	.143800	.147198	.150610	.154036	.157473	.164378	.171314	.178274	.185253
	-.40	.138953	.145520	.152184	.155547	.158929	.162326	.165739	.169164	.172602	.179506	.186442	.193403	.200381

5.0 YEAR HOLDING PERIOD
.140 EQUITY YIELD RATE
.750 LOAN RATIO

INTEREST RATE

TERM YEARS	APPR DEP	5.0	6.0	7.0	7.5	8.0	8.5	9.0	9.5	10.0	11.0	12.0	13.0	14.0
10	.40	.020254	.026099	.032053	.035069	.038111	.041179	.044272	.047389	.050530	.056884	.063328	.069860	.076476
	.30	.035383	.041228	.047181	.050197	.053240	.056307	.059400	.062517	.065659	.072012	.078457	.084989	.091604
	.20	.050511	.056356	.062309	.065326	.068368	.071436	.074528	.077646	.080787	.087140	.093585	.100117	.106733
	.10	.065639	.071484	.077438	.080454	.083496	.086564	.089657	.092774	.095915	.102269	.108713	.115245	.121861
	0.00	.080768	.086613	.092566	.095582	.098625	.101692	.104785	.107902	.111044	.117397	.123842	.130374	.136989
	-.10	.095896	.101741	.107695	.110711	.113753	.116821	.119913	.123031	.126172	.132525	.138970	.145502	.152118
	-.20	.111025	.116870	.122823	.125839	.128881	.131949	.135042	.138159	.141300	.147654	.154098	.160630	.167246
	-.30	.126153	.131998	.137951	.140968	.144010	.147077	.150170	.153287	.156429	.162782	.169227	.175759	.182375
	-.40	.141281	.147126	.153080	.156096	.159138	.162206	.165298	.168416	.171557	.177911	.184355	.190887	.197503
15	.40	.016790	.023213	.029753	.033065	.036403	.039767	.043155	.046567	.050002	.056937	.063953	.071043	.078199
	.30	.031918	.038341	.044881	.048193	.051531	.054895	.058283	.061696	.065131	.072066	.079082	.086171	.093327
	.20	.047047	.053470	.060010	.063321	.066660	.070023	.073412	.076824	.080259	.087194	.094210	.101299	.108456
	.10	.062175	.068598	.075138	.078450	.081788	.085152	.088540	.091952	.095387	.102323	.109338	.116428	.123584
	0.00	.077303	.083726	.090267	.093578	.096916	.100280	.103669	.107081	.110516	.117451	.124467	.131556	.138713
	-.10	.092432	.098855	.105395	.108707	.112045	.115408	.118797	.122209	.125644	.132579	.139595	.146684	.153841
	-.20	.107560	.113983	.120523	.123835	.127173	.130537	.133925	.137337	.140772	.147708	.154723	.161813	.168969
	-.30	.122688	.129111	.135652	.138963	.142301	.145665	.149054	.152466	.155901	.162836	.169852	.176941	.184098
	-.40	.137817	.144240	.150780	.154092	.157430	.160794	.164182	.167594	.171029	.177964	.184980	.192070	.199226
20	.40	.015110	.021832	.028670	.032129	.035612	.039119	.042649	.046199	.049768	.056961	.064217	.071529	.078887
	.30	.030238	.036960	.043798	.047257	.050741	.054248	.057777	.061327	.064896	.072089	.079346	.086657	.094016
	.20	.045367	.052089	.058927	.062385	.065869	.069376	.072905	.076455	.080025	.087217	.094474	.101785	.109144
	.10	.060495	.067217	.074055	.077514	.080997	.084505	.088034	.091584	.095153	.102346	.109602	.116914	.124272
	0.00	.075623	.082345	.089183	.092641	.096126	.099633	.103162	.106712	.110282	.117474	.124731	.132042	.139401
	-.10	.090752	.097474	.104312	.107771	.111254	.114761	.118290	.121840	.125410	.132603	.139859	.147170	.154529
	-.20	.105880	.112602	.119440	.122899	.126383	.129890	.133419	.136969	.140538	.147731	.154987	.162299	.169657
	-.30	.121009	.127731	.134568	.138027	.141511	.145018	.148547	.152097	.155667	.162859	.170116	.177427	.184786
	-.40	.136137	.142859	.149697	.153156	.156639	.160146	.163675	.167225	.170795	.177988	.185244	.192556	.199914
25	.40	.014142	.021050	.028069	.031615	.035184	.038773	.042381	.046006	.049648	.056972	.064345	.071756	.079197
	.30	.029271	.036179	.043197	.046744	.050312	.053901	.057509	.061135	.064776	.072101	.079473	.086884	.094326
	.20	.044399	.051307	.058326	.061872	.065441	.069030	.072638	.076263	.079904	.087229	.094601	.102012	.109454
	.10	.059528	.066435	.073454	.077000	.080569	.084158	.087766	.091391	.095033	.102357	.109730	.117141	.124582
	0.00	.074656	.081564	.088582	.092129	.095697	.099286	.102894	.106520	.110161	.117486	.124858	.132269	.139711
	-.10	.089784	.096692	.103711	.107257	.110826	.114415	.118023	.121648	.125289	.132614	.139987	.147397	.154839
	-.20	.104913	.111821	.118839	.122385	.125954	.129543	.133151	.136777	.140418	.147749	.155115	.162526	.169967
	-.30	.120041	.126949	.133968	.137514	.141082	.144671	.148279	.151905	.155546	.162871	.170243	.177654	.185096
	-.40	.135169	.142077	.149096	.152642	.156211	.159800	.163408	.167033	.170675	.177999	.185372	.192783	.200224
30	.40	.013529	.020565	.027705	.031309	.034932	.038572	.042228	.045898	.049581	.056979	.064410	.071868	.079345
	.30	.028658	.035694	.042834	.046437	.050060	.053700	.057356	.061027	.064710	.072107	.079539	.086996	.094473
	.20	.043786	.050822	.057962	.061565	.065188	.068829	.072445	.076155	.079838	.087235	.094667	.102125	.109601
	.10	.058914	.065950	.073090	.076694	.080317	.083957	.087613	.091283	.094966	.102364	.109795	.117253	.124730
	0.00	.074043	.081079	.088219	.091822	.095445	.099085	.102742	.106412	.110095	.117492	.124924	.132381	.139858
	-.10	.089171	.096207	.103347	.106950	.110573	.114214	.117870	.121540	.125223	.132620	.140052	.147510	.154986
	-.20	.104299	.111336	.118475	.122079	.125702	.129342	.132998	.136669	.140351	.147749	.155180	.162638	.170115
	-.30	.119428	.126464	.133604	.137207	.140830	.144470	.148127	.151797	.155480	.162877	.170309	.177766	.185243
	-.40	.134556	.141592	.148732	.152336	.155958	.159599	.163255	.166925	.170608	.178005	.185437	.192895	.200371

5.0 YEAR HOLDING PERIOD
.140 EQUITY YIELD RATE
.800 LOAN RATIO

INTEREST RATE

TERM YEARS	APPR DEP	5.0	6.0	7.0	7.5	8.0	8.5	9.0	9.5	10.0	11.0	12.0	13.0	14.0
10	.40	.016306	.022540	.028891	.032108	.035353	.038625	.041924	.045249	.048600	.055377	.062251	.069219	.076275
	.30	.031434	.037669	.044019	.047236	.050481	.053753	.057052	.060377	.063728	.070505	.077379	.084347	.091404
	.20	.046562	.052797	.059147	.062365	.065510	.068882	.072181	.075506	.078857	.085634	.092508	.099475	.106532
	.10	.061691	.067925	.074276	.077493	.080738	.084010	.087309	.090634	.093985	.100762	.107636	.114604	.121660
	0.00	.076819	.083054	.089404	.092621	.095866	.099138	.102437	.105762	.109113	.115890	.122764	.129732	.136789
	-.10	.091947	.098182	.104532	.107750	.110995	.114267	.117566	.120891	.124242	.131019	.137893	.144860	.151917
	-.20	.107076	.113310	.119661	.122878	.126123	.129395	.132694	.136019	.139370	.146147	.153021	.159989	.167046
	-.30	.122204	.128439	.134789	.138006	.141251	.144524	.147822	.151147	.154498	.161275	.168150	.175117	.182174
	-.40	.137332	.143567	.149917	.153135	.156380	.159652	.162951	.166276	.169627	.176404	.183278	.190245	.197302
15	.40	.012610	.019461	.026438	.029970	.033531	.037119	.040733	.044373	.048037	.055434	.062918	.070480	.078113
	.30	.027738	.034590	.041566	.045098	.048659	.052247	.055861	.059501	.063165	.070563	.078046	.085608	.093242
	.20	.042867	.049718	.056694	.060227	.063787	.067375	.070990	.074629	.078293	.085691	.093174	.100736	.108370
	.10	.057995	.064846	.071823	.075355	.078916	.082504	.086118	.089758	.093422	.100819	.108303	.115865	.123498
	0.00	.073123	.079975	.086951	.090483	.094044	.097632	.101246	.104886	.108550	.115948	.123431	.130993	.138627
	-.10	.088252	.095103	.102079	.105612	.109172	.112760	.116375	.120014	.123679	.131076	.138559	.146122	.153755
	-.20	.103380	.110232	.117208	.120740	.124301	.127889	.131503	.135143	.138807	.146204	.153688	.161250	.168883
	-.30	.118509	.125360	.132336	.135868	.139429	.143017	.146631	.150271	.153935	.161333	.168816	.176378	.184012
	-.40	.133637	.140488	.147464	.150997	.154557	.158146	.161760	.165400	.169064	.176461	.183944	.191507	.199140
20	.40	.010818	.017988	.025282	.028972	.032687	.036428	.040193	.043979	.047787	.055459	.063199	.070998	.078847
	.30	.025947	.033117	.040410	.044100	.047816	.051557	.055321	.059108	.062915	.070587	.078328	.086127	.093976
	.20	.041075	.048245	.055539	.059228	.062944	.066685	.070449	.074236	.078044	.085716	.093456	.101255	.109104
	.10	.056203	.063373	.070667	.074357	.078073	.081813	.085578	.089364	.093172	.100844	.108584	.116383	.124232
	0.00	.071332	.078502	.085796	.089485	.093201	.096942	.100706	.104493	.108300	.115972	.123713	.131512	.139361
	-.10	.086460	.093630	.100924	.104613	.108329	.112070	.115835	.119621	.123429	.131101	.138841	.146640	.154489
	-.20	.101588	.108759	.116052	.119742	.123458	.127198	.130963	.134750	.138557	.146229	.153969	.161768	.169617
	-.30	.116717	.123887	.131181	.134870	.138586	.142327	.146091	.149878	.153685	.161358	.169098	.176897	.184746
	-.40	.131845	.139015	.146309	.149998	.153714	.157455	.161220	.165006	.168814	.176486	.184226	.192025	.199874
25	.40	.009786	.017155	.024641	.028424	.032230	.036059	.039907	.043774	.047658	.055471	.063335	.071240	.079178
	.30	.024915	.032283	.039770	.043552	.047359	.051187	.055036	.058903	.062787	.070600	.078464	.086369	.094306
	.20	.040043	.047411	.054898	.058681	.062487	.066315	.070164	.074031	.077915	.085728	.093592	.101497	.109435
	.10	.055171	.062540	.070026	.073809	.077615	.081444	.085292	.089159	.093044	.100857	.108720	.116625	.124563
	0.00	.070300	.077668	.085155	.088937	.092744	.096572	.100421	.104288	.108172	.115985	.123849	.131754	.139691
	-.10	.085428	.092796	.100283	.104066	.107872	.111700	.115549	.119416	.123300	.131113	.138977	.146882	.154820
	-.20	.100556	.107925	.115411	.119194	.123000	.126829	.130677	.134545	.138429	.146242	.154105	.162010	.169948
	-.30	.115685	.123053	.130540	.134322	.138129	.141957	.145806	.149673	.153557	.161370	.169234	.177139	.185076
	-.40	.130813	.138181	.145668	.149451	.153257	.157086	.160934	.164801	.168685	.176498	.184362	.192267	.200205
30	.40	.009132	.016637	.024253	.028097	.031961	.035844	.039744	.043659	.047587	.055478	.063405	.071360	.079335
	.30	.024260	.031766	.039382	.043225	.047090	.050973	.054873	.058788	.062716	.070606	.078534	.086488	.094463
	.20	.039389	.046894	.054510	.058354	.062218	.066101	.070001	.073916	.077844	.085735	.093662	.101617	.109592
	.10	.054517	.062022	.069638	.073482	.077346	.081229	.085129	.089044	.092973	.100863	.108790	.116745	.124720
	0.00	.069645	.077151	.084767	.088610	.092475	.096358	.100258	.104173	.108101	.115992	.123919	.131873	.139849
	-.10	.084774	.092279	.099895	.103739	.107603	.111486	.115386	.119301	.123229	.131120	.139047	.147002	.154977
	-.20	.099902	.107407	.115023	.118867	.122731	.126614	.130514	.134429	.138358	.146248	.154175	.162130	.170105
	-.30	.115031	.122536	.130152	.133995	.137860	.141743	.145643	.149558	.153486	.161377	.169304	.177259	.185234
	-.40	.130159	.137664	.145280	.149124	.152988	.156871	.160771	.164686	.168614	.176505	.184432	.192387	.200362

5.0 YEAR HOLDING PERIOD
.140 EQUITY YIELD RATE
.900 LOAN RATIO

INTEREST RATE

TERM YEARS	APPR DEP	5.0	6.0	7.0	7.5	8.0	8.5	9.0	9.5	10.0	11.0	12.0	13.0	14.0
10	.40	.008408	.015422	.022566	.026186	.029836	.033517	.037229	.040969	.044739	.052363	.060097	.067935	.075874
	.30	.023536	.030550	.037694	.041314	.044965	.048646	.052357	.056098	.059867	.067491	.075225	.083063	.091002
	.20	.038665	.045679	.052823	.056442	.060093	.063774	.067485	.071226	.074996	.082620	.090353	.098192	.106131
	.10	.053793	.060807	.067951	.071571	.075221	.078902	.082614	.086354	.090124	.097748	.105482	.113320	.121259
	0.00	.068921	.075935	.083079	.086699	.090350	.094031	.097742	.101483	.105252	.112876	.120610	.128448	.136387
	-.10	.084050	.091064	.098208	.101827	.105478	.109159	.112870	.116611	.120381	.128005	.135738	.143577	.151516
	-.20	.099178	.106192	.113336	.116956	.120606	.124287	.127999	.131739	.135509	.143133	.150867	.158705	.166644
	-.30	.114306	.121320	.128464	.132084	.135735	.139416	.143127	.146868	.150637	.158262	.165995	.173834	.181772
	-.40	.129435	.136449	.143593	.147212	.150863	.154544	.158255	.161996	.165766	.173390	.181123	.188962	.196901
15	.40	.004250	.011958	.019806	.023780	.027786	.031823	.035889	.039983	.044106	.052428	.060847	.069354	.077942
	.30	.019379	.027087	.034935	.038909	.042915	.046951	.051017	.055112	.059234	.067556	.075975	.084482	.093070
	.20	.034507	.042215	.050063	.054037	.058043	.062079	.066146	.070240	.074362	.082684	.091103	.099611	.108198
	.10	.049636	.057343	.065191	.069165	.073171	.077208	.081274	.085369	.089491	.097813	.106232	.114739	.123327
	0.00	.064764	.072472	.080320	.084294	.088300	.092336	.096402	.100497	.104619	.112941	.121360	.129867	.138455
	-.10	.079892	.087600	.095448	.099422	.103428	.107464	.111531	.115625	.119747	.128069	.136488	.144996	.153583
	-.20	.095021	.102728	.110577	.114550	.118556	.122593	.126659	.130754	.134876	.143198	.151617	.160124	.168712
	-.30	.110149	.117857	.125705	.129679	.133685	.137721	.141787	.145882	.150004	.158326	.166745	.175252	.183840
	-.40	.125277	.132985	.140833	.144807	.148813	.152850	.156916	.161010	.165132	.173454	.181873	.190381	.198968
20	.40	.002235	.010301	.018507	.022657	.026838	.031046	.035281	.039541	.043824	.052456	.061163	.069937	.078767
	.30	.017363	.025430	.033635	.037786	.041966	.046174	.050409	.054669	.058953	.067584	.076292	.085065	.093896
	.20	.032491	.040558	.048763	.052914	.057094	.061303	.065538	.069798	.074081	.082712	.091420	.100192	.109024
	.10	.047620	.055686	.063892	.068042	.072223	.076431	.080666	.084926	.089209	.097841	.106548	.115322	.124152
	0.00	.062748	.070815	.079020	.083171	.087351	.091559	.095794	.100054	.104338	.112969	.121677	.130451	.139281
	-.10	.077877	.085943	.094148	.098299	.102479	.106688	.110923	.115183	.119466	.128097	.136805	.145579	.154409
	-.20	.093005	.101071	.109277	.113427	.117608	.121816	.126051	.130311	.134595	.143226	.151933	.160707	.169537
	-.30	.108133	.116200	.124405	.128556	.132736	.136945	.141180	.145439	.149723	.158354	.167062	.175836	.184666
	-.40	.123262	.131328	.139533	.143684	.147864	.152073	.156308	.160568	.164851	.173482	.182190	.190964	.199794
25	.40	.001074	.009363	.017786	.022041	.026323	.030630	.034960	.039310	.043680	.052470	.061316	.070209	.079139
	.30	.016202	.024492	.032914	.037169	.041452	.045759	.050088	.054439	.058808	.067598	.076444	.085338	.094268
	.20	.031330	.039620	.048042	.052298	.056580	.060887	.065217	.069567	.073937	.082726	.091573	.100466	.109396
	.10	.046459	.054748	.063171	.067426	.071708	.076015	.080345	.084695	.089065	.097855	.106701	.115595	.124524
	0.00	.061587	.069877	.078299	.082554	.086837	.091144	.095473	.099824	.104193	.112983	.121830	.130723	.139653
	-.10	.076715	.085005	.093427	.097683	.101965	.106272	.110602	.114952	.119322	.128111	.136958	.145851	.154781
	-.20	.091844	.100133	.108556	.112811	.117093	.121400	.125730	.130080	.134450	.143240	.152087	.160979	.169910
	-.30	.106972	.115262	.123684	.127940	.132222	.136529	.140858	.145209	.149579	.158369	.167215	.176108	.185038
	-.40	.122100	.130390	.138812	.143068	.147350	.151657	.155987	.160337	.164707	.173496	.182343	.191236	.200166
30	.40	.000338	.008781	.017349	.021673	.026021	.030389	.034776	.039181	.043600	.052477	.061395	.070344	.079316
	.30	.015466	.023910	.032477	.036801	.041149	.045517	.049905	.054309	.058728	.067605	.076523	.085473	.094445
	.20	.030594	.039038	.047606	.051930	.056277	.060646	.065033	.069438	.073856	.082734	.091652	.100601	.109573
	.10	.045723	.054166	.062734	.067058	.071406	.075774	.080161	.084566	.088985	.097862	.106780	.115729	.124701
	0.00	.060851	.069295	.077863	.082187	.086534	.090902	.095290	.099694	.104113	.112990	.121909	.130858	.139830
	-.10	.075979	.084423	.092991	.097315	.101662	.106031	.110418	.114823	.119242	.128119	.137037	.145986	.154958
	-.20	.091108	.099551	.108119	.112443	.116791	.121159	.125547	.129951	.134370	.143247	.152165	.161114	.170086
	-.30	.106236	.114680	.123248	.127572	.131919	.136287	.140675	.145079	.149499	.158376	.167294	.176243	.185215
	-.40	.121365	.129808	.138376	.142700	.147047	.151416	.155803	.160208	.164627	.173504	.182422	.191371	.200343

5.0 YEAR HOLDING PERIOD
.150 EQUITY YIELD RATE
.600 LOAN RATIO

INTEREST RATE

TERM YEARS	APPR DEP	5.0	6.0	7.0	7.5	8.0	8.5	9.0	9.5	10.0	11.0	12.0	13.0	14.0
10	.40	.038068	.042722	.047463	.049866	.052289	.054732	.057196	.059679	.062182	.067244	.072379	.077585	.082858
	.30	.052900	.057554	.062295	.064697	.067120	.069564	.072027	.074511	.077013	.082076	.087211	.092417	.097689
	.20	.067731	.072385	.077126	.079529	.081952	.084395	.086859	.089342	.091845	.096907	.102042	.107248	.112521
	.10	.082563	.087217	.091958	.094360	.096783	.099227	.101691	.104174	.106677	.111739	.116874	.122080	.127353
	0.00	.097394	.102048	.106790	.109192	.111615	.114058	.116522	.119005	.121508	.126570	.131706	.136911	.142184
	-.10	.112226	.116880	.121621	.124023	.126447	.128890	.131354	.133337	.136340	.141402	.146537	.151743	.157016
	-.20	.127057	.131712	.136453	.138885	.141278	.143722	.146185	.148669	.151171	.156233	.161369	.166554	.171847
	-.30	.141889	.146543	.151284	.153687	.156110	.158553	.161017	.163500	.166003	.171065	.176200	.181406	.186679
	-.40	.156720	.161375	.166116	.168518	.170941	.173385	.175848	.178332	.180834	.185896	.191032	.196237	.201510
15	.40	.034969	.040082	.045289	.047926	.050585	.053264	.055964	.058682	.061419	.066946	.072538	.078190	.083897
	.30	.049801	.054916	.060121	.062758	.065417	.068096	.070795	.073514	.076251	.081777	.087370	.093022	.098729
	.20	.064633	.069745	.074952	.077589	.080248	.082927	.085627	.088345	.091082	.096609	.102201	.107854	.113560
	.10	.079464	.084577	.089784	.092421	.095080	.097759	.100458	.103177	.105914	.111441	.117033	.122685	.128392
	0.00	.094296	.099408	.104615	.107253	.109911	.112590	.115290	.118008	.120745	.126272	.131864	.137517	.143223
	-.10	.109127	.114240	.119447	.122084	.124743	.127422	.130121	.132840	.135577	.141104	.146696	.152348	.158055
	-.20	.123959	.129071	.134279	.136916	.139574	.142254	.144953	.147671	.150408	.155935	.161528	.167180	.172887
	-.30	.138790	.143903	.149111	.151747	.154406	.157085	.159784	.162503	.165240	.170767	.176359	.182011	.187718
	-.40	.153622	.158735	.163942	.166579	.169237	.171917	.174616	.177335	.180072	.185598	.191191	.196843	.202550
20	.40	.033467	.038819	.044265	.047021	.049797	.052592	.055405	.058235	.061081	.066817	.072605	.078439	.084312
	.30	.048299	.053651	.059097	.061852	.064628	.067423	.070236	.073066	.075912	.081648	.087437	.093271	.099144
	.20	.063130	.068482	.073928	.076684	.079460	.082255	.085068	.087898	.090744	.096480	.102268	.108102	.113975
	.10	.077962	.083314	.088760	.091515	.094291	.097086	.099899	.102729	.105575	.111311	.117100	.122934	.128807
	0.00	.092793	.098145	.103591	.106347	.109123	.111918	.114731	.117561	.120407	.126143	.131932	.137766	.143638
	-.10	.107625	.112977	.118423	.121179	.123954	.126749	.129562	.132392	.135238	.140975	.146763	.152597	.158470
	-.20	.122457	.127808	.133254	.136010	.138786	.141581	.144394	.147224	.150070	.155806	.161595	.167429	.173302
	-.30	.137288	.142640	.148086	.150842	.153617	.156412	.159225	.162055	.164901	.170638	.176426	.182260	.188133
	-.40	.152120	.157472	.162918	.165673	.168449	.171244	.174057	.176887	.179733	.185469	.191258	.197092	.202965
25	.40	.032602	.038104	.043697	.046524	.049369	.052231	.055109	.058001	.060907	.066752	.072638	.078556	.084499
	.30	.047433	.052936	.058529	.061356	.064201	.067063	.069941	.072833	.075738	.081584	.087469	.093387	.099331
	.20	.062265	.067767	.073360	.076187	.079032	.081894	.084772	.087664	.090570	.096415	.102301	.108219	.114162
	.10	.077097	.082599	.088192	.091019	.093864	.096726	.099604	.102496	.105401	.111247	.117132	.123050	.128994
	0.00	.091928	.097430	.103023	.105850	.108695	.111558	.114435	.117327	.120233	.126079	.131964	.137882	.143825
	-.10	.106760	.112262	.117855	.120682	.123527	.126389	.129267	.132159	.135064	.140910	.146796	.152713	.158657
	-.20	.121591	.127093	.132686	.135513	.138359	.141221	.144098	.146991	.149896	.155742	.161627	.167545	.173489
	-.30	.136423	.141925	.147518	.150345	.153190	.156052	.158930	.161822	.164727	.170573	.176459	.182376	.188320
	-.40	.151254	.156757	.162350	.165176	.168022	.170884	.173762	.176654	.179559	.185405	.191292	.197208	.203152
30	.40	.032053	.037661	.043353	.046227	.049118	.052022	.054940	.057870	.060810	.066718	.072654	.078613	.084588
	.30	.046885	.052492	.058185	.061059	.063949	.066854	.069772	.072702	.075642	.081549	.087486	.093445	.099420
	.20	.061716	.067324	.073016	.075890	.078781	.081685	.084603	.087533	.090474	.096381	.102318	.108276	.114251
	.10	.076548	.082155	.087848	.090722	.093612	.096517	.099435	.102365	.105305	.111213	.117149	.123108	.129083
	0.00	.091380	.096987	.102680	.105554	.108444	.111349	.114267	.117196	.120137	.126044	.131981	.137939	.143914
	-.10	.106211	.111818	.117511	.120385	.123275	.126180	.129098	.132028	.134968	.140876	.146812	.152771	.158746
	-.20	.121043	.126650	.132343	.135217	.138107	.141012	.143930	.146859	.149800	.155707	.161644	.167602	.173577
	-.30	.135874	.141481	.147174	.150048	.152938	.155843	.158761	.161691	.164631	.170539	.176475	.182434	.188409
	-.40	.150706	.156313	.162006	.164880	.167770	.170675	.173593	.176523	.179463	.185370	.191307	.197265	.203241

5.0 YEAR HOLDING PERIOD
.150 EQUITY YIELD RATE
.667 LOAN RATIO

INTEREST RATE

TERM YEARS	APPR DEP	14.0	13.0	12.0	11.0	10.0	9.5	9.0	8.5	8.0	7.5	7.0	6.0	5.0
10	.40	.081989	.076131	.070347	.064641	.059016	.056235	.053476	.050739	.048024	.045331	.042662	.037394	.032223
	.30	.096821	.090962	.085178	.079472	.073848	.071067	.068307	.065572	.062855	.060163	.057493	.052226	.047054
	.20	.111652	.105794	.100010	.094304	.088679	.085898	.083139	.080402	.077687	.074994	.072325	.067057	.061886
	.10	.126484	.120625	.114841	.109135	.103511	.100730	.097971	.095233	.092518	.089826	.087157	.081889	.076717
	0.00	.141316	.135457	.129673	.123967	.118342	.115561	.112802	.110065	.107350	.104657	.101988	.096720	.091549
	-.10	.156147	.150288	.144504	.138798	.133174	.130393	.127634	.124896	.122181	.119489	.116820	.111552	.106380
	-.20	.170979	.165120	.159336	.153630	.148005	.145224	.142465	.139728	.137013	.134321	.131651	.126383	.121212
	-.30	.185810	.179951	.174167	.168461	.162837	.160056	.157297	.154559	.151844	.149152	.146483	.141215	.136043
	-.40	.200642	.194783	.188999	.183293	.177668	.174888	.172128	.169391	.166676	.163984	.161314	.156046	.150875
15	.40	.083144	.076803	.070523	.064309	.058168	.055127	.052107	.049107	.046130	.043176	.040246	.034461	.028780
	.30	.097976	.091635	.085355	.079141	.073000	.069959	.066938	.063939	.060962	.058008	.055078	.049292	.043611
	.20	.112807	.106466	.100186	.093972	.087832	.084790	.081770	.078771	.075794	.072840	.069909	.064124	.058443
	.10	.127639	.121298	.115018	.108804	.102663	.099622	.096601	.093602	.090625	.087671	.084741	.078955	.073274
	0.00	.142470	.136130	.129849	.123636	.117495	.114453	.111433	.108434	.105457	.102503	.099572	.093787	.088106
	-.10	.157302	.150961	.144681	.138467	.132326	.129285	.126264	.123265	.120288	.117334	.114404	.108618	.102938
	-.20	.172134	.165793	.159512	.153299	.147158	.144117	.141096	.138097	.135120	.132166	.129236	.123450	.117769
	-.30	.186965	.180624	.174344	.168130	.161989	.158948	.155928	.152928	.149951	.146997	.144067	.138281	.132601
	-.40	.201797	.195456	.189175	.182962	.176821	.173780	.170759	.167760	.164783	.161829	.158899	.153113	.147432
20	.40	.083605	.077080	.070598	.064166	.057792	.054630	.051486	.048360	.045254	.042170	.039108	.033057	.027111
	.30	.098437	.091911	.085429	.078997	.072624	.069462	.066317	.063191	.060086	.057002	.053940	.047889	.041942
	.20	.113268	.106743	.100261	.093829	.087455	.084293	.081149	.078023	.074918	.071833	.068772	.062720	.056774
	.10	.128100	.121575	.115092	.108660	.102287	.099125	.095980	.092855	.089749	.086665	.083603	.077552	.071605
	0.00	.142932	.136406	.129924	.123492	.117119	.113956	.110812	.107686	.104581	.101496	.098435	.092383	.086437
	-.10	.157763	.151238	.144755	.138324	.131950	.128788	.125643	.122518	.119412	.116328	.113266	.107215	.101268
	-.20	.172595	.166069	.159587	.153155	.146782	.143619	.140475	.137349	.134244	.131160	.128098	.122046	.116100
	-.30	.187426	.180901	.174418	.167987	.161613	.158451	.155306	.152181	.149075	.145991	.142929	.136878	.130931
	-.40	.202258	.195732	.189250	.182818	.176445	.173282	.170138	.167012	.163907	.160823	.157761	.151710	.145763
25	.40	.083813	.077209	.070634	.064094	.057599	.054371	.051157	.047960	.044780	.041618	.038477	.032263	.026149
	.30	.098645	.092041	.085465	.078926	.072431	.069202	.065989	.062791	.059611	.056450	.053309	.047094	.040981
	.20	.113476	.106872	.100297	.093757	.087262	.084034	.080820	.077623	.074443	.071281	.068140	.061926	.055812
	.10	.128308	.121704	.115128	.108589	.102094	.098865	.095652	.092454	.089274	.086113	.082972	.076757	.070644
	0.00	.143139	.136535	.129960	.123420	.116925	.113697	.110484	.107286	.104106	.100944	.097803	.091589	.085475
	-.10	.157971	.151367	.144791	.138252	.131757	.128529	.125315	.122118	.118937	.115776	.112635	.106421	.100307
	-.20	.172803	.166198	.159623	.153084	.146588	.143360	.140147	.136949	.133769	.130608	.127467	.121252	.115138
	-.30	.187634	.181030	.174455	.167915	.161420	.158192	.154978	.151781	.148600	.145439	.142298	.136084	.129970
	-.40	.202466	.195861	.189286	.182747	.176251	.173023	.169810	.166612	.163432	.160271	.157130	.150915	.144802
30	.40	.083912	.077273	.070652	.064056	.057492	.054225	.050970	.047728	.044500	.041289	.038095	.031770	.025540
	.30	.098743	.092104	.085484	.078888	.072324	.069057	.065801	.062559	.059331	.056120	.052927	.046601	.040371
	.20	.113575	.106936	.100315	.093719	.087155	.083888	.080633	.077391	.074163	.070952	.067758	.061433	.055203
	.10	.128407	.121768	.115147	.108551	.101987	.098720	.095464	.092222	.088995	.085783	.082590	.076265	.070034
	0.00	.143238	.136599	.129978	.123382	.116818	.113551	.110296	.107054	.103826	.100615	.097421	.091096	.084866
	-.10	.158070	.151431	.144810	.138214	.131650	.128383	.125128	.121885	.118658	.115446	.112253	.105928	.099697
	-.20	.172901	.166262	.159641	.153045	.146481	.143214	.139959	.136717	.133489	.130278	.127085	.120759	.114529
	-.30	.187733	.181094	.174473	.167877	.161313	.158046	.154791	.151548	.148321	.145109	.141916	.135591	.129361
	-.40	.202564	.195925	.189305	.182708	.176145	.172878	.169622	.166380	.163152	.159941	.156748	.150422	.144192

5.0 YEAR HOLDING PERIOD
.150 EQUITY YIELD RATE
.700 LOAN RATIO

INTEREST RATE

TERM YEARS	APPR DEP	5.0	6.0	7.0	7.5	8.0	8.5	9.0	9.5	10.0	11.0	12.0	13.0	14.0
10	.40	.029300	.034730	.040262	.043064	.045891	.048742	.051616	.054513	.057433	.063339	.069330	.075403	.081555
	.30	.044132	.049562	.055093	.057896	.060723	.063574	.066448	.069345	.072265	.078171	.084162	.090235	.095387
	.20	.058963	.064393	.069925	.072727	.075554	.078405	.081279	.084177	.087096	.093002	.098993	.105067	.111218
	.10	.073795	.079225	.084756	.087559	.090386	.093237	.096111	.099008	.101928	.107834	.113825	.119898	.126050
	0.00	.088627	.094056	.099588	.102391	.105217	.108068	.110942	.113840	.116759	.122665	.128657	.134730	.140881
	-.10	.103458	.108888	.114419	.117222	.120049	.122900	.125774	.128671	.131591	.137497	.143488	.149561	.155713
	-.20	.118290	.123720	.129251	.132054	.134881	.137731	.140606	.143503	.146423	.152328	.158320	.164393	.170545
	-.30	.133121	.138551	.144082	.146885	.149712	.152563	.155437	.158334	.161254	.167160	.173151	.179224	.185376
	-.40	.147953	.153383	.158914	.161717	.164544	.167394	.170269	.173166	.176086	.181991	.187983	.194056	.200208
15	.40	.025685	.031650	.037725	.040802	.043903	.047029	.050179	.053350	.056543	.062991	.069516	.076110	.082768
	.30	.040517	.046482	.052557	.055633	.058735	.061861	.065010	.068182	.071375	.077823	.084347	.090941	.097599
	.20	.055349	.061313	.067388	.070465	.073567	.076692	.079842	.083013	.086206	.092654	.099179	.105773	.112431
	.10	.070180	.076145	.082220	.085296	.088398	.091524	.094673	.097845	.101038	.107486	.114010	.120605	.127262
	0.00	.085012	.090976	.097051	.100128	.103230	.106356	.109505	.112676	.115870	.122317	.128842	.135436	.142094
	-.10	.099843	.105808	.111883	.114960	.118061	.121187	.124336	.127508	.130701	.137149	.143673	.150268	.156926
	-.20	.114675	.120640	.126714	.129791	.132893	.136019	.139168	.142339	.145533	.151981	.158505	.165099	.171757
	-.30	.129506	.135471	.141546	.144623	.147724	.150850	.153999	.157171	.160364	.166812	.173336	.179931	.186589
	-.40	.144338	.150303	.156378	.159454	.162556	.165682	.168831	.172003	.175196	.181644	.188168	.194762	.201420
20	.40	.023933	.030177	.036530	.039745	.042984	.046244	.049526	.052828	.056148	.062841	.069594	.076400	.083252
	.30	.038764	.045008	.051362	.054577	.057815	.061076	.064358	.067660	.070980	.077672	.084425	.091232	.098084
	.20	.053596	.059840	.066194	.069408	.072647	.075908	.079189	.082491	.085812	.092504	.099257	.106063	.112915
	.10	.068427	.074671	.081025	.084240	.087478	.090739	.094021	.097323	.100643	.107335	.114089	.120895	.127747
	0.00	.083259	.089503	.095857	.099071	.102310	.105571	.108853	.112154	.115475	.122167	.128920	.135726	.142578
	-.10	.098091	.104334	.110688	.113903	.117141	.120402	.123684	.126986	.130306	.136998	.143752	.150558	.157410
	-.20	.112922	.119166	.125520	.128735	.131973	.135234	.138516	.141817	.145138	.151830	.158583	.165390	.172241
	-.30	.127754	.133998	.140351	.143566	.146805	.150065	.153347	.156649	.159969	.166661	.173415	.180221	.187073
	-.40	.142585	.148829	.155183	.158398	.161636	.164897	.168179	.171480	.174801	.181493	.188246	.195053	.201904
25	.40	.022923	.029342	.035868	.039166	.042485	.045824	.049182	.052556	.055945	.062765	.069632	.076536	.083470
	.30	.037755	.044174	.050699	.053997	.057317	.060656	.064013	.067387	.070777	.077597	.084463	.091367	.098302
	.20	.052586	.059006	.065531	.068829	.072148	.075487	.078845	.082219	.085609	.092428	.099295	.106199	.113133
	.10	.067418	.073837	.080362	.083660	.086980	.090319	.093676	.097051	.100440	.107260	.114126	.121030	.127965
	0.00	.082249	.088669	.095194	.098492	.101811	.105150	.108508	.111882	.115272	.122092	.128958	.135862	.142796
	-.10	.097081	.103500	.110025	.113323	.116643	.119982	.123339	.126714	.130103	.136923	.143789	.150694	.157628
	-.20	.111913	.118332	.124857	.128155	.131474	.134814	.138171	.141545	.144935	.151755	.158621	.165525	.172460
	-.30	.126744	.133163	.139689	.142987	.146306	.149645	.153002	.156377	.159766	.166586	.173453	.180357	.187291
	-.40	.141576	.147995	.154520	.157818	.161138	.164477	.167834	.171208	.174598	.181418	.188284	.195188	.202123
30	.40	.022283	.028825	.035467	.038820	.042191	.045580	.048985	.052403	.055833	.062725	.069651	.076603	.083574
	.30	.037115	.043657	.050298	.053651	.057023	.060412	.063816	.067234	.070665	.077557	.084483	.091434	.098405
	.20	.051946	.058488	.065130	.068483	.071855	.075244	.078648	.082066	.085496	.092388	.099314	.106266	.113237
	.10	.066778	.073320	.079961	.083314	.086686	.090075	.093479	.096898	.100328	.107220	.114146	.121098	.128069
	0.00	.081610	.088151	.094793	.098146	.101518	.104907	.108311	.111729	.115159	.122051	.128977	.135929	.142900
	-.10	.096441	.102983	.109624	.112977	.116349	.119738	.123143	.126561	.129991	.136883	.143809	.150761	.157732
	-.20	.111273	.117814	.124456	.127809	.131181	.134570	.137974	.141393	.144823	.151715	.158641	.165592	.172563
	-.30	.126104	.132646	.139287	.142640	.146012	.149401	.152806	.156224	.159654	.166546	.173472	.180424	.187395
	-.40	.140936	.147477	.154119	.157472	.160844	.164233	.167637	.171055	.174486	.181378	.188304	.195255	.202226

5.0 YEAR HOLDING PERIOD
.150 EQUITY YIELD RATE
.750 LOAN RATIO

INTEREST RATE

TERM YEARS	APPR DEP	5.0	6.0	7.0	7.5	8.0	8.5	9.0	9.5	10.0	11.0	12.0	13.0	14.0
10	.40	.024916	.030734	.036661	.039664	.042692	.045747	.048826	.051931	.055059	.061387	.067806	.074313	.080904
	.30	.039748	.045566	.051492	.054495	.057724	.060578	.063658	.066762	.069890	.076218	.082637	.089144	.095735
	.20	.054580	.060397	.066324	.069327	.072356	.075410	.078489	.081594	.084722	.091050	.097469	.103976	.110567
	.10	.069411	.075229	.081155	.084158	.087187	.090242	.093321	.096425	.099554	.105881	.112300	.118807	.125399
	0.00	.084243	.090061	.095987	.098990	.102019	.105073	.108153	.111257	.114385	.120713	.127132	.133639	.140230
	-.10	.099074	.104892	.110818	.113821	.116850	.119905	.122984	.126088	.129217	.135544	.141964	.148471	.155062
	-.20	.113906	.119724	.125650	.128653	.131682	.134736	.137816	.140920	.144048	.150376	.156795	.163302	.169893
	-.30	.128737	.134555	.140482	.143485	.146513	.149568	.152647	.155751	.158880	.165207	.171627	.178134	.184725
	-.40	.143569	.149387	.155313	.158316	.161345	.164399	.167479	.170583	.173711	.180039	.186458	.192965	.199556
15	.40	.021043	.027434	.033943	.037240	.040563	.043912	.047286	.050684	.054105	.061014	.068004	.075070	.082203
	.30	.035875	.042266	.048775	.052071	.055394	.058743	.062118	.065516	.068937	.075846	.082836	.089901	.097035
	.20	.050706	.057097	.063606	.066903	.070226	.073575	.076949	.080347	.083769	.090677	.097667	.104733	.111866
	.10	.065538	.071929	.078438	.081734	.085057	.088407	.091781	.095179	.098600	.105509	.112499	.119564	.126698
	0.00	.080370	.086760	.093269	.096566	.099889	.103238	.106612	.110010	.113432	.120340	.127331	.134396	.141529
	-.10	.095201	.101592	.108101	.111397	.114721	.118070	.121444	.124842	.128263	.135172	.142162	.149227	.156361
	-.20	.110033	.116424	.122932	.126229	.129552	.132901	.136275	.139673	.143095	.150003	.156994	.164059	.171192
	-.30	.124864	.131255	.137764	.141060	.144384	.147733	.151107	.154505	.157926	.164835	.171825	.178890	.186024
	-.40	.139696	.146087	.152596	.155892	.159215	.162564	.165938	.169337	.172758	.179666	.186657	.193722	.200855
20	.40	.019166	.025855	.032663	.036107	.039577	.043071	.046587	.050125	.053682	.060852	.068088	.075381	.082722
	.30	.033997	.040687	.047495	.050939	.054409	.057902	.061419	.064956	.068514	.075684	.082920	.090212	.097553
	.20	.048829	.055519	.062326	.065771	.069240	.072734	.076250	.079788	.083345	.090516	.097751	.105044	.112385
	.10	.063660	.070350	.077158	.080602	.084072	.087566	.091082	.094619	.098177	.105347	.112583	.119875	.127216
	0.00	.078492	.085182	.091989	.095434	.098903	.102397	.105913	.109451	.113009	.120179	.127414	.134707	.142048
	-.10	.093323	.100013	.106821	.110265	.113735	.117229	.120745	.124283	.127840	.135010	.142246	.149538	.156880
	-.20	.108155	.114845	.121652	.125097	.128567	.132060	.135577	.139114	.142672	.149842	.157078	.164370	.171711
	-.30	.122986	.129676	.136484	.139928	.143398	.146891	.150408	.153946	.157503	.164673	.171909	.179202	.186543
	-.40	.137818	.144508	.151315	.154760	.158230	.161723	.165240	.168777	.172335	.179505	.186741	.194033	.201374
25	.40	.018084	.024962	.031953	.035487	.039043	.042621	.046218	.049833	.053465	.060772	.068129	.075526	.082956
	.30	.032915	.039793	.046785	.050318	.053875	.057452	.061049	.064665	.068296	.075603	.082960	.090358	.097787
	.20	.047747	.054625	.061616	.065150	.068706	.072284	.075881	.079496	.083128	.090435	.097792	.105189	.112619
	.10	.062579	.069456	.076448	.079981	.083538	.087115	.090713	.094328	.097959	.105267	.112623	.120021	.127450
	0.00	.077410	.084288	.091279	.094813	.098369	.101947	.105544	.109159	.112791	.120098	.127455	.134852	.142282
	-.10	.092242	.099119	.106111	.109644	.113201	.116778	.120376	.123991	.127623	.134930	.142286	.149684	.157113
	-.20	.107073	.113951	.120942	.124476	.128032	.131610	.135207	.138822	.142454	.149761	.157118	.164515	.171945
	-.30	.121905	.128783	.135774	.139307	.142864	.146442	.150039	.153654	.157286	.164593	.171950	.179347	.186777
	-.40	.136736	.143614	.150605	.154139	.157695	.161273	.164870	.168486	.172117	.179424	.186781	.194178	.201608
30	.40	.017398	.024407	.031523	.035116	.038728	.042360	.046007	.049669	.053345	.060729	.068150	.075598	.083067
	.30	.032230	.039239	.046355	.049947	.053560	.057191	.060839	.064501	.068176	.075560	.082981	.090429	.097898
	.20	.047061	.054070	.061186	.064779	.068392	.072023	.075670	.079332	.083008	.090392	.097813	.105261	.112730
	.10	.061893	.068902	.076018	.079610	.083223	.086854	.090502	.094164	.097839	.105224	.112644	.120092	.127561
	0.00	.076725	.083733	.090849	.094442	.098055	.101686	.105333	.108995	.112671	.120055	.127476	.134924	.142393
	-.10	.091556	.098565	.105681	.109273	.112886	.116517	.120165	.123827	.127502	.134887	.142307	.149756	.157224
	-.20	.106388	.113397	.120513	.124105	.127718	.131349	.134996	.138659	.142334	.149718	.157139	.164587	.172056
	-.30	.121219	.128228	.135344	.138937	.142550	.146180	.149828	.153490	.157165	.164550	.171970	.179419	.186888
	-.40	.136051	.143060	.150176	.153768	.157381	.161012	.164659	.168322	.171997	.179381	.186802	.194250	.201719

5.0 YEAR HOLDING PERIOD
.150 EQUITY YIELD RATE
.800 LOAN RATIO

INTEREST RATE

TERM YEARS	APPR DEP	5.0	6.0	7.0	7.5	8.0	8.5	9.0	9.5	10.0	11.0	12.0	13.0	14.0
10	.40	.020533	.026738	.033060	.036263	.039494	.042752	.046037	.049348	.052685	.059434	.066281	.073222	.080253
	.30	.035364	.041570	.047891	.051094	.054325	.057583	.060868	.064179	.067516	.074266	.081113	.088054	.095084
	.20	.050196	.056401	.062723	.065926	.069157	.072415	.075700	.079011	.082348	.089097	.095944	.102885	.109916
	.10	.065027	.071233	.077554	.080758	.083988	.087246	.090531	.093842	.097179	.103929	.110776	.117717	.124747
	0.00	.079859	.086065	.092386	.095589	.098820	.102078	.105363	.108674	.112011	.118760	.125607	.132548	.139579
	-.10	.094690	.100896	.107218	.110421	.113652	.116910	.120194	.123505	.126842	.133592	.140439	.147380	.154410
	-.20	.109522	.115728	.122049	.125252	.128483	.131741	.135026	.138337	.141674	.148423	.155271	.162211	.169242
	-.30	.124354	.130559	.136881	.140084	.143315	.146573	.149857	.153169	.156505	.163255	.170102	.177043	.184073
	-.40	.139185	.145391	.151712	.154915	.158146	.161404	.164689	.168000	.171337	.178087	.184934	.191874	.198905
15	.40	.016401	.023218	.030161	.033677	.037222	.040794	.044393	.048018	.051668	.059037	.066493	.074029	.081638
	.30	.031233	.038050	.044993	.048509	.052054	.055626	.059225	.062850	.066499	.073868	.081325	.088861	.096470
	.20	.046064	.052881	.059824	.063340	.066885	.070458	.074057	.077681	.081331	.088700	.096156	.103692	.111301
	.10	.060896	.067713	.074656	.078172	.081717	.085289	.088888	.092513	.096162	.103531	.110988	.118524	.126133
	0.00	.075728	.082544	.089487	.093003	.096548	.100121	.103720	.107344	.110994	.118363	.125819	.133356	.140965
	-.10	.090559	.097376	.104319	.107835	.111380	.114952	.118551	.122176	.125825	.133194	.140651	.148187	.155796
	-.20	.105391	.112208	.119150	.122667	.126211	.129784	.133383	.137008	.140657	.148026	.155482	.163019	.170628
	-.30	.120222	.127039	.133982	.137498	.141043	.144615	.148214	.151839	.155488	.162858	.170314	.177850	.185459
	-.40	.135054	.141871	.148813	.152330	.155874	.159447	.163046	.166671	.170320	.177689	.185145	.192682	.200291
20	.40	.014398	.021534	.028796	.032470	.036171	.039897	.043648	.047421	.051216	.058864	.066582	.074361	.082192
	.30	.029230	.036366	.043627	.047301	.051002	.054729	.058480	.062253	.066048	.073696	.081414	.089193	.097023
	.20	.044061	.051197	.058459	.062133	.065834	.069561	.073311	.077085	.080879	.088527	.096246	.104024	.111855
	.10	.058893	.066029	.073290	.076964	.080665	.084392	.088143	.091916	.095711	.103359	.111077	.118856	.126686
	0.00	.073725	.080860	.088122	.091796	.095497	.099224	.102974	.106748	.110542	.118191	.125909	.133687	.141518
	-.10	.088556	.095692	.102953	.106628	.110329	.114055	.117806	.121579	.125374	.133022	.140740	.148519	.156349
	-.20	.103388	.110523	.117785	.121459	.125160	.128887	.132637	.136411	.140206	.147854	.155572	.163350	.171181
	-.30	.118219	.125355	.132617	.136291	.139992	.143718	.147469	.151242	.155037	.162685	.170403	.178182	.186013
	-.40	.133051	.140187	.147448	.151122	.154823	.158550	.162301	.166074	.169869	.177517	.185235	.193014	.200844
25	.40	.013245	.020581	.028038	.031807	.035601	.039417	.043254	.047110	.050984	.058778	.066626	.074516	.082441
	.30	.028076	.035412	.042870	.046639	.050433	.054249	.058086	.061942	.065816	.073610	.081457	.089348	.097273
	.20	.042908	.050244	.057701	.061471	.065264	.069080	.072917	.076774	.080647	.088442	.096289	.104179	.112104
	.10	.057739	.065076	.072533	.076302	.080096	.083912	.087749	.091605	.095479	.103273	.111120	.119011	.126936
	0.00	.072571	.079907	.087364	.091134	.094927	.098743	.102580	.106437	.110310	.118105	.125952	.133842	.141767
	-.10	.087402	.094739	.102196	.105965	.109759	.113575	.117412	.121268	.125142	.132936	.140783	.148674	.156599
	-.20	.102234	.109570	.117028	.120797	.124590	.128407	.132244	.136100	.139974	.147768	.155615	.163505	.171430
	-.30	.117065	.124402	.131859	.135628	.139422	.143238	.147075	.150931	.154805	.162599	.170447	.178337	.186262
	-.40	.131897	.139233	.146691	.150460	.154253	.158070	.161907	.165763	.169637	.177431	.185278	.193169	.201094
30	.40	.012513	.019989	.027580	.031412	.035265	.039139	.043029	.046936	.050856	.058733	.066648	.074593	.082560
	.30	.027345	.034821	.042411	.046243	.050097	.053970	.057861	.061767	.065688	.073564	.081479	.089424	.097391
	.20	.042176	.049653	.057243	.061075	.064929	.068802	.072692	.076599	.080519	.088396	.096311	.104256	.112223
	.10	.057008	.064484	.072074	.075906	.079760	.083633	.087524	.091430	.095351	.103227	.111143	.119087	.127054
	0.00	.071839	.079316	.086906	.090738	.094592	.098465	.102355	.106262	.110182	.118059	.125974	.133919	.141886
	-.10	.086671	.094147	.101738	.105570	.109423	.113296	.117187	.121093	.125014	.132890	.140806	.148751	.156717
	-.20	.101502	.108979	.116569	.120401	.124255	.128128	.132019	.135925	.139845	.147722	.155637	.163582	.171549
	-.30	.116334	.123810	.131401	.135233	.139086	.142959	.146850	.150756	.154677	.162553	.170469	.178414	.186380
	-.40	.131166	.138642	.146232	.150064	.153918	.157791	.161682	.165588	.169508	.177385	.185300	.193245	.201212

5.0 YEAR HOLDING PERIOD
.150 EQUITY YIELD RATE
.900 LOAN RATIO

INTEREST RATE

TERM YEARS	APPR DEP	14.0	13.0	12.0	11.0	10.0	9.5	9.0	8.5	8.0	7.5	7.0	6.0	5.0
10	.40	.078950	.071041	.063232	.055529	.047936	.044182	.040457	.036761	.033096	.029462	.025858	.018746	.011765
	.30	.093781	.085872	.078064	.070361	.062767	.059013	.055288	.051593	.047928	.044293	.040690	.033578	.026597
	.20	.108613	.100704	.092895	.085192	.077599	.073845	.070120	.066425	.062759	.059125	.055521	.048410	.041428
	.10	.123445	.115535	.107727	.100024	.092431	.088677	.084952	.081256	.077591	.073956	.070353	.063241	.056260
	0.00	.138276	.130367	.122558	.114855	.107262	.103508	.099783	.096088	.092422	.088788	.085184	.078073	.071091
	-.10	.153108	.145198	.137390	.129687	.122094	.118340	.114615	.110919	.107254	.103619	.100016	.092904	.085923
	-.20	.167939	.160030	.152221	.144518	.136925	.133171	.129446	.125751	.122086	.118451	.114847	.107736	.100754
	-.30	.182771	.174861	.167053	.159350	.151757	.148003	.144278	.140582	.136917	.133282	.129679	.122567	.115586
	-.40	.197602	.189693	.181885	.174182	.166588	.162834	.159109	.155414	.151749	.148114	.144511	.137399	.130417
15	.40	.080509	.071949	.063470	.055082	.046792	.042686	.038608	.034560	.030541	.026553	.022597	.014786	.007117
	.30	.095340	.086780	.078302	.069914	.061623	.057518	.053440	.049391	.045372	.041384	.037428	.029618	.021949
	.20	.110172	.101612	.093134	.084745	.076455	.072349	.068272	.064223	.060204	.056216	.052260	.044449	.036780
	.10	.125004	.116443	.107965	.099577	.091286	.087181	.083103	.079054	.075035	.071047	.067092	.059281	.051612
	0.00	.139835	.131275	.122797	.114408	.106118	.102012	.097935	.093886	.089867	.085879	.081923	.074113	.066443
	-.10	.154667	.146107	.137628	.129240	.120950	.116844	.112766	.108717	.104698	.100710	.096755	.088944	.081275
	-.20	.169498	.160938	.152460	.144071	.135781	.131676	.127598	.123549	.119530	.115542	.111586	.103776	.096107
	-.30	.184330	.175770	.167291	.158903	.150613	.146507	.142429	.138380	.134361	.130374	.126418	.118607	.110938
	-.40	.199161	.190601	.182123	.173734	.165444	.161339	.157261	.153212	.149193	.145205	.141249	.133439	.125770
20	.40	.081131	.072322	.063571	.054888	.046284	.042015	.037770	.033550	.029358	.025194	.021061	.012892	.004864
	.30	.095963	.087154	.078403	.069720	.061116	.056847	.052601	.048382	.044190	.040026	.035892	.027723	.019695
	.20	.110795	.101985	.093234	.084551	.075947	.071678	.067433	.063213	.059021	.054857	.050724	.042555	.034527
	.10	.125626	.116817	.108066	.099383	.090779	.086510	.082265	.078045	.073853	.069689	.065556	.057386	.049359
	0.00	.140458	.131648	.122897	.114214	.105610	.101341	.097096	.092877	.088684	.084520	.080387	.072218	.064190
	-.10	.155289	.146480	.137729	.129046	.120442	.116173	.111928	.107708	.103516	.099352	.095219	.087049	.079022
	-.20	.170121	.161311	.152560	.143878	.135273	.131004	.126759	.122540	.118347	.114184	.110050	.101881	.093853
	-.30	.184952	.176143	.167392	.158703	.150105	.145836	.141591	.137371	.133179	.129015	.124882	.116713	.108685
	-.40	.199784	.190975	.182224	.173541	.164936	.160667	.156422	.152203	.148010	.143847	.139713	.131544	.123516
25	.40	.081442	.072496	.063620	.054792	.046023	.041665	.037327	.033010	.028717	.024449	.020209	.011819	.003566
	.30	.096244	.087328	.078451	.069623	.060855	.056497	.052158	.047842	.043548	.039281	.035040	.026651	.018397
	.20	.111075	.102160	.093283	.084455	.075686	.071328	.066990	.062673	.058380	.054112	.049872	.041482	.033229
	.10	.125907	.116991	.108114	.099286	.090518	.086160	.081821	.077505	.073212	.068944	.064703	.056314	.048061
	0.00	.140738	.131823	.122946	.114118	.105349	.100991	.096653	.092336	.088043	.083775	.079535	.071145	.062892
	-.10	.155570	.146654	.137777	.128949	.120181	.115823	.111485	.107168	.102875	.098607	.094367	.085977	.077724
	-.20	.170401	.161486	.152609	.143781	.135012	.130654	.126316	.121999	.117706	.113438	.109198	.100809	.092555
	-.30	.185233	.176317	.167441	.158612	.149844	.145486	.141148	.136831	.132538	.128270	.124030	.115640	.107387
	-.40	.200064	.191149	.182272	.173444	.164675	.160317	.155979	.151663	.147369	.143102	.138861	.130472	.122218
30	.40	.081545	.072583	.063645	.054740	.045879	.041468	.037074	.032697	.028339	.024004	.019693	.011154	.002743
	.30	.096377	.087414	.078476	.069572	.060710	.056300	.051905	.047528	.043171	.038836	.034525	.025985	.017575
	.20	.111208	.102246	.093308	.084403	.075542	.071131	.066737	.062360	.058003	.053667	.049356	.040817	.032406
	.10	.126040	.117077	.108139	.099235	.090373	.085963	.081568	.077191	.072834	.068499	.064188	.055649	.047238
	0.00	.140872	.131909	.122971	.114066	.105205	.100795	.096400	.092023	.087666	.083330	.079019	.070480	.062069
	-.10	.155703	.146740	.137802	.128898	.120037	.115626	.111231	.106854	.102497	.098162	.093851	.085312	.076901
	-.20	.170535	.161572	.152634	.143729	.134868	.130458	.126063	.121686	.117329	.112993	.108682	.100143	.091733
	-.30	.185366	.176404	.167466	.158561	.149700	.145289	.140895	.136518	.132160	.127825	.123514	.114975	.106564
	-.40	.200198	.191235	.182297	.173392	.164531	.160121	.155726	.151349	.146992	.142657	.138346	.129806	.121396

5.0 YEAR HOLDING PERIOD
.160 EQUITY YIELD RATE
.600 LOAN RATIO

INTEREST RATE

TERM YEARS	APPR DEP	5.0	6.0	7.0	7.5	8.0	8.5	9.0	9.5	10.0	11.0	12.0	13.0	14.0
10	.40	.043994	.048627	.053347	.055739	.058152	.060585	.063038	.065511	.068004	.073045	.078161	.083347	.088600
	.30	.058535	.063168	.067888	.070280	.072692	.075126	.077579	.080052	.082544	.087586	.092702	.097888	.103141
	.20	.073076	.077709	.082429	.084821	.087233	.089667	.092120	.094593	.097085	.102127	.107243	.112429	.117682
	.10	.087617	.092250	.096970	.099362	.101774	.104207	.106661	.109134	.111626	.116668	.121784	.126970	.132223
	0.00	.102158	.106791	.111511	.113903	.116315	.118748	.121202	.123675	.126167	.131209	.136325	.141511	.146764
	-.10	.116699	.121332	.126052	.128444	.130856	.133289	.135743	.138216	.140708	.145750	.150866	.156052	.161305
	-.20	.131240	.135873	.140593	.142985	.145397	.147830	.150284	.152757	.155249	.160291	.165407	.170593	.175846
	-.30	.145781	.150414	.155134	.157525	.159938	.162371	.164825	.167298	.169790	.174832	.179947	.185133	.190387
	-.40	.160322	.164955	.169675	.172066	.174479	.176912	.179365	.181839	.184331	.189373	.194488	.199674	.204928
15	.40	.040576	.045663	.050846	.053471	.056118	.058786	.061474	.064181	.066907	.072413	.077986	.083619	.089308
	.30	.055117	.060204	.065386	.068012	.070659	.073326	.076015	.078722	.081448	.086954	.092527	.098160	.103849
	.20	.069657	.074745	.079927	.082553	.085200	.087867	.090555	.093263	.095989	.101495	.107068	.112701	.118390
	.10	.084198	.089286	.094468	.097094	.099741	.102408	.105096	.107804	.110530	.116036	.121609	.127242	.132931
	0.00	.098739	.103827	.109009	.111635	.114281	.116949	.119637	.122345	.125071	.130577	.136149	.141783	.147472
	-.10	.113280	.118368	.123550	.126176	.128822	.131490	.134178	.136886	.139612	.145118	.150690	.156324	.162012
	-.20	.127821	.132909	.138091	.140716	.143363	.146031	.148719	.151427	.154153	.159659	.165231	.170865	.176553
	-.30	.142362	.147449	.152632	.155257	.157904	.160572	.163260	.165968	.168694	.174200	.179772	.185406	.191094
	-.40	.156903	.161990	.167173	.169798	.172445	.175113	.177801	.180509	.183235	.188741	.194313	.199947	.205635
20	.40	.038918	.044245	.049667	.052412	.055177	.057961	.060764	.063584	.066421	.072139	.077912	.083731	.089590
	.30	.053459	.058786	.064208	.066953	.069717	.072502	.075305	.078125	.080962	.086680	.092453	.098272	.104131
	.20	.068000	.073327	.078749	.081493	.084258	.087043	.089846	.092666	.095503	.101221	.106994	.112813	.118672
	.10	.082541	.087868	.093290	.096034	.098799	.101584	.104387	.107207	.110044	.115762	.121535	.127354	.133213
	0.00	.097082	.102409	.107831	.110575	.113340	.116125	.118928	.121748	.124585	.130303	.136075	.141895	.147754
	-.10	.111623	.116950	.122372	.125116	.127881	.130666	.133469	.136289	.139126	.144844	.150616	.156436	.162295
	-.20	.126164	.131490	.136913	.139657	.142422	.145207	.148010	.150830	.153667	.159385	.165157	.170976	.176836
	-.30	.140705	.146031	.151454	.154198	.156963	.159748	.162550	.165371	.168207	.173926	.179698	.185517	.191377
	-.40	.155246	.160572	.165995	.168739	.171504	.174289	.177091	.179912	.182748	.188467	.194239	.200058	.205918
25	.40	.037963	.043442	.049014	.051831	.054666	.057520	.060389	.063273	.066171	.072003	.077676	.083783	.089717
	.30	.052504	.057983	.063555	.066372	.069207	.072061	.074930	.077814	.080712	.086544	.092217	.098324	.104258
	.20	.067045	.072524	.078096	.080912	.083748	.086601	.089471	.092355	.095253	.101085	.106958	.112865	.118799
	.10	.081586	.087065	.092637	.095453	.098289	.101142	.104012	.106896	.109794	.115626	.121499	.127406	.133340
	0.00	.096127	.101606	.107177	.109994	.112830	.115683	.118553	.121437	.124335	.130166	.136040	.141947	.147881
	-.10	.110668	.116147	.121718	.124535	.127371	.130224	.133094	.135978	.138876	.144707	.150581	.156488	.162422
	-.20	.125209	.130688	.136259	.139076	.141912	.144765	.147635	.150519	.153416	.159248	.165122	.171029	.176963
	-.30	.139750	.145229	.150800	.153617	.156453	.159306	.162175	.165060	.167957	.173789	.179663	.185570	.191504
	-.40	.154291	.159770	.165341	.168158	.170994	.173847	.176716	.179601	.182498	.188330	.194203	.200111	.206045
30	.40	.037358	.042944	.048618	.051484	.054366	.057263	.060175	.063098	.066033	.071930	.077858	.083809	.089778
	.30	.051899	.057485	.063159	.066025	.068907	.071804	.074716	.077639	.080574	.086471	.092399	.098350	.104319
	.20	.066440	.072026	.077700	.080566	.083448	.086345	.089257	.092180	.095115	.101012	.106939	.112891	.118860
	.10	.080981	.086567	.092241	.095106	.097989	.100886	.103797	.106721	.109655	.115553	.121480	.127432	.133401
	0.00	.095522	.101108	.106782	.109647	.112530	.115427	.118338	.121262	.124196	.130094	.136021	.141973	.147942
	-.10	.110063	.115649	.121323	.124188	.127071	.129968	.132879	.135803	.138737	.144634	.150562	.156514	.162483
	-.20	.124604	.130190	.135864	.138729	.141612	.144509	.147420	.150344	.153278	.159175	.165103	.171055	.177024
	-.30	.139145	.144731	.150405	.153270	.156153	.159050	.161961	.164885	.167819	.173716	.179644	.185596	.191565
	-.40	.153686	.159272	.164946	.167811	.170693	.173591	.176502	.179426	.182360	.188257	.194185	.200136	.206105

5.0 YEAR HOLDING PERIOD
.160 EQUITY YIELD RATE
.667 LOAN RATIO

INTEREST RATE

TERM YEARS	APPR DEP	14.0	13.0	12.0	11.0	10.0	9.5	9.0	8.5	8.0	7.5	7.0	6.0	5.0
10	.40	.087130	.081292	.075530	.069846	.064244	.061475	.058727	.056001	.053297	.050617	.047959	.042715	.037567
	.30	.101671	.095833	.090071	.084387	.078785	.076016	.073268	.070542	.067838	.065158	.062500	.057256	.052108
	.20	.116212	.110374	.104612	.098928	.093326	.090557	.087809	.085083	.082379	.079699	.077041	.071796	.066649
	.10	.130753	.124915	.119153	.113469	.107867	.105097	.102350	.099624	.096920	.094240	.091582	.086337	.081190
	0.00	.145294	.139456	.133694	.128010	.122408	.119638	.116891	.114165	.111461	.108780	.106123	.100878	.095731
	-.10	.159834	.153997	.148235	.142551	.136949	.134179	.131431	.128706	.126002	.123321	.120664	.115419	.110272
	-.20	.174375	.168538	.162776	.157092	.151490	.148720	.145972	.143247	.140543	.137862	.135205	.129960	.124812
	-.30	.188916	.183079	.177317	.171633	.166031	.163261	.160513	.157788	.155084	.152403	.149746	.144501	.139353
	-.40	.203457	.197620	.191858	.186174	.180572	.177802	.175054	.172328	.169625	.166944	.164287	.159042	.153894
15	.40	.087916	.081595	.075336	.069144	.063026	.059997	.056989	.054002	.051038	.048097	.045180	.039421	.033768
	.30	.102457	.096136	.089876	.083685	.077567	.074538	.071530	.068543	.065579	.062638	.059721	.053962	.048309
	.20	.116998	.110677	.104417	.098226	.092108	.089079	.086070	.083084	.080119	.077178	.074261	.068503	.062850
	.10	.131538	.125218	.118958	.112767	.106649	.103620	.100611	.097625	.094660	.091719	.088802	.083044	.077391
	0.00	.146079	.139759	.133499	.127308	.121190	.118161	.115152	.112166	.109201	.106260	.103343	.097585	.091932
	-.10	.160620	.154299	.148040	.141849	.135731	.132702	.129693	.126707	.123742	.120801	.117884	.112126	.106473
	-.20	.175161	.168840	.162581	.156390	.150272	.147243	.144234	.141248	.138283	.135342	.132425	.126667	.121014
	-.30	.189702	.183381	.177122	.170931	.164813	.161784	.158775	.155788	.152824	.149883	.146966	.141208	.135555
	-.40	.204243	.197922	.191663	.185471	.179354	.176324	.173316	.170329	.167365	.164424	.161507	.155749	.150096
20	.40	.088229	.081719	.075253	.068840	.062486	.059334	.056200	.053086	.049992	.046924	.043870	.037845	.031927
	.30	.102770	.096260	.089794	.083380	.077027	.073875	.070741	.067627	.064533	.061461	.058411	.052386	.046468
	.20	.117311	.110801	.104335	.097921	.091568	.088416	.085282	.082168	.079074	.076002	.072952	.066927	.061009
	.10	.131852	.125342	.118876	.112462	.106108	.102957	.099823	.096709	.093615	.090543	.087493	.081468	.075550
	0.00	.146393	.139883	.133417	.127003	.120649	.117498	.114364	.111249	.108156	.105083	.102034	.096009	.090091
	-.10	.160934	.154424	.147958	.141544	.135190	.132038	.128905	.125790	.122697	.119624	.116575	.110550	.104632
	-.20	.175475	.168965	.162499	.156085	.149731	.146579	.143446	.140331	.137238	.134165	.131116	.125091	.119173
	-.30	.190016	.183506	.177040	.170626	.164272	.161120	.157987	.154872	.151778	.148706	.145657	.139632	.133713
	-.40	.204557	.198047	.191581	.185167	.178813	.175661	.172528	.169413	.166319	.163247	.160198	.154173	.148254
25	.40	.088371	.081777	.075214	.068688	.062208	.058988	.055783	.052595	.049425	.046274	.043144	.036954	.030866
	.30	.102912	.096318	.089755	.083229	.076749	.073529	.070324	.067136	.063966	.060815	.057685	.051495	.045407
	.20	.117453	.110859	.104295	.097770	.091290	.088070	.084865	.081677	.078507	.075356	.072226	.066035	.059948
	.10	.131994	.125400	.118836	.112311	.105831	.102611	.099406	.096218	.093048	.089897	.086767	.080576	.074489
	0.00	.146535	.139941	.133377	.126851	.120372	.117152	.113947	.110759	.107589	.104438	.101308	.095117	.089030
	-.10	.161076	.154482	.147918	.141392	.134913	.131693	.128488	.125300	.122130	.118979	.115849	.109658	.103571
	-.20	.175617	.169023	.162459	.155933	.149453	.146234	.143029	.139841	.136671	.133520	.130390	.124199	.118112
	-.30	.190157	.183564	.177000	.170474	.163994	.160775	.157570	.154382	.151212	.148061	.144931	.138740	.132653
	-.40	.204698	.198105	.191541	.185015	.178535	.175316	.172111	.168923	.165753	.162602	.159472	.153281	.147194
30	.40	.088438	.081806	.075193	.068607	.062054	.058794	.055545	.052311	.049091	.045889	.042705	.036400	.030194
	.30	.102979	.096347	.089734	.083148	.076595	.073335	.070086	.066852	.063632	.060430	.057246	.050941	.044735
	.20	.117520	.110888	.104275	.097689	.091136	.087876	.084627	.081393	.078173	.074971	.071787	.065482	.059276
	.10	.132061	.125429	.118816	.112230	.105677	.102417	.099168	.095934	.092714	.089511	.086327	.080023	.073817
	0.00	.146602	.139970	.133357	.126770	.120218	.116957	.113709	.110474	.107255	.104052	.100868	.094564	.088358
	-.10	.161143	.154510	.147898	.141311	.134759	.131498	.128250	.125015	.121796	.118593	.115409	.109105	.102898
	-.20	.175684	.169051	.162439	.155852	.149300	.146039	.142791	.139556	.136337	.133134	.129950	.123646	.117439
	-.30	.190225	.183592	.176980	.170393	.163841	.160580	.157332	.154097	.150878	.147675	.144491	.138187	.131980
	-.40	.204766	.198133	.191521	.184934	.178382	.175121	.171873	.168638	.165419	.162216	.159032	.152728	.146521

5.0 YEAR HOLDING PERIOD
.160 EQUITY YIELD RATE
.700 LOAN RATIO

INTEREST RATE

TERM YEARS	APPR DEP	5.0	6.0	7.0	7.5	8.0	8.5	9.0	9.5	10.0	11.0	12.0	13.0	14.0
10	.40	.034354	.039759	.045265	.048056	.050871	.053709	.056572	.059457	.062365	.068247	.074215	.080265	.086395
	.30	.048895	.054300	.059806	.062597	.065412	.068250	.071112	.073998	.076904	.082788	.088756	.094806	.100935
	.20	.063436	.068841	.074347	.077138	.079953	.082791	.085653	.088539	.091447	.097329	.103297	.109347	.115476
	.10	.077977	.083382	.088888	.091679	.094494	.097332	.100194	.103080	.105988	.111870	.117838	.123888	.130017
	0.00	.092517	.097923	.103429	.106220	.109035	.111873	.114735	.117621	.120528	.126411	.132379	.138429	.144558
	-.10	.107058	.112464	.117970	.120761	.123575	.126414	.129276	.132161	.135069	.140952	.146920	.152970	.159099
	-.20	.121599	.127004	.132511	.135302	.138116	.140955	.143817	.146702	.149610	.154493	.161461	.167511	.173640
	-.30	.136140	.141545	.147052	.149843	.152657	.155496	.158358	.161243	.164151	.170034	.176002	.182052	.188181
	-.40	.150681	.156086	.161593	.164383	.167198	.170037	.172899	.175784	.178692	.184574	.190542	.196693	.202722
15	.40	.030365	.036301	.042347	.045410	.048498	.051610	.054746	.057905	.061086	.067510	.074011	.080583	.087220
	.30	.044906	.050842	.056888	.059951	.063039	.066151	.069287	.072446	.075627	.082050	.088552	.095124	.101761
	.20	.059447	.065383	.071429	.074492	.077580	.080692	.083828	.086987	.090168	.096591	.103093	.109665	.116302
	.10	.073988	.079924	.085970	.089033	.092121	.095233	.098369	.101528	.104709	.111132	.117633	.124206	.130842
	0.00	.088529	.094464	.100511	.103574	.106662	.109774	.112910	.116069	.119250	.125673	.132174	.138747	.145383
	-.10	.103070	.109005	.115052	.118115	.121203	.124315	.127451	.130610	.133791	.140214	.146715	.153287	.159924
	-.20	.117611	.123546	.129593	.132656	.135744	.138856	.141992	.145151	.148332	.154755	.161256	.167828	.174465
	-.30	.132152	.138087	.144134	.147196	.150284	.153397	.156533	.159692	.162872	.169296	.175797	.182369	.189006
	-.40	.146693	.152628	.158675	.161737	.164825	.167937	.171074	.174233	.177413	.183837	.190338	.196910	.203547
20	.40	.028432	.034646	.040972	.044174	.047400	.050648	.053919	.057209	.060518	.067190	.073924	.080713	.087549
	.30	.042973	.049187	.055513	.058715	.061941	.065189	.068459	.071750	.075059	.081731	.088465	.095254	.102090
	.20	.057514	.063728	.070054	.073256	.076482	.079730	.083000	.086291	.089600	.096272	.103006	.109795	.116631
	.10	.072005	.078269	.084595	.087797	.091023	.094271	.097541	.100832	.104141	.110813	.117547	.124336	.131172
	0.00	.086596	.092810	.099136	.102338	.105564	.108812	.112082	.115373	.118682	.125354	.132088	.138877	.145713
	-.10	.101136	.107351	.113677	.116879	.120105	.123353	.126623	.129914	.133223	.139895	.146629	.153418	.160254
	-.20	.115677	.121892	.128218	.131420	.134646	.137894	.141164	.144455	.147764	.154436	.161170	.167959	.174795
	-.30	.130218	.136433	.142759	.145961	.149187	.152435	.155705	.158995	.162305	.168976	.175711	.182500	.189336
	-.40	.144759	.150974	.157300	.160502	.163727	.166976	.170246	.173536	.176846	.183517	.190252	.197041	.203877
25	.40	.027318	.033710	.040210	.043496	.046805	.050133	.053481	.056846	.060227	.067030	.073883	.080774	.087698
	.30	.041859	.048251	.054751	.058037	.061346	.064674	.068022	.071387	.074768	.081571	.088424	.095315	.102239
	.20	.056460	.062792	.069292	.072578	.075887	.079215	.082563	.085928	.089308	.096112	.102964	.109856	.116780
	.10	.070941	.077333	.083833	.087119	.090428	.093756	.097104	.100469	.103849	.110653	.117505	.124397	.131321
	0.00	.085482	.091874	.098374	.101660	.104968	.108297	.111645	.115010	.118390	.125194	.132046	.138938	.145861
	-.10	.100023	.106415	.112915	.116201	.119509	.122838	.126186	.129551	.132931	.139735	.146587	.153479	.160402
	-.20	.114564	.120955	.127456	.130742	.134050	.137379	.140727	.144091	.147472	.154276	.161128	.168020	.174943
	-.30	.129105	.135496	.141997	.145283	.148591	.151920	.155268	.158632	.162013	.168817	.175669	.182561	.189484
	-.40	.143645	.150037	.156537	.159824	.163132	.166461	.169808	.173173	.176554	.183358	.190210	.197102	.204025
30	.40	.026612	.033129	.039748	.043092	.046454	.049835	.053231	.056642	.060065	.066945	.073861	.080804	.087768
	.30	.041153	.047670	.054289	.057632	.060995	.064376	.067772	.071183	.074606	.081486	.088402	.095345	.102309
	.20	.055694	.062211	.068830	.072173	.075536	.078917	.082313	.085724	.089147	.096027	.102943	.109886	.116850
	.10	.070235	.076752	.083371	.086714	.090077	.093457	.096854	.100265	.103688	.110568	.117484	.124427	.131391
	0.00	.084776	.091293	.097912	.101255	.104618	.107998	.111395	.114806	.118229	.125109	.132025	.138968	.145932
	-.10	.099317	.105833	.112453	.115796	.119159	.122539	.125936	.129347	.132770	.139650	.146566	.153509	.160473
	-.20	.113858	.120374	.126994	.130337	.133700	.137080	.140477	.143887	.147311	.154191	.161107	.168050	.175014
	-.30	.128399	.134915	.141535	.144878	.148241	.151621	.155018	.158428	.161852	.168732	.175648	.182591	.189555
	-.40	.142940	.149456	.156076	.159419	.162782	.166162	.169559	.172969	.176393	.183273	.190189	.197132	.204096

5.0 YEAR HOLDING PERIOD
.160 EQUITY YIELD RATE
.750 LOAN RATIO

INTEREST RATE

TERM YEARS	APPR DEP	5.0	6.0	7.0	7.5	8.0	8.5	9.0	9.5	10.0	11.0	12.0	13.0	14.0
10	.40	.029534	.035325	.041225	.044215	.047230	.050272	.053338	.056430	.059545	.065848	.072242	.078725	.035292
	.30	.044074	.049866	.055766	.058755	.061771	.064813	.067879	.070971	.074086	.080389	.086783	.093265	.039832
	.20	.058615	.064407	.070307	.073296	.076312	.079354	.082420	.085512	.088627	.094930	.101324	.107806	.114373
	.10	.073156	.078948	.084848	.087837	.090853	.093895	.096961	.100053	.103168	.109471	.115865	.122347	.128914
	0.00	.087697	.093488	.099388	.102378	.105394	.108436	.111502	.114593	.117709	.124012	.130406	.136888	.143455
	-.10	.102238	.108029	.113929	.116919	.119935	.122976	.126043	.129134	.132250	.138552	.144947	.151429	.157996
	-.20	.116779	.122570	.128470	.131460	.134476	.137517	.140584	.143675	.146791	.153093	.159488	.165970	.172537
	-.30	.131320	.137111	.143011	.146001	.149017	.152058	.155125	.158216	.161332	.167634	.174029	.180511	.187078
	-.40	.145861	.151652	.157552	.160542	.163558	.166599	.169666	.172757	.175873	.182175	.188570	.195052	.201619
15	.40	.025260	.031620	.038098	.041379	.044688	.048023	.051383	.054767	.058175	.065058	.072023	.079065	.086176
	.30	.039801	.046161	.052639	.055920	.059229	.062564	.065924	.069308	.072716	.079599	.086564	.093606	.100717
	.20	.054342	.060701	.067180	.070461	.073770	.077105	.080465	.083849	.087257	.094139	.101105	.108147	.115258
	.10	.068883	.075242	.081721	.085002	.088311	.091646	.095006	.098390	.101798	.108680	.115646	.122688	.129798
	0.00	.083424	.089783	.096262	.099543	.102852	.106187	.109547	.112931	.116339	.123221	.130187	.137228	.144339
	-.10	.097965	.104324	.110803	.114084	.117393	.120728	.124088	.127472	.130880	.137762	.144728	.151769	.158880
	-.20	.112506	.118865	.125343	.128625	.131934	.135268	.138629	.142013	.145421	.152303	.159269	.166310	.173421
	-.30	.127047	.133406	.139884	.143166	.146475	.149809	.153169	.156554	.159962	.166844	.173810	.180851	.187962
	-.40	.141588	.147947	.154425	.157707	.161016	.164350	.167710	.171095	.174503	.181385	.188351	.195392	.202503
20	.40	.023189	.029847	.036625	.040055	.043512	.046992	.050496	.054021	.057567	.064715	.071931	.079205	.086529
	.30	.037730	.044388	.051166	.054596	.058053	.061533	.065037	.068562	.072108	.079256	.086472	.093745	.101070
	.20	.052271	.058929	.065707	.069137	.072594	.076074	.079578	.083103	.086649	.093797	.101012	.108286	.115611
	.10	.066811	.073470	.080248	.083678	.087134	.090615	.094119	.097644	.101190	.108338	.115553	.122827	.130152
	0.00	.081352	.088011	.094789	.098219	.101675	.105156	.108660	.112185	.115731	.122879	.130094	.137368	.144692
	-.10	.095893	.102552	.109330	.112760	.116216	.119697	.123201	.126726	.130272	.137420	.144635	.151909	.159233
	-.20	.110434	.117093	.123871	.127301	.130757	.134238	.137741	.141267	.144813	.151961	.159176	.166450	.173774
	-.30	.124975	.131634	.138412	.141842	.145298	.148779	.152282	.155808	.159354	.166502	.173717	.180991	.188315
	-.40	.139516	.146174	.152953	.156383	.159839	.163320	.166823	.170349	.173895	.181043	.188258	.195532	.202856
25	.40	.021995	.028844	.035808	.039329	.042874	.046440	.050027	.053632	.057254	.064544	.071886	.079270	.086688
	.30	.036536	.043385	.050349	.053870	.057415	.060981	.064568	.068173	.071795	.079085	.086427	.093811	.101229
	.20	.051077	.057925	.064890	.068411	.071956	.075522	.079109	.082714	.086336	.093626	.100968	.108352	.115770
	.10	.065618	.072466	.079431	.082952	.086497	.090063	.093650	.097255	.100877	.108167	.115509	.122893	.130311
	0.00	.080159	.087007	.093972	.097493	.101038	.104604	.108191	.111796	.115418	.122708	.130050	.137434	.144852
	-.10	.094700	.101548	.108513	.112034	.115579	.119145	.122732	.126337	.129959	.137249	.144591	.151975	.159392
	-.20	.109241	.116089	.123054	.126575	.130120	.133686	.137273	.140878	.144500	.151790	.159132	.166515	.173933
	-.30	.123782	.130630	.137595	.141116	.144660	.148227	.151814	.155419	.159041	.166331	.173672	.181056	.188474
	-.40	.138323	.145171	.152136	.155657	.159201	.162768	.166355	.169960	.173582	.180872	.188213	.195597	.203015
30	.40	.021239	.028221	.035314	.038895	.042498	.046120	.049759	.053414	.057082	.064453	.071863	.079302	.036763
	.30	.035780	.042762	.049854	.053436	.057039	.060661	.064300	.067955	.071623	.078994	.086404	.093843	.101304
	.20	.050321	.057303	.064395	.067977	.071580	.075202	.078841	.082496	.086164	.093535	.100945	.108384	.115845
	.10	.064862	.071844	.078936	.082518	.086121	.089743	.093382	.097036	.100705	.108076	.115486	.122925	.130386
	0.00	.079403	.086385	.093477	.097059	.100662	.104284	.107923	.111577	.115245	.122617	.130027	.137466	.144927
	-.10	.093944	.100926	.108018	.111600	.115203	.118825	.122464	.126118	.129786	.137158	.144568	.152007	.159468
	-.20	.108484	.115467	.122559	.126141	.129744	.133366	.137005	.140659	.144327	.151699	.159109	.166548	.174009
	-.30	.123025	.130008	.137100	.140682	.144285	.147907	.151546	.155200	.158868	.166240	.173650	.181089	.188550
	-.40	.137566	.144549	.151641	.155223	.158826	.162448	.166087	.169741	.173409	.180781	.188190	.195630	.203091

5.0 YEAR HOLDING PERIOD
.160 EQUITY YIELD RATE
.800 LOAN RATIO

INTEREST RATE

TERM YEARS	APPR DEP	5.0	6.0	7.0	7.5	8.0	8.5	9.0	9.5	10.0	11.0	12.0	13.0	14.0
10	.40	.024713	.030891	.037184	.040373	.043590	.046834	.050105	.053403	.056726	.063449	.070269	.077184	.084189
	.30	.039254	.045432	.051725	.054914	.058131	.061375	.064646	.067944	.071267	.077989	.084810	.091725	.098730
	.20	.053795	.059973	.066266	.069455	.072672	.075916	.079187	.082484	.085808	.092530	.099351	.106266	.113270
	.10	.068336	.074513	.080807	.083996	.087213	.090457	.093728	.097025	.100349	.107071	.113892	.120807	.127811
	0.00	.082877	.089054	.095348	.098537	.101754	.104998	.108269	.111566	.114890	.121612	.128433	.135348	.142352
	-.10	.097418	.103595	.109889	.113078	.116295	.119539	.122810	.126107	.129431	.136153	.142974	.149888	.156893
	-.20	.111959	.118136	.124430	.127619	.130836	.134080	.137351	.140648	.143972	.150694	.157515	.164429	.171434
	-.30	.126500	.132677	.138971	.142160	.145377	.148621	.151892	.155189	.158513	.165235	.172056	.178970	.185975
	-.40	.141041	.147218	.153511	.156701	.159917	.163162	.166433	.169730	.173053	.179776	.186597	.193511	.200516
15	.40	.020155	.026938	.033849	.037349	.040878	.044435	.048019	.051629	.055264	.062606	.070036	.077547	.085132
	.30	.034696	.041479	.048390	.051890	.055419	.058976	.062560	.066170	.069805	.077147	.084576	.092088	.099673
	.20	.049237	.056020	.062931	.066431	.069960	.073517	.077101	.080711	.084346	.091688	.099117	.106628	.114213
	.10	.063778	.070561	.077471	.080972	.084501	.088058	.091642	.095252	.098887	.106229	.113658	.121169	.128754
	0.00	.078319	.085102	.092012	.095513	.099042	.102599	.106183	.109793	.113428	.120769	.128199	.135710	.143295
	-.10	.092860	.099643	.106553	.110054	.113583	.117140	.120724	.124334	.127970	.135310	.142740	.150251	.157836
	-.20	.107401	.114184	.121094	.124595	.128124	.131681	.135265	.138875	.142510	.149851	.157281	.164792	.172377
	-.30	.121942	.128725	.135635	.139136	.142665	.146222	.149806	.153416	.157051	.164392	.171822	.179333	.186918
	-.40	.136483	.143266	.150176	.153676	.157206	.160763	.164347	.167957	.171592	.178933	.186363	.193874	.201459
20	.40	.017945	.025048	.032278	.035937	.039623	.043336	.047073	.050834	.054616	.062240	.069937	.077696	.085508
	.30	.032486	.039589	.046819	.050478	.054164	.057877	.061614	.065374	.069157	.076781	.084478	.092237	.100049
	.20	.047027	.054130	.061359	.065019	.068705	.072418	.076155	.079915	.083698	.091322	.099019	.106778	.114590
	.10	.061568	.068671	.075900	.079560	.083246	.086959	.090696	.094456	.098239	.105863	.113560	.121319	.129131
	0.00	.076110	.083211	.090441	.094100	.097787	.101500	.105237	.108997	.112780	.120404	.128101	.135859	.143672
	-.10	.090650	.097752	.104982	.108641	.112328	.116041	.119778	.123538	.127320	.134945	.142642	.150400	.158213
	-.20	.105191	.112293	.119523	.123182	.126869	.130582	.134319	.138079	.141861	.149486	.157183	.164941	.172754
	-.30	.119732	.126834	.134064	.137723	.141410	.145122	.148860	.152620	.156402	.164027	.171723	.179482	.187295
	-.40	.134273	.141375	.148605	.152264	.155951	.159663	.163401	.167161	.170943	.178568	.186264	.194023	.201836
25	.40	.016673	.023977	.031406	.035162	.038943	.042747	.046573	.050419	.054282	.062058	.069889	.077765	.085678
	.30	.031213	.038518	.045947	.049703	.053484	.057288	.061114	.064960	.068823	.076599	.084430	.092306	.100219
	.20	.045754	.053059	.060488	.064244	.068025	.071829	.075655	.079501	.083364	.091140	.098971	.106847	.114760
	.10	.060295	.067600	.075029	.078785	.082566	.086370	.090196	.094042	.097905	.105681	.113512	.121388	.129301
	0.00	.074836	.082141	.089570	.093326	.097107	.100911	.104737	.108582	.112446	.120222	.128053	.135929	.143842
	-.10	.089377	.096682	.104111	.107867	.111648	.115452	.119278	.123123	.126987	.134763	.142594	.150470	.158383
	-.20	.103918	.111223	.118652	.122408	.126189	.129993	.133819	.137664	.141528	.149304	.157135	.165011	.172924
	-.30	.118459	.125764	.133193	.136949	.140730	.144534	.148360	.152205	.156069	.163845	.171676	.179552	.187464
	-.40	.133000	.140305	.147734	.151490	.155271	.159075	.162901	.166746	.170610	.178386	.186217	.194093	.202005
30	.40	.015866	.023313	.030879	.034699	.038543	.042406	.046287	.050185	.054098	.061961	.069865	.077800	.085759
	.30	.030407	.037854	.045420	.049240	.053083	.056947	.060828	.064726	.068639	.076502	.084406	.092341	.100299
	.20	.044948	.052395	.059961	.063781	.067624	.071488	.075369	.079267	.083180	.091043	.098947	.106882	.114840
	.10	.059489	.066936	.074502	.078322	.082165	.086029	.089910	.093808	.097721	.105584	.113488	.121423	.129381
	0.00	.074029	.081477	.089042	.092863	.096706	.100570	.104451	.108349	.112262	.120125	.128029	.135964	.143922
	-.10	.088570	.096018	.103583	.107404	.111247	.115111	.118992	.122890	.126803	.134666	.142569	.150505	.158463
	-.20	.103111	.110559	.118124	.121945	.125788	.129652	.133533	.137431	.141344	.149207	.157110	.165045	.173004
	-.30	.117652	.125100	.132665	.136486	.140329	.144192	.148074	.151972	.155885	.163748	.171651	.179586	.187545
	-.40	.132193	.139641	.147206	.151027	.154870	.158733	.162615	.166513	.170426	.178289	.186192	.194127	.202086

5.0 YEAR HOLDING PERIOD
.160 EQUITY YIELD RATE
.900 LOAN RATIO

INTEREST RATE

TERM YEARS	APPR DEP	5.0	6.0	7.0	7.5	8.0	8.5	9.0	9.5	10.0	11.0	12.0	13.0	14.0
10	.40	.015073	.022022	.029102	.032690	.036309	.039959	.043639	.047348	.051087	.058650	.066323	.074102	.081983
	.30	.029614	.036563	.043643	.047231	.050850	.054500	.058180	.061889	.065628	.073191	.080864	.088643	.096524
	.20	.044155	.051104	.058184	.061772	.065391	.069041	.072721	.076430	.080169	.087732	.095405	.103184	.111064
	.10	.058696	.065645	.072725	.076313	.079932	.083582	.087262	.090710	.094710	.102273	.109946	.117725	.125605
	0.00	.073237	.080186	.087266	.090854	.094473	.098123	.101803	.105512	.109251	.116814	.124487	.132266	.140146
	-.10	.087778	.094727	.101807	.105395	.109014	.112664	.116343	.120053	.123792	.131355	.139028	.146807	.154687
	-.20	.102319	.109268	.116348	.119936	.123555	.127205	.130884	.134594	.138333	.145896	.153569	.161348	.169228
	-.30	.116860	.123809	.130889	.134477	.138096	.141745	.145425	.149135	.152874	.160437	.168110	.175889	.183769
	-.40	.131400	.138350	.145430	.149018	.152637	.156286	.159966	.163676	.167415	.174978	.182651	.190430	.198310
15	.40	.009945	.017576	.025350	.029288	.033258	.037260	.041292	.045354	.049443	.057702	.066060	.074510	.083044
	.30	.024486	.032217	.039891	.043829	.047799	.051801	.055833	.059894	.063984	.072243	.080601	.089051	.097584
	.20	.039027	.046658	.054432	.058370	.062340	.066342	.070374	.074435	.078525	.086784	.095142	.103592	.112125
	.10	.053568	.061199	.068973	.072911	.076881	.080883	.084915	.088976	.093066	.101325	.109683	.118133	.126666
	0.00	.068109	.075740	.083514	.087452	.091422	.095424	.099456	.103517	.107607	.115866	.124224	.132674	.141207
	-.10	.082650	.090281	.098055	.101993	.105963	.109965	.113997	.118058	.122148	.130407	.138765	.147215	.155748
	-.20	.097191	.104822	.112596	.116534	.120504	.124506	.128538	.132599	.136689	.144948	.153306	.161756	.170289
	-.30	.111732	.119363	.127137	.131075	.135045	.139047	.143079	.147140	.151230	.159488	.167847	.176297	.184830
	-.40	.126273	.133904	.141678	.145616	.149586	.153588	.157620	.161681	.165770	.174029	.182388	.190838	.199371
20	.40	.007459	.015449	.023583	.027699	.031847	.036023	.040228	.044458	.048713	.057291	.065949	.074678	.083467
	.30	.022000	.029990	.038124	.042240	.046388	.050564	.054769	.058999	.063254	.071832	.080490	.089219	.098008
	.20	.036541	.044531	.052665	.056781	.060929	.065105	.069310	.073540	.077795	.086373	.095031	.103760	.112549
	.10	.051082	.059072	.067206	.071322	.075470	.079646	.083851	.088081	.092336	.100914	.109572	.118301	.127060
	0.00	.065623	.073613	.081747	.085863	.090010	.094187	.098391	.102622	.106877	.115455	.124113	.132842	.141631
	-.10	.080164	.088154	.096287	.100404	.104551	.108728	.112932	.117163	.121418	.129996	.138654	.147383	.156172
	-.20	.094705	.102695	.110828	.114945	.119092	.123269	.127473	.131704	.135959	.144537	.153195	.161924	.170713
	-.30	.109246	.117236	.125369	.129486	.133633	.137810	.142014	.146245	.150500	.159077	.167736	.176465	.185254
	-.40	.123787	.131777	.139910	.144027	.148174	.152351	.156555	.160786	.165041	.173618	.182277	.191006	.199795
25	.40	.006027	.014245	.022602	.026828	.031081	.035361	.039665	.043991	.048338	.057086	.065896	.074757	.083658
	.30	.020568	.028786	.037143	.041369	.045622	.049902	.054206	.058532	.062893	.071627	.080437	.089297	.098199
	.20	.035109	.043327	.051684	.055910	.060163	.064443	.068747	.073073	.077420	.086168	.094978	.103838	.112740
	.10	.049650	.057868	.066225	.070451	.074704	.078984	.083288	.087614	.091961	.100709	.109519	.118379	.127281
	0.00	.064191	.072409	.080766	.084992	.089245	.093525	.097829	.102155	.106502	.115250	.124060	.132920	.141822
	-.10	.078732	.086950	.095307	.099533	.103786	.108066	.112370	.116696	.121043	.129791	.138601	.147461	.156363
	-.20	.093273	.101491	.109848	.114073	.118327	.122607	.126911	.131237	.135584	.144332	.153141	.162002	.170904
	-.30	.107814	.116032	.124389	.128614	.132868	.137148	.141452	.145778	.150125	.158873	.167682	.176543	.185443
	-.40	.122355	.130573	.138930	.143155	.147409	.151689	.155993	.160319	.164666	.173413	.182223	.191084	.199986
30	.40	.005119	.013498	.022009	.026307	.030631	.034977	.039344	.043729	.048131	.056977	.065868	.074795	.083749
	.30	.019660	.028039	.036550	.040848	.045172	.049518	.053885	.058270	.062672	.071518	.080409	.089336	.098290
	.20	.034201	.042580	.051091	.055389	.059713	.064059	.068426	.072811	.077213	.086058	.094950	.103877	.112831
	.10	.048742	.057121	.065632	.069930	.074254	.078600	.082967	.087352	.091754	.100599	.109491	.118418	.127372
	0.00	.063283	.071662	.080173	.084471	.088795	.093141	.097508	.101893	.106295	.115140	.124032	.132959	.141913
	-.10	.077824	.086203	.094714	.099012	.103336	.107682	.112049	.116434	.120836	.129681	.138573	.147500	.156454
	-.20	.092365	.100744	.109255	.113553	.117876	.122223	.126590	.130975	.135376	.144222	.153114	.162041	.170994
	-.30	.106906	.115285	.123796	.128094	.132417	.136764	.141130	.145516	.149917	.158763	.167655	.176582	.185535
	-.40	.121447	.129826	.138337	.142635	.146958	.151305	.155671	.160057	.164458	.173304	.182196	.191123	.200076

5.0 YEAR HOLDING PERIOD
.180 EQUITY YIELD RATE
.600 LOAN RATIO

INTEREST RATE

TERM YEARS	APPR DEP	5.0	6.0	7.0	7.5	8.0	8.5	9.0	9.5	10.0	11.0	12.0	13.0	14.0
10	.40	.055726	.060318	.064997	.067369	.069761	.072174	.074608	.077061	.079533	.084536	.089613	.094761	.099977
	.30	.069704	.074296	.078975	.081347	.083739	.086152	.088585	.091038	.093511	.098514	.103591	.108739	.113955
	.20	.083682	.088274	.092953	.095324	.097717	.100130	.102563	.105016	.107489	.112492	.117569	.122717	.127933
	.10	.097660	.102252	.106931	.109302	.111695	.114108	.116541	.118994	.121467	.126470	.131546	.136694	.141911
	0.00	.111638	.116229	.120908	.123280	.125672	.128085	.130519	.132972	.135445	.140447	.145524	.150672	.155888
	-.10	.125615	.130207	.134886	.137258	.139650	.142063	.144496	.146950	.149422	.154425	.159502	.164650	.169866
	-.20	.139593	.144185	.148864	.151236	.153628	.156041	.158474	.160927	.163400	.168403	.173480	.178628	.183844
	-.30	.153571	.158163	.162842	.165213	.167606	.170019	.172452	.174905	.177378	.182381	.187458	.192606	.197822
	-.40	.167549	.172140	.176820	.179191	.181584	.183997	.186430	.188883	.191356	.196359	.201435	.206583	.211800
15	.40	.051688	.056726	.061861	.064464	.067088	.069733	.072400	.075086	.077791	.083257	.088791	.094387	.100041
	.30	.065666	.070704	.075839	.078441	.081066	.083711	.086377	.089064	.091769	.097235	.102769	.108365	.114019
	.20	.079643	.084682	.089817	.092419	.095043	.097689	.100355	.103041	.105747	.111212	.116746	.122343	.127997
	.10	.093621	.098660	.103795	.106397	.109021	.111667	.114333	.117019	.119725	.125190	.130724	.136321	.141975
	0.00	.107599	.112637	.117772	.120375	.122999	.125645	.128311	.130997	.133702	.139168	.144702	.150298	.155952
	-.10	.121577	.126615	.131750	.134352	.136977	.139622	.142289	.144975	.147680	.153146	.158680	.164276	.169930
	-.20	.135555	.140593	.145728	.148330	.150954	.153600	.156266	.158953	.161658	.167124	.172657	.178254	.183908
	-.30	.149532	.154571	.159706	.162308	.164932	.167578	.170244	.172930	.175636	.181101	.186635	.192232	.197886
	-.40	.163510	.168548	.173684	.176286	.178910	.181556	.184222	.186908	.189614	.195079	.200613	.206210	.211863
20	.40	.049730	.055008	.060384	.063107	.065851	.068615	.071398	.074200	.077018	.082702	.088443	.094234	.100067
	.30	.063708	.068985	.074362	.077085	.079828	.082593	.085376	.088177	.090996	.096680	.102421	.108211	.114044
	.20	.077685	.082963	.088340	.091062	.093806	.096570	.099354	.102155	.104974	.110658	.116399	.122189	.128022
	.10	.091663	.096941	.102318	.105040	.107784	.110548	.113331	.116133	.118951	.124636	.130377	.136167	.142000
	0.00	.105641	.110919	.116295	.119018	.121762	.124526	.127309	.130111	.132929	.138614	.144354	.150145	.155978
	-.10	.119619	.124897	.130273	.132996	.135740	.138504	.141287	.144088	.146907	.152591	.158332	.164123	.169956
	-.20	.133597	.138874	.144251	.146973	.149717	.152482	.155265	.158066	.160885	.166569	.172310	.178100	.183933
	-.30	.147574	.152852	.158229	.160951	.163695	.166459	.169243	.172044	.174863	.180547	.186288	.192078	.197911
	-.40	.161552	.166830	.172207	.174929	.177673	.180437	.183220	.186022	.188840	.194525	.200266	.206056	.211889
25	.40	.048602	.054035	.059565	.062363	.065180	.068016	.070869	.073737	.076621	.082426	.088275	.094162	.100078
	.30	.062580	.068013	.073543	.076340	.079158	.081994	.084847	.087715	.090599	.096404	.102253	.108140	.114056
	.20	.076557	.081991	.087521	.090318	.093136	.095971	.098824	.101693	.104576	.110381	.116231	.122117	.128034
	.10	.090535	.095968	.101498	.104296	.107113	.109949	.112802	.115671	.118554	.124359	.130209	.136095	.142011
	0.00	.104513	.109946	.115476	.118274	.121091	.123927	.126780	.129649	.132532	.138337	.144187	.150073	.155989
	-.10	.118491	.123924	.129454	.132252	.135069	.137905	.140758	.143626	.146510	.152315	.158164	.164051	.169967
	-.20	.132469	.137902	.143432	.146229	.149047	.151883	.154736	.157604	.160487	.166293	.172142	.178029	.183945
	-.30	.146446	.151879	.157409	.160207	.163025	.165860	.168713	.171582	.174465	.180270	.186120	.192006	.197923
	-.40	.160424	.165857	.171387	.174185	.177002	.179838	.182691	.185560	.188443	.194248	.200098	.205984	.211900
30	.40	.047887	.053431	.059069	.061918	.064785	.067668	.070566	.073478	.076401	.082278	.088189	.094126	.100084
	.30	.061865	.067409	.073047	.075896	.078763	.081646	.084544	.087456	.090379	.096256	.102167	.108104	.114061
	.20	.075843	.081387	.087025	.089874	.092741	.095624	.098522	.101433	.104357	.110234	.116145	.122082	.128039
	.10	.089820	.095365	.101002	.103851	.106719	.109602	.112500	.115411	.118334	.124212	.130123	.136060	.142017
	0.00	.103798	.109343	.114980	.117829	.120696	.123580	.126478	.129389	.132312	.138189	.144100	.150038	.155995
	-.10	.117776	.123320	.128958	.131807	.134674	.137557	.140455	.143367	.146290	.152167	.158078	.164015	.169973
	-.20	.131754	.137298	.142936	.145785	.148652	.151535	.154433	.157345	.160268	.166145	.172056	.177993	.183950
	-.30	.145732	.151276	.156913	.159763	.162630	.165513	.168411	.171322	.174246	.180123	.186034	.191971	.197928
	-.40	.159709	.165254	.170891	.173740	.176607	.179491	.182389	.185300	.188223	.194101	.200011	.205949	.211906

5.0 YEAR HOLDING PERIOD
.180 EQUITY YIELD RATE
.667 LOAN RATIO

INTEREST RATE

TERM YEARS	APPR DEP	5.0	6.0	7.0	7.5	8.0	8.5	9.0	9.5	10.0	11.0	12.0	13.0	14.0
10	.40	.048130	.053232	.058431	.061066	.063725	.066406	.069109	.071835	.074583	.080141	.085782	.091502	.097298
	.30	.062108	.067210	.072409	.075044	.077702	.080384	.083087	.085813	.088561	.094119	.099760	.105480	.111276
	.20	.076086	.081188	.086387	.089022	.091680	.094361	.097065	.099791	.102538	.108097	.113738	.119458	.125254
	.10	.090064	.095166	.100365	.103000	.105658	.108339	.111043	.113768	.116516	.122075	.127716	.133436	.139231
	0.00	.104041	.109143	.114342	.116977	.119636	.122317	.125020	.127746	.130494	.136052	.141693	.147413	.153209
	-.10	.118019	.123121	.128320	.130955	.133613	.136295	.138998	.141724	.144472	.150030	.155671	.161391	.167187
	-.20	.131997	.137099	.142298	.144933	.147591	.150272	.152976	.155702	.158449	.164008	.169649	.175369	.181165
	-.30	.145975	.151077	.156276	.158911	.161569	.164250	.166954	.169680	.172427	.177986	.183627	.189347	.195143
	-.40	.159953	.165054	.170253	.172889	.175547	.178228	.180932	.183657	.186405	.191964	.197605	.203325	.209120
15	.40	.043643	.049241	.054947	.057838	.060754	.063694	.066656	.069641	.072647	.078720	.084869	.091087	.097369
	.30	.057621	.063219	.068925	.071816	.074732	.077671	.080634	.083619	.086625	.092698	.098846	.105065	.111347
	.20	.071598	.077197	.082902	.085794	.088710	.091649	.094612	.097596	.100602	.106675	.112824	.119043	.125325
	.10	.085576	.091174	.096880	.099772	.102687	.105627	.108590	.111574	.114580	.120653	.126802	.133020	.139302
	0.00	.099554	.105152	.110858	.113749	.116665	.119605	.122567	.125552	.128558	.134631	.140780	.146998	.153280
	-.10	.113532	.119130	.124836	.127727	.130643	.133583	.136545	.139530	.142536	.148609	.154757	.160976	.167258
	-.20	.127510	.133108	.138814	.141705	.144621	.147560	.150523	.153508	.156514	.162586	.168735	.174954	.181236
	-.30	.141487	.147086	.152791	.155683	.158598	.161538	.164501	.167485	.170491	.176564	.182713	.188931	.195214
	-.40	.155465	.161063	.166769	.169660	.172576	.175516	.178478	.181463	.184469	.190542	.196691	.202909	.209191
20	.40	.041467	.047332	.053306	.056331	.059379	.062451	.065543	.068656	.071788	.078104	.084482	.090916	.097397
	.30	.055445	.061309	.067283	.070308	.073357	.076428	.079521	.082634	.085766	.092081	.098460	.104894	.111375
	.20	.069423	.075287	.081261	.084286	.087335	.090406	.093498	.096612	.099743	.106059	.112438	.118872	.125353
	.10	.083401	.089265	.095239	.098264	.101313	.104384	.107477	.110589	.113721	.120037	.126416	.132850	.139331
	0.00	.097378	.103243	.109217	.112242	.115291	.118362	.121454	.124567	.127699	.134015	.140394	.146827	.153308
	-.10	.111356	.117221	.123195	.126220	.129268	.132340	.135432	.138545	.141677	.147993	.154371	.160805	.167286
	-.20	.125334	.131198	.137172	.140197	.143246	.146317	.149410	.152523	.155654	.161970	.168349	.174783	.181264
	-.30	.139312	.145176	.151150	.154175	.157224	.160295	.163388	.166500	.169632	.175948	.182327	.188761	.195242
	-.40	.153290	.159154	.165128	.168153	.171202	.174273	.177366	.180478	.183610	.189926	.196305	.202738	.209220
25	.40	.040214	.046251	.052395	.055504	.058634	.061785	.064955	.068143	.071346	.077796	.084296	.090836	.097410
	.30	.054192	.060229	.066373	.069482	.072612	.075763	.078933	.082120	.085324	.091774	.098274	.104814	.111388
	.20	.068170	.074206	.080351	.083459	.086590	.089741	.092911	.096098	.099302	.105752	.112252	.118792	.125366
	.10	.082147	.088184	.094329	.097437	.100568	.103719	.106889	.110076	.113280	.119730	.126229	.132770	.139344
	0.00	.096125	.102162	.108306	.111415	.114545	.117696	.120866	.124054	.127257	.133707	.140207	.146748	.153321
	-.10	.110103	.116140	.122284	.125393	.128523	.131674	.134844	.138032	.141235	.147685	.154185	.160725	.167299
	-.20	.124080	.130117	.136262	.139370	.142501	.145652	.148822	.152009	.155213	.161663	.168163	.174703	.181277
	-.30	.138059	.144095	.150240	.153348	.156479	.159630	.162800	.165987	.169191	.175641	.182141	.188681	.195255
	-.40	.152036	.158073	.164218	.167326	.170457	.173608	.176777	.179965	.183168	.189619	.196118	.202659	.209232
30	.40	.039420	.045580	.051844	.055010	.058196	.061399	.064619	.067854	.071102	.077632	.084200	.090797	.097416
	.30	.053398	.059558	.065822	.068988	.072173	.075377	.078597	.081832	.085080	.091610	.098178	.104775	.111394
	.20	.067375	.073536	.079800	.082965	.086151	.089355	.092575	.095810	.099058	.105588	.112156	.118753	.125372
	.10	.081353	.087514	.093778	.096943	.100129	.103333	.106553	.109787	.113035	.119566	.126133	.132730	.139350
	0.00	.095331	.101491	.107755	.110920	.114107	.117310	.120530	.123765	.127013	.133544	.140111	.146708	.153327
	-.10	.109309	.115469	.121733	.124899	.128084	.131288	.134508	.137743	.140991	.147521	.154089	.160686	.167305
	-.20	.123286	.129447	.135711	.138877	.142062	.145266	.148486	.151721	.154969	.161499	.168067	.174664	.181283
	-.30	.137264	.143425	.149689	.152854	.156040	.159244	.162464	.165699	.168947	.175477	.182045	.188642	.195261
	-.40	.151242	.157402	.163666	.166832	.170018	.173221	.176442	.179676	.182924	.189455	.196022	.202619	.209238

5.0 YEAR HOLDING PERIOD
.180 EQUITY YIELD RATE
.700 LOAN RATIO

INTEREST RATE

TERM YEARS	APPR DEP	5.0	6.0	7.0	7.5	8.0	8.5	9.0	9.5	10.0	11.0	12.0	13.0	14.0
10	.40	.044333	.049690	.055149	.057915	.060707	.063522	.066361	.069223	.072108	.077944	.083867	.089873	.095959
	.30	.058311	.063568	.069126	.071893	.074684	.077500	.080338	.083200	.086085	.091922	.097845	.103851	.109936
	.20	.072288	.077645	.083104	.085871	.088662	.091477	.094316	.097178	.100063	.105900	.111823	.117829	.123914
	.10	.086266	.091623	.097082	.099849	.102640	.105455	.108294	.111156	.114041	.119878	.125800	.131806	.137892
	0.00	.100244	.105601	.111060	.113827	.116618	.119433	.122272	.125134	.128019	.133855	.139778	.145784	.151870
	-.10	.114222	.119579	.125038	.127804	.130596	.133411	.136250	.139112	.141996	.147833	.153756	.159764	.165848
	-.20	.128199	.133556	.139015	.141782	.144573	.147389	.150227	.153089	.155974	.161811	.167734	.173740	.179825
	-.30	.142177	.147534	.152993	.155760	.158551	.161366	.164205	.167067	.169952	.175789	.181712	.187718	.193803
	-.40	.156155	.161512	.166971	.169738	.172529	.175344	.178183	.181045	.183930	.189766	.195689	.201695	.207781
15	.40	.039621	.045499	.051490	.054526	.057588	.060674	.063785	.066919	.070075	.076452	.082908	.089437	.096033
	.30	.053599	.059477	.065468	.068504	.071566	.074652	.077763	.080897	.084053	.090429	.096885	.103415	.110011
	.20	.067577	.073455	.079446	.082482	.085543	.088630	.091740	.094874	.098031	.104407	.110863	.117393	.123989
	.10	.081554	.087432	.093423	.096459	.099521	.102608	.105718	.108852	.112008	.118385	.124841	.131370	.137967
	0.00	.095532	.101410	.107401	.110437	.113499	.116585	.119696	.122830	.125986	.132363	.138819	.145348	.151944
	-.10	.109510	.115388	.121379	.124415	.127477	.130563	.133674	.136808	.139964	.146340	.152797	.159326	.165922
	-.20	.123488	.129366	.135357	.138393	.141454	.144541	.147652	.150785	.153942	.160318	.166774	.173304	.179900
	-.30	.137466	.143344	.149335	.152372	.155432	.158519	.161629	.164763	.167920	.174296	.180752	.187282	.193878
	-.40	.151443	.157321	.163312	.166348	.169410	.172496	.175607	.178741	.181897	.188274	.194730	.201259	.207855
20	.40	.037337	.043494	.049767	.052943	.056144	.059369	.062616	.065885	.069173	.075805	.082502	.089258	.096063
	.30	.051314	.057472	.063745	.066921	.070122	.073347	.076594	.079862	.083151	.089782	.096480	.103236	.110041
	.20	.065292	.071450	.077722	.080899	.084100	.087325	.090572	.093840	.097129	.103760	.110458	.117213	.124019
	.10	.079270	.085428	.091700	.094876	.098078	.101302	.104550	.107818	.111106	.117738	.124436	.131191	.137996
	0.00	.093248	.099405	.105678	.108854	.112055	.115280	.118527	.121796	.125084	.131716	.138414	.145169	.151974
	-.10	.107226	.113383	.119656	.122832	.126033	.129258	.132505	.135774	.139062	.145694	.152391	.159147	.165952
	-.20	.121203	.127361	.133634	.136810	.140011	.143236	.146483	.149751	.153040	.159671	.166369	.173124	.179930
	-.30	.135181	.141339	.147611	.150788	.153989	.157214	.160461	.163729	.167017	.173649	.180347	.187102	.193907
	-.40	.149159	.155316	.161589	.164765	.167967	.171191	.174439	.177707	.180995	.187627	.194325	.201080	.207885
25	.40	.036021	.042359	.048811	.052075	.055362	.058670	.061999	.065346	.068709	.075482	.082307	.089174	.096076
	.30	.049999	.056337	.062789	.066053	.069340	.072648	.075977	.079323	.082687	.089460	.096284	.103152	.110054
	.20	.063976	.070315	.076767	.080030	.083317	.086626	.089954	.093301	.096665	.103438	.110262	.117130	.124032
	.10	.077954	.084293	.090744	.094008	.097295	.100604	.103932	.107279	.110643	.117415	.124240	.131107	.138010
	0.00	.091932	.098270	.104722	.107986	.111273	.114582	.117910	.121257	.124620	.131393	.138218	.145085	.151987
	-.10	.105910	.112248	.118700	.121964	.125251	.128559	.131888	.135235	.138598	.145371	.152196	.159063	.165965
	-.20	.119887	.126226	.132678	.135942	.139229	.142537	.145866	.149212	.152576	.159349	.166173	.173041	.179943
	-.30	.133865	.140204	.146655	.149919	.153206	.156515	.159843	.163190	.166554	.173326	.180151	.187019	.193921
	-.40	.147843	.154182	.160633	.163897	.167184	.170493	.173821	.177168	.180532	.187304	.194129	.200996	.207899
30	.40	.035187	.041655	.048232	.051556	.054901	.058265	.061646	.065043	.068453	.075310	.082206	.089133	.096083
	.30	.049165	.055633	.062210	.065534	.068879	.072243	.075624	.079020	.082431	.089288	.096184	.103110	.110061
	.20	.063142	.069611	.076188	.079512	.082857	.086221	.089602	.092998	.096409	.103265	.110161	.117088	.124038
	.10	.077120	.083589	.090166	.093490	.096835	.100198	.103579	.106976	.110386	.117243	.124139	.131066	.138016
	0.00	.091098	.097566	.104143	.107467	.110812	.114176	.117557	.120954	.124364	.131221	.138117	.145044	.151994
	-.10	.105076	.111544	.118121	.121445	.124790	.128154	.131535	.134932	.138342	.145199	.152095	.159022	.165972
	-.20	.119053	.125522	.132099	.135423	.138768	.142132	.145513	.148909	.152320	.159176	.166073	.172999	.179972
	-.30	.133031	.139500	.146077	.149401	.152746	.156110	.159491	.162887	.166298	.173154	.180050	.186977	.193927
	-.40	.147009	.153477	.160055	.163379	.166723	.170087	.173468	.176865	.180275	.187132	.194028	.200955	.207905

5.0 YEAR HOLDING PERIOD
.180 EQUITY YIELD RATE
.750 LOAN RATIO

INTEREST RATE

TERM YEARS	APPR DEP	5.0	6.0	7.0	7.5	8.0	8.5	9.0	9.5	10.0	11.0	12.0	13.0	14.0
10	.40	.038636	.044376	.050224	.053189	.056179	.059196	.062237	.065304	.068395	.074648	.080994	.087429	.093949
	.30	.052614	.058353	.064202	.067167	.070157	.073173	.076215	.079281	.082372	.088626	.094972	.101407	.107927
	.20	.066591	.072331	.078180	.081144	.084135	.087151	.090193	.093259	.096350	.102604	.108950	.115385	.121905
	.10	.080569	.086309	.092158	.095122	.098113	.101129	.104171	.107237	.110328	.116581	.122928	.129363	.135883
	0.00	.094547	.100287	.106136	.109100	.112090	.115107	.118148	.121215	.124306	.130559	.136905	.143340	.149861
	-.10	.108525	.114264	.120113	.123078	.126068	.129085	.132126	.135193	.138284	.144537	.150883	.157318	.163838
	-.20	.122503	.128242	.134091	.137055	.140046	.143062	.146104	.149170	.152261	.158515	.164861	.171296	.177816
	-.30	.136480	.142220	.148069	.151033	.154024	.157040	.160082	.163148	.166239	.172493	.178839	.185274	.191794
	-.40	.150458	.156198	.162047	.165011	.168002	.171018	.174059	.177126	.180217	.186470	.192816	.199251	.205772
15	.40	.033588	.039886	.046304	.049557	.052838	.056145	.059477	.062835	.066217	.073049	.079966	.086962	.094029
	.30	.047565	.053863	.060282	.063535	.066815	.070122	.073455	.076813	.080195	.087027	.093944	.100940	.108007
	.20	.061543	.067841	.074260	.077513	.080793	.084100	.087433	.090791	.094172	.101004	.107922	.114917	.121985
	.10	.075521	.081819	.088238	.091491	.094771	.098078	.101411	.104768	.108150	.114982	.121900	.128895	.135963
	0.00	.089499	.095797	.102216	.105468	.108749	.112056	.115389	.118746	.122128	.128960	.135877	.142873	.149940
	-.10	.103477	.109774	.116193	.119446	.122726	.126033	.129366	.132724	.136106	.142938	.149855	.156851	.163918
	-.20	.117454	.123752	.130171	.133424	.136704	.140011	.143344	.146702	.150084	.156916	.163833	.170829	.177896
	-.30	.131432	.137730	.144149	.147402	.150682	.153989	.157322	.160680	.164061	.170893	.177811	.184806	.191874
	-.40	.145410	.151708	.158127	.161379	.164660	.167967	.171300	.174657	.178039	.184871	.191788	.198784	.205852
20	.40	.031140	.037737	.044458	.047861	.051291	.054746	.058225	.061727	.065250	.072356	.079532	.086770	.094061
	.30	.045118	.051715	.058436	.061839	.065269	.068724	.072203	.075705	.079228	.086334	.093510	.100748	.108039
	.20	.059096	.065693	.072414	.075817	.079247	.082702	.086181	.089683	.093206	.100311	.107487	.114725	.122017
	.10	.073073	.079671	.086391	.089795	.093224	.096680	.100159	.103661	.107184	.114289	.121465	.128703	.135994
	0.00	.087051	.093649	.100369	.103772	.107202	.110657	.114137	.117638	.121162	.128267	.135443	.142681	.149972
	-.10	.101029	.107626	.114347	.117750	.121180	.124635	.128114	.131616	.135139	.142245	.149421	.156659	.163950
	-.20	.115007	.121604	.128325	.131728	.135158	.138613	.142092	.145594	.149117	.156222	.163399	.170637	.177928
	-.30	.128985	.135582	.142303	.145706	.149136	.152591	.156070	.159572	.163095	.170200	.177376	.184614	.191906
	-.40	.142962	.149560	.156280	.159684	.163113	.166569	.170048	.173549	.177073	.184178	.191354	.198592	.205883
25	.40	.029730	.036521	.043434	.046931	.050453	.053998	.057564	.061150	.064754	.072010	.079322	.086680	.094075
	.30	.043708	.050499	.057412	.060909	.064431	.067975	.071542	.075127	.078731	.085988	.093300	.100658	.108053
	.20	.057686	.064477	.071390	.074887	.078408	.081953	.085519	.089105	.092709	.099966	.107278	.114636	.122031
	.10	.071664	.078455	.085367	.088864	.092386	.095931	.099497	.103083	.106687	.113943	.121255	.128613	.136009
	0.00	.085641	.092433	.099345	.102842	.106364	.109909	.113475	.117061	.120665	.127921	.135233	.142591	.149987
	-.10	.099619	.106410	.113323	.116820	.120342	.123887	.127453	.131039	.134643	.141899	.149211	.156569	.163964
	-.20	.113597	.120388	.127301	.130798	.134320	.137864	.141431	.145016	.148620	.155877	.163189	.170547	.177942
	-.30	.127575	.134366	.141278	.144776	.148297	.151842	.155408	.158994	.162598	.169855	.177167	.184525	.191920
	-.40	.141552	.148344	.155256	.158753	.162275	.165820	.169386	.172972	.176576	.183832	.191144	.198502	.205898
30	.40	.028837	.035767	.042814	.046375	.049959	.053563	.057186	.060825	.064479	.071826	.079214	.086636	.094082
	.30	.042814	.049745	.056792	.060353	.063937	.067541	.071164	.074803	.078457	.085803	.093192	.100614	.108060
	.20	.056792	.063723	.070770	.074331	.077915	.081519	.085142	.088781	.092435	.099781	.107170	.114591	.122038
	.10	.070770	.077700	.084747	.088309	.091893	.095497	.099119	.102758	.106412	.113759	.121148	.128569	.136016
	0.00	.084748	.091678	.098725	.102287	.105870	.109475	.113097	.116736	.120390	.127737	.135125	.142547	.149993
	-.10	.098726	.105656	.112703	.116264	.119848	.123452	.127075	.130714	.134368	.141714	.149103	.156525	.163971
	-.20	.112703	.119634	.126681	.130242	.133826	.137430	.141053	.144692	.148346	.155692	.163081	.170502	.177949
	-.30	.126681	.133612	.140659	.144220	.147804	.151408	.155030	.158670	.162324	.169670	.177059	.184480	.191927
	-.40	.140659	.147589	.154636	.158198	.161782	.165386	.169008	.172647	.176301	.183648	.191037	.198458	.205905

5.0 YEAR HOLDING PERIOD
.180 EQUITY YIELD RATE
.800 LOAN RATIO

INTEREST RATE

TERM YEARS	APPR DEP	5.0	6.0	7.0	7.5	8.0	8.5	9.0	9.5	10.0	11.0	12.0	13.0	14.0
10	.40	.032939	.039061	.045300	.048462	.051652	.054869	.058114	.061385	.064682	.071352	.078121	.084985	.091940
	.30	.046917	.053039	.059278	.062440	.065630	.068847	.072092	.075362	.078659	.085330	.092099	.098963	.105918
	.20	.060895	.067017	.073256	.076418	.079608	.082825	.086069	.089340	.092637	.099308	.106077	.112941	.119896
	.10	.074872	.080995	.087233	.090395	.093585	.096803	.100047	.103318	.106615	.113285	.120055	.126919	.133873
	0.00	.088850	.094972	.101211	.104373	.107563	.110781	.114025	.117296	.120593	.127263	.134032	.140898	.147851
	-.10	.102828	.108950	.115189	.118351	.121541	.124758	.128003	.131274	.134571	.141241	.148010	.154874	.161829
	-.20	.116806	.122928	.129167	.132329	.135519	.138736	.141980	.145251	.148548	.155219	.161988	.168852	.175807
	-.30	.130784	.136906	.143145	.146307	.149497	.152714	.155958	.159229	.162526	.169197	.175966	.182830	.189785
	-.40	.144761	.150884	.157122	.160284	.163474	.166692	.169936	.173207	.176504	.183174	.189943	.196807	.203762
15	.40	.027554	.034272	.041119	.044588	.048087	.051615	.055170	.058752	.062359	.069646	.077025	.084487	.092025
	.30	.041532	.048250	.055097	.058566	.062065	.065593	.069148	.072729	.076337	.083624	.091002	.098465	.106003
	.20	.055510	.062228	.069074	.072544	.076043	.079570	.083126	.086707	.090314	.097602	.104980	.112442	.119981
	.10	.069488	.076205	.083052	.086522	.090021	.093548	.097103	.100685	.104292	.111580	.118958	.126420	.133959
	0.00	.083465	.090183	.097030	.100500	.103999	.107526	.111081	.114663	.118270	.125557	.132936	.140398	.147936
	-.10	.097443	.104161	.111008	.114477	.117976	.121504	.125059	.128640	.132248	.139535	.146914	.154376	.161914
	-.20	.111421	.118139	.124986	.128455	.131954	.135482	.139037	.142618	.146225	.153513	.160891	.168353	.175892
	-.30	.125399	.132116	.138963	.142433	.145932	.149459	.153014	.156596	.160203	.167491	.174869	.182331	.189870
	-.40	.139376	.146094	.152941	.156411	.159910	.163437	.166992	.170574	.174181	.181468	.188847	.196309	.203848
20	.40	.024943	.031981	.039149	.042779	.046438	.050123	.053835	.057570	.061328	.068907	.076561	.084282	.092059
	.30	.038921	.045958	.053127	.056757	.060416	.064101	.067812	.071548	.075306	.082885	.090539	.098260	.106037
	.20	.052899	.059936	.067105	.070735	.074394	.078079	.081790	.085525	.089283	.096862	.104517	.112237	.120015
	.10	.066877	.073914	.081083	.084713	.088371	.092057	.095768	.099503	.103261	.110840	.118495	.126215	.133993
	0.00	.080855	.087892	.095061	.098691	.102349	.106035	.109746	.113481	.117239	.124818	.132473	.140193	.147970
	-.10	.094832	.101870	.109038	.112668	.116327	.120012	.123723	.127459	.131217	.138796	.146450	.154171	.161948
	-.20	.108810	.115847	.123016	.126646	.130305	.133990	.137701	.141436	.145195	.152774	.160428	.168149	.175926
	-.30	.122788	.129825	.136994	.140624	.144282	.147968	.151679	.155414	.159172	.166751	.174406	.182126	.189904
	-.40	.136766	.143803	.150972	.154602	.158260	.161946	.165657	.169392	.173150	.180729	.188384	.196104	.203882
25	.40	.023440	.030684	.038057	.041787	.045544	.049325	.053129	.056954	.060798	.068538	.076338	.084186	.092075
	.30	.037417	.044661	.052035	.055765	.059522	.063303	.067106	.070931	.074776	.082516	.090315	.098164	.106052
	.20	.051395	.058639	.066013	.069743	.073499	.077280	.081084	.084909	.088753	.096494	.104293	.112142	.120030
	.10	.065373	.072617	.079990	.083721	.087477	.091258	.095062	.098887	.102731	.110471	.118271	.126120	.134008
	0.00	.079351	.086595	.093968	.097698	.101455	.105236	.109040	.112865	.116709	.124449	.132249	.140097	.147986
	-.10	.093329	.100573	.107946	.111676	.115433	.119214	.123018	.126843	.130687	.138427	.146227	.154075	.161963
	-.20	.107306	.114550	.121924	.125654	.129410	.133192	.136996	.140820	.144665	.152405	.160204	.168053	.175941
	-.30	.121284	.128528	.135901	.139632	.143388	.147169	.150973	.154798	.158642	.166383	.174182	.182031	.189919
	-.40	.135262	.142506	.149879	.153609	.157366	.161147	.164951	.168776	.172620	.180360	.188160	.196008	.203897
30	.40	.022486	.029879	.037396	.041195	.045017	.048862	.052726	.056607	.060505	.068341	.076223	.084139	.092082
	.30	.036464	.043857	.051373	.055172	.058995	.062839	.066703	.070585	.074483	.082319	.090220	.098117	.106060
	.20	.050442	.057835	.065351	.069150	.072973	.076817	.080681	.084563	.088461	.096297	.104178	.112094	.120037
	.10	.064420	.071812	.079329	.083128	.086951	.090795	.094659	.098541	.102438	.110275	.118156	.126072	.134015
	0.00	.078398	.085790	.093307	.097106	.100928	.104773	.108637	.112519	.116416	.124252	.132134	.140050	.147993
	-.10	.092375	.099768	.107285	.111083	.114906	.118751	.122615	.126496	.130394	.138230	.146112	.154028	.161971
	-.20	.106353	.113746	.121262	.125061	.128884	.132728	.136592	.140474	.144372	.152208	.160089	.168006	.175949
	-.30	.120331	.127723	.135240	.139039	.142862	.146706	.150570	.154452	.158350	.166186	.174067	.181983	.189926
	-.40	.134309	.141701	.149218	.153017	.156840	.160684	.164548	.168430	.172327	.180164	.188045	.195961	.203904

5.0 YEAR HOLDING PERIOD
.180 EQUITY YIELD RATE
.900 LOAN RATIO

INTEREST RATE

TERM YEARS	APPR DEP	5.0	6.0	7.0	7.5	8.0	8.5	9.0	9.5	10.0	11.0	12.0	13.0	14.0
10	.40	.021545	.028433	.035451	.039009	.042597	.046217	.049867	.053547	.057256	.064760	.072375	.080097	.087922
	.30	.035523	.042411	.049429	.052987	.056575	.060195	.063845	.067524	.071234	.078738	.086353	.094075	.101899
	.20	.049501	.056388	.063407	.066964	.070553	.074173	.077822	.081502	.085211	.092716	.100331	.108053	.115677
	.10	.063479	.070366	.077385	.080942	.084531	.088150	.091800	.095480	.099189	.106693	.114309	.122031	.129855
	0.00	.077456	.084344	.091363	.094920	.098509	.102128	.105778	.109458	.113167	.120671	.128286	.136008	.143833
	-.10	.091434	.098322	.105340	.108898	.112486	.116106	.119756	.123436	.127145	.134649	.142264	.149986	.157810
	-.20	.105412	.112300	.119318	.122875	.126464	.130084	.133734	.137413	.141122	.148627	.156242	.163964	.171788
	-.30	.119390	.126277	.133296	.136853	.140442	.144061	.147711	.151391	.155100	.162604	.170220	.177942	.185766
	-.40	.133368	.140255	.147274	.150831	.154420	.158039	.161689	.165369	.169078	.176582	.184197	.191919	.199744
15	.40	.015487	.023045	.030748	.034651	.038587	.042556	.046555	.050584	.054643	.062841	.071142	.079536	.088017
	.30	.029465	.037023	.044725	.048629	.052565	.056533	.060533	.064562	.068620	.076819	.085119	.093514	.101995
	.20	.043443	.051001	.058703	.062606	.066543	.070511	.074511	.078540	.082598	.090797	.099097	.107492	.115973
	.10	.057421	.064978	.072681	.076584	.080521	.084489	.088488	.092518	.096576	.104774	.113075	.121470	.129951
	0.00	.071399	.078956	.086659	.090562	.094498	.098467	.102466	.106496	.110554	.118752	.127053	.135448	.143928
	-.10	.085376	.092934	.100637	.104540	.108477	.112445	.116444	.120473	.124531	.132730	.141031	.149425	.157906
	-.20	.099354	.106912	.114614	.118518	.122454	.126422	.130422	.134451	.138509	.146708	.155008	.163403	.171884
	-.30	.113332	.120889	.128592	.132495	.136432	.140400	.144400	.148429	.152487	.160685	.168986	.177381	.185862
	-.40	.127310	.134867	.142570	.146473	.150410	.154378	.158377	.162407	.166465	.174663	.182964	.191359	.199840
20	.40	.012550	.020467	.028532	.032616	.036732	.040878	.045053	.049255	.053483	.062009	.070621	.079306	.088056
	.30	.026528	.034445	.042510	.046594	.050709	.054856	.059031	.063233	.067460	.075987	.084598	.093284	.102033
	.20	.040506	.048423	.056488	.060571	.064687	.068833	.073008	.077210	.081438	.089965	.098576	.107262	.116011
	.10	.054484	.062400	.070465	.074549	.078665	.082811	.086986	.091188	.095416	.103942	.112554	.121239	.129989
	0.00	.068461	.076378	.084443	.088527	.092643	.096789	.100964	.105166	.109394	.117920	.126532	.135217	.143967
	-.10	.082439	.090356	.098421	.102505	.106620	.110767	.114942	.119144	.123372	.131898	.140509	.149195	.157944
	-.20	.096417	.104334	.112399	.116482	.120598	.124744	.128919	.133122	.137349	.145876	.154487	.163173	.171922
	-.30	.110395	.118312	.126376	.130460	.134576	.138722	.142897	.147099	.151327	.159854	.168465	.177150	.185900
	-.40	.124373	.132289	.140354	.144438	.148554	.152700	.156875	.161077	.165305	.173831	.182443	.191128	.199878
25	.40	.010858	.019008	.027303	.031499	.035726	.039979	.044259	.048562	.052887	.061594	.070369	.079198	.088073
	.30	.024836	.032986	.041281	.045477	.049703	.053957	.058237	.062540	.066864	.075572	.084347	.093176	.102051
	.20	.038814	.046964	.055259	.059455	.063682	.067935	.072214	.076517	.080842	.089550	.098324	.107154	.116028
	.10	.052792	.060941	.069236	.073433	.077659	.081913	.086192	.090495	.094820	.103528	.112302	.121132	.130006
	0.00	.066770	.074919	.083214	.087411	.091637	.095891	.100170	.104473	.108798	.117505	.126280	.135110	.143984
	-.10	.080747	.088897	.097192	.101388	.105615	.109868	.114148	.118451	.122775	.131483	.140258	.149087	.157962
	-.20	.094725	.102875	.111170	.115366	.119592	.123846	.128126	.132429	.136753	.145461	.154236	.163065	.171939
	-.30	.108703	.116852	.125147	.129344	.133570	.137824	.142103	.146406	.150731	.159439	.168213	.177043	.185917
	-.40	.122681	.130830	.139125	.143322	.147548	.151802	.156081	.160384	.164709	.173417	.182191	.191021	.199895
30	.40	.009786	.018103	.026559	.030833	.035133	.039458	.043305	.048172	.052557	.061373	.070239	.079145	.088081
	.30	.023764	.032080	.040537	.044811	.049111	.053436	.057783	.062150	.066535	.075351	.084217	.093123	.102059
	.20	.037742	.046058	.054515	.058788	.063089	.067414	.071761	.076128	.080513	.089328	.098195	.107101	.116037
	.10	.051719	.060036	.068492	.072766	.077067	.081392	.085739	.090106	.094490	.103306	.112173	.121078	.130014
	0.00	.065697	.074014	.082470	.086744	.091045	.095369	.099716	.104063	.108468	.117284	.126150	.135056	.143992
	-.10	.079675	.087992	.096448	.100722	.105022	.109347	.113694	.118061	.122446	.131262	.140128	.149034	.157970
	-.20	.093653	.101969	.110426	.114699	.119000	.123325	.127672	.132039	.136424	.145240	.154106	.163012	.171948
	-.30	.107631	.115947	.124404	.128677	.132998	.137303	.141650	.146017	.150402	.159217	.168084	.176990	.185925
	-.40	.121608	.129925	.138381	.142655	.146956	.151281	.155628	.159995	.164379	.173195	.182062	.190967	.199903

5.0 YEAR HOLDING PERIOD
.200 EQUITY YIELD RATE
.600 LOAN RATIO

INTEREST RATE

TERM YEARS	APPR DEP	5.0	6.0	7.0	7.5	8.0	8.5	9.0	9.5	10.0	11.0	12.0	13.0	14.0
10	.40	.067304	.071856	.076496	.078848	.081221	.083615	.086029	.088463	.090917	.095882	.100922	.106034	.111214
	.30	.080742	.085294	.089934	.092286	.094659	.097053	.099467	.101901	.104355	.109320	.114360	.119472	.124652
	.20	.094180	.098732	.103372	.105724	.108097	.110491	.112905	.115339	.117793	.122758	.127798	.132910	.138090
	.10	.107618	.112170	.116810	.119162	.121535	.123929	.126343	.128777	.131231	.136196	.141236	.146348	.151528
	0.00	.121056	.125608	.130248	.132600	.134973	.137367	.139781	.142215	.144669	.149634	.154674	.159786	.164966
	-.10	.134494	.139046	.143686	.146038	.148411	.150805	.153219	.155653	.158107	.163072	.168112	.173224	.178404
	-.20	.147932	.152484	.157124	.159476	.161849	.164243	.166657	.169091	.171545	.176510	.181550	.186662	.191842
	-.30	.161370	.165922	.170562	.172914	.175287	.177681	.180095	.182529	.184983	.189948	.194988	.200100	.205280
	-.40	.174808	.179360	.184000	.186352	.188725	.191119	.193533	.195967	.198421	.203386	.208426	.213538	.218718
15	.40	.062671	.067662	.072752	.075332	.077935	.080559	.083205	.085870	.088556	.093983	.099479	.105041	.110661
	.30	.076109	.081100	.086190	.088770	.091373	.093997	.096642	.099308	.101994	.107421	.112917	.118479	.124099
	.20	.089547	.094538	.099628	.102208	.104811	.107435	.110080	.112746	.115432	.120858	.126355	.131917	.137537
	.10	.102985	.107976	.113066	.115646	.118249	.120873	.123518	.126184	.128870	.134296	.139793	.145355	.150975
	0.00	.116423	.121414	.126504	.129084	.131687	.134311	.136956	.139622	.142308	.147734	.153231	.158793	.164413
	-.10	.129861	.134852	.139942	.142522	.145125	.147749	.150394	.153060	.155746	.161172	.166669	.172231	.177851
	-.20	.143299	.148290	.153380	.155960	.158563	.161187	.163832	.166498	.169184	.174610	.180107	.185669	.191289
	-.30	.156737	.161728	.166818	.169398	.172001	.174625	.177270	.179936	.182621	.188048	.193545	.199107	.204727
	-.40	.170175	.175166	.180256	.182836	.185439	.188063	.190708	.193374	.196059	.201486	.206983	.212545	.218165
20	.40	.060425	.065656	.070989	.073690	.076414	.079159	.081923	.084706	.087508	.093159	.098870	.104633	.110440
	.30	.073863	.079094	.084427	.087128	.089852	.092597	.095361	.098144	.100946	.106597	.112308	.118071	.123878
	.20	.087301	.092532	.097865	.100566	.103290	.106035	.108799	.111582	.114384	.120035	.125746	.131509	.137316
	.10	.100739	.105970	.111303	.114004	.116728	.119473	.122237	.125020	.127822	.133473	.139184	.144947	.150754
	0.00	.114177	.119408	.124741	.127442	.130166	.132910	.135675	.138458	.141259	.146911	.152622	.158385	.164192
	-.10	.127615	.132846	.138179	.140880	.143604	.146348	.149113	.151896	.154697	.160349	.166060	.171823	.177630
	-.20	.141053	.146284	.151616	.154318	.157042	.159786	.162551	.165334	.168135	.173787	.179498	.185260	.191068
	-.30	.154491	.159722	.165054	.167756	.170480	.173224	.175989	.178772	.181573	.187225	.192936	.198698	.204506
	-.40	.167929	.173160	.178492	.181194	.183918	.186662	.189427	.192210	.195011	.200663	.206374	.212136	.217944
25	.40	.059131	.064520	.070010	.072790	.075590	.078409	.081246	.084100	.086969	.092748	.098576	.104442	.110341
	.30	.072569	.077958	.083448	.086228	.089028	.091847	.094684	.097538	.100407	.106186	.112013	.117880	.123779
	.20	.086007	.091396	.096886	.099666	.102466	.105285	.108122	.110976	.113845	.119624	.125451	.131318	.137217
	.10	.099445	.104834	.110324	.113104	.115903	.118723	.121560	.124414	.127283	.133062	.138889	.144756	.150655
	0.00	.112883	.118272	.123762	.126541	.129341	.132161	.134998	.137852	.140721	.146500	.152327	.158194	.164093
	-.10	.126321	.131710	.137200	.139979	.142779	.145599	.148436	.151290	.154159	.159938	.165765	.171632	.177531
	-.20	.139759	.145148	.150638	.153417	.156217	.159037	.161874	.164728	.167597	.173376	.179203	.185070	.190969
	-.30	.153197	.158586	.164076	.166855	.169655	.172475	.175312	.178166	.181035	.186814	.192641	.198508	.204407
	-.40	.166635	.172024	.177514	.180293	.183093	.185913	.188750	.191604	.194473	.200252	.206079	.211946	.217845
30	.40	.058311	.063816	.069418	.072252	.075104	.077974	.080859	.083759	.086671	.092529	.098424	.104348	.110294
	.30	.071749	.077254	.082856	.085690	.088542	.091412	.094297	.097197	.100109	.105967	.111862	.117786	.123732
	.20	.085187	.090692	.096294	.099128	.101980	.104850	.107735	.110635	.113547	.119405	.125300	.131224	.137170
	.10	.098625	.104130	.109732	.112566	.115418	.118288	.121173	.124073	.126985	.132843	.138738	.144662	.150608
	0.00	.112063	.117568	.123170	.126004	.128856	.131726	.134611	.137511	.140423	.146281	.152176	.158100	.164046
	-.10	.125501	.131005	.136608	.139442	.142294	.145164	.148049	.150949	.153861	.159719	.165614	.171538	.177484
	-.20	.138939	.144443	.150046	.152880	.155732	.158602	.161487	.164387	.167299	.173157	.179052	.184976	.190922
	-.30	.152377	.157881	.163484	.166318	.169170	.172040	.174925	.177825	.180737	.186595	.192490	.198414	.204359
	-.40	.165815	.171319	.176922	.179755	.182608	.185478	.188363	.191263	.194175	.200033	.205928	.211852	.217797

5.0 YEAR HOLDING PERIOD
.200 EQUITY YIELD RATE
.667 LOAN RATIO

INTEREST RATE

TERM YEARS	APPR DEP	5.0	6.0	7.0	7.5	8.0	8.5	9.0	9.5	10.0	11.0	12.0	13.0	14.0
10	.40	.058532	.063590	.068746	.071359	.073996	.076655	.079338	.082042	.084769	.090286	.095886	.101565	.107321
	.30	.071970	.077028	.082184	.084797	.087434	.090093	.092776	.095480	.098207	.103724	.109324	.115003	.120759
	.20	.085408	.090466	.095622	.098235	.100872	.103531	.106214	.108918	.111645	.117162	.122762	.128441	.134197
	.10	.098846	.103904	.109060	.111673	.114310	.116969	.119652	.122356	.125083	.130600	.136200	.141879	.147635
	0.00	.112284	.117342	.122497	.125111	.127748	.130407	.133090	.135794	.138521	.144038	.149638	.155317	.161073
	-.10	.125722	.130780	.135935	.138549	.141186	.143845	.146528	.149232	.151959	.157476	.163076	.168755	.174511
	-.20	.139160	.144218	.149373	.151987	.154624	.157283	.159966	.162670	.165397	.170914	.176514	.182193	.187949
	-.30	.152598	.157656	.162811	.165425	.168062	.170721	.173404	.176108	.178835	.184352	.189952	.195631	.201387
	-.40	.166036	.171094	.176249	.178863	.181500	.184159	.186842	.189546	.192273	.197790	.203390	.209069	.214825
15	.40	.053384	.058930	.064586	.067452	.070344	.073260	.076199	.079161	.082145	.088175	.094283	.100462	.106707
	.30	.066822	.072368	.078024	.080890	.083782	.086698	.089637	.092599	.095583	.101613	.107721	.113900	.120145
	.20	.080260	.085806	.091462	.094328	.097220	.100136	.103075	.106037	.109021	.115051	.121159	.127338	.133583
	.10	.093698	.099244	.104899	.107766	.110658	.113574	.116513	.119475	.122459	.128489	.134597	.140776	.147021
	0.00	.107136	.112682	.118337	.121204	.124096	.127012	.129951	.132913	.135897	.141927	.148035	.154214	.160459
	-.10	.120574	.126120	.131775	.134642	.137534	.140450	.143389	.146351	.149335	.155365	.161473	.167652	.173897
	-.20	.134012	.139558	.145213	.148080	.150972	.153888	.156827	.159789	.162773	.168803	.174911	.181090	.187335
	-.30	.147450	.152996	.158651	.161518	.164410	.167326	.170265	.173227	.176211	.182241	.188348	.194528	.200773
	-.40	.160888	.166434	.172089	.174956	.177848	.180764	.183703	.186665	.189649	.195679	.201786	.207966	.214211
20	.40	.050889	.056701	.062626	.065628	.068654	.071704	.074776	.077868	.080981	.087260	.093605	.100008	.106462
	.30	.064327	.070139	.076064	.079066	.082092	.085142	.088214	.091306	.094419	.100698	.107043	.113446	.119900
	.20	.077765	.083577	.089502	.092504	.095530	.098580	.101651	.104744	.107856	.114136	.120481	.126884	.133338
	.10	.091202	.097015	.102940	.105942	.108968	.112018	.115089	.118182	.121294	.127574	.133919	.140322	.146776
	0.00	.104640	.110453	.116378	.119380	.122406	.125456	.128527	.131620	.134732	.141012	.147357	.153760	.160214
	-.10	.118078	.123891	.129816	.132818	.135844	.138894	.141965	.145058	.148170	.154450	.160795	.167198	.173651
	-.20	.131516	.137329	.143254	.146256	.149282	.152333	.155403	.158496	.161608	.167888	.174233	.180636	.187089
	-.30	.144954	.150767	.156692	.159694	.162720	.165770	.168841	.171934	.175046	.181326	.187671	.194074	.200527
	-.40	.158392	.164205	.170130	.173132	.176158	.179208	.182279	.185372	.188484	.194764	.201109	.207512	.213965
25	.40	.049451	.055439	.061539	.064627	.067738	.070871	.074023	.077194	.080382	.086804	.093278	.099797	.106351
	.30	.062889	.068877	.074977	.078065	.081176	.084309	.087461	.090632	.093820	.100242	.106716	.113235	.119789
	.20	.076327	.082315	.088415	.091503	.094614	.097747	.100900	.104070	.107258	.113680	.120154	.126673	.133227
	.10	.089765	.095753	.101853	.104941	.108052	.111185	.114337	.117508	.120696	.127118	.133592	.140111	.146665
	0.00	.103203	.109191	.115291	.118379	.121490	.124624	.127775	.130946	.134134	.140556	.147030	.153549	.160103
	-.10	.116641	.122629	.128729	.131817	.134928	.138061	.141213	.144384	.147572	.153994	.160468	.166987	.173541
	-.20	.130079	.136067	.142167	.145255	.148366	.151499	.154651	.157822	.161010	.167432	.173906	.180425	.186979
	-.30	.143517	.149505	.155605	.158693	.161804	.164936	.168089	.171260	.174448	.180870	.187344	.193862	.200417
	-.40	.156955	.162943	.169043	.172131	.175242	.178374	.181527	.184698	.187886	.194308	.200782	.207300	.213855
30	.40	.048540	.054656	.060881	.064029	.067199	.070387	.073593	.076815	.080051	.086560	.093110	.099692	.106299
	.30	.061978	.068094	.074319	.077467	.080637	.083825	.087031	.090253	.093489	.099998	.106548	.113130	.119737
	.20	.075416	.081532	.087757	.090905	.094075	.097263	.100469	.103691	.106927	.113436	.119986	.126568	.133174
	.10	.088854	.094970	.101195	.104343	.107513	.110701	.113907	.117129	.120365	.126874	.133424	.140006	.146612
	0.00	.102292	.108408	.114633	.117781	.120951	.124139	.127345	.130567	.133803	.140312	.146862	.153444	.160050
	-.10	.115730	.121846	.128071	.131219	.134389	.137577	.140783	.144005	.147241	.153750	.160300	.166882	.173488
	-.20	.129167	.135284	.141509	.144657	.147827	.151015	.154221	.157443	.160679	.167188	.173738	.180320	.186926
	-.30	.142605	.148722	.154947	.158095	.161265	.164453	.167659	.170881	.174117	.180626	.187176	.193758	.200364
	-.40	.156043	.162160	.168385	.171533	.174703	.177891	.181097	.184319	.187555	.194064	.200614	.207196	.213802

5.0 YEAR HOLDING PERIOD
.200 EQUITY YIELD RATE
.700 LOAN RATIO

INTEREST RATE

TERM YEARS	APPR DEP	5.0	6.0	7.0	7.5	8.0	8.5	9.0	9.5	10.0	11.0	12.0	13.0	14.0
10	.40	.054147	.059458	.064871	.067615	.070384	.073176	.075993	.078832	.081695	.087488	.093368	.099331	.105375
	.30	.067585	.072896	.078309	.081053	.083822	.086614	.089431	.092270	.095133	.100926	.106806	.112769	.118813
	.20	.081023	.086334	.091747	.094491	.097259	.100052	.102869	.105708	.108571	.114364	.120244	.126207	.132251
	.10	.094461	.099772	.105185	.107929	.110697	.113490	.116307	.119146	.122009	.127802	.133682	.139645	.145689
	0.00	.107899	.113210	.118623	.121367	.124135	.126928	.129745	.132584	.135447	.141240	.147120	.153083	.159127
	-.10	.121337	.126648	.132061	.134805	.137573	.140366	.143183	.146022	.148885	.154678	.160558	.166521	.172565
	-.20	.134775	.140086	.145499	.148243	.151011	.153804	.156621	.159460	.162323	.168116	.173996	.179959	.186003
	-.30	.148213	.153524	.158937	.161681	.164449	.167242	.170058	.172898	.175761	.181554	.187434	.193397	.199441
	-.40	.161651	.166962	.172375	.175119	.177887	.180680	.183496	.186336	.189199	.194992	.200872	.206835	.212879
15	.40	.048742	.054565	.060503	.063513	.066549	.069611	.072697	.075807	.078940	.085272	.091685	.098173	.104730
	.30	.062180	.068003	.073941	.076951	.079987	.083049	.086135	.089245	.092378	.098710	.105123	.111611	.118168
	.20	.075618	.081441	.087379	.090389	.093425	.096487	.099573	.102683	.105816	.112148	.118561	.125049	.131606
	.10	.089056	.094879	.100817	.103827	.106863	.109925	.113011	.116121	.119254	.125586	.131999	.138487	.145044
	0.00	.102494	.108317	.114255	.117265	.120301	.123363	.126449	.129559	.132692	.139024	.145437	.151925	.158482
	-.10	.115932	.121755	.127693	.130703	.133739	.136801	.139887	.142997	.146130	.152461	.158875	.165363	.171920
	-.20	.129370	.135193	.141131	.144141	.147177	.150239	.153325	.156435	.159568	.165899	.172313	.178801	.185358
	-.30	.142808	.148631	.154569	.157579	.160615	.163677	.166763	.169873	.173006	.179337	.185750	.192239	.198796
	-.40	.156245	.162069	.168007	.171017	.174053	.177115	.180201	.183311	.186444	.192775	.199188	.205677	.212234
20	.40	.046121	.052224	.058445	.061597	.064775	.067977	.071202	.074450	.077718	.084311	.090974	.097697	.104473
	.30	.059559	.065662	.071883	.075035	.078213	.081415	.084640	.087888	.091155	.097749	.104412	.111135	.117910
	.20	.072997	.079100	.085321	.088473	.091651	.094853	.098078	.101325	.104593	.111187	.117850	.124573	.131348
	.10	.086435	.092538	.098759	.101911	.105089	.108291	.111516	.114763	.118031	.124625	.131288	.138011	.144786
	0.00	.099873	.105976	.112197	.115349	.118527	.121729	.124954	.128201	.131469	.138063	.144725	.151449	.158224
	-.10	.113311	.119414	.125635	.128787	.131965	.135167	.138392	.141639	.144907	.151501	.158163	.164887	.171662
	-.20	.126749	.132852	.139073	.142225	.145403	.148605	.151830	.155077	.158345	.164939	.171601	.178325	.185100
	-.30	.140187	.146290	.152511	.155663	.158841	.162043	.165268	.168515	.171783	.178377	.185039	.191763	.198538
	-.40	.153625	.159728	.165949	.169101	.172279	.175481	.178706	.181953	.185221	.191815	.198477	.205201	.211976
25	.40	.044612	.050899	.057304	.060547	.063813	.067102	.070412	.073742	.077089	.083832	.090630	.097474	.104356
	.30	.058050	.064337	.070742	.073985	.077251	.080540	.083850	.087180	.090527	.097270	.104068	.110912	.117794
	.20	.071487	.077775	.084180	.087422	.090689	.093978	.097288	.100618	.103965	.110708	.117506	.124350	.131232
	.10	.084925	.091213	.097618	.100860	.104127	.107416	.110726	.114056	.117403	.124146	.130944	.137788	.144670
	0.00	.098363	.104651	.111056	.114298	.117565	.120854	.124164	.127494	.130841	.137584	.144382	.151226	.158108
	-.10	.111801	.118089	.124494	.127736	.131003	.134292	.137602	.140932	.144279	.151022	.157820	.164664	.171546
	-.20	.125239	.131527	.137932	.141174	.144441	.147730	.151040	.154370	.157717	.164460	.171258	.178102	.184984
	-.30	.138677	.144965	.151370	.154612	.157879	.161168	.164478	.167808	.171155	.177898	.184696	.191540	.198422
	-.40	.152115	.158403	.164808	.168050	.171317	.174606	.177916	.181245	.184593	.191336	.198134	.204978	.211860
30	.40	.043655	.050077	.056613	.059919	.063247	.066595	.069961	.073344	.076742	.083576	.090453	.097364	.104301
	.30	.057093	.063515	.070051	.073357	.076685	.080033	.083399	.086782	.090180	.097014	.103891	.110802	.117739
	.20	.070531	.076953	.083489	.086795	.090123	.093471	.096837	.100220	.103618	.110452	.117329	.124240	.131177
	.10	.083969	.090391	.096927	.100233	.103561	.106909	.110275	.113658	.117056	.123890	.130767	.137678	.144615
	0.00	.097407	.103829	.110365	.113671	.116999	.120347	.123713	.127096	.130494	.137328	.144205	.151116	.158053
	-.10	.110845	.117267	.123803	.127109	.130437	.133785	.137151	.140534	.143932	.150766	.157643	.164554	.171491
	-.20	.124283	.130705	.137241	.140547	.143875	.147223	.150589	.153972	.157370	.164204	.171081	.177992	.184929
	-.30	.137721	.144143	.150679	.153985	.157313	.160661	.164027	.167410	.170808	.177642	.184519	.191430	.198367
	-.40	.151159	.157581	.164117	.167423	.170751	.174098	.177465	.180848	.184246	.191080	.197957	.204868	.211805

```
5.0  YEAR HOLDING PERIOD
.200 EQUITY YIELD RATE
.750 LOAN RATIO
```

INTEREST RATE

TERM YEARS	APPR DEP	5.0	6.0	7.0	7.5	8.0	8.5	9.0	9.5	10.0	11.0	12.0	13.0	14.0
10	.40	.047568	.053258	.059058	.061998	.064965	.067957	.070974	.074017	.077084	.083291	.089591	.095980	.102456
	.30	.061006	.066696	.072496	.075436	.078403	.081395	.084412	.087455	.090522	.096729	.103029	.109418	.115894
	.20	.074444	.080134	.085934	.088874	.091841	.094833	.097850	.100893	.103960	.110167	.116467	.122856	.129332
	.10	.087882	.093572	.099372	.102312	.105279	.108271	.111288	.114331	.117398	.123605	.129905	.136294	.142770
	0.00	.101320	.107010	.112810	.115750	.118717	.121709	.124726	.127769	.130836	.137043	.143343	.149732	.156208
	-.10	.114758	.120448	.126248	.129188	.132154	.135147	.138164	.141207	.144274	.150481	.156781	.163170	.169646
	-.20	.128196	.133886	.139686	.142626	.145592	.148585	.151602	.154645	.157712	.163919	.170219	.176608	.183084
	-.30	.141634	.147324	.153124	.156064	.159030	.162023	.165040	.168083	.171150	.177357	.183657	.190046	.196521
	-.40	.155072	.160762	.166562	.169502	.172468	.175461	.178478	.181521	.184588	.190795	.197095	.203484	.209959
15	.40	.041777	.048016	.054378	.057603	.060856	.064137	.067444	.070776	.074133	.080916	.087787	.094739	.101765
	.30	.055215	.061454	.067816	.071041	.074294	.077575	.080882	.084214	.087571	.094354	.101225	.108177	.115203
	.20	.068653	.074892	.081254	.084479	.087732	.091013	.094320	.097652	.101009	.107792	.114663	.121615	.128640
	.10	.082091	.088330	.094662	.097917	.101170	.104451	.107758	.111090	.114446	.121230	.128101	.135053	.142078
	0.00	.095529	.101768	.108130	.111355	.114608	.117889	.121195	.124528	.127884	.134668	.141539	.148491	.155516
	-.10	.108967	.115206	.121568	.124793	.128046	.131327	.134633	.137966	.141322	.148106	.154977	.161929	.168954
	-.20	.122405	.128644	.135006	.138231	.141484	.144765	.148071	.151404	.154760	.161544	.168415	.175367	.182392
	-.30	.135843	.142082	.148444	.151669	.154922	.158203	.161509	.164842	.168198	.174982	.181853	.188805	.195830
	-.40	.149281	.155520	.161882	.165107	.168360	.171641	.174947	.178280	.181636	.188420	.195291	.202243	.209268
20	.40	.038969	.045508	.052174	.055551	.058955	.062386	.065842	.069321	.072822	.079887	.087025	.094229	.101489
	.30	.052407	.058946	.065612	.068989	.072393	.075824	.079280	.082759	.086260	.093325	.100463	.107667	.114927
	.20	.065845	.072384	.079050	.082427	.085831	.089262	.092718	.096197	.099698	.106763	.113901	.121105	.128364
	.10	.079283	.085822	.092488	.095865	.099269	.102700	.106156	.109635	.113136	.120201	.127339	.134543	.141802
	0.00	.092721	.099260	.105926	.109303	.112707	.116138	.119594	.123073	.126574	.133639	.140777	.147981	.155240
	-.10	.106159	.112698	.119364	.122741	.126145	.129576	.133032	.136511	.140012	.147077	.154215	.161419	.168678
	-.20	.119597	.126136	.132802	.136179	.139583	.143014	.146470	.149949	.153450	.160515	.167653	.174857	.182116
	-.30	.133035	.139574	.146240	.149617	.153021	.156452	.159908	.163387	.166888	.173953	.181091	.188295	.195554
	-.40	.146473	.153012	.159678	.163055	.166459	.169890	.173346	.176825	.180326	.187391	.194529	.201733	.208992
25	.40	.037352	.044088	.050951	.054425	.057925	.061449	.064995	.068563	.072149	.079374	.086657	.093991	.101364
	.30	.050790	.057526	.064389	.067863	.071363	.074887	.078433	.082001	.085587	.092812	.100095	.107428	.114802
	.20	.064228	.070964	.077827	.081301	.084801	.088325	.091871	.095439	.099025	.106250	.113533	.120866	.128240
	.10	.077666	.084402	.091265	.094739	.098239	.101763	.105309	.108877	.112463	.119687	.126971	.134304	.141678
	0.00	.091104	.097840	.104703	.108177	.111677	.115201	.118747	.122315	.125901	.133125	.140409	.147742	.155116
	-.10	.104542	.111278	.118141	.121615	.125115	.128639	.132185	.135753	.139339	.146563	.153847	.161180	.168554
	-.20	.117980	.124716	.131579	.135053	.138553	.142077	.145623	.149191	.152777	.160001	.167285	.174618	.181992
	-.30	.131418	.138154	.145017	.148491	.151991	.155515	.159061	.162628	.166215	.173439	.180723	.188056	.195430
	-.40	.144856	.151592	.158455	.161929	.165429	.168953	.172499	.176066	.179653	.186877	.194161	.201494	.208868
30	.40	.036327	.043208	.050211	.053753	.057318	.060905	.064512	.068136	.071777	.079100	.086468	.093873	.101305
	.30	.049765	.056645	.063649	.067191	.070756	.074343	.077950	.081574	.085215	.092538	.099906	.107311	.114743
	.20	.063203	.070083	.077087	.080629	.084194	.087781	.091388	.095012	.098653	.105976	.113344	.120749	.128181
	.10	.076641	.083521	.090525	.094067	.097632	.101219	.104826	.108450	.112091	.119414	.126782	.134187	.141619
	0.00	.090079	.096959	.103963	.107505	.111070	.114657	.118264	.121888	.125529	.132852	.140220	.147625	.155057
	-.10	.103517	.110397	.117401	.120942	.124508	.128095	.131702	.135326	.138967	.146289	.153658	.161063	.168495
	-.20	.116954	.123835	.130839	.134380	.137946	.141533	.145140	.148764	.152405	.159727	.167096	.174500	.181933
	-.30	.130392	.137273	.144277	.147818	.151384	.154971	.158578	.162202	.165843	.173165	.180534	.187938	.195371
	-.40	.143830	.150711	.157715	.161256	.164822	.168409	.172016	.175640	.179281	.186603	.193972	.201376	.208809

5.0 YEAR HOLDING PERIOD
.200 EQUITY YIELD RATE
.800 LOAN RATIO

INTEREST RATE

TERM YEARS	APPR DEP	5.0	6.0	7.0	7.5	8.0	8.5	9.0	9.5	10.0	11.0	12.0	13.0	14.0
10	.40	.040990	.047059	.053246	.056382	.059546	.062737	.065956	.069202	.072473	.079094	.085814	.092629	.099536
	.30	.054428	.060497	.066684	.069820	.072984	.076175	.079394	.082640	.085911	.092532	.099252	.106067	.112974
	.20	.067866	.073935	.080122	.083258	.086422	.089613	.092832	.096078	.099349	.105970	.112690	.119505	.126412
	.10	.081304	.087373	.093559	.096696	.099860	.103051	.106270	.109516	.112787	.119408	.126128	.132943	.139850
	0.00	.094741	.100811	.106997	.110134	.113298	.116489	.119708	.122954	.126225	.132846	.139566	.146381	.153288
	-.10	.108179	.114249	.120435	.123572	.126736	.129927	.133146	.136392	.139663	.146284	.153003	.159819	.166726
	-.20	.121617	.127687	.133873	.137009	.140174	.143365	.146584	.149830	.153101	.159722	.166441	.173257	.180164
	-.30	.135055	.141125	.147311	.150447	.153612	.156803	.160022	.163267	.166539	.173160	.179879	.186695	.193602
	-.40	.148493	.154563	.160749	.163885	.167049	.170241	.173460	.176705	.179977	.186598	.193317	.200133	.207040
15	.40	.034812	.041467	.048254	.051694	.055164	.058663	.062190	.065744	.069325	.076561	.083890	.091305	.098799
	.30	.048250	.054905	.061692	.065132	.068602	.072101	.075628	.079182	.082763	.089999	.097328	.104743	.112237
	.20	.061688	.068343	.075129	.078570	.082040	.085539	.089066	.092620	.096201	.103437	.110766	.118181	.125675
	.10	.075126	.081781	.088567	.092008	.095478	.098977	.102504	.106058	.109639	.116875	.124204	.131619	.139113
	0.00	.088564	.095219	.102005	.105445	.108916	.112415	.115942	.119496	.123077	.130313	.137642	.145057	.152551
	-.10	.102002	.108657	.115443	.118883	.122354	.125853	.129380	.132934	.136515	.143751	.151080	.158495	.165989
	-.20	.115440	.122095	.128881	.132321	.135791	.139291	.142818	.146372	.149953	.157189	.164518	.171933	.179427
	-.30	.128878	.135533	.142319	.145759	.149229	.152729	.156256	.159810	.163391	.170626	.177956	.185371	.192865
	-.40	.142316	.148971	.155757	.159197	.162667	.166167	.169694	.173248	.176829	.184064	.191394	.198809	.206303
20	.40	.031817	.038792	.045902	.049504	.053136	.056795	.060481	.064193	.067927	.075463	.083077	.090761	.098505
	.30	.045255	.052230	.059340	.062942	.066574	.070233	.073919	.077631	.081365	.088901	.096515	.104199	.111943
	.20	.058693	.065668	.072778	.076380	.080012	.083671	.087357	.091069	.094803	.102339	.109953	.117637	.125381
	.10	.072131	.079106	.086216	.089818	.093450	.097109	.100795	.104507	.108241	.115777	.123391	.131075	.138818
	0.00	.085569	.092544	.099654	.103256	.106888	.110547	.114233	.117944	.121679	.129215	.136829	.144513	.152256
	-.10	.099007	.105982	.113092	.116694	.120326	.123985	.127671	.131382	.135117	.142653	.150267	.157951	.165694
	-.20	.112445	.119420	.126530	.130132	.133764	.137423	.141109	.144820	.148555	.156091	.163705	.171389	.179132
	-.30	.125883	.132858	.139968	.143570	.147202	.150861	.154547	.158258	.161993	.169529	.177143	.184827	.192570
	-.40	.139321	.146296	.153406	.157008	.160640	.164299	.167985	.171696	.175431	.182967	.190581	.198265	.206008
25	.40	.030092	.037278	.044598	.048303	.052037	.055796	.059579	.063384	.067209	.074915	.082685	.090507	.098372
	.30	.043530	.050716	.058036	.061741	.065475	.069234	.073017	.076822	.080647	.088353	.096123	.103945	.111810
	.20	.056968	.064154	.071474	.075179	.078913	.082672	.086455	.090260	.094085	.101791	.109561	.117383	.125248
	.10	.070406	.077592	.084912	.088617	.092351	.096110	.099893	.103698	.107523	.115229	.122999	.130821	.138686
	0.00	.083844	.091030	.098350	.102055	.105789	.109548	.113330	.117136	.120961	.128667	.136437	.144259	.152124
	-.10	.097282	.104468	.111788	.115493	.119227	.122986	.126768	.130574	.134399	.142105	.149875	.157697	.165562
	-.20	.110720	.117906	.125226	.128931	.132664	.136423	.140206	.144011	.147837	.155543	.163312	.171135	.179000
	-.30	.124158	.131343	.138664	.142369	.146102	.149861	.153644	.157449	.161275	.168981	.176750	.184572	.192438
	-.40	.137596	.144781	.152102	.155807	.159540	.163299	.167082	.170887	.174713	.182419	.190188	.198010	.205876
30	.40	.028999	.036338	.043808	.047586	.051389	.055216	.059063	.062929	.066812	.074623	.082483	.090381	.098309
	.30	.042437	.049776	.057246	.061024	.064827	.068654	.072501	.076367	.080250	.088061	.095921	.103819	.111747
	.20	.055875	.063214	.070684	.074462	.078265	.082092	.085939	.089805	.093688	.101499	.109359	.117257	.125185
	.10	.069312	.076652	.084122	.087900	.091703	.095530	.099377	.103243	.107126	.114937	.122797	.130695	.138623
	0.00	.082750	.090090	.097560	.101338	.105141	.108968	.112815	.116681	.120564	.128375	.136235	.144133	.152061
	-.10	.096188	.103528	.110998	.114776	.118579	.122406	.126253	.130119	.134002	.141813	.149673	.157571	.165499
	-.20	.109626	.116966	.124436	.128214	.132017	.135844	.139691	.143557	.147440	.155251	.163111	.171009	.178937
	-.30	.123064	.130404	.137874	.141652	.145455	.149282	.153129	.156995	.160889	.168689	.176549	.184447	.192375
	-.40	.136502	.143842	.151312	.155090	.158893	.162719	.166567	.170433	.174316	.182127	.189987	.197885	.205813

5.0 YEAR HOLDING PERIOD
.200 EQUITY YIELD RATE
.900 LOAN RATIO

INTEREST RATE

TERM YEARS	APPR DEP	5.0	6.0	7.0	7.5	8.0	8.5	9.0	9.5	10.0	11.0	12.0	13.0	14.0
10	.40	.027832	.034660	.041620	.045148	.048708	.052299	.055920	.059571	.063252	.070700	.078259	.085927	.093697
	.30	.041270	.048098	.055058	.058566	.062146	.065737	.069358	.073109	.076690	.084137	.091967	.099365	.107135
	.20	.054708	.061536	.068496	.072024	.075584	.079174	.082796	.086447	.090128	.097575	.105135	.112803	.120573
	.10	.068146	.074974	.081934	.085462	.089022	.092612	.096234	.099885	.103566	.111013	.118573	.126241	.134011
	0.00	.081584	.088412	.095372	.098900	.102460	.106050	.109672	.113333	.117003	.124451	.132011	.139679	.147449
	-.10	.095022	.101850	.108810	.112338	.115898	.119488	.123110	.126761	.130441	.137889	.145449	.153116	.160887
	-.20	.108460	.115288	.122248	.125776	.129336	.132926	.136548	.140199	.143889	.151327	.158887	.166554	.174325
	-.30	.121898	.128726	.135686	.139214	.142774	.146364	.149985	.153637	.157317	.164765	.172325	.179992	.187763
	-.40	.135336	.142164	.149124	.152652	.156212	.159802	.163423	.167075	.170755	.178203	.185763	.193430	.201201
15	.40	.020883	.028370	.036004	.039874	.043778	.047715	.051683	.055681	.059709	.067850	.076095	.084437	.092868
	.30	.034321	.041808	.049442	.053312	.057216	.061153	.065121	.069119	.073147	.081288	.089533	.097875	.106306
	.20	.047759	.055246	.062880	.066750	.070654	.074591	.078559	.082557	.086585	.094726	.102971	.111313	.119744
	.10	.061197	.068684	.076318	.080188	.084092	.088029	.091997	.095995	.100023	.108164	.116409	.124751	.133182
	0.00	.074635	.082122	.089756	.093626	.097530	.101466	.105435	.109433	.113461	.121602	.129847	.138189	.146620
	-.10	.088073	.095559	.103194	.107064	.110968	.114904	.118873	.122899	.126899	.135040	.143285	.151627	.160058
	-.20	.101511	.108997	.116632	.120502	.124406	.128342	.132311	.136309	.140337	.148478	.156723	.165065	.173496
	-.30	.114949	.122435	.130070	.133940	.137844	.141780	.145749	.149747	.153775	.161916	.170161	.178503	.186934
	-.40	.128386	.135873	.143508	.147378	.151282	.155218	.159186	.163185	.167213	.175354	.183599	.191941	.200372
20	.40	.017513	.025360	.033359	.037411	.041497	.045614	.049761	.053936	.058137	.066615	.075181	.083825	.092537
	.30	.030951	.038798	.046797	.050849	.054935	.059052	.063199	.067374	.071575	.080053	.088619	.097263	.105975
	.20	.044389	.052236	.060235	.064287	.068373	.072490	.076637	.080812	.085013	.093491	.102057	.110701	.119413
	.10	.057827	.065674	.073673	.077725	.081811	.085928	.090075	.094250	.098451	.106929	.115495	.124139	.132851
	0.00	.071265	.079112	.087111	.091163	.095249	.099366	.103513	.107688	.111889	.120367	.128933	.137577	.146289
	-.10	.084703	.092550	.100549	.104601	.108687	.112804	.116950	.121126	.125327	.133805	.142371	.151015	.159726
	-.20	.098141	.105988	.113987	.118039	.122125	.126242	.130388	.134563	.138765	.147242	.155809	.164453	.173164
	-.30	.111579	.119426	.127425	.131477	.135563	.139680	.143826	.148001	.152203	.160680	.169247	.177891	.186602
	-.40	.125017	.132864	.140863	.144915	.149001	.153118	.157264	.161439	.165641	.174118	.182685	.191329	.200040
25	.40	.015573	.023656	.031892	.036060	.040260	.044489	.048745	.053026	.057329	.065999	.074739	.083539	.092387
	.30	.029010	.037094	.045330	.049498	.053698	.057927	.062183	.066464	.070767	.079437	.088177	.096977	.105825
	.20	.042448	.050532	.058768	.062936	.067136	.071365	.075621	.079902	.084205	.092875	.101615	.110415	.119263
	.10	.055886	.063970	.072206	.076374	.080574	.084803	.089059	.093340	.097643	.106313	.115053	.123853	.132701
	0.00	.069324	.077408	.085644	.089812	.094012	.098241	.102497	.106778	.111081	.119751	.128491	.137291	.146139
	-.10	.082762	.090846	.099081	.103250	.107450	.111679	.115935	.120215	.124519	.133189	.141929	.150729	.159577
	-.20	.096200	.104284	.112519	.116688	.120888	.125117	.129373	.133653	.137957	.146626	.155367	.164167	.173015
	-.30	.109638	.117722	.125957	.130126	.134326	.138555	.142811	.147091	.151395	.160064	.168805	.177605	.186453
	-.40	.123076	.131160	.139395	.143564	.147764	.151993	.156249	.160529	.164833	.173502	.182243	.191043	.199891
30	.40	.014342	.022599	.031003	.035254	.039532	.043837	.048165	.052514	.056883	.065670	.074512	.083398	.092316
	.30	.027780	.036037	.044441	.048691	.052970	.057275	.061603	.065952	.070321	.079108	.087950	.096836	.105754
	.20	.041218	.049475	.057879	.062129	.066408	.070713	.075041	.079390	.083759	.092546	.101388	.110274	.119192
	.10	.054656	.062913	.071317	.075567	.079846	.084151	.088479	.092828	.097197	.105984	.114826	.123711	.132630
	0.00	.068094	.076351	.084755	.089005	.093284	.097589	.101917	.106266	.110635	.119422	.128264	.137149	.146068
	-.10	.081532	.089789	.098193	.102443	.106722	.111026	.115355	.119704	.124073	.132860	.141702	.150587	.159506
	-.20	.094970	.103227	.111631	.115881	.120160	.124464	.128793	.133142	.137511	.146298	.155140	.164025	.172944
	-.30	.108408	.116665	.125069	.129319	.133598	.137902	.142231	.146580	.150949	.159736	.168578	.177463	.186382
	-.40	.121846	.130103	.138507	.142757	.147036	.151340	.155668	.160018	.164387	.173174	.182016	.190901	.199820

5.0 YEAR HOLDING PERIOD
.250 EQUITY YIELD RATE
.600 LOAN RATIO

INTEREST RATE

TERM YEARS	APPR DEP	5.0	6.0	7.0	7.5	8.0	8.5	9.0	9.5	10.0	11.0	12.0	13.0	14.0
10	.40	.095611	.100071	.104620	.106927	.109255	.111604	.113973	.116363	.118773	.123651	.128605	.133632	.138729
	.30	.107795	.112256	.116804	.119111	.121439	.123788	.126158	.128548	.130958	.135636	.140790	.145817	.150914
	.20	.119980	.124440	.128989	.131296	.133624	.135973	.138343	.140732	.143142	.148021	.152974	.158001	.163099
	.10	.132165	.136625	.141174	.143481	.145809	.148158	.150527	.152917	.155327	.160205	.165159	.170186	.175283
	0.00	.144349	.148810	.153358	.155665	.157993	.160342	.162712	.165102	.167512	.172390	.177344	.182371	.187468
	-.10	.156534	.160994	.165543	.167850	.170178	.172527	.174897	.177287	.179696	.184575	.189529	.194555	.199653
	-.20	.168719	.173179	.177728	.180035	.182363	.184712	.187081	.189471	.191881	.196759	.201713	.206740	.211837
	-.30	.180903	.185364	.189913	.192219	.194547	.196896	.199266	.201656	.204066	.208944	.213898	.218925	.224022
	-.40	.193088	.197548	.202097	.204404	.206732	.209081	.211451	.213841	.216250	.221129	.226083	.231110	.236207
15	.40	.089598	.094480	.099464	.101993	.104545	.107120	.109717	.112335	.114974	.120311	.125722	.131202	.136744
	.30	.101782	.106664	.111649	.114177	.116729	.119304	.121901	.124520	.127158	.132496	.137907	.143386	.148929
	.20	.113967	.118849	.123833	.126362	.128914	.131489	.134086	.136704	.139343	.144680	.150091	.155571	.161114
	.10	.126152	.131034	.136018	.138547	.141099	.143674	.146271	.148889	.151528	.156865	.162276	.167756	.173298
	0.00	.138336	.143218	.148203	.150731	.153283	.155858	.158455	.161074	.163713	.169050	.174461	.179940	.185483
	-.10	.150521	.155403	.160387	.162916	.165468	.168043	.170640	.173258	.175897	.181234	.186645	.192125	.197668
	-.20	.162706	.167588	.172572	.175101	.177653	.180228	.182825	.185443	.188082	.193419	.198830	.204310	.209852
	-.30	.174890	.179772	.184757	.187285	.189837	.192412	.195009	.197628	.200267	.205604	.211015	.216494	.222037
	-.40	.187075	.191957	.196941	.199470	.202022	.204597	.207194	.209812	.212451	.217788	.223199	.228679	.234222
20	.40	.086682	.091805	.097035	.099688	.102365	.105065	.107786	.110527	.113288	.118863	.124504	.130203	.135952
	.30	.098867	.103989	.109220	.111873	.114550	.117249	.119970	.122712	.125472	.131048	.136689	.142387	.148136
	.20	.111052	.116174	.121405	.124058	.126735	.129434	.132155	.134896	.137657	.143232	.148873	.154572	.160321
	.10	.123236	.128359	.133589	.136242	.138919	.141619	.144340	.147081	.149842	.155417	.161058	.166757	.172506
	0.00	.135421	.140543	.145774	.148427	.151104	.153803	.156524	.159266	.162026	.167602	.173243	.178941	.184690
	-.10	.147606	.152728	.157959	.160612	.163289	.165988	.168709	.171450	.174211	.179786	.185427	.191126	.196875
	-.20	.159790	.164913	.170143	.172796	.175473	.178173	.180894	.183635	.186396	.191971	.197612	.203311	.209060
	-.30	.171975	.177097	.182328	.184981	.187658	.190357	.193078	.195820	.198580	.204156	.209797	.215495	.221245
	-.40	.184160	.189282	.194513	.197166	.199843	.202542	.205263	.208004	.210765	.216341	.221981	.227680	.233429
25	.40	.085003	.090291	.095688	.098424	.101184	.103964	.106765	.109584	.112421	.118141	.123916	.129736	.135595
	.30	.097188	.102475	.107873	.110609	.113368	.116149	.118950	.121769	.124606	.130326	.136100	.141921	.147779
	.20	.109372	.114660	.120058	.122794	.125553	.128334	.131134	.133954	.136790	.142510	.148285	.154105	.159964
	.10	.121557	.126845	.132242	.134979	.137738	.140518	.143319	.146138	.148975	.154695	.160470	.166290	.172149
	0.00	.133742	.139029	.144427	.147163	.149922	.152703	.155504	.158323	.161160	.166880	.172654	.178475	.184333
	-.10	.145926	.151214	.156612	.159348	.162107	.164888	.167688	.170508	.173344	.179064	.184839	.190659	.196518
	-.20	.158111	.163399	.168796	.171533	.174292	.177072	.179873	.182692	.185529	.191249	.197024	.202844	.208703
	-.30	.170296	.175583	.180981	.183717	.186476	.189257	.192058	.194877	.197714	.203434	.209208	.215029	.220887
	-.40	.182480	.187768	.193166	.195902	.198661	.201442	.204242	.207062	.209898	.215618	.221393	.227213	.233072
30	.40	.083939	.089351	.094873	.097670	.100488	.103326	.106182	.109055	.111942	.117756	.123613	.129505	.135425
	.30	.096123	.101536	.107057	.109854	.112673	.115511	.118367	.121239	.124127	.129940	.135798	.141690	.147610
	.20	.108308	.113720	.119242	.122039	.124857	.127695	.130552	.133424	.136311	.142125	.147982	.153875	.159794
	.10	.120493	.125905	.131427	.134224	.137042	.139880	.142736	.145609	.148496	.154310	.160167	.166059	.171979
	0.00	.132677	.138090	.143611	.146408	.149227	.152065	.154921	.157793	.160681	.166494	.172352	.178244	.184164
	-.10	.144862	.150274	.155796	.158593	.161411	.164249	.167106	.169978	.172865	.178679	.184536	.190429	.196348
	-.20	.157047	.162459	.167981	.170778	.173596	.176434	.179291	.182163	.185050	.190864	.196721	.202613	.208533
	-.30	.169231	.174644	.180166	.182962	.185781	.188619	.191475	.194347	.197235	.203048	.208906	.214798	.220718
	-.40	.181416	.186829	.192350	.195147	.197965	.200803	.203660	.206532	.209419	.215233	.221090	.226983	.232902

5.0 YEAR HOLDING PERIOD
.250 EQUITY YIELD RATE
.667 LOAN RATIO

INTEREST RATE

TERM YEARS	APPR DEP	5.0	6.0	7.0	7.5	8.0	8.5	9.0	9.5	10.0	11.0	12.0	13.0	14.0
10	.40	.083871	.088827	.093881	.096444	.099031	.101641	.104274	.106930	.109607	.115027	.120532	.126117	.131781
	.30	.096056	.101012	.106066	.108629	.111216	.113826	.116459	.119114	.121792	.127212	.132717	.138302	.143966
	.20	.108241	.113196	.118251	.120814	.123401	.126011	.128643	.131299	.133976	.139397	.144901	.150487	.156150
	.10	.120425	.125381	.130435	.132998	.135585	.138195	.140828	.143484	.146161	.151581	.157086	.162671	.168335
	0.00	.132610	.137566	.142620	.145183	.147770	.150380	.153013	.155668	.158346	.163766	.169271	.174856	.180520
	-.10	.144795	.149750	.154805	.157368	.159955	.162565	.165197	.167853	.170531	.175951	.181455	.187041	.192704
	-.20	.156979	.161935	.166989	.169553	.172139	.174749	.177382	.180038	.182715	.188135	.193640	.199225	.204889
	-.30	.169164	.174120	.179174	.181737	.184324	.186934	.189567	.192222	.194900	.200320	.205825	.211410	.217074
	-.40	.181349	.186304	.191359	.193922	.196509	.199119	.201752	.204407	.207085	.212505	.218009	.223595	.229258
15	.40	.077190	.082615	.088152	.090962	.093798	.096659	.099544	.102454	.105386	.111316	.117328	.123417	.129576
	.30	.089375	.094799	.100337	.103147	.105983	.108844	.111729	.114638	.117571	.123501	.129513	.135601	.141760
	.20	.101559	.106984	.112522	.115331	.118167	.121028	.123914	.126823	.129755	.135685	.141698	.147786	.153945
	.10	.113744	.119169	.124707	.127516	.130352	.133213	.136098	.139008	.141940	.147870	.153882	.159971	.166130
	0.00	.125929	.131353	.136891	.139701	.142537	.145398	.148283	.151192	.154125	.160055	.166067	.172156	.178314
	-.10	.138113	.143538	.149076	.151886	.154721	.157582	.160468	.163377	.166309	.172239	.178252	.184340	.190499
	-.20	.150298	.155723	.161261	.164070	.166906	.169767	.172652	.175562	.178494	.184424	.190436	.196525	.202684
	-.30	.162483	.167907	.173445	.176255	.179091	.181952	.184837	.187746	.190679	.196609	.202621	.208710	.214868
	-.40	.174667	.180092	.185630	.188440	.191275	.194136	.197022	.199931	.202863	.208793	.214806	.220894	.227053
20	.40	.073951	.079642	.085454	.088402	.091376	.094376	.097399	.100445	.103512	.109707	.115975	.122307	.128695
	.30	.086135	.091827	.097639	.100587	.103561	.106560	.109583	.112629	.115697	.121892	.128160	.134491	.140879
	.20	.098320	.104012	.109823	.112771	.115746	.118745	.121768	.124814	.127882	.134077	.140344	.146676	.153064
	.10	.110505	.116196	.122008	.124956	.127930	.130930	.133953	.136999	.140066	.146261	.152529	.158861	.165249
	0.00	.122689	.128381	.134193	.137141	.140115	.143114	.146137	.149183	.152251	.158446	.164714	.171045	.177434
	-.10	.134874	.140566	.146377	.149325	.152300	.155299	.158322	.161368	.164436	.170631	.176898	.183230	.189618
	-.20	.147059	.152750	.158562	.161510	.164484	.167484	.170507	.173553	.176620	.182815	.189083	.195415	.201803
	-.30	.159243	.164935	.170747	.173695	.176669	.179668	.182692	.185737	.188805	.195000	.201268	.207599	.213988
	-.40	.171428	.177120	.182931	.185879	.188854	.191853	.194876	.197922	.200990	.207185	.213452	.219784	.226172
25	.40	.072085	.077960	.083957	.086998	.090063	.093153	.096265	.099398	.102549	.108905	.115321	.121788	.128298
	.30	.084269	.090145	.096142	.099182	.102248	.105338	.108450	.111582	.114734	.121090	.127506	.133973	.140483
	.20	.096454	.102329	.108327	.111367	.114433	.117522	.120634	.123767	.126919	.133274	.139691	.146158	.152667
	.10	.108639	.114514	.120511	.123552	.126617	.129707	.132819	.135952	.139103	.145459	.151875	.158342	.164852
	0.00	.120823	.126699	.132696	.135736	.138802	.141892	.145004	.148136	.151288	.157644	.164060	.170527	.177037
	-.10	.133008	.138883	.144881	.147921	.150987	.154076	.157188	.160321	.163473	.169828	.176245	.182712	.189221
	-.20	.145193	.151068	.157065	.160106	.163171	.166261	.169373	.172506	.175657	.182013	.188429	.194896	.201406
	-.30	.157377	.163253	.169250	.172290	.175356	.178446	.181558	.184690	.187842	.194198	.200614	.207081	.213591
	-.40	.169562	.175437	.181435	.184475	.187541	.190630	.193742	.196875	.200027	.206382	.212799	.219266	.225775
30	.40	.070902	.076916	.083051	.086159	.089290	.092444	.095617	.098809	.102017	.108477	.114985	.121532	.128109
	.30	.083087	.089101	.095236	.098344	.101475	.104629	.107802	.110994	.114202	.120662	.127170	.133717	.140294
	.20	.095271	.101285	.107421	.110528	.113660	.116813	.119987	.123178	.126386	.132846	.139354	.145901	.152479
	.10	.107456	.113470	.119605	.122713	.125844	.128998	.132171	.135363	.138571	.145031	.151539	.158086	.164663
	0.00	.119641	.125655	.131790	.134898	.138029	.141183	.144356	.147548	.150756	.157216	.163724	.170271	.176848
	-.10	.131825	.137839	.143975	.147082	.150214	.153367	.156541	.159732	.162941	.169400	.175908	.182455	.189033
	-.20	.144010	.150024	.156159	.159267	.162398	.165552	.168725	.171917	.175125	.181585	.188093	.194640	.201217
	-.30	.156195	.162209	.168344	.171452	.174583	.177737	.180910	.184102	.187310	.193770	.200278	.206825	.213402
	-.40	.168379	.174393	.180529	.183636	.186768	.189921	.193095	.196286	.199495	.205954	.212462	.219009	.225587

5.0 YEAR HOLDING PERIOD
.250 EQUITY YIELD RATE
.700 LOAN RATIO

INTEREST RATE

TERM YEARS	APPR DEP	5.0	6.0	7.0	7.5	8.0	8.5	9.0	9.5	10.0	11.0	12.0	13.0	14.0
10	.40	.078002	.083206	.088513	.091204	.093920	.096661	.099425	.102213	.105025	.110716	.116496	.122361	.128307
	.30	.090187	.095391	.100698	.103389	.106105	.108845	.111610	.114398	.117210	.122901	.128680	.134545	.140492
	.20	.102272	.107575	.112882	.115574	.118290	.121030	.123795	.126583	.129394	.135085	.140865	.146730	.152677
	.10	.114556	.119760	.125067	.127758	.130474	.133215	.135979	.138767	.141579	.147270	.153050	.158915	.164861
	0.00	.126741	.131945	.137252	.139943	.142659	.145399	.148164	.150952	.153764	.159455	.165234	.171099	.177046
	-.10	.138926	.144129	.149436	.152128	.154844	.157584	.160349	.163137	.165948	.171640	.177419	.183284	.189231
	-.20	.151111	.156314	.161621	.164312	.167028	.169769	.172533	.175321	.178133	.183824	.189604	.195469	.201415
	-.30	.163295	.168499	.173806	.176497	.179213	.181953	.184718	.187506	.190318	.196009	.201789	.207653	.213600
	-.40	.175480	.180683	.185990	.188682	.191398	.194138	.196903	.199691	.202502	.208194	.213973	.219838	.225785
15	.40	.070087	.076683	.082498	.085448	.088425	.091429	.094459	.097514	.100593	.106819	.113132	.119525	.125992
	.30	.083172	.088867	.094682	.097632	.100610	.103614	.106644	.109698	.112777	.119004	.125317	.131710	.138176
	.20	.095356	.101052	.106867	.109817	.112795	.115799	.118828	.121883	.124962	.131188	.137501	.143894	.150361
	.10	.107541	.113237	.119052	.122002	.124979	.127983	.131013	.134068	.137147	.143373	.149686	.156079	.162546
	0.00	.119726	.125421	.131236	.134186	.137164	.140168	.143198	.146252	.149331	.155558	.161871	.168264	.174730
	-.10	.131910	.137606	.143421	.146371	.149349	.152353	.155382	.158437	.161516	.167742	.174055	.180448	.186915
	-.20	.144095	.149791	.155606	.158556	.161533	.164537	.167567	.170622	.173701	.179927	.186240	.192633	.199100
	-.30	.156280	.161976	.167790	.170740	.173718	.176722	.179752	.182807	.185885	.192112	.198425	.204818	.211284
	-.40	.168464	.174160	.179975	.182925	.185903	.188907	.191936	.194991	.198070	.204296	.210609	.217002	.223469
20	.40	.067586	.073562	.079664	.082760	.085883	.089032	.092206	.095404	.098625	.105130	.111711	.118359	.125067
	.30	.079770	.085747	.091849	.094944	.098067	.101216	.104391	.107589	.110810	.117315	.123896	.130544	.137252
	.20	.091955	.097931	.104034	.107129	.110252	.113401	.116576	.119774	.122995	.129499	.136080	.142729	.149436
	.10	.104140	.110116	.116218	.119314	.122437	.125586	.128760	.131959	.135179	.141684	.148265	.154913	.161621
	0.00	.116324	.122301	.128403	.131498	.134621	.137771	.140945	.144143	.147364	.153869	.160450	.167098	.173806
	-.10	.128509	.134485	.140588	.143683	.146806	.149955	.153130	.156328	.159549	.166053	.172634	.179283	.185990
	-.20	.140694	.146670	.152772	.155868	.158991	.162140	.165315	.168513	.171733	.178238	.184819	.191467	.198175
	-.30	.152879	.158855	.164957	.168052	.171175	.174325	.177499	.180697	.183918	.190423	.197004	.203652	.210360
	-.40	.165063	.171039	.177142	.180237	.183360	.186509	.189684	.192882	.196103	.202607	.209188	.215837	.222544
25	.40	.065627	.071795	.078093	.081285	.084504	.087748	.091016	.094305	.097614	.104288	.111025	.117815	.124650
	.30	.077811	.083980	.090277	.093470	.096689	.099933	.103200	.106490	.109799	.116472	.123209	.130000	.136835
	.20	.089996	.096165	.102462	.105654	.108873	.112118	.115385	.118674	.121984	.128657	.135394	.142184	.149019
	.10	.102181	.108349	.114647	.117839	.121058	.124302	.127570	.130859	.134168	.140842	.147579	.154369	.161204
	0.00	.114365	.120534	.126831	.130024	.133243	.136487	.139754	.143044	.146353	.153026	.159763	.166554	.173389
	-.10	.126550	.132719	.139016	.142208	.145427	.148672	.151939	.155228	.158538	.165211	.171948	.178738	.185573
	-.20	.138735	.144903	.151201	.154393	.157612	.160856	.164124	.167413	.170722	.177396	.184133	.190923	.197758
	-.30	.150919	.157088	.163385	.166578	.169797	.173041	.176308	.179598	.182907	.189580	.196317	.203108	.209943
	-.40	.163104	.169273	.175570	.178762	.181981	.185226	.188493	.191782	.195092	.201765	.208502	.215292	.222128
30	.40	.064385	.070699	.077141	.080404	.083692	.087004	.090336	.093687	.097055	.103838	.110672	.117546	.124452
	.30	.076569	.082884	.089326	.092589	.095877	.099188	.102520	.105872	.109240	.116023	.122856	.129731	.136637
	.20	.088754	.095069	.101511	.104774	.108062	.111373	.114705	.118056	.121425	.128207	.135041	.141915	.148821
	.10	.100939	.107253	.113695	.116958	.120246	.123558	.126890	.130241	.133609	.140392	.147226	.154100	.161006
	0.00	.113124	.119438	.125880	.129143	.132431	.135742	.139074	.142426	.145794	.152577	.159410	.166285	.173191
	-.10	.125308	.131623	.138065	.141328	.144616	.147927	.151259	.154610	.157979	.164761	.171595	.178469	.185375
	-.20	.137493	.143807	.150249	.153512	.156801	.160112	.163444	.166795	.170164	.176946	.183780	.190654	.197560
	-.30	.149678	.155992	.162434	.165697	.168985	.172296	.175628	.178980	.182348	.189131	.195964	.202839	.209745
	-.40	.161862	.168177	.174619	.177882	.181170	.184481	.187813	.191164	.194533	.201316	.208149	.215023	.221930

5.0 YEAR HOLDING PERIOD
.250 EQUITY YIELD RATE
.750 LOAN RATIO

INTEREST RATE

TERM YEARS	APPR DEP	5.0	6.0	7.0	7.5	8.0	8.5	9.0	9.5	10.0	11.0	12.0	13.0	14.0
10	.40	.069198	.074773	.080459	.083363	.086253	.089189	.092151	.095139	.098151	.104249	.110441	.116725	.123096
	.30	.081383	.086958	.092644	.095528	.098438	.101374	.104336	.107323	.110336	.116433	.122626	.128910	.135281
	.20	.093567	.099143	.104829	.107712	.110622	.113559	.116521	.119508	.122520	.128618	.134810	.141194	.147466
	.10	.105752	.111327	.117013	.119697	.122807	.125743	.128705	.131693	.134705	.140803	.146995	.153279	.159650
	0.00	.117937	.123512	.129198	.132082	.134992	.137928	.140890	.143877	.146890	.152987	.159180	.165464	.171835
	-.10	.130121	.135697	.141383	.144266	.147176	.150113	.153075	.156062	.159074	.165172	.171364	.177648	.184020
	-.20	.142306	.147882	.153567	.156451	.159361	.162297	.165259	.168247	.171259	.177357	.183549	.189833	.196204
	-.30	.154491	.160066	.165752	.168636	.171546	.174482	.177444	.180431	.183444	.189541	.195734	.202018	.208389
	-.40	.166675	.172251	.177937	.180820	.183730	.186667	.189629	.192616	.195628	.201726	.207918	.214202	.220574
15	.40	.061682	.067784	.074015	.077175	.080366	.083584	.086830	.090103	.093402	.100073	.106837	.113687	.120615
	.30	.073866	.079969	.086199	.089360	.092550	.095769	.099015	.102288	.105587	.112258	.119022	.125871	.132800
	.20	.086051	.092154	.098384	.101545	.104735	.107954	.111200	.114473	.117771	.124443	.131206	.138056	.144985
	.10	.098236	.104338	.110569	.113730	.116920	.120138	.123384	.126657	.129956	.136627	.143391	.150241	.157166
	0.00	.110420	.116523	.122753	.125914	.129104	.132323	.135569	.138842	.142141	.148812	.155576	.162425	.169354
	-.10	.122605	.128708	.134938	.138099	.141289	.144508	.147754	.151027	.154325	.160997	.167760	.174610	.181539
	-.20	.134790	.140892	.147123	.150283	.153474	.156692	.159938	.163211	.166510	.173181	.179945	.186795	.193723
	-.30	.146974	.153077	.159307	.162468	.165658	.168877	.172123	.175396	.178695	.185366	.192130	.198979	.205908
	-.40	.159159	.165262	.171492	.174653	.177843	.181062	.184308	.187581	.190879	.197551	.204315	.211164	.218093
20	.40	.058038	.064441	.070979	.074295	.077641	.081015	.084417	.087843	.091294	.098264	.105315	.112438	.119624
	.30	.070222	.076625	.083163	.086480	.089826	.093200	.096601	.100028	.103479	.110448	.117499	.124623	.131809
	.20	.082407	.088810	.095348	.098665	.102011	.105385	.108786	.112213	.115664	.122633	.129684	.136807	.143994
	.10	.094592	.100995	.107533	.110849	.114195	.117569	.120971	.124397	.127848	.134818	.141869	.148992	.156178
	0.00	.106777	.113179	.119718	.123034	.126380	.129754	.133155	.136582	.140033	.147002	.154053	.161177	.168363
	-.10	.118961	.125364	.131902	.135219	.138565	.141939	.145340	.148767	.152218	.159187	.166238	.173361	.180548
	-.20	.131146	.137549	.144087	.147403	.150749	.154123	.157525	.160951	.164402	.171372	.178423	.185546	.192732
	-.30	.143330	.149733	.156272	.159588	.162934	.166308	.169709	.173136	.176587	.183556	.190607	.197731	.204917
	-.40	.155515	.161918	.168456	.171773	.175119	.178493	.181894	.185321	.188772	.195741	.202792	.209915	.217102
25	.40	.055938	.062548	.069295	.072715	.076164	.079640	.083141	.086665	.090211	.097361	.104579	.111855	.119178
	.30	.068123	.074733	.081480	.084900	.088349	.091825	.095326	.098850	.102396	.109546	.116764	.124039	.131363
	.20	.080308	.086917	.093664	.097085	.100534	.104009	.107510	.111034	.114580	.121730	.128949	.136224	.143547
	.10	.092492	.099102	.105849	.109269	.112718	.116194	.119695	.123219	.126765	.133915	.141133	.148409	.155732
	0.00	.104677	.111287	.118034	.121454	.124903	.128379	.131880	.135404	.138950	.146100	.153318	.160593	.167917
	-.10	.116862	.123471	.130218	.133639	.137088	.140564	.144064	.147589	.151134	.158284	.165503	.172778	.180101
	-.20	.129046	.135656	.142403	.145823	.149272	.152749	.156249	.159773	.163319	.170469	.177687	.184963	.192286
	-.30	.141231	.147841	.154588	.158008	.161457	.164933	.168434	.171958	.175504	.182654	.189872	.197147	.204471
	-.40	.153416	.160025	.166772	.170193	.173642	.177118	.180618	.184143	.187688	.194838	.202057	.209332	.216655
30	.40	.054608	.061374	.068276	.071772	.075295	.078842	.082412	.086003	.089612	.096879	.104201	.111566	.118966
	.30	.066793	.073558	.080460	.083956	.087479	.091027	.094597	.098188	.101797	.109064	.116386	.123751	.131150
	.20	.078977	.085743	.092645	.096141	.099664	.103212	.106782	.110372	.113982	.121249	.128570	.135936	.143335
	.10	.091162	.097928	.104830	.108326	.111849	.115396	.118966	.122557	.126166	.133433	.140755	.148120	.155520
	0.00	.103347	.110112	.117014	.120510	.124033	.127581	.131151	.134742	.138351	.145618	.152940	.160305	.167704
	-.10	.115531	.122297	.129199	.132695	.136218	.139766	.143336	.146926	.150536	.157803	.165124	.172490	.179889
	-.20	.127716	.134482	.141384	.144880	.148403	.151950	.155520	.159111	.162720	.169987	.177309	.184674	.192074
	-.30	.139901	.146666	.153568	.157064	.160587	.164135	.167705	.171296	.174905	.182172	.189494	.196859	.204258
	-.40	.152085	.158851	.165753	.169249	.172772	.176320	.179890	.183480	.187090	.194357	.201678	.209044	.216443

5.0 YEAR HOLDING PERIOD
.250 EQUITY YIELD RATE
.800 LOAN RATIO

INTEREST RATE

TERM YEARS	APPR DEP	5.0	6.0	7.0	7.5	8.0	8.5	9.0	9.5	10.0	11.0	12.0	13.0	14.0
10	.40	.060394	.066341	.072406	.075482	.078586	.081718	.084877	.088064	.091277	.097781	.104386	.111089	.117885
	.30	.072579	.078526	.084591	.087666	.090770	.093902	.097062	.100248	.103462	.109966	.116571	.123274	.130070
	.20	.084763	.090710	.096775	.099851	.102955	.106087	.109247	.112433	.115646	.122150	.128756	.135458	.142255
	.10	.096948	.102895	.108960	.112036	.115140	.118272	.121431	.124618	.127831	.134335	.140940	.147643	.154439
	0.00	.109133	.115080	.121145	.124220	.127325	.130456	.133616	.136802	.140016	.146520	.153125	.159828	.166624
	-.10	.121317	.127264	.133329	.136405	.139509	.142641	.145801	.148987	.152200	.158704	.165310	.172012	.178809
	-.20	.133502	.139449	.145514	.148590	.151694	.154826	.157985	.161172	.164385	.170889	.177494	.184197	.190993
	-.30	.145687	.151634	.157699	.160774	.163879	.167011	.170170	.173356	.176570	.183074	.189679	.196382	.203178
	-.40	.157871	.163818	.169883	.172959	.176063	.179195	.182355	.185541	.188754	.195259	.201864	.208566	.215363
15	.40	.052376	.058886	.065531	.068903	.072306	.075739	.079202	.082693	.086211	.093327	.100542	.107848	.115239
	.30	.064561	.071071	.077716	.081088	.084490	.087924	.091386	.094877	.098396	.105512	.112727	.120033	.127423
	.20	.076746	.083255	.089901	.093272	.096675	.100108	.103571	.107062	.110581	.117697	.124912	.132218	.139608
	.10	.088930	.095440	.102085	.105457	.108860	.112293	.115756	.119247	.122765	.129881	.137096	.144402	.151793
	0.00	.101115	.107625	.114270	.117642	.121045	.124478	.127940	.131431	.134950	.142066	.149281	.156587	.163977
	-.10	.113300	.119809	.126455	.129826	.133229	.136662	.140125	.143616	.147135	.154251	.161466	.168772	.176162
	-.20	.125484	.131994	.138639	.142011	.145414	.148847	.152310	.155801	.159319	.166435	.173650	.180956	.188347
	-.30	.137669	.144179	.150824	.154196	.157599	.161032	.164494	.167985	.171504	.178620	.185835	.193141	.200531
	-.40	.149854	.156363	.163009	.166380	.169783	.173216	.176679	.180170	.183689	.190805	.198020	.205326	.212716
20	.40	.048489	.055319	.062293	.065831	.069400	.072999	.076627	.080282	.083963	.091397	.098918	.106516	.114182
	.30	.060674	.067504	.074478	.078015	.081584	.085184	.088812	.092467	.096148	.103582	.111103	.118701	.126367
	.20	.072859	.079689	.086663	.090200	.093769	.097368	.100996	.104651	.108332	.115766	.123288	.130886	.138551
	.10	.085043	.091873	.098847	.102385	.105954	.109553	.113181	.116836	.120517	.127951	.135472	.143070	.150736
	0.00	.097228	.104058	.111032	.114569	.118139	.121738	.125366	.129021	.132702	.140136	.147657	.155255	.162921
	-.10	.109413	.116243	.123217	.126754	.130323	.133922	.137550	.141205	.144886	.152320	.159842	.167440	.175105
	-.20	.121597	.128427	.135401	.138939	.142508	.146107	.149735	.153390	.157071	.164505	.172026	.179624	.187290
	-.30	.133782	.140612	.147586	.151123	.154693	.158292	.161920	.165575	.169256	.176690	.184211	.191809	.199475
	-.40	.145967	.152797	.159771	.163308	.166877	.170476	.174104	.177759	.181440	.188874	.196396	.203994	.211659
25	.40	.046250	.053300	.060497	.064446	.067825	.071532	.075266	.079025	.082808	.090434	.098134	.105894	.113706
	.30	.058435	.065485	.072682	.076330	.080000	.083717	.087451	.091210	.094992	.102619	.110318	.118079	.125890
	.20	.070620	.077670	.084867	.088515	.092194	.095901	.099636	.103395	.107177	.114804	.122503	.130264	.138075
	.10	.082804	.089854	.097051	.100700	.104379	.108086	.111820	.115579	.119362	.126988	.134688	.142448	.150260
	0.00	.094989	.102039	.109236	.112884	.116563	.120271	.124005	.127764	.131546	.139173	.146872	.154633	.162444
	-.10	.107174	.114224	.121421	.125069	.128749	.132455	.136190	.139949	.143731	.151358	.159057	.166818	.174629
	-.20	.119358	.126408	.133605	.137254	.140933	.144640	.148374	.152133	.155916	.163542	.171242	.179002	.186814
	-.30	.131543	.138593	.145790	.149438	.153117	.156825	.160559	.164318	.168100	.175727	.183426	.191187	.198998
	-.40	.143728	.150778	.157975	.161623	.165302	.169009	.172744	.176503	.180285	.187912	.195611	.203372	.211183
30	.40	.044831	.052048	.059410	.063139	.066897	.070681	.074489	.078319	.082169	.089921	.097730	.105587	.113479
	.30	.057016	.064232	.071595	.075324	.079082	.082866	.086674	.090504	.094354	.102105	.109915	.117771	.125664
	.20	.069200	.076417	.083779	.087508	.091266	.095050	.098858	.102688	.106538	.114290	.122100	.129956	.137849
	.10	.081385	.088602	.095964	.099693	.103451	.107235	.111043	.114873	.118723	.126475	.134284	.142141	.150033
	0.00	.093570	.100786	.108149	.111878	.115636	.119420	.123228	.127058	.130908	.138659	.146469	.154325	.162218
	-.10	.105754	.112971	.120333	.124062	.127820	.131604	.135413	.139242	.143092	.150844	.158654	.166510	.174403
	-.20	.117939	.125156	.132518	.136247	.140005	.143789	.147597	.151427	.155277	.163029	.170838	.178695	.186587
	-.30	.130124	.137340	.144703	.148432	.152190	.155974	.159782	.163612	.167462	.175213	.183023	.190879	.198772
	-.40	.142308	.149525	.156887	.160617	.164374	.168158	.171967	.175797	.179646	.187398	.195208	.203064	.210957

5.0 YEAR HOLDING PERIOD
.250 EQUITY YIELD RATE
.900 LOAN RATIO

INTEREST RATE

TERM YEARS	APPR DEP	5.0	6.0	7.0	7.5	8.0	8.5	9.0	9.5	10.0	11.0	12.0	13.0	14.0
10	.40	.042785	.049476	.056299	.059759	.063251	.066775	.070329	.073914	.077529	.084846	.092277	.099818	.107463
	.30	.054970	.061661	.068484	.071944	.075436	.078960	.082514	.086099	.089713	.097031	.104462	.112002	.119648
	.20	.067155	.073845	.080668	.084129	.087621	.091144	.094699	.098283	.101898	.109215	.116646	.124187	.131833
	.10	.079339	.086030	.092853	.096313	.099805	.103329	.106883	.110468	.114083	.121400	.128831	.136372	.144017
	0.00	.091524	.098215	.105038	.108498	.111990	.115514	.119068	.122653	.126267	.133585	.141016	.148556	.156202
	-.10	.103709	.110399	.117222	.120683	.124175	.127698	.131253	.134837	.138452	.145769	.153200	.160741	.168387
	-.20	.115893	.122584	.129407	.132867	.136359	.139883	.143437	.147022	.150637	.157954	.165385	.172926	.180571
	-.30	.128078	.134769	.141592	.145052	.148544	.152068	.155622	.159207	.162822	.170139	.177570	.185110	.192756
	-.40	.140263	.146953	.153776	.157237	.160729	.164252	.167807	.171391	.175006	.182323	.189754	.197295	.204941
15	.40	.033766	.041089	.048565	.052358	.056186	.060049	.063944	.067872	.071830	.079836	.087952	.096172	.104486
	.30	.045950	.053274	.060750	.064543	.068371	.072233	.076129	.080056	.084015	.092020	.100137	.108356	.116671
	.20	.058135	.065458	.072935	.076728	.080556	.084418	.088314	.092241	.096199	.104205	.112322	.120541	.128855
	.10	.070320	.077643	.085119	.088912	.092740	.096603	.100498	.104426	.108384	.116390	.124506	.132726	.141040
	0.00	.082504	.089828	.097304	.101097	.104925	.108787	.112683	.116610	.120569	.128574	.136691	.144910	.153225
	-.10	.094689	.102012	.109489	.113282	.117110	.120972	.124868	.128795	.132753	.140759	.148876	.157095	.165409
	-.20	.106874	.114197	.121673	.125466	.129294	.133157	.137052	.140980	.144938	.152944	.161060	.169280	.177594
	-.30	.119059	.126382	.133858	.137651	.141479	.145341	.149237	.153164	.157123	.165128	.173245	.181464	.189779
	-.40	.131243	.138566	.146043	.149836	.153664	.157526	.161422	.165349	.169307	.177313	.185430	.193649	.201963
20	.40	.029393	.037076	.044922	.048902	.052917	.056966	.061048	.065160	.069301	.077664	.086125	.094673	.103297
	.30	.041577	.049261	.057107	.061087	.065102	.069151	.073232	.077344	.081485	.089849	.098310	.106858	.115482
	.20	.053762	.061446	.069292	.073271	.077286	.081336	.085417	.089529	.093670	.102033	.110495	.119042	.127666
	.10	.065947	.073630	.081476	.085456	.089471	.093520	.097602	.101714	.105855	.114218	.122679	.131227	.139851
	0.00	.078131	.085815	.093661	.097641	.101656	.105705	.109786	.113898	.118039	.126403	.134864	.143412	.152036
	-.10	.090316	.098000	.105846	.109825	.113840	.117890	.121971	.126083	.130224	.138587	.147049	.155597	.164220
	-.20	.102501	.110184	.118030	.122010	.126025	.130074	.134156	.138268	.142409	.150772	.159233	.167781	.176405
	-.30	.114686	.122369	.130215	.134195	.138210	.142259	.146340	.150452	.154594	.162957	.171418	.179966	.188590
	-.40	.126870	.134554	.142400	.146379	.150395	.154444	.158525	.162637	.166778	.175141	.183603	.192151	.200775
25	.40	.026874	.034805	.042902	.047006	.051145	.055316	.059517	.063746	.068001	.076581	.085243	.093973	.102761
	.30	.039059	.046990	.055086	.059191	.063330	.067501	.071702	.075931	.080186	.088766	.097427	.106158	.114946
	.20	.051243	.059175	.067271	.071375	.075514	.079685	.083886	.088115	.092370	.100950	.109612	.118343	.127131
	.10	.063428	.071359	.079456	.083560	.087699	.091870	.096071	.100300	.104555	.113135	.121797	.130527	.139315
	0.00	.075613	.083544	.091640	.095745	.099884	.104055	.108256	.112485	.116740	.125320	.133981	.142712	.151500
	-.10	.087797	.095729	.103825	.107929	.112068	.116239	.120440	.124669	.128924	.137504	.146166	.154897	.163685
	-.20	.099982	.107913	.116010	.120114	.124253	.128424	.132625	.136854	.141109	.149689	.158351	.167081	.175869
	-.30	.112167	.120098	.128194	.132299	.136438	.140609	.144810	.149039	.153294	.161874	.170535	.179266	.188054
	-.40	.124351	.132283	.140379	.144483	.148622	.152793	.156994	.161223	.165478	.174058	.182720	.191451	.200239
30	.40	.025277	.033396	.041679	.045874	.050101	.054358	.058643	.062951	.067282	.076003	.084789	.093627	.102507
	.30	.037462	.045581	.053863	.058059	.062286	.066543	.070827	.075136	.079467	.088188	.096974	.105812	.114691
	.20	.049647	.057765	.066048	.070243	.074471	.078728	.083012	.087321	.091652	.100372	.109158	.117997	.126876
	.10	.061831	.069950	.078233	.082428	.086655	.090913	.095197	.099505	.103836	.112557	.121343	.130181	.139061
	0.00	.074016	.082135	.090417	.094613	.098840	.103097	.107381	.111690	.116021	.124742	.133528	.142366	.151245
	-.10	.086201	.094319	.102602	.106797	.111025	.115282	.119566	.123875	.128206	.136926	.145712	.154551	.163430
	-.20	.098385	.106504	.114787	.118982	.123209	.127467	.131751	.136059	.140390	.149111	.157897	.166735	.175615
	-.30	.110570	.118689	.126971	.131167	.135394	.139651	.143935	.148244	.152575	.161296	.170082	.178920	.187799
	-.40	.122755	.130873	.139156	.143351	.147579	.151836	.156120	.160429	.164760	.173480	.182266	.191105	.199984

5.0 YEAR HOLDING PERIOD
.300 EQUITY YIELD RATE
.600 LOAN RATIO

INTEREST RATE

TERM YEARS	APPR DEP	5.0	6.0	7.0	7.5	8.0	8.5	9.0	9.5	10.0	11.0	12.0	13.0	14.0
10	.40	.123077	.127455	.131922	.134188	.136475	.138784	.141114	.143464	.145834	.150634	.155511	.160462	.165484
	.30	.134135	.138513	.142980	.145246	.147534	.149842	.152172	.154522	.156892	.161692	.166569	.171520	.176542
	.20	.145193	.149571	.154038	.156304	.158592	.160901	.163230	.165580	.167950	.172750	.177627	.182578	.187600
	.10	.156251	.160629	.165096	.167362	.169650	.171959	.174288	.176638	.179009	.183809	.188685	.193636	.198659
	0.00	.167310	.171687	.176154	.178420	.180708	.183017	.185346	.187696	.190067	.194867	.199744	.204694	.209717
	-.10	.178368	.182746	.187212	.189479	.191766	.194075	.196405	.198755	.201125	.205925	.210802	.215753	.220775
	-.20	.189426	.193804	.198271	.200537	.202824	.205133	.207463	.209813	.212183	.216983	.221860	.226811	.231833
	-.30	.200484	.204862	.209329	.211595	.213883	.216191	.218521	.220871	.223241	.228041	.232918	.237869	.242891
	-.40	.211542	.215920	.220387	.222653	.224941	.227249	.229579	.231929	.234299	.239099	.243976	.248927	.253949
15	.40	.115823	.120607	.125497	.127979	.130486	.133016	.135570	.138146	.140743	.145999	.151333	.156739	.162212
	.30	.126882	.131666	.136565	.139037	.141544	.144075	.146628	.149204	.151801	.157057	.162391	.167797	.173270
	.20	.137940	.142724	.147613	.150095	.152602	.155133	.157686	.160262	.162859	.168115	.173449	.178856	.184329
	.10	.148998	.153782	.158671	.161154	.163660	.166191	.168744	.171320	.173917	.179173	.184507	.189914	.195387
	0.00	.160056	.164840	.169729	.172212	.174719	.177249	.179802	.182378	.184975	.190232	.195566	.200972	.206445
	-.10	.171114	.175898	.180787	.183270	.185777	.188307	.190861	.193436	.196034	.201290	.206624	.212030	.217503
	-.20	.182172	.186956	.191846	.194328	.196835	.199365	.201919	.204494	.207092	.212348	.217682	.223088	.228561
	-.30	.193231	.198014	.202904	.205386	.207893	.210424	.212977	.215553	.218150	.223406	.228740	.234146	.239619
	-.40	.204289	.209073	.213962	.216444	.218951	.221482	.224035	.226611	.229208	.234464	.239798	.245204	.250677
20	.40	.112307	.117331	.122470	.125080	.127714	.130373	.133055	.135759	.138483	.143990	.149568	.155209	.160906
	.30	.123365	.128390	.133528	.136138	.138773	.141431	.144113	.146817	.149541	.155048	.160626	.166267	.171964
	.20	.134423	.139448	.144587	.147196	.149831	.152489	.155171	.157875	.160599	.166106	.171684	.177325	.183022
	.10	.145481	.150506	.155645	.158254	.160889	.163548	.166229	.168933	.171657	.177165	.182742	.188383	.194080
	0.00	.156539	.161564	.166703	.169312	.171947	.174606	.177288	.179991	.182716	.188223	.193801	.199442	.205138
	-.10	.167597	.172622	.177761	.180371	.183005	.185664	.188346	.191049	.193774	.199281	.204859	.210500	.216196
	-.20	.178656	.183680	.188819	.191429	.194063	.196722	.199404	.202107	.204832	.210339	.215917	.221558	.227255
	-.30	.189714	.194739	.199877	.202487	.205122	.207780	.210462	.213166	.215890	.221397	.226975	.232616	.238313
	-.40	.200772	.205797	.210936	.213545	.216180	.218838	.221520	.224224	.226948	.232455	.238033	.243674	.249371
25	.40	.110281	.115477	.120792	.123489	.126212	.128958	.131726	.134514	.137322	.142988	.148715	.154494	.160317
	.30	.121339	.126535	.131850	.134548	.137270	.140016	.142784	.145572	.148380	.154046	.159774	.165553	.171375
	.20	.132397	.137593	.142908	.145606	.148328	.151074	.153842	.156630	.159438	.165104	.170832	.176611	.182433
	.10	.143455	.148652	.153966	.156664	.159386	.162132	.164900	.167689	.170496	.176163	.181890	.187669	.193491
	0.00	.154514	.159710	.165024	.167722	.170445	.173191	.175958	.178747	.181554	.187221	.192948	.198727	.204549
	-.10	.165572	.170768	.176082	.178780	.181503	.184249	.187017	.189805	.192612	.198279	.204006	.209785	.215608
	-.20	.176630	.181826	.187141	.189838	.192561	.195307	.198075	.200863	.203670	.209337	.215064	.220843	.226666
	-.30	.187688	.192884	.198199	.200896	.203619	.206365	.209133	.211921	.214729	.220395	.226123	.231901	.237724
	-.40	.198746	.203942	.209257	.211955	.214677	.217423	.220191	.222979	.225787	.231453	.237181	.242960	.248782
30	.40	.108997	.114327	.119776	.122540	.125327	.128137	.130967	.133815	.136680	.142453	.148277	.154141	.160037
	.30	.120055	.125385	.130834	.133598	.136385	.139195	.142025	.144873	.147738	.153512	.159335	.165199	.171095
	.20	.131113	.136443	.141892	.144656	.147444	.150253	.153083	.155931	.158796	.164570	.170393	.176257	.182153
	.10	.142171	.147501	.152950	.155714	.158502	.161311	.164141	.166989	.169854	.175628	.181452	.187315	.193211
	0.00	.153230	.158559	.164008	.166772	.169560	.172370	.175199	.178047	.180912	.186686	.192510	.198374	.204270
	-.10	.164288	.169617	.175066	.177830	.180618	.183428	.186257	.189106	.191970	.197744	.203568	.209432	.215328
	-.20	.175346	.180676	.186124	.188888	.191676	.194486	.197316	.200164	.203029	.208802	.214626	.220490	.226386
	-.30	.186404	.191734	.197183	.199947	.202734	.205544	.208374	.211222	.214087	.219861	.225684	.231548	.237444
	-.40	.197462	.202792	.208241	.211005	.213793	.216602	.219432	.222280	.225145	.230919	.236742	.242606	.248502

281

5.0 YEAR HOLDING PERIOD
.300 EQUITY YIELD RATE
.667 LOAN RATIO

INTEREST RATE

TERM YEARS	APPR DEP	5.0	6.0	7.0	7.5	8.0	8.5	9.0	9.5	10.0	11.0	12.0	13.0	14.0
10	.40	.108333	.113197	.118160	.120678	.123220	.125785	.128374	.130985	.133619	.138952	.144371	.149872	.155452
	.30	.119391	.124255	.129218	.131736	.134278	.136844	.139432	.142043	.144677	.150010	.155429	.160930	.166510
	.20	.130449	.135313	.140277	.142795	.145336	.147902	.150490	.153101	.155735	.161068	.166487	.171988	.177569
	.10	.141507	.146372	.151335	.153853	.156395	.158960	.161548	.164160	.166793	.172126	.177545	.183046	.188627
	0.00	.152565	.157430	.162393	.164911	.167453	.170018	.172606	.175218	.177851	.183185	.188603	.194104	.199685
	-.10	.163624	.168488	.173451	.175969	.178511	.181076	.183665	.186276	.188910	.194243	.199661	.205163	.210743
	-.20	.174682	.179546	.184509	.187027	.189569	.192134	.194723	.197334	.199968	.205301	.210720	.216221	.221801
	-.30	.185740	.190604	.195567	.198085	.200627	.203192	.205781	.208392	.211026	.216359	.221778	.227279	.232859
	-.40	.196798	.201662	.206626	.209144	.211685	.214251	.216839	.219450	.222084	.227417	.232836	.238337	.243917
15	.40	.100273	.105589	.111021	.113780	.116565	.119377	.122214	.125076	.127962	.133802	.139729	.145736	.151817
	.30	.111331	.116647	.122080	.124838	.127623	.130435	.133272	.136134	.139020	.144860	.150787	.156794	.162875
	.20	.122390	.127705	.133138	.135896	.138681	.141493	.144330	.147192	.150078	.155918	.161845	.167852	.173933
	.10	.133448	.138763	.144196	.146954	.149740	.152551	.155388	.158250	.161136	.166976	.172903	.178910	.184991
	0.00	.144506	.149821	.155254	.158012	.160798	.163609	.166447	.169308	.172194	.178034	.183961	.189968	.196049
	-.10	.155564	.160880	.166312	.169071	.171856	.174668	.177505	.180367	.183252	.189093	.195019	.201026	.207107
	-.20	.166622	.171938	.177370	.180129	.182914	.185726	.188563	.191425	.194310	.200151	.206078	.212084	.218166
	-.30	.177680	.182996	.188428	.191187	.193972	.196784	.199621	.202483	.205369	.211209	.217136	.223143	.229224
	-.40	.188739	.194054	.199487	.202245	.205030	.207842	.210679	.213541	.216427	.222267	.228194	.234201	.240282
20	.40	.096366	.101949	.107659	.110558	.113486	.116440	.119419	.122424	.125451	.131570	.137768	.144035	.150365
	.30	.107424	.113007	.118717	.121616	.124544	.127498	.130478	.133482	.136509	.142628	.148826	.155093	.161423
	.20	.118482	.124065	.129775	.132674	.135602	.138556	.141536	.144540	.147567	.153686	.159884	.166152	.172481
	.10	.129540	.135123	.140833	.143733	.146660	.149614	.152594	.155598	.158625	.164744	.170942	.177210	.183539
	0.00	.140598	.146182	.151891	.154791	.157718	.160672	.163652	.166656	.169683	.175802	.182000	.188268	.194598
	-.10	.151657	.157240	.162950	.165849	.168776	.171731	.174710	.177714	.180741	.186861	.193058	.199326	.205656
	-.20	.162715	.168298	.174008	.176907	.179835	.182789	.185768	.188772	.191800	.197919	.204116	.210384	.216714
	-.30	.173773	.179356	.185066	.187965	.190893	.193847	.196827	.199831	.202858	.208977	.215175	.221442	.227772
	-.40	.184831	.190414	.196124	.199023	.201951	.204905	.207885	.210889	.213916	.220035	.226233	.232501	.238830
25	.40	.094115	.099889	.105794	.108791	.111816	.114867	.117943	.121041	.124160	.130456	.136820	.143241	.149711
	.30	.105173	.110947	.116852	.119849	.122874	.125925	.129001	.132099	.135218	.141515	.147878	.154299	.160769
	.20	.116231	.122005	.127910	.130907	.133933	.136984	.140059	.143157	.146277	.152573	.158937	.165358	.171827
	.10	.127289	.133063	.138968	.141966	.144991	.148042	.151117	.154215	.157335	.163631	.169995	.176416	.182885
	0.00	.138348	.144121	.150026	.153024	.156049	.159100	.162175	.165274	.168393	.174689	.181053	.187474	.193943
	-.10	.149406	.155179	.161084	.164082	.167107	.170158	.173234	.176332	.179451	.185747	.192111	.198532	.205001
	-.20	.160464	.166237	.172143	.175140	.178165	.181216	.184292	.187390	.190509	.196805	.203169	.209590	.216060
	-.30	.171522	.177296	.183201	.186198	.189223	.192274	.195350	.198448	.201567	.207864	.214227	.220648	.227118
	-.40	.182580	.188354	.194259	.197256	.200281	.203333	.206408	.209506	.212625	.218922	.225285	.231707	.238176
30	.40	.092688	.098610	.104665	.107736	.110833	.113955	.117099	.120264	.123447	.129862	.136333	.142849	.149400
	.30	.103747	.109668	.115723	.118794	.121891	.125013	.128157	.131322	.134505	.140921	.147391	.153907	.160458
	.20	.114805	.120727	.126781	.129852	.132950	.136071	.139216	.142380	.145563	.151979	.158449	.164965	.171516
	.10	.125863	.131785	.137839	.140910	.144008	.147130	.150274	.153438	.156621	.163037	.169508	.176023	.182574
	0.00	.136921	.142843	.148897	.151968	.155066	.158188	.161332	.164496	.167680	.174095	.180566	.187081	.193632
	-.10	.147979	.153901	.159955	.163026	.166124	.169246	.172390	.175555	.178738	.185153	.191624	.198139	.204691
	-.20	.159037	.164959	.171014	.174085	.177182	.180304	.183448	.186613	.189796	.196211	.202682	.209197	.215749
	-.30	.170095	.176017	.182072	.185143	.188240	.191362	.194506	.197671	.200854	.207269	.213740	.220256	.226807
	-.40	.181154	.187075	.193130	.196201	.199299	.202420	.205565	.208729	.211912	.218328	.224798	.231314	.237865

5.0 YEAR HOLDING PERIOD
.300 EQUITY YIELD RATE
.700 LOAN RATIO

INTEREST RATE

TERM YEARS	APPR DEP	5.0	6.0	7.0	7.5	8.0	8.5	9.0	9.5	10.0	11.0	12.0	13.0	14.0
10	.40	.100962	.106069	.111281	.113925	.116593	.119287	.122005	.124747	.127512	.133112	.138801	.144578	.150437
	.30	.112020	.117127	.122339	.124983	.127652	.130345	.133063	.135805	.138570	.144170	.149860	.155636	.161495
	.20	.123078	.128186	.133397	.136041	.138710	.141403	.144121	.146863	.149628	.155228	.160918	.166694	.172553
	.10	.134136	.139244	.144455	.147099	.149768	.152461	.155179	.157921	.160686	.166286	.171976	.177752	.183611
	0.00	.145194	.150302	.155513	.158157	.160826	.163520	.166237	.168979	.171745	.177345	.183034	.188810	.194670
	-.10	.156253	.161360	.166571	.169215	.171884	.174578	.177296	.180037	.182803	.188403	.194092	.199868	.205728
	-.20	.167311	.172418	.177630	.180273	.182942	.185636	.188354	.191096	.193861	.199461	.205150	.210927	.216786
	-.30	.178369	.183476	.188688	.191332	.194001	.196694	.199412	.202154	.204919	.210519	.216209	.221985	.227844
	-.40	.189427	.194535	.199746	.202390	.205059	.207752	.210470	.213212	.215977	.221577	.227267	.233043	.238902
15	.40	.092499	.098081	.103785	.106681	.109606	.112558	.115537	.118542	.121572	.127704	.133927	.140235	.146620
	.30	.103558	.109139	.114843	.117739	.120664	.123616	.126595	.129600	.132630	.138762	.144985	.151293	.157678
	.20	.114616	.120197	.125901	.128797	.131722	.134674	.137653	.140658	.143688	.149821	.156044	.162351	.168736
	.10	.125674	.131255	.136959	.139856	.142780	.145732	.148711	.151716	.154746	.160879	.167102	.173409	.179794
	0.00	.136732	.142313	.148017	.150914	.153838	.156791	.159770	.162774	.165805	.171937	.178160	.184467	.190852
	-.10	.147790	.153371	.159076	.161972	.164897	.167849	.170828	.173833	.176863	.182995	.189218	.195525	.201910
	-.20	.158848	.164430	.170134	.173030	.175955	.178907	.181886	.184891	.187921	.194053	.200276	.206583	.212969
	-.30	.169907	.175488	.181192	.184088	.187013	.189965	.192944	.195949	.198979	.205111	.211334	.217642	.224027
	-.40	.180965	.186546	.192250	.195146	.198071	.201023	.204002	.207007	.210037	.216169	.222392	.228700	.235085
20	.40	.088397	.094259	.100254	.103299	.106372	.109474	.112603	.115757	.118936	.125361	.131868	.138449	.145095
	.30	.099455	.105317	.111312	.114357	.117430	.120532	.123661	.126815	.129994	.136419	.142926	.149507	.156153
	.20	.110513	.116375	.122370	.125415	.128489	.131590	.134719	.137873	.141052	.147477	.153984	.160566	.167212
	.10	.121571	.127433	.133429	.136473	.139547	.142649	.145777	.148932	.152110	.158535	.165043	.171624	.178270
	0.00	.132629	.138491	.144487	.147531	.150605	.153707	.156835	.159990	.163168	.169593	.176101	.182682	.189328
	-.10	.143687	.149550	.155545	.158589	.161663	.164765	.167894	.171048	.174226	.180651	.187159	.193740	.200386
	-.20	.154745	.160608	.166603	.169647	.172721	.175823	.178952	.182106	.185284	.191709	.198217	.204798	.211444
	-.30	.165804	.171666	.177661	.180706	.183779	.186881	.190010	.193164	.196343	.202768	.209275	.215856	.222502
	-.40	.176862	.182724	.188719	.191764	.194838	.197939	.201068	.204222	.207401	.213826	.220333	.226914	.233561
25	.40	.086033	.092095	.098296	.101443	.104619	.107823	.111052	.114305	.117581	.124192	.130873	.137616	.144408
	.30	.097091	.103154	.109354	.112501	.115678	.118881	.122110	.125363	.128639	.135250	.141932	.148674	.155466
	.20	.108150	.114212	.120412	.123559	.126736	.129939	.133169	.136422	.139697	.146308	.152990	.159732	.166525
	.10	.119208	.125270	.131470	.134618	.137794	.140998	.144227	.147480	.150755	.157366	.164048	.170790	.177583
	0.00	.130266	.136328	.142528	.145676	.148852	.152056	.155285	.158538	.161813	.168424	.175106	.181848	.188641
	-.10	.141324	.147386	.153586	.156734	.159910	.163114	.166343	.169596	.172871	.179482	.186164	.192906	.199699
	-.20	.152382	.158444	.164645	.167792	.170968	.174172	.177401	.180654	.183930	.190541	.197222	.203965	.210757
	-.30	.163440	.169503	.175703	.178850	.182027	.185230	.188459	.191712	.194988	.201599	.208281	.215023	.221815
	-.40	.174498	.180561	.186761	.189908	.193085	.196288	.199518	.202771	.206046	.212657	.219339	.226081	.232874
30	.40	.084535	.090753	.097110	.100335	.103587	.106865	.110167	.113489	.116832	.123568	.130362	.137203	.144082
	.30	.095593	.101811	.108168	.111393	.114645	.117923	.121225	.124548	.127890	.134626	.141420	.148261	.155140
	.20	.106652	.112870	.119227	.122451	.125704	.128982	.132283	.135606	.138948	.145684	.152478	.159320	.166198
	.10	.117710	.123928	.130285	.133509	.136762	.140040	.143341	.146664	.150006	.156742	.163536	.170378	.177256
	0.00	.128768	.134986	.141343	.144568	.147820	.151098	.154399	.157722	.161064	.167800	.174595	.181436	.188315
	-.10	.139826	.146044	.152401	.155626	.158878	.162156	.165457	.168780	.172122	.178859	.185653	.192494	.199373
	-.20	.150884	.157102	.163459	.166684	.169936	.173214	.176516	.179838	.183181	.189917	.196711	.203552	.210431
	-.30	.161942	.168160	.174517	.177742	.180994	.184272	.187574	.190896	.194239	.200975	.207769	.214610	.221489
	-.40	.173000	.179218	.185575	.188800	.192053	.195330	.198632	.201955	.205297	.212033	.218827	.225668	.232547

5.0 YEAR HOLDING PERIOD
.300 EQUITY YIELD RATE
.750 LOAN RATIO

INTEREST RATE

TERM YEARS	APPR DEP	5.0	6.0	7.0	7.5	8.0	8.5	9.0	9.5	10.0	11.0	12.0	13.0	14.0
10	.40	.089904	.095377	.100960	.103793	.106652	.109538	.112450	.115388	.118351	.124351	.130447	.136635	.142913
	.30	.100962	.106435	.112018	.114851	.117711	.120597	.123509	.126446	.129409	.135409	.141505	.147694	.153972
	.20	.112021	.117493	.123077	.125909	.128769	.131655	.134567	.137504	.140467	.146467	.152563	.158752	.165030
	.10	.123079	.128551	.134135	.136967	.139827	.142713	.145625	.148562	.151525	.157525	.163621	.169810	.176088
	0.00	.134137	.139609	.145193	.148026	.150885	.153771	.156683	.159621	.162583	.168583	.174679	.180868	.187146
	-.10	.145195	.150667	.156251	.159084	.161943	.164829	.167741	.170679	.173642	.179642	.185738	.191926	.198204
	-.20	.156253	.161726	.167309	.170142	.173001	.175887	.178799	.181737	.184700	.190700	.196796	.202984	.209262
	-.30	.167311	.172784	.178367	.181200	.184060	.186945	.189857	.192795	.195758	.201758	.207854	.214043	.220320
	-.40	.178370	.183842	.189425	.192258	.195118	.198004	.200916	.203853	.206816	.212816	.218912	.225101	.231379
15	.40	.080837	.086817	.092929	.096032	.099166	.102329	.105520	.108740	.111987	.118557	.125224	.131982	.138823
	.30	.091896	.097876	.103987	.107090	.110224	.113387	.116579	.119798	.123045	.129615	.136283	.143040	.149882
	.20	.102954	.108934	.115045	.118148	.121282	.124445	.127637	.130856	.134103	.140673	.147341	.154098	.160940
	.10	.114012	.119992	.126103	.129207	.132340	.135503	.138695	.141915	.145162	.151731	.158399	.165157	.171998
	0.00	.125070	.131050	.137162	.140265	.143398	.146561	.149753	.152973	.156219	.162789	.169457	.176215	.183056
	-.10	.136128	.142108	.148220	.151323	.154456	.157619	.160811	.164031	.167277	.173848	.180515	.187273	.194114
	-.20	.147186	.153166	.159278	.162381	.165515	.168678	.171869	.175089	.178335	.184906	.191573	.198331	.205172
	-.30	.158245	.164224	.170336	.173439	.176573	.179736	.182928	.186147	.189394	.195964	.202631	.209389	.216231
	-.40	.169303	.175283	.181394	.184497	.187631	.190794	.193986	.197205	.200452	.207022	.213690	.220447	.227289
20	.40	.076441	.082722	.089146	.092408	.095701	.099025	.102377	.105756	.109162	.116046	.123018	.130069	.137190
	.30	.087500	.093781	.100204	.103466	.106759	.110083	.113435	.116814	.120220	.127104	.134076	.141128	.148248
	.20	.098558	.104839	.111262	.114524	.117817	.121141	.124493	.127873	.131278	.138162	.145135	.152186	.159306
	.10	.109616	.115897	.122321	.125582	.128876	.132199	.135551	.138931	.142336	.149220	.156193	.163244	.170365
	0.00	.120674	.126955	.133379	.136640	.139934	.143257	.146609	.149989	.153394	.160278	.167251	.174302	.181423
	-.10	.131732	.138013	.144437	.147699	.150992	.154315	.157668	.161047	.164453	.171337	.178309	.185360	.192481
	-.20	.142790	.149071	.155495	.158757	.162050	.165374	.168726	.172105	.175511	.182395	.189367	.196418	.203539
	-.30	.153849	.160130	.166553	.169815	.173108	.176432	.179784	.183163	.186569	.193453	.200425	.207476	.214597
	-.40	.164907	.171188	.177616	.180873	.184166	.187490	.190842	.194222	.197627	.204511	.211483	.218535	.225655
25	.40	.073909	.080405	.087048	.090420	.093823	.097256	.100715	.104201	.107710	.114793	.121952	.129176	.136454
	.30	.084967	.091463	.098106	.101478	.104881	.108314	.111774	.115259	.118768	.125851	.133011	.140234	.147512
	.20	.096026	.102521	.109164	.112536	.115939	.119372	.122832	.126317	.129826	.136910	.144069	.151292	.158570
	.10	.107084	.113579	.120222	.123594	.126998	.130430	.133890	.137375	.140885	.147968	.155127	.162351	.169629
	0.00	.118142	.124637	.131280	.134653	.138056	.141488	.144948	.148434	.151943	.159026	.166185	.173409	.180687
	-.10	.129200	.135695	.142339	.145711	.149114	.152546	.156006	.159492	.163001	.170084	.177243	.184467	.191745
	-.20	.140258	.146753	.153397	.156769	.160172	.163605	.167064	.170550	.174059	.181142	.188301	.195525	.202803
	-.30	.151316	.157812	.164455	.167827	.171230	.174663	.178123	.181608	.185117	.192200	.199360	.206583	.213861
	-.40	.162375	.168870	.175513	.178885	.182288	.185721	.189181	.192666	.196175	.203259	.210418	.217641	.224919
30	.40	.072304	.078966	.085778	.089233	.092717	.096229	.099767	.103327	.106908	.114125	.121404	.128734	.136104
	.30	.083363	.090025	.096836	.100291	.103775	.107288	.110825	.114385	.117966	.125183	.132463	.139792	.147163
	.20	.094421	.101083	.107894	.111349	.114834	.118346	.121883	.125443	.129024	.136241	.143521	.150851	.158221
	.10	.105479	.112141	.118952	.122407	.125892	.129404	.132941	.136501	.140082	.147299	.154579	.161909	.169279
	0.00	.116537	.123199	.130010	.133465	.136950	.140462	.143999	.147559	.151140	.158358	.165637	.172967	.180337
	-.10	.127595	.134257	.141068	.144523	.148008	.151520	.155057	.158617	.162198	.169416	.176695	.184025	.191395
	-.20	.138653	.145315	.152127	.155582	.159066	.162578	.166115	.169676	.173257	.180474	.187753	.195083	.202453
	-.30	.149711	.156374	.163185	.166640	.170124	.173636	.177174	.180734	.184315	.191532	.198812	.206141	.213511
	-.40	.160770	.167432	.174243	.177698	.181183	.184695	.188232	.191792	.195373	.202590	.209870	.217200	.224570

5.0 YEAR HOLDING PERIOD
.300 EQUITY YIELD RATE
.800 LOAN RATIO

INTEREST RATE

TERM YEARS	APPR DEP	5.0	6.0	7.0	7.5	8.0	8.5	9.0	9.5	10.0	11.0	12.0	13.0	14.0
10	.40	.078847	.084684	.090640	.093661	.096711	.099790	.102896	.106029	.109190	.115590	.122092	.128693	.135390
	.30	.089905	.095742	.101698	.104719	.107770	.110848	.113954	.117088	.120248	.126648	.133150	.139751	.146448
	.20	.100963	.106800	.112756	.115778	.118828	.121906	.125012	.128146	.131306	.137706	.144208	.150810	.157506
	.10	.112021	.117858	.123814	.126836	.129886	.132964	.136070	.139204	.142364	.148764	.155267	.161868	.168564
	0.00	.123079	.128916	.134872	.137894	.140944	.144022	.147129	.150262	.153422	.159822	.166325	.172926	.179622
	-.10	.134138	.139975	.145931	.148952	.152002	.155081	.158187	.161320	.164481	.170880	.177383	.183984	.190681
	-.20	.145196	.151033	.156989	.160010	.163060	.166139	.169245	.172378	.175539	.181939	.188441	.195042	.201739
	-.30	.156254	.162091	.168047	.171068	.174119	.177197	.180303	.183436	.186597	.192997	.199499	.206100	.212797
	-.40	.167312	.173149	.179105	.182127	.185177	.188255	.191361	.194495	.197655	.204055	.210557	.217159	.223855
15	.40	.069175	.075554	.082073	.085383	.088726	.092099	.095504	.098938	.102401	.109410	.116522	.123730	.131027
	.30	.080234	.086612	.093131	.096441	.099784	.103158	.106562	.109996	.113459	.120468	.127580	.134788	.142085
	.20	.091292	.097670	.104189	.107499	.110842	.114216	.117620	.121055	.124517	.131526	.138638	.145846	.153143
	.10	.102350	.108728	.115248	.118558	.121900	.125274	.128678	.132113	.135576	.142584	.149696	.156904	.164202
	0.00	.113408	.119787	.126306	.129616	.132958	.136332	.139737	.143171	.146634	.153642	.160754	.167962	.175260
	-.10	.124466	.130845	.137364	.140674	.144016	.147390	.150795	.154229	.157692	.164700	.171812	.179021	.186318
	-.20	.135524	.141903	.148422	.151732	.155074	.158448	.161853	.165287	.168750	.175758	.182870	.190079	.197376
	-.30	.146583	.152961	.159480	.162790	.166133	.169507	.172911	.176345	.179808	.186817	.193929	.201137	.208434
	-.40	.157641	.164019	.170538	.173848	.177191	.180565	.183969	.187403	.190866	.197875	.204987	.212195	.219492
20	.40	.064486	.071186	.078038	.081517	.085030	.088575	.092151	.095756	.099388	.106731	.114168	.121690	.129285
	.30	.075545	.082244	.089096	.092575	.096088	.099633	.103209	.106814	.110446	.117789	.125226	.132748	.140343
	.20	.086603	.093302	.100154	.103634	.107146	.110691	.114267	.117872	.121504	.128847	.136285	.143806	.151401
	.10	.097661	.104361	.111212	.114692	.118205	.121750	.125325	.128930	.132563	.139905	.147343	.154864	.162460
	0.00	.108719	.115419	.122271	.125750	.129263	.132808	.136383	.139988	.143621	.150964	.158401	.165922	.173518
	-.10	.119777	.126477	.133329	.136808	.140321	.143866	.147442	.151046	.154679	.162022	.169459	.176980	.184576
	-.20	.130835	.137535	.144387	.147866	.151379	.154924	.158500	.162105	.165737	.173080	.180517	.188038	.195634
	-.30	.141894	.148593	.155445	.158924	.162437	.165982	.169558	.173163	.176795	.184138	.191575	.199097	.206692
	-.40	.152952	.159651	.166503	.169982	.173495	.177040	.180616	.184221	.187853	.195196	.202633	.210155	.217750
25	.40	.061785	.068714	.075800	.079397	.083027	.086688	.090379	.094096	.097840	.105395	.113031	.120737	.128500
	.30	.072844	.079772	.086858	.090455	.094085	.097746	.101437	.105155	.108898	.116453	.124090	.131795	.139558
	.20	.083902	.090830	.097916	.101513	.105143	.108804	.112495	.116213	.119956	.127511	.135148	.142853	.150616
	.10	.094960	.101888	.108974	.112571	.116201	.119863	.123553	.127271	.131014	.138570	.146206	.153911	.161674
	0.00	.106018	.112946	.120032	.123629	.127259	.130921	.134611	.138329	.142072	.149628	.157264	.164969	.172733
	-.10	.117076	.124004	.131091	.134687	.138318	.141979	.145669	.149387	.153130	.160686	.168322	.176028	.183791
	-.20	.128134	.135063	.142149	.145746	.149376	.153037	.156728	.160445	.164189	.171744	.179380	.187086	.194849
	-.30	.139193	.146121	.153207	.156804	.160434	.164095	.167786	.171504	.175247	.182802	.190439	.198144	.205907
	-.40	.150251	.157179	.164265	.167862	.171492	.175153	.178844	.182562	.186305	.193860	.201497	.209202	.216965
30	.40	.060074	.067180	.074445	.078130	.081847	.085594	.089367	.093164	.096984	.104682	.112447	.120265	.128127
	.30	.071132	.078238	.085503	.089188	.092905	.096652	.100425	.104222	.108042	.115740	.123505	.131324	.139185
	.20	.082190	.089296	.096561	.100247	.103964	.107710	.111483	.115280	.119100	.126798	.134563	.142382	.150243
	.10	.093248	.100354	.107619	.111305	.115022	.118768	.122541	.126338	.130158	.137857	.145621	.153440	.161301
	0.00	.104306	.111412	.118678	.122363	.126080	.129826	.133599	.137397	.141216	.148915	.156680	.164498	.172360
	-.10	.115364	.122471	.129736	.133421	.137138	.140884	.144657	.148455	.152274	.159973	.167738	.175556	.183418
	-.20	.126422	.133529	.140794	.144479	.148196	.151942	.155715	.159513	.163333	.171031	.178796	.186614	.194476
	-.30	.137481	.144587	.151852	.155537	.159254	.163001	.166774	.170571	.174391	.182089	.189854	.197673	.205534
	-.40	.148539	.155645	.162910	.166596	.170313	.174059	.177832	.181629	.185449	.193147	.200912	.208731	.216592

5.0 YEAR HOLDING PERIOD
.300 EQUITY YIELD RATE
.900 LOAN RATIO

INTEREST RATE

TERM YEARS	APPR DEP	5.0	6.0	7.0	7.5	8.0	8.5	9.0	9.5	10.0	11.0	12.0	13.0	14.0
10	.40	.056732	.063298	.069999	.073398	.076829	.080293	.083787	.087312	.090868	.098067	.105383	.112809	.120343
	.30	.067790	.074357	.081057	.084456	.087888	.091351	.094845	.098370	.101926	.109126	.116441	.123867	.131401
	.20	.078848	.085415	.092115	.095514	.098946	.102409	.105903	.109428	.112984	.120184	.127499	.134925	.142459
	.10	.089906	.096473	.103173	.106573	.110004	.113467	.116961	.120487	.124042	.131242	.138557	.145984	.153517
	0.00	.100964	.107531	.114231	.117631	.121062	.124525	.128020	.131545	.135100	.142300	.149615	.157042	.164575
	-.10	.112023	.118589	.125290	.128689	.132120	.135583	.139078	.142603	.146158	.153358	.160673	.168100	.175633
	-.20	.123081	.129647	.136348	.139747	.143178	.146642	.150136	.153661	.157217	.164416	.171732	.179158	.186692
	-.30	.134139	.140705	.147406	.150805	.154237	.157700	.161194	.164719	.168275	.175475	.182790	.190216	.197750
	-.40	.145197	.151764	.158464	.161863	.165295	.168758	.172252	.175777	.179333	.186533	.193848	.201274	.208808
15	.40	.045851	.053027	.060361	.064085	.067845	.071641	.075471	.079335	.083230	.091115	.099116	.107225	.115435
	.30	.056910	.064086	.071419	.075143	.078903	.082699	.086529	.090393	.094289	.102173	.110174	.118283	.126493
	.20	.067968	.075144	.082478	.086201	.089962	.093757	.097587	.101451	.105347	.113231	.121232	.129341	.137551
	.10	.079026	.086202	.093536	.097259	.101020	.104815	.108646	.112509	.116405	.124289	.132290	.140400	.148609
	0.00	.090084	.097260	.104594	.108318	.112078	.115874	.119704	.123567	.127463	.135347	.143348	.151458	.159667
	-.10	.101142	.108318	.115652	.119376	.123136	.126932	.130762	.134625	.138521	.146406	.154407	.162516	.170725
	-.20	.112200	.119376	.126710	.130434	.134194	.137990	.141820	.145684	.149580	.157464	.165465	.173574	.181784
	-.30	.123259	.130434	.137768	.141492	.145252	.149048	.152878	.156742	.160637	.168522	.176523	.184632	.192842
	-.40	.134317	.141493	.148827	.152550	.156311	.160106	.163936	.167800	.171696	.179580	.187581	.195690	.203900
20	.40	.040576	.048114	.055822	.059736	.063688	.067676	.071699	.075754	.079841	.088101	.096468	.104930	.113475
	.30	.051634	.059172	.066880	.070794	.074746	.078734	.082757	.086812	.090899	.099160	.107527	.115988	.124533
	.20	.062693	.070230	.077938	.081852	.085804	.089792	.093815	.097870	.101957	.110218	.118585	.127046	.135591
	.10	.073751	.081288	.088996	.092910	.096862	.100851	.104873	.108929	.113015	.121276	.129643	.138104	.146649
	0.00	.084809	.092346	.100054	.103969	.107921	.111909	.115931	.119987	.124073	.132334	.140701	.149162	.157707
	-.10	.095867	.103404	.111113	.115027	.118979	.122967	.126989	.131045	.135132	.143392	.151759	.160221	.168766
	-.20	.106925	.114462	.122171	.126085	.130037	.134025	.138048	.142103	.146190	.154450	.162817	.171279	.179824
	-.30	.117983	.125521	.133229	.137143	.141095	.145083	.149106	.153161	.157248	.165509	.173875	.182337	.190882
	-.40	.129042	.136579	.144287	.148201	.152153	.156141	.160164	.164219	.168306	.176567	.184934	.193395	.201940
25	.40	.037538	.045332	.053304	.057350	.061434	.065553	.069705	.073888	.078099	.086599	.095190	.103858	.112591
	.30	.048596	.056390	.064362	.068409	.072492	.076611	.080763	.084946	.089157	.097657	.106248	.114916	.123650
	.20	.059654	.067448	.075420	.079467	.083551	.087670	.091821	.096004	.100215	.108715	.117306	.125974	.134708
	.10	.070712	.078506	.086478	.090525	.094609	.098728	.102880	.107062	.111273	.119773	.128364	.137032	.145766
	0.00	.081770	.089565	.097536	.101583	.105667	.109786	.113938	.118120	.122331	.130831	.139422	.148091	.156824
	-.10	.092828	.100623	.108595	.112641	.116725	.120844	.124996	.129178	.133389	.141889	.150480	.159149	.167882
	-.20	.103887	.111681	.119653	.123699	.127783	.131902	.136054	.140237	.144448	.152947	.161538	.170207	.178940
	-.30	.114945	.122739	.130711	.134757	.138841	.142960	.147112	.151295	.155506	.164006	.172597	.181265	.189999
	-.40	.126003	.133797	.141769	.145816	.149900	.154019	.158170	.162353	.166564	.175064	.183655	.192323	.201057
30	.40	.035612	.043606	.051780	.055926	.060107	.064322	.068566	.072839	.077136	.085796	.094532	.103328	.112172
	.30	.046670	.054664	.062838	.066984	.071165	.075380	.079625	.083897	.088194	.096855	.105590	.114386	.123230
	.20	.057728	.065723	.073896	.078042	.082224	.086438	.090683	.094955	.099252	.107913	.116648	.125444	.134288
	.10	.068786	.076781	.084954	.089100	.093282	.097496	.101741	.106013	.110310	.118971	.127706	.136502	.145346
	0.00	.079844	.087839	.095012	.100158	.104340	.108554	.112799	.117071	.121368	.130029	.138765	.147560	.156404
	-.10	.090903	.098897	.107060	.111216	.115398	.119613	.123857	.128129	.132427	.141087	.149823	.158618	.167463
	-.20	.101961	.109955	.118129	.122275	.126456	.130671	.134915	.139187	.143485	.152145	.160881	.169677	.178521
	-.30	.113019	.121013	.129181	.133333	.137514	.141729	.145973	.150246	.154543	.163204	.171939	.180735	.189579
	-.40	.124077	.132072	.140245	.144391	.148573	.152787	.157032	.161304	.165601	.174262	.182997	.191793	.200637

5.0 YEAR HOLDING PERIOD
.400 EQUITY YIELD RATE
.600 LOAN RATIO

INTEREST RATE

TERM YEARS	APPR DEP	5.0	6.0	7.0	7.5	8.0	8.5	9.0	9.5	10.0	11.0	12.0	13.0	14.0
10	.40	.175816	.180053	.184380	.186577	.188795	.191036	.193297	.195579	.197882	.202548	.207293	.212115	.217009
	.30	.184952	.189189	.193516	.195713	.197932	.200172	.202433	.204715	.207018	.211684	.216493	.221251	.226145
	.20	.194088	.198325	.202652	.204849	.207068	.209308	.211569	.213851	.216154	.220821	.225566	.230387	.235282
	.10	.203224	.207461	.211788	.213985	.216204	.218444	.220705	.222987	.225290	.229957	.234702	.239523	.244418
	0.00	.212360	.216597	.220924	.223121	.225340	.227580	.229841	.232123	.234426	.239093	.243838	.248659	.253554
	-.10	.221496	.225733	.230060	.232257	.234476	.236716	.238977	.241260	.243562	.248229	.252974	.257795	.262690
	-.20	.230632	.234869	.239197	.241393	.243612	.245852	.248113	.250396	.252699	.257365	.262110	.266931	.271826
	-.30	.239768	.244005	.248333	.250529	.252748	.254988	.257250	.259532	.261835	.266501	.271246	.276067	.280962
	-.40	.248905	.253142	.257469	.259666	.261884	.264124	.266386	.268668	.270971	.275637	.280382	.285203	.290098
15	.40	.166446	.171062	.175790	.178193	.180623	.183078	.185557	.188060	.190586	.195704	.200907	.206187	.211541
	.30	.175582	.180198	.184926	.187330	.189759	.192214	.194693	.197196	.199722	.204840	.210043	.215324	.220677
	.20	.184718	.189335	.194062	.196466	.198895	.201350	.203829	.206332	.208858	.213976	.219179	.224460	.229814
	.10	.193854	.198471	.203198	.205602	.208031	.210486	.212965	.215468	.217994	.223112	.228315	.233596	.238950
	0.00	.202990	.207607	.212334	.214738	.217167	.219622	.222101	.224604	.227130	.232248	.237451	.242732	.248086
	-.10	.212126	.216743	.221470	.223874	.226303	.228758	.231237	.233740	.236266	.241385	.246587	.251868	.257222
	-.20	.221262	.225879	.230606	.233010	.235440	.237894	.240373	.242876	.245402	.250521	.255723	.261004	.266358
	-.30	.230398	.235015	.239742	.242146	.244576	.247030	.249509	.252012	.254538	.259657	.264859	.270140	.275494
	-.40	.239535	.244151	.248878	.251282	.253712	.256166	.258645	.261148	.263674	.268793	.273995	.279276	.284630
20	.40	.161903	.166761	.171744	.174279	.176841	.179431	.182045	.184685	.187347	.192738	.198208	.203751	.209358
	.30	.171039	.175897	.180880	.183415	.185977	.188567	.191182	.193821	.196483	.201874	.207344	.212887	.218494
	.20	.180175	.185033	.190016	.192551	.195113	.197703	.200318	.202957	.205619	.211010	.216481	.222023	.227630
	.10	.189311	.194169	.199152	.201687	.204250	.206839	.209454	.212093	.214756	.220146	.225617	.231159	.236766
	0.00	.198447	.203306	.208288	.210823	.213386	.215975	.218590	.221229	.223892	.229282	.234753	.240295	.245902
	-.10	.207583	.212442	.217424	.219959	.222522	.225111	.227726	.230365	.233028	.238418	.243889	.249431	.255038
	-.20	.216720	.221578	.226560	.229096	.231658	.234247	.236862	.239501	.242164	.247554	.253028	.258568	.264174
	-.30	.225856	.230714	.235696	.238231	.240794	.243383	.245998	.248637	.251300	.256690	.262161	.267704	.273310
	-.40	.234992	.239850	.244832	.247367	.249930	.252519	.255134	.257773	.260436	.265826	.271297	.276840	.282447
25	.40	.159286	.164326	.169499	.172131	.174791	.177478	.180190	.182925	.185683	.191258	.196905	.202613	.208374
	.30	.168422	.173463	.178635	.181267	.183927	.186614	.189326	.192061	.194819	.200394	.206041	.211749	.217510
	.20	.177558	.182599	.187771	.190403	.193063	.195750	.198462	.201198	.203955	.209530	.215177	.220885	.226646
	.10	.186694	.191735	.196907	.199539	.202199	.204886	.207598	.210334	.213091	.218666	.224313	.230021	.235782
	0.00	.195830	.200871	.206043	.208675	.211336	.214022	.216734	.219470	.222227	.227803	.233449	.239158	.244918
	-.10	.204967	.210007	.215180	.217812	.220472	.223159	.225870	.228606	.231363	.236939	.242585	.248294	.254054
	-.20	.214103	.219143	.224316	.226948	.229608	.232295	.235007	.237742	.240499	.246075	.251722	.257430	.263190
	-.30	.223239	.228279	.233452	.236084	.238744	.241431	.244143	.246878	.249636	.255211	.260858	.266566	.272326
	-.40	.232375	.237415	.242588	.245220	.247880	.250567	.253279	.256014	.258772	.264347	.269994	.275702	.281462
30	.40	.157628	.162816	.168141	.170849	.173584	.176345	.179130	.181937	.184763	.190469	.196235	.202020	.207906
	.30	.166764	.171952	.177277	.179985	.182720	.185481	.188266	.191073	.193899	.199605	.205371	.211187	.217042
	.20	.175900	.181088	.186413	.189121	.191856	.194618	.197402	.200209	.203035	.208741	.214507	.220323	.226178
	.10	.185036	.190224	.195549	.198257	.200992	.203754	.206538	.209345	.212171	.217877	.223643	.229459	.235314
	0.00	.194172	.199360	.204685	.207393	.210129	.212890	.215674	.218481	.221307	.227013	.232779	.238595	.244451
	-.10	.203308	.208496	.213821	.216529	.219265	.222026	.224811	.227617	.230443	.236149	.241915	.247731	.253587
	-.20	.212444	.217632	.222957	.225665	.228441	.231162	.233947	.236753	.239579	.245285	.251051	.256867	.262723
	-.30	.221580	.226769	.232093	.234801	.237537	.240298	.243083	.245889	.248716	.254421	.260187	.266003	.271859
	-.40	.230716	.235905	.241229	.243937	.246673	.249434	.252219	.255025	.257852	.263557	.269324	.275139	.280995

287

5.0 YEAR HOLDING PERIOD
.400 EQUITY YIELD RATE
.667 LOAN RATIO

INTEREST RATE

TERM YEARS	APPR DEP	5.0	6.0	7.0	7.5	8.0	8.5	9.0	9.5	10.0	11.0	12.0	13.0	14.0
10	.40	.154966	.159674	.164482	.166923	.169388	.171877	.174389	.176925	.179484	.184669	.189941	.195298	.200737
	.30	.164102	.168810	.173618	.176050	.178524	.181013	.183526	.186061	.188620	.193805	.199077	.204434	.209873
	.20	.173238	.177946	.182754	.185195	.187660	.190149	.192662	.195197	.197756	.202941	.208213	.213570	.219009
	.10	.182374	.187082	.191890	.194331	.196796	.199285	.201798	.204334	.206892	.212077	.217349	.222706	.228145
	0.00	.191510	.196218	.201026	.203462	.205932	.208421	.210934	.213470	.216028	.221213	.226486	.231843	.237281
	-.10	.200646	.205354	.210162	.212603	.215068	.217557	.220070	.222606	.225164	.230349	.235622	.240979	.246417
	-.20	.209782	.214490	.219298	.221739	.224204	.226693	.229206	.231742	.234301	.239485	.244758	.250115	.255553
	-.30	.218919	.223626	.228434	.230875	.233340	.235829	.238342	.240878	.243437	.248622	.253894	.259251	.264689
	-.40	.228055	.232762	.237570	.240011	.242477	.244966	.247478	.250014	.252573	.257758	.263030	.268387	.273826
15	.40	.144555	.149684	.154937	.157608	.160307	.163035	.165789	.168570	.171377	.177064	.182845	.188712	.194661
	.30	.153691	.158820	.164073	.166744	.169443	.172171	.174925	.177706	.180513	.186200	.191981	.197848	.203797
	.20	.162827	.167956	.173209	.175880	.178579	.181307	.184061	.186842	.189649	.195336	.201117	.206985	.212933
	.10	.171963	.177093	.182346	.185016	.187716	.190443	.193197	.195978	.198785	.204472	.210253	.216121	.222069
	0.00	.181099	.186229	.191481	.194152	.196852	.199579	.202334	.205115	.207921	.213608	.219389	.225257	.231206
	-.10	.190235	.195365	.200617	.203288	.205988	.208715	.211470	.214251	.217057	.222745	.228525	.234393	.240342
	-.20	.199371	.204501	.209753	.212424	.215124	.217851	.220606	.223387	.226193	.231881	.237661	.243529	.249478
	-.30	.208507	.213637	.218890	.221560	.224260	.226987	.229742	.232523	.235330	.241017	.246797	.252665	.258614
	-.40	.217644	.222773	.228026	.230696	.233396	.236123	.238878	.241659	.244466	.250153	.255933	.261801	.267750
20	.40	.139507	.144905	.150441	.153258	.156105	.158982	.161888	.164820	.167779	.173768	.179847	.186005	.192235
	.30	.148643	.154041	.159577	.162394	.165241	.168118	.171024	.173956	.176915	.182904	.188983	.195141	.201371
	.20	.157779	.163177	.168713	.171530	.174377	.177255	.180160	.183092	.186051	.192040	.198119	.204277	.210507
	.10	.166915	.172313	.177849	.180666	.183514	.186391	.189296	.192229	.195187	.201176	.207255	.213413	.219643
	0.00	.176051	.181449	.186985	.189802	.192650	.195527	.198432	.201365	.204323	.210312	.216391	.222550	.228779
	-.10	.185188	.190586	.196122	.198938	.201786	.204663	.207568	.210501	.213459	.219449	.225527	.231686	.237915
	-.20	.194324	.199722	.205258	.208074	.210922	.213799	.216704	.219637	.222595	.228585	.234663	.240822	.247052
	-.30	.203460	.208858	.214394	.217210	.220058	.222935	.225840	.228773	.231731	.237721	.243799	.249958	.256188
	-.40	.212596	.217994	.223530	.226347	.229194	.232071	.234977	.237909	.240867	.246857	.252935	.259094	.265324
25	.40	.136600	.142200	.147947	.150872	.153827	.156813	.159826	.162865	.165929	.172124	.178398	.184741	.191142
	.30	.145736	.151336	.157083	.160008	.162964	.165949	.168962	.172002	.175065	.181260	.187535	.193877	.200278
	.20	.154872	.160472	.166220	.169144	.172100	.175085	.178098	.181138	.184202	.190396	.196671	.203013	.209414
	.10	.164008	.169608	.175356	.178280	.181236	.184221	.187234	.190274	.193338	.199532	.205807	.212149	.218550
	0.00	.173144	.178744	.184492	.187416	.190372	.193357	.196370	.199410	.202474	.208669	.214943	.221285	.227686
	-.10	.182280	.187880	.193628	.196552	.199508	.202493	.205507	.208546	.211610	.217805	.224079	.230421	.236822
	-.20	.191416	.197016	.202764	.205688	.208644	.211629	.214643	.217682	.220746	.226941	.233215	.239557	.245958
	-.30	.200552	.206153	.211900	.214824	.217780	.220765	.223779	.226818	.229882	.236077	.242351	.248694	.255094
	-.40	.209688	.215289	.221036	.223960	.226916	.229902	.232915	.235954	.239018	.245213	.251487	.257830	.264230
30	.40	.134757	.140521	.146438	.149447	.152486	.155554	.158648	.161767	.164907	.171247	.177654	.184116	.190622
	.30	.143893	.149658	.155574	.158584	.161622	.164690	.167785	.170903	.174043	.180383	.186790	.193252	.199758
	.20	.153029	.158794	.164710	.167719	.170758	.173826	.176921	.180039	.183179	.189519	.195926	.202388	.208894
	.10	.162165	.167930	.173846	.176855	.179895	.182963	.186057	.189175	.192315	.198655	.205062	.211524	.218030
	0.00	.171301	.177066	.182982	.185991	.189031	.192099	.195193	.198311	.201452	.207791	.214198	.220660	.227166
	-.10	.180437	.186202	.192118	.195127	.198167	.201235	.204329	.207447	.210588	.216927	.223334	.229796	.236303
	-.20	.189573	.195338	.201254	.204263	.207303	.210371	.213465	.216583	.219724	.226063	.232470	.238932	.245439
	-.30	.198709	.204474	.210390	.213399	.216439	.219507	.222601	.225719	.228860	.235200	.241606	.248068	.254575
	-.40	.207845	.213610	.219527	.222535	.225575	.228643	.231737	.234856	.237996	.244336	.250743	.257204	.263711

5.0 YEAR HOLDING PERIOD
.400 EQUITY YIELD RATE
.700 LOAN RATIO

INTEREST RATE

TERM YEARS	APPR DEP	5.0	6.0	7.0	7.5	8.0	8.5	9.0	9.5	10.0	11.0	12.0	13.0	14.0
10	.40	.144543	.149486	.154534	.157097	.159685	.162299	.164937	.167600	.170286	.175730	.181266	.186891	.192602
	.30	.153679	.158622	.163670	.166233	.168822	.171435	.174073	.176736	.179422	.184867	.190402	.196027	.201738
	.20	.162815	.167758	.172806	.175369	.177958	.180571	.183209	.185872	.188559	.194003	.199539	.205163	.210874
	.10	.171951	.176894	.181942	.184505	.187094	.189707	.192345	.195008	.197695	.203139	.208675	.214299	.220010
	0.00	.181087	.186030	.191078	.193641	.196230	.198843	.201481	.204144	.206831	.212275	.217811	.223436	.229146
	-.10	.190223	.195166	.200215	.202778	.205366	.207979	.210618	.213280	.215967	.221411	.226947	.232572	.238282
	-.20	.199359	.204302	.209351	.211914	.214502	.217115	.219754	.222416	.225103	.230547	.236083	.241708	.247418
	-.30	.208495	.213438	.218487	.221050	.223638	.226252	.228890	.231552	.234239	.239683	.245219	.250844	.256554
	-.40	.217631	.222574	.227623	.230186	.232774	.235388	.238026	.240688	.243375	.248819	.254355	.259980	.265690
15	.40	.133611	.138997	.144512	.147316	.150151	.153015	.155907	.158827	.161774	.167745	.173815	.179976	.186222
	.30	.142747	.148133	.153648	.156453	.159287	.162151	.165043	.167963	.170910	.176882	.182951	.189112	.195358
	.20	.151883	.157269	.162784	.165589	.168423	.171287	.174179	.177099	.180046	.186018	.192087	.198248	.204495
	.10	.161019	.166405	.171920	.174725	.177559	.180423	.183315	.186235	.189182	.195154	.201223	.207384	.213631
	0.00	.170155	.175541	.181056	.183861	.186695	.189559	.192451	.195371	.198318	.204290	.210359	.216520	.222767
	-.10	.179291	.184677	.190193	.192997	.195831	.198695	.201587	.204507	.207454	.213426	.219495	.225657	.231903
	-.20	.188427	.193813	.199329	.202133	.204967	.207831	.210723	.213644	.216590	.222562	.228632	.234793	.241039
	-.30	.197564	.202949	.208465	.211269	.214104	.216967	.219860	.222780	.225727	.231698	.237768	.243929	.250175
	-.40	.206700	.212086	.217601	.220405	.223240	.226103	.228996	.231916	.234863	.240834	.246904	.253065	.259311
20	.40	.128311	.133979	.139791	.142749	.145739	.148760	.151810	.154890	.157996	.164285	.170667	.177134	.183675
	.30	.137447	.143115	.148928	.151885	.154875	.157896	.160947	.164026	.167132	.173421	.179803	.186270	.192811
	.20	.146583	.152251	.158064	.161021	.164011	.167032	.170083	.173162	.176268	.182557	.188939	.195406	.201947
	.10	.155719	.161387	.167200	.170157	.173147	.176168	.179219	.182298	.185404	.191693	.198075	.204542	.211083
	0.00	.164855	.170523	.176336	.179293	.182283	.185304	.188355	.191434	.194540	.200829	.207212	.213678	.220219
	-.10	.173991	.179659	.185472	.188429	.191419	.194440	.197491	.200570	.203676	.209965	.216348	.222814	.229355
	-.20	.183127	.188795	.194608	.197566	.200555	.203576	.206627	.209706	.212812	.219101	.225484	.231950	.238491
	-.30	.192264	.197931	.203744	.206702	.209692	.212712	.215763	.218842	.221948	.228237	.234620	.241086	.247628
	-.40	.201400	.207067	.212880	.215838	.218828	.221849	.224899	.227978	.231085	.237373	.243756	.250222	.256764
25	.40	.125258	.131138	.137173	.140244	.143347	.146482	.149646	.152837	.156054	.162559	.169147	.175806	.182527
	.30	.134394	.140274	.146309	.149380	.152483	.155618	.158782	.161973	.165190	.171695	.178283	.184942	.191663
	.20	.143530	.149410	.155445	.158516	.161619	.164754	.167918	.171109	.174326	.180831	.187419	.194078	.200799
	.10	.152666	.158547	.164581	.167652	.170755	.173890	.177054	.180245	.183462	.189967	.196555	.203214	.209935
	0.00	.161802	.167683	.173717	.176788	.179892	.183026	.186190	.189381	.192598	.199103	.205691	.212351	.219071
	-.10	.170938	.176819	.182854	.185924	.189028	.192162	.195326	.198517	.201735	.208239	.214827	.221487	.228207
	-.20	.180074	.185955	.191990	.195060	.198164	.201298	.204462	.207654	.210871	.217375	.223963	.230623	.237343
	-.30	.189211	.195091	.201126	.204196	.207300	.210434	.213598	.216790	.220007	.226511	.233099	.239759	.246479
	-.40	.198347	.204227	.210262	.213332	.216436	.219571	.222734	.225926	.229143	.235647	.242235	.248895	.255615
30	.40	.123323	.129376	.135588	.138747	.141939	.145160	.148409	.151683	.154981	.161638	.168365	.175150	.181981
	.30	.132459	.138512	.144724	.147883	.151075	.154296	.157545	.160819	.164117	.170774	.177501	.184286	.191117
	.20	.141595	.147648	.153860	.157020	.160211	.163432	.166681	.169956	.173253	.179910	.186637	.193422	.200254
	.10	.150731	.156784	.162996	.166156	.169347	.172569	.175817	.179092	.182389	.189046	.195773	.202558	.209390
	0.00	.159867	.165920	.172132	.175292	.178483	.181705	.184954	.188228	.191525	.198182	.204909	.211694	.218526
	-.10	.169003	.175056	.181268	.184428	.187619	.190841	.194090	.197364	.200661	.207318	.214045	.220830	.227662
	-.20	.178139	.184193	.190405	.193564	.196755	.199977	.203226	.206500	.209797	.216454	.223181	.229966	.236799
	-.30	.187276	.193329	.199541	.202700	.205892	.209113	.212362	.215636	.218933	.225590	.232317	.239102	.245934
	-.40	.196412	.202465	.208677	.211836	.215028	.218249	.221498	.224772	.228070	.234726	.241453	.248238	.255070

5.0 YEAR HOLDING PERIOD
.400 EQUITY YIELD RATE
.750 LOAN RATIO

INTEREST RATE

TERM YEARS	APPR DEP	5.0	6.0	7.0	7.5	8.0	8.5	9.0	9.5	10.0	11.0	12.0	13.0	14.0
10	.40	.128906	.134202	.139611	.142357	.145130	.147931	.150757	.153610	.156489	.162322	.168253	.174279	.180398
	.30	.138042	.143338	.148747	.151493	.154267	.157067	.159893	.162746	.165625	.171458	.177389	.183416	.189534
	.20	.147178	.152474	.157883	.160629	.163403	.166203	.169029	.171882	.174761	.180594	.186525	.192552	.198670
	.10	.156314	.161610	.167019	.169765	.172539	.175339	.178165	.181018	.183897	.189730	.195661	.201688	.207806
	0.00	.165450	.170746	.176155	.178901	.181675	.184475	.187302	.190154	.193033	.198866	.204797	.210824	.216942
	-.10	.174586	.179883	.185292	.188038	.190811	.193611	.196438	.199290	.202169	.208002	.213933	.219960	.226078
	-.20	.183722	.189019	.194428	.197174	.199947	.202747	.205574	.208427	.211305	.217138	.223069	.229096	.235214
	-.30	.192859	.198155	.203564	.206310	.209083	.211883	.214710	.217563	.220441	.226274	.232206	.238232	.244350
	-.40	.201995	.207291	.212700	.215446	.218219	.221019	.223846	.226699	.229577	.235410	.241342	.247368	.253487
15	.40	.117193	.122964	.128873	.131878	.134915	.137983	.141082	.144211	.147368	.153766	.160269	.166870	.173563
	.30	.126329	.132100	.138009	.141014	.144051	.147119	.150218	.153347	.156504	.162902	.169405	.176006	.182699
	.20	.135466	.141236	.147145	.150150	.153187	.156255	.159354	.162483	.165640	.172038	.178541	.185143	.191835
	.10	.144602	.150372	.156282	.159286	.162323	.165391	.168490	.171619	.174776	.181174	.187678	.194279	.200971
	0.00	.153738	.159508	.165418	.168422	.171459	.174528	.177626	.180755	.183912	.190311	.196814	.203415	.210107
	-.10	.162874	.168644	.174554	.177558	.180595	.183664	.186762	.189891	.193049	.199447	.205950	.212551	.219243
	-.20	.172010	.177781	.183690	.186694	.189731	.192800	.195899	.199027	.202185	.208583	.215086	.221687	.228379
	-.30	.181146	.186917	.192826	.195831	.198867	.201936	.205035	.208163	.211321	.217719	.224222	.230823	.237515
	-.40	.190282	.196053	.201962	.204967	.208004	.211072	.214171	.217299	.220457	.226855	.233358	.239959	.246652
20	.40	.111515	.117588	.123815	.126984	.130188	.133424	.136693	.139992	.143320	.150058	.156897	.163825	.170833
	.30	.120651	.126724	.132952	.136120	.139324	.142560	.145829	.149128	.152456	.159194	.166033	.172961	.179969
	.20	.129787	.135860	.142088	.145256	.148460	.151697	.154965	.158264	.161592	.168330	.175169	.182097	.189106
	.10	.138923	.144996	.151224	.154393	.157596	.160833	.164101	.167400	.170728	.177467	.184305	.191233	.198242
	0.00	.148059	.154132	.160360	.163529	.166732	.169969	.173237	.176536	.179865	.186603	.193441	.200369	.207378
	-.10	.157195	.163268	.169496	.172665	.175868	.179105	.182373	.185672	.189001	.195739	.202577	.209505	.216514
	-.20	.166331	.172404	.178632	.181801	.185004	.188241	.191510	.194809	.198137	.204875	.211713	.218641	.225650
	-.30	.175467	.181540	.187768	.190937	.194140	.197377	.200646	.203945	.207273	.214011	.220849	.227777	.234786
	-.40	.184604	.190676	.196904	.200073	.203276	.206513	.209782	.213081	.216409	.223147	.229985	.236914	.243922
25	.40	.108244	.114544	.121010	.124300	.127625	.130984	.134374	.137793	.141240	.148209	.155267	.162403	.169603
	.30	.117380	.123680	.130146	.133436	.136761	.140120	.143510	.146929	.150376	.157345	.164403	.171539	.178739
	.20	.126516	.132816	.139282	.142572	.145897	.149256	.152646	.156065	.159512	.166481	.173540	.180675	.187875
	.10	.135652	.141952	.148418	.151708	.155033	.158392	.161782	.165201	.168648	.175617	.182676	.189811	.197012
	0.00	.144788	.151089	.157554	.160844	.164170	.167528	.170918	.174337	.177784	.184753	.191812	.198947	.206148
	-.10	.153924	.160225	.166690	.169980	.173306	.176664	.180054	.183473	.186920	.193889	.200948	.208083	.215284
	-.20	.163060	.169361	.175827	.179116	.182442	.185800	.189190	.192609	.196056	.203025	.210084	.217219	.224420
	-.30	.172196	.178497	.184963	.188253	.191578	.194936	.198326	.201745	.205192	.212161	.219220	.226355	.233556
	-.40	.181333	.187633	.194099	.197389	.200714	.204072	.207462	.210882	.214328	.221298	.228356	.235491	.242692
30	.40	.106171	.112656	.119312	.122697	.126116	.129568	.133049	.136557	.140090	.147222	.154430	.161699	.169019
	.30	.115307	.121792	.128448	.131833	.135252	.138704	.142185	.145693	.149226	.156358	.163566	.170835	.178155
	.20	.124443	.130928	.137584	.140969	.144388	.147840	.151321	.154829	.158362	.165494	.172702	.179971	.187291
	.10	.133579	.140064	.146720	.150105	.153525	.156976	.160457	.163965	.167498	.174630	.181838	.189107	.196427
	0.00	.142715	.149200	.155856	.159241	.162661	.166112	.169593	.173101	.176634	.183766	.190974	.198243	.205563
	-.10	.151851	.158336	.164992	.168377	.171797	.175248	.178729	.182237	.185770	.192902	.200110	.207380	.214699
	-.20	.160987	.167473	.174128	.177513	.180933	.184384	.187865	.191373	.194906	.202038	.209246	.216516	.223835
	-.30	.170123	.176609	.183264	.186649	.190069	.193520	.197001	.200509	.204042	.211175	.218382	.225652	.232972
	-.40	.179259	.185745	.192401	.195786	.199205	.202656	.206137	.209646	.213179	.220311	.227518	.234788	.242108

5.0 YEAR HOLDING PERIOD
.400 EQUITY YIELD RATE
.800 LOAN RATIO

INTEREST RATE

TERM YEARS	APPR DEP	5.0	6.0	7.0	7.5	8.0	8.5	9.0	9.5	10.0	11.0	12.0	13.0	14.0
10	.40	.113269	.118919	.124688	.127617	.130575	.133562	.136577	.139620	.142691	.148913	.155239	.161668	.168194
	.30	.122405	.128055	.133824	.136753	.139711	.142698	.145713	.148756	.151827	.158049	.164375	.170804	.177330
	.20	.131541	.137191	.142960	.145889	.148848	.151834	.154849	.157892	.160963	.167185	.173512	.179940	.186466
	.10	.140677	.146327	.152096	.155026	.157984	.160970	.163986	.167029	.170099	.176321	.182648	.189076	.195602
	0.00	.149814	.155463	.161233	.164162	.167120	.170107	.173122	.176165	.179235	.185457	.191784	.198212	.204738
	-.10	.158950	.164599	.170369	.173298	.176256	.179243	.182258	.185301	.188371	.194593	.200920	.207348	.213874
	-.20	.168086	.173735	.179505	.182434	.185392	.188379	.191394	.194437	.197507	.203729	.210056	.216484	.223011
	-.30	.177222	.182871	.188641	.191570	.194528	.197515	.200530	.203573	.206643	.212865	.219192	.225620	.232147
	-.40	.186358	.192007	.197777	.200706	.203664	.206651	.209666	.212709	.215780	.222001	.228328	.234756	.241283
15	.40	.100776	.106931	.113234	.116439	.119679	.122952	.126257	.129594	.132962	.139787	.146723	.153765	.160903
	.30	.109912	.116067	.122371	.125575	.128815	.132088	.135393	.138730	.142098	.148923	.155860	.162901	.170039
	.20	.119048	.125203	.131507	.134712	.137951	.141224	.144529	.147866	.151234	.158059	.164996	.172037	.179175
	.10	.128184	.134340	.140643	.143848	.147087	.150360	.153665	.157003	.160371	.167195	.174132	.181173	.188312
	0.00	.137320	.143476	.149779	.152984	.156223	.159496	.162801	.166139	.169507	.176331	.183268	.190309	.197448
	-.10	.146456	.152612	.158915	.162120	.165359	.168632	.171938	.175275	.178643	.185467	.192404	.199445	.206584
	-.20	.155592	.161749	.168051	.171256	.174495	.177768	.181074	.184411	.187779	.194603	.201540	.208581	.215720
	-.30	.164729	.170884	.177187	.180392	.183631	.186904	.190210	.193547	.196915	.203740	.210676	.217717	.224856
	-.40	.173865	.180020	.186323	.189528	.192767	.196040	.199346	.202683	.206051	.212876	.219812	.226853	.233992
20	.40	.094719	.101196	.107839	.111219	.114636	.118089	.121575	.125094	.128644	.135832	.143126	.150516	.157992
	.30	.103855	.110332	.116976	.120355	.123773	.127225	.130712	.134231	.137781	.144968	.152262	.159652	.167128
	.20	.112991	.119469	.126112	.129492	.132909	.136361	.139848	.143367	.146917	.154104	.161398	.168788	.176264
	.10	.122127	.128605	.135248	.138628	.142045	.145497	.148984	.152503	.156053	.163240	.170534	.177924	.185400
	0.00	.131263	.137741	.144384	.147764	.151181	.154633	.158120	.161639	.165189	.172376	.179670	.187060	.194535
	-.10	.140399	.146877	.153520	.156900	.160317	.163769	.167256	.170775	.174325	.181512	.188806	.196197	.203672
	-.20	.149535	.156013	.162656	.166036	.169453	.172906	.176392	.179911	.183461	.190648	.197942	.205333	.212808
	-.30	.158671	.165149	.171792	.175172	.178589	.182042	.185528	.189047	.192597	.199784	.207079	.214469	.221945
	-.40	.167807	.174285	.180928	.184308	.187725	.191178	.194664	.198183	.201733	.208920	.216215	.223605	.231081
25	.40	.091230	.097950	.104847	.108356	.111903	.115486	.119101	.122749	.126425	.133859	.141388	.148999	.156680
	.30	.100366	.107086	.113983	.117492	.121039	.124622	.128237	.131885	.135561	.142995	.150524	.158135	.165816
	.20	.109502	.116222	.123119	.126628	.130175	.133758	.137374	.141021	.144697	.152131	.159660	.167271	.174952
	.10	.118638	.125358	.132255	.135764	.139311	.142894	.146510	.150157	.153834	.161267	.168796	.176407	.184088
	0.00	.127774	.134494	.141391	.144901	.148447	.152030	.155646	.159293	.162970	.170403	.177932	.185543	.193224
	-.10	.136910	.143631	.150527	.154037	.157584	.161166	.164782	.168429	.172106	.179540	.187069	.194680	.202360
	-.20	.146046	.152767	.159663	.163173	.166720	.170302	.173918	.177565	.181242	.188676	.196205	.203816	.211496
	-.30	.155182	.161903	.168800	.172309	.175856	.179438	.183054	.186701	.190378	.197812	.205341	.212952	.220632
	-.40	.164318	.171039	.177936	.181445	.184992	.188574	.192190	.195837	.199514	.206948	.214477	.222088	.229769
30	.40	.089018	.095936	.103036	.106646	.110294	.113975	.117688	.121430	.125199	.132806	.140495	.148249	.156056
	.30	.098154	.105072	.112172	.115782	.119430	.123111	.126824	.130566	.134335	.141942	.149631	.157385	.165193
	.20	.107290	.114208	.121308	.124918	.128566	.132247	.135960	.139702	.143471	.151079	.158767	.166521	.174329
	.10	.116427	.123344	.130444	.134054	.137702	.141383	.145097	.148838	.152607	.160215	.167903	.175657	.183465
	0.00	.125563	.132480	.139580	.143191	.146838	.150520	.154233	.157975	.161743	.169351	.177039	.184793	.192601
	-.10	.134699	.141616	.148716	.152327	.155974	.159656	.163369	.167111	.170879	.178487	.186175	.193929	.201737
	-.20	.143835	.150753	.157852	.161463	.165110	.168792	.172505	.176247	.180015	.187623	.195311	.203065	.210873
	-.30	.152971	.159889	.166988	.170599	.174246	.177928	.181641	.185383	.189151	.196759	.204447	.212201	.220009
	-.40	.162107	.169025	.176124	.179735	.183382	.187064	.190777	.194519	.198287	.205895	.213583	.221337	.229145

5.0 YEAR HOLDING PERIOD
.400 EQUITY YIELD RATE
.900 LOAN RATIO

INTEREST RATE

TERM YEARS	APPR DEP	5.0	6.0	7.0	7.5	8.0	8.5	9.0	9.5	10.0	11.0	12.0	13.0	14.0
10	.40	.081996	.088351	.094842	.098137	.101465	.104826	.108218	.111641	.115095	.122095	.129212	.136444	.143786
	.30	.091132	.097487	.103978	.107274	.110601	.113962	.117354	.120777	.124231	.131231	.138348	.145580	.152922
	.20	.100268	.106624	.113114	.116410	.119738	.123098	.126490	.129913	.133367	.140367	.147485	.154716	.162058
	.10	.109404	.115760	.122250	.125546	.128874	.132234	.135626	.139049	.142503	.149503	.156620	.163852	.171195
	0.00	.118540	.124896	.131387	.134682	.138010	.141370	.144762	.148185	.151640	.158639	.165757	.172989	.180331
	-.10	.127676	.134032	.140523	.143818	.147146	.150506	.153898	.157321	.160776	.167775	.174892	.182125	.189467
	-.20	.136812	.143168	.149659	.152954	.156282	.159642	.163034	.166457	.169911	.176911	.184029	.191261	.198603
	-.30	.145949	.152304	.158795	.162090	.165418	.168778	.172170	.175593	.179048	.186047	.193165	.200397	.207739
	-.40	.155085	.161440	.167931	.171226	.174554	.177914	.181306	.184730	.188184	.195183	.202301	.209533	.216875
15	.40	.067941	.074866	.081957	.085562	.089207	.092889	.096607	.100362	.104151	.111828	.119632	.127553	.135584
	.30	.077077	.084002	.091093	.094698	.098343	.102025	.105743	.109498	.113287	.120964	.128768	.136689	.144720
	.20	.086213	.093138	.100229	.103835	.107479	.111161	.114879	.118634	.122423	.130100	.137904	.145826	.153856
	.10	.095349	.102274	.109365	.112971	.116615	.120297	.124016	.127770	.131559	.139237	.147040	.154962	.162993
	0.00	.104485	.111410	.118501	.122107	.125751	.129433	.133152	.136906	.140695	.148373	.156176	.164098	.172129
	-.10	.113621	.120546	.127637	.131243	.134887	.138569	.142288	.146042	.149831	.157509	.165312	.173234	.181265
	-.20	.122758	.129682	.136773	.140379	.144023	.147705	.151424	.155178	.158967	.166645	.174448	.182370	.190401
	-.30	.131894	.138818	.145909	.149515	.153159	.156841	.160560	.164314	.168103	.175781	.183584	.191506	.199537
	-.40	.141030	.147954	.155046	.158651	.162295	.165977	.169696	.173450	.177239	.184917	.192720	.200642	.208673
20	.40	.061127	.068414	.075887	.079690	.083534	.087418	.091340	.095299	.099293	.107379	.115585	.123899	.132309
	.30	.070263	.077550	.085024	.088826	.092670	.096554	.100477	.104435	.108429	.116515	.124721	.133035	.141445
	.20	.079399	.086686	.094160	.097962	.101806	.105690	.109613	.113571	.117565	.125651	.133857	.142171	.150581
	.10	.088535	.095822	.103296	.107098	.110942	.114827	.118749	.122707	.126701	.134787	.142993	.151307	.159717
	0.00	.097671	.104958	.112432	.116234	.120078	.123963	.127885	.131843	.135837	.143923	.152129	.160443	.168853
	-.10	.106807	.114094	.121568	.125370	.129215	.133099	.137021	.140980	.144974	.153059	.161265	.169579	.177989
	-.20	.115943	.123230	.130704	.134506	.138351	.142235	.146157	.150116	.154110	.162195	.170401	.178715	.187125
	-.30	.125079	.132366	.139840	.143643	.147487	.151371	.155293	.159252	.163246	.171331	.179537	.187851	.196261
	-.40	.134215	.141503	.148976	.152779	.156623	.160507	.164429	.168338	.172382	.180467	.188673	.196987	.205398
25	.40	.057201	.064762	.072521	.076469	.080459	.084489	.088557	.092660	.096796	.105159	.113630	.122192	.130833
	.30	.066338	.073898	.081657	.085605	.089595	.093625	.097693	.101796	.105933	.114296	.122766	.131328	.139969
	.20	.075474	.083034	.090793	.094741	.098731	.102761	.106829	.110932	.115069	.123432	.131902	.140464	.149105
	.10	.084610	.092170	.099929	.103877	.107867	.111898	.115965	.120069	.124205	.132568	.141038	.149600	.158241
	0.00	.093746	.101306	.109065	.113013	.117003	.121034	.125101	.129205	.133341	.141704	.150174	.158736	.167377
	-.10	.102882	.110442	.118201	.122149	.126140	.130170	.134238	.138341	.142477	.150840	.159310	.167872	.176513
	-.20	.112018	.119578	.127337	.131285	.135276	.139306	.143374	.147477	.151613	.159976	.168446	.177009	.185649
	-.30	.121154	.128715	.136474	.140421	.144412	.148442	.152510	.156613	.160749	.169112	.177582	.186145	.194785
	-.40	.130290	.137851	.145610	.149558	.153548	.157578	.161646	.165749	.169885	.178248	.186718	.195281	.203922
30	.40	.054714	.062496	.070483	.074545	.078648	.082790	.086967	.091177	.095417	.103975	.112624	.121348	.130132
	.30	.063850	.071632	.079619	.083681	.087784	.091926	.096103	.100313	.104553	.113111	.121760	.130484	.139268
	.20	.072986	.080768	.088755	.092817	.096921	.101062	.105240	.109449	.113689	.122247	.130897	.139620	.148404
	.10	.082122	.089040	.097891	.101953	.106057	.110198	.114376	.118585	.122825	.131383	.140033	.148756	.157540
	0.00	.091258	.099040	.107027	.111089	.115193	.119335	.123512	.127721	.131961	.140520	.149169	.157892	.166676
	-.10	.100394	.108177	.116163	.120225	.124329	.128471	.132648	.136857	.141097	.149656	.158305	.167028	.175812
	-.20	.109530	.117313	.125300	.129362	.133465	.137607	.141784	.145993	.150233	.158792	.167441	.176164	.184948
	-.30	.118666	.126449	.134436	.138498	.142601	.146743	.150920	.155130	.159369	.167928	.176577	.185300	.194084
	-.40	.127802	.135585	.143572	.147634	.151737	.155879	.160056	.164266	.168505	.177064	.185713	.194437	.203220

5.0 YEAR HOLDING PERIOD
.500 EQUITY YIELD RATE
.600 LOAN RATIO

INTEREST RATE

TERM YEARS	APPR DEP	14.0	13.0	12.0	11.0	10.0	9.5	9.0	8.5	8.0	7.5	7.0	6.0	5.0
10	.40	.266323	.261531	.256614	.252176	.247617	.245369	.243142	.240935	.238751	.236588	.234447	.230233	.226110
	.30	.273905	.269114	.264397	.259759	.255200	.252952	.250725	.248518	.246334	.244171	.242030	.237816	.233693
	.20	.281488	.276697	.271980	.267342	.262783	.260535	.258308	.256101	.253917	.251754	.249613	.245399	.241276
	.10	.289071	.284280	.279563	.274925	.270366	.268118	.265890	.263684	.261500	.259337	.257196	.252982	.248858
	0.00	.296654	.291863	.287146	.282508	.277949	.275701	.273473	.271267	.269083	.266920	.264779	.260565	.256441
	-.10	.304237	.299446	.294729	.290091	.285532	.283284	.281056	.278850	.276666	.274503	.272362	.268148	.264024
	-.20	.311820	.307029	.302312	.297673	.293115	.290867	.288639	.286433	.284248	.282086	.279945	.275730	.271607
	-.30	.319403	.314611	.309895	.305256	.300698	.298450	.296222	.294016	.291831	.289669	.287528	.283313	.279190
	-.40	.326986	.322194	.317478	.312839	.308281	.306033	.303805	.301599	.299414	.297252	.295111	.290896	.286773
15	.40	.259080	.253822	.248643	.243546	.238539	.236071	.233627	.231208	.228814	.226447	.224107	.219511	.215029
	.30	.266663	.261405	.256225	.251129	.246122	.243654	.241210	.238791	.236397	.234030	.231690	.227094	.222612
	.20	.274246	.268988	.263808	.258712	.253705	.251237	.248793	.246374	.243980	.241613	.239273	.234677	.230195
	.10	.281829	.276571	.271391	.266295	.261288	.258820	.256376	.253957	.251563	.249196	.246856	.242259	.237778
	0.00	.289412	.284154	.278974	.273878	.268871	.266403	.263959	.261539	.259146	.256779	.254439	.249842	.245361
	-.10	.296995	.291737	.286557	.281461	.276454	.273986	.271542	.269122	.266729	.264362	.262022	.257425	.252944
	-.20	.304578	.299320	.294140	.289044	.284037	.281569	.279124	.276705	.274312	.271945	.269605	.265008	.260527
	-.30	.312161	.306903	.301723	.296627	.291630	.289151	.286707	.284288	.281895	.279528	.277188	.272591	.268110
	-.40	.319743	.314486	.309306	.304210	.299203	.296734	.294290	.291871	.289478	.287111	.284771	.280174	.275693
20	.40	.256188	.250653	.245190	.239806	.234510	.231898	.229310	.226750	.224216	.221712	.219237	.214381	.209657
	.30	.263771	.258236	.252773	.247389	.242093	.239481	.236893	.234333	.231799	.229295	.226820	.221964	.217240
	.20	.271354	.265819	.260356	.254972	.249676	.247064	.244476	.241916	.239382	.236878	.234403	.229547	.224823
	.10	.278937	.273402	.267939	.262555	.257259	.254647	.252059	.249498	.246965	.244461	.241986	.237130	.232406
	0.00	.286520	.280985	.275522	.270138	.264842	.262229	.259642	.257081	.254548	.252043	.249569	.244713	.239989
	-.10	.294102	.288568	.283105	.277721	.272425	.269812	.267225	.264664	.262131	.259626	.257152	.252296	.247572
	-.20	.301685	.296151	.290668	.285304	.280008	.277395	.274808	.272247	.269714	.267209	.264734	.259879	.255155
	-.30	.309268	.303734	.298271	.292887	.287591	.284978	.282391	.279830	.277297	.274792	.272317	.267462	.262738
	-.40	.316851	.311317	.305854	.300470	.295174	.292561	.289974	.287413	.284880	.282375	.279900	.275044	.270321
25	.40	.254884	.249174	.243523	.237941	.232439	.229722	.227030	.224363	.221723	.219114	.216535	.211477	.206563
	.30	.262467	.256757	.251106	.245524	.240022	.237305	.234613	.231946	.229307	.226699	.224128	.219060	.214146
	.20	.270050	.264340	.258689	.253106	.247605	.244888	.242195	.239529	.236890	.234280	.231701	.226643	.221729
	.10	.277633	.271923	.266272	.260690	.255188	.252471	.249778	.247112	.244473	.241863	.239284	.234226	.229312
	0.00	.285216	.279506	.273854	.268273	.262771	.260054	.257361	.254695	.252056	.249446	.246867	.241809	.236895
	-.10	.292799	.287088	.281437	.275856	.270354	.267637	.264944	.262278	.259639	.257029	.254450	.249392	.244478
	-.20	.300382	.294671	.289020	.283439	.277937	.275220	.272527	.269860	.267221	.264612	.262033	.256975	.252061
	-.30	.307965	.302254	.296603	.291022	.285504	.282803	.280110	.277527	.274805	.272195	.269616	.264558	.259644
	-.40	.315548	.309837	.304186	.298604	.293103	.290386	.287693	.285026	.282387	.279778	.277199	.272141	.267226
30	.40	.254265	.248442	.242665	.236946	.231295	.228499	.225727	.222978	.220256	.217563	.214900	.209676	.204602
	.30	.261848	.256025	.250248	.244528	.238878	.236082	.233310	.230561	.227839	.225146	.222483	.217259	.212185
	.20	.269431	.263608	.257831	.252111	.246461	.243665	.240893	.238144	.235422	.232729	.230066	.224842	.219768
	.10	.277014	.271191	.265414	.259694	.254044	.251248	.248475	.245727	.243005	.240312	.237649	.232425	.227350
	0.00	.284597	.278774	.272997	.267277	.261627	.258831	.256058	.253310	.250588	.247895	.245232	.240008	.234933
	-.10	.292180	.286357	.280580	.274860	.269209	.266414	.263641	.260893	.258171	.255477	.252815	.247590	.242516
	-.20	.299763	.293939	.288163	.282443	.276792	.273997	.271224	.268476	.265754	.263060	.260398	.255173	.250099
	-.30	.307346	.301522	.295746	.290026	.284375	.281580	.278807	.276059	.273337	.270643	.267981	.262756	.257682
	-.40	.314929	.309105	.303329	.297609	.291958	.289163	.286390	.283642	.280920	.278226	.275564	.270339	.265265

5.0 YEAR HOLDING PERIOD
.500 EQUITY YIELD RATE
.667 LOAN RATIO

INTEREST RATE

TERM YEARS	APPR DEP	5.0	6.0	7.0	7.5	8.0	8.5	9.0	9.5	10.0	11.0	12.0	13.0	14.0
10	.40	.199046	.203628	.208310	.210689	.213092	.215519	.217971	.220446	.222944	.228009	.233163	.238403	.243727
	.30	.206629	.211211	.215893	.218272	.220675	.223102	.225554	.228029	.230527	.235593	.240746	.245986	.251110
	.20	.214212	.218793	.223476	.225855	.228258	.230685	.233137	.235612	.238110	.243175	.248329	.253569	.258893
	.10	.221795	.226376	.231059	.233438	.235841	.238268	.240720	.243194	.245693	.250758	.255912	.261152	.266476
	0.00	.229378	.233959	.238642	.241021	.243424	.245851	.248303	.250777	.253276	.258341	.263495	.268735	.274059
	-.10	.236961	.241542	.246225	.248604	.251007	.253434	.255885	.258360	.260859	.265923	.271078	.276318	.281642
	-.20	.244544	.249125	.253808	.256187	.258590	.261017	.263468	.265943	.268441	.273506	.278661	.283901	.289225
	-.30	.252127	.256708	.261391	.263769	.266173	.268600	.271051	.273526	.276024	.281089	.286243	.291484	.296808
	-.40	.259710	.264291	.268974	.271352	.273756	.276183	.278634	.281109	.283607	.288672	.293826	.299067	.304391
15	.40	.186735	.191714	.196821	.199421	.202051	.204711	.207399	.210114	.212857	.218420	.224083	.229838	.235680
	.30	.194318	.199297	.204404	.207004	.209634	.212294	.214982	.217697	.220440	.226003	.231666	.237421	.243263
	.20	.201901	.206880	.211987	.214587	.217217	.219877	.222565	.225280	.228023	.233586	.239249	.245004	.250846
	.10	.209484	.214463	.219570	.222170	.224800	.227460	.230147	.232863	.235606	.241169	.246832	.252587	.258429
	0.00	.217067	.222046	.227153	.229753	.232383	.235043	.237730	.240446	.243189	.248752	.254415	.260170	.266012
	-.10	.224650	.229629	.234736	.237336	.239966	.242625	.245313	.248029	.250772	.256335	.261998	.267753	.273595
	-.20	.232232	.237212	.242319	.244919	.247549	.250208	.252896	.255612	.258355	.263918	.269581	.275336	.281178
	-.30	.239815	.244795	.249902	.252502	.255132	.257791	.260479	.263195	.265938	.271501	.277163	.282919	.288761
	-.40	.247398	.252377	.257485	.260085	.262715	.265374	.268062	.270778	.273521	.279084	.284746	.290502	.296344
20	.40	.180766	.186014	.191410	.194160	.196943	.199757	.202603	.205477	.208380	.214265	.220247	.226317	.232467
	.30	.188349	.193597	.198993	.201743	.204526	.207340	.210186	.213060	.215963	.221848	.227830	.233900	.240049
	.20	.195932	.201180	.206576	.209325	.212108	.214923	.217769	.220643	.223546	.229431	.235413	.241483	.247632
	.10	.203515	.208763	.214159	.216908	.219691	.222506	.225352	.228226	.231129	.237014	.242996	.249066	.255215
	0.00	.211098	.216346	.221742	.224491	.227274	.230089	.232934	.235809	.238712	.244597	.250579	.256649	.262798
	-.10	.218681	.223929	.229324	.232074	.234857	.237672	.240517	.243392	.246295	.252180	.258162	.264232	.270381
	-.20	.226264	.231512	.236907	.239657	.242440	.245255	.248100	.250975	.253878	.259763	.265745	.271815	.277964
	-.30	.233846	.239095	.244490	.247240	.250023	.252838	.255683	.258558	.261461	.267345	.273328	.279398	.285547
	-.40	.241429	.246678	.252073	.254823	.257606	.260421	.263266	.266141	.269044	.274928	.280911	.286981	.293130
25	.40	.177328	.182788	.188408	.191273	.194173	.197105	.200068	.203060	.206079	.212192	.218394	.224673	.231018
	.30	.184911	.190371	.195991	.198856	.201756	.204688	.207651	.210643	.213662	.219775	.225977	.232256	.238601
	.20	.192493	.197954	.203574	.206439	.209339	.212271	.215234	.218226	.221245	.227358	.233560	.239839	.246184
	.10	.200076	.205537	.211157	.214022	.216922	.219854	.222817	.225809	.228828	.234941	.241143	.247422	.253767
	0.00	.207659	.213120	.218740	.221605	.224505	.227437	.230400	.233392	.236411	.242524	.248726	.255005	.261350
	-.10	.215242	.220703	.226323	.229188	.232088	.235020	.237983	.240975	.243994	.250107	.256309	.262588	.268933
	-.20	.222825	.228286	.233906	.236771	.239671	.242603	.245566	.248558	.251577	.257690	.263892	.270171	.276516
	-.30	.230408	.235869	.241489	.244354	.247254	.250186	.253149	.256141	.259160	.265273	.271475	.277754	.284099
	-.40	.237991	.243451	.249072	.251937	.254837	.257769	.260732	.263724	.266743	.272856	.279058	.285337	.291682
30	.40	.175148	.180786	.186591	.189550	.192542	.195567	.198621	.201702	.204808	.211086	.217441	.223860	.230330
	.30	.182731	.188369	.194174	.197133	.200125	.203150	.206204	.209285	.212390	.218669	.225024	.231443	.237913
	.20	.190314	.195952	.201757	.204716	.207708	.210733	.213787	.216867	.219973	.226252	.232607	.239026	.245496
	.10	.197897	.203535	.209340	.212298	.215291	.218316	.221369	.224450	.227556	.233835	.240190	.246609	.253079
	0.00	.205480	.211118	.216923	.219881	.222874	.225899	.228952	.232033	.235139	.241418	.247773	.254192	.260662
	-.10	.213063	.218701	.224506	.227464	.230457	.233482	.236535	.239616	.242722	.249001	.255356	.261775	.268245
	-.20	.220646	.226284	.232089	.235047	.238040	.241064	.244118	.247199	.250305	.256584	.262939	.269357	.275828
	-.30	.228229	.233867	.239672	.242630	.245623	.248647	.251701	.254782	.257888	.264167	.270522	.276941	.283411
	-.40	.235812	.241450	.247255	.250213	.253206	.256230	.259284	.262365	.265471	.271750	.278105	.284523	.290994

5.0 YEAR HOLDING PERIOD
.500 EQUITY YIELD RATE
.700 LOAN RATIO

INTEREST RATE

TERM YEARS	APPR DEP	5.0	6.0	7.0	7.5	8.0	8.5	9.0	9.5	10.0	11.0	12.0	13.0	14.0
10	.40	.185517	.190327	.195244	.197741	.200265	.202813	.205387	.207986	.210609	.215927	.221339	.226841	.232432
	.30	.193100	.197910	.202827	.205324	.207848	.210396	.212970	.215569	.218192	.223510	.228922	.234424	.240014
	.20	.200682	.205493	.210410	.212907	.215430	.217979	.220553	.223152	.225775	.231093	.236505	.242007	.247597
	.10	.208265	.213076	.217993	.220490	.223013	.225562	.228136	.230735	.233358	.238676	.244088	.249590	.255180
	0.00	.215848	.220659	.225575	.228073	.230596	.233145	.235719	.238318	.240941	.246259	.251671	.257173	.262763
	-.10	.223431	.228242	.233158	.235656	.238179	.240728	.243302	.245901	.248524	.253842	.259254	.264756	.270346
	-.20	.231014	.235825	.240741	.243239	.245762	.248311	.250885	.253483	.256107	.261425	.266837	.272339	.277929
	-.30	.238597	.243408	.248324	.250822	.253345	.255894	.258468	.261066	.263690	.269008	.274419	.279922	.285522
	-.40	.246180	.250990	.255907	.258405	.260928	.263477	.266051	.268649	.271272	.276591	.282002	.287505	.293095
15	.40	.172590	.177818	.183180	.185910	.188672	.191464	.194287	.197138	.200018	.205859	.211805	.217848	.223982
	.30	.180173	.185401	.190763	.193493	.196255	.199047	.201870	.204721	.207601	.213442	.219388	.225431	.231565
	.20	.187756	.192984	.198346	.201076	.203838	.206630	.209452	.212304	.215184	.221025	.226971	.233014	.239148
	.10	.195338	.200567	.205929	.208659	.211421	.214213	.217035	.219887	.222767	.228608	.234554	.240597	.246731
	0.00	.202921	.208149	.213512	.216242	.219004	.221796	.224618	.227470	.230350	.236191	.242137	.248180	.254314
	-.10	.210504	.215732	.221095	.223825	.226587	.229379	.232201	.235053	.237933	.243774	.249720	.255763	.261897
	-.20	.218087	.223315	.228678	.231408	.234170	.236962	.239784	.242636	.245516	.251357	.257303	.263346	.269480
	-.30	.225670	.230898	.236261	.238991	.241753	.244545	.247367	.250219	.253098	.258940	.264886	.270928	.277062
	-.40	.233253	.238481	.243844	.246574	.249336	.252128	.254950	.257802	.260681	.266523	.272468	.278511	.284645
20	.40	.166322	.171833	.177498	.180386	.183308	.186263	.189251	.192269	.195317	.201496	.207777	.214151	.220608
	.30	.173905	.179416	.185081	.187969	.190891	.193846	.196834	.199852	.202900	.209079	.215360	.221734	.228191
	.20	.181488	.186999	.192664	.195552	.198474	.201429	.204417	.207435	.210483	.216662	.222943	.229317	.235774
	.10	.189071	.194582	.200247	.203134	.206057	.209012	.212000	.215018	.218066	.224245	.230526	.236900	.243357
	0.00	.196654	.202165	.207830	.210717	.213639	.216595	.219583	.222601	.225649	.231828	.238109	.244483	.250939
	-.10	.204237	.209748	.215413	.218300	.221222	.224178	.227166	.230184	.233232	.239411	.245692	.252066	.258522
	-.20	.211820	.217331	.222996	.225883	.228805	.231761	.234748	.237767	.240815	.246994	.253275	.259649	.266105
	-.30	.219403	.224914	.230579	.233466	.236388	.239344	.242331	.245350	.248399	.254577	.260858	.267232	.273688
	-.40	.226986	.232497	.238162	.241049	.243971	.246927	.249914	.252933	.255981	.262160	.268441	.274815	.281271
25	.40	.162712	.168445	.174347	.177355	.180400	.183479	.186590	.189731	.192901	.199320	.205832	.212425	.219087
	.30	.170295	.176028	.181929	.184938	.187983	.191062	.194173	.197314	.200484	.206903	.213415	.220008	.226670
	.20	.177878	.183611	.189512	.192521	.195566	.198644	.201756	.204897	.208067	.214486	.220998	.227591	.234253
	.10	.185461	.191194	.197095	.200104	.203149	.206227	.209339	.212480	.215650	.222069	.228581	.235173	.241836
	0.00	.193044	.198777	.204678	.207687	.210732	.213810	.216921	.220063	.223233	.229652	.236164	.242756	.249419
	-.10	.200627	.206360	.212261	.215270	.218314	.221393	.224504	.227646	.230816	.237234	.243746	.250339	.257002
	-.20	.208210	.213943	.219844	.222853	.225897	.228976	.232087	.235229	.238399	.244817	.251329	.257922	.264585
	-.30	.215793	.221526	.227427	.230436	.233480	.236559	.239670	.242812	.245982	.252400	.258912	.265505	.272168
	-.40	.223376	.229109	.235010	.238019	.241063	.244142	.247253	.250395	.253565	.259983	.266495	.273088	.279751
30	.40	.160424	.166344	.172439	.175545	.178688	.181863	.185070	.188305	.191566	.198158	.204831	.211571	.218365
	.30	.168007	.173927	.180022	.183128	.186270	.189446	.192653	.195888	.199149	.205741	.212414	.219154	.225947
	.20	.175590	.181510	.187605	.190711	.193853	.197029	.200236	.203471	.206732	.213324	.219997	.226737	.233530
	.10	.183173	.189093	.195187	.198294	.201436	.204612	.207819	.211054	.214315	.220907	.227580	.234320	.241113
	0.00	.190756	.196675	.202770	.205877	.209019	.212195	.215401	.218636	.221898	.228490	.235163	.241902	.248696
	-.10	.198339	.204258	.210353	.213460	.216602	.219778	.222984	.226219	.229481	.236073	.242746	.249485	.256279
	-.20	.205922	.211841	.217936	.221043	.224185	.227361	.230567	.233802	.237064	.243656	.250329	.257068	.263862
	-.30	.213504	.219424	.225519	.228626	.231768	.234944	.238150	.241385	.244646	.251239	.257912	.264651	.271445
	-.40	.221087	.227007	.233102	.236209	.239351	.242527	.245733	.248968	.252229	.258822	.265495	.272234	.279028

5.0 YEAR HOLDING PERIOD
.500 EQUITY YIELD RATE
.750 LOAN RATIO

INTEREST RATE

TERM YEARS	APPR DEP	5.0	6.0	7.0	7.5	8.0	8.5	9.0	9.5	10.0	11.0	12.0	13.0	14.0
10	.40	.165220	.170374	.175642	.178318	.181021	.183752	.186510	.189294	.192105	.197803	.203601	.209497	.215486
	.30	.172803	.177957	.183225	.185901	.188604	.191335	.194093	.196877	.199688	.205386	.211184	.217080	.223069
	.20	.180386	.185540	.190808	.193484	.196187	.198918	.201676	.204460	.207271	.212969	.218767	.224662	.230652
	.10	.187969	.193123	.198391	.201067	.203707	.206501	.209259	.212043	.214854	.220552	.226350	.232245	.238235
	0.00	.195552	.200706	.205974	.208650	.211353	.214084	.216842	.219626	.222436	.228134	.233933	.239828	.245818
	-.10	.203135	.208289	.213557	.216233	.218936	.221667	.224425	.227209	.230019	.235717	.241516	.247411	.253401
	-.20	.210718	.215872	.221140	.223816	.226519	.229250	.232008	.234792	.237602	.243300	.249099	.254994	.260984
	-.30	.218301	.223455	.228723	.231399	.234102	.236833	.239591	.242375	.245185	.250883	.256682	.262577	.268567
	-.40	.225884	.231037	.236305	.238981	.241685	.244416	.247174	.249958	.252768	.258466	.264265	.270160	.276150
15	.40	.151370	.156971	.162717	.165642	.168601	.171593	.174616	.177672	.180757	.187016	.193386	.199861	.206433
	.30	.158953	.164554	.170300	.173225	.176184	.179176	.182199	.185255	.188340	.194599	.200969	.207444	.214016
	.20	.166536	.172137	.177883	.180808	.183767	.186758	.189782	.192837	.195923	.202182	.208552	.215027	.221599
	.10	.174119	.179720	.185466	.188391	.191350	.194341	.197365	.200420	.203506	.209765	.216135	.222610	.229182
	0.00	.181702	.187303	.193049	.195974	.198933	.201924	.204948	.208003	.211089	.217348	.223718	.230192	.236765
	-.10	.189284	.194886	.200632	.203557	.206516	.209507	.212531	.215586	.218672	.224931	.231301	.237775	.244348
	-.20	.196867	.202469	.208215	.211140	.214099	.217090	.220114	.223169	.226255	.232514	.238884	.245358	.251930
	-.30	.204450	.210052	.215798	.218723	.221681	.224673	.227697	.230752	.233838	.240097	.246467	.252941	.259513
	-.40	.212033	.217635	.223380	.226306	.229264	.232256	.235280	.238335	.241421	.247679	.254050	.260524	.267096
20	.40	.144655	.150559	.156629	.159723	.162853	.166020	.169221	.172455	.175721	.182341	.189071	.195900	.202818
	.30	.152238	.158142	.164212	.167306	.170436	.173603	.176804	.180038	.183304	.189924	.196654	.203483	.210401
	.20	.159821	.165725	.171795	.174888	.178019	.181186	.184387	.187621	.190887	.197507	.204237	.211066	.217984
	.10	.167404	.173308	.179378	.182471	.185602	.188769	.191970	.195204	.198469	.205090	.211820	.218649	.225566
	0.00	.174986	.180891	.186961	.190054	.193185	.196352	.199553	.202787	.206052	.212673	.219403	.226232	.233149
	-.10	.182569	.188474	.194544	.197637	.200768	.203935	.207136	.210370	.213635	.220256	.226986	.233814	.240732
	-.20	.190152	.196057	.202127	.205220	.208351	.211518	.214719	.217953	.221218	.227839	.234568	.241397	.248315
	-.30	.197735	.203640	.209710	.212803	.215934	.219101	.222302	.225536	.228801	.235421	.242151	.248980	.255898
	-.40	.205318	.211223	.217293	.220386	.223517	.226684	.229885	.233119	.236384	.243004	.249734	.256563	.263481
25	.40	.140787	.146930	.153252	.156476	.159738	.163036	.166370	.169736	.173132	.180009	.186986	.194050	.201188
	.30	.148370	.154512	.160835	.164059	.167321	.170619	.173953	.177319	.180715	.187592	.194569	.201633	.208771
	.20	.155953	.162095	.168418	.171641	.174904	.178202	.181536	.184902	.188298	.195175	.202152	.209216	.216354
	.10	.163535	.169678	.176001	.179224	.182487	.185785	.189119	.192485	.195881	.202758	.209735	.216799	.223937
	0.00	.171118	.177261	.183584	.186807	.190069	.193368	.196702	.200067	.203464	.210341	.217318	.224382	.231520
	-.10	.178701	.184844	.191167	.194390	.197652	.200951	.204285	.207650	.211047	.217924	.224901	.231965	.239103
	-.20	.186284	.192427	.198750	.201973	.205235	.208534	.211867	.215233	.218630	.225507	.232484	.239548	.246686
	-.30	.193867	.200010	.206333	.209556	.212818	.216117	.219450	.222816	.226213	.233090	.240067	.247131	.254269
	-.40	.201450	.207593	.213916	.217139	.220401	.223700	.227033	.230399	.233796	.240673	.247650	.254714	.261852
30	.40	.138335	.144678	.151208	.154536	.157903	.161306	.164741	.168207	.171701	.178765	.185914	.193135	.200414
	.30	.145918	.152261	.158791	.162119	.165486	.168889	.172324	.175790	.179284	.186348	.193497	.200718	.207997
	.20	.153501	.159844	.166374	.169702	.173069	.176472	.179907	.183373	.186867	.193931	.201080	.208301	.215580
	.10	.161084	.167426	.173957	.177285	.180652	.184054	.187490	.190956	.194450	.201514	.208663	.215884	.223163
	0.00	.168667	.175009	.181540	.184868	.188235	.191637	.195073	.198539	.202033	.209097	.216246	.223467	.230746
	-.10	.176250	.182592	.189123	.192451	.195818	.199220	.202656	.206122	.209616	.216680	.223829	.231050	.238329
	-.20	.183833	.190175	.196706	.200034	.203401	.206803	.210239	.213705	.217199	.224262	.231412	.238633	.245912
	-.30	.191416	.197758	.204289	.207617	.210984	.214386	.217822	.221288	.224782	.231845	.238995	.246216	.253495
	-.40	.198999	.205341	.211871	.215200	.218567	.221969	.225405	.228871	.232365	.239428	.246578	.253799	.261078

INTEREST RATE

5.0 YEAR HOLDING PERIOD
.500 EQUITY YIELD RATE
.800 LOAN RATIO

TERM YEARS	APPR DEP	5.0	6.0	7.0	7.5	8.0	8.5	9.0	9.5	10.0	11.0	12.0	13.0	14.0
10	.40	.144923	.150421	.156040	.158895	.161778	.164691	.167633	.170603	.173600	.179678	.185863	.192152	.198541
	.30	.152206	.158004	.163623	.166478	.169735	.172274	.175216	.178186	.181183	.187261	.193446	.199735	.206124
	.20	.160089	.165587	.171206	.174060	.176944	.179857	.182799	.185769	.188766	.194844	.201029	.207318	.213706
	.10	.167672	.173170	.178789	.181643	.184527	.187440	.190382	.193351	.196349	.202427	.208612	.214901	.221289
	0.00	.175255	.180753	.186372	.189226	.192110	.195023	.197965	.200934	.203932	.210010	.216195	.222484	.228872
	-.10	.182838	.188336	.193955	.196809	.199693	.202606	.205547	.208517	.211515	.217593	.223778	.230066	.236455
	-.20	.190421	.195919	.201538	.204392	.207276	.210189	.213130	.216100	.219098	.225176	.231361	.237649	.244038
	-.30	.198004	.203502	.209121	.211975	.214859	.217772	.220713	.223683	.226681	.232759	.238944	.245232	.251621
	-.40	.205587	.211085	.216704	.219558	.222442	.225355	.228296	.231266	.234264	.240342	.246527	.252815	.259204
15	.40	.130150	.136125	.142254	.145374	.148530	.151721	.154946	.158205	.161496	.168172	.174967	.181874	.188884
	.30	.137733	.143708	.149837	.152957	.156113	.159304	.162529	.165788	.169079	.175755	.182550	.189456	.196467
	.20	.145316	.151291	.157419	.160540	.163696	.166887	.170112	.173371	.176662	.183338	.190133	.197039	.204050
	.10	.152899	.158874	.165002	.168122	.171279	.174470	.177695	.180954	.184245	.190921	.197716	.204622	.211633
	0.00	.160482	.166457	.172585	.175705	.178861	.182053	.185278	.188537	.191828	.198504	.205299	.212205	.219216
	-.10	.168065	.174039	.180168	.183288	.186444	.189636	.192861	.196120	.199411	.206087	.212882	.219788	.226799
	-.20	.175648	.181622	.187751	.190871	.194027	.197219	.200444	.203703	.206994	.213670	.220465	.227371	.234381
	-.30	.183230	.189205	.195334	.198454	.201610	.204801	.208027	.211286	.214577	.221253	.228048	.234954	.241964
	-.40	.190813	.196788	.202917	.206037	.209193	.212384	.215610	.218869	.222160	.228836	.235631	.242537	.249547
20	.40	.122987	.129285	.135760	.139060	.142399	.145777	.149191	.152641	.156124	.163186	.170364	.177649	.185028
	.30	.130570	.136868	.143343	.146642	.149982	.153360	.156774	.160224	.163707	.170769	.177947	.185232	.192611
	.20	.138153	.144451	.150926	.154225	.157565	.160943	.164357	.167807	.171290	.178352	.185530	.192814	.200193
	.10	.145736	.152034	.158509	.161808	.165148	.168526	.171940	.175390	.178873	.185935	.193113	.200397	.207776
	0.00	.153319	.159617	.166091	.169391	.172731	.176109	.179523	.182973	.186456	.193517	.200696	.207980	.215359
	-.10	.160902	.167200	.173674	.176974	.180314	.183692	.187106	.190556	.194039	.201100	.208279	.215563	.222942
	-.20	.168485	.174783	.181257	.184557	.187897	.191274	.194689	.198138	.201622	.208683	.215862	.223146	.230525
	-.30	.176068	.182366	.188840	.192140	.195480	.198857	.202272	.205721	.209205	.216266	.223445	.230729	.238108
	-.40	.183651	.189949	.196423	.199723	.203063	.206440	.209855	.213304	.216788	.223849	.231028	.238312	.245691
25	.40	.118861	.125414	.132158	.135596	.139076	.142594	.146150	.149740	.153363	.160699	.168141	.175676	.183290
	.30	.126444	.132997	.139741	.143179	.146659	.150177	.153733	.157323	.160946	.168281	.175724	.183259	.190873
	.20	.134027	.140580	.147324	.150762	.154242	.157760	.161316	.164906	.168529	.175864	.183307	.190841	.198456
	.10	.141610	.148162	.154907	.158345	.161825	.165343	.168899	.172489	.176112	.183447	.190890	.198424	.206038
	0.00	.149193	.155745	.162489	.165928	.169407	.172926	.176482	.180072	.183695	.191030	.198473	.206007	.213621
	-.10	.156776	.163328	.170072	.173511	.176990	.180509	.184065	.187655	.191278	.198613	.206056	.213590	.221204
	-.20	.164359	.170911	.177655	.181094	.184573	.188092	.191648	.195238	.198861	.206196	.213638	.221173	.228787
	-.30	.171942	.178494	.185238	.188677	.192156	.195675	.199230	.202821	.206444	.213779	.221221	.228756	.236370
	-.40	.179525	.186077	.192821	.196260	.199739	.203258	.206813	.210404	.214027	.221362	.228804	.236339	.243953
30	.40	.116246	.123012	.129977	.133528	.137119	.140748	.144413	.148110	.151837	.159371	.166997	.174700	.182464
	.30	.123829	.130595	.137560	.141111	.144702	.148331	.151996	.155693	.159420	.166954	.174580	.182283	.190047
	.20	.131412	.138178	.145143	.148693	.152285	.155914	.159579	.163276	.167003	.174537	.182163	.189866	.197630
	.10	.138995	.145760	.152726	.156276	.159868	.163497	.167162	.170859	.174586	.182120	.189746	.197448	.205213
	0.00	.146578	.153343	.160309	.163859	.167451	.171080	.174745	.178442	.182169	.189703	.197329	.205031	.212796
	-.10	.154161	.160926	.167892	.171442	.175034	.178663	.182327	.186025	.189752	.197286	.204912	.212614	.220379
	-.20	.161744	.168509	.175475	.179025	.182616	.186246	.189910	.193608	.197335	.204869	.212495	.220197	.227962
	-.30	.169327	.176092	.183058	.186608	.190190	.193829	.197493	.201190	.204918	.212452	.220078	.227780	.235545
	-.40	.176910	.183675	.190641	.194191	.197782	.201412	.205076	.208773	.212500	.220035	.227661	.235363	.243128

5.0 YEAR HOLDING PERIOD
.500 EQUITY YIELD RATE
.900 LOAN RATIO

INTEREST RATE

TERM YEARS	APPR DEP	5.0	6.0	7.0	7.5	8.0	8.5	9.0	9.5	10.0	11.0	12.0	13.0	14.0
10	.40	.104330	.110515	.116837	.120048	.123292	.126569	.129878	.133219	.136592	.143430	.150388	.157462	.164650
	.30	.111913	.118098	.124420	.127631	.130875	.134152	.137461	.140802	.144175	.151013	.157971	.165045	.172233
	.20	.119496	.125681	.132003	.135214	.138458	.141735	.145044	.148385	.151758	.158596	.165553	.172628	.179816
	.10	.127079	.133264	.139586	.142797	.146041	.149318	.152627	.155968	.159341	.166178	.173136	.180211	.187398
	0.00	.134662	.140847	.147168	.150380	.153624	.156901	.160210	.163551	.166924	.173761	.180719	.187794	.194981
	-.10	.142245	.148430	.154751	.157963	.161207	.164484	.167793	.171134	.174507	.181344	.188302	.195377	.202564
	-.20	.149828	.156013	.162334	.165546	.168790	.172067	.175376	.178717	.182090	.188927	.195885	.202960	.210147
	-.30	.157411	.163596	.169917	.173128	.176373	.179650	.182959	.186300	.189673	.196510	.203468	.210543	.217730
	-.40	.164994	.171179	.177500	.180711	.183956	.187233	.190542	.193883	.197256	.204093	.211051	.218126	.225313
15	.40	.087710	.094432	.101327	.104837	.108387	.111977	.115606	.119272	.122975	.130485	.138130	.145899	.153786
	.30	.095293	.102015	.108910	.112420	.115970	.119560	.123189	.126855	.130558	.138068	.145713	.153482	.161369
	.20	.102876	.109598	.116493	.120003	.123553	.127143	.130772	.134438	.138141	.145651	.153296	.161065	.168952
	.10	.110459	.117181	.124076	.127586	.131136	.134726	.138355	.142021	.145724	.153234	.160879	.168648	.176535
	0.00	.118042	.124764	.131658	.135169	.138719	.142309	.145938	.149604	.153307	.160817	.168461	.176231	.184118
	-.10	.125625	.132347	.139241	.142752	.146302	.149892	.153521	.157187	.160890	.168400	.176044	.183814	.191700
	-.20	.133208	.139929	.146824	.150334	.153885	.157475	.161104	.164770	.168472	.175983	.183627	.191397	.199283
	-.30	.140791	.147512	.154407	.157917	.161468	.165058	.168687	.172353	.176055	.183566	.191210	.198980	.206866
	-.40	.148374	.155095	.161990	.165500	.169051	.172641	.176270	.179936	.183638	.191149	.198793	.206563	.214449
20	.40	.079652	.086737	.094021	.097733	.101490	.105290	.109132	.113012	.116931	.124875	.132951	.141146	.149448
	.30	.087235	.094320	.101604	.105316	.109073	.112873	.116715	.120595	.124514	.132458	.140534	.148729	.157030
	.20	.094818	.101903	.109187	.112899	.116656	.120456	.124297	.128178	.132097	.140041	.148117	.156312	.164613
	.10	.102401	.109486	.116770	.120482	.124239	.128039	.131880	.135761	.139680	.147624	.155700	.163895	.172196
	0.00	.109984	.117069	.124353	.128065	.131822	.135622	.139463	.143344	.147263	.155207	.163283	.171478	.179779
	-.10	.117567	.124652	.131936	.135648	.139405	.143205	.147046	.150927	.154846	.162790	.170866	.179061	.187362
	-.20	.125150	.132235	.139519	.143231	.146988	.150788	.154629	.158510	.162429	.170373	.178449	.186644	.194945
	-.30	.132733	.139818	.147102	.150814	.154571	.158371	.162212	.166093	.170012	.177956	.186032	.194227	.202528
	-.40	.140316	.147401	.154685	.158397	.162154	.165954	.169795	.173676	.177595	.185539	.193615	.201810	.210111
25	.40	.075010	.082382	.089969	.093837	.097752	.101710	.105710	.109749	.113825	.122077	.130450	.138926	.147492
	.30	.082593	.089965	.097552	.101420	.105335	.109293	.113293	.117332	.121408	.129660	.138033	.146509	.155075
	.20	.090176	.097548	.105135	.109003	.112918	.116876	.120876	.124915	.128991	.137243	.145616	.154092	.162658
	.10	.097759	.105131	.112718	.116586	.120500	.124459	.128459	.132498	.136574	.144826	.153199	.161675	.170241
	0.00	.105342	.112714	.120301	.124169	.128083	.132042	.136042	.140081	.144157	.152409	.160782	.169258	.177824
	-.10	.112925	.120296	.127884	.131752	.135666	.139625	.143625	.147664	.151740	.159999	.168365	.176841	.185407
	-.20	.120508	.127879	.135467	.139335	.143249	.147208	.151208	.155247	.159323	.167575	.175948	.184424	.192990
	-.30	.128091	.135462	.143049	.146918	.150832	.154791	.158791	.162830	.166905	.175158	.183530	.192007	.200573
	-.40	.135674	.143045	.150632	.154501	.158415	.162374	.166374	.170413	.174488	.182741	.191113	.199590	.208156
30	.40	.072068	.079680	.087516	.091510	.095550	.099633	.103756	.107915	.112108	.120584	.129164	.137829	.146563
	.30	.079651	.087262	.095099	.099093	.103133	.107216	.111339	.115498	.119691	.128167	.136747	.145442	.154146
	.20	.087234	.094845	.102682	.106676	.110716	.114799	.118922	.123081	.127274	.135750	.144330	.152994	.161729
	.10	.094817	.102428	.110265	.114259	.118299	.122382	.126505	.130664	.134857	.143333	.151912	.160577	.169312
	0.00	.102400	.110011	.117848	.121842	.125882	.129965	.134088	.138247	.142440	.150916	.159495	.168160	.176895
	-.10	.109983	.117594	.125431	.129425	.133465	.137548	.141671	.145830	.150023	.158499	.167078	.175743	.184478
	-.20	.117566	.125177	.133014	.137008	.141048	.145131	.149253	.153413	.157606	.166082	.174661	.183326	.192061
	-.30	.125149	.132760	.140597	.144591	.148631	.152714	.156836	.160996	.165189	.173665	.182244	.190909	.199644
	-.40	.132732	.140343	.148179	.152174	.156214	.160297	.164419	.168579	.172772	.181248	.189827	.198492	.207227

10.0 YEAR HOLDING PERIOD
.040 EQUITY YIELD RATE
.600 LOAN RATIO

INTEREST RATE

TERM YEARS	APPR DEP	5.0	6.0	7.0	7.5	8.0	8.5	9.0	9.5	10.0	11.0	12.0	13.0	14.0
10	.40	.009076	.012644	.016307	.018174	.020065	.021979	.023916	.025875	.027858	.031889	.036008	.040213	.044501
	.30	.017405	.020973	.024636	.026503	.028394	.030308	.032245	.034204	.036187	.040218	.044337	.048542	.052830
	.20	.025734	.029302	.032965	.034833	.036723	.038637	.040574	.042533	.044516	.048547	.052666	.056871	.061159
	.10	.034064	.037631	.041294	.043162	.045052	.046966	.048903	.050863	.052845	.056876	.060995	.065200	.069488
	0.00	.042393	.045960	.049624	.051491	.053381	.055295	.057232	.059192	.061174	.065205	.069325	.073529	.077817
	-.10	.050722	.054289	.057953	.059820	.061710	.063624	.065561	.067521	.069503	.073535	.077654	.081858	.086146
	-.20	.059051	.062618	.066282	.068149	.070039	.071953	.073890	.075850	.077832	.081864	.085983	.090187	.094475
	-.30	.067380	.070947	.074611	.076478	.078369	.080282	.082219	.084179	.086161	.090193	.094312	.098516	.102805
	-.40	.075709	.079277	.082940	.084807	.086698	.088612	.090548	.092508	.094490	.098522	.102641	.106846	.111134
15	.40	.010588	.015280	.020109	.022574	.025070	.027597	.030154	.032741	.035356	.040669	.046084	.051596	.057197
	.30	.018917	.023609	.028439	.030903	.033399	.035926	.038483	.041070	.043685	.048998	.054413	.059925	.065526
	.20	.027246	.031938	.036768	.039232	.041728	.044255	.046812	.049399	.052014	.057327	.062742	.068254	.073855
	.10	.035575	.040267	.045097	.047561	.050057	.052584	.055141	.057728	.060343	.065656	.071072	.076583	.082184
	0.00	.043904	.048597	.053426	.055890	.058386	.060913	.063471	.066057	.068672	.073985	.079401	.084912	.090513
	-.10	.052233	.056926	.061755	.064219	.066715	.069242	.071800	.074386	.077002	.082314	.087730	.093242	.098842
	-.20	.060562	.065255	.070084	.072548	.075044	.077571	.080129	.082715	.085331	.090643	.096059	.101571	.107172
	-.30	.068892	.073584	.078413	.080877	.083373	.085900	.088458	.091045	.093660	.098972	.104388	.109900	.115501
	-.40	.077221	.081913	.086742	.089206	.091702	.094230	.096787	.099374	.101989	.107301	.112717	.118229	.123830
20	.40	.011321	.016541	.021900	.024628	.027386	.030171	.032984	.035822	.038684	.044474	.050341	.056275	.062267
	.30	.019650	.024870	.030230	.032957	.035715	.038501	.041313	.044151	.047013	.052803	.058670	.064604	.070596
	.20	.027979	.033200	.038559	.041286	.044044	.046830	.049642	.052480	.055342	.061132	.066999	.072934	.078925
	.10	.036308	.041529	.046888	.049615	.052373	.055159	.057971	.060810	.063671	.069461	.075328	.081263	.087254
	0.00	.044637	.049858	.055217	.057944	.060702	.063488	.066301	.069139	.072001	.077790	.083657	.089592	.095583
	-.10	.052966	.058187	.063546	.066273	.069031	.071817	.074630	.077468	.080330	.086119	.091986	.097921	.103912
	-.20	.061295	.066516	.071875	.074603	.077360	.080146	.082959	.085797	.088659	.094448	.100315	.106250	.112241
	-.30	.069624	.074845	.080204	.082932	.085689	.088475	.091288	.094126	.096988	.102777	.108645	.114579	.120571
	-.40	.077954	.083174	.088533	.091261	.094018	.096804	.099617	.102455	.105317	.111106	.116974	.122908	.128900
25	.40	.011743	.017255	.022894	.025755	.028641	.031550	.034480	.037429	.040395	.046371	.052397	.058460	.064552
	.30	.020072	.025584	.031223	.034084	.036970	.039879	.042809	.045758	.048724	.054700	.060726	.066790	.072881
	.20	.028401	.033914	.039552	.042413	.045299	.048208	.051138	.054087	.057053	.063030	.069055	.075119	.081210
	.10	.036730	.042243	.047881	.050742	.053628	.056537	.059467	.062416	.065382	.071359	.077384	.083448	.089539
	0.00	.045059	.050572	.056210	.059071	.061957	.064866	.067796	.070745	.073711	.079688	.085713	.091777	.097868
	-.10	.053388	.058901	.064539	.067400	.070286	.073195	.076125	.079074	.082040	.088017	.094043	.100106	.106197
	-.20	.061718	.067230	.072868	.075729	.078616	.081524	.084454	.087403	.090369	.096346	.102372	.108435	.114526
	-.30	.070047	.075559	.081198	.084059	.086945	.089854	.092783	.095732	.098698	.104675	.110701	.116764	.122856
	-.40	.078376	.083888	.089527	.092388	.095274	.098183	.101113	.104061	.107027	.113004	.119030	.125093	.131185
30	.40	.012011	.017698	.023495	.026428	.029380	.032350	.035334	.038331	.041340	.047384	.053454	.059541	.065637
	.30	.020340	.026027	.031824	.034757	.037709	.040679	.043663	.046661	.049669	.055713	.061783	.067870	.073966
	.20	.028669	.034356	.040153	.043086	.046038	.049008	.051992	.054990	.057998	.064042	.070113	.076199	.082296
	.10	.036998	.042686	.048482	.051415	.054367	.057337	.060321	.063319	.066327	.072371	.078442	.084529	.090625
	0.00	.045327	.051015	.056812	.059744	.062697	.065666	.068650	.071648	.074656	.080701	.086771	.092858	.098954
	-.10	.053656	.059344	.065141	.068073	.071026	.073995	.076979	.079977	.082986	.089030	.095100	.101187	.107283
	-.20	.061985	.067673	.073470	.076402	.079355	.082324	.085309	.088306	.091315	.097359	.103429	.109516	.115612
	-.30	.070314	.076002	.081799	.084732	.087684	.090653	.093638	.096635	.099644	.105688	.111758	.117845	.123941
	-.40	.078643	.084331	.090128	.093061	.096013	.098982	.101967	.104964	.107973	.114017	.120087	.126174	.132270

10.0 YEAR HOLDING PERIOD
.040 EQUITY YIELD RATE
.667 LOAN RATIO

INTEREST RATE

TERM YEARS	APPR DEP	5.0	6.0	7.0	7.5	8.0	8.5	9.0	9.5	10.0	11.0	12.0	13.0	14.0
10	.40	.009342	.013306	.017376	.019451	.021552	.023678	.025830	.028008	.030210	.034690	.039267	.043938	.048703
	.30	.017671	.021635	.025706	.027780	.029981	.032007	.034159	.036337	.038539	.043019	.047596	.052268	.057032
	.20	.026000	.029964	.034035	.036109	.038202	.040336	.042489	.044666	.046869	.051348	.055925	.060597	.065361
	.10	.034329	.038293	.042364	.044438	.046539	.048666	.050818	.052995	.055198	.059677	.064254	.068926	.073690
	0.00	.042658	.046622	.050693	.052768	.054868	.056995	.059147	.061324	.063527	.068006	.072583	.077255	.082019
	-.10	.050988	.054952	.059022	.061097	.063197	.065324	.067476	.069653	.071856	.076335	.080912	.085584	.090348
	-.20	.059317	.063281	.067351	.069426	.071526	.073653	.075805	.077982	.080185	.084664	.089241	.093913	.098678
	-.30	.067646	.071610	.075680	.077755	.079855	.081982	.084134	.086311	.088514	.092993	.097570	.102242	.107007
	-.40	.075975	.079939	.084009	.086084	.088185	.090311	.092463	.094641	.096843	.101323	.105899	.110571	.115336
15	.40	.011022	.016235	.021601	.024339	.027113	.029921	.032762	.035636	.038542	.044445	.050462	.056587	.062810
	.30	.019351	.024564	.029930	.032668	.035442	.038250	.041091	.043965	.046871	.052774	.058791	.064916	.071139
	.20	.027680	.032894	.038259	.040997	.043771	.046579	.049420	.052294	.055200	.061103	.067120	.073245	.079468
	.10	.036009	.041223	.046589	.049327	.052101	.054908	.057749	.060624	.063529	.069432	.075450	.081574	.087797
	0.00	.044338	.049552	.054918	.057656	.060429	.063237	.066078	.068953	.071858	.077761	.083779	.089903	.096126
	-.10	.052667	.057881	.063247	.065985	.068758	.071566	.074408	.077282	.080188	.086090	.092108	.098232	.104455
	-.20	.060996	.066210	.071576	.074314	.077087	.079895	.082737	.085611	.088517	.094419	.100437	.106561	.112784
	-.30	.069325	.074539	.079905	.082643	.085416	.088224	.091066	.093940	.096846	.102748	.108766	.114890	.121114
	-.40	.077654	.082868	.088234	.090972	.093745	.096553	.099395	.102269	.105175	.111078	.117095	.123219	.129443
20	.40	.011836	.017637	.023591	.026622	.029686	.032781	.035907	.039060	.042240	.048673	.055192	.061786	.068443
	.30	.020165	.025966	.031920	.034951	.038015	.041110	.044236	.047389	.050569	.057002	.063521	.070115	.076772
	.20	.028494	.034295	.040249	.043280	.046344	.049440	.052565	.055718	.058898	.065331	.071850	.078444	.085101
	.10	.036823	.042624	.048578	.051609	.054673	.057769	.060894	.064047	.067227	.073660	.080179	.086773	.093430
	0.00	.045152	.050953	.056908	.059938	.063002	.066098	.069223	.072376	.075556	.081989	.088508	.095102	.101760
	-.10	.053482	.059282	.065237	.068267	.071332	.074427	.077552	.080705	.083885	.090318	.096837	.103431	.110089
	-.20	.061811	.067611	.073566	.076596	.079660	.082756	.085881	.089035	.092215	.098647	.105166	.111760	.118848
	-.30	.070140	.075940	.081895	.084926	.087990	.091085	.094210	.097364	.100544	.106976	.113496	.120089	.126747
	-.40	.078469	.084270	.090224	.093255	.096319	.099414	.102539	.105693	.108873	.115305	.121825	.128419	.135076
25	.40	.012305	.018430	.024695	.027874	.031081	.034313	.037568	.040845	.044141	.050781	.057477	.064214	.070982
	.30	.020634	.026759	.033024	.036203	.039410	.042642	.045897	.049174	.052470	.059110	.065806	.072543	.079311
	.20	.028963	.035088	.041353	.044532	.047739	.050971	.054227	.057503	.060799	.067440	.074135	.080872	.087640
	.10	.037292	.043417	.049682	.052861	.056068	.059300	.062556	.065832	.069128	.075769	.082464	.089201	.095969
	0.00	.045622	.051746	.058011	.061190	.064397	.067629	.070885	.074161	.077457	.084098	.090793	.097530	.104298
	-.10	.053951	.060075	.066341	.069520	.072726	.075958	.079214	.082490	.085786	.092427	.099122	.105859	.112627
	-.20	.062280	.068405	.074670	.077849	.081056	.084288	.087543	.090819	.094115	.100756	.107451	.114188	.120957
	-.30	.070609	.076734	.082999	.086178	.089384	.092617	.095872	.099149	.102444	.109085	.115780	.122517	.129286
	-.40	.078938	.085063	.091328	.094507	.097714	.100946	.104201	.107478	.110773	.117414	.124109	.130846	.137615
30	.40	.012602	.018922	.025363	.028622	.031902	.035201	.038518	.041848	.045191	.051907	.058651	.065415	.072188
	.30	.020932	.027251	.033692	.036951	.040231	.043531	.046847	.050177	.053520	.060236	.066981	.073744	.080517
	.20	.029261	.035580	.042021	.045280	.048560	.051860	.055176	.058506	.061849	.068565	.075310	.082073	.088846
	.10	.037590	.043909	.050351	.053609	.056889	.060189	.063505	.066835	.070178	.076894	.083639	.090402	.097175
	0.00	.045919	.052239	.058680	.061938	.065218	.068518	.071834	.075164	.078507	.085223	.091968	.098731	.105505
	-.10	.054248	.060568	.067009	.070267	.073548	.076847	.080163	.083494	.086836	.093552	.100297	.107060	.113834
	-.20	.062577	.068897	.075338	.078596	.081877	.085176	.088492	.091823	.095166	.101881	.108626	.115389	.122163
	-.30	.070906	.077226	.083667	.086926	.090206	.093505	.096821	.100152	.103495	.110210	.116955	.123718	.130492
	-.40	.079235	.085555	.091996	.095255	.098535	.101834	.105150	.108481	.111824	.118539	.125284	.132047	.138821

```
10.0 YEAR HOLDING PERIOD
 .040 EQUITY YIELD RATE
 .700 LOAN RATIO
```

INTEREST RATE

TERM YEARS	APPR DEP	5.0	6.0	7.0	7.5	8.0	8.5	9.0	9.5	10.0	11.0	12.0	13.0	14.0
10	.40	.009475	.013637	.017911	.020089	.022295	.024528	.026788	.029074	.031387	.036090	.040896	.045801	.050804
	.30	.017804	.021966	.026240	.028419	.030624	.032857	.035117	.037403	.039716	.044419	.049225	.054130	.059133
	.20	.026133	.030295	.034569	.036748	.038953	.041186	.043446	.045732	.048045	.052748	.057554	.062459	.067462
	.10	.034462	.038624	.042898	.045077	.047282	.049515	.051775	.054061	.056374	.061077	.065883	.070788	.075791
	0.00	.042791	.046954	.051227	.053406	.055612	.057844	.060104	.062390	.064703	.069406	.074212	.079117	.084120
	-.10	.051120	.055283	.059557	.061735	.063941	.066173	.068433	.070719	.073032	.077735	.082541	.087446	.092449
	-.20	.059450	.063612	.067886	.070064	.072270	.074503	.076762	.079048	.081361	.086065	.090871	.095776	.100778
	-.30	.067779	.071941	.076215	.078393	.080599	.082832	.085091	.087378	.089690	.094394	.099199	.104105	.109107
	-.40	.076108	.080270	.084544	.086722	.088928	.091161	.093420	.095707	.098019	.102723	.107528	.112434	.117437
15	.40	.011239	.016713	.022347	.025222	.028134	.031082	.034066	.037084	.040135	.046333	.052651	.059082	.065616
	.30	.019568	.025042	.030676	.033551	.036463	.039411	.042395	.045413	.048464	.054662	.060980	.067411	.073945
	.20	.027897	.033371	.039005	.041880	.044792	.047740	.050724	.053742	.056793	.062991	.069309	.075740	.082274
	.10	.036226	.041700	.047334	.050209	.053121	.056070	.059053	.062071	.065122	.071320	.077638	.084069	.090603
	0.00	.044555	.050029	.055663	.058538	.061450	.064399	.067382	.070400	.073451	.079649	.085967	.092398	.098932
	-.10	.052884	.058358	.063993	.066867	.069779	.072728	.075711	.078729	.081780	.087978	.094296	.100727	.107261
	-.20	.061213	.066687	.072322	.075196	.078109	.081057	.084040	.087058	.090109	.096307	.102626	.109056	.115590
	-.30	.069542	.075017	.080651	.083526	.086438	.089386	.092370	.095387	.098439	.104636	.110955	.117385	.123920
	-.40	.077871	.083346	.088980	.091855	.094767	.097715	.100699	.103717	.106768	.112965	.119284	.125714	.132249
20	.40	.012094	.018184	.024437	.027619	.030836	.034086	.037368	.040679	.044018	.050772	.057617	.064541	.071531
	.30	.020423	.026513	.032766	.035948	.039165	.042415	.045697	.049008	.052347	.059101	.065946	.072870	.079860
	.20	.028752	.034843	.041095	.044277	.047494	.050744	.054026	.057337	.060676	.067430	.074275	.081199	.088189
	.10	.037081	.043172	.049424	.052606	.055823	.059073	.062355	.065666	.069005	.075759	.082604	.089528	.096518
	0.00	.045410	.051501	.057753	.060935	.064153	.067402	.070684	.073995	.077334	.084088	.090933	.097857	.104847
	-.10	.053739	.059830	.066082	.069264	.072481	.075732	.079013	.082324	.085663	.092417	.099263	.106186	.113176
	-.20	.062068	.068159	.074411	.077593	.080810	.084061	.087342	.090653	.093992	.100746	.107592	.114515	.121505
	-.30	.070397	.076488	.082740	.085922	.089139	.092390	.095671	.098982	.102321	.109076	.115921	.122844	.129834
	-.40	.078726	.084817	.091069	.094251	.097469	.100719	.104000	.107311	.110650	.117405	.124250	.131173	.138164
25	.40	.012586	.019017	.025596	.028933	.032300	.035694	.039112	.042553	.046013	.052986	.060016	.067090	.074197
	.30	.020915	.027346	.033925	.037263	.040630	.044023	.047442	.050882	.054342	.061315	.068345	.075419	.082526
	.20	.029244	.035675	.042254	.045592	.048959	.052352	.055771	.059211	.062671	.069644	.076674	.083748	.090855
	.10	.037573	.044005	.050583	.053921	.057288	.060682	.064100	.067540	.071000	.077973	.085003	.092077	.099184
	0.00	.045903	.052334	.058912	.062250	.065617	.069011	.072429	.075869	.079330	.086302	.093332	.100406	.107513
	-.10	.054232	.060663	.067241	.070579	.073946	.077340	.080758	.084198	.087659	.094631	.101661	.108735	.115842
	-.20	.062561	.068992	.075570	.078908	.082275	.085669	.089087	.092527	.095988	.102961	.109991	.117065	.124171
	-.30	.070890	.077321	.083899	.087237	.090604	.093998	.097416	.100856	.104317	.111290	.118320	.125394	.132500
	-.40	.079219	.085650	.092228	.095566	.098933	.102327	.105745	.109186	.112646	.119619	.126649	.133723	.140829
30	.40	.012898	.019534	.026297	.029719	.033163	.036627	.040109	.043606	.047116	.054168	.061250	.068351	.075463
	.30	.021227	.027863	.034626	.038048	.041492	.044956	.048438	.051935	.055445	.062497	.069579	.076680	.083792
	.20	.029557	.036192	.042955	.046377	.049821	.053285	.056767	.060264	.063774	.070826	.077908	.085009	.092121
	.10	.037886	.044521	.051284	.054706	.058150	.061615	.065096	.068593	.072103	.079155	.086237	.093338	.100450
	0.00	.046215	.052850	.059614	.063035	.066479	.069944	.073425	.076922	.080433	.087484	.094566	.101667	.108779
	-.10	.054544	.061180	.067943	.071364	.074808	.078273	.081755	.085252	.088762	.095813	.102895	.109996	.117109
	-.20	.062873	.069509	.076272	.079693	.083137	.086602	.090084	.093581	.097091	.104142	.111224	.118325	.125438
	-.30	.071202	.077838	.084601	.088022	.091467	.094931	.098413	.101910	.105420	.112471	.119553	.126655	.133767
	-.40	.079531	.086167	.092930	.096351	.099796	.103260	.106742	.110239	.113749	.120800	.127882	.134984	.142096

10.0 YEAR HOLDING PERIOD
.040 EQUITY YIELD RATE
.750 LOAN RATIO

INTEREST RATE

TERM YEARS	APPR DEP	5.0	6.0	7.0	7.5	8.0	8.5	9.0	9.5	10.0	11.0	12.0	13.0	14.0
10	.40	.009674	.014134	.018713	.021047	.023410	.025803	.028224	.030673	.033151	.038190	.043339	.048595	.053955
	.30	.018003	.022463	.027042	.029376	.031739	.034132	.036553	.039002	.041480	.046520	.051668	.056924	.062284
	.20	.026333	.030792	.035371	.037705	.040068	.042461	.044882	.047331	.049809	.054849	.059997	.065253	.070613
	.10	.034662	.039121	.043700	.046034	.048398	.050790	.053211	.055660	.058138	.063178	.068327	.073582	.078942
	0.00	.042991	.047450	.052029	.054363	.056727	.059119	.061540	.063990	.066467	.071507	.076656	.081911	.087272
	-.10	.051320	.055779	.060359	.062692	.065056	.067448	.069869	.072319	.074797	.079836	.084985	.090241	.095601
	-.20	.059649	.064108	.068688	.071022	.073385	.075777	.078198	.080648	.083126	.088165	.093314	.098570	.103930
	-.30	.067978	.072438	.077017	.079351	.081714	.084106	.086527	.088977	.091455	.096494	.101643	.106899	.112259
	-.40	.076307	.080767	.085346	.087680	.090043	.092435	.094856	.097306	.099784	.104823	.109972	.115228	.120588
15	.40	.011564	.017429	.023466	.026546	.029666	.032825	.036022	.039255	.042524	.049165	.055934	.062824	.069825
	.30	.019893	.025758	.031795	.034875	.037995	.041154	.044351	.047584	.050853	.057494	.064263	.071153	.078154
	.20	.028222	.034087	.040124	.043204	.046324	.049483	.052680	.055913	.059182	.065823	.072593	.079482	.086484
	.10	.036551	.042417	.048453	.051533	.054653	.057812	.061009	.064242	.067512	.074152	.080922	.087812	.094813
	0.00	.044880	.050746	.056782	.059862	.062983	.066141	.069338	.072572	.075841	.082481	.089251	.096141	.103142
	-.10	.053209	.059075	.065111	.068192	.071312	.074471	.077667	.080901	.084170	.090810	.097580	.104470	.111471
	-.20	.061539	.067404	.073440	.076521	.079641	.082800	.085996	.089230	.092499	.099139	.105909	.112799	.119800
	-.30	.069868	.075733	.081770	.084850	.087970	.091129	.094325	.097559	.100828	.107468	.114238	.121128	.128129
	-.40	.078197	.084062	.090099	.093179	.096299	.099458	.102655	.105888	.109157	.115797	.122567	.129457	.136458
20	.40	.012480	.019006	.025705	.029114	.032561	.036043	.039559	.043107	.046684	.053921	.061255	.068673	.076163
	.30	.020809	.027335	.034034	.037443	.040890	.044372	.047888	.051436	.055013	.062250	.069584	.077002	.084492
	.20	.029138	.035664	.042363	.045772	.049219	.052702	.056218	.059765	.063343	.070579	.077913	.085331	.092821
	.10	.037467	.043993	.050692	.054101	.057548	.061031	.064547	.068094	.071672	.078908	.086242	.093661	.101150
	0.00	.045796	.052322	.059021	.062430	.065877	.069360	.072876	.076423	.080001	.087237	.094572	.101990	.109479
	-.10	.054126	.060651	.067350	.070760	.074206	.077689	.081205	.084752	.088330	.095567	.102901	.110319	.117808
	-.20	.062455	.068980	.075679	.079089	.082536	.086018	.089534	.093082	.096659	.103896	.111230	.118648	.126137
	-.30	.070784	.077309	.084008	.087418	.090865	.094347	.097863	.101411	.104988	.112225	.119559	.126977	.134466
	-.40	.079113	.085639	.092337	.095747	.099194	.102676	.106192	.109740	.113317	.120554	.127888	.135306	.142796
25	.40	.013008	.019898	.026946	.030523	.034130	.037766	.041429	.045115	.048822	.056293	.063825	.071405	.079019
	.30	.021337	.028227	.035276	.038852	.042459	.046096	.049758	.053444	.057152	.064622	.072155	.079734	.087348
	.20	.029666	.036556	.043605	.047181	.050788	.054425	.058087	.061773	.065481	.072952	.080484	.088063	.095677
	.10	.037995	.044886	.051934	.055510	.059118	.062754	.066416	.070102	.073810	.081281	.088813	.096392	.104006
	0.00	.046324	.053215	.060263	.063839	.067447	.071083	.074745	.078431	.082139	.089610	.097142	.104721	.112335
	-.10	.054653	.061544	.068592	.072168	.075776	.079412	.083074	.086760	.090468	.097939	.105471	.113050	.120664
	-.20	.062982	.069873	.076921	.080497	.084105	.087741	.091403	.095089	.098797	.106268	.113800	.121379	.128993
	-.30	.071311	.078202	.085250	.088826	.092434	.096070	.099732	.103419	.107126	.114597	.122129	.129708	.137323
	-.40	.079641	.086531	.093579	.097155	.100763	.104399	.108062	.111748	.115455	.122926	.130458	.138037	.145652
30	.40	.013342	.020452	.027698	.031364	.035065	.038766	.042497	.046243	.050004	.057559	.065147	.072756	.080376
	.30	.021671	.028781	.036027	.039693	.043383	.047095	.050826	.054573	.058333	.065888	.073476	.081085	.088705
	.20	.030000	.037110	.044356	.048022	.051712	.055424	.059155	.062901	.066662	.074217	.081805	.089414	.097034
	.10	.038330	.045439	.052685	.056351	.060042	.063753	.067484	.071231	.074991	.082547	.090135	.097743	.105363
	0.00	.046659	.053768	.061014	.064680	.068371	.072082	.075813	.079560	.083321	.090876	.098463	.106072	.113692
	-.10	.054988	.062097	.069344	.073009	.076700	.080412	.084142	.087889	.091650	.099205	.106793	.114401	.122021
	-.20	.063317	.070427	.077673	.081339	.085029	.088741	.092471	.096218	.099979	.107534	.115122	.122730	.130350
	-.30	.071646	.078756	.086002	.089668	.093358	.097070	.100800	.104547	.108308	.115863	.123451	.131059	.138680
	-.40	.079975	.087085	.094331	.097997	.101687	.105399	.109129	.112876	.116637	.124192	.131780	.139388	.147009

10.0 YEAR HOLDING PERIOD
.040 EQUITY YIELD RATE
.800 LOAN RATIO

INTEREST RATE

TERM YEARS	APPR DEP	5.0	6.0	7.0	7.5	8.0	8.5	9.0	9.5	10.0	11.0	12.0	13.0	14.0
10	.40	.009874	.014631	.019515	.022005	.024525	.027077	.029660	.032273	.034916	.040291	.045783	.051389	.057107
	.30	.018203	.022960	.027844	.030354	.032854	.035406	.037989	.040602	.043245	.048620	.054112	.059718	.065436
	.20	.026532	.031289	.036173	.038663	.041184	.043735	.046318	.048931	.051574	.056949	.062441	.068047	.073765
	.10	.034861	.039618	.044502	.046992	.049513	.052064	.054647	.057260	.059903	.065278	.070770	.076376	.082094
	0.00	.043190	.047947	.052831	.055321	.057842	.060394	.062976	.065589	.068232	.073607	.079099	.084706	.090423
	-.10	.051519	.056276	.061160	.063650	.066171	.068723	.071305	.073918	.076561	.081936	.087428	.093035	.098752
	-.20	.059848	.064605	.069490	.071979	.074500	.077052	.079634	.082247	.084890	.090265	.095758	.101364	.107081
	-.30	.068177	.072934	.077819	.080308	.082829	.085381	.087963	.090576	.093219	.098595	.104087	.109693	.115410
	-.40	.076507	.081263	.086148	.088637	.091158	.093710	.096292	.098905	.101548	.106924	.112416	.118022	.123739
15	.40	.011889	.018146	.024585	.027870	.031198	.034568	.037978	.041427	.044914	.051997	.059218	.066567	.074035
	.30	.020218	.026475	.032914	.036199	.039527	.042897	.046307	.049756	.053243	.060326	.067547	.074896	.082364
	.20	.028548	.034804	.041243	.044528	.047857	.051226	.054636	.058085	.061572	.068655	.075876	.083225	.090693
	.10	.036877	.043133	.049572	.052858	.056186	.059555	.062965	.066414	.069901	.076984	.084205	.091554	.099022
	0.00	.045206	.051462	.057901	.061187	.064515	.067884	.071294	.074743	.078230	.085313	.092534	.099883	.107351
	-.10	.053535	.059791	.066230	.069516	.072844	.076213	.079623	.083072	.086559	.093642	.100863	.108212	.115680
	-.20	.061864	.068120	.074559	.077845	.081173	.084542	.087952	.091401	.094888	.101971	.109192	.116542	.124009
	-.30	.070193	.076449	.082888	.086174	.089502	.092871	.096281	.099730	.103217	.110300	.117521	.124871	.132338
	-.40	.078522	.084778	.091217	.094503	.097831	.101201	.104610	.108059	.111546	.118630	.125851	.133200	.140668
20	.40	.012867	.019827	.026973	.030609	.034286	.038001	.041751	.045535	.049351	.057070	.064893	.072806	.080795
	.30	.021196	.028156	.035302	.038939	.042615	.046330	.050080	.053864	.057680	.065399	.073222	.081135	.089124
	.20	.029525	.036486	.043631	.047268	.050944	.054659	.058409	.062193	.066009	.073728	.081551	.089464	.097453
	.10	.037854	.044815	.051960	.055597	.059273	.062988	.066738	.070522	.074338	.082057	.089881	.097793	.105782
	0.00	.046183	.053144	.060289	.063926	.067603	.071317	.075067	.078852	.082667	.090387	.098210	.106122	.114111
	-.10	.054512	.061473	.068618	.072255	.075932	.079646	.083397	.087181	.090997	.098716	.106539	.114451	.122440
	-.20	.062841	.069802	.076947	.080584	.084261	.087975	.091726	.095510	.099326	.107045	.114868	.122780	.130769
	-.30	.071170	.078131	.085276	.088913	.092590	.096304	.100055	.103839	.107655	.115374	.123197	.131110	.139098
	-.40	.079499	.086460	.093605	.097242	.100919	.104633	.108384	.112168	.115984	.123703	.131526	.139439	.147427
25	.40	.013429	.020779	.028297	.032112	.035960	.039839	.043745	.047677	.051632	.059601	.067635	.075719	.083841
	.30	.021759	.029108	.036626	.040441	.044289	.048168	.052074	.056006	.059961	.067930	.075964	.084049	.092170
	.20	.030088	.037437	.044955	.048770	.052618	.056497	.060403	.064335	.068290	.076259	.084293	.092378	.100499
	.10	.038417	.045767	.053285	.057099	.060947	.064826	.068732	.072664	.076619	.084588	.092622	.100707	.108829
	0.00	.046746	.054096	.061614	.065428	.069276	.073155	.077062	.080993	.084948	.092917	.100951	.109036	.117158
	-.10	.055075	.062425	.069943	.073757	.077606	.081484	.085391	.089322	.093277	.101246	.109280	.117365	.125487
	-.20	.063404	.070754	.078272	.082087	.085935	.089813	.093720	.097652	.101606	.109575	.117609	.125694	.133816
	-.30	.071733	.079083	.086601	.090416	.094264	.098142	.102049	.105981	.109935	.117904	.125939	.134023	.142145
	-.40	.080062	.087412	.094930	.098743	.102593	.106471	.110378	.114310	.118264	.126233	.134268	.142352	.150474
30	.40	.013786	.021370	.029099	.033009	.036946	.040905	.044884	.048881	.052892	.060951	.069045	.077161	.085289
	.30	.022115	.029699	.037428	.041338	.045279	.049234	.053213	.057210	.061221	.069280	.077374	.085490	.093618
	.20	.030444	.038028	.045757	.049668	.053604	.057563	.061542	.065539	.069550	.077609	.085703	.093819	.101947
	.10	.038773	.046357	.054086	.057997	.061933	.065892	.069871	.073868	.077880	.085938	.094032	.102148	.110276
	0.00	.047103	.054686	.062415	.066326	.070262	.074221	.078201	.082197	.086209	.094267	.102361	.110477	.118605
	-.10	.055432	.063015	.070745	.074655	.078591	.082550	.086530	.090526	.094538	.102596	.110690	.118806	.126934
	-.20	.063761	.071344	.079074	.082984	.086920	.090879	.094859	.098855	.102867	.110926	.119019	.127135	.135263
	-.30	.072090	.079673	.087403	.091313	.095249	.099209	.103188	.107184	.111196	.119255	.127348	.135464	.143592
	-.40	.080419	.088003	.095732	.099642	.103578	.107538	.111517	.115514	.119525	.127584	.135677	.143793	.151921

10.0 YEAR HOLDING PERIOD
.040 EQUITY YIELD RATE
.900 LOAN RATIO

INTEREST RATE

TERM YEARS	APPR DEP	5.0	6.0	7.0	7.5	8.0	8.5	9.0	9.5	10.0	11.0	12.0	13.0	14.0
10	.40	.010273	.015624	.021119	.023920	.026756	.029626	.032532	.035471	.038445	.044492	.050670	.056977	.063410
	.30	.018602	.023953	.029448	.032249	.035085	.037955	.040861	.043800	.046774	.052821	.058999	.065306	.071739
	.20	.026931	.032282	.037777	.040578	.043414	.046285	.049190	.052129	.055103	.061150	.067329	.073636	.080068
	.10	.035260	.040611	.046106	.048907	.051743	.054614	.057519	.060458	.063432	.069479	.075658	.081965	.088397
	0.00	.043589	.048940	.054435	.057236	.060072	.062943	.065848	.068787	.071761	.077808	.083987	.090294	.096726
	-.10	.051918	.057269	.062764	.065565	.068401	.071272	.074177	.077117	.080090	.086137	.092316	.098623	.105055
	-.20	.060247	.065598	.071093	.073894	.076730	.079601	.082506	.085446	.088419	.094466	.100645	.106952	.113384
	-.30	.068576	.073927	.079423	.082223	.085059	.087930	.090835	.093775	.096748	.102795	.108974	.115281	.121713
	-.40	.076905	.082257	.087752	.090552	.093388	.096259	.099164	.102104	.105077	.111125	.117303	.123610	.130042
15	.40	.012540	.019578	.026822	.030519	.034263	.038053	.041889	.045770	.049692	.057661	.065785	.074052	.082454
	.30	.020869	.027907	.035151	.038848	.042592	.046382	.050218	.054099	.058021	.065990	.074114	.082381	.090783
	.20	.029198	.036237	.043481	.047177	.050921	.054712	.058548	.062428	.066351	.074319	.082443	.090711	.099112
	.10	.037527	.044566	.051810	.055506	.059250	.063041	.066877	.070757	.074680	.082648	.090772	.099040	.107441
	0.00	.045856	.052895	.060139	.063835	.067579	.071370	.075206	.079086	.083009	.090977	.099101	.107369	.115770
	-.10	.054186	.061224	.068468	.072164	.075908	.079699	.083535	.087415	.091338	.099306	.107430	.115698	.124099
	-.20	.062515	.069553	.076797	.080493	.084237	.088028	.091864	.095744	.099667	.107636	.115759	.124027	.132428
	-.30	.070844	.077882	.085126	.088822	.092566	.096357	.100193	.104073	.107996	.115965	.124088	.132356	.140757
	-.40	.079173	.086211	.093455	.097151	.100895	.104686	.108522	.112402	.116325	.124294	.132417	.140685	.149086
20	.40	.013639	.021470	.029509	.033600	.037736	.041915	.046134	.050392	.054684	.063369	.072170	.081071	.090059
	.30	.021968	.029799	.037838	.041929	.046066	.050244	.054464	.058721	.063014	.071698	.080499	.089400	.098388
	.20	.030298	.038128	.046167	.050258	.054395	.058574	.062793	.067050	.071343	.080027	.088828	.097729	.106717
	.10	.038627	.046458	.054496	.058587	.062724	.066903	.071122	.075379	.079672	.088356	.097157	.106058	.115046
	0.00	.046956	.054787	.062825	.066916	.071053	.075232	.079451	.083708	.088001	.096685	.105486	.114388	.123375
	-.10	.055285	.063116	.071154	.075246	.079382	.083561	.087780	.092037	.096330	.105014	.113815	.122717	.131704
	-.20	.063614	.071445	.079483	.083575	.087711	.091890	.096109	.100366	.104659	.113343	.122144	.131046	.140033
	-.30	.071943	.079774	.087812	.091904	.096040	.100219	.104438	.108695	.112988	.121672	.130473	.139375	.148362
	-.40	.080272	.088103	.096142	.100233	.104369	.108548	.112767	.117024	.121317	.130001	.138802	.147704	.156691
25	.40	.014273	.022541	.030999	.035291	.039620	.043983	.048378	.052801	.057250	.066215	.075254	.084349	.093486
	.30	.022602	.030870	.039328	.043620	.047949	.052312	.056707	.061130	.065579	.074544	.083583	.092678	.101815
	.20	.030931	.039199	.047657	.051949	.056278	.060641	.065036	.069459	.073908	.082873	.091912	.101007	.110144
	.10	.039260	.047528	.055986	.060278	.064607	.068970	.073365	.077788	.082237	.091203	.100241	.109336	.118473
	0.00	.047589	.055858	.064315	.068607	.072936	.077299	.081694	.086118	.090567	.099532	.108570	.117665	.126802
	-.10	.055918	.064187	.072644	.076936	.081265	.085628	.090023	.094447	.098896	.107861	.116899	.125994	.135131
	-.20	.064247	.072516	.080974	.085265	.089594	.093958	.098352	.102776	.107225	.116190	.125228	.134323	.143461
	-.30	.072576	.080845	.089303	.093594	.097923	.102287	.106681	.111105	.115554	.124519	.133557	.142653	.151790
	-.40	.080905	.089174	.097632	.101923	.106252	.110616	.115011	.119434	.123883	.132848	.141887	.150982	.160119
30	.40	.014674	.023206	.031901	.036300	.040728	.045183	.049659	.054155	.058668	.067734	.076840	.085970	.095114
	.30	.023003	.031535	.040230	.044629	.049058	.053512	.057988	.062484	.066997	.076064	.085169	.094299	.103443
	.20	.031332	.039864	.048559	.052958	.057387	.061841	.066317	.070814	.075327	.084393	.093498	.102628	.111772
	.10	.039661	.048193	.056888	.061287	.065716	.070170	.074646	.079143	.083656	.092722	.101827	.110957	.120102
	0.00	.047990	.056522	.065217	.069616	.074045	.078499	.082976	.087472	.091985	.101051	.110156	.119287	.128431
	-.10	.056319	.064851	.073546	.077946	.082374	.086828	.091305	.095801	.100314	.109380	.118485	.127616	.136760
	-.20	.064649	.073180	.081876	.086275	.090703	.095157	.099634	.104130	.108643	.117709	.126814	.135945	.145089
	-.30	.072978	.081509	.090205	.094604	.099032	.103486	.107963	.112459	.116972	.126038	.135143	.144274	.153418
	-.40	.081307	.089838	.098534	.102933	.107361	.111815	.116292	.120788	.125301	.134367	.143473	.152603	.161747

10.0 YEAR HOLDING PERIOD
.060 EQUITY YIELD RATE
.600 LOAN RATIO

INTEREST RATE

TERM YEARS	APPR DEP	5.0	6.0	7.0	7.5	8.0	8.5	9.0	9.5	10.0	11.0	12.0	13.0	14.0
10	.40	.024499	.028067	.031730	.033597	.035488	.037402	.039339	.041298	.043281	.047312	.051431	.055636	.059924
	.30	.032086	.035654	.039317	.041184	.043075	.044989	.046925	.048885	.050867	.054989	.059018	.063223	.067512
	.20	.039673	.043240	.046904	.048771	.050662	.052575	.054512	.056472	.058454	.062486	.066605	.070809	.075097
	.10	.047260	.050827	.054491	.056358	.058248	.060162	.062099	.064059	.066041	.070072	.074192	.078396	.082684
	0.00	.054846	.058414	.062077	.063944	.065835	.067749	.069686	.071645	.073628	.077659	.081778	.085983	.090271
	-.10	.062433	.066001	.069664	.071531	.073422	.075336	.077273	.079232	.081215	.085246	.089365	.093570	.097858
	-.20	.070020	.073588	.077251	.079118	.081009	.082923	.084859	.086819	.088801	.092833	.096952	.101157	.105445
	-.30	.077607	.081174	.084838	.086705	.088595	.090509	.092446	.094406	.096388	.100420	.104539	.108743	.113031
	-.40	.085194	.088761	.092425	.094292	.096182	.098096	.100033	.101993	.103975	.108006	.112125	.116630	.120618
15	.40	.024145	.028759	.033511	.035936	.038394	.040882	.043401	.045949	.048527	.053763	.059104	.064542	.070071
	.30	.031731	.036346	.041098	.043523	.045980	.048469	.050988	.053536	.056113	.061350	.066691	.072129	.077658
	.20	.039318	.043933	.048684	.051110	.053567	.056056	.058575	.061123	.063700	.068937	.074278	.079716	.085244
	.10	.046905	.051519	.056271	.058697	.061154	.063642	.066161	.068710	.071287	.076524	.081865	.087303	.092831
	0.00	.054492	.059106	.063858	.066283	.068741	.071229	.073748	.076297	.078874	.084110	.089451	.094890	.100418
	-.10	.062079	.066693	.071445	.073870	.076327	.078816	.081335	.083883	.086460	.091697	.097038	.102476	.108005
	-.20	.069665	.074280	.079032	.081457	.083914	.086403	.088922	.091470	.094047	.099284	.104625	.110063	.115592
	-.30	.077252	.081867	.086618	.089044	.091501	.093990	.096509	.099057	.101634	.106871	.112212	.117650	.123178
	-.40	.084839	.089453	.094205	.096631	.099088	.101576	.104095	.106644	.109221	.114458	.119799	.125237	.130765
20	.40	.023973	.029090	.034349	.037028	.039738	.042477	.045244	.048037	.050855	.056559	.062346	.068204	.074123
	.30	.031559	.036677	.041936	.044615	.047325	.050064	.052831	.055624	.058442	.064146	.069933	.075790	.081710
	.20	.039146	.044264	.049523	.052202	.054912	.057651	.060417	.063211	.066028	.071733	.077519	.083377	.089296
	.10	.046733	.051851	.057110	.059789	.062498	.065237	.068004	.070797	.073615	.079320	.085106	.090964	.096883
	0.00	.054320	.059437	.064697	.067376	.070085	.072824	.075591	.078384	.081202	.086906	.092693	.098551	.104470
	-.10	.061907	.067024	.072283	.074962	.077672	.080411	.083178	.085971	.088789	.094493	.100280	.106138	.112057
	-.20	.069494	.074611	.079870	.082549	.085259	.087998	.090765	.093558	.096376	.102080	.107867	.113725	.119644
	-.30	.077080	.082198	.087457	.090136	.092846	.095585	.098351	.101145	.103962	.109667	.115453	.121311	.127230
	-.40	.084667	.089785	.095044	.097723	.100432	.103171	.105938	.108731	.111549	.117254	.123040	.128898	.134817
25	.40	.023874	.029278	.034815	.037627	.040467	.043331	.046218	.049125	.052051	.057954	.063912	.069913	.075949
	.30	.031460	.036865	.042401	.045214	.048054	.050918	.053805	.056712	.059638	.065541	.071498	.077500	.083536
	.20	.039047	.044451	.049988	.052801	.055640	.058505	.061391	.064299	.067225	.073127	.079085	.085087	.091123
	.10	.046634	.052038	.057575	.060388	.063227	.066091	.068978	.071886	.074812	.080714	.086672	.092674	.098709
	0.00	.054221	.059625	.065162	.067975	.070814	.073678	.076565	.079472	.082399	.088301	.094259	.100261	.106296
	-.10	.061807	.067212	.072749	.075561	.078401	.081265	.084152	.087059	.089986	.095888	.101846	.107847	.113883
	-.20	.069394	.074799	.080335	.083148	.085988	.088852	.091738	.094646	.097572	.103475	.109432	.115434	.121470
	-.30	.076981	.082385	.087922	.090735	.093574	.096439	.099325	.102233	.105159	.111061	.117019	.123021	.129057
	-.40	.084568	.089972	.095509	.098322	.101161	.104025	.106911	.109820	.112746	.118648	.124606	.130608	.136643
30	.40	.023811	.029394	.035096	.037985	.040896	.043826	.046774	.049737	.052713	.058698	.064717	.070759	.076817
	.30	.031398	.036981	.042683	.045572	.048483	.051413	.054361	.057324	.060300	.066285	.072304	.078346	.084403
	.20	.038984	.044568	.050270	.053159	.056070	.059000	.061948	.064910	.067886	.073872	.079890	.085933	.091990
	.10	.046571	.052154	.057857	.060747	.063646	.066587	.069534	.072497	.075473	.081458	.087477	.093519	.099577
	0.00	.054158	.059741	.065443	.068332	.071243	.074174	.077121	.080084	.083060	.089045	.095064	.101106	.107164
	-.10	.061745	.067328	.073030	.075919	.078830	.081760	.084708	.087671	.090647	.096632	.102651	.108693	.114751
	-.20	.069332	.074915	.080617	.083506	.086417	.089347	.092295	.095258	.098234	.104219	.110238	.116280	.122337
	-.30	.076918	.082502	.088204	.091093	.094004	.096934	.099882	.102844	.105820	.111806	.117824	.123867	.129924
	-.40	.084505	.090088	.095791	.098680	.101590	.104521	.107468	.110431	.113407	.119392	.125411	.131453	.137511

10.0 YEAR HOLDING PERIOD
.060 EQUITY YIELD RATE
.667 LOAN RATIO

INTEREST RATE

TERM YEARS	APPR DEP	5.0	6.0	7.0	7.5	8.0	8.5	9.0	9.5	10.0	11.0	12.0	13.0	14.0
10	.40	.023927	.027891	.031961	.034036	.036136	.038263	.040415	.042592	.044795	.049274	.053851	.058523	.063287
	.30	.031513	.035477	.039548	.041622	.043723	.045850	.048002	.050179	.052382	.056861	.061438	.066110	.070874
	.20	.039100	.043064	.047135	.049209	.051310	.053436	.055588	.057766	.059968	.064448	.069025	.073697	.078461
	.10	.046687	.050651	.054721	.056796	.058897	.061023	.063175	.065353	.067555	.072035	.076611	.081283	.086048
	0.00	.054274	.058238	.062308	.064383	.066483	.068610	.070762	.072939	.075142	.079621	.084198	.088870	.093635
	-.10	.061861	.065825	.069895	.071970	.074070	.076197	.078349	.080526	.082729	.087208	.091785	.096457	.101221
	-.20	.069447	.073411	.077482	.079556	.081657	.083784	.085936	.088113	.090316	.094795	.099372	.104044	.108808
	-.30	.077034	.080998	.085069	.087143	.089244	.091370	.093522	.095700	.097902	.102382	.106959	.111630	.116395
	-.40	.084621	.088585	.092655	.094730	.096831	.098957	.101109	.103287	.105489	.109969	.114545	.119217	.123982
15	.40	.023532	.028660	.033939	.036634	.039365	.042130	.044929	.047760	.050624	.056442	.062377	.068419	.074562
	.30	.031119	.036247	.041526	.044221	.046952	.049717	.052515	.055347	.058210	.064029	.069964	.076006	.082149
	.20	.038706	.043833	.049113	.051808	.054538	.057303	.060102	.062934	.065797	.071616	.077550	.083593	.089736
	.10	.046293	.051420	.056700	.059395	.062125	.064890	.067689	.070521	.073384	.079203	.085137	.091180	.097322
	0.00	.053880	.059007	.064287	.066981	.069712	.072477	.075276	.078107	.080971	.086790	.092724	.098766	.104909
	-.10	.061466	.066594	.071873	.074568	.077299	.080064	.082863	.085694	.088558	.094377	.100311	.106353	.112496
	-.20	.069053	.074181	.079460	.082155	.084886	.087651	.090449	.093281	.096144	.101963	.107898	.113940	.120083
	-.30	.076640	.081767	.087047	.089742	.092472	.095237	.098036	.100868	.103731	.109550	.115484	.121527	.127670
	-.40	.084227	.089354	.094634	.097329	.100059	.102824	.105623	.108455	.111318	.117137	.123071	.129114	.135256
20	.40	.023341	.029028	.034871	.037848	.040859	.043902	.046976	.050081	.053211	.059549	.065978	.072487	.079064
	.30	.030928	.036615	.042458	.045435	.048445	.051489	.054563	.057667	.060798	.067136	.073565	.080074	.086651
	.20	.038515	.044201	.050045	.053021	.056032	.059076	.062150	.065253	.068384	.074723	.081152	.087661	.094238
	.10	.046102	.051788	.057632	.060608	.063619	.066662	.069737	.072840	.075971	.082309	.088739	.095248	.101825
	0.00	.053689	.059375	.065219	.068195	.071206	.074249	.077323	.080427	.083558	.089896	.096326	.102834	.109411
	-.10	.061275	.066962	.072805	.075782	.078793	.081836	.084910	.088014	.091145	.097483	.103912	.110421	.116998
	-.20	.068862	.074549	.080392	.083369	.086379	.089423	.092497	.095600	.098732	.105070	.111499	.118008	.124585
	-.30	.076449	.082135	.087979	.090955	.093966	.097010	.100084	.103187	.106318	.112657	.119086	.125595	.132172
	-.40	.084036	.089722	.095566	.098542	.101553	.104596	.107671	.110774	.113905	.120243	.126673	.133182	.139759
25	.40	.023231	.029236	.035388	.038514	.041669	.044851	.048058	.051289	.054540	.061098	.067718	.074387	.081093
	.30	.030818	.036823	.042975	.046100	.049255	.052438	.055645	.058876	.062127	.068685	.075305	.081974	.088680
	.20	.038405	.044410	.050562	.053687	.056842	.060024	.063232	.066462	.069714	.076272	.082892	.089561	.096267
	.10	.045992	.051996	.058149	.061274	.064429	.067611	.070819	.074049	.077301	.083859	.090479	.097147	.103854
	0.00	.053579	.059583	.065735	.068861	.072016	.075198	.078406	.081636	.084888	.091446	.098065	.104734	.111441
	-.10	.061165	.067170	.073322	.076448	.079602	.082785	.085992	.089223	.092474	.099032	.105652	.112321	.119027
	-.20	.068752	.074757	.080909	.084034	.087189	.090372	.093579	.096810	.100061	.106619	.113239	.119908	.126614
	-.30	.076339	.082344	.088496	.091621	.094776	.097958	.101166	.104396	.107648	.114206	.120826	.127495	.134201
	-.40	.083926	.089930	.096083	.099208	.102363	.105545	.108753	.111983	.115235	.121793	.128413	.135081	.141788
30	.40	.023162	.029365	.035701	.038911	.042145	.045401	.048676	.051968	.055275	.061925	.068613	.075327	.082057
	.30	.030748	.036952	.043288	.046498	.049732	.052988	.056263	.059555	.062862	.069512	.076200	.082913	.089644
	.20	.038335	.044539	.050875	.054085	.057319	.060575	.063850	.067142	.070449	.077099	.083787	.090500	.097231
	.10	.045922	.052126	.058462	.061671	.064906	.068162	.071437	.074729	.078036	.084686	.091373	.098087	.104818
	0.00	.053509	.059713	.066048	.069258	.072493	.075748	.079024	.082316	.085622	.092273	.098960	.105674	.112405
	-.10	.061096	.067299	.073635	.076845	.080079	.083335	.086610	.089902	.093209	.099859	.106547	.113261	.119991
	-.20	.068682	.074886	.081222	.084432	.087666	.090922	.094197	.097489	.100796	.107446	.114134	.120847	.127578
	-.30	.076269	.082473	.088809	.092019	.095253	.098509	.101784	.105076	.108383	.115033	.121721	.128434	.135165
	-.40	.083856	.090060	.096396	.099605	.102840	.106096	.109371	.112663	.115970	.122620	.129307	.136021	.142752

10.0 YEAR HOLDING PERIOD
.060 EQUITY YIELD RATE
.700 LOAN RATIO

INTEREST RATE

TERM YEARS	APPR DEP	5.0	6.0	7.0	7.5	8.0	8.5	9.0	9.5	10.0	11.0	12.0	13.0	14.0
10	.40	.023640	.027802	.032076	.034255	.036460	.038893	.040953	.043239	.045552	.050255	.055061	.059966	.064969
	.30	.031227	.035389	.039663	.041842	.044047	.046280	.048540	.050826	.053139	.057842	.062648	.067553	.072556
	.20	.038814	.042976	.047250	.049428	.051634	.053867	.056126	.058413	.060725	.065429	.070234	.075140	.080143
	.10	.046401	.050563	.054837	.057015	.059221	.061454	.063713	.066000	.068312	.073016	.077821	.082727	.087729
	0.00	.053987	.058150	.062424	.064602	.066808	.069040	.071300	.073586	.075899	.080602	.085408	.090313	.095316
	-.10	.061574	.065736	.070010	.072189	.074394	.076627	.078887	.081173	.083486	.088189	.092995	.097900	.102903
	-.20	.069161	.073323	.077597	.079776	.081981	.084214	.086474	.088760	.091073	.095776	.100582	.105487	.110490
	-.30	.076748	.080910	.085184	.087362	.089568	.091801	.094060	.096347	.098659	.103363	.108168	.113074	.118077
	-.40	.084335	.088497	.092771	.094949	.097155	.099388	.101647	.103934	.106246	.110950	.115755	.120661	.125663
15	.40	.023226	.028610	.034154	.036983	.039850	.042754	.045692	.048666	.051672	.057782	.064013	.070357	.076807
	.30	.030813	.036197	.041741	.044570	.047437	.050340	.053279	.056252	.059259	.065368	.071600	.077944	.084394
	.20	.038400	.043784	.049327	.052157	.055024	.057927	.060866	.063839	.066846	.072955	.079186	.085531	.091981
	.10	.045987	.051371	.056914	.059744	.062611	.065514	.068453	.071426	.074433	.080542	.086773	.093118	.099568
	0.00	.053574	.058957	.064501	.067331	.070197	.073101	.076040	.079013	.082019	.088129	.094360	.100705	.107154
	-.10	.061160	.066544	.072088	.074917	.077784	.080688	.083626	.086599	.089606	.095716	.101947	.108291	.114741
	-.20	.068747	.074131	.079675	.082504	.085371	.088274	.091213	.094186	.097193	.103302	.109534	.115878	.122328
	-.30	.076334	.081718	.087261	.090091	.092958	.095861	.098800	.101773	.104780	.110889	.117120	.123465	.129915
	-.40	.083921	.089304	.094848	.097678	.100545	.103448	.106387	.109360	.112366	.118476	.124707	.131052	.137502
20	.40	.023026	.028997	.035132	.038258	.041419	.044614	.047842	.051101	.054389	.061044	.067795	.074629	.081535
	.30	.030613	.036583	.042719	.045844	.049006	.052201	.055429	.058688	.061975	.068630	.075381	.082216	.089121
	.20	.038199	.044170	.050306	.053431	.056592	.059788	.063016	.066275	.069562	.076217	.082968	.089802	.096708
	.10	.045786	.051757	.057893	.061018	.064180	.067375	.070603	.073861	.077149	.083804	.090555	.097389	.104295
	0.00	.053373	.059344	.065479	.068605	.071766	.074962	.078190	.081448	.084736	.091391	.098142	.104976	.111882
	-.10	.060960	.066931	.073066	.076192	.079353	.082548	.085776	.089035	.092322	.098978	.105729	.112563	.119469
	-.20	.068547	.074517	.080653	.083778	.086940	.090135	.093363	.096622	.099909	.106564	.113315	.120150	.127055
	-.30	.076133	.082104	.088240	.091365	.094526	.097722	.100950	.104209	.107496	.114151	.120902	.127736	.134642
	-.40	.083720	.089691	.095827	.098952	.102113	.105309	.108537	.111795	.115083	.121738	.128489	.135323	.142229
25	.40	.022910	.029215	.035675	.038957	.042269	.045611	.048979	.052371	.055785	.062671	.069621	.076623	.083665
	.30	.030497	.036802	.043262	.046543	.049856	.053197	.056565	.059957	.063371	.070257	.077208	.084210	.091252
	.20	.038084	.044389	.050849	.054130	.057443	.060784	.064152	.067544	.070958	.077844	.084795	.091797	.098839
	.10	.045671	.051976	.058436	.061717	.065030	.068371	.071739	.075131	.078545	.085431	.092382	.099384	.106425
	0.00	.053257	.059562	.066022	.069304	.072616	.075958	.079326	.082718	.086132	.093018	.099969	.106971	.114012
	-.10	.060844	.067149	.073609	.076891	.080203	.083545	.086913	.090305	.093719	.100605	.107555	.114557	.121599
	-.20	.068431	.074736	.081196	.084477	.087790	.091131	.094499	.097891	.101305	.108191	.115142	.122144	.129186
	-.30	.076018	.082323	.088783	.092064	.095377	.098718	.102086	.105478	.108892	.115778	.122729	.129731	.136773
	-.40	.083605	.089910	.096370	.099651	.102964	.106305	.109673	.113065	.116479	.123365	.130316	.137318	.144359
30	.40	.022837	.029351	.036004	.039374	.042770	.046189	.049628	.053084	.056556	.063539	.070561	.077610	.084677
	.30	.030424	.036938	.043590	.046961	.050357	.053775	.057214	.060671	.064143	.071126	.078148	.085197	.092264
	.20	.038011	.044525	.051177	.054548	.057944	.061362	.064801	.068258	.071730	.078712	.085734	.092784	.099851
	.10	.045597	.052111	.058764	.062134	.065530	.068949	.072388	.075845	.079317	.086299	.093321	.100370	.107438
	0.00	.053184	.059698	.066351	.069721	.073117	.076536	.079975	.083431	.086903	.093886	.100908	.107957	.115024
	-.10	.060771	.067285	.073938	.077308	.080704	.084123	.087561	.091018	.094490	.101473	.108495	.115544	.122611
	-.20	.068358	.074872	.081524	.084895	.088291	.091709	.095148	.098605	.102077	.109060	.116082	.123131	.130198
	-.30	.075945	.082459	.089111	.092482	.095878	.099296	.102735	.106192	.109664	.116646	.123668	.130718	.137785
	-.40	.083531	.090045	.096698	.100068	.103464	.106883	.110322	.113778	.117251	.124233	.131255	.138304	.145372

10.0 YEAR HOLDING PERIOD
.060 EQUITY YIELD RATE
.750 LOAN RATIO

INTEREST RATE

TERM YEARS	APPR DEP	5.0	6.0	7.0	7.5	8.0	8.5	9.0	9.5	10.0	11.0	12.0	13.0	14.0
10	.40	.023211	.027670	.032249	.034583	.036947	.039339	.041760	.044210	.046688	.051727	.056876	.062132	.067492
	.30	.030798	.035257	.039836	.042170	.044533	.046926	.049347	.051796	.054278	.059347	.064462	.069718	.075078
	.20	.038384	.042844	.047423	.049757	.052120	.054513	.056934	.059383	.061861	.066900	.072049	.077305	.082665
	.10	.045971	.050431	.055010	.057344	.059707	.062099	.064520	.066970	.069448	.074487	.079636	.084892	.090252
	0.00	.053558	.058017	.062597	.064931	.067294	.069686	.072107	.074557	.077035	.082074	.087223	.092459	.097839
	-.10	.061145	.065604	.070183	.072517	.074881	.077273	.079694	.082144	.084621	.089661	.094810	.100065	.105426
	-.20	.068732	.073191	.077770	.080104	.082467	.084860	.087281	.089730	.092208	.097248	.102396	.107652	.113012
	-.30	.076318	.080778	.085357	.087691	.090054	.092447	.094868	.097317	.099795	.104834	.109983	.115239	.120599
	-.40	.083905	.088365	.092944	.095278	.097641	.100033	.102454	.104904	.107382	.112421	.117570	.122826	.128186
15	.40	.022767	.028536	.034475	.037507	.040579	.043689	.046838	.050024	.053245	.059791	.066467	.073265	.080175
	.30	.030354	.036122	.042062	.045094	.048165	.051276	.054425	.057610	.060832	.067378	.074054	.080852	.087762
	.20	.037941	.043709	.049649	.052681	.055772	.058863	.062012	.065197	.068419	.074964	.081641	.088438	.095349
	.10	.045528	.051296	.057236	.060267	.063339	.066450	.069598	.072784	.076005	.082551	.089227	.096025	.102936
	0.00	.053115	.058883	.064822	.067854	.070926	.074037	.077185	.080371	.083592	.090138	.096814	.103612	.110523
	-.10	.060701	.066470	.072409	.075441	.078513	.081623	.084772	.087958	.091179	.097725	.104401	.111199	.118109
	-.20	.068288	.074056	.079996	.083028	.086099	.089210	.092359	.095544	.098766	.105312	.111988	.118786	.125696
	-.30	.075875	.081643	.087583	.090615	.093686	.096797	.099946	.103131	.106353	.112898	.119575	.126372	.133283
	-.40	.083462	.089230	.095170	.098201	.101273	.104384	.107532	.110718	.113939	.120485	.127161	.133959	.140870
20	.40	.022553	.028950	.035524	.038872	.042259	.045683	.049142	.052633	.056155	.063286	.070519	.077841	.085240
	.30	.030139	.036536	.043110	.046459	.049846	.053270	.056728	.060220	.063742	.070873	.078106	.085428	.092827
	.20	.037726	.044123	.050697	.054046	.057433	.060857	.064315	.067807	.071329	.078459	.085693	.093015	.100414
	.10	.045313	.051710	.058284	.061633	.065020	.068443	.071902	.075393	.078916	.086046	.093279	.100602	.108001
	0.00	.052900	.059297	.065871	.069219	.072607	.076030	.079489	.082980	.086503	.093633	.100866	.108189	.115588
	-.10	.060486	.066884	.073458	.076806	.080193	.083617	.087076	.090567	.094089	.101220	.108453	.115775	.123174
	-.20	.068073	.074470	.081044	.084393	.087780	.091204	.094662	.098154	.101676	.108807	.116040	.123362	.130761
	-.30	.075660	.082057	.088631	.091980	.095367	.098791	.102249	.105741	.109263	.116393	.123627	.130949	.138348
	-.40	.083247	.089644	.096218	.099567	.102954	.106377	.109836	.113327	.116850	.123980	.131213	.138536	.145935
25	.40	.022429	.029184	.036105	.039621	.043170	.046751	.050359	.053993	.057651	.065029	.072476	.079978	.087523
	.30	.030015	.036771	.043692	.047208	.050757	.054337	.057946	.061580	.065238	.072616	.080063	.087565	.095110
	.20	.037602	.044358	.051279	.054795	.058344	.061924	.065533	.069167	.072825	.080203	.087650	.095152	.102697
	.10	.045189	.051944	.058866	.062381	.065931	.069511	.073119	.076754	.080412	.087789	.095237	.102739	.110284
	0.00	.052776	.059531	.066452	.069968	.073518	.077098	.080706	.084340	.087998	.095376	.102823	.110326	.117870
	-.10	.060363	.067118	.074040	.077555	.081104	.084685	.088293	.091927	.095585	.102963	.110410	.117912	.125457
	-.20	.067949	.074705	.081626	.085142	.088691	.092271	.095880	.099514	.103172	.110550	.117997	.125499	.133044
	-.30	.075536	.082292	.089213	.092729	.096278	.099858	.103467	.107101	.110759	.118137	.125584	.133086	.140631
	-.40	.083123	.089878	.096800	.100315	.103865	.107445	.111053	.114688	.118346	.125723	.133171	.140673	.148217
30	.40	.022350	.029329	.036457	.040068	.043707	.047370	.051054	.054758	.058478	.065959	.073483	.081036	.088608
	.30	.029937	.036916	.044044	.047655	.051294	.054957	.058641	.062345	.066065	.073546	.081070	.088622	.096194
	.20	.037524	.044503	.051631	.055242	.058880	.062543	.066228	.069931	.073651	.081133	.088656	.096209	.103781
	.10	.045111	.052090	.059218	.062829	.066467	.070130	.073815	.077518	.081238	.088720	.096243	.103796	.111368
	0.00	.052697	.059677	.066804	.070416	.074054	.077717	.081401	.085105	.088825	.096412	.103830	.111383	.118955
	-.10	.060284	.067263	.074391	.078002	.081641	.085304	.088988	.092692	.096412	.103893	.111417	.118970	.126542
	-.20	.067871	.074850	.081978	.085589	.089228	.092891	.096575	.100279	.103999	.111480	.119004	.126556	.134128
	-.30	.075458	.082437	.089565	.093176	.096814	.100477	.104162	.107865	.111585	.119067	.126590	.134143	.141715
	-.40	.083045	.090024	.097152	.100763	.104401	.108064	.111749	.115452	.119172	.126654	.134177	.141730	.149302

10.0 YEAR HOLDING PERIOD
.060 EQUITY YIELD RATE
.800 LOAN RATIO

INTEREST RATE

TERM YEARS	APPR DEP	14.0	13.0	12.0	11.0	10.0	9.5	9.0	8.5	8.0	7.5	7.0	6.0	5.0
10	.40	.070014	.064297	.058691	.053198	.047823	.045180	.042567	.039985	.037433	.034912	.032423	.027538	.022781
	.30	.077684	.071684	.066277	.060785	.055440	.052767	.050154	.047572	.045020	.042499	.040009	.035125	.030358
	.20	.085188	.079470	.073864	.068372	.062997	.060354	.057741	.055158	.052607	.050086	.047596	.042712	.037955
	.10	.092775	.087057	.081451	.075959	.070584	.067940	.065328	.062745	.060193	.057673	.055183	.050299	.045542
	0.00	.100361	.094644	.089038	.083546	.078170	.075527	.072914	.070332	.067780	.065259	.062770	.057885	.053129
	-.10	.107948	.102231	.096625	.091132	.085757	.083114	.080501	.077919	.075367	.072846	.070357	.065472	.060715
	-.20	.115535	.109818	.104211	.098719	.093344	.090701	.088088	.085505	.082954	.080433	.077943	.073059	.068302
	-.30	.123122	.117404	.111798	.106306	.100931	.098288	.095675	.093092	.090541	.088020	.085530	.080646	.075889
	-.40	.130709	.124991	.119385	.113893	.108518	.105874	.103262	.100679	.098127	.095607	.093117	.088232	.083476
15	.40	.083544	.076172	.068921	.061800	.054818	.051382	.047984	.044625	.041307	.038031	.034797	.028461	.022308
	.30	.091130	.083759	.076508	.069387	.062405	.058968	.055570	.052212	.048894	.045617	.042384	.036048	.029895
	.20	.098717	.091346	.084095	.076974	.069991	.066555	.063157	.059799	.056481	.053204	.049970	.043635	.037482
	.10	.106304	.098933	.091682	.084560	.077578	.074142	.070744	.067386	.064067	.060791	.057557	.051222	.045069
	0.00	.113891	.106520	.099269	.092147	.085165	.081729	.078331	.074972	.071654	.068378	.065144	.058808	.052656
	-.10	.121478	.114106	.106855	.099734	.092752	.089316	.085918	.082559	.079241	.075965	.072731	.066395	.060242
	-.20	.129064	.121693	.114442	.107321	.100339	.096902	.093504	.090146	.086828	.083551	.080318	.073982	.067829
	-.30	.136651	.129280	.122029	.114908	.107925	.104489	.101091	.097733	.094415	.091138	.087904	.081569	.075416
	-.40	.144238	.136867	.129616	.122494	.115512	.112076	.108678	.105320	.102001	.098725	.095491	.089156	.083003
20	.40	.088946	.081054	.073243	.065528	.057922	.054165	.050441	.046752	.043100	.039487	.035915	.028903	.022079
	.30	.096533	.088641	.080830	.073115	.065509	.061752	.058028	.054339	.050687	.047074	.043502	.036490	.029666
	.20	.104120	.096228	.088417	.080702	.073096	.069339	.065614	.061925	.058273	.054660	.051089	.044076	.037253
	.10	.111707	.103814	.096004	.088288	.080683	.076925	.073201	.069512	.065860	.062247	.058675	.051663	.044840
	0.00	.119293	.111401	.103591	.095875	.088269	.084512	.080788	.077099	.073447	.069834	.066262	.059250	.052426
	-.10	.126880	.118988	.111177	.103462	.095856	.092099	.088375	.084686	.081034	.077421	.073849	.066837	.060013
	-.20	.134467	.126575	.118764	.111049	.103443	.099686	.095962	.092273	.088621	.085008	.081436	.074424	.067600
	-.30	.142054	.134161	.126351	.118636	.111030	.107273	.103548	.099859	.096207	.092594	.089023	.082010	.075187
	-.40	.149641	.141748	.133938	.126222	.118617	.114859	.111135	.107446	.103794	.100181	.096609	.089597	.082774
25	.40	.091381	.083334	.075331	.067387	.059518	.055616	.051739	.047890	.044072	.040286	.036535	.029153	.021947
	.30	.098968	.090920	.082918	.074974	.067105	.063203	.059326	.055477	.051658	.047872	.044122	.036740	.029534
	.20	.106555	.098507	.090505	.082561	.074691	.070790	.066913	.063064	.059245	.055459	.051709	.044326	.037121
	.10	.114142	.106094	.098092	.090148	.082278	.078376	.074500	.070651	.066832	.063046	.059296	.051913	.044707
	0.00	.121728	.113681	.105678	.097735	.089865	.085963	.082087	.078238	.074419	.070633	.066882	.059500	.052294
	-.10	.129315	.121268	.113265	.105321	.097452	.093550	.089673	.085824	.082006	.078220	.074469	.067087	.059881
	-.20	.136902	.128854	.120852	.112908	.105038	.101137	.097260	.093411	.089592	.085806	.082056	.074674	.067468
	-.30	.144489	.136441	.128439	.120495	.112625	.108724	.104847	.100998	.097179	.093393	.089643	.082260	.075055
	-.40	.152076	.144028	.136026	.128082	.120212	.116310	.112434	.108585	.104766	.100980	.097230	.089847	.082641
30	.40	.092538	.084461	.076405	.068380	.060440	.056431	.052481	.048551	.044644	.040763	.036911	.029308	.021863
	.30	.100125	.092048	.083992	.075966	.067986	.064018	.060068	.056138	.052231	.048350	.044498	.036895	.029450
	.20	.107712	.099635	.091578	.083553	.075573	.071605	.067655	.063724	.059817	.055936	.052084	.044481	.037037
	.10	.115298	.107221	.099165	.091140	.083160	.079192	.075241	.071311	.067404	.063523	.059671	.052068	.044624
	0.00	.122885	.114808	.106752	.098727	.090747	.086779	.082828	.078898	.074991	.071110	.067258	.059655	.052211
	-.10	.130472	.122395	.114339	.106314	.098334	.094365	.090415	.086485	.082578	.078697	.074845	.067242	.059797
	-.20	.138059	.129982	.121926	.113900	.105920	.101952	.098002	.094072	.090165	.086283	.082432	.074829	.067384
	-.30	.145646	.137569	.129512	.121487	.113507	.109539	.105589	.101658	.097751	.093870	.090018	.082415	.074971
	-.40	.153232	.145155	.137099	.129074	.121094	.117126	.113175	.109245	.105338	.101457	.097605	.090002	.082558

10.0 YEAR HOLDING PERIOD
.060 EQUITY YIELD RATE
.900 LOAN RATIO

INTEREST RATE

TERM YEARS	APPR DEP	5.0	6.0	7.0	7.5	8.0	8.5	9.0	9.5	10.0	11.0	12.0	13.0	14.0
10	.40	.021922	.027274	.032769	.035570	.038405	.041276	.044181	.047121	.050094	.056142	.062320	.068627	.075059
	.30	.029509	.034861	.040356	.043356	.045992	.048863	.051768	.054708	.057681	.063728	.069907	.076214	.082646
	.20	.037096	.042447	.047942	.050743	.053579	.056450	.059355	.062295	.065268	.071315	.077494	.083801	.090233
	.10	.044683	.050034	.055529	.058330	.061166	.064037	.066942	.069881	.072855	.078902	.085081	.091388	.097820
	0.00	.052220	.057621	.063116	.065917	.068753	.071623	.074529	.077468	.080442	.086489	.092667	.098974	.105407
	-.10	.059856	.065208	.070703	.073504	.076339	.079210	.082115	.085055	.088028	.094076	.100254	.106561	.112993
	-.20	.067443	.072795	.078290	.081090	.083926	.086797	.089702	.092642	.095615	.101662	.107841	.114148	.120580
	-.30	.075030	.080381	.085876	.088677	.091513	.094384	.097289	.100229	.103202	.109249	.115428	.121322	.128167
	-.40	.082617	.087968	.093463	.096264	.099100	.101971	.104876	.107815	.110789	.116836	.123015	.129322	.135754
15	.40	.021390	.028312	.035440	.039078	.042764	.046497	.050275	.054098	.057963	.065818	.073830	.081987	.090280
	.30	.028977	.035899	.043027	.046665	.050351	.054083	.057862	.061685	.065550	.073405	.081417	.089574	.097867
	.20	.036564	.043486	.050613	.054251	.057937	.061670	.065449	.069271	.073137	.080992	.089000	.097161	.105454
	.10	.044151	.051073	.058200	.061838	.065524	.069257	.073035	.076858	.080724	.088579	.096590	.104748	.113040
	0.00	.051738	.058659	.065787	.069425	.073111	.076844	.080622	.084445	.088311	.096166	.104177	.112334	.120627
	-.10	.059324	.066246	.073374	.077012	.080698	.084431	.088209	.092032	.095897	.103752	.111764	.119921	.128214
	-.20	.066911	.073833	.080960	.084599	.088285	.092017	.095796	.099618	.103484	.111339	.119351	.127508	.135801
	-.30	.074498	.081420	.088547	.092185	.095871	.099604	.103383	.107205	.111071	.118926	.126938	.135095	.143388
	-.40	.082085	.089007	.096134	.099772	.103458	.107191	.110969	.114792	.118658	.126513	.134524	.142682	.150974
20	.40	.021132	.028809	.036698	.040716	.044781	.048889	.053039	.057229	.061456	.070012	.078692	.087479	.096358
	.30	.028719	.036396	.044285	.048303	.052367	.056476	.060626	.064816	.069043	.077599	.086279	.095066	.103945
	.20	.036306	.043983	.051871	.055890	.059954	.064063	.068213	.072403	.076629	.085186	.093866	.102653	.111532
	.10	.043893	.051569	.059458	.063476	.067541	.071650	.075800	.079989	.084216	.092773	.101453	.110239	.119118
	0.00	.051480	.059156	.067045	.071063	.075128	.079236	.083387	.087576	.091803	.100360	.109039	.117626	.126705
	-.10	.059066	.066743	.074632	.078650	.082715	.086823	.090973	.095163	.099390	.107946	.116626	.125413	.134292
	-.20	.066653	.074330	.082219	.086237	.090301	.094410	.098560	.102750	.106977	.115533	.124213	.133000	.141879
	-.30	.074240	.081917	.089805	.093824	.097888	.101997	.106147	.110337	.114563	.123120	.131800	.140587	.149466
	-.40	.081827	.089503	.097392	.101410	.105475	.109584	.113734	.117923	.122150	.130707	.139387	.148173	.157052
25	.40	.020984	.029090	.037396	.041615	.045874	.050170	.054500	.058861	.063251	.072104	.081041	.090044	.099097
	.30	.028571	.036677	.044982	.049202	.053461	.057757	.062087	.066448	.070838	.079691	.088628	.097630	.106684
	.20	.036157	.044264	.052569	.056788	.061048	.065344	.069674	.074035	.078424	.087278	.096215	.105217	.114271
	.10	.043744	.051851	.060156	.064375	.068634	.072930	.077261	.081622	.086011	.094865	.103801	.112804	.121858
	0.00	.051331	.059437	.067743	.071962	.076221	.080517	.084847	.089209	.093598	.102451	.111388	.120391	.129444
	-.10	.058918	.067024	.075330	.079549	.083808	.088104	.092434	.096795	.101185	.110038	.118975	.127978	.137031
	-.20	.066505	.074611	.082916	.087135	.091395	.095691	.100021	.104382	.108772	.117625	.126562	.135564	.144618
	-.30	.074091	.082198	.090503	.094722	.098982	.103278	.107608	.111969	.116358	.125212	.134149	.143151	.152205
	-.40	.081678	.089785	.098090	.102309	.106568	.110864	.115195	.119556	.123945	.132799	.141735	.150738	.159792
30	.40	.020890	.029265	.037818	.042151	.046518	.050913	.055335	.059779	.064243	.073221	.082249	.091312	.100399
	.30	.028476	.036851	.045405	.049738	.054104	.058500	.062921	.067366	.071830	.080807	.089836	.098899	.107985
	.20	.036063	.044438	.052992	.057325	.061691	.066087	.070508	.074952	.079417	.088394	.097422	.106486	.115572
	.10	.043650	.052025	.060578	.064912	.069278	.073674	.078095	.082539	.087003	.095981	.105009	.114073	.123159
	0.00	.051237	.059612	.068166	.072499	.076865	.081260	.085682	.090126	.094590	.103568	.112596	.121659	.130746
	-.10	.058824	.067199	.075752	.080085	.084452	.088847	.093269	.097713	.102177	.111155	.120183	.129246	.138333
	-.20	.066410	.074785	.083339	.087672	.092038	.096434	.100855	.105300	.109764	.118741	.127769	.136833	.145919
	-.30	.073997	.082372	.090926	.095259	.099626	.104021	.108442	.112886	.117350	.126328	.135356	.144420	.153506
	-.40	.081584	.089959	.098512	.102846	.107212	.111608	.116029	.120473	.124937	.133915	.142943	.152007	.161093

10.0 YEAR HOLDING PERIOD
.080 EQUITY YIELD RATE
.600 LOAN RATIO

INTEREST RATE

TERM YEARS	APPR DEP	5.0	6.0	7.0	7.5	8.0	8.5	9.0	9.5	10.0	11.0	12.0	13.0	14.0
10	.40	.039338	.042905	.045569	.048436	.050326	.052240	.054177	.056137	.058119	.062151	.066270	.070474	.074762
	.30	.046241	.049808	.053472	.055339	.057229	.059143	.061080	.063040	.065022	.069053	.073173	.077377	.081665
	.20	.053144	.056711	.060375	.062242	.064132	.066046	.067983	.069943	.071925	.075956	.080075	.084280	.088568
	.10	.060047	.063614	.067277	.069145	.071035	.072949	.074886	.076846	.078828	.082859	.086978	.091183	.095471
	0.00	.066949	.070517	.074180	.076048	.077938	.079852	.081789	.083749	.085731	.089762	.093881	.098086	.102374
	-.10	.073852	.077420	.081083	.082951	.084841	.086755	.088692	.090651	.092634	.096665	.100784	.104989	.109277
	-.20	.080755	.084323	.087986	.089853	.091744	.093658	.095595	.097554	.099537	.103568	.107687	.111892	.116180
	-.30	.087658	.091226	.094889	.096756	.098647	.100561	.102498	.104457	.106440	.110471	.114590	.118795	.123083
	-.40	.094561	.098129	.101792	.103659	.105550	.107464	.109401	.111360	.113343	.117374	.121493	.125698	.129986
15	.40	.037264	.041807	.046487	.048876	.051298	.053751	.056235	.058748	.061290	.066457	.071729	.077099	.082561
	.30	.044167	.048710	.053390	.055779	.058201	.060654	.063138	.065651	.068193	.073360	.078632	.084002	.089464
	.20	.051070	.055612	.060293	.062682	.065104	.067557	.070041	.072554	.075096	.080263	.085535	.090905	.096367
	.10	.057972	.062515	.067196	.069585	.072007	.074460	.076944	.079457	.081999	.087166	.092438	.097808	.103270
	0.00	.064875	.069418	.074099	.076488	.078910	.081363	.083846	.086360	.088902	.094069	.099341	.104711	.110173
	-.10	.071778	.076321	.081001	.083391	.085813	.088266	.090749	.093263	.095805	.100972	.106244	.111614	.117076
	-.20	.078681	.083224	.087904	.090294	.092716	.095169	.097652	.100165	.102707	.107875	.113147	.118517	.123979
	-.30	.085584	.090127	.094807	.097197	.099619	.102072	.104555	.107068	.109610	.114777	.120050	.125420	.130882
	-.40	.092487	.097030	.101710	.104100	.106522	.108975	.111458	.113971	.116513	.121680	.126953	.132323	.137785
20	.40	.036258	.041281	.046448	.049082	.051748	.054444	.057168	.059920	.062697	.068323	.074035	.079823	.085675
	.30	.043161	.048184	.053351	.055985	.058651	.061347	.064071	.066823	.069600	.075226	.080938	.086726	.092578
	.20	.050064	.055087	.060254	.062888	.065554	.068250	.070974	.073726	.076503	.082129	.087841	.093629	.099481
	.10	.056967	.061990	.067157	.069791	.072457	.075152	.077877	.080629	.083406	.089032	.094744	.100531	.106384
	0.00	.063870	.068893	.074060	.076694	.079360	.082055	.084780	.087531	.090309	.095935	.101647	.107434	.113287
	-.10	.070773	.075796	.080963	.083597	.086263	.088958	.091683	.094434	.097212	.102838	.108550	.114337	.120190
	-.20	.077676	.082699	.087866	.090500	.093166	.095861	.098586	.101337	.104115	.109741	.115453	.121240	.127093
	-.30	.084579	.089602	.094769	.097403	.100068	.102764	.105489	.108240	.111018	.116644	.122356	.128143	.133996
	-.40	.091482	.096505	.101672	.104306	.106971	.109667	.112392	.115143	.117921	.123547	.129259	.135046	.140899
25	.40	.035679	.040983	.046427	.049195	.051992	.054814	.057661	.060531	.063420	.069254	.075149	.081094	.087079
	.30	.042582	.047886	.053330	.056098	.058895	.061717	.064564	.067434	.070323	.076157	.082052	.087997	.093982
	.20	.049485	.054789	.060233	.063001	.065798	.068620	.071467	.074337	.077226	.083060	.088955	.094900	.100885
	.10	.056388	.061692	.067136	.069904	.072700	.075523	.078370	.081239	.084129	.089963	.095858	.101803	.107788
	0.00	.063291	.068595	.074039	.076807	.079603	.082426	.085273	.088142	.091032	.096866	.102761	.108706	.114691
	-.10	.070194	.075498	.080941	.083710	.086506	.089329	.092176	.095045	.097935	.103769	.109664	.115609	.121594
	-.20	.077097	.082401	.087844	.090613	.093409	.096232	.099079	.101948	.104838	.110672	.116567	.122512	.128496
	-.30	.083999	.089304	.094747	.097516	.100312	.103135	.105982	.108851	.111741	.117575	.123470	.129415	.135399
	-.40	.090902	.096207	.101650	.104419	.107215	.110038	.112885	.115754	.118644	.124478	.130373	.136318	.142302
30	.40	.035312	.040799	.046414	.049262	.052135	.055029	.057943	.060874	.063820	.069751	.075722	.081723	.087746
	.30	.042215	.047702	.053317	.056165	.059038	.061932	.064846	.067777	.070723	.076654	.082625	.088626	.094649
	.20	.049118	.054605	.060220	.063068	.065941	.068835	.071749	.074680	.077626	.083557	.089528	.095529	.101551
	.10	.056021	.061508	.067123	.069971	.072844	.075738	.078652	.081583	.084529	.090460	.096431	.102432	.108454
	0.00	.062923	.068411	.074026	.076874	.079747	.082641	.085555	.088486	.091432	.097363	.103334	.109335	.115357
	-.10	.069826	.075314	.080929	.083777	.086650	.089544	.092458	.095389	.098335	.104266	.110237	.116238	.122260
	-.20	.076729	.082217	.087831	.090680	.093553	.096447	.099361	.102292	.105238	.111169	.117140	.123141	.129163
	-.30	.083632	.089119	.094734	.097583	.100456	.103350	.106264	.109195	.112141	.118071	.124043	.130044	.136066
	-.40	.090535	.096022	.101637	.104486	.107359	.110253	.113167	.116098	.119044	.124974	.130946	.136947	.142969

10.0 YEAR HOLDING PERIOD
.080 EQUITY YIELD RATE
.667 LOAN RATIO

INTEREST RATE

TERM YEARS	APPR DEP	5.0	6.0	7.0	7.5	8.0	8.5	9.0	9.5	10.0	11.0	12.0	13.0	14.0
10	.40	.037888	.041852	.045922	.047997	.050097	.052224	.054376	.056553	.058756	.063235	.067812	.072484	.077248
	.30	.044791	.048755	.052825	.054900	.057000	.059127	.061279	.063456	.065659	.070138	.074715	.079387	.084151
	.20	.051693	.055657	.059728	.061803	.063903	.066030	.068182	.070359	.072562	.077041	.081618	.086290	.091054
	.10	.058596	.062560	.066631	.068705	.070806	.072933	.075085	.077262	.079465	.083944	.088521	.093193	.097957
	0.00	.065499	.069463	.073534	.075608	.077709	.079836	.081988	.084165	.086368	.090847	.095424	.100096	.104860
	-.10	.072402	.076366	.080437	.082511	.084612	.086739	.088891	.091068	.093271	.097750	.102327	.106999	.111763
	-.20	.079305	.083269	.087340	.089414	.091515	.093641	.095794	.097971	.100174	.104653	.109230	.113902	.118666
	-.30	.086208	.090172	.094243	.096317	.098418	.100544	.102696	.104874	.107076	.111556	.116133	.120805	.125569
	-.40	.093111	.097075	.101146	.103220	.105323	.107447	.109599	.111777	.113979	.118459	.123036	.127707	.132472
15	.40	.035583	.040631	.045831	.048486	.051177	.053903	.056662	.059454	.062279	.068020	.073878	.079845	.085914
	.30	.042486	.047534	.052734	.055389	.058080	.060806	.063565	.066357	.069182	.074923	.080781	.086748	.092817
	.20	.049389	.054437	.059637	.062292	.064983	.067709	.070468	.073260	.076085	.081826	.087684	.093651	.099720
	.10	.056292	.061340	.066540	.069195	.071886	.074611	.077371	.080163	.082988	.088729	.094587	.100554	.106623
	0.00	.063195	.068243	.073443	.076098	.078789	.081514	.084274	.087066	.089891	.095632	.101490	.107457	.113526
	-.10	.070098	.075146	.080346	.083001	.085692	.088417	.091177	.093969	.096794	.102535	.108393	.114360	.120428
	-.20	.077001	.082049	.087249	.089904	.092595	.095320	.098080	.100872	.103697	.109438	.115296	.121263	.127331
	-.30	.083904	.088951	.094152	.096807	.099498	.102223	.104983	.107775	.110600	.116341	.122199	.128166	.134234
	-.40	.090807	.095854	.101055	.103710	.106401	.109126	.111886	.114678	.117502	.123244	.129102	.135069	.141137
20	.40	.034466	.040047	.045788	.048715	.051677	.054672	.057699	.060757	.063843	.070094	.076441	.082871	.089374
	.30	.041369	.046950	.052691	.055618	.058580	.061575	.064602	.067660	.070745	.076997	.083344	.089774	.096277
	.20	.048272	.053853	.059594	.062521	.065483	.068478	.071505	.074562	.077648	.083900	.090246	.096677	.103180
	.10	.055175	.060756	.066497	.069424	.072386	.075381	.078408	.081465	.084551	.090803	.097149	.103580	.110083
	0.00	.062078	.067659	.073400	.076327	.079288	.082284	.085311	.088368	.091454	.097706	.104052	.110483	.116986
	-.10	.068980	.074562	.080303	.083230	.086191	.089187	.092214	.095271	.098357	.104609	.110955	.117386	.123889
	-.20	.075883	.081464	.087206	.090133	.093094	.096090	.099117	.102174	.105260	.111512	.117858	.124289	.130792
	-.30	.082786	.088367	.094109	.097035	.099997	.102993	.106020	.109077	.112163	.118414	.124761	.131192	.137695
	-.40	.089689	.095270	.101012	.103938	.106900	.109896	.112923	.115980	.119066	.125317	.131664	.138095	.144598
25	.40	.033822	.039716	.045764	.048840	.051948	.055084	.058247	.061435	.064646	.071128	.077678	.084284	.090933
	.30	.040725	.046619	.052667	.055743	.058850	.061987	.065150	.068338	.071549	.078031	.084581	.091187	.097836
	.20	.047628	.053522	.059570	.062646	.065753	.068890	.072053	.075241	.078452	.084934	.091484	.098090	.104739
	.10	.054531	.060425	.066473	.069549	.072656	.075793	.078956	.082144	.085355	.091837	.098387	.104993	.111642
	0.00	.061434	.067328	.073376	.076452	.079559	.082696	.085859	.089047	.092258	.098740	.105290	.111896	.118545
	-.10	.068337	.074231	.080279	.083355	.086462	.089599	.092762	.095950	.099161	.105643	.112193	.118799	.125448
	-.20	.075240	.081134	.087182	.090258	.093365	.096502	.099665	.102853	.106064	.112546	.119096	.125702	.132351
	-.30	.082143	.088037	.094085	.097161	.100268	.103405	.106568	.109756	.112967	.119449	.125999	.132605	.139254
	-.40	.089046	.094940	.100988	.104064	.107171	.110308	.113471	.116659	.119870	.126352	.132902	.139508	.146157
30	.40	.033414	.039511	.045750	.048915	.052107	.055323	.058560	.061817	.065090	.071680	.078315	.084983	.091674
	.30	.040317	.046414	.052653	.055818	.059010	.062226	.065463	.068720	.071993	.078583	.085218	.091886	.098577
	.20	.047220	.053317	.059556	.062721	.065913	.069129	.072366	.075623	.078896	.085486	.092121	.098789	.105480
	.10	.054123	.060220	.066459	.069624	.072816	.076032	.079269	.082526	.085799	.092389	.099024	.105692	.112383
	0.00	.061026	.067123	.073362	.076527	.079719	.082935	.086172	.089429	.092702	.099292	.105927	.112595	.119286
	-.10	.067929	.074026	.080265	.083430	.086622	.089838	.093075	.096332	.099605	.106195	.112830	.119498	.126189
	-.20	.074832	.080929	.087168	.090333	.093525	.096741	.099978	.103235	.106508	.113098	.119733	.126401	.133092
	-.30	.081735	.087832	.094071	.097236	.100428	.103644	.106881	.110138	.113411	.120001	.126636	.133304	.139995
	-.40	.088638	.094735	.100974	.104139	.107331	.110546	.113784	.117040	.120314	.126904	.133539	.140207	.146898

10.0 YEAR HOLDING PERIOD
.080 EQUITY YIELD RATE
.700 LOAN RATIO

INTEREST RATE

TERM YEARS	APPR DEP	5.0	6.0	7.0	7.5	8.0	8.5	9.0	9.5	10.0	11.0	12.0	13.0	14.0
10	.40	.037163	.041325	.045599	.047777	.049983	.052216	.054475	.056762	.059074	.063778	.068583	.073489	.078491
	.30	.044066	.048228	.052502	.054680	.056886	.059118	.061378	.063664	.065977	.070681	.075486	.080392	.085394
	.20	.050968	.055131	.059405	.061583	.063789	.066021	.068281	.070567	.072880	.077583	.082389	.087294	.092297
	.10	.057871	.062034	.066308	.068486	.070692	.072924	.075184	.077470	.079783	.084486	.089292	.094197	.099200
	0.00	.064774	.068937	.073210	.075389	.077595	.079827	.082087	.084373	.086686	.091389	.096195	.101100	.106103
	-.10	.071677	.075840	.080113	.082292	.084497	.086730	.088990	.091276	.093589	.098292	.103098	.108003	.113006
	-.20	.078580	.082742	.087016	.089195	.091400	.093633	.095893	.098179	.100492	.105195	.110001	.114906	.119909
	-.30	.085483	.089645	.093919	.096098	.098303	.100536	.102796	.105082	.107395	.112098	.116904	.121809	.126812
	-.40	.092386	.096548	.100822	.103001	.105206	.107439	.109699	.111985	.114298	.119001	.123807	.128712	.133715
15	.40	.034743	.040043	.045503	.048291	.051116	.053978	.056876	.059808	.062773	.068802	.074952	.081218	.087590
	.30	.041646	.046946	.052406	.055194	.058019	.060881	.063779	.066711	.069676	.075705	.081855	.088121	.094494
	.20	.048549	.053849	.059309	.062097	.064922	.067784	.070682	.073614	.076579	.082607	.088758	.095024	.101396
	.10	.055452	.060752	.066212	.069000	.071825	.074687	.077585	.080517	.083482	.089510	.095661	.101927	.108299
	0.00	.062355	.067655	.073115	.075903	.078728	.081590	.084488	.087420	.090385	.096414	.102564	.108830	.115202
	-.10	.069258	.074558	.080018	.082806	.085631	.088493	.091390	.094322	.097288	.103316	.109467	.115733	.122105
	-.20	.076161	.081461	.086921	.089709	.092534	.095396	.098293	.101225	.104191	.110219	.116370	.122636	.129007
	-.30	.083063	.088364	.093823	.096612	.099437	.102299	.105196	.108128	.111094	.117122	.123273	.129538	.135910
	-.40	.089966	.095267	.100727	.103515	.106340	.109202	.112099	.115031	.117997	.124025	.130176	.136441	.142813
20	.40	.033570	.039430	.045458	.048531	.051641	.054786	.057965	.061175	.064415	.070979	.077643	.084395	.091223
	.30	.040473	.046333	.052361	.055434	.058544	.061689	.064868	.068078	.071318	.077882	.084546	.091298	.098126
	.20	.047376	.053236	.059264	.062337	.065447	.068592	.071771	.074981	.078221	.084785	.091449	.098201	.105029
	.10	.054279	.060139	.066167	.069240	.072350	.075495	.078674	.081884	.085124	.091688	.098352	.105104	.111932
	0.00	.061181	.067042	.073070	.076143	.079253	.082398	.085577	.088787	.092027	.098591	.105255	.112007	.118835
	-.10	.068084	.073945	.079973	.083046	.086156	.089301	.092480	.095690	.098930	.105494	.112158	.118910	.125738
	-.20	.074987	.080847	.086876	.089949	.093059	.096204	.099382	.102593	.105833	.112397	.119061	.125813	.132641
	-.30	.081890	.087750	.093779	.096852	.099962	.103107	.106285	.109496	.112736	.119300	.125964	.132716	.139544
	-.40	.088793	.094653	.100682	.103755	.106865	.110010	.113188	.116399	.119639	.126203	.132867	.139619	.146447
25	.40	.032894	.039083	.045433	.048663	.051925	.055219	.058540	.061888	.065259	.072065	.078943	.085879	.092861
	.30	.039797	.045986	.052336	.055566	.058828	.062122	.065443	.068791	.072162	.078968	.085846	.092782	.099763
	.20	.046700	.052889	.059239	.062469	.065731	.069025	.072346	.075694	.079065	.085871	.092749	.099685	.106666
	.10	.053603	.059791	.066142	.069372	.072634	.075928	.079249	.082597	.085968	.092774	.099652	.106588	.113569
	0.00	.060506	.066694	.073045	.076275	.079537	.082830	.086152	.089499	.092871	.099677	.106555	.113490	.120472
	-.10	.067409	.073597	.079948	.083178	.086440	.089734	.093055	.096402	.099774	.106580	.113458	.120393	.127375
	-.20	.074312	.080500	.086851	.090081	.093343	.096636	.099958	.103305	.106677	.113483	.120361	.127296	.134278
	-.30	.081215	.087403	.093754	.096983	.100246	.103539	.106861	.110208	.113580	.120386	.127263	.134199	.141181
	-.40	.088117	.094306	.100657	.103886	.107149	.110442	.113764	.117111	.120483	.127289	.134166	.141102	.148084
30	.40	.032466	.038867	.045418	.048741	.052093	.055470	.058869	.062288	.065725	.072645	.079611	.086613	.093638
	.30	.039369	.045770	.052321	.055644	.058996	.062373	.065772	.069191	.072628	.079548	.086514	.093516	.100541
	.20	.046271	.052673	.059224	.062547	.065899	.069276	.072675	.076094	.079531	.086459	.093417	.100418	.107444
	.10	.053174	.059576	.066127	.069450	.072802	.076178	.079578	.082997	.086434	.093353	.100320	.107321	.114347
	0.00	.060077	.066479	.073030	.076353	.079705	.083081	.086481	.089900	.093337	.100256	.107223	.114224	.121250
	-.10	.066980	.073382	.079933	.083256	.086608	.089984	.093384	.096803	.100240	.107159	.114126	.121127	.128153
	-.20	.073883	.080285	.086836	.090159	.093511	.096887	.100287	.103706	.107143	.114062	.121029	.128030	.135056
	-.30	.080786	.087188	.093739	.097062	.100414	.103790	.107190	.110609	.114046	.120965	.127932	.134933	.141959
	-.40	.087689	.094091	.100642	.103965	.107317	.110693	.114092	.117512	.120949	.127868	.134835	.141836	.148862

10.0 YEAR HOLDING PERIOD
.080 EQUITY YIELD RATE
.750 LOAN RATIO

INTEREST RATE

TERM YEARS	APPR DEP	5.0	6.0	7.0	7.5	8.0	8.5	9.0	9.5	10.0	11.0	12.0	13.0	14.0
10	.40	.036075	.040535	.045114	.047448	.049811	.052203	.054624	.057074	.059552	.064591	.069740	.074996	.080356
	.30	.042978	.047437	.052017	.054351	.056714	.059106	.061527	.063977	.066455	.071494	.076643	.081899	.087259
	.20	.049881	.054340	.058920	.061254	.063617	.066009	.068430	.070880	.073358	.078397	.083546	.088802	.094162
	.10	.056784	.061243	.065823	.068157	.070520	.072912	.075333	.077783	.080261	.085300	.090449	.095705	.101065
	0.00	.063687	.068146	.072726	.075059	.077423	.079815	.082236	.084686	.087164	.092203	.097352	.102608	.107968
	-.10	.070590	.075049	.079628	.081962	.084326	.086718	.089139	.091589	.094066	.099106	.104255	.109510	.114871
	-.20	.077493	.081952	.086531	.088865	.091229	.093621	.096042	.098492	.100969	.106009	.111158	.116413	.121774
	-.30	.084396	.088855	.093434	.095768	.098132	.100524	.102945	.105395	.107872	.112912	.118061	.123316	.128677
	-.40	.091299	.095758	.100337	.102671	.105035	.107427	.109848	.112297	.114775	.119815	.124964	.130219	.135579
15	.40	.033482	.039161	.045011	.047998	.051026	.054092	.057196	.060338	.063515	.069974	.076564	.083277	.090104
	.30	.040385	.046064	.051914	.054901	.057929	.060995	.064099	.067241	.070418	.076877	.083467	.090180	.097007
	.20	.047288	.052967	.058817	.061804	.064832	.067898	.071002	.074144	.077321	.083780	.090370	.097083	.103910
	.10	.054191	.059870	.065720	.068707	.071734	.074801	.077905	.081047	.084224	.090683	.097273	.103986	.110810
	0.00	.061094	.066773	.072623	.075610	.078637	.081704	.084808	.087950	.091127	.097586	.104176	.110889	.117716
	-.10	.067997	.073676	.079526	.082513	.085540	.088607	.091711	.094852	.098030	.104489	.111079	.117792	.124619
	-.20	.074900	.080579	.086429	.089416	.092443	.095510	.098614	.101755	.104933	.111392	.117982	.124695	.131522
	-.30	.081803	.087482	.093332	.096319	.099346	.102413	.105517	.108658	.111836	.118295	.124885	.131598	.138425
	-.40	.088706	.094385	.100235	.103222	.106249	.109315	.112420	.115561	.118739	.125198	.131788	.138501	.145328
20	.40	.032226	.038504	.044963	.048256	.051588	.054957	.058363	.061803	.065274	.072307	.079447	.086681	.093997
	.30	.039128	.045407	.051866	.055159	.058491	.061860	.065266	.068706	.072177	.079210	.086353	.093584	.100900
	.20	.046031	.052310	.058769	.062062	.065394	.068763	.072169	.075608	.079080	.086113	.093253	.100487	.107803
	.10	.052934	.059213	.065672	.068964	.072297	.075666	.079072	.082511	.085983	.093016	.100156	.107390	.114706
	0.00	.059837	.066116	.072575	.075867	.079200	.082569	.085975	.089414	.092886	.099919	.107059	.114293	.121609
	-.10	.066740	.073019	.079478	.082770	.086103	.089472	.092878	.096317	.099789	.106822	.113962	.121196	.128512
	-.20	.073643	.079922	.086381	.089673	.093005	.096375	.099781	.103220	.106692	.113725	.120865	.128099	.135415
	-.30	.080546	.086825	.093284	.096576	.099908	.103278	.106684	.110123	.113595	.120628	.127768	.135002	.142318
	-.40	.087449	.093728	.100187	.103479	.106811	.110181	.113587	.117026	.120498	.127531	.134671	.141905	.149221
25	.40	.031501	.038132	.044936	.048397	.051892	.055421	.058980	.062566	.066178	.073471	.080840	.088271	.095751
	.30	.038404	.045035	.051839	.055300	.058795	.062324	.065883	.069469	.073081	.080373	.087743	.095174	.102654
	.20	.045307	.051938	.058742	.062203	.065698	.069227	.072786	.076372	.079984	.087276	.094645	.102077	.109557
	.10	.052210	.058841	.065645	.069106	.072601	.076130	.079688	.083275	.086887	.094180	.101548	.108980	.116460
	0.00	.059113	.065744	.072548	.076009	.079504	.083033	.086591	.090177	.093790	.101082	.108451	.115883	.123363
	-.10	.066016	.072647	.079451	.082911	.086407	.089936	.093494	.097081	.100693	.107985	.115354	.122786	.130266
	-.20	.072919	.079550	.086354	.089814	.093310	.096839	.100397	.103984	.107596	.114888	.122257	.129689	.137169
	-.30	.079822	.086453	.093257	.096717	.100213	.103742	.107300	.110887	.114499	.121791	.129160	.136592	.144072
	-.40	.086725	.093356	.100160	.103620	.107116	.110644	.114203	.117790	.121402	.128694	.136063	.143494	.150975
30	.40	.031043	.037902	.044920	.048481	.052072	.055690	.059332	.062995	.066678	.074091	.081556	.089057	.096585
	.30	.037945	.044804	.051823	.055384	.058975	.062593	.066235	.069898	.073581	.080994	.088459	.095960	.103488
	.20	.044848	.051707	.058726	.062287	.065878	.069496	.073138	.076801	.080484	.087897	.095362	.102863	.110391
	.10	.051751	.058610	.065629	.069190	.072781	.076399	.080041	.083704	.087387	.094800	.102265	.109766	.117294
	0.00	.058654	.065513	.072532	.076093	.079684	.083302	.086944	.090607	.094290	.101703	.109167	.116669	.124197
	-.10	.065557	.072416	.079435	.082996	.086587	.090204	.093847	.097510	.101193	.108606	.116070	.123572	.131100
	-.20	.072460	.079319	.086338	.089899	.093490	.097107	.100749	.104413	.108096	.115509	.122973	.130475	.138003
	-.30	.079363	.086222	.093241	.096802	.100392	.104010	.107652	.111316	.114999	.122412	.129876	.137378	.144906
	-.40	.086266	.093125	.100144	.103705	.107295	.110913	.114555	.118219	.121902	.129315	.136779	.144281	.151808

INTEREST RATE

10.0 YEAR HOLDING PERIOD
.080 EQUITY YIELD RATE
.800 LOAN RATIO

TERM YEARS	APPR DEP	5.0	6.0	7.0	7.5	8.0	8.5	9.0	9.5	10.0	11.0	12.0	13.0	14.0
10	.40	.034988	.039744	.044629	.047118	.049639	.052191	.054773	.057386	.060029	.065405	.070897	.076503	.082220
	.30	.041890	.046647	.051532	.054021	.056542	.059094	.061676	.064289	.066932	.072308	.077800	.083406	.089123
	.20	.048793	.053550	.058435	.060924	.063445	.065997	.068579	.071192	.073835	.079211	.084703	.090309	.096026
	.10	.055696	.060453	.065338	.067827	.070348	.072900	.075482	.078095	.080738	.086113	.091606	.097212	.102929
	0.00	.062599	.067356	.072241	.074730	.077251	.079803	.082385	.084998	.087641	.093016	.098509	.104415	.109832
	-.10	.069502	.074259	.079143	.081633	.084154	.086706	.089288	.091901	.094544	.099919	.105411	.111018	.116735
	-.20	.076405	.081162	.086046	.088536	.091057	.093609	.096191	.098804	.101447	.106822	.112314	.117921	.123638
	-.30	.083308	.088065	.092949	.095439	.097960	.100512	.103094	.105707	.108350	.113725	.119217	.124824	.130541
	-.40	.090211	.094968	.099852	.102342	.104863	.107414	.109997	.112610	.115253	.120628	.126120	.131727	.137444
15	.40	.032222	.038279	.044520	.047706	.050935	.054205	.057517	.060868	.064257	.071146	.078176	.085336	.092619
	.30	.039125	.045182	.051423	.054609	.057838	.061108	.064420	.067771	.071160	.078049	.085079	.092239	.099522
	.20	.046028	.052085	.058325	.061512	.064741	.068011	.071323	.074674	.078063	.084952	.091982	.099142	.106425
	.10	.052931	.058988	.065228	.068415	.071644	.074914	.078226	.081577	.084966	.091855	.098885	.106045	.113327
	0.00	.059834	.065891	.072131	.075318	.078547	.081817	.085129	.088480	.091869	.098758	.105788	.112948	.120230
	-.10	.066737	.072794	.079034	.082221	.085450	.088720	.092032	.095382	.098772	.105661	.112691	.119851	.127133
	-.20	.073640	.079697	.085937	.089123	.092352	.095623	.098935	.102285	.105675	.112564	.119594	.126754	.134036
	-.30	.080543	.086600	.092840	.096026	.099255	.102526	.105838	.109188	.112578	.119467	.126497	.133657	.140939
	-.40	.087446	.093503	.099743	.102929	.106158	.109429	.112740	.116091	.119481	.126370	.133399	.140560	.147842
20	.40	.030881	.037579	.044468	.047980	.051534	.055129	.058761	.062430	.066133	.073635	.081251	.088967	.096771
	.30	.037784	.044482	.051371	.054883	.058437	.062032	.065664	.069333	.073036	.080538	.088154	.095870	.103674
	.20	.044687	.051384	.058274	.061786	.065340	.068935	.072567	.076236	.079939	.087441	.095057	.102773	.110577
	.10	.051590	.058287	.065177	.068689	.072243	.075838	.079470	.083139	.086842	.094344	.101960	.109676	.117480
	0.00	.058493	.065190	.072080	.075592	.079146	.082741	.086373	.090042	.093745	.101247	.108863	.116579	.124383
	-.10	.065396	.072093	.078983	.082495	.086049	.089643	.093276	.096945	.100648	.108150	.115766	.123482	.131286
	-.20	.072299	.078996	.085886	.089398	.092952	.096546	.100179	.103848	.107551	.115053	.122669	.130385	.138189
	-.30	.079202	.085899	.092789	.096301	.099855	.103449	.107082	.110751	.114454	.121955	.129572	.137288	.145092
	-.40	.086105	.092802	.099692	.103204	.106758	.110352	.113985	.117654	.121357	.128858	.136475	.144191	.151994
25	.40	.030109	.037182	.044440	.048131	.051859	.055623	.059419	.063245	.067098	.074876	.082736	.090663	.098642
	.30	.037012	.044085	.051343	.055034	.058762	.062526	.066322	.070148	.074001	.081779	.089639	.097566	.105545
	.20	.043915	.050988	.058245	.061937	.065665	.069429	.073225	.077051	.080904	.088682	.096542	.104469	.112448
	.10	.050818	.057891	.065148	.068839	.072568	.076332	.080128	.083954	.087807	.095585	.103445	.111372	.119351
	0.00	.057721	.064794	.072051	.075742	.079471	.083235	.087031	.090857	.094710	.102488	.110348	.118275	.126254
	-.10	.064624	.071697	.078954	.082645	.086374	.090138	.093934	.097759	.101612	.109391	.117251	.125178	.133157
	-.20	.071527	.078600	.085857	.089548	.093277	.097041	.100837	.104662	.108515	.116294	.124154	.132081	.140060
	-.30	.078430	.085502	.092760	.096451	.100180	.103944	.107740	.111565	.115418	.123197	.131057	.138984	.146963
	-.40	.085333	.092405	.099663	.103354	.107083	.110847	.114643	.118468	.122321	.130100	.137960	.145887	.153866
30	.40	.029619	.036936	.044422	.048221	.052051	.055910	.059795	.063703	.067631	.075538	.083500	.091502	.099531
	.30	.036522	.043839	.051325	.055123	.058954	.062813	.066698	.070606	.074534	.082441	.090403	.098405	.106434
	.20	.043425	.050742	.058228	.062026	.065857	.069716	.073601	.077508	.081437	.089344	.097306	.105308	.113337
	.10	.050328	.057645	.065131	.068929	.072760	.076619	.080504	.084411	.088340	.096247	.104209	.112211	.120240
	0.00	.057231	.064548	.072034	.075832	.079663	.083522	.087406	.091314	.095243	.103150	.111112	.119114	.127143
	-.10	.064134	.071450	.078937	.082735	.086565	.090425	.094309	.098217	.102145	.110053	.118015	.126017	.134046
	-.20	.071037	.078353	.085840	.089638	.093468	.097328	.101212	.105120	.109048	.116956	.124918	.132919	.140949
	-.30	.077940	.085256	.092743	.096541	.100371	.104230	.108115	.112023	.115951	.123859	.131821	.139822	.147852
	-.40	.084843	.092159	.099646	.103444	.107274	.111133	.115018	.118926	.122854	.130762	.138724	.146725	.154755

10.0 YEAR HOLDING PERIOD
.080 EQUITY YIELD RATE
.900 LOAN RATIO

INTEREST RATE

TERM YEARS	APPR DEP	5.0	6.0	7.0	7.5	8.0	8.5	9.0	9.5	10.0	11.0	12.0	13.0	14.0
10	.40	.032812	.038164	.043659	.046460	.049295	.052166	.055072	.058011	.060984	.067032	.073210	.079517	.085949
	.30	.039715	.045067	.050562	.053363	.056198	.059069	.061974	.064914	.067887	.073935	.080113	.086420	.092852
	.20	.046618	.051970	.057465	.060265	.063101	.065972	.068877	.071817	.074790	.080838	.087016	.093323	.099755
	.10	.053521	.058873	.064368	.067168	.070004	.072875	.075780	.078720	.081693	.087741	.093919	.100226	.106658
	0.00	.060424	.065776	.071271	.074071	.076907	.079778	.082683	.085623	.088596	.094643	.100822	.107129	.113561
	-.10	.067327	.072679	.078174	.080974	.083810	.086681	.089586	.092526	.095499	.101546	.107725	.114032	.120464
	-.20	.074230	.079582	.085077	.087877	.090713	.093584	.096489	.099429	.102402	.108449	.114628	.120935	.127367
	-.30	.081133	.086484	.091979	.094780	.097616	.100487	.103392	.106332	.109305	.115352	.121531	.127838	.134270
	-.40	.088036	.093387	.098882	.101683	.104519	.107390	.110295	.113235	.116208	.122255	.128434	.134741	.141173
15	.40	.029701	.036516	.043536	.047120	.050753	.054433	.058158	.061928	.065741	.073491	.081399	.089455	.097647
	.30	.036604	.043419	.050439	.054023	.057656	.061336	.065061	.068831	.072644	.080394	.088302	.096358	.104550
	.20	.043507	.050322	.057342	.060926	.064559	.068239	.071964	.075734	.079546	.087297	.095205	.103261	.111453
	.10	.050410	.057225	.064245	.067829	.071462	.075141	.078867	.082636	.086449	.094200	.102108	.110164	.118356
	0.00	.057313	.064128	.071148	.074732	.078365	.082044	.085770	.089539	.093352	.101103	.109011	.117067	.125259
	-.10	.064216	.071031	.078051	.081635	.085268	.088947	.092673	.096442	.100255	.108006	.115914	.123970	.132162
	-.20	.071119	.077933	.084954	.088538	.092171	.095850	.099576	.103345	.107157	.114909	.122817	.130873	.139065
	-.30	.078022	.084836	.091857	.095441	.099074	.102753	.106479	.110248	.114061	.121812	.129720	.137775	.145968
	-.40	.084925	.091739	.098760	.102344	.105977	.109656	.113381	.117151	.120964	.128715	.136623	.144678	.152871
20	.40	.028193	.035727	.043478	.047429	.051428	.055471	.059558	.063685	.067851	.076291	.084859	.093540	.102319
	.30	.035096	.042630	.050381	.054332	.058331	.062374	.066461	.070588	.074754	.083194	.091762	.100443	.109222
	.20	.041999	.049533	.057284	.061235	.065234	.069277	.073364	.077491	.081657	.090097	.098665	.107346	.116125
	.10	.048902	.056436	.064187	.068138	.072137	.076180	.080267	.084394	.088560	.097000	.105568	.114249	.123028
	0.00	.055805	.063339	.071090	.075041	.079039	.083083	.087170	.091297	.095463	.103902	.112471	.121152	.129931
	-.10	.062708	.070242	.077993	.081944	.085942	.089986	.094073	.098200	.102366	.110805	.119374	.128055	.136833
	-.20	.069611	.077145	.084896	.088847	.092845	.096889	.100976	.105103	.109269	.117708	.126276	.134957	.143736
	-.30	.076514	.084048	.091799	.095750	.099748	.103792	.107879	.112006	.116172	.124611	.133179	.141860	.150639
	-.40	.083417	.090951	.098702	.102653	.106651	.110695	.114782	.118909	.123075	.131514	.140082	.148763	.157542
25	.40	.027324	.035281	.043446	.047598	.051793	.056027	.060298	.064602	.068936	.077687	.086530	.095447	.104424
	.30	.034227	.042184	.050349	.054501	.058696	.062930	.067201	.071505	.075839	.084590	.093433	.102350	.111327
	.20	.041130	.049087	.057252	.061404	.065599	.069833	.074104	.078408	.082742	.091493	.100336	.109253	.118230
	.10	.048033	.055990	.064155	.068307	.072502	.076736	.081007	.085311	.089645	.098396	.107239	.116156	.125133
	0.00	.054936	.062893	.071058	.075210	.079405	.083639	.087910	.092214	.096548	.105299	.114142	.123059	.132036
	-.10	.061839	.069796	.077961	.082113	.086308	.090542	.094813	.099117	.103451	.112202	.121045	.129962	.138939
	-.20	.068742	.076699	.084864	.089016	.093211	.097445	.101716	.106020	.110354	.119105	.127948	.136865	.145842
	-.30	.075645	.083602	.091767	.095919	.100114	.104348	.108619	.112922	.117257	.126008	.134851	.143768	.152745
	-.40	.082548	.090505	.098670	.102822	.107017	.111251	.115521	.119825	.124160	.132911	.141753	.150671	.159648
30	.40	.026773	.035004	.043427	.047700	.052009	.056350	.060721	.065117	.069536	.078432	.087389	.096391	.105424
	.30	.033676	.041907	.050330	.054603	.058912	.063253	.067623	.072020	.076439	.085335	.094292	.103294	.112327
	.20	.040579	.048810	.057232	.061505	.065814	.070156	.074526	.078923	.083342	.092238	.101195	.110197	.119230
	.10	.047482	.055713	.064135	.068408	.072717	.077059	.081429	.085826	.090245	.099141	.108098	.117100	.126133
	0.00	.054385	.062616	.071038	.075311	.079620	.083962	.088332	.092729	.097148	.106044	.115001	.124003	.133036
	-.10	.061288	.069519	.077941	.082214	.086523	.090865	.095235	.099632	.104051	.112947	.121904	.130906	.139939
	-.20	.068191	.076422	.084844	.089117	.093426	.097768	.102138	.106535	.110954	.119850	.128807	.137809	.146842
	-.30	.075094	.083325	.091747	.096020	.100329	.104671	.109041	.113437	.117857	.126753	.135710	.144712	.153745
	-.40	.081997	.090228	.098650	.102923	.107232	.111574	.115944	.120340	.124760	.133656	.142613	.151615	.160648

10.0 YEAR HOLDING PERIOD
.100 EQUITY YIELD RATE
.600 LOAN RATIO

INTEREST RATE

TERM YEARS	APPR DEP	5.0	6.0	7.0	7.5	8.0	8.5	9.0	9.5	10.0	11.0	12.0	13.0	14.0
10	.40	.053622	.057189	.060853	.062720	.064610	.066524	.068461	.070421	.072403	.076435	.080554	.084758	.089046
	.30	.059896	.063464	.067127	.068994	.070885	.072799	.074736	.076695	.078678	.082709	.086828	.091033	.095321
	.20	.066171	.069738	.073402	.075269	.077160	.079073	.081010	.082970	.084952	.088984	.093103	.097307	.101596
	.10	.072445	.076013	.079676	.081543	.083434	.085348	.087285	.089244	.091227	.095258	.099377	.103582	.107870
	0.00	.078720	.082288	.085951	.087818	.089709	.091622	.093559	.095519	.097501	.101533	.105652	.109856	.114445
	-.10	.084994	.088562	.092225	.094093	.095983	.097897	.099834	.101794	.103776	.107807	.111926	.116131	.120419
	-.20	.091269	.094837	.098500	.100367	.102258	.104172	.106108	.108068	.110050	.114082	.118201	.122406	.126694
	-.30	.097544	.101111	.104774	.106642	.108532	.110446	.112383	.114343	.116325	.120356	.124475	.128680	.132968
	-.40	.103818	.107386	.111049	.112916	.114807	.116721	.118657	.120617	.122599	.126631	.130750	.134955	.139243
15	.40	.049968	.054445	.059059	.061416	.063805	.066226	.068676	.071157	.073667	.077870	.083979	.089287	.094687
	.30	.056242	.060719	.065334	.067691	.070080	.072500	.074951	.077432	.079941	.085044	.090253	.095561	.100962
	.20	.062517	.066994	.071608	.073965	.076354	.078775	.081226	.083706	.086216	.091319	.096528	.101836	.107236
	.10	.068791	.073269	.077883	.080240	.082629	.085049	.087500	.089981	.092491	.097593	.102802	.108110	.113511
	0.00	.075066	.079543	.084157	.086514	.088903	.091324	.093775	.096255	.098765	.103868	.109077	.114385	.119785
	-.10	.081340	.085818	.090432	.092789	.095178	.097598	.100049	.102530	.105040	.110143	.115351	.120659	.126060
	-.20	.087615	.092092	.096707	.099063	.101452	.103873	.106324	.108804	.111314	.116417	.121626	.126934	.132334
	-.30	.093889	.098367	.102981	.105338	.107727	.110147	.112598	.115079	.117589	.122692	.127901	.133209	.138609
	-.40	.100164	.104641	.109256	.111612	.114001	.116422	.118873	.121354	.123863	.128966	.134175	.139483	.144883
20	.40	.048196	.053132	.058215	.060807	.063433	.066089	.068774	.071488	.074228	.079782	.085426	.091148	.096940
	.30	.054471	.059406	.064489	.067082	.069707	.072363	.075049	.077762	.080502	.086057	.091700	.097423	.103214
	.20	.060745	.065681	.070764	.073356	.075982	.078638	.081323	.084037	.086777	.092331	.097975	.103697	.109489
	.10	.067020	.071956	.077038	.079631	.082256	.084912	.087598	.090311	.093051	.098606	.104249	.109972	.115763
	0.00	.073294	.078230	.083313	.085906	.088531	.091187	.093872	.096586	.099326	.104880	.110524	.116246	.122038
	-.10	.079569	.084505	.089587	.092180	.094805	.097461	.100147	.102860	.105600	.111155	.116798	.122521	.128312
	-.20	.085843	.090779	.095862	.098455	.101080	.103736	.106421	.109135	.111875	.117429	.123073	.128795	.134587
	-.30	.092118	.097054	.102136	.104729	.107354	.110010	.112696	.115409	.118150	.123704	.129347	.135070	.140861
	-.40	.098392	.103328	.108411	.111004	.113629	.116285	.118970	.121684	.124424	.129978	.135622	.141345	.147136
25	.40	.047176	.052389	.057746	.060473	.063231	.066015	.068826	.071660	.074516	.080287	.086125	.092017	.097955
	.30	.053450	.058663	.064021	.066748	.069505	.072290	.075100	.077935	.080791	.086561	.092399	.098292	.104229
	.20	.059725	.064938	.070295	.073022	.075780	.078564	.081375	.084209	.087065	.092836	.098674	.104567	.110504
	.10	.065999	.071212	.076570	.079297	.082054	.084839	.087649	.090484	.093340	.099110	.104948	.110841	.116778
	0.00	.072274	.077487	.082844	.085572	.088329	.091113	.093924	.096758	.099614	.105385	.111223	.117116	.123053
	-.10	.078548	.083761	.089119	.091846	.094603	.097388	.100198	.103033	.105889	.111660	.117497	.123390	.129327
	-.20	.084823	.090036	.095393	.098121	.100878	.103663	.106473	.109307	.112163	.117934	.123772	.129665	.135602
	-.30	.091097	.096310	.101668	.104395	.107152	.109937	.112748	.115582	.118438	.124209	.130046	.135939	.141877
	-.40	.097372	.102585	.107942	.110670	.113427	.116212	.119022	.121856	.124712	.130483	.136321	.142214	.148151
30	.40	.046529	.051928	.057462	.060274	.063112	.065973	.068855	.071757	.074675	.080556	.086484	.092447	.098437
	.30	.052803	.058202	.063737	.066549	.069386	.072247	.075130	.078031	.080950	.086831	.092759	.098722	.104712
	.20	.059078	.064477	.070011	.072823	.075661	.078522	.081404	.084306	.087224	.093105	.099033	.104996	.110986
	.10	.065352	.070751	.076286	.079098	.081935	.084796	.087679	.090580	.093499	.099380	.105308	.111271	.117261
	0.00	.071627	.077026	.082561	.085372	.088210	.091071	.093953	.096855	.099774	.105654	.111582	.117546	.123535
	-.10	.077901	.083300	.088835	.091647	.094484	.097345	.100228	.103130	.106048	.111929	.117857	.123820	.129810
	-.20	.084176	.089575	.095110	.097921	.100759	.103620	.106502	.109404	.112323	.118203	.124131	.130095	.136084
	-.30	.090451	.095849	.101384	.104196	.107033	.109895	.112777	.115679	.118597	.124478	.130406	.136369	.142359
	-.40	.096725	.102124	.107659	.110470	.113308	.116169	.119052	.121953	.124872	.130753	.136680	.142644	.148633

10.0 YEAR HOLDING PERIOD
.100 EQUITY YIELD RATE
.667 LOAN RATIO

INTEREST RATE

TERM YEARS	APPR DEP	5.0	6.0	7.0	7.5	8.0	8.5	9.0	9.5	10.0	11.0	12.0	13.0	14.0
10	.40	.051257	.055221	.059292	.061366	.063467	.065593	.067745	.069923	.072125	.076605	.081182	.085854	.090618
	.30	.057532	.061496	.065566	.067641	.069741	.071868	.074020	.076197	.078400	.082879	.087456	.092128	.096893
	.20	.063806	.067770	.071841	.073915	.076016	.078142	.080295	.082472	.084675	.089154	.093731	.098403	.103167
	.10	.070081	.074045	.078115	.080190	.082291	.084417	.086569	.088747	.090949	.095429	.100005	.104677	.109442
	0.00	.076355	.080319	.084390	.086465	.088565	.090692	.092844	.095021	.097224	.101703	.106294	.110992	.115716
	-.10	.082630	.086594	.090564	.092739	.094840	.096966	.099118	.101296	.103498	.107978	.112554	.117226	.121991
	-.20	.088904	.092868	.096939	.099013	.101114	.103241	.105393	.107570	.109773	.114252	.118829	.123501	.128265
	-.30	.095179	.099143	.103213	.105288	.107389	.109515	.111667	.113845	.116047	.120527	.125053	.129775	.134540
	-.40	.101454	.105418	.109488	.111563	.113663	.115790	.117942	.120119	.122322	.126801	.131378	.136050	.140814
15	.40	.047197	.052172	.057299	.059918	.062572	.065261	.067985	.070741	.073530	.079200	.084987	.090885	.096886
	.30	.053472	.058446	.063573	.066192	.068847	.071536	.074259	.077016	.079804	.085474	.091262	.097160	.103160
	.20	.059746	.064721	.069848	.072467	.075121	.077811	.080534	.083290	.086079	.091749	.097536	.103434	.109435
	.10	.066021	.070995	.076123	.078741	.081396	.084086	.086808	.089565	.092353	.098023	.103811	.109709	.115709
	0.00	.072295	.077270	.082397	.085016	.087670	.090360	.093083	.095839	.098628	.104298	.110085	.115983	.121984
	-.10	.078570	.083545	.088672	.091290	.093945	.096634	.099357	.102114	.104902	.110572	.116360	.122258	.128258
	-.20	.084844	.089819	.094946	.097565	.100219	.102909	.105632	.108388	.111177	.116847	.122635	.128532	.134533
	-.30	.091119	.096094	.101221	.103839	.106494	.109183	.111907	.114663	.117451	.123121	.128909	.134807	.140807
	-.40	.097393	.102368	.107495	.110114	.112768	.115458	.118181	.120937	.123726	.129396	.135184	.141081	.147082
20	.40	.045229	.050713	.056360	.059241	.062158	.065109	.068093	.071108	.074153	.080324	.086595	.092953	.099388
	.30	.051503	.056987	.062635	.065516	.068433	.071384	.074368	.077383	.080427	.086599	.092870	.099228	.105663
	.20	.057778	.063262	.068909	.071790	.074707	.077658	.080642	.083657	.086702	.092873	.099144	.105503	.111937
	.10	.064052	.069537	.075184	.078065	.080982	.083933	.086917	.089932	.092977	.099148	.105419	.111777	.118212
	0.00	.070327	.075811	.081458	.084339	.087256	.090207	.093191	.096206	.099251	.105422	.111693	.118052	.124486
	-.10	.076601	.082086	.087733	.090614	.093531	.096482	.099466	.102481	.105526	.111697	.117968	.124326	.130761
	-.20	.082876	.088360	.094008	.096888	.099805	.102757	.105741	.108756	.111800	.117972	.124242	.130601	.137036
	-.30	.089150	.094635	.100282	.103163	.106080	.109031	.112015	.115030	.118075	.124246	.130517	.136875	.143310
	-.40	.095425	.100909	.106557	.109438	.112354	.115306	.118290	.121305	.124349	.130521	.136791	.143150	.149585
25	.40	.044095	.049887	.055840	.058870	.061934	.065028	.068151	.071300	.074473	.080885	.087372	.093919	.100516
	.30	.050369	.056162	.062114	.065145	.068208	.071302	.074425	.077574	.080748	.087160	.093646	.100194	.106791
	.20	.056644	.062436	.068389	.071419	.074483	.077577	.080700	.083849	.087022	.093434	.099921	.106468	.113065
	.10	.062919	.068711	.074663	.077694	.080757	.083851	.086974	.090123	.093297	.099709	.106195	.112743	.119340
	0.00	.069193	.074985	.080938	.083968	.087032	.090126	.093249	.096398	.099571	.105983	.112470	.119017	.125614
	-.10	.075467	.081260	.087212	.090243	.093306	.096401	.099523	.102672	.105846	.112258	.118744	.125292	.131889
	-.20	.081742	.087534	.093487	.096517	.099581	.102675	.105798	.108947	.112121	.118532	.125019	.131567	.138164
	-.30	.088017	.093809	.099761	.102792	.105855	.108950	.112072	.115222	.118395	.124807	.131293	.137841	.144438
	-.40	.094291	.100083	.106036	.109066	.112130	.115224	.118347	.121496	.124670	.131081	.137568	.144116	.150713
30	.40	.043376	.049375	.055525	.058649	.061801	.064981	.068183	.071407	.074650	.081184	.087771	.094397	.101052
	.30	.049651	.055649	.061799	.064923	.068076	.071255	.074458	.077682	.080925	.087459	.094046	.100672	.107327
	.20	.055925	.061924	.068074	.071198	.074351	.077530	.080732	.083956	.087199	.093734	.100320	.106946	.113601
	.10	.062200	.068198	.074348	.077472	.080625	.083804	.087007	.090231	.093474	.100008	.106595	.113221	.119876
	0.00	.068474	.074473	.080623	.083747	.086900	.090079	.093282	.096506	.099748	.106283	.112869	.119495	.126150
	-.10	.074749	.080747	.086897	.090021	.093174	.096353	.099556	.102780	.106023	.112557	.119144	.125770	.132425
	-.20	.081023	.087022	.093172	.096296	.099449	.102628	.105831	.109055	.112297	.118832	.125418	.132044	.138699
	-.30	.087298	.093297	.099446	.102570	.105723	.108902	.112105	.115329	.118572	.125106	.131693	.138319	.144974
	-.40	.093572	.099571	.105721	.108845	.111998	.115177	.118380	.121604	.124847	.131381	.137967	.144593	.151248

318

10.0 YEAR HOLDING PERIOD
.100 EQUITY YIELD RATE
.700 LOAN RATIO

INTEREST RATE

TERM YEARS	APPR DEP	5.0	6.0	7.0	7.5	8.0	8.5	9.0	9.5	10.0	11.0	12.0	13.0	14.0
10	.40	.050075	.054237	.058511	.060690	.062895	.065128	.067388	.069674	.071987	.076690	.081496	.086401	.091404
	.30	.056350	.060512	.064786	.066964	.069170	.071403	.073662	.075949	.078261	.082965	.087770	.092676	.097678
	.20	.062624	.066786	.071060	.073239	.075444	.077677	.079937	.082223	.084536	.089239	.094045	.098950	.103953
	.10	.068899	.073061	.077335	.079513	.081719	.083952	.086211	.088498	.090810	.095514	.100319	.105225	.110227
	0.00	.075173	.079335	.083609	.085788	.087993	.090226	.092486	.094772	.097085	.101788	.106594	.111499	.116502
	-.10	.081448	.085610	.089884	.092062	.094268	.096501	.098760	.101047	.103359	.108063	.112868	.117774	.122777
	-.20	.087722	.091885	.096158	.098337	.100542	.102775	.105035	.107321	.109634	.114337	.119143	.124048	.129051
	-.30	.093997	.098159	.102433	.104611	.106817	.109050	.111309	.113596	.115908	.120612	.125417	.130323	.135326
	-.40	.100271	.104434	.108708	.110886	.113092	.115324	.117584	.119870	.122183	.126886	.131692	.136597	.141600
15	.40	.045812	.051035	.056419	.059169	.061956	.064779	.067639	.070533	.073461	.079415	.085492	.091684	.097985
	.30	.052087	.057310	.062693	.065443	.068230	.071054	.073913	.076808	.079736	.085689	.091766	.097959	.104259
	.20	.058361	.063585	.068968	.071718	.074505	.077329	.080188	.083082	.086010	.091964	.098041	.104233	.110534
	.10	.064636	.069859	.075243	.077992	.080779	.083603	.086463	.089357	.092285	.098238	.104315	.110508	.116808
	0.00	.070910	.076134	.081517	.084267	.087054	.089878	.092737	.095631	.098559	.104513	.110590	.116782	.123083
	-.10	.077185	.082408	.087792	.090541	.093328	.096152	.099012	.101906	.104834	.110787	.116864	.123057	.129357
	-.20	.083459	.088683	.094066	.096816	.099603	.102427	.105286	.108180	.111108	.117062	.123139	.129331	.135632
	-.30	.089734	.094957	.100341	.103090	.105878	.108701	.111561	.114455	.117383	.123336	.129413	.135606	.141906
	-.40	.096008	.101232	.106615	.109365	.112152	.114976	.117835	.120729	.123657	.129611	.135688	.141881	.148181
20	.40	.043745	.049504	.055433	.058458	.061521	.064620	.067753	.070919	.074115	.080595	.087180	.093856	.100613
	.30	.050020	.055778	.061708	.064733	.067796	.070894	.074027	.077193	.080390	.086870	.093454	.100130	.106887
	.20	.056294	.062053	.067982	.071007	.074070	.077169	.080302	.083468	.086665	.093144	.099729	.106405	.113162
	.10	.062569	.068327	.074257	.077282	.080345	.083443	.086577	.089742	.092939	.099419	.106003	.112680	.119436
	0.00	.068843	.074602	.080532	.083556	.086619	.089718	.092851	.096017	.099214	.105694	.112278	.118954	.125711
	-.10	.075118	.080876	.086806	.089831	.092894	.095992	.099126	.102291	.105488	.111968	.118552	.125229	.131985
	-.20	.081392	.087151	.093081	.096106	.099168	.102267	.105400	.108566	.111763	.118243	.124827	.131503	.138260
	-.30	.087667	.093425	.099355	.102380	.105443	.108541	.111675	.114840	.118037	.124517	.131101	.137778	.144534
	-.40	.093941	.099700	.105630	.108655	.111717	.114816	.117949	.121115	.124312	.130792	.137376	.144052	.150809
25	.40	.042555	.048637	.054887	.058069	.061285	.064534	.067813	.071120	.074452	.081184	.087995	.094870	.101797
	.30	.048829	.054911	.061161	.064343	.067560	.070809	.074088	.077394	.080726	.087459	.094270	.101145	.108071
	.20	.055104	.061186	.067436	.070618	.073834	.077083	.080362	.083669	.087001	.093733	.100544	.107419	.114346
	.10	.061378	.067460	.073710	.076892	.080109	.083358	.086637	.089943	.093275	.100008	.106819	.113694	.120621
	0.00	.067653	.073735	.079985	.083167	.086383	.089632	.092911	.096218	.099550	.106282	.113093	.119968	.126895
	-.10	.073927	.080009	.086259	.089441	.092658	.095907	.099186	.102492	.105824	.112557	.119368	.126243	.133170
	-.20	.080202	.086284	.092534	.095716	.098933	.102181	.105460	.108767	.112099	.118832	.125642	.132517	.139444
	-.30	.086476	.092558	.098808	.101990	.105207	.108456	.111735	.115041	.118374	.125106	.131917	.138792	.145719
	-.40	.092751	.098833	.105083	.108265	.111482	.114731	.118010	.121316	.124648	.131381	.138191	.145066	.151993
30	.40	.041800	.048099	.054556	.057836	.061147	.064485	.067847	.071233	.074638	.081499	.088414	.095372	.102360
	.30	.048075	.054373	.060830	.064111	.067421	.070759	.074122	.077507	.080912	.087773	.094689	.101646	.108634
	.20	.054349	.060648	.067105	.070385	.073696	.077034	.080397	.083782	.087187	.094048	.100963	.107921	.114909
	.10	.060624	.066922	.073379	.076660	.079970	.083308	.086671	.090056	.093461	.100322	.107238	.114195	.121183
	0.00	.066898	.073197	.079654	.082934	.086245	.089583	.092946	.096331	.099736	.106597	.113513	.120470	.127458
	-.10	.073173	.079471	.085928	.089209	.092519	.095857	.099220	.102605	.106010	.112871	.119787	.126744	.133732
	-.20	.079448	.085746	.092203	.095483	.098794	.102132	.105495	.108880	.112285	.119146	.126062	.133019	.140007
	-.30	.085722	.092020	.098478	.101758	.105068	.108406	.111769	.115154	.118559	.125420	.132336	.139293	.146281
	-.40	.091996	.098295	.104752	.108032	.111343	.114681	.118044	.121429	.124834	.131695	.138611	.145568	.152556

10.0 YEAR HOLDING PERIOD
.100 EQUITY YIELD RATE
.750 LOAN RATIO

INTEREST RATE

TERM YEARS	APPR DEP	5.0	6.0	7.0	7.5	8.0	8.5	9.0	9.5	10.0	11.0	12.0	13.0	14.0
10	.40	.048302	.052761	.057340	.059674	.062038	.064430	.066851	.069301	.071778	.076818	.081967	.087222	.092583
	.30	.054576	.059036	.063615	.065949	.068312	.070704	.073126	.075575	.078053	.083092	.088241	.093497	.098857
	.20	.060851	.065310	.069890	.072223	.074587	.076979	.079400	.081850	.084328	.089367	.094516	.099772	.105132
	.10	.067125	.071585	.076164	.078498	.080861	.083254	.085675	.088124	.090602	.095644	.100790	.106046	.111406
	0.00	.073400	.077859	.082439	.084773	.087136	.089528	.091949	.094399	.096877	.101916	.107065	.112321	.117681
	-.10	.079674	.084134	.088713	.091047	.093410	.095803	.098224	.100673	.103151	.108191	.113339	.118595	.123955
	-.20	.085949	.090408	.094988	.097322	.099685	.102077	.104498	.106948	.109426	.114465	.119614	.124870	.130230
	-.30	.092224	.096683	.101262	.103596	.105959	.108352	.110773	.113222	.115700	.120740	.125888	.131144	.136504
	-.40	.098498	.102958	.107537	.109871	.112234	.114626	.117047	.119497	.121975	.127014	.132163	.137419	.142779
15	.40	.043734	.049331	.055099	.058045	.061031	.064056	.067120	.070221	.073358	.079737	.086248	.092883	.099633
	.30	.050009	.055605	.061373	.064319	.067306	.070331	.073395	.076496	.079633	.086011	.092523	.099158	.105908
	.20	.056283	.061880	.067648	.070594	.073580	.076606	.079669	.082770	.085907	.092286	.098797	.105432	.112183
	.10	.062558	.068154	.073922	.076868	.079855	.082880	.085944	.089045	.092182	.098561	.105072	.111707	.118457
	0.00	.068832	.074429	.080197	.083143	.086129	.089155	.092218	.095319	.098456	.104835	.111346	.117981	.124732
	-.10	.075107	.080703	.086471	.089417	.092404	.095429	.098493	.101594	.104731	.111110	.117621	.124256	.131006
	-.20	.081381	.086978	.092746	.095692	.098678	.101704	.104767	.107868	.111005	.117384	.123895	.130530	.137281
	-.30	.087656	.093252	.099020	.101967	.104953	.107978	.111042	.114143	.117280	.123659	.130170	.136805	.143555
	-.40	.093930	.099527	.105295	.108241	.111227	.114256	.117316	.120417	.123554	.129933	.136444	.143079	.149830
20	.40	.041520	.047689	.054043	.057284	.060565	.063885	.067242	.070634	.074059	.081005	.088057	.095210	.102449
	.30	.047794	.053964	.060317	.063558	.066840	.070160	.073517	.076909	.080334	.087277	.094331	.101484	.108724
	.20	.054069	.060239	.066592	.069833	.073114	.076434	.079791	.083183	.086608	.093551	.100606	.107759	.114998
	.10	.060343	.066513	.072866	.076107	.079389	.082709	.086066	.089458	.092883	.099826	.106880	.114033	.121273
	0.00	.066618	.072788	.079141	.082382	.085663	.088983	.092340	.095732	.099157	.106100	.113155	.120308	.127547
	-.10	.072892	.079062	.085415	.088656	.091938	.095258	.098615	.102007	.105432	.112375	.119429	.126582	.133822
	-.20	.079167	.085337	.091690	.094931	.098212	.101533	.104889	.108281	.111707	.118649	.125704	.132857	.140096
	-.30	.085441	.091611	.097965	.101206	.104487	.107807	.111164	.114556	.117981	.124924	.131978	.139132	.146371
	-.40	.091716	.097886	.104239	.107480	.110762	.114082	.117439	.120830	.124256	.131198	.138253	.145406	.152645
25	.40	.040244	.046760	.053457	.056866	.060313	.063794	.067307	.070850	.074420	.081633	.088930	.096296	.103718
	.30	.046519	.053035	.059732	.063141	.066587	.070068	.073581	.077124	.080694	.087908	.095205	.102571	.109993
	.20	.052793	.059309	.066006	.069415	.072862	.076343	.079856	.083399	.086969	.094182	.101479	.108845	.116267
	.10	.059068	.065584	.072281	.075690	.079136	.082617	.086130	.089673	.093243	.100457	.107754	.115120	.122542
	0.00	.065342	.071859	.078555	.081964	.085411	.088892	.092405	.095948	.099518	.106731	.114028	.121395	.128816
	-.10	.071617	.078133	.084830	.088239	.091685	.095166	.098679	.102222	.105792	.113006	.120303	.127669	.135091
	-.20	.077891	.084408	.091104	.094514	.097960	.101441	.104954	.108497	.112067	.119280	.126578	.133944	.141365
	-.30	.084166	.090682	.097379	.100788	.104234	.107715	.111229	.114771	.118341	.125555	.132852	.140218	.147640
	-.40	.090440	.096957	.103653	.107063	.110509	.113990	.117503	.121046	.124616	.131829	.139127	.146493	.153914
30	.40	.039436	.046184	.053103	.056617	.060164	.063741	.067344	.070971	.074619	.081970	.089380	.096834	.104321
	.30	.045710	.052459	.059377	.062892	.066439	.070015	.073618	.077245	.080893	.088244	.095654	.103108	.110595
	.20	.051985	.058733	.065652	.069166	.072713	.076290	.079893	.083520	.087168	.094519	.101929	.109383	.116870
	.10	.058259	.065008	.071926	.075441	.078988	.082564	.086167	.089794	.093442	.100793	.108203	.115657	.123144
	0.00	.064534	.071282	.078201	.081715	.085262	.088838	.092442	.096069	.099717	.107068	.114478	.121932	.129419
	-.10	.070808	.077557	.084475	.087990	.091537	.095113	.098716	.102343	.105991	.113342	.120752	.128207	.135694
	-.20	.077083	.083831	.090750	.094264	.097811	.101388	.104991	.108618	.112266	.119617	.127027	.134481	.141968
	-.30	.083357	.090106	.097024	.100539	.104086	.107662	.111265	.114892	.118541	.125892	.133301	.140756	.148243
	-.40	.089632	.096380	.103299	.106813	.110360	.113937	.117540	.121167	.124815	.132166	.139576	.147030	.154517

10.0 YEAR HOLDING PERIOD
.100 EQUITY YIELD RATE
.800 LOAN RATIO

INTEREST RATE

TERM 10 YEARS

APPR DEP	5.0	6.0	7.0	7.5	8.0	8.5	9.0	9.5	10.0	11.0	12.0	13.0	14.0
.40	.046528	.051285	.056170	.058659	.061180	.063732	.066314	.068927	.071570	.076946	.082438	.088044	.093761
.30	.052803	.057560	.062444	.064934	.067455	.070006	.072589	.075202	.077845	.083220	.088712	.094318	.100036
.20	.059077	.063834	.068719	.071208	.073729	.076281	.078863	.081476	.084119	.089495	.094987	.100593	.106310
.10	.065352	.070109	.074993	.077483	.080004	.082555	.085138	.087751	.090394	.095769	.101261	.106867	.112585
0.00	.071627	.076383	.081268	.083757	.086278	.088830	.091412	.094025	.096668	.102044	.107536	.113142	.118859
-.10	.077901	.082658	.087542	.090032	.092553	.095104	.097687	.100300	.102943	.108318	.113810	.119417	.125134
-.20	.084176	.088932	.093817	.096306	.098827	.101379	.103962	.106574	.109217	.114593	.120085	.125691	.131409
-.30	.090450	.095207	.100091	.102581	.105102	.107654	.110236	.112849	.115492	.120867	.126359	.131966	.137683
-.40	.096725	.101482	.106366	.108856	.111376	.113928	.116511	.119123	.121767	.127142	.132634	.138240	.143958

TERM 15 YEARS

APPR DEP	5.0	6.0	7.0	7.5	8.0	8.5	9.0	9.5	10.0	11.0	12.0	13.0	14.0
.40	.041656	.047626	.053778	.056921	.060106	.063333	.066601	.069909	.073255	.080059	.087004	.094082	.101282
.30	.047931	.053900	.060053	.063195	.066381	.069608	.072876	.076184	.079530	.086334	.093279	.100356	.107557
.20	.054205	.060175	.066328	.069470	.072655	.075883	.079150	.082458	.085804	.092608	.099553	.106631	.113831
.10	.060480	.066450	.072602	.075745	.078930	.082157	.085425	.088733	.092079	.098883	.105828	.112905	.120106
0.00	.066754	.072724	.078877	.082019	.085204	.088432	.091700	.095007	.098353	.105157	.112103	.119180	.126380
-.10	.073029	.078999	.085151	.088294	.091479	.094706	.097974	.101282	.104628	.111432	.118377	.125454	.132655
-.20	.079304	.085273	.091426	.094568	.097754	.100981	.104249	.107556	.110902	.117706	.124652	.131729	.138929
-.30	.085578	.091548	.097700	.100843	.104028	.107255	.110523	.113831	.117177	.123981	.130926	.138003	.145204
-.40	.091853	.097822	.103975	.107117	.110303	.113530	.116798	.120105	.123452	.130256	.137201	.144278	.151479

TERM 20 YEARS

APPR DEP	5.0	6.0	7.0	7.5	8.0	8.5	9.0	9.5	10.0	11.0	12.0	13.0	14.0
.40	.039294	.045875	.052652	.056109	.059609	.063151	.066732	.070350	.074003	.081409	.088934	.096564	.104285
.30	.045569	.052150	.058927	.062384	.065884	.069425	.073006	.076624	.080278	.087683	.095208	.102838	.110560
.20	.051843	.058424	.065201	.068658	.072159	.075700	.079281	.082899	.086552	.093958	.101483	.109113	.116835
.10	.058118	.064699	.071476	.074933	.078433	.081974	.085555	.089173	.092827	.100232	.107757	.115387	.123109
0.00	.064392	.070973	.077750	.081207	.084707	.088249	.091830	.095448	.099101	.106507	.114032	.121662	.129384
-.10	.070667	.077248	.084025	.087482	.090982	.094524	.098104	.101722	.105376	.112781	.120306	.127936	.135658
-.20	.076941	.083523	.090299	.093756	.097257	.100798	.104379	.107997	.111650	.119056	.126581	.134211	.141933
-.30	.083216	.089797	.096574	.100031	.103531	.107073	.110653	.114271	.117925	.125330	.132855	.140485	.148207
-.40	.089491	.096072	.102848	.106306	.109806	.113347	.116928	.120546	.124199	.131605	.139130	.146760	.154482

TERM 25 YEARS

APPR DEP	5.0	6.0	7.0	7.5	8.0	8.5	9.0	9.5	10.0	11.0	12.0	13.0	14.0
.40	.037934	.044884	.052027	.055664	.059340	.063053	.066800	.070579	.074387	.082082	.089866	.097723	.105639
.30	.044208	.051159	.058302	.061938	.065615	.069328	.073075	.076854	.080662	.088356	.096140	.103997	.111914
.20	.050483	.057433	.064576	.068213	.071889	.075602	.079350	.083128	.086937	.094631	.102415	.110272	.118188
.10	.056757	.063708	.070851	.074488	.078164	.081877	.085624	.089403	.093211	.100905	.108689	.116546	.124463
0.00	.063032	.069983	.077126	.080762	.084438	.088151	.091899	.095678	.099486	.107180	.114964	.122821	.130737
-.10	.069306	.076257	.083400	.087037	.090713	.094426	.098173	.101952	.105760	.113454	.121238	.129095	.137012
-.20	.075581	.082532	.089675	.093311	.096987	.100700	.104448	.108227	.112035	.119729	.127513	.135370	.143286
-.30	.081855	.088806	.095949	.099586	.103262	.106975	.110722	.114501	.118309	.126004	.133787	.141644	.149561
-.40	.088130	.095081	.102224	.105860	.109536	.113249	.116997	.120776	.124584	.132278	.140062	.147919	.155835

TERM 30 YEARS

APPR DEP	5.0	6.0	7.0	7.5	8.0	8.5	9.0	9.5	10.0	11.0	12.0	13.0	14.0
.40	.037071	.044270	.051649	.055398	.059181	.062996	.066840	.070708	.074600	.082441	.090345	.098296	.106282
.30	.043346	.050544	.057924	.061673	.065456	.069271	.073114	.076983	.080874	.088716	.096619	.104570	.112557
.20	.049620	.056819	.064198	.067947	.071731	.075546	.079389	.083258	.087149	.094990	.102894	.110845	.118831
.10	.055895	.063093	.070473	.074222	.078005	.081820	.085663	.089532	.093424	.101265	.109168	.117120	.125106
0.00	.062169	.069368	.076747	.080496	.084280	.088095	.091938	.095807	.099698	.107539	.115443	.123394	.131380
-.10	.068444	.075642	.083022	.086771	.090554	.094369	.098212	.102081	.105973	.113814	.121717	.129669	.137655
-.20	.074718	.081917	.089296	.093045	.096829	.100644	.104487	.108356	.112247	.120088	.127992	.135943	.143929
-.30	.080993	.088191	.095571	.099320	.103103	.106918	.110762	.114630	.118522	.126363	.134267	.142218	.150204
-.40	.087267	.094466	.101846	.105594	.109378	.113193	.117036	.120905	.124796	.132637	.140541	.148492	.156478

10.0 YEAR HOLDING PERIOD
.100 EQUITY YIELD RATE
.900 LOAN RATIO

INTEREST RATE

TERM YEARS	APPR DEP	5.0	6.0	7.0	7.5	8.0	8.5	9.0	9.5	10.0	11.0	12.0	13.0	14.0
10	.40	.042982	.048333	.053828	.056629	.059465	.062336	.065241	.068180	.071154	.077201	.083380	.089687	.096119
	.30	.049256	.054608	.060103	.062903	.065739	.068610	.071515	.074455	.077428	.083476	.089654	.095961	.102393
	.20	.055531	.060882	.066377	.069178	.072014	.074885	.077790	.080729	.083703	.089750	.095929	.102236	.108668
	.10	.061805	.067157	.072652	.075453	.078288	.081159	.084064	.087004	.089977	.096025	.102203	.108510	.114942
	0.00	.068080	.073431	.078926	.081727	.084563	.087434	.090339	.093279	.096252	.102299	.108478	.114785	.121217
	-.10	.074354	.079706	.085201	.088002	.090837	.093708	.096614	.099553	.102526	.108574	.114752	.121059	.127491
	-.20	.080629	.085980	.091475	.094276	.097112	.099983	.102888	.105828	.108801	.114848	.121027	.127334	.133766
	-.30	.086904	.092255	.097750	.100551	.103387	.106257	.109163	.112102	.115076	.121123	.127301	.133608	.140041
	-.40	.093178	.098529	.104024	.106825	.109661	.112532	.115437	.118377	.121350	.127397	.133576	.139883	.146315
15	.40	.037501	.044216	.051138	.054673	.058257	.061887	.065564	.069285	.073049	.080704	.088517	.096479	.104580
	.30	.043775	.050491	.057413	.060948	.064531	.068162	.071838	.075559	.079324	.086978	.094792	.102754	.110854
	.20	.050050	.056766	.063687	.067222	.070806	.074436	.078113	.081834	.085599	.093253	.101066	.109028	.117129
	.10	.056324	.063040	.069962	.073497	.077080	.080711	.084387	.088109	.091873	.099528	.107341	.115303	.123403
	0.00	.062599	.069315	.076236	.079771	.083355	.086986	.090662	.094383	.098148	.105802	.113615	.121577	.129678
	-.10	.068873	.075589	.082511	.086046	.089630	.093260	.096936	.100658	.104422	.112077	.119890	.127852	.135952
	-.20	.075148	.081864	.088785	.092321	.095904	.099535	.103211	.106932	.110697	.118351	.126164	.134126	.142227
	-.30	.081422	.088138	.095060	.098595	.102179	.105809	.109486	.113207	.116971	.124626	.132439	.140401	.148502
	-.40	.087697	.094413	.101334	.104870	.108453	.112084	.115760	.119481	.123246	.130900	.138714	.146676	.154776
20	.40	.034843	.042247	.049871	.053760	.057698	.061682	.065711	.069739	.073781	.082247	.090688	.099271	.107958
	.30	.041118	.048522	.056145	.060035	.063972	.067957	.071985	.076013	.080055	.088521	.096962	.105546	.114233
	.20	.047392	.054796	.062420	.066309	.070247	.074231	.078259	.082288	.086330	.094796	.103237	.111820	.120508
	.10	.053667	.061071	.068695	.072584	.076521	.080506	.084534	.088562	.092604	.101070	.109511	.118095	.126782
	0.00	.059941	.067345	.074969	.078858	.082796	.086780	.090808	.094837	.098879	.107345	.115786	.124370	.133057
	-.10	.066216	.073620	.081244	.085133	.089071	.093055	.097083	.101111	.105153	.113619	.122060	.130644	.139331
	-.20	.072490	.079894	.087518	.091407	.095345	.099329	.103358	.107385	.111428	.119893	.128335	.136919	.145606
	-.30	.078765	.086169	.093793	.097682	.101620	.105604	.109632	.113660	.117702	.126168	.134609	.143193	.151880
	-.40	.085040	.092443	.100067	.103956	.107894	.111878	.115907	.119934	.123977	.132442	.140884	.149468	.158155
25	.40	.033312	.041132	.049168	.053259	.057395	.061572	.065788	.070039	.074323	.082979	.091736	.100575	.109481
	.30	.039587	.047407	.055443	.059534	.063669	.067847	.072062	.076314	.080598	.089254	.098011	.106850	.115756
	.20	.045862	.053681	.061717	.065808	.069944	.074121	.078337	.082588	.086872	.095528	.104285	.113124	.122030
	.10	.052136	.059956	.067992	.072083	.076218	.080396	.084611	.088863	.093147	.101803	.110560	.119399	.128305
	0.00	.058411	.066230	.074266	.078357	.082493	.086670	.090886	.095137	.099421	.108077	.116834	.125673	.134579
	-.10	.064685	.072505	.080541	.084632	.088768	.092945	.097160	.101412	.105696	.114352	.123109	.131948	.140854
	-.20	.070960	.078779	.086815	.090906	.095042	.099219	.103435	.107686	.111970	.120627	.129383	.138222	.147128
	-.30	.077234	.085054	.093090	.097181	.101317	.105494	.109710	.113961	.118245	.126901	.135658	.144497	.153403
	-.40	.083509	.091328	.099364	.103456	.107591	.111768	.115984	.120235	.124520	.133176	.141932	.150772	.159678
30	.40	.032342	.040440	.048743	.052960	.057216	.061541	.065832	.070184	.074542	.083383	.092275	.101220	.110205
	.30	.038617	.046715	.055017	.059235	.063491	.067783	.072107	.076459	.080837	.089658	.098550	.107495	.116479
	.20	.044891	.052990	.061292	.065509	.069766	.074057	.078381	.082733	.087111	.095932	.104824	.113769	.122754
	.10	.051166	.059264	.067566	.071784	.076040	.080332	.084656	.089008	.093386	.102207	.111099	.120044	.129028
	0.00	.057440	.065539	.073841	.078058	.082315	.086606	.090930	.095282	.099660	.108482	.117373	.126318	.135303
	-.10	.063715	.071813	.080115	.084333	.088589	.092881	.097205	.101557	.105935	.114756	.123648	.132593	.141577
	-.20	.069990	.078088	.086390	.090607	.094864	.099155	.103479	.107832	.112209	.121031	.129922	.138867	.147852
	-.30	.076264	.084362	.092664	.096882	.101138	.105430	.109754	.114106	.118484	.127305	.136197	.145142	.154126
	-.40	.082539	.090637	.098939	.103156	.107413	.111705	.116028	.120381	.124759	.133580	.142471	.151417	.160401

10.0 YEAR HOLDING PERIOD
.120 EQUITY YIELD RATE
.600 LOAN RATIO

INTEREST RATE

TERM YEARS	APPR DEP	5.0	6.0	7.0	7.5	8.0	8.5	9.0	9.5	10.0	11.0	12.0	13.0	14.0
10	.40	.067383	.070951	.074614	.076481	.078372	.080286	.082222	.084182	.086164	.090196	.094315	.098520	.102808
	.30	.073081	.076649	.080312	.082180	.084070	.085984	.087921	.089880	.091863	.095894	.100013	.104218	.108506
	.20	.078760	.082347	.086011	.087878	.089769	.091682	.093619	.095579	.097561	.101593	.105712	.109916	.114205
	.10	.084478	.088046	.091709	.093576	.095467	.097381	.099318	.101277	.103260	.107291	.111410	.115615	.119903
	0.00	.090177	.093744	.097408	.099275	.101165	.103079	.105016	.106976	.108958	.112990	.117109	.121313	.125601
	-.10	.095875	.099443	.103106	.104973	.106864	.108778	.110714	.112674	.114656	.118688	.122807	.127012	.131300
	-.20	.101574	.105141	.108804	.110672	.112562	.114476	.116413	.118373	.120355	.124386	.128505	.132710	.136998
	-.30	.107272	.110840	.114503	.116367	.118261	.120174	.122111	.124071	.126053	.130085	.134204	.138408	.142697
	-.40	.112970	.116538	.120201	.122068	.123959	.125873	.127810	.129769	.131752	.135783	.139902	.144107	.148395
15	.40	.062280	.066697	.071251	.073578	.075937	.078328	.080749	.083200	.085680	.090724	.095875	.101126	.106470
	.30	.067979	.072396	.076950	.079277	.081636	.084026	.086447	.088898	.091378	.096422	.101573	.106824	.112168
	.20	.073677	.078094	.082648	.084975	.087334	.089724	.092146	.094597	.097077	.102121	.107272	.112523	.117867
	.10	.079376	.083793	.088347	.090673	.093032	.095423	.097844	.100295	.102775	.107819	.112970	.118221	.123565
	0.00	.085074	.089491	.094045	.096372	.098731	.101121	.103542	.105993	.108473	.113518	.118669	.123919	.129264
	-.10	.090772	.095189	.099744	.102070	.104429	.106820	.109241	.111692	.114172	.119216	.124367	.129618	.134962
	-.20	.096471	.100888	.105442	.107769	.110128	.112518	.114939	.117390	.119870	.124914	.130065	.135316	.140660
	-.30	.102169	.106586	.111140	.113467	.115826	.118217	.120638	.123089	.125569	.130613	.135764	.141015	.146359
	-.40	.107868	.112285	.116839	.119166	.121525	.123915	.126336	.128787	.131267	.136311	.141462	.146713	.152057
20	.40	.059806	.064662	.069668	.072223	.074811	.077430	.080080	.082759	.085465	.090953	.096534	.102197	.107932
	.30	.065505	.070361	.075366	.077921	.080509	.083129	.085778	.088457	.091163	.096651	.102232	.107895	.113631
	.20	.071203	.076059	.081064	.083619	.086207	.088827	.091477	.094156	.096862	.102350	.107931	.113594	.119329
	.10	.076902	.081758	.086763	.089318	.091906	.094526	.097175	.099854	.102560	.108048	.113629	.119292	.125028
	0.00	.082600	.087456	.092461	.095016	.097604	.100224	.102874	.105552	.108258	.113746	.119328	.124991	.130726
	-.10	.088299	.093155	.098160	.100715	.103303	.105922	.108572	.111251	.113957	.119445	.125026	.130689	.136424
	-.20	.093997	.098853	.103858	.106413	.109001	.111621	.114271	.116949	.119655	.125144	.130724	.136388	.142123
	-.30	.099695	.104551	.109557	.112112	.114700	.117319	.119969	.122648	.125354	.130842	.136423	.142086	.147821
	-.40	.105394	.110250	.115255	.117810	.120398	.123018	.125668	.128346	.131052	.136540	.142121	.147784	.153520
25	.40	.058381	.063511	.068789	.071479	.074200	.076950	.079727	.082529	.085354	.091067	.096852	.102697	.108591
	.30	.064080	.069209	.074488	.077177	.079898	.082648	.085425	.088227	.091053	.096766	.102551	.108396	.114290
	.20	.069778	.074907	.080186	.082876	.085597	.088347	.091124	.093926	.096751	.102464	.108249	.114094	.119988
	.10	.075477	.080606	.085884	.088574	.091295	.094045	.096822	.099624	.102449	.108162	.113948	.119793	.125687
	0.00	.081175	.086304	.091583	.094273	.096994	.099744	.102521	.105323	.108148	.113861	.119646	.125491	.131385
	-.10	.086874	.092003	.097281	.099971	.102692	.105442	.108219	.111021	.113846	.119559	.125344	.131189	.137084
	-.20	.092572	.097701	.102980	.105670	.108390	.111140	.113917	.116719	.119545	.125258	.131043	.136888	.142782
	-.30	.098270	.103400	.108678	.111368	.114089	.116839	.119616	.122418	.125243	.130956	.136741	.142586	.148480
	-.40	.103969	.109098	.114376	.117066	.119787	.122537	.125314	.128116	.130942	.136655	.142440	.148285	.154179
30	.40	.057478	.062796	.068257	.071035	.073840	.076671	.079525	.082400	.085293	.091128	.097016	.102945	.108905
	.30	.063177	.068494	.073956	.076733	.079539	.082370	.085224	.088098	.090992	.096827	.102714	.108643	.114603
	.20	.068875	.074193	.079654	.082432	.085237	.088068	.090922	.093797	.096690	.102525	.108413	.114342	.120301
	.10	.074573	.079891	.085353	.088130	.090936	.093767	.096620	.099495	.102388	.108223	.114111	.120040	.126000
	0.00	.080272	.085590	.091051	.093829	.096634	.099465	.102319	.105193	.108087	.113922	.119810	.125738	.131698
	-.10	.085970	.091288	.096749	.099527	.102332	.105163	.108017	.110892	.113785	.119620	.125508	.131437	.137397
	-.20	.091669	.096987	.102448	.105225	.108031	.110862	.113716	.116590	.119484	.125319	.131207	.137135	.143095
	-.30	.097367	.102685	.108146	.110924	.113729	.116560	.119414	.122289	.125182	.131017	.136905	.142834	.148793
	-.40	.103066	.108383	.113845	.116622	.119428	.122259	.125112	.127987	.130880	.136715	.142603	.148532	.154492

10.0 YEAR HOLDING PERIOD
.120 EQUITY YIELD RATE
.667 LOAN RATIO

INTEREST RATE

TERM YEARS	APPR DEP	14.0	13.0	12.0	11.0	10.0	9.5	9.0	8.5	8.0	7.5	7.0	6.0	5.0
10	.40	.103430	.098665	.093994	.089417	.084937	.082735	.080557	.078405	.076279	.074178	.072104	.068033	.064069
	.30	.109128	.104364	.099692	.095115	.090636	.088433	.086256	.084104	.081977	.079877	.077802	.073732	.069768
	.20	.114827	.110062	.105390	.100814	.096334	.094132	.091954	.089802	.087676	.085575	.083500	.079430	.075466
	.10	.120525	.115761	.111089	.106512	.102033	.099830	.097653	.095501	.093374	.091273	.089199	.085128	.081164
	0.00	.126224	.121459	.116787	.112211	.107731	.105528	.103351	.101199	.099073	.096972	.094897	.090827	.086863
	-.10	.131922	.127158	.122486	.117909	.113430	.111227	.109050	.106897	.104771	.102670	.100596	.096525	.092561
	-.20	.137621	.132856	.128184	.123607	.119128	.116925	.114748	.112596	.110469	.108369	.106294	.102224	.098260
	-.30	.143319	.138554	.133883	.129306	.124826	.122624	.120446	.118294	.116168	.114067	.111992	.107922	.103958
	-.40	.149017	.144253	.139581	.135004	.130525	.128322	.126145	.123993	.121866	.119766	.117691	.113620	.109656
15	.40	.107499	.101561	.095727	.090004	.084399	.081643	.078920	.076230	.073574	.070953	.068367	.063307	.058400
	.30	.113198	.107260	.101425	.095702	.090097	.087342	.084618	.081928	.079272	.076651	.074066	.069006	.064098
	.20	.118896	.112958	.107124	.101401	.095796	.093040	.090317	.087627	.084971	.082350	.079764	.074704	.069796
	.10	.124594	.118657	.112822	.107099	.101494	.098739	.096015	.093325	.090669	.088048	.085463	.080403	.075495
	0.00	.130293	.124355	.118521	.112797	.107193	.104437	.101714	.099024	.096368	.093746	.091161	.086101	.081193
	-.10	.135991	.130053	.124219	.118496	.112891	.110135	.107412	.104722	.102066	.099445	.096859	.091799	.086892
	-.20	.141690	.135752	.129918	.124194	.118590	.115834	.113111	.110420	.107764	.105143	.102558	.097498	.092590
	-.30	.147388	.141450	.135616	.129893	.124288	.121532	.118809	.116119	.113463	.110842	.108256	.103196	.098288
	-.40	.153087	.147149	.141314	.135591	.129986	.127231	.124507	.121817	.119161	.116540	.113955	.108895	.103987
20	.40	.109124	.102752	.096459	.090258	.084160	.081153	.078177	.075233	.072322	.069447	.066608	.061046	.055651
	.30	.114823	.108450	.102158	.095957	.089859	.086852	.083876	.080931	.078021	.075145	.072306	.066745	.061349
	.20	.120521	.114148	.107856	.101655	.095557	.092550	.089574	.086630	.083719	.080843	.078004	.072443	.067048
	.10	.126219	.119847	.113555	.107353	.101255	.098249	.095272	.092328	.089417	.086542	.083703	.078142	.072746
	0.00	.131918	.125545	.119253	.113052	.106954	.103947	.100971	.098027	.095116	.092240	.089401	.083840	.078444
	-.10	.137616	.131244	.124951	.118750	.112652	.109646	.106669	.103725	.100814	.097939	.095100	.089538	.084143
	-.20	.143315	.136942	.130650	.124449	.118351	.115344	.112368	.109423	.106513	.103637	.100798	.095237	.089841
	-.30	.149013	.142641	.136348	.130147	.124049	.121042	.118066	.115122	.112211	.109335	.106497	.100935	.095540
	-.40	.154711	.148339	.142047	.135846	.129747	.126741	.123765	.120820	.117909	.115034	.112195	.106634	.101238
25	.40	.109856	.103307	.096813	.090385	.084037	.080898	.077785	.074699	.071644	.068620	.065631	.059767	.054067
	.30	.115555	.109006	.102511	.096083	.089736	.086597	.083483	.080398	.077342	.074319	.071330	.065465	.059766
	.20	.121253	.114704	.108210	.101782	.095434	.092295	.089182	.086096	.083040	.080017	.077028	.071163	.065464
	.10	.126952	.120403	.113908	.107480	.101133	.097993	.094880	.091794	.088739	.085716	.082727	.076862	.071163
	0.00	.132650	.126101	.119607	.113179	.106831	.103692	.100578	.097493	.094437	.091414	.088425	.082560	.076861
	-.10	.138349	.131800	.125305	.118877	.112529	.109390	.106277	.103191	.100136	.097112	.094124	.088259	.082559
	-.20	.144047	.137498	.131003	.124576	.118228	.115089	.111975	.108890	.105834	.102811	.099822	.093957	.088258
	-.30	.149745	.143196	.136702	.130274	.123926	.120787	.117674	.114588	.111533	.108509	.105520	.099655	.093956
	-.40	.155444	.148895	.142400	.135972	.129625	.126485	.123372	.120286	.117231	.114208	.111219	.105354	.099655
30	.40	.110204	.103582	.096995	.090453	.083969	.080755	.077560	.074389	.071244	.068127	.065041	.058972	.053064
	.30	.115903	.109281	.102693	.096151	.089668	.086454	.083259	.080088	.076942	.073825	.070739	.064671	.058762
	.20	.121601	.114979	.108392	.101850	.095366	.092151	.088957	.085786	.082641	.079524	.076437	.070369	.064461
	.10	.127300	.120678	.114090	.107548	.101065	.097850	.094656	.091485	.088339	.085222	.082136	.076068	.070159
	0.00	.132998	.126376	.119789	.113246	.106763	.103548	.100354	.097183	.094038	.090921	.087834	.081766	.075857
	-.10	.138696	.132075	.125487	.118945	.112461	.109247	.106053	.102882	.099736	.096619	.093533	.087465	.081556
	-.20	.144395	.137773	.131185	.124643	.118160	.114945	.111751	.108580	.105435	.102317	.099231	.093163	.087254
	-.30	.150093	.143471	.136884	.130342	.123858	.120643	.117449	.114278	.111133	.108016	.104929	.098861	.092953
	-.40	.155792	.149170	.142582	.136040	.129557	.126342	.123148	.119977	.116831	.113714	.110628	.104560	.098651

```
10.0 YEAR HOLDING PERIOD
 .120 EQUITY YIELD RATE
 .700 LOAN RATIO
```

INTEREST RATE

TERM YEARS	APPR DEP	5.0	6.0	7.0	7.5	8.0	8.5	9.0	9.5	10.0	11.0	12.0	13.0	14.0
10	.40	.062412	.066575	.070849	.073027	.075233	.077465	.079725	.082211	.084324	.089027	.093833	.098738	.103741
	.30	.068111	.072273	.076547	.078725	.080931	.083164	.085423	.087710	.090022	.094726	.099531	.104437	.109440
	.20	.073809	.077971	.082245	.084424	.086629	.088862	.091122	.093408	.095721	.100424	.105230	.110135	.115138
	.10	.079508	.083670	.087944	.090122	.092328	.094561	.096820	.099107	.101419	.106123	.110928	.115834	.120836
	0.00	.085206	.089368	.093642	.095821	.098026	.100259	.102519	.104805	.107118	.111821	.116627	.121532	.126535
	-.10	.090905	.095067	.099341	.101519	.103725	.105957	.108217	.110503	.112816	.117520	.122325	.127231	.132233
	-.20	.096603	.100765	.105039	.107217	.109423	.111656	.113916	.116202	.118515	.123218	.128024	.132929	.137932
	-.30	.102301	.106464	.110737	.112916	.115122	.117354	.119614	.121900	.124213	.128916	.133722	.138627	.143630
	-.40	.108000	.112162	.116436	.118614	.120820	.123053	.125312	.127599	.129911	.134615	.139420	.144326	.149329
15	.40	.056459	.061612	.066926	.069640	.072392	.075181	.078006	.080865	.083759	.089644	.095653	.101779	.108014
	.30	.062158	.067311	.072624	.075339	.078091	.080880	.083704	.086564	.089457	.095342	.101351	.107477	.113712
	.20	.067856	.073009	.078322	.081037	.083789	.086578	.089403	.092262	.095156	.101041	.107050	.113176	.119411
	.10	.073555	.078708	.084021	.086735	.089488	.092276	.095101	.097961	.100854	.106739	.112748	.118874	.125109
	0.00	.079253	.084406	.089719	.092434	.095186	.097975	.100799	.103659	.106552	.112437	.118447	.124573	.130807
	-.10	.084952	.090105	.095418	.098132	.100884	.103673	.106498	.109357	.112251	.118136	.124145	.130271	.136506
	-.20	.090650	.095803	.101116	.103831	.106583	.109372	.112196	.115056	.117949	.123834	.129844	.135969	.142204
	-.30	.096348	.101501	.106815	.109529	.112281	.115070	.117895	.120754	.123648	.129533	.135542	.141668	.147903
	-.40	.102047	.107200	.112513	.115228	.117980	.120769	.123593	.126453	.129346	.135231	.141240	.147366	.153601
20	.40	.053573	.059239	.065078	.068059	.071078	.074134	.077226	.080351	.083508	.089911	.096422	.103029	.109720
	.30	.059272	.064937	.070776	.073757	.076776	.079833	.082924	.086049	.089206	.095609	.102120	.108727	.115418
	.20	.064970	.070635	.076475	.079455	.082475	.085531	.088623	.091748	.094905	.101308	.107819	.114426	.121117
	.10	.070668	.076334	.082173	.085154	.088173	.091230	.094321	.097446	.100603	.107006	.113516	.120124	.126815
	0.00	.076367	.082032	.087871	.090852	.093872	.096928	.100020	.103145	.106302	.112704	.119216	.125823	.132514
	-.10	.082065	.087731	.093570	.096551	.099570	.102626	.105718	.108843	.112000	.118403	.124914	.131521	.138212
	-.20	.087764	.093429	.099268	.102249	.105269	.108325	.111416	.114541	.117698	.124101	.130612	.137219	.143910
	-.30	.093462	.099128	.104967	.107948	.110967	.114023	.117115	.120240	.123397	.129800	.136311	.142918	.149609
	-.40	.099161	.104826	.110665	.113646	.116665	.119722	.122813	.125938	.129095	.135498	.142009	.148616	.155307
25	.40	.051911	.057895	.064053	.067191	.070366	.073574	.076814	.080083	.083379	.090044	.096793	.103613	.110489
	.30	.057609	.063593	.069751	.072890	.076064	.079272	.082512	.085781	.089077	.095742	.102492	.109311	.116187
	.20	.063307	.069292	.075450	.078588	.081762	.084971	.088211	.091480	.094776	.101441	.108190	.115009	.121886
	.10	.069006	.074990	.081148	.084286	.087461	.090669	.093909	.097178	.100474	.107139	.113889	.120708	.127584
	0.00	.074704	.080688	.086847	.089985	.093159	.096368	.099607	.102876	.106173	.112838	.119587	.126406	.133283
	-.10	.080403	.086387	.092545	.095683	.098858	.102066	.105306	.108575	.111871	.118536	.125285	.132105	.138981
	-.20	.086101	.092085	.098243	.101382	.104556	.107764	.111004	.114273	.117569	.124235	.130984	.137803	.144679
	-.30	.091800	.097784	.103942	.107080	.110255	.113463	.116703	.119972	.123268	.129933	.136682	.143501	.150378
	-.40	.097498	.103482	.109640	.112778	.115953	.119161	.122401	.125670	.128966	.135631	.142381	.149200	.156076
30	.40	.050857	.057061	.063432	.066673	.069946	.073249	.076578	.079932	.083308	.090115	.096984	.103901	.110854
	.30	.056555	.062759	.069131	.072371	.075644	.078947	.082277	.085630	.089006	.095814	.102683	.109600	.116553
	.20	.062254	.068458	.074829	.078070	.081343	.084646	.087975	.091329	.094704	.101512	.108381	.115298	.122251
	.10	.067952	.074156	.080528	.083768	.087041	.090344	.093674	.097027	.100403	.107210	.114080	.120996	.127950
	0.00	.073651	.079855	.086226	.089467	.092740	.096042	.099372	.102726	.106101	.112909	.119778	.126695	.133648
	-.10	.079349	.085553	.091925	.095165	.098438	.101741	.105070	.108424	.111800	.118607	.125476	.132393	.139346
	-.20	.085047	.091251	.097623	.100864	.104137	.107439	.110769	.114123	.117498	.124306	.131175	.138092	.145045
	-.30	.090746	.096950	.103321	.106562	.109835	.113138	.116467	.119821	.123197	.130004	.136873	.143790	.150743
	-.40	.096444	.102648	.109020	.112260	.115533	.118836	.122166	.125519	.128895	.135702	.142572	.149489	.156442

10.0 YEAR HOLDING PERIOD
.120 EQUITY YIELD RATE
.750 LOAN RATIO

INTEREST RATE

TERM YEARS	APPR DEP	5.0	6.0	7.0	7.5	8.0	8.5	9.0	9.5	10.0	11.0	12.0	13.0	14.0
10	.40	.059927	.064387	.068966	.071300	.073663	.076055	.078476	.080926	.083304	.088443	.093592	.098848	.104208
	.30	.065626	.070005	.074664	.076998	.079361	.081754	.084175	.086624	.089102	.094142	.099290	.104546	.109906
	.20	.071324	.075783	.080363	.082697	.085060	.087452	.089873	.092323	.094801	.099840	.104989	.110245	.115605
	.10	.077022	.081482	.086061	.088395	.090758	.093151	.095572	.098021	.100499	.105538	.110687	.115943	.121303
	0.00	.082721	.087180	.091760	.094093	.096457	.098849	.101270	.103720	.106198	.111237	.116386	.121642	.127002
	-.10	.088419	.092879	.097458	.099792	.102155	.104547	.106968	.109418	.111896	.116935	.122084	.127340	.132700
	-.20	.094118	.098577	.103156	.105490	.107854	.110246	.112667	.115117	.117594	.122634	.127783	.133038	.138399
	-.30	.099816	.104276	.108855	.111189	.113552	.115944	.118365	.120815	.123293	.128332	.133481	.138737	.144097
	-.40	.105515	.109974	.114553	.116887	.119250	.121643	.124064	.126513	.128991	.134031	.139179	.144435	.149795
15	.40	.053549	.059070	.064763	.067671	.070620	.073608	.076634	.079698	.082798	.089104	.095542	.102106	.108786
	.30	.059247	.064768	.070461	.073370	.076318	.079306	.082333	.085396	.088497	.094802	.101241	.107804	.114484
	.20	.064946	.070467	.076160	.079068	.082017	.085005	.088031	.091095	.094195	.100500	.106939	.113502	.120183
	.10	.070644	.076165	.081858	.084766	.087715	.090703	.093730	.096793	.099893	.106199	.112637	.119201	.125881
	0.00	.076343	.081864	.087556	.090465	.093414	.096402	.099428	.102492	.105592	.111897	.118336	.124899	.131579
	-.10	.082041	.087562	.093255	.096163	.099112	.102100	.105126	.108190	.111290	.117596	.124034	.130598	.137278
	-.20	.087739	.093261	.098953	.101862	.104810	.107798	.110825	.113889	.116989	.123294	.129733	.136296	.142976
	-.30	.093438	.098959	.104652	.107560	.110509	.113497	.116523	.119587	.122687	.128992	.135431	.141995	.148675
	-.40	.099136	.104657	.110350	.113259	.116207	.119195	.122222	.125285	.128386	.134691	.141129	.147693	.154373
20	.40	.050457	.056527	.062783	.065977	.069212	.072486	.075799	.079147	.082529	.089390	.096366	.103445	.110614
	.30	.056155	.062225	.068481	.071675	.074910	.078185	.081497	.084845	.088228	.095088	.102064	.109143	.116312
	.20	.061853	.067923	.074180	.077374	.080609	.083883	.087196	.090544	.093926	.100787	.107763	.114842	.122011
	.10	.067552	.073622	.079878	.083072	.086307	.089582	.092894	.096242	.099625	.106485	.113461	.120540	.127709
	0.00	.073250	.079320	.085577	.088770	.092006	.095280	.098592	.101941	.105323	.112183	.119160	.126238	.133407
	-.10	.078949	.085019	.091275	.094469	.097704	.100978	.104291	.107639	.111021	.117882	.124858	.131937	.139106
	-.20	.084647	.090717	.096973	.100167	.103402	.106677	.109989	.113337	.116720	.123580	.130556	.137635	.144804
	-.30	.090345	.096415	.102672	.105866	.109101	.112375	.115688	.119036	.122418	.129279	.136255	.143334	.150503
	-.40	.096044	.102114	.108370	.111564	.114799	.118074	.121386	.124734	.128117	.134977	.141953	.149032	.156201
25	.40	.048675	.055087	.061685	.065047	.068448	.071886	.075357	.078860	.082391	.089532	.096764	.104070	.111438
	.30	.054374	.060785	.067383	.070746	.074147	.077584	.081055	.084558	.088090	.095231	.102462	.109769	.117136
	.20	.060072	.066484	.073082	.076444	.079845	.083283	.086754	.090256	.093788	.100929	.108161	.115467	.122835
	.10	.065770	.072182	.078780	.082142	.085544	.088981	.092452	.095955	.099486	.106628	.113859	.121165	.128533
	0.00	.071469	.077880	.084478	.087841	.091242	.094680	.098151	.101653	.105185	.112326	.119557	.126864	.134231
	-.10	.077167	.083579	.090177	.093539	.096940	.100378	.103849	.107352	.110883	.118025	.125256	.132562	.139930
	-.20	.082866	.089277	.095875	.099238	.102639	.106076	.109548	.113050	.116582	.123723	.130954	.138261	.145628
	-.30	.088564	.094976	.101574	.104936	.108337	.111775	.115246	.118749	.122280	.129421	.136653	.143959	.151327
	-.40	.094263	.100674	.107272	.110635	.114036	.117473	.120944	.124447	.127979	.135120	.142351	.149657	.157025
30	.40	.047546	.054193	.061020	.064492	.067999	.071537	.075105	.078698	.082315	.089609	.096968	.104379	.111829
	.30	.053245	.059892	.066718	.070190	.073697	.077236	.080803	.084397	.088013	.095307	.102667	.110078	.117528
	.20	.058943	.065590	.072417	.075889	.079396	.082934	.086502	.090095	.093712	.101005	.108365	.115776	.123226
	.10	.064641	.071289	.078115	.081587	.085094	.088633	.092200	.095793	.099410	.106704	.114064	.121475	.128924
	0.00	.070340	.076987	.083814	.087286	.090793	.094331	.097899	.101492	.105109	.112402	.119762	.127173	.134623
	-.10	.076038	.082686	.089512	.092984	.096491	.100030	.103597	.107190	.110807	.118101	.125461	.132872	.140321
	-.20	.081737	.088384	.095211	.098683	.102189	.105728	.109295	.112889	.116505	.123799	.131159	.138570	.146020
	-.30	.087435	.094082	.100909	.104381	.107888	.111426	.114994	.118587	.122204	.129498	.136857	.144268	.151718
	-.40	.093134	.099781	.106607	.110079	.113586	.117125	.120692	.124286	.127902	.135196	.142556	.149967	.157416

10.0 YEAR HOLDING PERIOD
.120 EQUITY YIELD RATE
.800 LOAN RATIO

INTEREST RATE

TERM YEARS	APPR DEP	5.0	6.0	7.0	7.5	8.0	8.5	9.0	9.5	10.0	11.0	12.0	13.0	14.0
10	.40	.057442	.062199	.067083	.069573	.072093	.074645	.077228	.079841	.082484	.087859	.093351	.098957	.104675
	.30	.063140	.067897	.072782	.075271	.077792	.080344	.082926	.085539	.088182	.093557	.099050	.104656	.110373
	.20	.068839	.073596	.078480	.080970	.083490	.086042	.088625	.091237	.093881	.099256	.104748	.110354	.116072
	.10	.074537	.079294	.084178	.086668	.089189	.091741	.094323	.096936	.099579	.104954	.110446	.116053	.121770
	0.00	.080236	.084992	.089877	.092366	.094887	.097439	.100021	.102634	.105277	.110653	.116145	.121751	.127468
	-.10	.085934	.090691	.095575	.098065	.100586	.103137	.105720	.108333	.110976	.116351	.121843	.127449	.133167
	-.20	.091632	.096389	.101274	.103763	.106284	.108836	.111418	.114034	.116674	.122050	.127542	.133148	.138865
	-.30	.097331	.102088	.106972	.109462	.111982	.114534	.117117	.119730	.122373	.127748	.133240	.138846	.144564
	-.40	.103029	.107786	.112670	.115160	.117681	.120233	.122815	.125428	.128071	.133446	.138938	.144545	.150262
15	.40	.050638	.056528	.062600	.065702	.068847	.072035	.075263	.078531	.081838	.088563	.095431	.102432	.109558
	.30	.056337	.062226	.068298	.071401	.074546	.077733	.080961	.084229	.087536	.094262	.101130	.108131	.115256
	.20	.062035	.067924	.073997	.077099	.080244	.083432	.086660	.089928	.093234	.099960	.106828	.113829	.120955
	.10	.067734	.073623	.079695	.082797	.085943	.089130	.092358	.095626	.098933	.105659	.112526	.119527	.126653
	0.00	.073432	.079321	.085393	.088496	.091641	.094828	.098057	.101325	.104631	.111357	.118225	.125226	.132351
	-.10	.079131	.085020	.091092	.094194	.097340	.100527	.103755	.107023	.110330	.117055	.123923	.130924	.138050
	-.20	.084829	.090718	.096790	.099893	.103038	.106225	.109453	.112721	.116028	.122754	.129622	.136623	.143748
	-.30	.090527	.096417	.102489	.105591	.108736	.111924	.115152	.118420	.121727	.128452	.135320	.142321	.149447
	-.40	.096226	.102115	.108187	.111290	.114435	.117622	.120850	.124118	.127425	.134151	.141018	.148020	.155145
20	.40	.047340	.053815	.060488	.063895	.067345	.070838	.074372	.077943	.081551	.088869	.096310	.103861	.111538
	.30	.053038	.059513	.066186	.069593	.073044	.076537	.080070	.083641	.087249	.094567	.102008	.109559	.117206
	.20	.058737	.065211	.071885	.075292	.078742	.082235	.085768	.089340	.092948	.100265	.107707	.115257	.122904
	.10	.064435	.070910	.077583	.080990	.084441	.087934	.091467	.095038	.098646	.105964	.113405	.120956	.128603
	0.00	.070134	.076608	.083282	.086688	.090139	.093632	.097165	.100737	.104345	.111662	.119104	.126654	.134301
	-.10	.075832	.082307	.088980	.092387	.095838	.099330	.102864	.106435	.110043	.117361	.124802	.132353	.140000
	-.20	.081531	.088005	.094679	.098085	.101536	.105028	.108562	.112133	.115741	.123059	.130500	.138051	.145698
	-.30	.087229	.093703	.100377	.103784	.107234	.110727	.114260	.117832	.121440	.128758	.136199	.143750	.151397
	-.40	.092927	.099402	.106075	.109482	.112933	.116426	.119959	.123530	.127138	.134456	.141897	.149448	.157095
25	.40	.045440	.052279	.059317	.062903	.066531	.070198	.073900	.077637	.081404	.089021	.096734	.104528	.112386
	.30	.051138	.057977	.065015	.068601	.072230	.075896	.079599	.083335	.087102	.094719	.102433	.110226	.118085
	.20	.056837	.063676	.070714	.074300	.077928	.081595	.085297	.089033	.092800	.100418	.108131	.115925	.123783
	.10	.062535	.069374	.076412	.079998	.083626	.087293	.090995	.094732	.098499	.106116	.113830	.121623	.129481
	0.00	.068234	.075072	.082110	.085697	.089325	.092992	.096694	.100430	.104197	.111815	.119528	.127321	.135180
	-.10	.073932	.080771	.087809	.091395	.095023	.098690	.102393	.106129	.109896	.117513	.125226	.133020	.140878
	-.20	.079630	.086469	.093507	.097094	.100722	.104388	.108091	.111827	.115594	.123211	.130925	.138718	.146577
	-.30	.085329	.092168	.099206	.102792	.106420	.110087	.113789	.117525	.121292	.128910	.136623	.144417	.152275
	-.40	.091027	.097866	.104904	.108491	.112119	.115785	.119488	.123224	.126991	.134608	.142322	.150115	.157974
30	.40	.044236	.051326	.058608	.062311	.066052	.069826	.073631	.077464	.081322	.089102	.096953	.104858	.112804
	.30	.049934	.057024	.064306	.068010	.071750	.075524	.079330	.083162	.087020	.094801	.102651	.110556	.118502
	.20	.055632	.062723	.070004	.073708	.077449	.081223	.085028	.088861	.092719	.100499	.108349	.116254	.124201
	.10	.061331	.068421	.075703	.079406	.083147	.086921	.090726	.094560	.098417	.106197	.114048	.121953	.129899
	0.00	.067029	.074120	.081401	.085105	.088845	.092620	.096425	.100258	.104116	.111896	.119746	.127651	.135598
	-.10	.072728	.079818	.087100	.090803	.094544	.098318	.102123	.105956	.109814	.117594	.125445	.133350	.141296
	-.20	.078426	.085516	.092798	.096501	.100242	.104016	.107822	.111654	.115512	.123292	.131143	.139048	.146994
	-.30	.084124	.091215	.098497	.102200	.105941	.109715	.113520	.117353	.121211	.128991	.136841	.144747	.152693
	-.40	.089823	.096913	.104195	.107898	.111639	.115414	.119219	.123052	.126909	.134689	.142540	.150445	.158391

10.0 YEAR HOLDING PERIOD
.120 EQUITY YIELD RATE
.900 LOAN RATIO

INTEREST RATE

TERM YEARS	APPR DEP	5.0	6.0	7.0	7.5	8.0	8.5	9.0	9.5	10.0	11.0	12.0	13.0	14.0
10	.40	.052471	.057823	.063318	.066118	.068954	.071825	.074730	.077670	.080643	.086691	.092869	.099176	.105608
	.30	.058170	.063521	.069016	.071817	.074653	.077524	.080429	.083368	.086342	.092389	.098568	.104875	.111307
	.20	.063868	.069220	.074715	.077515	.080351	.083222	.086127	.089067	.092040	.098087	.104266	.110573	.117005
	.10	.069567	.074918	.080413	.083214	.086050	.088920	.091826	.094765	.097739	.103786	.109964	.116271	.122704
	0.00	.075265	.080616	.086111	.088912	.091748	.094619	.097524	.100464	.103437	.109484	.115663	.121970	.128402
	-.10	.080963	.086315	.091810	.094611	.097446	.100317	.103223	.106162	.109135	.115183	.121361	.127668	.134100
	-.20	.086662	.092013	.097508	.100309	.103145	.106016	.108921	.111860	.114834	.120881	.127060	.133367	.139799
	-.30	.092360	.097712	.103207	.106007	.108843	.111714	.114619	.117559	.120532	.126580	.132758	.139065	.145497
	-.40	.098059	.103410	.108905	.111706	.114542	.117412	.120318	.123257	.126231	.132278	.138457	.144764	.151196
15	.40	.044817	.051443	.058274	.061764	.065303	.068888	.072520	.076196	.079917	.087483	.095209	.103085	.111102
	.30	.050516	.057141	.063972	.067463	.071001	.074587	.078218	.081895	.085615	.093181	.100908	.108784	.116800
	.20	.056214	.062840	.069671	.073161	.076699	.080285	.083917	.087593	.091313	.098880	.106606	.114482	.122499
	.10	.061913	.068538	.075369	.078859	.082398	.085984	.089615	.093292	.097012	.104578	.112304	.120181	.128197
	0.00	.067611	.074236	.081068	.084558	.088096	.091682	.095314	.098990	.102710	.110277	.118003	.125879	.133895
	-.10	.073310	.079935	.086766	.090256	.093795	.097380	.101012	.104689	.108408	.115975	.123701	.131578	.139594
	-.20	.079008	.085633	.092464	.095955	.099493	.103079	.106710	.110387	.114107	.121673	.129400	.137276	.145292
	-.30	.084706	.091332	.098163	.101653	.105192	.108777	.112409	.116085	.119805	.127372	.135098	.142974	.150991
	-.40	.090405	.097030	.103861	.107351	.110890	.114476	.118107	.121784	.125504	.133070	.140797	.148673	.156689
20	.40	.041107	.048391	.055898	.059731	.063613	.067542	.071517	.075535	.079594	.087826	.096198	.104692	.113295
	.30	.046805	.054089	.061597	.065429	.069311	.073241	.077216	.081233	.085292	.093525	.101896	.110391	.118994
	.20	.052503	.059787	.067295	.071128	.075010	.078939	.082914	.086932	.090991	.099223	.107595	.116089	.124692
	.10	.058202	.065486	.072993	.076826	.080708	.084638	.088612	.092630	.096689	.104922	.113293	.121788	.130391
	0.00	.063900	.071184	.078692	.082524	.086406	.090336	.094311	.098329	.102388	.110620	.118991	.127486	.136089
	-.10	.069599	.076883	.084390	.088223	.092105	.096034	.100009	.104027	.108086	.116318	.124690	.133185	.141787
	-.20	.075297	.082581	.090089	.093921	.097803	.101733	.105708	.109726	.113784	.122017	.130388	.138883	.147486
	-.30	.080995	.088279	.095787	.099620	.103502	.107431	.111406	.115424	.119483	.127715	.136087	.144581	.153184
	-.40	.086694	.093978	.101486	.105318	.109200	.113130	.117104	.121122	.125181	.133414	.141785	.150280	.158883
25	.40	.038969	.046663	.054580	.058615	.062697	.066822	.070987	.075190	.079428	.087998	.096675	.105443	.114284
	.30	.044667	.052361	.060279	.064314	.068395	.072520	.076686	.080889	.085127	.093696	.102374	.111141	.119982
	.20	.050366	.058060	.065977	.070012	.074094	.078219	.082384	.086587	.090825	.099394	.108072	.116840	.125681
	.10	.056064	.063758	.071676	.075711	.079792	.083917	.088082	.092286	.096523	.105093	.113771	.122538	.131379
	0.00	.061763	.069456	.077374	.081409	.085490	.089615	.093781	.097984	.102222	.110791	.119469	.128237	.137078
	-.10	.067461	.075155	.083073	.087107	.091189	.095314	.099479	.103682	.107920	.116490	.125167	.133935	.142776
	-.20	.073160	.080853	.088771	.092806	.096887	.101012	.105178	.109381	.113619	.122188	.130866	.139633	.148474
	-.30	.078858	.086552	.094469	.098504	.102586	.106711	.110876	.115079	.119317	.127887	.136564	.145332	.154173
	-.40	.084556	.092250	.100168	.104203	.108284	.112409	.116575	.120778	.125016	.133585	.142263	.151030	.159871
30	.40	.037413	.045591	.053783	.057949	.062157	.066404	.070685	.074997	.079337	.088089	.096921	.105814	.114754
	.30	.043313	.051289	.059481	.063646	.067856	.072102	.076383	.080695	.085035	.093787	.102619	.111512	.120452
	.20	.049011	.056988	.065180	.069346	.073554	.077801	.082081	.086393	.090733	.099486	.108318	.117211	.126150
	.10	.054709	.062686	.070878	.075044	.079253	.083499	.087780	.092092	.096432	.105184	.114016	.122909	.131849
	0.00	.060408	.068385	.076576	.080743	.084951	.089197	.093478	.097790	.102130	.110883	.119715	.128608	.137547
	-.10	.066106	.074083	.082275	.086441	.090650	.094896	.099177	.103489	.107829	.116581	.125413	.134306	.143246
	-.20	.071805	.079781	.087973	.092140	.096348	.100594	.104875	.109187	.113527	.122280	.131111	.140005	.148944
	-.30	.077503	.085480	.093672	.097838	.102046	.106293	.110573	.114885	.119225	.127978	.136810	.145703	.154643
	-.40	.083202	.091178	.099370	.103537	.107745	.111991	.116272	.120584	.124924	.133676	.142508	.151401	.160341

10.0 YEAR HOLDING PERIOD
.140 EQUITY YIELD RATE
.600 LOAN RATIO

INTEREST RATE

TERM YEARS	APPR DEP	5.0	6.0	7.0	7.5	8.0	8.5	9.0	9.5	10.0	11.0	12.0	13.0	14.0
10	.40	.080654	.084221	.087885	.089752	.091642	.093556	.095493	.097453	.099435	.103466	.107586	.111790	.116078
	.30	.085825	.089393	.093056	.094923	.096814	.098728	.100664	.102624	.104606	.108638	.112757	.116962	.121250
	.20	.090996	.094464	.098227	.100094	.101985	.103899	.105836	.107795	.109778	.113809	.117928	.122133	.126421
	.10	.096168	.099735	.103399	.105266	.107156	.109070	.111007	.112967	.114949	.118981	.123100	.127304	.131592
	0.00	.101339	.104907	.108570	.110437	.112328	.114242	.116178	.118138	.120120	.124152	.128271	.132476	.136764
	-.10	.106510	.110078	.113741	.115609	.117499	.119413	.121350	.123309	.125292	.129323	.133442	.137647	.141935
	-.20	.111682	.115249	.118943	.120780	.122671	.124584	.126521	.128481	.130463	.134495	.138614	.142818	.147106
	-.30	.116853	.120421	.124084	.125951	.127842	.129756	.131692	.133652	.135634	.139666	.143785	.147990	.152278
	-.40	.122024	.125592	.129255	.131123	.133013	.134927	.136864	.138824	.140806	.144837	.148956	.153161	.157449
15	.40	.074226	.078588	.083087	.085386	.087717	.090080	.092474	.094898	.097351	.102342	.107439	.112638	.117931
	.30	.079397	.083759	.088258	.090557	.092889	.095252	.097646	.100069	.102522	.107513	.112611	.117809	.123102
	.20	.084569	.088930	.093429	.095729	.098060	.100423	.102817	.105241	.107694	.112684	.117782	.122981	.128273
	.10	.089740	.094102	.098601	.100900	.103231	.105594	.107988	.110412	.112865	.117856	.122953	.128152	.133445
	0.00	.094911	.099273	.103772	.106071	.108403	.110766	.113160	.115583	.118036	.123027	.128125	.133323	.138616
	-.10	.100083	.104444	.108943	.111243	.113574	.115937	.118331	.120755	.123208	.128198	.133296	.138495	.143787
	-.20	.105254	.109616	.114115	.116414	.118745	.121109	.123502	.125926	.128379	.133370	.138467	.143666	.148959
	-.30	.110425	.114787	.119286	.121585	.123917	.126280	.128674	.131097	.133551	.138541	.143639	.148837	.154130
	-.40	.115597	.119958	.124457	.126757	.129088	.131451	.133845	.136269	.138722	.143712	.148810	.154009	.159301
20	.40	.071109	.075892	.080827	.083347	.085901	.088468	.091105	.093751	.096426	.101854	.107378	.112986	.118670
	.30	.076281	.081064	.085998	.088518	.091072	.093669	.096276	.098923	.101597	.107025	.112549	.118158	.123842
	.20	.081452	.086235	.091169	.093690	.096244	.098830	.101447	.104094	.106769	.112197	.117720	.123329	.129013
	.10	.086624	.091406	.096341	.098861	.101415	.104002	.106619	.109265	.111940	.117368	.122892	.128500	.134184
	0.00	.091795	.096578	.101512	.104032	.106587	.109173	.111790	.114437	.117112	.122559	.128063	.133672	.139356
	-.10	.096966	.101749	.106683	.109204	.111758	.114344	.116961	.119608	.122283	.127711	.133234	.138843	.144527
	-.20	.102138	.106921	.111855	.114375	.116929	.119516	.122133	.124780	.127454	.132882	.138406	.144014	.149698
	-.30	.107309	.112092	.117026	.119547	.122101	.124687	.127304	.129951	.132626	.138053	.143577	.149186	.154870
	-.40	.112480	.117263	.122197	.124718	.127272	.129858	.132476	.135122	.137797	.143225	.148748	.154357	.160041
25	.40	.069314	.074367	.079573	.082229	.084917	.087635	.090381	.093154	.095951	.101611	.107348	.113149	.119004
	.30	.074486	.079538	.084744	.087400	.090088	.092806	.095552	.098325	.101122	.106782	.112519	.118320	.124175
	.20	.079657	.084709	.089916	.092571	.095259	.097977	.100724	.103496	.106293	.111954	.117690	.123492	.129346
	.10	.084828	.089881	.095087	.097743	.100431	.103149	.105895	.108668	.111465	.117125	.122862	.128663	.134518
	0.00	.090000	.095052	.100258	.102914	.105602	.108320	.111066	.113839	.116636	.122296	.128033	.133834	.139689
	-.10	.095171	.100224	.105430	.108085	.110773	.113491	.116238	.119010	.121807	.127468	.133204	.139006	.144860
	-.20	.100342	.105395	.110601	.113257	.115945	.118663	.121409	.124182	.126979	.132639	.138376	.144177	.150032
	-.30	.105514	.110566	.115773	.118428	.121116	.123834	.126581	.129353	.132150	.137810	.143547	.149349	.155203
	-.40	.110685	.115738	.120944	.123600	.126287	.129006	.131752	.134525	.137322	.142982	.148719	.154520	.160374
30	.40	.068177	.073420	.078814	.081561	.084337	.087140	.089968	.092818	.095688	.101481	.107332	.113230	.119162
	.30	.073348	.078592	.083986	.086732	.089508	.092311	.095139	.097989	.100859	.106652	.112504	.118401	.124333
	.20	.078519	.083763	.089157	.091903	.094680	.097483	.100310	.103160	.106031	.111824	.117675	.123572	.129505
	.10	.083691	.088934	.094328	.097075	.099851	.102654	.105482	.108332	.111202	.116995	.122846	.128744	.134676
	0.00	.088862	.094116	.099500	.102246	.105022	.107825	.110653	.113503	.116373	.122167	.128018	.133915	.139847
	-.10	.094033	.099277	.104671	.107418	.110194	.112997	.115824	.118674	.121545	.127338	.133189	.139086	.145019
	-.20	.099205	.104449	.109842	.112589	.115365	.118168	.120996	.123846	.126716	.132509	.138361	.144258	.150190
	-.30	.104376	.109620	.115014	.117760	.120536	.123339	.126167	.129017	.131887	.137681	.143532	.149429	.155361
	-.40	.109547	.114791	.120185	.122932	.125708	.128511	.131338	.134189	.137059	.142852	.148703	.154600	.160533

10.0 YEAR HOLDING PERIOD
.140 EQUITY YIELD RATE
.667 LOAN RATIO

INTEREST RATE

TERM YEARS	APPR DEP	5.0	6.0	7.0	7.5	8.0	8.5	9.0	9.5	10.0	11.0	12.0	13.0	14.0
10	.40	.076358	.080322	.084392	.086467	.088567	.090694	.092846	.095023	.097226	.101705	.106282	.110954	.115719
	.30	.081529	.085493	.089564	.091638	.093739	.095865	.098017	.100195	.102397	.106877	.111454	.116125	.120890
	.20	.086700	.090664	.094735	.096810	.098910	.101037	.103189	.105366	.107569	.112048	.116625	.121297	.126061
	.10	.091872	.095836	.099906	.101981	.104082	.106208	.108360	.110538	.112740	.117220	.121796	.126468	.131233
	0.00	.097043	.101007	.105078	.107152	.109253	.111379	.113531	.115709	.117911	.122391	.126968	.131640	.136404
	-.10	.102215	.106179	.110249	.112324	.114424	.116551	.118703	.120880	.123083	.127562	.132139	.136811	.141575
	-.20	.107386	.111350	.115420	.117495	.119596	.121722	.123874	.126052	.128254	.132734	.137310	.141982	.146747
	-.30	.112557	.116521	.120592	.122666	.124767	.126893	.129046	.131223	.133426	.137905	.142482	.147154	.151918
	-.40	.117729	.121693	.125763	.127838	.129938	.132065	.134217	.136394	.138597	.143076	.147653	.152325	.157090
15	.40	.069216	.074062	.079061	.081616	.084206	.086832	.089492	.092185	.094911	.100456	.106120	.111896	.117777
	.30	.074387	.079234	.084232	.086787	.089378	.092003	.094663	.097356	.100082	.105627	.111291	.117067	.122948
	.20	.079558	.084405	.089404	.091958	.094549	.097175	.099834	.102528	.105253	.110798	.116463	.122239	.128119
	.10	.084730	.089576	.094575	.097130	.099720	.102346	.105006	.107699	.110425	.115970	.121634	.127410	.133291
	0.00	.089901	.094748	.099746	.102301	.104892	.107517	.110177	.112870	.115596	.121141	.126805	.132581	.138462
	-.10	.095073	.099919	.104918	.107473	.110063	.112689	.115349	.118042	.120767	.126312	.131977	.137753	.143634
	-.20	.100244	.105090	.110089	.112644	.115235	.117860	.120520	.123213	.125939	.131484	.137148	.142924	.148805
	-.30	.105415	.110262	.115261	.117815	.120406	.123031	.125691	.128384	.131110	.136655	.142319	.148095	.153976
	-.40	.110587	.115433	.120432	.122987	.125577	.128203	.130863	.133556	.136281	.141826	.147491	.153267	.159148
20	.40	.065753	.071067	.076550	.079350	.082188	.085062	.087970	.090911	.093883	.099914	.106051	.112283	.118599
	.30	.070924	.076239	.081721	.084522	.087360	.090233	.093141	.096082	.099054	.105085	.111223	.117454	.123770
	.20	.076096	.081410	.086893	.089693	.092531	.095405	.098313	.101254	.104226	.110257	.116394	.122626	.128941
	.10	.081267	.086582	.092064	.094864	.097702	.100576	.103484	.106425	.109397	.115428	.121565	.127797	.134113
	0.00	.086438	.091753	.097235	.100036	.102874	.105748	.108656	.111596	.114568	.120599	.126737	.132969	.139284
	-.10	.091610	.096924	.102407	.105207	.108045	.110919	.113827	.116768	.119740	.125771	.131908	.138140	.144455
	-.20	.096781	.102096	.107578	.110378	.113216	.116090	.118998	.121939	.124911	.130942	.137079	.143311	.149627
	-.30	.101953	.107267	.112749	.115550	.118388	.121262	.124170	.127110	.130082	.136113	.142251	.148483	.154798
	-.40	.107124	.112438	.117921	.120721	.123559	.126433	.129341	.132282	.135254	.141285	.147422	.153654	.159969
25	.40	.063758	.069372	.075157	.078108	.081094	.084115	.087166	.090247	.093355	.099644	.106018	.112464	.118969
	.30	.068930	.074544	.080328	.083279	.086266	.089286	.092337	.095418	.098526	.104815	.111189	.117635	.124140
	.20	.074101	.079715	.085500	.088451	.091437	.094457	.097509	.100589	.103697	.109986	.116361	.122807	.129312
	.10	.079273	.084886	.090671	.093622	.096608	.099629	.102680	.105761	.108869	.115158	.121532	.127978	.134483
	0.00	.084444	.090058	.095842	.098793	.101780	.104800	.107851	.110932	.114040	.120329	.126703	.133149	.139654
	-.10	.089615	.095229	.101014	.103965	.106951	.109971	.113023	.116104	.119211	.125500	.131875	.138321	.144826
	-.20	.094787	.100400	.106185	.109136	.112122	.115143	.118194	.121275	.124383	.130672	.137046	.143492	.149997
	-.30	.099958	.105572	.111357	.114307	.117294	.120314	.123366	.126446	.129554	.135843	.142218	.148663	.155168
	-.40	.105129	.110743	.116528	.119479	.122465	.125485	.128537	.131618	.134725	.141015	.147389	.153835	.160340
30	.40	.062494	.068321	.074314	.077366	.080450	.083565	.086707	.089873	.093063	.099499	.106001	.112553	.119145
	.30	.067666	.073492	.079485	.082537	.085622	.088736	.091878	.095045	.098234	.104671	.111172	.117725	.124316
	.20	.072837	.078663	.084657	.087708	.090793	.093908	.097049	.100216	.103405	.109842	.116344	.122896	.129488
	.10	.078008	.083835	.089828	.092880	.095964	.099079	.102221	.105388	.108577	.115014	.121515	.128067	.134659
	0.00	.083180	.089006	.094999	.098051	.101136	.104250	.107392	.110559	.113748	.120185	.126686	.133239	.139830
	-.10	.088351	.094177	.100171	.103222	.106307	.109422	.112563	.115730	.118919	.125356	.131858	.138410	.145002
	-.20	.093522	.099349	.105342	.108394	.111478	.114593	.117735	.120902	.124091	.130528	.137029	.143581	.150173
	-.30	.098694	.104520	.110513	.113565	.116650	.119764	.122906	.126073	.129262	.135699	.142200	.148753	.155344
	-.40	.103865	.109691	.115685	.118737	.121821	.124936	.128078	.131244	.134433	.140870	.147372	.153924	.160516

10.0 YEAR HOLDING PERIOD
.140 EQUITY YIELD RATE
.700 LOAN RATIO

INTEREST RATE

TERM YEARS	APPR DEP	5.0	6.0	7.0	7.5	8.0	8.5	9.0	9.5	10.0	11.0	12.0	13.0	14.0
10	.40	.074210	.078372	.082646	.084825	.087030	.089263	.091523	.093809	.096122	.100825	.105631	.110536	.115539
	.30	.079381	.083543	.087818	.089996	.092202	.094434	.096694	.098980	.101293	.105996	.110802	.115707	.120710
	.20	.084553	.088715	.092989	.095167	.097373	.099606	.101865	.104152	.106464	.111168	.115973	.120879	.125882
	.10	.089724	.093886	.098160	.100339	.102544	.104777	.107037	.109323	.111636	.116339	.121145	.126050	.131053
	0.00	.094896	.099058	.103332	.105510	.107716	.109949	.112208	.114495	.116807	.121511	.126316	.131222	.136225
	-.10	.100067	.104229	.108503	.110681	.112887	.115120	.117380	.119666	.121978	.126682	.131487	.136393	.141396
	-.20	.105238	.109400	.113674	.115853	.118058	.120291	.122551	.124837	.127150	.131853	.136659	.141564	.146567
	-.30	.110410	.114572	.118846	.121024	.123230	.125463	.127722	.130009	.132321	.137025	.141830	.146736	.151739
	-.40	.115581	.119743	.124017	.126195	.128401	.130634	.132894	.135180	.137493	.142196	.147002	.151907	.156910
15	.40	.066711	.071800	.077049	.079731	.082451	.085208	.088001	.090829	.093690	.099513	.105460	.111525	.117700
	.30	.071882	.076971	.082220	.084902	.087623	.090379	.093172	.096000	.098862	.104684	.110631	.116696	.122871
	.20	.077054	.082142	.087391	.090074	.092794	.095551	.098344	.101171	.104033	.109855	.115803	.121868	.128043
	.10	.082225	.087314	.092563	.095245	.097965	.100722	.103515	.106343	.109204	.115027	.120974	.127039	.133214
	0.00	.087396	.092485	.097734	.100416	.103137	.105894	.108686	.111514	.114376	.120198	.126146	.132210	.138385
	-.10	.092568	.097657	.102905	.105588	.108308	.111065	.113858	.116685	.119547	.125369	.131317	.137382	.143557
	-.20	.097739	.102828	.108077	.110759	.113479	.116236	.119029	.121857	.124719	.130540	.136488	.142553	.148728
	-.30	.102911	.107999	.113248	.115931	.118651	.121408	.124200	.127028	.129890	.135712	.141660	.147725	.153899
	-.40	.108082	.113171	.118419	.121102	.123822	.126579	.129372	.132199	.135061	.140884	.146831	.152896	.159071
20	.40	.063075	.068655	.074412	.077352	.080332	.083350	.086403	.089491	.092611	.098944	.105388	.111932	.118563
	.30	.068247	.073826	.079583	.082524	.085503	.088521	.091574	.094662	.097783	.104115	.110559	.117103	.123734
	.20	.073418	.078998	.084755	.087695	.090675	.093692	.096746	.099834	.102954	.109287	.115731	.122274	.128906
	.10	.078589	.084169	.089926	.092866	.095846	.098864	.101917	.105005	.108125	.114458	.120902	.127446	.134077
	0.00	.083761	.089341	.095097	.098038	.101018	.104035	.107089	.110176	.113297	.119629	.126074	.132617	.139248
	-.10	.088932	.094512	.100269	.103209	.106189	.109206	.112260	.115348	.118468	.124801	.131245	.137788	.144420
	-.20	.094103	.099683	.105440	.108381	.111360	.114378	.117431	.120519	.123639	.129972	.136416	.142960	.149591
	-.30	.099275	.104855	.110611	.113552	.116532	.119549	.122603	.125691	.128811	.135143	.141588	.148131	.154762
	-.40	.104446	.110026	.115783	.118723	.121703	.124720	.127774	.130862	.133982	.140315	.146759	.153302	.159934
25	.40	.060981	.066875	.072949	.076048	.079184	.082355	.085559	.088794	.092057	.098660	.105353	.112121	.118952
	.30	.066152	.072046	.078121	.081219	.084355	.087526	.090730	.093965	.097228	.103832	.110525	.117293	.124123
	.20	.071324	.077218	.083292	.086390	.089526	.092697	.095901	.099136	.102399	.109003	.115696	.122464	.129294
	.10	.076495	.082389	.088463	.091562	.094698	.097869	.101073	.104308	.107571	.114174	.120867	.127636	.134466
	0.00	.081666	.087561	.093635	.096733	.099869	.103040	.106244	.109479	.112742	.119346	.126039	.132807	.139637
	-.10	.086838	.092732	.098806	.101906	.105040	.108211	.111416	.114650	.117914	.124517	.131210	.137978	.144809
	-.20	.092009	.097903	.103978	.107076	.110212	.113383	.116587	.119822	.123085	.129688	.136381	.143150	.149980
	-.30	.097180	.103075	.109149	.112247	.115383	.118554	.121758	.124993	.128256	.134860	.141553	.148321	.155151
	-.40	.102352	.108246	.114320	.117419	.120554	.123726	.126930	.130164	.133428	.140031	.146724	.153492	.160323
30	.40	.059654	.065771	.072064	.075268	.078507	.081777	.085077	.088402	.091750	.098509	.105335	.112215	.119137
	.30	.064825	.070942	.077236	.080439	.083678	.086949	.090248	.093573	.096922	.103680	.110507	.117387	.124308
	.20	.069996	.076114	.082407	.085611	.088850	.092120	.095419	.098744	.102093	.108852	.115678	.122558	.129479
	.10	.075168	.081285	.087578	.090782	.094021	.097292	.100591	.103916	.107264	.114023	.120849	.127729	.134651
	0.00	.080339	.086457	.092749	.095954	.099193	.102463	.105762	.109087	.112436	.119194	.126021	.132901	.139822
	-.10	.085510	.091628	.097921	.101125	.104364	.107634	.110933	.114258	.117607	.124366	.131192	.138072	.144993
	-.20	.090682	.096799	.103092	.106296	.109535	.112806	.116105	.119430	.122778	.129537	.136364	.143243	.150165
	-.30	.095853	.101971	.108264	.111468	.114707	.117977	.121276	.124601	.127950	.134709	.141535	.148415	.155336
	-.40	.101024	.107142	.113435	.116639	.119878	.123148	.126447	.129772	.133121	.139880	.146706	.153586	.160507

10.0 YEAR HOLDING PERIOD
.140 EQUITY YIELD RATE
.750 LOAN RATIO

INTEREST RATE

TERM YEARS	APPR DEP	5.0	6.0	7.0	7.5	8.0	8.5	9.0	9.5	10.0	11.0	12.0	13.0	14.0
10	.40	.070988	.075448	.080027	.082361	.084724	.087117	.089538	.091987	.094465	.099504	.104653	.109909	.115269
	.30	.076160	.080619	.085198	.087532	.089896	.092288	.094709	.097159	.099636	.104676	.109825	.115080	.120441
	.20	.081331	.085791	.090370	.092704	.095067	.097459	.099880	.102330	.104808	.109847	.114996	.120252	.125612
	.10	.086502	.090962	.095541	.097875	.100238	.102631	.105052	.107501	.109979	.115019	.120167	.125423	.130783
	0.00	.091674	.096133	.100712	.103046	.105410	.107802	.110223	.112673	.115151	.120190	.125339	.130595	.135955
	-.10	.096845	.101305	.105884	.108218	.110581	.112973	.115394	.117844	.120322	.125361	.130510	.135766	.141126
	-.20	.102017	.106476	.111055	.113389	.115752	.118145	.120566	.123015	.125493	.130533	.135681	.140937	.146297
	-.30	.107188	.111647	.116227	.118560	.120924	.123316	.125737	.128187	.130665	.135704	.140853	.146109	.151469
	-.40	.112359	.116819	.121398	.123732	.126095	.128487	.130908	.133358	.135836	.140875	.146024	.151280	.156640
15	.40	.062954	.068406	.074030	.076904	.079818	.082772	.085764	.088794	.091860	.098098	.104471	.110969	.117585
	.30	.068125	.073577	.079201	.082075	.084989	.087943	.090935	.093965	.097031	.103270	.109642	.116140	.122756
	.20	.073296	.078749	.084372	.087246	.090161	.093115	.096107	.099137	.102203	.108441	.114813	.121311	.127927
	.10	.078468	.083920	.089544	.092418	.095332	.098286	.101278	.104308	.107374	.113612	.119985	.126483	.133099
	0.00	.083639	.089091	.094715	.097589	.100503	.103457	.106450	.109480	.112546	.118784	.125156	.131654	.138270
	-.10	.088810	.094263	.099886	.102760	.105675	.108629	.111621	.114651	.117717	.123955	.130327	.136825	.143441
	-.20	.093982	.099434	.105058	.107932	.110846	.113800	.116792	.119822	.122888	.129126	.135499	.141997	.148613
	-.30	.099153	.104605	.110229	.113103	.116018	.118971	.121964	.124993	.128060	.134298	.140670	.147168	.153784
	-.40	.104324	.109777	.115400	.118274	.121189	.124143	.127135	.130165	.133231	.139469	.145841	.152340	.158955
20	.40	.059058	.065037	.071205	.074355	.077548	.080781	.084052	.087361	.090704	.097489	.104393	.111404	.118509
	.30	.064230	.070208	.076376	.079526	.082719	.085952	.089224	.092532	.095875	.102660	.109565	.116576	.123680
	.20	.069401	.075380	.081547	.084698	.087890	.091123	.094395	.097703	.101047	.107832	.114736	.121747	.128852
	.10	.074572	.080551	.086719	.089869	.093062	.096295	.099566	.102875	.106218	.113003	.119907	.126918	.134023
	0.00	.079744	.085722	.091890	.095041	.098233	.101466	.104738	.108046	.111389	.118174	.125079	.132090	.139195
	-.10	.084915	.090894	.097061	.100212	.103405	.106638	.109909	.113217	.116561	.123346	.130250	.137261	.144366
	-.20	.090086	.096065	.102233	.105383	.108576	.111809	.115080	.118389	.121732	.128517	.135421	.142432	.149537
	-.30	.095258	.101236	.107404	.110555	.113747	.116980	.120252	.123560	.126903	.133688	.140593	.147604	.154709
	-.40	.100429	.106408	.112575	.115726	.118919	.122152	.125423	.128731	.132075	.138860	.145764	.152775	.159880
25	.40	.056814	.063130	.069638	.072957	.076317	.079715	.083148	.086613	.090110	.097185	.104356	.111608	.118926
	.30	.061986	.068301	.074809	.078129	.081488	.084886	.088319	.091785	.095281	.102356	.109527	.116779	.124097
	.20	.067157	.073472	.079980	.083300	.086660	.090057	.093490	.096956	.100452	.107528	.114699	.121950	.129269
	.10	.072328	.078644	.085152	.088471	.091831	.095229	.098662	.102128	.105624	.112699	.119870	.127122	.134440
	0.00	.077500	.083815	.090323	.093643	.097002	.100400	.103833	.107299	.110795	.117870	.125041	.132293	.139611
	-.10	.082671	.088987	.095494	.098814	.102174	.105571	.109004	.112470	.115967	.123042	.130213	.137464	.144783
	-.20	.087842	.094158	.100666	.103985	.107345	.110743	.114176	.117642	.121138	.128213	.135384	.142636	.149954
	-.30	.093014	.099329	.105837	.109157	.112517	.115914	.119347	.122813	.126309	.133384	.140556	.147807	.155125
	-.40	.098185	.104501	.111008	.114328	.117688	.121086	.124518	.127984	.131481	.138556	.145727	.152978	.160297
30	.40	.055392	.061947	.068689	.072122	.075592	.079096	.082631	.086194	.089781	.097023	.104337	.111708	.119124
	.30	.060563	.067118	.073860	.077294	.080764	.084268	.087802	.091365	.094953	.102194	.109508	.116880	.124295
	.20	.065735	.072289	.079032	.082465	.085935	.089439	.092974	.096536	.100124	.107365	.114680	.122051	.129466
	.10	.070906	.077461	.084203	.087636	.091106	.094610	.098145	.101708	.105295	.112537	.119851	.127222	.134638
	0.00	.076077	.082632	.089375	.092808	.096278	.099782	.103316	.106879	.110467	.117708	.125022	.132394	.139809
	-.10	.081249	.087803	.094546	.097979	.101449	.104953	.108488	.112050	.115638	.122879	.130194	.137565	.144981
	-.20	.086420	.092975	.099717	.103150	.106621	.110124	.113659	.117222	.120809	.128051	.135365	.142736	.150152
	-.30	.091591	.098146	.104889	.108322	.111792	.115296	.118830	.122393	.125981	.133222	.140536	.147908	.155323
	-.40	.096763	.103317	.110060	.113493	.116963	.120467	.124002	.127564	.131152	.138394	.145708	.153079	.160495

10.0 YEAR HOLDING PERIOD
.140 EQUITY YIELD RATE
.800 LOAN RATIO

INTEREST RATE

TERM 10 YEARS

APPR DEP	5.0	6.0	7.0	7.5	8.0	8.5	9.0	9.5	10.0	11.0	12.0	13.0	14.0
.40	.067767	.072523	.077408	.079897	.082418	.084970	.087552	.090165	.092808	.098184	.103676	.109282	.115000
.30	.072938	.077695	.082579	.085069	.087590	.090141	.092724	.095337	.097980	.103355	.108847	.114453	.120171
.20	.078109	.082866	.087751	.090240	.092761	.095313	.097895	.100508	.103151	.108526	.114019	.119625	.125342
.10	.083281	.088037	.092922	.095412	.097932	.100484	.103067	.105679	.108323	.113698	.119190	.124796	.130514
0.00	.088452	.093209	.098093	.100583	.103104	.105655	.108238	.110851	.113494	.118869	.124361	.129967	.135685
-.10	.093623	.098380	.103265	.105754	.108275	.110827	.113409	.116022	.118665	.124041	.129533	.135139	.140856
-.20	.098795	.103552	.108436	.110926	.113446	.115998	.118581	.121194	.123837	.129212	.134704	.140310	.146028
-.30	.103966	.108723	.113607	.116097	.118618	.121169	.123752	.126365	.129008	.134383	.139875	.145482	.151199
-.40	.109137	.113894	.118779	.121268	.123789	.126341	.128923	.131536	.134179	.139555	.145047	.150653	.156370

TERM 15 YEARS

APPR DEP	5.0	6.0	7.0	7.5	8.0	8.5	9.0	9.5	10.0	11.0	12.0	13.0	14.0
.40	.059196	.065012	.071011	.074076	.077185	.080336	.083527	.086759	.090030	.096684	.103481	.110412	.117469
.30	.064368	.070183	.076182	.079248	.082356	.085507	.088699	.091930	.095201	.101855	.108652	.115584	.122641
.20	.069539	.075355	.081353	.084419	.087528	.090678	.093870	.097101	.100373	.107027	.113824	.120755	.127812
.10	.074710	.080526	.086524	.089590	.092699	.095850	.099041	.102273	.105544	.112198	.118995	.125926	.132983
0.00	.079882	.085697	.091696	.094762	.097870	.101021	.104213	.107445	.110715	.117369	.124166	.131098	.138155
-.10	.085053	.090869	.096867	.099933	.103042	.106192	.109384	.112616	.115887	.122541	.129338	.136269	.143326
-.20	.090224	.096040	.102039	.105104	.108213	.111364	.114556	.117787	.121058	.127712	.134509	.141440	.148497
-.30	.095396	.101211	.107210	.110276	.113384	.116535	.119727	.122959	.126229	.132883	.139680	.146612	.153669
-.40	.100567	.106383	.112381	.115447	.118556	.121706	.124898	.128130	.131401	.138055	.144852	.151783	.158840

TERM 20 YEARS

APPR DEP	5.0	6.0	7.0	7.5	8.0	8.5	9.0	9.5	10.0	11.0	12.0	13.0	14.0
.40	.055041	.061418	.067997	.071358	.074763	.078212	.081701	.085230	.088797	.096034	.103399	.110877	.118455
.30	.060212	.066590	.073169	.076529	.079935	.083383	.086873	.090402	.093968	.101205	.108570	.116048	.123627
.20	.065384	.071761	.078340	.081701	.085106	.088555	.092044	.095573	.099139	.106377	.113741	.121220	.128798
.10	.070555	.076932	.083511	.086872	.090277	.093726	.097216	.100744	.104311	.111548	.118913	.126391	.133969
0.00	.075726	.082104	.088683	.092043	.095449	.098897	.102387	.105916	.109482	.116719	.124084	.131562	.139141
-.10	.080898	.087275	.093854	.097215	.100620	.104069	.107558	.111087	.114653	.121891	.129255	.136734	.144312
-.20	.086069	.092446	.099025	.102386	.105791	.109240	.112730	.116258	.119825	.127062	.134427	.141905	.149484
-.30	.091241	.097618	.104197	.107557	.110963	.114411	.117901	.121430	.124996	.132233	.139598	.147076	.154655
-.40	.096412	.102789	.109368	.112729	.116134	.119583	.123072	.126601	.130167	.137405	.144769	.152248	.159826

TERM 25 YEARS

APPR DEP	5.0	6.0	7.0	7.5	8.0	8.5	9.0	9.5	10.0	11.0	12.0	13.0	14.0
.40	.052648	.059384	.066326	.069867	.073451	.077075	.080737	.084433	.088163	.095710	.103359	.111094	.118900
.30	.057819	.064555	.071497	.075038	.078622	.082246	.085908	.089605	.093334	.100881	.108530	.116265	.124071
.20	.062990	.069727	.076669	.080209	.083793	.087417	.091079	.094776	.098505	.106052	.113702	.121437	.129243
.10	.068162	.074898	.081840	.085381	.088965	.092589	.096251	.099947	.103677	.111224	.118873	.126608	.134414
0.00	.073333	.080070	.087011	.090552	.094136	.097760	.101422	.105119	.108848	.116395	.124044	.131779	.139585
-.10	.078504	.085241	.092183	.095723	.099307	.102931	.106593	.110290	.114020	.121566	.129216	.136951	.144757
-.20	.083676	.090412	.097354	.100895	.104479	.108103	.111765	.115461	.119191	.126738	.134387	.142122	.149928
-.30	.088847	.095584	.102525	.106066	.109650	.113274	.116936	.120633	.124362	.131909	.139558	.147293	.155099
-.40	.094018	.100755	.107697	.111238	.114821	.118446	.122107	.125804	.129534	.137080	.144730	.152465	.160271

TERM 30 YEARS

APPR DEP	5.0	6.0	7.0	7.5	8.0	8.5	9.0	9.5	10.0	11.0	12.0	13.0	14.0
.40	.051131	.058122	.065314	.068976	.072678	.076415	.080185	.083985	.087812	.095537	.103338	.111201	.119111
.30	.056302	.063293	.070485	.074148	.077849	.081586	.085357	.089157	.092984	.100708	.108510	.116373	.124282
.20	.061473	.068465	.075657	.079319	.083020	.086758	.090528	.094328	.098155	.105879	.113681	.121544	.129454
.10	.066645	.073636	.080828	.084490	.088192	.091929	.095699	.099499	.103326	.111051	.118852	.126715	.134625
0.00	.071816	.078807	.086000	.089662	.093363	.097100	.100871	.104671	.108498	.116222	.124024	.131887	.139796
-.10	.076987	.083979	.091171	.094833	.098534	.102272	.106042	.109842	.113669	.121393	.129195	.137058	.144968
-.20	.082159	.089150	.096342	.100004	.103706	.107443	.111213	.115014	.118841	.126565	.134366	.142229	.150139
-.30	.087330	.094322	.101514	.105176	.108877	.112615	.116385	.120185	.124012	.131736	.139538	.147401	.155311
-.40	.092501	.099493	.106685	.110347	.114048	.117786	.121556	.125356	.129183	.136907	.144709	.152572	.160482

10.0 YEAR HOLDING PERIOD
.140 EQUITY YIELD RATE
.900 LOAN RATIO

INTEREST RATE

TERM YEARS	APPR DEP	5.0	6.0	7.0	7.5	8.0	8.5	9.0	9.5	10.0	11.0	12.0	13.0	14.0
10	.40	.061323	.066675	.072170	.074970	.077806	.080677	.083582	.086522	.089495	.095542	.101721	.108028	.114460
	.30	.066495	.071846	.077341	.080142	.082978	.085848	.088754	.091693	.094667	.100714	.106892	.113199	.119632
	.20	.071666	.077017	.082512	.085313	.088149	.091020	.093925	.096864	.099838	.105885	.112064	.118371	.124803
	.10	.076637	.082149	.087684	.090484	.093320	.096191	.099096	.102036	.105009	.111056	.117235	.123542	.129974
	0.00	.082009	.087360	.092855	.095656	.098492	.101362	.104268	.107207	.110181	.116228	.122406	.128713	.135146
	-.10	.087180	.092531	.098026	.100827	.103663	.106534	.109439	.112379	.115352	.121399	.127578	.133885	.140317
	-.20	.092351	.097703	.103198	.105998	.108834	.111705	.114610	.117550	.120523	.126571	.132749	.139056	.145488
	-.30	.097523	.102874	.108369	.111170	.114006	.116876	.119782	.122721	.125695	.131742	.137920	.144227	.150660
	-.40	.102694	.108045	.113540	.116341	.119177	.122048	.124953	.127893	.130866	.136913	.143092	.149399	.155831
15	.40	.051681	.058224	.064973	.068421	.071919	.075463	.079054	.082690	.086369	.093855	.101502	.109300	.117239
	.30	.056853	.063395	.070144	.073593	.077090	.080635	.084225	.087861	.091541	.099026	.106673	.114471	.122410
	.20	.062024	.068567	.075315	.078764	.082261	.085806	.089397	.093032	.096712	.104198	.111844	.119642	.127581
	.10	.067196	.073738	.080487	.083936	.087433	.090977	.094568	.098204	.101883	.109369	.117016	.124814	.132753
	0.00	.072367	.078910	.085658	.089107	.092604	.096149	.099739	.103375	.107055	.114540	.122187	.129985	.137924
	-.10	.077538	.084081	.090829	.094278	.097776	.101320	.104911	.108546	.112226	.119712	.127359	.135156	.143095
	-.20	.082710	.089252	.096001	.099450	.102947	.106491	.110082	.113718	.117397	.124883	.132530	.140328	.148267
	-.30	.087881	.094424	.101172	.104621	.108119	.111663	.115253	.118889	.122569	.130055	.137701	.145499	.153438
	-.40	.093052	.099595	.106343	.109792	.113290	.116834	.120425	.124061	.127740	.135226	.142873	.150670	.158609
20	.40	.047007	.054181	.061583	.065363	.069194	.073074	.077000	.080970	.084982	.093124	.101409	.109822	.118348
	.30	.052178	.059353	.066754	.070535	.074366	.078245	.082171	.086141	.090153	.098295	.106580	.114994	.123519
	.20	.057350	.064524	.071925	.075706	.079537	.083417	.087343	.091313	.095325	.103466	.111752	.120165	.128691
	.10	.062521	.069695	.077097	.080877	.084708	.088588	.092514	.096484	.100496	.108638	.116923	.125336	.133862
	0.00	.067692	.074867	.082268	.086049	.089880	.093759	.097685	.101655	.105667	.113809	.122095	.130508	.139033
	-.10	.072864	.080038	.087439	.091220	.095051	.098931	.102857	.106827	.110839	.118981	.127266	.135679	.144205
	-.20	.078035	.085209	.092611	.096391	.100223	.104102	.108028	.111998	.116010	.124152	.132437	.140850	.149376
	-.30	.083206	.090381	.097782	.101563	.105394	.109273	.113199	.117169	.121181	.129323	.137609	.146022	.154548
	-.40	.088378	.095552	.102953	.106734	.110565	.114445	.118371	.122341	.126353	.134495	.142780	.151193	.159719
25	.40	.044314	.051893	.059702	.063686	.067718	.071795	.075914	.080073	.084269	.092759	.101364	.110066	.118848
	.30	.049486	.057064	.064874	.068857	.072889	.076966	.081086	.085245	.089440	.097930	.106536	.115238	.124019
	.20	.054657	.062236	.070045	.074028	.078060	.082137	.086257	.090416	.094611	.103102	.111707	.120409	.129191
	.10	.059828	.067407	.075216	.079200	.083232	.087309	.091428	.095587	.099783	.108273	.116878	.125580	.134362
	0.00	.065000	.072578	.080388	.084371	.088403	.092480	.096600	.100759	.104954	.113444	.122050	.130752	.139533
	-.10	.070171	.077750	.085559	.089542	.093574	.097652	.101771	.105930	.110126	.118616	.127221	.135923	.144705
	-.20	.075342	.082921	.090730	.094714	.098746	.102823	.106942	.111101	.115297	.123787	.132392	.141094	.149876
	-.30	.080514	.088092	.095902	.099885	.103917	.107994	.112114	.116273	.120468	.128958	.137564	.146266	.155048
	-.40	.085685	.093264	.101073	.105057	.109088	.113166	.117285	.121444	.125640	.134130	.142735	.151437	.160219
30	.40	.042608	.050473	.058564	.062684	.066848	.071053	.075294	.079569	.083875	.092564	.101341	.110187	.119086
	.30	.047779	.055644	.063735	.067855	.072019	.076224	.080466	.084741	.089046	.097736	.106513	.115358	.124257
	.20	.052950	.060816	.068907	.073027	.077191	.081395	.085637	.089912	.094217	.102907	.111684	.120530	.129428
	.10	.058122	.065987	.074078	.078198	.082362	.086567	.090808	.095083	.099389	.108078	.116855	.125701	.134600
	0.00	.063293	.071158	.079249	.083369	.087533	.091738	.095980	.100255	.104560	.113250	.122027	.130872	.139771
	-.10	.068464	.076330	.084421	.088541	.092705	.096909	.101151	.105426	.109731	.118421	.127198	.136044	.144942
	-.20	.073636	.081501	.089592	.093712	.097876	.102081	.106322	.110597	.114903	.123592	.132369	.141215	.150114
	-.30	.078807	.086672	.094764	.098883	.103047	.107252	.111494	.115769	.120074	.128764	.137541	.146386	.155285
	-.40	.083978	.091844	.099935	.104055	.108219	.112423	.116665	.120940	.125246	.133935	.142712	.151558	.160456

INTEREST RATE

10.0 YEAR HOLDING PERIOD
.150 EQUITY YIELD RATE
.600 LOAN RATIO

TERM YEARS	APPR DEP	5.0	6.0	7.0	7.5	8.0	8.5	9.0	9.5	10.0	11.0	12.0	13.0	14.0
10	.40	.087115	.090683	.094346	.096213	.098104	.100018	.101954	.103314	.105896	.109928	.114047	.118252	.122540
	.30	.092040	.095608	.099271	.101138	.103029	.104943	.106880	.108839	.110822	.114853	.118972	.123177	.127465
	.20	.096966	.100533	.104196	.106064	.107954	.109868	.111805	.113765	.115747	.119778	.123897	.128102	.132390
	.10	.101891	.105458	.109122	.110989	.112879	.114793	.116730	.118690	.120672	.124704	.128823	.133027	.137315
	0.00	.106816	.110384	.114047	.115914	.117805	.119718	.121655	.123615	.125597	.129629	.133748	.137952	.142241
	-.10	.111741	.115309	.118972	.120839	.122730	.124644	.126581	.128540	.130522	.134554	.138673	.142878	.147166
	-.20	.116666	.120234	.123897	.125764	.127655	.129569	.131506	.133465	.135448	.139479	.143598	.147803	.152091
	-.30	.121592	.125159	.128822	.130690	.132580	.134494	.136431	.138391	.140373	.144404	.148523	.152728	.157016
	-.40	.126517	.130084	.133748	.135615	.137505	.139419	.141356	.143316	.145298	.149330	.153449	.157653	.161941
15	.40	.080068	.084404	.088878	.091164	.093483	.095833	.098214	.100625	.103066	.108031	.113104	.118278	.123547
	.30	.084994	.089330	.093803	.096089	.098408	.100758	.103139	.105550	.107991	.112956	.118029	.123203	.128472
	.20	.089919	.094255	.098728	.101014	.103333	.105683	.108064	.110476	.112916	.117881	.122954	.128128	.133397
	.10	.094844	.099180	.103653	.105940	.108258	.110609	.112990	.115401	.117841	.122807	.127880	.133054	.138322
	0.00	.099769	.104105	.108578	.110865	.113184	.115534	.117915	.120326	.122766	.127732	.132805	.137979	.143248
	-.10	.104694	.109030	.113504	.115790	.118109	.120459	.122840	.125251	.127692	.132657	.137730	.142904	.148173
	-.20	.109620	.113956	.118429	.120715	.123034	.125384	.127765	.130176	.132617	.137582	.142655	.147829	.153098
	-.30	.114545	.118881	.123354	.125641	.127959	.130309	.132690	.135102	.137542	.142507	.147580	.152755	.158023
	-.40	.119470	.123806	.128279	.130566	.132884	.135235	.137616	.140027	.142467	.147433	.152506	.157680	.162948
20	.40	.076652	.081401	.086302	.088806	.091344	.093915	.096517	.099149	.101809	.107209	.112706	.118289	.123949
	.30	.081577	.086326	.091227	.093731	.096270	.098840	.101442	.104074	.106734	.112134	.117631	.123214	.128874
	.20	.086502	.091251	.096152	.098657	.101195	.103766	.106368	.108999	.111659	.117059	.122556	.128139	.133799
	.10	.091428	.096176	.101078	.103582	.106120	.108691	.111293	.113925	.116585	.121984	.127481	.133065	.138724
	0.00	.096353	.101102	.106003	.108507	.111045	.113616	.116218	.118850	.121510	.126910	.132406	.137990	.143650
	-.10	.101278	.106027	.110928	.113432	.115970	.118541	.121143	.123775	.126435	.131835	.137332	.142915	.148575
	-.20	.106203	.110952	.115853	.118357	.120896	.123466	.126068	.128700	.131360	.136760	.142257	.147840	.153500
	-.30	.111128	.115877	.120778	.123283	.125821	.128392	.130994	.133625	.136286	.141685	.147182	.152765	.158425
	-.40	.116054	.120802	.125704	.128208	.130746	.133317	.135919	.138551	.141211	.146610	.152107	.157691	.163351
25	.40	.074684	.079701	.084873	.087513	.090185	.092889	.095621	.098379	.101163	.106799	.112513	.118294	.124130
	.30	.079609	.084626	.089798	.092438	.095110	.097814	.100546	.103305	.106089	.111724	.117438	.123219	.129055
	.20	.084534	.089551	.094724	.097363	.100036	.102739	.105471	.108230	.111014	.116649	.122364	.128144	.133981
	.10	.089460	.094476	.099649	.102288	.104961	.107664	.110396	.113155	.115939	.121574	.127289	.133070	.138906
	0.00	.094385	.099401	.104574	.107214	.109886	.112589	.115321	.118080	.120865	.126500	.132214	.137995	.143831
	-.10	.099310	.104327	.109499	.112139	.114811	.117515	.120247	.123005	.125789	.131425	.137139	.142920	.148756
	-.20	.104235	.109252	.114424	.117064	.119736	.122440	.125172	.127931	.130715	.136350	.142064	.147845	.153681
	-.30	.109160	.114177	.119350	.121989	.124662	.127365	.130097	.132856	.135640	.141275	.146990	.152770	.158607
	-.40	.114086	.119102	.124275	.126914	.129587	.132290	.135022	.137781	.140565	.146200	.151915	.157696	.163532
30	.40	.073437	.078646	.084008	.086740	.089503	.092293	.095108	.097947	.100806	.106580	.112414	.118297	.124216
	.30	.078362	.083571	.088934	.091666	.094428	.097218	.100034	.102872	.105732	.111505	.117339	.123222	.129141
	.20	.083287	.088496	.093859	.096591	.099353	.102143	.104959	.107797	.110657	.116430	.122265	.128147	.134067
	.10	.088212	.093421	.098784	.101516	.104278	.107068	.109884	.112723	.115582	.121356	.127190	.133072	.138992
	0.00	.093138	.098347	.103709	.106441	.109204	.111994	.114809	.117648	.120507	.126281	.132115	.137997	.143917
	-.10	.098063	.103272	.108634	.111366	.114129	.116919	.119734	.122573	.125432	.131206	.137040	.142923	.148842
	-.20	.102988	.108197	.113560	.116292	.119054	.121844	.124660	.127498	.130358	.136131	.141965	.147848	.153767
	-.30	.107913	.113122	.118485	.121217	.123979	.126769	.129585	.132423	.135283	.141056	.146891	.152773	.158693
	-.40	.112838	.118047	.123410	.126142	.128904	.131695	.134510	.137349	.140208	.145982	.151816	.157698	.163618

10.0 YEAR HOLDING PERIOD
.150 EQUITY YIELD RATE
.667 LOAN RATIO

INTEREST RATE

TERM YEARS	APPR DEP	5.0	6.0	7.0	7.5	8.0	8.5	9.0	9.5	10.0	11.0	12.0	13.0	14.0
10	.40	.082317	.086281	.090351	.092426	.094526	.096653	.098805	.100982	.103185	.107664	.112241	.116913	.121678
	.30	.087242	.091206	.095276	.097351	.099452	.101578	.103730	.105908	.108110	.112590	.117166	.121838	.126603
	.20	.092167	.096131	.100201	.102276	.104377	.106503	.108655	.110833	.113035	.117515	.122092	.126763	.131528
	.10	.097092	.101056	.105127	.107201	.109302	.111428	.113581	.115758	.117961	.122440	.127017	.131689	.136453
	0.00	.102017	.105981	.110052	.112127	.114227	.116354	.118506	.120683	.122886	.127365	.131942	.136614	.141378
	-.10	.106943	.110907	.114977	.117052	.119152	.121279	.123431	.125608	.127811	.132290	.136867	.141539	.146304
	-.20	.111868	.115832	.119902	.121977	.124078	.126204	.128356	.130534	.132736	.137216	.141792	.146464	.151229
	-.30	.116793	.120757	.124827	.126902	.129003	.131129	.133281	.135459	.137661	.142141	.146718	.151389	.156154
	-.40	.121718	.125682	.129753	.131827	.133928	.136054	.138207	.140384	.142587	.147066	.151643	.156315	.161079
15	.40	.074487	.079305	.084275	.086816	.089392	.092003	.094649	.097328	.100039	.105557	.111193	.116942	.122796
	.30	.079412	.084230	.089200	.091741	.094317	.096928	.099574	.102253	.104965	.110482	.116119	.121868	.127722
	.20	.084337	.089155	.094125	.096666	.099242	.101854	.104499	.107178	.109890	.115407	.121044	.126793	.132647
	.10	.089263	.094080	.099051	.101591	.104167	.106779	.109424	.112104	.114815	.120332	.125969	.131718	.137572
	0.00	.094188	.099006	.103976	.106516	.109093	.111704	.114350	.117029	.119740	.125257	.130894	.136643	.142497
	-.10	.099113	.103931	.108901	.111442	.114018	.116629	.119275	.121954	.124665	.130183	.135819	.141568	.147422
	-.20	.104038	.108856	.113826	.116367	.118943	.121554	.124200	.126879	.129591	.135108	.140745	.146494	.152347
	-.30	.108963	.113781	.118751	.121292	.123868	.126480	.129125	.131804	.134516	.140033	.145670	.151419	.157273
	-.40	.113889	.118706	.123677	.126217	.128793	.131405	.134051	.136730	.139441	.144958	.150595	.156344	.162198
20	.40	.070691	.075967	.081413	.084196	.087016	.089872	.092763	.095688	.098643	.104643	.110751	.116954	.123243
	.30	.075616	.080893	.086338	.089121	.091941	.094798	.097689	.100613	.103569	.109568	.115676	.121880	.128168
	.20	.080541	.085818	.091263	.094046	.096866	.099723	.102614	.105538	.108494	.114494	.120601	.126805	.133094
	.10	.085467	.090743	.096189	.098971	.101792	.104648	.107539	.110463	.113419	.119419	.125526	.131730	.138019
	0.00	.090392	.095668	.101114	.103896	.106717	.109573	.112464	.115388	.118344	.124344	.130452	.136655	.142944
	-.10	.095317	.100593	.106039	.108822	.111642	.114499	.117390	.120314	.123269	.129269	.135377	.141580	.147869
	-.20	.100242	.105519	.110964	.113747	.116567	.119424	.122315	.125239	.128195	.134194	.140302	.146506	.152794
	-.30	.105167	.110444	.115890	.118673	.121492	.124349	.127240	.130164	.133120	.139120	.145227	.151431	.157720
	-.40	.110093	.115369	.120815	.123597	.126418	.129274	.132165	.135089	.138045	.144045	.150152	.156356	.162645
25	.40	.068504	.074078	.079826	.082759	.085728	.088732	.091767	.094833	.097926	.104187	.110537	.116960	.123445
	.30	.073429	.079003	.084751	.087684	.090653	.093657	.096692	.099758	.102851	.109113	.115462	.121885	.128370
	.20	.078355	.083929	.089676	.092609	.095578	.098582	.101618	.104683	.107776	.114038	.120387	.126810	.133295
	.10	.083280	.088854	.094601	.097534	.100543	.103507	.106543	.109608	.112701	.118963	.125312	.131736	.138220
	0.00	.088205	.093779	.099526	.102459	.105429	.108432	.111468	.114533	.117627	.123888	.130238	.136661	.143145
	-.10	.093130	.098704	.104452	.107385	.110354	.113358	.116393	.119459	.122552	.128814	.135163	.141586	.148071
	-.20	.098055	.103629	.109377	.112310	.115279	.118283	.121318	.124383	.127477	.133739	.140088	.146511	.152996
	-.30	.102981	.108555	.114302	.117235	.120204	.123208	.126244	.129309	.132402	.138664	.145013	.151436	.157921
	-.40	.107906	.113480	.119227	.122160	.125130	.128133	.131169	.134234	.137327	.143589	.149939	.156362	.162846
30	.40	.067118	.072906	.078865	.081900	.084970	.088070	.091198	.094352	.097529	.103944	.110427	.116963	.123540
	.30	.072044	.077831	.083790	.086825	.089895	.092995	.096123	.099277	.102454	.108870	.115352	.121888	.128465
	.20	.076969	.082757	.088715	.091751	.094820	.097920	.101043	.104202	.107380	.113795	.120277	.126813	.133391
	.10	.081894	.087682	.093640	.096676	.099745	.102845	.105974	.109128	.112305	.118720	.125203	.131738	.138316
	0.00	.086819	.092607	.098565	.101601	.104670	.107771	.110899	.114053	.117230	.123645	.130128	.136664	.143241
	-.10	.091744	.097532	.103491	.106526	.109596	.112696	.115824	.118978	.122155	.128570	.135053	.141589	.148166
	-.20	.096670	.102457	.108416	.111452	.114521	.117621	.120749	.123903	.127080	.133496	.139978	.146514	.153092
	-.30	.101595	.107383	.113341	.116377	.119446	.122546	.125675	.128829	.132006	.138421	.144903	.151439	.158017
	-.40	.106520	.112308	.118266	.121302	.124371	.127471	.130600	.133754	.136931	.143346	.149829	.156364	.162942

10.0 YEAR HOLDING PERIOD
.150 EQUITY YIELD RATE
.700 LOAN RATIO

INTEREST RATE

TERM YEARS	APPR DEP	5.0	6.0	7.0	7.5	8.0	8.5	9.0	9.5	10.0	11.0	12.0	13.0	14.0
10	.40	.079918	.084080	.088354	.090532	.092738	.094971	.097230	.099517	.101829	.106533	.111338	.116244	.121247
	.30	.084443	.089005	.093279	.095457	.097663	.099896	.102156	.104442	.106755	.111458	.116172	.121156	.126172
	.20	.089768	.093330	.098204	.100383	.102588	.104821	.107081	.109367	.111680	.116383	.121189	.126094	.131097
	.10	.094693	.098856	.103129	.105308	.107514	.109746	.112006	.114292	.116605	.121308	.126114	.131019	.136022
	0.00	.099619	.103761	.108055	.110233	.112439	.114672	.116931	.119218	.121530	.126234	.131039	.135945	.140947
	-.10	.104544	.108706	.112980	.115158	.117364	.119597	.121856	.124143	.126455	.131159	.135964	.140870	.145873
	-.20	.109469	.113631	.117905	.120083	.122289	.124522	.126782	.129068	.131381	.136084	.140890	.145795	.150798
	-.30	.114394	.118556	.122830	.125009	.127214	.129447	.131707	.133993	.136306	.141009	.145815	.150720	.155723
	-.40	.119319	.123482	.127756	.129934	.132140	.134372	.136632	.138918	.141231	.145934	.150740	.155645	.160648
15	.40	.071697	.076755	.081974	.084642	.087347	.090089	.092867	.095679	.098527	.104320	.110238	.116275	.122421
	.30	.076622	.081681	.086899	.089567	.092272	.095014	.097792	.100605	.103452	.109245	.115163	.121200	.127347
	.20	.081547	.086606	.091824	.094492	.097197	.099939	.102717	.105530	.108377	.114170	.120089	.126125	.132272
	.10	.086472	.091531	.096750	.099417	.102122	.104864	.107642	.110455	.113302	.119095	.125014	.131050	.137197
	0.00	.091397	.096456	.101675	.104342	.107048	.109789	.112567	.115380	.118227	.124020	.129939	.135975	.142122
	-.10	.096323	.101381	.106600	.109268	.111973	.114715	.117493	.120306	.123153	.128946	.134864	.140901	.147047
	-.20	.101248	.106307	.111525	.114193	.116898	.119640	.122418	.125231	.128078	.133871	.139789	.145826	.151973
	-.30	.106173	.111232	.116451	.119118	.121823	.124565	.127343	.130156	.133003	.138796	.144715	.150751	.156898
	-.40	.111098	.116157	.121376	.124044	.126748	.129490	.132268	.135081	.137928	.143721	.149640	.155676	.161823
20	.40	.067711	.073251	.078969	.081891	.084852	.087851	.090887	.093957	.097061	.103360	.109773	.116287	.122890
	.30	.072636	.078176	.083894	.086816	.089777	.092776	.095812	.098882	.101986	.108286	.114699	.121212	.127816
	.20	.077561	.083101	.088819	.091741	.094702	.097702	.100737	.103808	.106911	.113211	.119624	.126138	.132741
	.10	.082486	.088027	.093745	.096666	.099627	.102627	.105663	.108733	.111836	.118136	.124549	.131063	.137666
	0.00	.087411	.092952	.098670	.101592	.104553	.107552	.110588	.113658	.116762	.123061	.129474	.135988	.142591
	-.10	.092337	.097877	.103595	.106517	.109478	.112477	.115513	.118583	.121687	.127986	.134399	.140913	.147517
	-.20	.097262	.102802	.108520	.111442	.114403	.117403	.120438	.123509	.126612	.132912	.139325	.145838	.152442
	-.30	.102187	.107728	.113445	.116367	.119328	.122328	.125363	.128434	.131537	.137837	.144250	.150764	.157367
	-.40	.107112	.112653	.118371	.121292	.124254	.127253	.130289	.133359	.136462	.142762	.149175	.155689	.162292
25	.40	.065415	.071267	.077302	.080382	.083500	.086653	.089841	.093059	.096307	.102882	.109549	.116293	.123102
	.30	.070340	.076193	.082227	.085307	.088425	.091579	.094766	.097985	.101233	.107807	.114474	.121218	.128027
	.20	.075265	.081118	.087153	.090232	.093350	.096504	.099691	.102910	.106158	.112732	.119399	.126144	.132952
	.10	.080190	.086043	.092078	.095157	.098275	.101429	.104616	.107835	.111083	.117658	.124324	.131069	.137878
	0.00	.085116	.090968	.097003	.100083	.103200	.106354	.109542	.112760	.116008	.122583	.129250	.135994	.142803
	-.10	.090041	.095894	.101928	.105008	.108126	.111279	.114467	.117686	.120933	.127508	.134175	.140919	.147728
	-.20	.094966	.100819	.106853	.109933	.113051	.116205	.119392	.122611	.125859	.132433	.139100	.145844	.152653
	-.30	.099891	.105744	.111779	.114858	.117976	.121130	.124317	.127536	.130784	.137358	.144025	.150770	.157578
	-.40	.104816	.110669	.116704	.119783	.122901	.126055	.129242	.132461	.135709	.142284	.148950	.155695	.162504
30	.40	.063960	.070037	.076293	.079481	.082703	.085958	.089243	.092555	.095891	.102627	.109433	.116296	.123202
	.30	.068885	.074962	.081218	.084406	.087629	.090884	.094168	.097480	.100816	.107552	.114359	.121221	.128128
	.20	.073810	.079887	.086144	.089331	.092554	.095809	.099094	.102405	.105741	.112477	.119284	.126146	.133053
	.10	.078735	.084812	.091069	.094256	.097479	.100734	.104019	.107331	.110667	.117402	.124209	.131072	.137978
	0.00	.083660	.089738	.095994	.099181	.102404	.105659	.108944	.112256	.115592	.122328	.129134	.135997	.142903
	-.10	.088586	.094663	.100919	.104107	.107329	.110585	.113869	.117181	.120517	.127253	.134059	.140922	.147828
	-.20	.093511	.099588	.105844	.109032	.112255	.115510	.118794	.122106	.125442	.132178	.138985	.145847	.152754
	-.30	.098436	.104513	.110770	.113957	.117180	.120435	.123720	.127031	.130367	.137103	.143910	.150773	.157679
	-.40	.103361	.109438	.115695	.118882	.122105	.125360	.128645	.131957	.135293	.142028	.148835	.155698	.162604

10.0 YEAR HOLDING PERIOD
.150 EQUITY YIELD RATE
.750 LOAN RATIO

INTEREST RATE

TERM YEARS	APPR DEP	5.0	6.0	7.0	7.5	8.0	8.5	9.0	9.5	10.0	11.0	12.0	13.0	14.0
10	.40	.076319	.080779	.085358	.087692	.090055	.092447	.094868	.097318	.099796	.104835	.109984	.115240	.120600
	.30	.081244	.085704	.090283	.092617	.094980	.097372	.099794	.102243	.104721	.109760	.114909	.120165	.125525
	.20	.086170	.090629	.095208	.097542	.099905	.102298	.104719	.107168	.109646	.114686	.119834	.125090	.130450
	.10	.091095	.095554	.100133	.102467	.104831	.107223	.109644	.112094	.114571	.119611	.124760	.130015	.135376
	0.00	.096020	.100479	.105059	.107393	.109756	.112148	.114569	.117019	.119497	.124536	.129685	.134941	.140301
	-.10	.100945	.105405	.109984	.112318	.114681	.117073	.119494	.121944	.124422	.129461	.134610	.139866	.145226
	-.20	.105870	.110330	.114909	.117243	.119606	.121998	.124420	.126869	.129347	.134386	.139535	.144791	.150151
	-.30	.110796	.115255	.119834	.122168	.124531	.126924	.129345	.131794	.134272	.139312	.144460	.149716	.155076
	-.40	.115721	.120180	.124759	.127093	.129457	.131849	.134270	.136720	.139197	.144237	.149386	.154641	.160002
15	.40	.067511	.072931	.078522	.081380	.084279	.087216	.090193	.093207	.096257	.102464	.108805	.115273	.121859
	.30	.072436	.077856	.083447	.086305	.089204	.092142	.095118	.098132	.101182	.107389	.113730	.120198	.126784
	.20	.077361	.082781	.088373	.091231	.094129	.097067	.100043	.103057	.106108	.112314	.118656	.125123	.131709
	.10	.082286	.087706	.093298	.096156	.099054	.101992	.104968	.107982	.111033	.117240	.123581	.130048	.136634
	0.00	.087212	.092632	.098223	.101081	.103979	.106917	.109894	.112907	.115958	.122165	.128506	.134974	.141559
	-.10	.092137	.097557	.103148	.106006	.108905	.111842	.114819	.117833	.120883	.127090	.133431	.139899	.146485
	-.20	.097062	.102482	.108074	.110932	.113830	.116768	.119744	.122758	.125808	.132015	.138356	.144824	.151410
	-.30	.101987	.107407	.112999	.115857	.118755	.121693	.124669	.127683	.130734	.136940	.143282	.149749	.156335
	-.40	.106912	.112332	.117924	.120782	.123680	.126618	.129594	.132608	.135659	.141866	.148207	.154674	.161260
20	.40	.063240	.069176	.075303	.078433	.081606	.084819	.088072	.091361	.094687	.101436	.108307	.115286	.122361
	.30	.068165	.074101	.080228	.083358	.086531	.089744	.092997	.096287	.099612	.106361	.113232	.120212	.127286
	.20	.073091	.079027	.085153	.088283	.091456	.094670	.097922	.101212	.104537	.111287	.118158	.125137	.132212
	.10	.078016	.083952	.090078	.093209	.096381	.099595	.102847	.106137	.109462	.116212	.123083	.130062	.137137
	0.00	.082941	.088877	.095003	.098134	.101307	.104520	.107773	.111062	.114387	.121137	.128008	.134987	.142062
	-.10	.087866	.093802	.099929	.103059	.106232	.109445	.112698	.115987	.119313	.126062	.132933	.139912	.146987
	-.20	.092791	.098727	.104854	.107984	.111157	.114371	.117623	.120913	.124238	.130987	.137858	.144838	.151913
	-.30	.097717	.103653	.109779	.112909	.116082	.119296	.122548	.125838	.129163	.135913	.142784	.149763	.156838
	-.40	.102642	.108578	.114704	.117835	.121007	.124221	.127473	.130763	.134088	.140838	.147709	.154688	.161763
25	.40	.060780	.067051	.073517	.076816	.080157	.083536	.086951	.090400	.093879	.100924	.108067	.115293	.122588
	.30	.065705	.071976	.078442	.081741	.085082	.088461	.091876	.095325	.098805	.105849	.112992	.120218	.127513
	.20	.070631	.076901	.083367	.086667	.090007	.093386	.096801	.100250	.103730	.110774	.117917	.125143	.132438
	.10	.075556	.081827	.088292	.091592	.094932	.098311	.101727	.105175	.108655	.115699	.122842	.130068	.137363
	0.00	.080481	.086752	.093218	.096517	.099858	.103237	.106652	.110100	.113580	.120625	.127767	.134994	.142289
	-.10	.085406	.091677	.098143	.101442	.104783	.108162	.111577	.115026	.118505	.125550	.132693	.139919	.147214
	-.20	.090331	.096602	.103068	.106367	.109708	.113087	.116502	.119951	.123431	.130475	.137618	.144844	.152139
	-.30	.095257	.101527	.107993	.111293	.114633	.118012	.121427	.124876	.128356	.135400	.142543	.149769	.157064
	-.40	.100182	.106453	.112918	.116218	.119558	.122937	.126353	.129801	.133281	.140325	.147468	.154694	.161989
30	.40	.059221	.065732	.072436	.075851	.079304	.082791	.086311	.089859	.093433	.100650	.107943	.115296	.122695
	.30	.064146	.070658	.077361	.080776	.084229	.087716	.091236	.094784	.098358	.105575	.112868	.120221	.127621
	.20	.069071	.075583	.082286	.085701	.089154	.092642	.096161	.099709	.103283	.110501	.117793	.125146	.132546
	.10	.073997	.080508	.087211	.090626	.094079	.097567	.101086	.104634	.108209	.115426	.122719	.130071	.137471
	0.00	.078922	.085433	.092136	.095551	.099004	.102492	.106011	.109560	.113134	.120351	.127644	.134997	.142396
	-.10	.083847	.090358	.097062	.100477	.103930	.107417	.110937	.114485	.118059	.125276	.132569	.139922	.147321
	-.20	.088772	.095284	.101987	.105402	.108855	.112343	.115862	.119410	.122984	.130201	.137494	.144847	.152247
	-.30	.093698	.100209	.106912	.110327	.113780	.117268	.120787	.124335	.127910	.135127	.142419	.149772	.157172
	-.40	.098623	.105134	.111837	.115252	.118705	.122193	.125712	.129261	.132835	.140052	.147345	.154698	.162097

10.0 YEAR HOLDING PERIOD
.150 EQUITY YIELD RATE
.800 LOAN RATIO

INTEREST RATE

TERM YEARS	APPR DEP	5.0	6.0	7.0	7.5	8.0	8.5	9.0	9.5	10.0	11.0	12.0	13.0	14.0
10	.40	.072720	.077477	.082362	.084851	.087372	.089924	.092506	.095119	.097762	.103138	.108630	.114236	.119953
	.30	.077646	.082402	.087287	.089776	.092297	.094849	.097431	.100044	.102687	.108063	.113555	.119161	.124879
	.20	.082571	.087328	.092212	.094702	.097222	.099774	.102357	.104970	.107613	.112988	.118480	.124086	.129804
	.10	.087496	.092253	.097137	.099627	.102148	.104699	.107282	.109895	.112538	.117913	.123405	.129011	.134729
	0.00	.092421	.097178	.102062	.104552	.107073	.109625	.112207	.114820	.117463	.122838	.128330	.133937	.139654
	-.10	.097346	.102103	.106988	.109477	.111998	.114550	.117132	.119745	.122388	.127764	.133256	.138862	.144505
	-.20	.102272	.107028	.111913	.114402	.116923	.119475	.122058	.124670	.127313	.132689	.138181	.143787	.149505
	-.30	.107197	.111954	.116838	.119328	.121848	.124400	.126983	.129596	.132239	.137614	.143106	.148712	.154430
	-.40	.112122	.116879	.121763	.124253	.126774	.129325	.131908	.134521	.137164	.142539	.148031	.153637	.159355
15	.40	.063325	.069106	.075070	.078119	.081211	.084344	.087519	.090734	.093988	.100608	.107372	.114271	.121296
	.30	.068250	.074031	.079996	.083044	.086136	.089269	.092444	.095659	.098913	.105533	.112297	.119196	.126221
	.20	.073175	.078957	.084921	.087969	.091061	.094195	.097369	.100584	.103838	.110459	.117223	.124121	.131146
	.10	.078100	.083882	.089846	.092895	.095986	.099120	.102295	.105509	.108763	.115384	.122148	.129047	.136072
	0.00	.083026	.088807	.094771	.097820	.100911	.104045	.107220	.110435	.113688	.120309	.127073	.133972	.140997
	-.10	.087951	.093732	.099697	.102745	.105837	.108970	.112145	.115360	.118614	.125234	.131998	.138897	.145922
	-.20	.092876	.098657	.104622	.107670	.110762	.113896	.117070	.120285	.123539	.130159	.136924	.143822	.150847
	-.30	.097801	.103583	.109547	.112595	.115687	.118821	.121995	.125210	.128464	.135085	.141849	.148748	.155772
	-.40	.102727	.108508	.114472	.117521	.120612	.123746	.126921	.130135	.133389	.140010	.146774	.153673	.160698
20	.40	.058770	.065101	.071636	.074975	.078360	.081787	.085257	.088766	.092312	.099512	.106841	.114286	.121832
	.30	.063695	.070027	.076561	.079900	.083285	.086712	.090182	.093691	.097238	.104437	.111766	.119211	.126757
	.20	.068620	.074952	.081487	.084826	.088211	.091638	.095108	.098616	.102163	.109362	.116692	.124136	.131683
	.10	.073545	.079877	.086412	.089751	.093135	.096563	.100032	.103541	.107088	.114288	.121617	.129061	.136608
	0.00	.078471	.084802	.091337	.094676	.098060	.101488	.104957	.108466	.112013	.119213	.126542	.133986	.141533
	-.10	.083396	.089727	.096262	.099601	.102986	.106413	.109883	.113392	.116938	.124138	.131467	.138912	.146458
	-.20	.088321	.094653	.101187	.104526	.107911	.111339	.114808	.118317	.121864	.129063	.136392	.143837	.151383
	-.30	.093246	.099578	.106113	.109452	.112836	.116264	.119733	.123242	.126789	.133988	.141318	.148762	.156309
	-.40	.098171	.104503	.111038	.114377	.117761	.121189	.124658	.128167	.131714	.138914	.146243	.153687	.161234
25	.40	.056146	.062834	.069731	.073251	.076814	.080418	.084061	.087740	.091451	.098965	.106585	.114292	.122074
	.30	.061071	.067760	.074656	.078176	.081739	.085343	.088986	.092665	.096377	.103891	.111510	.119218	.126999
	.20	.065996	.072685	.079582	.083101	.086664	.090269	.093911	.097590	.101302	.108816	.116435	.124143	.131924
	.10	.070921	.077610	.084507	.088026	.091590	.095194	.098837	.102515	.106227	.113741	.121360	.129068	.136849
	0.00	.075846	.082535	.089432	.092952	.096515	.100119	.103762	.107441	.111152	.118666	.126285	.133993	.141775
	-.10	.080772	.087460	.094357	.097877	.101440	.105044	.108687	.112366	.116077	.123591	.131211	.138918	.146700
	-.20	.085697	.092386	.099283	.102802	.106365	.109969	.113612	.117291	.121003	.128517	.136136	.143844	.151625
	-.30	.090622	.097311	.104208	.107727	.111290	.114895	.118537	.122216	.125928	.133442	.141061	.148769	.156550
	-.40	.095547	.102236	.109133	.112652	.116216	.119820	.123463	.127141	.130853	.138367	.145986	.153694	.161475
30	.40	.054483	.061428	.068578	.072221	.075904	.079624	.083378	.087163	.090975	.098674	.106453	.114296	.122189
	.30	.059408	.066353	.073503	.077146	.080829	.084549	.088303	.092088	.095901	.103599	.111378	.119221	.127114
	.20	.064333	.071278	.078428	.082071	.085754	.089474	.093229	.097013	.100826	.108524	.116303	.124146	.132039
	.10	.069258	.076204	.083354	.086996	.090680	.094400	.098154	.101939	.105751	.113449	.121228	.129071	.136964
	0.00	.074183	.081129	.088279	.091922	.095605	.099325	.103079	.106864	.110676	.118374	.126153	.133996	.141889
	-.10	.079109	.086054	.093204	.096847	.100530	.104250	.108004	.111789	.115602	.123300	.131079	.138922	.146815
	-.20	.084034	.090979	.098129	.101772	.105455	.109175	.112929	.116714	.120527	.128225	.136004	.143847	.151740
	-.30	.088959	.095904	.103055	.106697	.110380	.114101	.117855	.121639	.125452	.133150	.140929	.148772	.156665
	-.40	.093884	.100830	.107980	.111622	.115306	.119026	.122780	.126565	.130377	.138075	.145854	.153697	.161590

10.0 YEAR HOLDING PERIOD
.150 EQUITY YIELD RATE
.900 LOAN RATIO

INTEREST RATE

TERM YEARS	APPR DEP	5.0	6.0	7.0	7.5	8.0	8.5	9.0	9.5	10.0	11.0	12.0	13.0	14.0
10	.40	.065523	.070874	.076369	.079170	.082006	.084877	.087782	.090722	.093695	.099742	.105921	.112228	.118660
	.30	.070448	.075800	.081295	.084095	.086931	.089802	.092707	.095647	.098620	.104668	.110846	.117153	.123585
	.20	.075373	.080725	.086220	.089021	.091857	.094727	.097633	.100572	.103546	.109593	.115771	.122078	.128510
	.10	.080299	.085650	.091145	.093946	.096782	.099652	.102558	.105497	.108471	.114518	.120697	.127004	.133436
	0.00	.085224	.090575	.096070	.098871	.101707	.104578	.107483	.110423	.113396	.119443	.125622	.131929	.138361
	-.10	.090149	.095500	.100996	.103796	.106632	.109503	.112408	.115348	.118321	.124368	.130547	.136854	.143286
	-.20	.095074	.100426	.105921	.108721	.111557	.114428	.117333	.120273	.123246	.129294	.135472	.141779	.148211
	-.30	.100000	.105351	.110846	.113647	.116483	.119353	.122259	.125198	.128172	.134219	.140397	.146704	.153137
	-.40	.104925	.110276	.115771	.118572	.121408	.124279	.127184	.130123	.133097	.139144	.145323	.151630	.158062
15	.40	.054953	.061457	.068167	.071597	.075075	.078600	.082171	.085788	.089449	.096897	.104506	.112268	.120171
	.30	.059878	.066382	.073092	.076522	.080000	.083525	.087097	.090713	.094374	.101822	.109432	.117193	.125096
	.20	.064803	.071307	.078017	.081447	.084925	.088450	.092022	.095639	.099299	.106747	.114357	.122118	.130021
	.10	.069729	.076233	.082943	.086372	.089850	.093376	.096947	.100564	.104224	.111673	.119282	.127043	.134946
	0.00	.074654	.081158	.087868	.091297	.094775	.098301	.101872	.105489	.109150	.116598	.124207	.131968	.139871
	-.10	.079579	.086083	.092793	.096223	.099701	.103226	.106798	.110414	.114075	.121523	.129132	.136894	.144797
	-.20	.084504	.091008	.097718	.101148	.104626	.108151	.111723	.115339	.119000	.126448	.134058	.141819	.149722
	-.30	.089430	.095934	.102643	.106073	.109551	.113076	.116648	.120265	.123925	.131373	.138983	.146744	.154647
	-.40	.094355	.100859	.107569	.110998	.114476	.118002	.121573	.125190	.128850	.136299	.143908	.151669	.159572
20	.40	.049828	.056952	.064303	.068060	.071867	.075723	.079626	.083574	.087564	.095664	.103909	.112284	.120774
	.30	.054754	.061877	.069228	.072985	.076792	.080648	.084551	.088499	.092489	.100589	.108834	.117209	.125699
	.20	.059679	.066802	.074154	.077910	.081717	.085573	.089477	.093424	.097414	.105514	.113759	.122134	.130624
	.10	.064604	.071727	.079079	.082835	.086643	.090499	.094402	.098350	.102340	.110439	.118684	.127059	.135549
	0.00	.069529	.076652	.084004	.087761	.091568	.095424	.099327	.103275	.107265	.115364	.123610	.131985	.140475
	-.10	.074454	.081578	.088929	.092686	.096493	.100349	.104252	.108200	.112190	.120290	.128535	.136910	.145400
	-.20	.079380	.086503	.093855	.097611	.101418	.105275	.109178	.113125	.117115	.125215	.133460	.141835	.150325
	-.30	.084305	.091428	.098780	.102536	.106344	.110200	.114103	.118050	.122040	.130140	.138385	.146760	.155250
	-.40	.089230	.096353	.103705	.107461	.111269	.115125	.119028	.122976	.126966	.135065	.143310	.151685	.160175
25	.40	.046876	.054401	.062160	.066120	.070128	.074183	.078281	.082420	.086595	.095049	.103620	.112291	.121046
	.30	.051802	.059327	.067085	.071045	.075054	.079108	.083206	.087345	.091521	.099974	.108545	.117217	.125971
	.20	.056727	.064252	.072011	.075970	.079979	.084034	.088132	.092270	.096446	.104899	.113471	.122142	.130896
	.10	.061652	.069177	.076936	.080895	.084904	.088959	.093057	.097195	.101371	.109824	.118396	.127067	.135821
	0.00	.066577	.074102	.081861	.085820	.089829	.093884	.097982	.102120	.106296	.114749	.123321	.131992	.140746
	-.10	.071502	.079027	.086786	.090746	.094754	.098809	.102907	.107046	.111221	.119675	.128246	.136917	.145672
	-.20	.076428	.083953	.091711	.095671	.099680	.103734	.107832	.111971	.116147	.124600	.133171	.141843	.150597
	-.30	.081353	.088878	.096637	.100596	.104605	.108660	.112758	.116896	.121072	.129525	.138097	.146768	.155522
	-.40	.086278	.093803	.101562	.105521	.109530	.113585	.117683	.121821	.125997	.134450	.143022	.151693	.160447
30	.40	.045005	.052819	.060863	.064961	.069104	.073290	.077513	.081771	.086060	.094720	.103472	.112295	.121175
	.30	.049931	.057744	.065788	.069886	.074030	.078215	.082438	.086696	.090985	.099646	.108397	.117220	.126100
	.20	.054856	.062669	.070713	.074811	.078955	.083141	.087363	.091621	.095910	.104571	.113322	.122146	.131025
	.10	.059781	.067595	.075639	.079737	.083880	.088065	.092289	.096546	.100836	.109496	.118247	.127071	.135950
	0.00	.064706	.072520	.080564	.084662	.088805	.092991	.097214	.101472	.105761	.114421	.123173	.131996	.140876
	-.10	.069631	.077445	.085489	.089587	.093731	.097916	.102139	.106397	.110686	.119346	.128098	.136921	.145801
	-.20	.074557	.082370	.090414	.094512	.098656	.102841	.107064	.111322	.115611	.124272	.133023	.141846	.150726
	-.30	.079482	.087295	.095339	.099437	.103581	.107766	.111989	.116247	.120536	.129197	.137948	.146772	.155651
	-.40	.084407	.092221	.100265	.104363	.108506	.112691	.116915	.121172	.125462	.134122	.142873	.151697	.160576

10.0 YEAR HOLDING PERIOD
.160 EQUITY YIELD RATE
.600 LOAN RATIO

INTEREST RATE

TERM YEARS	APPR DEP	5.0	6.0	7.0	7.5	8.0	8.5	9.0	9.5	10.0	11.0	12.0	13.0	14.0
10	.40	.093466	.097034	.100697	.102564	.104455	.106369	.108305	.110265	.112247	.116279	.120398	.124603	.128891
	.30	.096156	.101724	.105387	.107254	.109145	.111059	.112996	.114955	.116938	.120969	.125088	.129293	.133581
	.20	.102846	.106414	.110077	.111944	.113835	.115749	.117686	.119645	.121628	.125659	.129778	.133983	.138271
	.10	.107536	.111104	.114767	.116635	.118525	.120439	.122376	.124335	.126318	.130349	.134468	.138673	.142961
	0.00	.112227	.115794	.119457	.121325	.123215	.125129	.127066	.129026	.131008	.135039	.139158	.143363	.147651
	-.10	.116917	.120484	.124148	.126015	.127905	.129819	.131756	.133716	.135698	.139729	.143849	.148053	.152341
	-.20	.121607	.125174	.128838	.130705	.132595	.134509	.136446	.138406	.140388	.144420	.148539	.152743	.157031
	-.30	.126297	.129864	.133528	.135395	.137286	.139199	.141136	.143096	.145078	.149110	.153229	.157433	.161722
	-.40	.130987	.134555	.138218	.140085	.141976	.143889	.145826	.147786	.149768	.153800	.157919	.162124	.166412
15	.40	.085828	.090140	.094588	.096862	.099169	.101507	.103876	.106275	.108703	.113645	.118694	.123845	.129090
	.30	.090518	.094830	.099278	.101553	.103859	.106197	.108566	.110965	.113393	.118335	.123384	.128535	.133781
	.20	.095209	.099520	.103969	.106243	.108549	.110887	.113256	.115655	.118083	.123025	.128074	.133225	.138471
	.10	.099899	.104210	.108659	.110933	.113239	.115577	.117946	.120345	.122773	.127715	.132764	.137915	.143161
	0.00	.104589	.108900	.113349	.115623	.117929	.120267	.122636	.125035	.127464	.132405	.137454	.142605	.147851
	-.10	.109279	.113590	.118039	.120313	.122619	.124957	.127326	.129725	.132154	.137095	.142144	.147295	.152541
	-.20	.113969	.118280	.122729	.125003	.127310	.129648	.132016	.134415	.136844	.141785	.146835	.151985	.157231
	-.30	.118659	.122970	.127419	.129693	.131999	.134338	.136707	.139106	.141534	.146475	.151525	.156675	.161921
	-.40	.123349	.127661	.132109	.134383	.136690	.139028	.141397	.143796	.146224	.151165	.156215	.161366	.166611
20	.40	.082125	.086842	.091711	.094200	.096723	.099279	.101866	.104484	.107130	.112503	.117974	.123533	.129170
	.30	.086815	.091532	.096401	.098890	.101413	.103969	.106556	.109174	.111820	.117193	.122664	.128223	.133860
	.20	.091505	.096222	.101091	.103580	.106103	.108659	.111247	.113864	.116510	.121883	.127354	.132913	.138550
	.10	.096196	.100912	.105781	.108270	.110793	.113349	.115937	.118554	.121200	.126573	.132044	.137603	.143240
	0.00	.100886	.105602	.110471	.112960	.115483	.118039	.120627	.123244	.125890	.131263	.136734	.142294	.147931
	-.10	.105576	.110292	.115162	.117650	.120173	.122729	.125317	.127934	.130581	.135953	.141425	.146984	.152621
	-.20	.110266	.114982	.119852	.122340	.124864	.127420	.130007	.132624	.135271	.140643	.146115	.151674	.157311
	-.30	.114956	.119672	.124542	.127031	.129554	.132110	.134697	.137315	.139961	.145334	.150806	.156364	.162001
	-.40	.119646	.124362	.129232	.131721	.134244	.136800	.139387	.142005	.144651	.150024	.155495	.161054	.166691
25	.40	.079992	.084975	.090115	.092739	.095397	.098086	.100804	.103550	.106321	.111933	.117626	.123388	.129206
	.30	.084682	.089665	.094805	.097429	.100087	.102776	.105495	.108240	.111012	.116623	.122316	.128078	.133896
	.20	.089372	.094355	.099495	.102120	.104777	.107466	.110185	.112930	.115702	.121314	.127006	.132768	.138586
	.10	.094063	.099045	.104185	.106810	.109467	.112156	.114875	.117621	.120392	.126004	.131697	.137458	.143276
	0.00	.098753	.103735	.108875	.111500	.114157	.116846	.119565	.122311	.125082	.130694	.136387	.142148	.147966
	-.10	.103443	.108425	.113566	.116190	.118848	.121537	.124225	.127001	.129772	.135384	.141077	.146838	.152657
	-.20	.108133	.113115	.118256	.120880	.123538	.126227	.128945	.131691	.134462	.140074	.145767	.151528	.157347
	-.30	.112823	.117805	.122946	.125570	.128228	.130917	.133635	.136381	.139152	.144764	.150457	.156218	.162037
	-.40	.117513	.122495	.127636	.130260	.132918	.135607	.138325	.141071	.143842	.149454	.155147	.160908	.166727
30	.40	.078640	.083816	.089149	.091867	.094616	.097394	.100198	.103025	.105875	.111629	.117447	.123316	.129223
	.30	.083336	.088506	.093839	.096557	.099306	.102084	.104888	.107716	.110565	.116320	.122138	.128006	.133913
	.20	.088020	.093196	.098529	.101247	.103996	.106774	.109578	.112406	.115255	.121010	.126828	.132696	.138603
	.10	.092711	.097887	.103219	.105937	.108687	.111464	.114268	.117096	.119945	.125700	.131518	.137386	.143293
	0.00	.097401	.102577	.107909	.110627	.113377	.116154	.118958	.121786	.124635	.130390	.136208	.142076	.147984
	-.10	.102091	.107267	.112599	.115318	.118067	.120845	.123648	.126476	.129325	.135080	.140898	.146766	.152674
	-.20	.106781	.111957	.117290	.120008	.122747	.125535	.128339	.131166	.134015	.139770	.145588	.151456	.157364
	-.30	.111471	.116647	.121980	.124698	.127447	.130225	.133029	.135856	.138705	.144460	.150278	.156146	.162054
	-.40	.116161	.121337	.126670	.129388	.132137	.134915	.137719	.140546	.143395	.149150	.154968	.160836	.166744

10.0 YEAR HOLDING PERIOD
.160 EQUITY YIELD RATE
.667 LOAN RATIO

INTEREST RATE

TERM YEARS	APPR DEP	5.0	6.0	7.0	7.5	8.0	8.5	9.0	9.5	10.0	11.0	12.0	13.0	14.0
10	.40	.088158	.092122	.096192	.098267	.100367	.102494	.104646	.106823	.109026	.113505	.118082	.122754	.127519
	.30	.092848	.096812	.100882	.102957	.105057	.107184	.109336	.111513	.113716	.118195	.122772	.127444	.132209
	.20	.097538	.101502	.105572	.107647	.109748	.111874	.114026	.116204	.118406	.122886	.127462	.132134	.136899
	.10	.102228	.106192	.110262	.112337	.114438	.116564	.118716	.120894	.123096	.127576	.132152	.136824	.141589
	0.00	.106918	.110882	.114953	.117027	.119128	.121254	.123406	.125584	.127786	.132266	.136843	.141514	.146279
	-.10	.111608	.115572	.119643	.121717	.123818	.125944	.128096	.130274	.132476	.136956	.141533	.146205	.150969
	-.20	.116298	.120262	.124333	.126407	.128508	.130635	.132787	.134964	.137167	.141646	.146223	.150895	.155659
	-.30	.120988	.124952	.129023	.131097	.133198	.135325	.137477	.139654	.141857	.146336	.150913	.155585	.160349
	-.40	.125679	.129643	.133713	.135788	.137888	.140015	.142167	.144344	.146547	.151026	.155603	.160275	.165039
15	.40	.079671	.084462	.089405	.091931	.094494	.097092	.099724	.102390	.105088	.110578	.116189	.121912	.127740
	.30	.084361	.089152	.094095	.096622	.099184	.101782	.104414	.107080	.109778	.115268	.120879	.126602	.132431
	.20	.089051	.093842	.098785	.101312	.103874	.106472	.109104	.111770	.114468	.119959	.125569	.131292	.137121
	.10	.093742	.098532	.103475	.106002	.108564	.111162	.113794	.116460	.119158	.124649	.130259	.135982	.141811
	0.00	.098432	.103222	.108165	.110692	.113255	.115852	.118485	.121150	.123848	.129339	.134949	.140672	.146501
	-.10	.103122	.107912	.112855	.115382	.117945	.120543	.123175	.125840	.128538	.134029	.139639	.145362	.151191
	-.20	.107812	.112602	.117545	.120072	.122635	.125233	.127865	.130530	.133228	.138719	.144329	.150052	.155881
	-.30	.112502	.117292	.122235	.124762	.127325	.129923	.132555	.135220	.137919	.143409	.149019	.154743	.160571
	-.40	.117192	.121983	.126925	.129452	.132015	.134613	.137245	.139910	.142609	.148099	.153710	.159433	.165261
20	.40	.075557	.080797	.086208	.088973	.091776	.094616	.097491	.100400	.103340	.109310	.115389	.121566	.127829
	.30	.080247	.085487	.090898	.093663	.096467	.099306	.102181	.105090	.108030	.114000	.120079	.126256	.132519
	.20	.084937	.090177	.095588	.098353	.101157	.103997	.106872	.109780	.112720	.118690	.124769	.130946	.137209
	.10	.089627	.094867	.100278	.103043	.105847	.108687	.111562	.114470	.117410	.123380	.129459	.135636	.141899
	0.00	.094317	.099557	.104968	.107733	.110537	.113377	.116252	.119160	.122100	.128070	.134149	.140326	.146589
	-.10	.099007	.104248	.109658	.112423	.115227	.118067	.120942	.123850	.126790	.132760	.138839	.145016	.151280
	-.20	.103697	.108938	.114348	.117114	.119917	.122757	.125632	.128540	.131480	.137450	.143529	.149706	.155970
	-.30	.108387	.113628	.119038	.121804	.124607	.127447	.130322	.133230	.136171	.142140	.148220	.154396	.160660
	-.40	.113078	.118318	.123728	.126494	.129297	.132137	.135012	.137921	.140861	.146831	.152910	.159086	.165350
25	.40	.073187	.078723	.084434	.087350	.090303	.093291	.096311	.099362	.102442	.108677	.115002	.121404	.127869
	.30	.077877	.083413	.089124	.092040	.094993	.097981	.101002	.104052	.107132	.113367	.119693	.126094	.132559
	.20	.082567	.088103	.093814	.096730	.099683	.102671	.105692	.108742	.111822	.118057	.124383	.130784	.137249
	.10	.087257	.092793	.098504	.101420	.104373	.107361	.110382	.113433	.116512	.122747	.129073	.135474	.141939
	0.00	.091947	.097483	.103195	.106111	.109064	.112051	.115072	.118123	.121202	.127437	.133763	.140164	.146629
	-.10	.096637	.102173	.107885	.110801	.113754	.116741	.119762	.122813	.125892	.132128	.138453	.144854	.151319
	-.20	.101327	.106863	.112575	.115491	.118444	.121432	.124452	.127503	.130582	.136818	.143143	.149545	.156010
	-.30	.106017	.111553	.117265	.120181	.123134	.126122	.129142	.132193	.135272	.141508	.147833	.154235	.160700
	-.40	.110707	.116243	.121955	.124871	.127824	.130812	.133832	.136883	.139962	.146198	.152523	.158925	.165390
30	.40	.071684	.077436	.083361	.086381	.089436	.092522	.095637	.098779	.101945	.108339	.114804	.121324	.127888
	.30	.076375	.082126	.088051	.091071	.094126	.097212	.100328	.103469	.106635	.113029	.119494	.126014	.132578
	.20	.081065	.086816	.092741	.095761	.098816	.101902	.105018	.108159	.111325	.117720	.124184	.130704	.137268
	.10	.085755	.091506	.097431	.100451	.103506	.106592	.109708	.112850	.116015	.122410	.128874	.135394	.141958
	0.00	.090445	.096196	.102121	.105141	.108196	.111282	.114398	.117540	.120705	.127100	.133564	.140084	.146648
	-.10	.095135	.100886	.106811	.109831	.112886	.115973	.119088	.122230	.125396	.131790	.138254	.144775	.151338
	-.20	.099825	.105576	.111501	.114522	.117576	.120663	.123778	.126920	.130086	.136480	.142944	.149465	.156029
	-.30	.104515	.110266	.116191	.119212	.122266	.125353	.128468	.131610	.134776	.141170	.147635	.154155	.160719
	-.40	.109205	.114956	.120882	.123902	.126957	.130043	.133158	.136300	.139466	.145860	.152325	.158845	.165409

10.0 YEAR HOLDING PERIOD
.160 EQUITY YIELD RATE
.700 LOAN RATIO

INTEREST RATE

TERM YEARS	APPR DEP	5.0	6.0	7.0	7.5	8.0	8.5	9.0	9.5	10.0	11.0	12.0	13.0	14.0
10	.40	.085504	.089666	.093940	.096118	.098324	.100557	.102816	.105103	.107415	.112119	.116924	.121830	.126833
	.30	.090194	.094356	.098630	.100808	.103014	.105247	.107507	.109793	.112106	.116809	.121615	.126520	.131523
	.20	.094884	.099046	.103320	.105499	.107704	.109937	.112197	.114483	.116796	.121499	.126305	.131210	.136213
	.10	.099574	.103736	.108010	.110189	.112394	.114627	.116887	.119173	.121486	.126189	.130995	.135900	.140903
	0.00	.104264	.108426	.112700	.114879	.117084	.119317	.121577	.123863	.126176	.130879	.135685	.140590	.145593
	-.10	.108954	.113117	.117390	.119569	.121775	.124007	.126267	.128553	.130866	.135569	.140375	.145280	.150283
	-.20	.113644	.117807	.122081	.124259	.126465	.128697	.130957	.133243	.135556	.140259	.145065	.149970	.154973
	-.30	.118335	.122497	.126771	.128949	.131155	.133388	.135647	.137934	.140246	.144950	.149755	.154661	.159663
	-.40	.123025	.127187	.131461	.133639	.135845	.138078	.140337	.142624	.144936	.149640	.154445	.159351	.164353
15	.40	.076593	.081623	.086813	.089466	.092157	.094885	.097649	.100447	.103280	.109045	.114936	.120946	.127066
	.30	.081283	.086313	.091503	.094156	.096847	.099575	.102339	.105137	.107970	.113736	.119626	.125636	.131756
	.20	.085973	.091003	.096193	.098847	.101537	.104265	.107029	.109828	.112661	.118426	.124317	.130326	.136446
	.10	.090663	.095693	.100883	.103537	.106227	.108955	.111719	.114518	.117351	.123116	.129007	.135016	.141136
	0.00	.095354	.100384	.105573	.108227	.110918	.113645	.116409	.119208	.122041	.127806	.133697	.139706	.145826
	-.10	.100044	.105074	.110264	.112917	.115608	.118335	.121099	.123898	.126731	.132496	.138387	.144396	.150516
	-.20	.104734	.109764	.114954	.117607	.120298	.123025	.125789	.128588	.131421	.137186	.143077	.149086	.155206
	-.30	.109424	.114454	.119644	.122297	.124988	.127716	.130479	.133278	.136111	.141876	.147767	.153776	.159896
	-.40	.114114	.119144	.124334	.126987	.129678	.132406	.135169	.137968	.140801	.146566	.152457	.158466	.164586
20	.40	.072273	.077775	.083456	.086360	.089304	.092285	.095304	.098358	.101445	.107713	.114096	.120582	.127159
	.30	.076963	.082465	.088146	.091050	.093994	.096976	.099994	.103048	.106135	.112403	.118787	.125272	.131849
	.20	.081653	.087155	.092836	.095740	.098684	.101666	.104684	.107738	.110825	.117094	.123477	.129962	.136539
	.10	.086343	.091845	.097527	.100430	.103374	.106356	.109374	.112428	.115515	.121784	.128167	.134652	.141229
	0.00	.091033	.096536	.102217	.105120	.108064	.111046	.114065	.117118	.120205	.126474	.132857	.139342	.145919
	-.10	.095723	.101226	.106907	.109810	.112754	.115736	.118755	.121808	.124896	.131164	.137547	.144033	.150609
	-.20	.100414	.105916	.111597	.114501	.117444	.120426	.123445	.126499	.129586	.135854	.142237	.148723	.155299
	-.30	.105104	.110606	.116287	.119191	.122134	.125116	.128135	.131189	.134276	.140544	.146927	.153413	.159989
	-.40	.109794	.115296	.120977	.123881	.126824	.129806	.132825	.135879	.138966	.145234	.151617	.158103	.164679
25	.40	.069784	.075597	.081594	.084656	.087757	.090894	.094065	.097269	.100502	.107049	.113691	.120412	.127200
	.30	.074474	.080287	.086284	.089346	.092447	.095584	.098755	.101959	.105192	.111739	.118381	.125102	.131891
	.20	.079165	.084977	.090974	.094036	.097137	.100274	.103445	.106649	.109882	.116429	.123071	.129792	.136581
	.10	.083855	.089667	.095665	.098726	.101827	.104964	.108136	.111339	.114572	.121119	.127761	.134483	.141271
	0.00	.088545	.094357	.100355	.103416	.106517	.109654	.112826	.116029	.119262	.125809	.132451	.139173	.145961
	-.10	.093235	.099048	.105045	.108106	.111207	.114344	.117516	.120719	.123952	.130500	.137141	.143863	.150651
	-.20	.097925	.103738	.109735	.112797	.115897	.119034	.122206	.125409	.128642	.135190	.141831	.148553	.155341
	-.30	.102615	.108428	.114425	.117487	.120587	.123725	.126896	.130099	.133333	.139880	.146521	.153243	.160031
	-.40	.107305	.113118	.119115	.122177	.125277	.128415	.131586	.134789	.138023	.144570	.151212	.157933	.164721
30	.40	.068207	.074246	.080467	.083638	.086846	.090086	.093358	.096656	.099980	.106694	.113482	.120328	.127220
	.30	.072897	.078936	.085157	.088328	.091536	.094777	.098048	.101347	.104671	.111385	.118172	.125018	.131910
	.20	.077587	.083626	.089847	.093018	.096226	.099467	.102738	.106037	.109361	.116075	.122862	.129709	.136601
	.10	.082277	.088316	.094537	.097709	.100916	.104157	.107428	.110727	.114051	.120765	.127552	.134399	.141291
	0.00	.086967	.093006	.099228	.102399	.105606	.108847	.112118	.115417	.118741	.125455	.132243	.139089	.145981
	-.10	.091658	.097696	.103918	.107089	.110296	.113537	.116808	.120107	.123431	.130145	.136933	.143779	.150671
	-.20	.096348	.102386	.108608	.111779	.114986	.118227	.121498	.124797	.128121	.134835	.141623	.148469	.155361
	-.30	.101038	.107076	.113298	.116469	.119676	.122917	.126188	.129487	.132811	.139525	.146313	.153159	.160051
	-.40	.105728	.111767	.117988	.121159	.124367	.127607	.130878	.134177	.137501	.144215	.151003	.157849	.164741

```
10.0 YEAR HOLDING PERIOD
 .160 EQUITY YIELD RATE
 .750 LOAN RATIO
```

INTEREST RATE

TERM YEARS	APPR DEP	5.0	6.0	7.0	7.5	8.0	8.5	9.0	9.5	10.0	11.0	12.0	13.0	14.0
10	.40	.081523	.085982	.090561	.092895	.095259	.097651	.100072	.102522	.104999	.110039	.115188	.120443	.125804
	.30	.086213	.090672	.095251	.097585	.099949	.102341	.104762	.107212	.109690	.114729	.119878	.125134	.130494
	.20	.090903	.095362	.099942	.102276	.104640	.107031	.109452	.111902	.114380	.119419	.124568	.129824	.135184
	.10	.095593	.100053	.104632	.106966	.109329	.111721	.114142	.116592	.119070	.124109	.129258	.134514	.139874
	0.00	.100283	.104743	.109322	.111656	.114019	.116411	.118832	.121282	.123760	.128799	.133948	.139204	.144564
	-.10	.104973	.109433	.114012	.116346	.118709	.121101	.123522	.125972	.128450	.133489	.138638	.143894	.149254
	-.20	.109663	.114123	.118702	.121036	.123399	.125792	.128213	.130662	.133140	.138179	.143328	.148584	.153944
	-.30	.114353	.118813	.123392	.125726	.128089	.130482	.132903	.135352	.137830	.142870	.148018	.153274	.158634
	-.40	.119044	.123503	.128082	.130416	.132779	.135172	.137593	.140042	.142520	.147560	.152708	.157964	.163324
15	.40	.071976	.077365	.082926	.085768	.088651	.091574	.094535	.097534	.100569	.106746	.113057	.119496	.126053
	.30	.076666	.082055	.087616	.090458	.093341	.096264	.099225	.102224	.105259	.111436	.117748	.124186	.130743
	.20	.081356	.086745	.092306	.095148	.098031	.100954	.103915	.106914	.109949	.116126	.122438	.128876	.135433
	.10	.086046	.091435	.096996	.099839	.102722	.105644	.108605	.111604	.114639	.120816	.127128	.133566	.140123
	0.00	.090736	.096125	.101686	.104529	.107412	.110334	.113295	.116294	.119329	.125506	.131818	.138256	.144814
	-.10	.095426	.100815	.106376	.109219	.112102	.115024	.117985	.120984	.124020	.130196	.136508	.142946	.149504
	-.20	.100116	.105505	.111066	.113909	.116792	.119714	.122676	.125674	.128710	.134886	.141198	.147637	.154194
	-.30	.104806	.110196	.115756	.118599	.121482	.124405	.127366	.130364	.133400	.139577	.145888	.152327	.158884
	-.40	.109496	.114886	.120446	.123289	.126172	.129095	.132056	.135054	.138090	.144267	.150578	.157017	.163574
20	.40	.067347	.073242	.079329	.082440	.085594	.088789	.092023	.095295	.098603	.105319	.112158	.119106	.126153
	.30	.072037	.077932	.084019	.087130	.090284	.093479	.096713	.099985	.103293	.110009	.116848	.123797	.130843
	.20	.076727	.082622	.088709	.091820	.094974	.098169	.101403	.104675	.107983	.114699	.121538	.128487	.135533
	.10	.081417	.087312	.093399	.096510	.099664	.102859	.106093	.109365	.112673	.119389	.126228	.133177	.140223
	0.00	.086107	.092002	.098089	.101200	.104354	.107549	.110783	.114055	.117363	.124079	.130918	.137867	.144913
	-.10	.090797	.096693	.102779	.105890	.109044	.112239	.115474	.118745	.122053	.128769	.135608	.142557	.149603
	-.20	.095487	.101383	.107469	.110581	.113734	.116929	.120164	.123436	.126743	.133459	.140298	.147247	.154293
	-.30	.100177	.106073	.112160	.115271	.118425	.121619	.124854	.128126	.131433	.138149	.144988	.151937	.158984
	-.40	.104868	.110763	.116850	.119961	.123115	.126310	.129544	.132816	.136123	.142840	.149678	.156627	.163674
25	.40	.064680	.070908	.077334	.080614	.083936	.087298	.090696	.094128	.097592	.104607	.111723	.118925	.126198
	.30	.069371	.075598	.082024	.085304	.088626	.091988	.095386	.098818	.102282	.109297	.116413	.123615	.130888
	.20	.074061	.080289	.086714	.089994	.093317	.096678	.100076	.103508	.106972	.113987	.121103	.128305	.135578
	.10	.078751	.084979	.091404	.094685	.098007	.101368	.104766	.108198	.111662	.118677	.125793	.132995	.140268
	0.00	.083441	.089669	.096094	.099375	.102697	.106058	.109456	.112888	.116352	.123367	.130483	.137685	.144958
	-.10	.088131	.094359	.100784	.104065	.107387	.110748	.114146	.117578	.121043	.128057	.135173	.142375	.149648
	-.20	.092821	.099049	.105474	.108755	.112077	.115438	.118836	.122268	.125733	.132747	.139864	.147065	.154338
	-.30	.097511	.103739	.110165	.113445	.116767	.120128	.123526	.126959	.130423	.137438	.144554	.151755	.159028
	-.40	.102201	.108429	.114855	.118135	.121457	.124819	.128216	.131649	.135113	.142128	.149244	.156445	.163719
30	.40	.062990	.069460	.076126	.079524	.082960	.086433	.089937	.093472	.097033	.104227	.111499	.118835	.126219
	.30	.067681	.074151	.080816	.084214	.087651	.091123	.094628	.098162	.101723	.108917	.116190	.123525	.130909
	.20	.072371	.078841	.085506	.088904	.092341	.095813	.099318	.102852	.106414	.113607	.120880	.128215	.135599
	.10	.077061	.083531	.090197	.093594	.097031	.100503	.104008	.107542	.111104	.118297	.125570	.132905	.140289
	0.00	.081751	.088221	.094887	.098284	.101721	.105193	.108698	.112232	.115794	.122987	.130260	.137595	.144979
	-.10	.086441	.092911	.099577	.102974	.106411	.109883	.113388	.116922	.120484	.127678	.134950	.142285	.149670
	-.20	.091131	.097601	.104267	.107665	.111101	.114573	.118078	.121613	.125174	.132368	.139640	.146975	.154360
	-.30	.095821	.102291	.108957	.112355	.115791	.119263	.122768	.126303	.129864	.137058	.144330	.151665	.159050
	-.40	.100511	.106981	.113647	.117045	.120481	.123953	.127458	.130993	.134554	.141748	.149020	.156356	.163740

10.0 YEAR HOLDING PERIOD
.160 EQUITY YIELD RATE
.800 LOAN RATIO

INTEREST RATE

TERM YEARS	APPR DEP	5.0	6.0	7.0	7.5	8.0	8.5	9.0	9.5	10.0	11.0	12.0	13.0	14.0
10	.40	.077542	.082298	.087183	.089672	.092193	.094745	.097327	.099940	.102583	.107959	.113451	.119057	.124774
	.30	.082232	.086988	.091873	.094363	.096883	.099435	.102018	.104630	.107274	.112649	.118141	.123747	.129465
	.20	.086922	.091679	.096563	.099053	.101573	.104125	.106708	.109321	.111964	.117339	.122831	.128437	.134155
	.10	.091612	.096369	.101253	.103743	.106264	.108815	.111398	.114011	.116654	.122029	.127521	.133127	.138845
	0.00	.096302	.101059	.105943	.108433	.110954	.113505	.116088	.118701	.121344	.126719	.132211	.137817	.143535
	-.10	.100992	.105749	.110633	.113123	.115644	.118196	.120778	.123391	.126034	.131409	.136901	.142508	.148225
	-.20	.105682	.110439	.115323	.117813	.120334	.122886	.125468	.128081	.130724	.136099	.141591	.147198	.152915
	-.30	.110372	.115129	.120014	.122503	.125024	.127576	.130158	.132771	.135414	.140789	.146282	.151888	.157605
	-.40	.115062	.119819	.124704	.127193	.129714	.132266	.134848	.137461	.140104	.145480	.150972	.156578	.162295
15	.40	.067358	.073106	.079038	.082070	.085145	.088263	.091421	.094620	.097858	.104446	.111179	.118046	.125041
	.30	.072048	.077797	.083728	.086760	.089835	.092953	.096111	.099310	.102548	.109136	.115869	.122736	.129731
	.20	.076738	.082487	.088418	.091450	.094526	.097643	.100801	.104000	.107238	.113826	.120559	.127427	.134421
	.10	.081428	.087177	.093108	.096140	.099216	.102333	.105492	.108690	.111928	.118517	.125249	.132117	.139111
	0.00	.086118	.091867	.097798	.100831	.103906	.107023	.110182	.113380	.116618	.123207	.129939	.136807	.143801
	-.10	.090808	.096557	.102488	.105521	.108596	.111713	.114872	.118070	.121308	.127897	.134629	.141497	.148491
	-.20	.095499	.101247	.107179	.110211	.113286	.116403	.119562	.122761	.125998	.132587	.139319	.146187	.153181
	-.30	.100189	.105937	.111869	.114901	.117976	.121093	.124252	.127451	.130688	.137277	.144009	.150877	.157871
	-.40	.104879	.110627	.116559	.119591	.122666	.125784	.128942	.132141	.135378	.141967	.148700	.155567	.162562
20	.40	.062421	.068709	.075201	.078520	.081884	.085292	.088742	.092232	.095760	.102924	.110219	.117631	.125147
	.30	.067111	.073399	.079892	.083210	.086574	.089982	.093432	.096922	.100450	.107614	.114909	.122321	.129837
	.20	.071801	.078089	.084582	.087900	.091264	.094672	.098122	.101612	.105140	.112304	.119599	.127011	.134527
	.10	.076491	.082779	.089272	.092590	.095954	.099362	.102812	.106302	.109830	.116994	.124289	.131701	.139217
	0.00	.081181	.087469	.093962	.097280	.100645	.104052	.107502	.110992	.114521	.121684	.128979	.136391	.143907
	-.10	.085871	.092159	.098652	.101970	.105335	.108743	.112192	.115682	.119211	.126374	.133669	.141081	.148598
	-.20	.090561	.096849	.103342	.106661	.110025	.113433	.116883	.120373	.123901	.131065	.138359	.145772	.153288
	-.30	.095251	.101540	.108032	.111351	.114715	.118123	.121573	.125063	.128591	.135755	.143050	.150462	.157978
	-.40	.099941	.106230	.112722	.116041	.119405	.122813	.126263	.129753	.133281	.140445	.147740	.155152	.162668
25	.40	.059576	.066220	.073073	.076573	.080016	.083702	.087326	.090987	.094682	.102165	.109755	.117437	.125195
	.30	.064267	.070910	.077764	.081263	.084806	.088392	.092016	.095677	.099372	.106855	.114445	.122127	.129885
	.20	.068957	.075600	.082454	.085953	.089496	.093082	.096706	.100367	.104062	.111545	.119135	.126817	.134575
	.10	.073647	.080290	.087144	.090643	.094186	.097772	.101396	.105057	.108752	.116235	.123826	.131507	.139265
	0.00	.078337	.084980	.091834	.095333	.098877	.102462	.106086	.109748	.113443	.120925	.128516	.136197	.143955
	-.10	.083027	.089670	.096524	.100023	.103567	.107152	.110777	.114438	.118133	.125615	.133206	.140887	.148645
	-.20	.087717	.094360	.101214	.104713	.108257	.111842	.115467	.119128	.122823	.130305	.137896	.145578	.153336
	-.30	.092407	.099050	.105904	.109403	.112947	.116532	.120157	.123818	.127513	.134995	.142586	.150268	.158026
	-.40	.097097	.103740	.110594	.114093	.117637	.121222	.124847	.128508	.132203	.139686	.147276	.154958	.162716
30	.40	.057774	.064675	.071785	.075410	.079075	.082779	.086517	.090287	.094086	.101759	.109517	.117341	.125218
	.30	.062464	.069365	.076475	.080100	.083765	.087469	.091207	.094978	.098776	.106450	.114207	.122031	.129908
	.20	.067154	.074055	.081166	.084790	.088455	.092159	.095898	.099668	.103467	.111140	.118897	.126721	.134598
	.10	.071844	.078745	.085856	.089480	.093145	.096849	.100588	.104358	.108157	.115830	.123587	.131411	.139288
	0.00	.076534	.083436	.090546	.094170	.097836	.101539	.105278	.109048	.112847	.120520	.128277	.136101	.143978
	-.10	.081224	.088126	.095236	.098860	.102526	.106229	.109968	.113738	.117537	.125210	.132967	.140792	.148668
	-.20	.085914	.092816	.099926	.103550	.107216	.110919	.114658	.118428	.122227	.129900	.137657	.145482	.153358
	-.30	.090605	.097506	.104616	.108240	.111906	.115610	.119348	.123118	.126917	.134590	.142348	.150172	.158048
	-.40	.095295	.102196	.109306	.112930	.116596	.120300	.124038	.127808	.131607	.139280	.147038	.154862	.162738

10.0 YEAR HOLDING PERIOD
.160 EQUITY YIELD RATE
.900 LOAN RATIO

INTEREST RATE

TERM YEARS	APPR DEP	5.0	6.0	7.0	7.5	8.0	8.5	9.0	9.5	10.0	11.0	12.0	13.0	14.0
10	.40	.069579	.074931	.080426	.083227	.086062	.088933	.091838	.094778	.097751	.103799	.109977	.116284	.122716
	.30	.074269	.079621	.085116	.087917	.090753	.093623	.096529	.099468	.102441	.108489	.114667	.120974	.127406
	.20	.078960	.084311	.089806	.092607	.095443	.098313	.101219	.104158	.107132	.113179	.119357	.125664	.132097
	.10	.083650	.089001	.094496	.097297	.100133	.103003	.105909	.108848	.111822	.117869	.124048	.130355	.136787
	0.00	.088340	.093691	.099186	.101987	.104823	.107694	.110599	.113538	.116512	.122559	.128738	.135045	.141467
	-.10	.093030	.098381	.103876	.106677	.109513	.112384	.115289	.118228	.121202	.127249	.133428	.139735	.146167
	-.20	.097720	.103071	.108566	.111367	.114203	.117074	.119979	.122919	.125892	.131939	.138118	.144425	.150857
	-.30	.102410	.107761	.113257	.116057	.118893	.121764	.124669	.127609	.130582	.136629	.142808	.149115	.155547
	-.40	.107100	.112452	.117947	.120747	.123583	.126454	.129359	.132299	.135272	.141319	.147498	.153805	.160237
15	.40	.058123	.064590	.071263	.074674	.078134	.081641	.085194	.088792	.092435	.099847	.107421	.115147	.123016
	.30	.062813	.069280	.075953	.079364	.082824	.086331	.089884	.093483	.097125	.104537	.112111	.119837	.127706
	.20	.067503	.073970	.080643	.084054	.087514	.091021	.094574	.098173	.101815	.109227	.116801	.124527	.132396
	.10	.072193	.078660	.085333	.088744	.092204	.095711	.099264	.102863	.106505	.113917	.121491	.129218	.137086
	0.00	.076883	.083350	.090023	.093434	.096894	.100401	.103954	.107553	.111195	.118608	.126182	.133908	.141776
	-.10	.081573	.088040	.094713	.098124	.101584	.105091	.108644	.112243	.115885	.123298	.130872	.138598	.146466
	-.20	.086263	.092730	.099403	.102815	.106274	.109781	.113335	.116933	.120576	.127988	.135562	.143288	.151156
	-.30	.090953	.097421	.104093	.107505	.110964	.114471	.118025	.121623	.125266	.132678	.140252	.147978	.155847
	-.40	.095644	.102111	.108784	.112195	.115654	.119161	.122715	.126313	.129956	.137368	.144942	.152668	.160537
20	.40	.052568	.059642	.066947	.070680	.074465	.078299	.082180	.086106	.090075	.098134	.106341	.114680	.123135
	.30	.057258	.064333	.071637	.075370	.079155	.082969	.086870	.090796	.094765	.102825	.111031	.119370	.127825
	.20	.061948	.069023	.076327	.080060	.083845	.087679	.091560	.095486	.099455	.107515	.115721	.124060	.132516
	.10	.066638	.073713	.081017	.084750	.088535	.092369	.096270	.100176	.104146	.112205	.120412	.128750	.137206
	0.00	.071329	.078403	.085707	.089440	.093225	.097059	.100940	.104866	.108836	.116895	.125102	.133440	.141896
	-.10	.076019	.083093	.090397	.094131	.097915	.101749	.105630	.109556	.113526	.121585	.129792	.138130	.146586
	-.20	.080709	.087783	.095087	.098821	.102605	.106439	.110320	.114247	.118216	.126275	.134482	.142821	.151276
	-.30	.085399	.092473	.099777	.103511	.107295	.111129	.115010	.118937	.122906	.130965	.139172	.147511	.155966
	-.40	.090089	.097163	.104468	.108201	.111985	.115819	.119701	.123627	.127596	.135655	.143862	.152201	.160656
25	.40	.049369	.056842	.064553	.068489	.072476	.076509	.080587	.084706	.088862	.097280	.105820	.114462	.123189
	.30	.054059	.061532	.069243	.073179	.077166	.081199	.085277	.089396	.093553	.101970	.110510	.119152	.127879
	.20	.058749	.066222	.073933	.077869	.081856	.085889	.089967	.094086	.098243	.106660	.115200	.123842	.132570
	.10	.063439	.070912	.078623	.082560	.086546	.090580	.094657	.098776	.102933	.111351	.119890	.128532	.137260
	0.00	.068129	.075602	.083313	.087250	.091236	.095270	.099347	.103466	.107623	.116041	.124580	.133222	.141950
	-.10	.072819	.080293	.088003	.091940	.095926	.099960	.104037	.108156	.112313	.120731	.129270	.137912	.146640
	-.20	.077509	.084983	.092693	.096630	.100616	.104650	.108727	.112846	.117003	.125421	.133960	.142602	.151330
	-.30	.082199	.089673	.097383	.101320	.105306	.109340	.113418	.117536	.121693	.130111	.138650	.147292	.156020
	-.40	.086889	.094363	.102074	.106010	.109997	.114030	.118108	.122226	.126383	.134801	.143340	.151982	.160710
30	.40	.047341	.055105	.063104	.067181	.071305	.075471	.079677	.083918	.088192	.096824	.105551	.114354	.123215
	.30	.052031	.059795	.067794	.071871	.075995	.080161	.084367	.088609	.092882	.101515	.110242	.119044	.127905
	.20	.056721	.064485	.072484	.076561	.080685	.084851	.089057	.093299	.097572	.106205	.114932	.123734	.132595
	.10	.061411	.069175	.077174	.081251	.085375	.089542	.093747	.097989	.102262	.110895	.119622	.128424	.137285
	0.00	.066101	.073865	.081864	.085941	.090065	.094232	.098437	.102679	.106952	.115585	.124312	.133114	.141975
	-.10	.070791	.078555	.086554	.090631	.094755	.098922	.103128	.107369	.111643	.120275	.129002	.137804	.146665
	-.20	.075481	.083245	.091244	.095321	.099445	.103612	.107818	.112059	.116333	.124965	.133692	.142494	.151356
	-.30	.080171	.087935	.095934	.100011	.104135	.108302	.112508	.116749	.121023	.129625	.138382	.147184	.156046
	-.40	.084861	.092625	.100624	.104702	.108825	.112992	.117198	.121439	.125713	.134345	.143072	.151875	.160736

10.0 YEAR HOLDING PERIOD
.180 EQUITY YIELD RATE
.600 LOAN RATIO

INTEREST RATE

TERM YEARS	APPR DEP	5.0	6.0	7.0	7.5	8.0	8.5	9.0	9.5	10.0	11.0	12.0	13.0	14.0
10	.40	.105853	.109420	.113083	.114951	.116841	.118755	.120692	.122652	.124634	.128665	.132784	.136989	.141277
	.30	.110104	.113672	.117335	.119202	.121093	.123007	.124943	.126903	.128885	.132917	.137036	.141241	.145529
	.20	.114355	.117923	.121586	.123454	.125344	.127258	.129195	.131155	.133137	.137168	.141287	.145492	.149780
	.10	.118607	.122175	.125838	.127705	.129596	.131509	.133446	.135406	.137388	.141420	.145539	.149743	.154032
	0.00	.122858	.126426	.130089	.131956	.133847	.135761	.137698	.139657	.141640	.145671	.149790	.153995	.158283
	-.10	.127110	.130677	.134341	.136208	.138099	.140012	.141949	.143909	.145891	.149923	.154042	.158246	.162535
	-.20	.131361	.134929	.138592	.140459	.142350	.144264	.146201	.148160	.150143	.154174	.158293	.162498	.166786
	-.30	.135613	.139180	.142844	.144711	.146601	.148515	.150452	.152412	.154394	.158426	.162545	.166749	.171037
	-.40	.139864	.143432	.147095	.148962	.150853	.152767	.154704	.156663	.158646	.162677	.166796	.171001	.175289
15	.40	.097112	.101377	.105780	.108031	.110315	.112630	.114976	.117353	.119758	.124655	.129660	.134768	.139971
	.30	.101363	.105629	.110032	.112283	.114566	.116882	.119228	.121604	.124010	.128907	.133912	.139019	.144222
	.20	.105615	.109880	.114283	.116534	.118818	.121133	.123479	.125856	.128261	.133158	.138163	.143271	.148473
	.10	.109866	.114132	.118534	.120786	.123069	.125385	.127731	.130107	.132513	.137410	.142415	.147522	.152725
	0.00	.114118	.118383	.122786	.125037	.127321	.129636	.131982	.134359	.136764	.141661	.146666	.151773	.156976
	-.10	.118369	.122635	.127037	.129289	.131572	.133887	.136234	.138610	.141016	.145913	.150918	.156025	.161228
	-.20	.122621	.126886	.131289	.133540	.135824	.138139	.140485	.142861	.145267	.150164	.155169	.160276	.165479
	-.30	.126872	.131138	.135540	.137792	.140075	.142390	.144737	.147113	.149519	.154416	.159421	.164528	.169731
	-.40	.131124	.135389	.139792	.142043	.144327	.146642	.148988	.151364	.153770	.158667	.163672	.168779	.173982
20	.40	.092874	.097530	.102340	.104800	.107295	.109823	.112383	.114974	.117595	.122917	.128341	.133854	.139449
	.30	.097126	.101781	.106591	.109052	.111546	.114075	.116635	.119226	.121846	.127169	.132592	.138106	.143700
	.20	.101377	.106033	.110843	.113303	.115798	.118326	.120886	.123477	.126097	.131420	.136844	.142357	.147952
	.10	.105629	.110284	.115094	.117555	.120049	.122578	.125138	.127729	.130349	.135672	.141095	.146609	.152203
	0.00	.109880	.114535	.119346	.121806	.124301	.126829	.129389	.131980	.134600	.139923	.145346	.150860	.156455
	-.10	.114131	.118787	.123597	.126058	.128552	.131081	.133641	.136232	.138852	.144174	.149598	.155112	.160706
	-.20	.118383	.123038	.127849	.130309	.132804	.135332	.137892	.140483	.143103	.148426	.153849	.159363	.164957
	-.30	.122634	.127290	.132100	.134560	.137055	.139583	.142144	.144735	.147355	.152677	.158101	.163615	.169209
	-.40	.126886	.131541	.136352	.138812	.141307	.143835	.146395	.148986	.151606	.156929	.162352	.167866	.173460
25	.40	.090433	.095352	.100432	.103028	.105658	.108320	.111013	.113735	.116482	.122050	.127703	.133428	.139214
	.30	.094685	.099603	.104683	.107279	.109900	.112572	.115265	.117986	.120734	.126302	.131955	.137679	.143465
	.20	.098936	.103854	.108935	.111531	.114161	.116823	.119516	.122237	.124985	.130553	.136206	.141931	.147716
	.10	.103187	.108106	.113186	.115782	.118412	.121075	.123768	.126489	.129237	.134805	.140457	.146182	.151968
	0.00	.107439	.112357	.117438	.120034	.122664	.125326	.128019	.130740	.133488	.139056	.144709	.150434	.156219
	-.10	.111690	.116609	.121689	.124285	.126915	.129578	.132271	.134992	.137740	.143308	.148960	.154685	.160471
	-.20	.115942	.120860	.125941	.128536	.131167	.133829	.136522	.139243	.141991	.147559	.153212	.158937	.164722
	-.30	.120193	.125112	.130192	.132788	.135418	.138081	.140774	.143495	.146243	.151811	.157463	.163188	.168974
	-.40	.124445	.129363	.134444	.137039	.139670	.142332	.145025	.147746	.150494	.156062	.161715	.167440	.173225
30	.40	.088886	.094000	.099277	.101969	.104694	.107449	.110231	.113038	.115868	.121588	.127375	.133217	.139102
	.30	.093137	.098252	.103528	.106221	.108945	.111700	.114482	.117289	.120119	.125839	.131627	.137469	.143353
	.20	.097389	.102503	.107780	.110472	.113197	.115951	.118734	.121541	.124371	.130091	.135878	.141720	.147605
	.10	.101640	.106755	.112031	.114724	.117448	.120203	.122985	.125792	.128622	.134342	.140130	.145971	.151856
	0.00	.105892	.111006	.116283	.118975	.121700	.124454	.127236	.130044	.132874	.138594	.144381	.150223	.156108
	-.10	.110143	.115258	.120534	.123226	.125951	.128706	.131488	.134295	.137125	.142845	.148633	.154474	.160359
	-.20	.114395	.119509	.124786	.127478	.130203	.132957	.135739	.138547	.141376	.147096	.152884	.158726	.164611
	-.30	.118646	.123760	.129037	.131729	.134454	.137209	.139991	.142798	.145628	.151348	.157136	.162977	.168862
	-.40	.122898	.128012	.133289	.135981	.138706	.141460	.144242	.147049	.149879	.155599	.161387	.167229	.173114

10.0 YEAR HOLDING PERIOD
.180 EQUITY YIELD RATE
.667 LOAN RATIO

INTEREST RATE

TERM YEARS	APPR DEP	5.0	6.0	7.0	7.5	8.0	8.5	9.0	9.5	10.0	11.0	12.0	13.0	14.0
10	.40	.099503	.103467	.107538	.109612	.111713	.113839	.115991	.118169	.120371	.124851	.129428	.134099	.138864
	.30	.103755	.107719	.111789	.113864	.115964	.118091	.120243	.122420	.124623	.129102	.133679	.138351	.143116
	.20	.108006	.111970	.116040	.118115	.120216	.122342	.124494	.126672	.128874	.133354	.137931	.142602	.147367
	.10	.112258	.116222	.120292	.122367	.124467	.126594	.128746	.130923	.133126	.137605	.142182	.146854	.151618
	0.00	.116509	.120473	.124543	.126618	.128719	.130845	.132997	.135175	.137377	.141857	.146433	.151105	.155870
	-.10	.120760	.124724	.128795	.130870	.132970	.135097	.137249	.139426	.141629	.146108	.150685	.155357	.160121
	-.20	.125012	.128976	.133046	.135121	.137222	.139348	.141500	.143678	.145880	.150360	.154936	.159608	.164373
	-.30	.129263	.133227	.137298	.139372	.141473	.143600	.145752	.147929	.150132	.154611	.159188	.163860	.168624
	-.40	.133515	.137479	.141549	.143624	.145725	.147851	.150003	.152181	.154383	.158863	.163439	.168111	.172876
15	.40	.089791	.094531	.099423	.101924	.104461	.107034	.109641	.112281	.114954	.120395	.125956	.131631	.137412
	.30	.094043	.098782	.103674	.106176	.108713	.111285	.113892	.116533	.119206	.124647	.130208	.135883	.141664
	.20	.098294	.103034	.107926	.110427	.112964	.115537	.118144	.120784	.123457	.128898	.134459	.140134	.145915
	.10	.102546	.107285	.112177	.114679	.117216	.119788	.122395	.125036	.127709	.133149	.138711	.144386	.150167
	0.00	.106797	.111537	.116429	.118930	.121467	.124040	.126647	.129287	.131960	.137401	.142962	.148637	.154418
	-.10	.111049	.115788	.120680	.123181	.125719	.128291	.130898	.133538	.136212	.141652	.147214	.152888	.158670
	-.20	.115300	.120040	.124931	.127433	.129970	.132543	.135150	.137790	.140463	.145904	.151465	.157140	.162921
	-.30	.119552	.124291	.129183	.131684	.134222	.136794	.139401	.142041	.144714	.150155	.155717	.161391	.167172
	-.40	.123803	.128542	.133434	.135936	.138473	.141046	.143652	.146293	.148966	.154407	.159968	.165643	.171424
20	.40	.085083	.090255	.095600	.098334	.101106	.103915	.106760	.109639	.112550	.118464	.124490	.130617	.136832
	.30	.089334	.094507	.099852	.102585	.105357	.108166	.111011	.113890	.116801	.122715	.128741	.134868	.141084
	.20	.093586	.098758	.104103	.106837	.109609	.112418	.115263	.118142	.121053	.126967	.132993	.139119	.145335
	.10	.097837	.103010	.108355	.111088	.113860	.116669	.119514	.122393	.125304	.131218	.137244	.143371	.149587
	0.00	.102088	.107261	.112606	.115340	.118112	.120921	.123766	.126644	.129556	.135470	.141496	.147622	.153838
	-.10	.106340	.111513	.116858	.119591	.122363	.125172	.128017	.130896	.133807	.139721	.145747	.151874	.158090
	-.20	.110591	.115764	.121109	.123843	.126615	.129424	.132269	.135147	.138059	.143973	.149999	.156125	.162341
	-.30	.114843	.120016	.125361	.128094	.130866	.133675	.136520	.139399	.142310	.148224	.154250	.160377	.166593
	-.40	.119094	.124267	.129612	.132345	.135118	.137927	.140771	.143650	.146562	.152476	.158502	.164628	.170844
25	.40	.082370	.087835	.093480	.096364	.099287	.102245	.105237	.108261	.111314	.117501	.123782	.130143	.136571
	.30	.086622	.092087	.097732	.100616	.103538	.106497	.109489	.112512	.115566	.121752	.128033	.134394	.140823
	.20	.090873	.096338	.101983	.104867	.107790	.110748	.113740	.116764	.119817	.126004	.132285	.138646	.145074
	.10	.095125	.100590	.106235	.109119	.112041	.115000	.117992	.121015	.124069	.130255	.136536	.142897	.149326
	0.00	.099376	.104841	.110486	.113370	.116293	.119251	.122243	.125267	.128320	.134507	.140788	.147149	.153577
	-.10	.103628	.109093	.114737	.117622	.120544	.123503	.126495	.129518	.132571	.138758	.145039	.151400	.157828
	-.20	.107879	.113344	.118989	.121873	.124796	.127754	.130746	.133770	.136823	.143010	.149290	.155651	.162080
	-.30	.112131	.117596	.123240	.126125	.129047	.132005	.134998	.138021	.141074	.147261	.153542	.159903	.166331
	-.40	.116382	.121847	.127492	.130376	.133299	.136257	.139249	.142273	.145326	.151512	.157793	.164154	.170583
30	.40	.080651	.086334	.092197	.095188	.098216	.101277	.104368	.107487	.110631	.116987	.123417	.129908	.136447
	.30	.084903	.090585	.096448	.099440	.102467	.105528	.108619	.111738	.114883	.121238	.127669	.134160	.140698
	.20	.089154	.094837	.100700	.103691	.106719	.109779	.112871	.115990	.119134	.125490	.131920	.138411	.144950
	.10	.093406	.099088	.104951	.107943	.110970	.114031	.117122	.120241	.123386	.129741	.136172	.142663	.149201
	0.00	.097657	.103340	.109203	.112194	.115222	.118282	.121374	.124493	.127637	.133993	.140423	.146914	.153453
	-.10	.101909	.107591	.113454	.116446	.119473	.122534	.125625	.128744	.131888	.138244	.144675	.151166	.157704
	-.20	.106160	.111843	.117706	.120697	.123725	.126785	.129877	.132996	.136140	.142496	.148926	.155417	.161956
	-.30	.110411	.116094	.121957	.124949	.127976	.131037	.134128	.137247	.140391	.146747	.153178	.159669	.166207
	-.40	.114663	.120346	.126208	.129200	.132227	.135288	.138379	.141498	.144643	.150998	.157429	.163920	.170459

10.0 YEAR HOLDING PERIOD
.180 EQUITY YIELD RATE
.700 LOAN RATIO

INTEREST RATE

TERM YEARS	APPR DEP	5.0	6.0	7.0	7.5	8.0	8.5	9.0	9.5	10.0	11.0	12.0	13.0	14.0
10	.40	.096329	.100491	.104765	.106943	.109149	.111382	.113642	.115928	.118241	.122944	.127749	.132655	.137658
	.30	.100580	.104743	.109016	.111195	.113401	.115633	.117893	.120179	.122492	.127195	.132001	.136906	.141909
	.20	.104832	.108994	.113268	.115446	.117652	.119885	.122144	.124431	.126743	.131447	.136252	.141158	.146161
	.10	.109083	.113246	.117519	.119698	.121903	.124136	.126396	.128682	.130995	.135698	.140504	.145409	.150412
	0.00	.113335	.117497	.121771	.123949	.126155	.128388	.130647	.132934	.135246	.139950	.144755	.149661	.154664
	-.10	.117586	.121748	.126022	.128201	.130406	.132639	.134899	.137185	.139498	.144201	.149007	.153912	.158915
	-.20	.121838	.126000	.130274	.132452	.134658	.136891	.139150	.141437	.143749	.148453	.153258	.158164	.163166
	-.30	.126089	.130251	.134525	.136704	.138909	.141142	.143402	.145688	.148001	.152704	.157510	.162415	.167418
	-.40	.130341	.134503	.138777	.140955	.143161	.145394	.147653	.149940	.152252	.156956	.161761	.166667	.171669
15	.40	.086132	.091108	.096244	.098871	.101535	.104236	.106973	.109746	.112552	.118265	.124105	.130063	.136133
	.30	.090383	.095359	.100496	.103122	.105787	.108488	.111225	.113997	.116804	.122517	.128356	.134315	.140385
	.20	.094634	.099611	.104747	.107374	.110038	.112739	.115476	.118249	.121055	.126768	.132608	.138566	.144636
	.10	.098886	.103862	.108999	.111625	.114289	.116991	.119728	.122500	.125307	.131020	.136859	.142818	.148888
	0.00	.103137	.108114	.113250	.115877	.118541	.121242	.123979	.126752	.129558	.135271	.141111	.147069	.153139
	-.10	.107389	.112365	.117502	.120128	.122792	.125493	.128231	.131003	.133810	.139523	.145362	.151320	.157391
	-.20	.111640	.116617	.121753	.124380	.127044	.129745	.132482	.135255	.138061	.143774	.149614	.155572	.161642
	-.30	.115892	.120868	.126005	.128631	.131295	.133996	.136734	.139506	.142313	.148026	.153865	.159823	.165893
	-.40	.120143	.125120	.130256	.132883	.135547	.138248	.140985	.143757	.146564	.152277	.158116	.164075	.170145
20	.40	.081187	.086619	.092231	.095101	.098012	.100961	.103948	.106971	.110028	.116238	.122565	.128998	.135524
	.30	.085439	.090870	.096482	.099353	.102263	.105213	.108200	.111223	.114279	.120489	.126816	.133249	.139776
	.20	.089690	.095122	.100734	.103604	.106515	.109464	.112451	.115474	.118531	.124741	.131068	.137501	.144027
	.10	.093942	.099373	.104985	.107856	.110766	.113716	.116703	.119725	.122782	.128992	.135319	.141752	.148279
	0.00	.098193	.103625	.109237	.112107	.115018	.117967	.120954	.123977	.127034	.133244	.139571	.146004	.152530
	-.10	.102445	.107876	.113488	.116358	.119269	.122219	.125206	.128228	.131285	.137495	.143822	.150255	.156782
	-.20	.106696	.112128	.117740	.120610	.123521	.126470	.129457	.132480	.135537	.141746	.148074	.154507	.161033
	-.30	.110948	.116379	.121991	.124861	.127772	.130722	.133709	.136731	.139788	.145998	.152325	.158758	.165285
	-.40	.115199	.120631	.126243	.129113	.132023	.134973	.137960	.140983	.144040	.150249	.156577	.163010	.169536
25	.40	.078340	.084078	.090005	.093033	.096102	.099208	.102350	.105525	.108730	.115226	.121821	.128500	.135250
	.30	.082591	.088329	.094256	.097285	.100353	.103460	.106601	.109776	.112982	.119478	.126073	.132752	.139502
	.20	.086842	.092581	.098508	.101536	.104605	.107711	.110853	.114028	.117233	.123729	.130324	.137003	.143753
	.10	.091094	.096832	.102759	.105788	.108856	.111962	.115104	.118279	.121485	.127981	.134576	.141255	.148005
	0.00	.095345	.101084	.107011	.110039	.113108	.116214	.119356	.122530	.125736	.132232	.138827	.145506	.152256
	-.10	.099597	.105335	.111262	.114291	.117359	.120465	.123607	.126782	.129988	.136484	.143079	.149758	.156507
	-.20	.103848	.109587	.115514	.118542	.121611	.124717	.127859	.131033	.134239	.140735	.147330	.154009	.160759
	-.30	.108100	.113838	.119765	.122794	.125862	.128968	.132110	.135285	.138491	.144987	.151581	.158261	.165010
	-.40	.112351	.118089	.124017	.127045	.130114	.133220	.136362	.139536	.142742	.149238	.155833	.162512	.169262
30	.40	.076535	.082501	.088657	.091798	.094977	.098191	.101437	.104712	.108013	.114687	.121439	.128254	.135120
	.30	.080786	.086753	.092909	.096050	.099229	.102442	.105688	.108963	.112265	.118938	.125690	.132506	.139371
	.20	.085037	.091004	.097160	.100301	.103480	.106694	.109940	.113215	.116516	.123190	.129942	.136757	.143623
	.10	.089289	.095256	.101412	.104553	.107732	.110945	.114191	.117466	.120768	.127441	.134193	.141009	.147874
	0.00	.093540	.099507	.105663	.108804	.111983	.115197	.118443	.121718	.125019	.131692	.138445	.145260	.152126
	-.10	.097792	.103759	.109915	.113056	.116235	.119448	.122694	.125969	.129271	.135944	.142696	.149512	.156377
	-.20	.102043	.108010	.114166	.117307	.120486	.123700	.126945	.130220	.133522	.140195	.146948	.153763	.160629
	-.30	.106295	.112261	.118418	.121559	.124737	.127951	.131197	.134472	.137774	.144447	.151199	.158014	.164880
	-.40	.110546	.116513	.122669	.125810	.128989	.132203	.135448	.138723	.142025	.148698	.155450	.162266	.169131

10.0 YEAR HOLDING PERIOD
.180 EQUITY YIELD RATE
.750 LOAN RATIO

INTEREST RATE

TERM YEARS	APPR DEP	5.0	6.0	7.0	7.5	8.0	8.5	9.0	9.5	10.0	11.0	12.0	13.0	14.0
10	.40	.091567	.096027	.100606	.102940	.105303	.107695	.110116	.112566	.115044	.120083	.125232	.130488	.135848
	.30	.095819	.100278	.104857	.107191	.109554	.111947	.114368	.116817	.119295	.124335	.129483	.134739	.140099
	.20	.100070	.104530	.109109	.111443	.113806	.116198	.118619	.121069	.123547	.128586	.133735	.138991	.144351
	.10	.104322	.108781	.113360	.115694	.118057	.120450	.122871	.125320	.127798	.132838	.137986	.143242	.148602
	0.00	.108573	.113032	.117612	.119946	.122309	.124701	.127122	.129572	.132050	.137089	.142238	.147494	.152854
	-.10	.112824	.117284	.121863	.124197	.126560	.128953	.131374	.133823	.136301	.141340	.146489	.151745	.157105
	-.20	.117076	.121535	.126115	.128449	.130812	.133204	.135625	.138075	.140553	.145592	.150741	.155997	.161357
	-.30	.121327	.125787	.130366	.132700	.135063	.137456	.139877	.142326	.144804	.149843	.154992	.160248	.165608
	-.40	.125579	.130038	.134618	.136951	.139315	.141707	.144128	.146578	.149056	.154095	.159244	.164500	.169860
15	.40	.080641	.085973	.091477	.094291	.097145	.100039	.102972	.105942	.108949	.115070	.121327	.127711	.134215
	.30	.084893	.090225	.095728	.098542	.101397	.104291	.107223	.110194	.113201	.119322	.125578	.131962	.138466
	.20	.089144	.094476	.099980	.102794	.105648	.108542	.111475	.114445	.117452	.123573	.129830	.136214	.142718
	.10	.093396	.098728	.104231	.107045	.109900	.112794	.115726	.118697	.121704	.127825	.134081	.140465	.146969
	0.00	.097647	.102979	.108482	.111296	.114151	.117045	.119978	.122948	.125955	.132076	.138333	.144717	.151220
	-.10	.101899	.107230	.112734	.115548	.118402	.121296	.124229	.127200	.130207	.136328	.142584	.148968	.155472
	-.20	.106150	.111482	.116985	.119799	.122654	.125548	.128481	.131451	.134458	.140579	.146836	.153220	.159723
	-.30	.110402	.115733	.121237	.124051	.126905	.129799	.132732	.135703	.138710	.144831	.151087	.157471	.163975
	-.40	.114653	.119985	.125488	.128302	.131157	.134051	.136984	.139954	.142961	.149082	.155339	.161723	.168226
20	.40	.075344	.081163	.087177	.090252	.093370	.096530	.099731	.102969	.106245	.112898	.119677	.126570	.133562
	.30	.079596	.085415	.091428	.094503	.097622	.100782	.103982	.107221	.110496	.117149	.123929	.130821	.137814
	.20	.083847	.089666	.095679	.098755	.101873	.105033	.108234	.111472	.114748	.121401	.128180	.135072	.142065
	.10	.088099	.093918	.099931	.103006	.106125	.109285	.112485	.115724	.118999	.125652	.132432	.139324	.146317
	0.00	.092350	.098169	.104182	.107257	.110376	.113536	.116737	.119975	.123250	.129904	.136683	.143575	.150568
	-.10	.096601	.102421	.108434	.111509	.114627	.117788	.120988	.124227	.127502	.134155	.140935	.147827	.154680
	-.20	.100853	.106672	.112685	.115760	.118879	.122039	.125240	.128478	.131753	.138407	.145186	.152078	.159071
	-.30	.105104	.110924	.116937	.120012	.123130	.126291	.129491	.132730	.136005	.142658	.149437	.156330	.163323
	-.40	.109356	.115175	.121188	.124263	.127382	.130542	.133744	.136981	.140256	.146910	.153689	.160581	.167574
25	.40	.072293	.078441	.084791	.088036	.091334	.094652	.098018	.101420	.104854	.111814	.118880	.126036	.133268
	.30	.076564	.082692	.089043	.092288	.095575	.098903	.102270	.105671	.109106	.116066	.123132	.130288	.137520
	.20	.080796	.086944	.093294	.096539	.099827	.103155	.106521	.109923	.113357	.120317	.127383	.134539	.141771
	.10	.085047	.091195	.097546	.100790	.104078	.107406	.110772	.114174	.117609	.124569	.131635	.138791	.146023
	0.00	.089299	.095447	.101797	.105042	.108330	.111658	.115024	.118426	.121860	.128820	.135886	.143042	.150274
	-.10	.093550	.099698	.106049	.109293	.112581	.115909	.119275	.122677	.126111	.133072	.140138	.147294	.154526
	-.20	.097802	.103950	.110300	.113545	.116833	.120161	.123527	.126928	.130363	.137323	.144389	.151545	.158777
	-.30	.102053	.108201	.114552	.117796	.121084	.124412	.127778	.131180	.134615	.141575	.148641	.155797	.163029
	-.40	.106305	.112453	.118803	.122048	.125336	.128664	.132030	.135431	.138866	.145826	.152892	.160048	.167280
30	.40	.070259	.076752	.083348	.086713	.090119	.093562	.097040	.100549	.104086	.111236	.118471	.125773	.133129
	.30	.074610	.081003	.087599	.090964	.094370	.097814	.101291	.104800	.108338	.115488	.122722	.130024	.137380
	.20	.078862	.085255	.091850	.095216	.098622	.102065	.105543	.109052	.112589	.119739	.126973	.134276	.141632
	.10	.083113	.089506	.096102	.099467	.102873	.106317	.109794	.113303	.116840	.123990	.131225	.138527	.145883
	0.00	.087365	.093758	.100353	.103719	.107125	.110568	.114046	.117555	.121092	.128242	.135476	.142779	.150135
	-.10	.091616	.098009	.104605	.107970	.111376	.114819	.118297	.121806	.125343	.132493	.139728	.147030	.154386
	-.20	.095868	.102261	.108856	.112222	.115628	.119071	.122549	.126057	.129595	.136745	.143979	.151282	.158638
	-.30	.100119	.106512	.113108	.116473	.119879	.123322	.126800	.130309	.133846	.140996	.148231	.155533	.162889
	-.40	.104371	.110763	.117359	.120725	.124131	.127574	.131051	.134560	.138098	.145248	.152482	.159785	.167140

10.0 YEAR HOLDING PERIOD
.180 EQUITY YIELD RATE
.800 LOAN RATIO

INTEREST RATE

TERM YEARS	APPR DEP	5.0	6.0	7.0	7.5	8.0	8.5	9.0	9.5	10.0	11.0	12.0	13.0	14.0
10	.40	.086805	.091562	.096447	.098936	.101457	.104009	.106591	.109204	.111847	.117222	.122715	.128321	.134038
	.30	.091057	.095814	.100698	.103188	.105708	.108260	.110843	.113456	.116099	.121474	.126966	.132522	.138290
	.20	.095308	.100065	.104949	.107439	.109960	.112512	.115094	.117707	.120350	.125725	.131217	.136624	.142541
	.10	.099560	.104317	.109201	.111691	.114211	.116763	.119346	.121958	.124602	.129977	.135469	.141075	.146793
	0.00	.103811	.108568	.113452	.115942	.118463	.121015	.123597	.126210	.128853	.134228	.139720	.145327	.151044
	-.10	.108063	.112819	.117704	.120193	.122714	.125266	.127848	.130461	.133104	.138480	.143972	.149578	.155296
	-.20	.112314	.117071	.121955	.124445	.126966	.129517	.132100	.134713	.137356	.142731	.148223	.153830	.159547
	-.30	.116566	.121322	.126207	.128696	.131217	.133769	.136351	.138964	.141607	.146983	.152475	.158081	.163798
	-.40	.120817	.125574	.130458	.132948	.135469	.138020	.140603	.143216	.145859	.151234	.156726	.162332	.168050
15	.40	.075151	.080838	.086709	.089710	.092755	.095842	.098970	.102139	.105347	.111876	.118549	.125359	.132296
	.30	.079403	.085090	.090960	.093962	.097007	.100094	.103222	.106390	.109598	.116127	.122801	.129610	.136547
	.20	.083654	.089341	.095212	.098213	.101258	.104345	.107473	.110642	.113849	.120378	.127052	.133862	.140799
	.10	.087906	.093593	.099463	.102465	.105510	.108597	.111725	.114893	.118101	.124630	.131304	.138113	.145050
	0.00	.092157	.097844	.103715	.106716	.109761	.112848	.115976	.119145	.122352	.128881	.135555	.142365	.149302
	-.10	.096408	.102096	.107966	.110968	.114013	.117099	.120228	.123396	.126604	.133133	.139806	.146616	.153553
	-.20	.100660	.106347	.112218	.115219	.118264	.121351	.124479	.127648	.130855	.137384	.144058	.150868	.157805
	-.30	.104911	.110599	.116469	.119471	.122516	.125602	.128731	.131899	.135107	.141636	.148309	.155119	.162056
	-.40	.109163	.114850	.120720	.123722	.126767	.129854	.132982	.136151	.139358	.145887	.152561	.159370	.166308
20	.40	.069501	.075708	.082122	.085402	.088729	.092100	.095513	.098968	.102461	.109558	.116789	.124141	.131600
	.30	.073752	.079960	.086373	.089654	.092980	.096351	.099765	.103219	.106713	.113810	.121041	.128393	.135852
	.20	.078004	.084211	.090625	.093905	.097231	.100602	.104016	.107471	.110964	.118061	.125292	.132644	.140103
	.10	.082255	.088462	.094876	.098156	.101483	.104854	.108268	.111722	.115216	.122313	.129544	.136896	.144356
	0.00	.086507	.092714	.099128	.102408	.105734	.109105	.112519	.115974	.119467	.126564	.133795	.141147	.148606
	-.10	.090758	.096965	.103379	.106659	.109986	.113357	.116771	.120225	.123719	.130815	.138047	.145399	.152858
	-.20	.095010	.101217	.107631	.110911	.114237	.117608	.121022	.124477	.127970	.135067	.142298	.149650	.157109
	-.30	.099261	.105468	.111882	.115162	.118489	.121860	.125273	.128728	.132222	.139318	.146550	.153901	.161360
	-.40	.103512	.109720	.116134	.119414	.122740	.126111	.129525	.132979	.136473	.143570	.150801	.158153	.165612
25	.40	.066246	.072804	.079578	.083039	.086546	.090096	.093686	.097315	.100978	.108402	.115939	.123573	.131287
	.30	.070498	.077055	.083829	.087290	.090797	.094347	.097938	.101566	.105230	.112654	.120191	.127824	.135538
	.20	.074749	.081307	.088081	.091542	.095049	.098599	.102189	.105818	.109481	.116905	.124442	.132076	.139790
	.10	.079000	.085558	.092332	.095793	.099300	.102850	.106441	.110069	.113733	.121157	.128694	.136327	.144041
	0.00	.083252	.089810	.096584	.100045	.103552	.107102	.110692	.114321	.117984	.125408	.132945	.140578	.148293
	-.10	.087503	.094061	.100835	.104296	.107803	.111353	.114944	.118572	.122236	.129660	.137197	.144830	.152544
	-.20	.091755	.098313	.105087	.108548	.112055	.115605	.119195	.122823	.126487	.133911	.141448	.149081	.156795
	-.30	.096006	.102564	.109338	.112799	.116306	.119856	.123447	.127075	.130739	.138163	.145700	.153333	.161047
	-.40	.100258	.106816	.113590	.117051	.120557	.124108	.127698	.131326	.134990	.142414	.149951	.157584	.165298
30	.40	.064183	.071002	.078038	.081627	.085261	.088933	.092643	.096386	.100159	.107786	.115502	.123291	.131138
	.30	.068435	.075254	.082289	.085879	.089512	.093185	.096894	.100637	.104410	.112037	.119754	.127543	.135389
	.20	.072686	.079505	.086541	.090130	.093763	.097436	.101146	.104889	.108662	.116288	.124005	.131794	.139641
	.10	.076938	.083757	.090792	.094382	.098015	.101688	.105397	.109140	.112913	.120540	.128257	.136046	.143892
	0.00	.081189	.088008	.095044	.098633	.102266	.105939	.109649	.113391	.117165	.124791	.132508	.140297	.148144
	-.10	.085440	.092260	.099295	.102885	.106518	.110191	.113900	.117643	.121416	.129043	.136760	.144549	.152395
	-.20	.089692	.096511	.103547	.107136	.110769	.114442	.118152	.121894	.125668	.133294	.141011	.148800	.156646
	-.30	.093943	.100762	.107798	.111388	.115021	.118694	.122403	.126146	.129919	.137546	.145263	.153052	.160898
	-.40	.098195	.105014	.112049	.115639	.119272	.122945	.126655	.130397	.134171	.141797	.149514	.157303	.165149

10.0 YEAR HOLDING PERIOD
.180 EQUITY YIELD RATE
.900 LOAN RATIO

INTEREST RATE

TERM YEARS	APPR DEP	5.0	6.0	7.0	7.5	8.0	8.5	9.0	9.5	10.0	11.0	12.0	13.0	14.0
10	.40	.077282	.082633	.088128	.090929	.093765	.096636	.099541	.102480	.105454	.111501	.117680	.123987	.130419
	.30	.081633	.086885	.092380	.095180	.098016	.100887	.103792	.106732	.109705	.115752	.121931	.128238	.134670
	.20	.085785	.091136	.096631	.099432	.102268	.105138	.108044	.110983	.113957	.120004	.126183	.132489	.138922
	.10	.090036	.095388	.100883	.103683	.106519	.109390	.112295	.115235	.118208	.124255	.130434	.136741	.143173
	0.00	.094288	.099639	.105134	.107935	.110771	.113641	.116547	.119486	.122460	.128507	.134685	.140992	.147425
	-.10	.098539	.103890	.109385	.112186	.115022	.117893	.120798	.123738	.126711	.132758	.138937	.145244	.151676
	-.20	.102791	.108142	.113637	.116438	.119274	.122144	.125050	.127989	.130963	.137010	.143188	.149495	.155928
	-.30	.107042	.112393	.117888	.120689	.123525	.126396	.129301	.132241	.135214	.141261	.147440	.153747	.160109
	-.40	.111293	.116645	.122140	.124941	.127776	.130647	.133553	.136492	.139465	.145513	.151691	.157998	.164430
15	.40	.064171	.070569	.077173	.080550	.083975	.087448	.090967	.094532	.098141	.105486	.112993	.120654	.128459
	.30	.068422	.074820	.081425	.084801	.088227	.091700	.095219	.098783	.102392	.109737	.117245	.124906	.132710
	.20	.072674	.079072	.085676	.089053	.092478	.095951	.099470	.103035	.106643	.113989	.121496	.129157	.136962
	.10	.076925	.083323	.089927	.093304	.096730	.100203	.103722	.107286	.110895	.118240	.125748	.133409	.141213
	0.00	.081177	.087575	.094179	.097556	.100981	.104454	.107973	.111538	.115146	.122492	.129999	.137660	.145465
	-.10	.085428	.091826	.098430	.101807	.105233	.108705	.112225	.115789	.119398	.126743	.134251	.141912	.149716
	-.20	.089680	.096078	.102682	.106059	.109484	.112957	.116476	.120041	.123649	.130995	.138502	.146163	.153967
	-.30	.093931	.100329	.106933	.110310	.113736	.117208	.120728	.124292	.127901	.135246	.142754	.150415	.158219
	-.40	.098182	.104581	.111185	.114562	.117987	.121460	.124979	.128544	.132152	.139497	.147005	.154666	.162470
20	.40	.057814	.064797	.072013	.075703	.079445	.083238	.087078	.090964	.094895	.102879	.111014	.119285	.127676
	.30	.062066	.069049	.076264	.079955	.083697	.087489	.091330	.095216	.099146	.107130	.115265	.123536	.131927
	.20	.066317	.073300	.080516	.084206	.087948	.091741	.095581	.099467	.103398	.111382	.119517	.127788	.136179
	.10	.070569	.077552	.084767	.088457	.092200	.095992	.099833	.103719	.107649	.115633	.123768	.132039	.140430
	0.00	.074820	.081803	.089019	.092709	.096451	.100244	.104084	.107970	.111901	.119885	.128020	.136290	.144682
	-.10	.079071	.086055	.093270	.096960	.100703	.104495	.108335	.112222	.116152	.124136	.132271	.140542	.148933
	-.20	.083323	.090306	.097522	.101212	.104954	.108747	.112587	.116473	.120404	.128387	.136523	.144793	.153185
	-.30	.087574	.094558	.101773	.105463	.109206	.112998	.116838	.120725	.124655	.132639	.140774	.149045	.157436
	-.40	.091826	.098809	.106025	.109715	.113457	.117249	.121090	.124976	.128906	.136890	.145026	.153296	.161688
25	.40	.054153	.061530	.069151	.073044	.076990	.080984	.085023	.089105	.093227	.101578	.110058	.118645	.127323
	.30	.058404	.065782	.073402	.077296	.081241	.085235	.089274	.093356	.097478	.105830	.114309	.122896	.131575
	.20	.062655	.070033	.077654	.081547	.085493	.089486	.093526	.097608	.101729	.110081	.118560	.127148	.135826
	.10	.066907	.074285	.081905	.085799	.089744	.093738	.097777	.101859	.105981	.114333	.122812	.131399	.140078
	0.00	.071158	.078536	.086157	.090050	.093996	.097989	.102029	.106111	.110232	.118584	.127063	.135651	.144329
	-.10	.075410	.082788	.090408	.094302	.098247	.102241	.106280	.110362	.114484	.122836	.131315	.139902	.148581
	-.20	.079661	.087039	.094660	.098553	.102499	.106492	.110532	.114614	.118735	.127087	.135566	.144154	.152832
	-.30	.083913	.091290	.098911	.102805	.106750	.110744	.114783	.118865	.122987	.131339	.139818	.148405	.157083
	-.40	.088164	.095542	.103162	.107056	.111001	.114995	.119035	.123116	.127238	.135590	.144069	.152657	.161335
30	.40	.051832	.059503	.067418	.071457	.075544	.079676	.083849	.088060	.092304	.100884	.109566	.118329	.127156
	.30	.056083	.063755	.071670	.075709	.079795	.083927	.088100	.092311	.096555	.105136	.113817	.122580	.131407
	.20	.060335	.068006	.075921	.079960	.084047	.088178	.092352	.096562	.100807	.109387	.118069	.126831	.135659
	.10	.064586	.072258	.080173	.084211	.088298	.092430	.096603	.100814	.105059	.113639	.122320	.131083	.139910
	0.00	.068838	.076509	.084424	.088463	.092550	.096682	.100855	.105065	.109310	.117890	.126572	.135334	.144162
	-.10	.073089	.080761	.088676	.092714	.096801	.100933	.105106	.109317	.113562	.122142	.130823	.139586	.148413
	-.20	.077341	.085012	.092927	.096965	.101053	.105185	.109358	.113568	.117813	.126393	.135075	.143837	.152664
	-.30	.081592	.089263	.097178	.101217	.105304	.109436	.113609	.117820	.122065	.130645	.139326	.148089	.156916
	-.40	.085843	.093515	.101430	.105468	.109556	.113687	.117861	.122071	.126316	.134896	.143578	.152340	.161167

10.0 YEAR HOLDING PERIOD
.200 EQUITY YIELD RATE
.600 LOAN RATIO

INTEREST RATE

TERM YEARS	APPR DEP	5.0	6.0	7.0	7.5	8.0	8.5	9.0	9.5	10.0	11.0	12.0	13.0	14.0
10	.40	.117844	.121412	.125075	.126943	.128833	.130747	.132684	.134643	.136626	.140657	.144776	.148981	.153269
	.30	.121697	.125264	.128928	.130795	.132685	.134599	.136536	.138496	.140478	.144510	.148629	.152833	.157121
	.20	.125549	.129117	.132780	.134647	.136538	.138451	.140388	.142348	.144330	.148362	.152481	.156686	.160974
	.10	.129401	.132969	.136632	.138499	.140390	.142304	.144241	.146200	.148183	.152214	.156333	.160538	.164826
	0.00	.133254	.136821	.140484	.142352	.144242	.146156	.148093	.150053	.152035	.156066	.160185	.164390	.168678
	-.10	.137106	.140673	.144337	.146204	.148094	.150008	.151945	.153905	.155887	.159919	.164038	.168242	.172530
	-.20	.140958	.144526	.148189	.150056	.151947	.153861	.155799	.157757	.159739	.163771	.167890	.172095	.176383
	-.30	.144810	.148378	.152041	.153908	.155799	.157713	.159650	.161609	.163592	.167623	.171742	.175947	.180235
	-.40	.148663	.152230	.155894	.157761	.159651	.161565	.163502	.165462	.167444	.171475	.175595	.179799	.184087
15	.40	.108100	.112324	.116685	.118915	.121178	.123472	.125798	.128154	.130539	.135395	.140360	.145428	.150592
	.30	.111952	.116176	.120537	.122767	.125040	.127325	.129650	.132006	.134391	.139247	.144212	.149280	.154444
	.20	.115805	.120028	.124389	.126620	.128883	.131177	.133502	.135858	.138243	.143100	.148065	.153132	.158296
	.10	.119657	.123881	.128242	.130472	.132735	.135029	.137355	.139710	.142096	.146952	.151917	.156984	.162148
	0.00	.123509	.127733	.132094	.134324	.136587	.138882	.141207	.143563	.145948	.150804	.155769	.160837	.166001
	-.10	.127361	.131585	.135946	.138177	.140439	.142734	.145059	.147415	.149800	.154656	.159621	.164689	.169853
	-.20	.131214	.135437	.139798	.142029	.144292	.146586	.148912	.151267	.153653	.158509	.163474	.168541	.173705
	-.30	.135066	.139290	.143651	.145881	.148144	.150438	.152764	.155120	.157505	.162361	.167326	.172394	.177557
	-.40	.138918	.143142	.147503	.149733	.151996	.154291	.156616	.158972	.161357	.166213	.171178	.176246	.181410
20	.40	.103376	.107976	.112733	.115166	.117636	.120139	.122674	.125241	.127837	.133114	.138494	.143967	.149522
	.30	.107228	.111828	.116585	.119019	.121488	.123991	.126526	.129093	.131690	.136967	.142347	.147819	.153375
	.20	.111080	.115680	.120437	.122871	.125340	.127843	.130379	.132945	.135542	.140819	.146199	.151672	.157227
	.10	.114933	.119533	.124289	.126723	.129192	.131695	.134231	.136798	.139394	.144671	.150051	.155524	.161079
	0.00	.118785	.123385	.128142	.130576	.133045	.135548	.138083	.140650	.143246	.148523	.153903	.159376	.164931
	-.10	.122637	.127237	.131994	.134428	.136897	.139400	.141936	.144502	.147099	.152376	.157756	.163228	.168784
	-.20	.126489	.131090	.135846	.138280	.140749	.143252	.145788	.148355	.150951	.156228	.161608	.167081	.172636
	-.30	.130342	.134942	.139699	.142132	.144602	.147105	.149640	.152207	.154803	.160080	.165460	.170933	.176488
	-.40	.134194	.138794	.143551	.145985	.148454	.150957	.153492	.156059	.158656	.163933	.169313	.174785	.180341
25	.40	.100654	.105515	.110540	.113110	.115715	.118354	.121023	.123722	.126449	.131977	.137593	.143285	.149040
	.30	.104507	.109367	.114393	.116963	.119568	.122206	.124876	.127575	.130301	.135829	.141445	.147137	.152893
	.20	.108359	.113219	.118245	.120815	.123420	.126058	.128728	.131427	.134153	.139681	.145298	.150989	.156745
	.10	.112211	.117072	.122097	.124667	.127272	.129911	.132580	.135279	.138006	.143534	.149150	.154842	.160597
	0.00	.116063	.120924	.125949	.128519	.131124	.133763	.136433	.139132	.141858	.147386	.153002	.158694	.164450
	-.10	.119916	.124776	.129802	.132372	.134977	.137615	.140285	.142984	.145710	.151238	.156854	.162546	.168302
	-.20	.123768	.128628	.133654	.136224	.138829	.141467	.144137	.146836	.149563	.155090	.160707	.166399	.172154
	-.30	.127620	.132481	.137506	.140076	.142681	.145320	.147989	.150688	.153415	.158943	.164559	.170251	.176006
	-.40	.131473	.136333	.141359	.143928	.146534	.149172	.151842	.154541	.157267	.162795	.168411	.174103	.179859
30	.40	.098930	.103988	.109213	.111882	.114585	.117318	.120081	.122869	.125681	.131370	.137130	.142947	.148812
	.30	.102782	.107840	.113066	.115734	.118437	.121171	.123933	.126721	.129534	.135222	.140982	.146800	.152664
	.20	.106634	.111692	.116918	.119587	.122289	.125023	.127785	.130574	.133386	.139074	.144834	.150652	.156516
	.10	.110486	.115544	.120770	.123439	.126142	.128875	.131637	.134426	.137238	.142927	.148686	.154504	.160368
	0.00	.114339	.119397	.124623	.127291	.129994	.132727	.135490	.138278	.141091	.146779	.152539	.158357	.164221
	-.10	.118191	.123249	.128475	.131144	.133846	.136580	.139342	.142130	.144943	.150631	.156391	.162209	.168073
	-.20	.122043	.127101	.132327	.134996	.137698	.140432	.143194	.145983	.148795	.154483	.160243	.166061	.171925
	-.30	.125895	.130954	.136179	.138848	.141551	.144284	.147046	.149835	.152647	.158336	.164096	.169913	.175777
	-.40	.129748	.134806	.140032	.142700	.145403	.148137	.150899	.153687	.156500	.162188	.167948	.173766	.179630

```
10.0  YEAR HOLDING PERIOD
.200  EQUITY YIELD RATE
.667  LOAN RATIO
```

INTEREST RATE

TERM YEARS	APPR DEP	5.0	6.0	7.0	7.5	8.0	8.5	9.0	9.5	10.0	11.0	12.0	13.0	14.0
10	.40	.110428	.114392	.118462	.120537	.122637	.124764	.126916	.129093	.131296	.135775	.140352	.145024	.149789
	.30	.114280	.118244	.122314	.124389	.126490	.128616	.130768	.132946	.135148	.139628	.144205	.148876	.153641
	.20	.118132	.122096	.126167	.128241	.130342	.133469	.134621	.136798	.139001	.143480	.148057	.152729	.157493
	.10	.121985	.125949	.130019	.132094	.134194	.136321	.138473	.140650	.142853	.147332	.151909	.156581	.161346
	0.00	.125837	.129801	.133871	.135946	.138047	.140173	.142325	.144503	.146705	.151185	.155761	.160433	.165198
	-.10	.129689	.133653	.137724	.139798	.141899	.144025	.146177	.148355	.150557	.155037	.159614	.164285	.169050
	-.20	.133541	.137505	.141576	.143650	.145751	.147878	.150030	.152207	.154410	.158889	.163466	.168138	.172902
	-.30	.137394	.141358	.145428	.147503	.149603	.151730	.153882	.156059	.158262	.162741	.167318	.171990	.176755
	-.40	.141246	.145210	.149280	.151355	.153456	.155582	.157734	.159912	.162114	.166594	.171170	.175842	.180607
15	.40	.099601	.104294	.109139	.111617	.114132	.116681	.119265	.121883	.124533	.129929	.135445	.141076	.146814
	.30	.103453	.108146	.112992	.115470	.117984	.120533	.123117	.125735	.128385	.133781	.139297	.144928	.150666
	.20	.107305	.111998	.116844	.119322	.121836	.124386	.126970	.129587	.132237	.137633	.143150	.148780	.154518
	.10	.111158	.115851	.120696	.123174	.125689	.128238	.130822	.133439	.136090	.141485	.147002	.152633	.158370
	0.00	.115010	.119703	.124548	.127027	.129541	.132090	.134674	.137292	.139942	.145338	.150854	.156485	.162223
	-.10	.118862	.123555	.128401	.130879	.133393	.135943	.138526	.141144	.143794	.149190	.154707	.160337	.166075
	-.20	.122714	.127407	.132253	.134731	.137245	.139795	.142379	.144996	.147647	.153042	.158559	.164190	.169927
	-.30	.126567	.131260	.136105	.138583	.141098	.143647	.146231	.148848	.151499	.156894	.162411	.168042	.173780
	-.40	.130419	.135112	.139957	.142436	.144950	.147499	.150083	.152701	.155351	.160747	.166263	.171894	.177632
20	.40	.094351	.099463	.104748	.107452	.110196	.112977	.115794	.118646	.121531	.127394	.133372	.139453	.145626
	.30	.098204	.103315	.108600	.111305	.114048	.116829	.119646	.122498	.125383	.131247	.137224	.143305	.149478
	.20	.102056	.107167	.112452	.115157	.117900	.120681	.123499	.126351	.129236	.135099	.141077	.147158	.153330
	.10	.105908	.111019	.116305	.119009	.121753	.124534	.127351	.130203	.133088	.138951	.144929	.151010	.157182
	0.00	.109760	.114872	.120157	.122861	.125605	.128386	.131203	.134055	.136940	.142804	.148781	.154862	.161035
	-.10	.113613	.118724	.124009	.126714	.129457	.132238	.135056	.137907	.140793	.146656	.152634	.158714	.164887
	-.20	.117465	.122576	.127862	.130566	.133309	.136091	.138908	.141760	.144645	.150508	.156486	.162567	.168739
	-.30	.121317	.126429	.131714	.134418	.137162	.139943	.142760	.145612	.148497	.154360	.160338	.166419	.172592
	-.40	.125170	.130281	.135566	.138270	.141014	.143795	.146612	.149464	.152349	.158213	.164190	.170271	.176444
25	.40	.091328	.096728	.102312	.105168	.108062	.110994	.113960	.116959	.119988	.126131	.132371	.138695	.145090
	.30	.095180	.100580	.106164	.109020	.111914	.114846	.117812	.120811	.123841	.129983	.136223	.142547	.148943
	.20	.099032	.104433	.110017	.112872	.115767	.118698	.121665	.124664	.127693	.133835	.140075	.146400	.152795
	.10	.102884	.108285	.113869	.116724	.119619	.122551	.125517	.128516	.131545	.137687	.143928	.150252	.156647
	0.00	.106737	.112137	.117721	.120577	.123471	.126403	.129369	.132368	.135397	.141540	.147780	.154104	.160499
	-.10	.110589	.115989	.121574	.124429	.127324	.130255	.133221	.136220	.139250	.145392	.151632	.157956	.164352
	-.20	.114441	.119842	.125426	.128281	.131176	.134107	.137074	.140073	.143102	.149244	.155485	.161809	.168204
	-.30	.118294	.123694	.129278	.132133	.135028	.137960	.140926	.143925	.146954	.153096	.159337	.165661	.172056
	-.40	.122146	.127546	.133130	.135986	.138880	.141812	.144778	.147777	.150807	.156949	.163189	.169513	.175908
30	.40	.089411	.095031	.100838	.103803	.106806	.109843	.112912	.116011	.119136	.125456	.131856	.138320	.144836
	.30	.093263	.098884	.104690	.107655	.110658	.113695	.116765	.119863	.122988	.129308	.135708	.142172	.148688
	.20	.097116	.102736	.108542	.111508	.114510	.117548	.120617	.123715	.126840	.133161	.139560	.146025	.152540
	.10	.100968	.106588	.112395	.115360	.118363	.121400	.124469	.127568	.130693	.137013	.143413	.149877	.156393
	0.00	.104820	.110440	.116247	.119212	.122215	.125252	.128321	.131420	.134545	.140865	.147265	.153729	.160245
	-.10	.108672	.114293	.120099	.123064	.126067	.129105	.132174	.135272	.138397	.144717	.151117	.157582	.164097
	-.20	.112525	.118145	.123951	.126917	.129919	.132957	.136026	.139124	.142249	.148570	.154970	.161434	.167950
	-.30	.116377	.121997	.127804	.130769	.133772	.136809	.139878	.142977	.146102	.152422	.158822	.165286	.171802
	-.40	.120229	.125850	.131656	.134621	.137624	.140661	.143731	.146829	.149954	.156274	.162674	.169138	.175654

10.0 YEAR HOLDING PERIOD
.200 EQUITY YIELD RATE
.700 LOAN RATIO

INTEREST RATE

TERM YEARS	APPR DEP	5.0	6.0	7.0	7.5	8.0	8.5	9.0	9.5	10.0	11.0	12.0	13.0	14.0
10	.40	.106720	.110882	.115156	.117334	.119540	.121773	.124033	.126319	.128632	.133335	.138141	.143046	.148049
	.30	.110572	.114734	.119008	.121187	.123392	.125625	.127885	.130171	.132484	.137187	.141993	.146898	.151901
	.20	.114425	.118587	.122861	.125039	.127245	.129477	.131737	.134023	.136336	.141040	.145845	.150751	.155753
	.10	.118277	.122439	.126713	.128891	.131097	.133330	.135589	.137876	.140188	.144892	.149697	.154603	.159606
	0.00	.122129	.126291	.130565	.132744	.134949	.137182	.139442	.141728	.144041	.148744	.153550	.158455	.163458
	-.10	.125981	.130144	.134417	.136596	.138802	.141034	.143294	.145580	.147893	.152596	.157402	.162307	.167310
	-.20	.129834	.133996	.138270	.140448	.142654	.144887	.147146	.149433	.151745	.156449	.161254	.166160	.171162
	-.30	.133686	.137848	.142122	.144300	.146506	.148739	.150999	.153285	.155598	.160301	.165160	.170012	.175015
	-.40	.137538	.141700	.145974	.148153	.150358	.152591	.154851	.157137	.159450	.164153	.168959	.173864	.178867
15	.40	.095352	.100279	.105367	.107969	.110609	.113286	.115999	.118747	.121530	.127196	.132988	.138900	.144925
	.30	.099204	.104132	.109219	.111821	.114461	.117138	.119851	.122600	.125383	.131048	.136840	.142753	.148777
	.20	.103056	.107984	.113072	.115674	.118314	.120991	.123704	.126452	.129235	.134900	.140693	.146605	.152630
	.10	.106908	.111836	.116924	.119526	.122166	.124843	.127556	.130304	.133087	.138753	.144545	.150457	.156482
	0.00	.110761	.115688	.120776	.123378	.126018	.128695	.131408	.134157	.136939	.142605	.148397	.154309	.160334
	-.10	.114613	.119541	.124628	.127231	.129871	.132547	.135260	.138009	.140792	.146457	.152250	.158162	.164186
	-.20	.118465	.123393	.128481	.131083	.133723	.136400	.139113	.141861	.144644	.150309	.156102	.162014	.168039
	-.30	.122318	.127245	.132333	.134935	.137575	.140252	.142965	.145713	.148496	.154162	.159954	.165866	.171891
	-.40	.126170	.131097	.136185	.138787	.141427	.144104	.146817	.149566	.152348	.158014	.163806	.169719	.175743
20	.40	.089840	.095207	.100756	.103596	.106476	.109397	.112355	.115349	.118378	.124535	.130812	.137196	.143678
	.30	.093692	.099059	.104608	.107448	.110329	.113249	.116207	.119202	.122231	.128387	.134664	.141049	.147530
	.20	.097544	.102911	.108461	.111300	.114181	.117101	.120059	.123054	.126083	.132239	.138516	.144901	.151382
	.10	.101397	.106764	.112313	.115153	.118033	.120953	.123912	.126906	.129935	.136092	.142368	.148753	.155234
	0.00	.105249	.110616	.116165	.119005	.121886	.124806	.127764	.130758	.133788	.139944	.146221	.152605	.159087
	-.10	.109101	.114468	.120018	.122857	.125738	.128658	.131616	.134611	.137640	.143796	.150073	.156458	.162939
	-.20	.112954	.118320	.123870	.126709	.129590	.132510	.135468	.138463	.141492	.147649	.153925	.160310	.166791
	-.30	.116806	.122173	.127722	.130562	.133443	.136363	.139321	.142315	.145344	.151501	.157777	.164162	.170644
	-.40	.120658	.126025	.131574	.134414	.137295	.140215	.143173	.146167	.149197	.155353	.161630	.168015	.174496
25	.40	.086665	.092335	.098199	.101197	.104236	.107314	.110429	.113578	.116759	.123208	.129760	.136401	.143115
	.30	.090517	.096188	.102051	.105049	.108088	.111167	.114281	.117430	.120611	.127060	.133612	.140253	.146968
	.20	.094370	.100040	.105903	.108901	.111941	.115019	.118133	.121282	.124463	.130912	.137465	.144105	.150820
	.10	.098222	.103892	.109755	.112754	.115793	.118871	.121986	.125135	.128315	.134765	.141317	.147957	.154672
	0.00	.102074	.107744	.113608	.116606	.119645	.122723	.125838	.128987	.132168	.138617	.145169	.151810	.158525
	-.10	.105926	.111597	.117460	.120458	.123497	.126576	.129690	.132839	.136020	.142469	.149021	.155662	.162377
	-.20	.109779	.115449	.121313	.124311	.127350	.130428	.133543	.136691	.139872	.146321	.152874	.159514	.166229
	-.30	.113631	.119301	.125165	.128163	.131202	.134280	.137395	.140544	.143725	.150174	.156726	.163366	.170081
	-.40	.117483	.123154	.129017	.132015	.135054	.138132	.141247	.144396	.147577	.154026	.160578	.167219	.173934
30	.40	.084653	.090554	.096650	.099764	.102917	.106106	.109329	.112584	.115863	.122500	.129219	.136007	.142849
	.30	.088505	.094406	.100503	.103616	.106769	.109958	.113181	.116434	.119716	.126352	.133072	.139859	.146701
	.20	.092357	.098258	.104355	.107469	.110622	.113811	.117033	.120287	.123568	.130204	.136924	.143711	.150553
	.10	.096209	.102111	.108207	.111321	.114474	.117663	.120886	.124139	.127420	.134056	.140776	.147564	.154405
	0.00	.100062	.105963	.112060	.115173	.118326	.121515	.124738	.127991	.131272	.137909	.144629	.151416	.158257
	-.10	.103914	.109815	.115912	.119025	.122178	.125368	.128590	.131843	.135125	.141761	.148481	.155268	.162110
	-.20	.107766	.113667	.119764	.122878	.126031	.129220	.132442	.135696	.138977	.145613	.152333	.159121	.165962
	-.30	.111619	.117520	.123616	.126730	.129883	.133072	.136295	.139548	.142829	.149466	.156185	.162973	.169814
	-.40	.115471	.121372	.127469	.130582	.133735	.136924	.140147	.143400	.146681	.153318	.160038	.166825	.173667

10.0 YEAR HOLDING PERIOD
.200 EQUITY YIELD RATE
.750 LOAN RATIO

INTEREST RATE

TERM YEARS	APPR DEP	5.0	6.0	7.0	7.5	8.0	8.5	9.0	9.5	10.0	11.0	12.0	13.0	14.0
10	.40	.101158	.105617	.110196	.112530	.114894	.117286	.119707	.122157	.124634	.129674	.134823	.140078	.145439
	.30	.105010	.109470	.114049	.116383	.118746	.121138	.123559	.126009	.128487	.133526	.138675	.143931	.149291
	.20	.108862	.113322	.117901	.120235	.122598	.124991	.127412	.129861	.132339	.137378	.142527	.147783	.153143
	.10	.112715	.117174	.121753	.124087	.126450	.128843	.131264	.133713	.136191	.141231	.146380	.151635	.156995
	0.00	.116567	.121026	.125606	.127940	.130303	.132695	.135116	.137566	.140044	.145083	.150232	.155488	.160848
	-.10	.120419	.124879	.129458	.131792	.134155	.136547	.138968	.141418	.143896	.148935	.154084	.159340	.164700
	-.20	.124271	.128731	.133310	.135644	.138007	.140400	.142821	.145270	.147748	.152787	.157936	.163192	.168552
	-.30	.128124	.132583	.137162	.139496	.141860	.144252	.146673	.149123	.151600	.156640	.161789	.167044	.172405
	-.40	.131976	.136435	.141015	.143349	.145712	.148104	.150525	.152975	.155453	.160492	.165641	.170897	.176257
15	.40	.088977	.094257	.099708	.102496	.105325	.108193	.111100	.114044	.117026	.123096	.129302	.135637	.142092
	.30	.092830	.098109	.103561	.106349	.109177	.112045	.114952	.117897	.120878	.126948	.133155	.139489	.145944
	.20	.096682	.101962	.107413	.110201	.113029	.115897	.118804	.121749	.124730	.130801	.137007	.143341	.149796
	.10	.100534	.105814	.111265	.114053	.116882	.119750	.122656	.125601	.128583	.134653	.140859	.147194	.153649
	0.00	.104386	.109666	.115117	.117905	.120734	.123602	.126509	.129453	.132435	.138505	.144711	.151046	.157501
	-.10	.108239	.113518	.118970	.121758	.124586	.127454	.130361	.133306	.136287	.142357	.148564	.154898	.161353
	-.20	.112091	.117371	.122822	.125610	.128438	.131306	.134213	.137158	.140140	.146210	.152416	.158750	.165205
	-.30	.115943	.121223	.126674	.129462	.132291	.135159	.138066	.141010	.143992	.150062	.156268	.162603	.169058
	-.40	.119796	.125075	.130526	.133314	.136141	.139011	.141918	.144863	.147844	.153914	.160120	.166455	.172910
20	.40	.083072	.088822	.094768	.097810	.100897	.104026	.107195	.110403	.113649	.120245	.126970	.133811	.140755
	.30	.086924	.092074	.098620	.101663	.104749	.107878	.111047	.114256	.117501	.124097	.130822	.137663	.144607
	.20	.090776	.096527	.102473	.105515	.108601	.111730	.114900	.118108	.121354	.127950	.134675	.141516	.148460
	.10	.094629	.100379	.106325	.109367	.112454	.115582	.118752	.121960	.125206	.131802	.138527	.145368	.152312
	0.00	.098481	.104231	.110177	.113219	.116306	.119435	.122604	.125812	.129058	.135654	.142379	.149220	.156164
	-.10	.102333	.108083	.114029	.117072	.120158	.123287	.126456	.129665	.132910	.139507	.146232	.153072	.160017
	-.20	.106186	.111936	.117882	.120924	.124010	.127139	.130309	.133517	.136763	.143359	.150084	.156925	.163869
	-.30	.110038	.115788	.121734	.124776	.127863	.130992	.134161	.137369	.140615	.147211	.153936	.160777	.167721
	-.40	.113890	.119640	.125586	.128629	.131715	.134844	.138013	.141222	.144467	.151063	.157788	.164629	.171573
25	.40	.079670	.085746	.092028	.095240	.098496	.101794	.105132	.108505	.111913	.118823	.125844	.132958	.140153
	.30	.083523	.089598	.095880	.099092	.102349	.105647	.108984	.112358	.115766	.122676	.129696	.136811	.144005
	.20	.087375	.093450	.099732	.102945	.106201	.109499	.112836	.116210	.119618	.126528	.133548	.140663	.147857
	.10	.091227	.097302	.103585	.106797	.110053	.113351	.116688	.120062	.123470	.130380	.137400	.144515	.151710
	0.00	.095079	.101155	.107437	.110649	.113906	.117204	.120541	.123914	.127323	.134232	.141253	.148367	.155562
	-.10	.098932	.105007	.111289	.114501	.117758	.121056	.124393	.127767	.131175	.138085	.145105	.152220	.159414
	-.20	.102784	.108859	.115141	.118354	.121610	.124908	.128245	.131619	.135027	.141937	.148957	.156072	.163267
	-.30	.106636	.112712	.118994	.122206	.125462	.128760	.132098	.135471	.138879	.145789	.152810	.159924	.167119
	-.40	.110488	.116564	.122846	.126058	.129315	.132613	.135950	.139324	.142732	.149641	.156662	.163777	.170971
30	.40	.077514	.083537	.090369	.093705	.097083	.100500	.103953	.107439	.110954	.118064	.125264	.132537	.139867
	.30	.081366	.087689	.094221	.097557	.100935	.104352	.107805	.111291	.114806	.121917	.129117	.136389	.143719
	.20	.085219	.091541	.098074	.101410	.104788	.108205	.111658	.115143	.118659	.125769	.132969	.140241	.147571
	.10	.089071	.095394	.101926	.105262	.108640	.112057	.115510	.118995	.122511	.129621	.136821	.144093	.151424
	0.00	.092923	.099246	.105778	.109114	.112492	.115909	.119362	.122848	.126363	.133474	.140673	.147946	.155276
	-.10	.096776	.103098	.109630	.112966	.116345	.119762	.123214	.126700	.130216	.137326	.144526	.151798	.159128
	-.20	.100628	.106951	.113483	.116819	.120197	.123614	.127067	.130552	.134068	.141178	.148378	.155650	.162980
	-.30	.104480	.110803	.117335	.120671	.124049	.127466	.130919	.134405	.137920	.145030	.152230	.159503	.166833
	-.40	.108332	.114655	.121187	.124523	.127901	.131318	.134771	.138257	.141772	.148883	.156083	.163355	.170685

10.0 YEAR HOLDING PERIOD
.200 EQUITY YIELD RATE
.800 LOAN RATIO

INTEREST RATE

TERM YEARS	APPR DEP	5.0	6.0	7.0	7.5	8.0	8.5	9.0	9.5	10.0	11.0	12.0	13.0	14.0
10	.40	.095596	.100352	.105237	.107726	.110247	.112799	.115381	.117994	.120637	.126013	.131505	.137111	.142828
	.30	.099448	.104205	.109089	.111579	.114090	.116651	.119234	.121847	.124490	.129865	.135357	.140963	.146661
	.20	.103300	.108057	.112941	.115431	.117952	.120504	.123086	.125699	.128342	.133717	.139209	.144816	.150533
	.10	.107152	.111909	.116794	.119283	.121804	.124356	.126938	.129551	.132194	.137570	.143062	.148668	.154385
	0.00	.111005	.115761	.120646	.123135	.125656	.128208	.130791	.133403	.136047	.141422	.146914	.152520	.158238
	-.10	.114857	.119614	.124498	.126988	.129509	.132060	.134643	.137256	.139899	.145274	.150766	.156372	.162090
	-.20	.118709	.123466	.128350	.130840	.133361	.135913	.138495	.141108	.143751	.149126	.154618	.160225	.165942
	-.30	.122562	.127318	.132203	.134692	.137213	.139765	.142347	.144960	.147603	.152979	.158471	.164077	.169794
	-.40	.126414	.131171	.136055	.138545	.141065	.143617	.146200	.148813	.151456	.156831	.162323	.167929	.173647
15	.40	.082603	.088235	.094049	.097023	.100040	.103100	.106200	.109341	.112522	.118996	.125616	.132373	.139258
	.30	.086455	.092087	.097902	.100876	.103893	.106952	.110053	.113194	.116374	.122849	.129469	.136225	.143111
	.20	.090308	.095939	.101754	.104728	.107745	.110804	.113905	.117046	.120226	.126701	.133321	.140078	.146963
	.10	.094160	.099792	.105606	.108580	.111597	.114656	.117757	.120898	.124078	.130553	.137173	.143930	.150815
	0.00	.098012	.103644	.109458	.112432	.115449	.118509	.121609	.124750	.127931	.134405	.141025	.147782	.154668
	-.10	.101865	.107496	.113311	.116285	.119302	.122361	.125462	.128603	.131783	.138258	.144878	.151635	.158520
	-.20	.105717	.111348	.117163	.120137	.123154	.126213	.129314	.132455	.135635	.142110	.148730	.155487	.162372
	-.30	.109569	.115201	.121015	.123989	.127006	.130066	.133166	.136307	.139488	.145962	.152582	.159339	.166224
	-.40	.113421	.119053	.124868	.127841	.130859	.133918	.137018	.140159	.143340	.149815	.156435	.163191	.170077
20	.40	.076304	.082437	.088780	.092025	.095317	.098655	.102035	.105458	.108920	.115955	.123129	.130426	.137833
	.30	.080156	.086290	.092632	.095877	.099169	.102507	.105888	.109310	.112772	.119808	.126981	.134278	.141685
	.20	.084009	.090142	.096484	.099730	.103022	.106359	.109740	.113162	.116624	.123660	.130833	.138130	.145537
	.10	.087861	.093994	.100337	.103582	.106874	.110212	.113592	.117014	.120476	.127512	.134686	.141982	.149390
	0.00	.091713	.097847	.104189	.107434	.110726	.114064	.117444	.120867	.124329	.131365	.138538	.145835	.153242
	-.10	.095565	.101699	.108041	.111286	.114579	.117916	.121297	.124719	.128181	.135217	.142390	.149687	.157094
	-.20	.099418	.105551	.111893	.115139	.118431	.121768	.125149	.128571	.132033	.139069	.146242	.153539	.160946
	-.30	.103270	.109403	.115746	.118991	.122283	.125620	.129001	.132423	.135885	.142921	.150095	.157392	.164799
	-.40	.107122	.113256	.119598	.122843	.126135	.129473	.132853	.136276	.139738	.146774	.153947	.161244	.168651
25	.40	.072676	.079156	.085857	.089283	.092757	.096275	.099834	.103433	.107068	.114439	.121927	.129516	.137190
	.30	.076528	.083008	.089709	.093136	.096609	.100127	.103687	.107285	.110921	.118291	.125779	.133368	.141043
	.20	.080380	.086860	.093561	.096988	.100461	.103979	.107539	.111138	.114773	.122143	.129632	.137221	.144895
	.10	.084232	.090713	.097414	.100840	.104314	.107832	.111391	.114990	.118625	.125996	.133484	.141073	.148747
	0.00	.088085	.094565	.101266	.104692	.108166	.111684	.115243	.118842	.122477	.129848	.137336	.144925	.152599
	-.10	.091937	.098417	.105118	.108545	.112018	.115536	.119096	.122694	.126330	.133700	.141189	.148778	.156452
	-.20	.095789	.102270	.108971	.112397	.115871	.119388	.122948	.126547	.130182	.137552	.145041	.152630	.160304
	-.30	.099641	.106122	.112823	.116249	.119723	.123241	.126800	.130399	.134034	.141405	.148893	.156482	.164156
	-.40	.103494	.109974	.116675	.120102	.123575	.127093	.130652	.134251	.137886	.145257	.152745	.160334	.168009
30	.40	.070376	.077120	.084088	.087646	.091249	.094894	.098577	.102295	.106045	.113629	.121309	.129066	.136885
	.30	.074228	.080972	.087940	.091498	.095102	.098746	.102429	.106147	.109897	.117482	.125162	.132919	.140737
	.20	.078080	.084825	.091792	.095350	.098954	.102599	.106282	.110000	.113750	.121334	.129014	.136771	.144590
	.10	.081933	.088677	.095644	.099203	.102806	.106451	.110134	.113852	.117602	.125186	.132866	.140623	.148442
	0.00	.085785	.092529	.099497	.103055	.106658	.110303	.113986	.117704	.121454	.129039	.136718	.144475	.152294
	-.10	.089637	.096381	.103349	.106907	.110511	.114155	.117838	.121556	.125306	.132891	.140571	.148328	.156146
	-.20	.093489	.100234	.107201	.110760	.114363	.118008	.121691	.125409	.129159	.136743	.144423	.152180	.159999
	-.30	.097342	.104086	.111053	.114612	.118215	.121860	.125543	.129261	.133011	.140595	.148275	.156032	.163851
	-.40	.101194	.107938	.114906	.118464	.122067	.125712	.129395	.133113	.136863	.144448	.152127	.159885	.167703

10.0 YEAR HOLDING PERIOD
.200 EQUITY YIELD RATE
.900 LOAN RATIO

INTEREST RATE

TERM YEARS	APPR DEP	5.0	6.0	7.0	7.5	8.0	8.5	9.0	9.5	10.0	11.0	12.0	13.0	14.0
10	.40	.084471	.089823	.095318	.098118	.100954	.103825	.106730	.109670	.112643	.118690	.124869	.131176	.137608
	.30	.088323	.093675	.099170	.101971	.104806	.107677	.110583	.113522	.116495	.122693	.128721	.135028	.141460
	.20	.092176	.097527	.103022	.105823	.108659	.111530	.114435	.117374	.120348	.126395	.132574	.138881	.145313
	.10	.096028	.101379	.106874	.109675	.112511	.115382	.118287	.121227	.124200	.130247	.136426	.142733	.149165
	0.00	.099880	.105232	.110727	.113527	.116363	.119234	.122139	.125079	.128052	.134100	.140278	.146585	.153017
	-.10	.103733	.109084	.114579	.117380	.120216	.123086	.125992	.128931	.131905	.137952	.144130	.150437	.156870
	-.20	.107585	.112936	.118431	.121232	.124068	.126939	.129844	.132783	.135757	.141804	.147983	.154290	.160722
	-.30	.111437	.116788	.122284	.125084	.127920	.130791	.133696	.136636	.139609	.145656	.151835	.158142	.164574
	-.40	.115289	.120641	.126136	.128937	.131772	.134643	.137548	.140488	.143461	.149509	.155687	.161994	.168426
15	.40	.069855	.076190	.082732	.086077	.089471	.092913	.096401	.099935	.103513	.110797	.118245	.125846	.133592
	.30	.073707	.080043	.086584	.089930	.093324	.096765	.100254	.103787	.107365	.114649	.122097	.129698	.137444
	.20	.077559	.083895	.090436	.093782	.097176	.100618	.104106	.107640	.111218	.118502	.125949	.133555	.141296
	.10	.081412	.087747	.094288	.097634	.101028	.104470	.107958	.111492	.115070	.122354	.129801	.137403	.145149
	0.00	.085264	.091599	.098141	.101486	.104881	.108322	.111811	.115344	.118922	.126206	.133654	.141255	.149001
	-.10	.089116	.095452	.101993	.105339	.108733	.112175	.115663	.119196	.122774	.130058	.137506	.145107	.152853
	-.20	.092968	.099304	.105845	.109191	.112585	.116027	.119515	.123049	.126627	.133911	.141358	.148960	.156706
	-.30	.096821	.103156	.109698	.113043	.116437	.119879	.123367	.126901	.130479	.137763	.145210	.152812	.160558
	-.40	.100673	.107008	.113550	.116896	.120290	.123731	.127220	.130753	.134331	.141615	.149063	.156664	.164410
20	.40	.062768	.069668	.076803	.080454	.084158	.087913	.091716	.095566	.099461	.107376	.115446	.123655	.131988
	.30	.066620	.073521	.080656	.084307	.088010	.091765	.095568	.099418	.103313	.111228	.119298	.127507	.135840
	.20	.070473	.077373	.084508	.088159	.091863	.095617	.099420	.103270	.107165	.115081	.123151	.131360	.139693
	.10	.074325	.081225	.088360	.092011	.095715	.099469	.103273	.107123	.111017	.118933	.127003	.135212	.143545
	0.00	.078177	.085077	.092213	.095863	.099567	.103322	.107125	.110975	.114870	.122785	.130855	.139064	.147397
	-.10	.082030	.088930	.096065	.099716	.103419	.107174	.110977	.114827	.118722	.126637	.134707	.142916	.151249
	-.20	.085882	.092782	.099917	.103568	.107272	.111026	.114829	.118680	.122574	.130490	.138560	.146769	.155102
	-.30	.089734	.096634	.103769	.107420	.111124	.114878	.118682	.122532	.126427	.134342	.142412	.150621	.158954
	-.40	.093586	.100487	.107622	.111272	.114976	.118731	.122534	.126384	.130279	.138194	.146264	.154473	.162806
25	.40	.058686	.065977	.073515	.077370	.081278	.085235	.089240	.093288	.097378	.105670	.114094	.122632	.131265
	.30	.062538	.069829	.077367	.081222	.085130	.089087	.093092	.097141	.101230	.109522	.117946	.126484	.135118
	.20	.066391	.073681	.081220	.085074	.088982	.092940	.096944	.100993	.105082	.113374	.121799	.130336	.138970
	.10	.070243	.077533	.085072	.088927	.092834	.096792	.100797	.104845	.108935	.117227	.125651	.134189	.142822
	0.00	.074095	.081386	.088924	.092779	.096687	.100644	.104649	.108697	.112787	.121079	.129503	.138041	.146674
	-.10	.077947	.085238	.092777	.096631	.100539	.104497	.108501	.112550	.116639	.124931	.133356	.141893	.150527
	-.20	.081800	.089090	.096629	.100484	.104391	.108349	.112353	.116402	.120492	.128783	.137208	.145746	.154379
	-.30	.085652	.092942	.100481	.104336	.108244	.112201	.116206	.120254	.124344	.132636	.141060	.149598	.158231
	-.40	.089504	.096795	.104333	.108188	.112096	.116053	.120058	.124106	.128196	.136488	.144912	.153450	.162083
30	.40	.056099	.063686	.071525	.075528	.079582	.083682	.087825	.092008	.096227	.104759	.113399	.122126	.130922
	.30	.059951	.067538	.075377	.079380	.083434	.087534	.091678	.095860	.100079	.108611	.117251	.125978	.134774
	.20	.063803	.071391	.079229	.083232	.087286	.091387	.095530	.099713	.103931	.112464	.121104	.129830	.138626
	.10	.067656	.075243	.083081	.087085	.091138	.095239	.099382	.103565	.107784	.116316	.124956	.133683	.142479
	0.00	.071508	.079095	.086933	.090937	.094991	.099091	.103234	.107417	.111636	.120168	.128808	.137535	.146331
	-.10	.075360	.082947	.090786	.094789	.098843	.102943	.107087	.111269	.115488	.124021	.132660	.141387	.150183
	-.20	.079212	.086800	.094638	.098641	.102695	.106796	.110939	.115122	.119340	.127873	.136513	.145239	.154036
	-.30	.083065	.090652	.098491	.102494	.106547	.110648	.114791	.118974	.123193	.131725	.140365	.149092	.157888
	-.40	.086917	.094504	.102343	.106346	.110400	.114500	.118644	.122826	.127045	.135577	.144217	.152944	.161740

```
10.0  YEAR HOLDING PERIOD
 .250  EQUITY YIELD RATE
 .600  LOAN RATIO
```

INTEREST RATE

TERM YEARS	APPR DEP	5.0	6.0	7.0	7.5	8.0	8.5	9.0	9.5	10.0	11.0	12.0	13.0	14.0
10	.40	.146295	.149862	.153526	.155393	.157283	.159197	.161134	.163094	.165076	.169107	.173227	.177431	.181719
	.30	.149302	.152862	.156533	.158400	.160291	.162204	.164141	.166101	.168083	.172115	.176234	.180438	.184727
	.20	.152309	.155877	.159540	.161407	.163298	.165212	.167149	.169108	.171090	.175122	.179241	.183446	.187734
	.10	.155316	.158884	.162547	.164414	.166305	.168219	.170156	.172115	.174098	.178129	.182248	.186453	.190741
	0.00	.158324	.161891	.165555	.167422	.169312	.171226	.173163	.175123	.177105	.181136	.185256	.189460	.193748
	-.10	.161331	.164898	.168562	.170429	.172320	.174233	.176170	.178130	.180112	.184144	.188263	.192467	.196756
	-.20	.164338	.167906	.171569	.173436	.175327	.177241	.179178	.181137	.183120	.187151	.191270	.195475	.199763
	-.30	.167345	.170913	.174576	.176444	.178334	.180248	.182185	.184144	.186127	.190158	.194277	.198482	.202770
	-.40	.170353	.173920	.177584	.179451	.181341	.183255	.185192	.187152	.189134	.193165	.197285	.201489	.205777
15	.40	.134426	.138561	.142834	.145020	.147239	.149489	.151771	.154083	.156425	.161195	.166075	.171058	.176140
	.30	.137433	.141568	.145841	.148027	.150246	.152496	.154778	.157090	.159432	.164202	.169082	.174066	.179147
	.20	.140440	.144575	.148848	.151034	.153253	.155504	.157785	.160097	.162439	.167209	.172089	.177073	.182154
	.10	.143447	.147583	.151855	.154042	.156260	.158511	.160793	.163105	.165447	.170217	.175096	.180080	.185162
	0.00	.146455	.150590	.154863	.157049	.159268	.161518	.163800	.166112	.168454	.173224	.178104	.183087	.188169
	-.10	.149462	.153597	.157870	.160056	.162275	.164525	.166807	.169119	.171461	.176231	.181111	.186095	.191176
	-.20	.152469	.156604	.160877	.163063	.165282	.167533	.169814	.172127	.174468	.179238	.184118	.189102	.194183
	-.30	.155476	.159612	.163884	.166071	.168289	.170540	.172822	.175134	.177476	.182246	.187125	.192109	.197191
	-.40	.158484	.162619	.166892	.169078	.171297	.173547	.175829	.178141	.180483	.185253	.190133	.195116	.200198
20	.40	.128671	.133154	.137797	.140176	.142590	.145040	.147523	.150039	.152585	.157765	.163053	.168439	.173912
	.30	.131678	.136161	.140805	.143183	.145598	.148047	.150531	.153046	.155592	.160773	.166061	.171446	.176919
	.20	.134686	.139169	.143812	.146190	.148605	.151055	.153538	.156053	.158600	.163780	.169068	.174453	.179926
	.10	.137693	.142176	.146819	.149198	.151612	.154062	.156545	.159061	.161607	.166787	.172075	.177461	.182934
	0.00	.140700	.145183	.149826	.152205	.154619	.157069	.159552	.162068	.164614	.169794	.175082	.180468	.185941
	-.10	.143707	.148191	.152834	.155212	.157627	.160076	.162560	.165075	.167621	.172802	.178090	.183475	.188948
	-.20	.146715	.151198	.155841	.158219	.160634	.163084	.165567	.168082	.170629	.175809	.181097	.186482	.191955
	-.30	.149722	.154205	.158848	.161227	.163641	.166091	.168574	.171090	.173636	.178816	.184104	.189490	.194963
	-.40	.152729	.157212	.161855	.164234	.166649	.169098	.171581	.174097	.176643	.181823	.187111	.192497	.197970
25	.40	.125357	.130094	.135004	.137519	.140071	.142658	.145279	.147931	.150612	.156055	.161594	.167216	.172908
	.30	.128364	.133101	.138011	.140526	.143078	.145665	.148286	.150938	.153619	.159062	.164601	.170223	.175915
	.20	.131371	.136108	.141018	.143533	.146085	.148673	.151293	.153945	.156626	.162069	.167608	.173237	.178922
	.10	.134378	.139116	.144026	.146540	.149093	.151680	.154300	.156952	.159633	.165077	.170616	.176237	.181930
	0.00	.137386	.142123	.147033	.149548	.152100	.154687	.157308	.159960	.162641	.168084	.173623	.179245	.184937
	-.10	.140393	.145130	.150040	.152555	.155107	.157694	.160315	.162967	.165648	.171091	.176630	.182252	.187944
	-.20	.143400	.148137	.153047	.155562	.158114	.160702	.163322	.165974	.168655	.174098	.179637	.185259	.190951
	-.30	.146407	.151145	.156055	.158569	.161122	.163709	.166329	.168981	.171663	.177106	.182645	.188266	.193959
	-.40	.149415	.154152	.159062	.161577	.164129	.166716	.169337	.171989	.174670	.180113	.185652	.191274	.196966
30	.40	.123256	.128195	.133313	.135932	.138587	.141276	.143997	.146746	.149521	.155142	.160843	.166610	.172431
	.30	.126263	.131202	.136320	.138939	.141594	.144283	.147004	.149753	.152528	.158149	.163851	.169618	.175438
	.20	.129270	.134209	.139327	.141946	.144602	.147291	.150011	.152760	.155536	.161157	.166858	.172625	.178445
	.10	.132277	.137217	.142335	.144954	.147609	.150298	.153018	.155767	.158543	.164164	.169865	.175632	.181453
	0.00	.135285	.140224	.145342	.147961	.150616	.153305	.156026	.158775	.161551	.167171	.172872	.178640	.184460
	-.10	.138292	.143231	.148349	.150968	.153623	.156313	.159033	.161782	.164557	.170178	.175880	.181647	.187467
	-.20	.141299	.146238	.151356	.153975	.156631	.159320	.162040	.164789	.167564	.173186	.178887	.184654	.190474
	-.30	.144306	.149246	.154364	.156983	.159638	.162327	.165047	.167796	.170572	.176193	.181894	.187661	.193482
	-.40	.147314	.152253	.157371	.159990	.162645	.165334	.168055	.170804	.173579	.179200	.184902	.190669	.196489

10.0 YEAR HOLDING PERIOD
.250 EQUITY YIELD RATE
.667 LOAN RATIO

INTEREST RATE

TERM YEARS	APPR DEP	5.0	6.0	7.0	7.5	8.0	8.5	9.0	9.5	10.0	11.0	12.0	13.0	14.0
10	.40	.136108	.140072	.144142	.146217	.148818	.150444	.152596	.154774	.156976	.161456	.166032	.170704	.175469
	.30	.139115	.143079	.147150	.149224	.151325	.153451	.155603	.157781	.159983	.164463	.169040	.173711	.178476
	.20	.142122	.146086	.150157	.152231	.154332	.156459	.158611	.160788	.162991	.167470	.172047	.176719	.181483
	.10	.145130	.149094	.153164	.155229	.157339	.159466	.161618	.163795	.165998	.170477	.175054	.179726	.184491
	0.00	.148137	.152101	.156171	.158246	.160347	.162473	.164625	.166803	.169005	.173485	.178061	.182733	.187498
	-.10	.151144	.155108	.159179	.161253	.163354	.165480	.167632	.169810	.172012	.176492	.181069	.185740	.190505
	-.20	.154151	.158115	.162186	.164260	.166361	.168488	.170640	.172817	.175020	.179499	.184076	.188748	.193512
	-.30	.157159	.161123	.165193	.167268	.169368	.171495	.173647	.175824	.178027	.182506	.187083	.191755	.196520
	-.40	.160166	.164130	.168200	.170275	.172376	.174502	.176654	.178832	.181034	.185514	.190090	.194762	.199527
15	.40	.122920	.127515	.132262	.134691	.137157	.139657	.142193	.144762	.147364	.152664	.158086	.163623	.169269
	.30	.125927	.130522	.135269	.137699	.140164	.142665	.145200	.147769	.150371	.155671	.161093	.166631	.172277
	.20	.128935	.133529	.138277	.140706	.143171	.145672	.148207	.150776	.153378	.158678	.164100	.169638	.175284
	.10	.131942	.136537	.141284	.143713	.146178	.148679	.151214	.153783	.156385	.161685	.167108	.172645	.178291
	0.00	.134949	.139544	.144291	.146720	.149186	.151686	.154222	.156791	.159393	.164693	.170115	.175652	.181298
	-.10	.137956	.142551	.147298	.149728	.152193	.154694	.157229	.159798	.162400	.167700	.173122	.178660	.184306
	-.20	.140964	.145558	.150306	.152735	.155200	.157701	.160236	.162805	.165407	.170707	.176129	.181667	.187313
	-.30	.143971	.148566	.153313	.155742	.158207	.160708	.163243	.165812	.168414	.173714	.179137	.184674	.190320
	-.40	.146978	.151573	.156320	.158749	.161215	.163715	.166251	.168820	.171422	.176722	.182144	.187681	.193327
20	.40	.116526	.121507	.126666	.129309	.131992	.134714	.137473	.140268	.143097	.148853	.154729	.160713	.166794
	.30	.119533	.124515	.129674	.132316	.134999	.137721	.140480	.143275	.146105	.151860	.157736	.163720	.169801
	.20	.122541	.127522	.132681	.135324	.138007	.140728	.143488	.146283	.149112	.154868	.160743	.166727	.172808
	.10	.125548	.130529	.135688	.138331	.141014	.143736	.146495	.149290	.152119	.157875	.163751	.169734	.175816
	0.00	.128555	.133536	.138695	.141338	.144021	.146743	.149502	.152297	.155126	.160882	.166758	.172742	.178823
	-.10	.131562	.136544	.141703	.144345	.147028	.149750	.152509	.155304	.158134	.163889	.169765	.175749	.181830
	-.20	.134570	.139551	.144710	.147353	.150036	.152757	.155517	.158312	.161141	.166897	.172772	.178756	.184837
	-.30	.137577	.142558	.147717	.150360	.153043	.155765	.158524	.161319	.164148	.169904	.175780	.181763	.187845
	-.40	.140584	.145565	.150724	.153367	.156050	.158772	.161531	.164326	.167155	.172911	.178787	.184771	.190852
25	.40	.112843	.118107	.123562	.126357	.129192	.132067	.134979	.137926	.140905	.146953	.153107	.159353	.165678
	.30	.115850	.121114	.126570	.129364	.132200	.135074	.137986	.140933	.143912	.149960	.156114	.162361	.168685
	.20	.118858	.124121	.129577	.132371	.135207	.138082	.140994	.143940	.146919	.152967	.159122	.165368	.171693
	.10	.121865	.127129	.132584	.135379	.138214	.141089	.144001	.146947	.149926	.155974	.162129	.168375	.174700
	0.00	.124872	.130136	.135591	.138386	.141221	.144096	.147008	.149955	.152934	.158982	.165136	.171382	.177707
	-.10	.127879	.133143	.138599	.141393	.144229	.147104	.150015	.152962	.155941	.161989	.168143	.174390	.180714
	-.20	.130887	.136150	.141606	.144400	.147236	.150111	.153023	.155969	.158948	.164996	.171151	.177397	.183722
	-.30	.133894	.139158	.144613	.147408	.150243	.153118	.156030	.158976	.161955	.168003	.174158	.180404	.186729
	-.40	.136901	.142165	.147620	.150415	.153250	.156125	.159037	.161984	.164963	.171011	.177165	.183412	.189736
30	.40	.110509	.115997	.121684	.124594	.127544	.130532	.133554	.136609	.139693	.145938	.152273	.158681	.165148
	.30	.113316	.119004	.124691	.127601	.130551	.133539	.136562	.139616	.142700	.148946	.155281	.161688	.168155
	.20	.116523	.122012	.127698	.130608	.133558	.136546	.139569	.142623	.145707	.151953	.158288	.164696	.171163
	.10	.119531	.125020	.130705	.133615	.136566	.139554	.142576	.145631	.148715	.154960	.161295	.167703	.174170
	0.00	.122538	.128026	.133713	.136623	.139573	.142561	.145583	.148638	.151722	.157968	.164302	.170710	.177177
	-.10	.125545	.131033	.136720	.139630	.142580	.145568	.148591	.151645	.154729	.160975	.167310	.173717	.180184
	-.20	.128552	.134041	.139727	.142637	.145587	.148575	.151598	.154652	.157736	.163982	.170317	.176725	.183192
	-.30	.131560	.137048	.142734	.145644	.148595	.151583	.154605	.157660	.160744	.166989	.173324	.179732	.186199
	-.40	.134567	.140055	.145742	.148652	.151602	.154590	.157612	.160667	.163751	.169997	.176331	.182739	.189206

10.0 YEAR HOLDING PERIOD
.250 EQUITY YIELD RATE
.700 LOAN RATIO

INTEREST RATE

TERM YEARS	APPR DEP	5.0	6.0	7.0	7.5	8.0	8.5	9.0	9.5	10.0	11.0	12.0	13.0	14.0
10	.40	.131015	.135177	.139451	.141630	.143835	.146068	.148328	.150614	.152927	.157630	.162436	.167341	.172344
	.30	.134022	.138185	.142459	.144637	.146843	.149075	.151335	.153621	.155934	.160637	.165443	.170348	.175351
	.20	.137030	.141192	.145466	.147644	.149850	.152083	.154342	.156629	.158941	.163645	.168450	.173356	.178358
	.10	.140037	.144199	.148473	.150651	.152857	.155090	.157350	.159636	.161949	.166652	.171458	.176363	.181356
	0.00	.143044	.147206	.151480	.153659	.155864	.158097	.160357	.162643	.164956	.169659	.174465	.179370	.184373
	-.10	.146051	.150214	.154488	.156666	.158872	.161104	.163364	.165650	.167963	.172666	.177472	.182377	.187380
	-.20	.149059	.153221	.157495	.159673	.161879	.164112	.166371	.168658	.170970	.175674	.180479	.185385	.190388
	-.30	.152066	.156228	.160502	.162680	.164886	.167119	.169379	.171665	.173978	.178681	.183487	.188392	.193395
	-.40	.155073	.159235	.163509	.165688	.167893	.170126	.172386	.174672	.176985	.181688	.186494	.191399	.196402
15	.40	.117168	.121993	.126977	.129528	.132116	.134742	.137404	.140102	.142834	.148399	.154092	.159906	.165835
	.30	.120175	.125000	.129985	.132535	.135124	.137749	.140411	.143109	.145841	.151406	.157099	.162914	.168842
	.20	.123183	.128007	.132992	.135542	.138131	.140757	.143419	.146116	.148848	.154413	.160106	.165921	.171849
	.10	.126190	.131014	.135999	.138550	.141138	.143764	.146426	.149123	.151856	.157421	.163114	.168928	.174856
	0.00	.129197	.134022	.139006	.141557	.144146	.146771	.149433	.152131	.154863	.160428	.166121	.171935	.177864
	-.10	.132204	.137029	.142014	.144564	.147153	.149778	.152440	.155138	.157870	.163435	.169128	.174943	.180871
	-.20	.135212	.140036	.145021	.147571	.150160	.152786	.155448	.158145	.160877	.166442	.172135	.177950	.183878
	-.30	.138219	.143043	.148028	.150579	.153167	.155793	.158455	.161152	.163885	.169450	.175143	.180957	.186886
	-.40	.141226	.146051	.151035	.153586	.156175	.158800	.161462	.164160	.166892	.172457	.178150	.183964	.189893
20	.40	.110455	.115685	.121102	.123877	.126694	.129552	.132449	.135383	.138354	.144398	.150567	.156850	.163235
	.30	.113462	.118692	.124109	.126884	.129701	.132559	.135456	.138391	.141361	.147405	.153574	.159857	.166263
	.20	.116469	.121699	.127116	.129891	.132708	.135566	.138463	.141398	.144369	.150412	.156582	.162865	.169250
	.10	.119476	.124707	.130123	.132898	.135715	.138573	.141470	.144405	.147376	.153420	.159589	.165872	.172257
	0.00	.122484	.127714	.133131	.135906	.138723	.141581	.144478	.147412	.150383	.156427	.162596	.168879	.175264
	-.10	.125491	.130721	.136138	.138913	.141730	.144588	.147485	.150420	.153390	.159434	.165603	.171886	.178272
	-.20	.128498	.133728	.139145	.141920	.144737	.147595	.150492	.153427	.156398	.162441	.168611	.174894	.181279
	-.30	.131505	.136736	.142152	.144927	.147744	.150602	.153499	.156434	.159405	.165449	.171618	.177901	.184286
	-.40	.134513	.139743	.145160	.147935	.150752	.153610	.156507	.159441	.162412	.168456	.174625	.180908	.187293
25	.40	.106587	.112114	.117843	.120777	.123754	.126773	.129830	.132924	.136052	.142402	.148864	.155423	.162064
	.30	.109595	.115121	.120850	.123784	.126761	.129780	.132837	.135931	.139059	.145410	.151872	.158430	.165071
	.20	.112602	.118129	.123857	.126791	.129769	.132787	.135844	.138938	.142066	.148417	.154879	.161438	.168078
	.10	.115609	.121136	.126864	.129798	.132776	.135794	.138852	.141946	.145074	.151424	.157886	.164445	.171086
	0.00	.118616	.124143	.129872	.132806	.135783	.138802	.141859	.144953	.148081	.154431	.160893	.167452	.174093
	-.10	.121624	.127150	.132879	.135813	.138790	.141809	.144866	.147960	.151088	.157439	.163901	.170459	.177100
	-.20	.124631	.130158	.135886	.138820	.141798	.144816	.147873	.150967	.154095	.160446	.166908	.173467	.180107
	-.30	.127638	.133165	.138893	.141827	.144805	.147823	.150881	.153975	.157103	.163453	.169915	.176474	.183115
	-.40	.130645	.136172	.141901	.144835	.147812	.150831	.153888	.156982	.160110	.166460	.172922	.179481	.186122
30	.40	.104136	.109899	.115870	.118925	.122023	.125160	.128334	.131541	.134779	.141337	.147989	.154717	.161507
	.30	.107144	.112906	.118877	.121932	.125030	.128168	.131341	.134549	.137787	.144345	.150996	.157724	.164515
	.20	.110151	.115913	.121884	.124940	.128038	.131175	.134349	.137556	.140794	.147352	.154003	.160732	.167522
	.10	.113158	.118921	.124892	.127947	.131045	.134182	.137356	.140563	.143801	.150359	.157011	.163739	.170529
	0.00	.116165	.121928	.127899	.130954	.134052	.137189	.140363	.143570	.146808	.153366	.160018	.166746	.173536
	-.10	.119173	.124935	.130906	.133962	.137059	.140197	.143370	.146578	.149816	.156374	.163025	.169753	.176544
	-.20	.122180	.127942	.133913	.136969	.140067	.143204	.146378	.149585	.152823	.159381	.166032	.172761	.179551
	-.30	.125187	.130950	.136921	.139976	.143074	.146211	.149385	.152592	.155830	.162388	.169040	.175768	.182558
	-.40	.128194	.133957	.139928	.142983	.146081	.149219	.152392	.155599	.158837	.165395	.172047	.178775	.185565

10.0 YEAR HOLDING PERIOD
.250 EQUITY YIELD RATE
.750 LOAN RATIO

INTEREST RATE

TERM YEARS	APPR DEP	14.0	13.0	12.0	11.0	10.0	9.5	9.0	8.5	8.0	7.5	7.0	6.0	5.0
10	.40	.167656	.162296	.157040	.151892	.146852	.144374	.141925	.139504	.137111	.134748	.132414	.127835	.123376
	.30	.170664	.165303	.160048	.154899	.149859	.147382	.144932	.142511	.140119	.137755	.135421	.130842	.126383
	.20	.173671	.168311	.163055	.157906	.152867	.150389	.147939	.145518	.143126	.140763	.138429	.133850	.129390
	.10	.176678	.171318	.166062	.160913	.155874	.153396	.150947	.148525	.146133	.143770	.141436	.136857	.132397
	0.00	.179685	.174325	.169069	.163921	.158881	.156403	.153954	.151533	.149140	.146777	.144443	.139864	.135405
	-.10	.182693	.177333	.172077	.166928	.161888	.159411	.156961	.154540	.152148	.149784	.147450	.142871	.138412
	-.20	.185700	.180340	.175084	.169935	.164896	.162418	.159968	.157547	.155155	.152792	.150458	.145879	.141419
	-.30	.188707	.183347	.178091	.172942	.167903	.165425	.162976	.160554	.158162	.155799	.153465	.148886	.144426
	-.40	.191714	.186354	.181098	.175950	.170910	.168432	.165983	.163562	.161169	.158806	.156472	.151893	.147434
15	.40	.160682	.154330	.148101	.142001	.136038	.133111	.130221	.127369	.124555	.121782	.119049	.113708	.108539
	.30	.163689	.157338	.151108	.145008	.139046	.136118	.133228	.130376	.127563	.124789	.122056	.116716	.111547
	.20	.166697	.160345	.154115	.148015	.142053	.139125	.136235	.133383	.130570	.127796	.125064	.119723	.114554
	.10	.169704	.163352	.157122	.151022	.145060	.142133	.139243	.136390	.133577	.130804	.128071	.122730	.117561
	0.00	.172711	.166359	.160130	.154030	.148067	.145140	.142250	.139398	.136584	.133811	.131079	.125737	.120568
	-.10	.175718	.169367	.163137	.157037	.151075	.148147	.145257	.142405	.139592	.136818	.134085	.128745	.123576
	-.20	.178726	.172374	.166144	.160044	.154082	.151155	.148264	.145412	.142599	.139826	.137093	.131752	.126583
	-.30	.181733	.175381	.169151	.163052	.157089	.154162	.151272	.148419	.145606	.142833	.140100	.134759	.129590
	-.40	.184740	.178388	.172159	.166059	.160096	.157169	.154279	.151427	.148613	.145840	.143107	.137766	.132597
20	.40	.157897	.151056	.144324	.137714	.131239	.128056	.124911	.121807	.118745	.115727	.112754	.106950	.101346
	.30	.160904	.154063	.147331	.140721	.134246	.131063	.127919	.124815	.121753	.118734	.115761	.109957	.104354
	.20	.163912	.157070	.150338	.143729	.137253	.134070	.130926	.127822	.124760	.121741	.118768	.112965	.107361
	.10	.166919	.160078	.153346	.146736	.140260	.137077	.133933	.130829	.127767	.124749	.121776	.115972	.110368
	0.00	.169926	.163085	.156353	.149743	.143268	.140085	.136940	.133836	.130774	.127756	.124783	.118979	.113375
	-.10	.172933	.166092	.159360	.152750	.146275	.143092	.139948	.136844	.133782	.130763	.127790	.121986	.116383
	-.20	.175941	.169099	.162368	.155758	.149282	.146099	.142955	.139851	.136789	.133771	.130797	.124994	.119390
	-.30	.178948	.172107	.165375	.158765	.152290	.149107	.145962	.142858	.139796	.136778	.133805	.128001	.122397
	-.40	.181955	.175114	.168382	.161772	.155297	.152114	.148969	.145865	.142803	.139785	.136812	.131008	.125404
25	.40	.156642	.149527	.142500	.135576	.128772	.125420	.122106	.118830	.115596	.112406	.109262	.103124	.097203
	.30	.159649	.152534	.145507	.138583	.131779	.128428	.125113	.121837	.118603	.115413	.112269	.106132	.100210
	.20	.162657	.155541	.148514	.141590	.134786	.131435	.128120	.124844	.121610	.118420	.115277	.109139	.103217
	.10	.165664	.158548	.151521	.144598	.137794	.134442	.131127	.127852	.124617	.121427	.118284	.112146	.106225
	0.00	.168671	.161556	.154529	.147605	.140801	.137449	.134135	.130859	.127625	.124435	.121291	.115153	.109232
	-.10	.171678	.164563	.157536	.150612	.143808	.140457	.137142	.133866	.130632	.127442	.124298	.118161	.112239
	-.20	.174686	.167570	.160543	.153619	.146815	.143464	.140149	.136873	.133639	.130449	.127306	.121168	.115246
	-.30	.177693	.170578	.163550	.156627	.149823	.146471	.143156	.139881	.136647	.133456	.130313	.124175	.118254
	-.40	.180700	.173585	.166558	.159634	.152830	.149478	.146164	.142888	.139654	.136464	.133320	.127182	.121261
30	.40	.156046	.148770	.141562	.134435	.127409	.123939	.120503	.117103	.113741	.110422	.107148	.100751	.094577
	.30	.159053	.151778	.144569	.137442	.130416	.126947	.123510	.120110	.116748	.113429	.110156	.103758	.097584
	.20	.162060	.154785	.147576	.140449	.133423	.129954	.126517	.123117	.119756	.116436	.113163	.106765	.100591
	.10	.165067	.157792	.150583	.143457	.136430	.132962	.129525	.126124	.122763	.119444	.116170	.109773	.103599
	0.00	.168075	.160799	.153591	.146464	.139438	.135968	.132532	.129132	.125770	.122451	.119177	.112780	.106606
	-.10	.171082	.163807	.156598	.149471	.142445	.138976	.135539	.132139	.128777	.125458	.122185	.115787	.109613
	-.20	.174089	.166814	.159605	.152478	.145452	.141983	.138546	.135146	.131784	.128466	.125192	.118794	.112620
	-.30	.177096	.169821	.162612	.155486	.148459	.144990	.141554	.138153	.134792	.131473	.128199	.121802	.115628
	-.40	.180104	.172828	.165620	.158493	.151467	.147997	.144561	.141161	.137799	.134480	.131206	.124809	.118635

10.0 YEAR HOLDING PERIOD
.250 EQUITY YIELD RATE
.800 LOAN RATIO

INTEREST RATE

TERM YEARS	APPR DEP	5.0	6.0	7.0	7.5	8.0	8.5	9.0	9.5	10.0	11.0	12.0	13.0	14.0
10	.40	.115736	.120493	.125377	.127867	.130387	.132939	.135522	.138135	.140778	.146153	.151645	.157251	.162969
	.30	.118743	.123500	.128384	.130874	.133395	.135946	.138529	.141142	.143785	.149160	.154652	.160258	.165976
	.20	.121750	.126507	.131392	.133881	.136402	.138954	.141536	.144149	.146792	.152167	.157660	.163266	.168983
	.10	.124758	.129514	.134399	.136888	.139409	.141961	.144543	.147156	.149799	.155175	.160667	.166273	.171990
	0.00	.127765	.132522	.137406	.139896	.142416	.144968	.147551	.150164	.152807	.158182	.163674	.169280	.174998
	-.10	.130772	.135529	.140413	.142903	.145424	.147975	.150558	.153171	.155814	.161189	.166681	.172288	.178005
	-.20	.133779	.138536	.143421	.145910	.148431	.150983	.153565	.156178	.158821	.164196	.169689	.175295	.181012
	-.30	.136787	.141543	.146428	.148918	.151438	.153990	.156572	.159185	.161828	.167204	.172696	.178302	.184019
	-.40	.139794	.144551	.149435	.151925	.154445	.156997	.159580	.162193	.164836	.170211	.175703	.181309	.187027
15	.40	.099911	.105424	.111121	.114036	.116994	.119995	.123037	.126120	.129243	.135603	.142109	.148754	.155530
	.30	.102918	.108432	.114128	.117043	.120002	.123002	.126045	.129128	.132250	.138610	.145116	.151762	.158537
	.20	.105925	.111439	.117136	.120051	.123009	.126010	.129052	.132135	.135257	.141617	.148124	.154769	.161544
	.10	.108932	.114446	.120143	.123058	.126016	.129017	.132059	.135142	.138265	.144624	.151131	.157776	.164551
	0.00	.111940	.117453	.123150	.126065	.129023	.132024	.135066	.138149	.141272	.147632	.154138	.160783	.167559
	-.10	.114947	.120461	.126157	.129072	.132031	.135031	.138074	.141157	.144279	.150639	.157146	.163791	.170566
	-.20	.117954	.123468	.129165	.132080	.135038	.138039	.141081	.144164	.147286	.153646	.160153	.166798	.173573
	-.30	.120961	.126475	.132172	.135087	.138045	.141046	.144088	.147171	.150294	.156654	.163160	.169805	.176580
	-.40	.123969	.129482	.135179	.138094	.141052	.144053	.147095	.150178	.153301	.159661	.166167	.172812	.179588
20	.40	.092238	.098215	.104406	.107577	.110797	.114063	.117374	.120728	.124123	.131030	.138081	.145261	.152559
	.30	.095245	.101223	.107413	.110585	.113804	.117070	.120381	.123735	.127130	.134037	.141088	.148269	.155566
	.20	.098252	.104230	.110421	.113592	.116811	.120078	.123389	.126743	.130138	.137045	.144095	.151276	.158573
	.10	.101260	.107237	.113428	.116599	.119819	.123085	.126396	.129750	.133145	.140052	.147103	.154283	.161581
	0.00	.104267	.110244	.116435	.119606	.122826	.126092	.129403	.132757	.136152	.143059	.150110	.157291	.164588
	-.10	.107274	.113252	.119442	.122614	.125833	.129099	.132411	.135764	.139160	.146066	.153117	.160298	.167595
	-.20	.110281	.116259	.122450	.125621	.128840	.132107	.135418	.138772	.142167	.149074	.156124	.163305	.170602
	-.30	.113289	.119266	.125457	.128628	.131848	.135114	.138425	.141779	.145174	.152081	.159132	.166312	.173610
	-.40	.116296	.122273	.128464	.131636	.134855	.138121	.141432	.144786	.148181	.155088	.162139	.169320	.176617
25	.40	.087818	.094135	.100681	.104035	.107437	.110887	.114381	.117917	.121492	.128750	.136135	.143630	.151220
	.30	.090826	.097142	.103689	.107042	.110445	.113894	.117388	.120924	.124499	.131757	.139142	.146638	.154227
	.20	.093833	.100149	.106696	.110049	.113452	.116902	.120396	.123932	.127507	.134764	.142149	.149645	.157235
	.10	.096840	.103156	.109703	.113056	.116459	.119909	.123403	.126939	.130514	.137771	.145157	.152652	.160242
	0.00	.099847	.106164	.112710	.116064	.119466	.122916	.126410	.129946	.133521	.140779	.148164	.155659	.163249
	-.10	.102855	.109171	.115718	.119071	.122474	.125923	.129418	.132953	.136528	.143786	.151171	.158667	.166256
	-.20	.105862	.112178	.118725	.122078	.125481	.128931	.132425	.135961	.139536	.146793	.154178	.161674	.169264
	-.30	.108869	.115185	.121732	.125085	.128488	.131938	.135432	.138968	.142543	.149800	.157186	.164681	.172271
	-.40	.111876	.118193	.124739	.128093	.131495	.134945	.138439	.141975	.145550	.152808	.160193	.167688	.175278
30	.40	.085017	.091603	.098427	.101919	.105459	.109045	.112672	.116337	.120038	.127533	.135134	.142824	.150584
	.30	.088024	.094610	.101434	.104924	.108466	.112052	.115679	.119344	.123045	.130540	.138142	.145831	.153591
	.20	.091032	.097617	.104441	.107933	.111474	.115059	.118686	.122352	.126052	.133547	.141149	.148838	.156599
	.10	.094039	.100625	.107449	.110940	.114481	.118066	.121694	.125359	.129059	.136554	.144156	.151845	.159606
	0.00	.097046	.103632	.110456	.113948	.117488	.121074	.124701	.128366	.132067	.139562	.147163	.154853	.162613
	-.10	.100053	.106639	.113463	.116955	.120495	.124081	.127708	.131373	.135074	.142569	.150171	.157860	.165620
	-.20	.103061	.109646	.116470	.119962	.123503	.127088	.130715	.134381	.138081	.145576	.153178	.160867	.168628
	-.30	.106068	.112654	.119478	.122969	.126510	.130095	.133723	.137388	.141089	.148583	.156185	.163874	.171635
	-.40	.109075	.115661	.122485	.125977	.129517	.133103	.136730	.140395	.144096	.151591	.159192	.166882	.174642

10.0 YEAR HOLDING PERIOD
.250 EQUITY YIELD RATE
.900 LOAN RATIO

INTEREST RATE

TERM YEARS	APPR DEP	5.0	6.0	7.0	7.5	8.0	8.5	9.0	9.5	10.0	11.0	12.0	13.0	14.0
10	.40	.100456	.105808	.111303	.114104	.116939	.119810	.122716	.125655	.128628	.134676	.140854	.147161	.153593
	.30	.103464	.108815	.114310	.117111	.119947	.122817	.125723	.128662	.131636	.137683	.143862	.150169	.156601
	.20	.106471	.111822	.117317	.120118	.122954	.125825	.128730	.131670	.134643	.140690	.146869	.153176	.159608
	.10	.109478	.114830	.120325	.123125	.125961	.128832	.131737	.134677	.137650	.143697	.149876	.156183	.162615
	0.00	.112485	.117837	.123332	.126133	.128968	.131839	.134745	.137684	.140657	.146705	.152883	.159190	.165622
	-.10	.115493	.120844	.126339	.129140	.131976	.134846	.137752	.140691	.143665	.149712	.155891	.162198	.168630
	-.20	.118500	.123851	.129346	.132147	.134983	.137854	.140759	.143699	.146672	.152719	.158898	.165205	.171637
	-.30	.121507	.126859	.132354	.135154	.137990	.140861	.143766	.146706	.149679	.155726	.161905	.168212	.174644
	-.40	.124514	.129866	.135361	.138162	.140998	.143868	.146774	.149713	.152687	.158734	.164912	.171219	.177651
15	.40	.082653	.088856	.095265	.098544	.101872	.105248	.108671	.112139	.115652	.122807	.130127	.137602	.145224
	.30	.085660	.091863	.098272	.101551	.104880	.108255	.111678	.115146	.118659	.125814	.133134	.140609	.148232
	.20	.088668	.094870	.101279	.104559	.107887	.111263	.114685	.118153	.121666	.128821	.136141	.143617	.151239
	.10	.091675	.097878	.104287	.107566	.110894	.114270	.117693	.121161	.124674	.131828	.139148	.146624	.154246
	0.00	.094682	.100885	.107294	.110573	.113901	.117277	.120700	.124168	.127681	.134836	.142156	.149631	.157253
	-.10	.097689	.103892	.110301	.113580	.116909	.120284	.123707	.127175	.130688	.137843	.145163	.152638	.160261
	-.20	.100697	.106899	.113308	.116588	.119916	.123292	.126714	.130182	.133695	.140850	.148170	.155646	.163268
	-.30	.103704	.109907	.116316	.119595	.122923	.126299	.129722	.133190	.136703	.143857	.151177	.158653	.166275
	-.40	.106711	.112914	.119323	.122602	.125930	.129306	.132729	.136197	.139710	.146865	.154185	.161660	.169282
20	.40	.074021	.080746	.087710	.091278	.094900	.098575	.102299	.106073	.109892	.117663	.125595	.133673	.141882
	.30	.077029	.083753	.090718	.094285	.097907	.101582	.105307	.109080	.112900	.120670	.128602	.136680	.144890
	.20	.080036	.086760	.093725	.097293	.100915	.104589	.108314	.112087	.115907	.123677	.131609	.139687	.147897
	.10	.083043	.089768	.096732	.100300	.103922	.107596	.111321	.115094	.118914	.126684	.134616	.142695	.150904
	0.00	.086050	.092775	.099739	.103307	.106929	.110604	.114328	.118102	.121921	.129692	.137624	.145702	.153911
	-.10	.089058	.095782	.102747	.106314	.109936	.113611	.117336	.121109	.124929	.132699	.140631	.148709	.156919
	-.20	.092065	.098789	.105754	.109322	.112944	.116618	.120343	.124116	.127936	.135706	.143638	.151716	.159926
	-.30	.095072	.101797	.108761	.112329	.115951	.119625	.123350	.127123	.130943	.138713	.146645	.154724	.162933
	-.40	.098079	.104804	.111769	.115336	.118958	.122633	.126357	.130131	.133950	.141721	.149653	.157731	.165940
25	.40	.069049	.076155	.083520	.087293	.091121	.095002	.098933	.102910	.106932	.115097	.123405	.131838	.140376
	.30	.072057	.079162	.086528	.090300	.094128	.098010	.101940	.105918	.109939	.118104	.126413	.134845	.143383
	.20	.075064	.082170	.089535	.093307	.097135	.101016	.104947	.108925	.112947	.121111	.129420	.137852	.146391
	.10	.078071	.085177	.092542	.096314	.100142	.104023	.107954	.111932	.115954	.124119	.132427	.140860	.149398
	0.00	.081078	.088184	.095549	.099322	.103150	.107031	.110962	.114939	.118961	.127126	.135434	.143867	.152405
	-.10	.084086	.091191	.098556	.102329	.106157	.110038	.113969	.117947	.121968	.130133	.138442	.146874	.155412
	-.20	.087093	.094199	.101564	.105336	.109164	.113045	.116976	.120954	.124976	.133140	.141449	.149881	.158420
	-.30	.090100	.097206	.104571	.108343	.112172	.116052	.119983	.123961	.127983	.136148	.144456	.152889	.161427
	-.40	.093107	.100213	.107578	.111351	.115179	.119060	.122991	.126968	.130990	.139155	.147463	.155896	.164434
30	.40	.065898	.073307	.080984	.084912	.088895	.092929	.097009	.101133	.105296	.113728	.122280	.130930	.139661
	.30	.068905	.076314	.083991	.087919	.091902	.095936	.100017	.104140	.108303	.116735	.125287	.133937	.142668
	.20	.071912	.079321	.086998	.090927	.094910	.098943	.103024	.107147	.111311	.119742	.128294	.136945	.145675
	.10	.074920	.082329	.090005	.093934	.097917	.101951	.106031	.110155	.114318	.122750	.131301	.139952	.148683
	0.00	.077927	.085336	.093013	.096941	.100924	.104958	.109038	.113162	.117325	.125757	.134309	.142959	.151690
	-.10	.080934	.088343	.096020	.099948	.103931	.107965	.112046	.116169	.120332	.128764	.137316	.145967	.154697
	-.20	.083941	.091350	.099027	.102956	.106939	.110972	.115053	.119176	.123340	.131771	.140323	.148974	.157704
	-.30	.086949	.094358	.102035	.105963	.109946	.113980	.118060	.122184	.126347	.134779	.143330	.151981	.160711
	-.40	.089956	.097365	.105042	.108970	.112953	.116987	.121067	.125191	.129354	.137786	.146338	.154988	.163719

10.0 YEAR HOLDING PERIOD
.300 EQUITY YIELD RATE
.600 LOAN RATIO

INTEREST RATE

TERM YEARS	APPR DEP	5.0	6.0	7.0	7.5	8.0	8.5	9.0	9.5	10.0	11.0	12.0	13.0	14.0
10	.40	.172904	.176471	.180135	.182002	.183892	.185806	.187743	.189703	.191685	.195717	.199836	.204040	.208328
	.30	.175250	.178818	.182481	.184348	.186239	.188153	.190089	.192049	.194031	.198063	.202182	.206387	.210625
	.20	.177596	.181164	.184827	.186695	.188585	.190499	.192436	.194395	.196378	.200409	.204528	.208733	.213021
	.10	.179943	.183510	.187174	.189041	.190931	.192845	.194782	.196742	.198724	.202756	.206875	.211079	.215367
	0.00	.182289	.185857	.189520	.191387	.193278	.195192	.197128	.199088	.201070	.205102	.209221	.213426	.217714
	-.10	.184635	.188203	.191866	.193734	.195624	.197538	.199475	.201435	.203417	.207448	.211567	.215772	.220060
	-.20	.186982	.190549	.194213	.196080	.197970	.199884	.201821	.203781	.205763	.209795	.213914	.218118	.222406
	-.30	.189328	.192896	.196559	.198426	.200317	.202231	.204168	.206127	.208109	.212141	.216260	.220465	.224753
	-.40	.191674	.195242	.198905	.200773	.202663	.204577	.206514	.208474	.210456	.214487	.218606	.222811	.227099
15	.40	.159373	.163439	.167643	.169794	.171979	.174195	.176442	.178720	.181028	.185731	.190544	.195462	.200479
	.30	.161719	.165786	.169989	.172141	.174325	.176541	.178789	.181067	.183375	.188077	.192891	.197809	.202826
	.20	.164066	.168132	.172335	.174487	.176671	.178888	.181135	.183413	.185721	.190424	.195237	.200155	.205172
	.10	.166412	.170478	.174682	.176833	.179018	.181234	.183481	.185759	.188067	.192770	.197583	.202501	.207518
	0.00	.168758	.172825	.177028	.179180	.181364	.183580	.185828	.188106	.190414	.195116	.199930	.204848	.209865
	-.10	.171105	.175171	.179374	.181526	.183710	.185927	.188174	.190452	.192760	.197463	.202276	.207194	.212211
	-.20	.173451	.177517	.181721	.183872	.186057	.188273	.190520	.192798	.195106	.199809	.204622	.209541	.214557
	-.30	.175797	.179864	.184067	.186219	.188403	.190619	.192867	.195145	.197453	.202155	.206969	.211887	.216904
	-.40	.178144	.182210	.186413	.188565	.190749	.192966	.195213	.197491	.199799	.204502	.209315	.214233	.219250
20	.40	.152813	.157204	.161759	.164094	.166466	.168874	.171316	.173791	.176299	.181403	.186619	.191936	.197345
	.30	.155159	.159551	.164105	.166440	.168812	.171220	.173662	.176138	.178645	.183749	.188965	.194283	.199691
	.20	.157506	.161897	.166451	.168786	.171158	.173566	.176009	.178484	.180991	.186096	.191312	.196629	.202038
	.10	.159852	.164243	.168798	.171133	.173505	.175913	.178355	.180830	.183338	.188442	.193658	.198975	.204384
	0.00	.162198	.166590	.171144	.173479	.175851	.178259	.180701	.183177	.185684	.190788	.196005	.201322	.206730
	-.10	.164545	.168936	.173490	.175825	.178197	.180605	.183048	.185523	.188030	.193135	.198351	.203668	.209077
	-.20	.166891	.171282	.175837	.178172	.180544	.182952	.185394	.187869	.190377	.195481	.200697	.206015	.211423
	-.30	.169237	.173629	.178183	.180518	.182890	.185298	.187740	.190216	.192723	.197828	.203044	.208361	.213770
	-.40	.171584	.175975	.180529	.182864	.185237	.187644	.190087	.192562	.195069	.200174	.205390	.210707	.216116
25	.40	.149034	.153675	.158495	.160967	.163477	.166025	.168607	.171222	.173868	.179245	.184723	.190290	.195933
	.30	.151381	.156021	.160841	.163313	.165824	.168371	.170953	.173568	.176214	.181591	.187069	.192636	.198279
	.20	.153727	.158368	.163187	.165659	.168170	.170717	.173299	.175914	.178560	.183937	.189416	.194983	.200625
	.10	.156073	.160714	.165534	.168006	.170516	.173064	.175646	.178261	.180907	.186284	.191762	.197329	.202972
	0.00	.158420	.163061	.167880	.170352	.172863	.175410	.177992	.180607	.183253	.188630	.194108	.199675	.205318
	-.10	.160766	.165407	.170226	.172698	.175209	.177756	.180338	.182953	.185599	.190976	.196455	.202022	.207664
	-.20	.163112	.167753	.172573	.175045	.177555	.180103	.182685	.185300	.187946	.193323	.198801	.204368	.210011
	-.30	.165459	.170100	.174919	.177391	.179902	.182449	.185031	.187646	.190292	.195669	.201148	.206714	.212357
	-.40	.167805	.172446	.177265	.179737	.182248	.184795	.187378	.189993	.192638	.198015	.203494	.209061	.214703
30	.40	.146639	.151486	.156519	.159099	.161718	.164372	.167059	.169778	.172524	.178093	.183748	.189475	.195261
	.30	.148985	.153832	.158865	.161445	.164064	.166718	.169406	.172124	.174870	.180439	.186094	.191822	.197608
	.20	.151332	.156178	.161212	.163792	.166410	.169065	.171752	.174470	.177217	.182785	.188441	.194168	.199954
	.10	.153678	.158525	.163558	.166138	.168757	.171411	.174098	.176817	.179563	.185132	.190787	.196514	.202300
	0.00	.156024	.160871	.165904	.168484	.171103	.173757	.176445	.179163	.181909	.187478	.193133	.198861	.204647
	-.10	.158371	.163217	.168251	.170831	.173449	.176104	.178791	.181509	.184256	.189824	.195480	.201207	.206993
	-.20	.160717	.165564	.170597	.173177	.175796	.178450	.181137	.183856	.186602	.192171	.197826	.203553	.209339
	-.30	.163064	.167910	.172943	.175523	.178142	.180796	.183484	.186202	.188948	.194517	.200173	.205900	.211686
	-.40	.165410	.170256	.175290	.177870	.180488	.183143	.185830	.188548	.191295	.196863	.202519	.208246	.214032

10.0 YEAR HOLDING PERIOD
.300 EQUITY YIELD RATE
.667 LOAN RATIO

INTEREST RATE

TERM YEARS	APPR DEP	5.0	6.0	7.0	7.5	8.0	8.5	9.0	9.5	10.0	11.0	12.0	13.0	14.0
10	.40	.159824	.163788	.167859	.169933	.172034	.174160	.176312	.178490	.180692	.185172	.189749	.194420	.199185
	.30	.162170	.166134	.170205	.172279	.174380	.176507	.178659	.180836	.183039	.187518	.192095	.196767	.201531
	.20	.164517	.168481	.172551	.174626	.176727	.178853	.181005	.183183	.185385	.189865	.194441	.199113	.203878
	.10	.166863	.170827	.174898	.176972	.179073	.181199	.183351	.185529	.187731	.192211	.196788	.201459	.206224
	0.00	.169209	.173173	.177244	.179319	.181419	.183546	.185698	.187875	.190078	.194557	.199134	.203806	.208570
	-.10	.171556	.175520	.179590	.181665	.183766	.185892	.188044	.190222	.192424	.196904	.201480	.206152	.210917
	-.20	.173902	.177866	.181937	.184011	.186112	.188238	.190390	.192568	.194770	.199250	.203827	.208499	.213263
	-.30	.176248	.180213	.184283	.186358	.188458	.190585	.192737	.194914	.197117	.201596	.206173	.210845	.215609
	-.40	.178595	.182559	.186629	.188704	.190805	.192931	.195083	.197261	.199463	.203943	.208519	.213191	.217956
15	.40	.144790	.149308	.153978	.156369	.158796	.161259	.163756	.166287	.168851	.174077	.179425	.184889	.190464
	.30	.147136	.151654	.156325	.158716	.161143	.163605	.166102	.168633	.171198	.176423	.181771	.187236	.192810
	.20	.149483	.154001	.158671	.161062	.163489	.165951	.168449	.170980	.173544	.178769	.184117	.189582	.195157
	.10	.151829	.156347	.161017	.163408	.165835	.168298	.170795	.173326	.175891	.181116	.186464	.191929	.197503
	0.00	.154175	.158693	.163364	.165755	.168182	.170644	.173141	.175672	.178237	.183462	.188810	.194275	.199849
	-.10	.156522	.161040	.165710	.168101	.170528	.172990	.175488	.178019	.180583	.185808	.191157	.196621	.202196
	-.20	.158868	.163386	.168056	.170447	.172874	.175337	.177834	.180365	.182930	.188155	.193503	.198968	.204542
	-.30	.161214	.165732	.170403	.172794	.175221	.177683	.180181	.182712	.185276	.190501	.195849	.201314	.206888
	-.40	.163561	.168079	.172749	.175140	.177567	.180029	.182527	.185058	.187622	.192847	.198196	.203660	.209235
20	.40	.137501	.142380	.147440	.150035	.152671	.155346	.158060	.160810	.163596	.169268	.175064	.180972	.186981
	.30	.139847	.144727	.149787	.152381	.155017	.157692	.160406	.163157	.165942	.171614	.177410	.183318	.189328
	.20	.142194	.147073	.152133	.154728	.157363	.160039	.162753	.165503	.168289	.173961	.179756	.185664	.191674
	.10	.144540	.149419	.154479	.157074	.159709	.162385	.165099	.167849	.170635	.176307	.182103	.188010	.194020
	0.00	.146886	.151766	.156826	.159420	.162056	.164732	.167445	.170196	.172981	.178653	.184449	.190357	.196367
	-.10	.149233	.154112	.159172	.161767	.164402	.167078	.169792	.172542	.175328	.181000	.186795	.192703	.198713
	-.20	.151579	.156458	.161519	.164113	.166749	.169424	.172138	.174888	.177674	.183346	.189142	.195050	.201059
	-.30	.153925	.158805	.163865	.166459	.169095	.171771	.174484	.177235	.180021	.185692	.191488	.197396	.203406
	-.40	.156272	.161151	.166211	.168806	.171441	.174117	.176831	.179581	.182367	.188039	.193834	.199742	.205752
25	.40	.133302	.138459	.143814	.146561	.149350	.152181	.155050	.157955	.160895	.166869	.172957	.179142	.185412
	.30	.135649	.140805	.146160	.148907	.151696	.154527	.157396	.160302	.163241	.169216	.175303	.181488	.187758
	.20	.137995	.143152	.148507	.151253	.154043	.156873	.159742	.162648	.165588	.171562	.177649	.183835	.190104
	.10	.140341	.145498	.150853	.153600	.156389	.159220	.162089	.164994	.167934	.173908	.179996	.186181	.192451
	0.00	.142688	.147844	.153199	.155946	.158736	.161566	.164435	.167341	.170280	.176255	.182342	.188527	.194797
	-.10	.145034	.150191	.155546	.158292	.161082	.163912	.166781	.169687	.172627	.178601	.184689	.190874	.197143
	-.20	.147380	.152537	.157892	.160639	.163428	.166259	.169128	.172033	.174973	.180948	.187035	.193220	.199490
	-.30	.149727	.154883	.160238	.162985	.165775	.168605	.171474	.174380	.177319	.183294	.189381	.195567	.201836
	-.40	.152073	.157230	.162585	.165331	.168121	.170951	.173820	.176726	.179666	.185640	.191728	.197913	.204183
30	.40	.130641	.136026	.141619	.144485	.147395	.150344	.153344	.156351	.159402	.165590	.171873	.178237	.184666
	.30	.132987	.138372	.143965	.146832	.149741	.152691	.155677	.158697	.161749	.167936	.174220	.180583	.187012
	.20	.135334	.140719	.146311	.149178	.152088	.155037	.158023	.161043	.164095	.170282	.176566	.182930	.189359
	.10	.137680	.143065	.148658	.151525	.154434	.157383	.160369	.163390	.166441	.172629	.178912	.185276	.191705
	0.00	.140026	.145411	.151004	.153871	.156780	.159730	.162716	.165736	.168788	.174975	.181259	.187623	.194051
	-.10	.142373	.147758	.153351	.156217	.159127	.162076	.165062	.168082	.171134	.177321	.183605	.189969	.196398
	-.20	.144719	.150104	.155697	.158564	.161473	.164422	.167408	.170429	.173480	.179668	.185952	.192315	.198744
	-.30	.147065	.152450	.158043	.160910	.163819	.166769	.169755	.172775	.175827	.182014	.188298	.194662	.201090
	-.40	.149412	.154797	.160390	.163256	.166166	.169115	.172101	.175121	.178173	.184360	.190644	.197008	.203437

```
10.0 YEAR HOLDING PERIOD
.300 EQUITY YIELD RATE
.700 LOAN RATIO
```

INTEREST RATE

TERM YEARS	APPR DEP	5.0	6.0	7.0	7.5	8.0	8.5	9.0	9.5	10.0	11.0	12.0	13.0	14.0
10	.40	.153285	.157447	.161721	.163900	.166105	.168338	.170598	.172884	.175197	.179900	.184706	.189611	.194614
	.30	.155632	.159794	.164068	.166246	.168452	.170685	.172944	.175231	.177543	.182247	.187052	.191958	.196960
	.20	.157978	.162140	.166414	.168592	.170798	.173031	.175291	.177577	.179890	.184593	.189399	.194304	.199307
	.10	.160324	.164486	.168760	.170939	.173144	.175377	.177637	.179923	.182236	.186939	.191745	.196650	.201653
	0.00	.162671	.166833	.171107	.173285	.175491	.177724	.179983	.182270	.184582	.189286	.194091	.198997	.203999
	-.10	.165017	.169179	.173453	.175631	.177837	.180070	.182330	.184616	.186929	.191632	.196438	.201343	.206346
	-.20	.167363	.171526	.175799	.177978	.180183	.182416	.184676	.186962	.189275	.193978	.198784	.203689	.208692
	-.30	.169710	.173372	.178146	.180324	.182530	.184763	.187022	.189309	.191621	.196325	.201130	.206036	.211038
	-.40	.172056	.176218	.180492	.182670	.184876	.187109	.189369	.191655	.193968	.198671	.203477	.208382	.213385
15	.40	.137499	.142243	.147147	.149658	.152206	.154792	.157414	.160071	.162764	.168250	.173866	.179604	.185457
	.30	.139846	.144590	.149494	.152004	.154552	.157138	.159760	.162418	.165110	.170597	.176212	.181950	.187803
	.20	.142192	.146936	.151840	.154350	.156899	.159484	.162106	.164764	.167457	.172943	.178559	.184296	.190150
	.10	.144539	.149282	.154186	.156697	.159245	.161831	.164453	.167110	.169803	.175289	.180905	.186643	.192496
	0.00	.146885	.151629	.156533	.159043	.161591	.164177	.166799	.169457	.172149	.177636	.183251	.188989	.194842
	-.10	.149231	.153975	.158879	.161389	.163938	.166523	.169145	.171803	.174496	.179982	.185598	.191335	.197189
	-.20	.151578	.156321	.161225	.163736	.166284	.168870	.171492	.174149	.176842	.182328	.187944	.193682	.199535
	-.30	.153924	.158668	.163572	.166082	.168630	.171216	.173838	.176496	.179188	.184675	.190290	.196028	.201881
	-.40	.156270	.161014	.165918	.168428	.170976	.173562	.176184	.178842	.181535	.187021	.192637	.198375	.204228
20	.40	.129846	.134969	.140283	.143007	.145774	.148583	.151433	.154323	.157246	.163201	.169287	.175490	.181800
	.30	.132192	.137316	.142629	.145353	.148121	.150930	.153779	.156667	.159592	.165547	.171633	.177836	.184147
	.20	.134539	.139662	.144975	.147699	.150467	.153276	.156125	.159013	.161939	.167894	.173979	.180183	.186493
	.10	.136885	.142008	.147322	.150046	.152813	.155622	.158472	.161360	.164285	.170240	.176326	.182529	.188839
	0.00	.139231	.144355	.149668	.152392	.155160	.157969	.160818	.163706	.166631	.172587	.178672	.184875	.191186
	-.10	.141578	.146701	.152014	.154739	.157506	.160315	.163164	.166052	.168978	.174933	.181018	.187222	.193532
	-.20	.143924	.149047	.154361	.157085	.159852	.162662	.165511	.168399	.171324	.177279	.183365	.189568	.195878
	-.30	.146270	.151394	.156707	.159431	.162198	.165008	.167857	.170745	.173670	.179626	.185711	.191914	.198225
	-.40	.148617	.153740	.159053	.161778	.164545	.167354	.170204	.173092	.176017	.181972	.188057	.194261	.200571
25	.40	.125437	.130852	.136475	.139359	.142288	.145260	.148272	.151323	.154410	.160683	.167075	.173569	.180152
	.30	.127784	.133198	.138821	.141705	.144634	.147606	.150618	.153669	.156756	.163029	.169421	.175915	.182499
	.20	.130130	.135545	.141167	.144051	.146980	.149952	.152965	.156016	.159102	.165376	.171767	.178262	.184845
	.10	.132476	.137891	.143514	.146398	.149327	.152299	.155311	.158362	.161449	.167722	.174114	.180608	.187191
	0.00	.134823	.140237	.145860	.148744	.151673	.154645	.157658	.160708	.163795	.170068	.176460	.182954	.189538
	-.10	.137169	.142584	.148206	.151090	.154019	.156991	.160004	.163055	.166142	.172415	.178806	.185301	.191884
	-.20	.139516	.144930	.150553	.153437	.156366	.159338	.162350	.165401	.168488	.174761	.181153	.187647	.194230
	-.30	.141862	.147276	.152899	.155783	.158712	.161684	.164697	.167747	.170834	.177107	.183499	.189993	.196577
	-.40	.144208	.149623	.155245	.158129	.161058	.164030	.167043	.170094	.173181	.179454	.185845	.192340	.198923
30	.40	.122643	.128297	.134170	.137180	.140235	.143331	.146467	.149638	.152842	.159339	.165937	.172619	.179369
	.30	.124990	.130644	.136516	.139526	.142581	.145678	.148813	.151984	.155189	.161685	.168283	.174965	.181716
	.20	.127336	.132990	.138862	.141872	.144927	.148024	.151160	.154331	.157535	.164032	.170630	.177312	.184062
	.10	.129682	.135336	.141209	.144219	.147274	.150370	.153506	.156677	.159881	.166378	.172976	.179658	.186408
	0.00	.132029	.137683	.143555	.146565	.149620	.152717	.155852	.159023	.162228	.168724	.175322	.182004	.188755
	-.10	.134375	.140029	.145902	.148912	.151966	.155063	.158199	.161370	.164574	.171071	.177669	.184351	.191101
	-.20	.136721	.142375	.148248	.151258	.154313	.157409	.160545	.163716	.166920	.173417	.180015	.186697	.193447
	-.30	.139068	.144722	.150594	.153604	.156659	.159756	.162891	.166062	.169267	.175763	.182361	.189043	.195794
	-.40	.141414	.147068	.152941	.155951	.159005	.162102	.165238	.168409	.171613	.178110	.184708	.191390	.198140

10.0 YEAR HOLDING PERIOD
.300 EQUITY YIELD RATE
.750 LOAN RATIO

INTEREST RATE

TERM YEARS	APPR DEP	5.0	6.0	7.0	7.5	8.0	8.5	9.0	9.5	10.0	11.0	12.0	13.0	14.0
10	.40	.143476	.147935	.152515	.154849	.157212	.159604	.162025	.164475	.166953	.171992	.177141	.182397	.187757
	.30	.145822	.150282	.154861	.157195	.159558	.161951	.164372	.166821	.169299	.174338	.179487	.184743	.190103
	.20	.148169	.152628	.157207	.159541	.161905	.164297	.166718	.169168	.171645	.176685	.181834	.187089	.192450
	.10	.150515	.154975	.159554	.161888	.164251	.166643	.169064	.171514	.173992	.179031	.184180	.189436	.194796
	0.00	.152861	.157321	.161900	.164234	.166597	.168990	.171411	.173860	.176338	.181377	.186526	.191782	.197142
	-.10	.155208	.159667	.164246	.166580	.168944	.171336	.173757	.176207	.178684	.183724	.188873	.194128	.199489
	-.20	.157554	.162014	.166593	.168927	.171290	.173682	.176103	.178553	.181031	.186070	.191219	.196475	.201835
	-.30	.159900	.164360	.168939	.171273	.173636	.176029	.178450	.180899	.183377	.188416	.193565	.198821	.204181
	-.40	.162247	.166706	.171285	.173619	.175983	.178375	.180796	.183246	.185723	.190763	.195912	.201167	.206528
15	.40	.126563	.131645	.136900	.139589	.142320	.145090	.147899	.150747	.153632	.159910	.165527	.171674	.177946
	.30	.128909	.133992	.139246	.141936	.144666	.147436	.150246	.153093	.155978	.161856	.167873	.174021	.180292
	.20	.131255	.136338	.141592	.144282	.147012	.149783	.152592	.155440	.158324	.164203	.170219	.176367	.182638
	.10	.133602	.138684	.143939	.146628	.149359	.152129	.154938	.157786	.160671	.166549	.172566	.178713	.184985
	0.00	.135948	.141031	.146285	.148975	.151705	.154475	.157285	.160132	.163017	.168895	.174912	.181060	.187331
	-.10	.138294	.143377	.148631	.151321	.154051	.156822	.159631	.162479	.165363	.171242	.177258	.183406	.189677
	-.20	.140641	.145723	.150978	.153667	.156398	.159168	.161977	.164825	.167710	.173588	.179605	.185752	.192024
	-.30	.142987	.148070	.153324	.156014	.158744	.161514	.164324	.167171	.170056	.175934	.181951	.188099	.194370
	-.40	.145333	.150416	.155670	.158360	.161090	.163861	.166670	.169518	.172403	.178281	.184297	.190445	.196716
20	.40	.118363	.123852	.129544	.132463	.135429	.138438	.141491	.144585	.147720	.154100	.160620	.167267	.174028
	.30	.120709	.126198	.131891	.134810	.137775	.140785	.143838	.146932	.150066	.156447	.162967	.169613	.176374
	.20	.123055	.128544	.134237	.137156	.140121	.143131	.146184	.149278	.152412	.158793	.165313	.171960	.178720
	.10	.125402	.130891	.136584	.139502	.142468	.145477	.148530	.151625	.154759	.161139	.167659	.174306	.181067
	0.00	.127748	.133237	.138930	.141849	.144814	.147824	.150877	.153971	.157105	.163486	.170006	.176652	.183413
	-.10	.130094	.135584	.141276	.144195	.147160	.150170	.153223	.156317	.159451	.165832	.172352	.178999	.185759
	-.20	.132441	.137930	.143623	.146541	.149507	.152516	.155569	.158664	.161798	.168178	.174698	.181345	.188106
	-.30	.134787	.140276	.145969	.148888	.151853	.154863	.157916	.161010	.164144	.170525	.177045	.183691	.190452
	-.40	.137133	.142623	.148315	.151234	.154199	.157209	.160262	.163356	.166490	.172871	.179391	.186038	.192798
25	.40	.113639	.119440	.125465	.128555	.131693	.134877	.138105	.141374	.144681	.151402	.158250	.165209	.172262
	.30	.115985	.121787	.127811	.130901	.134039	.137223	.140451	.143720	.147027	.153748	.160597	.167555	.174608
	.20	.118332	.124133	.130157	.133247	.136386	.139570	.142798	.146066	.149374	.156095	.162943	.169901	.176955
	.10	.120678	.126479	.132504	.135594	.138732	.141916	.145144	.148413	.151720	.158441	.165289	.172248	.179301
	0.00	.123024	.128826	.134850	.137940	.141078	.144262	.147490	.150759	.154066	.160787	.167636	.174594	.181647
	-.10	.125371	.131172	.137196	.140286	.143425	.146609	.149837	.153105	.156413	.163134	.169982	.176940	.183994
	-.20	.127717	.133518	.139543	.142633	.145771	.148955	.152183	.155452	.158759	.165480	.172328	.179287	.186340
	-.30	.130063	.135865	.141889	.144979	.148117	.151302	.154529	.157798	.161105	.167826	.174675	.181633	.188686
	-.40	.132410	.138211	.144235	.147325	.150464	.153648	.156876	.160144	.163452	.170173	.177021	.183979	.191033
30	.40	.110645	.116703	.122995	.126220	.129493	.132811	.136171	.139568	.143001	.149962	.157031	.164191	.171423
	.30	.112992	.119050	.125342	.128567	.131840	.135158	.138517	.141915	.145348	.152308	.159378	.166537	.173769
	.20	.115338	.121396	.127688	.130913	.134186	.137504	.140863	.144261	.147695	.154655	.161724	.168883	.176116
	.10	.117684	.123742	.130034	.133259	.136532	.139850	.143210	.146607	.150040	.157001	.164071	.171230	.178462
	0.00	.120031	.126089	.132381	.135605	.138879	.142197	.145556	.148954	.152387	.159347	.166417	.173576	.180808
	-.10	.122377	.128435	.134727	.137952	.141225	.144543	.147902	.151300	.154733	.161694	.168763	.175922	.183155
	-.20	.124723	.130781	.137073	.140298	.143571	.146889	.150249	.153646	.157079	.164040	.171110	.178269	.185501
	-.30	.127070	.133128	.139420	.142645	.145918	.149236	.152595	.155993	.159426	.166387	.173456	.180615	.187848
	-.40	.129416	.135474	.141766	.144991	.148264	.151582	.154941	.158339	.161772	.168733	.175802	.182961	.190194

10.0 YEAR HOLDING PERIOD
.300 EQUITY YIELD RATE
.800 LOAN RATIO

INTEREST RATE

TERM YEARS	APPR DEP	5.0	6.0	7.0	7.5	8.0	8.5	9.0	9.5	10.0	11.0	12.0	13.0	14.0
10	.40	.133667	.138424	.143308	.145798	.148318	.150870	.153453	.156066	.158709	.164084	.169576	.175182	.180900
	.30	.136013	.140770	.145654	.148144	.150665	.153216	.155799	.158412	.161055	.166430	.171922	.177529	.183546
	.20	.138359	.143116	.148001	.150490	.153011	.155563	.158145	.160758	.163401	.168777	.174269	.179875	.185592
	.10	.140706	.145463	.150347	.152837	.155357	.157909	.160492	.163105	.165748	.171123	.176615	.182221	.187939
	0.00	.143052	.147809	.152693	.155183	.157704	.160256	.162838	.165451	.168094	.173469	.178961	.184568	.190285
	-.10	.145398	.150155	.155040	.157529	.160050	.162602	.165184	.167797	.170440	.175816	.181308	.186914	.192631
	-.20	.147745	.152502	.157386	.159876	.162396	.164948	.167531	.170144	.172787	.178162	.183654	.189260	.194978
	-.30	.150091	.154848	.159732	.162222	.164743	.167295	.169877	.172490	.175133	.180508	.186000	.191607	.197324
	-.40	.152438	.157194	.162079	.164568	.167089	.169641	.172223	.174836	.177479	.182855	.188347	.193953	.199670
15	.40	.115626	.121047	.126652	.129521	.132433	.135388	.138385	.141422	.144500	.150770	.157188	.163745	.170434
	.30	.117972	.123394	.128998	.131867	.134780	.137735	.140731	.143769	.146846	.153116	.159534	.166091	.172781
	.20	.120319	.125740	.131345	.134214	.137126	.140081	.143077	.146115	.149192	.155462	.161880	.168438	.175127
	.10	.122665	.128086	.133691	.136560	.139472	.142427	.145424	.148461	.151539	.157809	.164227	.170784	.177473
	0.00	.125011	.130433	.136037	.138906	.141819	.144774	.147770	.150808	.153885	.160155	.166573	.173130	.179820
	-.10	.127358	.132779	.138384	.141253	.144165	.147120	.150117	.153154	.156231	.162501	.168920	.175477	.182166
	-.20	.129704	.135125	.140730	.143599	.146511	.149466	.152463	.155500	.158578	.164848	.171266	.177823	.184512
	-.30	.132050	.137472	.143076	.145945	.148858	.151813	.154809	.157847	.160924	.167194	.173612	.180169	.186859
	-.40	.134397	.139818	.145423	.148292	.151204	.154159	.157156	.160193	.163270	.169540	.175958	.182516	.189205
20	.40	.106879	.112734	.118806	.121920	.125083	.128293	.131550	.134850	.138193	.144999	.151954	.159044	.162255
	.30	.109225	.115081	.121153	.124266	.127429	.130640	.133896	.137197	.140540	.147346	.154300	.161390	.168602
	.20	.111572	.117427	.123499	.126613	.129775	.132986	.136242	.139543	.142886	.149692	.156647	.163736	.170948
	.10	.113918	.119773	.125846	.128959	.132122	.135332	.138589	.141889	.145232	.152038	.158993	.166083	.173294
	0.00	.116264	.122120	.128192	.131305	.134468	.137679	.140935	.144236	.147579	.154385	.161339	.168429	.175641
	-.10	.118611	.124466	.130538	.133652	.136815	.140025	.143281	.146582	.149925	.156731	.163686	.170775	.177987
	-.20	.120957	.126812	.132885	.135998	.139161	.142371	.145628	.148928	.152271	.159077	.166032	.173122	.180333
	-.30	.123303	.129159	.135231	.138344	.141507	.144718	.147974	.151275	.154618	.161424	.168378	.175468	.182680
	-.40	.125650	.131505	.137577	.140691	.143854	.147064	.150320	.153621	.156964	.163770	.170725	.177814	.185026
25	.40	.101841	.108029	.114455	.117751	.121098	.124495	.127937	.131424	.134952	.142121	.149426	.156848	.164372
	.30	.104187	.110375	.116801	.120097	.123444	.126841	.130284	.133770	.137298	.144468	.151772	.159195	.166718
	.20	.106533	.112721	.119147	.122443	.125791	.129187	.132630	.136117	.139645	.146814	.154119	.161541	.169065
	.10	.108880	.115068	.121494	.124790	.128137	.131534	.134977	.138463	.141991	.149160	.156465	.163887	.171411
	0.00	.111226	.117414	.123840	.127136	.130483	.133880	.137323	.140810	.144337	.151507	.158811	.166234	.173757
	-.10	.113572	.119760	.126186	.129482	.132830	.136226	.139669	.143156	.146684	.153853	.161158	.168580	.176104
	-.20	.115919	.122107	.128533	.131829	.135176	.138573	.142016	.145502	.149030	.156199	.163504	.170926	.178450
	-.30	.118265	.124453	.130879	.134175	.137523	.140919	.144362	.147849	.151376	.158546	.165850	.173273	.180796
	-.40	.120611	.126799	.133226	.136521	.139869	.143265	.146708	.150195	.153723	.160892	.168197	.175619	.183143
30	.40	.098647	.105109	.111821	.115261	.118752	.122291	.125874	.129499	.133160	.140585	.148126	.155762	.163477
	.30	.100994	.107456	.114167	.117607	.121098	.124637	.128221	.131845	.135507	.142932	.150472	.158109	.165823
	.20	.103340	.109802	.116513	.119953	.123445	.126984	.130567	.134191	.137853	.145278	.152819	.160455	.168170
	.10	.105686	.112148	.118860	.122300	.125791	.129330	.132913	.136538	.140200	.147624	.155165	.162801	.170516
	0.00	.108033	.114495	.121206	.124646	.128137	.131676	.135260	.138884	.142546	.149971	.157511	.165148	.172862
	-.10	.110379	.116841	.123552	.126992	.130484	.134023	.137606	.141230	.144892	.152317	.159858	.167494	.175209
	-.20	.112725	.119187	.125899	.129339	.132830	.136369	.139952	.143577	.147239	.154663	.162204	.169840	.177555
	-.30	.115072	.121534	.128245	.131685	.135176	.138715	.142299	.145923	.149585	.157010	.164550	.172187	.179901
	-.40	.117418	.123880	.130591	.134031	.137523	.141062	.144645	.148269	.151931	.159356	.166897	.174533	.182248

10.0 YEAR HOLDING PERIOD
.300 EQUITY YIELD RATE
.900 LOAN RATIO

INTEREST RATE

TERM YEARS	APPR .DEP	5.0	6.0	7.0	7.5	8.0	8.5	9.0	9.5	10.0	11.0	12.0	13.0	14.0
10	.40	.114048	.119400	.124895	.127695	.130531	.133402	.136307	.139247	.142220	.148268	.154446	.160753	.167185
	.30	.116395	.121746	.127241	.130042	.132878	.135748	.138654	.141593	.144567	.150614	.156792	.163099	.169532
	.20	.118741	.124092	.129587	.132388	.135224	.138095	.141000	.143940	.146913	.152960	.159139	.165446	.171878
	.10	.121087	.126439	.131934	.134734	.137570	.140441	.143346	.146286	.149259	.155307	.161485	.167792	.174224
	0.00	.123434	.128785	.134280	.137081	.139917	.142787	.145693	.148632	.151606	.157653	.163832	.170139	.176571
	-.10	.125780	.131131	.136626	.139427	.142263	.145134	.148039	.150979	.153952	.159999	.166178	.172485	.178917
	-.20	.128126	.133478	.138973	.141774	.144609	.147480	.150385	.153325	.156298	.162346	.168524	.174831	.181263
	-.30	.130473	.135824	.141319	.144120	.146956	.149826	.152732	.155671	.158645	.164692	.170871	.177178	.183610
	-.40	.132819	.138170	.143665	.146466	.149302	.152173	.155078	.158018	.160991	.167038	.173217	.179524	.185956
15	.40	.093752	.099851	.106157	.109384	.112661	.115985	.119356	.122773	.126235	.133289	.140509	.147886	.155412
	.30	.096099	.102198	.108503	.111731	.115007	.118331	.121703	.125120	.128582	.135635	.142855	.150233	.157758
	.20	.098445	.104544	.110849	.114077	.117353	.120678	.124049	.127466	.130928	.137982	.145202	.152579	.160105
	.10	.100791	.106890	.113196	.116423	.119700	.123024	.126395	.129812	.133274	.140328	.147548	.154925	.162451
	0.00	.103138	.109237	.115542	.118770	.122046	.125370	.128742	.132159	.135621	.142674	.149894	.157272	.164797
	-.10	.105484	.111583	.117888	.121116	.124392	.127717	.131088	.134505	.137967	.145021	.152241	.159618	.167144
	-.20	.107830	.113930	.120235	.123462	.126739	.130063	.133434	.136851	.140313	.147367	.154587	.161964	.169490
	-.30	.110177	.116276	.122581	.125809	.129085	.132409	.135781	.139198	.142660	.149713	.156934	.164311	.171836
	-.40	.112523	.118622	.124927	.128155	.131431	.134756	.138127	.141544	.145006	.152060	.159280	.166657	.174183
20	.40	.083912	.090499	.097330	.100833	.104391	.108003	.111667	.115380	.119140	.126797	.134621	.142597	.150710
	.30	.086258	.092846	.099677	.103179	.106738	.110349	.114013	.117726	.121487	.129144	.136968	.144944	.153057
	.20	.088605	.095192	.102023	.105526	.109084	.112696	.116359	.120072	.123833	.131490	.139314	.147290	.155403
	.10	.090951	.097538	.104370	.107872	.111430	.115042	.118706	.122419	.126180	.133836	.141660	.149636	.157749
	0.00	.093298	.099885	.106716	.110219	.113777	.117388	.121052	.124765	.128526	.136183	.144007	.151983	.160096
	-.10	.095644	.102231	.109062	.112565	.116123	.119735	.123398	.127111	.130872	.138529	.146353	.154329	.162442
	-.20	.097990	.104577	.111409	.114911	.118469	.122081	.125745	.129458	.133219	.140875	.148699	.156675	.164788
	-.30	.100337	.106924	.113755	.117258	.120816	.124428	.128091	.131804	.135565	.143222	.151046	.159022	.167135
	-.40	.102683	.109270	.116101	.119604	.123162	.126774	.130437	.134150	.137911	.145568	.153392	.161368	.169481
25	.40	.078244	.085205	.092435	.096143	.099909	.103730	.107603	.111525	.115494	.123559	.131777	.140127	.148591
	.30	.080590	.087552	.094781	.098489	.102255	.106076	.109949	.113872	.117840	.125906	.134124	.142474	.150938
	.20	.082937	.089898	.097127	.100835	.104601	.108422	.112296	.116218	.120187	.128252	.136470	.144820	.153284
	.10	.085283	.092244	.099474	.103182	.106948	.110769	.114642	.118564	.122533	.130599	.138816	.147167	.155630
	0.00	.087629	.094591	.101820	.105528	.109294	.113115	.116988	.120911	.124879	.132945	.141163	.149513	.157977
	-.10	.089976	.096937	.104166	.107874	.111640	.115461	.119335	.123257	.127226	.135291	.143509	.151859	.160323
	-.20	.092322	.099283	.106513	.110221	.113987	.117808	.121681	.125603	.129572	.137638	.145855	.154206	.162670
	-.30	.094668	.101630	.108859	.112567	.116333	.120154	.124027	.127950	.131919	.139984	.148202	.156552	.165016
	-.40	.097015	.103976	.111206	.114913	.118679	.122500	.126374	.130296	.134265	.142330	.150548	.158898	.167362
30	.40	.074651	.081921	.089471	.093341	.097269	.101250	.105282	.109359	.113479	.121832	.130315	.138906	.147585
	.30	.076998	.084267	.091818	.095688	.099615	.103597	.107628	.111705	.115825	.124178	.132661	.141252	.149931
	.20	.079344	.086614	.094164	.098034	.101962	.105943	.109974	.114052	.118171	.126524	.135008	.143598	.152278
	.10	.081690	.088960	.096510	.100380	.104308	.108290	.112321	.116398	.120518	.128871	.137354	.145945	.154624
	0.00	.084037	.091306	.098857	.102727	.106654	.110636	.114667	.118744	.122864	.131217	.139700	.148291	.156970
	-.10	.086383	.093653	.101203	.105073	.109001	.112982	.117013	.121091	.125210	.133563	.142047	.150638	.159317
	-.20	.088729	.095999	.103549	.107419	.111347	.115329	.119360	.123437	.127557	.135910	.144393	.152984	.161663
	-.30	.091076	.098345	.105896	.109766	.113693	.117675	.121706	.125783	.129903	.138256	.146739	.155330	.164009
	-.40	.093422	.100692	.108242	.112112	.116040	.120021	.124052	.128130	.132249	.140602	.149086	.157677	.166356

10.0 YEAR HOLDING PERIOD
.400 EQUITY YIELD RATE
.600 LOAN RATIO

INTEREST RATE

TERM YEARS	APPR DEP	5.0	6.0	7.0	7.5	8.0	8.5	9.0	9.5	10.0	11.0	12.0	13.0	14.0
10	.40	.222043	.225611	.229274	.231141	.233032	.234946	.236883	.238842	.240825	.244856	.248975	.253180	.257468
	.30	.223476	.227043	.230707	.232574	.234464	.236378	.238315	.240275	.242257	.246289	.250408	.254612	.258900
	.20	.224908	.228476	.232139	.234006	.235897	.237811	.239747	.241707	.243689	.247721	.251840	.256045	.260333
	.10	.226340	.229908	.233571	.235439	.237329	.239243	.241180	.243140	.245122	.249153	.253272	.257477	.261765
	0.00	.227773	.231340	.235004	.236871	.238762	.240675	.242612	.244572	.246554	.250586	.254705	.258909	.263198
	-.10	.229205	.232773	.236436	.238303	.240194	.242108	.244045	.246004	.247987	.252018	.256137	.260342	.264630
	-.20	.230638	.234205	.237869	.239736	.241626	.243540	.245477	.247437	.249419	.253459	.257570	.261774	.266062
	-.30	.232070	.235638	.239301	.241168	.243059	.244973	.246909	.248869	.250851	.254883	.259002	.263207	.267495
	-.40	.233502	.237070	.240733	.242601	.244491	.246405	.248342	.250301	.252284	.256315	.260434	.264639	.268927
15	.40	.206215	.210185	.214293	.216397	.218534	.220702	.222903	.225133	.227394	.232004	.236725	.241553	.246480
	.30	.207647	.211618	.215725	.217829	.219966	.222135	.224335	.226566	.228827	.233436	.238158	.242985	.247913
	.20	.209079	.213050	.217158	.219262	.221398	.223567	.225767	.227998	.230259	.234869	.239590	.244417	.249345
	.10	.210512	.214482	.218590	.220694	.222831	.225000	.227200	.229431	.231692	.236301	.241022	.245850	.250778
	0.00	.211944	.215915	.220023	.222127	.224263	.226432	.228632	.230863	.233124	.237733	.242455	.247282	.252210
	-.10	.213377	.217347	.221455	.223559	.225696	.227864	.230065	.232295	.234556	.239166	.243887	.248715	.253642
	-.20	.214809	.218779	.222887	.224991	.227128	.229297	.231497	.233728	.235989	.240598	.245320	.250147	.255075
	-.30	.216241	.220212	.224320	.226424	.228560	.230729	.232929	.235160	.237421	.242031	.246752	.251579	.256507
	-.40	.217674	.221644	.225752	.227856	.229993	.232162	.234362	.236593	.238854	.243463	.248184	.253012	.257939
20	.40	.198540	.202805	.207236	.209512	.211825	.214175	.216561	.218981	.221434	.226434	.231550	.236773	.242093
	.30	.199973	.204238	.208669	.210944	.213257	.215607	.217993	.220413	.222866	.227866	.232983	.238206	.243525
	.20	.201405	.205670	.210101	.212376	.214690	.217040	.219425	.221845	.224298	.229298	.234415	.239638	.244958
	.10	.202838	.207102	.211534	.213809	.216122	.218472	.220858	.223278	.225731	.230731	.235847	.241070	.246390
	0.00	.204270	.208535	.212966	.215241	.217554	.219904	.222290	.224710	.227163	.232163	.237280	.242503	.247822
	-.10	.205702	.209967	.214398	.216673	.218987	.221337	.223723	.226143	.228596	.233596	.238712	.243935	.249255
	-.20	.207135	.211400	.215831	.218106	.220419	.222769	.225155	.227575	.230028	.235028	.240144	.245367	.250687
	-.30	.208567	.212832	.217263	.219538	.221852	.224202	.226587	.229007	.231460	.236460	.241577	.246800	.252119
	-.40	.210000	.214264	.218695	.220971	.223284	.225634	.228020	.230440	.232893	.237893	.243009	.248232	.253552
25	.40	.194120	.198628	.203322	.205735	.208188	.210680	.213209	.215773	.218370	.223655	.229050	.234541	.240115
	.30	.195552	.200060	.204755	.207167	.209620	.212113	.214642	.217206	.219802	.225088	.230483	.235974	.241548
	.20	.196985	.201493	.206187	.208599	.211053	.213545	.216074	.218638	.221235	.226520	.231915	.237406	.242980
	.10	.198417	.202925	.207619	.210032	.212485	.214977	.217506	.220070	.222667	.227953	.233348	.238838	.244412
	0.00	.199849	.204357	.209052	.211464	.213917	.216410	.218939	.221503	.224100	.229385	.234780	.240271	.245845
	-.10	.201282	.205790	.210484	.212897	.215350	.217842	.220371	.222935	.225532	.230817	.236212	.241703	.247277
	-.20	.202714	.207222	.211917	.214329	.216782	.219274	.221803	.224367	.226964	.232250	.237645	.243136	.248710
	-.30	.204147	.208655	.213349	.215761	.218215	.220707	.223236	.225800	.228397	.233682	.239077	.244568	.250142
	-.40	.205579	.210087	.214781	.217194	.219647	.222139	.224668	.227232	.229829	.235114	.240509	.246000	.251574
30	.40	.191318	.196036	.200953	.203479	.206047	.208653	.211295	.213970	.216677	.222173	.227765	.233437	.239176
	.30	.192750	.197468	.202385	.204911	.207479	.210085	.212727	.215403	.218109	.223605	.229197	.234870	.240608
	.20	.194183	.198901	.203818	.206344	.208911	.211517	.214160	.216835	.219542	.225038	.230630	.236302	.242041
	.10	.195615	.200333	.205250	.207776	.210344	.212950	.215592	.218268	.220974	.226470	.232062	.237734	.243473
	0.00	.197048	.201766	.206682	.209209	.211776	.214382	.217024	.219700	.222406	.227902	.233494	.239167	.244905
	-.10	.198480	.203198	.208115	.210641	.213208	.215815	.218457	.221132	.223839	.229335	.234927	.240599	.246338
	-.20	.199912	.204630	.209547	.212073	.214641	.217247	.219889	.222565	.225271	.230767	.236359	.242032	.247770
	-.30	.201345	.206063	.210980	.213506	.216073	.218679	.221322	.223997	.226703	.232199	.237792	.243464	.249203
	-.40	.202777	.207495	.212412	.214938	.217506	.220112	.222754	.225429	.228136	.233632	.239224	.244896	.250635

10.0 YEAR HOLDING PERIOD
.400 EQUITY YIELD RATE
.667 LOAN RATIO

INTEREST RATE

TERM YEARS	APPR DEP	5.0	6.0	7.0	7.5	8.0	8.5	9.0	9.5	10.0	11.0	12.0	13.0	14.0
10	.40	.202906	.206870	.210940	.213015	.215116	.217242	.219394	.221572	.223774	.228254	.232831	.237502	.242267
	.30	.204338	.208302	.212373	.214447	.216548	.218675	.220827	.223004	.225207	.229686	.234263	.238935	.243699
	.20	.205771	.209735	.213805	.215880	.217981	.220107	.222259	.224437	.226639	.231119	.235695	.240367	.245132
	.10	.207203	.211167	.215238	.217312	.219413	.221539	.223691	.225869	.228071	.232551	.237128	.241800	.246564
	0.00	.208636	.212600	.216670	.218745	.220845	.222972	.225124	.227301	.229504	.233983	.238560	.243232	.247996
	-.10	.210068	.214032	.218102	.220177	.222278	.224404	.226556	.228734	.230936	.235416	.239992	.244664	.249429
	-.20	.211500	.215464	.219535	.221609	.223710	.225837	.227989	.230166	.232369	.236848	.241425	.246097	.250861
	-.30	.212933	.216897	.220967	.223042	.225142	.227269	.229421	.231598	.233801	.238280	.242857	.247529	.252294
	-.40	.214365	.218329	.222400	.224474	.226575	.228701	.230853	.233031	.235233	.239713	.244290	.248961	.253726
15	.40	.185319	.189730	.194294	.196632	.199006	.201416	.203861	.206340	.208852	.213973	.219219	.224583	.230058
	.30	.186751	.191163	.195727	.198065	.200439	.202849	.205293	.207772	.210284	.215406	.220652	.226016	.231491
	.20	.188183	.192595	.197159	.199497	.201871	.204281	.206726	.209204	.211717	.216838	.222084	.227448	.232923
	.10	.189616	.194028	.198592	.200929	.203304	.205713	.208158	.210637	.213149	.218270	.223516	.228880	.234356
	0.00	.191048	.195460	.200024	.202362	.204736	.207146	.209590	.212069	.214581	.219703	.224949	.230313	.235788
	-.10	.192481	.196892	.201456	.203794	.206168	.208578	.211023	.213501	.216014	.221135	.226381	.231745	.237220
	-.20	.193913	.198325	.202889	.205227	.207601	.210010	.212455	.214934	.217446	.222568	.227814	.233177	.238653
	-.30	.195345	.199757	.204321	.206659	.209033	.211443	.213887	.216366	.218878	.224000	.229246	.234610	.240085
	-.40	.196778	.201189	.205754	.208091	.210466	.212875	.215320	.217799	.220311	.225432	.230678	.236042	.241518
20	.40	.176792	.181530	.186454	.188982	.191552	.194163	.196814	.199503	.202229	.207784	.213469	.219273	.225183
	.30	.178224	.182963	.187886	.190414	.192984	.195596	.198246	.200935	.203661	.209217	.214902	.220705	.226616
	.20	.179656	.184395	.189319	.191847	.194417	.197028	.199679	.202368	.205093	.210649	.216334	.222137	.228048
	.10	.181089	.185827	.190751	.193279	.195849	.198460	.201111	.203800	.206526	.212081	.217766	.223570	.229480
	0.00	.182521	.187260	.192183	.194711	.197282	.199893	.202544	.205233	.207958	.213514	.219199	.225002	.230913
	-.10	.183954	.188692	.193616	.196144	.198714	.201325	.203976	.206665	.209391	.214946	.220631	.226435	.232345
	-.20	.185386	.190125	.195048	.197576	.200146	.202758	.205408	.208097	.210823	.216378	.222064	.227867	.233778
	-.30	.186818	.191557	.196481	.199008	.201579	.204190	.206841	.209530	.212255	.217811	.223496	.229299	.235210
	-.40	.188251	.192989	.197913	.200441	.203011	.205622	.208273	.210962	.213688	.219243	.224928	.230732	.236642
25	.40	.171880	.176889	.182105	.184785	.187511	.190280	.193090	.195939	.198825	.204697	.210692	.216793	.222986
	.30	.173312	.178321	.183537	.186218	.188943	.191713	.194523	.197371	.200257	.206130	.212124	.218225	.224419
	.20	.174745	.179753	.184969	.187650	.190376	.193145	.195955	.198804	.201689	.207562	.213556	.219657	.225851
	.10	.176177	.181186	.186402	.189082	.191808	.194577	.197387	.200236	.203122	.208994	.214989	.221090	.227283
	0.00	.177609	.182618	.187834	.190515	.193241	.196010	.198820	.201669	.204554	.210427	.216421	.222522	.228716
	-.10	.179042	.184051	.189267	.191947	.194673	.197442	.200252	.203101	.205987	.211859	.217854	.223955	.230148
	-.20	.180474	.185483	.190699	.193380	.196105	.198874	.201685	.204533	.207419	.213291	.219286	.225387	.231580
	-.30	.181907	.186915	.192131	.194812	.197538	.200307	.203117	.205966	.208851	.214724	.220718	.226819	.233013
	-.40	.183339	.188348	.193564	.196244	.198970	.201739	.204549	.207398	.210284	.216156	.222151	.228252	.234445
30	.40	.168767	.174009	.179472	.182279	.185132	.188027	.190963	.193936	.196943	.203050	.209263	.215566	.221942
	.30	.170199	.175441	.180904	.183711	.186564	.189460	.192396	.195368	.198376	.204482	.210696	.216998	.223375
	.20	.171631	.176873	.182337	.185144	.187996	.190892	.193828	.196801	.199808	.205915	.212128	.218431	.224807
	.10	.173064	.178306	.183769	.186576	.189429	.192325	.195260	.198233	.201240	.207347	.213561	.219863	.226239
	0.00	.174496	.179738	.185202	.188008	.190861	.193757	.196693	.199666	.202673	.208779	.214993	.221296	.227672
	-.10	.175929	.181171	.186634	.189441	.192294	.195189	.198125	.201098	.204105	.210212	.216425	.222728	.229104
	-.20	.177361	.182603	.188066	.190873	.193726	.196622	.199558	.202530	.205537	.211644	.217858	.224160	.230537
	-.30	.178793	.184036	.189499	.192306	.195158	.198054	.200990	.203963	.206970	.213077	.219290	.225593	.231969
	-.40	.180226	.185468	.190931	.193738	.196591	.199487	.202422	.205395	.208402	.214509	.220722	.227025	.233401

10.0 YEAR HOLDING PERIOD
.400 EQUITY YIELD RATE
.700 LOAN RATIO

INTEREST RATE

TERM YEARS	APPR DEP	5.0	6.0	7.0	7.5	8.0	8.5	9.0	9.5	10.0	11.0	12.0	13.0	14.0
10	.40	.193339	.197501	.201775	.203953	.206159	.208392	.210651	.212938	.215250	.219954	.224759	.229665	.234668
	.30	.194771	.198933	.203207	.205386	.207591	.209824	.212084	.214370	.216683	.221386	.226192	.231097	.236100
	.20	.196204	.200366	.204640	.206818	.209024	.211257	.213516	.215802	.218115	.222819	.227624	.232530	.237532
	.10	.197636	.201798	.206072	.208250	.210456	.212689	.214949	.217235	.219548	.224251	.229057	.233962	.238965
	0.00	.199068	.203231	.207504	.209683	.211888	.214121	.216381	.218667	.220980	.225683	.230489	.235394	.240397
	-.10	.200501	.204663	.208937	.211115	.213321	.215554	.217813	.220100	.222412	.227116	.231921	.236827	.241829
	-.20	.201933	.206095	.210369	.212548	.214753	.216986	.219246	.221532	.223845	.228548	.233354	.238259	.243262
	-.30	.203365	.207528	.211802	.213980	.216186	.218418	.220678	.222964	.225277	.229980	.234746	.239691	.244694
	-.40	.204798	.208960	.213234	.215412	.217618	.219851	.222110	.224397	.226709	.231413	.236218	.241124	.246127
15	.40	.174872	.179504	.184297	.186751	.189244	.191774	.194341	.196944	.199582	.204959	.210468	.216100	.221849
	.30	.176304	.180937	.185729	.188184	.190677	.193207	.195774	.198376	.201014	.206392	.211900	.217532	.223281
	.20	.177737	.182369	.187162	.189616	.192109	.194639	.197206	.199809	.202447	.207824	.213332	.218964	.224714
	.10	.179169	.183801	.188594	.191049	.193541	.196072	.198638	.201241	.203879	.209257	.214765	.220397	.226146
	0.00	.180602	.185234	.190026	.192481	.194974	.197504	.200071	.202674	.205311	.210689	.216197	.221829	.227578
	-.10	.182034	.186666	.191459	.193913	.196406	.198936	.201503	.204106	.206744	.212121	.217630	.223262	.229011
	-.20	.183466	.188099	.192891	.195346	.197839	.200369	.202936	.205538	.208176	.213554	.219062	.224694	.230443
	-.30	.184899	.189531	.194323	.196778	.199271	.201801	.204368	.206971	.209608	.214986	.220494	.226126	.231875
	-.40	.186331	.190963	.195756	.198211	.200703	.203233	.205800	.208403	.211041	.216418	.221927	.227559	.233308
20	.40	.165919	.170894	.176064	.178718	.181417	.184159	.186942	.189766	.192628	.198461	.204430	.210524	.216730
	.30	.167351	.172327	.177496	.180151	.182850	.185591	.188375	.191198	.194060	.199893	.205863	.211956	.218162
	.20	.168784	.173759	.178929	.181583	.184282	.187024	.189807	.192630	.195492	.201326	.207295	.213388	.219595
	.10	.170216	.175191	.180361	.183016	.185714	.188456	.191239	.194063	.196925	.202758	.208727	.214821	.221027
	0.00	.171648	.176624	.181794	.184448	.187147	.189889	.192672	.195495	.198357	.204190	.210160	.216253	.222459
	-.10	.173081	.178056	.183226	.185880	.188579	.191321	.194104	.196928	.199789	.205623	.211592	.217686	.223892
	-.20	.174513	.179489	.184658	.187313	.190012	.192753	.195537	.198360	.201222	.207055	.213024	.219118	.225324
	-.30	.175946	.180921	.186091	.188745	.191444	.194186	.196969	.199792	.202654	.208487	.214457	.220550	.226757
	-.40	.177378	.182353	.187523	.190177	.192876	.195618	.198401	.201225	.204087	.209920	.215889	.221983	.228189
25	.40	.160762	.166021	.171498	.174312	.177174	.180082	.183032	.186024	.189053	.195220	.201514	.207920	.214423
	.30	.162194	.167453	.172930	.175744	.178607	.181514	.184465	.187456	.190486	.196652	.202946	.209352	.215855
	.20	.163626	.168885	.174362	.177177	.180039	.182946	.185897	.188888	.191918	.198084	.204378	.210784	.217288
	.10	.165059	.170318	.175795	.178609	.181471	.184379	.187329	.190321	.193350	.199517	.205811	.212217	.218720
	0.00	.166491	.171750	.177227	.180042	.182904	.185811	.188762	.191753	.194783	.200949	.207243	.213649	.220152
	-.10	.167923	.173183	.178659	.181474	.184336	.187244	.190194	.193185	.196215	.202381	.208676	.215082	.221585
	-.20	.169356	.174615	.180092	.182906	.185769	.188676	.191627	.194618	.197648	.203814	.210108	.216514	.223017
	-.30	.170788	.176047	.181524	.184339	.187201	.190108	.193059	.196050	.199080	.205246	.211540	.217946	.224450
	-.40	.172221	.177480	.182957	.185771	.188633	.191541	.194491	.197483	.200512	.206679	.212973	.219379	.225882
30	.40	.157493	.162997	.168733	.171680	.174676	.177716	.180799	.183920	.187078	.193490	.200014	.206632	.213327
	.30	.158925	.164429	.170166	.173113	.176108	.179148	.182231	.185353	.188510	.194922	.201446	.208064	.214759
	.20	.160357	.165862	.171598	.174545	.177541	.180581	.183664	.186785	.189943	.196355	.202879	.209496	.216192
	.10	.161790	.167294	.173030	.175978	.178973	.182014	.185096	.188218	.191375	.197787	.204311	.210929	.217624
	0.00	.163222	.168726	.174463	.177410	.180405	.183446	.186528	.189650	.192807	.199219	.205744	.212361	.219056
	-.10	.164655	.170159	.175895	.178842	.181838	.184878	.187961	.191082	.194240	.200652	.207176	.213794	.220489
	-.20	.166087	.171591	.177328	.180275	.183270	.186311	.189393	.192515	.195672	.202084	.208608	.215226	.221921
	-.30	.167519	.173024	.178760	.181707	.184703	.187743	.190826	.193947	.197105	.203517	.210041	.216658	.223353
	-.40	.168952	.174456	.180192	.183140	.186135	.189175	.192258	.195379	.198537	.204949	.211473	.218091	.224786

10.0 YEAR HOLDING PERIOD
.400 EQUITY YIELD RATE
.750 LOAN RATIO

INTEREST RATE

TERM YEARS	APPR DEP	5.0	6.0	7.0	7.5	8.0	8.5	9.0	9.5	10.0	11.0	12.0	13.0	14.0
10	.40	.178987	.183446	.188025	.190359	.192722	.195115	.197536	.199985	.202463	.207503	.212651	.217907	.223267
	.30	.180419	.184878	.189458	.191792	.194155	.196547	.198968	.201418	.203896	.208935	.214084	.219340	.224700
	.20	.181851	.186311	.190890	.193224	.195587	.197979	.200401	.202850	.205328	.210367	.215516	.220772	.226132
	.10	.183284	.187743	.192322	.194656	.197020	.199412	.201833	.204283	.206760	.211800	.216949	.222204	.227565
	0.00	.184716	.189176	.193755	.196089	.198452	.200844	.203265	.205715	.208193	.213232	.218381	.223637	.228997
	-.10	.186148	.190608	.195187	.197521	.199884	.202277	.204698	.207147	.209625	.214665	.219813	.225069	.230429
	-.20	.187581	.192040	.196620	.198953	.201317	.203709	.206130	.208580	.211058	.216097	.221246	.226502	.231862
	-.30	.189013	.193473	.198052	.200386	.202749	.205141	.207562	.210012	.212490	.217529	.222678	.227934	.233294
	-.40	.190446	.194905	.199484	.201818	.204181	.206574	.208995	.211444	.213922	.218962	.224111	.229366	.234726
15	.40	.159201	.164164	.169299	.171929	.174600	.177310	.180061	.182849	.185675	.191437	.197339	.203373	.209533
	.30	.160633	.165596	.170731	.173361	.176032	.178743	.181493	.184282	.187108	.192870	.198771	.204806	.210965
	.20	.162066	.167029	.172163	.174793	.177464	.180175	.182925	.185714	.188540	.194302	.200204	.206238	.212398
	.10	.163498	.168461	.173596	.176226	.178897	.181608	.184358	.187146	.189973	.195734	.201636	.207670	.213830
	0.00	.164930	.169893	.175028	.177658	.180329	.183040	.185790	.188579	.191405	.197167	.203068	.209103	.215262
	-.10	.166363	.171326	.176461	.179091	.181761	.184472	.187223	.190011	.192837	.198599	.204501	.210535	.216695
	-.20	.167795	.172758	.177893	.180523	.183194	.185905	.188655	.191444	.194270	.200032	.205933	.211968	.218127
	-.30	.169227	.174191	.179325	.181955	.184626	.187337	.190087	.192876	.195702	.201464	.207366	.213400	.219560
	-.40	.170660	.175623	.180758	.183388	.186059	.188770	.191520	.194308	.197135	.202896	.208798	.214832	.220992
20	.40	.149608	.154939	.160478	.163322	.166213	.169151	.172133	.175158	.178224	.184474	.190870	.197399	.204048
	.30	.151040	.156371	.161910	.164754	.167646	.170583	.173566	.176591	.179657	.185907	.192302	.198831	.205481
	.20	.152473	.157804	.163343	.166187	.169078	.172016	.174998	.178023	.181089	.187339	.193735	.200264	.206913
	.10	.153905	.159236	.164775	.167619	.170511	.173448	.176430	.179455	.182522	.188772	.195167	.201696	.208346
	0.00	.155338	.160668	.166207	.169051	.171943	.174881	.177863	.180888	.183954	.190204	.196600	.203128	.209778
	-.10	.156770	.162101	.167640	.170484	.173375	.176313	.179295	.182320	.185386	.191636	.198032	.204561	.211210
	-.20	.158202	.163533	.169072	.171916	.174808	.177745	.180727	.183752	.186819	.193069	.199464	.205993	.212643
	-.30	.159635	.164966	.170505	.173349	.176240	.179178	.182160	.185185	.188251	.194501	.200897	.207426	.214075
	-.40	.161067	.166398	.171937	.174781	.177672	.180610	.183592	.186617	.189684	.195933	.202329	.208858	.215507
25	.40	.144082	.149717	.155585	.158601	.161667	.164783	.167944	.171149	.174395	.181002	.187745	.194609	.201577
	.30	.145515	.151149	.157018	.160033	.163100	.166215	.169376	.172581	.175827	.182434	.189178	.196041	.203009
	.20	.146947	.152582	.158450	.161466	.164532	.167647	.170809	.174014	.177260	.183866	.190610	.197474	.204441
	.10	.148379	.154014	.159882	.162898	.165964	.169080	.172241	.175446	.178692	.185299	.192042	.198906	.205874
	0.00	.149812	.155447	.161315	.164330	.167397	.170512	.173673	.176878	.180125	.186731	.193475	.200338	.207306
	-.10	.151244	.156879	.162747	.165763	.168829	.171944	.175106	.178311	.181557	.188164	.194907	.201771	.208738
	-.20	.152677	.158311	.164180	.167195	.170262	.173377	.176538	.179743	.182989	.189596	.196340	.203203	.210171
	-.30	.154109	.159744	.165612	.168627	.171694	.174809	.177971	.181175	.184422	.191028	.197772	.204636	.211603
	-.40	.155541	.161176	.167044	.170060	.173126	.176242	.179403	.182608	.185854	.192461	.199204	.206068	.213036
30	.40	.140580	.146477	.152624	.155781	.158991	.162248	.165551	.168895	.172278	.179148	.186138	.193229	.200402
	.30	.142012	.147910	.154056	.157214	.160423	.163681	.166983	.170328	.173711	.180581	.187571	.194661	.201835
	.20	.143445	.149342	.155488	.158646	.161855	.165113	.168416	.171760	.175143	.182013	.189003	.196094	.203267
	.10	.144877	.150775	.156921	.160078	.163288	.166545	.169848	.173193	.176576	.183445	.190436	.197526	.204699
	0.00	.146310	.152207	.158353	.161511	.164720	.167978	.171280	.174625	.178008	.184878	.191868	.198958	.206132
	-.10	.147742	.153639	.159785	.162943	.166152	.169410	.172713	.176057	.179440	.186310	.193300	.200391	.207564
	-.20	.149174	.155072	.161218	.164375	.167585	.170843	.174145	.177490	.180873	.187743	.194733	.201823	.208997
	-.30	.150607	.156504	.162650	.165808	.169017	.172275	.175578	.178922	.182305	.189175	.196165	.203256	.210429
	-.40	.152039	.157936	.164083	.167240	.170450	.173707	.177010	.180354	.183737	.190607	.197598	.204688	.211861

```
10.0 YEAR HOLDING PERIOD
 .400 EQUITY YIELD RATE
 .800 LOAN RATIO
```

INTEREST RATE

TERM YEARS	APPR DEP	5.0	6.0	7.0	7.5	8.0	8.5	9.0	9.5	10.0	11.0	12.0	13.0	14.0
10	.40	.164634	.169391	.174276	.176765	.179286	.181838	.184420	.187033	.189676	.195051	.200543	.206150	.211867
	.30	.166067	.170823	.175708	.178197	.180718	.183270	.185853	.188465	.191108	.196484	.201976	.207582	.213300
	.20	.167499	.172256	.177140	.179630	.182151	.184702	.187285	.189898	.192541	.197916	.203408	.209014	.214732
	.10	.168931	.173688	.178573	.181062	.183583	.186135	.188717	.191330	.193973	.199349	.204841	.210447	.216164
	0.00	.170364	.175121	.180005	.182495	.185015	.187567	.190150	.192763	.195406	.200781	.206273	.211879	.217597
	-.10	.171796	.176553	.181437	.183927	.186448	.189000	.191582	.194195	.196838	.202213	.207705	.213312	.219029
	-.20	.173229	.177985	.182870	.185359	.187880	.190432	.193014	.195627	.198270	.203646	.209138	.214744	.220461
	-.30	.174661	.179418	.184302	.186792	.189313	.191864	.194447	.197060	.199703	.205078	.210570	.216176	.221894
	-.40	.176093	.180850	.185735	.188224	.190745	.193297	.195879	.198492	.201135	.206510	.212003	.217609	.223326
15	.40	.143529	.148823	.154300	.157106	.159955	.162846	.165780	.168754	.171769	.177915	.184210	.190647	.197217
	.30	.144962	.150256	.155733	.158538	.161387	.164279	.167212	.170187	.173201	.179347	.185642	.192079	.198649
	.20	.146394	.151688	.157165	.159971	.162820	.165711	.168645	.171619	.174634	.180780	.187075	.193512	.200082
	.10	.147827	.153121	.158598	.161403	.164252	.167144	.170077	.173052	.176066	.182212	.188507	.194944	.201514
	0.00	.149259	.154553	.160030	.162835	.165684	.168576	.171509	.174484	.177499	.183645	.189940	.196376	.202947
	-.10	.150691	.155985	.161462	.164268	.167117	.170008	.172942	.175916	.178931	.185077	.191372	.197809	.204379
	-.20	.152124	.157418	.162895	.165700	.168549	.171441	.174374	.177349	.180363	.186509	.192804	.199241	.205811
	-.30	.153556	.158850	.164327	.167133	.169981	.172873	.175807	.178781	.181796	.187942	.194237	.200673	.207244
	-.40	.154989	.160282	.165760	.168565	.171414	.174306	.177239	.180214	.183228	.189374	.195669	.202106	.208676
20	.40	.133297	.138983	.144892	.147925	.151010	.154143	.157324	.160551	.163821	.170488	.177310	.184274	.191367
	.30	.134730	.140416	.146324	.149358	.152442	.155575	.158756	.161983	.165254	.171920	.178742	.185706	.192799
	.20	.136162	.141848	.147756	.150790	.153874	.157008	.160189	.163415	.166686	.173353	.180175	.187139	.194232
	.10	.137594	.143281	.149189	.152222	.155307	.158440	.161621	.164848	.168119	.174785	.181607	.188571	.195664
	0.00	.139027	.144713	.150621	.153655	.156739	.159873	.163054	.166280	.169551	.176218	.183040	.190004	.197096
	-.10	.140459	.146145	.152053	.155087	.158172	.161305	.164486	.167713	.170983	.177650	.184472	.191436	.198529
	-.20	.141891	.147578	.153486	.156520	.159604	.162737	.165918	.169145	.172416	.179082	.185904	.192868	.199961
	-.30	.143324	.149010	.154918	.157952	.161036	.164170	.167351	.170577	.173848	.180515	.187337	.194301	.201394
	-.40	.144756	.150443	.156351	.159384	.162469	.165602	.168783	.172010	.175280	.181947	.188769	.195733	.202826
25	.40	.127403	.133444	.139673	.142889	.146160	.149483	.152855	.156274	.159737	.166784	.173977	.181298	.188730
	.30	.128835	.134846	.141105	.144322	.147593	.150916	.154288	.157706	.161169	.168216	.175409	.182731	.190163
	.20	.130268	.136278	.142538	.145754	.149025	.152348	.155720	.159139	.162601	.169648	.176842	.184163	.191595
	.10	.131700	.137711	.143970	.147187	.150458	.153780	.157153	.160571	.164034	.171081	.178274	.185595	.193027
	0.00	.133133	.139143	.145402	.148619	.151890	.155213	.158585	.162004	.165466	.172513	.179707	.187028	.194460
	-.10	.134565	.140575	.146835	.150051	.153332	.156645	.160017	.163436	.166899	.173946	.181139	.188460	.195892
	-.20	.135997	.142008	.148267	.151484	.154755	.158078	.161450	.164868	.168331	.175378	.182571	.189892	.197325
	-.30	.137430	.143440	.149700	.152916	.156187	.159510	.162882	.166301	.169763	.176810	.184004	.191325	.198757
	-.40	.138862	.144873	.151132	.154349	.157620	.160942	.164314	.167733	.171196	.178243	.185436	.192757	.200189
30	.40	.123667	.129958	.136514	.139882	.143305	.146780	.150303	.153870	.157479	.164807	.172263	.179826	.187478
	.30	.125100	.131390	.137946	.141314	.144738	.148212	.151735	.155303	.158911	.166239	.173695	.181259	.188910
	.20	.126532	.132823	.139379	.142747	.146170	.149645	.153168	.156735	.160344	.167672	.175128	.182691	.190342
	.10	.127964	.134255	.140811	.144179	.147602	.151077	.154600	.158168	.161776	.169104	.176560	.184123	.191775
	0.00	.129397	.135687	.142243	.145611	.149035	.152510	.156033	.159600	.163208	.170536	.177993	.185556	.193207
	-.10	.130829	.137120	.143676	.147044	.150467	.153942	.157465	.161032	.164641	.171969	.179425	.186988	.194640
	-.20	.132262	.138552	.145108	.148476	.151900	.155374	.158897	.162465	.166073	.173401	.180857	.188420	.196072
	-.30	.133694	.139985	.146540	.149909	.153332	.156807	.160330	.163897	.167506	.174834	.182290	.189853	.197504
	-.40	.135126	.141417	.147973	.151341	.154764	.158239	.161762	.165329	.168938	.176266	.183722	.191285	.198937

10.0 YEAR HOLDING PERIOD
.400 EQUITY YIELD RATE
.900 LOAN RATIO

INTEREST RATE

TERM YEARS	APPR DEP	5.0	6.0	7.0	7.5	8.0	8.5	9.0	9.5	10.0	11.0	12.0	13.0	14.0
10	.40	.135930	.141281	.146776	.149577	.152413	.155284	.158189	.161128	.164102	.170149	.176328	.182635	.189067
	.30	.137362	.142714	.148209	.151009	.153845	.156716	.159621	.162561	.165534	.171581	.177760	.184067	.190499
	.20	.138795	.144146	.149641	.152424	.155278	.158148	.161054	.163993	.166967	.173014	.179192	.185499	.191932
	.10	.140227	.145578	.151073	.153874	.156710	.159581	.162486	.165426	.168399	.174446	.180625	.186932	.193364
	0.00	.141659	.147011	.152506	.155306	.158142	.161013	.163918	.166858	.169831	.175879	.182057	.188364	.194796
	-.10	.143092	.148443	.153938	.156739	.159575	.162445	.165351	.168290	.171264	.177311	.183490	.189797	.196229
	-.20	.144524	.149875	.155370	.158171	.161007	.163878	.166783	.169723	.172696	.178743	.184922	.191229	.197661
	-.30	.145956	.151308	.156803	.159604	.162439	.165310	.168226	.171155	.174128	.180176	.186354	.192661	.199093
	-.40	.147389	.152740	.158235	.161036	.163872	.166743	.169648	.172587	.175561	.181608	.187787	.194094	.200526
15	.40	.112187	.118143	.124304	.127460	.130665	.133918	.137219	.140565	.143956	.150871	.157953	.165194	.172585
	.30	.113619	.119575	.125737	.128893	.132098	.135351	.138651	.141997	.145388	.152303	.159385	.166626	.174018
	.20	.115052	.121007	.127169	.130325	.133530	.136783	.140083	.143430	.146821	.153735	.160817	.168059	.175450
	.10	.116484	.122440	.128601	.131757	.134962	.138216	.141516	.144862	.148254	.155168	.162250	.169491	.176883
	0.00	.117916	.123872	.130034	.133190	.136395	.139648	.142948	.146295	.149686	.156600	.163682	.170923	.178315
	-.10	.119349	.125304	.131466	.134622	.137827	.141080	.144381	.147727	.151118	.158032	.165114	.172356	.179747
	-.20	.120781	.126737	.132899	.136055	.139260	.142513	.145813	.149159	.152551	.159465	.166547	.173788	.181180
	-.30	.122214	.128169	.134331	.137487	.140692	.143945	.147245	.150592	.153983	.160897	.167979	.175220	.182612
	-.40	.123646	.129602	.135763	.138919	.142124	.145378	.148678	.152024	.155416	.162330	.169412	.176653	.184044
20	.40	.100675	.107073	.113719	.117132	.120602	.124127	.127706	.131336	.135015	.142515	.150190	.158025	.166004
	.30	.102108	.108505	.115152	.118564	.122034	.125560	.129138	.132768	.136448	.143948	.151622	.159457	.167436
	.20	.103540	.109937	.116584	.119997	.123467	.126992	.130570	.134200	.137880	.145380	.153055	.160889	.168869
	.10	.104973	.111370	.118017	.121429	.124899	.128424	.132003	.135633	.139312	.146812	.154487	.162322	.170301
	0.00	.106405	.112802	.119449	.122862	.126332	.129857	.133435	.137065	.140745	.148245	.155920	.163754	.171733
	-.10	.107837	.114235	.120881	.124294	.127764	.131289	.134868	.138498	.142177	.149677	.157352	.165186	.173166
	-.20	.109270	.115667	.122314	.125726	.129196	.132721	.136300	.139930	.143610	.151109	.158784	.166619	.174598
	-.30	.110702	.117099	.123746	.127159	.130629	.134154	.137732	.141362	.145042	.152542	.160217	.168051	.176031
	-.40	.112135	.118532	.125178	.128591	.132061	.135586	.139165	.142795	.146474	.153974	.161649	.169483	.177463
25	.40	.094045	.100806	.107848	.111467	.115147	.118885	.122679	.126524	.130420	.138348	.146440	.154677	.163038
	.30	.095477	.102239	.109281	.112899	.116579	.120317	.124111	.127957	.131852	.139780	.147873	.156110	.164470
	.20	.096909	.103671	.110713	.114332	.118011	.121750	.125543	.129389	.133285	.141213	.149305	.157542	.165903
	.10	.098342	.105104	.112145	.115764	.119444	.123182	.126976	.130822	.134717	.142645	.150737	.158974	.167335
	0.00	.099774	.106536	.113578	.117196	.120876	.124614	.128408	.132254	.136149	.144077	.152170	.160406	.168767
	-.10	.101207	.107968	.115010	.118629	.122309	.126047	.129840	.133686	.137582	.145510	.153602	.161839	.170200
	-.20	.102639	.109401	.116442	.120061	.123741	.127479	.131273	.135119	.139014	.146942	.155035	.163271	.171632
	-.30	.104071	.110833	.117875	.121493	.125173	.128912	.132705	.136551	.140447	.148375	.156467	.164703	.173064
	-.40	.105504	.112266	.119307	.122926	.126606	.130344	.134138	.137984	.141879	.149807	.157899	.166136	.174497
30	.40	.089842	.096919	.104294	.108083	.111935	.115844	.119807	.123820	.127880	.136124	.144512	.153021	.161629
	.30	.091274	.098351	.105727	.109516	.113367	.117276	.121239	.125253	.129312	.137556	.145944	.154453	.163061
	.20	.092707	.099784	.107159	.110948	.114799	.118709	.122672	.126686	.130745	.138989	.147377	.155885	.164493
	.10	.094139	.101216	.108591	.112380	.116232	.120141	.124104	.128118	.132177	.140421	.148809	.157318	.165926
	0.00	.095571	.102648	.110024	.113813	.117664	.121573	.125537	.129550	.133610	.141853	.150242	.158750	.167358
	-.10	.097004	.104081	.111456	.115245	.119096	.123006	.126969	.130982	.135042	.143286	.151674	.160183	.168791
	-.20	.098436	.105513	.112888	.116678	.120529	.124438	.128401	.132415	.136474	.144718	.153106	.161615	.170223
	-.30	.099869	.106945	.114321	.118110	.121961	.125871	.129834	.133847	.137907	.146151	.154539	.163047	.171655
	-.40	.101301	.108378	.115753	.119542	.123394	.127303	.131266	.135279	.139339	.147583	.155971	.164480	.173088

376

```
10.0 YEAR HOLDING PERIOD
 .500 EQUITY YIELD RATE
 .600 LOAN RATIO
```

INTEREST RATE

TERM YEARS	APPR DEP	5.0	6.0	7.0	7.5	8.0	8.5	9.0	9.5	10.0	11.0	12.0	13.0	14.0
10	.40	.267543	.271111	.274774	.276641	.278532	.280446	.282383	.284342	.286325	.290356	.294475	.298680	.302968
	.30	.268426	.271993	.275657	.277524	.279414	.281328	.283265	.285225	.287207	.291239	.295358	.299562	.303850
	.20	.269308	.272876	.276539	.278406	.280297	.282211	.284148	.286107	.288090	.292121	.296240	.300445	.304733
	.10	.270191	.273758	.277421	.279289	.281179	.283093	.285030	.286990	.288972	.293003	.297122	.301327	.305615
	0.00	.271073	.274640	.278304	.280171	.282062	.283975	.285912	.287872	.289854	.293886	.298005	.302209	.306498
	-.10	.271955	.275523	.279186	.281053	.282944	.284858	.286795	.288754	.290737	.294768	.298887	.303092	.307380
	-.20	.272838	.276405	.280069	.281936	.283826	.285740	.287677	.289637	.291619	.295650	.299770	.303973	.308262
	-.30	.273720	.277288	.280951	.282818	.284709	.286623	.288559	.290519	.292501	.296533	.300652	.304857	.309145
	-.40	.274602	.278170	.281833	.283701	.285591	.287505	.289442	.291401	.293384	.297415	.301534	.305739	.310027
15	.40	.250332	.254245	.258295	.260370	.262478	.264619	.266790	.268993	.271225	.275779	.280445	.285218	.290092
	.30	.251214	.255127	.259177	.261253	.263361	.265501	.267673	.269875	.272108	.276661	.281327	.286100	.290974
	.20	.252097	.256010	.260060	.262135	.264243	.266383	.268555	.270757	.272990	.277544	.282210	.286982	.291856
	.10	.252979	.256892	.260942	.263018	.265126	.267266	.269437	.271640	.273873	.278426	.283092	.287865	.292739
	0.00	.253861	.257774	.261825	.263900	.266008	.268148	.270320	.272522	.274755	.279308	.283974	.288747	.293621
	-.10	.254744	.258657	.262707	.264782	.266890	.269030	.271202	.273405	.275637	.280191	.284857	.289630	.294504
	-.20	.255626	.259539	.263589	.265665	.267773	.269913	.272084	.274287	.276520	.281073	.285739	.290512	.295386
	-.30	.256509	.260421	.264472	.266547	.268655	.270795	.272967	.275169	.277402	.281955	.286621	.291394	.296268
	-.40	.257391	.261304	.265354	.267429	.269537	.271678	.273849	.276052	.278284	.282838	.287504	.292277	.297151
20	.40	.241987	.246176	.250533	.252772	.255050	.257365	.259717	.262103	.264524	.269461	.274518	.279684	.284950
	.30	.242870	.247058	.251415	.253654	.255932	.258248	.260599	.262986	.265406	.270343	.275400	.280566	.285832
	.20	.243752	.247940	.252298	.254537	.256815	.259130	.261482	.263868	.266289	.271226	.276282	.281449	.286715
	.10	.244634	.248823	.253180	.255419	.257697	.260012	.262364	.264751	.267171	.272108	.277165	.282331	.287597
	0.00	.245517	.249705	.254062	.256302	.258579	.260895	.263246	.265633	.268053	.272990	.278047	.283213	.288479
	-.10	.246399	.250588	.254945	.257184	.259462	.261777	.264129	.266515	.268936	.273873	.278929	.284096	.289362
	-.20	.247281	.251470	.255827	.258066	.260344	.262659	.265011	.267398	.269818	.274755	.279812	.284978	.290244
	-.30	.248164	.252352	.256710	.258949	.261226	.263542	.265893	.268280	.270701	.275638	.280694	.285860	.291127
	-.40	.249046	.253235	.257592	.259831	.262109	.264424	.266776	.269162	.271583	.276520	.281577	.286743	.292009
25	.40	.237180	.241608	.246227	.248604	.251023	.253482	.255979	.258512	.261080	.266310	.271654	.277100	.282633
	.30	.238063	.242491	.247110	.249486	.251905	.254364	.256861	.259394	.261962	.267192	.272537	.277982	.283515
	.20	.238945	.243373	.247992	.250369	.252788	.255246	.257744	.260277	.262844	.268074	.273419	.278864	.284397
	.10	.239828	.244255	.248875	.251251	.253670	.256129	.258626	.261159	.263727	.268957	.274302	.279747	.285280
	0.00	.240710	.245138	.249757	.252134	.254552	.257011	.259508	.262042	.264609	.269839	.275184	.280629	.286162
	-.10	.241592	.246020	.250639	.253016	.255435	.257894	.260391	.262924	.265491	.270722	.276066	.281512	.287044
	-.20	.242475	.246902	.251522	.253898	.256317	.258776	.261273	.263806	.266374	.271604	.276949	.282394	.287927
	-.30	.243357	.247785	.252404	.254781	.257199	.259658	.262155	.264689	.267256	.272486	.277831	.283276	.288809
	-.40	.244239	.248667	.253286	.255663	.258082	.260541	.263038	.265571	.268139	.273369	.278713	.284159	.289692
30	.40	.234134	.238774	.243621	.246115	.248652	.251229	.253844	.256494	.259176	.264628	.270182	.275821	.281532
	.30	.235016	.239657	.244504	.246997	.249534	.252111	.254726	.257376	.260058	.265511	.271065	.276704	.282414
	.20	.235899	.240539	.245386	.247880	.250416	.252994	.255608	.258258	.260941	.266393	.271947	.277586	.283296
	.10	.236781	.241422	.246268	.248762	.251299	.253876	.256491	.259141	.261823	.267275	.272829	.278469	.284179
	0.00	.237663	.242304	.247151	.249644	.252181	.254758	.257373	.260023	.262705	.268158	.273712	.279351	.285061
	-.10	.238546	.243186	.248033	.250527	.253064	.255641	.258256	.260905	.263588	.269040	.274594	.280233	.285943
	-.20	.239428	.244069	.248915	.251409	.253946	.256523	.259138	.261788	.264470	.269922	.275476	.281116	.286825
	-.30	.240310	.244951	.249798	.252291	.254828	.257405	.260020	.262670	.265353	.270805	.276359	.281998	.287708
	-.40	.241193	.245833	.250680	.253174	.255711	.258288	.260903	.263553	.266235	.271687	.277241	.282880	.288591

10.0 YEAR HOLDING PERIOD
.500 EQUITY YIELD RATE
.667 LOAN RATIO

INTEREST RATE

TERM YEARS	APPR DEP	5.0	6.0	7.0	7.5	8.0	8.5	9.0	9.5	10.0	11.0	12.0	13.0	14.0
10	.40	.242106	.246070	.250140	.252215	.254315	.256442	.258594	.260771	.262974	.267453	.272030	.276702	.281467
	.30	.242988	.246952	.251023	.253097	.255198	.257324	.259476	.261654	.263856	.268336	.272913	.277585	.282349
	.20	.243871	.247835	.251905	.253980	.256080	.258207	.260359	.262536	.264739	.269218	.273795	.278467	.283231
	.10	.244753	.248717	.252787	.254862	.256963	.259089	.261241	.263419	.265621	.270101	.274677	.279349	.284114
	0.00	.245635	.249599	.253670	.255744	.257845	.259971	.262124	.264301	.266504	.270983	.275560	.280231	.284996
	-.10	.246518	.250482	.254552	.256627	.258727	.260854	.263006	.265183	.267386	.271865	.276442	.281114	.285879
	-.20	.247400	.251364	.255434	.257509	.259610	.261736	.263888	.266066	.268268	.272748	.277325	.281996	.286761
	-.30	.248282	.252246	.256317	.258391	.260492	.262619	.264771	.266948	.269151	.273630	.278207	.282879	.287643
	-.40	.249165	.253129	.257199	.259274	.261375	.263501	.265653	.267831	.270033	.274513	.279089	.283761	.288526
15	.40	.222982	.227329	.231830	.234136	.236478	.238856	.241269	.243716	.246197	.251256	.256441	.261744	.267160
	.30	.223864	.228212	.232712	.235018	.237360	.239738	.242151	.244599	.247079	.252139	.257323	.262626	.268042
	.20	.224747	.229094	.233595	.235900	.238243	.240621	.243034	.245481	.247962	.253021	.258205	.263509	.268924
	.10	.225629	.229977	.234477	.236783	.239125	.241503	.243916	.246363	.248844	.253903	.259088	.264391	.269807
	0.00	.226511	.230859	.235359	.237665	.240008	.242385	.244798	.247246	.249726	.254786	.259970	.265273	.270689
	-.10	.227394	.231741	.236242	.238548	.240890	.243268	.245681	.248128	.250609	.255668	.260853	.266156	.271572
	-.20	.228276	.232624	.237124	.239430	.241772	.244150	.246563	.249010	.251491	.256551	.261735	.267038	.272454
	-.30	.229158	.233506	.238006	.240312	.242655	.245033	.247446	.249893	.252374	.257433	.262617	.267921	.273336
	-.40	.230041	.234389	.238889	.241195	.243537	.245915	.248328	.250775	.253256	.258315	.263500	.268803	.274219
20	.40	.213710	.218364	.223205	.225693	.228224	.230797	.233410	.236061	.238751	.244236	.249855	.255595	.261446
	.30	.214592	.219246	.224088	.226575	.229106	.231679	.234292	.236944	.239633	.245119	.250737	.256478	.262329
	.20	.215475	.220129	.224970	.227458	.229989	.232561	.235174	.237826	.240516	.246001	.251620	.257360	.263211
	.10	.216357	.221011	.225852	.228340	.230871	.233444	.236057	.238709	.241398	.246883	.252502	.258242	.264094
	0.00	.217239	.221893	.226735	.229223	.231753	.234326	.236939	.239591	.242280	.247766	.253384	.259125	.264976
	-.10	.218122	.222776	.227617	.230105	.232636	.235208	.237821	.240473	.243163	.248648	.254267	.260007	.265858
	-.20	.219004	.223658	.228499	.230987	.233518	.236091	.238704	.241356	.244045	.249531	.255149	.260890	.266741
	-.30	.219887	.224540	.229382	.231870	.234401	.236973	.239586	.242238	.244927	.250413	.256032	.261772	.267623
	-.40	.220769	.225423	.230264	.232752	.235283	.237856	.240469	.243120	.245810	.251295	.256914	.262654	.268505
25	.40	.208369	.213289	.218421	.221062	.223749	.226482	.229256	.232071	.234924	.240735	.246674	.252724	.258872
	.30	.209251	.214171	.219304	.221944	.224632	.227364	.230139	.232953	.235806	.241617	.247556	.253606	.259754
	.20	.210134	.215054	.220186	.222827	.225514	.228246	.231021	.233836	.236688	.242500	.248438	.254489	.260636
	.10	.211016	.215936	.221068	.223709	.226397	.229129	.231903	.234718	.237571	.243382	.249321	.255371	.261519
	0.00	.211899	.216818	.221951	.224591	.227279	.230011	.232786	.235600	.238453	.244265	.250203	.256253	.262401
	-.10	.212781	.217701	.222833	.225474	.228161	.230894	.233668	.236483	.239336	.245147	.251085	.257136	.263283
	-.20	.213663	.218583	.223715	.226356	.229044	.231776	.234550	.237365	.240218	.246029	.251968	.258018	.264166
	-.30	.214546	.219465	.224598	.227239	.229926	.232658	.235433	.238248	.241100	.246912	.252850	.258901	.265048
	-.40	.215428	.220348	.225480	.228121	.230809	.233541	.236315	.239130	.241983	.247794	.253733	.259783	.265931
30	.40	.204984	.210140	.215525	.218296	.221115	.223978	.226884	.229828	.232808	.238867	.245038	.251304	.257648
	.30	.205866	.211022	.216408	.219179	.221997	.224861	.227766	.230711	.233691	.239749	.245920	.252186	.258531
	.20	.206749	.211905	.217290	.220061	.222880	.225743	.228649	.231593	.234573	.240631	.246802	.253068	.259413
	.10	.207631	.212787	.218172	.220943	.223762	.226626	.229531	.232475	.235456	.241514	.247685	.253951	.260295
	0.00	.208513	.213670	.219055	.221826	.224644	.227508	.230413	.233358	.236338	.242396	.248567	.254833	.261178
	-.10	.209396	.214552	.219937	.222708	.225527	.228390	.231296	.234240	.237220	.243278	.249450	.255716	.262060
	-.20	.210278	.215434	.220820	.223590	.226409	.229273	.232178	.235122	.238103	.244161	.250332	.256598	.262943
	-.30	.211161	.216317	.221702	.224473	.227291	.230155	.233060	.236005	.238985	.245043	.251214	.257480	.263825
	-.40	.212043	.217199	.222584	.225355	.228174	.231037	.233943	.236887	.239868	.245926	.252097	.258363	.264707

10.0 YEAR HOLDING PERIOD
.500 EQUITY YIELD RATE
.700 LOAN RATIO

INTEREST RATE

TERM YEARS	APPR DEP	5.0	6.0	7.0	7.5	8.0	8.5	9.0	9.5	10.0	11.0	12.0	13.0	14.0
10	.40	.229389	.233551	.237825	.240003	.242209	.244442	.246701	.248988	.251300	.256004	.260809	.265715	.270718
	.30	.230271	.234433	.238707	.240886	.243091	.245324	.247584	.249870	.252183	.256886	.261692	.266597	.271600
	.20	.231154	.235316	.239590	.241768	.243974	.246207	.248466	.250753	.253065	.257769	.262574	.267480	.272482
	.10	.232036	.236198	.240472	.242650	.244856	.247089	.249349	.251635	.253948	.258651	.263457	.268362	.273365
	0.00	.232918	.237081	.241354	.243533	.245739	.247971	.250231	.252517	.254830	.259533	.264339	.269244	.274247
	-.10	.233801	.237963	.242237	.244415	.246621	.248854	.251113	.253400	.255712	.260416	.265221	.270127	.275130
	-.20	.234683	.238845	.243119	.245298	.247503	.249736	.251996	.254282	.256595	.261298	.266104	.271009	.276012
	-.30	.235566	.239728	.244002	.246180	.248386	.250618	.252878	.255164	.257477	.262180	.266986	.271892	.276894
	-.40	.236448	.240610	.244884	.247062	.249268	.251501	.253761	.256047	.258359	.263063	.267868	.272774	.277777
15	.40	.209309	.213874	.218599	.221020	.223480	.225977	.228510	.231080	.233685	.238997	.244440	.250009	.255695
	.30	.210191	.214756	.219482	.221903	.224362	.226859	.229393	.231962	.234567	.239879	.245323	.250891	.256578
	.20	.211074	.215639	.220364	.222785	.225245	.227741	.230275	.232845	.235449	.240762	.246205	.251774	.257460
	.10	.211956	.216521	.221246	.223668	.226127	.228624	.231157	.233727	.236332	.241644	.247088	.252656	.258342
	0.00	.212838	.217403	.222129	.224550	.227009	.229506	.232040	.234609	.237214	.242526	.247970	.253538	.259225
	-.10	.213721	.218286	.223011	.225432	.227892	.230388	.232922	.235492	.238097	.243409	.248852	.254421	.260107
	-.20	.214603	.219168	.223893	.226315	.228774	.231271	.233804	.236374	.238979	.244291	.249735	.255303	.260990
	-.30	.215485	.220051	.224776	.227197	.229656	.232153	.234687	.237256	.239861	.245174	.250617	.256186	.261872
	-.40	.216368	.220933	.225658	.228079	.230539	.233036	.235569	.238139	.240744	.246056	.251500	.257068	.262754
20	.40	.199573	.204460	.209543	.212156	.214813	.217514	.220258	.223042	.225866	.231626	.237525	.243553	.249696
	.30	.200456	.205342	.210426	.213038	.215695	.218397	.221140	.223925	.226748	.232508	.238408	.244435	.250579
	.20	.201338	.206225	.211308	.213920	.216578	.219279	.222023	.224807	.227631	.233391	.239290	.245317	.251461
	.10	.202221	.207107	.212190	.214803	.217460	.220161	.222905	.225689	.228513	.234273	.240173	.246200	.252344
	0.00	.203103	.207989	.213073	.215685	.218343	.221044	.223787	.226572	.229396	.235155	.241055	.247082	.253226
	-.10	.203985	.208872	.213955	.216567	.219225	.221926	.224670	.227454	.230278	.236038	.241937	.247965	.254108
	-.20	.204868	.209754	.214838	.217450	.220107	.222809	.225552	.228337	.231160	.236920	.242820	.248847	.254991
	-.30	.205750	.210637	.215720	.218332	.220990	.223691	.226434	.229219	.232043	.237803	.243702	.249729	.255873
	-.40	.206632	.211519	.216602	.219215	.221872	.224573	.227317	.230101	.232925	.238685	.244584	.250612	.256755
25	.40	.193965	.199131	.204520	.207293	.210115	.212984	.215897	.218852	.221848	.227950	.234185	.240538	.246993
	.30	.194848	.200014	.205403	.208175	.210997	.213866	.216779	.219735	.222730	.228832	.235067	.241420	.247875
	.20	.195730	.200896	.206285	.209058	.211880	.214748	.217662	.220617	.223613	.229714	.235950	.242303	.248758
	.10	.196613	.201778	.207167	.209940	.212762	.215631	.218544	.221499	.224495	.230597	.236832	.243185	.249640
	0.00	.197495	.202661	.208050	.210822	.213644	.216513	.219426	.222382	.225377	.231479	.237715	.244067	.250522
	-.10	.198377	.203543	.208932	.211705	.214527	.217395	.220309	.223264	.226260	.232361	.238597	.244950	.251405
	-.20	.199260	.204425	.209814	.212587	.215409	.218278	.221191	.224147	.227142	.233244	.239479	.245832	.252287
	-.30	.200142	.205308	.210697	.213470	.216292	.219160	.222073	.225029	.228024	.234126	.240362	.246715	.253169
	-.40	.201024	.206190	.211579	.214352	.217174	.220043	.222956	.225911	.228907	.235009	.241244	.247597	.254052
30	.40	.190411	.195825	.201480	.204389	.207349	.210355	.213406	.216497	.219627	.225988	.232467	.239047	.245708
	.30	.191293	.196707	.202362	.205271	.208231	.211238	.214288	.217380	.220509	.226870	.233350	.239929	.246591
	.20	.192176	.197590	.203244	.206154	.209113	.212120	.215171	.218262	.221392	.227752	.234232	.240811	.247473
	.10	.193058	.198472	.204127	.207036	.209996	.213002	.216053	.219145	.222274	.228635	.235115	.241694	.248356
	0.00	.193941	.199355	.205009	.207918	.210878	.213885	.216935	.220027	.223156	.229517	.235997	.242576	.249238
	-.10	.194823	.200237	.205891	.208801	.211760	.214767	.217818	.220909	.224039	.230400	.236879	.243458	.250120
	-.20	.195705	.201119	.206774	.209683	.212643	.215650	.218700	.221792	.224921	.231282	.237762	.244341	.251003
	-.30	.196588	.202002	.207656	.210566	.213525	.216532	.219583	.222674	.225803	.232164	.238644	.245223	.251885
	-.40	.197470	.202884	.208539	.211448	.214408	.217414	.220465	.223556	.226686	.233047	.239526	.246106	.252767

10.0 YEAR HOLDING PERIOD
.500 EQUITY YIELD RATE
.750 LOAN RATIO

INTEREST RATE

TERM YEARS	APPR DEP	5.0	6.0	7.0	7.5	8.0	8.5	9.0	9.5	10.0	11.0	12.0	13.0	14.0
10	.40	.210312	.214771	.219350	.221684	.224047	.226440	.228861	.231310	.233788	.238828	.243977	.249232	.254592
	.30	.211194	.215653	.220233	.222567	.224930	.227322	.229743	.232193	.234671	.239710	.244859	.250115	.255475
	.20	.212076	.216536	.221115	.223449	.225812	.228205	.230626	.233075	.235553	.240592	.245741	.250997	.256357
	.10	.212959	.217418	.221997	.224331	.226695	.229087	.231508	.233958	.236435	.241475	.246624	.251879	.257240
	0.00	.213841	.218301	.222880	.225214	.227577	.229969	.232390	.234840	.237318	.242357	.247506	.252762	.258122
	-.10	.214724	.219183	.223762	.226096	.228459	.230852	.233273	.235722	.238200	.243240	.248388	.253644	.259004
	-.20	.215606	.220065	.224645	.226979	.229342	.231734	.234155	.236605	.239083	.244122	.249271	.254527	.259887
	-.30	.216488	.220948	.225527	.227861	.230224	.232616	.235037	.237487	.239965	.245004	.250153	.255409	.260769
	-.40	.217371	.221830	.226409	.228743	.231107	.233499	.235920	.238369	.240847	.245887	.251036	.256291	.261651
15	.40	.188797	.193688	.198751	.201345	.203980	.206656	.209370	.212123	.214914	.220606	.226438	.232404	.238497
	.30	.189680	.194571	.199634	.202228	.204863	.207538	.210253	.213006	.215797	.221488	.227321	.233287	.239379
	.20	.190562	.195453	.200516	.203110	.205745	.208420	.211135	.213888	.216679	.222371	.228203	.234169	.240262
	.10	.191444	.196336	.201398	.203992	.206628	.209303	.212017	.214770	.217561	.223253	.229085	.235052	.241144
	0.00	.192327	.197218	.202281	.204875	.207510	.210185	.212900	.215653	.218444	.224135	.229968	.235934	.242027
	-.10	.193209	.198100	.203163	.205757	.208392	.211067	.213782	.216535	.219326	.225018	.230850	.236816	.242909
	-.20	.194092	.198983	.204045	.206640	.209275	.211950	.214664	.217418	.220208	.225900	.231733	.237699	.243791
	-.30	.194974	.199865	.204928	.207522	.210157	.212832	.215547	.218300	.221091	.226783	.232615	.238581	.244674
	-.40	.195856	.200747	.205810	.208404	.211039	.213715	.216429	.219182	.221973	.227665	.233497	.239463	.245556
20	.40	.178366	.183602	.189049	.191847	.194695	.197589	.200528	.203512	.206537	.212708	.219029	.225487	.232070
	.30	.179249	.184484	.189931	.192730	.195577	.198471	.201411	.204394	.207420	.213591	.219912	.226369	.232952
	.20	.180131	.185367	.190813	.193612	.196459	.199354	.202293	.205276	.208302	.214473	.220794	.227252	.233834
	.10	.181014	.186249	.191696	.194494	.197342	.200236	.203175	.206159	.209184	.215356	.221676	.228134	.234717
	0.00	.181896	.187132	.192578	.195377	.198224	.201118	.204058	.207041	.210067	.216239	.222559	.229017	.235599
	-.10	.182778	.188014	.193460	.196259	.199107	.202001	.204940	.207924	.210949	.217120	.223441	.229899	.236482
	-.20	.183661	.188896	.194343	.197142	.199989	.202883	.205823	.208806	.211831	.218003	.224324	.230781	.237364
	-.30	.184543	.189778	.195225	.198024	.200871	.203765	.206705	.209688	.212714	.218885	.225206	.231664	.238246
	-.40	.185425	.190661	.196108	.198906	.201754	.204648	.207587	.210571	.213596	.219768	.226088	.232546	.239129
25	.40	.172358	.177893	.183667	.186637	.189661	.192735	.195856	.199022	.202232	.208770	.215450	.222257	.229173
	.30	.173240	.178775	.184549	.187520	.190543	.193617	.196738	.199905	.203114	.209652	.216333	.223139	.230055
	.20	.174123	.179657	.185431	.188402	.191426	.194499	.197621	.200787	.203997	.210534	.217215	.224022	.230938
	.10	.175005	.180540	.186314	.189285	.192308	.195382	.198503	.201670	.204879	.211417	.218098	.224904	.231820
	0.00	.175887	.181422	.187196	.190167	.193190	.196264	.199385	.202552	.205761	.212299	.218980	.225786	.232703
	-.10	.176770	.182305	.188078	.191049	.194073	.197146	.200268	.203434	.206644	.213181	.219862	.226669	.233585
	-.20	.177652	.183187	.188961	.191931	.194955	.198029	.201150	.204317	.207526	.214064	.220745	.227551	.234467
	-.30	.178535	.184069	.189843	.192814	.195838	.198911	.202033	.205199	.208408	.214946	.221627	.228434	.235350
	-.40	.179417	.184952	.190726	.193696	.196720	.199794	.202915	.206081	.209291	.215829	.222509	.229316	.236232
30	.40	.168550	.174350	.180409	.183526	.186697	.189918	.193187	.196499	.199852	.206668	.213610	.220659	.227797
	.30	.169432	.175233	.181291	.184408	.187579	.190801	.194069	.197382	.200735	.207550	.214492	.221542	.228679
	.20	.170314	.176115	.182174	.185291	.188462	.191683	.194952	.198264	.201617	.208432	.215375	.222424	.229562
	.10	.171197	.176998	.183056	.186173	.189344	.192566	.195834	.199146	.202499	.209315	.216257	.223306	.230444
	0.00	.172079	.177880	.183938	.187055	.190226	.193448	.196717	.200029	.203382	.210197	.217140	.224189	.231326
	-.10	.172962	.178762	.184821	.187938	.191109	.194330	.197599	.200911	.204264	.211079	.218022	.225071	.232209
	-.20	.173844	.179645	.185703	.188820	.191991	.195213	.198481	.201794	.205146	.211962	.218904	.225953	.233091
	-.30	.174726	.180527	.186585	.189703	.192874	.196095	.199364	.202676	.206029	.212844	.219787	.226836	.233973
	-.40	.175609	.181409	.187468	.190585	.193756	.196977	.200246	.203558	.206911	.213727	.220669	.227718	.234856

10.0 YEAR HOLDING PERIOD
.500 EQUITY YIELD RATE
.800 LOAN RATIO

INTEREST RATE

TERM YEARS	APPR DEP	5.0	6.0	7.0	7.5	8.0	8.5	9.0	9.5	10.0	11.0	12.0	13.0	14.0
10	.40	.191234	.195991	.200876	.203365	.205886	.208438	.211020	.213633	.216276	.221651	.227144	.232750	.238467
	.30	.192117	.196874	.201758	.204248	.206768	.209320	.211903	.214515	.217159	.222534	.228026	.233632	.239350
	.20	.192999	.197756	.202640	.205130	.207651	.210202	.212785	.215398	.218041	.223416	.228908	.234515	.240232
	.10	.193881	.198638	.203523	.206012	.208533	.211085	.213667	.216280	.218923	.224299	.229791	.235397	.241114
	0.00	.194764	.199521	.204405	.206695	.209415	.211967	.214550	.217163	.219806	.225181	.230673	.236279	.241997
	-.10	.195646	.200403	.205287	.207777	.210298	.212850	.215432	.218045	.220688	.226063	.231555	.237162	.242879
	-.20	.196529	.201285	.206170	.208659	.211180	.213732	.216314	.218927	.221570	.226946	.232438	.238044	.243762
	-.30	.197411	.202168	.207052	.209542	.212063	.214614	.217197	.219810	.222453	.227828	.233320	.238926	.244644
	-.40	.198293	.203050	.207935	.210424	.212945	.215497	.218079	.220692	.223335	.228710	.234203	.239809	.245526
15	.40	.168286	.173503	.178903	.181670	.184481	.187335	.190230	.193167	.196144	.202215	.208436	.214800	.221299
	.30	.169168	.174385	.179786	.182553	.185363	.188217	.191113	.194049	.197026	.203097	.209319	.215682	.222181
	.20	.170050	.175268	.180668	.183435	.186246	.189099	.191995	.194932	.197909	.203980	.210201	.216565	.223064
	.10	.170933	.176150	.181550	.184317	.187128	.189982	.192877	.195814	.198791	.204862	.211083	.217447	.223946
	0.00	.171815	.177032	.182433	.185200	.188011	.190864	.193760	.196696	.199673	.205744	.211966	.218330	.224828
	-.10	.172698	.177915	.183315	.186082	.188893	.191746	.194642	.197579	.200556	.206627	.212848	.219212	.225711
	-.20	.173580	.178797	.184198	.186965	.189775	.192629	.195524	.198461	.201438	.207509	.213730	.220094	.226593
	-.30	.174462	.179680	.185080	.187847	.190658	.193511	.196407	.199343	.202320	.208392	.214613	.220977	.227475
	-.40	.175345	.180562	.185962	.188729	.191540	.194394	.197289	.200226	.203203	.209274	.215495	.221859	.228358
20	.40	.157159	.162744	.168554	.171539	.174576	.177663	.180799	.183981	.187208	.193791	.200533	.207422	.214443
	.30	.158042	.163627	.169436	.172422	.175459	.178546	.181681	.184863	.188091	.194673	.201416	.208304	.215325
	.20	.158924	.164509	.170318	.173304	.176341	.179428	.182564	.185746	.188973	.195556	.202298	.209186	.216208
	.10	.159807	.165391	.171201	.174186	.177223	.180311	.183446	.186628	.189855	.196438	.203180	.210069	.217090
	0.00	.160689	.166274	.172083	.175069	.178106	.181193	.184328	.187511	.190738	.197321	.204063	.210951	.217973
	-.10	.161571	.167156	.172966	.175951	.178988	.182075	.185211	.188393	.191620	.198203	.204945	.211834	.218855
	-.20	.162454	.168038	.173848	.176833	.179871	.182958	.186093	.189275	.192503	.199085	.205828	.212716	.219737
	-.30	.163336	.168921	.174730	.177716	.180753	.183840	.186976	.190158	.193385	.199968	.206710	.213598	.220620
	-.40	.164218	.169803	.175613	.178598	.181635	.184722	.187858	.191040	.194267	.200850	.207592	.214481	.221502
25	.40	.150750	.156654	.162813	.165982	.169207	.172485	.175815	.179193	.182616	.189589	.196716	.203976	.211353
	.30	.151633	.157536	.163695	.166864	.170089	.173368	.176697	.180075	.183498	.190472	.197598	.204858	.212236
	.20	.152515	.158419	.164578	.167747	.170972	.174250	.177580	.180957	.184381	.191354	.198480	.205741	.213118
	.10	.153398	.159301	.165460	.168629	.171854	.175133	.178462	.181840	.185263	.192237	.199363	.206623	.214000
	0.00	.154280	.160184	.166343	.169511	.172736	.176015	.179344	.182722	.186145	.193119	.200245	.207506	.214883
	-.10	.155162	.161066	.167225	.170394	.173619	.176897	.180227	.183604	.187028	.194001	.201128	.208388	.215765
	-.20	.156045	.161948	.168107	.171276	.174501	.177780	.181109	.184487	.187910	.194884	.202010	.209270	.216647
	-.30	.156927	.162831	.168990	.172159	.175384	.178662	.181992	.185369	.188793	.195766	.202892	.210153	.217530
	-.40	.157809	.163713	.169872	.173041	.176266	.179544	.182874	.186252	.189675	.196648	.203775	.211035	.218412
30	.40	.146688	.152876	.159338	.162663	.166045	.169482	.172968	.176501	.180078	.187347	.194753	.202272	.209885
	.30	.147571	.153758	.160220	.163545	.166928	.170364	.173850	.177384	.180960	.188230	.195635	.203154	.210768
	.20	.148453	.154640	.161103	.164428	.167810	.171246	.174733	.178266	.181842	.189112	.196517	.204036	.211650
	.10	.149335	.155523	.161985	.165310	.168693	.172129	.175615	.179148	.182725	.189994	.197400	.204919	.212532
	0.00	.150218	.156405	.162868	.166192	.169575	.173011	.176498	.180031	.183607	.190877	.198282	.205801	.213415
	-.10	.151100	.157288	.163750	.167075	.170457	.173894	.177380	.180913	.184490	.191759	.199165	.206684	.214297
	-.20	.151983	.158170	.164632	.167957	.171340	.174776	.178262	.181796	.185372	.192642	.200047	.207566	.215180
	-.30	.152865	.159052	.165515	.168840	.172222	.175658	.179145	.182678	.186254	.193524	.200929	.208448	.216062
	-.40	.153747	.159935	.166397	.169722	.173104	.176541	.180027	.183560	.187137	.194406	.201812	.209331	.216944

10.0 YEAR HOLDING PERIOD
.500 EQUITY YIELD RATE
.900 LOAN RATIO

INTEREST RATE

TERM YEARS	APPR DEP	5.0	6.0	7.0	7.5	8.0	8.5	9.0	9.5	10.0	11.0	12.0	13.0	14.0
10	.40	.153080	.158431	.163926	.166727	.169563	.172434	.175339	.178278	.181252	.187299	.193478	.199785	.206217
	.30	.153962	.159314	.164809	.167609	.170445	.173316	.176221	.179161	.182134	.188181	.194360	.200667	.207099
	.20	.154845	.160196	.165691	.168492	.171328	.174198	.177104	.180043	.183017	.189064	.195242	.201549	.207982
	.10	.155727	.161078	.166573	.169374	.172210	.175081	.177986	.180926	.183899	.189946	.196125	.202432	.208864
	0.00	.156609	.161961	.167456	.170257	.173092	.175963	.178868	.181808	.184781	.190829	.197007	.203314	.209746
	-.10	.157492	.162843	.168338	.171139	.173975	.176846	.179751	.182690	.185664	.191711	.197890	.204197	.210629
	-.20	.158374	.163725	.169221	.172021	.174857	.177728	.180633	.183573	.186546	.192593	.198772	.205079	.211511
	-.30	.159256	.164608	.170103	.172904	.175740	.178610	.181516	.184455	.187429	.193476	.199654	.205961	.212393
	-.40	.160139	.165490	.170985	.173786	.176622	.179493	.182398	.185337	.188311	.194358	.200537	.206844	.213276
15	.40	.127263	.133132	.139207	.142320	.145482	.148693	.151950	.155254	.158603	.165433	.172432	.179591	.186902
	.30	.128145	.134014	.140090	.143203	.146365	.149575	.152832	.156136	.159485	.166315	.173314	.180474	.187785
	.20	.129027	.134897	.140972	.144085	.147247	.150457	.153715	.157019	.160368	.167198	.174197	.181356	.188667
	.10	.129910	.135779	.141854	.144967	.148130	.151340	.154597	.157901	.161250	.168080	.175079	.182238	.189549
	0.00	.130792	.136661	.142737	.145850	.149012	.152222	.155480	.158783	.162132	.168962	.175961	.183121	.190432
	-.10	.131675	.137544	.143619	.146732	.149894	.153105	.156362	.159666	.163015	.169845	.176844	.184003	.191314
	-.20	.132557	.138426	.144502	.147615	.150777	.153987	.157244	.160548	.163897	.170727	.177726	.184886	.192197
	-.30	.133439	.139309	.145384	.148497	.151659	.154869	.158127	.161431	.164780	.171610	.178609	.185768	.193079
	-.40	.134322	.140191	.146266	.149379	.152541	.155752	.159009	.162313	.165662	.172492	.179491	.186650	.193961
20	.40	.114746	.121028	.127564	.130923	.134339	.137812	.141340	.144920	.148551	.155956	.163541	.171291	.179190
	.30	.115628	.121911	.128447	.131805	.135222	.138695	.142222	.145802	.149433	.156838	.164423	.172173	.180072
	.20	.116510	.122793	.129329	.132687	.136104	.139577	.143105	.146685	.150315	.157721	.165306	.173055	.180954
	.10	.117393	.123675	.130211	.133570	.136987	.140460	.143987	.147567	.151198	.158603	.166188	.173938	.181837
	0.00	.118275	.124558	.131094	.134452	.137869	.141342	.144869	.148449	.152080	.159486	.167071	.174820	.182719
	-.10	.119157	.125440	.131976	.135335	.138751	.142224	.145752	.149332	.152962	.160368	.167953	.175702	.183601
	-.20	.120040	.126323	.132858	.136217	.139634	.143107	.146634	.150214	.153845	.161250	.168835	.176585	.184484
	-.30	.120922	.127205	.133741	.137099	.140516	.143989	.147517	.151097	.154727	.162133	.169718	.177467	.185366
	-.40	.121805	.128087	.134623	.137982	.141398	.144872	.148399	.151979	.155610	.163015	.170600	.178350	.186249
25	.40	.107535	.114177	.121106	.124671	.128299	.131987	.135733	.139533	.143384	.151229	.159246	.167414	.175714
	.30	.108418	.115059	.121988	.125553	.129181	.132870	.136615	.140415	.144267	.152112	.160129	.168297	.176596
	.20	.109300	.115942	.122871	.126436	.130064	.133752	.137498	.141298	.145149	.152994	.161011	.169179	.177478
	.10	.110183	.116824	.123753	.127318	.130946	.134634	.138380	.142180	.146031	.153876	.161894	.170061	.178361
	0.00	.111065	.117707	.124635	.128200	.131828	.135517	.139262	.143062	.146914	.154759	.162776	.170944	.179243
	-.10	.111947	.118589	.125518	.129083	.132711	.136399	.140145	.143945	.147796	.155641	.163658	.171826	.180125
	-.20	.112830	.119471	.126400	.129965	.133593	.137282	.141027	.144827	.148678	.156524	.164541	.172709	.181008
	-.30	.113712	.120354	.127282	.130847	.134476	.138164	.141910	.145709	.149561	.157406	.165423	.173591	.181890
	-.40	.114594	.121236	.128165	.131730	.135358	.139046	.142792	.146592	.150443	.158288	.166305	.174473	.182773
30	.40	.102966	.109926	.117196	.120937	.124742	.128608	.132530	.136505	.140529	.148707	.157038	.165497	.174062
	.30	.103848	.110809	.118079	.121819	.125625	.129490	.133413	.137387	.141411	.149589	.157920	.166379	.174944
	.20	.104730	.111691	.118961	.122702	.126507	.130373	.134295	.138270	.142293	.150472	.158803	.167262	.175827
	.10	.105613	.112573	.119844	.123584	.127389	.131255	.135177	.139152	.143176	.151354	.159685	.168144	.176709
	0.00	.106495	.113456	.120726	.124467	.128272	.132138	.136060	.140035	.144058	.152236	.160567	.169026	.177592
	-.10	.107377	.114338	.121608	.125349	.129154	.133020	.136942	.140917	.144940	.153119	.161450	.169909	.178474
	-.20	.108260	.115221	.122491	.126231	.130036	.133902	.137825	.141799	.145823	.154001	.162332	.170791	.179356
	-.30	.109142	.116103	.123373	.127114	.130919	.134785	.138707	.142682	.146705	.154884	.163215	.171674	.180239
	-.40	.110025	.116985	.124255	.127996	.131801	.135667	.139589	.143564	.147588	.155766	.164097	.172556	.181121

15.0 YEAR HOLDING PERIOD
.040 EQUITY YIELD RATE
.600 LOAN RATIO

INTEREST RATE

TERM YEARS	APPR DEP	5.0	6.0	7.0	7.5	8.0	8.5	9.0	9.5	10.0	11.0	12.0	13.0	14.0
15	.40	.022996	.026817	.030775	.032804	.034866	.036960	.039086	.041243	.043430	.047894	.052471	.057156	.061944
	.30	.027990	.031811	.035769	.037798	.039860	.041954	.044080	.046237	.048425	.052888	.057465	.062150	.066938
	.20	.032984	.036805	.040763	.042792	.044854	.046948	.049074	.051231	.053419	.057882	.062459	.067145	.071932
	.10	.037978	.041799	.045757	.047786	.049848	.051942	.054068	.056225	.058413	.062876	.067453	.072139	.076927
	0.00	.042972	.046793	.050751	.052780	.054842	.056937	.059063	.061220	.063407	.067870	.072447	.077133	.081921
	-.10	.047967	.051787	.055745	.057774	.059836	.061931	.064057	.066214	.068401	.072864	.077442	.082127	.086915
	-.20	.052961	.056781	.060739	.062768	.064831	.066925	.069051	.071208	.073395	.077859	.082436	.087121	.091909
	-.30	.057955	.061775	.065733	.067763	.069825	.071919	.074045	.076202	.078389	.082853	.087430	.092115	.096903
	-.40	.062949	.066769	.070727	.072757	.074819	.076913	.079039	.081196	.083383	.087847	.092424	.097109	.101897
20	.40	.024055	.028746	.033613	.036108	.038644	.041217	.043827	.046472	.049150	.054602	.060169	.065841	.071606
	.30	.029049	.033740	.038607	.041103	.043638	.046211	.048821	.051466	.054144	.059596	.065164	.070836	.076600
	.20	.034043	.038734	.043601	.046097	.048632	.051205	.053815	.056460	.059138	.064590	.070158	.075830	.081595
	.10	.039037	.043729	.048595	.051091	.053626	.056199	.058809	.061454	.064132	.069584	.075152	.080824	.086589
	0.00	.044031	.048723	.053589	.056085	.058620	.061193	.063803	.066448	.069127	.074578	.080146	.085818	.091583
	-.10	.049025	.053717	.058583	.061079	.063614	.066187	.068797	.071442	.074121	.079572	.085140	.090812	.096577
	-.20	.054019	.058711	.063577	.066073	.068608	.071182	.073791	.076436	.079115	.084566	.090134	.095806	.101571
	-.30	.059014	.063705	.068572	.071067	.073602	.076176	.078785	.081430	.084109	.089560	.095128	.100800	.106565
	-.40	.064008	.068699	.073566	.076061	.078596	.081170	.083780	.086425	.089103	.094555	.100122	.105794	.111559
25	.40	.024665	.029838	.035187	.037921	.040691	.043496	.046332	.049197	.052090	.057947	.063888	.069897	.075961
	.30	.029659	.034833	.040181	.042915	.045686	.048490	.051326	.054191	.057084	.062941	.068882	.074891	.080955
	.20	.034653	.039827	.045175	.047909	.050680	.053484	.056320	.059186	.062078	.067936	.073876	.079885	.085949
	.10	.039647	.044821	.050170	.052903	.055674	.058478	.061314	.064180	.067072	.072930	.078871	.084880	.090943
	0.00	.044641	.049815	.055164	.057898	.060668	.063472	.066308	.069174	.072066	.077924	.083865	.089874	.095937
	-.10	.049635	.054809	.060158	.062892	.065662	.068466	.071302	.074168	.077060	.082918	.088859	.094868	.100931
	-.20	.054629	.059803	.065152	.067886	.070656	.073460	.076297	.079162	.082054	.087912	.093853	.099862	.105926
	-.30	.059623	.064797	.070146	.072880	.075650	.078455	.081291	.084156	.087049	.092906	.098847	.104856	.110920
	-.40	.064618	.069791	.075140	.077874	.080644	.083449	.086285	.089150	.092043	.097900	.103841	.109850	.115914
30	.40	.025051	.030516	.036140	.039004	.041897	.044818	.047763	.050729	.053715	.059733	.065800	.071903	.078030
	.30	.030045	.035510	.041134	.043998	.046891	.049812	.052757	.055723	.058709	.064727	.070795	.076897	.083024
	.20	.035039	.040504	.046128	.048992	.051886	.054806	.057751	.060717	.063703	.069721	.075789	.081892	.088018
	.10	.040034	.045498	.051123	.053986	.056880	.059800	.062745	.065712	.068697	.074715	.080783	.086886	.093012
	0.00	.045028	.050493	.056117	.058980	.061874	.064794	.067739	.070706	.073691	.079709	.085777	.091880	.098006
	-.10	.050022	.055487	.061111	.063974	.066868	.069789	.072733	.075700	.078685	.084703	.090771	.096874	.103000
	-.20	.055016	.060481	.066105	.068968	.071862	.074783	.077727	.080694	.083679	.089697	.095765	.101868	.107994
	-.30	.060010	.065475	.071099	.073962	.076856	.079777	.082722	.085688	.088673	.094692	.100759	.106862	.112988
	-.40	.065004	.070469	.076093	.078957	.081850	.084771	.087716	.090682	.093667	.099686	.105753	.111856	.117983
40	.40	.025493	.031263	.037148	.040123	.043116	.046122	.049139	.052166	.055198	.061277	.067363	.073450	.079534
	.30	.030487	.036257	.042142	.045118	.048110	.051116	.054134	.057160	.060192	.066271	.072357	.078445	.084528
	.20	.035481	.041251	.047136	.050112	.053104	.056110	.059128	.062154	.065186	.071265	.077351	.083439	.089522
	.10	.040476	.046246	.052131	.055106	.058098	.061104	.064122	.067148	.070181	.076259	.082345	.088433	.094516
	0.00	.045470	.051240	.057125	.060100	.063092	.066099	.069116	.072142	.075175	.081253	.087340	.093427	.099510
	-.10	.050464	.056234	.062119	.065094	.068086	.071093	.074110	.077137	.080169	.086247	.092334	.098421	.104504
	-.20	.055458	.061228	.067113	.070088	.073080	.076087	.079104	.082130	.085163	.091241	.097328	.103415	.109498
	-.30	.060452	.066222	.072107	.075082	.078075	.081081	.084098	.087124	.090157	.096235	.102322	.108409	.114492
	-.40	.065446	.071216	.077101	.080076	.083069	.086075	.089092	.092118	.095151	.101229	.107316	.113403	.119487

15.0 YEAR HOLDING PERIOD
.040 EQUITY YIELD RATE
.667 LOAN RATIO

INTEREST RATE

TERM YEARS	APPR DEP	5.0	6.0	7.0	7.5	8.0	8.5	9.0	9.5	10.0	11.0	12.0	13.0	14.0
15	.40	.023326	.027571	.031969	.034224	.036515	.038842	.041204	.043601	.046031	.050991	.056076	.061282	.066602
	.30	.028320	.032566	.036963	.039218	.041509	.043836	.046198	.048595	.051029	.055985	.061071	.066277	.071596
	.20	.033315	.037560	.041957	.044212	.046503	.048830	.051192	.053589	.056020	.060979	.066065	.071271	.076591
	.10	.038309	.042554	.046951	.049206	.051497	.053824	.056187	.058583	.061014	.065973	.071059	.076265	.081585
	0.00	.043303	.047548	.051946	.054200	.056492	.058819	.061181	.063577	.066008	.070967	.076053	.081259	.086579
	-.10	.048297	.052542	.056940	.059194	.061486	.063813	.066175	.068571	.071002	.075961	.081047	.086253	.091573
	-.20	.053291	.057536	.061934	.064189	.066480	.068807	.071169	.073566	.075996	.080955	.086041	.091247	.096567
	-.30	.058285	.062530	.066928	.069183	.071474	.073801	.076163	.078560	.080990	.085950	.091035	.096241	.101561
	-.40	.063279	.067524	.071922	.074177	.076468	.078795	.081157	.083554	.085984	.090944	.096029	.101235	.106555
20	.40	.024503	.029715	.035123	.037896	.040713	.043572	.046472	.049410	.052387	.058444	.064630	.070933	.077338
	.30	.029997	.034710	.040117	.042890	.045707	.048566	.051466	.054405	.057381	.063438	.069624	.075927	.082332
	.20	.034491	.039704	.045111	.047884	.050701	.053560	.056460	.059399	.062375	.068432	.074619	.080921	.087326
	.10	.039485	.044698	.050105	.052878	.055695	.058554	.061454	.064393	.067369	.073426	.079613	.085915	.092320
	0.00	.044479	.049692	.055099	.057872	.060689	.063548	.066448	.069387	.072363	.078420	.084607	.090909	.097315
	-.10	.049473	.054686	.060093	.062866	.065683	.068542	.071442	.074381	.077357	.083414	.089601	.095903	.102309
	-.20	.054467	.059680	.065087	.067860	.070677	.073536	.076436	.079375	.082351	.088409	.094595	.100897	.107303
	-.30	.059462	.064674	.070082	.072854	.075671	.078531	.081430	.084369	.087345	.093403	.099589	.105891	.112297
	-.40	.064456	.069668	.075076	.077849	.080665	.083525	.086425	.089363	.092339	.098397	.104583	.110885	.117291
25	.40	.025180	.030929	.036872	.039910	.042988	.046104	.049255	.052439	.055653	.062161	.068762	.075439	.082176
	.30	.030175	.035923	.041866	.044904	.047982	.051098	.054249	.057433	.060647	.067155	.073756	.080433	.087171
	.20	.035169	.040917	.046860	.049898	.052976	.056092	.059243	.062427	.065641	.072150	.078750	.085427	.092165
	.10	.040163	.045911	.051854	.054892	.057970	.061086	.064238	.067421	.070635	.077144	.083745	.090421	.097159
	0.00	.045157	.050905	.056849	.059886	.062964	.066080	.069232	.072415	.075629	.082138	.088739	.095415	.102153
	-.10	.050151	.055900	.061843	.064880	.067959	.071075	.074226	.077410	.080623	.087132	.093733	.100410	.107147
	-.20	.055145	.060894	.066837	.069874	.072953	.076069	.079220	.082404	.085618	.092126	.098727	.105404	.112141
	-.30	.060139	.065888	.071831	.074869	.077947	.081063	.084214	.087398	.090612	.097120	.103721	.110398	.117135
	-.40	.065133	.070882	.076825	.079863	.082941	.086057	.089208	.092392	.095606	.102114	.108715	.115392	.122129
30	.40	.025610	.031682	.037931	.041113	.044328	.047573	.050845	.054141	.057458	.064145	.070887	.077668	.084475
	.30	.030604	.036676	.042925	.046107	.049322	.052567	.055839	.059135	.062452	.069139	.075881	.082662	.089469
	.20	.035598	.041670	.047919	.051101	.054316	.057561	.060833	.064129	.067446	.074133	.080875	.087656	.094463
	.10	.040592	.046664	.052913	.056095	.059310	.062555	.065827	.069123	.072441	.079127	.085869	.092650	.099457
	0.00	.045586	.051658	.057907	.061089	.064304	.067549	.070822	.074118	.077435	.084122	.090863	.097644	.104452
	-.10	.050580	.056653	.062902	.066084	.069298	.072544	.075816	.079112	.082429	.089116	.095858	.102639	.109446
	-.20	.055575	.061647	.067896	.071077	.074292	.077538	.080810	.084106	.087423	.094110	.100852	.107633	.114440
	-.30	.060569	.066641	.072890	.076071	.079287	.082532	.085804	.089100	.092417	.099104	.105846	.112627	.119434
	-.40	.065563	.071635	.077884	.081066	.084281	.087526	.090798	.094094	.097411	.104098	.110840	.117621	.124428
40	.40	.026101	.032512	.039051	.042357	.045682	.049022	.052375	.055737	.059107	.065860	.072623	.079387	.086146
	.30	.031095	.037506	.044045	.047351	.050676	.054016	.057369	.060731	.064101	.070855	.077617	.084381	.091140
	.20	.036089	.042500	.049039	.052345	.055670	.059010	.062363	.065725	.069095	.075849	.082612	.089375	.096134
	.10	.041083	.047494	.054033	.057339	.060664	.064004	.067357	.070719	.074089	.080843	.087606	.094369	.101129
	0.00	.046077	.052488	.059027	.062333	.065658	.068998	.072351	.075713	.079083	.085837	.092600	.099363	.106123
	-.10	.051072	.057483	.064022	.067327	.070652	.073993	.077345	.080708	.084077	.090831	.097594	.104358	.111117
	-.20	.056066	.062477	.069016	.072322	.075646	.078987	.082339	.085702	.089071	.095825	.102588	.109352	.116111
	-.30	.061060	.067471	.074010	.077316	.080641	.083981	.087333	.090696	.094060	.100819	.107582	.114346	.121105
	-.40	.066054	.072465	.079004	.082310	.085635	.088975	.092328	.095690	.099060	.105813	.112576	.119340	.126099

15.0 YEAR HOLDING PERIOD
.040 EQUITY YIELD RATE
.700 LOAN RATIO

INTEREST RATE

TERM YEARS	APPR DEP	5.0	6.0	7.0	7.5	8.0	8.5	9.0	9.5	10.0	11.0	12.0	13.0	14.0
15	.40	.023491	.027949	.032566	.034934	.037340	.039783	.042263	.044780	.047332	.052539	.057579	.063345	.068931
	.30	.028486	.033943	.037560	.039928	.042334	.044757	.047257	.049774	.052533	.057533	.062873	.068339	.073925
	.20	.033480	.037937	.042555	.044922	.047328	.049771	.052251	.054768	.057320	.062527	.067867	.073333	.078919
	.10	.038474	.042931	.047549	.049916	.052322	.054765	.057246	.059762	.062314	.067521	.072861	.078327	.083913
	0.00	.043468	.047925	.052543	.054910	.057316	.059759	.062240	.064756	.067308	.072515	.077855	.083322	.088908
	-.10	.048462	.052919	.057537	.059904	.062310	.064753	.067234	.069750	.072302	.077509	.082849	.088316	.093902
	-.20	.053456	.057913	.062531	.064898	.067304	.069748	.072228	.074744	.077296	.082504	.087844	.093310	.098896
	-.30	.058450	.062908	.067525	.069893	.072298	.074742	.077222	.079738	.082290	.087498	.092838	.098304	.103890
	-.40	.063444	.067902	.072519	.074887	.077292	.079736	.082216	.084733	.087284	.092492	.097832	.103298	.108884
20	.40	.024727	.030200	.035878	.038789	.041747	.044749	.047794	.050880	.054005	.060365	.066860	.073478	.080203
	.30	.029721	.035194	.040872	.043783	.046741	.049743	.052788	.055874	.058999	.065359	.071855	.078472	.085198
	.20	.034715	.040188	.045866	.048777	.051735	.054737	.057782	.060868	.063993	.070353	.076849	.083466	.090192
	.10	.039709	.045182	.050860	.053772	.056729	.059731	.062776	.065862	.068987	.075347	.081843	.088460	.095186
	0.00	.044703	.050176	.055854	.058766	.061723	.064725	.067770	.070856	.073981	.080341	.086837	.093454	.100180
	-.10	.049697	.055170	.060848	.063760	.066717	.069720	.072764	.075850	.078975	.085335	.091831	.098448	.105174
	-.20	.054691	.060165	.065842	.068754	.071712	.074714	.077759	.080844	.083969	.090329	.096825	.103442	.110168
	-.30	.059685	.065159	.070836	.073748	.076706	.079708	.082753	.085838	.088963	.095324	.101819	.108436	.115162
	-.40	.064680	.070153	.075831	.078742	.081700	.084702	.087747	.090833	.093957	.100318	.106613	.113431	.120156
25	.40	.025438	.031474	.037714	.040904	.044136	.047408	.050717	.054060	.057434	.064268	.071199	.078209	.085284
	.30	.030432	.036468	.042709	.045898	.049130	.052402	.055711	.059054	.062428	.069262	.076193	.083204	.090278
	.20	.035426	.041462	.047703	.050892	.054124	.057396	.060705	.064048	.067422	.074256	.081187	.088198	.095272
	.10	.040421	.046456	.052697	.055886	.059118	.062390	.065699	.069042	.072416	.079250	.086181	.093192	.100266
	0.00	.045415	.051451	.057691	.060880	.064113	.067384	.070693	.074036	.077411	.084244	.091175	.098186	.105260
	-.10	.050409	.056445	.062685	.065875	.069107	.072378	.075687	.079030	.082405	.089239	.096169	.103180	.110254
	-.20	.055403	.061439	.067679	.070869	.074101	.077373	.080681	.084024	.087399	.094233	.101164	.108174	.115248
	-.30	.060397	.066433	.072673	.075863	.079095	.082367	.085675	.089018	.092393	.099227	.106158	.113168	.120243
	-.40	.065391	.071427	.077667	.080857	.084089	.087361	.090670	.094012	.097387	.104221	.111152	.118162	.125237
30	.40	.025889	.032265	.038826	.042167	.045543	.048950	.052386	.055847	.059330	.066351	.073430	.080550	.087697
	.30	.030883	.037259	.043820	.047161	.050537	.053944	.057380	.060841	.064324	.071345	.078424	.085544	.092692
	.20	.035877	.042253	.048815	.052155	.055531	.058939	.062374	.065835	.069318	.076339	.083418	.090538	.097686
	.10	.040872	.047247	.053809	.057149	.060525	.063933	.067368	.070829	.074312	.081333	.088412	.095532	.102680
	0.00	.045866	.052241	.058803	.062143	.065519	.068927	.072362	.075823	.079306	.086327	.093406	.100526	.107674
	-.10	.050860	.057235	.063797	.067138	.070513	.073921	.077357	.080817	.084300	.091321	.098400	.105521	.112668
	-.20	.055854	.062229	.068791	.072132	.075508	.078915	.082351	.085811	.089294	.096316	.103395	.110515	.117662
	-.30	.060848	.067224	.073785	.077126	.080502	.083909	.087345	.090806	.094288	.101310	.108389	.115509	.122656
	-.40	.065842	.072218	.078779	.082120	.085496	.088903	.092339	.095800	.099283	.106304	.113383	.120503	.127650
40	.40	.026405	.033136	.040002	.043473	.046965	.050472	.053992	.057523	.061061	.068152	.075253	.082355	.089452
	.30	.031399	.038131	.044996	.048468	.051959	.055466	.058986	.062517	.066055	.073146	.080247	.087349	.094446
	.20	.036393	.043125	.049991	.053462	.056953	.060460	.063980	.067511	.071049	.078140	.085241	.092343	.099440
	.10	.041387	.048119	.054985	.058456	.061947	.065454	.068974	.072505	.076043	.083134	.090235	.097337	.104434
	0.00	.046381	.053113	.059979	.063450	.066941	.070448	.073969	.077499	.081037	.088128	.095230	.102331	.109428
	-.10	.051375	.058107	.064973	.068445	.071935	.075442	.078963	.082493	.086031	.093123	.100224	.107325	.114423
	-.20	.056370	.063101	.069967	.073438	.076929	.080436	.083957	.087487	.091025	.098117	.105218	.112320	.119417
	-.30	.061364	.068095	.074961	.078432	.081923	.085431	.088951	.092481	.096019	.103111	.110212	.117314	.124411
	-.40	.066358	.073089	.079955	.083426	.086917	.090425	.093945	.097475	.101014	.108105	.115206	.122308	.129405

15.0 YEAR HOLDING PERIOD
.040 EQUITY YIELD RATE
.750 LOAN RATIO RATE

INTEREST RATE

TERM YEARS	APPR DEP	5.0	6.0	7.0	7.5	8.0	8.5	9.0	9.5	10.0	11.0	12.0	13.0	14.0
15	.40	.023739	.028515	.033462	.035999	.038576	.041194	.043852	.046548	.049282	.054861	.060583	.066440	.072424
	.30	.028733	.033509	.038456	.040993	.043571	.046188	.048846	.051542	.054276	.059856	.065577	.071434	.077419
	.20	.033727	.038503	.043450	.045987	.048565	.051183	.053840	.056536	.059270	.064850	.070571	.076428	.082413
	.10	.038721	.043497	.048445	.050981	.053559	.056177	.058834	.061530	.064265	.069844	.075565	.081422	.087407
	0.00	.043716	.048491	.053439	.055975	.058553	.061171	.063828	.066524	.069259	.074838	.080559	.086416	.092401
	-.10	.048710	.053485	.058433	.060969	.063547	.066165	.068822	.071519	.074253	.079832	.085553	.091410	.097395
	-.20	.053704	.058480	.063427	.065964	.068541	.071159	.073816	.076513	.079247	.084826	.090548	.096404	.102389
	-.30	.058698	.063474	.068421	.070958	.073535	.076153	.078810	.081507	.084241	.089820	.095542	.101398	.107383
	-.40	.063692	.068468	.073415	.075952	.078529	.081147	.083805	.086501	.089235	.094814	.100536	.106392	.112377
20	.40	.025063	.030927	.037010	.040130	.043299	.046515	.049777	.053084	.056432	.063246	.070206	.077296	.084502
	.30	.030057	.035921	.042004	.045124	.048293	.051509	.054772	.058078	.061426	.068240	.075200	.082290	.089496
	.20	.035051	.040915	.046998	.050118	.053287	.056503	.059766	.063072	.066420	.073234	.080194	.087284	.094490
	.10	.040045	.045909	.051992	.055112	.058281	.061497	.064760	.068066	.071414	.078229	.085188	.092278	.099484
	0.00	.045039	.050903	.056987	.060106	.063275	.066492	.069754	.073060	.076408	.083223	.090182	.097272	.104478
	-.10	.050033	.055897	.061981	.065100	.068269	.071486	.074748	.078054	.081402	.088217	.095176	.102266	.109473
	-.20	.055027	.060891	.066975	.070094	.073263	.076480	.079742	.083048	.086396	.093211	.100171	.107261	.114467
	-.30	.060021	.065886	.071969	.075088	.078257	.081474	.084736	.088042	.091391	.098205	.105165	.112255	.119461
	-.40	.065016	.070880	.076963	.080083	.083251	.086468	.089730	.093037	.096385	.103199	.110159	.117249	.124455
25	.40	.025825	.032292	.038978	.042395	.045858	.049364	.052909	.056491	.060106	.067428	.074854	.082366	.089945
	.30	.030819	.037286	.043972	.047390	.050853	.054358	.057903	.061485	.065100	.072422	.079848	.087360	.094939
	.20	.035813	.042280	.048966	.052384	.055847	.059352	.062897	.066479	.070095	.077417	.084843	.092354	.099933
	.10	.040807	.047274	.053960	.057378	.060841	.064346	.067891	.071473	.075089	.082411	.089837	.097348	.104928
	0.00	.045801	.052269	.058955	.062372	.065835	.069341	.072885	.076467	.080083	.087405	.094831	.102342	.109922
	-.10	.050796	.057263	.063949	.067366	.070829	.074334	.077880	.081461	.085077	.092399	.099825	.107336	.114916
	-.20	.055790	.062257	.068943	.072360	.075823	.079329	.082874	.086455	.090071	.097393	.104819	.112330	.119910
	-.30	.060784	.067251	.073937	.077354	.080817	.084323	.087868	.091450	.095065	.102387	.109813	.117324	.124904
	-.40	.065778	.072245	.078931	.082348	.085811	.089317	.092862	.096444	.100059	.107381	.114807	.122318	.129898
30	.40	.026308	.033139	.040169	.043749	.047366	.051017	.054698	.058406	.062137	.069660	.077245	.084873	.092531
	.30	.031302	.038133	.045163	.048743	.052360	.056011	.059692	.063400	.067131	.074654	.082239	.089867	.097525
	.20	.036296	.043127	.050158	.053737	.057354	.061005	.064686	.068394	.072126	.079648	.087233	.094861	.102519
	.10	.041290	.048121	.055152	.058731	.062348	.065999	.069680	.073388	.077120	.084642	.092227	.099856	.107514
	0.00	.046285	.053116	.060146	.063725	.067342	.070993	.074674	.078382	.082114	.089636	.097221	.104850	.112508
	-.10	.051279	.058110	.065140	.068719	.072336	.075987	.079668	.083376	.087108	.094631	.102215	.109844	.117502
	-.20	.056273	.063104	.070134	.073713	.077330	.080981	.084662	.088370	.092102	.099625	.107209	.114838	.122496
	-.30	.061267	.068098	.075128	.078707	.082324	.085975	.089656	.093364	.097096	.104619	.112203	.119832	.127490
	-.40	.066261	.073092	.080122	.083702	.087319	.090969	.094651	.098359	.102090	.109613	.117198	.124826	.132484
40	.40	.026861	.034073	.041429	.045148	.048889	.052647	.056418	.060201	.063992	.071590	.079198	.086807	.094411
	.30	.031855	.039067	.046423	.050143	.053883	.057641	.061413	.065195	.068986	.076584	.084192	.091801	.099405
	.20	.036849	.044061	.051418	.055137	.058877	.062635	.066407	.070189	.073980	.081578	.089186	.096795	.104399
	.10	.041843	.049055	.056412	.060131	.063871	.067629	.071401	.075183	.078974	.086572	.094180	.101790	.109393
	0.00	.046837	.054050	.061406	.065125	.068865	.072623	.076395	.080177	.083968	.091566	.099174	.106784	.114388
	-.10	.051831	.059044	.066400	.070119	.073859	.077617	.081389	.085172	.088962	.096560	.104169	.111778	.119382
	-.20	.056825	.064038	.071394	.075113	.078854	.082611	.086383	.090166	.093957	.101554	.109163	.116772	.124376
	-.30	.061819	.069032	.076388	.080107	.083848	.087605	.091377	.095160	.098951	.106549	.114157	.121766	.129370
	-.40	.066814	.074026	.081382	.085101	.088842	.092600	.096371	.100154	.103945	.111543	.119151	.126760	.134364

15.0 YEAR HOLDING PERIOD
.040 EQUITY YIELD RATE
.800 LOAN RATIO

INTEREST RATE

TERM YEARS	APPR DEP	5.0	6.0	7.0	7.5	8.0	8.5	9.0	9.5	10.0	11.0	12.0	13.0	14.0
15	.40	.023987	.029081	.034358	.037064	.039813	.042606	.045440	.048316	.051233	.057184	.063287	.069534	.075918
	.30	.028981	.034025	.039352	.042058	.044807	.047600	.050434	.053310	.056227	.062178	.068281	.074528	.080912
	.20	.033975	.039069	.044346	.047052	.049801	.052594	.055428	.058304	.061221	.067172	.073275	.079522	.085906
	.10	.038969	.044063	.049341	.052046	.054796	.057588	.060423	.063299	.066215	.072166	.078269	.084516	.090900
	0.00	.043963	.049057	.054335	.057040	.059790	.062582	.065417	.068293	.071209	.077160	.083263	.089510	.095894
	-.10	.048957	.054051	.059329	.062034	.064784	.067576	.070411	.073287	.076203	.082155	.088257	.094504	.100888
	-.20	.053952	.059046	.064323	.067029	.069778	.072570	.075405	.078281	.081197	.087149	.093251	.099499	.105883
	-.30	.058946	.064040	.069317	.072023	.074772	.077564	.080399	.083275	.086192	.092143	.098246	.104493	.110877
	-.40	.063940	.069034	.074311	.077017	.079766	.082559	.085393	.088269	.091186	.097137	.103240	.109487	.115871
20	.40	.025399	.031654	.038143	.041470	.044850	.048281	.051761	.055288	.058859	.066128	.073551	.081114	.088801
	.30	.030393	.036648	.043137	.046464	.049844	.053275	.056755	.060282	.063853	.071122	.078545	.086108	.093795
	.20	.035387	.041642	.048131	.051458	.054838	.058269	.061749	.065276	.068847	.076116	.083540	.091102	.098789
	.10	.040381	.046636	.053125	.056452	.059833	.063264	.066743	.070270	.073841	.081110	.088534	.096096	.103783
	0.00	.045375	.051630	.058119	.061446	.064827	.068258	.071738	.075264	.078835	.086104	.093528	.101090	.108777
	-.10	.050369	.056624	.063113	.066441	.069821	.073252	.076732	.080258	.083830	.091098	.098522	.106085	.113771
	-.20	.055363	.061618	.068107	.071435	.074815	.078246	.081726	.085252	.088824	.096092	.103516	.111079	.118765
	-.30	.060357	.066612	.073101	.076429	.079809	.083240	.086720	.090246	.093818	.101087	.108510	.116073	.123759
	-.40	.065351	.071607	.078095	.081423	.084803	.088234	.091714	.095241	.098812	.106081	.113504	.121067	.128754
25	.40	.026212	.033110	.040242	.043887	.047581	.051320	.055101	.058922	.062779	.070589	.078510	.086522	.094607
	.30	.031206	.038104	.045236	.048881	.052575	.056314	.060095	.063916	.067773	.075583	.083504	.091516	.099601
	.20	.036200	.043098	.050230	.053875	.057569	.061308	.065090	.068910	.072767	.080577	.088498	.096510	.104595
	.10	.041194	.048092	.055224	.058869	.062563	.066302	.070084	.073904	.077761	.085571	.093492	.101504	.109589
	0.00	.046188	.053086	.060218	.063863	.067557	.071296	.075078	.078898	.082755	.090565	.098486	.106498	.114583
	-.10	.051182	.058081	.065212	.068857	.072551	.076290	.080072	.083892	.087749	.095559	.103480	.111492	.119577
	-.20	.056176	.063075	.070206	.073852	.077545	.081285	.085066	.088887	.092743	.100553	.108474	.116486	.124571
	-.30	.061170	.068069	.075200	.078846	.082540	.086279	.090060	.093881	.097737	.105547	.113468	.121480	.129565
	-.40	.066165	.073063	.080195	.083840	.087534	.091273	.095054	.098875	.102731	.110542	.118463	.126475	.134560
30	.40	.026727	.034014	.041512	.045330	.049189	.053083	.057009	.060964	.064945	.072969	.081059	.089197	.097365
	.30	.031721	.039008	.046506	.050325	.054183	.058077	.062003	.065959	.069939	.077963	.086053	.094191	.102359
	.20	.036715	.044002	.051501	.055319	.059177	.063071	.066997	.070953	.074933	.082957	.091048	.099185	.107353
	.10	.041709	.048996	.056495	.060313	.064171	.068065	.071992	.075947	.079927	.087951	.096042	.104179	.112347
	0.00	.046704	.053990	.061489	.065307	.069165	.073059	.076986	.080941	.084921	.092946	.101036	.109173	.117342
	-.10	.051698	.058984	.066483	.070301	.074159	.078053	.081980	.085935	.089915	.097940	.106030	.114167	.122336
	-.20	.056692	.063978	.071477	.075295	.079153	.083047	.086974	.090929	.094910	.102934	.111024	.119161	.127330
	-.30	.061686	.068972	.076471	.080289	.084147	.088042	.091968	.095923	.099904	.107928	.116018	.124155	.132324
	-.40	.066680	.073966	.081465	.085283	.089141	.093036	.096962	.100917	.104898	.112922	.121012	.129149	.137318
40	.40	.027317	.035010	.042856	.046823	.050813	.054822	.058845	.062880	.066923	.075028	.083143	.091259	.099370
	.30	.032311	.040004	.047851	.051817	.055807	.059816	.063839	.067874	.071917	.080022	.088137	.096254	.104364
	.20	.037305	.044998	.052845	.056812	.060801	.064810	.068833	.072868	.076911	.085016	.093131	.101248	.109359
	.10	.042299	.049992	.057839	.061806	.065796	.069804	.073827	.077862	.081905	.090010	.098125	.106242	.114353
	0.00	.047293	.054986	.062833	.066800	.070790	.074798	.078821	.082856	.086900	.095004	.103119	.111236	.119347
	-.10	.052287	.059980	.067827	.071794	.075784	.079792	.083815	.087850	.091894	.099998	.108114	.116230	.124341
	-.20	.057281	.064974	.072821	.076788	.080778	.084786	.088809	.092844	.096888	.104992	.113108	.121224	.129335
	-.30	.062275	.069968	.077815	.081782	.085772	.089780	.093804	.097838	.101882	.109986	.118102	.126218	.134329
	-.40	.067269	.074963	.082809	.086776	.090766	.094774	.098798	.102832	.106876	.114980	.123096	.131212	.139323

15.0 YEAR HOLDING PERIOD
.040 EQUITY YIELD RATE
.900 LOAN RATIO

INTEREST RATE

TERM YEARS	APPR DEP	5.0	6.0	7.0	7.5	8.0	8.5	9.0	9.5	10.0	11.0	12.0	13.0	14.0
15	.40	.024482	.030213	.036150	.039194	.042287	.045428	.048617	.051853	.055134	.061829	.068695	.075723	.082905
	.30	.029476	.035207	.041144	.044188	.047281	.050423	.053611	.056847	.060128	.066823	.073689	.080717	.087899
	.20	.034471	.040201	.046138	.049182	.052275	.055417	.058606	.061841	.065122	.071817	.078683	.085711	.092893
	.10	.039465	.045195	.051132	.054176	.057269	.060411	.063600	.066835	.070116	.076811	.083677	.090705	.097887
	0.00	.044459	.050190	.056126	.059170	.062263	.065405	.068594	.071829	.075110	.081805	.088671	.095695	.102881
	-.10	.049453	.055184	.061121	.064164	.067258	.070399	.073588	.076823	.080104	.086800	.093665	.100693	.107875
	-.20	.054447	.060178	.066115	.069159	.072252	.075393	.078582	.081817	.085099	.091794	.098659	.105687	.112863
	-.30	.059441	.065172	.071109	.074153	.077246	.080387	.083576	.086812	.090093	.096788	.103663	.110681	.117863
	-.40	.064435	.070166	.076103	.079147	.082240	.085381	.088570	.091806	.095087	.101782	.108648	.115676	.122858
20	.40	.026070	.033107	.040407	.044151	.047954	.051813	.055728	.059696	.063713	.071891	.080242	.088750	.097398
	.30	.031065	.038102	.045402	.049145	.052948	.056808	.060722	.064690	.068708	.076885	.085236	.093744	.102392
	.20	.036059	.043096	.050396	.054139	.057942	.061802	.065716	.069684	.073702	.081879	.090231	.098739	.107386
	.10	.041053	.048090	.055390	.059133	.062936	.066796	.070711	.074678	.078696	.086873	.095225	.103733	.112380
	0.00	.046047	.053084	.060384	.064127	.067930	.071790	.075705	.079672	.083690	.091867	.100219	.108727	.117374
	-.10	.051041	.058078	.065378	.069121	.072924	.076784	.080699	.084666	.088684	.096861	.105213	.113721	.122368
	-.20	.056035	.063072	.070372	.074116	.077918	.081778	.085693	.089660	.093678	.101855	.110207	.118715	.127362
	-.30	.061029	.068066	.075366	.079110	.082912	.086772	.090687	.094654	.098672	.106850	.115201	.123709	.132357
	-.40	.066023	.073060	.080360	.084104	.087906	.091766	.095681	.099649	.103666	.111844	.120195	.128703	.137351
25	.40	.026985	.034746	.042769	.046870	.051025	.055232	.059486	.063784	.068123	.076909	.085820	.094834	.103930
	.30	.031979	.039740	.047763	.051864	.056020	.060226	.064480	.068778	.073117	.081903	.090815	.099828	.108924
	.20	.036973	.044734	.052757	.056858	.061014	.065220	.069474	.073772	.078111	.086897	.095809	.104822	.113918
	.10	.041968	.049728	.057751	.061852	.066008	.070214	.074468	.078766	.083105	.091892	.100803	.109816	.118912
	0.00	.046962	.054722	.062745	.066846	.071002	.075208	.079463	.083761	.088099	.096886	.105797	.114810	.123906
	-.10	.051956	.059716	.067740	.071840	.075996	.080203	.084457	.088755	.093093	.101880	.110791	.119805	.128900
	-.20	.056950	.064711	.072734	.076835	.080990	.085197	.089451	.093749	.098088	.106874	.115785	.124799	.133894
	-.30	.061944	.069705	.077728	.081829	.085984	.090191	.094445	.098743	.103082	.111868	.120779	.129793	.138888
	-.40	.066938	.074699	.082722	.086823	.090978	.095185	.099439	.103737	.108076	.116862	.125773	.134787	.143882
30	.40	.027565	.035762	.044198	.048494	.052834	.057215	.061632	.066082	.070560	.079587	.088689	.097843	.107033
	.30	.032559	.040756	.049193	.053488	.057828	.062209	.066627	.071076	.075554	.084581	.093683	.102837	.112027
	.20	.037553	.045751	.054187	.058482	.062822	.067203	.071621	.076070	.080548	.089576	.098677	.107831	.117021
	.10	.042547	.050745	.059181	.063476	.067816	.072197	.076615	.081064	.085542	.094570	.103671	.112826	.122015
	0.00	.047542	.055739	.064175	.068470	.072811	.077192	.081609	.086058	.090537	.099564	.108665	.117820	.127009
	-.10	.052536	.060733	.069169	.073464	.077805	.082186	.086603	.091053	.095531	.104558	.113659	.122814	.132003
	-.20	.057530	.065727	.074163	.078458	.082799	.087180	.091597	.096047	.100525	.109552	.118654	.127808	.136997
	-.30	.062524	.070721	.079157	.083453	.087793	.092174	.096591	.101041	.105519	.114546	.123648	.132802	.141992
	-.40	.067518	.075715	.084151	.088447	.092787	.097168	.101585	.106035	.110513	.119540	.128642	.137796	.146986
40	.40	.028228	.036883	.045711	.050173	.054662	.059171	.063697	.068237	.072786	.081903	.091033	.100164	.109289
	.30	.033222	.041877	.050705	.055168	.059656	.064165	.068692	.073231	.077780	.086897	.096027	.105158	.114283
	.20	.038216	.046871	.055699	.060162	.064650	.069160	.073686	.078225	.082774	.091891	.101021	.110152	.119277
	.10	.043210	.051865	.060693	.065156	.069644	.074154	.078680	.083219	.087768	.096885	.106015	.115146	.124271
	0.00	.048205	.056859	.065687	.070150	.074638	.079148	.083674	.088213	.092762	.101879	.111009	.120140	.129265
	-.10	.053199	.061854	.070681	.075144	.079633	.084142	.088668	.093207	.097756	.106874	.116003	.125134	.134259
	-.20	.058193	.066848	.075675	.080138	.084627	.089136	.093662	.098201	.102750	.111868	.120998	.130129	.139253
	-.30	.063187	.071842	.080669	.085132	.089621	.094130	.098656	.103199	.107744	.116862	.125992	.135123	.144247
	-.40	.068181	.076836	.085663	.090126	.094615	.099124	.103650	.108189	.112738	.121856	.130986	.140117	.149242

15.0 YEAR HOLDING PERIOD
.060 EQUITY YIELD RATE
.600 LOAN RATIO

INTEREST RATE

TERM YEARS	APPR DEP	5.0	6.0	7.0	7.5	8.0	8.5	9.0	9.5	10.0	11.0	12.0	13.0	14.0
15	.40	.037974	.041795	.045753	.047782	.049844	.051938	.054064	.056221	.058409	.062872	.067449	.072135	.076923
	.30	.042271	.046091	.050049	.052078	.054140	.056235	.058361	.060518	.062705	.067168	.071746	.076431	.081219
	.20	.046567	.050387	.054345	.056375	.058437	.060531	.062657	.064814	.067001	.071465	.076042	.080727	.085515
	.10	.050863	.054684	.058642	.060671	.062733	.064827	.066953	.069110	.071298	.075761	.080338	.085024	.089811
	0.00	.055159	.058980	.062938	.064967	.067029	.069124	.071250	.073407	.075594	.080057	.084634	.089320	.094108
	-.10	.059456	.063276	.067234	.069264	.071326	.073420	.075546	.077703	.079890	.084354	.088931	.093616	.098404
	-.20	.063752	.067573	.071531	.073560	.075622	.077716	.079842	.081999	.084186	.088650	.093227	.097912	.102700
	-.30	.068048	.071869	.075827	.077856	.079918	.082012	.084138	.086295	.088483	.092946	.097523	.102209	.106997
	-.40	.072345	.076165	.080123	.082152	.084214	.086309	.088435	.090592	.092779	.097242	.101820	.106505	.111293
20	.40	.037569	.042173	.046952	.049403	.051895	.054424	.056990	.059592	.062227	.067592	.073075	.078664	.084347
	.30	.041865	.046469	.051248	.053700	.056191	.058720	.061287	.063888	.066523	.071889	.077371	.082960	.088643
	.20	.046161	.050765	.055544	.057996	.060487	.063017	.065583	.068184	.070819	.076185	.081668	.087256	.092940
	.10	.050458	.055062	.059841	.062292	.064784	.067313	.069879	.072480	.075116	.080481	.085964	.091553	.097236
	0.00	.054754	.059358	.064137	.066589	.069080	.071609	.074175	.076777	.079412	.084777	.090260	.095849	.101532
	-.10	.059050	.063654	.068433	.070885	.073376	.075906	.078472	.081073	.083708	.089074	.094557	.100145	.105828
	-.20	.063347	.067951	.072729	.075181	.077672	.080202	.082768	.085369	.088004	.093370	.098853	.104441	.110125
	-.30	.067643	.072247	.077026	.079477	.081969	.084498	.087064	.089666	.092301	.097666	.103149	.108738	.114421
	-.40	.071939	.076543	.081322	.083774	.086265	.088794	.091360	.093962	.096597	.101963	.107445	.113034	.118717
25	.40	.037335	.042387	.047617	.050293	.053006	.055755	.058536	.061349	.064189	.069947	.075793	.081713	.087693
	.30	.041632	.046683	.051913	.054589	.057303	.060051	.062833	.065645	.068485	.074243	.080089	.086009	.091989
	.20	.045928	.050979	.056209	.058885	.061599	.064347	.067129	.069941	.072782	.078539	.084385	.090305	.096286
	.10	.050224	.055276	.060506	.063182	.065895	.068644	.071425	.074237	.077078	.082835	.088682	.094602	.100582
	0.00	.054520	.059572	.064802	.067478	.070191	.072940	.075722	.078534	.081374	.087132	.092978	.098898	.104878
	-.10	.058817	.063868	.069098	.071774	.074488	.077236	.080018	.082830	.085670	.091428	.097274	.103194	.109175
	-.20	.063113	.068165	.073394	.076070	.078784	.081533	.084314	.087126	.089967	.095724	.101570	.107490	.113471
	-.30	.067409	.072461	.077691	.080367	.083080	.085829	.088610	.091422	.094263	.100021	.105867	.111787	.117767
	-.40	.071706	.076757	.081987	.084663	.087376	.090125	.092907	.095719	.098559	.104317	.110163	.116083	.122063
30	.40	.037187	.042520	.048019	.050824	.053661	.056527	.059420	.062336	.065274	.071203	.077190	.083221	.089283
	.30	.041484	.046816	.052316	.055120	.057957	.060823	.063716	.066632	.069570	.075499	.081487	.087517	.093579
	.20	.045780	.051112	.056612	.059416	.062253	.065120	.068012	.070929	.073866	.079795	.085783	.091814	.097875
	.10	.050076	.055408	.060908	.063713	.066550	.069416	.072308	.075225	.078162	.084092	.090079	.096110	.102172
	0.00	.054372	.059705	.065204	.068009	.070846	.073712	.076605	.079521	.082459	.088388	.094375	.100406	.106468
	-.10	.058669	.064001	.069501	.072305	.075142	.078008	.080901	.083817	.086755	.092684	.098672	.104702	.110764
	-.20	.062965	.068297	.073797	.076602	.079438	.082305	.085197	.088114	.091051	.096981	.102968	.108999	.115060
	-.30	.067261	.072594	.078093	.080898	.083735	.086601	.089494	.092410	.095348	.101277	.107264	.113295	.119357
	-.40	.071557	.076890	.082390	.085194	.088031	.090897	.093790	.096706	.099644	.105573	.111560	.117591	.123653
40	.40	.037018	.042666	.048445	.051373	.054322	.057288	.060269	.063262	.066264	.072289	.078332	.084384	.090438
	.30	.041314	.046962	.052741	.055670	.058618	.061585	.064566	.067558	.070560	.076586	.082629	.088680	.094735
	.20	.045611	.051259	.057038	.059966	.062915	.065881	.068862	.071854	.074857	.080882	.086925	.092977	.099031
	.10	.049907	.055555	.061334	.064262	.067211	.070177	.073158	.076151	.079153	.085178	.091221	.097273	.103327
	0.00	.054203	.059851	.065630	.068558	.071507	.074474	.077454	.080447	.083449	.089474	.095517	.101569	.107624
	-.10	.058499	.064147	.069927	.072855	.075804	.078770	.081751	.084743	.087745	.093771	.099814	.105865	.111920
	-.20	.062796	.068444	.074223	.077151	.080100	.083066	.086047	.089039	.092042	.098067	.104110	.110162	.116216
	-.30	.067092	.072740	.078519	.081447	.084396	.087362	.090343	.093336	.096338	.102363	.108406	.114458	.120512
	-.40	.071388	.077036	.082815	.085744	.088692	.091659	.094639	.097632	.100634	.106659	.112702	.118754	.124809

15.0 YEAR HOLDING PERIOD
.060 EQUITY YIELD RATE
.667 LOAN RATIO

INTEREST RATE

TERM YEARS	APPR DEP	5.0	6.0	7.0	7.5	8.0	8.5	9.0	9.5	10.0	11.0	12.0	13.0	14.0
15	.40	.037437	.041682	.046079	.048334	.050625	.052952	.055314	.057711	.060142	.065101	.070187	.075393	.080713
	.30	.041733	.045978	.050376	.052630	.054922	.057249	.059611	.062007	.064438	.069397	.074483	.079689	.085009
	.20	.046029	.050274	.054672	.056927	.059218	.061545	.063907	.066304	.068734	.073693	.078779	.083985	.089305
	.10	.050325	.054570	.058968	.061223	.063514	.065841	.068203	.070600	.073030	.077990	.083075	.088281	.093601
	0.00	.054622	.058867	.063264	.065519	.067810	.070137	.072500	.074896	.077327	.082286	.087392	.092578	.097898
	-.10	.058918	.063163	.067561	.069815	.072107	.074434	.076796	.079192	.081623	.086582	.091668	.096874	.102194
	-.20	.063214	.067459	.071857	.074112	.076403	.078730	.081092	.083489	.085919	.090879	.095964	.101170	.106490
	-.30	.067510	.071756	.076153	.078408	.080699	.083026	.085388	.087785	.090215	.095175	.100261	.105467	.110786
	-.40	.071807	.076052	.080450	.082704	.084995	.087322	.089685	.092081	.094512	.099471	.104557	.109763	.115083
20	.40	.036986	.042102	.047411	.050136	.052904	.055714	.058565	.061456	.064384	.070346	.076438	.082647	.088962
	.30	.041282	.046398	.051708	.054432	.057200	.060010	.062862	.065752	.068680	.074642	.080734	.086944	.093258
	.20	.045579	.050694	.056004	.058728	.061496	.064307	.067158	.070048	.072976	.078938	.085030	.091240	.097555
	.10	.049875	.054990	.060300	.063024	.065792	.068603	.071454	.074345	.077273	.083234	.089326	.095536	.101851
	0.00	.054171	.059287	.064597	.067321	.070089	.072899	.075750	.078641	.081569	.087531	.093623	.099832	.106147
	-.10	.058467	.063583	.068893	.071617	.074385	.077195	.080047	.082937	.085865	.091827	.097919	.104129	.110443
	-.20	.062764	.067879	.073189	.075913	.078681	.081492	.084343	.087233	.090161	.096123	.102215	.108425	.114740
	-.30	.067060	.072176	.077485	.080209	.082978	.085788	.088639	.091530	.094458	.100419	.106512	.112721	.119036
	-.40	.071356	.076472	.081782	.084506	.087274	.090084	.092936	.095826	.098754	.104716	.110808	.117017	.123332
25	.40	.036726	.042339	.048150	.051124	.054139	.057193	.060283	.063408	.066564	.072961	.079457	.086035	.092680
	.30	.041023	.046636	.052447	.055420	.058435	.061489	.064580	.067704	.070860	.077258	.083753	.090331	.096976
	.20	.045319	.050932	.056743	.059716	.062731	.065785	.068876	.072001	.075157	.081554	.088050	.094628	.101272
	.10	.049615	.055228	.061039	.064013	.067028	.070082	.073172	.076297	.079453	.085850	.092346	.098924	.105569
	0.00	.053912	.059524	.065335	.068309	.071324	.074378	.077468	.080593	.083749	.090146	.096642	.103220	.109865
	-.10	.058208	.063821	.069632	.072605	.075620	.078674	.081765	.084889	.088045	.094443	.100939	.107516	.114161
	-.20	.062504	.068117	.073928	.076901	.079916	.082970	.086061	.089186	.092342	.098739	.105235	.111813	.118458
	-.30	.066800	.072413	.078224	.081198	.084213	.087267	.090357	.093482	.096638	.103035	.109531	.116116	.122754
	-.40	.071097	.076710	.082521	.085494	.088509	.091563	.094654	.097778	.100934	.107332	.113827	.120405	.127050
30	.40	.036562	.042487	.048598	.051714	.054866	.058051	.061265	.064505	.067769	.074357	.081010	.087711	.094446
	.30	.040858	.046783	.052894	.056010	.059162	.062347	.065561	.068801	.072065	.078654	.085306	.092007	.098742
	.20	.045155	.051079	.057190	.060306	.063458	.066643	.069857	.073098	.076362	.082950	.089602	.096303	.103039
	.10	.049451	.055376	.061486	.064603	.067755	.070939	.074153	.077394	.080658	.087246	.093899	.100600	.107335
	0.00	.053747	.059672	.065783	.068899	.072051	.075236	.078450	.081690	.084954	.091542	.098195	.104896	.111631
	-.10	.058043	.063968	.070079	.073195	.076347	.079532	.082746	.085987	.089251	.095839	.102491	.109192	.115928
	-.20	.062340	.068264	.074375	.077492	.080644	.083828	.087042	.090283	.093547	.100135	.106788	.113468	.120224
	-.30	.066636	.072561	.078672	.081788	.084940	.088125	.091339	.094579	.097843	.104431	.111084	.117785	.124520
	-.40	.070932	.076857	.082968	.086084	.089236	.092421	.095635	.098875	.102139	.108728	.115380	.122081	.128816
40	.40	.036374	.042649	.049071	.052324	.055601	.058897	.062209	.065534	.068870	.075564	.082279	.089003	.095730
	.30	.040670	.046946	.053367	.056621	.059897	.063193	.066505	.069830	.073166	.079861	.086575	.093299	.100026
	.20	.044966	.051242	.057663	.060917	.064193	.067489	.070801	.074126	.077462	.084157	.090871	.097596	.104323
	.10	.049263	.055538	.061960	.065213	.068490	.071786	.075098	.078423	.081758	.088453	.095168	.101892	.108619
	0.00	.053559	.059835	.066256	.069509	.072786	.076082	.079394	.082719	.086055	.092749	.099464	.106188	.112915
	-.10	.057855	.064131	.070552	.073806	.077082	.080378	.083690	.087015	.090351	.097046	.103760	.110484	.117212
	-.20	.062152	.068427	.074848	.078102	.081378	.084674	.087986	.091311	.094647	.101342	.108056	.114781	.121508
	-.30	.066448	.072724	.079145	.082398	.085675	.088971	.092283	.095608	.098943	.105638	.112353	.119077	.125804
	-.40	.070744	.077020	.083441	.086694	.089971	.093267	.096579	.099904	.103240	.109935	.116649	.123373	.130100

15.0 YEAR HOLDING PERIOD
.060 EQUITY YIELD RATE
.700 LOAN RATIO

INTEREST RATE

TERM YEARS	APPR DEP	5.0	6.0	7.0	7.5	8.0	8.5	9.0	9.5	10.0	11.0	12.0	13.0	14.0
15	.40	.037168	.041625	.046243	.048610	.051016	.053459	.055939	.058456	.061008	.066215	.071555	.077021	.082607
	.30	.041464	.045921	.050539	.052906	.055312	.057755	.060236	.062752	.065304	.070511	.075851	.081318	.086904
	.20	.045760	.050217	.054835	.057203	.059608	.062052	.064532	.067048	.069600	.074808	.080148	.085614	.091200
	.10	.050056	.054514	.059131	.061499	.063905	.066348	.068828	.071345	.073897	.079104	.084444	.089910	.095496
	0.00	.054353	.058810	.063428	.065795	.068201	.070644	.073124	.075641	.078193	.083400	.088740	.094206	.099792
	-.10	.058649	.063106	.067724	.070091	.072497	.074940	.077421	.079937	.082489	.087696	.093036	.098503	.104089
	-.20	.062945	.067403	.072020	.074388	.076793	.079237	.081717	.084233	.086785	.091993	.097333	.102799	.108385
	-.30	.067242	.071699	.076316	.078684	.081090	.083533	.086013	.088530	.091082	.096289	.101629	.107095	.112681
	-.40	.071538	.075995	.080613	.082980	.085386	.087829	.090310	.092826	.095378	.100585	.105925	.111392	.116977
20	.40	.036695	.042066	.047641	.050502	.053408	.056359	.059353	.062388	.065462	.071722	.078119	.084639	.091269
	.30	.040991	.046362	.051938	.054798	.057704	.060655	.063649	.066684	.069758	.076018	.082415	.088935	.095565
	.20	.045287	.050658	.056234	.059094	.062001	.064952	.067945	.070980	.074055	.080314	.086711	.093231	.099862
	.10	.049583	.054955	.060530	.063390	.066297	.069248	.072242	.075277	.078351	.084611	.091007	.097527	.104158
	0.00	.053880	.059251	.064826	.067687	.070593	.073544	.076538	.079573	.082647	.088907	.095304	.101824	.108454
	-.10	.058176	.063547	.069123	.071983	.074889	.077840	.080834	.083869	.086943	.093203	.099600	.106120	.112750
	-.20	.062472	.067844	.073419	.076279	.079186	.082137	.085130	.088165	.091240	.097500	.103896	.110416	.117047
	-.30	.066768	.072140	.077715	.080575	.083482	.086433	.089427	.092462	.095536	.101796	.108193	.114713	.121343
	-.40	.071065	.076436	.082011	.084872	.087778	.090729	.093723	.096758	.099832	.106092	.112489	.119009	.125639
25	.40	.036422	.042316	.048417	.051539	.054705	.057912	.061157	.064438	.067751	.074469	.081289	.088196	.095173
	.30	.040718	.046612	.052713	.055835	.059001	.062208	.065453	.068734	.072048	.078765	.085585	.092492	.099469
	.20	.045015	.050908	.057010	.060132	.063297	.066504	.069749	.073030	.076344	.083061	.089882	.096788	.103765
	.10	.049311	.055204	.061306	.064428	.067594	.070800	.074046	.077326	.080640	.087357	.094178	.101085	.108062
	0.00	.053607	.059501	.065602	.068724	.071890	.075097	.078342	.081623	.084936	.091654	.098474	.105381	.112358
	-.10	.057903	.063797	.069898	.073020	.076186	.079393	.082638	.085919	.089233	.095950	.102771	.109677	.116654
	-.20	.062200	.068093	.074195	.077317	.080482	.083689	.086934	.090215	.093529	.100246	.107067	.113973	.120950
	-.30	.066496	.072389	.078491	.081613	.084779	.087986	.091231	.094511	.097825	.104542	.111363	.118270	.125247
	-.40	.070792	.076686	.082787	.085909	.089075	.092282	.095527	.098808	.102122	.108839	.115659	.122566	.129543
30	.40	.036249	.042470	.048887	.052159	.055468	.058812	.062187	.065590	.069017	.075934	.082919	.089955	.097027
	.30	.040546	.046767	.053183	.056455	.059765	.063109	.066483	.069886	.073313	.080231	.087216	.094252	.101324
	.20	.044842	.051063	.057479	.060751	.064061	.067405	.070780	.074182	.077609	.084527	.091512	.098548	.105620
	.10	.049138	.055359	.061776	.065048	.068357	.071701	.075076	.078478	.081906	.088823	.095808	.102844	.109916
	0.00	.053434	.059655	.066072	.069344	.072654	.075997	.079372	.082775	.086202	.093119	.100105	.107140	.114213
	-.10	.057731	.063952	.070368	.073640	.076950	.080294	.083668	.087071	.090498	.097416	.104401	.111437	.118509
	-.20	.062027	.068248	.074664	.077936	.081246	.084590	.087965	.091367	.094794	.101712	.108697	.115733	.122805
	-.30	.066323	.072544	.078961	.082233	.085542	.088886	.092261	.095663	.099091	.106008	.112993	.120029	.127101
	-.40	.070620	.076841	.083257	.086529	.089839	.093183	.096557	.099960	.103387	.110304	.117290	.124326	.131398
40	.40	.036052	.042641	.049384	.052800	.056240	.059701	.063178	.066670	.070172	.077202	.084252	.091312	.098376
	.30	.040348	.046937	.053680	.057096	.060536	.063997	.067475	.070966	.074468	.081498	.088548	.095609	.102672
	.20	.044644	.051234	.057976	.061392	.064833	.068293	.071771	.075262	.078765	.085794	.092844	.099905	.106968
	.10	.048941	.055530	.062272	.065689	.069129	.072590	.076067	.079558	.083061	.090090	.097141	.104201	.111265
	0.00	.053237	.059826	.066569	.069985	.073425	.076886	.080363	.083855	.087357	.094387	.101437	.108497	.115561
	-.10	.057533	.064123	.070865	.074281	.077721	.081182	.084660	.088151	.091654	.098683	.105733	.112794	.119857
	-.20	.061829	.068419	.075161	.078577	.082018	.085478	.088956	.092447	.095950	.102980	.110029	.117090	.124153
	-.30	.066126	.072715	.079457	.082874	.086314	.089775	.093252	.096744	.100246	.107276	.114326	.121386	.128450
	-.40	.070422	.077011	.083754	.087170	.090610	.094071	.097549	.101040	.104542	.111572	.118622	.125682	.132746

15.0 YEAR HOLDING PERIOD
.060 EQUITY YIELD RATE
.750 LOAN RATIO

INTEREST RATE

TERM YEARS	APPR DEP	5.0	6.0	7.0	7.5	8.0	8.5	9.0	9.5	10.0	11.0	12.0	13.0	14.0
15	.40	.036764	.041540	.046487	.049024	.051602	.054219	.056877	.059573	.062307	.067887	.073608	.079465	.085450
	.30	.041061	.045836	.050784	.053320	.055898	.058516	.061173	.063869	.066604	.072183	.077904	.083761	.089746
	.20	.045357	.050132	.055080	.057616	.060194	.062812	.065469	.068166	.070899	.076479	.082200	.088057	.094042
	.10	.049653	.054429	.059376	.061913	.064490	.067108	.069766	.072462	.075196	.080775	.086497	.092353	.098338
	0.00	.053949	.058725	.063672	.066209	.068787	.071404	.074062	.076758	.079492	.085072	.090793	.096650	.102635
	-.10	.058246	.063021	.067969	.070505	.073083	.075701	.078358	.081054	.083789	.089368	.095089	.100946	.106931
	-.20	.062542	.067318	.072265	.074802	.077379	.079997	.082654	.085351	.088085	.093664	.099386	.105242	.111227
	-.30	.066838	.071614	.076561	.079098	.081675	.084293	.086951	.089647	.092381	.097960	.103682	.109539	.115523
	-.40	.071134	.075910	.080858	.083394	.085972	.088590	.091247	.093943	.096677	.102257	.107978	.113835	.119820
20	.40	.036257	.042012	.047986	.051051	.054165	.057326	.060534	.063786	.067080	.073787	.080640	.087626	.094730
	.30	.040554	.046309	.052282	.055347	.058461	.061623	.064830	.068082	.071376	.078083	.084937	.091922	.099026
	.20	.044850	.050605	.056579	.059643	.062757	.065919	.069127	.072379	.075672	.082379	.089233	.096219	.103323
	.10	.049146	.054901	.060875	.063939	.067053	.070215	.073423	.076675	.079969	.086676	.093529	.100515	.107619
	0.00	.053442	.059198	.065171	.068236	.071350	.074512	.077719	.080971	.084265	.090972	.097825	.104811	.111915
	-.10	.057739	.063494	.069467	.072532	.075646	.078808	.082015	.085267	.088561	.095268	.102122	.109107	.116211
	-.20	.062035	.067790	.073764	.076828	.079942	.083104	.086312	.089563	.092857	.099564	.106418	.113404	.120508
	-.30	.066331	.072086	.078060	.081125	.084239	.087400	.090608	.093860	.097154	.103861	.110714	.117700	.124804
	-.40	.070628	.076383	.082356	.085421	.088535	.091697	.094904	.098156	.101450	.108157	.115011	.121996	.129100
25	.40	.035965	.042280	.048817	.052162	.055554	.058990	.062467	.065982	.069533	.076730	.084037	.091437	.098913
	.30	.040262	.046576	.053114	.056459	.059850	.063286	.066763	.070278	.073829	.081026	.088334	.095734	.103209
	.20	.044558	.050872	.057410	.060755	.064147	.067582	.071059	.074575	.078125	.085322	.092630	.100030	.107505
	.10	.048854	.055169	.061706	.065051	.068443	.071879	.075356	.078871	.082421	.089618	.096926	.104326	.111802
	0.00	.053151	.059465	.066002	.069347	.072739	.076175	.079652	.083167	.086718	.093915	.101222	.108622	.116098
	-.10	.057447	.063761	.070299	.073644	.077035	.080471	.083948	.087463	.091014	.098211	.105519	.112919	.120394
	-.20	.061743	.068058	.074595	.077940	.081332	.084768	.088244	.091760	.095310	.102507	.109815	.117215	.124690
	-.30	.066039	.072354	.078891	.082236	.085628	.089064	.092541	.096056	.099607	.106803	.114111	.121511	.128987
	-.40	.070336	.076650	.083187	.086532	.089924	.093360	.096837	.100352	.103903	.111100	.118408	.125808	.133283
30	.40	.035780	.042446	.049320	.052826	.056372	.059955	.063571	.067216	.070888	.078300	.085784	.093322	.100900
	.30	.040077	.046742	.053617	.057122	.060669	.064251	.067867	.071513	.075185	.082596	.090080	.097619	.105196
	.20	.044373	.051038	.057913	.061419	.064965	.068548	.072164	.075809	.079481	.086892	.094377	.101915	.109492
	.10	.048669	.055335	.062209	.065715	.069261	.072844	.076460	.080105	.083777	.091189	.098673	.106211	.113789
	0.00	.052965	.059631	.066506	.070011	.073557	.077140	.080756	.084401	.088073	.095485	.102969	.110508	.118085
	-.10	.057262	.063927	.070802	.074308	.077854	.081436	.085052	.088698	.092369	.099781	.107265	.114804	.122381
	-.20	.061558	.068223	.075098	.078604	.082150	.085733	.089348	.092994	.096666	.104078	.111562	.119100	.126677
	-.30	.065854	.072520	.079394	.082900	.086446	.090029	.093645	.097290	.100962	.108374	.115858	.123396	.130974
	-.40	.070151	.076816	.083691	.087196	.090742	.094325	.097941	.101586	.105258	.112670	.120154	.127693	.135270
40	.40	.035569	.042629	.049853	.053513	.057199	.060907	.064633	.068374	.072126	.079658	.087212	.094776	.102344
	.30	.039865	.046925	.054149	.057809	.061495	.065203	.068929	.072670	.076423	.083954	.091508	.099073	.106641
	.20	.044161	.051221	.058445	.062105	.065792	.069499	.073225	.076966	.080719	.088250	.095804	.103369	.110937
	.10	.048458	.055518	.062742	.066402	.070088	.073796	.077522	.081262	.085015	.092547	.100100	.107665	.115233
	0.00	.052754	.059814	.067038	.070698	.074384	.078092	.081818	.085559	.089311	.096843	.104397	.111961	.119529
	-.10	.057050	.064110	.071334	.074994	.078680	.082388	.086114	.089855	.093608	.101139	.108693	.116258	.123826
	-.20	.061346	.068406	.075630	.079290	.082976	.086685	.090410	.094151	.097904	.105435	.112989	.120554	.128122
	-.30	.065643	.072703	.079927	.083587	.087273	.090981	.094707	.098447	.102200	.109732	.117286	.124850	.132418
	-.40	.069939	.076999	.084223	.087883	.091569	.095277	.099003	.102744	.106496	.114028	.121582	.129147	.136715

15.0 YEAR HOLDING PERIOD
.060 EQUITY YIELD RATE
.800 LOAN RATIO

INTEREST RATE

TERM YEARS	APPR DEP	5.0	6.0	7.0	7.5	8.0	8.5	9.0	9.5	10.0	11.0	12.0	13.0	14.0
15	.40	.036361	.041455	.046732	.049438	.052187	.054980	.057814	.060690	.063607	.069558	.075661	.081908	.088292
	.30	.040657	.045751	.051128	.053734	.056484	.059276	.062111	.064947	.067903	.073854	.079957	.086204	.092588
	.20	.044953	.050047	.055325	.058030	.060780	.063572	.066407	.069283	.072199	.078151	.084253	.090500	.096884
	.10	.049250	.054344	.059621	.062327	.065076	.067869	.070703	.073579	.076496	.082447	.088550	.094797	.101181
	0.00	.053546	.058640	.063621	.066623	.069372	.072165	.074999	.077875	.080792	.086743	.092846	.099093	.105477
	-.10	.057842	.062936	.068214	.070919	.073669	.076461	.079296	.082172	.085088	.091039	.097142	.103389	.109773
	-.20	.062139	.067233	.072510	.075216	.077965	.080757	.083592	.086468	.089384	.095336	.101438	.107686	.114070
	-.30	.066435	.071529	.076806	.079512	.082261	.085054	.087888	.090764	.093681	.099632	.105735	.111982	.118366
	-.40	.070731	.075825	.081102	.083808	.086557	.089350	.092184	.095060	.097977	.103928	.110031	.116278	.122662
20	.40	.035820	.041959	.048331	.051600	.054921	.058294	.061715	.065184	.068697	.075852	.083162	.090613	.098191
	.30	.040116	.046255	.052627	.055896	.059218	.062590	.066012	.069480	.072994	.080148	.087458	.094910	.102487
	.20	.044413	.050551	.056923	.060192	.063514	.066886	.070308	.073776	.077290	.084444	.091755	.099206	.106784
	.10	.048709	.054848	.061220	.064488	.067810	.071183	.074604	.078073	.081586	.088740	.096051	.103502	.111080
	0.00	.053005	.059144	.065516	.068785	.072106	.075479	.078901	.082369	.085883	.093037	.100347	.107799	.115376
	-.10	.057302	.063440	.069812	.073081	.076403	.079775	.083197	.086665	.090179	.097333	.104643	.112095	.119672
	-.20	.061598	.067737	.074108	.077377	.080699	.084072	.087493	.090962	.094475	.101629	.108940	.116391	.123969
	-.30	.065894	.072033	.078405	.081674	.084995	.088368	.091789	.095258	.098771	.105925	.113236	.120687	.128265
	-.40	.070190	.076329	.082701	.085970	.089292	.092664	.096086	.099554	.103068	.110222	.117532	.124984	.132561
25	.40	.035509	.042244	.049217	.052785	.056403	.060048	.063777	.067526	.071314	.078990	.086785	.094679	.102653
	.30	.039805	.046540	.053514	.057082	.060700	.064365	.068073	.071823	.075610	.083287	.091082	.098975	.106949
	.20	.044101	.050837	.057810	.061378	.064996	.068661	.072370	.076119	.079906	.087583	.095378	.103271	.111245
	.10	.048398	.055133	.062106	.065674	.069292	.072957	.076666	.080415	.084203	.091879	.099674	.107568	.115541
	0.00	.052694	.059429	.066403	.069971	.073588	.077253	.080962	.084712	.088499	.096176	.103971	.111864	.119838
	-.10	.056990	.063726	.070699	.074267	.077885	.081550	.085258	.089008	.092795	.100472	.108267	.116160	.124134
	-.20	.061286	.068022	.074995	.078563	.082181	.085846	.089555	.093304	.097091	.104768	.112563	.120456	.128430
	-.30	.065583	.072318	.079291	.082859	.086477	.090142	.093851	.097600	.101388	.109064	.116859	.124753	.132726
	-.40	.069879	.076614	.083588	.087156	.090774	.094438	.098147	.101897	.105684	.113361	.121156	.129049	.137023
30	.40	.035311	.042421	.049754	.053494	.057276	.061098	.064955	.068843	.072760	.080666	.088649	.096690	.104772
	.30	.039608	.046717	.054050	.057790	.061572	.065394	.069251	.073139	.077056	.084962	.092945	.100986	.109068
	.20	.043904	.051014	.058347	.062086	.065869	.069690	.073547	.077436	.081352	.089258	.097241	.105282	.113365
	.10	.048200	.055310	.062643	.066382	.070165	.073986	.077843	.081732	.085649	.093554	.101538	.109578	.117661
	0.00	.052497	.059606	.066939	.070679	.074461	.078283	.082140	.086028	.089945	.097851	.105834	.113875	.121957
	-.10	.056793	.063903	.071236	.074975	.078757	.082579	.086436	.090324	.094241	.102147	.110130	.118171	.126253
	-.20	.061089	.068199	.075532	.079271	.083054	.086875	.090732	.094621	.098537	.106443	.114426	.122467	.130550
	-.30	.065385	.072495	.079828	.083568	.087350	.091172	.095028	.098917	.102834	.110740	.118723	.126764	.134846
	-.40	.069682	.076791	.084124	.087864	.091646	.095468	.099325	.103213	.107130	.115036	.123019	.131060	.139142
40	.40	.035086	.042616	.050322	.054226	.058158	.062113	.066087	.070077	.074080	.082114	.090171	.098240	.106313
	.30	.039382	.046913	.054618	.058522	.062454	.066409	.070384	.074374	.078377	.086410	.094468	.102537	.110609
	.20	.043678	.051209	.058914	.062819	.066751	.070706	.074680	.078670	.082673	.090707	.098764	.106833	.114905
	.10	.047975	.055505	.063211	.067115	.071047	.075002	.078976	.082966	.086969	.095003	.103060	.111129	.119202
	0.00	.052271	.059801	.067507	.071411	.075343	.079298	.083272	.087263	.091265	.099299	.107356	.115426	.123498
	-.10	.056567	.064098	.071803	.075707	.079639	.083594	.087569	.091559	.095562	.103595	.111653	.119722	.127794
	-.20	.060863	.068394	.076100	.080004	.083936	.087891	.091865	.095855	.099858	.107892	.115949	.124018	.132091
	-.30	.065160	.072690	.080396	.084300	.088232	.092187	.096161	.100151	.104154	.112188	.120245	.128314	.136387
	-.40	.069456	.076987	.084692	.088596	.092528	.096483	.100458	.104448	.108451	.116484	.124542	.132611	.140683

15.0 YEAR HOLDING PERIOD
.060 EQUITY YIELD RATE
.900 LOAN RATIO

INTEREST RATE

TERM YEARS	APPR DEP	5.0	6.0	7.0	7.5	8.0	8.5	9.0	9.5	10.0	11.0	12.0	13.0	14.0
15	.40	.035554	.041285	.047222	.050266	.053359	.056500	.059689	.062925	.066206	.072901	.079767	.086795	.093976
	.30	.039850	.045581	.051518	.054562	.057655	.060797	.063985	.067221	.070502	.077197	.084063	.091091	.098273
	.20	.044147	.049877	.055814	.058858	.061951	.065093	.068282	.071517	.074798	.081493	.088359	.095387	.102569
	.10	.048443	.054174	.060111	.063155	.066248	.069389	.072578	.075814	.079095	.085790	.092655	.099683	.106865
	0.00	.052739	.058470	.064407	.067451	.070544	.073685	.076874	.080110	.083391	.090086	.096952	.103980	.111162
	-.10	.057036	.062766	.068703	.071747	.074840	.077982	.081171	.084406	.087687	.094382	.101248	.108276	.115458
	-.20	.061332	.067063	.073000	.076043	.079136	.082278	.085467	.088702	.091983	.098679	.105544	.112572	.119754
	-.30	.065628	.071359	.077296	.080340	.083433	.086575	.089763	.092999	.096280	.102975	.109840	.116868	.124050
	-.40	.069924	.075655	.081592	.084636	.087729	.090870	.094059	.097295	.100576	.107271	.114137	.121165	.128347
20	.40	.034946	.041852	.049020	.052698	.056435	.060229	.064078	.067980	.071933	.079981	.088205	.096588	.105113
	.30	.039242	.046148	.053316	.056994	.060731	.064525	.068374	.072276	.076229	.084277	.092502	.100885	.109409
	.20	.043538	.050444	.057613	.061290	.065027	.068821	.072671	.076573	.080525	.088574	.096798	.105181	.113706
	.10	.047835	.054741	.061909	.065587	.069323	.073118	.076967	.080869	.084822	.092870	.101094	.109477	.118002
	0.00	.052131	.059037	.066205	.069883	.073620	.077414	.081263	.085165	.089118	.097166	.105390	.113773	.122298
	-.10	.056427	.063333	.070502	.074179	.077916	.081711	.085559	.089461	.093414	.101462	.109687	.118070	.126594
	-.20	.060724	.067630	.074798	.078475	.082212	.086006	.089856	.093758	.097710	.105759	.113983	.122366	.130891
	-.30	.065020	.071926	.079094	.082772	.086509	.090303	.094152	.098054	.102007	.110055	.118279	.126662	.135187
	-.40	.069316	.076222	.083390	.087068	.090805	.094599	.098448	.102350	.106303	.114351	.122576	.130959	.139483
25	.40	.034596	.042173	.050018	.054032	.058102	.062225	.066397	.070615	.074876	.083512	.092282	.101162	.110132
	.30	.038892	.046469	.054314	.058328	.062398	.066521	.070694	.074912	.079172	.087809	.096578	.105458	.114429
	.20	.043188	.050765	.058610	.062624	.066695	.070817	.074990	.079208	.083469	.092105	.100874	.109754	.118725
	.10	.047484	.055062	.062907	.066921	.070991	.075114	.079286	.083504	.087765	.096401	.105171	.114051	.123021
	0.00	.051781	.059358	.067203	.071217	.075287	.079410	.083582	.087800	.092061	.100698	.109467	.118347	.127317
	-.10	.056077	.063654	.071499	.075513	.079583	.083706	.087879	.092097	.096357	.104994	.113763	.122643	.131614
	-.20	.060373	.067951	.075795	.079809	.083880	.088003	.092175	.096393	.100654	.109290	.118059	.126939	.135910
	-.30	.064669	.072247	.080092	.084106	.088176	.092299	.096471	.100689	.104950	.113586	.122356	.131236	.140206
	-.40	.068966	.076543	.084388	.088402	.092472	.096595	.100767	.104986	.109246	.117883	.126652	.135532	.144502
30	.40	.034373	.042372	.050622	.054828	.059084	.063383	.067722	.072097	.076503	.085397	.094378	.103424	.112517
	.30	.038670	.046668	.054918	.059125	.063380	.067679	.072018	.076393	.080799	.089693	.098674	.107720	.116813
	.20	.042966	.050965	.059214	.063421	.067676	.071976	.076315	.080689	.085096	.093989	.102971	.112017	.121109
	.10	.047262	.055261	.063510	.067717	.071973	.076272	.080611	.084985	.089392	.098286	.107267	.116313	.125406
	0.00	.051559	.059557	.067807	.072014	.076269	.080568	.084907	.089282	.093688	.102582	.111563	.120609	.129702
	-.10	.055855	.063854	.072103	.076310	.080565	.084864	.089203	.093578	.097984	.106878	.115859	.124905	.133998
	-.20	.060151	.068150	.076399	.080606	.084861	.089161	.093500	.097874	.102281	.111175	.120156	.129202	.138294
	-.30	.064447	.072446	.080696	.084902	.089158	.093457	.097796	.102170	.106577	.115471	.124452	.133498	.142591
	-.40	.068744	.076742	.084992	.089199	.093454	.097753	.102092	.106467	.110873	.119767	.128748	.137794	.146887
40	.40	.034120	.042591	.051260	.055653	.060076	.064525	.068996	.073485	.077989	.087026	.096091	.105169	.114250
	.30	.038416	.046888	.055557	.059949	.064372	.068822	.073293	.077782	.082285	.091323	.100387	.109465	.118546
	.20	.042712	.051184	.059853	.064245	.068668	.073118	.077589	.082078	.086581	.095619	.104684	.113761	.122843
	.10	.047008	.055480	.064149	.068541	.072965	.077414	.081885	.086374	.090877	.099915	.108980	.118057	.127139
	0.00	.051305	.059777	.068445	.072838	.077261	.081710	.086182	.090670	.095174	.104211	.113276	.122354	.131435
	-.10	.055601	.064073	.072742	.077134	.081557	.086007	.090478	.094967	.099470	.108508	.117572	.126650	.135732
	-.20	.059897	.068369	.077038	.081430	.085853	.090303	.094774	.099263	.103766	.112804	.121869	.130946	.140028
	-.30	.064193	.072665	.081334	.085726	.090150	.094599	.099070	.103559	.108062	.117100	.126165	.135243	.144324
	-.40	.068490	.076962	.085630	.090023	.094446	.098895	.103367	.107856	.112359	.121397	.130461	.139539	.148620

15.0 YEAR HOLDING PERIOD
.080 EQUITY YIELD RATE
.600 LOAN RATIO

INTEREST RATE

TERM YEARS	APPR DEP	5.0	6.0	7.0	7.5	8.0	8.5	9.0	9.5	10.0	11.0	12.0	13.0	14.0
15	.40	.052108	.055928	.059886	.061915	.063977	.066072	.068198	.070355	.072542	.077005	.081583	.086268	.091056
	.30	.055791	.059611	.063569	.065598	.067660	.069755	.071881	.074038	.076225	.080668	.085266	.089951	.094739
	.20	.059474	.063294	.067252	.069281	.071343	.073438	.075564	.077721	.079908	.084371	.088948	.093634	.098422
	.10	.063156	.066977	.070935	.072964	.075026	.077121	.079247	.081403	.083591	.088054	.092631	.097317	.102105
	0.00	.066839	.070660	.074618	.076647	.078709	.080804	.082929	.085086	.087274	.091737	.096314	.101000	.105788
	-.10	.070522	.074343	.078301	.080330	.082392	.084486	.086612	.088769	.090957	.095420	.099997	.104683	.109471
	-.20	.074205	.078026	.081984	.084013	.086075	.088169	.090295	.092452	.094640	.099103	.103680	.108366	.113154
	-.30	.077888	.081709	.085667	.087696	.089758	.091852	.093978	.096135	.098323	.102786	.107363	.112049	.116837
	-.40	.081571	.085392	.089350	.091379	.093441	.095535	.097661	.099818	.102006	.106469	.111046	.115732	.120519
20	.40	.050415	.054942	.059644	.062057	.064510	.067001	.069529	.072092	.074689	.079979	.085387	.090902	.096514
	.30	.054098	.058625	.063327	.065740	.068193	.070684	.073211	.075775	.078372	.083662	.089070	.094585	.100197
	.20	.057781	.062308	.067010	.069423	.071876	.074367	.076894	.079458	.082055	.087344	.092753	.098268	.103880
	.10	.061464	.065991	.070693	.073106	.075559	.078050	.080577	.083140	.085737	.091027	.096436	.101951	.107562
	0.00	.065147	.069674	.074376	.076789	.079242	.081733	.084260	.086823	.089420	.094710	.100119	.105634	.111245
	-.10	.068830	.073357	.078059	.080472	.082925	.085416	.087943	.090506	.093103	.098393	.103802	.109317	.114928
	-.20	.072513	.077040	.081742	.084155	.086608	.089099	.091626	.094189	.096786	.102076	.107485	.113000	.118611
	-.30	.076196	.080723	.085425	.087838	.090291	.092781	.095309	.097872	.100469	.105759	.111168	.116683	.122294
	-.40	.079879	.084406	.089108	.091521	.093974	.096464	.098992	.101555	.104152	.109442	.114851	.120366	.125977
25	.40	.049440	.053384	.059510	.062135	.064799	.067498	.070232	.072997	.075792	.081461	.087225	.093066	.098973
	.30	.053123	.057067	.063193	.065818	.068481	.071181	.073915	.076680	.079475	.085144	.090908	.096749	.102656
	.20	.056806	.060750	.066876	.069501	.072164	.074864	.077598	.080363	.083158	.088827	.094591	.100432	.106339
	.10	.060489	.064433	.070559	.073184	.075847	.078547	.081281	.084046	.086841	.092510	.098273	.104115	.110022
	0.00	.064172	.068116	.074242	.076867	.079530	.082230	.084964	.087729	.090524	.096193	.101956	.107798	.113705
	-.10	.067855	.071799	.077925	.080550	.083213	.085913	.088647	.091412	.094207	.099876	.105639	.111481	.117388
	-.20	.071538	.075482	.081608	.084233	.086896	.089596	.092330	.095095	.097890	.103559	.109322	.115164	.121071
	-.30	.075221	.079165	.085291	.087916	.090579	.093279	.096012	.098778	.101573	.107242	.113005	.118847	.124754
	-.40	.078904	.082848	.088974	.091599	.094262	.096962	.099695	.102461	.105255	.110925	.116688	.122530	.128437
30	.40	.048822	.054038	.059429	.062181	.064968	.067787	.070634	.073506	.076402	.082253	.088170	.094137	.100142
	.30	.052505	.057721	.063112	.065864	.068651	.071470	.074316	.077189	.080085	.085936	.091853	.097820	.103825
	.20	.056188	.061404	.066795	.069547	.072334	.075153	.077999	.080872	.083768	.089619	.095535	.101503	.107508
	.10	.059871	.065087	.070478	.073230	.076017	.078836	.081682	.084555	.087450	.093302	.099218	.105186	.111191
	0.00	.063554	.068770	.074161	.076913	.079700	.082519	.085365	.088238	.091133	.096985	.102901	.108869	.114874
	-.10	.067237	.072453	.077843	.080596	.083383	.086202	.089048	.091921	.094816	.100668	.106584	.112552	.118557
	-.20	.070920	.076136	.081526	.084279	.087066	.089885	.092731	.095604	.098499	.104351	.110267	.116235	.122240
	-.30	.074603	.079819	.085209	.087962	.090749	.093567	.096414	.099287	.102182	.108034	.113950	.119918	.125923
	-.40	.078286	.083502	.088892	.091645	.094432	.097250	.100097	.102970	.105865	.111716	.117633	.123600	.129606
40	.40	.048116	.053657	.059343	.062230	.065140	.068071	.071020	.073983	.076958	.082937	.088942	.094962	.100991
	.30	.051799	.057340	.063026	.065913	.068823	.071754	.074703	.077666	.080641	.086620	.092625	.098645	.104674
	.20	.055482	.061023	.066709	.069595	.072506	.075437	.078386	.081349	.084324	.090303	.096308	.102328	.108357
	.10	.059165	.064705	.070392	.073278	.076189	.079120	.082069	.085032	.088007	.093986	.099991	.106011	.112040
	0.00	.062848	.068388	.074075	.076961	.079872	.082803	.085752	.088715	.091690	.097669	.103674	.109694	.115723
	-.10	.066531	.072071	.077758	.080644	.083555	.086486	.089435	.092398	.095373	.101352	.107357	.113377	.119406
	-.20	.070214	.075754	.081441	.084327	.087238	.090169	.093118	.096081	.099056	.105035	.111040	.117060	.123089
	-.30	.073897	.079437	.085124	.088010	.090921	.093852	.096801	.099764	.102739	.108718	.114723	.120743	.126772
	-.40	.077579	.083120	.088806	.091693	.094604	.097535	.100484	.103447	.106422	.112401	.118405	.124426	.130455

15.0 YEAR HOLDING PERIOD
.080 EQUITY YIELD RATE
.667 LOAN RATIO

INTEREST RATE

TERM YEARS	APPR DEP	5.0	6.0	7.0	7.5	8.0	8.5	9.0	9.5	10.0	11.0	12.0	13.0	14.0
15	.40	.050645	.054890	.059288	.061543	.063834	.066161	.068523	.070920	.073350	.078310	.083395	.088601	.093921
	.30	.054328	.058973	.062971	.065226	.067517	.069844	.072206	.074603	.077033	.081993	.087078	.092284	.097604
	.20	.058011	.062256	.066654	.068909	.071200	.073527	.075889	.078286	.080716	.085676	.090761	.095967	.101287
	.10	.061694	.065939	.070337	.072592	.074883	.077210	.079572	.081969	.084399	.089359	.094444	.099650	.104970
	0.00	.065377	.069622	.074020	.076275	.078566	.080893	.083255	.085652	.088082	.093041	.098127	.103333	.108653
	-.10	.069060	.073305	.077703	.079958	.082249	.084576	.086938	.089335	.091765	.096724	.101810	.107016	.112336
	-.20	.072743	.076988	.081386	.083641	.085932	.088259	.090621	.093018	.095448	.100407	.105493	.110699	.116019
	-.30	.076426	.080671	.085069	.087323	.089615	.091942	.094304	.096701	.099131	.104090	.109176	.114382	.119702
	-.40	.080109	.084354	.088752	.091006	.093298	.095625	.097987	.100383	.102814	.107773	.112859	.118065	.123385
20	.40	.048765	.053795	.059019	.061700	.064426	.067193	.070002	.072850	.075735	.081613	.087622	.093751	.099985
	.30	.052448	.057478	.062702	.065383	.068109	.070876	.073685	.076533	.079418	.085296	.091305	.097434	.103668
	.20	.056131	.061161	.066385	.069066	.071792	.074559	.077368	.080216	.083101	.088979	.094988	.101116	.107351
	.10	.059814	.064844	.070068	.072749	.075474	.078242	.081051	.083899	.086784	.092662	.098671	.104799	.111034
	0.00	.063497	.068527	.073751	.076432	.079157	.081925	.084734	.087582	.090467	.096345	.102354	.108482	.114717
	-.10	.067180	.072211	.077434	.080115	.082840	.085608	.088417	.091265	.094150	.100028	.106037	.112165	.118400
	-.20	.070862	.075893	.081117	.083798	.086523	.089291	.092100	.094948	.097833	.103711	.109720	.115848	.122083
	-.30	.074545	.079576	.084800	.087481	.089206	.092974	.095783	.098630	.101516	.107394	.113403	.119531	.125766
	-.40	.078228	.083259	.088483	.091164	.093889	.096657	.099466	.102313	.105199	.111077	.117086	.123214	.129449
25	.40	.047682	.053175	.058870	.061787	.064746	.067746	.070783	.073856	.076961	.083261	.089664	.096155	.102719
	.30	.051365	.056858	.062553	.065470	.068429	.071429	.074466	.077539	.080644	.086944	.093347	.099838	.106401
	.20	.055047	.060541	.066236	.069153	.072112	.075112	.078149	.081222	.084327	.090627	.097030	.103521	.110084
	.10	.058730	.064224	.069919	.072836	.075795	.078795	.081832	.084905	.088010	.094310	.100713	.107204	.113767
	0.00	.062413	.067907	.073602	.076519	.079478	.082478	.085515	.088588	.091693	.097993	.104396	.110887	.117450
	-.10	.066096	.071590	.077285	.080202	.083161	.086161	.089198	.092271	.095376	.101676	.108079	.114570	.121133
	-.20	.069779	.075273	.080968	.083885	.086844	.089844	.092881	.095954	.099059	.105359	.111762	.118253	.124816
	-.30	.073462	.078956	.084651	.087568	.090527	.093527	.096564	.099637	.102742	.109042	.115445	.121936	.128499
	-.40	.077145	.082639	.088334	.091250	.094210	.097210	.100247	.103320	.106425	.112724	.119128	.125619	.132182
30	.40	.046995	.052790	.058780	.061838	.064935	.068067	.071230	.074421	.077639	.084140	.090714	.097345	.104017
	.30	.050678	.056473	.062463	.065521	.068618	.071750	.074913	.078104	.081322	.087823	.094397	.101028	.107700
	.20	.054361	.060156	.066146	.069204	.072301	.075433	.078596	.081787	.085005	.091506	.098080	.104711	.111383
	.10	.058044	.063839	.069829	.072887	.075984	.079115	.082279	.085470	.088688	.095189	.101763	.108393	.115066
	0.00	.061727	.067522	.073512	.076570	.079667	.082798	.085962	.089153	.092371	.098872	.105446	.112076	.118749
	-.10	.065410	.071205	.077195	.080253	.083350	.086481	.089644	.092836	.096054	.102555	.109129	.115759	.122432
	-.20	.069093	.074888	.080878	.083936	.087033	.090164	.093327	.096519	.099736	.106238	.112812	.119442	.126115
	-.30	.072776	.078571	.084561	.087619	.090716	.093847	.097010	.100202	.103419	.109921	.116495	.123125	.129798
	-.40	.076459	.082254	.088243	.091302	.094399	.097530	.100693	.103885	.107102	.113604	.120178	.126808	.133481
40	.40	.046210	.052366	.058684	.061892	.065126	.068383	.071659	.074952	.078257	.084900	.091572	.098262	.104961
	.30	.049893	.056049	.062367	.065575	.068809	.072066	.075342	.078634	.081940	.088583	.095255	.101945	.108644
	.20	.053576	.059732	.066050	.069258	.072492	.075749	.079025	.082317	.085623	.092266	.098938	.105628	.112327
	.10	.057259	.063415	.069733	.072941	.076175	.079432	.082708	.086000	.089306	.095949	.102621	.109311	.116010
	0.00	.060942	.067098	.073416	.076624	.079858	.083115	.086391	.089683	.092989	.099632	.106304	.112994	.119693
	-.10	.064625	.070781	.077099	.080307	.083541	.086798	.090074	.093366	.096672	.103315	.109987	.116677	.123376
	-.20	.068308	.074464	.080782	.083990	.087224	.090481	.093757	.097049	.100355	.106998	.113670	.120360	.127059
	-.30	.071991	.078147	.084465	.087673	.090907	.094164	.097440	.100732	.104038	.110681	.117353	.124043	.130742
	-.40	.075674	.081830	.088148	.091356	.094590	.097847	.101123	.104415	.107721	.114364	.121036	.127726	.134425

15.0 YEAR HOLDING PERIOD
.080 EQUITY YIELD RATE
.700 LOAN RATIO

INTEREST RATE

TERM YEARS	APPR DEP	5.0	6.0	7.0	7.5	8.0	8.5	9.0	9.5	10.0	11.0	12.0	13.0	14.0
15	.40	.049914	.054371	.058989	.061357	.063762	.066206	.068686	.071202	.073754	.078962	.084302	.089768	.095354
	.30	.053597	.058054	.062672	.065039	.067445	.069889	.072369	.074885	.077437	.082645	.087985	.093451	.099037
	.20	.057280	.061737	.066355	.068722	.071128	.073572	.076052	.078568	.081120	.086328	.091668	.097134	.102720
	.10	.060963	.065420	.070038	.072405	.074811	.077254	.079735	.082251	.084803	.090011	.095350	.100817	.106403
	0.00	.064646	.069103	.073721	.076088	.078494	.080937	.083418	.085934	.088486	.093693	.099033	.104500	.110086
	-.10	.068329	.072786	.077404	.079771	.082177	.084620	.087101	.089617	.092169	.097376	.102716	.108183	.113769
	-.20	.072012	.076469	.081087	.083454	.085860	.088303	.090784	.093300	.095852	.101059	.106399	.111866	.117452
	-.30	.075695	.080152	.084770	.087137	.089543	.091986	.094467	.096983	.099535	.104742	.110082	.115549	.121134
	-.40	.079378	.083835	.088453	.090820	.093226	.095669	.098150	.100666	.103218	.108425	.113765	.119231	.124817
20	.40	.047940	.053221	.058707	.061522	.064383	.067290	.070239	.073229	.076259	.082430	.088740	.095175	.101721
	.30	.051623	.056904	.062390	.065205	.068066	.070973	.073922	.076912	.079942	.086113	.092423	.098858	.105404
	.20	.055306	.060587	.066073	.068888	.071749	.074655	.077604	.080595	.083625	.089796	.096106	.102540	.109087
	.10	.058989	.064270	.069756	.072571	.075432	.078338	.081287	.084278	.087308	.093479	.099789	.106223	.112770
	0.00	.062671	.067953	.073439	.076254	.079115	.082021	.084970	.087961	.090990	.097162	.103472	.109906	.116453
	-.10	.066354	.071636	.077122	.079937	.082798	.085704	.088653	.091644	.094673	.100845	.107155	.113589	.120136
	-.20	.070037	.075319	.080805	.083620	.086481	.089387	.092336	.095327	.098356	.104528	.110838	.117272	.123819
	-.30	.073720	.079002	.084487	.087303	.090164	.093070	.096019	.099010	.102039	.108211	.114521	.120955	.127502
	-.40	.077403	.082685	.088170	.090986	.093847	.096753	.099702	.102692	.105722	.111894	.118204	.124638	.131185
25	.40	.046802	.052570	.058550	.061613	.064720	.067870	.071059	.074285	.077546	.084160	.090884	.097699	.104591
	.30	.050485	.056253	.062233	.065296	.068403	.071553	.074742	.077968	.081229	.087843	.094567	.101382	.108274
	.20	.054168	.059936	.065916	.068979	.072086	.075236	.078425	.081651	.084912	.091526	.098250	.105065	.111957
	.10	.057851	.063619	.069599	.072662	.075769	.078919	.082108	.085334	.088595	.095209	.101933	.108748	.115640
	0.00	.061534	.067302	.073282	.076345	.079452	.082602	.085791	.089017	.092278	.098892	.105616	.112431	.119323
	-.10	.065217	.070985	.076965	.080028	.083135	.086285	.089474	.092700	.095961	.102575	.109299	.116114	.123006
	-.20	.068900	.074668	.080648	.083711	.086818	.089968	.093157	.096383	.099644	.106258	.112982	.119797	.126689
	-.30	.072583	.078351	.084331	.087393	.090501	.093651	.096840	.100066	.103326	.109941	.116665	.123480	.130372
	-.40	.076266	.082034	.088014	.091076	.094184	.097334	.100523	.103749	.107009	.113624	.120348	.127163	.134055
30	.40	.046081	.052167	.058455	.061667	.064919	.068207	.071528	.074879	.078257	.085084	.091986	.098948	.105954
	.30	.049764	.055850	.062138	.065350	.068601	.071889	.075211	.078562	.081940	.088767	.095669	.102631	.109637
	.20	.053447	.059533	.065821	.069033	.072284	.075572	.078894	.082245	.085623	.092450	.099352	.106314	.113320
	.10	.057130	.063215	.069504	.072716	.075967	.079255	.082577	.085928	.089306	.096132	.103035	.109997	.117003
	0.00	.060813	.066898	.073187	.076399	.079650	.082938	.086260	.089611	.092989	.099815	.106718	.113680	.120686
	-.10	.064496	.070581	.076870	.080082	.083333	.086621	.089943	.093294	.096672	.103498	.110401	.117363	.124369
	-.20	.068179	.074264	.080553	.083765	.087016	.090304	.093625	.096977	.100355	.107181	.114084	.121046	.128052
	-.30	.071862	.077947	.084236	.087448	.090699	.093987	.097308	.100660	.104038	.110864	.117767	.124729	.131735
	-.40	.075545	.081630	.087919	.091131	.094382	.097670	.100991	.104343	.107721	.114547	.121450	.128412	.135418
40	.40	.045257	.051721	.058355	.061723	.065119	.068539	.071979	.075436	.078907	.085882	.092887	.099911	.106945
	.30	.048940	.055404	.062038	.065406	.068802	.072222	.075662	.079119	.082590	.089565	.096570	.103594	.110628
	.20	.052623	.059087	.065721	.069089	.072485	.075905	.079345	.082802	.086273	.093248	.100253	.107277	.114311
	.10	.056306	.062770	.069404	.072772	.076168	.079587	.083027	.086484	.089956	.096931	.103936	.110960	.117994
	0.00	.059989	.066453	.073087	.076455	.079851	.083270	.086710	.090167	.093639	.100614	.107619	.114643	.121677
	-.10	.063672	.070136	.076770	.080138	.083534	.086953	.090393	.093850	.097322	.104297	.111302	.118326	.125360
	-.20	.067355	.073819	.080453	.083821	.087217	.090636	.094076	.097533	.101005	.107980	.114985	.122009	.129043
	-.30	.071038	.077502	.084136	.087504	.090900	.094319	.097759	.101216	.104687	.111663	.118668	.125692	.132726
	-.40	.074721	.081185	.087819	.091187	.094583	.098002	.101442	.104899	.108370	.115346	.122351	.129375	.136409

397

15.0 YEAR HOLDING PERIOD
.080 EQUITY YIELD RATE
.750 LOAN RATIO

INTEREST RATE

TERM YEARS	APPR DEP	5.0	6.0	7.0	7.5	8.0	8.5	9.0	9.5	10.0	11.0	12.0	13.0	14.0
15	.40	.048817	.053593	.058541	.061077	.063655	.066273	.068930	.071626	.074360	.079940	.085661	.091518	.097503
	.30	.052500	.057276	.062224	.064760	.067338	.069956	.072613	.075309	.078043	.083623	.089344	.095201	.101186
	.20	.056183	.060959	.065906	.068443	.071021	.073638	.076296	.078992	.081726	.087306	.093027	.098884	.104869
	.10	.059866	.064642	.069589	.072126	.074704	.077321	.079979	.082675	.085409	.090989	.096710	.102567	.108552
	0.00	.063549	.068325	.073272	.075809	.078387	.081004	.083662	.086358	.089092	.094672	.100393	.106250	.112235
	-.10	.067232	.072008	.076955	.079492	.082069	.084687	.087345	.090041	.092775	.098355	.104076	.109933	.115918
	-.20	.070915	.075691	.080638	.083175	.085752	.088370	.091028	.093724	.096458	.102037	.107759	.113616	.119600
	-.30	.074598	.079374	.084321	.086858	.089435	.092053	.094711	.097407	.100141	.105720	.111442	.117298	.123283
	-.40	.078281	.083057	.088004	.090541	.093118	.095736	.098394	.101090	.103824	.109403	.115125	.120981	.126966
20	.40	.046702	.052361	.058238	.061254	.064320	.067434	.070594	.073797	.077044	.083656	.090417	.097311	.104325
	.30	.050385	.056044	.061921	.064937	.068003	.071117	.074277	.077480	.080727	.087339	.094100	.100994	.108008
	.20	.054068	.059727	.065604	.068620	.071686	.074800	.077959	.081163	.084410	.091022	.097782	.104677	.111691
	.10	.057751	.063410	.069287	.072303	.075369	.078483	.081642	.084846	.088093	.094705	.101465	.108360	.115374
	0.00	.061434	.067093	.072970	.075986	.079052	.082166	.085325	.088529	.091776	.098388	.105148	.112043	.119057
	-.10	.065117	.070776	.076653	.079669	.082735	.085849	.089008	.092212	.095458	.102071	.108831	.115726	.122740
	-.20	.068800	.074459	.080336	.083352	.086418	.089532	.092691	.095895	.099141	.105754	.112514	.119408	.126423
	-.30	.072483	.078142	.084019	.087035	.090101	.093215	.096374	.099578	.102824	.109437	.116197	.123091	.130106
	-.40	.076166	.081825	.087702	.090718	.093784	.096898	.100057	.103261	.106507	.113120	.119880	.126774	.133789
25	.40	.045483	.051664	.058070	.061352	.064681	.068056	.071473	.074929	.078423	.085510	.092714	.100016	.107400
	.30	.049166	.055346	.061753	.065035	.068364	.071739	.075156	.078612	.082106	.089193	.096397	.103699	.111083
	.20	.052849	.059029	.065436	.068718	.072047	.075422	.078839	.082295	.085789	.092876	.100080	.107382	.114766
	.10	.056532	.062712	.069119	.072401	.075730	.079105	.082522	.085978	.089472	.096559	.103763	.111065	.118448
	0.00	.060215	.066395	.072802	.076084	.079413	.082788	.086205	.089661	.093155	.100242	.107446	.114748	.122131
	-.10	.063898	.070078	.076485	.079766	.083096	.086470	.089887	.093344	.096838	.103925	.111128	.118431	.125814
	-.20	.067581	.073761	.080168	.083449	.086779	.090153	.093570	.097027	.100520	.107608	.114811	.122114	.129497
	-.30	.071264	.077444	.083851	.087132	.090462	.093836	.097253	.100710	.104203	.111290	.118494	.125797	.133180
	-.40	.074947	.081127	.087534	.090815	.094145	.097519	.100936	.104393	.107886	.114973	.122177	.129480	.136863
30	.40	.044711	.051231	.057969	.061410	.064894	.068416	.071975	.075565	.079185	.086499	.093895	.101354	.108860
	.30	.048394	.054914	.061652	.065093	.068577	.072099	.075658	.079248	.082868	.090182	.097578	.105037	.112543
	.20	.052077	.058597	.065335	.068776	.072259	.075782	.079341	.082931	.086551	.093865	.101261	.108720	.116226
	.10	.055760	.062280	.069018	.072459	.075942	.079465	.083024	.086614	.090234	.097548	.104944	.112403	.119909
	0.00	.059443	.065963	.072701	.076142	.079625	.083148	.086707	.090297	.093917	.101231	.108627	.116086	.123592
	-.10	.063126	.069646	.076384	.079825	.083308	.086831	.090390	.093980	.097600	.104914	.112310	.119769	.127275
	-.20	.066809	.073329	.080067	.083508	.086991	.090514	.094073	.097663	.101283	.108597	.115993	.123452	.130958
	-.30	.070492	.077011	.083750	.087190	.090674	.094197	.097756	.101346	.104966	.112280	.119676	.127135	.134641
	-.40	.074175	.080694	.087432	.090873	.094357	.097880	.101438	.105029	.108649	.115963	.123359	.130818	.138324
40	.40	.043828	.050754	.057861	.061470	.065108	.068772	.072458	.076162	.079881	.087354	.094860	.102386	.109922
	.30	.047511	.054437	.061544	.065153	.068791	.072455	.076141	.079845	.083564	.091037	.098543	.106069	.113605
	.20	.051194	.058120	.065227	.068836	.072474	.076138	.079824	.083528	.087247	.094720	.102226	.109752	.117288
	.10	.054877	.061803	.068910	.072519	.076157	.079821	.083507	.087211	.090930	.098403	.105909	.113435	.120971
	0.00	.058560	.065486	.072593	.076202	.079840	.083504	.087190	.090894	.094613	.102086	.109592	.117118	.124654
	-.10	.062243	.069168	.076276	.079885	.083523	.087187	.090873	.094577	.098296	.105769	.113275	.120801	.128337
	-.20	.065925	.072851	.079959	.083568	.087206	.090870	.094556	.098260	.101979	.109452	.116958	.124484	.132020
	-.30	.069608	.076534	.083642	.087251	.090889	.094553	.098239	.101943	.105662	.113135	.120641	.128167	.135703
	-.40	.073291	.080217	.087325	.090934	.094572	.098236	.101922	.105626	.109345	.116818	.124324	.131850	.139386

15.0 YEAR HOLDING PERIOD
.080 EQUITY YIELD RATE
.800 LOAN RATIO

INTEREST RATE

TERM YEARS	APPR DEP	5.0	6.0	7.0	7.5	8.0	8.5	9.0	9.5	10.0	11.0	12.0	13.0	14.0
15	.40	.047721	.052815	.058092	.060798	.063547	.066340	.069174	.072050	.074967	.080918	.087021	.093268	.099652
	.30	.051404	.056498	.061775	.064481	.067230	.070022	.072857	.075733	.078650	.084601	.090704	.096951	.103335
	.20	.055087	.060181	.065458	.068164	.070913	.073705	.076540	.079416	.082333	.088284	.094387	.100634	.107018
	.10	.058770	.063864	.069141	.071847	.074596	.077388	.080223	.083099	.086016	.091967	.098070	.104317	.110701
	0.00	.062453	.067547	.072824	.075530	.078279	.081071	.083906	.086782	.089698	.095650	.101752	.108000	.114384
	-.10	.066136	.071230	.076507	.079213	.081962	.084754	.087589	.090465	.093381	.099333	.105435	.111683	.118066
	-.20	.069818	.074913	.080190	.082895	.085645	.088437	.091272	.094148	.097064	.103016	.109118	.115366	.121749
	-.30	.073501	.078595	.083550	.086578	.089328	.092120	.094955	.097831	.100747	.106699	.112801	.119048	.125432
	-.40	.077184	.082278	.087556	.090261	.093011	.095803	.098638	.101514	.104430	.110381	.116484	.122731	.129115
20	.40	.045464	.051501	.057769	.060987	.064257	.067578	.070949	.074366	.077829	.084882	.092093	.099447	.106929
	.30	.049147	.055183	.061452	.064670	.067940	.071261	.074632	.078049	.081512	.088565	.095776	.103130	.110612
	.20	.052830	.058866	.065135	.068353	.071623	.074944	.078315	.081732	.085195	.092248	.099459	.106813	.114295
	.10	.056513	.062549	.068818	.072036	.075306	.078627	.081997	.085415	.088878	.095931	.103142	.110496	.117978
	0.00	.060196	.066232	.072501	.075719	.078989	.082310	.085680	.089098	.092561	.099614	.106825	.114179	.121661
	-.10	.063879	.069915	.076184	.079402	.082672	.085993	.089363	.092781	.096244	.103297	.110508	.117862	.125344
	-.20	.067562	.073598	.079867	.083085	.086355	.089676	.093046	.096464	.099926	.106980	.114191	.121545	.129026
	-.30	.071245	.077281	.083550	.086768	.090038	.093359	.096729	.100147	.103609	.110663	.117874	.125228	.132709
	-.40	.074928	.080964	.087233	.090451	.093721	.097042	.100412	.103830	.107292	.114346	.121557	.128911	.136392
25	.40	.044164	.050757	.057591	.061091	.064642	.068242	.071886	.075573	.079300	.086859	.094543	.102332	.110208
	.30	.047847	.054439	.061274	.064774	.068325	.071925	.075569	.079256	.082983	.090542	.098226	.106015	.113891
	.20	.051530	.058122	.064956	.068457	.072008	.075607	.079252	.082939	.086666	.094225	.101909	.109698	.117574
	.10	.055213	.061805	.068639	.072139	.075691	.079290	.082935	.086618	.090349	.097908	.105592	.113381	.121257
	0.00	.058896	.065488	.072322	.075822	.078989	.082973	.086618	.090301	.094032	.101591	.109275	.117064	.124940
	-.10	.062579	.069171	.076005	.079505	.083057	.086656	.090301	.093984	.097715	.105274	.112958	.120747	.128623
	-.20	.066262	.072854	.079688	.083188	.086740	.090339	.093984	.097671	.101397	.108957	.116641	.124430	.132306
	-.30	.069945	.076537	.083371	.086871	.090423	.094022	.097667	.101354	.105080	.112640	.120324	.128113	.135989
	-.40	.073628	.080220	.087054	.090554	.094106	.097705	.101350	.105037	.108763	.116323	.124007	.131796	.139672
30	.40	.043340	.050295	.057482	.061153	.064869	.068626	.072422	.076252	.080113	.087914	.095803	.103760	.111767
	.30	.047023	.053978	.061165	.064836	.068552	.072309	.076105	.079935	.083796	.091597	.099486	.107443	.115449
	.20	.050706	.057661	.064848	.068518	.072234	.075992	.079788	.083618	.087479	.095280	.103169	.111126	.119132
	.10	.054389	.061344	.068531	.072201	.075917	.079675	.083471	.087301	.091162	.098963	.106852	.114809	.122815
	0.00	.058072	.065027	.072214	.075884	.079600	.083358	.087154	.090984	.094845	.102646	.110535	.118492	.126498
	-.10	.061755	.068710	.075897	.079567	.083283	.087041	.090837	.094667	.098528	.106329	.114218	.122174	.130181
	-.20	.065438	.072393	.079580	.083250	.086966	.090724	.094520	.098350	.102210	.110012	.117901	.125857	.133864
	-.30	.069121	.076076	.083263	.086933	.090649	.094407	.098203	.102033	.105893	.113695	.121584	.129540	.137547
	-.40	.072804	.079759	.086946	.090616	.094332	.098090	.101886	.105716	.109576	.117378	.125267	.133223	.141230
40	.40	.042398	.049786	.057368	.061217	.065098	.069006	.072937	.076888	.080855	.088827	.096633	.104860	.112899
	.30	.046081	.053469	.061051	.064900	.068781	.072689	.076620	.080571	.084538	.092510	.100516	.108543	.116582
	.20	.049764	.057152	.064734	.068583	.072463	.076372	.080303	.084254	.088221	.096193	.104199	.112226	.120265
	.10	.053447	.060835	.068417	.072266	.076146	.080055	.083986	.087937	.091904	.099876	.107882	.115909	.123948
	0.00	.057130	.064518	.072099	.075948	.079829	.083738	.087669	.091620	.095587	.103559	.111565	.119592	.127631
	-.10	.060813	.068201	.075782	.079631	.083512	.087421	.091352	.095303	.099270	.107241	.115248	.123275	.131314
	-.20	.064496	.071884	.079465	.083314	.087195	.091104	.095035	.098986	.102953	.110924	.118931	.126958	.134997
	-.30	.068179	.075567	.083148	.086997	.090878	.094787	.098718	.102669	.106636	.114607	.122614	.130641	.138680
	-.40	.071862	.079250	.086831	.090680	.094561	.098469	.102401	.106352	.110319	.118290	.126297	.134324	.142363

15.0 YEAR HOLDING PERIOD
.080 EQUITY YIELD RATE
.900 LOAN RATIO

INTEREST RATE

TERM YEARS	APPR DEP	5.0	6.0	7.0	7.5	8.0	8.5	9.0	9.5	10.0	11.0	12.0	13.0	14.0
15	.40	.045527	.051258	.057195	.060239	.063332	.066473	.069662	.072898	.076179	.082874	.089740	.096768	.103950
	.30	.049210	.054941	.060878	.063922	.067015	.070156	.073345	.076581	.079862	.086557	.093423	.100451	.107633
	.20	.052893	.058624	.064561	.067605	.070698	.073839	.077028	.080264	.083545	.090240	.097106	.104134	.111316
	.10	.056576	.062307	.068244	.071288	.074381	.077522	.080711	.083947	.087228	.093923	.100789	.107817	.114999
	0.00	.060259	.065990	.071927	.074971	.078064	.081205	.084394	.087630	.090911	.097606	.104472	.111500	.118681
	-.10	.063942	.069673	.075610	.078654	.081747	.084888	.088077	.091313	.094594	.101289	.108155	.115183	.122364
	-.20	.067625	.073356	.079293	.082337	.085430	.088571	.091760	.094996	.098277	.104972	.111837	.118865	.126047
	-.30	.071308	.077039	.082976	.086020	.089113	.092254	.095443	.098679	.101960	.108655	.115520	.122548	.129730
	-.40	.074991	.080722	.086659	.089703	.092796	.095937	.099126	.102361	.105643	.112338	.119203	.126231	.133413
20	.40	.042989	.049780	.056832	.060452	.064131	.067867	.071659	.075503	.079399	.087334	.095446	.103719	.112136
	.30	.046672	.053462	.060515	.064135	.067814	.071550	.075342	.079186	.083082	.091017	.099129	.107402	.115819
	.20	.050355	.057145	.064198	.067818	.071497	.075233	.079025	.082869	.086765	.094700	.102812	.111085	.119502
	.10	.054038	.060828	.067881	.071501	.075180	.078916	.082708	.086552	.090448	.098383	.106495	.114768	.123185
	0.00	.057720	.064511	.071564	.075184	.078863	.082599	.086390	.090235	.094131	.102066	.110178	.118451	.126868
	-.10	.061403	.068194	.075247	.078866	.082546	.086282	.090073	.093918	.097814	.105749	.113861	.122134	.130551
	-.20	.065086	.071877	.078930	.082549	.086228	.089965	.093756	.097601	.101497	.109432	.117544	.125817	.134234
	-.30	.068769	.075560	.082613	.086232	.089911	.093648	.097439	.101284	.105179	.113114	.121227	.129500	.137917
	-.40	.072452	.079243	.086296	.089915	.093594	.097331	.101122	.104967	.108862	.116797	.124910	.133183	.141600
25	.40	.041526	.048943	.056631	.060568	.064564	.068613	.072714	.076862	.081054	.089558	.098203	.106965	.115826
	.30	.045209	.052626	.060314	.064251	.068247	.072296	.076397	.080544	.084737	.093241	.101886	.110648	.119509
	.20	.048892	.056308	.063997	.067934	.071930	.075979	.080080	.084227	.088420	.096924	.105569	.114331	.123192
	.10	.052575	.059991	.067680	.071617	.075613	.079662	.083762	.087910	.092103	.100607	.109252	.118014	.126875
	0.00	.056258	.063674	.071363	.075300	.079296	.083345	.087445	.091593	.095785	.104290	.112935	.121697	.130558
	-.10	.059941	.067357	.075046	.078983	.082978	.087028	.091128	.095276	.099468	.107973	.116618	.125380	.134241
	-.20	.063624	.071040	.078729	.082666	.086661	.090711	.094811	.098959	.103151	.111656	.120301	.129063	.137924
	-.30	.067307	.074723	.082412	.086349	.090344	.094394	.098494	.102642	.106834	.115339	.123983	.132746	.141607
	-.40	.070990	.078406	.086094	.090032	.094027	.098077	.102177	.106325	.110517	.119022	.127666	.136429	.145290
30	.40	.040600	.048423	.056509	.060638	.064819	.069046	.073316	.077625	.081968	.090745	.099620	.108571	.117579
	.30	.044282	.052106	.060192	.064321	.068502	.072729	.076999	.081308	.085651	.094428	.103303	.112254	.121262
	.20	.047965	.055789	.063875	.068004	.072185	.076412	.080682	.084991	.089334	.098111	.106986	.115937	.124945
	.10	.051648	.059472	.067558	.071687	.075867	.080095	.084365	.088674	.093017	.101794	.110669	.119620	.128628
	0.00	.055331	.063155	.071241	.075370	.079550	.083778	.088048	.092357	.096700	.105477	.114352	.123303	.132311
	-.10	.059014	.066838	.074924	.079053	.083233	.087461	.091731	.096040	.100383	.109160	.118035	.126986	.135994
	-.20	.062697	.070521	.078607	.082736	.086916	.091144	.095414	.099723	.104066	.112843	.121718	.130669	.139677
	-.30	.066380	.074204	.082290	.086419	.090599	.094827	.099097	.103406	.107749	.116526	.125401	.134352	.143359
	-.40	.070063	.077887	.085973	.090102	.094282	.098510	.102780	.107089	.111432	.120209	.129084	.138035	.147042
40	.40	.039540	.047851	.056380	.060779	.065076	.069473	.073896	.078341	.082804	.091772	.100779	.109809	.118853
	.30	.043223	.051534	.060063	.064393	.068759	.073156	.077579	.082024	.086487	.095454	.104462	.113492	.122536
	.20	.046906	.055217	.063746	.068076	.072442	.076839	.081262	.085707	.090169	.099137	.108145	.117175	.126219
	.10	.050589	.058900	.067429	.071759	.076125	.080522	.084945	.089389	.093852	.102820	.111828	.120858	.129902
	0.00	.054271	.062583	.071112	.075442	.079808	.084205	.088628	.093072	.097535	.106503	.115510	.124541	.133585
	-.10	.057954	.066266	.074795	.079125	.083491	.087888	.092311	.096755	.101218	.110186	.119193	.128224	.137268
	-.20	.061637	.069949	.078478	.082808	.087174	.091571	.095994	.100438	.104901	.113869	.122876	.131907	.140951
	-.30	.065320	.073632	.082161	.086491	.090857	.095254	.099677	.104121	.108584	.117552	.126559	.135590	.144634
	-.40	.069003	.077314	.085844	.090174	.094540	.098937	.103360	.107804	.112267	.121235	.130242	.139273	.148317

15.0 YEAR HOLDING PERIOD
.100 EQUITY YIELD RATE
.600 LOAN RATIO

INTEREST RATE

TERM YEARS	APPR DEP	5.0	6.0	7.0	7.5	8.0	8.5	9.0	9.5	10.0	11.0	12.0	13.0	14.0
15	.40	.065463	.069284	.073242	.075271	.077333	.079427	.081553	.083710	.085898	.090361	.094938	.099624	.104412
	.30	.068611	.072431	.076389	.078418	.080481	.082575	.084701	.086858	.089045	.093509	.098086	.102771	.107559
	.20	.071758	.075579	.079537	.081566	.083628	.085722	.087848	.090005	.092193	.096656	.101233	.105918	.110706
	.10	.074905	.078726	.082684	.084713	.086775	.088870	.090996	.093153	.095340	.099803	.104380	.109066	.113854
	0.00	.078053	.081873	.085831	.087861	.089923	.092017	.094143	.096300	.098487	.102951	.107528	.112213	.117001
	-.10	.081200	.085021	.088979	.091008	.093070	.095164	.097290	.099447	.101635	.106098	.110675	.115361	.120148
	-.20	.084348	.088168	.092126	.094155	.096217	.098312	.100438	.102595	.104782	.109245	.113823	.118508	.123296
	-.30	.087495	.091316	.095274	.097303	.099365	.101459	.103585	.105742	.107929	.112393	.116970	.121656	.126443
	-.40	.090642	.094463	.098421	.100450	.102512	.104606	.106732	.108889	.111077	.115540	.120117	.124803	.129591
20	.40	.062647	.067107	.071742	.074121	.076540	.078997	.081491	.084021	.086585	.091809	.097152	.102603	.108152
	.30	.065795	.070255	.074889	.077268	.079687	.082145	.084639	.087169	.089732	.094956	.100299	.105751	.111299
	.20	.068942	.073402	.078036	.080416	.082835	.085292	.087786	.090316	.092880	.098104	.103447	.108898	.114447
	.10	.072089	.076549	.081184	.083563	.085982	.088439	.090934	.093463	.096027	.101251	.106594	.112045	.117594
	0.00	.075237	.079697	.084331	.086711	.089130	.091587	.094081	.096611	.099174	.104398	.109742	.115193	.120742
	-.10	.078384	.082844	.087479	.089858	.092277	.094734	.097228	.099758	.102322	.107546	.112889	.118340	.123889
	-.20	.081531	.085992	.090626	.093005	.095424	.097882	.100376	.102905	.105469	.110693	.116036	.121488	.127036
	-.30	.084679	.089139	.093773	.096153	.098572	.101029	.103523	.106053	.108616	.113840	.119184	.124635	.130184
	-.40	.087826	.092286	.096921	.099300	.101719	.104176	.106670	.109200	.111764	.116988	.122331	.127782	.133331
25	.40	.061025	.065875	.070910	.073490	.076110	.078767	.081459	.084183	.086938	.092531	.098221	.103995	.109838
	.30	.064172	.069023	.074057	.076638	.079257	.081914	.084606	.087330	.090085	.095678	.101369	.107142	.112985
	.20	.067320	.072170	.077204	.079785	.082405	.085062	.087753	.090478	.093233	.098826	.104516	.110290	.116133
	.10	.070467	.075317	.080352	.082932	.085552	.088209	.090901	.093625	.096380	.101973	.107663	.113437	.119280
	0.00	.073614	.078465	.083499	.086080	.088700	.091357	.094048	.096773	.099527	.105120	.110811	.116584	.122427
	-.10	.076762	.081612	.086647	.089227	.091847	.094504	.097196	.099920	.102675	.108268	.113958	.119732	.125575
	-.20	.079909	.084760	.089794	.092374	.094994	.097651	.100343	.103067	.105822	.111415	.117106	.122879	.128722
	-.30	.083057	.087907	.092941	.095522	.098142	.100799	.103490	.106215	.108970	.114562	.120253	.126026	.131869
	-.40	.086204	.091054	.096089	.098669	.101289	.103946	.106638	.109362	.112117	.117710	.123400	.129174	.135017
30	.40	.059997	.065111	.070406	.073113	.075857	.078633	.081440	.084274	.087133	.092916	.098771	.104683	.110639
	.30	.063144	.068258	.073553	.076261	.079004	.081781	.084587	.087422	.090281	.096063	.101919	.107830	.113786
	.20	.066292	.071406	.076701	.079408	.082152	.084928	.087735	.090569	.093428	.099211	.105066	.110978	.116933
	.10	.069439	.074553	.079848	.082556	.085299	.088076	.090882	.093716	.096575	.102358	.108213	.114125	.120081
	0.00	.072586	.077700	.082995	.085703	.088446	.091223	.094030	.096864	.099723	.105506	.111361	.117273	.123228
	-.10	.075734	.080848	.086143	.088850	.091594	.094370	.097177	.100011	.102870	.108653	.114508	.120420	.126376
	-.20	.078881	.083995	.089290	.091998	.094741	.097518	.100324	.103158	.106017	.111800	.117655	.123567	.129523
	-.30	.082028	.087143	.092438	.095145	.097889	.100665	.103472	.106306	.109165	.114948	.120803	.126715	.132670
	-.40	.085176	.090290	.095585	.098292	.101036	.103812	.106619	.109453	.112312	.118095	.123950	.129862	.135818
40	.40	.058821	.064268	.069873	.072724	.075601	.078502	.081422	.084359	.087311	.093249	.099221	.105214	.111221
	.30	.061968	.067416	.073021	.075871	.078748	.081649	.084569	.087507	.090459	.096397	.102368	.108361	.114368
	.20	.065116	.070563	.076168	.079018	.081896	.084796	.087717	.090654	.093606	.099544	.105515	.111509	.117516
	.10	.068263	.073710	.079315	.082166	.085043	.087944	.090864	.093802	.096753	.102691	.108663	.114656	.120663
	0.00	.071410	.076858	.082463	.085313	.088191	.091091	.094012	.096949	.099901	.105839	.111810	.117803	.123810
	-.10	.074558	.080005	.085610	.088461	.091338	.094238	.097159	.100096	.103048	.108986	.114957	.120951	.126958
	-.20	.077705	.083152	.088757	.091608	.094485	.097386	.100306	.103244	.106196	.112134	.118105	.124098	.130105
	-.30	.080853	.086300	.091905	.094755	.097633	.100533	.103454	.106391	.109343	.115281	.121252	.127246	.133252
	-.40	.084000	.089447	.095052	.097903	.100780	.103681	.106601	.109539	.112490	.118428	.124400	.130393	.136400

15.0 YEAR HOLDING PERIOD
.100 EQUITY YIELD RATE
.667 LOAN RATIO

INTEREST RATE

TERM YEARS	APPR DEP	5.0	6.0	7.0	7.5	8.0	8.5	9.0	9.5	10.0	11.0	12.0	13.0	14.0
15	.40	.063025	.067270	.071667	.073922	.076213	.078540	.080903	.083299	.085730	.090689	.095775	.100981	.106301
	.30	.066172	.070417	.074815	.077070	.079361	.081688	.084050	.086447	.088877	.093836	.098922	.104128	.109448
	.20	.069319	.073565	.077962	.080217	.082508	.084835	.087197	.089594	.092024	.096984	.102070	.107276	.112595
	.10	.072467	.076712	.081110	.083364	.085656	.087983	.090345	.092741	.095217	.100131	.105217	.110423	.115743
	0.00	.075614	.079859	.084257	.086512	.088803	.091130	.093492	.095889	.098319	.103279	.108364	.113570	.118890
	-.10	.078762	.083007	.087404	.089659	.091950	.094277	.096639	.099036	.101467	.106426	.111512	.116718	.122038
	-.20	.081909	.086154	.090552	.092806	.095098	.097425	.099787	.102184	.104614	.109573	.114659	.119865	.125185
	-.30	.085056	.089301	.093699	.095954	.098245	.100572	.102934	.105331	.107761	.112721	.117806	.123012	.128332
	-.40	.088204	.092449	.096847	.099101	.101392	.103719	.106082	.108478	.110909	.115868	.120954	.126160	.131480
20	.40	.059896	.064851	.070001	.072644	.075332	.078062	.080834	.083645	.086493	.092298	.098234	.104292	.110457
	.30	.063043	.067999	.073148	.075792	.078480	.081210	.083981	.086792	.089640	.095445	.101382	.107439	.113604
	.20	.066190	.071146	.076295	.078939	.081627	.084357	.087129	.089939	.092788	.098592	.104529	.110586	.116751
	.10	.069338	.074293	.079443	.082087	.084774	.087505	.090276	.093087	.095935	.101740	.107677	.113734	.119899
	0.00	.072485	.077441	.082590	.085234	.087922	.090652	.093423	.096234	.099083	.104887	.110824	.116881	.123046
	-.10	.075632	.080588	.085738	.088381	.091069	.093799	.096571	.099381	.102230	.108034	.113971	.120028	.126194
	-.20	.078780	.083736	.088885	.091529	.094216	.096947	.099718	.102529	.105377	.111182	.117119	.123176	.129341
	-.30	.081927	.086883	.092032	.094676	.097364	.100094	.102865	.105676	.108525	.114329	.120266	.126323	.132488
	-.40	.085075	.090030	.095180	.097823	.100511	.103241	.106013	.108824	.111672	.117477	.123413	.129471	.135636
25	.40	.058093	.063482	.069076	.071943	.074854	.077807	.080797	.083824	.086885	.093100	.099423	.105838	.112330
	.30	.061240	.066630	.072223	.075091	.078002	.080954	.083945	.086972	.090033	.096247	.102570	.108985	.115477
	.20	.064388	.069777	.075371	.078238	.081149	.084101	.087092	.090119	.093180	.099395	.105717	.112132	.118625
	.10	.067535	.072925	.078518	.081386	.084297	.087249	.090240	.093267	.096328	.102542	.108865	.115280	.121772
	0.00	.070683	.076072	.081666	.084533	.087444	.090396	.093387	.096414	.099475	.105689	.112012	.118427	.124919
	-.10	.073830	.079219	.084813	.087680	.090591	.093543	.096534	.099561	.102622	.108837	.115160	.121574	.128067
	-.20	.076977	.082367	.087960	.090828	.093739	.096691	.099682	.102709	.105770	.111984	.118307	.124722	.131214
	-.30	.080125	.085514	.091108	.093975	.096886	.099838	.102829	.105856	.108917	.115131	.121454	.127869	.134361
	-.40	.083272	.088661	.094255	.097122	.100033	.102986	.105976	.109004	.112064	.118279	.124602	.131017	.137509
30	.40	.056951	.062633	.068516	.071525	.074573	.077658	.080777	.083926	.087102	.093528	.100034	.106602	.113220
	.30	.060098	.065780	.071664	.074672	.077720	.080805	.083924	.087073	.090250	.096675	.103181	.109750	.116367
	.20	.063245	.068928	.074811	.077820	.080868	.083953	.087071	.090220	.093397	.099823	.106328	.112897	.119514
	.10	.066393	.072075	.077959	.080967	.084015	.087100	.090219	.093368	.096544	.102970	.109476	.116044	.122662
	0.00	.069540	.075223	.081106	.084114	.087163	.090248	.093366	.096515	.099692	.106117	.112623	.119192	.125809
	-.10	.072688	.078370	.084253	.087262	.090310	.093395	.096514	.099663	.102839	.109265	.115770	.122339	.128957
	-.20	.075835	.081517	.087401	.090409	.093457	.096542	.099661	.102810	.105987	.112412	.118918	.125487	.132104
	-.30	.078982	.084665	.090548	.093556	.096605	.099690	.102808	.105957	.109134	.115560	.122065	.128634	.135251
	-.40	.082130	.087812	.093695	.096704	.099752	.102837	.105956	.109105	.112281	.118707	.125213	.131781	.138399
40	.40	.055644	.061697	.067924	.071092	.074286	.077512	.080757	.084020	.087300	.093898	.100533	.107192	.113867
	.30	.058792	.064844	.071072	.074239	.077436	.080659	.083904	.087168	.090448	.097045	.103680	.110339	.117014
	.20	.061939	.067991	.074219	.077387	.080584	.083806	.087051	.090315	.093595	.100193	.106828	.113487	.120161
	.10	.065086	.071139	.077367	.080534	.083731	.086954	.090199	.093463	.096742	.103340	.109975	.116634	.123309
	0.00	.068234	.074286	.080514	.083681	.086878	.090101	.093346	.096610	.099890	.106488	.113122	.119782	.126456
	-.10	.071381	.077434	.083661	.086829	.090026	.093249	.096494	.099757	.103037	.109635	.116270	.122929	.129603
	-.20	.074528	.080581	.086809	.089976	.093173	.096396	.099641	.102905	.106185	.112782	.119417	.126076	.132751
	-.30	.077676	.083728	.089956	.093123	.096320	.099543	.102788	.106052	.109332	.115930	.122565	.129224	.135898
	-.40	.080823	.086876	.093103	.096271	.099468	.102691	.105936	.109200	.112479	.119077	.125712	.132371	.139046

15.0 YEAR HOLDING PERIOD
.100 EQUITY YIELD RATE
.700 LOAN RATIO

INTEREST RATE

TERM YEARS	APPR DEP	5.0	6.0	7.0	7.5	8.0	8.5	9.0	9.5	10.0	11.0	12.0	13.0	14.0
15	.40	.061806	.066263	.070880	.073248	.075654	.078097	.080577	.083094	.085646	.090853	.096193	.101659	.107245
	.30	.064953	.069410	.074028	.076395	.078801	.081244	.083725	.086241	.088793	.094000	.099340	.104807	.110392
	.20	.068100	.072558	.077175	.079543	.081948	.084392	.086872	.089388	.091940	.097148	.102488	.107954	.113540
	.10	.071248	.075705	.080323	.082690	.085096	.087539	.090019	.092536	.095088	.100295	.105635	.111101	.116687
	0.00	.074395	.078852	.083470	.085837	.088243	.090686	.093167	.095683	.098235	.103442	.108782	.114249	.119835
	-.10	.077542	.082000	.086617	.088985	.091391	.093834	.096314	.098831	.101383	.106590	.111930	.117396	.122982
	-.20	.080690	.085147	.089765	.092132	.094538	.096981	.099462	.101978	.104530	.109737	.115077	.120543	.126129
	-.30	.083837	.088294	.092912	.095280	.097685	.100129	.102609	.105125	.107677	.112885	.118225	.123691	.129277
	-.40	.086985	.091442	.096059	.098427	.100833	.103276	.105756	.108273	.110825	.116032	.121372	.126838	.132424
20	.40	.058520	.063723	.069130	.071906	.074728	.077595	.080505	.083456	.086447	.092542	.098776	.105135	.111609
	.30	.061667	.066871	.072278	.075054	.077876	.080742	.083652	.086604	.089595	.095689	.101923	.108283	.114756
	.20	.064815	.070018	.075425	.078201	.081023	.083890	.086800	.089751	.092742	.098837	.105070	.111430	.117904
	.10	.067962	.073166	.078572	.081348	.084170	.087037	.089947	.092898	.095889	.101984	.108218	.114578	.121051
	0.00	.071109	.076313	.081720	.084496	.087318	.090185	.093094	.096046	.099037	.105131	.111365	.117725	.124198
	-.10	.074257	.079460	.084867	.087643	.090465	.093332	.096242	.099193	.102184	.108279	.114512	.120872	.127346
	-.20	.077404	.082608	.088015	.090790	.093613	.096479	.099389	.102340	.105332	.111426	.117660	.124020	.130493
	-.30	.080552	.085755	.091162	.093938	.096760	.099627	.102537	.105488	.108479	.114574	.120807	.127167	.133641
	-.40	.083699	.088903	.094309	.097085	.099907	.102774	.105684	.108635	.111626	.117721	.123955	.130315	.136788
25	.40	.056627	.062286	.068159	.071170	.074227	.077326	.080467	.083645	.086859	.093384	.100023	.106759	.113576
	.30	.059775	.065433	.071307	.074318	.077374	.080474	.083614	.086793	.090007	.096532	.103171	.109906	.116723
	.20	.062922	.068581	.074454	.077465	.080521	.083621	.086762	.089940	.093154	.099679	.106318	.113054	.119870
	.10	.066069	.071728	.077602	.080612	.083669	.086769	.089909	.093087	.096301	.102826	.109465	.116201	.123018
	0.00	.069217	.074876	.080749	.083760	.086816	.089916	.093056	.096235	.099449	.105974	.112613	.119348	.126165
	-.10	.072364	.078023	.083896	.086907	.089964	.093063	.096204	.099382	.102596	.109121	.115760	.122496	.129313
	-.20	.075512	.081170	.087044	.090054	.093111	.096211	.099351	.102529	.105743	.112268	.118907	.125643	.132460
	-.30	.078659	.084318	.090191	.093202	.096258	.099358	.102498	.105677	.108891	.115416	.122055	.128791	.135607
	-.40	.081806	.087465	.093338	.096349	.099406	.102505	.105646	.108824	.112038	.118563	.125202	.131938	.138755
30	.40	.055428	.061394	.067572	.070731	.073931	.077171	.080445	.083751	.087087	.093834	.100665	.107562	.114510
	.30	.058575	.064542	.070719	.073878	.077079	.080318	.083592	.086899	.090234	.096981	.103812	.110709	.117657
	.20	.061723	.067689	.073867	.077025	.080226	.083465	.086740	.090046	.093382	.100128	.106959	.113857	.120805
	.10	.064870	.070836	.077014	.080173	.083373	.086613	.089887	.093194	.096529	.103276	.110107	.117004	.123952
	0.00	.068017	.073984	.080161	.083320	.086521	.089760	.093034	.096341	.099676	.106423	.113254	.120151	.127099
	-.10	.071165	.077131	.083309	.086668	.089668	.092907	.096182	.099488	.102824	.109571	.116402	.123299	.130247
	-.20	.074312	.080279	.086456	.089615	.092816	.096055	.099329	.102636	.105971	.112718	.119549	.126446	.133394
	-.30	.077459	.083426	.089603	.092762	.095963	.099202	.102477	.105783	.109119	.115865	.122696	.129593	.136542
	-.40	.080607	.086573	.092751	.095910	.099110	.102350	.105624	.108930	.112266	.119013	.125844	.132741	.139689
40	.40	.054056	.060411	.066950	.070276	.073633	.077017	.080424	.083851	.087295	.094222	.101189	.108181	.115189
	.30	.057203	.063559	.070098	.073443	.076780	.080164	.083571	.086998	.090442	.097370	.104336	.111328	.118337
	.20	.060351	.066706	.073245	.076571	.079928	.083312	.086719	.090146	.093590	.100517	.107484	.114476	.121484
	.10	.063498	.069853	.076392	.079718	.083075	.086459	.089866	.093293	.096737	.103665	.110631	.117623	.124631
	0.00	.066646	.073001	.079540	.082865	.086222	.089606	.093013	.096441	.099884	.106812	.113778	.120771	.127779
	-.10	.069793	.076148	.082687	.086013	.089370	.092754	.096161	.099588	.103032	.109959	.116926	.123918	.130926
	-.20	.072940	.079295	.085835	.089160	.092517	.095901	.099308	.102735	.106179	.113107	.120073	.127065	.134073
	-.30	.076088	.082443	.088982	.092308	.095664	.099048	.102456	.105883	.109326	.116254	.123221	.130213	.137221
	-.40	.079235	.085590	.092129	.095455	.098812	.102196	.105603	.109030	.112474	.119401	.126368	.133360	.140368

15.0 YEAR HOLDING PERIOD
.100 EQUITY YIELD RATE
.750 LOAN RATIO

INTEREST RATE

TERM YEARS	APPR DEP	5.0	6.0	7.0	7.5	8.0	8.5	9.0	9.5	10.0	11.0	12.0	13.0	14.0
15	.40	.059977	.064752	.069700	.072236	.074814	.077432	.080089	.082785	.085520	.091099	.096820	.102677	.108662
	.30	.063124	.067900	.072847	.075384	.077961	.080579	.083237	.085933	.088667	.094246	.099968	.105824	.111809
	.20	.066271	.071047	.075994	.078531	.081109	.083726	.086384	.089080	.091814	.097394	.103115	.108972	.114957
	.10	.069419	.074194	.079142	.081678	.084256	.086874	.089531	.092228	.094962	.100541	.106262	.112119	.118104
	0.00	.072566	.077342	.082289	.084826	.087403	.090021	.092679	.095375	.098109	.103688	.109410	.115266	.121251
	-.10	.075713	.080489	.085437	.087973	.090551	.093169	.095826	.098522	.101257	.106836	.112557	.118414	.124399
	-.20	.078861	.083637	.088584	.091121	.093698	.096316	.098973	.101670	.104404	.109983	.115705	.121561	.127546
	-.30	.082008	.086784	.091731	.094268	.096845	.099463	.102121	.104817	.107551	.113131	.118852	.124709	.130694
	-.40	.085156	.089931	.094879	.097415	.099993	.102611	.105268	.107964	.110699	.116278	.121999	.127856	.133841
20	.40	.056456	.062032	.067825	.070799	.073822	.076894	.080012	.083174	.086378	.092908	.099587	.106402	.113337
	.30	.059604	.065179	.070972	.073946	.076970	.080041	.083159	.086321	.089526	.096056	.102735	.109549	.116485
	.20	.062751	.068326	.074119	.077093	.080117	.083189	.086306	.089469	.092673	.099203	.105882	.112696	.119632
	.10	.065898	.071474	.077267	.080241	.083265	.086336	.089454	.092616	.095821	.102351	.109030	.115844	.122780
	0.00	.069046	.074621	.080414	.083388	.086412	.089484	.092601	.095763	.098968	.105498	.112177	.118991	.125927
	-.10	.072193	.077768	.083561	.086536	.089559	.092631	.095749	.098911	.102115	.108645	.115324	.122138	.129074
	-.20	.075341	.080916	.086709	.089683	.092707	.095778	.098896	.102058	.105263	.111793	.118472	.125286	.132222
	-.30	.078488	.084063	.089856	.092830	.095854	.098926	.102043	.105205	.108410	.114940	.121619	.128433	.135369
	-.40	.081635	.087211	.093004	.095978	.099001	.102073	.105191	.108353	.111557	.118087	.124766	.131581	.138516
25	.40	.054429	.060492	.066784	.070010	.073285	.076606	.079971	.083376	.086820	.093811	.100924	.108141	.115445
	.30	.057576	.063639	.069932	.073158	.076432	.079753	.083118	.086524	.089967	.096958	.104071	.111288	.118592
	.20	.060723	.066786	.073079	.076305	.079580	.082901	.086266	.089671	.093115	.100106	.107219	.114436	.121739
	.10	.063871	.069934	.076227	.079452	.082727	.086048	.089413	.092818	.096262	.103253	.110366	.117583	.124887
	0.00	.067018	.073081	.079374	.082600	.085874	.089196	.092560	.095966	.099409	.106400	.113514	.120730	.128034
	-.10	.070165	.076228	.082521	.085747	.089022	.092343	.095708	.099113	.102557	.109548	.116661	.123878	.131181
	-.20	.073313	.079376	.085669	.088894	.092169	.095490	.098855	.102261	.105704	.112695	.119808	.127025	.134329
	-.30	.076460	.082523	.088816	.092042	.095317	.098638	.102002	.105408	.108851	.115843	.122956	.130173	.137476
	-.40	.079608	.085671	.091963	.095189	.098464	.101785	.105150	.108555	.111999	.118990	.126103	.133320	.140624
30	.40	.053143	.059536	.066155	.069539	.072969	.076439	.079947	.083490	.087064	.094293	.101611	.109001	.116446
	.30	.056291	.062683	.069302	.072687	.076116	.079586	.083095	.086637	.090211	.097440	.104759	.112149	.119593
	.20	.059438	.065831	.072450	.075834	.079263	.082734	.086242	.089785	.093359	.100587	.107906	.115296	.122740
	.10	.062585	.068978	.075597	.078981	.082411	.085881	.089390	.092932	.096506	.103735	.111054	.118443	.125888
	0.00	.065733	.072126	.078744	.082129	.085558	.089029	.092537	.096080	.099653	.106882	.114201	.121591	.129035
	-.10	.068880	.075273	.081892	.085276	.088705	.092176	.095684	.099227	.102801	.110029	.117348	.124738	.132183
	-.20	.072028	.078420	.085039	.088423	.091853	.095323	.098832	.102374	.105948	.113177	.120496	.127885	.135330
	-.30	.075175	.081568	.088186	.091571	.095000	.098471	.101979	.105522	.109095	.116324	.123643	.131033	.138477
	-.40	.078322	.084715	.091334	.094718	.098148	.101618	.105126	.108669	.112243	.119472	.126790	.134180	.141625
40	.40	.051674	.058483	.065489	.069052	.072649	.076274	.079925	.083597	.087287	.094709	.102173	.109665	.117173
	.30	.054821	.061630	.068636	.072199	.075796	.079422	.083072	.086744	.090434	.097856	.105320	.112812	.120321
	.20	.057968	.064777	.071784	.075347	.078943	.082569	.086220	.089892	.093581	.101004	.108468	.115959	.123468
	.10	.061116	.067925	.074931	.078494	.082091	.085717	.089367	.093039	.096729	.104151	.111615	.119107	.126616
	0.00	.064263	.071072	.078078	.081642	.085238	.088864	.092514	.096186	.099876	.107298	.114763	.122254	.129763
	-.10	.067410	.074220	.081226	.084789	.088386	.092011	.095662	.099334	.103023	.110446	.117910	.125402	.132910
	-.20	.070558	.077367	.084373	.087936	.091533	.095159	.098809	.102481	.106171	.113593	.121057	.128549	.136058
	-.30	.073705	.080514	.087520	.091084	.094680	.098306	.101957	.105628	.109318	.116741	.124205	.131696	.139205
	-.40	.076853	.083662	.090668	.094231	.097828	.101453	.105104	.108776	.112466	.119888	.127352	.134844	.142352

15.0 YEAR HOLDING PERIOD
.100 EQUITY YIELD RATE
.800 LOAN RATIO RATE

INTEREST RATE

TERM YEARS	APPR DEP	5.0	6.0	7.0	7.5	8.0	8.5	9.0	9.5	10.0	11.0	12.0	13.0	14.0
15	.40	.058448	.063242	.068519	.071225	.073974	.076766	.079601	.082477	.085394	.091345	.097448	.103595	.110079
	.30	.061295	.066389	.071666	.074372	.077121	.079914	.082748	.085524	.088541	.094492	.100595	.106642	.113226
	.20	.064442	.069536	.074814	.077519	.080269	.083061	.085896	.088772	.091688	.097640	.103742	.109989	.116373
	.10	.067590	.072684	.077961	.080667	.083416	.086209	.089043	.091919	.094836	.100787	.106890	.113137	.119521
	0.00	.070737	.075831	.081108	.083814	.086564	.089356	.092191	.095067	.097983	.103934	.110037	.116284	.122668
	-.10	.073885	.078979	.084256	.086962	.089711	.092503	.095338	.098214	.101130	.107082	.113184	.119432	.125816
	-.20	.077032	.082126	.087403	.090109	.092858	.095651	.098485	.101361	.104278	.110229	.116332	.122579	.128963
	-.30	.080179	.085273	.090551	.093256	.096006	.098798	.101633	.104509	.107425	.113376	.119479	.125726	.132110
	-.40	.083327	.088421	.093698	.096404	.099153	.101945	.104780	.107656	.110573	.116524	.122627	.128874	.135258
20	.40	.054393	.060340	.066519	.069691	.072917	.076193	.079518	.082891	.086310	.093275	.100399	.107668	.115066
	.30	.057540	.063487	.069666	.072839	.076064	.079340	.082666	.086039	.089457	.096422	.103547	.110815	.118213
	.20	.060687	.066634	.072814	.075986	.079211	.082488	.085813	.089186	.092604	.099570	.106694	.113962	.121361
	.10	.063835	.069782	.075961	.079133	.082359	.085635	.088961	.092333	.095752	.102717	.109841	.117110	.124508
	0.00	.066982	.072929	.079108	.082281	.085506	.088782	.092108	.095481	.098899	.105864	.112989	.120257	.127655
	-.10	.070130	.076077	.082256	.085428	.088653	.091930	.095255	.098628	.102047	.109012	.116136	.123405	.130803
	-.20	.073277	.079224	.085403	.088575	.091801	.095077	.098403	.101776	.105194	.112159	.119283	.126552	.133950
	-.30	.076424	.082371	.088550	.091723	.094948	.098225	.101550	.104923	.108341	.115307	.122431	.129699	.137097
	-.40	.079572	.085519	.091698	.094871	.098096	.101372	.104697	.108070	.111489	.118454	.125578	.132847	.140245
25	.40	.052230	.058697	.065409	.068850	.072343	.075886	.079475	.083107	.086780	.094238	.101825	.109523	.117314
	.30	.055377	.061844	.068557	.071997	.075491	.079033	.082622	.086255	.089928	.097385	.104972	.112670	.120461
	.20	.058525	.064992	.071704	.075145	.078638	.082181	.085770	.089402	.093075	.100532	.108120	.115818	.123608
	.10	.061672	.068139	.074851	.078292	.081785	.085328	.088917	.092549	.096223	.103680	.111267	.118965	.126756
	0.00	.064819	.071286	.077999	.081440	.084933	.088475	.092064	.095697	.099370	.106827	.114414	.122112	.129903
	-.10	.067967	.074434	.081146	.084587	.088080	.091623	.095212	.098844	.102517	.109974	.117562	.125260	.133050
	-.20	.071114	.077581	.084294	.087734	.091228	.094770	.098359	.101992	.105665	.113122	.120709	.128407	.136198
	-.30	.074261	.080729	.087441	.090882	.094375	.097917	.101506	.105139	.108812	.116269	.123857	.131555	.139345
	-.40	.077409	.083876	.090588	.094029	.097522	.101065	.104654	.108286	.111959	.119417	.127004	.134702	.142493
30	.40	.050859	.057678	.064738	.068348	.072006	.075708	.079450	.083229	.087041	.094751	.102558	.110441	.118381
	.30	.054006	.060825	.067885	.071495	.075153	.078855	.082597	.086376	.090188	.097899	.105706	.113588	.121529
	.20	.057154	.063972	.071032	.074643	.078300	.082002	.085745	.089523	.093335	.101046	.108853	.116735	.124676
	.10	.060301	.067120	.074180	.077790	.081448	.085150	.088892	.092671	.096483	.104193	.112000	.119883	.127823
	0.00	.063448	.070267	.077327	.080937	.084595	.088297	.092039	.095818	.099630	.107341	.115148	.123030	.130971
	-.10	.066596	.073415	.080475	.084085	.087743	.091445	.095187	.098966	.102778	.110488	.118295	.126177	.134118
	-.20	.069743	.076562	.083622	.087232	.090890	.094592	.098334	.102113	.105925	.113636	.121442	.129325	.137266
	-.30	.072890	.079709	.086769	.090379	.094037	.097739	.101482	.105260	.109072	.116783	.124590	.132472	.140413
	-.40	.076038	.082857	.089917	.093527	.097185	.100887	.104629	.108408	.112220	.119930	.127737	.135620	.143560
40	.40	.049291	.056554	.064027	.067828	.071665	.075532	.079426	.083343	.087278	.095196	.103157	.111148	.119158
	.30	.052439	.059701	.067175	.070976	.074812	.078679	.082573	.086490	.090426	.098343	.106305	.114296	.122305
	.20	.055586	.062849	.070322	.074123	.077959	.081827	.085721	.089637	.093573	.101490	.109452	.117443	.125452
	.10	.058733	.065996	.073470	.077270	.081107	.084974	.088868	.092785	.096720	.104638	.112599	.120590	.128600
	0.00	.061881	.069144	.076617	.080418	.084254	.088121	.092015	.095932	.099868	.107785	.115747	.123738	.131747
	-.10	.065028	.072291	.079764	.083565	.087401	.091269	.095163	.099079	.103015	.110932	.118894	.126885	.134894
	-.20	.068175	.075438	.082912	.086712	.090549	.094416	.098310	.102227	.106163	.114080	.122042	.130033	.138042
	-.30	.071323	.078586	.086059	.089860	.093696	.097564	.101458	.105374	.109310	.117227	.125189	.133180	.141189
	-.40	.074470	.081733	.089206	.093007	.096844	.100711	.104605	.108522	.112457	.120375	.128336	.136327	.144337

15.0 YEAR HOLDING PERIOD
.100 EQUITY YIELD RATE
.900 LOAN RATIO

INTEREST RATE

TERM YEARS	APPR DEP	5.0	6.0	7.0	7.5	8.0	8.5	9.0	9.5	10.0	11.0	12.0	13.0	14.0
15	.40	.054490	.060221	.066158	.069201	.072295	.075436	.078625	.081860	.085141	.091837	.098702	.105730	.112912
	.30	.057637	.063368	.069305	.072349	.075442	.078583	.081772	.085000	.088289	.094984	.101850	.108877	.116060
	.20	.060785	.066515	.072452	.075496	.078589	.081731	.084920	.088155	.091436	.098131	.104997	.112025	.119207
	.10	.063932	.069663	.075600	.078644	.081737	.084878	.088067	.091302	.094584	.101279	.108144	.115172	.122354
	0.00	.067079	.072810	.078747	.081791	.084884	.088025	.091214	.094450	.097731	.104426	.111292	.118320	.125502
	-.10	.070227	.075958	.081894	.084938	.088031	.091173	.094362	.097597	.100878	.107573	.114439	.121467	.128649
	-.20	.073374	.079105	.085042	.088086	.091179	.094320	.097509	.100745	.104026	.110721	.117587	.124615	.131796
	-.30	.076521	.082252	.088189	.091233	.094326	.097468	.100657	.103892	.107173	.113868	.120734	.127762	.134944
	-.40	.079669	.085400	.091337	.094380	.097474	.100615	.103804	.107039	.110320	.117016	.123881	.130909	.138091
20	.40	.050265	.056956	.063907	.067476	.071105	.074791	.078532	.082326	.086172	.094008	.102023	.110200	.118523
	.30	.053413	.060103	.067055	.070624	.074252	.077938	.081679	.085474	.089319	.097155	.105170	.113347	.121670
	.20	.056560	.063251	.070202	.073771	.077400	.081085	.084827	.088621	.092467	.100303	.108318	.116495	.124818
	.10	.059708	.066398	.073349	.076918	.080547	.084233	.087974	.091769	.095614	.103450	.111465	.119642	.127965
	0.00	.062855	.069545	.076497	.080066	.083694	.087380	.091121	.094916	.098762	.106597	.114612	.122789	.131112
	-.10	.066002	.072693	.079644	.083213	.086842	.090528	.094269	.098063	.101909	.109745	.117760	.125937	.134260
	-.20	.069150	.075840	.082792	.086361	.089989	.093675	.097416	.101211	.105056	.112892	.120907	.129084	.137407
	-.30	.072297	.078987	.085939	.089508	.093136	.096822	.100564	.104358	.108204	.116040	.124054	.132231	.140554
	-.40	.075445	.082135	.089086	.092655	.096284	.099970	.103711	.107505	.111351	.119187	.127202	.135379	.143702
25	.40	.047832	.055108	.062659	.066530	.070460	.074445	.078483	.082569	.086702	.095091	.103627	.112287	.121051
	.30	.050980	.058255	.065807	.069677	.073607	.077593	.081630	.085717	.089849	.098238	.106774	.115434	.124199
	.20	.054127	.061402	.068954	.072825	.076755	.080740	.084778	.088864	.092996	.101386	.109922	.118582	.127346
	.10	.057274	.064550	.072101	.075972	.079902	.083887	.087925	.092012	.096144	.104533	.113069	.121729	.130494
	0.00	.060422	.067697	.075249	.079120	.083049	.087035	.091072	.095159	.099291	.107680	.116216	.124876	.133641
	-.10	.063569	.070845	.078396	.082267	.086197	.090182	.094220	.098306	.102439	.110828	.119364	.128024	.136788
	-.20	.066716	.073992	.081543	.085414	.089344	.093330	.097367	.101454	.105586	.113975	.122511	.131171	.139936
	-.30	.069864	.077139	.084691	.088562	.092492	.096477	.100514	.104601	.108733	.117123	.125658	.134319	.143083
	-.40	.073011	.080287	.087838	.091709	.095639	.099624	.103662	.107748	.111881	.120270	.128806	.137466	.146230
30	.40	.046290	.053961	.061904	.065965	.070080	.074245	.078455	.082706	.086994	.095669	.104452	.113319	.122253
	.30	.049437	.057109	.065051	.069112	.073227	.077392	.081602	.085853	.090142	.098816	.107599	.116467	.125400
	.20	.052585	.060256	.068198	.072260	.076375	.080540	.084750	.089001	.093289	.101964	.110746	.119614	.128547
	.10	.055732	.063403	.071346	.075407	.079522	.083687	.087897	.092148	.096437	.105111	.113894	.122762	.131695
	0.00	.058879	.066551	.074493	.078554	.082670	.086834	.091044	.095295	.099584	.108258	.117041	.125909	.134842
	-.10	.062027	.069698	.077641	.081702	.085817	.089982	.094192	.098443	.102731	.111406	.120188	.129056	.137990
	-.20	.065174	.072845	.080788	.084849	.088964	.093129	.097339	.101590	.105879	.114553	.123336	.132204	.141137
	-.30	.068322	.075993	.083935	.087997	.092112	.096276	.100486	.104738	.109026	.117701	.126483	.135351	.144284
	-.40	.071469	.079140	.087083	.091144	.095259	.099424	.103634	.107885	.112173	.120848	.129631	.138498	.147432
40	.40	.044526	.052697	.061104	.065380	.069696	.074047	.078428	.082834	.087262	.096169	.105126	.114116	.123126
	.30	.047674	.055844	.064252	.068528	.072844	.077195	.081575	.085981	.090409	.099316	.108273	.117263	.126273
	.20	.050821	.058992	.067399	.071675	.075991	.080342	.084723	.089129	.093557	.102463	.111420	.120410	.129421
	.10	.053968	.062139	.070547	.074822	.079138	.083489	.087870	.092276	.096704	.105611	.114568	.123558	.132568
	0.00	.057116	.065287	.073694	.077970	.082286	.086637	.091017	.095424	.099851	.108758	.117715	.126705	.135716
	-.10	.060263	.068434	.076841	.081117	.085433	.089784	.094165	.098571	.102999	.111906	.120863	.129852	.138863
	-.20	.063410	.071581	.079989	.084265	.088581	.092931	.097312	.101718	.106146	.115053	.124010	.133000	.142010
	-.30	.066558	.074729	.083136	.087412	.091728	.096079	.100459	.104866	.109293	.118200	.127157	.136147	.145158
	-.40	.069705	.077876	.086284	.090559	.094875	.099226	.103607	.108013	.112441	.121348	.130305	.139295	.148305

15.0 YEAR HOLDING PERIOD
.120 EQUITY YIELD RATE
.600 LOAN RATIO

INTEREST RATE

TERM YEARS	APPR DEP	5.0	6.0	7.0	7.5	8.0	8.5	9.0	9.5	10.0	11.0	12.0	13.0	14.0
15	.40	.078113	.081933	.085891	.087921	.089983	.092077	.094203	.096360	.098547	.103011	.107588	.112273	.117061
	.30	.080795	.084616	.088574	.090603	.092665	.094759	.096885	.099042	.101230	.105693	.110270	.114956	.119744
	.20	.083478	.087298	.091256	.093285	.095348	.097442	.099568	.101725	.103912	.108376	.112953	.117638	.122426
	.10	.086160	.089981	.093939	.095968	.098030	.100124	.102250	.104407	.106595	.111058	.115635	.120320	.125108
	0.00	.088843	.092663	.096621	.098650	.100712	.102807	.104933	.107090	.109277	.113740	.118318	.123003	.127791
	-.10	.091525	.095346	.099304	.101333	.103395	.105489	.107615	.109772	.111959	.116423	.121000	.125685	.130473
	-.20	.094207	.098028	.101986	.104015	.106077	.108172	.110297	.112454	.114642	.119105	.123682	.128368	.133156
	-.30	.096890	.100710	.104668	.106698	.108760	.110854	.112980	.115137	.117324	.121788	.126365	.131050	.135838
	-.40	.099572	.103393	.107351	.109380	.111442	.113536	.115662	.117819	.120007	.124470	.129047	.133733	.138521
20	.40	.074321	.078723	.083299	.085649	.088039	.090467	.092932	.095432	.097967	.103134	.108421	.113816	.119311
	.30	.077004	.081406	.085981	.088331	.090721	.093149	.095614	.098115	.100650	.105816	.111113	.116499	.121993
	.20	.079686	.084088	.088664	.091014	.093404	.095832	.098297	.100797	.103332	.108499	.113786	.119181	.124675
	.10	.082368	.086770	.091346	.093696	.096086	.098514	.100979	.103480	.106015	.111181	.116468	.121864	.127358
	0.00	.085051	.089453	.094029	.096379	.098768	.101197	.103662	.106162	.108697	.113864	.119150	.124546	.130040
	-.10	.087733	.092135	.096711	.099061	.101451	.103879	.106344	.108845	.111379	.116546	.121833	.127229	.132723
	-.20	.090416	.094818	.099394	.101744	.104133	.106561	.109026	.111527	.114062	.119229	.124515	.129911	.135405
	-.30	.093098	.097500	.102076	.104426	.106816	.109244	.111709	.114209	.116744	.121911	.127198	.132593	.138088
	-.40	.095780	.100182	.104758	.107108	.109498	.111926	.114391	.116892	.119427	.124593	.129880	.135276	.140770
25	.40	.072137	.076906	.081861	.084403	.086985	.089605	.092260	.094949	.097669	.103195	.108823	.114537	.120324
	.30	.074819	.079588	.084543	.087085	.089667	.092287	.094943	.097631	.100352	.105878	.111505	.117220	.123007
	.20	.077502	.082271	.087226	.089768	.092350	.094970	.097625	.100314	.103034	.108560	.114188	.119902	.125689
	.10	.080184	.084953	.089908	.092450	.095032	.097652	.100307	.102996	.105716	.111243	.116870	.122584	.128372
	0.00	.082867	.087636	.092591	.095133	.097715	.100334	.102990	.105679	.108399	.113925	.119553	.125267	.131054
	-.10	.085549	.090318	.095273	.097815	.100397	.103017	.105672	.108361	.111081	.116608	.122235	.127949	.133737
	-.20	.088231	.093000	.097956	.100498	.103079	.105699	.108355	.111044	.113764	.119290	.124917	.130632	.136419
	-.30	.090914	.095683	.100638	.103180	.105762	.108382	.111037	.113726	.116446	.121972	.127600	.133314	.139101
	-.40	.093596	.098365	.103320	.105862	.108444	.111064	.113720	.116408	.119129	.124655	.130282	.135996	.141784
30	.40	.070753	.075778	.080991	.083659	.086364	.089105	.091876	.094677	.097504	.103228	.109030	.114894	.120806
	.30	.073435	.078461	.083673	.086342	.089047	.091787	.094559	.097360	.100187	.105911	.111712	.117576	.123489
	.20	.076117	.081143	.086355	.089024	.091729	.094469	.097241	.100042	.102869	.108593	.114395	.120258	.126171
	.10	.078800	.083826	.089038	.091706	.094412	.097152	.099924	.102725	.105552	.111275	.117077	.122941	.128853
	0.00	.081482	.086508	.091720	.094388	.097094	.099834	.102606	.105407	.108234	.113958	.119760	.125623	.131536
	-.10	.084165	.089191	.094403	.097071	.099777	.102517	.105289	.108089	.110917	.116640	.122442	.128306	.134218
	-.20	.086847	.091873	.097085	.099753	.102459	.105199	.107971	.110772	.113599	.119323	.125124	.130988	.136901
	-.30	.089529	.094555	.099768	.102436	.105141	.107881	.110653	.113454	.116281	.122005	.127807	.133671	.139583
	-.40	.092212	.097238	.102450	.105118	.107824	.110564	.113336	.116137	.118964	.124688	.130469	.136353	.142265
40	.40	.069169	.074635	.080070	.082889	.085737	.088611	.091507	.094423	.097354	.103257	.109199	.115168	.121156
	.30	.071852	.077218	.082752	.085571	.088420	.091294	.094190	.097105	.100036	.105939	.111881	.117851	.123839
	.20	.074534	.079900	.085435	.088254	.091102	.093976	.096872	.099787	.102719	.108621	.114564	.120533	.126521
	.10	.077217	.082583	.088117	.090936	.093785	.096659	.099555	.102470	.105401	.111304	.117246	.123216	.129204
	0.00	.079899	.085265	.090800	.093619	.096467	.099341	.102237	.105152	.108084	.113986	.119929	.125898	.131886
	-.10	.082582	.087948	.093482	.096301	.099150	.102023	.104919	.107835	.110766	.116669	.122611	.128581	.134568
	-.20	.085264	.090630	.096164	.098984	.101832	.104706	.107602	.110517	.113449	.119351	.125293	.131263	.137251
	-.30	.087946	.093312	.098847	.101666	.104514	.107388	.110284	.113199	.116131	.122034	.127976	.133945	.139933
	-.40	.090629	.095995	.101529	.104348	.107197	.110071	.112967	.115882	.118813	.124716	.130658	.136628	.142616

15.0 YEAR HOLDING PERIOD
.120 EQUITY YIELD RATE
.667 LOAN RATIO

INTEREST RATE

TERM YEARS	APPR DEP	5.0	6.0	7.0	7.5	8.0	8.5	9.0	9.5	10.0	11.0	12.0	13.0	14.0
15	.40	.074651	.078896	.083294	.085548	.087840	.090167	.092529	.094925	.097356	.102315	.107401	.112607	.117927
	.30	.077333	.081578	.085976	.088231	.090322	.092849	.095221	.097608	.100038	.105083	.110083	.115289	.120609
	.20	.080016	.084261	.088658	.090913	.093204	.095531	.097894	.100290	.102721	.107680	.112766	.117972	.123292
	.10	.082698	.086943	.091341	.093596	.095887	.098214	.100576	.102973	.105403	.110362	.115448	.120654	.125974
	0.00	.085380	.089626	.094023	.096278	.098569	.100896	.103258	.105655	.108086	.113045	.118131	.123337	.128657
	-.10	.088063	.092308	.096706	.098960	.101252	.103579	.105941	.108338	.110768	.115727	.120813	.126019	.131339
	-.20	.090745	.094990	.099388	.101643	.103934	.106261	.108623	.111020	.113450	.118410	.123495	.128701	.134021
	-.30	.093428	.097673	.102071	.104325	.106617	.108944	.111306	.113702	.116133	.121092	.126178	.131384	.136704
	-.40	.096110	.100355	.104753	.107008	.109299	.111626	.113988	.116385	.118815	.123775	.128860	.134066	.139386
20	.40	.070438	.075329	.080413	.083024	.085680	.088377	.091116	.093895	.096711	.102452	.108326	.114322	.120426
	.30	.073120	.078011	.083096	.085707	.088362	.091060	.093799	.096577	.099394	.105135	.111009	.117004	.123109
	.20	.075802	.080694	.085778	.088389	.091044	.093742	.096481	.099260	.102076	.107817	.113691	.119686	.125791
	.10	.078485	.083376	.088460	.091072	.093727	.096425	.099164	.101942	.104759	.110499	.116374	.122369	.128474
	0.00	.081167	.086058	.091143	.093754	.096409	.099107	.101846	.104625	.107441	.113182	.119056	.125051	.131156
	-.10	.083850	.088741	.093825	.096436	.099092	.101790	.104529	.107307	.110123	.115864	.121738	.127734	.133838
	-.20	.086532	.091423	.096508	.099119	.101774	.104472	.107211	.109989	.112806	.118547	.124421	.130416	.136521
	-.30	.089215	.094106	.099190	.101801	.104457	.107154	.109893	.112672	.115488	.121229	.127103	.133099	.139203
	-.40	.091897	.096788	.101873	.104484	.107139	.109837	.112576	.115354	.118171	.123912	.129786	.135781	.141886
25	.40	.068011	.073310	.078815	.081640	.084509	.087420	.090370	.093358	.096380	.102520	.108773	.115122	.121553
	.30	.070693	.075992	.081498	.084322	.087191	.090102	.093052	.096040	.099063	.105203	.111456	.117805	.124235
	.20	.073376	.078674	.084180	.087005	.089874	.092785	.095735	.098723	.101745	.107885	.114138	.120487	.126918
	.10	.076058	.081357	.086863	.089687	.092556	.095467	.098417	.101405	.104427	.110568	.116821	.123170	.129600
	0.00	.078740	.084039	.089545	.092369	.095238	.098149	.101100	.104087	.107110	.113250	.119503	.125852	.132282
	-.10	.081423	.086722	.092227	.095052	.097921	.100832	.103782	.106770	.109792	.115933	.122185	.128534	.134965
	-.20	.084105	.089404	.094910	.097734	.100603	.103514	.106465	.109452	.112475	.118615	.124868	.131217	.137647
	-.30	.086788	.092087	.097592	.100417	.103286	.106197	.109147	.112135	.115157	.121297	.127550	.133899	.140330
	-.40	.089470	.094769	.100275	.103099	.105968	.108879	.111829	.114817	.117840	.123980	.130233	.136582	.143012
30	.40	.066473	.072057	.077848	.080813	.083819	.086864	.089944	.093056	.096197	.102557	.109003	.115518	.122088
	.30	.069155	.074739	.080531	.083495	.086502	.089546	.092626	.095738	.098879	.105239	.111686	.118201	.124770
	.20	.071837	.077422	.083213	.086178	.089184	.092229	.095309	.098421	.101562	.107922	.114368	.120883	.127453
	.10	.074520	.080104	.085895	.088860	.091867	.094911	.097991	.101103	.104244	.110604	.117050	.123566	.130135
	0.00	.077202	.082787	.088578	.091543	.094549	.097594	.100673	.103785	.106927	.113287	.119733	.126248	.132818
	-.10	.079885	.085469	.091260	.094225	.097231	.100276	.103356	.106468	.109609	.115969	.122415	.128931	.135500
	-.20	.082567	.088151	.093943	.096907	.099914	.102958	.106038	.109150	.112292	.118651	.125098	.131613	.138182
	-.30	.085250	.090834	.096625	.099590	.102596	.105641	.108721	.111833	.114974	.121334	.127780	.134295	.140865
	-.40	.087932	.093516	.099308	.102272	.105279	.108323	.111403	.114515	.117656	.124016	.130462	.136978	.143547
40	.40	.064714	.070676	.076825	.079958	.083123	.086316	.089534	.092773	.096030	.102588	.109191	.115824	.122477
	.30	.067396	.073358	.079508	.082640	.085805	.088998	.092216	.095455	.098712	.105271	.111873	.118506	.125159
	.20	.070078	.076041	.082190	.085322	.088487	.091681	.094898	.098138	.101395	.107953	.114556	.121189	.127842
	.10	.072761	.078723	.084872	.088005	.091170	.094363	.097581	.100820	.104077	.110636	.117238	.123871	.130524
	0.00	.075443	.081405	.087555	.090687	.093852	.097045	.100263	.103502	.106760	.113318	.119921	.126554	.133207
	-.10	.078126	.084088	.090237	.093370	.096535	.099728	.102946	.106185	.109442	.116000	.122603	.129236	.135889
	-.20	.080808	.086770	.092920	.096052	.099217	.102410	.105628	.108867	.112124	.118683	.125285	.131918	.138572
	-.30	.083491	.089453	.095602	.098735	.101899	.105093	.108311	.111550	.114807	.121365	.127968	.134601	.141254
	-.40	.086173	.092135	.098285	.101417	.104582	.107775	.110993	.114232	.117489	.124048	.130650	.137283	.143936

15.0 YEAR HOLDING PERIOD
.120 EQUITY YIELD RATE
.700 LOAN RATIO

INTEREST RATE

TERM YEARS	APPR DEP	5.0	6.0	7.0	7.5	8.0	8.5	9.0	9.5	10.0	11.0	12.0	13.0	14.0
15	.40	.072920	.077377	.081995	.084362	.086768	.089211	.091692	.094208	.096760	.101967	.107307	.112774	.118360
	.30	.075602	.080060	.084677	.087045	.089451	.091894	.094374	.096891	.099443	.104650	.109990	.115456	.121042
	.20	.078285	.082742	.087360	.089727	.092133	.094576	.097057	.099573	.102125	.107332	.112672	.118139	.123724
	.10	.080967	.085425	.090042	.092410	.094815	.097259	.099739	.102255	.104807	.110015	.115355	.120821	.126407
	0.00	.083650	.088107	.092725	.095092	.097498	.099941	.102421	.104938	.107490	.112697	.118037	.123503	.129089
	-.10	.086332	.090789	.095407	.097774	.100180	.102624	.105104	.107620	.110172	.115380	.120720	.126186	.131772
	-.20	.089015	.093472	.098089	.100457	.102863	.105306	.107786	.110303	.112855	.118062	.123402	.128868	.134454
	-.30	.091697	.096154	.100772	.103139	.105545	.107988	.110469	.112985	.115537	.120744	.126084	.131551	.137137
	-.40	.094379	.098837	.103454	.105822	.108228	.110671	.113151	.115668	.118220	.123427	.128767	.134233	.139819
20	.40	.068496	.073632	.078970	.081712	.084500	.087333	.090209	.093126	.096083	.102111	.108279	.114574	.120984
	.30	.071179	.076314	.081653	.084395	.087183	.090015	.092891	.095809	.098766	.104794	.110961	.117257	.123666
	.20	.073861	.078997	.084335	.087077	.089865	.092698	.095574	.098491	.101448	.107476	.113644	.119939	.126349
	.10	.076543	.081679	.087018	.089759	.092547	.095380	.098256	.101173	.104131	.110159	.116326	.122621	.129031
	0.00	.079226	.084362	.089700	.092442	.095230	.098063	.100938	.103856	.106813	.112841	.119009	.125304	.131714
	-.10	.081908	.087044	.092383	.095124	.097912	.100745	.103621	.106538	.109496	.115523	.121691	.127986	.134396
	-.20	.084591	.089726	.095065	.097807	.100595	.103427	.106303	.109221	.112178	.118206	.124374	.130669	.137079
	-.30	.087273	.092409	.097747	.100489	.103277	.106110	.108986	.111903	.114860	.120888	.127056	.133351	.139761
	-.40	.089956	.095091	.100430	.103172	.105960	.108792	.111668	.114586	.117543	.123571	.129738	.136034	.142443
25	.40	.065948	.071512	.077293	.080258	.083271	.086327	.089425	.092562	.095736	.102183	.108748	.115415	.122167
	.30	.068630	.074194	.079975	.082941	.085953	.089010	.092108	.095245	.098418	.104865	.111431	.118097	.124849
	.20	.071313	.076877	.082658	.085623	.088636	.091692	.094790	.097927	.101101	.107548	.114113	.120780	.127532
	.10	.073995	.079559	.085340	.088306	.091318	.094374	.097472	.100609	.103783	.110230	.116796	.123462	.130214
	0.00	.076678	.082241	.088022	.090988	.094000	.097057	.100155	.103292	.106465	.112913	.119478	.126145	.132897
	-.10	.079360	.084924	.090705	.093671	.096683	.099739	.102837	.105974	.109148	.115595	.122161	.128827	.135579
	-.20	.082043	.087606	.093387	.096353	.099365	.102422	.105520	.108657	.111830	.118277	.124843	.131509	.138261
	-.30	.084725	.090289	.096070	.099035	.102048	.105104	.108202	.111339	.114513	.120960	.127525	.134192	.140944
	-.40	.087407	.092971	.098752	.101718	.104730	.107787	.110885	.114022	.117195	.123642	.130208	.136874	.143626
30	.40	.064333	.070196	.076277	.079390	.082547	.085744	.088977	.092245	.095543	.102221	.108990	.115831	.122729
	.30	.067015	.072879	.078960	.082073	.085229	.088426	.091660	.094928	.098226	.104904	.111672	.118513	.125411
	.20	.069698	.075561	.081642	.084755	.087912	.091109	.094342	.097610	.100908	.107586	.114355	.121196	.128094
	.10	.072380	.078244	.084325	.087437	.090594	.093791	.097025	.100292	.103591	.110268	.117037	.123878	.130776
	0.00	.075063	.080926	.087007	.090120	.093277	.096473	.099707	.102975	.106273	.112951	.119719	.126560	.133458
	-.10	.077745	.083609	.089689	.092802	.095959	.099156	.102390	.105657	.108956	.115633	.122402	.129243	.136141
	-.20	.080427	.086291	.092372	.095485	.098641	.101838	.105072	.108340	.111638	.118316	.125084	.131925	.138823
	-.30	.083110	.088973	.095054	.098167	.101324	.104521	.107754	.111022	.114320	.120998	.127767	.134608	.141506
	-.40	.085792	.091656	.097737	.100850	.104006	.107203	.110437	.113704	.117003	.123681	.130449	.137290	.144188
40	.40	.062486	.068746	.075203	.078492	.081815	.085168	.088547	.091948	.095368	.102254	.109187	.116151	.123137
	.30	.065168	.071429	.077886	.081175	.084498	.087851	.091229	.094630	.098050	.104937	.111869	.118834	.125820
	.20	.067851	.074111	.080568	.083857	.087180	.090533	.093912	.097313	.100733	.107619	.114552	.121516	.128502
	.10	.070533	.076794	.083250	.086539	.089863	.093215	.096594	.099995	.103415	.110302	.117234	.124199	.131185
	0.00	.073216	.079476	.085933	.089222	.092545	.095898	.099277	.102678	.106098	.112984	.119917	.126881	.133867
	-.10	.075898	.082158	.088615	.091904	.095227	.098580	.101959	.105360	.108780	.115666	.122599	.129564	.136549
	-.20	.078580	.084841	.091298	.094587	.097910	.101263	.104641	.108042	.111462	.118349	.125281	.132246	.139232
	-.30	.081263	.087523	.093980	.097269	.100592	.103945	.107324	.110725	.114145	.121031	.127964	.134928	.141914
	-.40	.083945	.090206	.096662	.099952	.103275	.106628	.110006	.113407	.116827	.123714	.130646	.137611	.144597

15.0 YEAR HOLDING PERIOD
.120 EQUITY YIELD RATE
.750 LOAN RATIO

INTEREST RATE

TERM YEARS	APPR DEP	5.0	6.0	7.0	7.5	8.0	8.5	9.0	9.5	10.0	11.0	12.0	13.0	14.0
15	.40	.070324	.075099	.080047	.082583	.085161	.087779	.090436	.093132	.095867	.101446	.107167	.113024	.119009
	.30	.073006	.077782	.082729	.085266	.087843	.090461	.093118	.095815	.098549	.104128	.109850	.115706	.121691
	.20	.075688	.080464	.085412	.087948	.090526	.093144	.095801	.098497	.101231	.106811	.112532	.118389	.124374
	.10	.078371	.083147	.088094	.090631	.093208	.095826	.098483	.101180	.103914	.109493	.115215	.121071	.127056
	0.00	.081053	.085829	.090776	.093313	.095890	.098508	.101166	.103862	.106596	.112176	.117897	.123754	.129739
	-.10	.083736	.088511	.093459	.095995	.098572	.101191	.103848	.106544	.109279	.114858	.120579	.126436	.132421
	-.20	.086418	.091194	.096141	.098678	.101255	.103873	.106531	.109227	.111961	.117540	.123262	.129118	.135103
	-.30	.089101	.093876	.098824	.101360	.103938	.106556	.109213	.111909	.114644	.120223	.125944	.131801	.137786
	-.40	.091783	.096559	.101506	.104043	.106620	.109238	.111896	.114592	.117326	.122905	.128627	.134483	.140468
20	.40	.065584	.071086	.076806	.079744	.082731	.085766	.088847	.091973	.095142	.101600	.108208	.114953	.121821
	.30	.068266	.073769	.079489	.082426	.085413	.088448	.091530	.094655	.097824	.104282	.110891	.117635	.124503
	.20	.070949	.076451	.082171	.085109	.088096	.091131	.094212	.097338	.100506	.106965	.113573	.120318	.127186
	.10	.073631	.079134	.084853	.087791	.090778	.093813	.096895	.100020	.103189	.109647	.116256	.123000	.129868
	0.00	.076313	.081816	.087536	.090473	.093461	.096496	.099577	.102703	.105871	.112330	.118938	.125683	.132550
	-.10	.078996	.084498	.090218	.093156	.096143	.099178	.102259	.105385	.108554	.115012	.121620	.128365	.135233
	-.20	.081678	.087181	.092901	.095838	.098825	.101860	.104942	.108068	.111236	.117694	.124303	.131048	.137915
	-.30	.084361	.089863	.095583	.098521	.101508	.104543	.107624	.110750	.113919	.120377	.126985	.133730	.140598
	-.40	.087043	.092546	.098266	.101203	.104190	.107225	.110307	.113432	.116601	.123059	.129668	.136412	.143280
25	.40	.062854	.068815	.075009	.078186	.081414	.084688	.088008	.091369	.094769	.101677	.108711	.115854	.123088
	.30	.065536	.071497	.077691	.080869	.084096	.087371	.090690	.094051	.097451	.104359	.111394	.118536	.125770
	.20	.068218	.074180	.080374	.083551	.086778	.090053	.093372	.096734	.100134	.107042	.114076	.121219	.128453
	.10	.070901	.076862	.083056	.086233	.089461	.092736	.096055	.099416	.102816	.109724	.116758	.123901	.131135
	0.00	.073583	.079544	.085738	.088916	.092143	.095418	.098737	.102098	.105499	.112406	.119441	.126583	.133818
	-.10	.076266	.082227	.088421	.091599	.094826	.098101	.101420	.104781	.108181	.115089	.122123	.129266	.136500
	-.20	.078948	.084909	.091103	.094281	.097508	.100783	.104102	.107463	.110863	.117771	.124806	.131948	.139183
	-.30	.081631	.087592	.093786	.096963	.100191	.103465	.106785	.110146	.113546	.120454	.127488	.134631	.141866
	-.40	.084313	.090274	.096468	.099646	.102873	.106148	.109467	.112828	.116228	.123136	.130170	.137313	.144547
30	.40	.061123	.067405	.073921	.077256	.080638	.084063	.087528	.091029	.094563	.101718	.108970	.116299	.123690
	.30	.063806	.070088	.076603	.079938	.083320	.086746	.090210	.093711	.097245	.104400	.111652	.118982	.126372
	.20	.066488	.072770	.079285	.082621	.086003	.089428	.092893	.096394	.099928	.107083	.114335	.121664	.129055
	.10	.069170	.075453	.081968	.085303	.088685	.092111	.095575	.099076	.102610	.109765	.117017	.124347	.131737
	0.00	.071853	.078135	.084650	.087986	.091368	.094793	.098258	.101759	.105293	.112447	.119699	.127029	.134420
	-.10	.074535	.080818	.087333	.090668	.094050	.097475	.100940	.104441	.107975	.115130	.122382	.129711	.137102
	-.20	.077218	.083500	.090015	.093350	.096733	.100158	.103623	.107124	.110658	.117812	.125064	.132394	.139785
	-.30	.079900	.086182	.092698	.096033	.099415	.102840	.106305	.109806	.113340	.120495	.127747	.135076	.142467
	-.40	.082582	.088865	.095380	.098715	.102097	.105523	.108987	.112488	.116022	.123177	.130429	.137759	.145149
40	.40	.059144	.065852	.072770	.076294	.079854	.083447	.087067	.090711	.094375	.101753	.109181	.116643	.124128
	.30	.061827	.068534	.075452	.078976	.082537	.086129	.089749	.093393	.097057	.104436	.111863	.119325	.126810
	.20	.064509	.071217	.078135	.081659	.085219	.088811	.092431	.096075	.099740	.107118	.114546	.122008	.129493
	.10	.067191	.073899	.080817	.084341	.087901	.091494	.095114	.098758	.102422	.109800	.117228	.124690	.132175
	0.00	.069874	.076581	.083499	.087023	.090584	.094176	.097796	.101440	.105105	.112483	.119911	.127373	.134857
	-.10	.072556	.079264	.086182	.089706	.093266	.096859	.100479	.104123	.107787	.115165	.122593	.130055	.137540
	-.20	.075239	.081946	.088864	.092388	.095949	.099541	.103161	.106805	.110469	.117848	.125276	.132738	.140222
	-.30	.077921	.084629	.091547	.095071	.098631	.102224	.105844	.109488	.113152	.120530	.127958	.135420	.142905
	-.40	.080604	.087311	.094229	.097753	.101314	.104906	.108526	.112170	.115834	.123213	.130640	.138102	.145587

15.0 YEAR HOLDING PERIOD
.120 EQUITY YIELD RATE
.800 LOAN RATIO

INTEREST RATE

TERM YEARS	APPR DEP	5.0	6.0	7.0	7.5	8.0	8.5	9.0	9.5	10.0	11.0	12.0	13.0	14.0
15	.40	.067727	.072821	.078098	.080804	.083554	.086346	.089181	.092056	.094973	.100924	.107027	.113274	.119658
	.30	.070410	.075504	.080781	.083487	.086236	.089028	.091863	.094739	.097655	.103607	.109709	.115957	.122341
	.20	.073092	.078186	.083463	.086169	.088918	.091711	.094545	.097421	.100338	.106289	.112392	.118639	.125023
	.10	.075774	.080868	.086146	.088851	.091601	.094393	.097228	.100104	.103020	.108971	.115074	.121321	.127705
	0.00	.078457	.083551	.088828	.091534	.094283	.097076	.099910	.102786	.105703	.111654	.117757	.124004	.130388
	-.10	.081139	.086233	.091511	.094216	.096966	.099758	.102593	.105469	.108385	.114336	.120439	.126686	.133070
	-.20	.083822	.088916	.094193	.096899	.099648	.102440	.105275	.108151	.111068	.117019	.123122	.129369	.135753
	-.30	.086504	.091598	.096875	.099581	.102330	.105123	.107957	.110833	.113750	.119701	.125804	.132051	.138435
	-.40	.089186	.094281	.099558	.102263	.105013	.107805	.110640	.113516	.116432	.122384	.128486	.134734	.141117
20	.40	.062671	.068541	.074642	.077775	.080962	.084199	.087486	.090820	.094200	.101089	.108137	.115332	.122657
	.30	.065354	.071223	.077324	.080458	.083644	.086881	.090168	.093502	.096882	.103771	.110820	.118014	.125340
	.20	.068036	.073906	.080007	.083140	.086326	.089564	.092851	.096185	.099565	.106453	.113502	.120697	.128022
	.10	.070719	.076588	.082689	.085823	.089009	.092246	.095533	.098867	.102247	.109136	.116185	.123379	.130705
	0.00	.073401	.079270	.085372	.088505	.091691	.094929	.098215	.101550	.104930	.111818	.118867	.126062	.133387
	-.10	.076083	.081953	.088054	.091187	.094374	.097611	.100898	.104232	.107612	.114501	.121550	.128744	.136070
	-.20	.078766	.084635	.090736	.093870	.097056	.100294	.103580	.106914	.110295	.117183	.124232	.131426	.138752
	-.30	.081448	.087318	.093419	.096552	.099739	.102976	.106263	.109597	.112977	.119865	.126914	.134109	.141434
	-.40	.084131	.090000	.096101	.099235	.102421	.105658	.108945	.112279	.115659	.122548	.129597	.136791	.144117
25	.40	.059759	.066118	.072725	.076114	.079556	.083050	.086590	.090175	.093802	.101170	.108674	.116293	.124009
	.30	.062442	.068800	.075407	.078796	.082239	.085732	.089273	.092858	.096485	.103853	.111356	.118975	.126692
	.20	.065124	.071483	.078089	.081479	.084921	.088414	.091955	.095540	.099167	.106535	.114039	.121658	.129374
	.10	.067806	.074165	.080772	.084161	.087604	.091097	.094637	.098223	.101849	.109218	.116721	.124340	.132056
	0.00	.070489	.076847	.083454	.086844	.090286	.093779	.097320	.100905	.104532	.111900	.119404	.127022	.134739
	-.10	.073171	.079530	.086137	.089526	.092969	.096462	.100002	.103587	.107214	.114583	.122086	.129705	.137421
	-.20	.075854	.082212	.088819	.092208	.095651	.099144	.102685	.106270	.109897	.117265	.124768	.132387	.140104
	-.30	.078536	.084895	.091502	.094891	.098333	.101827	.105367	.108952	.112579	.119947	.127451	.135070	.142786
	-.40	.081218	.087577	.094184	.097573	.101016	.104509	.108049	.111635	.115262	.122630	.130133	.137752	.145469
30	.40	.057913	.064614	.071564	.075122	.078729	.082383	.086079	.089813	.093583	.101214	.108950	.116768	.124651
	.30	.060596	.067297	.074246	.077804	.081412	.085065	.088761	.092495	.096265	.103897	.111632	.119450	.127334
	.20	.063278	.069979	.076929	.080486	.084094	.087748	.091443	.095178	.098947	.106579	.114314	.122133	.130016
	.10	.065961	.072662	.079611	.083169	.086776	.090430	.094126	.097860	.101630	.109261	.116997	.124815	.132699
	0.00	.068643	.075344	.082294	.085851	.089459	.093112	.096808	.100543	.104312	.111944	.119679	.127498	.135381
	-.10	.071325	.078027	.084976	.088534	.092141	.095795	.099491	.103225	.106995	.114626	.122362	.130180	.138063
	-.20	.074008	.080709	.087658	.091216	.094824	.098477	.102173	.105907	.109677	.117309	.125044	.132863	.140746
	-.30	.076690	.083391	.090341	.093899	.097506	.101160	.104855	.108590	.112359	.119991	.127727	.135545	.143428
	-.40	.079373	.086074	.093023	.096581	.100189	.103842	.107538	.111272	.115042	.122674	.130409	.138227	.146111
40	.40	.055802	.062957	.070336	.074095	.077893	.081725	.085586	.089473	.093382	.101252	.109175	.117135	.125118
	.30	.058485	.065640	.073019	.076778	.080576	.084407	.088269	.092156	.096064	.103934	.111857	.119817	.127801
	.20	.061167	.068322	.075701	.079460	.083258	.087090	.090951	.094838	.098747	.106617	.114540	.122499	.130483
	.10	.063850	.071004	.078384	.082143	.085940	.089772	.093634	.097521	.101429	.109299	.117222	.125182	.133165
	0.00	.066532	.073687	.081066	.084825	.088623	.092455	.096316	.100203	.104112	.111982	.119905	.127864	.135848
	-.10	.069215	.076369	.083748	.087507	.091305	.095137	.098998	.102885	.106794	.114664	.122587	.130547	.138530
	-.20	.071897	.079051	.086431	.090190	.093988	.097820	.101681	.105568	.109477	.117347	.125270	.133229	.141213
	-.30	.074579	.081734	.089113	.092872	.096670	.100502	.104363	.108250	.112159	.120029	.127952	.135911	.143895
	-.40	.077262	.084416	.091796	.095555	.099353	.103184	.107046	.110933	.114841	.122711	.130634	.138594	.146578

15.0 YEAR HOLDING PERIOD
.120 EQUITY YIELD RATE
.900 LOAN RATIO

INTEREST RATE

TERM YEARS	APPR DEP	5.0	6.0	7.0	7.5	8.0	8.5	9.0	9.5	10.0	11.0	12.0	13.0	14.0
15	.40	.062534	.068265	.074202	.077246	.080339	.083480	.086669	.089905	.093186	.099881	.106747	.113775	.120957
	.30	.065217	.070947	.076884	.079928	.083021	.086163	.089352	.092587	.095868	.102563	.109429	.116457	.123639
	.20	.067899	.073630	.079567	.082611	.085704	.088845	.092034	.095270	.098551	.105246	.112121	.119139	.126321
	.10	.070581	.076312	.082249	.085293	.088386	.091528	.094717	.097952	.101233	.107928	.114794	.121822	.129004
	0.00	.073264	.078995	.084932	.087976	.091069	.094210	.097399	.100634	.103916	.110611	.117476	.124504	.131686
	-.10	.075946	.081677	.087614	.090658	.093751	.096892	.100081	.103317	.106598	.113293	.120159	.127187	.134369
	-.20	.078629	.084360	.090296	.093340	.096433	.099575	.102764	.105999	.109280	.115976	.122841	.129869	.137051
	-.30	.081311	.087042	.092979	.096023	.099116	.102257	.105446	.108682	.111963	.118658	.125524	.132552	.139734
	-.40	.083994	.089724	.095669	.098705	.101798	.104940	.108129	.111364	.114645	.121340	.128206	.135234	.142416
20	.40	.056846	.063449	.070313	.073838	.077423	.081065	.084763	.088514	.092316	.100066	.107996	.116089	.124331
	.30	.059529	.066132	.072996	.076521	.080105	.083748	.087445	.091196	.094998	.102748	.110678	.118772	.127013
	.20	.062211	.068814	.075678	.079203	.082788	.086430	.090127	.093878	.097681	.105431	.113361	.121454	.129696
	.10	.064894	.071497	.078361	.081886	.085470	.089112	.092810	.096561	.100363	.108113	.116043	.124137	.132378
	0.00	.067576	.074179	.081043	.084568	.088153	.091795	.095492	.099243	.103046	.110795	.118726	.126819	.135060
	-.10	.070259	.076862	.083725	.087250	.090835	.094477	.098175	.101926	.105728	.113478	.121408	.129502	.137743
	-.20	.072941	.079544	.086408	.089933	.093518	.097160	.100857	.104608	.108410	.116160	.124090	.132184	.140425
	-.30	.075623	.082226	.089090	.092615	.096200	.099842	.103540	.107291	.111093	.118843	.126773	.134866	.143108
	-.40	.078306	.084909	.091773	.095298	.098882	.102524	.106222	.109973	.113775	.121525	.129455	.137549	.145790
25	.40	.053570	.060724	.068156	.071969	.075842	.079772	.083755	.087788	.091869	.100158	.108599	.117170	.125852
	.30	.056253	.063406	.070839	.074652	.078525	.082454	.086437	.090471	.094551	.102840	.111282	.119853	.128534
	.20	.058935	.066088	.073521	.077334	.081207	.085137	.089120	.093153	.097234	.105523	.113964	.122535	.131216
	.10	.061617	.068771	.076204	.080017	.083890	.087819	.091802	.095836	.099916	.108205	.116647	.125218	.133899
	0.00	.064300	.071453	.078886	.082699	.086572	.090502	.094485	.098518	.102598	.110888	.119329	.127900	.136581
	-.10	.066982	.074136	.081568	.085381	.089254	.093184	.097167	.101200	.105281	.113570	.122011	.130583	.139264
	-.20	.069665	.076818	.084251	.088064	.091937	.095866	.099850	.103883	.107963	.116253	.124694	.133265	.141946
	-.30	.072347	.079501	.086933	.090746	.094619	.098549	.102532	.106565	.110646	.118935	.127376	.135947	.144628
	-.40	.075030	.082183	.089616	.093429	.097302	.101231	.105214	.109248	.113328	.121617	.130059	.138630	.147311
30	.40	.051494	.059032	.066851	.070853	.074912	.079022	.083180	.087381	.091622	.100207	.108910	.117705	.126574
	.30	.054176	.061715	.069533	.073535	.077594	.081704	.085862	.090063	.094304	.102890	.111592	.120388	.129256
	.20	.056858	.064397	.072216	.076218	.080276	.084387	.088544	.092746	.096986	.105572	.114274	.123070	.131939
	.10	.059541	.067080	.074898	.078900	.082959	.087069	.091227	.095428	.099669	.108254	.116957	.125752	.134621
	0.00	.062223	.069762	.077580	.081583	.085641	.089751	.093909	.098111	.102351	.110937	.119639	.128435	.137304
	-.10	.064906	.072445	.080263	.084265	.088324	.092434	.096592	.100793	.105034	.113619	.122322	.131117	.139986
	-.20	.067588	.075127	.082945	.086949	.091006	.095116	.099274	.103475	.107716	.116302	.125000	.133800	.142669
	-.30	.070271	.077809	.085628	.089630	.093688	.097799	.101957	.106158	.110398	.118984	.127687	.136482	.145351
	-.40	.072953	.080492	.088310	.092312	.096371	.100481	.104639	.108840	.113081	.121667	.130369	.139165	.148033
40	.40	.049119	.057168	.065470	.069698	.073971	.078282	.082626	.086999	.091396	.100250	.109163	.118118	.127099
	.30	.051801	.059850	.068152	.072381	.076653	.080964	.085308	.089681	.094078	.102932	.111846	.120800	.129782
	.20	.054484	.062533	.070834	.075063	.079336	.083647	.087991	.092363	.096761	.105615	.114528	.123482	.132464
	.10	.057166	.065215	.073517	.077746	.082018	.086329	.090673	.095046	.099443	.108297	.117210	.126165	.135146
	0.00	.059849	.067898	.076199	.080428	.084701	.089012	.093356	.097728	.102126	.110979	.119893	.128847	.137829
	-.10	.062531	.070580	.078882	.083111	.087383	.091694	.096038	.100411	.104808	.113662	.122575	.131530	.140511
	-.20	.065214	.073262	.081564	.085793	.090066	.094376	.098720	.103093	.107490	.116344	.125258	.134212	.143194
	-.30	.067896	.075945	.084247	.088475	.092748	.097059	.101403	.105776	.110173	.119027	.127940	.136895	.145876
	-.40	.070578	.078627	.086929	.091158	.095430	.099741	.104085	.108458	.112855	.121709	.130623	.139577	.148859

15.0 YEAR HOLDING PERIOD
.140 EQUITY YIELD RATE
.600 LOAN RATIO

INTEREST RATE

TERM YEARS	APPR DEP	5.0	6.0	7.0	7.5	8.0	8.5	9.0	9.5	10.0	11.0	12.0	13.0	14.0
15	.40	.090128	.093949	.097907	.099936	.101998	.104092	.106218	.108375	.110563	.115026	.119603	.124288	.129076
	.30	.092409	.096230	.100188	.102217	.104279	.106373	.108499	.110656	.112844	.117307	.121884	.126569	.131357
	.20	.094690	.098511	.102468	.104498	.106560	.108654	.110780	.112937	.115124	.119588	.124165	.128850	.133638
	.10	.096971	.100791	.104749	.106779	.108841	.110935	.113061	.115218	.117405	.121869	.126446	.131131	.135919
	0.00	.099252	.103072	.107030	.109060	.111122	.113216	.115342	.117499	.119686	.124150	.128727	.133412	.138200
	-.10	.101533	.105353	.109311	.111340	.113402	.115497	.117623	.119780	.121967	.126430	.131008	.135693	.140481
	-.20	.103814	.107634	.111592	.113621	.115683	.117778	.119904	.122061	.124248	.128711	.133289	.137974	.142762
	-.30	.106094	.109915	.113873	.115902	.117964	.120059	.122185	.124341	.126529	.130992	.135569	.140255	.145043
	-.40	.108375	.112196	.116154	.118183	.120245	.122339	.124465	.126622	.128810	.133273	.137850	.142536	.147324
20	.40	.085494	.089846	.094371	.096696	.099060	.101463	.103903	.106379	.108888	.114006	.119243	.124591	.130038
	.30	.087775	.092126	.096652	.098977	.101341	.103744	.106184	.108659	.111169	.116286	.121524	.126872	.132319
	.20	.090056	.094407	.098933	.101258	.103622	.106025	.108465	.110940	.113450	.118567	.123805	.129153	.134600
	.10	.092337	.096688	.101214	.103538	.105903	.108306	.110746	.113221	.115731	.120848	.126086	.131434	.136881
	0.00	.094617	.098969	.103495	.105819	.108184	.110587	.113027	.115502	.118012	.123129	.128367	.133715	.139162
	-.10	.096898	.101250	.105775	.108100	.110465	.112868	.115307	.117783	.120293	.125410	.130648	.135996	.141443
	-.20	.099179	.103531	.108056	.110381	.112746	.115148	.117588	.120064	.122574	.127691	.132929	.138277	.143724
	-.30	.101460	.105812	.110337	.112662	.115026	.117429	.119869	.122345	.124855	.129972	.135210	.140557	.146005
	-.40	.103741	.108093	.112618	.114943	.117307	.119710	.122150	.124626	.127136	.132253	.137491	.142838	.148286
25	.40	.082824	.087523	.092410	.094918	.097468	.100055	.102679	.105338	.108028	.113497	.119070	.124733	.130472
	.30	.085105	.089804	.094691	.097199	.099749	.102336	.104960	.107619	.110309	.115777	.121351	.127013	.132753
	.20	.087386	.092085	.096972	.099480	.102029	.104617	.107241	.109899	.112590	.118058	.123631	.129294	.135034
	.10	.089667	.094366	.099252	.101761	.104310	.106898	.109522	.112180	.114871	.120339	.125912	.131575	.137315
	0.00	.091948	.096647	.101533	.104042	.106591	.109179	.111803	.114461	.117151	.122620	.128193	.133856	.139596
	-.10	.094229	.098927	.103814	.106323	.108872	.111460	.114084	.116742	.119432	.124901	.130474	.136137	.141876
	-.20	.096510	.101208	.106095	.108604	.111153	.113740	.116365	.119023	.121713	.127182	.132755	.138418	.144157
	-.30	.098791	.103489	.108376	.110885	.113434	.116022	.118646	.121304	.123994	.129463	.135036	.140699	.146438
	-.40	.101072	.105770	.110657	.113166	.115715	.118303	.120927	.123585	.126275	.131744	.137317	.142980	.148719
30	.40	.081132	.086082	.091223	.093857	.096530	.099239	.101981	.104753	.107552	.113225	.118980	.124803	.130678
	.30	.083413	.088363	.093503	.096138	.098811	.101520	.104261	.107033	.109833	.115506	.121261	.127083	.132959
	.20	.085694	.090644	.095784	.098419	.101092	.103801	.106542	.109314	.112114	.117787	.123542	.129364	.135240
	.10	.087975	.092925	.098065	.100700	.103373	.106081	.108823	.111595	.114395	.120068	.125823	.131645	.137521
	0.00	.090256	.095206	.100346	.102981	.105654	.108373	.111104	.113876	.116676	.122349	.128104	.133926	.139801
	-.10	.092537	.097486	.102627	.105261	.107934	.110643	.113385	.116157	.118957	.124629	.130385	.136207	.142082
	-.20	.094818	.099767	.104908	.107542	.110215	.112924	.115666	.118438	.121238	.126910	.132666	.138488	.144363
	-.30	.097099	.102048	.107189	.109823	.112496	.115204	.117947	.120719	.123519	.129191	.134947	.140769	.146644
	-.40	.099380	.104329	.109470	.112104	.114777	.117486	.120228	.123000	.125799	.131472	.137227	.143050	.148925
40	.40	.079198	.084493	.089967	.092759	.095582	.098433	.101308	.104204	.107118	.112990	.118907	.124856	.130828
	.30	.081478	.086774	.092248	.095040	.097863	.100714	.103589	.106485	.109399	.115271	.121188	.127137	.133109
	.20	.083759	.089055	.094529	.097321	.100144	.102995	.105870	.108766	.111680	.117552	.123469	.129418	.135389
	.10	.086040	.091336	.096810	.099602	.102425	.105276	.108151	.111047	.113961	.119833	.125750	.131699	.137670
	0.00	.088321	.093617	.099090	.101883	.104706	.107557	.110432	.113328	.116242	.122114	.128031	.133980	.139951
	-.10	.090602	.095898	.101371	.104163	.106987	.109838	.112713	.115609	.118522	.124395	.130312	.136261	.142232
	-.20	.092883	.098179	.103652	.106444	.109268	.112119	.114994	.117889	.120803	.126675	.132593	.138542	.144513
	-.30	.095164	.100460	.105933	.108725	.111549	.114400	.117274	.120170	.123084	.128956	.134874	.140823	.146794
	-.40	.097445	.102740	.108214	.111006	.113829	.116680	.119555	.122451	.125365	.131237	.137154	.143104	.149075

15.0 YEAR HOLDING PERIOD
.140 EQUITY YIELD RATE
.667 LOAN RATIO

INTEREST RATE

TERM YEARS	APPR DEP	5.0	6.0	7.0	7.5	8.0	8.5	9.0	9.5	10.0	11.0	12.0	13.0	14.0
15	.40	.085600	.089845	.094243	.096498	.098789	.101116	.103478	.105875	.108305	.113265	.118350	.123556	.128876
	.30	.087881	.092126	.096524	.098779	.101070	.103397	.105759	.108156	.110586	.115546	.120631	.125837	.131157
	.20	.090162	.094407	.098805	.101060	.103351	.105678	.108040	.110437	.112867	.117827	.122912	.128118	.133438
	.10	.092443	.096688	.101086	.103341	.105632	.107959	.110321	.112718	.115148	.120107	.125193	.130399	.135719
	0.00	.094724	.098969	.103367	.105622	.107913	.110240	.112602	.114999	.117429	.122388	.127474	.132680	.138000
	-.10	.097005	.101250	.105648	.107902	.110194	.112521	.114883	.117279	.119710	.124669	.129755	.134961	.140281
	-.20	.099286	.103531	.107929	.110183	.112474	.114801	.117164	.119560	.121991	.126950	.132036	.137242	.142562
	-.30	.101567	.105812	.110209	.112464	.114755	.117082	.119445	.121841	.124272	.129231	.134317	.139523	.144843
	-.40	.103848	.108093	.112490	.114745	.117036	.119363	.121725	.124122	.126553	.131512	.136598	.141804	.147124
20	.40	.080451	.085286	.090315	.092898	.095525	.098195	.100906	.103656	.106445	.112131	.117951	.123893	.129945
	.30	.082732	.087567	.092595	.095179	.097806	.100476	.103187	.105937	.108726	.114412	.120232	.126174	.132226
	.20	.085013	.089848	.094876	.097459	.100087	.102757	.105468	.108218	.111007	.116693	.122513	.128455	.134507
	.10	.087294	.092129	.097157	.099740	.102368	.105037	.107748	.110499	.113288	.118974	.124793	.130736	.136788
	0.00	.089575	.094410	.099438	.102021	.104648	.107318	.110029	.112780	.115569	.121254	.127074	.133016	.139069
	-.10	.091856	.096691	.101719	.104302	.106929	.109599	.112310	.115061	.117850	.123535	.129355	.135297	.141350
	-.20	.094136	.098972	.104000	.106583	.109210	.111880	.114591	.117342	.120131	.125816	.131636	.137578	.143631
	-.30	.096417	.101253	.106281	.108864	.111491	.114161	.116872	.119623	.122411	.128097	.133917	.139859	.145912
	-.40	.098698	.103534	.108562	.111145	.113772	.116442	.119153	.121904	.124692	.130378	.136198	.142140	.148192
25	.40	.077485	.082706	.088135	.090923	.093755	.096631	.099546	.102500	.105489	.111565	.117758	.124050	.130427
	.30	.079766	.084987	.090416	.093204	.096036	.098912	.101827	.104781	.107770	.113846	.120039	.126331	.132708
	.20	.082047	.087267	.092697	.095485	.098317	.101192	.104108	.107062	.110051	.116127	.122320	.128612	.134989
	.10	.084328	.089548	.094978	.097766	.100598	.103473	.106389	.109343	.112332	.118408	.124600	.130893	.137270
	0.00	.086609	.091829	.097259	.100046	.102879	.105754	.108670	.111623	.114613	.120689	.126881	.133173	.139551
	-.10	.088889	.094110	.099540	.102327	.105160	.108035	.110951	.113904	.116894	.122970	.129162	.135454	.141831
	-.20	.091170	.096391	.101821	.104608	.107441	.110316	.113232	.116185	.119174	.125251	.131443	.137735	.144112
	-.30	.093451	.098672	.104102	.106889	.109722	.112597	.115513	.118466	.121455	.127532	.133724	.140016	.146393
	-.40	.095732	.100953	.106383	.109170	.112003	.114878	.117793	.120747	.123736	.129813	.136005	.142297	.148674
30	.40	.075605	.081105	.086816	.089743	.092713	.095723	.098770	.101850	.104961	.111264	.117658	.124128	.130656
	.30	.077886	.083385	.089097	.092024	.094994	.098004	.101051	.104131	.107241	.113544	.119939	.126408	.132937
	.20	.080167	.085666	.091378	.094305	.097275	.100285	.103332	.106412	.109522	.115825	.122220	.128689	.135218
	.10	.082448	.087947	.093659	.096586	.099556	.102566	.105612	.108692	.111803	.118106	.124501	.130970	.137499
	0.00	.084729	.090228	.095940	.098867	.101837	.104847	.107893	.110973	.114084	.120387	.126782	.133251	.139779
	-.10	.087009	.092509	.098221	.101148	.104118	.107128	.110174	.113254	.116365	.122668	.129063	.135532	.142060
	-.20	.089290	.094790	.100502	.103429	.106399	.109409	.112455	.115535	.118646	.124949	.131344	.137813	.144341
	-.30	.091571	.097071	.102783	.105710	.108680	.111690	.114736	.117816	.120927	.127230	.133625	.140094	.146622
	-.40	.093852	.099352	.105064	.107991	.110961	.113970	.117017	.120097	.123208	.129511	.135906	.142375	.148903
40	.40	.073455	.079339	.085421	.088523	.091661	.094828	.098023	.101240	.104478	.111003	.117577	.124188	.130822
	.30	.075736	.081620	.087702	.090804	.093941	.097109	.100304	.103521	.106759	.113283	.119858	.126468	.133103
	.20	.078017	.083901	.089983	.093085	.096222	.099390	.102584	.105802	.109040	.115564	.122139	.128749	.135384
	.10	.080298	.086182	.092264	.095366	.098503	.101671	.104865	.108083	.111321	.117845	.124420	.131030	.137665
	0.00	.082579	.088463	.094545	.097647	.100784	.103952	.107146	.110364	.113602	.120126	.126701	.133311	.139946
	-.10	.084860	.090744	.096826	.099928	.103065	.106233	.109427	.112645	.115883	.122407	.128982	.135592	.142227
	-.20	.087141	.093025	.099107	.102209	.105346	.108514	.111708	.114926	.118163	.124688	.131263	.137873	.144508
	-.30	.089421	.095306	.101387	.104490	.107627	.110795	.113989	.117207	.120444	.126969	.133544	.140154	.146788
	-.40	.091702	.097587	.103668	.106771	.109908	.113075	.116270	.119488	.122725	.129250	.135824	.142435	.149069

15.0 YEAR HOLDING PERIOD
.140 EQUITY YIELD RATE
.700 LOAN RATIO

INTEREST RATE

TERM YEARS	APPR DEP	5.0	6.0	7.0	7.5	8.0	8.5	9.0	9.5	10.0	11.0	12.0	13.0	14.0
15	.40	.083337	.087794	.092412	.094779	.097185	.099628	.102109	.104625	.107177	.112384	.117724	.123190	.128776
	.30	.085618	.090075	.094693	.097060	.099466	.101909	.104389	.106906	.109458	.114665	.120005	.125471	.131058
	.20	.087899	.092356	.096974	.099341	.101747	.104190	.106670	.109187	.111739	.116946	.122286	.127752	.133338
	.10	.090179	.094637	.099254	.101622	.104028	.106471	.108951	.111468	.114020	.119227	.124567	.130033	.135619
	0.00	.092460	.096918	.101535	.103903	.106309	.108752	.111232	.113749	.116301	.121508	.126848	.132334	.137900
	-.10	.094741	.099199	.103816	.106184	.108589	.111033	.113513	.116029	.118581	.123789	.129129	.134595	.140181
	-.20	.097022	.101479	.106097	.108465	.110870	.113314	.115794	.118310	.120862	.126070	.131410	.136876	.142462
	-.30	.099303	.103760	.108378	.110745	.113151	.115595	.118075	.120591	.123143	.128351	.133691	.139157	.144743
	-.40	.101584	.106041	.110659	.113026	.115432	.117875	.120356	.122872	.125424	.130631	.135971	.141438	.147024
20	.40	.077930	.083007	.088287	.090999	.093758	.096561	.099407	.102296	.105224	.111194	.117305	.123544	.129899
	.30	.080211	.085288	.090568	.093280	.096038	.098842	.101688	.104576	.107505	.113475	.119585	.125825	.132180
	.20	.082492	.087569	.092849	.095561	.098319	.101123	.103969	.106857	.109785	.115756	.121866	.128105	.134461
	.10	.084773	.089850	.095129	.097842	.100600	.103404	.106250	.109138	.112066	.118036	.124147	.130386	.136741
	0.00	.087054	.092131	.097410	.100123	.102881	.105684	.108531	.111419	.114347	.120317	.126428	.132667	.139022
	-.10	.089335	.094412	.099691	.102403	.105162	.107965	.110812	.113700	.116628	.122598	.128709	.134948	.141303
	-.20	.091615	.096692	.101972	.104684	.107443	.110246	.113093	.115981	.118909	.124879	.130990	.137229	.143584
	-.30	.093896	.098973	.104253	.106965	.109724	.112527	.115374	.118262	.121190	.127160	.133271	.139510	.145865
	-.40	.096177	.101254	.106534	.109246	.112005	.114808	.117655	.120543	.123471	.129441	.135552	.141791	.148146
25	.40	.074816	.080297	.085999	.088925	.091900	.094919	.097980	.101081	.104220	.110600	.117102	.123709	.130405
	.30	.077097	.082578	.088280	.091206	.094180	.097199	.100261	.103362	.106501	.112881	.119383	.125990	.132685
	.20	.079377	.084859	.090560	.093487	.096461	.099480	.102542	.105643	.108782	.115162	.121664	.128270	.134966
	.10	.081658	.087140	.092841	.095768	.098742	.101761	.104823	.107924	.111062	.117443	.123945	.130551	.137247
	0.00	.083939	.089421	.095122	.098049	.101023	.104042	.107103	.110205	.113343	.119723	.126225	.132832	.139528
	-.10	.086220	.091702	.097403	.100330	.103304	.106323	.109384	.112486	.115624	.122004	.128506	.135113	.141809
	-.20	.088501	.093983	.099684	.102611	.105585	.108604	.111665	.114767	.117905	.124285	.130787	.137394	.144090
	-.30	.090782	.096264	.101965	.104892	.107866	.110885	.113946	.117047	.120186	.126566	.133068	.139675	.146371
	-.40	.093063	.098545	.104246	.107173	.110147	.113166	.116227	.119328	.122467	.128847	.135349	.141956	.148652
30	.40	.072842	.078616	.084614	.087687	.090806	.093966	.097165	.100399	.103665	.110283	.116998	.123790	.130645
	.30	.075123	.080897	.086895	.089968	.093086	.096247	.099445	.102680	.105946	.112564	.119279	.126071	.132926
	.20	.077403	.083178	.089175	.092249	.095367	.098528	.101726	.104960	.108227	.114845	.121559	.128352	.135207
	.10	.079684	.085459	.091456	.094530	.097648	.100808	.104007	.107241	.110508	.117126	.123840	.130633	.137488
	0.00	.081965	.087740	.093737	.096811	.099929	.103089	.106288	.109522	.112789	.119407	.126121	.132914	.139768
	-.10	.084246	.090021	.096018	.099091	.102210	.105370	.108569	.111803	.115069	.121687	.128402	.135195	.142049
	-.20	.086527	.092302	.098299	.101372	.104491	.107651	.110850	.114084	.117350	.123968	.130683	.137476	.144330
	-.30	.088808	.094583	.100580	.103653	.106772	.109932	.113131	.116365	.119631	.126249	.132964	.139756	.146611
	-.40	.091089	.096863	.102861	.105934	.109053	.112213	.115412	.118646	.121912	.128530	.135245	.142037	.148892
40	.40	.070584	.076763	.083149	.086406	.089700	.093026	.096380	.099759	.103158	.110009	.116912	.123853	.130820
	.30	.072865	.079044	.085430	.088687	.091981	.095307	.098661	.102040	.105439	.112290	.119193	.126134	.133100
	.20	.075146	.081325	.087710	.090968	.094262	.097588	.100942	.104320	.107720	.114571	.121474	.128415	.135381
	.10	.077427	.083605	.089991	.093249	.096543	.099869	.103223	.106601	.110001	.116852	.123755	.130696	.137662
	0.00	.079708	.085886	.092272	.095530	.098824	.102150	.105504	.108882	.112282	.119133	.126036	.132977	.139943
	-.10	.081989	.088167	.094553	.097811	.101104	.104431	.107785	.111163	.114563	.121413	.128317	.135258	.142224
	-.20	.084270	.090448	.096834	.100091	.103385	.106711	.110066	.113444	.116844	.123694	.130598	.137538	.144505
	-.30	.086551	.092729	.099115	.102372	.105666	.108992	.112346	.115725	.119125	.125975	.132879	.139819	.146786
	-.40	.088832	.095010	.101396	.104653	.107947	.111273	.114627	.118006	.121405	.128256	.135160	.142100	.149067

15.0 YEAR HOLDING PERIOD
.140 EQUITY YIELD RATE
.750 LOAN RATIO

INTEREST RATE

TERM YEARS	APPR DEP	5.0	6.0	7.0	7.5	8.0	8.5	9.0	9.5	10.0	11.0	12.0	13.0	14.0
15	.40	.079941	.084717	.089664	.092201	.094778	.097396	.100054	.102750	.105484	.111063	.116785	.122641	.128626
	.30	.082222	.086998	.091945	.094482	.097059	.099677	.102335	.105031	.107765	.113334	.119066	.124922	.130907
	.20	.084503	.089279	.094226	.096763	.099340	.101958	.104615	.107312	.110046	.115625	.121347	.127203	.133188
	.10	.086784	.091559	.096507	.099043	.101621	.104239	.106896	.109593	.112327	.117906	.123628	.129484	.135469
	0.00	.089065	.093840	.098788	.101324	.103902	.106520	.109177	.111873	.114608	.120187	.125908	.131765	.137750
	-.10	.091346	.096121	.101069	.103605	.106183	.108801	.111458	.114154	.116889	.122468	.128189	.134046	.140031
	-.20	.093626	.098402	.103350	.105886	.108464	.111082	.113739	.116435	.119170	.124749	.130470	.136327	.142312
	-.30	.095907	.100683	.105631	.108167	.110745	.113363	.116020	.118716	.121450	.127030	.132751	.138608	.144593
	-.40	.098188	.102964	.107911	.110448	.113026	.115643	.118301	.120997	.123731	.129311	.135032	.140889	.146874
20	.40	.074148	.079588	.085245	.088151	.091106	.094110	.097160	.100254	.103391	.109788	.116335	.123020	.129829
	.30	.076429	.081869	.087525	.090431	.093387	.096391	.099440	.102535	.105672	.112069	.118616	.125301	.132110
	.20	.078710	.084150	.089806	.092712	.095668	.098672	.101721	.104816	.107953	.114350	.120897	.127582	.134391
	.10	.080991	.086431	.092087	.094993	.097949	.100952	.104002	.107097	.110234	.116630	.123178	.129863	.136672
	0.00	.083272	.088711	.094368	.097274	.100230	.103233	.106283	.109378	.112515	.118911	.125459	.132143	.138952
	-.10	.085553	.090992	.096649	.099555	.102511	.105514	.108564	.111659	.114796	.121192	.127740	.134424	.141233
	-.20	.087834	.093273	.098930	.101836	.104792	.107795	.110845	.113939	.117077	.123473	.130021	.136705	.143514
	-.30	.090114	.095554	.101211	.104117	.107072	.110076	.113126	.116220	.119358	.125754	.132301	.138986	.145795
	-.40	.092395	.097835	.103492	.106398	.109353	.112357	.115407	.118501	.121639	.128035	.134582	.141267	.148076
25	.40	.070811	.076685	.082793	.085929	.089115	.092350	.095630	.098953	.102316	.109152	.116118	.123197	.130371
	.30	.073092	.078966	.085074	.088210	.091396	.094631	.097911	.101234	.104597	.111432	.118399	.125478	.132652
	.20	.075373	.081246	.087355	.090491	.093677	.096912	.100192	.103515	.106878	.113713	.120680	.127758	.134933
	.10	.077654	.083527	.089636	.092771	.095958	.099193	.102473	.105796	.109158	.115994	.122961	.130039	.137214
	0.00	.079935	.085808	.091917	.095052	.098239	.101474	.104754	.108076	.111439	.118275	.125242	.132320	.139494
	-.10	.082216	.088089	.094198	.097333	.100520	.103755	.107035	.110357	.113720	.120556	.127522	.134601	.141775
	-.20	.084497	.090370	.096478	.099614	.102801	.106035	.109316	.112638	.116001	.122837	.129803	.136882	.144056
	-.30	.086778	.092651	.098759	.101895	.105082	.108316	.111596	.114919	.118282	.125118	.132084	.139163	.146337
	-.40	.089058	.094932	.101040	.104176	.107363	.110597	.113877	.117200	.120563	.127399	.134365	.141444	.148618
30	.40	.068696	.074883	.081309	.084602	.087943	.091329	.094757	.098222	.101721	.108812	.116006	.123284	.130628
	.30	.070977	.077164	.083590	.086883	.090224	.093610	.097037	.100503	.104002	.111093	.118287	.125565	.132909
	.20	.073258	.079445	.085871	.089164	.092505	.095891	.099318	.102783	.106283	.113374	.120568	.127846	.135190
	.10	.075539	.081726	.088152	.091445	.094786	.098172	.101599	.105064	.108564	.115655	.122849	.130127	.137471
	0.00	.077820	.084007	.090433	.093726	.097067	.100453	.103880	.107345	.110845	.117936	.125130	.132408	.139752
	-.10	.080101	.086288	.092714	.096007	.099348	.102734	.106161	.109626	.113126	.120217	.127411	.134689	.142033
	-.20	.082382	.088569	.094994	.098287	.101629	.105015	.108442	.111907	.115407	.122497	.129692	.136969	.144314
	-.30	.084663	.090850	.097275	.100568	.103910	.107296	.110723	.114188	.117688	.124778	.131973	.139250	.146595
	-.40	.086944	.093131	.099556	.102849	.106190	.109577	.113004	.116469	.119968	.127059	.134253	.141531	.148875
40	.40	.066278	.072898	.079739	.083230	.086759	.090322	.093916	.097536	.101178	.108518	.115915	.123351	.130815
	.30	.068559	.075178	.082020	.085510	.089040	.092603	.096197	.099817	.103459	.110799	.118196	.125632	.133096
	.20	.070840	.077459	.084301	.087791	.091321	.094884	.098478	.102098	.105740	.113080	.120477	.127913	.135377
	.10	.073120	.079740	.086582	.090072	.093601	.097165	.100759	.104379	.108021	.115361	.122758	.130194	.137658
	0.00	.075401	.082020	.088863	.092353	.095882	.099446	.103040	.106660	.110302	.117642	.125039	.132475	.139939
	-.10	.077682	.084302	.091144	.094634	.098163	.101727	.105321	.108940	.112583	.119923	.127319	.134756	.142220
	-.20	.079963	.086583	.093425	.096915	.100444	.104008	.107602	.111221	.114864	.122204	.129600	.137037	.144501
	-.30	.082244	.088864	.095706	.099196	.102725	.106289	.109882	.113502	.117145	.124485	.131881	.139318	.146782
	-.40	.084525	.091145	.097987	.101477	.105006	.108570	.112163	.115783	.119426	.126766	.134162	.141599	.149063

416

INTEREST RATE

15.0 YEAR HOLDING PERIOD
.140 EQUITY YIELD RATE
.800 LOAN RATIO

TERM YEARS	APPR DEP	5.0	6.0	7.0	7.5	8.0	8.5	9.0	9.5	10.0	11.0	12.0	13.0	14.0
15	.40	.076545	.081639	.086917	.089622	.092372	.095164	.097999	.100875	.103791	.109743	.115845	.122092	.128476
	.30	.078826	.083920	.089198	.091903	.094653	.097445	.100280	.103156	.106072	.112023	.118126	.124373	.130757
	.20	.081107	.086201	.091479	.094184	.096934	.099726	.102561	.105437	.108353	.114304	.120407	.126654	.133038
	.10	.083388	.088482	.093759	.096465	.099215	.102007	.104842	.107718	.110634	.116585	.122688	.128935	.135319
	0.00	.085669	.090763	.096040	.098746	.101495	.104288	.107122	.109998	.112915	.118866	.124969	.131216	.137600
	-.10	.087950	.093044	.098321	.101027	.103776	.106569	.109403	.112279	.115196	.121147	.127250	.133497	.139881
	-.20	.090231	.095325	.100602	.103308	.106057	.108850	.111684	.114560	.117477	.123428	.129531	.135778	.142162
	-.30	.092512	.097606	.102883	.105589	.108338	.111131	.113965	.116841	.119758	.125709	.131812	.138059	.144443
	-.40	.094793	.099887	.105164	.107870	.110619	.113411	.116246	.119122	.122039	.127990	.134093	.140340	.146724
20	.40	.070366	.076169	.082202	.085302	.088455	.091659	.094912	.098213	.101559	.108382	.115366	.122496	.129759
	.30	.072647	.078450	.084483	.087583	.090736	.093939	.097193	.100493	.103840	.110663	.117647	.124777	.132040
	.20	.074928	.080730	.086764	.089864	.093017	.096220	.099474	.102774	.106121	.112944	.119928	.127058	.134321
	.10	.077209	.083011	.089045	.092145	.095297	.098501	.101754	.105055	.108402	.115225	.122208	.129339	.136602
	0.00	.079490	.085292	.091326	.094426	.097578	.100782	.104035	.107336	.110683	.117505	.124489	.131620	.138883
	-.10	.081771	.087573	.093607	.096707	.099859	.103063	.106316	.109617	.112964	.119786	.126770	.133901	.141164
	-.20	.084052	.089854	.095888	.098988	.102140	.105344	.108597	.111898	.115244	.122067	.129051	.136182	.143444
	-.30	.086333	.092135	.098169	.101268	.104421	.107625	.110878	.114179	.117525	.124348	.131332	.138462	.145725
	-.40	.088613	.094416	.100450	.103549	.106702	.109906	.113159	.116460	.119806	.126629	.133613	.140743	.148006
25	.40	.066807	.073072	.079588	.082932	.086331	.089782	.093280	.096825	.100412	.107703	.115134	.122685	.130337
	.30	.069088	.075353	.081868	.085213	.088612	.092063	.095561	.099106	.102693	.109984	.117415	.124966	.132618
	.20	.071369	.077634	.084149	.087494	.090893	.094343	.097842	.101386	.104974	.112265	.119696	.127246	.134899
	.10	.073650	.079915	.086430	.089775	.093174	.096624	.100123	.103667	.107255	.114546	.121977	.129527	.137180
	0.00	.075931	.082195	.088711	.092056	.095455	.098905	.102404	.105948	.109535	.116827	.124258	.131808	.139461
	-.10	.078211	.084476	.090992	.094337	.097736	.101186	.104685	.108229	.111816	.119108	.126539	.134089	.141742
	-.20	.080492	.086757	.093273	.096618	.100017	.103467	.106966	.110510	.114097	.121389	.128819	.136370	.144022
	-.30	.082773	.089038	.095554	.098899	.102298	.105748	.109247	.112791	.116378	.123670	.131100	.138651	.146303
	-.40	.085054	.091319	.097835	.101180	.104579	.108029	.111528	.115072	.118659	.125950	.133381	.140932	.148584
30	.40	.064551	.071150	.078005	.081517	.085081	.088693	.092349	.096045	.099778	.107341	.115015	.122778	.130612
	.30	.066832	.073431	.080286	.083798	.087362	.090974	.094629	.098326	.102058	.109622	.117296	.125059	.132893
	.20	.069113	.075712	.082566	.086079	.089643	.093255	.096910	.100606	.104339	.111903	.119577	.127340	.135174
	.10	.071394	.077993	.084847	.088360	.091924	.095536	.099191	.102887	.106620	.114184	.121858	.129621	.137454
	0.00	.073675	.080274	.087128	.090641	.094205	.097816	.101472	.105168	.108901	.116465	.124139	.131901	.139735
	-.10	.075955	.082555	.089409	.092922	.096486	.100097	.103753	.107449	.111182	.118746	.126419	.134182	.142016
	-.20	.078236	.084836	.091690	.095202	.098766	.102378	.106034	.109730	.113463	.121026	.128700	.136463	.144297
	-.30	.080517	.087117	.093971	.097483	.101047	.104659	.108315	.112011	.115744	.123307	.130981	.138744	.146578
	-.40	.082798	.089398	.096252	.099764	.103328	.106940	.110596	.114292	.118025	.125588	.133262	.141025	.148859
40	.40	.061971	.069032	.076330	.080053	.083818	.087619	.091452	.095313	.099199	.107028	.114918	.122850	.130811
	.30	.064252	.071313	.078611	.082334	.086099	.089900	.093733	.097594	.101479	.109309	.117198	.125131	.133092
	.20	.066533	.073594	.080892	.084615	.088379	.092181	.096014	.099875	.103760	.111590	.119479	.127412	.135373
	.10	.068814	.075875	.083173	.086896	.090660	.094462	.098295	.102156	.106041	.113871	.121760	.129693	.137654
	0.00	.071095	.078156	.085454	.089177	.092941	.096742	.100576	.104437	.108322	.116152	.124041	.131973	.139935
	-.10	.073376	.080437	.087735	.091458	.095222	.099023	.102857	.106718	.110603	.118432	.126322	.134254	.142216
	-.20	.075657	.082718	.090016	.093738	.097503	.101304	.105138	.108999	.112884	.120713	.128603	.136535	.144497
	-.30	.077937	.084999	.092297	.096019	.099784	.103585	.107418	.111280	.115165	.122994	.130884	.138816	.146778
	-.40	.080218	.087279	.094578	.098300	.102065	.105866	.109699	.113560	.117446	.125275	.133165	.141097	.149059

15.0 YEAR HOLDING PERIOD
.140 EQUITY YIELD RATE
.900 LOAN RATIO

INTEREST RATE

TERM YEARS	APPR DEP	5.0	6.0	7.0	7.5	8.0	8.5	9.0	9.5	10.0	11.0	12.0	13.0	14.0
15	.40	.069754	.075485	.081422	.084466	.087559	.090700	.093889	.097125	.100406	.107101	.113966	.120995	.128176
	.30	.072035	.077766	.083703	.086747	.089840	.092981	.096170	.099406	.102687	.109382	.116247	.123275	.130457
	.20	.074316	.080047	.085984	.089027	.092121	.095262	.098451	.101686	.104967	.111663	.118528	.125556	.132738
	.10	.076597	.082328	.088264	.091308	.094401	.097543	.100732	.103967	.107248	.113944	.120809	.127837	.135019
	0.00	.078878	.084608	.090545	.093589	.096682	.099824	.103013	.106248	.109529	.116224	.123090	.130118	.137300
	-.10	.081159	.086889	.092826	.095870	.098963	.102105	.105294	.108529	.111810	.118505	.125371	.132399	.139581
	-.20	.083439	.089170	.095107	.098151	.101244	.104386	.107575	.110810	.114091	.120786	.127652	.134680	.141862
	-.30	.085720	.091451	.097388	.100432	.103525	.106666	.109855	.113091	.116372	.123067	.129933	.136961	.144143
	-.40	.088001	.093732	.099669	.102713	.105806	.108947	.112136	.115372	.118653	.125348	.132214	.139242	.146424
20	.40	.062803	.069330	.076118	.079605	.083152	.086756	.090416	.094130	.097894	.105570	.113427	.121449	.129619
	.30	.065083	.071611	.078399	.081886	.085433	.089037	.092697	.096410	.100175	.107851	.115708	.123730	.131900
	.20	.067364	.073892	.080680	.084167	.087714	.091318	.094978	.098691	.102456	.110132	.117989	.126010	.134181
	.10	.069645	.076173	.082961	.086448	.089995	.093599	.097259	.100972	.104737	.112413	.120270	.128291	.136462
	0.00	.071926	.078454	.085242	.088729	.092276	.095880	.099540	.103253	.107018	.114694	.122550	.130572	.138743
	-.10	.074207	.080735	.087523	.091010	.094557	.098161	.101821	.105534	.109299	.116975	.124831	.132853	.141024
	-.20	.076488	.083016	.089804	.093291	.096837	.100442	.104102	.107815	.111580	.119255	.127112	.135134	.143305
	-.30	.078769	.085296	.092084	.095572	.099118	.102723	.106382	.110096	.113861	.121536	.129393	.137415	.145586
	-.40	.081050	.087577	.094365	.097853	.101399	.105004	.108663	.112377	.116142	.123817	.131674	.139696	.147867
25	.40	.058798	.065846	.073176	.076939	.080763	.084645	.088581	.092568	.096604	.104807	.113166	.121661	.130270
	.30	.061079	.068127	.075457	.079220	.083044	.086926	.090862	.094849	.098885	.107088	.115447	.123942	.132551
	.20	.063360	.070408	.077738	.081501	.085325	.089207	.093143	.097130	.101165	.109368	.117728	.126222	.134831
	.10	.065641	.072689	.080019	.083782	.087606	.091488	.095424	.099411	.103446	.111649	.120009	.128503	.137112
	0.00	.067922	.074970	.082300	.086063	.089887	.093768	.097704	.101692	.105727	.113930	.122290	.130784	.139393
	-.10	.070203	.077251	.084581	.088344	.092168	.096049	.099985	.103973	.108008	.116211	.124571	.133065	.141674
	-.20	.072484	.079532	.086862	.090625	.094449	.098330	.102266	.106254	.110289	.118492	.126852	.135346	.143955
	-.30	.074765	.081813	.089143	.092906	.096730	.100611	.104547	.108534	.112570	.120773	.129133	.137627	.146236
	-.40	.077045	.084093	.091424	.095187	.099010	.102892	.106828	.110815	.114851	.123054	.131413	.139908	.148517
30	.40	.056260	.063685	.071396	.075347	.079357	.083420	.087533	.091691	.095890	.104399	.113032	.121766	.130579
	.30	.058541	.065966	.073677	.077628	.081638	.085701	.089814	.093972	.098171	.106680	.115313	.124046	.132860
	.20	.060822	.068247	.075957	.079909	.083918	.087982	.092094	.096252	.100452	.108961	.117594	.126327	.135140
	.10	.063103	.070528	.078238	.082190	.086199	.090263	.094375	.098533	.102733	.111242	.119875	.128608	.137421
	0.00	.065384	.072808	.080519	.084471	.088480	.092544	.096656	.100814	.105014	.113523	.122156	.130889	.139702
	-.10	.067665	.075089	.082800	.086752	.090761	.094824	.098937	.103095	.107295	.115804	.124437	.133170	.141983
	-.20	.069946	.077370	.085081	.089033	.093042	.097105	.101218	.105376	.109576	.118085	.126718	.135451	.144264
	-.30	.072227	.079651	.087362	.091313	.095323	.099386	.103499	.107657	.111857	.120365	.128999	.137732	.146545
	-.40	.074508	.081932	.089643	.093594	.097604	.101667	.105780	.109938	.114137	.122646	.131279	.140013	.148826
40	.40	.053358	.061302	.069512	.073700	.077935	.082212	.086524	.090868	.095239	.104047	.112923	.121846	.130803
	.30	.055639	.063583	.071793	.075981	.080216	.084493	.088805	.093149	.097520	.106328	.115204	.124127	.133084
	.20	.057920	.065864	.074074	.078262	.082497	.086773	.091086	.095430	.099801	.108609	.117484	.126408	.135365
	.10	.060201	.068144	.076355	.080543	.084778	.089054	.093367	.097711	.102081	.110890	.119765	.128689	.137646
	0.00	.062482	.070425	.078636	.082824	.087059	.091335	.095648	.099992	.104362	.113170	.122046	.130970	.139927
	-.10	.064763	.072706	.080917	.085105	.089340	.093616	.097929	.102272	.106643	.115451	.124327	.133251	.142208
	-.20	.067043	.074987	.083197	.087386	.091621	.095897	.100209	.104553	.108924	.117732	.126608	.135532	.144489
	-.30	.069324	.077268	.085478	.089666	.093902	.098178	.102490	.106834	.111205	.120013	.128889	.137813	.146770
	-.40	.071605	.079549	.087759	.091947	.096182	.100459	.104771	.109115	.113486	.122294	.131170	.140094	.149050

15.0 YEAR HOLDING PERIOD
.150 EQUITY YIELD RATE
.600 LOAN RATIO

INTEREST RATE

TERM YEARS	APPR DEP	5.0	6.0	7.0	7.5	8.0	8.5	9.0	9.5	10.0	11.0	12.0	13.0	14.0
15	.40	.095920	.099741	.103699	.105728	.107790	.109884	.112010	.114167	.116355	.120818	.125395	.130080	.134868
	.30	.098022	.101842	.105800	.107830	.109892	.111986	.114112	.116269	.118456	.122920	.127497	.132182	.136970
	.20	.100123	.103944	.107902	.109931	.111993	.114088	.116214	.118371	.120558	.125021	.129598	.134284	.139072
	.10	.102225	.106046	.110004	.112033	.114095	.116189	.118315	.120472	.122660	.127123	.131700	.136385	.141173
	0.00	.104327	.108147	.112105	.114135	.116197	.118291	.120417	.122574	.124761	.129225	.133802	.138487	.143275
	-.10	.106429	.110249	.114207	.116236	.118298	.120393	.122519	.124676	.126863	.131326	.135904	.140589	.145377
	-.20	.108530	.112351	.116309	.118338	.120400	.122494	.124620	.126777	.128965	.133428	.138006	.142691	.147479
	-.30	.110632	.114453	.118411	.120440	.122502	.124596	.126722	.128879	.131066	.135530	.140107	.144792	.149580
	-.40	.112734	.116554	.120512	.122541	.124604	.126698	.128824	.130981	.133168	.137632	.142209	.146894	.151682
20	.40	.090910	.095239	.099742	.102055	.104409	.106800	.109229	.111693	.114192	.119287	.124503	.129830	.135256
	.30	.093011	.097341	.101844	.104157	.106510	.108902	.111331	.113795	.116294	.121389	.126605	.131931	.137357
	.20	.095113	.099442	.103945	.106259	.108612	.111004	.113432	.115897	.118395	.123490	.128707	.134033	.139459
	.10	.097215	.101544	.106047	.108361	.110714	.113105	.115534	.117998	.120497	.125592	.130808	.136135	.141561
	0.00	.099317	.103646	.108149	.110462	.112815	.115207	.117636	.120100	.122599	.127694	.132910	.138236	.143663
	-.10	.101418	.105748	.110250	.112564	.114917	.117309	.119737	.122202	.124700	.129796	.135012	.140338	.145764
	-.20	.103520	.107849	.112352	.114666	.117019	.119410	.121839	.124303	.126802	.131897	.137113	.142440	.147866
	-.30	.105622	.109951	.114454	.116767	.119121	.121512	.123941	.126405	.128904	.133999	.139215	.144541	.149968
	-.40	.107723	.112053	.116556	.118869	.121222	.123614	.126042	.128507	.131006	.136101	.141317	.146643	.152069
25	.40	.088024	.092691	.097547	.100143	.102576	.105149	.107759	.110404	.113081	.118523	.124072	.129712	.135430
	.30	.090125	.094793	.099649	.102244	.104677	.107251	.109861	.112505	.115182	.120625	.126174	.131814	.137532
	.20	.092227	.096894	.101751	.104346	.106779	.109352	.111962	.114607	.117284	.122727	.128276	.133916	.139634
	.10	.094329	.098996	.103852	.106447	.108881	.111454	.114064	.116709	.119386	.124829	.130377	.136017	.141735
	0.00	.096430	.101098	.105954	.108549	.110982	.113556	.116166	.118810	.121487	.126930	.132479	.138119	.143837
	-.10	.098532	.103199	.108056	.110651	.113084	.115658	.118268	.120912	.123589	.129032	.134581	.140221	.145939
	-.20	.100634	.105301	.110157	.112752	.115186	.117759	.120369	.123014	.125691	.131134	.136683	.142323	.148041
	-.30	.102736	.107403	.112259	.114854	.117288	.119861	.122471	.125116	.127792	.133235	.138784	.144424	.150142
	-.40	.104837	.109505	.114361	.116955	.119389	.121963	.124573	.127217	.129894	.135337	.140886	.146526	.152244
30	.40	.086194	.091110	.096219	.098838	.101496	.104191	.106920	.109679	.112466	.118116	.123851	.129654	.135513
	.30	.088296	.093212	.098320	.100940	.103598	.106293	.109021	.111780	.114568	.120218	.125952	.131756	.137615
	.20	.090398	.095313	.100422	.103041	.105700	.108395	.111123	.113882	.116670	.122319	.128054	.133858	.139717
	.10	.092500	.097415	.102524	.105143	.107801	.110496	.113225	.115984	.118771	.124421	.130156	.135960	.141818
	0.00	.094601	.099517	.104625	.107245	.109903	.112598	.115326	.118086	.120873	.126523	.132258	.138061	.143920
	-.10	.096703	.101619	.106727	.109346	.112005	.114700	.117428	.120187	.122975	.128625	.134359	.140163	.146022
	-.20	.098805	.103720	.108829	.111448	.114107	.116801	.119530	.122289	.125076	.130726	.136461	.142265	.148123
	-.30	.100906	.105822	.110931	.113550	.116208	.118903	.121631	.124391	.127178	.132828	.138563	.144366	.150225
	-.40	.103008	.107924	.113032	.115652	.118310	.121005	.123733	.126492	.129280	.134930	.140664	.146468	.152327
40	.40	.084103	.089367	.094813	.097593	.100406	.103246	.106112	.108999	.111905	.117764	.123670	.129610	.135574
	.30	.086204	.091469	.096915	.099695	.102507	.105348	.108214	.111101	.114007	.119865	.125771	.131711	.137675
	.20	.088306	.093570	.099017	.101797	.104609	.107450	.110315	.113203	.116109	.121967	.127873	.133813	.139777
	.10	.090408	.095672	.101119	.103899	.106711	.109551	.112417	.115304	.118210	.124069	.129975	.135915	.141879
	0.00	.092509	.097774	.103220	.106000	.108812	.111653	.114519	.117406	.120312	.126170	.132077	.138017	.143980
	-.10	.094611	.099876	.105322	.108102	.110914	.113755	.116620	.119508	.122414	.128272	.134178	.140118	.146082
	-.20	.096713	.101977	.107424	.110204	.113016	.115857	.118722	.121609	.124515	.130374	.136280	.142220	.148184
	-.30	.098815	.104079	.109525	.112305	.115117	.117958	.120824	.123711	.126617	.132475	.138382	.144322	.150285
	-.40	.100916	.106181	.111627	.114407	.117219	.120060	.122926	.125813	.128719	.134577	.140483	.146423	.152387

15.0 YEAR HOLDING PERIOD
.150 EQUITY YIELD RATE
.667 LOAN RATIO

INTEREST RATE

TERM YEARS	APPR DEP	5.0	6.0	7.0	7.5	8.0	8.5	9.0	9.5	10.0	11.0	12.0	13.0	14.0
15	.40	.090845	.095090	.099488	.101743	.104034	.106361	.108723	.111120	.113550	.118509	.123595	.128801	.134121
	.30	.092947	.097192	.101590	.103844	.106135	.108463	.110825	.113221	.115652	.120611	.125697	.130903	.136223
	.20	.095048	.099294	.103691	.105946	.108237	.110564	.112926	.115323	.117753	.122713	.127799	.133005	.138324
	.10	.097150	.101395	.105793	.108048	.110339	.112666	.115028	.117425	.119855	.124815	.129900	.135106	.140426
	0.00	.099252	.103497	.107895	.110150	.112441	.114768	.117130	.119526	.121957	.126916	.132002	.137208	.142528
	-.10	.101354	.105599	.109996	.112251	.114542	.116869	.119231	.121628	.124059	.129018	.134104	.139310	.144630
	-.20	.103455	.107700	.112098	.114353	.116644	.118971	.121333	.123730	.126160	.131120	.136205	.141411	.146731
	-.30	.105557	.109802	.114200	.116455	.118746	.121073	.123435	.125832	.128262	.133221	.138307	.143513	.148833
	-.40	.107659	.111904	.116302	.118556	.120847	.123174	.125537	.127933	.130364	.135323	.140409	.145615	.150935
20	.40	.085278	.090088	.095092	.097662	.100277	.102934	.105633	.108371	.111147	.116808	.122604	.128522	.134552
	.30	.087380	.092190	.097193	.099764	.102378	.105036	.107734	.110473	.113249	.118910	.124706	.130624	.136653
	.20	.089481	.094292	.099295	.101866	.104480	.107138	.109836	.112574	.115351	.121012	.126808	.132726	.138755
	.10	.091583	.096393	.101397	.103967	.106582	.109239	.111938	.114676	.117452	.123114	.128909	.134827	.140857
	0.00	.093685	.098495	.103498	.106069	.108684	.111341	.114039	.116778	.119554	.125215	.131011	.136929	.142958
	-.10	.095787	.100597	.105600	.108171	.110785	.113443	.116141	.118879	.121656	.127317	.133113	.139031	.145060
	-.20	.097888	.102699	.107702	.110272	.112887	.115544	.118243	.120981	.123757	.129419	.135214	.141133	.147162
	-.30	.099990	.104800	.109803	.112374	.114989	.117646	.120345	.123083	.125859	.131520	.137316	.143234	.149263
	-.40	.102092	.106902	.111905	.114476	.117090	.119748	.122446	.125184	.127961	.133622	.139418	.145336	.151365
25	.40	.082071	.087257	.092653	.095424	.098260	.101099	.104000	.106938	.109912	.115960	.122125	.128392	.134745
	.30	.084173	.089359	.094755	.097526	.100362	.103201	.106101	.109040	.112014	.118062	.124227	.130494	.136847
	.20	.086275	.091460	.096856	.099627	.102464	.105303	.108203	.111141	.114116	.120163	.126329	.132596	.138949
	.10	.088376	.093562	.098958	.101729	.104545	.107405	.110305	.113243	.116217	.122265	.128431	.134697	.141051
	0.00	.090478	.095664	.101060	.103831	.106647	.109506	.112406	.115345	.118319	.124367	.130532	.136799	.143152
	-.10	.092580	.097766	.103161	.105932	.108749	.111608	.114508	.117446	.120421	.126469	.132634	.138901	.145254
	-.20	.094681	.099867	.105263	.108034	.110850	.113710	.116610	.119548	.122523	.128570	.134736	.141002	.147356
	-.30	.096783	.101969	.107365	.110136	.112952	.115811	.118711	.121650	.124624	.130672	.136837	.143104	.149457
	-.40	.098885	.104071	.109467	.112237	.115054	.117913	.120813	.123752	.126726	.132774	.138939	.145206	.151559
30	.40	.080039	.085500	.091177	.094087	.097041	.100035	.103067	.106133	.109230	.115507	.121879	.128328	.134838
	.30	.082140	.087602	.093279	.096189	.099143	.102137	.105168	.108234	.111331	.117609	.123981	.130430	.136939
	.20	.084242	.089704	.095380	.098290	.101244	.104239	.107270	.110336	.113433	.119711	.126083	.132531	.139041
	.10	.086344	.091806	.097482	.100392	.103346	.106340	.109372	.112438	.115535	.121812	.128184	.134633	.141143
	0.00	.088446	.093907	.099584	.102494	.105448	.108442	.111474	.114539	.117637	.123914	.130286	.136735	.143244
	-.10	.090547	.096009	.101685	.104596	.107549	.110544	.113575	.116641	.119738	.126016	.132388	.138836	.145346
	-.20	.092649	.098111	.103787	.106697	.109651	.112645	.115677	.118743	.121840	.128118	.134489	.140938	.147448
	-.30	.094751	.100212	.105889	.108799	.111753	.114747	.117779	.120844	.123942	.130219	.136591	.143040	.149550
	-.40	.096852	.102314	.107990	.110901	.113855	.116849	.119880	.122946	.126043	.132321	.138693	.145141	.151651
40	.40	.077714	.083564	.089615	.092704	.095829	.098985	.102169	.105377	.108606	.115116	.121678	.128278	.134905
	.30	.079816	.085666	.091717	.094806	.097931	.101087	.104271	.107479	.110708	.117218	.123780	.130380	.137006
	.20	.081918	.087767	.093819	.096908	.100032	.103189	.106373	.109581	.112810	.119319	.125882	.132482	.139108
	.10	.084020	.089869	.095921	.099009	.102134	.105290	.108474	.111683	.114912	.121421	.127983	.134583	.141210
	0.00	.086121	.091971	.098023	.101111	.104236	.107392	.110576	.113784	.117013	.123523	.130085	.136685	.143311
	-.10	.088223	.094072	.100124	.103213	.106338	.109494	.112678	.115886	.119115	.125624	.132187	.138787	.145413
	-.20	.090325	.096174	.102226	.105315	.108439	.111596	.114780	.117988	.121217	.127726	.134288	.140888	.147515
	-.30	.092426	.098276	.104327	.107416	.110541	.113697	.116881	.120089	.123318	.129828	.136390	.142990	.149617
	-.40	.094528	.100378	.106429	.109518	.112643	.115799	.118983	.122191	.125420	.131929	.138492	.145092	.151718

15.0 YEAR HOLDING PERIOD
.150 EQUITY YIELD RATE
.700 LOAN RATIO

INTEREST RATE

TERM YEARS	APPR DEP	5.0	6.0	7.0	7.5	8.0	8.5	9.0	9.5	10.0	11.0	12.0	13.0	14.0
15	.40	.088308	.092765	.097383	.099750	.102156	.104599	.107080	.109596	.112148	.117355	.122695	.128162	.133748
	.30	.090410	.094867	.099485	.101852	.104258	.106701	.109181	.111698	.114250	.119487	.124797	.130263	.135849
	.20	.092511	.096969	.101586	.103954	.106359	.108803	.111283	.113800	.116351	.121559	.126899	.132365	.137951
	.10	.094613	.099070	.103688	.106055	.108461	.110904	.113385	.115901	.118453	.123661	.129000	.134467	.140053
	0.00	.096715	.101172	.105790	.108157	.110563	.113006	.115486	.118003	.120555	.125762	.131102	.136568	.142154
	-.10	.098816	.103274	.107891	.110259	.112665	.115108	.117588	.120105	.122657	.127864	.133204	.138670	.144256
	-.20	.100918	.105375	.109993	.112361	.114766	.117210	.119690	.122206	.124758	.129966	.135306	.140772	.146358
	-.30	.103020	.107477	.112095	.114462	.116868	.119311	.121792	.124308	.126860	.132067	.137407	.142874	.148459
	-.40	.105122	.109579	.114196	.116564	.118970	.121413	.123893	.126410	.128962	.134169	.139509	.144975	.150561
20	.40	.082463	.087513	.092767	.095466	.098211	.101001	.103835	.106710	.109625	.115569	.121655	.127869	.134199
	.30	.084564	.089615	.094868	.097567	.100313	.103103	.105936	.108812	.111727	.117671	.123756	.129971	.136301
	.20	.086666	.091717	.096970	.099669	.102415	.105205	.108038	.110913	.113828	.119773	.125858	.132072	.138403
	.10	.088768	.093818	.099072	.101771	.104516	.107306	.110140	.113015	.115930	.121874	.127960	.134174	.140505
	0.00	.090869	.095920	.101174	.103873	.106618	.109408	.112242	.115117	.118032	.123976	.130062	.136276	.142606
	-.10	.092971	.098022	.103275	.105974	.108720	.111510	.114343	.117218	.120134	.126078	.132163	.138377	.144708
	-.20	.095073	.100124	.105377	.108076	.110821	.113612	.116445	.119320	.122235	.128180	.134265	.140479	.146810
	-.30	.097174	.102225	.107479	.110178	.112923	.115713	.118547	.121422	.124337	.130281	.136367	.142581	.148911
	-.40	.099276	.104327	.109581	.112279	.115025	.117815	.120648	.123524	.126439	.132383	.138468	.144683	.151013
25	.40	.079095	.084541	.090206	.093116	.096073	.099075	.102122	.105205	.108328	.114679	.121152	.127732	.134403
	.30	.081197	.086642	.092308	.095217	.098174	.101177	.104222	.107307	.110430	.116780	.123254	.129834	.136505
	.20	.083299	.088744	.094410	.097319	.100276	.103278	.106323	.109409	.112532	.118882	.125356	.131936	.138607
	.10	.085401	.090846	.096511	.099421	.102378	.105380	.108425	.111510	.114634	.120984	.127457	.134037	.140708
	0.00	.087502	.092947	.098613	.101522	.104480	.107482	.110527	.113612	.116735	.123085	.129559	.136139	.142810
	-.10	.089604	.095049	.100715	.103624	.106581	.109584	.112629	.115714	.118837	.125187	.131661	.138241	.144912
	-.20	.091705	.097151	.102816	.105726	.108683	.111685	.114730	.117816	.120939	.127289	.133762	.140342	.147013
	-.30	.093807	.099252	.104918	.107828	.110785	.113787	.116832	.119917	.123040	.129390	.135864	.142444	.149115
	-.40	.095909	.101354	.107020	.109929	.112886	.115889	.118934	.122019	.125142	.131492	.137966	.144546	.151217
30	.40	.076961	.082696	.088656	.091712	.094814	.097957	.101141	.104360	.107612	.114203	.120894	.127665	.134500
	.30	.079063	.084798	.090758	.093814	.096915	.100059	.103242	.106461	.109713	.116305	.122995	.129766	.136602
	.20	.081165	.086900	.092860	.095915	.099017	.102161	.105344	.108563	.111815	.118407	.125097	.131868	.138703
	.10	.083266	.089001	.094961	.098017	.101119	.104263	.107446	.110665	.113917	.120508	.127199	.133970	.140805
	0.00	.085368	.091103	.097063	.100119	.103220	.106364	.109547	.112766	.116019	.122610	.129300	.136071	.142907
	-.10	.087470	.093205	.099165	.102221	.105322	.108466	.111649	.114868	.118120	.124712	.131402	.138173	.145008
	-.20	.089572	.095306	.101266	.104322	.107424	.110568	.113751	.116970	.120222	.126813	.133504	.140275	.147110
	-.30	.091673	.097408	.103368	.106424	.109525	.112669	.115853	.119072	.122324	.128915	.135606	.142377	.149212
	-.40	.093775	.099510	.105470	.108526	.111627	.114771	.117954	.121173	.124425	.131017	.137707	.144478	.151314
40	.40	.074521	.080663	.087017	.090260	.093541	.096855	.100198	.103567	.106957	.113792	.120682	.127612	.134570
	.30	.076623	.082764	.089119	.092362	.095643	.098957	.102300	.105669	.109059	.115894	.122784	.129714	.136672
	.20	.078724	.084866	.091220	.094464	.097744	.101059	.104402	.107770	.111161	.117995	.124886	.131816	.138774
	.10	.080826	.086968	.093322	.096565	.099846	.103160	.106503	.109872	.113262	.120097	.126988	.133918	.140875
	0.00	.082928	.089070	.095424	.098667	.101948	.105262	.108605	.111974	.115364	.122199	.129089	.136019	.142977
	-.10	.085029	.091171	.097525	.100769	.104050	.107364	.110707	.114075	.117466	.124301	.131191	.138121	.145079
	-.20	.087131	.093273	.099627	.102870	.106151	.109465	.112809	.116177	.119567	.126402	.133293	.140223	.147180
	-.30	.089233	.095375	.101729	.104972	.108253	.111567	.114910	.118279	.121669	.128504	.135394	.142324	.149282
	-.40	.091334	.097476	.103830	.107074	.110355	.113669	.117012	.120380	.123771	.130606	.137496	.144426	.151384

15.0 YEAR HOLDING PERIOD
.150 EQUITY YIELD RATE
.750 LOAN RATIO

INTEREST RATE

TERM YEARS	APPR DEP	5.0	6.0	7.0	7.5	8.0	8.5	9.0	9.5	10.0	11.0	12.0	13.0	14.0
15	.40	.084502	.089278	.094225	.096762	.099339	.101957	.104614	.107311	.110045	.115624	.121346	.127202	.133187
	.30	.086604	.091379	.096327	.098863	.101441	.104059	.106716	.109412	.112147	.117726	.123447	.129304	.135289
	.20	.088705	.093481	.098428	.100965	.103542	.106160	.108818	.111514	.114248	.119828	.125549	.131406	.137391
	.10	.090807	.095583	.100530	.103067	.105644	.108262	.110919	.113616	.116350	.121929	.127651	.133507	.139492
	0.00	.092909	.097684	.102632	.105168	.107746	.110364	.113021	.115717	.118452	.124031	.129752	.135609	.141594
	-.10	.095010	.099786	.104733	.107270	.109848	.112465	.115123	.117819	.120553	.126133	.131854	.137711	.143696
	-.20	.097112	.101888	.106835	.109372	.111949	.114567	.117225	.119921	.122655	.128234	.133956	.139812	.145797
	-.30	.099214	.103989	.108937	.111473	.114051	.116669	.119326	.122023	.124757	.130336	.136057	.141914	.147899
	-.40	.101315	.106091	.111039	.113575	.116153	.118771	.121428	.124124	.126858	.132438	.138159	.144016	.150001
20	.40	.078239	.083651	.089279	.092171	.095112	.098102	.101138	.104218	.107342	.113710	.120231	.126889	.133671
	.30	.080341	.085752	.091381	.094273	.097214	.100204	.103239	.106320	.109443	.115812	.122332	.128990	.135773
	.20	.082442	.087854	.093482	.096375	.099316	.102305	.105341	.108422	.111545	.117914	.124434	.131092	.137875
	.10	.084544	.089956	.095584	.098476	.101418	.104407	.107443	.110523	.113647	.120016	.126536	.133194	.139976
	0.00	.086646	.092057	.097686	.100578	.103519	.106509	.109545	.112625	.115748	.122117	.128637	.135295	.142078
	-.10	.088747	.094159	.099788	.102679	.105621	.108610	.111646	.114727	.117850	.124219	.130739	.137397	.144180
	-.20	.090849	.096261	.101889	.104781	.107723	.110712	.113748	.116828	.119952	.126321	.132841	.139499	.146282
	-.30	.092951	.098362	.103991	.106883	.109824	.112814	.115850	.118930	.122054	.128422	.134943	.141601	.148383
	-.40	.095053	.100464	.106093	.108985	.111926	.114916	.117951	.121032	.124155	.130524	.137044	.143702	.150485
25	.40	.074631	.080465	.086536	.089653	.092821	.096038	.099301	.102606	.105952	.112756	.119692	.126742	.133890
	.30	.076733	.082567	.088637	.091755	.094923	.098140	.101402	.104708	.108054	.114858	.121794	.128844	.135991
	.20	.078835	.084669	.090739	.093856	.097025	.100241	.103504	.106810	.110156	.116959	.123895	.130946	.138093
	.10	.080936	.086770	.092841	.095958	.099126	.102343	.105606	.108911	.112257	.119061	.125997	.133047	.140195
	0.00	.083038	.088872	.094943	.098060	.101228	.104445	.107707	.111013	.114359	.121163	.128099	.135149	.142296
	-.10	.085140	.090974	.097044	.100161	.103330	.106547	.109809	.113115	.116461	.123265	.130201	.137251	.144398
	-.20	.087242	.093076	.099146	.102263	.105431	.108648	.111911	.115216	.118563	.125366	.132302	.139352	.146500
	-.30	.089343	.095177	.101248	.104365	.107533	.110750	.114012	.117318	.120664	.127468	.134404	.141454	.148602
	-.40	.091445	.097279	.103349	.106467	.109635	.112852	.116114	.119420	.122766	.129570	.136506	.143556	.150703
30	.40	.072345	.078489	.084875	.088149	.091472	.094841	.098251	.101700	.105184	.112247	.119415	.126670	.133993
	.30	.074446	.080591	.086977	.090251	.093574	.096942	.100353	.103802	.107286	.114348	.121517	.128771	.136095
	.20	.076548	.082693	.089078	.092352	.095676	.099044	.102455	.105904	.109388	.116450	.123619	.130873	.138197
	.10	.078650	.084794	.091180	.094454	.097777	.101146	.104556	.108005	.111490	.118552	.125720	.132975	.140298
	0.00	.080752	.086896	.093282	.096556	.099879	.103247	.106658	.110107	.113591	.120654	.127822	.135077	.142400
	-.10	.082853	.088998	.095384	.098658	.101981	.105349	.108760	.112209	.115693	.122755	.129924	.137180	.144502
	-.20	.084955	.091099	.097485	.100759	.104082	.107451	.110861	.114310	.117795	.124857	.132025	.139280	.146603
	-.30	.087057	.093201	.099587	.102861	.106184	.109553	.112963	.116412	.119896	.126959	.134127	.141382	.148705
	-.40	.089158	.095303	.101689	.104963	.108286	.111654	.115065	.118514	.121998	.129060	.136229	.143483	.150807
40	.40	.069730	.076311	.083119	.086593	.090109	.093660	.097242	.100851	.104483	.111806	.119189	.126614	.134069
	.30	.071832	.078412	.085220	.088695	.092210	.095761	.099343	.102952	.106585	.113908	.121291	.128716	.136170
	.20	.073933	.080514	.087322	.090797	.094312	.097863	.101445	.105054	.108687	.116010	.123392	.130817	.138272
	.10	.076035	.082616	.089424	.092899	.096414	.099965	.103547	.107156	.110788	.118111	.125494	.132919	.140374
	0.00	.078137	.084717	.091525	.095000	.098516	.102066	.105648	.109257	.112890	.120213	.127596	.135021	.142475
	-.10	.080238	.086819	.093627	.097102	.100617	.104168	.107750	.111359	.114992	.122315	.129697	.137122	.144577
	-.20	.082340	.088921	.095729	.099204	.102719	.106270	.109852	.113461	.117093	.124417	.131799	.139224	.146679
	-.30	.084442	.091022	.097830	.101305	.104821	.108372	.111953	.115563	.119195	.126518	.133901	.141326	.148781
	-.40	.086544	.093124	.099932	.103407	.106922	.110473	.114055	.117664	.121297	.128620	.136002	.143428	.150882

15.0 YEAR HOLDING PERIOD
.150 EQUITY YIELD RATE
.800 LOAN RATIO

INTEREST RATE

TERM YEARS	APPR DEP	5.0	6.0	7.0	7.5	8.0	8.5	9.0	9.5	10.0	11.0	12.0	13.0	14.0
15	.40	.080696	.085790	.091067	.093773	.096522	.099315	.102149	.105025	.107942	.113893	.119996	.126243	.132627
	.30	.082797	.087891	.093169	.095874	.098624	.101416	.104251	.107127	.110043	.115995	.122097	.128344	.134728
	.20	.084499	.089993	.095270	.097976	.100726	.103518	.106353	.109229	.112145	.118096	.124199	.130446	.136830
	.10	.087001	.092095	.097372	.100078	.102827	.105620	.108454	.111330	.114247	.120198	.126301	.132548	.138932
	0.00	.089103	.094197	.099474	.102180	.104929	.107721	.110556	.113432	.116348	.122300	.128402	.134650	.141034
	-.10	.091204	.096298	.101576	.104281	.107031	.109823	.112658	.115534	.118450	.124401	.130504	.136751	.143135
	-.20	.093306	.098400	.103677	.106383	.109132	.111925	.114759	.117635	.120552	.126503	.132606	.138853	.145237
	-.30	.095408	.100502	.105779	.108485	.111234	.114026	.116861	.119737	.122654	.128605	.134708	.140955	.147339
	-.40	.097509	.102603	.107881	.110586	.113336	.116128	.118963	.121839	.124755	.130706	.136809	.143056	.149440
20	.40	.074015	.079788	.085791	.088876	.092014	.095203	.098441	.101727	.105058	.111852	.118806	.125908	.133143
	.30	.076117	.081889	.087893	.090978	.094115	.097304	.100542	.103828	.107160	.113953	.120908	.128010	.135245
	.20	.078219	.083991	.089995	.093080	.096217	.099406	.102644	.105930	.109262	.116055	.123010	.130112	.137347
	.10	.080320	.086093	.092097	.095181	.098319	.101508	.104746	.108032	.111363	.118157	.125112	.132213	.139448
	0.00	.082422	.088195	.094198	.097283	.100421	.103609	.106848	.110133	.113465	.120258	.127213	.134315	.141550
	-.10	.084524	.090296	.096300	.099385	.102522	.105711	.108949	.112235	.115567	.122360	.129315	.136417	.143652
	-.20	.086626	.092398	.098402	.101486	.104624	.107813	.111051	.114337	.117668	.124462	.131417	.138519	.145753
	-.30	.088727	.094500	.100503	.103588	.106726	.109914	.113153	.116439	.119770	.126564	.133518	.140620	.147855
	-.40	.090829	.096601	.102605	.105690	.108827	.112016	.115254	.118540	.121872	.128665	.135620	.142722	.149957
25	.40	.070167	.076390	.082865	.086190	.089570	.093001	.096481	.100007	.103576	.110834	.118232	.125752	.133376
	.30	.072269	.078492	.084967	.088292	.091671	.095103	.098583	.102109	.105678	.112935	.120334	.127854	.135478
	.20	.074371	.080594	.087069	.090394	.093773	.097204	.100684	.104210	.107780	.115037	.122435	.129956	.137579
	.10	.076472	.082695	.089172	.092495	.095875	.099306	.102786	.106312	.109881	.117139	.124537	.132057	.139681
	0.00	.078574	.084797	.091272	.094597	.097977	.101408	.104888	.108414	.111983	.119240	.126639	.134159	.141783
	-.10	.080676	.086899	.093374	.096699	.100078	.103510	.106990	.110516	.114085	.121342	.128741	.136261	.143885
	-.20	.082777	.089000	.095475	.098800	.102180	.105611	.109091	.112617	.116187	.123444	.130842	.138362	.145986
	-.30	.084879	.091102	.097577	.100902	.104282	.107713	.111193	.114719	.118288	.125546	.132944	.140464	.148088
	-.40	.086981	.093204	.099679	.103004	.106383	.109815	.113295	.116821	.120390	.127647	.135046	.142566	.150190
30	.40	.067728	.074282	.081094	.084586	.088131	.091724	.095362	.099041	.102757	.110290	.117937	.125675	.133487
	.30	.069830	.076384	.083196	.086688	.090232	.093826	.097463	.101142	.104859	.112392	.120038	.127777	.135588
	.20	.071932	.078486	.085297	.088790	.092334	.095927	.099565	.103244	.106961	.114494	.122140	.129878	.137690
	.10	.074033	.080587	.087399	.090891	.094436	.098029	.101667	.105346	.109062	.116595	.124242	.131980	.139792
	0.00	.076135	.082689	.089501	.092993	.096538	.100131	.103768	.107447	.111164	.118697	.126343	.134082	.141893
	-.10	.078237	.084791	.091602	.095095	.098639	.102232	.105870	.109549	.113266	.120799	.128445	.136183	.143995
	-.20	.080338	.086893	.093704	.097196	.100741	.104334	.107972	.111651	.115367	.122901	.130547	.138285	.146097
	-.30	.082440	.088994	.095806	.099298	.102843	.106436	.110074	.113753	.117469	.125002	.132649	.140387	.148199
	-.40	.084542	.091096	.097907	.101400	.104944	.108537	.112175	.115854	.119571	.127104	.134750	.142488	.150300
40	.40	.064939	.071958	.079220	.082927	.086676	.090464	.094285	.098134	.102009	.109821	.117695	.125615	.133567
	.30	.067041	.074060	.081322	.085029	.088778	.092565	.096386	.100236	.104111	.111924	.119797	.127717	.135669
	.20	.069142	.076162	.083424	.087130	.090880	.094667	.098488	.102338	.106213	.114024	.121899	.129819	.137770
	.10	.071244	.078263	.085525	.089232	.092982	.096769	.100590	.104440	.108314	.116126	.124000	.131920	.139872
	0.00	.073336	.080365	.087627	.091334	.095083	.098871	.102692	.106541	.110416	.118227	.126102	.134022	.141974
	-.10	.075448	.082467	.089729	.093435	.097185	.100973	.104793	.108643	.112518	.120329	.128204	.136124	.144076
	-.20	.077549	.084569	.091830	.095537	.099288	.103075	.106895	.110745	.114619	.122431	.130305	.138225	.146177
	-.30	.079651	.086670	.093932	.097639	.101388	.105176	.108997	.112846	.116721	.124532	.132407	.140327	.148279
	-.40	.081753	.088772	.096034	.099740	.103490	.107278	.111098	.114948	.118823	.126634	.134509	.142429	.150381

15.0 YEAR HOLDING PERIOD
.150 EQUITY YIELD RATE
.900 LOAN RATIO

INTEREST RATE

TERM YEARS	APPR DEP	5.0	6.0	7.0	7.5	8.0	8.5	9.0	9.5	10.0	11.0	12.0	13.0	14.0
15	.40	.073084	.078814	.084751	.087795	.090888	.094030	.097219	.100454	.103735	.110430	.117296	.124324	.131506
	.30	.075185	.080916	.086853	.089897	.092990	.096131	.099320	.102556	.105837	.112532	.119398	.126426	.133608
	.20	.077287	.083018	.088955	.091999	.095092	.098233	.101422	.104658	.107939	.114634	.121499	.128527	.135709
	.10	.079389	.085121	.091056	.094100	.097193	.100335	.103524	.106759	.110040	.116735	.123601	.130629	.137811
	0.00	.081490	.087221	.093158	.096202	.099295	.102437	.105625	.108861	.112142	.118837	.125703	.132731	.139913
	-.10	.083592	.089323	.095260	.098304	.101397	.104538	.107727	.110963	.114244	.120939	.127805	.134833	.142014
	-.20	.085694	.091425	.097362	.100406	.103498	.106640	.109829	.113064	.116345	.123041	.129906	.136934	.144116
	-.30	.087795	.093526	.099463	.102507	.105600	.108742	.111931	.115166	.118447	.125142	.132008	.139036	.146218
	-.40	.089897	.095628	.101565	.104609	.107702	.110843	.114032	.117268	.120549	.127244	.134110	.141138	.148320
20	.40	.065568	.072062	.078816	.082287	.085816	.089404	.093047	.096743	.100491	.108134	.115958	.123948	.132087
	.30	.067670	.074164	.080918	.084388	.087918	.091505	.095148	.098845	.102593	.110236	.118060	.126049	.134189
	.20	.069771	.076265	.083020	.086490	.090020	.093607	.097250	.100947	.104695	.112337	.120162	.128151	.136290
	.10	.071873	.078367	.085121	.088592	.092121	.095709	.099352	.103048	.106796	.114439	.122263	.130253	.138392
	0.00	.073975	.080469	.087223	.090693	.094223	.097811	.101454	.105150	.108898	.116541	.124365	.132355	.140494
	-.10	.076077	.082571	.089325	.092795	.096325	.099912	.103555	.107252	.111000	.118642	.126467	.134456	.142595
	-.20	.078178	.084672	.091426	.094897	.098427	.102014	.105657	.109353	.113102	.120744	.128568	.136558	.144697
	-.30	.080280	.086774	.093528	.096998	.100528	.104116	.107759	.111455	.115203	.122846	.130670	.138660	.146799
	-.40	.082382	.088876	.095630	.099100	.102630	.106217	.109860	.113557	.117305	.124948	.132772	.140761	.148901
25	.40	.061239	.068240	.075524	.079265	.083067	.086927	.090842	.094809	.098824	.106989	.115312	.123772	.132349
	.30	.063341	.070342	.077626	.081367	.085169	.089029	.092944	.096910	.100926	.109090	.117414	.125874	.134451
	.20	.065442	.072443	.079728	.083468	.087270	.091130	.095045	.099012	.103028	.111192	.119515	.127975	.136552
	.10	.067544	.074545	.081829	.085570	.089372	.093232	.097147	.101114	.105129	.113294	.121617	.130077	.138654
	0.00	.069646	.076647	.083931	.087672	.091474	.095334	.099249	.103216	.107231	.115395	.123719	.132179	.140756
	-.10	.071747	.078748	.086033	.089773	.093575	.097435	.101351	.105317	.109333	.117497	.125820	.134280	.142857
	-.20	.073849	.080850	.088134	.091875	.095677	.099537	.103452	.107419	.111434	.119599	.127922	.136382	.144959
	-.30	.075951	.082951	.090236	.093977	.097779	.101639	.105554	.109521	.113536	.121701	.130024	.138484	.147061
	-.40	.078053	.085053	.092338	.096078	.099880	.103741	.107656	.111622	.115638	.123802	.132125	.140586	.149162
30	.40	.058495	.065868	.073531	.077460	.081448	.085490	.089583	.093722	.097903	.106377	.114980	.123685	.132473
	.30	.060597	.067970	.075633	.079562	.083550	.087592	.091684	.095823	.100004	.108479	.117081	.125787	.134575
	.20	.062698	.070072	.077735	.081664	.085651	.089694	.093786	.097925	.102106	.110581	.119183	.127888	.136676
	.10	.064800	.072174	.079837	.083765	.087753	.091795	.095888	.100027	.104208	.112683	.121285	.129990	.138778
	0.00	.066902	.074275	.081938	.085867	.089855	.093897	.097990	.102128	.106310	.114784	.123386	.132092	.140880
	-.10	.069004	.076377	.084040	.087969	.091956	.095999	.100091	.104230	.108411	.116886	.125488	.134194	.142982
	-.20	.071105	.078479	.086142	.090070	.094058	.098100	.102193	.106332	.110513	.118988	.127590	.136295	.145084
	-.30	.073207	.080580	.088243	.092172	.096160	.100202	.104295	.108433	.112615	.121089	.129691	.138397	.147185
	-.40	.075309	.082682	.090345	.094274	.098262	.102304	.106396	.110535	.114716	.123191	.131793	.140499	.149287
40	.40	.055357	.063254	.071424	.075594	.079814	.084073	.088371	.092702	.097061	.105849	.114708	.123618	.132564
	.30	.057459	.065356	.073525	.077695	.081914	.086175	.090473	.094804	.099163	.107951	.116810	.125720	.134665
	.20	.059561	.067457	.075627	.079797	.084015	.088276	.092575	.096906	.101265	.110052	.118911	.127821	.136767
	.10	.061662	.069559	.077729	.081899	.086117	.090378	.094676	.099007	.103366	.112154	.121013	.129923	.138869
	0.00	.063764	.071661	.079830	.084000	.088219	.092480	.096778	.101109	.105468	.114256	.123115	.132025	.140971
	-.10	.065866	.073763	.081932	.086102	.090320	.094581	.098880	.103211	.107570	.116357	.125216	.134127	.143072
	-.20	.067968	.075864	.084034	.088204	.092422	.096683	.100981	.105312	.109671	.118459	.127318	.136228	.145174
	-.30	.070069	.077966	.086136	.090306	.094524	.098785	.103083	.107414	.111773	.120561	.129420	.138330	.147276
	-.40	.072171	.080068	.088237	.092407	.096626	.100887	.105185	.109516	.113875	.122663	.131522	.140432	.149377

15.0 YEAR HOLDING PERIOD
.160 EQUITY YIELD RATE
.600 LOAN RATIO

INTEREST RATE

TERM YEARS	APPR DEP	5.0	6.0	7.0	7.5	8.0	8.5	9.0	9.5	10.0	11.0	12.0	13.0	14.0
15	.40	.101580	.105400	.109358	.111387	.113449	.115544	.117670	.119827	.122014	.126477	.131055	.135740	.140528
	.30	.103515	.107336	.111294	.113323	.115385	.117479	.119605	.121762	.123990	.128413	.132990	.137676	.142464
	.20	.105451	.109272	.113230	.115259	.117321	.119415	.121541	.123698	.125886	.130349	.134926	.139611	.144399
	.10	.107387	.111207	.115165	.117195	.119257	.121351	.123477	.125634	.127821	.132285	.136862	.141547	.146335
	0.00	.109323	.113143	.117101	.119130	.121192	.123287	.125413	.127570	.129757	.134220	.138798	.143483	.148271
	-.10	.111258	.115079	.119037	.121066	.123128	.125222	.127348	.129505	.131693	.136156	.140733	.145419	.150207
	-.20	.113194	.117015	.120973	.123002	.125064	.127158	.129284	.131441	.133629	.138092	.142669	.147354	.152142
	-.30	.115130	.118950	.122908	.124938	.127000	.129094	.131220	.133377	.135564	.140028	.144605	.149290	.154078
	-.40	.117066	.120886	.124844	.126873	.128935	.131030	.133156	.135313	.137500	.141963	.146541	.151226	.156014
20	.40	.096221	.100530	.105012	.107315	.109657	.112039	.114457	.116911	.119399	.124474	.129670	.134976	.140383
	.30	.098157	.102465	.106947	.109250	.111593	.113974	.116393	.118847	.121335	.126410	.131606	.136912	.142319
	.20	.100093	.104401	.108883	.111186	.113529	.115910	.118328	.120782	.123271	.128345	.133541	.138848	.144255
	.10	.102028	.106337	.110819	.113122	.115465	.117846	.120264	.122718	.125207	.130281	.135477	.140784	.146190
	0.00	.103964	.108273	.112755	.115058	.117400	.119782	.122200	.124654	.127142	.132217	.137413	.142719	.148126
	-.10	.105900	.110208	.114690	.116993	.119336	.121717	.124136	.126590	.129078	.134153	.139349	.144655	.150062
	-.20	.107836	.112144	.116626	.118929	.121272	.123653	.126071	.128525	.131014	.136088	.141284	.146591	.151998
	-.30	.109771	.114080	.118562	.120865	.123208	.125589	.128007	.130461	.132950	.138024	.143220	.148527	.153933
	-.40	.111707	.116016	.120498	.122801	.125143	.127525	.129943	.132397	.134885	.139960	.145156	.150462	.155869
25	.40	.093134	.097773	.102601	.105081	.107602	.110162	.112759	.115391	.118055	.123475	.129001	.134620	.140318
	.30	.095070	.099708	.104536	.107016	.109537	.112098	.114695	.117327	.119991	.125410	.130937	.136556	.142254
	.20	.097006	.101644	.106472	.108952	.111473	.114033	.116630	.119262	.121927	.127346	.132872	.138491	.144189
	.10	.098942	.103580	.108408	.110888	.113409	.115969	.118566	.121198	.123863	.129282	.134808	.140427	.146125
	0.00	.100877	.105516	.110344	.112824	.115345	.117905	.120502	.123134	.125798	.131218	.136744	.142363	.148061
	-.10	.102813	.107451	.112279	.114759	.117280	.119841	.122438	.125070	.127734	.133153	.138680	.144299	.149997
	-.20	.104749	.109387	.114215	.116695	.119216	.121776	.124373	.127005	.129670	.135089	.140615	.146234	.151932
	-.30	.106685	.111323	.116151	.118631	.121152	.123712	.126309	.128941	.131606	.137025	.142551	.148170	.153868
	-.40	.108620	.113259	.118087	.120567	.123088	.125648	.128245	.130877	.133541	.138961	.144487	.150106	.155804
30	.40	.091178	.096062	.101141	.103746	.106391	.109073	.111789	.114536	.117313	.122941	.128657	.134443	.140287
	.30	.093114	.097998	.103077	.105682	.108327	.111009	.113725	.116472	.119248	.124877	.130593	.136379	.142223
	.20	.095050	.099934	.105013	.107618	.110263	.112945	.115661	.118408	.121184	.126813	.132528	.138315	.144158
	.10	.096985	.101869	.106948	.109554	.112199	.114880	.117596	.120344	.123120	.128749	.134464	.140251	.146094
	0.00	.098921	.103805	.108884	.111489	.114134	.116816	.119532	.122279	.125056	.130684	.136400	.142186	.148030
	-.10	.100857	.105741	.110820	.113425	.116070	.118752	.121468	.124215	.126991	.132620	.138336	.144122	.149966
	-.20	.102793	.107677	.112756	.115361	.118006	.120688	.123404	.126151	.128927	.134556	.140272	.146058	.151901
	-.30	.104728	.109612	.114691	.117297	.119942	.122623	.125339	.128087	.130863	.136492	.142207	.147994	.153837
	-.40	.106664	.111548	.116627	.119232	.121877	.124559	.127275	.130022	.132799	.138427	.144143	.149929	.155773
40	.40	.088941	.094176	.099598	.102366	.105168	.107999	.110856	.113735	.116634	.122480	.128376	.134307	.140264
	.30	.090877	.096112	.101533	.104302	.107104	.109935	.112792	.115671	.118570	.124416	.130312	.136243	.142200
	.20	.092812	.098048	.103469	.106238	.109040	.111871	.114728	.117607	.120506	.126352	.132247	.138179	.144136
	.10	.094748	.099984	.105405	.108174	.110975	.113807	.116663	.119543	.122442	.128287	.134183	.140115	.146072
	0.00	.096684	.101919	.107341	.110109	.112911	.115742	.118599	.121478	.124377	.130223	.136119	.142050	.148007
	-.10	.098620	.103855	.109276	.112045	.114847	.117678	.120535	.123414	.126313	.132159	.138055	.143986	.149943
	-.20	.100555	.105791	.111212	.113981	.116783	.119614	.122471	.125350	.128249	.134095	.139990	.145922	.151879
	-.30	.102491	.107727	.113148	.115917	.118718	.121550	.124406	.127286	.130185	.136030	.141926	.147858	.153815
	-.40	.104427	.109662	.115084	.117852	.120654	.123485	.126342	.129222	.132120	.137966	.143862	.149793	.155750

15.0 YEAR HOLDING PERIOD
.160 EQUITY YIELD RATE
.667 LOAN RATIO

INTEREST RATE

TERM YEARS	APPR DEP	5.0	6.0	7.0	7.5	8.0	8.5	9.0	9.5	10.0	11.0	12.0	13.0	14.0
15	.40	.095949	.100194	.104591	.106846	.109137	.111464	.113826	.116223	.118654	.123613	.128699	.133905	.139225
	.30	.097884	.102129	.106527	.108782	.111073	.113400	.115762	.118159	.120589	.125549	.130634	.135840	.141160
	.20	.099820	.104065	.108463	.110718	.113009	.115336	.117698	.120095	.122525	.127484	.132570	.137776	.143096
	.10	.101756	.106001	.110399	.112653	.114944	.117272	.119634	.122030	.124461	.129420	.134506	.139712	.145032
	0.00	.103692	.107937	.112334	.114589	.116880	.119207	.121569	.123966	.126397	.131356	.136442	.141648	.146968
	-.10	.105627	.109872	.114270	.116525	.118816	.121143	.123505	.125902	.128332	.133292	.138377	.143583	.148903
	-.20	.107563	.111808	.116206	.118461	.120752	.123079	.125441	.127838	.130268	.135227	.140313	.145519	.150839
	-.30	.109499	.113744	.118142	.120396	.122688	.125015	.127377	.129773	.132204	.137163	.142249	.147455	.152775
	-.40	.111435	.115680	.120077	.122332	.124623	.126950	.129312	.131709	.134140	.139099	.144185	.149391	.154711
20	.40	.089995	.094782	.099762	.102321	.104924	.107570	.110257	.112983	.115748	.121387	.127160	.133056	.139064
	.30	.091930	.096718	.101698	.104257	.106860	.109505	.112192	.114919	.117684	.123322	.129096	.134992	.140999
	.20	.093866	.098653	.103633	.106192	.108795	.111441	.114128	.116855	.119620	.125258	.131031	.136928	.142935
	.10	.095802	.100589	.105569	.108128	.110731	.113377	.116064	.118791	.121555	.127194	.132967	.138863	.144871
	0.00	.097738	.102525	.107505	.110064	.112667	.115313	.118000	.120726	.123491	.129130	.134903	.140799	.146807
	-.10	.099673	.104461	.109441	.112000	.114603	.117248	.119935	.122662	.125427	.131065	.136839	.142735	.148742
	-.20	.101609	.106396	.111376	.113935	.116538	.119184	.121871	.124598	.127363	.133001	.138774	.144671	.150678
	-.30	.103545	.108332	.113312	.115871	.118474	.121120	.123807	.126534	.129298	.134937	.140710	.146606	.152614
	-.40	.105481	.110268	.115248	.117807	.120410	.123056	.125743	.128469	.131234	.136873	.142646	.148542	.154550
25	.40	.086565	.091718	.097083	.099839	.102640	.105484	.108370	.111294	.114255	.120276	.126417	.132660	.138991
	.30	.088501	.093654	.099019	.101774	.104576	.107420	.110306	.113230	.116191	.122212	.128352	.134596	.140927
	.20	.090436	.095590	.100954	.103710	.106511	.109356	.112242	.115166	.118126	.124148	.130288	.136531	.142863
	.10	.092372	.097526	.102890	.105646	.108447	.111292	.114177	.117102	.120062	.126084	.132224	.138467	.144798
	0.00	.094308	.099461	.104826	.107582	.110383	.113227	.116113	.119037	.121998	.128019	.134160	.140403	.146734
	-.10	.096244	.101397	.106762	.109517	.112319	.115163	.118049	.120973	.123934	.129955	.136095	.142339	.148670
	-.20	.098179	.103333	.108697	.111453	.114254	.117099	.119985	.122909	.125869	.131891	.138031	.144274	.150606
	-.30	.100115	.105269	.110633	.113389	.116190	.119035	.121920	.124845	.127805	.133827	.139967	.146210	.152541
	-.40	.102051	.107204	.112569	.115325	.118126	.120970	.123856	.126780	.129741	.135762	.141903	.148146	.154477
30	.40	.084391	.089818	.095461	.098356	.101295	.104275	.107293	.110345	.113430	.119684	.126035	.132464	.138957
	.30	.086327	.091754	.097397	.100292	.103231	.106211	.109228	.112281	.115365	.121620	.127970	.134400	.140893
	.20	.088263	.093689	.099333	.102228	.105166	.108146	.111164	.114217	.117301	.123555	.129906	.136336	.142828
	.10	.090198	.095625	.101269	.104163	.107102	.110082	.113100	.116152	.119237	.125491	.131842	.138271	.144764
	0.00	.092134	.097561	.103204	.106099	.109038	.112018	.115036	.118088	.121173	.127427	.133778	.140207	.146700
	-.10	.094070	.099497	.105140	.108035	.110974	.113954	.116971	.120024	.123108	.129363	.135713	.142143	.148636
	-.20	.096006	.101432	.107076	.109971	.112909	.115889	.118907	.121960	.125044	.131298	.137649	.144079	.150571
	-.30	.097941	.103368	.109012	.111906	.114845	.117825	.120843	.123895	.126980	.133234	.139585	.146014	.152507
	-.40	.099877	.105304	.110947	.113842	.116781	.119761	.122779	.125831	.128916	.135170	.141521	.147950	.154443
40	.40	.081905	.087723	.093746	.096823	.099936	.103082	.106256	.109455	.112676	.119171	.125722	.132313	.138932
	.30	.083841	.089658	.095682	.098758	.101872	.105017	.108192	.111391	.114612	.121107	.127658	.134249	.140867
	.20	.085777	.091594	.097618	.100694	.103807	.106953	.110127	.113327	.116548	.123043	.129594	.136184	.142803
	.10	.087713	.093530	.099553	.102630	.105743	.108889	.112063	.115263	.118483	.124979	.131529	.138120	.144739
	0.00	.089648	.095466	.101489	.104566	.107679	.110825	.113999	.117198	.120419	.126914	.133465	.140056	.146675
	-.10	.091584	.097401	.103425	.106501	.109615	.112760	.115935	.119134	.122355	.128850	.135401	.141992	.148611
	-.20	.093520	.099337	.105361	.108437	.111550	.114696	.117870	.121070	.124291	.130786	.137337	.143927	.150546
	-.30	.095456	.101273	.107296	.110373	.113486	.116632	.119806	.123005	.126226	.132722	.139272	.145863	.152482
	-.40	.097391	.103209	.109232	.112309	.115422	.118568	.121742	.124941	.128162	.134657	.141208	.147799	.154418

```
15.0 YEAR HOLDING PERIOD
 .160 EQUITY YIELD RATE
 .700 LOAN RATIO
```

INTEREST RATE

TERM YEARS	APPR DEP	5.0	6.0	7.0	7.5	8.0	8.5	9.0	9.5	10.0	11.0	12.0	13.0	14.0
15	.40	.093133	.097591	.102208	.104576	.106982	.109425	.111905	.114422	.116974	.122181	.127521	.132987	.138573
	.30	.095069	.099526	.104144	.106512	.108917	.111361	.113841	.116357	.118909	.124117	.129457	.134923	.140509
	.20	.097005	.101462	.106080	.108447	.110853	.113296	.115777	.118293	.120845	.126052	.131392	.136859	.142445
	.10	.098941	.103398	.108016	.110383	.112789	.115232	.117712	.120229	.122781	.127988	.133328	.138794	.144380
	0.00	.100876	.105334	.109951	.112319	.114725	.117168	.119648	.122165	.124717	.129924	.135264	.140730	.146316
	-.10	.102812	.107269	.111887	.114255	.116660	.119104	.121584	.124100	.126652	.131860	.137200	.142666	.148252
	-.20	.104748	.109205	.113823	.116190	.118596	.121039	.123520	.126036	.128588	.133795	.139135	.144602	.150188
	-.30	.106684	.111141	.115759	.118126	.120532	.122975	.125455	.127972	.130524	.135731	.141071	.146537	.152123
	-.40	.108619	.113077	.117694	.120062	.122468	.124911	.127391	.129908	.132460	.137667	.143007	.148473	.154059
20	.40	.086682	.091908	.097137	.099824	.102557	.105335	.108157	.111020	.113923	.119843	.125905	.132096	.138404
	.30	.088817	.093844	.099073	.101760	.104493	.107271	.110093	.112956	.115859	.121779	.127841	.134032	.140340
	.20	.090753	.095780	.101009	.103696	.106429	.109143	.112028	.114891	.117794	.123715	.129777	.135968	.142276
	.10	.092689	.097716	.102945	.105631	.108365	.111143	.113964	.116827	.119730	.125651	.131713	.137903	.144211
	0.00	.094625	.099651	.104880	.107567	.110300	.113078	.115900	.118763	.121666	.127586	.133648	.139839	.146147
	-.10	.096561	.101587	.106816	.109503	.112236	.115014	.117836	.120699	.123602	.129522	.135584	.141775	.148083
	-.20	.098496	.103523	.108752	.111439	.114172	.116950	.119771	.122634	.125537	.131458	.137520	.143711	.150019
	-.30	.100432	.105459	.110688	.113374	.116108	.118886	.121707	.124570	.127473	.133394	.139456	.145647	.151954
	-.40	.102368	.107394	.112623	.115310	.118043	.120821	.123643	.126506	.129409	.135329	.141391	.147582	.153890
25	.40	.083281	.088692	.094325	.097218	.100159	.103146	.106176	.109246	.112355	.118677	.125125	.131680	.138328
	.30	.085216	.090628	.096260	.099154	.102095	.105082	.108112	.111182	.114291	.120613	.127061	.133616	.140264
	.20	.087152	.092563	.098196	.101089	.104031	.107018	.110047	.113118	.116227	.122549	.128996	.135552	.142200
	.10	.089088	.094499	.100132	.103025	.105966	.108953	.111983	.115054	.118162	.124485	.130932	.137487	.144135
	0.00	.091024	.096435	.102068	.104961	.107902	.110889	.113919	.116989	.120098	.126420	.132868	.139423	.146071
	-.10	.092959	.098371	.104003	.106897	.109838	.112825	.115855	.118925	.122034	.128356	.134804	.141359	.148007
	-.20	.094895	.100306	.105939	.108832	.111774	.114761	.117790	.120861	.123970	.130292	.136739	.143295	.149943
	-.30	.096831	.102242	.107875	.110768	.113709	.116696	.119726	.122797	.125905	.132228	.138675	.145231	.151878
	-.40	.098767	.104178	.109811	.112704	.115645	.118632	.121662	.124732	.127841	.134163	.140611	.147166	.153814
30	.40	.080998	.086696	.092622	.095661	.098747	.101876	.105045	.108250	.111489	.118055	.124724	.131474	.138292
	.30	.082934	.088632	.094558	.097597	.100683	.103812	.106980	.110185	.113424	.119991	.126659	.133410	.140228
	.20	.084870	.090568	.096493	.099533	.102619	.105747	.108916	.112121	.115360	.121927	.128595	.135346	.142163
	.10	.086805	.092504	.098429	.101469	.104554	.107683	.110852	.114057	.117296	.123863	.130531	.137282	.144099
	0.00	.088741	.094439	.100365	.103404	.106490	.109619	.112788	.115993	.119232	.125798	.132467	.139217	.146035
	-.10	.090677	.096375	.102301	.105340	.108426	.111555	.114723	.117928	.121167	.127734	.134402	.141153	.147971
	-.20	.092613	.098311	.104236	.107276	.110362	.113490	.116659	.119864	.123103	.129670	.136338	.143089	.149906
	-.30	.094548	.100247	.106172	.109212	.112297	.115426	.118595	.121800	.125039	.131606	.138274	.145025	.151842
	-.40	.096484	.102182	.108108	.111147	.114233	.117362	.120531	.123736	.126975	.133541	.140210	.146960	.153778
40	.40	.078388	.084496	.090821	.094051	.097320	.100623	.103956	.107315	.110697	.117517	.124396	.131316	.138266
	.30	.080324	.086432	.092757	.095987	.099256	.102559	.105892	.109251	.112633	.119453	.126331	.133252	.140201
	.20	.082263	.088368	.094692	.097923	.101192	.104495	.107828	.111187	.114569	.121389	.128267	.135187	.142137
	.10	.084195	.090303	.096628	.099858	.103127	.106430	.109763	.113122	.116504	.123325	.130203	.137123	.144073
	0.00	.086131	.092239	.098564	.101794	.105063	.108366	.111699	.115058	.118440	.125260	.132139	.139059	.146009
	-.10	.088067	.094175	.100500	.103730	.106999	.110302	.113635	.116994	.120376	.127196	.134074	.140995	.147944
	-.20	.090003	.096111	.102435	.105666	.108935	.112238	.115571	.118930	.122312	.129132	.136010	.142930	.149880
	-.30	.091938	.098046	.104371	.107601	.110870	.114173	.117506	.120865	.124247	.131058	.137946	.144866	.151816
	-.40	.093874	.099982	.106307	.109537	.112806	.116109	.119442	.122801	.126183	.133003	.139882	.146802	.153752

15.0 YEAR HOLDING PERIOD
.160 EQUITY YIELD RATE
.750 LOAN RATIO

INTEREST RATE

TERM YEARS	APPR DEP	5.0	6.0	7.0	7.5	8.0	8.5	9.0	9.5	10.0	11.0	12.0	13.0	14.0
15	.40	.088910	.093686	.098633	.101170	.103748	.106365	.109023	.111719	.114453	.120033	.125754	.131611	.137596
	.30	.090846	.095622	.100569	.103106	.105683	.108301	.110959	.113655	.116389	.121968	.127690	.133546	.139531
	.20	.092782	.097557	.102505	.105041	.107619	.110237	.112894	.115591	.118325	.123904	.129625	.135482	.141467
	.10	.094718	.099493	.104441	.106977	.109555	.112173	.114830	.117526	.120261	.125840	.131561	.137418	.143403
	0.00	.096653	.101429	.106376	.108913	.111491	.114108	.116766	.119462	.122196	.127776	.133497	.139354	.145339
	-.10	.098589	.103365	.108312	.110849	.113426	.116044	.118702	.121398	.124132	.129711	.135433	.141289	.147274
	-.20	.100525	.105300	.110248	.112784	.115362	.117980	.120637	.123334	.126068	.131647	.137368	.143225	.149210
	-.30	.102461	.107236	.112184	.114720	.117298	.119916	.122573	.125269	.128004	.133583	.139304	.145161	.151146
	-.40	.104396	.109172	.114119	.116656	.119234	.121851	.124509	.127205	.129939	.135519	.141240	.147097	.153082
20	.40	.082212	.087598	.093200	.096079	.099007	.101984	.105007	.108074	.111185	.117528	.124023	.130656	.137415
	.30	.084148	.089534	.095136	.098015	.100943	.103920	.106943	.110010	.113121	.119464	.125959	.132592	.139350
	.20	.086084	.091469	.097072	.099951	.102879	.105855	.108878	.111946	.115056	.121400	.127894	.134528	.141286
	.10	.088019	.093405	.099007	.101886	.104815	.107791	.110814	.113882	.116992	.123335	.129830	.136463	.143222
	0.00	.089955	.095341	.100943	.103822	.106750	.109727	.112750	.115817	.118928	.125271	.131766	.138399	.145158
	-.10	.091891	.097277	.102879	.105758	.108686	.111663	.114686	.117753	.120864	.127207	.133702	.140335	.147093
	-.20	.093827	.099212	.104815	.107694	.110622	.113598	.116621	.119689	.122799	.129143	.135638	.142271	.149029
	-.30	.095762	.101148	.106750	.109629	.112558	.115534	.118557	.121625	.124735	.131078	.137573	.144206	.150965
	-.40	.097698	.103084	.108686	.111565	.114493	.117470	.120493	.123560	.126671	.133014	.139509	.146142	.152901
25	.40	.078354	.084151	.090187	.093286	.096438	.099638	.102884	.106174	.109505	.116279	.123187	.130210	.137333
	.30	.080290	.086087	.092122	.095222	.098374	.101574	.104820	.108110	.111441	.118215	.125123	.132146	.139269
	.20	.082225	.088023	.094058	.097158	.100309	.103510	.106756	.110046	.113376	.120150	.127058	.134082	.141205
	.10	.084161	.089959	.095994	.099094	.102245	.105446	.108692	.111982	.115312	.122086	.128994	.136018	.143140
	0.00	.086097	.091895	.097930	.101029	.104181	.107381	.110627	.113917	.117248	.124022	.130930	.137953	.145076
	-.10	.088033	.093830	.099865	.102965	.106117	.109317	.112563	.115853	.119184	.125958	.132866	.139889	.147012
	-.20	.089968	.095766	.101801	.104901	.108052	.111253	.114499	.117789	.121119	.127893	.134801	.141825	.148948
	-.30	.091904	.097702	.103737	.106837	.109988	.113188	.116435	.119725	.123055	.129829	.136737	.143761	.150883
	-.40	.093840	.099638	.105673	.108773	.111924	.115124	.118370	.121660	.124991	.131765	.138673	.145696	.152819
30	.40	.075908	.082013	.088362	.091619	.094925	.098277	.101672	.105106	.108576	.115612	.122757	.129990	.137294
	.30	.077844	.083949	.090298	.093554	.096861	.100213	.103608	.107042	.110512	.117548	.124693	.131926	.139230
	.20	.079780	.085885	.092234	.095490	.098796	.102149	.105544	.108978	.112448	.119484	.126628	.133862	.141166
	.10	.081716	.087821	.094169	.097426	.100732	.104085	.107479	.110914	.114384	.121420	.128564	.135797	.143102
	0.00	.083651	.089756	.096105	.099362	.102668	.106020	.109415	.112849	.116319	.123355	.130500	.137733	.145037
	-.10	.085587	.091692	.098041	.101297	.104604	.107956	.111351	.114785	.118255	.125291	.132436	.139669	.146973
	-.20	.087523	.093628	.099977	.103233	.106539	.109892	.113287	.116721	.120191	.127227	.134371	.141605	.148909
	-.30	.089459	.095564	.101913	.105169	.108475	.111828	.115222	.118657	.122127	.129163	.136307	.143540	.150845
	-.40	.091394	.097499	.103848	.107105	.110411	.113763	.117158	.120592	.124062	.131098	.138243	.145476	.152780
40	.40	.073112	.079656	.086433	.089894	.093396	.096935	.100506	.104105	.107729	.115036	.122405	.129820	.137266
	.30	.075048	.081592	.088368	.091829	.095332	.098871	.102442	.106041	.109664	.116972	.124341	.131756	.139202
	.20	.076983	.083528	.090304	.093765	.097267	.100806	.104377	.107977	.111600	.118907	.126277	.133691	.141138
	.10	.078919	.085463	.092240	.095701	.099203	.102742	.106313	.109912	.113536	.120843	.128213	.135627	.143073
	0.00	.080855	.087399	.094176	.097637	.101139	.104678	.108249	.111848	.115472	.122779	.130148	.137563	.145009
	-.10	.082791	.089335	.096111	.099572	.103075	.106614	.110185	.113784	.117407	.124715	.132084	.139499	.146945
	-.20	.084726	.091271	.098047	.101508	.105010	.108549	.112120	.115720	.119343	.126650	.134020	.141434	.148881
	-.30	.086662	.093206	.099983	.103444	.106946	.110485	.114056	.117655	.121279	.128586	.135956	.143370	.150816
	-.40	.088598	.095142	.101919	.105380	.108882	.112421	.115992	.119591	.123215	.130522	.137892	.145306	.152752

15.0 YEAR HOLDING PERIOD
.160 EQUITY YIELD RATE
.800 LOAN RATIO

INTEREST RATE

TERM YEARS	APPR DEP	5.0	6.0	7.0	7.5	8.0	8.5	9.0	9.5	10.0	11.0	12.0	13.0	14.0
15	.40	.084687	.089781	.095058	.097764	.100514	.103306	.106141	.109017	.111933	.117884	.123987	.130234	.136618
	.30	.086623	.091717	.096994	.099720	.102449	.105242	.108076	.110952	.113869	.119820	.125923	.132170	.138554
	.20	.088559	.093653	.098930	.101636	.104385	.107177	.110012	.112888	.115805	.121756	.127859	.134106	.140490
	.10	.090494	.095588	.100866	.103571	.106321	.109113	.111948	.114824	.117740	.123692	.129794	.136041	.142425
	0.00	.092430	.097524	.102801	.105507	.108257	.111049	.113884	.116760	.119676	.125627	.131730	.137797	.144361
	-.10	.094366	.099460	.104737	.107443	.110192	.112985	.115819	.118695	.121612	.127563	.133666	.139913	.146297
	-.20	.096302	.101396	.106673	.109379	.112128	.114920	.117755	.120631	.123548	.129499	.135502	.141849	.148233
	-.30	.098237	.103331	.108609	.111314	.114064	.116856	.119691	.122567	.125483	.131435	.137437	.143784	.150168
	-.40	.100173	.105267	.110545	.113250	.116000	.118792	.121627	.124503	.127419	.133370	.139473	.145720	.152104
20	.40	.077542	.083287	.089263	.092334	.095457	.098632	.101857	.105129	.108447	.115213	.122141	.129216	.136425
	.30	.079478	.085223	.091199	.094270	.097393	.100568	.103792	.107065	.110382	.117149	.124076	.131152	.138361
	.20	.081414	.087159	.093135	.096205	.099329	.102504	.105728	.109000	.112318	.119084	.126012	.133088	.140297
	.10	.083350	.089094	.095070	.098141	.101265	.104440	.107664	.110936	.114254	.121020	.127948	.135023	.142232
	0.00	.085285	.091030	.097006	.100077	.103201	.106375	.109600	.112872	.116190	.122956	.129884	.136959	.144168
	-.10	.087221	.092966	.098942	.102013	.105136	.108311	.111536	.114808	.118125	.124892	.131819	.138895	.146104
	-.20	.089157	.094902	.100878	.103948	.107072	.110247	.113471	.116743	.120061	.126827	.133755	.140831	.148040
	-.30	.091093	.096837	.102813	.105884	.109008	.112183	.115407	.118679	.121997	.128763	.135691	.142766	.149975
	-.40	.093028	.098773	.104749	.107820	.110944	.114118	.117343	.120615	.123933	.130699	.137627	.144702	.151911
25	.40	.073427	.079611	.086048	.089355	.092717	.096116	.099593	.103102	.106655	.113880	.121249	.128741	.136338
	.30	.075363	.081547	.087984	.091291	.094652	.098066	.101529	.105038	.108591	.115816	.123185	.130676	.138274
	.20	.077298	.083483	.089920	.093227	.096588	.100002	.103464	.106974	.110526	.117752	.125120	.132612	.140210
	.10	.079234	.085418	.091856	.095162	.098524	.101937	.105400	.108909	.112462	.119688	.127056	.134548	.142145
	0.00	.081170	.087354	.093791	.097098	.100460	.103873	.107336	.110845	.114398	.121623	.128992	.136484	.144081
	-.10	.083106	.089290	.095727	.099034	.102395	.105809	.109272	.112781	.116334	.123559	.130928	.138419	.146017
	-.20	.085041	.091226	.097663	.100970	.104331	.107745	.111207	.114717	.118269	.125495	.132863	.140355	.147953
	-.30	.086977	.093161	.099599	.102905	.106267	.109680	.113143	.116652	.120205	.127431	.134799	.142291	.149888
	-.40	.088913	.095097	.101534	.104841	.108203	.111616	.115079	.118588	.122141	.129366	.136735	.144227	.151824
30	.40	.070818	.077330	.084103	.087576	.091103	.094679	.098300	.101963	.105664	.113169	.120790	.128506	.136297
	.30	.072754	.079266	.086038	.089512	.093039	.096614	.100236	.103899	.107600	.115105	.122726	.130441	.138233
	.20	.074690	.081202	.087974	.091448	.094974	.098550	.102171	.105834	.109536	.117041	.124662	.132377	.140168
	.10	.076626	.083138	.089910	.093383	.096910	.100486	.104107	.107770	.111472	.118977	.126597	.134313	.142104
	0.00	.078561	.085073	.091846	.095319	.098846	.102422	.106043	.109706	.113407	.120912	.128533	.136249	.144040
	-.10	.080497	.087009	.093781	.097255	.100782	.104358	.107979	.111642	.115343	.122848	.130469	.138184	.145976
	-.20	.082433	.088945	.095717	.099191	.102717	.106293	.109914	.113577	.117279	.124784	.132405	.140120	.147911
	-.30	.084369	.090881	.097653	.101126	.104653	.108229	.111850	.115513	.119215	.126720	.134340	.142056	.149847
	-.40	.086304	.092816	.099589	.103062	.106589	.110165	.113786	.117449	.121150	.128655	.136276	.143992	.151783
40	.40	.067835	.074816	.082044	.085736	.089472	.093247	.097056	.100895	.104760	.112555	.120415	.128324	.136267
	.30	.069771	.076752	.083980	.087672	.091408	.095183	.098992	.102831	.106696	.114491	.122351	.130260	.138203
	.20	.071707	.078688	.085916	.089608	.093343	.097118	.100927	.104766	.108632	.116426	.124287	.132196	.140138
	.10	.073643	.080623	.087852	.091543	.095279	.099054	.102863	.106702	.110567	.118362	.126223	.134131	.142074
	0.00	.075578	.082559	.089787	.093479	.097215	.100990	.104799	.108638	.112503	.120298	.128158	.136067	.144010
	-.10	.077514	.084495	.091723	.095415	.099151	.102926	.106735	.110574	.114439	.122233	.130094	.138003	.145946
	-.20	.079450	.086431	.093659	.097351	.101086	.104861	.108670	.112510	.116375	.124169	.132030	.139939	.147881
	-.30	.081386	.088366	.095595	.099286	.103022	.106797	.110606	.114445	.118310	.126105	.133966	.141874	.149817
	-.40	.083321	.090302	.097530	.101222	.104958	.108733	.112542	.116381	.120246	.128041	.135901	.143810	.151753

15.0 YEAR HOLDING PERIOD
.160 EQUITY YIELD RATE
.900 LOAN RATIO

INTEREST RATE

TERM YEARS	APPR DEP	5.0	6.0	7.0	7.5	8.0	8.5	9.0	9.5	10.0	11.0	12.0	13.0	14.0
15	.40	.076241	.081972	.087909	.090953	.094046	.097187	.100376	.103611	.106893	.113588	.120453	.127481	.134663
	.30	.078177	.083908	.089844	.092888	.095981	.099123	.102312	.105547	.108828	.115523	.122389	.129417	.136599
	.20	.080112	.085843	.091780	.094824	.097917	.101059	.104248	.107483	.110764	.117459	.124325	.131353	.138535
	.10	.082048	.087779	.093716	.096760	.099853	.102994	.106183	.109419	.112700	.119395	.126261	.133289	.140471
	0.00	.083984	.089715	.095652	.098696	.101789	.104930	.108119	.111354	.114636	.121331	.128196	.135224	.142406
	-.10	.085920	.091651	.097587	.100631	.103724	.106866	.110055	.113290	.116571	.123266	.130132	.137160	.144342
	-.20	.087855	.093586	.099523	.102567	.105660	.108802	.111991	.115226	.118507	.125202	.132068	.139096	.146278
	-.30	.089791	.095522	.101459	.104503	.107596	.110737	.113926	.117162	.120443	.127138	.134004	.141032	.148214
	-.40	.091727	.097458	.103395	.106439	.109532	.112673	.115862	.119098	.122379	.129074	.135939	.142967	.150149
20	.40	.068203	.074666	.081389	.084843	.088358	.091929	.095557	.099238	.102970	.110582	.118376	.126336	.134446
	.30	.070139	.076602	.083325	.086779	.090293	.093865	.097492	.101173	.104906	.112518	.120312	.128272	.136382
	.20	.072075	.078537	.085260	.088715	.092229	.095801	.099428	.103109	.106842	.114454	.122248	.130208	.138318
	.10	.074010	.080473	.087196	.090651	.094165	.097737	.101364	.105045	.108778	.116390	.124183	.132143	.140253
	0.00	.075946	.082409	.089131	.092586	.096101	.099672	.103300	.106981	.110713	.118325	.126119	.134079	.142189
	-.10	.077882	.084345	.091068	.094522	.098036	.101608	.105235	.108917	.112649	.120261	.128055	.136015	.144125
	-.20	.079818	.086280	.093003	.096458	.099972	.103544	.107171	.110852	.114585	.122197	.129991	.137951	.146061
	-.30	.081753	.088216	.094939	.098394	.101908	.105480	.109107	.112788	.116521	.124133	.131926	.139886	.147996
	-.40	.083689	.090152	.096875	.100329	.103844	.107415	.111043	.114724	.118456	.126068	.133862	.141822	.149932
25	.40	.063573	.070530	.077772	.081492	.085274	.089114	.093010	.096958	.100955	.109083	.117373	.125801	.134348
	.30	.065509	.072466	.079708	.083428	.087210	.091050	.094946	.098893	.102890	.111019	.119309	.127737	.136284
	.20	.067445	.074402	.081644	.085364	.089146	.092986	.096881	.100829	.104826	.112955	.121244	.129673	.138220
	.10	.069380	.076338	.083580	.087300	.091081	.094922	.098817	.102765	.106762	.114891	.123180	.131608	.140156
	0.00	.071316	.078273	.085515	.089235	.093017	.096857	.100753	.104701	.108698	.116826	.125116	.133544	.142091
	-.10	.073252	.080209	.087451	.091171	.094953	.098793	.102689	.106636	.110633	.118762	.127052	.135480	.144027
	-.20	.075188	.082145	.089387	.093107	.096889	.100729	.104624	.108572	.112569	.120698	.128987	.137416	.145963
	-.30	.077123	.084081	.091323	.095043	.098824	.102665	.106560	.110508	.114505	.122634	.130923	.139351	.147899
	-.40	.079059	.086016	.093258	.096978	.100760	.104600	.108496	.112444	.116441	.124569	.132859	.141287	.149834
30	.40	.060639	.067965	.075583	.079491	.083459	.087481	.091555	.095676	.099840	.108283	.116857	.125537	.134302
	.30	.062574	.069900	.077519	.081427	.085394	.089417	.093491	.097612	.101776	.110219	.118793	.127472	.136238
	.20	.064510	.071836	.079455	.083363	.087330	.091353	.095427	.099548	.103712	.112155	.120728	.129408	.138173
	.10	.066446	.073772	.081391	.085298	.089266	.093289	.097362	.101483	.105648	.114091	.122664	.131344	.140109
	0.00	.068382	.075708	.083326	.087234	.091202	.095224	.099298	.103419	.107583	.116026	.124600	.133280	.142045
	-.10	.070317	.077643	.085262	.089170	.093137	.097160	.101234	.105355	.109519	.117962	.126536	.135215	.143981
	-.20	.072253	.079579	.087198	.091106	.095073	.099096	.103170	.107291	.111455	.119898	.128471	.137151	.145916
	-.30	.074189	.081515	.089134	.093041	.097009	.101032	.105106	.109226	.113391	.121834	.130407	.139087	.147852
	-.40	.076125	.083451	.091069	.094977	.098945	.102967	.107041	.111162	.115326	.123769	.132343	.141023	.149788
40	.40	.057283	.065136	.073268	.077421	.081624	.085870	.090156	.094475	.098823	.107592	.116435	.125333	.134268
	.30	.059218	.067072	.075204	.079357	.083560	.087806	.092092	.096410	.100759	.109527	.118371	.127268	.136204
	.20	.061154	.069007	.077139	.081292	.085495	.089742	.094027	.098346	.102694	.111463	.120307	.129204	.138140
	.10	.063090	.070943	.079075	.083228	.087431	.091678	.095963	.100282	.104630	.113399	.122242	.131140	.140075
	0.00	.065026	.072879	.081011	.085164	.089367	.093614	.097899	.102218	.106566	.115335	.124178	.133076	.142011
	-.10	.066961	.074815	.082947	.087100	.091303	.095549	.099835	.104153	.108502	.117270	.126114	.135011	.143947
	-.20	.068897	.076750	.084882	.089035	.093238	.097485	.101770	.106089	.110437	.119206	.128050	.136947	.145883
	-.30	.070833	.078686	.086818	.090971	.095174	.099421	.103706	.108025	.112373	.121142	.129985	.138883	.147818
	-.40	.072769	.080622	.088754	.092907	.097110	.101357	.105642	.109961	.114309	.123078	.131921	.140819	.149754

15.0 YEAR HOLDING PERIOD
.180 EQUITY YIELD RATE
.600 LOAN RATIO

INTEREST RATE

TERM YEARS	APPR DEP	14.0	13.0	12.0	11.0	10.0	9.5	9.0	8.5	8.0	7.5	7.0	6.0	5.0
15	.40	.151483	.146695	.142009	.137432	.132969	.130781	.128624	.126498	.124404	.122342	.120313	.116355	.112534
	.30	.153123	.148335	.143650	.139072	.134609	.132422	.130265	.128139	.126044	.123982	.121953	.117995	.114175
	.20	.154763	.149975	.145290	.140713	.136249	.134062	.131905	.129779	.127685	.125623	.123593	.119635	.115815
	.10	.156403	.151615	.146930	.142353	.137890	.135702	.133545	.131419	.129325	.127263	.125234	.121276	.117455
	0.00	.158044	.153256	.148570	.143993	.139530	.137343	.135186	.133060	.130965	.128903	.126874	.122916	.119095
	-.10	.159684	.154896	.150211	.145634	.141170	.138983	.136826	.134700	.132606	.130543	.128514	.124556	.120736
	-.20	.161324	.156536	.151851	.147274	.142810	.140623	.138466	.136340	.134246	.132184	.130155	.126197	.122376
	-.30	.162965	.158176	.153491	.148914	.144451	.142263	.140106	.137980	.135886	.133824	.131795	.127837	.124016
	-.40	.164605	.159817	.155132	.150554	.146091	.143904	.141747	.139621	.137526	.135464	.133435	.129477	.125657
20	.40	.150390	.145018	.139747	.134587	.129549	.127079	.124643	.122243	.119881	.117557	.115272	.110827	.106556
	.30	.152031	.146659	.141387	.136227	.131189	.128719	.126283	.123884	.121521	.119197	.116912	.112468	.108196
	.20	.153671	.148299	.143028	.137868	.132829	.130359	.127924	.125524	.123161	.120837	.118553	.114108	.109836
	.10	.155311	.149939	.144668	.139508	.134470	.132000	.129564	.127164	.124802	.122477	.120193	.115748	.111477
	0.00	.156951	.151579	.146308	.141148	.136110	.133640	.131204	.128805	.126442	.124118	.121833	.117388	.113117
	-.10	.158592	.153220	.147948	.142788	.137750	.135280	.132845	.130445	.128082	.125758	.123474	.119029	.114757
	-.20	.160232	.154860	.149589	.144429	.139390	.136920	.134485	.132085	.129722	.127398	.125114	.120669	.116397
	-.30	.161872	.156500	.151229	.146069	.141031	.138561	.136125	.133725	.131363	.129039	.126754	.122309	.118038
	-.40	.163513	.158140	.152869	.147709	.142671	.140201	.137765	.135366	.133003	.130679	.128394	.123950	.119678
25	.40	.149898	.144235	.138654	.133168	.127791	.125149	.122539	.119965	.117429	.114932	.112476	.107698	.103112
	.30	.151538	.145876	.140294	.134808	.129431	.126789	.124180	.121606	.119069	.116572	.114116	.109339	.104752
	.20	.153179	.147516	.141935	.136448	.131072	.128429	.125820	.123246	.120709	.118212	.115757	.110979	.106393
	.10	.154819	.149156	.143575	.138089	.132712	.130069	.127460	.124886	.122350	.119852	.117397	.112619	.108033
	0.00	.156459	.150796	.145215	.139729	.134352	.131710	.129100	.126526	.123990	.121493	.119037	.114260	.109673
	-.10	.158100	.152437	.146856	.141369	.135992	.133350	.130741	.128167	.125630	.123133	.120678	.115900	.111313
	-.20	.159740	.154077	.148496	.143010	.137633	.134990	.132381	.129807	.127270	.124773	.122318	.117540	.112954
	-.30	.161380	.155717	.150136	.144650	.139273	.136630	.134021	.131447	.128911	.126413	.123958	.119180	.114594
	-.40	.163020	.157358	.151776	.146290	.140913	.138271	.135661	.133087	.130551	.128054	.125598	.120821	.116234
30	.40	.149664	.143848	.138092	.132411	.126820	.124064	.121337	.118644	.115985	.113364	.110784	.105757	.100929
	.30	.151305	.145488	.139732	.134051	.128460	.125704	.122978	.120284	.117625	.115004	.112424	.107398	.102570
	.20	.152945	.147129	.141373	.135691	.130100	.127344	.124618	.121924	.119265	.116644	.114064	.109038	.104210
	.10	.154585	.148769	.143013	.137331	.131740	.128984	.126258	.123564	.120906	.118285	.115705	.110678	.105850
	0.00	.156225	.150409	.144653	.138972	.133381	.130625	.127899	.125205	.122546	.119925	.117345	.112318	.107490
	-.10	.157866	.152050	.146294	.140612	.135021	.132265	.129539	.126845	.124186	.121565	.118985	.113959	.109131
	-.20	.159506	.153690	.147934	.142252	.136661	.133905	.131179	.128485	.125827	.123205	.120625	.115599	.110771
	-.30	.161146	.155330	.149574	.143893	.138301	.135546	.132819	.130126	.127467	.124846	.122266	.117239	.112411
	-.40	.162787	.156970	.151214	.145533	.139942	.137186	.134460	.131766	.129107	.126486	.123906	.118879	.114052
40	.40	.149494	.143550	.137633	.131756	.125932	.123047	.120181	.117340	.114526	.111742	.108993	.103617	.098433
	.30	.151135	.145190	.139273	.133396	.127573	.124687	.121822	.118980	.116166	.113383	.110634	.105257	.100074
	.20	.152775	.146830	.140914	.135036	.129213	.126327	.123462	.120621	.117806	.115023	.112274	.106898	.101714
	.10	.154415	.148470	.142554	.136677	.130853	.127967	.125102	.122261	.119447	.116663	.113914	.108538	.103354
	0.00	.156055	.150111	.144194	.138317	.132493	.129608	.126742	.123901	.121087	.118303	.115555	.110178	.104994
	-.10	.157696	.151751	.145834	.139957	.134134	.131248	.128383	.125541	.122727	.119944	.117195	.111818	.106635
	-.20	.159336	.153391	.147475	.141597	.135774	.132888	.130023	.127182	.124367	.121584	.118835	.113459	.108275
	-.30	.160976	.155031	.149115	.143238	.137414	.134528	.131663	.128822	.126008	.123224	.120475	.115099	.109915
	-.40	.162616	.156672	.150755	.144878	.139055	.136169	.133304	.130462	.127648	.124865	.122116	.116739	.111555

15.0 YEAR HOLDING PERIOD
.180 EQUITY YIELD RATE
.667 LOAN RATIO

INTEREST RATE

TERM YEARS	APPR DEP	5.0	6.0	7.0	7.5	8.0	8.5	9.0	9.5	10.0	11.0	12.0	13.0	14.0
15	.40	.105767	.110012	.114410	.116664	.118956	.121283	.123645	.126041	.128472	.133431	.138517	.143723	.149043
	.30	.107407	.111652	.116050	.118305	.120596	.122923	.125285	.127682	.130112	.135072	.140157	.145363	.150683
	.20	.109047	.113292	.117690	.119945	.122236	.124563	.126925	.129322	.131752	.136712	.141798	.147003	.152323
	.10	.110688	.114933	.119330	.121585	.123876	.126203	.128566	.130962	.133392	.138352	.143438	.148644	.153964
	0.00	.112328	.116573	.120971	.123226	.125517	.127844	.130206	.132603	.135033	.139992	.145078	.150284	.155604
	-.10	.113968	.118213	.122611	.124866	.127157	.129484	.131846	.134243	.136673	.141633	.146718	.151924	.157244
	-.20	.115609	.119854	.124251	.126506	.128797	.131124	.133486	.135883	.138314	.143273	.148359	.153565	.158885
	-.30	.117249	.121494	.125892	.128146	.130438	.132765	.135127	.137523	.139954	.144913	.149999	.155205	.160525
	-.40	.118889	.123134	.127532	.129787	.132078	.134405	.136767	.139164	.141594	.146553	.151639	.156845	.162165
20	.40	.099124	.103870	.108809	.111347	.113930	.116555	.119221	.121927	.124672	.130270	.136003	.141860	.147829
	.30	.100764	.105510	.110449	.112987	.115570	.118195	.120861	.123568	.126312	.131910	.137644	.143501	.149470
	.20	.102405	.107151	.112089	.114628	.117210	.119835	.122502	.125208	.127952	.133550	.139284	.145141	.151110
	.10	.104045	.108791	.113730	.116268	.118850	.121476	.124142	.126848	.129593	.135191	.140924	.146781	.152750
	0.00	.105685	.110431	.115370	.117908	.120491	.123116	.125782	.128488	.131233	.136831	.142564	.148421	.154390
	-.10	.107325	.112072	.117010	.119549	.122131	.124756	.127423	.130129	.132873	.138471	.144205	.150062	.156031
	-.20	.108966	.113712	.118651	.121189	.123771	.126396	.129063	.131769	.134514	.140112	.145845	.151702	.157671
	-.30	.110606	.115352	.120291	.122829	.125412	.128037	.130703	.133409	.136154	.141752	.147485	.153342	.159311
	-.40	.112246	.116992	.121931	.124469	.127052	.129677	.132343	.135050	.137794	.143392	.149125	.154982	.160952
25	.40	.095298	.100394	.105702	.108430	.111205	.114023	.116883	.119783	.122719	.128693	.134789	.140990	.147282
	.30	.096938	.102034	.107342	.110071	.112845	.115664	.118524	.121423	.124359	.130333	.136429	.142631	.148923
	.20	.098578	.103674	.108983	.111711	.114486	.117304	.120164	.123063	.125999	.131974	.138070	.144271	.150563
	.10	.100218	.105314	.110623	.113351	.116126	.118944	.121804	.124703	.127640	.133614	.139710	.145911	.152203
	0.00	.101859	.106955	.112263	.114992	.117766	.120585	.123445	.126344	.129280	.135254	.141350	.147551	.153843
	-.10	.103499	.108595	.113904	.116632	.119406	.122225	.125085	.127984	.130920	.136894	.142990	.149192	.155484
	-.20	.105139	.110235	.115544	.118272	.121047	.123865	.126725	.129624	.132560	.138535	.144631	.150832	.157124
	-.30	.106779	.111876	.117184	.119912	.122687	.125505	.128365	.131265	.134201	.140175	.146271	.152472	.158764
	-.40	.108420	.113516	.118824	.121553	.124327	.127146	.130006	.132905	.135841	.141815	.147911	.154113	.160405
30	.40	.092872	.098237	.103822	.106689	.109601	.112555	.115548	.118577	.121639	.127852	.134165	.140560	.147023
	.30	.094513	.099877	.105462	.108329	.111241	.114195	.117188	.120218	.123280	.129492	.135805	.142200	.148663
	.20	.096153	.101517	.107102	.109969	.112881	.115836	.118829	.121858	.124920	.131132	.137445	.143841	.150303
	.10	.097793	.103158	.108742	.111609	.114522	.117476	.120469	.123498	.126560	.132772	.139085	.145481	.151943
	0.00	.099433	.104798	.110383	.113250	.116162	.119116	.122109	.125138	.128200	.134413	.140726	.147121	.153584
	-.10	.101074	.106438	.112023	.114890	.117802	.120756	.123750	.126779	.129841	.136053	.142366	.148762	.155224
	-.20	.102714	.108078	.113663	.116530	.119442	.122397	.125390	.128419	.131481	.137693	.144006	.150402	.156864
	-.30	.104354	.109719	.115304	.118171	.121083	.124037	.127030	.130059	.133121	.139334	.145647	.152042	.158504
	-.40	.105994	.111359	.116944	.119811	.122723	.125677	.128670	.131699	.134762	.140974	.147287	.153682	.160145
40	.40	.090099	.095859	.101833	.104887	.107980	.111107	.114264	.117447	.120654	.127124	.133654	.140228	.146834
	.30	.091739	.097499	.103473	.106527	.109620	.112747	.115904	.119087	.122294	.128764	.135294	.141869	.148474
	.20	.093379	.099139	.105113	.108167	.111260	.114387	.117544	.120728	.123934	.130405	.136935	.143509	.150114
	.10	.095020	.100780	.106753	.109808	.112900	.116027	.119184	.122368	.125574	.132045	.138575	.145149	.151754
	0.00	.096660	.102420	.108394	.111448	.114541	.117668	.120825	.124008	.127215	.133685	.140215	.146789	.153395
	-.10	.098300	.104060	.110034	.113088	.116181	.119308	.122465	.125648	.128855	.135325	.141856	.148430	.155035
	-.20	.099941	.105700	.111674	.114728	.117821	.120948	.124105	.127289	.130495	.136966	.143496	.150070	.156675
	-.30	.101581	.107341	.113314	.116369	.119462	.122588	.125746	.128929	.132136	.138606	.145136	.151710	.158316
	-.40	.103221	.108981	.114955	.118009	.121102	.124229	.127386	.130569	.133776	.140246	.146777	.153351	.159956

15.0 YEAR HOLDING PERIOD
.180 EQUITY YIELD RATE
.700 LOAN RATIO

INTEREST RATE

TERM YEARS	APPR DEP	5.0	6.0	7.0	7.5	8.0	8.5	9.0	9.5	10.0	11.0	12.0	13.0	14.0
15	.40	.102384	.106841	.111459	.113826	.116232	.118675	.121155	.123672	.126224	.131431	.136771	.142237	.147823
	.30	.104024	.108481	.113099	.115466	.117872	.120315	.122796	.125312	.127864	.133071	.138411	.143878	.149463
	.20	.105664	.110121	.114739	.117107	.119512	.121956	.124436	.126952	.129504	.134712	.140052	.145558	.151104
	.10	.107304	.111762	.116379	.118747	.121153	.123596	.126076	.128593	.131145	.136352	.141692	.147158	.152744
	0.00	.108945	.113402	.118020	.120387	.122793	.125236	.127716	.130233	.132785	.137992	.143332	.148798	.154384
	-.10	.110585	.115042	.119660	.122027	.124433	.126876	.129357	.131873	.134425	.139632	.144972	.150439	.156025
	-.20	.112225	.116683	.121300	.123668	.126073	.128517	.130997	.133513	.136065	.141273	.146613	.152079	.157665
	-.30	.113866	.118323	.122940	.125308	.127714	.130157	.132637	.135154	.137706	.142913	.148253	.153719	.159305
	-.40	.115506	.119963	.124581	.126948	.129354	.131797	.134278	.136794	.139346	.144553	.149893	.155360	.160945
20	.40	.095409	.100392	.105578	.108243	.110954	.113711	.116511	.119352	.122234	.128112	.134132	.140281	.146549
	.30	.097049	.102032	.107218	.109883	.112595	.115351	.118151	.120992	.123874	.129752	.135772	.141922	.148189
	.20	.098689	.103673	.108858	.111523	.114235	.116991	.119791	.122633	.125514	.131392	.137412	.143562	.149830
	.10	.100329	.105313	.110499	.113164	.115875	.118632	.121431	.124273	.127155	.133032	.139053	.145202	.151470
	0.00	.101970	.106953	.112139	.114804	.117516	.120272	.123072	.125913	.128795	.134673	.140693	.146843	.153110
	-.10	.103610	.108593	.113779	.116444	.119156	.121912	.124712	.127553	.130435	.136313	.142333	.148483	.154750
	-.20	.105250	.110234	.115419	.118085	.120796	.123552	.126352	.129194	.132075	.137953	.143973	.150123	.156391
	-.30	.106891	.111874	.117060	.119725	.122436	.125193	.127992	.130834	.133716	.139594	.145614	.151763	.158031
	-.40	.108531	.113514	.118700	.121365	.124077	.126833	.129633	.132474	.135356	.141234	.147254	.153404	.159671
25	.40	.091391	.096742	.102316	.105180	.108094	.111053	.114056	.117100	.120183	.126456	.132857	.139368	.145975
	.30	.093031	.098382	.103956	.106821	.109734	.112693	.115696	.118740	.121823	.128096	.134497	.141008	.147615
	.20	.094671	.100022	.105596	.108461	.111374	.114334	.117337	.120381	.123464	.129737	.136137	.142649	.149255
	.10	.096312	.101663	.107237	.110101	.113014	.115974	.118977	.122021	.125104	.131377	.137778	.144289	.150896
	0.00	.097952	.103303	.108877	.111742	.114655	.117614	.120617	.123661	.126744	.133017	.139418	.145929	.152536
	-.10	.099592	.104943	.110517	.113382	.116295	.119254	.122257	.125301	.128384	.134657	.141058	.147570	.154176
	-.20	.101233	.106583	.112157	.115022	.117935	.120895	.123898	.126942	.130025	.136298	.142698	.149210	.155816
	-.30	.102873	.108224	.113798	.116662	.119576	.122535	.125538	.128582	.131665	.137938	.144339	.150850	.157457
	-.40	.104513	.109864	.115438	.118303	.121216	.124175	.127178	.130222	.133305	.139578	.145979	.152490	.159097
30	.40	.088844	.094477	.100341	.103351	.106409	.109511	.112654	.115834	.119050	.125573	.132201	.138916	.145702
	.30	.090485	.096117	.101981	.104992	.108049	.111151	.114294	.117475	.120690	.127213	.133841	.140557	.147342
	.20	.092125	.097758	.103622	.106632	.109690	.112792	.115934	.119115	.122330	.128853	.135482	.142197	.148982
	.10	.093765	.099398	.105262	.108272	.111330	.114432	.117575	.120755	.123970	.130493	.137122	.143837	.150623
	0.00	.095405	.101038	.106902	.109913	.112970	.116072	.119215	.122396	.125611	.132134	.138762	.145477	.152263
	-.10	.097046	.102678	.108543	.111553	.114611	.117713	.120855	.124036	.127251	.133774	.140402	.147118	.153903
	-.20	.098686	.104319	.110183	.113193	.116251	.119353	.122496	.125676	.128891	.135414	.142043	.148758	.155544
	-.30	.100326	.105959	.111823	.114833	.117891	.120993	.124136	.127316	.130532	.137054	.143683	.150398	.157184
	-.40	.101967	.107599	.113463	.116474	.119531	.122633	.125776	.128957	.132172	.138695	.145323	.152039	.158824
40	.40	.085932	.091980	.098253	.101460	.104707	.107990	.111305	.114648	.118015	.124809	.131665	.138568	.145504
	.30	.087573	.093620	.099893	.103100	.106347	.109631	.112945	.116288	.119655	.126449	.133306	.140208	.147144
	.20	.089213	.095261	.101533	.104740	.107988	.111271	.114586	.117928	.121295	.128089	.134946	.141849	.148784
	.10	.090853	.096901	.103173	.106380	.109628	.112911	.116226	.119569	.122935	.129729	.136586	.143489	.150424
	0.00	.092493	.098541	.104814	.108021	.111268	.114551	.117866	.121209	.124576	.131370	.138226	.145129	.152065
	-.10	.094134	.100182	.106454	.109661	.112908	.116192	.119507	.122849	.126216	.133010	.139867	.146769	.153705
	-.20	.095774	.101822	.108094	.111301	.114549	.117832	.121147	.124489	.127856	.134650	.141507	.148410	.155345
	-.30	.097414	.103462	.109735	.112941	.116189	.119472	.122787	.126130	.129497	.136291	.143147	.150050	.156985
	-.40	.099055	.105102	.111375	.114582	.117829	.121112	.124427	.127770	.131137	.137931	.144788	.151690	.158626

15.0 YEAR HOLDING PERIOD
.180 EQUITY YIELD RATE
.750 LOAN RATIO

INTEREST RATE

TERM YEARS	APPR DEP	5.0	6.0	7.0	7.5	8.0	8.5	9.0	9.5	10.0	11.0	12.0	13.0	14.0
15	.40	.097308	.102084	.107031	.109568	.112145	.114763	.117421	.120117	.122851	.128431	.134152	.140009	.145994
	.30	.098949	.103724	.108672	.111208	.113786	.116404	.119061	.121757	.124492	.130071	.135792	.141649	.147634
	.20	.100569	.105364	.110312	.112848	.115426	.118044	.120701	.123398	.126132	.131711	.137432	.143289	.149274
	.10	.102229	.107005	.111952	.114489	.117066	.119684	.122342	.125038	.127772	.133351	.139073	.144929	.150914
	0.00	.103869	.108645	.113592	.116129	.118707	.121324	.123982	.126678	.129412	.134992	.140713	.146570	.152555
	-.10	.105510	.110285	.115233	.117769	.120347	.122965	.125622	.128318	.131053	.136632	.142353	.148210	.154195
	-.20	.107150	.111926	.116873	.119410	.121987	.124605	.127262	.129959	.132693	.138272	.143994	.149850	.155835
	-.30	.108790	.113566	.118513	.121050	.123627	.126245	.128903	.131599	.134333	.139912	.145634	.151491	.157475
	-.40	.110430	.115206	.120154	.122690	.125268	.127886	.130543	.133239	.135973	.141553	.147274	.153131	.159116
20	.40	.089835	.095174	.100730	.103586	.106491	.109445	.112444	.115489	.118576	.124874	.131324	.137913	.144628
	.30	.091475	.096815	.102371	.105226	.108132	.111085	.114084	.117129	.120217	.126514	.132964	.139553	.146269
	.20	.093116	.098455	.104011	.106867	.109772	.112725	.115725	.118769	.121857	.128155	.134605	.141194	.147909
	.10	.094756	.100095	.105651	.108507	.111412	.114365	.117365	.120410	.123497	.129795	.136245	.142834	.149549
	0.00	.096396	.101736	.107292	.110147	.113052	.116006	.119005	.122050	.125137	.131435	.137885	.144474	.151189
	-.10	.098036	.103376	.108932	.111787	.114693	.117646	.120646	.123690	.126778	.133075	.139525	.146114	.152830
	-.20	.099677	.105016	.110572	.113428	.116333	.119286	.122286	.125330	.128418	.134716	.141166	.147755	.154470
	-.30	.101317	.106656	.112212	.115068	.117973	.120926	.123926	.126971	.130058	.136356	.142806	.149395	.156110
	-.40	.102957	.108297	.113853	.116708	.119613	.122567	.125566	.128611	.131698	.137996	.144446	.151035	.157750
25	.40	.085530	.091263	.097235	.100305	.103426	.106597	.109814	.113076	.116379	.123100	.129958	.136934	.144013
	.30	.087171	.092904	.098876	.101945	.105066	.108237	.111455	.114716	.118019	.124740	.131598	.138575	.145653
	.20	.088811	.094544	.100516	.103585	.106707	.109877	.113095	.116356	.119660	.126381	.133239	.140215	.147294
	.10	.090451	.096184	.102156	.105226	.108347	.111518	.114735	.117997	.121300	.128021	.134879	.141855	.148934
	0.00	.092091	.097824	.103797	.106866	.109987	.113158	.116375	.119637	.122940	.129661	.136519	.143496	.150574
	-.10	.093732	.099465	.105437	.108506	.111628	.114798	.118016	.121277	.124580	.131301	.138159	.145136	.152214
	-.20	.095372	.101105	.107077	.110146	.113268	.116439	.119656	.122918	.126221	.132942	.139800	.146776	.153855
	-.30	.097012	.102745	.108717	.111787	.114908	.118079	.121296	.124558	.127861	.134582	.141440	.148416	.155495
	-.40	.098653	.104386	.110358	.113427	.116548	.119719	.122937	.126198	.129501	.136222	.143080	.150057	.157135
30	.40	.082802	.088837	.095120	.098345	.101621	.104945	.108312	.111720	.115165	.122153	.129256	.136450	.143721
	.30	.084442	.090477	.096760	.099985	.103262	.106585	.109952	.113360	.116805	.123794	.130896	.138091	.145361
	.20	.086082	.092117	.098400	.101626	.104902	.108225	.111593	.115000	.118445	.125434	.132536	.139731	.147001
	.10	.087723	.093758	.100041	.103266	.106542	.109866	.113233	.116641	.120086	.127074	.134176	.141371	.148641
	0.00	.089363	.095398	.101681	.104906	.108182	.111506	.114873	.118281	.121726	.128715	.135817	.143012	.150282
	-.10	.091003	.097038	.103321	.106547	.109823	.113146	.116514	.119921	.123366	.130355	.137457	.144652	.151922
	-.20	.092644	.098679	.104962	.108187	.111463	.114787	.118154	.121562	.125006	.131995	.139097	.146292	.153562
	-.30	.094284	.100319	.106602	.109827	.113103	.116427	.119794	.123202	.126647	.133635	.140737	.147932	.155203
	-.40	.095924	.101959	.108242	.111467	.114744	.118067	.121434	.124842	.128287	.135276	.142378	.149573	.156843
40	.40	.079682	.086162	.092882	.096318	.099798	.103315	.106867	.110448	.114056	.121335	.128681	.136077	.143508
	.30	.081322	.087802	.094522	.097958	.101438	.104956	.108507	.112088	.115696	.122975	.130322	.137717	.145148
	.20	.082962	.089442	.096163	.099599	.103078	.106596	.110148	.113729	.117336	.124616	.131962	.139358	.146789
	.10	.084603	.091082	.097803	.101239	.104718	.108236	.111788	.115369	.118977	.126256	.133602	.140998	.148429
	0.00	.086243	.092723	.099443	.102879	.106359	.109876	.113428	.117010	.120617	.127896	.135243	.142638	.150069
	-.10	.087883	.094363	.101084	.104520	.107999	.111517	.115068	.118650	.122257	.129536	.136883	.144279	.151710
	-.20	.089523	.096003	.102724	.106160	.109639	.113157	.116709	.120290	.123898	.131177	.138523	.145919	.153350
	-.30	.091164	.097644	.104364	.107800	.111279	.114797	.118349	.121930	.125538	.132817	.140163	.147559	.154990
	-.40	.092804	.099284	.106004	.109440	.112920	.116438	.119989	.123571	.127178	.134457	.141804	.149199	.156630

15.0 YEAR HOLDING PERIOD
.180 EQUITY YIELD RATE
.800 LOAN RATIO

INTEREST RATE

TERM YEARS	APPR DEP	5.0	6.0	7.0	7.5	8.0	8.5	9.0	9.5	10.0	11.0	12.0	13.0	14.0
15	.40	.092233	.097327	.102604	.105310	.108059	.110852	.113686	.116562	.119479	.125430	.131533	.137780	.144164
	.30	.093873	.098967	.104244	.106950	.109700	.112492	.115327	.118203	.121119	.127070	.133173	.139420	.145804
	.20	.095513	.100607	.105885	.108590	.111340	.114132	.116967	.119843	.122759	.128711	.134813	.141060	.147444
	.10	.097154	.102248	.107525	.110231	.112980	.115772	.118607	.121483	.124400	.130351	.136454	.142701	.149085
	0.00	.098794	.103888	.109165	.111871	.114620	.117413	.120247	.123123	.126040	.131991	.138094	.144341	.150725
	-.10	.100434	.105528	.110806	.113511	.116261	.119053	.121888	.124764	.127680	.133631	.139734	.145981	.152365
	-.20	.102075	.107169	.112446	.115152	.117901	.120693	.123528	.126404	.129320	.135272	.141374	.147622	.154006
	-.30	.103715	.108809	.114086	.116792	.119541	.122334	.125168	.128044	.130961	.136912	.143015	.149262	.155646
	-.40	.105355	.110449	.115726	.118432	.121181	.123974	.126608	.129684	.132601	.138552	.144655	.150902	.157286
20	.40	.084261	.089957	.095883	.098929	.102028	.105178	.108378	.111625	.114919	.121636	.128516	.135545	.142708
	.30	.085902	.091597	.097524	.100569	.103668	.106819	.110018	.113266	.116559	.123277	.130157	.137185	.144348
	.20	.087542	.093237	.099164	.102210	.105309	.108459	.111658	.114906	.118199	.124917	.131797	.138825	.145988
	.10	.089182	.094878	.100804	.103850	.106949	.110099	.113299	.116546	.119840	.126557	.133437	.140466	.147628
	0.00	.090823	.096518	.102444	.105490	.108589	.111739	.114939	.118186	.121480	.128197	.135077	.142106	.149269
	-.10	.092463	.098158	.104085	.107131	.110229	.113380	.116579	.119827	.123120	.129838	.136718	.143746	.150909
	-.20	.094103	.099799	.105725	.108771	.111870	.115020	.118220	.121467	.124760	.131478	.138358	.145386	.152549
	-.30	.095743	.101439	.107365	.110411	.113510	.116660	.119860	.123107	.126401	.133118	.139998	.147027	.154189
	-.40	.097384	.103079	.109005	.112051	.115150	.118300	.121500	.124748	.128041	.134759	.141639	.148667	.155830
25	.40	.079670	.085785	.092155	.095429	.098759	.102141	.105573	.109052	.112575	.119744	.127059	.134501	.142051
	.30	.081310	.087425	.093796	.097069	.100399	.103781	.107213	.110692	.114215	.121384	.128700	.136141	.143691
	.20	.082950	.089066	.095436	.098710	.102039	.105421	.108853	.112332	.115856	.123025	.130340	.137781	.145332
	.10	.084591	.090706	.097076	.100350	.103679	.107062	.110494	.113973	.117496	.124665	.131980	.139422	.146972
	0.00	.086231	.092346	.098716	.101990	.105320	.108702	.112134	.115613	.119136	.126305	.133620	.141062	.148612
	-.10	.087871	.093986	.100357	.103631	.106960	.110342	.113774	.117253	.120776	.127946	.135261	.142702	.150253
	-.20	.089511	.095627	.101997	.105271	.108600	.111982	.115414	.118893	.122417	.129586	.136901	.144343	.151893
	-.30	.091152	.097267	.103637	.106911	.110241	.113623	.117055	.120534	.124057	.131226	.138541	.145983	.153533
	-.40	.092792	.098907	.105277	.108551	.111881	.115263	.118695	.122174	.125697	.132866	.140181	.147623	.155173
30	.40	.076759	.083197	.089899	.093339	.096834	.100379	.103970	.107605	.111280	.118734	.126310	.133985	.141739
	.30	.078400	.084837	.091539	.094979	.098474	.102019	.105611	.109246	.112920	.120375	.127950	.135625	.143380
	.20	.080040	.086477	.093179	.096619	.100114	.103659	.107251	.110886	.114560	.122015	.129591	.137265	.145020
	.10	.081680	.088118	.094819	.098260	.101754	.105299	.108891	.112526	.116201	.123655	.131231	.138905	.146660
	0.00	.083321	.089758	.096460	.099900	.103395	.106940	.110531	.114166	.117841	.125296	.132871	.140546	.148301
	-.10	.084961	.091398	.098100	.101540	.105035	.108580	.112172	.115807	.119481	.126936	.134511	.142186	.149941
	-.20	.086601	.093038	.099740	.103181	.106675	.110220	.113812	.117447	.121121	.128576	.136152	.143826	.151581
	-.30	.088241	.094679	.101381	.104821	.108315	.111861	.115452	.119087	.122762	.130216	.137792	.145467	.153221
	-.40	.089882	.096319	.103021	.106461	.109956	.113501	.117093	.120727	.124402	.131857	.139432	.147107	.154862
40	.40	.073431	.080343	.087512	.091177	.094888	.098640	.102423	.106249	.110097	.117861	.125698	.133586	.141513
	.30	.075072	.081983	.089152	.092817	.096528	.100281	.104069	.107909	.111737	.119502	.127338	.135227	.143153
	.20	.076712	.083624	.090792	.094457	.098169	.101921	.105709	.109530	.113377	.121142	.128978	.136867	.144793
	.10	.078352	.085264	.092433	.096098	.099810	.103561	.107350	.111170	.115018	.122782	.130618	.138507	.146434
	0.00	.079992	.086904	.094073	.097738	.101449	.105202	.108990	.112810	.116658	.124422	.132259	.140147	.148074
	-.10	.081633	.088545	.095713	.099378	.103089	.106842	.110630	.114450	.118298	.126063	.133899	.141788	.149714
	-.20	.083273	.090185	.097353	.101018	.104730	.108482	.112270	.116091	.119939	.127703	.135539	.143428	.151354
	-.30	.084913	.091825	.098994	.102659	.106370	.110122	.113911	.117731	.121579	.129343	.137180	.145068	.152995
	-.40	.086554	.093465	.100634	.104299	.108010	.111763	.115551	.119371	.123219	.130984	.138820	.146709	.154635

15.0 YEAR HOLDING PERIOD
.180 EQUITY YIELD RATE
.900 LOAN RATIO

INTEREST RATE

TERM YEARS	APPR DEP	5.0	6.0	7.0	7.5	8.0	8.5	9.0	9.5	10.0	11.0	12.0	13.0	14.0
15	.40	.082082	.087813	.093750	.096794	.099887	.103028	.106217	.109453	.112734	.119429	.126295	.133323	.140504
	.30	.083722	.089453	.095390	.098434	.101527	.104669	.107857	.111093	.114374	.121069	.127935	.134963	.142145
	.20	.085363	.091093	.097030	.100074	.103167	.106309	.109498	.112733	.116014	.122709	.129575	.136603	.143785
	.10	.087003	.092734	.098671	.101715	.104808	.107949	.111138	.114373	.117655	.124350	.131215	.138243	.145425
	0.00	.088643	.094374	.100311	.103355	.106448	.109589	.112778	.116014	.119295	.125990	.132856	.139884	.147066
	-.10	.090283	.096014	.101951	.104995	.108088	.111230	.114419	.117654	.120935	.127630	.134496	.141524	.148706
	-.20	.091924	.097655	.103592	.106635	.109728	.112870	.116059	.119294	.122575	.129271	.136136	.143164	.150346
	-.30	.093564	.099295	.105232	.108276	.111369	.114510	.117699	.120935	.124216	.130911	.137776	.144804	.151986
	-.40	.095204	.100935	.106872	.109916	.113009	.116150	.119339	.122575	.125856	.132551	.139417	.146445	.153627
20	.40	.073114	.079522	.086189	.089615	.093102	.096646	.100245	.103899	.107604	.115161	.122901	.130808	.138866
	.30	.074755	.081162	.087829	.091256	.094742	.098286	.101886	.105539	.109244	.116801	.124541	.132448	.140506
	.20	.076395	.082802	.089469	.092896	.096382	.099926	.103526	.107179	.110884	.118442	.126182	.134088	.142147
	.10	.078035	.084442	.091110	.094536	.098023	.101566	.105166	.108819	.112525	.120082	.127822	.135729	.143787
	0.00	.079675	.086083	.092750	.096177	.099663	.103207	.106806	.110460	.114165	.121722	.129462	.137369	.145427
	-.10	.081316	.087723	.094390	.097817	.101303	.104847	.108447	.112100	.115805	.123362	.131102	.139009	.147068
	-.20	.082956	.089363	.096030	.099457	.102943	.106487	.110087	.113740	.117445	.125003	.132743	.140650	.148708
	-.30	.084596	.091004	.097671	.101097	.104584	.108128	.111727	.115381	.119086	.126643	.134383	.142290	.150348
	-.40	.086237	.092644	.099311	.102738	.106224	.109768	.113367	.117021	.120726	.128283	.136023	.143930	.151988
25	.40	.067949	.074828	.081995	.085678	.089424	.093228	.097089	.101003	.104967	.113032	.121262	.129634	.138128
	.30	.069589	.076469	.083635	.087318	.091064	.094869	.098730	.102644	.106607	.114673	.122902	.131274	.139768
	.20	.071229	.078109	.085275	.088959	.092704	.096509	.100370	.104284	.108248	.116313	.124542	.132914	.141408
	.10	.072869	.079749	.086916	.090599	.094344	.098149	.102010	.105924	.109888	.117953	.126183	.134554	.143049
	0.00	.074510	.081389	.088556	.092239	.095985	.099790	.103651	.107564	.111528	.119593	.127823	.136195	.144689
	-.10	.076150	.083030	.090196	.093879	.097625	.101430	.105291	.109205	.113169	.121234	.129463	.137835	.146329
	-.20	.077790	.084670	.091836	.095520	.099265	.103070	.106931	.110845	.114809	.122874	.131103	.139475	.147969
	-.30	.079431	.086310	.093477	.097160	.100906	.104710	.108571	.112485	.116449	.124514	.132744	.141116	.149610
	-.40	.081071	.087950	.095117	.098800	.102546	.106351	.110212	.114126	.118089	.126155	.134384	.142756	.151250
30	.40	.064674	.071916	.079456	.083326	.087258	.091246	.095287	.099376	.103510	.111896	.120419	.129053	.137777
	.30	.066315	.073557	.081096	.084967	.088898	.092886	.096927	.101016	.105150	.113537	.122059	.130693	.139417
	.20	.067955	.075197	.082737	.086607	.090538	.094527	.098567	.102657	.106790	.115177	.123699	.132333	.141058
	.10	.069595	.076837	.084377	.088247	.092179	.096167	.100208	.104297	.108431	.116817	.125340	.133974	.142698
	0.00	.071236	.078478	.086017	.089888	.093819	.097807	.101848	.105937	.110071	.118458	.126980	.135614	.144338
	-.10	.072876	.080118	.087657	.091528	.095459	.099447	.103488	.107577	.111711	.120098	.128620	.137254	.145978
	-.20	.074516	.081758	.089298	.093168	.097100	.101088	.105128	.109218	.113352	.121738	.130261	.138894	.147619
	-.30	.076156	.083398	.090938	.094808	.098740	.102728	.106769	.110858	.114992	.123378	.131901	.140535	.149259
	-.40	.077797	.085039	.092578	.096449	.100380	.104368	.108409	.112498	.116632	.125019	.133541	.142175	.150899
40	.40	.060930	.068706	.076771	.080894	.085069	.089291	.093553	.097850	.102179	.110914	.119730	.128605	.137522
	.30	.062571	.070346	.078411	.082534	.086710	.090931	.095193	.099491	.103819	.112554	.121370	.130245	.139162
	.20	.064211	.071987	.080051	.084175	.088350	.092571	.096833	.101131	.105460	.114195	.123011	.131885	.140803
	.10	.065851	.073627	.081692	.085815	.089990	.094211	.098473	.102771	.107100	.115835	.124651	.133526	.142443
	0.00	.067492	.075267	.083332	.087455	.091630	.095852	.100114	.104411	.108740	.117475	.126291	.135166	.144083
	-.10	.069132	.076908	.084972	.089095	.093271	.097492	.101754	.106052	.110381	.119116	.127931	.136806	.145723
	-.20	.070772	.078548	.086612	.090736	.094911	.099132	.103394	.107692	.112021	.120756	.129572	.138446	.147364
	-.30	.072412	.080188	.088253	.092376	.096551	.100773	.105035	.109332	.113661	.122396	.131212	.140087	.149004
	-.40	.074053	.081828	.089893	.094016	.098191	.102413	.106675	.110973	.115301	.124036	.132852	.141727	.150644

15.0 YEAR HOLDING PERIOD
.200 EQUITY YIELD RATE
.600 LOAN RATIO

INTEREST RATE

TERM YEARS	APPR DEP	5.0	6.0	7.0	7.5	8.0	8.5	9.0	9.5	10.0	11.0	12.0	13.0	14.0
15	.40	.123055	.126876	.130834	.132863	.134925	.137019	.139145	.141302	.143489	.147953	.152530	.157215	.162003
	.30	.124443	.128264	.132222	.134251	.136313	.138407	.140533	.142690	.144878	.149341	.153918	.158604	.163391
	.20	.125831	.129652	.133610	.135639	.137701	.139796	.141921	.144078	.146266	.150729	.155306	.159992	.164780
	.10	.127220	.131040	.134998	.137027	.139089	.141184	.143310	.145467	.147654	.152117	.156695	.161380	.166168
	0.00	.128608	.132428	.136386	.138416	.140478	.142572	.144698	.146855	.149042	.153506	.158083	.162768	.167556
	-.10	.129996	.133817	.137775	.139804	.141866	.143960	.146086	.148243	.150431	.154894	.159471	.164156	.168944
	-.20	.131384	.135205	.139163	.141192	.143254	.145348	.147474	.149631	.151819	.156282	.160859	.165545	.170333
	-.30	.132773	.136593	.140551	.142580	.144642	.146737	.148863	.151020	.153207	.157670	.162247	.166933	.171721
	-.40	.134161	.137981	.141939	.143968	.146031	.148125	.150251	.152408	.154595	.159059	.163636	.168321	.173109
20	.40	.116548	.120788	.125201	.127469	.129778	.132124	.134508	.136928	.139383	.144390	.149519	.154760	.160103
	.30	.117936	.122176	.126589	.128857	.131166	.133513	.135897	.138316	.140771	.145778	.150907	.156148	.161491
	.20	.119324	.123564	.127977	.130246	.132554	.134901	.137285	.139705	.142159	.147166	.152295	.157537	.162879
	.10	.120712	.124952	.129365	.131634	.133942	.136289	.138673	.141093	.143547	.148554	.153684	.158925	.164267
	0.00	.122100	.126340	.130754	.133022	.135330	.137677	.140061	.142481	.144935	.149942	.155072	.160313	.165656
	-.10	.123489	.127729	.132142	.134410	.136719	.139065	.141449	.143869	.146324	.151331	.156460	.161701	.167044
	-.20	.124877	.129117	.133530	.135799	.138107	.140454	.142838	.145257	.147712	.152719	.157848	.163089	.168432
	-.30	.126265	.130505	.134918	.137187	.139495	.141842	.144226	.146646	.149100	.154107	.159237	.164478	.169820
	-.40	.127653	.131893	.136306	.138575	.140883	.143230	.145614	.148034	.150488	.155495	.160625	.165866	.171208
25	.40	.112799	.117341	.122076	.124511	.126987	.129504	.132058	.134648	.137272	.142612	.148065	.153614	.159246
	.30	.114187	.118730	.123464	.125899	.128375	.130892	.133446	.136036	.138660	.144001	.149453	.155002	.160634
	.20	.115576	.120118	.124853	.127287	.129764	.132280	.134834	.137424	.140048	.145389	.150841	.156390	.162023
	.10	.116964	.121506	.126241	.128675	.131152	.133668	.136223	.138813	.141436	.146777	.152229	.157778	.163411
	0.00	.118352	.122894	.127629	.130064	.132540	.135057	.137611	.140201	.142825	.148165	.153617	.159166	.164799
	-.10	.119740	.124282	.129017	.131452	.133928	.136445	.138999	.141589	.144213	.149553	.155006	.160555	.166187
	-.20	.121128	.125671	.130405	.132840	.135317	.137833	.140387	.142977	.145601	.150942	.156394	.161943	.167576
	-.30	.122517	.127059	.131794	.134228	.136705	.139221	.141775	.144365	.146989	.152330	.157782	.163331	.168964
	-.40	.123905	.128447	.133182	.135616	.138093	.140609	.143164	.145754	.148377	.153718	.159170	.164719	.170352
30	.40	.110423	.115203	.120185	.122744	.125344	.127983	.130658	.133366	.136105	.141664	.147317	.153047	.158839
	.30	.111811	.116592	.121573	.124132	.126732	.129372	.132047	.134755	.137493	.143052	.148705	.154435	.160228
	.20	.113200	.117980	.122961	.125520	.128121	.130760	.133435	.136143	.138882	.144440	.150093	.155823	.161616
	.10	.114588	.119368	.124350	.126908	.129509	.132148	.134823	.137531	.140270	.145829	.151481	.157211	.163004
	0.00	.115976	.120756	.125738	.128297	.130897	.133536	.136211	.138919	.141658	.147217	.152869	.158599	.164392
	-.10	.117364	.122144	.127126	.129685	.132285	.134924	.137599	.140308	.143046	.148605	.154258	.159988	.165780
	-.20	.118753	.123533	.128514	.131073	.133674	.136313	.138988	.141696	.144434	.149993	.155646	.161376	.167169
	-.30	.120141	.124921	.129902	.132461	.135062	.137701	.140376	.143084	.145823	.151382	.157034	.162764	.168557
	-.40	.121529	.126309	.131291	.133850	.136450	.139089	.141764	.144472	.147211	.152770	.158422	.164152	.169945
40	.40	.107706	.112846	.118184	.120916	.123684	.126484	.129312	.132165	.135040	.140844	.146705	.152609	.158544
	.30	.109095	.114234	.119573	.122304	.125072	.127872	.130700	.133553	.136428	.142232	.148094	.153997	.159932
	.20	.110483	.115623	.120961	.123693	.126460	.129260	.132088	.134941	.137816	.143620	.149482	.155386	.161320
	.10	.111871	.117011	.122349	.125081	.127849	.130648	.133476	.136330	.139204	.145009	.150870	.156774	.162708
	0.00	.113259	.118399	.123737	.126469	.129237	.132037	.134865	.137718	.140593	.146397	.152258	.158162	.164096
	-.10	.114647	.119787	.125125	.127857	.130625	.133425	.136253	.139106	.141981	.147785	.153647	.159550	.165485
	-.20	.116036	.121175	.126514	.129245	.132013	.134813	.137641	.140494	.143369	.149173	.155035	.160938	.166873
	-.30	.117424	.122564	.127902	.130634	.133401	.136201	.139029	.141882	.144757	.150561	.156423	.162327	.168261
	-.40	.118812	.123952	.129290	.132022	.134790	.137589	.140418	.143271	.146145	.151950	.157811	.163715	.169649

15.0 YEAR HOLDING PERIOD
.200 EQUITY YIELD RATE
.667 LOAN RATIO

INTEREST RATE

TERM YEARS	APPR DEP	5.0	6.0	7.0	7.5	8.0	8.5	9.0	9.5	10.0	11.0	12.0	13.0	14.0
15	.40	.115122	.119367	.123765	.126020	.128311	.130638	.133000	.135397	.137827	.142787	.147872	.153078	.158398
	.30	.116510	.120755	.125153	.127408	.129699	.132026	.134388	.136785	.139215	.144175	.149260	.154466	.159786
	.20	.117499	.122144	.126541	.128796	.131087	.133414	.135777	.138173	.140604	.145563	.150649	.155855	.161175
	.10	.119287	.123532	.127930	.130184	.132476	.134803	.137165	.139561	.141992	.146951	.152037	.157243	.162563
	0.00	.120675	.124920	.129318	.131573	.133864	.136191	.138553	.140950	.143380	.148339	.153425	.158631	.163951
	-.10	.122063	.126308	.130706	.132961	.135252	.137579	.139941	.142338	.144768	.149728	.154813	.160019	.165339
	-.20	.123451	.127697	.132094	.134349	.136640	.138967	.141329	.143726	.146156	.151116	.156202	.161408	.166727
	-.30	.124840	.129085	.133482	.135737	.138028	.140355	.142718	.145114	.147545	.152504	.157590	.162796	.168116
	-.40	.126228	.130473	.134871	.137125	.139417	.141744	.144106	.146502	.148933	.153892	.158978	.164184	.169504
20	.40	.107892	.112603	.117506	.120027	.122592	.125199	.127848	.130537	.133264	.138827	.144527	.150350	.156287
	.30	.109280	.113991	.118894	.121415	.123980	.126587	.129236	.131925	.134652	.140216	.145915	.151738	.157675
	.20	.110668	.115379	.120283	.122803	.125368	.127976	.130625	.133313	.136040	.141604	.147303	.153127	.159063
	.10	.112056	.116767	.121671	.124192	.126756	.129364	.132013	.134701	.137429	.142992	.148691	.154515	.160451
	0.00	.113444	.118156	.123059	.125580	.128145	.130752	.133401	.136090	.138817	.144380	.150080	.155903	.161839
	-.10	.114833	.119544	.124447	.126968	.129533	.132140	.134789	.137478	.140205	.145768	.151468	.157291	.163228
	-.20	.116221	.120932	.125835	.128356	.130921	.133528	.136177	.138866	.141593	.147157	.152856	.158680	.164616
	-.30	.117609	.122320	.127224	.129744	.132309	.134917	.137566	.140254	.142981	.148545	.154244	.160068	.166004
	-.40	.118997	.123708	.128612	.131133	.133697	.136305	.138954	.141643	.144370	.149933	.155632	.161456	.167392
25	.40	.103727	.108774	.114035	.116740	.119491	.122287	.125125	.128003	.130919	.136853	.142911	.149076	.155335
	.30	.105115	.110162	.115423	.118128	.120880	.123676	.126514	.129392	.132307	.138241	.144299	.150465	.156723
	.20	.106503	.111550	.116811	.119516	.122268	.125064	.127902	.130780	.133695	.139629	.145687	.151853	.158111
	.10	.107891	.112938	.118199	.120904	.123656	.126452	.129290	.132168	.135083	.141017	.147075	.153241	.159499
	0.00	.109280	.114327	.119587	.122292	.125044	.127840	.130678	.133556	.136471	.142406	.148464	.154629	.160888
	-.10	.110668	.115715	.120976	.123681	.126432	.129228	.132067	.134944	.137860	.143794	.149852	.156017	.162276
	-.20	.112056	.117103	.122364	.125069	.127821	.130617	.133455	.136333	.139248	.145182	.151240	.157406	.163664
	-.30	.113444	.118491	.123752	.126457	.129209	.132005	.134843	.137721	.140636	.146570	.152628	.158794	.165052
	-.40	.114832	.119879	.125140	.127845	.130597	.133393	.136231	.139109	.142024	.147958	.154016	.160182	.166441
30	.40	.101087	.106398	.111933	.114776	.117666	.120598	.123570	.126579	.129622	.135799	.142080	.148446	.154883
	.30	.102475	.107786	.113321	.116165	.119054	.121986	.124959	.127968	.131011	.137187	.143468	.149834	.156271
	.20	.103863	.109174	.114710	.117553	.120442	.123375	.126347	.129356	.132399	.138575	.144856	.151223	.157659
	.10	.105251	.110563	.116098	.118941	.121830	.124763	.127735	.130744	.133787	.139964	.146244	.152611	.159047
	0.00	.106640	.111951	.117486	.120329	.123219	.126151	.129123	.132132	.135175	.141352	.147633	.153999	.160436
	-.10	.108028	.113339	.118874	.121717	.124607	.127539	.130511	.133520	.136563	.142740	.149021	.155367	.161824
	-.20	.109416	.114727	.120262	.123106	.125995	.128927	.131900	.134909	.137952	.144128	.150409	.156775	.163212
	-.30	.110804	.116116	.121651	.124494	.127383	.130316	.133288	.136297	.139340	.145516	.151797	.158164	.164600
	-.40	.112193	.117504	.123039	.125882	.128771	.131704	.134676	.137685	.140728	.146905	.153185	.159552	.165988
40	.40	.098068	.103779	.109710	.112746	.115821	.118932	.122074	.125244	.128439	.134888	.141401	.147960	.154554
	.30	.099456	.105167	.111099	.114134	.117209	.120320	.123462	.126633	.129827	.136276	.142789	.149348	.155942
	.20	.100844	.106555	.112487	.115522	.118597	.121708	.124851	.128021	.131215	.137664	.144177	.150737	.157330
	.10	.102233	.107944	.113875	.116910	.119986	.123097	.126239	.129409	.132603	.139052	.145565	.152125	.158719
	0.00	.103621	.109332	.115263	.118299	.121374	.124485	.127627	.130797	.133991	.140441	.146953	.153513	.160107
	-.10	.105009	.110720	.116651	.119687	.122762	.125873	.129015	.132185	.135380	.141829	.148342	.154901	.161495
	-.20	.106397	.112108	.118040	.121075	.124150	.127261	.130404	.133574	.136768	.143217	.149730	.156290	.162883
	-.30	.107786	.113496	.119428	.122463	.125538	.128649	.131792	.134962	.138156	.144605	.151118	.157678	.164272
	-.40	.109174	.114885	.120816	.123851	.126927	.130038	.133180	.136350	.139544	.145993	.152506	.159066	.165660

15.0 YEAR HOLDING PERIOD
.200 EQUITY YIELD RATE
.700 LOAN RATIO

INTEREST RATE

TERM YEARS	APPR DEP	5.0	6.0	7.0	7.5	8.0	8.5	9.0	9.5	10.0	11.0	12.0	13.0	14.0
15	.40	.111156	.115614	.120231	.122599	.125004	.127448	.129928	.132445	.134996	.140204	.145544	.151010	.156596
	.30	.112545	.117002	.121619	.123987	.126393	.128836	.131316	.133833	.136385	.141592	.146932	.152398	.157984
	.20	.113933	.118390	.123008	.125375	.127781	.130224	.132704	.135221	.137773	.142980	.148320	.153786	.159372
	.10	.115321	.119778	.124396	.126763	.129169	.131612	.134093	.136609	.139161	.144368	.149708	.155175	.160761
	0.00	.116709	.121166	.125784	.128152	.130557	.133001	.135481	.137997	.140549	.145757	.151097	.156563	.162149
	-.10	.118097	.122555	.127172	.129540	.131946	.134389	.136869	.139386	.141938	.147145	.152485	.157951	.163537
	-.20	.119486	.123943	.128561	.130928	.133334	.135777	.138257	.140774	.143326	.148533	.153873	.159339	.164925
	-.30	.120874	.125331	.129949	.132316	.134722	.137165	.139646	.142162	.144714	.149921	.155261	.160727	.166313
	-.40	.122262	.126719	.131337	.133704	.136110	.138553	.141034	.143550	.146102	.151310	.156649	.162116	.167702
20	.40	.103564	.108511	.113660	.116306	.118999	.121737	.124518	.127342	.130205	.136047	.142031	.148146	.154379
	.30	.104953	.109899	.115048	.117694	.120387	.123125	.125907	.128730	.131593	.137435	.143419	.149534	.155767
	.20	.106341	.111287	.116436	.119083	.121776	.124514	.127295	.130118	.132982	.138823	.144807	.150922	.157155
	.10	.107729	.112676	.117824	.120471	.123164	.125902	.128683	.131506	.134370	.140211	.146196	.152310	.158543
	0.00	.109117	.114064	.119212	.121859	.124552	.127290	.130071	.132894	.135758	.141600	.147584	.153698	.159932
	-.10	.110505	.115452	.120601	.123247	.125940	.128678	.131460	.134283	.137146	.142988	.148972	.155087	.161320
	-.20	.111894	.116840	.121989	.124636	.127329	.130066	.132848	.135671	.138534	.144376	.150360	.156475	.162708
	-.30	.113282	.118228	.123377	.126024	.128717	.131455	.134236	.137059	.139923	.145764	.151748	.157863	.164096
	-.40	.114670	.119617	.124765	.127412	.130105	.132843	.135624	.138447	.141311	.147152	.153137	.159251	.165484
25	.40	.099191	.104490	.110014	.112855	.115744	.118680	.121660	.124681	.127743	.133973	.140334	.146808	.153379
	.30	.100579	.105879	.111403	.114243	.117132	.120068	.123048	.126070	.129131	.135362	.141722	.148196	.154768
	.20	.101968	.107267	.112791	.115631	.118520	.121456	.124436	.127458	.130519	.136750	.143111	.149584	.156156
	.10	.103356	.108655	.114179	.117019	.119909	.122844	.125824	.128846	.131907	.138138	.144499	.150973	.157544
	0.00	.104744	.110043	.115567	.118408	.121297	.124233	.127213	.130234	.133295	.139526	.145887	.152361	.158932
	-.10	.106132	.111432	.116955	.119796	.122685	.125621	.128601	.131623	.134684	.140914	.147275	.153749	.160320
	-.20	.107520	.112820	.118344	.121184	.124073	.127009	.129989	.133011	.136072	.142303	.148663	.155137	.161709
	-.30	.108909	.114208	.119732	.122572	.125461	.128397	.131377	.134399	.137460	.143691	.150052	.156526	.163097
	-.40	.110297	.115596	.121120	.123960	.126850	.129785	.132765	.135787	.138848	.145079	.151440	.157914	.164485
30	.40	.096419	.101996	.107808	.110793	.113827	.116906	.120027	.123186	.126381	.132867	.139462	.146146	.152905
	.30	.097808	.103384	.109196	.112181	.115215	.118294	.121415	.124575	.127770	.134255	.140850	.147535	.154293
	.20	.099196	.104772	.110584	.113570	.116604	.119683	.122803	.125963	.129158	.135643	.142238	.148923	.155681
	.10	.100584	.106161	.111972	.114958	.117992	.121071	.124192	.127351	.130546	.137031	.143626	.150311	.157069
	0.00	.101972	.107549	.113361	.116346	.119380	.122459	.125580	.128739	.131934	.138420	.145014	.151699	.158458
	-.10	.103360	.108937	.114749	.117734	.120768	.123847	.126968	.130127	.133322	.139808	.146403	.153087	.159846
	-.20	.104749	.110325	.116137	.119123	.122156	.125235	.128356	.131516	.134711	.141196	.147791	.154476	.161234
	-.30	.106137	.111714	.117525	.120511	.123545	.126624	.129744	.132904	.136099	.142584	.149179	.155864	.162622
	-.40	.107525	.113102	.118914	.121899	.124933	.128012	.131133	.134292	.137487	.143973	.150567	.157252	.164010
40	.40	.093250	.099246	.105474	.108661	.111890	.115157	.118456	.121785	.125139	.131910	.138749	.145636	.152560
	.30	.094638	.100634	.106862	.110049	.113278	.116545	.119844	.123173	.126527	.133298	.140137	.147024	.153948
	.20	.096026	.102022	.108250	.111437	.114667	.117933	.121232	.124561	.127915	.134687	.141525	.148413	.155336
	.10	.097414	.103411	.109639	.112826	.116055	.119321	.122621	.125949	.129303	.136075	.142913	.149801	.156724
	0.00	.098802	.104799	.111027	.114214	.117443	.120709	.124009	.127337	.130691	.137463	.144301	.151189	.158112
	-.10	.100191	.106187	.112415	.115602	.118831	.122098	.125397	.128726	.132080	.138851	.145690	.152577	.159501
	-.20	.101579	.107575	.113803	.116990	.120219	.123486	.126785	.130114	.133468	.140239	.147078	.153965	.160889
	-.30	.102967	.108964	.115191	.118379	.121608	.124874	.128174	.131502	.134856	.141628	.148466	.155354	.162277
	-.40	.104355	.110352	.116580	.119767	.122996	.126262	.129562	.132890	.136244	.143016	.149854	.156742	.163665

15.0 YEAR HOLDING PERIOD
.200 EQUITY YIELD RATE
.750 LOAN RATIO

INTEREST RATE

TERM YEARS	APPR DEP	14.0	13.0	12.0	11.0	10.0	9.5	9.0	8.5	8.0	7.5	7.0	6.0	5.0
15	.40	.153892	.147907	.142051	.136329	.130750	.128016	.125320	.122662	.120044	.117467	.114930	.109983	.105207
	.30	.155280	.149296	.143439	.137717	.132138	.129404	.126708	.124050	.121432	.118855	.116318	.111371	.106595
	.20	.156669	.150684	.144827	.139106	.133526	.130792	.128096	.125439	.122821	.120243	.117707	.112759	.107983
	.10	.158057	.152072	.146215	.140494	.134915	.132180	.129484	.126827	.124209	.121631	.119095	.114147	.109372
	0.00	.159445	.153460	.147603	.141882	.136303	.133569	.130872	.128215	.125597	.123020	.120483	.115536	.110760
	-.10	.160833	.154848	.148992	.143270	.137691	.134957	.132261	.129603	.126985	.124408	.121871	.116924	.112148
	-.20	.162222	.156237	.150380	.144659	.139079	.136345	.133649	.130991	.128374	.125796	.123259	.118312	.113536
	-.30	.163610	.157625	.151768	.146047	.140468	.137733	.135037	.132380	.129762	.127184	.124648	.119700	.114924
	-.40	.164998	.159013	.153156	.147435	.141856	.139121	.136425	.133768	.131150	.128572	.126036	.121088	.116313
20	.40	.151517	.144838	.138287	.131875	.125616	.122548	.119524	.116544	.113610	.110725	.107889	.102373	.097073
	.30	.152905	.146227	.139675	.133263	.127005	.123937	.120912	.117932	.114998	.112113	.109277	.103761	.098461
	.20	.154293	.147615	.141063	.134652	.128393	.125325	.122300	.119320	.116387	.113501	.110665	.105149	.099849
	.10	.155681	.149003	.142452	.136040	.129781	.126713	.123688	.120708	.117775	.114889	.112054	.106537	.101237
	0.00	.157070	.150391	.143840	.137428	.131169	.128101	.125076	.122096	.119163	.116278	.113442	.107926	.102626
	-.10	.158458	.151779	.145228	.138816	.132557	.129489	.126465	.123485	.120551	.117666	.114830	.109314	.104014
	-.20	.159846	.153168	.146616	.140205	.133946	.130878	.127853	.124873	.121939	.119054	.116218	.110702	.105402
	-.30	.161234	.154556	.148004	.141593	.135334	.132266	.129241	.126261	.123328	.120442	.117607	.112090	.106790
	-.40	.162622	.155944	.149393	.142981	.136722	.133654	.130629	.127649	.124716	.121830	.118995	.113478	.108178
25	.40	.150446	.143405	.136469	.129654	.122978	.119698	.116461	.113268	.110122	.107027	.103983	.098065	.092387
	.30	.151834	.144793	.137857	.131042	.124366	.121086	.117849	.114656	.111510	.108415	.105372	.099453	.093775
	.20	.153222	.146182	.139245	.132430	.125754	.122475	.119237	.116044	.112899	.109803	.106760	.100841	.095164
	.10	.154611	.147570	.140634	.133818	.127143	.123863	.120625	.117432	.114287	.111191	.108148	.102230	.096552
	0.00	.155999	.148958	.142022	.135207	.128531	.125251	.122014	.118821	.115675	.112579	.109536	.103618	.097940
	-.10	.157387	.150346	.143410	.136595	.129919	.126639	.123402	.120209	.117063	.113968	.110925	.105006	.099328
	-.20	.158775	.151735	.144798	.137983	.131307	.128027	.124790	.121597	.118452	.115356	.112313	.106394	.100716
	-.30	.160164	.153123	.146186	.139371	.132695	.129416	.126178	.122985	.119840	.116744	.113701	.107782	.102105
	-.40	.161552	.154511	.147575	.140759	.134084	.130804	.127566	.124374	.121228	.118132	.115089	.109171	.103493
30	.40	.149937	.142696	.135534	.128468	.121520	.118096	.114711	.111367	.108069	.104818	.101619	.095392	.089417
	.30	.151326	.144085	.136922	.129856	.122908	.119485	.116099	.112756	.109457	.106206	.103008	.096781	.090806
	.20	.152714	.145473	.138310	.131245	.124296	.120873	.117488	.114144	.110845	.107594	.104396	.098169	.092194
	.10	.154102	.146861	.139699	.132633	.125684	.122261	.118876	.115532	.112233	.108983	.105784	.099557	.093582
	0.00	.155490	.148249	.141087	.134021	.127072	.123649	.120264	.116920	.113621	.110371	.107172	.100945	.094970
	-.10	.156878	.149637	.142475	.135409	.128461	.125037	.121652	.118309	.115010	.111759	.108560	.102333	.096358
	-.20	.158267	.151026	.143863	.136798	.129849	.126426	.123040	.119697	.116398	.113147	.109949	.103722	.097747
	-.30	.159655	.152414	.145252	.138186	.131237	.127814	.124429	.121085	.117786	.114535	.111337	.105110	.099135
	-.40	.161043	.153802	.146640	.139574	.132625	.129202	.125817	.122473	.119174	.115924	.112725	.106498	.100523
40	.40	.149568	.142150	.134770	.127443	.120188	.116594	.113028	.109493	.105993	.102533	.099119	.092446	.086021
	.30	.150956	.143538	.136158	.128831	.121576	.117983	.114416	.110881	.107381	.103922	.100507	.093834	.087409
	.20	.152344	.144926	.137546	.130220	.122964	.119371	.115805	.112269	.108770	.105310	.101895	.095222	.088798
	.10	.153732	.146314	.138935	.131608	.124353	.120759	.117193	.113658	.110158	.106698	.103283	.096611	.090186
	0.00	.155120	.147703	.140323	.132996	.125741	.122147	.118581	.115046	.111546	.108086	.104672	.097999	.091574
	-.10	.156509	.149091	.141711	.134384	.127129	.123535	.119969	.116434	.112934	.109474	.106060	.099387	.092962
	-.20	.157897	.150479	.143099	.135772	.128517	.124924	.121357	.117822	.114322	.110863	.107448	.100775	.094350
	-.30	.159285	.151867	.144488	.137161	.129905	.126312	.122746	.119210	.115711	.112251	.108836	.102163	.095739
	-.40	.160673	.153255	.145876	.138549	.131294	.127700	.124134	.120599	.117099	.113639	.110224	.103552	.097127

15.0 YEAR HOLDING PERIOD
.200 EQUITY YIELD RATE
.800 LOAN RATIO

INTEREST RATE

TERM YEARS	APPR DEP	5.0	6.0	7.0	7.5	8.0	8.5	9.0	9.5	10.0	11.0	12.0	13.0	14.0
15	.40	.099258	.104352	.109629	.112335	.115084	.117876	.120711	.123587	.126504	.132455	.138858	.144805	.151189
	.30	.100646	.105740	.111017	.113723	.116472	.119265	.122099	.124975	.127892	.133843	.139996	.146193	.152577
	.20	.102034	.107128	.112405	.115111	.117860	.120653	.123487	.126363	.129280	.135231	.141134	.147581	.153965
	.10	.103422	.108516	.113794	.116499	.119249	.122041	.124876	.127752	.130668	.136619	.142722	.148969	.155353
	0.00	.104810	.109905	.115182	.117887	.120637	.123429	.126264	.129140	.132056	.138008	.144110	.150358	.156741
	-.10	.106199	.111293	.116570	.119276	.122025	.124818	.127652	.130528	.133445	.139396	.145499	.151746	.158130
	-.20	.107587	.112681	.117958	.120664	.123413	.126206	.129040	.131916	.134833	.140784	.146887	.153134	.159518
	-.30	.108975	.114069	.119346	.122052	.124802	.127594	.130429	.133305	.136221	.142172	.148275	.154522	.160906
	-.40	.110363	.115457	.120735	.123440	.126190	.128982	.131817	.134693	.137609	.143560	.149663	.155910	.162294
20	.40	.090581	.096234	.102118	.105143	.108221	.111350	.114529	.117755	.121028	.127704	.134543	.141531	.148655
	.30	.091969	.097623	.103507	.106531	.109609	.112738	.115917	.119143	.122416	.129092	.135931	.142919	.150043
	.20	.093357	.099011	.104895	.107920	.110997	.114126	.117305	.120532	.123804	.130480	.137319	.144308	.151431
	.10	.094746	.100399	.106283	.109308	.112386	.115515	.118693	.121920	.125192	.131868	.138708	.145696	.152819
	0.00	.096134	.101787	.107671	.110696	.113774	.116903	.120082	.123308	.126580	.133257	.140096	.147084	.154207
	-.10	.097522	.103175	.109060	.112084	.115162	.118291	.121470	.124696	.127969	.134645	.141484	.148472	.155596
	-.20	.098910	.104564	.110448	.113473	.116550	.119679	.122858	.126084	.129357	.136033	.142872	.149860	.156984
	-.30	.100299	.105952	.111836	.114861	.117938	.121068	.124246	.127473	.130745	.137421	.144260	.151249	.158372
	-.40	.101687	.107340	.113224	.116249	.119327	.122456	.125634	.128861	.132133	.138809	.145649	.152637	.159760
25	.40	.085583	.091640	.097953	.101199	.104501	.107856	.111262	.114715	.118213	.125334	.132604	.140002	.147513
	.30	.086971	.093028	.099341	.102587	.105889	.109244	.112650	.116103	.119601	.126722	.133992	.141391	.148901
	.20	.088360	.094416	.100729	.103975	.107277	.110632	.114038	.117491	.120990	.128111	.135380	.142779	.150289
	.10	.089748	.095804	.102117	.105363	.108665	.112020	.115426	.118880	.122378	.129499	.136768	.144167	.151677
	0.00	.091136	.097192	.103505	.106751	.110053	.113409	.116814	.120268	.123766	.130887	.138157	.145555	.153065
	-.10	.092524	.098581	.104894	.108140	.111442	.114797	.118203	.121656	.125154	.132275	.139545	.146944	.154454
	-.20	.093912	.099969	.106282	.109528	.112830	.116185	.119591	.123044	.126543	.133663	.140933	.148332	.155842
	-.30	.095301	.101357	.107670	.110916	.114218	.117573	.120979	.124432	.127931	.135052	.142321	.149720	.157230
	-.40	.096689	.102745	.109058	.112304	.115606	.118962	.122367	.125821	.129319	.136440	.143709	.151108	.158618
30	.40	.082415	.088789	.095431	.098843	.102310	.105829	.109395	.113006	.116658	.124070	.131606	.139246	.146970
	.30	.083804	.090177	.096819	.100231	.103698	.107217	.110784	.114394	.118046	.125458	.132995	.140635	.148358
	.20	.085192	.091565	.098207	.101619	.105086	.108605	.112172	.115783	.119434	.126846	.134383	.142023	.149746
	.10	.086580	.092953	.099595	.103007	.106475	.109993	.113560	.117171	.120822	.128234	.135771	.143411	.151135
	0.00	.087968	.094342	.100984	.104396	.107863	.111382	.114948	.118559	.122211	.129623	.137159	.144799	.152523
	-.10	.089356	.095730	.102372	.105784	.109251	.112770	.116336	.119947	.123599	.131011	.138548	.146187	.153911
	-.20	.090745	.097118	.103760	.107172	.110639	.114158	.117725	.121336	.124987	.132399	.139936	.147576	.155299
	-.30	.092133	.098506	.105148	.108560	.112028	.115546	.119113	.122724	.126375	.133787	.141324	.148964	.156688
	-.40	.093521	.099894	.106537	.109948	.113416	.116934	.120501	.124112	.127763	.135175	.142712	.150352	.158076
40	.40	.078793	.085646	.092763	.096406	.100096	.103829	.107600	.111404	.115237	.122976	.130792	.138663	.146576
	.30	.080181	.087034	.094152	.097794	.101484	.105218	.108988	.112792	.116626	.124364	.132180	.140051	.147964
	.20	.081569	.088422	.095540	.099182	.102873	.106606	.110377	.114181	.118014	.125753	.133568	.141440	.149352
	.10	.082957	.089811	.096928	.100570	.104261	.107994	.111765	.115569	.119402	.127141	.134956	.142828	.150740
	0.00	.084346	.091199	.098316	.101959	.105649	.109382	.113153	.116957	.120790	.128529	.136344	.144216	.152128
	-.10	.085734	.092587	.099705	.103347	.107037	.110770	.114541	.118345	.122178	.129917	.137733	.145604	.153517
	-.20	.087122	.093975	.101093	.104735	.108426	.112159	.115929	.119733	.123567	.131306	.139121	.146992	.154905
	-.30	.088510	.095363	.102481	.106123	.109814	.113547	.117318	.121122	.124955	.132694	.140509	.148381	.156293
	-.40	.089899	.096752	.103869	.107512	.111202	.114935	.118706	.122510	.126343	.134082	.141897	.149769	.157681

15.0 YEAR HOLDING PERIOD
.200 EQUITY YIELD RATE
.900 LOAN RATIO

INTEREST RATE

TERM YEARS	APPR DEP	5.0	6.0	7.0	7.5	8.0	8.5	9.0	9.5	10.0	11.0	12.0	13.0	14.0
15	.40	.087359	.093090	.099027	.102071	.105164	.108305	.111494	.114730	.118011	.124706	.131571	.138599	.145781
	.30	.088747	.094478	.100415	.103459	.106552	.109693	.112882	.116118	.119399	.126094	.132960	.139988	.147170
	.20	.090135	.095866	.101803	.104847	.107940	.111082	.114270	.117506	.120787	.127482	.134348	.141376	.148558
	.10	.091524	.097254	.103191	.106235	.109328	.112470	.115659	.118894	.122175	.128870	.135736	.142764	.149946
	0.00	.092912	.098643	.104580	.107623	.110717	.113858	.117047	.120282	.123563	.130259	.137124	.144152	.151334
	-.10	.094300	.100031	.105968	.109012	.112105	.115246	.118435	.121671	.124952	.131647	.138512	.145540	.152722
	-.20	.095688	.101419	.107356	.110400	.113493	.116634	.119823	.123059	.126340	.133035	.139901	.146929	.154111
	-.30	.097076	.102807	.108744	.111788	.114881	.118023	.121212	.124447	.127728	.134423	.141289	.148317	.155499
	-.40	.098465	.104195	.110132	.113176	.116269	.119411	.122600	.125835	.129116	.135811	.142677	.149705	.156887
20	.40	.077598	.083958	.090577	.093980	.097443	.100963	.104539	.108169	.111850	.119361	.127055	.134917	.142931
	.30	.078986	.085346	.091966	.095368	.098831	.102351	.105927	.109557	.113238	.120749	.128443	.136305	.144319
	.20	.080374	.086734	.093354	.096757	.100219	.103739	.107315	.110945	.114627	.122137	.129831	.137693	.145707
	.10	.081762	.088122	.094742	.098145	.101607	.105128	.108703	.112333	.116015	.123526	.131220	.139081	.147095
	0.00	.083151	.089511	.096130	.099533	.102996	.106516	.110092	.113721	.117403	.124914	.132608	.140469	.148483
	-.10	.084539	.090899	.097518	.100921	.104384	.107904	.111480	.115110	.118791	.126302	.133996	.141858	.149872
	-.20	.085927	.092287	.098907	.102310	.105772	.109292	.112868	.116498	.120179	.127690	.135384	.143246	.151260
	-.30	.087315	.093675	.100295	.103698	.107160	.110680	.114256	.117886	.121568	.129078	.136772	.144634	.152648
	-.40	.088703	.095063	.101683	.105086	.108548	.112069	.115645	.119274	.122956	.130467	.138161	.146022	.154036
25	.40	.071975	.078789	.085891	.089543	.093257	.097032	.100863	.104748	.108684	.116695	.124873	.133197	.141646
	.30	.073363	.080177	.087279	.090931	.094646	.098420	.102252	.106137	.110072	.118083	.126261	.134585	.143034
	.20	.074752	.081565	.088667	.092319	.096034	.099808	.103640	.107525	.111460	.119471	.127650	.135973	.144422
	.10	.076140	.082953	.090055	.093707	.097422	.101197	.105028	.108913	.112849	.120860	.129038	.137362	.145810
	0.00	.077528	.084341	.091444	.095095	.098810	.102585	.106416	.110301	.114237	.122248	.130426	.138750	.147199
	-.10	.078916	.085730	.092832	.096484	.100198	.103973	.107804	.111689	.115625	.123636	.131814	.140138	.148587
	-.20	.080304	.087118	.094220	.097872	.101587	.105361	.109193	.113078	.117013	.125024	.133203	.141526	.149975
	-.30	.081693	.088506	.095608	.099260	.102975	.106749	.110581	.114466	.118402	.126413	.134591	.142914	.151363
	-.40	.083081	.089894	.096996	.100648	.104363	.108138	.111969	.115854	.119790	.127801	.135979	.144303	.152752
30	.40	.068411	.075581	.083054	.086892	.090793	.094752	.098764	.102826	.106934	.115272	.123751	.132346	.141035
	.30	.069800	.076970	.084442	.088280	.092181	.096140	.100152	.104214	.108322	.116661	.125140	.133734	.142424
	.20	.071188	.078358	.085830	.089669	.093569	.097528	.101540	.105603	.109710	.118049	.126528	.135123	.143812
	.10	.072576	.079746	.087218	.091057	.094957	.098916	.102929	.106991	.111099	.119437	.127916	.136511	.145200
	0.00	.073964	.081134	.088607	.092445	.096346	.100304	.104317	.108379	.112487	.120825	.129304	.137899	.146588
	-.10	.075352	.082523	.089995	.093833	.097734	.101693	.105705	.109767	.113875	.122214	.130692	.139287	.147976
	-.20	.076741	.083911	.091383	.095221	.099122	.103081	.107093	.111155	.115263	.123602	.132081	.140675	.149365
	-.30	.078129	.085299	.092771	.096610	.100510	.104469	.108481	.112544	.116652	.124990	.133469	.142064	.150753
	-.40	.079517	.086687	.094159	.097998	.101899	.105857	.109870	.113932	.118040	.126378	.134857	.143452	.152141
40	.40	.064336	.072046	.080053	.084151	.088302	.092502	.096744	.101024	.105336	.114042	.122835	.131690	.140592
	.30	.065724	.073434	.081441	.085539	.089691	.093890	.098132	.102413	.106724	.115431	.124223	.133078	.141980
	.20	.067112	.074822	.082829	.086927	.091079	.095279	.099521	.103800	.108113	.116819	.125611	.134467	.143368
	.10	.068501	.076210	.084218	.088315	.092467	.096667	.100909	.105188	.109501	.118207	.126999	.135855	.144756
	0.00	.069889	.077599	.085606	.089704	.093855	.098055	.102297	.106576	.110889	.119595	.128387	.137243	.146145
	-.10	.071277	.078987	.086994	.091092	.095243	.099443	.103685	.107965	.112277	.120983	.129776	.138631	.147533
	-.20	.072665	.080375	.088382	.092480	.096632	.100831	.105074	.109353	.113665	.122372	.131164	.140019	.148921
	-.30	.074054	.081763	.089770	.093868	.098020	.102220	.106462	.110741	.115054	.123760	.132552	.141408	.150309
	-.40	.075442	.083151	.091159	.095256	.099408	.103608	.107850	.112130	.116442	.125148	.133940	.142796	.151697

15.0 YEAR HOLDING PERIOD
.250 EQUITY YIELD RATE
.600 LOAN RATIO

INTEREST RATE

TERM YEARS	APPR DEP	5.0	6.0	7.0	7.5	8.0	8.5	9.0	9.5	10.0	11.0	12.0	13.0	14.0
15	.40	.147820	.151641	.155599	.157628	.159690	.151784	.163910	.166067	.168255	.172718	.177295	.181981	.186769
	.30	.148732	.152553	.156510	.158540	.160602	.162696	.164822	.166979	.169166	.173630	.178207	.182892	.187680
	.20	.149644	.153464	.157422	.159451	.161513	.163608	.165734	.167891	.170078	.174541	.179119	.183804	.188592
	.10	.150555	.154376	.158334	.160363	.162425	.164519	.166645	.168802	.170990	.175453	.180030	.184716	.189504
	0.00	.151467	.155288	.159246	.161275	.163337	.165431	.167557	.169714	.171901	.176365	.180942	.185627	.190415
	-.10	.152379	.156199	.160157	.162186	.164249	.166343	.168469	.170626	.172813	.177277	.181854	.186539	.191327
	-.20	.153290	.157111	.161069	.163098	.165160	.167255	.169380	.171537	.173725	.178188	.182765	.187451	.192329
	-.30	.154202	.158023	.161981	.164010	.166072	.168166	.170292	.172449	.174637	.179100	.183677	.188362	.193150
	-.40	.155114	.158934	.162892	.164922	.166984	.169078	.171204	.173361	.175548	.180012	.184589	.189274	.194062
20	.40	.140313	.144493	.148846	.151085	.153363	.155680	.158034	.160424	.162849	.167798	.172869	.178053	.183340
	.30	.141225	.145405	.149758	.151997	.154275	.156592	.158946	.161336	.163761	.168709	.173781	.178965	.184252
	.20	.142136	.146317	.150670	.152908	.155187	.157504	.159858	.162248	.164673	.169621	.174692	.179877	.185163
	.10	.143048	.147228	.151581	.153820	.156098	.158415	.160769	.163159	.165584	.170533	.175604	.180788	.186075
	0.00	.143960	.148140	.152493	.154732	.157010	.159327	.161681	.164071	.166496	.171444	.176516	.181700	.186987
	-.10	.144871	.149052	.153405	.155643	.157922	.160239	.162593	.164983	.167408	.172356	.177427	.182612	.187898
	-.20	.145783	.149963	.154317	.156555	.158833	.161150	.163504	.165895	.168319	.173268	.178339	.183523	.188810
	-.30	.146695	.150875	.155228	.157467	.159745	.162062	.164416	.166806	.169231	.174180	.179251	.184435	.189722
	-.40	.147606	.151787	.156140	.158379	.160657	.162974	.165328	.167718	.170143	.175091	.180163	.185347	.190634
25	.40	.135989	.140447	.145101	.147496	.149934	.152412	.154929	.157483	.160071	.165343	.170731	.176219	.181795
	.30	.136900	.141359	.146013	.148408	.150845	.153324	.155841	.158394	.160983	.166255	.171643	.177131	.182707
	.20	.137812	.142271	.146924	.149319	.151757	.154235	.156752	.159306	.161894	.167167	.172554	.178043	.183618
	.10	.138724	.143182	.147836	.150231	.152669	.155147	.157664	.160218	.162806	.168078	.173466	.178954	.184530
	0.00	.139635	.144094	.148748	.151143	.153580	.156059	.158576	.161129	.163718	.168990	.174378	.179866	.185442
	-.10	.140547	.145006	.149659	.152054	.154492	.156970	.159488	.162041	.164629	.169902	.175289	.180778	.186353
	-.20	.141459	.145918	.150571	.152966	.155404	.157882	.160399	.162953	.165541	.170813	.176201	.181689	.187265
	-.30	.142370	.146829	.151483	.153878	.156315	.158794	.161311	.163865	.166453	.171725	.177113	.182601	.188177
	-.40	.143282	.147741	.152395	.154789	.157227	.159706	.162223	.164776	.167364	.172637	.178024	.183513	.189088
30	.40	.133248	.137937	.142834	.145353	.147914	.150516	.153155	.155829	.158535	.164034	.169631	.175312	.181061
	.30	.134159	.138848	.143746	.146264	.148826	.151428	.154067	.156741	.159447	.164945	.170543	.176224	.181972
	.20	.135071	.139761	.144657	.147176	.149738	.152340	.154979	.157653	.160359	.165857	.171455	.177135	.182884
	.10	.135983	.140672	.145569	.148088	.150649	.153251	.155890	.158564	.161270	.166769	.172367	.178047	.183796
	0.00	.136894	.141584	.146481	.148999	.151561	.154163	.156802	.159476	.162182	.167680	.173278	.178959	.184708
	-.10	.137806	.142496	.147392	.149911	.152473	.155075	.157714	.160388	.163094	.168592	.174190	.179870	.185619
	-.20	.138718	.143407	.148304	.150823	.153384	.155986	.158626	.161300	.164006	.169504	.175102	.180782	.186531
	-.30	.139629	.144319	.149216	.151734	.154296	.156898	.159537	.162211	.164917	.170415	.176013	.181694	.187443
	-.40	.140541	.145231	.150127	.152646	.155208	.157810	.160449	.163123	.165829	.171327	.176925	.182606	.188354
40	.40	.130113	.135170	.140436	.143135	.145873	.148646	.151449	.154279	.157133	.162901	.168733	.174612	.180527
	.30	.131025	.136082	.141347	.144047	.146785	.149558	.152361	.155191	.158045	.163813	.169645	.175524	.181439
	.20	.131937	.136993	.142259	.144959	.147697	.150469	.153272	.156103	.158957	.164725	.170556	.176436	.182350
	.10	.132848	.137905	.143171	.145870	.148609	.151382	.154184	.157014	.159868	.165636	.171468	.177347	.183262
	0.00	.133760	.138817	.144083	.146782	.149520	.152293	.155096	.157926	.160780	.166548	.172380	.178259	.184174
	-.10	.134672	.139728	.144994	.147694	.150432	.153204	.156008	.158838	.161692	.167460	.173291	.179171	.185086
	-.20	.135583	.140640	.145906	.148605	.151344	.154116	.156919	.159749	.162603	.168371	.174202	.180083	.185997
	-.30	.136495	.141552	.146818	.149517	.152255	.155028	.157831	.160661	.163515	.169283	.175115	.180994	.186909
	-.40	.137407	.142463	.147729	.150429	.153167	.155940	.158743	.161573	.164427	.170195	.176026	.181906	.187821

15.0 YEAR HOLDING PERIOD
.250 EQUITY YIELD RATE
.667 LOAN RATIO

INTEREST RATE

TERM YEARS	APPR DEP	5.0	6.0	7.0	7.5	8.0	8.5	9.0	9.5	10.0	11.0	12.0	13.0	14.0
15	.40	.136872	.141117	.145514	.147769	.150060	.152387	.154750	.157146	.159577	.164536	.169622	.174828	.180148
	.30	.137783	.142028	.146426	.148681	.150972	.153299	.155661	.158058	.160488	.165448	.170533	.175739	.181059
	.20	.138695	.142940	.147338	.149593	.151884	.154211	.156573	.158970	.161400	.166359	.171445	.176651	.181971
	.10	.139607	.143852	.148249	.150504	.152795	.155122	.157485	.159881	.162312	.167271	.172357	.177563	.182883
	0.00	.140518	.144763	.149161	.151416	.153707	.156034	.158396	.160793	.163223	.168183	.173268	.178474	.183794
	-.10	.141430	.145675	.150073	.152328	.154619	.156946	.159308	.161705	.164135	.169094	.174180	.179386	.184706
	-.20	.142342	.146587	.150985	.153239	.155530	.157857	.160220	.162616	.165047	.170006	.175092	.180298	.185618
	-.30	.143253	.147499	.151896	.154151	.156442	.158769	.161131	.163528	.165958	.170918	.176004	.181209	.186529
	-.40	.144165	.148410	.152808	.155063	.157354	.159681	.162043	.164440	.166870	.171830	.176915	.182121	.187441
20	.40	.128530	.133175	.138012	.140499	.143031	.145605	.148221	.150876	.153570	.159069	.164704	.170464	.176338
	.30	.129442	.134087	.138923	.141411	.143942	.146517	.149132	.151788	.154482	.159980	.165615	.171376	.177250
	.20	.130353	.134998	.139835	.142323	.144854	.147428	.150044	.152700	.155394	.160892	.166527	.172287	.178162
	.10	.131265	.135910	.140747	.143234	.145766	.148340	.150956	.153611	.156306	.161804	.167439	.173199	.179073
	0.00	.132177	.136822	.141659	.144146	.146677	.149252	.151867	.154523	.157217	.162715	.168350	.174111	.179985
	-.10	.133089	.137733	.142570	.145058	.147589	.150163	.152779	.155435	.158129	.163627	.169262	.175022	.180897
	-.20	.134000	.138645	.143482	.145969	.148501	.151075	.153691	.156346	.159041	.164539	.170174	.175934	.181808
	-.30	.134912	.139557	.144394	.146881	.149412	.151987	.154602	.157258	.159952	.165451	.171085	.176846	.182720
	-.40	.135824	.140468	.145305	.147793	.150324	.152898	.155514	.158170	.160864	.166362	.171997	.177757	.183632
25	.40	.123725	.128679	.133850	.136511	.139220	.141974	.144770	.147608	.150484	.156342	.162328	.168426	.174621
	.30	.124637	.129591	.134762	.137423	.140132	.142885	.145682	.148519	.151395	.157253	.163240	.169338	.175533
	.20	.125549	.130503	.135674	.138335	.141043	.143797	.146594	.149431	.152307	.158165	.164151	.170250	.176445
	.10	.126460	.131415	.136585	.139246	.141955	.144709	.147505	.150343	.153219	.159077	.165063	.171161	.177356
	0.00	.127372	.132326	.137497	.140158	.142867	.145620	.148417	.151254	.154130	.159989	.165975	.172073	.178268
	-.10	.128284	.133238	.138409	.141070	.143778	.146532	.149329	.152166	.155042	.160900	.166886	.172985	.179180
	-.20	.129195	.134150	.139320	.141981	.144690	.147444	.150240	.153078	.155954	.161812	.167798	.173896	.180091
	-.30	.130107	.135061	.140232	.142893	.145602	.148355	.151152	.153990	.156865	.162724	.168710	.174808	.181003
	-.40	.131019	.135973	.141144	.143805	.146513	.149267	.152064	.154901	.157777	.163635	.169621	.175720	.181915
30	.40	.120680	.125890	.131331	.134130	.136976	.139867	.142800	.145771	.148777	.154887	.161106	.167418	.173806
	.30	.121591	.126802	.132243	.135041	.137888	.140779	.143711	.146682	.149689	.155798	.162018	.168330	.174717
	.20	.122503	.127714	.133154	.135953	.138799	.141690	.144623	.147594	.150601	.156710	.162930	.169242	.175629
	.10	.123415	.128625	.134066	.136865	.139711	.142602	.145535	.148506	.151512	.157622	.163841	.170153	.176541
	0.00	.124326	.129537	.134978	.137776	.140623	.143514	.146446	.149417	.152424	.158533	.164753	.171065	.177452
	-.10	.125238	.130449	.135890	.138688	.141534	.144425	.147358	.150329	.153336	.159445	.165665	.171977	.178364
	-.20	.126150	.131361	.136801	.139600	.142446	.145337	.148270	.151241	.154248	.160357	.166576	.172888	.179276
	-.30	.127062	.132272	.137713	.140511	.143358	.146249	.149181	.152153	.155159	.161268	.167488	.173800	.180187
	-.40	.127973	.133184	.138625	.141423	.144270	.147161	.150093	.153064	.156071	.162180	.168400	.174712	.181099
40	.40	.117197	.122816	.128667	.131666	.134709	.137789	.140904	.144048	.147219	.153628	.160108	.166641	.173213
	.30	.118109	.123727	.129578	.132578	.135620	.138701	.141815	.144960	.148131	.154540	.161020	.167552	.174124
	.20	.119020	.124639	.130490	.133490	.136532	.139612	.142727	.145872	.149043	.155452	.161931	.168464	.175036
	.10	.119932	.125551	.131402	.134401	.137444	.140524	.143639	.146783	.149954	.156363	.162843	.169376	.175948
	0.00	.120844	.126462	.132313	.135313	.138355	.141436	.144550	.147695	.150866	.157275	.163755	.170288	.176859
	-.10	.121756	.127374	.133225	.136225	.139267	.142348	.145462	.148607	.151778	.158187	.164666	.171199	.177771
	-.20	.122667	.128286	.134137	.137136	.140179	.143259	.146374	.149518	.152690	.159098	.165578	.172111	.178683
	-.30	.123579	.129197	.135048	.138048	.141090	.144171	.147285	.150430	.153601	.160010	.166490	.173023	.179595
	-.40	.124491	.130109	.135960	.138960	.142002	.145083	.148197	.151342	.154513	.160922	.167402	.173934	.180506

15.0 YEAR HOLDING PERIOD
.250 EQUITY YIELD RATE
.700 LOAN RATIO

INTEREST RATE

TERM YEARS	APPR DEP	5.0	6.0	7.0	7.5	8.0	8.5	9.0	9.5	10.0	11.0	12.0	13.0	14.0
15	.40	.131398	.135855	.140473	.142840	.145246	.147690	.150170	.152686	.155238	.160446	.165786	.171252	.176838
	.30	.132310	.136767	.141375	.143752	.146158	.148601	.151082	.153598	.156150	.161357	.166697	.172163	.177749
	.20	.133221	.137679	.142296	.144664	.147070	.149513	.151993	.154510	.157062	.162269	.167609	.173075	.178661
	.10	.134133	.138590	.143208	.145576	.147981	.150425	.152905	.155421	.157973	.163181	.168521	.173987	.179573
	0.00	.135045	.139502	.144120	.146487	.148893	.151336	.153817	.156333	.158885	.164092	.169432	.174899	.180484
	-.10	.135957	.140414	.145031	.147399	.149805	.152248	.154728	.157245	.159797	.165004	.170344	.175810	.181396
	-.20	.136868	.141326	.145943	.148311	.150716	.153160	.155640	.158156	.160708	.165916	.171256	.176722	.182308
	-.30	.137780	.142237	.146855	.149222	.151628	.154071	.156552	.159068	.161620	.166827	.172167	.177634	.183220
	-.40	.138692	.143149	.147767	.150134	.152540	.154983	.157463	.159980	.162532	.167739	.173079	.178545	.184131
20	.40	.122640	.127517	.132595	.135207	.137865	.140568	.143314	.146103	.148932	.154705	.160622	.166670	.172838
	.30	.123551	.128428	.133507	.136119	.138777	.141480	.144226	.147015	.149844	.155617	.161533	.167582	.173750
	.20	.124463	.129340	.134419	.137030	.139688	.142391	.145138	.147926	.150755	.156528	.162445	.168493	.174661
	.10	.125375	.130252	.135330	.137942	.140600	.143303	.146050	.148838	.151667	.157440	.163357	.169405	.175573
	0.00	.126286	.131163	.136242	.138854	.141512	.144215	.146961	.149750	.152579	.158352	.164268	.170317	.176485
	-.10	.127198	.132075	.137154	.139765	.142423	.145126	.147873	.150661	.153490	.159263	.165180	.171228	.177396
	-.20	.128110	.132987	.138065	.140677	.143335	.146038	.148785	.151573	.154402	.160175	.166092	.172140	.178308
	-.30	.129021	.133898	.138977	.141589	.144247	.146950	.149696	.152485	.155314	.161087	.167003	.173052	.179220
	-.40	.129933	.134810	.139889	.142500	.145159	.147862	.150608	.153396	.156225	.161998	.167915	.173963	.180131
25	.40	.117594	.122796	.128226	.131020	.133864	.136755	.139692	.142671	.145691	.151842	.158127	.164530	.171035
	.30	.118506	.123708	.129137	.131931	.134775	.137667	.140603	.143583	.146602	.152753	.159039	.165442	.171947
	.20	.119418	.124620	.130049	.132843	.135687	.138579	.141515	.144494	.147514	.153665	.159951	.166354	.172858
	.10	.120329	.125531	.130961	.133755	.136599	.139490	.142427	.145406	.148426	.154577	.160862	.167265	.173770
	0.00	.121241	.126443	.131872	.134667	.137510	.140402	.143338	.146318	.149337	.155468	.161774	.168177	.174682
	-.10	.122153	.127355	.132784	.135578	.138422	.141314	.144250	.147229	.150249	.156400	.162686	.169089	.175594
	-.20	.123065	.128267	.133696	.136490	.139334	.142225	.145162	.148141	.151161	.157312	.163597	.170001	.176505
	-.30	.123976	.129178	.134607	.137402	.140246	.143137	.146074	.149053	.152072	.158224	.164509	.170912	.177417
	-.40	.124888	.130090	.135519	.138313	.141157	.144049	.146985	.149964	.152984	.159135	.165421	.171824	.178329
30	.40	.114397	.119868	.125581	.128519	.131508	.134543	.137622	.140742	.143899	.150314	.156844	.163472	.170179
	.30	.115308	.120780	.126492	.129431	.132419	.135455	.138534	.141654	.144811	.151225	.157756	.164383	.171090
	.20	.116220	.121691	.127404	.130342	.133331	.136367	.139446	.142565	.145723	.152137	.158668	.165295	.172002
	.10	.117132	.122603	.128316	.131254	.134243	.137278	.140358	.143477	.146634	.153049	.159580	.166207	.172914
	0.00	.118043	.123515	.129227	.132166	.135154	.138190	.141269	.144389	.147546	.153960	.160491	.167119	.173825
	-.10	.118955	.124426	.130139	.133077	.136066	.139102	.142181	.145301	.148458	.154872	.161403	.168030	.174737
	-.20	.119867	.125338	.131051	.133989	.136978	.140013	.143093	.146212	.149369	.155784	.162315	.168942	.175649
	-.30	.120778	.126250	.131962	.134901	.137890	.140925	.144004	.147124	.150281	.156696	.163226	.169854	.176560
	-.40	.121690	.127161	.132874	.135813	.138801	.141837	.144916	.148036	.151193	.157607	.164138	.170765	.177472
40	.40	.110740	.116639	.122783	.125932	.129127	.132361	.135632	.138934	.142263	.148993	.155796	.162656	.169556
	.30	.111652	.117551	.123695	.126844	.130039	.133273	.136543	.139845	.143175	.149904	.156708	.163567	.170468
	.20	.112563	.118463	.124606	.127756	.130950	.134185	.137455	.140757	.144087	.150816	.157620	.164479	.171379
	.10	.113475	.119374	.125518	.128667	.131862	.135097	.138367	.141669	.144998	.151728	.158531	.165391	.172291
	0.00	.114387	.120286	.126430	.129579	.132774	.136008	.139279	.142581	.145910	.152639	.159443	.166302	.173203
	-.10	.115298	.121198	.127341	.130491	.133685	.136920	.140190	.143492	.146822	.153551	.160355	.167214	.174115
	-.20	.116210	.122109	.128253	.131402	.134597	.137832	.141102	.144404	.147733	.154463	.161266	.168126	.175026
	-.30	.117122	.123021	.129165	.132314	.135509	.138743	.142014	.145315	.148645	.155374	.162178	.169037	.175938
	-.40	.118033	.123933	.130076	.133226	.136420	.139655	.142925	.146227	.149557	.156286	.163090	.169949	.176850

15.0 YEAR HOLDING PERIOD
.250 EQUITY YIELD RATE
.750 LOAN RATIO

INTEREST RATE

TERM YEARS	APPR DEP	5.0	6.0	7.0	7.5	8.0	8.5	9.0	9.5	10.0	11.0	12.0	13.0	14.0
15	.40	.123187	.127963	.132910	.135447	.138024	.140642	.143300	.145996	.148730	.154309	.160031	.165887	.171872
	.30	.124099	.128874	.133822	.136358	.138936	.141554	.144211	.146908	.149908	.155221	.160942	.166799	.172784
	.20	.125010	.129786	.134734	.137270	.139848	.142466	.145123	.147819	.150553	.156133	.161854	.167711	.173696
	.10	.125922	.130698	.135645	.138182	.140759	.143377	.146035	.148731	.151465	.157044	.162766	.168622	.174607
	0.00	.126834	.131609	.136557	.139093	.141671	.144289	.146946	.149643	.152377	.157956	.163677	.169534	.175519
	-.10	.127745	.132521	.137469	.140005	.142583	.145201	.147858	.150554	.153288	.158868	.164589	.170446	.176431
	-.20	.128657	.133433	.138380	.140917	.143494	.146112	.148770	.151466	.154200	.159779	.165501	.171358	.177342
	-.30	.129569	.134345	.139292	.141829	.144406	.147024	.149681	.152378	.155112	.160691	.166413	.172269	.178254
	-.40	.130481	.135256	.140204	.142740	.145318	.147936	.150593	.153289	.156024	.161603	.167324	.173181	.179166
20	.40	.113803	.119028	.124470	.127268	.130116	.133012	.135955	.138942	.141973	.148159	.154498	.160978	.167587
	.30	.114715	.119940	.125381	.128180	.131028	.133924	.136866	.139854	.142885	.149070	.155410	.161890	.168498
	.20	.115626	.120852	.126293	.129091	.131939	.134835	.137778	.140766	.143797	.149982	.156321	.162802	.169410
	.10	.116538	.121763	.127205	.130003	.132851	.135747	.138690	.141677	.144708	.150894	.157233	.163713	.170322
	0.00	.117450	.122675	.128116	.130915	.133763	.136659	.139601	.142589	.145620	.151805	.158145	.164625	.171233
	-.10	.118361	.123587	.129028	.131826	.134674	.137570	.140513	.143501	.146532	.152717	.159056	.165537	.172145
	-.20	.119273	.124498	.129940	.132738	.135586	.138482	.141425	.144412	.147443	.153629	.159968	.166448	.173057
	-.30	.120185	.125410	.130852	.133650	.136498	.139394	.142336	.145324	.148355	.154540	.160880	.167360	.173969
	-.40	.121096	.126322	.131763	.134561	.137409	.140305	.143248	.146236	.149267	.155452	.161791	.168272	.174880
25	.40	.108397	.113971	.119788	.122782	.125829	.128927	.132073	.135265	.138500	.145091	.151825	.158686	.165655
	.30	.109309	.114883	.120700	.123693	.126740	.129838	.132985	.136177	.139412	.146003	.152737	.159597	.166567
	.20	.110221	.115794	.121611	.124605	.127652	.130750	.133896	.137088	.140324	.146914	.153649	.160509	.167479
	.10	.111132	.116706	.122523	.125517	.128564	.131662	.134808	.138000	.141235	.147826	.154560	.161421	.168390
	0.00	.112044	.117618	.123435	.126428	.129476	.132574	.135720	.138912	.142147	.148738	.155472	.162332	.169302
	-.10	.112956	.118529	.124346	.127340	.130387	.133485	.136631	.139824	.143059	.149649	.156384	.163244	.170214
	-.20	.113867	.119441	.125258	.128252	.131299	.134397	.137543	.140735	.143971	.150561	.157295	.164156	.171125
	-.30	.114779	.120353	.126170	.129163	.132211	.135309	.138455	.141647	.144882	.151473	.158207	.165067	.172037
	-.40	.115691	.121264	.127081	.130075	.133122	.136220	.139367	.142559	.145794	.152384	.159119	.165979	.172949
30	.40	.104971	.110833	.116954	.120102	.123304	.126557	.129856	.133198	.136581	.143454	.150451	.157552	.164738
	.30	.105883	.111745	.117866	.121014	.124216	.127469	.130768	.134110	.137493	.144365	.151363	.158463	.165649
	.20	.106795	.112657	.118777	.121926	.125128	.128380	.131679	.135022	.138404	.145277	.152274	.159375	.166561
	.10	.107706	.113568	.119689	.122837	.126040	.129292	.132591	.135934	.139316	.146189	.153186	.160287	.167473
	0.00	.108618	.114480	.120601	.123749	.126951	.130204	.133503	.136845	.140228	.147101	.154098	.161198	.168384
	-.10	.109530	.115392	.121512	.124661	.127863	.131115	.134414	.137757	.141139	.148012	.155009	.162110	.169296
	-.20	.110441	.116303	.122424	.125572	.128775	.132027	.135326	.138669	.142051	.148924	.155921	.163022	.170208
	-.30	.111353	.117215	.123336	.126484	.129686	.132939	.136238	.139580	.142963	.149836	.156833	.163934	.171119
	-.40	.112265	.118127	.124247	.127396	.130598	.133850	.137149	.140492	.143874	.150747	.157744	.164845	.172031
40	.40	.101053	.107374	.113956	.117331	.120754	.124219	.127723	.131261	.134828	.142038	.149328	.156677	.164071
	.30	.101965	.108286	.114868	.118243	.121666	.125131	.128635	.132172	.135740	.142950	.150240	.157589	.164982
	.20	.102877	.109197	.115780	.119154	.122577	.126043	.129546	.133084	.136652	.143862	.151151	.158501	.165894
	.10	.103788	.110109	.116691	.120066	.123489	.126954	.130458	.133996	.137563	.144773	.152063	.159412	.166806
	0.00	.104700	.111021	.117603	.120978	.124400	.127866	.131370	.134908	.138475	.145685	.152975	.160324	.167717
	-.10	.105612	.111932	.118515	.121889	.125312	.128778	.132282	.135819	.139387	.146597	.153886	.161236	.168629
	-.20	.106523	.112844	.119427	.122801	.126224	.129689	.133193	.136731	.140298	.147508	.154798	.162147	.169541
	-.30	.107435	.113756	.120338	.123713	.127135	.130601	.134105	.137643	.141210	.148420	.155710	.163059	.170452
	-.40	.108347	.114667	.121250	.124624	.128047	.131513	.135017	.138554	.142122	.149332	.156621	.163971	.171364

15.0 YEAR HOLDING PERIOD
.250 EQUITY YIELD RATE
.800 LOAN RATIO

INTEREST RATE

TERM YEARS	APPR DEP	5.0	6.0	7.0	7.5	8.0	8.5	9.0	9.5	10.0	11.0	12.0	13.0	14.0
15	.40	.114976	.120070	.125347	.128053	.130802	.133595	.136429	.139305	.142222	.148173	.154276	.160523	.166907
	.30	.115888	.120982	.126259	.128965	.131714	.134506	.137341	.140217	.143134	.149085	.155188	.161435	.167819
	.20	.116799	.121893	.127171	.129876	.132626	.135418	.138253	.141129	.144045	.149996	.156099	.162346	.168730
	.10	.117711	.122805	.128082	.130788	.133537	.136330	.139164	.142040	.144957	.150908	.157011	.163258	.169642
	0.00	.118623	.123717	.128994	.131700	.134449	.137242	.140076	.142952	.145869	.151820	.157923	.164170	.170554
	-.10	.119534	.124628	.129906	.132611	.135361	.138153	.140988	.143864	.146780	.152732	.158834	.165081	.171465
	-.20	.120446	.125540	.130817	.133523	.136272	.139065	.141899	.144775	.147692	.153643	.159746	.165993	.172377
	-.30	.121358	.126452	.131729	.134435	.137184	.139977	.142811	.145687	.148604	.154555	.160658	.166905	.173289
	-.40	.122269	.127364	.132641	.135346	.138096	.140888	.143723	.146599	.149515	.155467	.161569	.167817	.174200
20	.40	.104966	.110540	.116344	.119329	.122367	.125456	.128595	.131781	.135014	.141612	.148374	.155287	.162336
	.30	.105878	.111452	.117256	.120241	.123278	.126368	.129506	.132693	.135926	.142524	.149286	.156198	.163247
	.20	.106790	.112363	.118168	.121152	.124190	.127279	.130418	.133605	.136838	.143436	.150198	.157110	.164159
	.10	.107701	.113275	.119079	.122064	.125102	.128191	.131330	.134517	.137750	.144347	.151109	.158022	.165071
	0.00	.108613	.114187	.119991	.122976	.126013	.129103	.132241	.135428	.138661	.145259	.152021	.158933	.165982
	-.10	.109525	.115098	.120903	.123887	.126925	.130014	.133153	.136340	.139573	.146171	.152933	.159845	.166894
	-.20	.110436	.116010	.121814	.124799	.127837	.130926	.134065	.137252	.140485	.147082	.153844	.160757	.167806
	-.30	.111348	.116922	.122726	.125711	.128749	.131838	.134976	.138163	.141396	.147994	.154756	.161668	.168717
	-.40	.112260	.117833	.123638	.126622	.129660	.132749	.135888	.139075	.142308	.148906	.155668	.162580	.169629
25	.40	.099200	.105145	.111350	.114544	.117794	.121098	.124454	.127859	.131310	.138340	.145523	.152841	.160275
	.30	.100112	.106057	.112262	.115455	.118706	.122010	.125366	.128771	.132222	.139252	.146435	.153753	.161187
	.20	.101024	.106969	.113174	.116367	.119617	.122922	.126278	.129683	.133134	.140163	.147347	.154665	.162099
	.10	.101935	.107880	.114085	.117279	.120529	.123833	.127189	.130594	.134046	.141075	.148259	.155576	.163010
	0.00	.102847	.108792	.114997	.118190	.121441	.124745	.128101	.131506	.134957	.141987	.149170	.156488	.163922
	-.10	.103759	.109704	.115909	.119102	.122352	.125657	.129013	.132418	.135869	.142898	.150082	.157400	.164834
	-.20	.104670	.110616	.116820	.120014	.123264	.126568	.129924	.133329	.136780	.143810	.150994	.158311	.165745
	-.30	.105582	.111527	.117732	.120925	.124176	.127480	.130836	.134241	.137692	.144722	.151905	.159223	.166657
	-.40	.106494	.112439	.118644	.121837	.125087	.128392	.131748	.135153	.138604	.145634	.152817	.160135	.167569
30	.40	.095546	.101799	.108327	.111686	.115101	.118570	.122089	.125655	.129263	.136594	.144058	.151632	.159297
	.30	.096457	.102710	.109239	.112597	.116013	.119482	.123001	.126566	.130175	.137506	.144969	.152543	.160208
	.20	.097369	.103622	.110151	.113509	.116925	.120394	.123913	.127478	.131086	.138417	.145881	.153455	.161120
	.10	.098281	.104534	.111062	.114421	.117836	.121305	.124825	.128390	.131998	.139329	.146793	.154367	.162032
	0.00	.099192	.105445	.111974	.115332	.118748	.122217	.125736	.129302	.132910	.140241	.147704	.155278	.162943
	-.10	.100104	.106357	.112886	.116244	.119660	.123129	.126648	.130213	.133821	.141152	.148616	.156190	.163855
	-.20	.101016	.107269	.113797	.117156	.120571	.124041	.127560	.131125	.134733	.142064	.149528	.157102	.164767
	-.30	.101928	.108180	.114709	.118067	.121483	.124952	.128471	.132037	.135645	.142976	.150439	.158013	.165678
	-.40	.102839	.109092	.115621	.118979	.122395	.125864	.129383	.132948	.136556	.143887	.151351	.158925	.166590
40	.40	.091367	.098109	.105130	.108729	.112380	.116077	.119814	.123588	.127393	.135084	.142860	.150699	.158585
	.30	.092278	.099020	.106042	.109641	.113292	.116989	.120726	.124500	.128305	.135996	.143771	.151610	.159497
	.20	.093190	.099932	.106953	.110553	.114204	.117900	.121638	.125411	.129217	.136907	.144683	.152522	.160408
	.10	.094102	.100844	.107865	.111464	.115115	.118812	.122549	.126323	.130128	.137819	.145595	.153434	.161320
	0.00	.095013	.101755	.108777	.112376	.116027	.119724	.123461	.127235	.131040	.138731	.146506	.154346	.162232
	-.10	.095925	.102667	.109688	.113288	.116939	.120635	.124373	.128146	.131952	.139642	.147418	.155257	.163143
	-.20	.096837	.103579	.110600	.114200	.117850	.121547	.125285	.129058	.132863	.140554	.148330	.156169	.164055
	-.30	.097748	.104490	.111512	.115111	.118762	.122459	.126196	.129970	.133775	.141466	.149241	.157081	.164967
	-.40	.098660	.105402	.112423	.116023	.119674	.123370	.127108	.130881	.134687	.142377	.150153	.157992	.165879

15.0 YEAR HOLDING PERIOD
.250 EQUITY YIELD RATE
.900 LOAN RATIO

INTEREST RATE

TERM YEARS	APPR DEP	14.0	13.0	12.0	11.0	10.0	9.5	9.0	8.5	8.0	7.5	7.0	6.0	5.0
15	.40	.155976	.149794	.142766	.135901	.129205	.125924	.122689	.119500	.116359	.113265	.110222	.104285	.098554
	.30	.157888	.150706	.143678	.136812	.130117	.126836	.123601	.120412	.117270	.114177	.111133	.105196	.099465
	.20	.158800	.151618	.144590	.137724	.131029	.127748	.124512	.121323	.118182	.115089	.112045	.106108	.100377
	.10	.159711	.152529	.145501	.138636	.131940	.128659	.125424	.122235	.119094	.116000	.112957	.107020	.101289
	0.00	.160623	.153441	.146413	.139547	.132852	.129571	.126336	.123147	.120005	.116912	.113868	.107931	.102201
	-.10	.161535	.154353	.147325	.140459	.133764	.130483	.127247	.124058	.120917	.117824	.114780	.108843	.103112
	-.20	.162446	.155264	.148236	.141371	.134676	.131394	.128159	.124970	.121829	.118736	.115692	.109755	.104024
	-.30	.163358	.156176	.149148	.142282	.135587	.132306	.129071	.125882	.122740	.119647	.116603	.110666	.104936
	-.40	.164270	.157088	.150060	.143194	.136499	.133218	.129982	.126793	.123652	.120559	.117515	.111578	.105847
20	.40	.151833	.143903	.136127	.128520	.121097	.117460	.113875	.110344	.106868	.103451	.100093	.093563	.087293
	.30	.152745	.144815	.137039	.129431	.122009	.118372	.114787	.111255	.107780	.104363	.101005	.094475	.088204
	.20	.153657	.145727	.137950	.130343	.122921	.119283	.115698	.112167	.108692	.105274	.101916	.095387	.089116
	.10	.154568	.146638	.138862	.131255	.123832	.120195	.116610	.113079	.109603	.106186	.102828	.096298	.090028
	0.00	.155480	.147550	.139774	.132166	.124744	.121107	.117522	.113990	.110515	.107098	.103740	.097210	.090940
	-.10	.156392	.148462	.140685	.133078	.125656	.122018	.118433	.114902	.111427	.108009	.104651	.098122	.091851
	-.20	.157304	.149373	.141597	.133990	.126567	.122930	.119345	.115814	.112339	.108921	.105563	.099033	.092763
	-.30	.158215	.150285	.142509	.134902	.127479	.123842	.120257	.116725	.113250	.109833	.106475	.099945	.093675
	-.40	.159127	.151197	.143420	.135813	.128391	.124753	.121168	.117637	.114162	.110744	.107387	.100857	.094586
25	.40	.149516	.141152	.132920	.124838	.116930	.113047	.109217	.105441	.101724	.098067	.094475	.087494	.080806
	.30	.150427	.142064	.133831	.125750	.117842	.113959	.110129	.106353	.102636	.098979	.095387	.088406	.081718
	.20	.151339	.142976	.134743	.126662	.118753	.114871	.111040	.107265	.103547	.099891	.096298	.089318	.082630
	.10	.152251	.143887	.135655	.127573	.119665	.115783	.111952	.108177	.104459	.100802	.097210	.090230	.083541
	0.00	.153162	.144799	.136566	.128485	.120577	.116694	.112864	.109088	.105371	.101714	.098122	.091141	.084453
	-.10	.154074	.145711	.137478	.129397	.121488	.117606	.113775	.110000	.106282	.102626	.099033	.092053	.085365
	-.20	.154986	.146622	.138390	.130309	.122400	.118518	.114687	.110912	.107194	.103537	.099945	.092965	.086276
	-.30	.155897	.147534	.139302	.131220	.123312	.119429	.115599	.111823	.108106	.104449	.100857	.093876	.087188
	-.40	.156809	.148446	.140213	.132132	.124223	.120341	.116511	.112735	.109017	.105361	.101768	.094788	.088100
30	.40	.148415	.139791	.131271	.122874	.114627	.110567	.106557	.102598	.098695	.094852	.091074	.083729	.076695
	.30	.149326	.140703	.132182	.123786	.115538	.111479	.107468	.103509	.099606	.095764	.091986	.084641	.077606
	.20	.150238	.141615	.133094	.124697	.116450	.112391	.108380	.104421	.100518	.096676	.092897	.085553	.078518
	.10	.151150	.142526	.134006	.125609	.117362	.113303	.109292	.105333	.101430	.097587	.093809	.086464	.079430
	0.00	.152061	.143438	.134917	.126521	.118273	.114214	.110203	.106244	.102341	.098499	.094721	.087376	.080342
	-.10	.152973	.144350	.135829	.127432	.119185	.115126	.111115	.107156	.103253	.099411	.095633	.088288	.081253
	-.20	.153885	.145262	.136741	.128344	.120097	.116038	.112027	.108068	.104165	.100322	.096544	.089199	.082165
	-.30	.154796	.146173	.137652	.129256	.121008	.116949	.112938	.108979	.105077	.101234	.097456	.090111	.083077
	-.40	.155708	.147085	.138564	.130167	.121920	.117861	.113850	.109891	.105988	.102146	.098368	.091023	.083988
40	.40	.147614	.138742	.129923	.121175	.112523	.108242	.103997	.099792	.095634	.091526	.087477	.079578	.071993
	.30	.148526	.139654	.130835	.122087	.113435	.109154	.104909	.100704	.096545	.092438	.088389	.080490	.072905
	.20	.149437	.140565	.131746	.122999	.114347	.110066	.105820	.101616	.097457	.093350	.089300	.081401	.073817
	.10	.150349	.141477	.132658	.123910	.115258	.110977	.106732	.102527	.098369	.094261	.090212	.082313	.074728
	0.00	.151261	.142389	.133570	.124822	.116170	.111889	.107644	.103439	.099280	.095173	.091124	.083225	.075640
	-.10	.152172	.143300	.134481	.125734	.117082	.112801	.108555	.104351	.100192	.096085	.092035	.084137	.076552
	-.20	.153084	.144212	.135393	.126645	.117993	.113712	.109467	.105263	.101104	.096997	.092947	.085048	.077463
	-.30	.153996	.145124	.136305	.127557	.118905	.114624	.110379	.106174	.102015	.097909	.093859	.085960	.078375
	-.40	.154908	.146035	.137216	.128469	.119817	.115536	.111291	.107086	.102927	.098820	.094770	.086872	.079287

448

15.0 YEAR HOLDING PERIOD
.300 EQUITY YIELD RATE
.600 LOAN RATIO

INTEREST RATE

TERM YEARS	APPR DEP	5.0	6.0	7.0	7.5	8.0	8.5	9.0	9.5	10.0	11.0	12.0	13.0	14.0
15	.40	.170959	.174780	.178738	.180767	.182829	.184923	.187049	.189206	.191394	.195857	.200434	.205120	.209908
	.30	.171557	.175378	.179336	.181365	.183427	.185521	.187647	.189804	.191992	.196455	.201032	.205717	.210505
	.20	.172155	.175975	.179933	.181963	.184025	.186119	.188245	.190402	.192589	.197053	.201630	.206315	.211103
	.10	.172753	.176573	.180531	.182560	.184623	.186717	.188843	.191000	.193187	.197651	.202228	.206913	.211701
	0.00	.173350	.177171	.181129	.183158	.185220	.187315	.189441	.191598	.193785	.198248	.202825	.207511	.212299
	-.10	.173948	.177769	.181727	.183756	.185818	.187912	.190038	.192195	.194383	.198846	.203423	.208109	.212896
	-.20	.174546	.178367	.182325	.184354	.186416	.188510	.190636	.192793	.194980	.199444	.204021	.208706	.213494
	-.30	.175144	.178964	.182922	.184952	.187014	.189108	.191234	.193391	.195578	.200042	.204619	.209304	.214092
	-.40	.175742	.179562	.183520	.185549	.187611	.189706	.191832	.193989	.196176	.200639	.205217	.209902	.214690
20	.40	.162793	.166934	.171248	.173467	.175725	.178023	.180357	.182728	.185133	.190043	.195076	.200222	.205473
	.30	.163391	.167532	.171846	.174065	.176323	.178620	.180955	.183325	.185731	.190640	.195674	.200820	.206070
	.20	.163989	.168130	.172444	.174662	.176921	.179218	.181553	.183923	.186328	.191238	.196271	.201418	.206668
	.10	.164587	.168728	.173041	.175260	.177519	.179816	.182150	.184521	.186926	.191836	.196869	.202016	.207266
	0.00	.165184	.169326	.173639	.175858	.178117	.180414	.182748	.185119	.187524	.192434	.197467	.202614	.207864
	-.10	.165782	.169923	.174237	.176456	.178714	.181011	.183346	.185716	.188122	.193031	.198065	.203211	.208461
	-.20	.166380	.170521	.174835	.177054	.179312	.181609	.183944	.186314	.188719	.193629	.198662	.203809	.209059
	-.30	.166978	.171119	.175433	.177651	.179910	.182207	.184541	.186912	.189317	.194227	.199260	.204407	.209657
	-.40	.167576	.171717	.176030	.178249	.180508	.182805	.185139	.187510	.189915	.194825	.199858	.205005	.210255
25	.40	.158090	.162493	.167094	.169463	.171875	.174328	.176820	.179350	.181915	.187142	.192487	.197936	.203474
	.30	.158687	.163091	.167691	.170060	.172472	.174926	.177418	.179948	.182513	.187740	.193085	.198533	.204071
	.20	.159285	.163689	.168289	.170658	.173070	.175523	.178016	.180546	.183111	.188338	.193683	.199131	.204669
	.10	.159883	.164287	.168887	.171256	.173668	.176121	.178614	.181143	.183708	.188936	.194281	.199729	.205267
	0.00	.160481	.164885	.169485	.171854	.174266	.176719	.179212	.181741	.184306	.189533	.194878	.200327	.205865
	-.10	.161078	.165482	.170083	.172451	.174864	.177317	.179809	.182339	.184904	.190131	.195476	.200924	.206463
	-.20	.161676	.166080	.170680	.173049	.175461	.177915	.180407	.182937	.185502	.190729	.196074	.201522	.207060
	-.30	.162274	.166678	.171278	.173647	.176059	.178512	.181005	.183535	.186099	.191327	.196672	.202120	.207658
	-.40	.162872	.167276	.171876	.174245	.176657	.179110	.181603	.184132	.186697	.191925	.197270	.202718	.208256
30	.40	.155108	.159738	.164579	.167071	.169607	.172185	.174800	.177452	.180136	.185595	.191156	.196804	.202524
	.30	.155706	.160336	.165177	.167669	.170205	.172782	.175398	.178050	.180734	.186192	.191754	.197402	.203122
	.20	.156304	.160934	.165774	.168267	.170803	.173380	.175996	.178647	.181332	.186790	.192352	.198000	.203720
	.10	.156901	.161531	.166372	.168864	.171401	.173978	.176594	.179245	.181930	.187388	.192950	.198598	.204317
	0.00	.157499	.162129	.166970	.169462	.171998	.174576	.177191	.179843	.182528	.187986	.193547	.199196	.204915
	-.10	.158097	.162727	.167568	.170060	.172596	.175173	.177789	.180441	.183125	.188584	.194145	.199793	.205513
	-.20	.158695	.163325	.168165	.170658	.173194	.175771	.178387	.181039	.183723	.189181	.194743	.200391	.206111
	-.30	.159293	.163923	.168763	.171255	.173792	.176369	.178985	.181636	.184321	.189779	.195341	.200989	.206709
	-.40	.159890	.164520	.169361	.171853	.174389	.176967	.179583	.182234	.184919	.190377	.195939	.201587	.207306
40	.40	.151699	.156701	.161919	.164597	.167316	.170070	.172857	.175672	.178512	.184256	.190069	.195932	.201834
	.30	.152297	.157298	.162517	.165195	.167914	.170668	.173455	.176270	.179110	.184854	.190666	.196530	.202432
	.20	.152894	.157896	.163114	.165793	.168511	.171266	.174053	.176868	.179708	.185452	.191264	.197128	.203029
	.10	.153492	.158494	.163712	.166391	.169109	.171864	.174650	.177465	.180306	.186050	.191862	.197725	.203627
	0.00	.154090	.159092	.164310	.166988	.169707	.172461	.175248	.178063	.180903	.186648	.192460	.198323	.204225
	-.10	.154688	.159689	.164908	.167586	.170305	.173059	.175846	.178661	.181501	.187245	.193057	.198921	.204823
	-.20	.155285	.160287	.165505	.168184	.170902	.173657	.176444	.179259	.182099	.187843	.193655	.199519	.205420
	-.30	.155883	.160885	.166103	.168782	.171500	.174255	.177041	.179857	.182697	.188441	.194253	.200116	.206018
	-.40	.156481	.161483	.166701	.169379	.172098	.174853	.177639	.180454	.183295	.189039	.194851	.200714	.206616

15.0 YEAR HOLDING PERIOD
.300 EQUITY YIELD RATE
.667 LOAN RATIO

INTEREST RATE

TERM YEARS	APPR DEP	5.0	6.0	7.0	7.5	8.0	8.5	9.0	9.5	10.0	11.0	12.0	13.0	14.0
15	.40	.156886	.161132	.165529	.167784	.170075	.172402	.174764	.177161	.179592	.184551	.189637	.194843	.200163
	.30	.157484	.161729	.166127	.168382	.170673	.173000	.175362	.177759	.180189	.185149	.190234	.195440	.200760
	.20	.158082	.162327	.166725	.168980	.171271	.173598	.175960	.178357	.180787	.185746	.190832	.196038	.201358
	.10	.158680	.162925	.167323	.169577	.171869	.174196	.176558	.178954	.181385	.186344	.191430	.196636	.201956
	0.00	.159278	.163523	.167920	.170175	.172466	.174793	.177156	.179552	.181983	.186942	.192028	.197234	.202554
	-.10	.159875	.164120	.168518	.170773	.173064	.175391	.177753	.180150	.182580	.187540	.192625	.197831	.203151
	-.20	.160473	.164718	.169116	.171371	.173662	.175989	.178351	.180748	.183178	.188138	.193223	.198429	.203749
	-.30	.161071	.165316	.169714	.171968	.174260	.176587	.178949	.181346	.183776	.188735	.193821	.199027	.204347
	-.40	.161669	.165914	.170312	.172566	.174857	.177184	.179547	.181943	.184374	.189333	.194419	.199625	.204945
20	.40	.147813	.152414	.157207	.159673	.162182	.164735	.167328	.169962	.172635	.178090	.183683	.189401	.195235
	.30	.148411	.153012	.157805	.160270	.162780	.165332	.167926	.170560	.173233	.178688	.184280	.189999	.195832
	.20	.149009	.153610	.158403	.160868	.163378	.165930	.168524	.171158	.173830	.179286	.184878	.190597	.196430
	.10	.149606	.154208	.159001	.161466	.163976	.166528	.169122	.171756	.174428	.179883	.185476	.191195	.197028
	0.00	.150204	.154805	.159598	.162064	.164573	.167126	.169720	.172353	.175026	.180481	.186074	.191792	.197626
	-.10	.150802	.155403	.160196	.162662	.165171	.167723	.170317	.172951	.175624	.181079	.186672	.192390	.198224
	-.20	.151400	.156001	.160794	.163259	.165769	.168321	.170915	.173549	.176222	.181677	.187269	.192988	.198821
	-.30	.151998	.156599	.161392	.163857	.166367	.168919	.171513	.174147	.176819	.182275	.187867	.193586	.199419
	-.40	.152595	.157197	.161990	.164455	.166964	.169517	.172111	.174745	.177417	.182872	.188465	.194183	.200017
25	.40	.142587	.147480	.152591	.155223	.157903	.160629	.163399	.166207	.169059	.174868	.180807	.186860	.193014
	.30	.143184	.148078	.153189	.155821	.158501	.161227	.163997	.166805	.169657	.175465	.181404	.187458	.193612
	.20	.143782	.148675	.153787	.156419	.159099	.161825	.164594	.167403	.170255	.176063	.182002	.188056	.194209
	.10	.144380	.149273	.154385	.157017	.159697	.162423	.165192	.168001	.170853	.176661	.182600	.188654	.194807
	0.00	.144978	.149871	.154982	.157614	.160295	.163020	.165790	.168599	.171451	.177259	.183198	.189251	.195405
	-.10	.145575	.150469	.155580	.158212	.160892	.163618	.166388	.169197	.172048	.177857	.183795	.189849	.196003
	-.20	.146173	.151067	.156178	.158810	.161490	.164216	.166985	.169795	.172646	.178454	.184393	.190447	.196600
	-.30	.146771	.151664	.156776	.159408	.162088	.164814	.167583	.170393	.173244	.179052	.184991	.191044	.197198
	-.40	.147369	.152262	.157373	.160006	.162686	.165412	.168181	.170992	.173842	.179650	.185589	.191642	.197796
30	.40	.139274	.144418	.149797	.152566	.155384	.158248	.161154	.164100	.167083	.173148	.179328	.185603	.191959
	.30	.139872	.145016	.150395	.153164	.155982	.158846	.161752	.164698	.167681	.173746	.179925	.186201	.192556
	.20	.140469	.145614	.150993	.153762	.156580	.159443	.162350	.165296	.168279	.174344	.180523	.186799	.193154
	.10	.141067	.146212	.151590	.154359	.157177	.160041	.162948	.165894	.168877	.174941	.181121	.187397	.193752
	0.00	.141665	.146810	.152188	.154957	.157775	.160639	.163545	.166492	.169474	.175539	.181719	.187994	.194350
	-.10	.142263	.147407	.152786	.155555	.158373	.161237	.164143	.167089	.170072	.176137	.182317	.188592	.194947
	-.20	.142861	.148005	.153384	.156153	.158971	.161835	.164741	.167687	.170670	.176735	.182914	.189190	.195545
	-.30	.143458	.148603	.153981	.156750	.159568	.162432	.165339	.168285	.171268	.177332	.183512	.189788	.196143
	-.40	.144056	.149201	.154579	.157348	.160166	.163030	.165937	.168883	.171865	.177930	.184110	.190386	.196741
40	.40	.135486	.141043	.146841	.149817	.152838	.155899	.158995	.162123	.165279	.171661	.178119	.184634	.191192
	.30	.136084	.141641	.147439	.150415	.153436	.156496	.159593	.162721	.165876	.172259	.178717	.185232	.191789
	.20	.136681	.142239	.148037	.151013	.154034	.157094	.160191	.163318	.166474	.172857	.179315	.185830	.192387
	.10	.137279	.142837	.148635	.151611	.154631	.157692	.160788	.163916	.167072	.173454	.179912	.186427	.192985
	0.00	.137877	.143434	.149232	.152208	.155229	.158290	.161386	.164514	.167670	.174052	.180510	.187025	.193583
	-.10	.138475	.144032	.149830	.152806	.155827	.158888	.161984	.165112	.168268	.174650	.181108	.187623	.194180
	-.20	.139072	.144630	.150428	.153404	.156425	.159485	.162582	.165710	.168865	.175248	.181706	.188221	.194778
	-.30	.139670	.145228	.151026	.154002	.157023	.160083	.163179	.166307	.169463	.175846	.182304	.188818	.195376
	-.40	.140268	.145825	.151624	.154600	.157620	.160681	.163777	.166905	.170061	.176443	.182901	.189416	.195974

15.0 YEAR HOLDING PERIOD
.300 EQUITY YIELD RATE
.700 LOAN RATIO

INTEREST RATE

TERM YEARS	APPR DEP	5.0	6.0	7.0	7.5	8.0	8.5	9.0	9.5	10.0	11.0	12.0	13.0	14.0
15	.40	.149851	.154308	.158926	.161293	.163699	.166143	.168623	.171139	.173691	.178899	.184239	.189705	.195291
	.30	.150449	.154906	.159524	.161891	.164297	.166740	.169221	.171737	.174289	.179496	.184836	.190303	.195889
	.20	.151047	.155504	.160122	.162489	.164895	.167338	.169818	.172335	.174887	.180094	.185434	.190900	.196486
	.10	.151644	.156102	.160722	.163087	.165493	.167936	.170416	.172933	.175485	.180692	.186032	.191498	.197084
	0.00	.152242	.156700	.161317	.163685	.166090	.168534	.171014	.173530	.176082	.181290	.186630	.192096	.197682
	-.10	.152840	.157297	.161915	.164282	.166688	.169131	.171612	.174128	.176680	.181887	.187227	.192694	.198280
	-.20	.153438	.157895	.162513	.164880	.167286	.169729	.172210	.174726	.177279	.182485	.187825	.193291	.198877
	-.30	.154036	.158493	.163110	.165478	.167884	.170327	.172807	.175324	.177876	.183083	.188423	.193889	.199475
	-.40	.154633	.159091	.163708	.166076	.168481	.170925	.173405	.175922	.178473	.183681	.189021	.194487	.200073
20	.40	.140324	.145155	.150188	.152777	.155412	.158092	.160815	.163581	.166387	.172115	.177987	.183991	.190116
	.30	.140922	.145753	.150786	.153374	.156009	.158689	.161413	.164178	.166985	.172713	.178585	.184589	.190714
	.20	.141520	.146351	.151383	.153972	.156607	.159287	.162011	.164776	.167582	.173310	.179183	.185187	.191312
	.10	.142117	.146949	.151981	.154570	.157205	.159885	.162608	.165374	.168180	.173908	.179780	.185785	.191910
	0.00	.142715	.147546	.152579	.155168	.157803	.160483	.163206	.165972	.168778	.174506	.180378	.186383	.192508
	-.10	.143313	.148144	.153177	.155765	.158400	.161080	.163804	.166570	.169376	.175104	.180976	.186980	.193105
	-.20	.143911	.148742	.153775	.156363	.158998	.161678	.164402	.167167	.169973	.175701	.181574	.187578	.193703
	-.30	.144509	.149340	.154372	.156961	.159596	.162276	.165000	.167765	.170571	.176299	.182171	.188176	.194301
	-.40	.145106	.149938	.154970	.157559	.160194	.162874	.165597	.168363	.171169	.176897	.182769	.188774	.194899
25	.40	.134836	.139974	.145341	.148105	.150919	.153781	.156689	.159640	.162633	.168731	.174967	.181323	.187785
	.30	.135434	.140572	.145939	.148703	.151517	.154379	.157287	.160238	.163230	.169329	.175565	.181921	.188382
	.20	.136032	.141170	.146537	.149300	.152114	.154977	.157885	.160836	.163828	.169927	.176163	.182519	.188980
	.10	.136630	.141768	.147134	.149898	.152712	.155574	.158482	.161434	.164426	.170525	.176760	.183117	.189578
	0.00	.137227	.142365	.147732	.150496	.153310	.156172	.159080	.162031	.165024	.171122	.177358	.183714	.190176
	-.10	.137825	.142963	.148330	.151094	.153908	.156770	.159678	.162629	.165622	.171720	.177956	.184312	.190773
	-.20	.138423	.143561	.148928	.151691	.154506	.157368	.160276	.163227	.166219	.172318	.178554	.184910	.191371
	-.30	.139021	.144159	.149526	.152289	.155103	.157966	.160873	.163825	.166817	.172916	.179152	.185508	.191969
	-.40	.139619	.144756	.150123	.152887	.155701	.158563	.161471	.164423	.167415	.173513	.179749	.186106	.192567
30	.40	.131358	.136760	.142407	.145315	.148274	.151281	.154332	.157426	.160558	.166926	.173414	.180004	.186677
	.30	.131956	.137357	.143005	.145912	.148871	.151878	.154930	.158023	.161155	.167523	.174012	.180601	.187274
	.20	.132554	.137955	.143603	.146510	.149469	.152476	.155528	.158621	.161753	.168121	.174610	.181199	.187872
	.10	.133151	.138553	.144200	.147108	.150067	.153074	.156126	.159219	.162351	.168719	.175208	.181797	.188470
	0.00	.133749	.139151	.144798	.147706	.150665	.153672	.156723	.159817	.162949	.169317	.175805	.182395	.189068
	-.10	.134347	.139749	.145396	.148304	.151262	.154269	.157321	.160415	.163547	.169915	.176403	.182993	.189666
	-.20	.134945	.140346	.145994	.148901	.151860	.154867	.157919	.161012	.164144	.170512	.177001	.183590	.190263
	-.30	.135542	.140944	.146592	.149499	.152458	.155465	.158517	.161610	.164742	.171110	.177599	.184188	.190861
	-.40	.136140	.141542	.147189	.150097	.153056	.156063	.159115	.162208	.165340	.171708	.178196	.184786	.191459
40	.40	.127380	.133216	.139304	.142429	.145604	.148814	.152065	.155349	.158663	.165364	.172145	.178986	.185871
	.30	.127978	.133814	.139902	.143026	.146198	.149412	.152663	.155947	.159261	.165962	.172743	.179584	.186469
	.20	.128576	.134411	.140499	.143624	.146796	.150010	.153261	.156545	.159858	.166560	.173341	.180181	.187067
	.10	.129174	.135009	.141097	.144222	.147394	.150607	.153858	.157143	.160456	.167158	.173939	.180779	.187665
	0.00	.129772	.135607	.141695	.144820	.147991	.151205	.154456	.157740	.161054	.167755	.174536	.181377	.188262
	-.10	.130369	.136205	.142293	.145418	.148589	.151803	.155054	.158338	.161652	.168353	.175134	.181975	.188860
	-.20	.130967	.136802	.142890	.146015	.149187	.152401	.155652	.158936	.162250	.168951	.175732	.182573	.189458
	-.30	.131565	.137400	.143488	.146613	.149785	.152998	.156249	.159534	.162847	.169549	.176330	.183170	.190056
	-.40	.132163	.137998	.144086	.147211	.150383	.153596	.156847	.160132	.163445	.170147	.176927	.183768	.190653

15.0 YEAR HOLDING PERIOD
.300 EQUITY YIELD RATE
.750 LOAN RATIO

INTEREST RATE

TERM YEARS	APPR DEP	5.0	6.0	7.0	7.5	8.0	8.5	9.0	9.5	10.0	11.0	12.0	13.0	14.0
15	.40	.139297	.144073	.149020	.151557	.154134	.156752	.159410	.162106	.164840	.170419	.176141	.181997	.187982
	.30	.139895	.144670	.149618	.152154	.154732	.157350	.160007	.162704	.165438	.171017	.176738	.182595	.188580
	.20	.140493	.145268	.150216	.152752	.155330	.157948	.160605	.163301	.166036	.171615	.177336	.183193	.189178
	.10	.141090	.145866	.150813	.153350	.155928	.158545	.161203	.163899	.166633	.172213	.177934	.183791	.189776
	0.00	.141688	.146464	.151411	.153948	.156525	.159143	.161801	.164497	.167231	.172811	.178532	.184388	.190373
	-.10	.142286	.147062	.152009	.154546	.157123	.159741	.162398	.165095	.167829	.173408	.179130	.184986	.190971
	-.20	.142884	.147659	.152607	.155143	.157721	.160339	.162996	.165692	.168427	.174006	.179727	.185584	.191569
	-.30	.143481	.148257	.153205	.155741	.158319	.160937	.163594	.166290	.169024	.174604	.180325	.186182	.192167
	-.40	.144079	.148855	.153802	.156339	.158916	.161534	.164192	.166888	.169622	.175202	.180923	.186780	.192765
20	.40	.129089	.134266	.139658	.142431	.145255	.148126	.151044	.154007	.157014	.163151	.169443	.175876	.182438
	.30	.129687	.134864	.140256	.143029	.145852	.148724	.151642	.154605	.157612	.163749	.170040	.176474	.183036
	.20	.130285	.135461	.140853	.143627	.146450	.149322	.152240	.155203	.158209	.164346	.170638	.177071	.183634
	.10	.130883	.136059	.141451	.144225	.147048	.149919	.152837	.155801	.158807	.164944	.171236	.177669	.184232
	0.00	.131481	.136657	.142049	.144823	.147646	.150517	.153435	.156398	.159405	.165542	.171834	.178267	.184830
	-.10	.132078	.137255	.142647	.145420	.148244	.151115	.154033	.156996	.160003	.166140	.172431	.178865	.185427
	-.20	.132676	.137852	.143245	.146018	.148841	.151713	.154631	.157594	.160600	.166738	.173029	.179463	.186025
	-.30	.133274	.138450	.143842	.146616	.149439	.152310	.155229	.158192	.161198	.167335	.173627	.180060	.186623
	-.40	.133872	.139048	.144440	.147214	.150037	.152908	.155826	.158789	.161796	.167933	.174225	.180658	.187221
25	.40	.123210	.128715	.134465	.137426	.140441	.143508	.146623	.149785	.152991	.159526	.166207	.173017	.179940
	.30	.123807	.129312	.135063	.138024	.141038	.144105	.147221	.150383	.153589	.160123	.166805	.173615	.180538
	.20	.124405	.129910	.135660	.138621	.141637	.144703	.147819	.150981	.154187	.160721	.167403	.174213	.181135
	.10	.125003	.130508	.136258	.139219	.142234	.145301	.148417	.151579	.154785	.161319	.168000	.174811	.181733
	0.00	.125601	.131106	.136856	.139817	.142832	.145899	.149014	.152177	.155383	.161917	.168598	.175408	.182331
	-.10	.126199	.131703	.137454	.140415	.143430	.146497	.149612	.152774	.155980	.162515	.169196	.176006	.182929
	-.20	.126796	.132301	.138051	.141013	.144028	.147094	.150210	.153372	.156578	.163112	.169794	.176604	.183527
	-.30	.127394	.132899	.138649	.141611	.144625	.147692	.150808	.153970	.157176	.163710	.170391	.177202	.184124
	-.40	.127992	.133497	.139247	.142208	.145223	.148290	.151406	.154568	.157774	.164308	.170989	.177799	.184722
30	.40	.119483	.125270	.131321	.134436	.137607	.140828	.144098	.147413	.150768	.157591	.164543	.171603	.178753
	.30	.120081	.125868	.131919	.135034	.138205	.141426	.144696	.148010	.151366	.158189	.165141	.172201	.179351
	.20	.120679	.126466	.132517	.135632	.138802	.142024	.145294	.148608	.151964	.158787	.165739	.172799	.179948
	.10	.121276	.127064	.133115	.136230	.139400	.142622	.145892	.149206	.152562	.159384	.166336	.173397	.180546
	0.00	.121874	.127662	.133712	.136828	.139998	.143220	.146489	.149804	.153159	.159982	.166934	.173994	.181144
	-.10	.122472	.128259	.134310	.137425	.140596	.143817	.147087	.150401	.153757	.160580	.167532	.174592	.181742
	-.20	.123070	.128857	.134908	.138023	.141193	.144415	.147685	.150999	.154355	.161178	.168130	.175190	.182340
	-.30	.123667	.129455	.135506	.138621	.141791	.145013	.148283	.151597	.154953	.161776	.168728	.175788	.182937
	-.40	.124265	.130053	.136104	.139219	.142389	.145611	.148880	.152195	.155551	.162373	.169325	.176386	.183535
40	.40	.115221	.121473	.127996	.131344	.134743	.138186	.141669	.145188	.148738	.155918	.163184	.170513	.177890
	.30	.115819	.122071	.128594	.131942	.135340	.138784	.142267	.145786	.149336	.156516	.163781	.171111	.178488
	.20	.116417	.122669	.129192	.132540	.135938	.139381	.142865	.146383	.149934	.157114	.164379	.171708	.179086
	.10	.117015	.123267	.129790	.133138	.136536	.139979	.143462	.146981	.150532	.157712	.164977	.172306	.179683
	0.00	.117612	.123865	.130387	.133735	.137134	.140577	.144060	.147579	.151129	.158309	.165575	.172904	.180281
	-.10	.118210	.124462	.130985	.134333	.137731	.141175	.144658	.148177	.151727	.158907	.166172	.173502	.180879
	-.20	.118808	.125060	.131583	.134931	.138329	.141772	.145256	.148775	.152325	.159505	.166770	.174099	.181477
	-.30	.119406	.125658	.132181	.135529	.138927	.142370	.145853	.149372	.152923	.160103	.167368	.174697	.182074
	-.40	.120004	.126256	.132779	.136127	.139525	.142968	.146451	.149970	.153520	.160701	.167966	.175295	.182672

15.0 YEAR HOLDING PERIOD
.300 EQUITY YIELD RATE
.800 LOAN RATIO

INTEREST RATE

TERM YEARS	APPR DEP	5.0	6.0	7.0	7.5	8.0	8.5	9.0	9.5	10.0	11.0	12.0	13.0	14.0
15	.40	.128743	.133837	.139114	.141820	.144569	.147362	.150196	.153072	.155989	.161940	.168043	.174290	.180674
	.30	.129341	.134435	.139712	.142418	.145167	.147959	.150794	.153670	.156587	.162538	.168641	.174888	.181272
	.20	.129938	.135032	.140310	.143015	.145765	.148557	.151392	.154268	.157184	.163136	.169238	.175485	.181869
	.10	.130536	.135630	.140908	.143613	.146363	.149155	.151990	.154866	.157782	.163733	.169836	.176083	.182467
	0.00	.131134	.136228	.141505	.144211	.146960	.149753	.152587	.155463	.158380	.164331	.170434	.176681	.183065
	-.10	.131732	.136826	.142103	.144809	.147558	.150351	.153185	.156061	.158978	.164929	.171032	.177279	.183663
	-.20	.132330	.137424	.142701	.145407	.148156	.150948	.153783	.156659	.159575	.165527	.171629	.177877	.184261
	-.30	.132927	.138021	.143299	.146004	.148754	.151546	.154381	.157257	.160173	.166124	.172227	.178474	.184858
	-.40	.133525	.138619	.143896	.146602	.149351	.152144	.154978	.157854	.160771	.166722	.172825	.179072	.185456
20	.40	.117855	.123376	.129128	.132086	.135098	.138161	.141273	.144434	.147641	.154187	.160898	.167760	.174760
	.30	.118453	.123974	.129726	.132684	.135695	.138758	.141871	.145032	.148239	.154785	.161496	.168358	.175358
	.20	.119050	.124572	.130323	.133282	.136293	.139356	.142469	.145629	.148836	.155383	.162094	.168956	.175956
	.10	.119648	.125170	.130921	.133880	.136891	.139954	.143066	.146227	.149434	.155980	.162691	.169554	.176554
	0.00	.120246	.125767	.131519	.134477	.137489	.140552	.143664	.146825	.150032	.156578	.163289	.170151	.177152
	-.10	.120844	.126365	.132117	.135075	.138087	.141149	.144262	.147423	.150630	.157176	.163887	.170749	.177752
	-.20	.121442	.126963	.132714	.135673	.138684	.141747	.144860	.148020	.151227	.157774	.164485	.171347	.178347
	-.30	.122039	.127561	.133312	.136271	.139282	.142345	.145458	.148618	.151825	.158371	.165083	.171945	.178945
	-.40	.122637	.128158	.133910	.136868	.139880	.142943	.146055	.149216	.152423	.158969	.165680	.172543	.179543
25	.40	.111583	.117455	.123589	.126747	.129963	.133234	.136558	.139931	.143350	.150320	.157447	.164711	.172095
	.30	.112181	.118053	.124186	.127345	.130561	.133832	.137155	.140528	.143948	.150918	.158045	.165309	.172693
	.20	.112779	.118650	.124784	.127943	.131159	.134430	.137753	.141126	.144546	.151516	.158642	.165907	.173291
	.10	.113376	.119248	.125382	.128540	.131757	.135028	.138351	.141724	.145144	.152114	.159240	.166504	.173889
	0.00	.113974	.119846	.125980	.129138	.132354	.135625	.138949	.142322	.145741	.152711	.159838	.167102	.174486
	-.10	.114572	.120444	.126577	.129736	.132952	.136223	.139547	.142919	.146339	.153309	.160436	.167700	.175084
	-.20	.115170	.121042	.127175	.130334	.133550	.136821	.140144	.143517	.146937	.153907	.161033	.168298	.175682
	-.30	.115768	.121639	.127773	.130931	.134148	.137419	.140742	.144115	.147535	.154505	.161631	.168896	.176280
	-.40	.116365	.122237	.128371	.131529	.134745	.138017	.141340	.144713	.148133	.155102	.162229	.169493	.176878
30	.40	.107608	.113781	.120235	.123558	.126940	.130376	.133864	.137400	.140979	.148257	.155672	.163203	.170829
	.30	.108206	.114379	.120833	.124156	.127538	.130974	.134462	.137997	.141577	.148854	.156270	.163801	.171427
	.20	.108803	.114977	.121431	.124754	.128135	.131572	.135060	.138595	.142174	.149452	.156868	.164398	.172025
	.10	.109401	.115575	.122029	.125352	.128733	.132170	.135658	.139193	.142772	.150050	.157465	.164996	.172623
	0.00	.109999	.116172	.122627	.125949	.129331	.132768	.136255	.139791	.143370	.150648	.158063	.165594	.173220
	-.10	.110597	.116770	.123225	.126547	.129929	.133365	.136853	.140388	.143968	.151245	.158661	.166192	.173818
	-.20	.111195	.117368	.123822	.127145	.130527	.133963	.137451	.140986	.144566	.151843	.159259	.166790	.174416
	-.30	.111792	.117966	.124420	.127743	.131124	.134561	.138049	.141584	.145163	.152441	.159857	.167387	.175014
	-.40	.112390	.118563	.125018	.128341	.131722	.135159	.138646	.142182	.145761	.153039	.160454	.167985	.175611
40	.40	.103062	.109731	.116689	.120260	.123885	.127558	.131273	.135026	.138813	.146472	.154222	.162040	.169909
	.30	.103660	.110329	.117287	.120858	.124483	.128155	.131871	.135624	.139411	.147070	.154820	.162638	.170507
	.20	.104258	.110927	.117884	.121456	.125080	.128753	.132469	.136222	.140009	.147668	.155417	.163235	.171104
	.10	.104855	.111524	.118482	.122053	.125678	.129351	.133066	.136820	.140607	.148266	.156015	.163833	.171702
	0.00	.105453	.112122	.119080	.122651	.126276	.129949	.133664	.137418	.141205	.148863	.156613	.164431	.172300
	-.10	.106051	.112720	.119678	.123249	.126874	.130546	.134262	.138015	.141802	.149461	.157211	.165029	.172898
	-.20	.106648	.113318	.120275	.123847	.127471	.131144	.134860	.138613	.142400	.150059	.157808	.165626	.173496
	-.30	.107247	.113915	.120873	.124444	.128069	.131742	.135457	.139211	.142998	.150657	.158406	.166224	.174093
	-.40	.107844	.114513	.121471	.125042	.128667	.132340	.136055	.139809	.143596	.151255	.159004	.166822	.174691

15.0 YEAR HOLDING PERIOD
.300 EQUITY YIELD RATE
.900 LOAN RATIO

INTEREST RATE

TERM YEARS	APPR DEP	5.0	6.0	7.0	7.5	8.0	8.5	9.0	9.5	10.0	11.0	12.0	13.0	14.0
15	.40	.107635	.113365	.119302	.122346	.125439	.128581	.131770	.135005	.138286	.144981	.151847	.158875	.166057
	.30	.108232	.113963	.119900	.122944	.126037	.129179	.132367	.135603	.138884	.145579	.152445	.159473	.166655
	.20	.108830	.114561	.120498	.123542	.126635	.129776	.132965	.136201	.139482	.146177	.153043	.160071	.167253
	.10	.109428	.115159	.121096	.124140	.127233	.130374	.133563	.136798	.140080	.146775	.153640	.160668	.167850
	0.00	.110026	.115757	.121693	.124737	.127830	.130972	.134161	.137396	.140677	.147372	.154238	.161266	.168448
	-.10	.110623	.116354	.122291	.125335	.128428	.131570	.134759	.137994	.141275	.147970	.154836	.161864	.169046
	-.20	.111221	.116952	.122889	.125933	.129026	.132167	.135356	.138592	.141873	.148568	.155434	.162462	.169644
	-.30	.111819	.117550	.123487	.126531	.129624	.132765	.135954	.139190	.142471	.149166	.156031	.163059	.170241
	-.40	.112417	.118148	.124085	.127128	.130222	.133363	.136552	.139787	.143068	.149764	.156629	.163657	.170839
20	.40	.095386	.101597	.108068	.111396	.114784	.118229	.121731	.125287	.128895	.136259	.143809	.151529	.159404
	.30	.095983	.102195	.108665	.111994	.115382	.118827	.122329	.125885	.129493	.136857	.144407	.152127	.160002
	.20	.096581	.102793	.109263	.112591	.115979	.119425	.122927	.126482	.130090	.137455	.145005	.152725	.160600
	.10	.097179	.103390	.109861	.113189	.116577	.120023	.123524	.127080	.130688	.138053	.145603	.153323	.161198
	0.00	.097777	.103988	.110459	.113787	.117175	.120621	.124122	.127678	.131286	.138650	.146200	.153920	.161795
	-.10	.098374	.104586	.111057	.114385	.117773	.121218	.124720	.128276	.131884	.139248	.146798	.154518	.162393
	-.20	.098972	.105184	.111654	.114983	.118370	.121816	.125318	.128874	.132481	.139846	.147396	.155116	.162991
	-.30	.099570	.105782	.112252	.115580	.118968	.122414	.125916	.129471	.133079	.140444	.147994	.155714	.163589
	-.40	.100168	.106379	.112850	.116178	.119566	.123012	.126513	.130069	.133677	.141042	.148591	.156311	.164187
25	.40	.088330	.094936	.101836	.105389	.109007	.112687	.116426	.120221	.124068	.131909	.139927	.148099	.156406
	.30	.088928	.095533	.102434	.105987	.109605	.113285	.117024	.120819	.124666	.132507	.140524	.148697	.157004
	.20	.089525	.096131	.103032	.106585	.110203	.113883	.117622	.121416	.125264	.133105	.141122	.149295	.157602
	.10	.090123	.096729	.103629	.107183	.110801	.114481	.118220	.122014	.125861	.133702	.141720	.149892	.158199
	0.00	.090721	.097327	.104227	.107780	.111399	.115079	.118817	.122612	.126459	.134300	.142318	.150490	.158797
	-.10	.091319	.097925	.104825	.108378	.111996	.115676	.119415	.123210	.127057	.134898	.142915	.151088	.159395
	-.20	.091917	.098522	.105423	.108976	.112594	.116274	.120013	.123807	.127655	.135496	.143513	.151686	.159993
	-.30	.092514	.099120	.106020	.109574	.113192	.116872	.120611	.124405	.128252	.136094	.144111	.152283	.160591
	-.40	.093112	.099718	.106618	.110172	.113790	.117470	.121208	.125003	.128850	.136691	.144709	.152881	.161188
30	.40	.083858	.090803	.098064	.101802	.105606	.109472	.113396	.117373	.121400	.129588	.137930	.146402	.154982
	.30	.084456	.091401	.098662	.102400	.106204	.110070	.113994	.117971	.121998	.130185	.138528	.147000	.155579
	.20	.085053	.091998	.099259	.102998	.106802	.110668	.114592	.118569	.122596	.130783	.139126	.147598	.156177
	.10	.085651	.092596	.099857	.103595	.107400	.111266	.115189	.119167	.123194	.131381	.139724	.148195	.156775
	0.00	.086249	.093194	.100455	.104193	.107997	.111864	.115787	.119764	.123791	.131979	.140321	.148793	.157373
	-.10	.086847	.093792	.101053	.104791	.108595	.112461	.116385	.120362	.124389	.132576	.140919	.149391	.157971
	-.20	.087444	.094389	.101650	.105389	.109193	.113059	.116983	.120960	.124987	.133174	.141517	.149989	.158568
	-.30	.088042	.094987	.102248	.105986	.109791	.113657	.117581	.121558	.125585	.133772	.142114	.150587	.159166
	-.40	.088640	.095585	.102846	.106584	.110389	.114255	.118178	.122156	.126182	.134370	.142712	.151184	.159764
40	.40	.078744	.086246	.094074	.098091	.102169	.106301	.110481	.114704	.118964	.127580	.136298	.145094	.153946
	.30	.079342	.086844	.094672	.098689	.102767	.106899	.111079	.115301	.119562	.128178	.136896	.145691	.154544
	.20	.079939	.087442	.095269	.099287	.103365	.107497	.111677	.115899	.120160	.128776	.137494	.146289	.155142
	.10	.080537	.088040	.095867	.099885	.103963	.108094	.112274	.116497	.120757	.129374	.138092	.146887	.155740
	0.00	.081135	.088637	.096465	.100483	.104560	.108692	.112872	.117095	.121355	.129971	.138690	.147485	.156337
	-.10	.081733	.089235	.097063	.101080	.105158	.109290	.113470	.117693	.121953	.130569	.139287	.148083	.156935
	-.20	.082330	.089833	.097660	.101678	.105756	.109888	.114068	.118290	.122551	.131167	.139885	.148680	.157533
	-.30	.082928	.090431	.098258	.102276	.106354	.110486	.114665	.118888	.123148	.131765	.140483	.149278	.158131
	-.40	.083526	.091029	.098856	.102874	.106951	.111083	.115263	.119486	.123746	.132362	.141081	.149876	.158728

```
15.0 YEAR HOLDING PERIOD
.400 EQUITY YIELD RATE
.600 LOAN RATIO
```

INTEREST RATE

TERM YEARS	APPR DEP	5.0	6.0	7.0	7.5	8.0	8.5	9.0	9.5	10.0	11.0	12.0	13.0	14.0
15	.40	.214349	.218170	.222128	.224157	.226219	.228313	.230439	.232596	.234784	.239247	.243824	.248510	.253298
	.30	.214608	.218429	.222387	.224416	.226478	.228572	.230698	.232855	.235042	.239506	.244083	.248768	.253557
	.20	.214867	.218687	.222645	.224675	.226737	.228831	.230957	.233114	.235301	.239765	.244342	.249027	.253815
	.10	.215126	.218946	.222904	.224933	.226995	.229090	.231216	.233373	.235560	.240023	.244601	.249286	.254074
	0.00	.215384	.219205	.223163	.225192	.227254	.229349	.231474	.233631	.235819	.240282	.244859	.249545	.254333
	-.10	.215643	.219464	.223422	.225451	.227513	.229607	.231733	.233890	.236078	.240541	.245118	.249804	.254591
	-.20	.215902	.219723	.223680	.225710	.227772	.229866	.231992	.234149	.236336	.240800	.245377	.250062	.254850
	-.30	.216161	.219981	.223939	.225969	.228031	.230125	.232251	.234408	.236595	.241059	.245636	.250321	.255109
	-.40	.216420	.220240	.224198	.226227	.228289	.230384	.232510	.234667	.236854	.241317	.245895	.250580	.255368
20	.40	.205472	.209571	.213842	.216039	.218276	.220552	.222865	.225215	.227599	.232467	.237459	.242565	.247775
	.30	.205731	.209829	.214100	.216298	.218535	.220811	.223124	.225474	.227858	.232726	.237718	.242824	.248034
	.20	.205990	.210088	.214359	.216557	.218794	.221070	.223383	.225732	.228117	.232984	.237977	.243083	.248293
	.10	.206248	.210347	.214618	.216815	.219053	.221329	.223642	.225991	.228375	.233243	.238235	.243341	.248552
	0.00	.206507	.210606	.214877	.217074	.219311	.221587	.223901	.226250	.228634	.233502	.238494	.243600	.248811
	-.10	.206766	.210865	.215136	.217333	.219570	.221846	.224159	.226509	.228893	.233761	.238753	.243859	.249069
	-.20	.207025	.211123	.215394	.217592	.219829	.222105	.224418	.226767	.229152	.234020	.239012	.244118	.249328
	-.30	.207283	.211382	.215653	.217851	.220088	.222364	.224677	.227026	.229410	.234278	.239270	.244377	.249587
	-.40	.207542	.211641	.215912	.218110	.220347	.222622	.224936	.227285	.229669	.234537	.239529	.244635	.249846
25	.40	.200358	.204703	.209245	.211586	.213971	.216397	.218863	.221367	.223906	.229085	.234384	.239789	.245287
	.30	.200617	.204962	.209504	.211845	.214229	.216656	.219122	.221625	.224165	.229344	.234643	.240048	.245546
	.20	.200876	.205221	.209763	.212104	.214488	.216914	.219380	.221884	.224424	.229603	.234902	.240307	.245804
	.10	.201135	.205479	.210022	.212363	.214747	.217173	.219639	.222143	.224683	.229861	.235161	.240566	.246063
	0.00	.201394	.205738	.210281	.212621	.215006	.217432	.219898	.222402	.224941	.230120	.235419	.240824	.246322
	-.10	.201652	.205997	.210539	.212880	.215265	.217691	.220157	.222661	.225200	.230379	.235678	.241083	.246581
	-.20	.201911	.206256	.210798	.213139	.215523	.217950	.220416	.222919	.225459	.230638	.235937	.241342	.246839
	-.30	.202170	.206514	.211057	.213398	.215782	.218208	.220674	.223178	.225718	.230897	.236196	.241601	.247098
	-.40	.202429	.206773	.211316	.213656	.216041	.218467	.220933	.223437	.225977	.231155	.236454	.241859	.247357
30	.40	.197117	.201683	.206463	.208927	.211435	.213986	.216577	.219204	.221865	.227280	.232803	.238416	.244104
	.30	.197376	.201942	.206722	.209186	.211694	.214245	.216836	.219463	.222124	.227539	.233062	.238675	.244363
	.20	.197635	.202201	.206981	.209444	.211953	.214504	.217094	.219722	.222383	.227798	.233321	.238934	.244622
	.10	.197894	.202459	.207240	.209703	.212212	.214763	.217353	.219980	.222642	.228057	.233579	.239192	.244881
	0.00	.198152	.202718	.207498	.209962	.212471	.215021	.217612	.220239	.222900	.228316	.233838	.239451	.245140
	-.10	.198411	.202977	.207757	.210221	.212729	.215280	.217871	.220498	.223159	.228574	.234097	.239710	.245398
	-.20	.198670	.203236	.208016	.210479	.212988	.215539	.218129	.220757	.223418	.228833	.234356	.239969	.245657
	-.30	.198929	.203494	.208275	.210738	.213247	.215798	.218388	.221015	.223677	.229092	.234615	.240228	.245916
	-.40	.199188	.203753	.208533	.210997	.213506	.216057	.218647	.221274	.223936	.229351	.234873	.240486	.246175
40	.40	.193411	.198353	.203520	.206176	.208873	.211609	.214377	.217176	.220002	.225720	.231511	.237357	.243245
	.30	.193670	.198612	.203779	.206435	.209132	.211867	.214636	.217435	.220260	.225979	.231770	.237616	.243504
	.20	.193929	.198871	.204038	.206693	.209391	.212126	.214895	.217694	.220519	.226238	.232028	.237875	.243762
	.10	.194187	.199130	.204297	.206952	.209649	.212385	.215154	.217953	.220778	.226496	.232287	.238133	.244021
	0.00	.194446	.199389	.204556	.207211	.209909	.212644	.215413	.218212	.221037	.226755	.232546	.238392	.244280
	-.10	.194705	.199647	.204814	.207470	.210167	.212902	.215671	.218470	.221296	.227014	.232805	.238651	.244539
	-.20	.194964	.199906	.205073	.207729	.210426	.213161	.215930	.218729	.221554	.227273	.233063	.238910	.244798
	-.30	.195223	.200165	.205332	.207987	.210685	.213420	.216189	.218988	.221813	.227531	.233322	.239169	.245056
	-.40	.195481	.200424	.205591	.208246	.210944	.213679	.216448	.219246	.222072	.227790	.233581	.239427	.245315

15.0 YEAR HOLDING PERIOD
.400 EQUITY YIELD RATE
.667 LOAN RATIO

INTEREST RATE

TERM YEARS	APPR DEP	5.0	6.0	7.0	7.5	8.0	8.5	9.0	9.5	10.0	11.0	12.0	13.0	14.0
15	.40	.193835	.198080	.202478	.204733	.207024	.209351	.211713	.214110	.216540	.221500	.226586	.231791	.237111
	.30	.194094	.198339	.202737	.204992	.207283	.209610	.211972	.214369	.216799	.221759	.226844	.232050	.237370
	.20	.194353	.198598	.202996	.205251	.207542	.209869	.212231	.214628	.217058	.222017	.227103	.232309	.237629
	.10	.194612	.198857	.203255	.205509	.207801	.210128	.212490	.214886	.217317	.222276	.227362	.232568	.237888
	0.00	.194871	.199116	.203513	.205768	.208059	.210386	.212748	.215145	.217576	.222535	.227621	.232827	.238147
	-.10	.195129	.199374	.203772	.206027	.208318	.210645	.213007	.215404	.217834	.222794	.227879	.233085	.238405
	-.20	.195388	.199633	.204031	.206286	.208577	.210904	.213266	.215663	.218093	.223053	.228138	.233344	.238664
	-.30	.195647	.199892	.204290	.206544	.208836	.211163	.213525	.215922	.218352	.223311	.228397	.233603	.238923
	-.40	.195906	.200151	.204549	.206803	.209094	.211421	.213784	.216180	.218611	.223570	.228656	.233862	.239182
20	.40	.183972	.188526	.193271	.195713	.198199	.200728	.203298	.205908	.208557	.213966	.219513	.225186	.230976
	.30	.184230	.188785	.193530	.195972	.198458	.200986	.203557	.206167	.208816	.214225	.219772	.225445	.231235
	.20	.184489	.189043	.193789	.196231	.198716	.201245	.203815	.206426	.209075	.214484	.220030	.225704	.231493
	.10	.184748	.189302	.194048	.196489	.198975	.201504	.204074	.206685	.209334	.214742	.220289	.225963	.231752
	0.00	.185007	.189561	.194306	.196748	.199234	.201763	.204333	.206943	.209592	.215001	.220548	.226222	.232011
	-.10	.185266	.189820	.194565	.197007	.199493	.202022	.204592	.207202	.209851	.215260	.220807	.226480	.232270
	-.20	.185524	.190078	.194824	.197266	.199752	.202280	.204851	.207461	.210110	.215519	.221066	.226739	.232529
	-.30	.185783	.190337	.195083	.197524	.200010	.202539	.205109	.207720	.210369	.215778	.221324	.226998	.232787
	-.40	.186042	.190596	.195342	.197783	.200269	.202798	.205368	.207978	.210628	.216036	.221583	.227257	.233046
25	.40	.178290	.183117	.188164	.190765	.193415	.196111	.198851	.201633	.204454	.210209	.216096	.222102	.228211
	.30	.178549	.183376	.188423	.191024	.193674	.196369	.199109	.201891	.204713	.210467	.216355	.222361	.228469
	.20	.178808	.183635	.188682	.191283	.193932	.196628	.199368	.202150	.204972	.210726	.216614	.222620	.228728
	.10	.179066	.183894	.188941	.191542	.194191	.196886	.199627	.202409	.205231	.210985	.216873	.222878	.228987
	0.00	.179325	.184152	.189200	.191800	.194450	.197146	.199886	.202668	.205489	.211244	.217132	.223137	.229246
	-.10	.179584	.184411	.189458	.192059	.194709	.197404	.200145	.202927	.205748	.211503	.217390	.223396	.229504
	-.20	.179843	.184670	.189717	.192318	.194967	.197663	.200403	.203185	.206007	.211761	.217649	.223655	.229763
	-.30	.180101	.184929	.189976	.192577	.195226	.197921	.200662	.203444	.206266	.212020	.217908	.223914	.230022
	-.40	.180360	.185188	.190235	.192836	.195485	.198181	.200921	.203703	.206525	.212279	.218167	.224172	.230281
30	.40	.174689	.179762	.185073	.187810	.190598	.193432	.196310	.199230	.202187	.208203	.214340	.220576	.226897
	.30	.174948	.180020	.185332	.188069	.190857	.193691	.196569	.199488	.202445	.208462	.214598	.220835	.227156
	.20	.175206	.180279	.185591	.188328	.191115	.193950	.196828	.199747	.202704	.208721	.214857	.221094	.227414
	.10	.175465	.180538	.185849	.188587	.191374	.194208	.197087	.200006	.202963	.208980	.215116	.221353	.227673
	0.00	.175724	.180797	.186108	.188846	.191633	.194467	.197346	.200265	.203222	.209239	.215375	.221612	.227932
	-.10	.175983	.181056	.186367	.189104	.191892	.194726	.197604	.200523	.203481	.209497	.215634	.221870	.228191
	-.20	.176241	.181315	.186626	.189363	.192150	.194985	.197863	.200782	.203739	.209756	.215892	.222129	.228450
	-.30	.176500	.181573	.186885	.189622	.192409	.195244	.198122	.201041	.203998	.210015	.216151	.222388	.228708
	-.40	.176759	.181832	.187143	.189881	.192668	.195502	.198381	.201300	.204257	.210274	.216410	.222647	.228967
40	.40	.170571	.176062	.181803	.184754	.187751	.190749	.193867	.196976	.200116	.206470	.212904	.219400	.225942
	.30	.170829	.176321	.182062	.185013	.188010	.191049	.194125	.197235	.200375	.206728	.213163	.219659	.226201
	.20	.171088	.176580	.182321	.185271	.188269	.191308	.194384	.197494	.200633	.206987	.213422	.219917	.226459
	.10	.171347	.176839	.182580	.185530	.188527	.191566	.194643	.197753	.200892	.207246	.213680	.220176	.226718
	0.00	.171606	.177097	.182838	.185789	.188786	.191825	.194902	.198012	.201151	.207505	.213939	.220435	.226977
	-.10	.171865	.177356	.183097	.186048	.189045	.192084	.195161	.198270	.201410	.207763	.214198	.220694	.227236
	-.20	.172123	.177615	.183356	.186307	.189304	.192343	.195419	.198529	.201669	.208022	.214457	.220953	.227494
	-.30	.172382	.177874	.183615	.186565	.189563	.192602	.195678	.198788	.201927	.208281	.214715	.221211	.227753
	-.40	.172641	.178133	.183874	.186824	.189821	.192860	.195937	.199047	.202186	.208540	.214974	.221470	.228012

15.0 YEAR HOLDING PERIOD
.400 EQUITY YIELD RATE
.700 LOAN RATIO

INTEREST RATE

TERM YEARS	APPR DEP	5.0	6.0	7.0	7.5	8.0	8.5	9.0	9.5	10.0	11.0	12.0	13.0	14.0
15	.40	.183580	.188037	.192655	.195022	.197428	.199871	.202352	.204868	.207420	.212628	.217967	.223434	.229020
	.30	.183839	.188296	.192914	.195281	.197687	.200130	.202611	.205127	.207679	.212886	.218226	.223692	.229278
	.20	.184098	.188555	.193173	.195540	.197946	.200389	.202869	.205386	.207938	.213145	.218485	.223951	.229537
	.10	.184356	.188814	.193431	.195799	.198204	.200648	.203128	.205645	.208197	.213404	.218744	.224210	.229796
	0.00	.184615	.189072	.193690	.196058	.198463	.200907	.203387	.205903	.208455	.213663	.219003	.224469	.230055
	-.10	.184874	.189331	.193949	.196316	.198722	.201165	.203646	.206162	.208714	.213921	.219261	.224728	.230314
	-.20	.185133	.189590	.194208	.196575	.198981	.201424	.203904	.206421	.208973	.214180	.219520	.224986	.230573
	-.30	.185392	.189849	.194466	.196834	.199240	.201683	.204163	.206680	.209232	.214439	.219779	.225245	.230831
	-.40	.185650	.190108	.194725	.197093	.199498	.201942	.204422	.206939	.209490	.214698	.220038	.225504	.231090
20	.40	.173223	.178005	.182988	.185551	.188162	.190817	.193515	.196256	.199038	.204717	.210541	.216498	.222577
	.30	.173482	.178264	.183247	.185810	.188420	.191076	.193774	.196515	.199297	.204976	.210800	.216757	.222836
	.20	.173741	.178522	.183505	.186069	.188679	.191334	.194033	.196774	.199556	.205235	.211059	.217016	.223095
	.10	.174000	.178781	.183764	.186328	.188938	.191593	.194292	.197033	.199814	.205494	.211318	.217275	.223354
	0.00	.174258	.179040	.184023	.186587	.189197	.191852	.194551	.197292	.200073	.205752	.211576	.217534	.223612
	-.10	.174517	.179299	.184282	.186845	.189455	.192111	.194809	.197550	.200332	.206011	.211835	.217792	.223871
	-.20	.174776	.179558	.184540	.187104	.189714	.192369	.195068	.197809	.200591	.206270	.212094	.218051	.224130
	-.30	.175035	.179816	.184799	.187363	.189973	.192628	.195327	.198068	.200849	.206529	.212353	.218310	.224389
	-.40	.175293	.180075	.185058	.187622	.190232	.192887	.195586	.198327	.201108	.206787	.212612	.218569	.224648
25	.40	.167257	.172326	.177626	.180356	.183138	.185969	.188846	.191767	.194730	.200772	.206954	.213260	.219674
	.30	.167516	.172585	.177884	.180615	.183397	.186228	.189105	.192026	.194989	.201031	.207213	.213519	.219933
	.20	.167775	.172844	.178143	.180874	.183656	.186486	.189363	.192285	.195247	.201289	.207472	.213777	.220191
	.10	.168034	.173102	.178402	.181132	.183915	.186745	.189622	.192543	.195506	.201548	.207730	.214036	.220450
	0.00	.168292	.173361	.178661	.181392	.184173	.187004	.189881	.192802	.195765	.201807	.207989	.214295	.220709
	-.10	.168551	.173620	.178919	.181650	.184432	.187263	.190140	.193061	.196024	.202066	.208248	.214554	.220968
	-.20	.168810	.173879	.179178	.181909	.184691	.187522	.190399	.193320	.196283	.202324	.208507	.214813	.221226
	-.30	.169069	.174137	.179437	.182168	.184950	.187780	.190657	.193578	.196541	.202583	.208766	.215071	.221485
	-.40	.169328	.174396	.179696	.182427	.185209	.188039	.190916	.193837	.196800	.202842	.209024	.215330	.221744
30	.40	.163476	.168803	.174380	.177254	.180180	.183157	.186179	.189244	.192349	.198666	.205109	.211658	.218294
	.30	.163735	.169061	.174638	.177513	.180439	.183415	.186438	.189503	.192608	.198925	.205368	.211917	.218553
	.20	.163994	.169320	.174897	.177771	.180698	.183674	.186696	.189761	.192866	.199184	.205627	.212175	.218812
	.10	.164252	.169579	.175156	.178030	.180957	.183933	.186955	.190020	.193125	.199443	.205886	.212434	.219071
	0.00	.164511	.169838	.175415	.178289	.181216	.184192	.187214	.190279	.193384	.199701	.206145	.212693	.219329
	-.10	.164770	.170097	.175674	.178548	.181474	.184450	.187473	.190538	.193643	.199960	.206403	.212952	.219588
	-.20	.165029	.170355	.175932	.178806	.181733	.184709	.187731	.190797	.193901	.200219	.206662	.213211	.219847
	-.30	.165288	.170614	.176191	.179065	.181992	.184968	.187990	.191055	.194160	.200478	.206921	.213469	.220106
	-.40	.165546	.170873	.176450	.179324	.182251	.185227	.188249	.191314	.194419	.200737	.207180	.213728	.220365
40	.40	.159152	.164918	.170946	.174044	.177191	.180382	.183613	.186878	.190174	.196846	.203602	.210422	.217292
	.30	.159411	.165177	.171205	.174303	.177450	.180641	.183872	.187137	.190433	.197105	.203861	.210681	.217550
	.20	.159670	.165436	.171464	.174562	.177709	.180900	.184130	.187396	.190692	.197363	.204120	.210940	.217809
	.10	.159928	.165695	.171723	.174821	.177968	.181159	.184389	.187654	.190951	.197622	.204378	.211199	.218068
	0.00	.160187	.165953	.171981	.175080	.178227	.181418	.184648	.187913	.191210	.197881	.204637	.211458	.218327
	-.10	.160446	.166212	.172240	.175338	.178485	.181676	.184907	.188172	.191468	.198140	.204896	.211716	.218585
	-.20	.160705	.166471	.172499	.175597	.178744	.181935	.185166	.188431	.191727	.198399	.205155	.211975	.218844
	-.30	.160964	.166730	.172758	.175856	.179003	.182194	.185424	.188690	.191986	.198657	.205413	.212234	.219103
	-.40	.161222	.166989	.173017	.176115	.179262	.182453	.185683	.188948	.192245	.198916	.205672	.212493	.219362

15.0 YEAR HOLDING PERIOD
.400 EQUITY YIELD RATE
.750 LOAN RATIO

INTEREST RATE

TERM YEARS	APPR DEP	5.0	6.0	7.0	7.5	8.0	8.5	9.0	9.5	10.0	11.0	12.0	13.0	14.0
15	.40	.168195	.172971	.177919	.180455	.183033	.185651	.188308	.191004	.193738	.199318	.205039	.210896	.216881
	.30	.168454	.173230	.178177	.180714	.183291	.185909	.188567	.191263	.193997	.199576	.205298	.211155	.217139
	.20	.168713	.173489	.178436	.180973	.183550	.186168	.188826	.191522	.194256	.199835	.205557	.211413	.217398
	.10	.168972	.173747	.178695	.181231	.183809	.186427	.189084	.191781	.194515	.200094	.205815	.211672	.217657
	0.00	.169231	.174006	.178954	.181490	.184068	.186686	.189343	.192039	.194774	.200353	.206074	.211931	.217916
	-.10	.169489	.174265	.179212	.181749	.184327	.186944	.189602	.192298	.195032	.200612	.206333	.212190	.218175
	-.20	.169748	.174524	.179471	.182008	.184585	.187203	.189861	.192557	.195291	.200870	.206592	.212448	.218433
	-.30	.170007	.174783	.179730	.182267	.184844	.187462	.190119	.192816	.195550	.201129	.206851	.212707	.218692
	-.40	.170266	.175041	.179989	.182525	.185103	.187721	.190378	.193074	.195809	.201388	.207109	.212966	.218951
20	.40	.157099	.162222	.167561	.170308	.173104	.175949	.178841	.181777	.184757	.190842	.197082	.203465	.209978
	.30	.157358	.162481	.167820	.170566	.173363	.176208	.179099	.182036	.185016	.191101	.197341	.203724	.210237
	.20	.157616	.162740	.168079	.170825	.173622	.176467	.179358	.182295	.185275	.191360	.197600	.203983	.210496
	.10	.157875	.162998	.168337	.171084	.173881	.176725	.179617	.182554	.185534	.191619	.197859	.204242	.210754
	0.00	.158134	.163257	.168596	.171343	.174139	.176984	.179876	.182813	.185793	.191877	.198118	.204500	.211013
	-.10	.158393	.163516	.168855	.171602	.174398	.177243	.180134	.183071	.186051	.192136	.198376	.204759	.211272
	-.20	.158651	.163775	.169114	.171860	.174657	.177502	.180393	.183330	.186310	.192395	.198635	.205018	.211531
	-.30	.158910	.164034	.169373	.172119	.174916	.177761	.180652	.183589	.186569	.192654	.198894	.205277	.211790
	-.40	.159169	.164292	.169631	.172378	.175175	.178019	.180911	.183847	.186828	.192913	.199153	.205535	.212048
25	.40	.150707	.156137	.161816	.164741	.167722	.170755	.173837	.176967	.180142	.186615	.193239	.199995	.206867
	.30	.150966	.156396	.162074	.165000	.167981	.171014	.174096	.177226	.180400	.186874	.193498	.200254	.207126
	.20	.151224	.156655	.162333	.165259	.168240	.171272	.174355	.177485	.180659	.187133	.193757	.200513	.207385
	.10	.151483	.156914	.162592	.165518	.168498	.171531	.174614	.177744	.180918	.187391	.194015	.200772	.207644
	0.00	.151742	.157173	.162851	.165777	.168757	.171790	.174873	.178002	.181177	.187650	.194274	.201030	.207902
	-.10	.152001	.157431	.163109	.166035	.169016	.172049	.175131	.178261	.181436	.187909	.194533	.201289	.208161
	-.20	.152260	.157690	.163368	.166294	.169275	.172308	.175390	.178520	.181694	.188168	.194792	.201548	.208420
	-.30	.152518	.157949	.163627	.166553	.169534	.172566	.175649	.178779	.181953	.188427	.195050	.201807	.208679
	-.40	.152777	.158208	.163886	.166812	.169792	.172825	.175908	.179037	.182212	.188685	.195309	.202066	.208937
30	.40	.146655	.152362	.158338	.161417	.164553	.167742	.170980	.174264	.177590	.184359	.191263	.198279	.205389
	.30	.146914	.152621	.158597	.161676	.164812	.168000	.171239	.174523	.177849	.184618	.191521	.198538	.205648
	.20	.147173	.152880	.158855	.161935	.165071	.168259	.171498	.174781	.178108	.184877	.191780	.198796	.205907
	.10	.147432	.153139	.159114	.162194	.165329	.168518	.171756	.175040	.178367	.185136	.192039	.199055	.206166
	0.00	.147691	.153398	.159373	.162452	.165588	.168777	.172015	.175299	.178626	.185394	.192298	.199314	.206424
	-.10	.147949	.153656	.159632	.162711	.165847	.169036	.172274	.175558	.178884	.185653	.192556	.199573	.206683
	-.20	.148208	.153915	.159891	.162970	.166106	.169294	.172532	.175816	.179143	.185912	.192815	.199832	.206942
	-.30	.148467	.154174	.160149	.163229	.166365	.169553	.172791	.176075	.179402	.186171	.193074	.200090	.207201
	-.40	.148726	.154433	.160408	.163488	.166623	.169811	.173050	.176334	.179661	.186430	.193333	.200349	.207460
40	.40	.142023	.148201	.154659	.157979	.161351	.164769	.168231	.171729	.175261	.182409	.189647	.196955	.204315
	.30	.142281	.148459	.154918	.158237	.161609	.165028	.168489	.171988	.175520	.182668	.189906	.197214	.204574
	.20	.142540	.148718	.155177	.158496	.161868	.165287	.168748	.172247	.175778	.182926	.190165	.197473	.204832
	.10	.142799	.148977	.155436	.158755	.162127	.165546	.169007	.172505	.176037	.183185	.190424	.197732	.205091
	0.00	.143058	.149236	.155694	.159014	.162386	.165805	.169266	.172764	.176296	.183444	.190683	.197990	.205350
	-.10	.143317	.149495	.155953	.159273	.162644	.166063	.169524	.173023	.176555	.183703	.190941	.198249	.205609
	-.20	.143575	.149753	.156212	.159531	.162902	.166322	.169783	.173282	.176815	.183961	.191200	.198508	.205868
	-.30	.143834	.150012	.156471	.159790	.163162	.166581	.170042	.173541	.177072	.184220	.191459	.198767	.206126
	-.40	.144093	.150271	.156730	.160049	.163421	.166840	.170301	.173799	.177331	.184479	.191718	.199025	.206385

```
15.0 YEAR HOLDING PERIOD
.400 EQUITY YIELD RATE
.800 LOAN RATIO RATE
```

INTEREST RATE

TERM YEARS	APPR DEP	5.0	6.0	7.0	7.5	8.0	8.5	9.0	9.5	10.0	11.0	12.0	13.0	14.0
15	.40	.152811	.157905	.163182	.165888	.168637	.171430	.174264	.177140	.180057	.186008	.192111	.198358	.204742
	.30	.153070	.158164	.163441	.166147	.168896	.171688	.174523	.177399	.180315	.186267	.192369	.198617	.205001
	.20	.153328	.158422	.163700	.166405	.169155	.171947	.174782	.177658	.180574	.186525	.192628	.198875	.205259
	.10	.153587	.158681	.163958	.166664	.169414	.172206	.175041	.177916	.180833	.186784	.192887	.199134	.205518
	0.00	.153846	.158940	.164217	.166923	.169672	.172465	.175299	.178175	.181092	.187043	.193146	.199393	.205777
	-.10	.154105	.159199	.164476	.167182	.169931	.172723	.175558	.178434	.181351	.187302	.193405	.199652	.206036
	-.20	.154363	.159458	.164735	.167440	.170190	.172982	.175817	.178693	.181609	.187561	.193663	.199911	.206294
	-.30	.154622	.159716	.164994	.167699	.170449	.173241	.176076	.178952	.181869	.187819	.193922	.200169	.206553
	-.40	.154881	.159975	.165252	.167958	.170707	.173500	.176334	.179210	.182127	.188078	.194181	.200428	.206812
20	.40	.140974	.146439	.152134	.155064	.158047	.161081	.164166	.167298	.170477	.176967	.183624	.190432	.197379
	.30	.141233	.146698	.152393	.155323	.158306	.161340	.164424	.167557	.170736	.177226	.183882	.190691	.197638
	.20	.141492	.146957	.152651	.155581	.158564	.161599	.164683	.167816	.170995	.177485	.184141	.190950	.197897
	.10	.141751	.147216	.152910	.155840	.158823	.161858	.164942	.168074	.171253	.177744	.184400	.191208	.198155
	0.00	.142009	.147474	.153169	.156099	.159082	.162116	.165201	.168333	.171512	.178003	.184659	.191467	.198414
	-.10	.142268	.147733	.153428	.156358	.159341	.162375	.165460	.168592	.171771	.178261	.184918	.191726	.198673
	-.20	.142527	.147992	.153687	.156617	.159600	.162634	.165718	.168851	.172030	.178520	.185176	.191985	.198932
	-.30	.142786	.148251	.153945	.156875	.159858	.162893	.165977	.169110	.172288	.178779	.185435	.192243	.199190
	-.40	.143045	.148509	.154204	.157134	.160117	.163152	.166236	.169368	.172547	.179038	.185694	.192502	.199449
25	.40	.134156	.139949	.146006	.149127	.152306	.155541	.158829	.162167	.165553	.172458	.179524	.186731	.194061
	.30	.134415	.140208	.146264	.149385	.152565	.155800	.159088	.162426	.165812	.172717	.179783	.186989	.194319
	.20	.134674	.140467	.146523	.149644	.152823	.156058	.159347	.162685	.166071	.172976	.180041	.187248	.194578
	.10	.134933	.140725	.146782	.149903	.153082	.156317	.159605	.162944	.166330	.173235	.180300	.187507	.194837
	0.00	.135191	.140984	.147041	.150162	.153341	.156576	.159864	.163202	.166589	.173494	.180559	.187766	.195096
	-.10	.135450	.141243	.147300	.150421	.153600	.156835	.160123	.163461	.166847	.173752	.180818	.188025	.195355
	-.20	.135709	.141502	.147559	.150679	.153859	.157094	.160382	.163720	.167106	.174011	.181077	.188283	.195613
	-.30	.135968	.141760	.147817	.150938	.154117	.157352	.160640	.163979	.167365	.174270	.181335	.188542	.195872
	-.40	.136227	.142019	.148076	.151197	.154376	.157611	.160899	.164238	.167624	.174529	.181594	.188801	.196131
30	.40	.129835	.135922	.142296	.145581	.148926	.152327	.155781	.159284	.162832	.170052	.177416	.184900	.192484
	.30	.130094	.136181	.142555	.145839	.149184	.152586	.156039	.159542	.163091	.170311	.177675	.185159	.192743
	.20	.130352	.136440	.142814	.146098	.149443	.152844	.156298	.159801	.163350	.170570	.177933	.185417	.193002
	.10	.130611	.136699	.143072	.146357	.149702	.153103	.156557	.160060	.163608	.170829	.178192	.185676	.193261
	0.00	.130870	.136957	.143331	.146616	.149961	.153362	.156816	.160319	.163867	.171087	.178451	.185935	.193519
	-.10	.131129	.137216	.143590	.146875	.150219	.153621	.157075	.160578	.164126	.171346	.178710	.186194	.193778
	-.20	.131388	.137475	.143849	.147133	.150478	.153880	.157333	.160836	.164385	.171605	.178968	.186452	.194037
	-.30	.131646	.137734	.144108	.147392	.150737	.154138	.157592	.161095	.164644	.171864	.179227	.186711	.194296
	-.40	.131905	.137993	.144366	.147651	.150996	.154397	.157851	.161354	.164902	.172123	.179486	.186970	.194555
40	.40	.124893	.131483	.138372	.141913	.145156	.149156	.152848	.156580	.160347	.167972	.175693	.183488	.191338
	.30	.125152	.131742	.138631	.142172	.145415	.149415	.153107	.156839	.160606	.168230	.175952	.183747	.191597
	.20	.125411	.132001	.138890	.142431	.145674	.149674	.153366	.157098	.160865	.168489	.176211	.184005	.191856
	.10	.125669	.132259	.139149	.142689	.145933	.149933	.153625	.157356	.161124	.168748	.176469	.184264	.192115
	0.00	.125928	.132518	.139407	.142948	.146192	.150192	.153884	.157615	.161382	.169007	.176728	.184523	.192373
	-.10	.126187	.132777	.139666	.143207	.146451	.150450	.154142	.157874	.161641	.169266	.176987	.184782	.192632
	-.20	.126446	.133036	.139925	.143466	.146710	.150709	.154401	.158133	.161900	.169524	.177246	.185041	.192891
	-.30	.126705	.133295	.140184	.143724	.146969	.150968	.154660	.158391	.162159	.169783	.177504	.185299	.193150
	-.40	.126963	.133553	.140443	.143983	.147228	.151227	.154918	.158650	.162417	.170042	.177763	.185558	.193408

459

15.0 YEAR HOLDING PERIOD
.400 EQUITY YIELD RATE
.900 LOAN RATIO

INTEREST RATE

TERM YEARS	APPR DEP	5.0	6.0	7.0	7.5	8.0	8.5	9.0	9.5	10.0	11.0	12.0	13.0	14.0
15	.40	.122041	.127772	.133709	.136753	.139846	.142988	.146177	.149412	.152693	.159388	.166254	.173282	.180464
	.30	.122300	.128031	.133968	.137012	.140105	.143246	.146435	.149671	.152952	.159647	.166513	.173541	.180723
	.20	.122559	.128290	.134227	.137271	.140364	.143505	.146694	.149930	.153211	.159906	.166772	.173800	.180981
	.10	.122818	.128549	.134486	.137529	.140623	.143764	.146953	.150188	.153469	.160165	.167030	.174058	.181240
	0.00	.123077	.128807	.134744	.137788	.140881	.144023	.147212	.150447	.153728	.160423	.167289	.174317	.181499
	-.10	.123335	.129066	.135003	.138047	.141140	.144282	.147471	.150706	.153987	.160682	.167548	.174576	.181758
	-.20	.123594	.129325	.135262	.138306	.141399	.144540	.147729	.150965	.154246	.160941	.167807	.174835	.182017
	-.30	.123853	.129584	.135521	.138565	.141658	.144799	.147988	.151224	.154505	.161200	.168065	.175093	.182275
	-.40	.124112	.129843	.135780	.138823	.141916	.145058	.148247	.151482	.154763	.161459	.168324	.175352	.182534
20	.40	.108726	.114873	.121280	.124576	.127932	.131346	.134816	.138340	.141916	.149218	.156706	.164365	.172181
	.30	.108984	.115132	.121539	.124835	.128191	.131605	.135074	.138598	.142175	.149477	.156965	.164624	.172440
	.20	.109243	.115391	.121798	.125094	.128450	.131863	.135333	.138857	.142434	.149735	.157224	.164883	.172698
	.10	.109502	.115650	.122056	.125353	.128708	.132122	.135592	.139116	.142692	.149994	.157482	.165142	.172957
	0.00	.109761	.115909	.122315	.125611	.128967	.132381	.135851	.139375	.142951	.150253	.157741	.165400	.173216
	-.10	.110019	.116167	.122574	.125870	.129226	.132640	.136110	.139634	.143210	.150512	.158000	.165659	.173475
	-.20	.110278	.116426	.122833	.126129	.129485	.132899	.136368	.139892	.143469	.150771	.158259	.165918	.173733
	-.30	.110537	.116685	.123091	.126388	.129744	.133157	.136627	.140151	.143727	.151029	.158517	.166177	.173992
	-.40	.110796	.116944	.123350	.126647	.130002	.133416	.136886	.140410	.143986	.151288	.158776	.166436	.174251
25	.40	.101055	.107572	.114386	.117897	.121474	.125113	.128812	.132568	.136377	.144145	.152094	.160201	.168448
	.30	.101314	.107831	.114644	.118156	.121732	.125372	.129071	.132826	.136636	.144404	.152353	.160460	.168706
	.20	.101573	.108090	.114903	.118414	.121991	.125631	.129330	.133085	.136895	.144663	.152611	.160719	.168965
	.10	.101832	.108348	.115162	.118673	.122250	.125889	.129588	.133344	.137153	.144922	.152870	.160978	.169224
	0.00	.102090	.108607	.115421	.118932	.122509	.126148	.129847	.133603	.137412	.145180	.153129	.161236	.169483
	-.10	.102349	.108866	.115680	.119191	.122767	.126407	.130106	.133862	.137671	.145439	.153388	.161495	.169742
	-.20	.102608	.109125	.115938	.119450	.123026	.126666	.130365	.134120	.137930	.145698	.153646	.161754	.170000
	-.30	.102867	.109384	.116197	.119708	.123285	.126924	.130623	.134379	.138188	.145957	.153905	.162013	.170259
	-.40	.103125	.109642	.116456	.119967	.123544	.127183	.130882	.134638	.138447	.146215	.154164	.162272	.170518
30	.40	.096194	.103042	.110212	.113908	.117671	.121497	.125383	.129324	.133316	.141438	.149722	.158142	.166674
	.30	.096452	.103301	.110471	.114166	.117929	.121756	.125641	.129582	.133574	.141697	.149981	.158400	.166933
	.20	.096711	.103560	.110730	.114425	.118188	.122015	.125900	.129841	.133833	.141956	.150240	.158659	.167192
	.10	.096970	.103818	.110989	.114684	.118447	.122273	.126159	.130100	.134092	.142215	.150498	.158918	.167451
	0.00	.097229	.104077	.111248	.114943	.118706	.122532	.126418	.130359	.134351	.142473	.150757	.159177	.167709
	-.10	.097488	.104336	.111506	.115202	.118965	.122791	.126677	.130617	.134609	.142732	.151016	.159436	.167968
	-.20	.097746	.104595	.111765	.115460	.119223	.123050	.126935	.130876	.134868	.142991	.151275	.159694	.168227
	-.30	.098005	.104854	.112024	.115719	.119482	.123309	.127194	.131135	.135127	.143250	.151534	.159953	.168486
	-.40	.098264	.105112	.112283	.115978	.119741	.123567	.127453	.131394	.135386	.143508	.151792	.160212	.168744
40	.40	.090634	.098048	.105798	.109781	.113828	.117930	.122084	.126282	.130520	.139098	.147784	.156553	.165385
	.30	.090893	.098307	.106057	.110040	.114086	.118189	.122342	.126541	.130779	.139356	.148043	.156812	.165644
	.20	.091152	.098565	.106316	.110299	.114345	.118448	.122601	.126799	.131038	.139615	.148302	.157071	.165902
	.10	.091411	.098824	.106575	.110558	.114604	.118707	.122860	.127058	.131296	.139874	.148560	.157330	.166161
	0.00	.091669	.099083	.106833	.110817	.114863	.118966	.123119	.127317	.131555	.140133	.148819	.157588	.166420
	-.10	.091928	.099342	.107092	.111075	.115122	.119224	.123378	.127576	.131814	.140391	.149078	.157847	.166679
	-.20	.092187	.099601	.107351	.111334	.115380	.119483	.123636	.127835	.132073	.140650	.149337	.158106	.166938
	-.30	.092446	.099859	.107610	.111593	.115639	.119742	.123895	.128093	.132331	.140909	.149595	.158365	.167196
	-.40	.092704	.100118	.107868	.111852	.115898	.120001	.124154	.128352	.132590	.141168	.149854	.158624	.167455

15.0 YEAR HOLDING PERIOD
.500 EQUITY YIELD RATE
.600 LOAN RATIO

INTEREST RATE

TERM YEARS	APPR DEP	5.0	6.0	7.0	7.5	8.0	8.5	9.0	9.5	10.0	11.0	12.0	13.0	14.0
15	.40	.255793	.259613	.263571	.265600	.267663	.269757	.271883	.274040	.276227	.280691	.285268	.289953	.294741
	.30	.255907	.259728	.263686	.265715	.267777	.269871	.271997	.274154	.276342	.280805	.285382	.290067	.294855
	.20	.256022	.259842	.263800	.265829	.267891	.269986	.272112	.274269	.276456	.280919	.285497	.290182	.294970
	.10	.256136	.259957	.263915	.265944	.268006	.270100	.272226	.274383	.276570	.281034	.285611	.290296	.295084
	0.00	.256250	.260071	.264029	.266058	.268120	.270215	.272341	.274498	.276685	.281148	.285725	.290411	.295199
	-.10	.256365	.260185	.264143	.266173	.268235	.270329	.272455	.274612	.276799	.281263	.285840	.290525	.295313
	-.20	.256479	.260300	.264258	.266287	.268349	.270443	.272569	.274726	.276913	.281377	.285954	.290640	.295428
	-.30	.256594	.260414	.264372	.266402	.268464	.270558	.272684	.274841	.277028	.281492	.286069	.290754	.295542
	-.40	.256708	.260529	.264487	.266516	.268578	.270672	.272798	.274955	.277143	.281606	.286183	.290869	.295656
20	.40	.246613	.250693	.254946	.257134	.259363	.261629	.263933	.266274	.268649	.273499	.278474	.283563	.288756
	.30	.246727	.250808	.255060	.257249	.259477	.261744	.264048	.266388	.268763	.273614	.278588	.283677	.288870
	.20	.246841	.250922	.255175	.257363	.259591	.261858	.264162	.266503	.268878	.273728	.278703	.283791	.288985
	.10	.246956	.251036	.255289	.257478	.259706	.261973	.264277	.266617	.268992	.273842	.278817	.283906	.289099
	0.00	.247070	.251151	.255404	.257592	.259820	.262087	.264391	.266732	.269107	.273957	.278931	.284020	.289214
	-.10	.247185	.251265	.255518	.257706	.259935	.262202	.264506	.266846	.269221	.274071	.279046	.284135	.289328
	-.20	.247299	.251380	.255633	.257821	.260049	.262316	.264620	.266960	.269336	.274186	.279160	.284249	.289443
	-.30	.247414	.251494	.255747	.257935	.260164	.262430	.264735	.267075	.269450	.274300	.279275	.284364	.289557
	-.40	.247528	.251609	.255861	.258050	.260278	.262545	.264849	.267189	.269565	.274415	.279389	.284478	.289672
25	.40	.241325	.245644	.250162	.252490	.254863	.257278	.259733	.262225	.264754	.269192	.275192	.280578	.286059
	.30	.241439	.245758	.250276	.252605	.254978	.257392	.259847	.262340	.264869	.270027	.275306	.280693	.286173
	.20	.241553	.245873	.250391	.252719	.255092	.257507	.259961	.262454	.264983	.270141	.275421	.280807	.286288
	.10	.241668	.245987	.250505	.252834	.255206	.257621	.260076	.262569	.265098	.270256	.275535	.280922	.286402
	0.00	.241782	.246102	.250619	.252948	.255321	.257736	.260190	.262683	.265212	.270370	.275650	.281036	.286516
	-.10	.241897	.246216	.250734	.253063	.255435	.257850	.260305	.262798	.265326	.270484	.275764	.281151	.286631
	-.20	.242011	.246330	.250848	.253177	.255550	.257965	.260419	.262912	.265441	.270599	.275878	.281265	.286745
	-.30	.242126	.246445	.250963	.253292	.255664	.258079	.260534	.263026	.265555	.270713	.275993	.281379	.286860
	-.40	.242240	.246559	.251077	.253406	.255779	.258193	.260648	.263141	.265670	.270828	.276107	.281494	.286974
30	.40	.237973	.242511	.247266	.249717	.252214	.254753	.257333	.259950	.262601	.267998	.273504	.279102	.284777
	.30	.238087	.242626	.247380	.249831	.252328	.254868	.257448	.260064	.262716	.268113	.273619	.279217	.284892
	.20	.238202	.242740	.247494	.249946	.252443	.254982	.257562	.260179	.262830	.268227	.273733	.279331	.285006
	.10	.238316	.242854	.247609	.250060	.252557	.255097	.257676	.260293	.262945	.268342	.273848	.279446	.285121
	0.00	.238431	.242969	.247723	.250175	.252672	.255211	.257791	.260408	.263059	.268456	.273962	.279560	.285235
	-.10	.238545	.243083	.247838	.250289	.252786	.255326	.257905	.260522	.263174	.268570	.274076	.279674	.285349
	-.20	.238660	.243198	.247952	.250404	.252901	.255440	.258020	.260637	.263288	.268685	.274191	.279789	.285464
	-.30	.238774	.243312	.248067	.250518	.253015	.255555	.258134	.260751	.263403	.268799	.274305	.279903	.285578
	-.40	.238888	.243427	.248181	.250632	.253129	.255669	.258249	.260866	.263517	.268914	.274420	.280018	.285693
40	.40	.234140	.239057	.244202	.246848	.249537	.252263	.255025	.257817	.260636	.266343	.272125	.277964	.283846
	.30	.234255	.239172	.244317	.246963	.249651	.252378	.255139	.257931	.260750	.266458	.272240	.278078	.283960
	.20	.234369	.239286	.244431	.247077	.249765	.252492	.255254	.258046	.260865	.266572	.272354	.278193	.284075
	.10	.234483	.239401	.244546	.247191	.249880	.252607	.255368	.258160	.260979	.266686	.272468	.278307	.284189
	0.00	.234598	.239515	.244660	.247306	.249994	.252721	.255483	.258274	.261094	.266801	.272583	.278422	.284303
	-.10	.234712	.239630	.244775	.247420	.250109	.252836	.255597	.258389	.261208	.266915	.272697	.278536	.284418
	-.20	.234827	.239744	.244889	.247535	.250223	.252950	.255711	.258503	.261322	.267030	.272812	.278651	.284532
	-.30	.234941	.239858	.245003	.247649	.250338	.253065	.255826	.258618	.261437	.267144	.272926	.278765	.284647
	-.40	.235056	.239973	.245118	.247764	.250452	.253179	.255940	.258732	.261551	.267259	.273041	.278879	.284761

15.0 YEAR HOLDING PERIOD
.500 EQUITY YIELD RATE
.667 LOAN RATIO

INTEREST RATE

TERM YEARS	APPR DEP	5.0	6.0	7.0	7.5	8.0	8.5	9.0	9.5	10.0	11.0	12.0	13.0	14.0
15	.40	.228708	.232953	.237351	.239606	.241897	.244224	.246586	.248983	.251413	.256372	.261458	.266664	.271984
	.30	.228823	.233068	.237465	.239720	.242011	.244338	.246700	.249097	.251528	.256487	.261573	.266779	.272099
	.20	.228937	.233182	.237580	.239835	.242126	.244453	.246815	.249212	.251642	.256601	.261687	.266893	.272213
	.10	.229051	.233296	.237695	.239949	.242240	.244567	.246929	.249326	.251756	.256716	.261802	.267007	.272327
	0.00	.229166	.233411	.237809	.240063	.242355	.244682	.247044	.249440	.251871	.256830	.261916	.267122	.272442
	-.10	.229280	.233525	.237923	.240178	.242469	.244796	.247158	.249555	.251985	.256945	.262031	.267236	.272556
	-.20	.229395	.233640	.238038	.240292	.242583	.244910	.247273	.249669	.252100	.257059	.262145	.267351	.272671
	-.30	.229509	.233754	.238152	.240407	.242698	.245025	.247387	.249784	.252214	.257174	.262259	.267465	.272785
	-.40	.229624	.233869	.238266	.240521	.242812	.245139	.247502	.249898	.252329	.257288	.262374	.267580	.272900
20	.40	.218508	.223042	.227767	.230199	.232675	.235193	.237753	.240354	.242993	.248382	.253909	.259564	.265334
	.30	.218622	.223156	.227882	.230313	.232789	.235308	.237868	.240468	.243107	.248496	.254024	.259678	.265449
	.20	.218737	.223271	.227996	.230428	.232903	.235422	.237982	.240583	.243222	.248611	.254138	.259793	.265563
	.10	.218851	.223385	.228111	.230542	.233018	.235537	.238097	.240697	.243336	.248725	.254253	.259907	.265678
	0.00	.218966	.223500	.228225	.230657	.233132	.235651	.238211	.240812	.243451	.248840	.254367	.260021	.265792
	-.10	.219080	.223614	.228339	.230771	.233247	.235765	.238326	.240926	.243565	.248954	.254481	.260136	.265906
	-.20	.219194	.223728	.228454	.230885	.233361	.235880	.238440	.241040	.243680	.249069	.254596	.260250	.266021
	-.30	.219309	.223843	.228568	.231000	.233476	.235994	.238554	.241155	.243794	.249183	.254710	.260365	.266135
	-.40	.219423	.223957	.228683	.231114	.233590	.236109	.238669	.241269	.243908	.249298	.254825	.260479	.266250
25	.40	.212632	.217431	.222451	.225039	.227675	.230358	.233086	.235855	.238665	.244397	.250263	.256248	.262337
	.30	.212747	.217546	.222566	.225153	.227790	.230473	.233200	.235970	.238780	.244511	.250377	.256362	.262452
	.20	.212861	.217660	.222680	.225268	.227904	.230587	.233315	.236084	.238894	.244625	.250492	.256477	.262566
	.10	.212976	.217775	.222795	.225382	.228019	.230702	.233429	.236199	.239009	.244740	.250606	.256591	.262680
	0.00	.213090	.217889	.222909	.225497	.228133	.230816	.233544	.236313	.239123	.244854	.250720	.256706	.262795
	-.10	.213204	.218004	.223024	.225611	.228247	.230930	.233658	.236428	.239238	.244969	.250835	.256820	.262909
	-.20	.213319	.218118	.223138	.225726	.228362	.231045	.233772	.236542	.239352	.245083	.250949	.256935	.263024
	-.30	.213433	.218233	.223252	.225840	.228476	.231159	.233887	.236657	.239466	.245198	.251064	.257049	.263138
	-.40	.213548	.218347	.223367	.225954	.228591	.231274	.234001	.236771	.239581	.245312	.251178	.257163	.263253
30	.40	.208908	.213951	.219233	.221957	.224732	.227553	.230420	.233327	.236273	.242270	.248388	.254608	.260913
	.30	.209023	.214065	.219348	.222072	.224846	.227668	.230534	.233442	.236388	.242384	.248502	.254722	.261028
	.20	.209137	.214180	.219462	.222186	.224960	.227782	.230649	.233556	.236502	.242499	.248616	.254837	.261142
	.10	.209251	.214294	.219577	.222301	.225075	.227897	.230763	.233671	.236617	.242613	.248731	.254951	.261257
	0.00	.209366	.214408	.219691	.222415	.225189	.228011	.230877	.233785	.236731	.242728	.248845	.255065	.261371
	-.10	.209480	.214523	.219806	.222529	.225304	.228126	.230992	.233900	.236846	.242842	.248960	.255180	.261486
	-.20	.209595	.214637	.219920	.222644	.225418	.228240	.231106	.234014	.236960	.242956	.249074	.255294	.261600
	-.30	.209709	.214752	.220035	.222758	.225533	.228354	.231221	.234128	.237075	.243071	.249189	.255409	.261714
	-.40	.209824	.214866	.220149	.222873	.225647	.228469	.231335	.234243	.237189	.243185	.249303	.255523	.261829
40	.40	.204650	.210113	.215830	.218770	.221757	.224787	.227855	.230957	.234089	.240431	.246855	.253343	.259878
	.30	.204764	.210228	.215944	.218884	.221871	.224901	.227969	.231071	.234204	.240545	.246970	.253457	.259993
	.20	.204878	.210342	.216059	.218998	.221986	.225016	.228084	.231186	.234318	.240660	.247084	.253572	.260107
	.10	.204993	.210456	.216173	.219113	.222100	.225130	.228198	.231300	.234433	.240774	.247199	.253686	.260222
	0.00	.205107	.210571	.216288	.219227	.222215	.225244	.228313	.231415	.234547	.240889	.247313	.253801	.260336
	-.10	.205222	.210685	.216402	.219342	.222329	.225359	.228427	.231529	.234661	.241003	.247427	.253915	.260450
	-.20	.205336	.210800	.216517	.219456	.222443	.225473	.228541	.231644	.234776	.241117	.247542	.254030	.260565
	-.30	.205451	.210914	.216631	.219571	.222558	.225588	.228656	.231758	.234890	.241232	.247656	.254144	.260679
	-.40	.205565	.211029	.216745	.219685	.222672	.225702	.228770	.231872	.235005	.241346	.247771	.254258	.260794

15.0 YEAR HOLDING PERIOD
.500 EQUITY YIELD RATE
.700 LOAN RATIO

INTEREST RATE

TERM YEARS	APPR DEP	5.0	6.0	7.0	7.5	8.0	8.5	9.0	9.5	10.0	11.0	12.0	13.0	14.0
15	.40	.215168	.219625	.224243	.226610	.229016	.231459	.233940	.236456	.239008	.244215	.249555	.255021	.260607
	.30	.215282	.219740	.224357	.226725	.229129	.231574	.234054	.236570	.239122	.244330	.249670	.255136	.260722
	.20	.215397	.219854	.224472	.226839	.229245	.231688	.234168	.236685	.239237	.244444	.249784	.255250	.260836
	.10	.215511	.219968	.224586	.226953	.229359	.231803	.234283	.236799	.239351	.244559	.249899	.255365	.260951
	0.00	.215626	.220083	.224700	.227068	.229474	.231917	.234397	.236914	.239466	.244673	.250013	.255479	.261065
	-.10	.215740	.220197	.224815	.227182	.229588	.232031	.234512	.237028	.239580	.244787	.250127	.255594	.261180
	-.20	.215854	.220312	.224929	.227297	.229703	.232146	.234626	.237143	.239695	.244902	.250242	.255708	.261294
	-.30	.215969	.220426	.225044	.227411	.229817	.232260	.234741	.237257	.239809	.245016	.250356	.255823	.261408
	-.40	.216083	.220541	.225158	.227526	.229931	.232375	.234855	.237372	.239923	.245131	.250471	.255937	.261523
20	.40	.204458	.209218	.214180	.216733	.219333	.221977	.224665	.227396	.230167	.235825	.241629	.247566	.253625
	.30	.204572	.209333	.214294	.216847	.219447	.222092	.224780	.227510	.230281	.235940	.241743	.247680	.253739
	.20	.204686	.209448	.214409	.216962	.219561	.222206	.224894	.227625	.230396	.236054	.241858	.247795	.253854
	.10	.204801	.209562	.214523	.217076	.219676	.222320	.225009	.227739	.230510	.236169	.241972	.247909	.253968
	0.00	.204915	.209676	.214638	.217191	.219790	.222435	.225123	.227853	.230625	.236283	.242087	.248024	.254083
	-.10	.205030	.209790	.214752	.217305	.219905	.222549	.225238	.227968	.230739	.236397	.242201	.248138	.254197
	-.20	.205144	.209905	.214867	.217420	.220019	.222664	.225352	.228082	.230853	.236512	.242316	.248253	.254312
	-.30	.205259	.210019	.214981	.217534	.220134	.222778	.225466	.228197	.230968	.236626	.242430	.248367	.254426
	-.40	.205373	.210134	.215095	.217649	.220248	.222893	.225581	.228311	.231082	.236741	.242544	.248482	.254541
25	.40	.198288	.203327	.208598	.211315	.214083	.216900	.219764	.222673	.225623	.231641	.237800	.244084	.250478
	.30	.198403	.203442	.208713	.211430	.214198	.217015	.219879	.222787	.225737	.231755	.237914	.244199	.250593
	.20	.198517	.203556	.208827	.211544	.214312	.217129	.219993	.222901	.225852	.231870	.238029	.244313	.250707
	.10	.198632	.203671	.208942	.211658	.214427	.217244	.220108	.223016	.225966	.231984	.238143	.244428	.250821
	0.00	.198746	.203785	.209056	.211773	.214541	.217358	.220222	.223130	.226081	.232098	.238258	.244542	.250936
	-.10	.198860	.203900	.209170	.211887	.214656	.217473	.220337	.223245	.226195	.232213	.238372	.244657	.251050
	-.20	.198975	.204014	.209285	.212002	.214770	.217587	.220451	.223359	.226310	.232327	.238487	.244771	.251165
	-.30	.199089	.204128	.209399	.212116	.214884	.217702	.220565	.223474	.226424	.232442	.238601	.244886	.251279
	-.40	.199204	.204243	.209514	.212231	.214999	.217816	.220680	.223588	.226538	.232556	.238716	.245000	.251394
30	.40	.194378	.199673	.205219	.208079	.210992	.213955	.216965	.220018	.223111	.229408	.235831	.242362	.248983
	.30	.194492	.199787	.205334	.208194	.211107	.214070	.217079	.220132	.223226	.229522	.235946	.242477	.249098
	.20	.194607	.199902	.205448	.208308	.211221	.214184	.217194	.220247	.223340	.229636	.236060	.242591	.249212
	.10	.194721	.200016	.205563	.208423	.211336	.214299	.217308	.220361	.223455	.229751	.236175	.242706	.249326
	0.00	.194836	.200130	.205677	.208537	.211450	.214413	.217423	.220476	.223569	.229865	.236289	.242820	.249441
	-.10	.194950	.200245	.205792	.208652	.211565	.214528	.217537	.220590	.223684	.229980	.236403	.242935	.249555
	-.20	.195065	.200359	.205906	.208766	.211679	.214642	.217652	.220705	.223798	.230094	.236518	.243049	.249670
	-.30	.195179	.200474	.206021	.208880	.211794	.214756	.217766	.220819	.223912	.230209	.236632	.243163	.249784
	-.40	.195294	.200588	.206135	.208995	.211908	.214871	.217880	.220934	.224027	.230323	.236747	.243278	.249899
40	.40	.189906	.195643	.201646	.204732	.207869	.211050	.214272	.217529	.220818	.227477	.234222	.241034	.247896
	.30	.190021	.195758	.201760	.204847	.207983	.211165	.214386	.217643	.220932	.227591	.234337	.241149	.248011
	.20	.190135	.195872	.201875	.204961	.208098	.211279	.214501	.217758	.221047	.227705	.234451	.241263	.248125
	.10	.190250	.195987	.201989	.205076	.208212	.211394	.214615	.217872	.221161	.227820	.234566	.241378	.248240
	0.00	.190364	.196101	.202103	.205190	.208327	.211508	.214730	.217987	.221276	.227934	.234680	.241492	.248354
	-.10	.190479	.196215	.202218	.205305	.208441	.211623	.214844	.218101	.221390	.228049	.234794	.241606	.248469
	-.20	.190593	.196330	.202332	.205419	.208556	.211737	.214958	.218216	.221505	.228163	.234909	.241721	.248583
	-.30	.190708	.196444	.202447	.205534	.208670	.211851	.215073	.218330	.221619	.228278	.235023	.241835	.248697
	-.40	.190822	.196559	.202561	.205648	.208785	.211966	.215187	.218445	.221734	.228392	.235138	.241950	.248812

15.0 YEAR HOLDING PERIOD
.500 EQUITY YIELD RATE
.750 LOAN RATIO

INTEREST RATE

TERM YEARS	APPR DEP	5.0	6.0	7.0	7.5	8.0	8.5	9.0	9.5	10.0	11.0	12.0	13.0	14.0
15	.40	.194855	.199631	.204578	.207115	.209693	.212310	.214968	.217664	.220398	.225978	.231699	.237556	.243541
	.30	.194970	.199745	.204693	.207229	.209807	.212425	.215082	.217779	.220513	.226092	.231813	.237670	.243655
	.20	.195084	.199860	.204807	.207344	.209921	.212539	.215197	.217893	.220627	.226207	.231928	.237785	.243770
	.10	.195199	.199974	.204922	.207458	.210036	.212654	.215311	.218007	.220742	.226321	.232042	.237899	.243884
	0.00	.195313	.200089	.205036	.207573	.210150	.212768	.215426	.218122	.220856	.226435	.232157	.238013	.243998
	-.10	.195428	.200203	.205151	.207687	.210265	.212883	.215540	.218236	.220971	.226550	.232271	.238128	.244113
	-.20	.195542	.200318	.205265	.207802	.210379	.212997	.215655	.218351	.221085	.226664	.232386	.238242	.244227
	-.30	.195656	.200432	.205380	.207916	.210494	.213112	.215769	.218465	.221199	.226779	.232500	.238357	.244342
	-.40	.195771	.200547	.205494	.208031	.210608	.213226	.215883	.218580	.221314	.226893	.232615	.238471	.244456
20	.40	.183380	.188481	.193797	.196532	.199318	.202151	.205031	.207957	.210926	.216988	.223207	.229568	.236059
	.30	.183495	.188595	.193911	.196647	.199432	.202265	.205146	.208071	.211040	.217103	.223321	.229682	.236174
	.20	.183609	.188710	.194026	.196761	.199547	.202380	.205260	.208186	.211155	.217217	.223435	.229797	.236288
	.10	.183723	.188824	.194140	.196876	.199661	.202494	.205375	.208300	.211269	.217332	.223550	.229911	.236403
	0.00	.183838	.188939	.194255	.196990	.199775	.202609	.205489	.208414	.211383	.217446	.223664	.230025	.236517
	-.10	.183952	.189053	.194369	.197105	.199890	.202723	.205603	.208529	.211498	.217561	.223779	.230140	.236632
	-.20	.184067	.189167	.194484	.197219	.200004	.202838	.205718	.208643	.211612	.217675	.223893	.230254	.236746
	-.30	.184181	.189282	.194598	.197333	.200119	.202952	.205832	.208758	.211727	.217789	.224008	.230369	.236861
	-.40	.184296	.189396	.194712	.197448	.200233	.203067	.205947	.208872	.211841	.217904	.224122	.230483	.236975
25	.40	.176770	.182169	.187817	.190727	.193693	.196712	.199780	.202896	.206057	.212505	.219104	.225837	.232688
	.30	.176885	.182284	.187931	.190842	.193808	.196826	.199895	.203011	.206172	.212619	.219219	.225952	.232802
	.20	.176999	.182398	.188045	.190956	.193922	.196941	.200009	.203125	.206286	.212734	.219333	.226066	.232917
	.10	.177113	.182512	.188160	.191071	.194037	.197055	.200124	.203239	.206401	.212848	.219448	.226181	.233031
	0.00	.177228	.182627	.188274	.191185	.194151	.197170	.200238	.203354	.206515	.212963	.219562	.226295	.233146
	-.10	.177342	.182741	.188389	.191300	.194266	.197284	.200352	.203468	.206629	.213077	.219676	.226410	.233260
	-.20	.177457	.182856	.188503	.191414	.194380	.197398	.200467	.203583	.206744	.213191	.219791	.226524	.233375
	-.30	.177571	.182970	.188618	.191529	.194494	.197513	.200581	.203697	.206858	.213306	.219905	.226639	.233489
	-.40	.177686	.183085	.188732	.191643	.194609	.197627	.200696	.203812	.206973	.213420	.220020	.226753	.233603
30	.40	.172581	.178253	.184196	.187261	.190382	.193556	.196781	.200052	.203366	.210112	.216995	.223992	.231086
	.30	.172695	.178368	.184311	.187375	.190496	.193671	.196895	.200166	.203481	.210227	.217109	.224107	.231200
	.20	.172809	.178482	.184425	.187489	.190611	.193785	.197010	.200281	.203595	.210341	.217224	.224221	.231315
	.10	.172924	.178597	.184540	.187604	.190725	.193900	.197124	.200395	.203710	.210456	.217338	.224336	.231429
	0.00	.173038	.178711	.184654	.187718	.190840	.194014	.197239	.200510	.203824	.210570	.217452	.224450	.231544
	-.10	.173153	.178825	.184769	.187833	.190954	.194129	.197353	.200624	.203939	.210684	.217567	.224565	.231658
	-.20	.173267	.178940	.184883	.187947	.191068	.194243	.197468	.200739	.204053	.210799	.217681	.224679	.231773
	-.30	.173382	.179054	.184998	.188062	.191183	.194357	.197582	.200853	.204167	.210913	.217796	.224793	.231887
	-.40	.173496	.179169	.185112	.188176	.191297	.194472	.197696	.200967	.204282	.211028	.217910	.224908	.232002
40	.40	.167790	.173936	.180367	.183675	.187035	.190444	.193895	.197385	.200909	.208043	.215271	.222569	.229922
	.30	.167904	.174051	.180482	.183789	.187150	.190558	.194010	.197500	.201024	.208158	.215385	.222684	.230036
	.20	.168018	.174165	.180596	.183903	.187264	.190673	.194124	.197614	.201138	.208272	.215500	.222798	.230150
	.10	.168133	.174279	.180711	.184018	.187379	.190787	.194239	.197729	.201252	.208387	.215614	.222913	.230265
	0.00	.168247	.174394	.180825	.184132	.187493	.190902	.194353	.197843	.201367	.208501	.215729	.223027	.230379
	-.10	.168362	.174508	.180940	.184247	.187607	.191016	.194468	.197957	.201481	.208616	.215843	.223142	.230494
	-.20	.168476	.174623	.181054	.184361	.187722	.191130	.194582	.198072	.201596	.208730	.215957	.223256	.230608
	-.30	.168591	.174737	.181168	.184476	.187836	.191245	.194696	.198186	.201710	.208844	.216072	.223370	.230723
	-.40	.168705	.174852	.181283	.184590	.187951	.191359	.194811	.198301	.201825	.208959	.216186	.223485	.230837

15.0 YEAR HOLDING PERIOD
.500 EQUITY YIELD RATE
.800 LOAN RATIO

INTEREST RATE

TERM YEARS	APPR DEP	5.0	6.0	7.0	7.5	8.0	8.5	9.0	9.5	10.0	11.0	12.0	13.0	14.0
15	.40	.174543	.179637	.184914	.187620	.190369	.193162	.195996	.198872	.201789	.207740	.213843	.220090	.226474
	.30	.174657	.179751	.185029	.187734	.190484	.193276	.196111	.198987	.201903	.207854	.213957	.220204	.226588
	.20	.174772	.179866	.185143	.187849	.190598	.193391	.196225	.199101	.202018	.207969	.214072	.220319	.226703
	.10	.174886	.179980	.185258	.187963	.190713	.193505	.196340	.199216	.202132	.208083	.214186	.220433	.226817
	0.00	.175001	.180095	.185372	.188078	.190827	.193619	.196454	.199330	.202247	.208198	.214301	.220548	.226932
	-.10	.175115	.180209	.185486	.188192	.190941	.193734	.196568	.199444	.202361	.208312	.214415	.220662	.227046
	-.20	.175230	.180324	.185601	.188307	.191056	.193848	.196683	.199559	.202475	.208427	.214529	.220777	.227161
	-.30	.175344	.180438	.185715	.188421	.191170	.193963	.196797	.199673	.202590	.208541	.214644	.220891	.227275
	-.40	.175458	.180552	.185830	.188535	.191285	.194077	.196912	.199788	.202704	.208656	.214758	.221005	.227389
20	.40	.162303	.167743	.173414	.176332	.179303	.182325	.185397	.188518	.191685	.198151	.204784	.211569	.218494
	.30	.162417	.167858	.173528	.176446	.179417	.182439	.185512	.188632	.191799	.198266	.204899	.211684	.218608
	.20	.162531	.167972	.173643	.176561	.179531	.182554	.185626	.188747	.191913	.198380	.205013	.211798	.218723
	.10	.162646	.168087	.173757	.176675	.179646	.182668	.185741	.188861	.192028	.198495	.205127	.211913	.218837
	0.00	.162760	.168201	.173872	.176789	.179760	.182783	.185855	.188975	.192142	.198609	.205242	.212027	.218952
	-.10	.162875	.168316	.173986	.176904	.179875	.182897	.185969	.189090	.192257	.198724	.205356	.212142	.219066
	-.20	.162989	.168430	.174101	.177018	.179989	.183012	.186084	.189204	.192371	.198838	.205471	.212256	.219181
	-.30	.163104	.168544	.174215	.177133	.180104	.183126	.186198	.189319	.192486	.198953	.205585	.212370	.219295
	-.40	.163218	.168659	.174329	.177247	.180218	.183241	.186313	.189433	.192600	.199067	.205700	.212485	.219410
25	.40	.155252	.161011	.167035	.170140	.173303	.176523	.179796	.183120	.186491	.193369	.200408	.207590	.214898
	.30	.155366	.161125	.167149	.170254	.173418	.176638	.179910	.183234	.186606	.193483	.200523	.207705	.215012
	.20	.155481	.161240	.167264	.170369	.173532	.176752	.180025	.183349	.186720	.193598	.200637	.207819	.215126
	.10	.155595	.161354	.167378	.170483	.173647	.176866	.180139	.183463	.186835	.193712	.200752	.207934	.215241
	0.00	.155710	.161469	.167493	.170598	.173761	.176981	.180254	.183578	.186949	.193827	.200866	.208048	.215355
	-.10	.155824	.161583	.167607	.170712	.173876	.177095	.180368	.183692	.187064	.193941	.200981	.208163	.215470
	-.20	.155939	.161698	.167721	.170826	.173990	.177210	.180483	.183806	.187178	.194056	.201095	.208277	.215584
	-.30	.156053	.161812	.167836	.170941	.174105	.177324	.180597	.183921	.187293	.194170	.201209	.208392	.215699
	-.40	.156167	.161926	.167950	.171055	.174219	.177439	.180712	.184035	.187407	.194285	.201324	.208506	.215813
30	.40	.150783	.156834	.163173	.166442	.169771	.173157	.176597	.180086	.183621	.190817	.198158	.205622	.213189
	.30	.150898	.156948	.163288	.166556	.169885	.173272	.176711	.180200	.183736	.190931	.198273	.205737	.213303
	.20	.151012	.157063	.163402	.166671	.170000	.173386	.176826	.180315	.183850	.191046	.198387	.205851	.213418
	.10	.151126	.157177	.163517	.166785	.170114	.173501	.176940	.180429	.183965	.191160	.198501	.205966	.213532
	0.00	.151241	.157292	.163631	.166900	.170229	.173615	.177055	.180544	.184079	.191275	.198616	.206080	.213647
	-.10	.151355	.157406	.163746	.167014	.170343	.173729	.177169	.180658	.184193	.191389	.198730	.206195	.213761
	-.20	.151470	.157521	.163860	.167128	.170458	.173844	.177283	.180773	.184308	.191503	.198845	.206309	.213876
	-.30	.151584	.157635	.163975	.167243	.170572	.173958	.177398	.180887	.184422	.191618	.198959	.206423	.213990
	-.40	.151699	.157750	.164089	.167357	.170687	.174073	.177512	.181001	.184537	.191732	.199074	.206538	.214104
40	.40	.145673	.152229	.159089	.162617	.166201	.169837	.173519	.177241	.181000	.188610	.196319	.204104	.211947
	.30	.145787	.152343	.159204	.162731	.166316	.169952	.173633	.177356	.181115	.188725	.196434	.204219	.212061
	.20	.145902	.152458	.159318	.162846	.166430	.170066	.173748	.177470	.181229	.188839	.196548	.204333	.212176
	.10	.146016	.152572	.159432	.162960	.166545	.170181	.173862	.177585	.181344	.188953	.196663	.204448	.212290
	0.00	.146131	.152687	.159547	.163075	.166659	.170295	.173977	.177699	.181458	.189068	.196777	.204562	.212405
	-.10	.146245	.152801	.159661	.163189	.166774	.170409	.174091	.177814	.181572	.189182	.196892	.204677	.212519
	-.20	.146359	.152916	.159776	.163303	.166888	.170524	.174206	.177928	.181687	.189297	.197006	.204791	.212634
	-.30	.146474	.153030	.159890	.163418	.167003	.170638	.174320	.178043	.181801	.189411	.197120	.204906	.212748
	-.40	.146588	.153145	.160005	.163532	.167117	.170753	.174434	.178157	.181916	.189526	.197235	.205020	.212862

15.0 YEAR HOLDING PERIOD
.500 EQUITY YIELD RATE
.900 LOAN RATIO

INTEREST RATE

TERM YEARS	APPR DEP	14.0	13.0	12.0	11.0	10.0	9.5	9.0	8.5	8.0	7.5	7.0	6.0	5.0
15	.40	.192340	.185158	.178130	.171265	.164570	.161288	.158053	.154864	.151723	.148630	.145586	.139649	.133918
	.30	.192455	.185273	.178245	.171379	.164684	.161403	.158167	.154979	.151837	.148744	.145700	.139763	.134032
	.20	.192569	.185387	.178359	.171494	.164798	.161517	.158282	.155093	.151952	.148858	.145815	.139878	.134147
	.10	.192694	.185616	.178474	.171608	.164913	.161746	.158396	.155207	.152180	.149087	.145929	.139992	.134261
	0.00	.192798	.185731	.178588	.171722	.165027	.161861	.158511	.155322	.152295	.149202	.146043	.140107	.134376
	-.10	.192913	.185845	.178703	.171837	.165142	.161975	.158625	.155436	.152409	.149316	.146158	.140221	.134490
	-.20	.193027	.185959	.178817	.171951	.165256	.162090	.158740	.155551	.152524	.149431	.146272	.140335	.134605
	-.30	.193141	.186074	.178931	.172066	.165371	.162204	.158854	.155665	.152638	.149545	.146387	.140450	.134719
	-.40	.193256	.186188	.179046	.172180	.165485	.162319	.158969	.155780	.152753	.149660	.146501	.140564	.134833
20	.40	.183363	.175573	.167939	.160478	.153202	.149640	.146129	.142673	.139273	.135930	.132648	.126268	.120148
	.30	.183477	.175687	.168054	.160592	.153317	.149754	.146244	.142787	.139387	.136045	.132762	.126383	.120262
	.20	.183592	.175802	.168168	.160706	.153431	.149868	.146358	.142902	.139502	.136159	.132877	.126497	.120377
	.10	.183706	.175916	.168283	.160821	.153546	.149983	.146472	.143016	.139616	.136274	.132991	.126612	.120491
	0.00	.183821	.176031	.168397	.160935	.153660	.150097	.146587	.143131	.139730	.136388	.133106	.126726	.120605
	-.10	.183935	.176145	.168512	.161050	.153775	.150212	.146701	.143245	.139845	.136503	.133220	.126841	.120720
	-.20	.184050	.176259	.168626	.161164	.153889	.150326	.146816	.143359	.139959	.136617	.133334	.126955	.120834
	-.30	.184164	.176374	.168740	.161279	.154003	.150441	.146930	.143474	.140074	.136731	.133449	.127070	.120949
	-.40	.184278	.176488	.168855	.161393	.154118	.150555	.147045	.143588	.140188	.136846	.133563	.127184	.121063
25	.40	.179317	.171096	.163017	.155097	.147360	.143567	.139828	.136146	.132524	.128965	.125471	.118695	.112216
	.30	.179431	.171211	.163131	.155212	.147475	.143681	.139942	.136260	.132638	.129079	.125586	.118809	.112330
	.20	.179546	.171325	.163245	.155326	.147589	.143796	.140057	.136375	.132752	.129193	.125700	.118923	.112445
	.10	.179660	.171440	.163360	.155441	.147703	.143910	.140171	.136489	.132867	.129308	.125815	.119038	.112559
	0.00	.179775	.171554	.163474	.155555	.147818	.144025	.140286	.136603	.132981	.129422	.125929	.119152	.112673
	-.10	.179889	.171669	.163589	.155670	.147932	.144139	.140400	.136718	.133096	.129537	.126044	.119267	.112788
	-.20	.180004	.171783	.163703	.155784	.148047	.144254	.140514	.136832	.133210	.129651	.126158	.119381	.112902
	-.30	.180118	.171898	.163818	.155898	.148161	.144368	.140629	.136947	.133325	.129766	.126272	.119496	.113017
	-.40	.180233	.172012	.163932	.156013	.148276	.144482	.140743	.137061	.133439	.129880	.126387	.119610	.113131
30	.40	.177395	.168882	.160485	.152226	.144131	.140154	.136229	.132359	.128550	.124804	.121127	.113995	.107188
	.30	.177509	.168997	.160600	.152341	.144246	.140268	.136343	.132474	.128664	.124919	.121242	.114110	.107303
	.20	.177624	.169111	.160714	.152455	.144360	.140383	.136457	.132588	.128779	.125033	.121356	.114224	.107417
	.10	.177738	.169226	.160828	.152569	.144474	.140497	.136572	.132702	.128893	.125148	.121471	.114339	.107531
	0.00	.177853	.169340	.160943	.152684	.144589	.140612	.136686	.132817	.129007	.125262	.121585	.114453	.107646
	-.10	.177967	.169455	.161057	.152798	.144703	.140726	.136801	.132931	.129122	.125377	.121700	.114568	.107760
	-.20	.178081	.169569	.161172	.152913	.144818	.140841	.136915	.133046	.129236	.125491	.121814	.114682	.107875
	-.30	.178196	.169683	.161286	.153027	.144932	.140955	.137030	.133160	.129351	.125605	.121928	.114797	.107989
	-.40	.178310	.169798	.161401	.153142	.145047	.141069	.137144	.133275	.129465	.125720	.122043	.114911	.108104
40	.40	.175997	.167175	.158416	.149744	.141182	.136954	.132766	.128624	.124534	.120501	.116532	.108815	.101439
	.30	.176112	.167289	.158531	.149858	.141297	.137068	.132880	.128739	.124648	.120616	.116647	.108929	.101553
	.20	.176226	.167404	.158645	.149972	.141411	.137183	.132995	.128853	.124763	.120730	.116761	.109044	.101668
	.10	.176341	.167518	.158760	.150087	.141526	.137297	.133109	.128967	.124877	.120844	.116876	.109158	.101782
	0.00	.176455	.167633	.158874	.150201	.141640	.137412	.133223	.129082	.124992	.120959	.116990	.109273	.101897
	-.10	.176570	.167747	.158989	.150316	.141755	.137526	.133338	.129196	.125106	.121073	.117105	.109387	.102011
	-.20	.176684	.167861	.159103	.150430	.141869	.137641	.133453	.129311	.125220	.121188	.117219	.109502	.102126
	-.30	.176799	.167976	.159218	.150545	.141984	.137755	.133567	.129425	.125335	.121302	.117334	.109616	.102240
	-.40	.176913	.168090	.159332	.150659	.142098	.137869	.133682	.129540	.125449	.121417	.117448	.109730	.102355

Appendix

Conversion of Simple Interest to Compound Interest
Computation of Compound Interest Factors with a Mini-Calculator
Multiple Interpolation Within the OAR Tables (Example)
Multiple Financing—15-Point Investment Analysis
Negative Cash Flow—15-Point Investment Analysis
Operating Statements Before and After Reconstruction (Example)

Conversion of Simple Interest to Compound Interest

Simple Interest (Annual Rate)	Compound Interest					
	5 yrs	10 yrs	15 yrs	20 yrs	25 yrs	30 yrs
3%	2 13/16%	2 11/16%	2 1/2%	2 3/8%	2 1/4%	2 3/16%
4	3 3/4	3 3/8	3 3/16	3	2 13/16	2 11/16
5	4 9/16	4 1/8	3 13/16	3 1/2	3 5/16	3 1/8
6	5 3/8	4 7/8	4 3/8	4	3 3/4	3 1/2
7	6 3/16	5 1/2	4 7/8	4 1/2	4 1/8	3 13/16
8	7	6 1/16	5 3/8	4 7/8	4 1/2	4 3/16
9	7 11/16	6 5/8	5 7/8	5 5/16	4 13/16	4 7/16
10	8 1/2	7 3/16	6 5/16	5 5/8	5 1/8	4 3/4
12	9 13/16	8 3/16	7 1/8	6 5/16	5 11/16	5 3/16
15	11 13/16	9 5/8	8 3/16	7 3/16	6 7/16	5 7/8
18	13 11/16	10 7/8	9 1/8	7 15/16	7 1/16	6 3/8
20	14 7/8	11 5/8	9 11/16	8 3/8	7 7/16	6 11/16
25	17 5/8	13 3/8	10 15/16	9 3/8	8 1/4	7 3/8
30	20 1/8	14 7/8	12 1/16	10 3/16	8 15/16	8
35	22 7/16	16 1/4	13	11	9 9/16	8 1/2
40	24 5/8	17 1/2	13 7/8	11 5/8	10 1/16	8 15/16
45	26 9/16	18 9/16	14 9/16	12 1/4	10 9/16	9 5/16
50	28 1/2	19 5/8	15 5/16	12 3/4	11	9 11/16
60	32	21 1/2	16 9/16	13 11/16	11 3/4	10 5/16
70	35 1/8	23 1/8	17 11/16	14 1/2	12 3/8	10 7/8
75	36 9/16	23 7/8	18 3/16	14 7/8	12 11/16	11 1/8
80	38	24 9/16	18 5/8	15 3/16	12 15/16	11 5/16
90	40 5/8	25 7/8	19 1/2	15 7/8	13 7/16	11 3/4
100	43 1/8	27 1/8	20 5/16	16 7/16	13 15/16	12 1/8

(Compound interest rates in the chart have been rounded to the nearest one-sixteenth of one percent.)

467

Rate of simple interest, converted to compound interest

- *Procedure:*
    a. Calculate the total percent of increase for the full time period.
    b. Divide *a* by the number of years in which the increase occurred. Quotient is the annual rate of simple interest.
    c. Change simple to compound interest by the Conversion Chart, interpolating if necessary.

Problem:
Wooded parcels of undeveloped land in Lake County were generally sold for $500 an acre ten years ago. Values continued to increase, and now the "going price" is $2,500 per acre. What has been the average rate of increase, compounded annually?

Solution:
    a. Amount of increase (per acre): $2,500 − $500 = $2,000
       Total percent of increase: $2,000 ÷ $500 = 4.0 or 400%
    b. Simple interest, annual rate of increase: 400% ÷ 10 years = 40%
    c. Rate of increase, compounded annually: 17½%
       (Note: A deposit of $500 would grow to $2,500 in 10 years in an account paying 17½% compounded annually.)

Notes:
— While the author has attempted in his textbooks to make compound interest simple, he has in one sense "reversed the field" in this chart by which simple interest is made compound. To be significant, growth in numbers should be expressed in terms of a compound rate, whether dealing with population increase, inflation, appreciation of a growth investment, et cetera.
— Statistical data can be misleading, if growth is expressed as a simple rate. For example, presume that school enrollment within a specified district has increased 150% in the past 10 years. Growth rate should not be interpreted as being 15% per year (150% ÷ 10 years). The Conversion Chart shows the rate to be 9 5/8%, compounded annually.
— Observe on any horizontal line of the table the decrease in rate as the term is extended. The time value of money is evident.
— If an investment doubles in value, has it actually generated earnings of 100%? The answer is yes only if the increase occurred in the first year of ownership. The pertinent question is not "Has the investment doubled in value?" Instead, ask "*How long* has it taken for the investment to double in value? What has been the compound rate of growth?" Answers can be read from the chart:

If an investment doubles in value—

    a. in 5 years, rate of simple interest is 20% (100% ÷ 5); however, rate of growth compounded annually is 14 7/8%.

    b. in 10 years, simple interest rate is 10%; conversion indicates rate of 7 3/16% compounded annually.

    c. in 20 years, simple interest rate is 5%; compound, 3½%.

— When either rate of simple interest or time period falls in an interval not given in the table, the analyst can calculate a close approximation, interpolating by simple proportion.

— For ease in interpolation and other calculations, express fractions appearing in the tables as decimals:

1/16 = .0625%	9/16 = .5625%
1/8 = .125	5/8 = .625
3/16 = .1875	11/16 = .6875
1/4 = .25	3/4 = .75
5/16 = .3125	13/16 = .8125
3/8 = .375	7/8 = .875
7/16 = .4375	15/16 = .9375
1/2 = .5	

To illustrate: 9 11/16% = .096875, or 9.6875%.

Computation of Compound Interest Factors with a Mini-Calculator

The six standard compound interest factors can be calculated readily at any interest rate for any period of time with a thirty-dollar pocket calculator that possesses a few basic capabilities. This can be done in a chain operation by pressing a few keys in specified sequence. It is not necessary to enter any figure into a memory bank or to record a number, clear the calculator, then reenter the figure subsequently in order to compute all six factors.

Specific procedures that follow have been prepared for the "Sharp Elsi 122." However, the basic patterns depicted can be adapted to other brands of mini-calculators. In addition to performing the four basic functions of arithmetic, the calculator should have the following characteristics or capabilities: floating decimal; constant multiplier and divisor; and ability to calculate a reciprocal, handle negative numbers, clear a minus sign, and perform chain operations. Slight changes from the programs that follow may be required, due to differences in circuitry between various makes. A bit of exploratory experimentation on the part of the user could be productive.

Direct calculation of factors is particularly advantageous to the analyst when dealing with a nontypical interest or yield rate, such as 9.6123%, or 120%. Computation of the factors eliminates the necessity of interpolation within the prepared compound interest and annuity tables or of extending the tables by extrapolation. Further, the calculations will be precise.

Following are symbols and abbreviations used in the subsequent programs:

FW 1: Future Worth Of 1 (Amount Of 1)
FW 1/P: Future Worth Of 1 Per Period
(Amount Of 1 Per Period)
SF: Sinking Fund
PW 1: Present Worth Of 1 (Reversionary Factor)
PW 1/P: Present Worth Of 1 Per Period
(Inwood Coefficient; Annuity Factor)
PR: Periodic Repayment (Partial Payment.;
Loan Amortization Factor)
i: Interest Rate

Route I: Calculate in order: FW 1, PW 1, PW 1/P, PR, SF, and FW 1/P.

Example: Compute each of the six factors at 9½%, interest compounded annually, for 10 years (periods). Use chain steps without removing and reentering any figure.

Solution: Follow in order each numbered step in each horizontal line. Take all lines in the sequence listed.

Steps in Calculation (enter number or press key):

	(1)	(2)	(3)	(4)	(5)	(6)	(7)	(8)	(9)	(10)	Factor Computed:
FW 1	1.095	×	=	=	=	=	×	=			2.4782276
PW 1	÷	=	=								.4035141
PW 1/P	−	1	=	÷	.095	=	÷	−	=	=	6.2787980
PR	÷	=	=								.1592661
SF	−	.095	=								.0642661
FW 1/P	÷	=	=								15.5602907

Note: If the number of periods is changed, only steps FW 1 (4) through (8) would be altered. Note that step FW 1 (1) is the FW 1 factor for year or period 1; FW 1 (3), for year or period 2; and so on. Step FW 1 (6) is the factor for year or period 5; Steps FW 1 (7) and (8) then *square* the 5 year factor, thereby calculating the factor for year or period 10. The same result could have been obtained by merely continuing to strike the "=" key from step FW 1 (6) on to 10 periods.

Route II: Calculate in order: PW 1, PW 1/P, PR, SF, and FW 1/P.

Example: Compute each of the five factors listed at 9½% interest compounded annually for 10 years (periods). Use chain steps only.

Solution: Follow in order each numbered step in each horizontal line. Take all lines in the sequence listed.

Steps in Calculation (enter number or press key):

	(1)	(2)	(3)	(4)	(5)	(6)	(7)	(8)	(9)	(10)	*Factor Computed:*
PW 1	1	÷	1.095	=	=	=	=	=	×	=	.4035141
PW 1/P	−	1	=	÷	.095	=	÷	−	=	=	6.2787980
PR	÷	=	=								.1592661
SF	−	.095	=								.0642661
FW 1/P	÷	=	=								15.5602907

Route III: Calculate in order: FW 1, FW 1/P, SF, PR, and PW 1/P.

Example: Compute each of the five factors listed at 9½% interest compounded annually for 10 years (periods). Use chain steps only.

Solution: Follow in order each numbered step in each horizontal line. Take all lines in the sequence listed.

Steps in Calculation (enter number or press key):

	(1)	(2)	(3)	(4)	(5)	(6)	(7)	(8)	*Factor Computed:*
FW 1	1.095	×	=	=	=	=	×	=	2.4782276
FW 1/P	−	1	=	÷	.095	=			15.5602907
SF	÷	=	=						.0642661
PR	+	.095	=						.1592661
PW 1/P	÷	=	=						6.2787980

Notes:
— Selection of Route I, II, or III, in any given situation, depends on the factor or factors sought. Calculate by means of the shortest, most direct procedure. It goes without saying that the analyst is not obligated to go full circuit on any of the three routes. He stops when he

has calculated the factors sought. To illustrate the most direct
course: If the student needs only the FW 1/P factor at any interest
rate for any given period of time, he should employ the program
outlined in Route III; for the second line of entries in the calculator
will compute the required factor.

— Refer to page 33 for an explanation of the principal functions of the
Compound Interest and Annuity Tables; pages 67 to 69 for interpolation within the tables, and pages 112 and 113 for extension of the
tables.

— Calculations used in Routes I, II, and III are based on the following
equations and relationships:

Equations of derivation:

$$FW\ 1 = (1 + i)^n$$

$$FW\ 1/P = \frac{(FW\ 1 - 1)}{i}$$

$$SF = \frac{i}{(FW\ 1 - 1)}$$

$$PW\ 1 = \frac{1}{FW\ 1}$$

$$PW\ 1/P = \frac{(1 - PW\ 1)}{i}$$

$$PR = \frac{i}{(1 - PW\ 1)}$$

Reciprocals:

FW 1 and PW 1
FW 1/P and SF
PW 1/P and PR

Many calculators are equipped with a reciprocal key: "1/x".
With less sophisticated calculators, the reciprocal of a number
already in the machine can be found by pressing the "÷" key
once and the "=" key twice.

Relationship between PR and SF factors:

$$SF = PR - i$$
$$PR = SF + i$$

Multiple Interpolation Within the OAR Tables (Example)

Problem:

A loan commitment on a new shopping center is made as follows: loan
ratio, 65%; interest rate, 10½%; and term, 20 years, monthly payments to

amortize. The prospective purchaser projects a holding period of 10 years, 15% appreciation, and an equity yield rate of 12%. Net annual income is calculated to be $660,235. Compute an indicator of value by the mortgage-equity technique.

Solution:
   Summary and analysis of six significant variables:

Holding period: 10 years	Loan ratio: 65%
Equity yield rate: 12%	Loan interest rate: 10½%
Appreciation: 15%	Loan term: 20 years

Note that interpolation is required for three of the variables, in relating to the precomputed Overall Rates: 15% appreciation, 65% loan ratio, and 10½% loan interest rate. Interpolation for each of the three will be made to a midpoint:

	Appreciation	Loan Interest Rate		
		10%	11%	10½%
60% Loan Ratio:	+.10	.102560	.102350	
	+.20	.096862	.108048	
	+.15	.099711	.105199	.102455
70% Loan Ratio:	+.10	.100603	.101308	
	+.20	.094905	.107006	
	+.15	.097754	.104157	.100955
65% Loan Ratio:	+.15			.101705

   OAR by multiple interpolation is .101705.
   Indicated value: $660,235 ÷ .101705 = $6,491,667

Check: How accurate is the OAR of .101705, arrived at by multiple interpolation? A precise calculation by a longer route using the compound interest tables gives an OAR of .1016923. (See procedure, page 73.) Using the computed OAR in the problem:
   Value = $660,235 ÷ .1016923
       = $6,492,478
The slight difference of $811 is insignificant and would be "washed out" completely in rounding to a value conclusion of possibly $6,490,000.

Multiple Financing—15-Point Investment Analysis

• *Procedure:*
   If the subject property is financed by more than one loan, the regular

15-point analysis form can be used, with a few slight adaptations:

Item 4: List loan ratios and calculate separately the dollar amount of each loan.

Item 5: Enter loan constant for each loan, calculate annual debt service, and add to determine total debt service.

Item 9: For each loan, enter percent of loan unpaid at the end of the holding period, calculate dollar amounts, and find combined loan balance.

Problem:

Commercial property produces net annual income of $72,000 and can be financed on these terms:

Down payment: 10% of purchase price

First mortgage:

Loan ratio: 75%

Interest rate: 8%

Term: 25 years, monthly payments to amortize

Second mortgage:

Loan ratio: 15%

Interest rate: 9%

Term: 15 years, monthly payments to amortize

Projections include a 10-year holding period, 20% equity yield rate, and 15% appreciation within the holding period.

OAR is computed to be .09343. (See procedure, page 75.)

Calculate the indicated property value and prepare a 15-point analysis.

Solution:

Value = Income ÷ Rate

= $72,000 ÷ .09343

= $770,630

(See following Investment Analysis.)

Investment Analysis and Proof of Computations
Fifteen-Point Summary of Calculations

1.	Over-all Rate Selected from OAR Tables or Computed				.09343
2.	Property Value	$72,000 (INCOME)	÷	.09343 (OAR)	= $770,630
3.	Original Equity (Down Payment)	.10 (Equity Ratio)	x	$770,630 (Value)	= 77,063
4.	Amount of Loan (Original Principal)	1st: .75 2nd: .15 (Loan Ratio)	x x	770,630 770,630 (Value)	577,972 = 115,595

Investment Analysis and Proof of Computations
Fifteen-Point Summary of Calculations
(cont.)

#						
5.	Debt Service (Yearly Payments)	1st: .092618 2nd: .121712 (Loan Constant)	x	577,972 115,595 (Principal)	=	53,531 14,069 —————— 67,600
6.	Cash Flow (Annuity)	72,000 (Net Income)	−	67,600 (Debt Service)	=	4,400
7.	Debt Coverage Ratio	72,000 (Net Income)	÷	67,600 (Debt Service)	=	1.0651
8.	Rate of Current Yield On Equity	4,400 (Cash Flow)	÷	77,063 (Orig. Equity)	=	.0571
9.	Loan Balance (End Holding Period)	1st: .807633 2nd: .488606 (% Unpaid)	x	577,972 115,595 (Principal)	=	466,789 56,480 —————— 523,269
10.	Resale Value as % of Original Value	100 (Orig. Val. as %)	+ −	15 (% Appr/Dep)	=	115%
11.	Resale Value as a Dollar Amount	115% (Resale Val. as %)	x	770,630 (Original Value)	=	886,225
12.	Reversion, Net (Terminal Equity)	886,225 (Resale Value)	−	523,269 (Loan Balance)	=	362,956
13.	Deferred Yield (Amount)	362,956 (Reversion Net)	−	77,063 (Down Payment)	=	285,893
14.	Terminal Equity Ratio	362,956 (Reversion Net)	÷	886,225 (Resale Value)	=	.40955

15. Proof of Yield on Equity

Equity Yield Rate: __20%__ (Percent) Term in Years: __10__ (Holding Period)

Present Worth of 1 Per Period: __4.192472__ (PW 1/P) Present Worth of 1: __.161506__ (PW 1)

Equation of Proof

Present Worth = (__$4,400__ (Cash Flow) x __4.192472__ (PW 1/P)) + (__$362,956__ (Net Reversion) x __.161506__ (PW 1))

= __$18,447__ + __$58,620__ = __$77,067__

Final Check Target Figure = __$77,063__ (Down Payment, Orig. Equity)

__$77,063__ (Target Figure) − __$77,067__ (Present Worth) = __− $4__ (Rounding Adjustment)

Notes:
— The investor, using a high degree of leverage, realizes a high equity yield rate of 20%. Equity ratio increases from 10% at the time of

purchase to about 41% within the 10-year holding period, and equity grows from $77,063 to $362,956. Deferred yield dollars, generated by debt reduction and appreciation, may be freed for reinvestment by resale or refinancing.

— If the purchaser pays 25% down to a first mortgage for 75% of value, all other problem data remaining unchanged, the Overall Rate would be .108127 (see the OAR Tables and interpolate for 15% appreciation). Indicated value: $72,000 ÷ .108127 = $665,884, say $665,900. Investment value drops over $100,000, based on an equity yield requirement of 20%.

— Assume the investor purchases the property for $770,630 and pays 25% down to the first mortgage of $577,972, all other problem data unchanged. Rate of yield on equity drops to about 15.3%. (Refer to procedures, pages 81 to 84.)

Negative Cash Flow—15-Point Investment Analysis

The following analysis relates to the illustrative problem in the patterned procedure "Extrapolation in OAR Tables—100% Loan Ratio," pages 71 and 72.

As a matter of immediate reference, here is a summary of both problem and solution:

Holding Period: 10 years
Equity Yield Rate: 25%
Financing Data:
    Loan Ratio: 100%
    Term: 20 years, monthly payments to amortize
    Interest Rate: 9%
Appreciation/Depreciation: 0%
Net Annual Income: $7,940
OAR (by extrapolation): .09926
Value: $7,940 ÷ .09926 = $80,000 (rounded)

Investment Analysis and Proof of Computations
Fifteen-Point Summary of Calculations

1.	Over-all Rate Selected from OAR Tables or Computed					.09926
2.	Property Value	$7,940 (INCOME)	÷	.09926 (OAR)	=	$80,000 (rounded)
3.	Original Equity (Down Payment)	0	×	$80,000 (Value)	=	0
		(Equity Ratio)				
4.	Amount of Loan (Original Principal)	1.0 (Loan Ratio)	×	80,000 (Value)	=	80,000

Investment Analysis and Proof of Computations
Fifteen-Point Summary of Calculations
(cont.)

5. **Debt Service** (Yearly Payments)

$$\underline{.107967}_{\text{(Loan Constant)}} \times \underline{80,000}_{\text{(Principal)}} = \underline{8,637}$$

6. **Cash Flow** (Annuity)

$$\underline{7,940}_{\text{(Net Income)}} - \underline{8,637}_{\text{(Debt Service)}} = \underline{(697)}$$

7. **Debt Coverage Ratio**

$$\underline{7,940}_{\text{(Net Income)}} \div \underline{8,637}_{\text{(Debt Service)}} = \underline{.9193}$$

8. **Rate of Current Yield On Equity**

$$\underline{(697)}_{\text{(Cash Flow)}} \div \underline{0}_{\text{(Orig. Equity)}} = \underline{0}$$

9. **Loan Balance** (End Holding Period)

$$\underline{.710259}_{\text{(\% Unpaid)}} \times \underline{80,000}_{\text{(Principal)}} = \underline{56,821}$$

10. **Resale Value as % of Original Value**

$$\underline{100}_{\text{(Orig. Val. as \%)}} \stackrel{+}{_-} \underline{0}_{\text{(\% Appr/Dep)}} = \underline{100\%}$$

11. **Resale Value as a Dollar Amount**

$$\underline{100\%}_{\text{(Resale Val. as \%)}} \times \underline{80,000}_{\text{(Original Value)}} = \underline{80,000}$$

12. **Reversion, Net** (Terminal Equity)

$$\underline{80,000}_{\text{(Resale Value)}} - \underline{56,821}_{\text{(Loan Balance)}} = \underline{23,179}$$

13. **Deferred Yield** (Amount)

$$\underline{23,179}_{\text{(Reversion Net)}} - \underline{6,970}_{\text{(Total negative cash flow)}} = \underline{16,209}$$

14. **Terminal Equity Ratio**

$$\underline{23,179}_{\text{(Reversion Net)}} \div \underline{80,000}_{\text{(Resale Value)}} = \underline{.29}$$

15. **Proof of Yield on Equity**

Equity Yield Rate: __25__ (Percent)   Term in Years: __10__ (Holding Period)

Present Worth of 1 Per Period: __3.570503__ (PW 1/P)   Present Worth of 1: __.107374__ (PW 1)

Equation of Proof

Present Worth = (__(697)__ (Cash Flow) × __3.570503__ (PW 1/P)) + (__23,179__ (Net Reversion) × __.107374__ (PW 1))

= __(2,489)__ + __2,489__ = __0__

Final Check Target Figure = __0__ (Down Payment, Orig. Equity)

$$\underline{0}_{\text{Target Figure}} - \underline{0}_{\text{(Present Worth)}} = \underline{0}_{\text{(Rounding Adjustment)}}$$

Notes:
— Debt service exceeds net annual income, resulting in a negative cash flow of $697 per year. Such a situation is quite typical in a 100% loan ratio transaction. Here is where the "equity" comes in. The buyer

invests $697 out of pocket each year and builds up an equity by installments.

— Original equity or down payment of zero in Line 3 of the 15-point analysis becomes the "target figure" in Item 15. The negative present worth of the negative cash flow offsets the positive present worth of the net reversion, canceling out to the original zero equity.

— From the net reversion of $23,179 the investor recaptures his cash investment of $697 each year for 10 years, a total of $6,970. The remainder of $16,209 represents 25% yield on the series of annual investments. All yield is deferred until the time of reversion. The investment generates no current yield.

— If the investor obtains 100% financing, a yield rate of 25% or more is not unusual. Maximum leverage (the use of other people's money) makes it possible.

— As a further check on the analysis, calculate the growth of $697 invested at the end of each year for 10 years, at a yield rate of 25% compounded annually. (See procedure, page 114.)

    PR factor at 25% for 10 years is .280073.
    PR − i (PR minus the interest rate) is .280073 − .25, or .030073.
        $697 ÷ .030073 = $23,177.

As calculated, an annual investment of $697 would grow in 10 years at a yield rate of 25% to $23,177, which is within $2 of the computed net reversion of $23,179.

Operating Statements Before and After Reconstruction (Examples)

The following set of statements is taken from *Income Property Valuation*, by William N. Kinnard, Jr., Copyright 1971 by D.C. Heath and Company. The reconstructed statement demonstrates an exclusion of a number of inappropriate entries and "stabilized figures for the appropriate items."

Apartment Property Owner's Income Statement

Total Receipts:
  Rent Collections $395,400
  Parking and Concession Receipts   10,600
                                                    _____
                                                    $406,000

Expenses:
  Property Taxes: $ 54,652.00

Mortgage Payments:	219,517.20	
Management Fee (4%):	15,816.00	
Resident Manager—Salary:	11,400.00	
Water:	11,898.77	
Electricity:	611.43	
Legal Fees:	12,000.00	
Insurance Premium (3 years):	8,550.00	
Supplies:	1,000.00	
Pool and grounds maintenance:	4,500.00	
Advertising:	1,500.00	
Repairs and maintenance—building:	27,865.00	
Replace two range-oven combinations:	540.00	
Replace three refrigerators:	630.00	
Depreciation:	84,000.00	
	$454,480.40	− 454,480.40
Income for the year (loss):		−$ 48,480.40

Reconstruction of Income Property Operating Statement

Potential Gross Income:		
160 2-bedroom units, $180 per month:		$345,600
40 1-bedroom units, $140 per month:		67,200
		$412,800
Less Allowance for Vacancy and Income Loss:		− 20,976
Rent Collections		$391,824
Plus Other Income:		
Parking Space Rentals:	$ 9,600	
Concession Income::	1.140	10,740
	$10,740	
Effective Gross Income:		$402,564
Less Operating Expenses:		
Property Tax (.05 × $1,100,000	$55,000	
Insurance (1/3 × $8,550):	2,850	
Management (.04 × $391,824):	15,816	
Resident Manager ($5 × 12 × 190):	11,400	
Resident Manager—Apartment:	2,160	
Water ($5 × 200 × 12):*	12,000	
Electricity ($50 × 12):	600	
Supplies:	1,000	

*Subject property is a 200-unit apartment house.

Advertising and Legal Fees:	5,500	
Pool and Grounds Maintenance:	3,500	
Repairs and Maintenance:	30,000	
Replacements:**		
Dishwashers ($150/12 × 200):	2,500	
Refrigerators ($210/12 × 200):	3,500	
Disposals ($102/12 × 200):	1,700	
Stoves ($270/12 × 200):	4,500	−152,026
	$152,026	
Net Operating Income (annual forecast):		$250,538

Following examples are furnished courtesy of Sheldon A. Leveston, Analyst, Avon, Connecticut. Subject property is a 500-unit luxury apartment complex.

Apartment Property Owner's Operating Statement

Income:

Scheduled Rental Income:		$1,409,670
Miscellaneous Income:		9,920
Laundry Income:		11,904
Scheduled Gross Income:		$1,431,494
Less Vacancy and Credit Loss:		− 71,575
Gross Operating Income:		$1,359,919

Less Operating Expenses:

Property Taxes:	$102,819
Insurance:	20,800
Electricity:	123,000
Gas:	9,000
Water and Sewer:	23,000
Rubbish:	6,000
Other Payroll:	28,000
Legal:	2,600
Services:	1,905
Advertising:	8,300
Telephone (includes cable TV):	4,150
Professional Management:	53,567

**Useful life of appliances furnished is estimated to be 12 years; 1/12 estimated replacement cost is charged each year to stabilize the annual expense statement.

Repairs and Maintenance:	88,620		
Miscellaneous:	3,650		
	$475,411	–	475,411
Net Operating Income			$ 884,508

Percentage of Expenses to Gross Operating Income: 34.96%

Reconstruction of Apartment Operating Statement

Income:

Scheduled Rental Income:		$1,409,670
Miscellaneous Income:		9,920
Laundry Income:		11,904
Scheduled Gross Income:		$1,431,494
Less Vacancy and Credit Loss:		– 71,575
Gross Operating Income:		$1,359,919

Less Operating Expenses:

Property Taxes:	$150,951	
Insurance:	33,998	
Electitricity:	141,432	
Gas:	14,959	
Water and Sewer:	23,119	
Rubbish:	5,440	
Other Payroll:	81,595	
Accounting and Legal:	3,400	
Supplies:	2,040	
Services	2,040	
Advertising:	10,063	
Telephone:	1,632	
Professional Management:	68,000	
Resident Manager:	3,400	
Repairs and Maintenance:	38,078	
Pool and Recreation Area:	9,519	
Replacement Reserves:	27,200	
	$616,866	– 616,866
Net Operating Income		$ 743,053

Percentage of Expenses to Gross Operating Income: 45.36%

Note: Again, it must be emphasized: *Watch that bottom line!*
The owner's statement: $884,508 net operating income.
The reconstructed statement: $743,053 net operating income.
If each figure were capitalized by an Overall Rate of .105 (for purposes of illustration) the differences in value estimate would be substantial:

$884,508 ÷ .105 = $8,423,886
$743,053 ÷ .105 = $7,076,695

By Way of Reference

Textbooks:

Appraisal of Income Properties:
  Income Property Valuation, William N. Kinnard, Jr.; first edition, 1971; Lexington Books, D.C. Heath and Company, Lexington, Massachusetts.

Basic Appraisal:
  The Appraisal of Real Estate, A.I.R.E.A.; sixth edition, 1973; American Institute of Real Estate Appraisers, Chicago, Illinois.
  The Valuation of Real Estate, Alfred A. Ring; second edition, 1970; Prentice-Hall, Inc., Englewood Cliffs, New Jersey.

Mathematics of Valuation:
  Mini-Math For Appraisers, Irvin E. Johnson; first edition, 1972; International Association of Assessing Officers, Chicago, Illinois.

Real Estate Investment Analysis:
  Real Estate Investment Analysis, James R. Cooper; first edition, 1974; Lexington Books, D.C. Heath and Company, Lexington, Massachusetts.

Publications:

Analysis of Income and Expenses:
  Dollars and Cents of Shopping Centers, U.L.I., annual; Urban Land Institute, Washington, D.C.
  Income/Expense Analysis–Apartments, Condominiums, and Cooperatives, I.R.E.M, annual; Institute of Real Estate Management, Chicago, Illinois.
  Office Building Experience Exchange Report, annual; Building Owners and Managers Association, International, Chicago, Illinois.
  Rental Housing, quarterly; National Apartment Owners Association, Washington, D.C.

Compound Interest Tables (extensive range):
  Financial Compound Interest and Annuity Tables; Financial Publishing Company, Boston, Massachusetts.

Terminology and Sources of Information:
  Real Estate Appraisal Terminology, Byrl N. Boyce, for A.I.R.E.A. and S.R.E.A., first edition, 1975; Ballinger Publishing Company, Cambridge, Massachusetts.

Problems and Suggested Solutions

Selection of Overall Rates from OAR Tables:

For each set of variables given, select the proper OAR and identify the page where found.

	1	2	3	4	5
Holding period:	10 yrs.	15 yrs.	5 yrs.	10 yrs.	10 yrs
Equity yield rate:	15%	12%	14%	14%	25%
Loan ratio:	70%	66.7%	80%	80%	90%
Loan term:	25 yrs.	20 yrs.	30 yrs.	30 yrs.	25 yrs.
Loan interest rate:	9%	8½%	9½%	9½%	10%
Appreciation/depreciation:	+30%	−20%	0%	−10%	+20%

The "Basic Five:"

1. Income required to meet equity yield rate demands:
An investor is considering purchasing Sherwood Apartments listed at $1,500,000. Financing is available for 75% of value on a loan at 9% interest for a term of 20 years. The investor anticipates appreciation of 10% in market value during a 10-year holding period and expects a yield of 15% on equity. Make the following calculations:
   a. Net annual income required to justify a purchase price of $1,500,000, based on an equity yield rate of 15%.
   b. Feasible offering price, if a reconstructed operating statement shows net income of $135,000.

2. Rate of yield on equity:
A recently constructed mobile home park, well-designed, well-managed, and well-maintained, was sold for $600,000. The purchaser paid $180,000 down and financed the balance on a 15-year loan at an interest rate of 10%. Net annual income from space rentals and related services is estimated to be $68,000. Calculate the rate of yield on equity, assuming 0% appreciation during a 10-year holding period.

3. Appreciation required to generate a specified rate of yield on equity:
An office building, purchased for $930,000, produces net annual income of $97,700. It is financed for 80% of value at 9½% interest, monthly payments

to amortize in 25 years. The investor projects a holding period of 10 years and expects a yield on equity of 16%. What percent of appreciation would be required within the holding period in order to produce a yield of 16% to maturity?

4. Estimate of market value by using the mortgage-equity technique:
Country Corners, a neighborhood shopping center, offered for sale, will support a loan commitment for 70% of value at 9% interest on a 20-year term. Net annual income is calculated to be $120,000. Based on projections of a 10-year holding period, 10% depreciation, and 15% equity yield rate, compute an indicator of value by using the mortgage-equity technique.

5. Fifteen-point investment analysis:
Prepare a 15-point investment analysis of the Country Corners neighborhood shopping center in the preceding problem.

Interpolation in the OAR Tables:

Calculate the OAR for each of the following sets of variables, interpolating by simple proportion. (The component for which interpolation is required has been noted in italics.)

	1	2	3	4	5	6
Holding period:	10 yrs.	*7 yrs.*	15 yrs.	10 yrs.	5 yrs.	10 yrs.
Equity yield rate:	15%	14%	12%	*17%*	18%	14%
Loan ratio:	85%	75%	70%	75%	90%	75%
Loan term:	20 yrs.	25 yrs.	25 yrs.	30 yrs.	15 yrs.	*24 yrs.*
Loan interest rate:	9%	8½%	*8¼%*	8%	9½%	7½%
Appreciation/ depreciation:	0%	+20%	−10%	+30%	*+5%*	+20%

Extension of the OAR Tables by extrapolation:

Calculate by extrapolation the OAR for each of the following sets of variables. (The item for which extension is required has been noted in italics.)

	1	2	3
Holding period:	10 yrs.	10 yrs.	10 yrs.
Equity yield rate:	16%	12%	20%
Loan ratio:	80%	50%	*100%*
Loan term:	*40 yrs.*	25 yrs.	20 yrs.
Loan interest rate:	8½%	9%	10%
Appreciation/depreciation:	+10%	−20%	0%

Calculation of OAR's from the Compound Interest Tables:

1. OAR, one loan only:
   Given:
   > Holding period: 12 years
   > Equity yield rate: 18%
   > Loan ratio: 65%
   > Loan term: 22 years
   > Loan interest rate: 9½%
   > Appreciation: 15%

   Calculate the mortgage-equity Overall Rate.

2. OAR, multiple financing:
   Given:
   > Holding period: 10 years
   > Equity yield rate: 20%
   > Appreciation: 5%
   > First mortgage:
   > > Loan ratio: 70%
   > > Loan term: 25 years
   > > Loan interest rate; 9½%
   > Second mortgage:
   > > Loan ratio: 20%
   > > Loan term: 20 years
   > > Loan interest rate: 8½%

   a. Calculate the mortgage-equity Overall Rate.
   b. Assume net annual income of $132,000. Compute an indicator of property value, and prove the validity of the OAR by completing a 15-point investment analysis.

3. OAR, holding period exceeding loan term:
   Given:
   > Holding period: 15 years
   > Equity yield rate: 15%
   > Loan ratio: 80%
   > Loan term: 12 years
   > Loan interest rate: 10½%
   > Appreciation: 5%

   a. Calculate the mortgage-equity Overall Rate.
   b. Based on net annual income of $60,000, value the property and prepare a 15-point investment analysis.

Special Capitalization Rates:

1. OAR, based on current yield requirements:
Calculate Overall Capitalization Rates, based on the following loan data and the investor's current yield requirements.

	1	2	3
Loan ratio:	75%	90%	80%
Loan term:	20 years	25 years	15 years
Loan interest rate:	9½%	9%	10%
Current equity yield rate:	10%	12%	9%

2. OAR, based on debt coverage ratio requirements:
Calculate Overall Capitalization Rates, based on the following financing data and the lender's debt coverage ratio requirements.

	1	2	3
Loan ratio:	80%	70%	75%
Loan term:	20 years	30 years	25 years
Loan interest rate:	10%	9%	9½%
Debt coverage ratio:	1.4	1.3	1.5

Loan Constants (from Compound Interest Tables):

Calculate the annual loan constant for each of the following (monthly payments to amortize):

	Interest Rate	Term
1.	10%	22 years
2.	9%	14 years
3.	12%	17 years
4.	9½%	29 years
5.	11%	18 years

Annual Debt Service (from Supplemental Tables):

Select the precomputed loan constant and calculate annual debt service for each of the following (monthly payments to amortize):

	Interest Rate	Term	Original Principal
1.	8½%	25 years	$ 450,000
2.	8%	30 years	80,000

3.	10%	15 years	130,000
4.	12%	20 years	1,500,000
5.	9%	20 years	1,500,000

Loan Balances and Debt Reduction (from Supplemental Tables):

Calculate for each of the following:

    a. Principal amount of loan remaining unpaid at the end of 10 years.
    b. Dollar amount by which the principal has been reduced in 10 years.

	Interest Rate	Term	Original Principal
1.	8½%	25 years	$ 450,000
2.	8%	30 years	80,000
3.	10%	15 years	130,000
4.	12%	20 years	1,500,000
5.	9%	20 years	1,500,000

Principal Balance Unpaid, Percent of (from Compound Interest Tables):

Calculate the percent of original principal unpaid at the end of the specified holding period for each of the following (monthly payments to amortize):

	Interest Rate	Term	Holding Period
1.	10%	25 years	7 years
2.	9%	27 years	12 years
3.	9½%	16 years	10 years

Cash Flow (Current Yield):

1. As a percent of value:
For each of the following sets of variables, calculate cash flow as a percent of total property value.

	1	2	3	4	5
Holding period:	10 yrs.	5 yrs.	15 yrs.	5 yrs.	10 yrs.
Equity yield rate:	14%	12%	10%	6%	30%
Loan ratio:	70%	75%	60%	66.7%	90%
Loan term:	25 yrs.	30 yrs.	20 yrs.	10 yrs.	15 yrs.
Loan interest rate:	8%	9%	8½%	9½%	10%
Appreciation/depreciation:	0%	−20%	+20%	+40%	+30%

2. As a percent of equity:

Compute cash flow as a percent of equity for each set of variables in the preceding problem.

Processing the Income Stream to an Ordinary Annuity Equivalent

1. Deferred annuity:

During a two-year incubation period prior to full occupancy, a newly completed apartment house is expected to meet operating expenses only. For the following 8 years it is anticipated that the property will generate a net annual income of $180,000, considered to be an ordinary annuity. Using a yield rate of 12% and a holding period of 10 years, calculate the present worth of the income stream and the level ordinary annuity equivalent for the full term.

2. Graduated annuity:

Terms of a net-net-net lease are as follows:
  First 5 years: $100,000 per year.
  Next 7 years: $120,000 per year.
  Final 8 years: $130,000 per year.
Calculate the level ordinary annuity equivalent for the first 15 years at a yield rate of 9%.

3. Increasing income:

Net annual income from a recreational vehicle park was $65,000 last year. It is expected to increase $5,000 in the current year and each subsequent year over the next 7 years. What is the level ordinary annuity equivalent at a yield rate of 15%?

4. Irregular income:

Estimated net annual income during the first 3 years' operation of a mobile home park is as follows:
  First year: $30,000
  Second year: $70,000
  Third year: $120,000
Compute the level ordinary annuity equivalent at a yield rate of 14%.

5. Negative income during build-up period:

Income from a new regional shopping center is estimated for the next 12 years:
  Year 1:   ⟨$200,000⟩
  Year 2:   ⟨ 120,000⟩

Year 3:	0	
Year 4:	300,000	
Year 5:	550,000	
Years 6-12:	800,000	per year

Calculate present worth and level ordinary annuity equivalent at a yield rate of 12%.

Nonproducing Properties Purchased For Appreciation

1. A tract of wooded acreage, located in a potential year-round second home recreational area, is offered for sale on these terms: Purchase price, $350,000; down payment, $50,000; balance of $300,000 to be carried by the seller on a first mortgage at 9% interest. The loan schedule specifies annual payments of interest only for 9 years, total principal amount due and payable at the end of 10 years. Property taxes amount to $4,500 per year. An interested client anticipates purchasing the property, holding it for appreciation, and reselling to a developer. The prospective investor requests the following analysis, which you as broker/counsellor now prepare:
   a. Sales price required to return 20% on equity, if the property is resold at the end of:
      1. Three years.
      2. Five years.
      3. Eight years.
   b. Rate of yield on equity, if property is resold for $700,000 at the end of:
      1. Three years.
      2. Five years.
      3. Eight years.

Make the calculations required and draw up a summary of your analysis.

2. A parcel of land, with 200 feet frontage and depth of 250 feet, located on a busy boulevard in a developing neighborhood, has been placed on the market at a price of $600 per front foot. There are presently two buildings on the lot: a 35-year-old single story office building and a 40-year-old masonry single family dwelling. Gross income from the office and the house is $310 per month. Net annual income is estimated to be $1,500. The owner offers to carry a loan of $75,000 at 8½% interest, with annual payments to amortize in 12 years. A developer interested in the parcel anticipates a holding period of 4 years before clearing the land in preparation for constructing a new commercial building which will represent highest and best use of the site. He estimates the value of the land, if vacant, to be $140,000 in 4 years, when, according to a feasibility study, redevelopment is due. Cost of demolishing and removing existing structures is calculated to be $5,000. Both buildings will, however, continue to be rented

for the next 4 years. Based on the seller's carrying $75,000 under the loan terms specified and on the investor's anticipation of 12% yield on dollars invested, calculate a feasible offering price. Prove your computations.

Valuation and Analysis

1. Net annual income for a new office building is projected as follows:

Year 1:	0
Year 2:	$100,000
Year 3:	225,000
Year 4:	475,000
Year 5:	700,000
Years 6-25:	900,000 per year

The property can be financed for 75% of value at an interest rate of 9½% for a term of 30 years. Assume a holding period of 15 years; appreciation, 20%; equity yield rate, 14%. Make these calculations:
   a. Level ordinary annuity equivalent for the first 15 years.
   b. Property value as indicated by the mortgage-equity technique.
   c. Fifteen-point investment analysis.

2. A commercial building, offered for sale, is encumbered by an assumable loan: principal balance, $420,000; interest rate, 7%; remaining loan term, 18 years; monthly payments to amortize. Net annual income is estimated to be $60,000. Assume a holding period of 10 years, 15% appreciation, and 16% equity yield rate. Calculate a feasible offering price and prepare a 15-point investment analysis. (Suggestion: Follow procedure "Investment value, when loan ratio is unknown," pages 100-103.)

3. Assume the property in the preceding problem is purchased for $615,000 and is refinanced on these terms: 80% loan ratio; 10% interest rate; 25-year loan term; monthly payments to amortize. Anticipated holding period remains at 10 years; and projected appreciation, 15%. What is the rate of yield on equity? (Compare to 16% in preceding problem.)

ANSWERS AND SUGGESTED SOLUTIONS

Selection of Overall Rates from OAR Tables:

	OAR	Page
1.	.094766	336
2.	.104472	407
3.	.104173	248

4. .109842   332
5. .112947   363
(Procedure: pages 65-67.)

The "Basic Five":

1. Income required to meet equity yield rate demands:
   a. .102847 × $1,500,000 = $154,270
      (I = R × V)
   b. $135,000 ÷ .102847 = $1,312,630 (rounded)
      (V = I ÷ R)
   (Procedure: pages 61-62.)
2. Rate of yield on equity:
      Amount of loan: $600,000 − $180,000 = $420,000
      Loan ratio: $420,000 ÷ $600,000 = 70%
      Overall Rate: $68,600 ÷ $600,000 = .114333
      (R = I ÷ V)
      Variables (arrayed):
         Holding period: 10 years   Loan term: 15 years
         Equity yield rate: ?   Loan interest rate: 10%
         Loan ratio: 70%   Appreciation: 0%
      Target figure is .114333 (the calculated Overall Rate).
      A search in the OAR Tables shows an Overall Rate of .114376 at 14%
         equity yield rate (page 330).
      (Procedure: pages 81, 82.)

3. Appreciation required to generate a specified rate of yield on equity:
      Overall Rate: $97,700 ÷ $930,000 = .105054
      Variables (arrayed):
         Holding period: 10 years   Loan term: 25 years
         Equity yield rate: 16%   Loan interest rate: 9½%
         Loan ratio: 80%   Appreciation: ?
      Target figure is .105054 (the calculated Overall Rate).
      Variables given indicate search will be confined to page 344.
      OAR at 10% appreciation is .105057—so close to .105054 that in-
         terpolation is not required.
      (Procedure: page 107.)

4. Estimate of market value by the mortgage-equity technique:
      Variables (arrayed):
         Holding period: 10 years   Loan term: 20 years
         Equity yield rate: 15%   Loan interest rate: 9%
         Loan ratio: 70%   Depreciation: 10%

OAR: .115513 (Page 336)

Value = Income ÷ Rate

= $120,000 ÷ .115513

= $1,038,844 (unrounded)

(Procedure: pages 98, 99.)

5. Fifteen-point investment analysis:

(Form, pages 150, 151. Examples and explanations, pages 10-14 and pages 154-161.)

Investment Analysis and Proof of Computations
Fifteen-Point Summary of Calculations

1.	Over-all Rate Selected from OAR Tables or Computed						.115513
2.	Property Value	$120,000 (INCOME)	÷	.115513 (OAR)	=	$1,038,844	
3.	Original Equity (Down Payment)	.30 (Equity Ratio)	x	$1,038,844 (Value)	=	311,653	
4.	Amount of Loan (Original Principal)	.70 (Loan Ratio)	x	1,038,844 (Value)	=	727,191	
5.	Debt Service (Yearly Payments)	.107967 (Loan Constant)	x	727,191 (Principal)	=	78,513	
6.	Cash Flow (Annuity)	120,000 (Net Income)	−	78,513 (Debt Service)	=	41,487	
7.	Debt Coverage Ratio	120,000 (Net Income)	÷	78,513 (Debt Service)	=	1.5284	
8.	Rate of Current Yield On Equity	41,487 (Cash Flow)	÷	311,653 (Orig. Equity)	=	.13312	
9.	Loan Balance (End Holding Period)	.710259 (% Unpaid)	x	727,191 (Principal)	=	516,494	
10.	Resale Value as % of Original Value	100 (Orig. Val. as %)	+−	−10 (% Appr/Dep)	=	90%	
11.	Resale Value as a Dollar Amount	90% (Resale Val. as %)	x	1,038,844 (Original Value)	=	934,960	
12.	Reversion, Net (Terminal Equity)	934,960 (Resale Value)	−	516,494 (Loan Balance)	=	418,466	
13.	Deferred Yield (Amount)	418,466 (Reversion Net)	−	311,653 (Down Payment)	=	106,813	

Investment Analysis and Proof of Computations
Fifteen-Point Summary of Calculations
(cont.)

14. Terminal Equity Ratio $\dfrac{418,466}{\text{(Reversion Net)}} \div \dfrac{934,960}{\text{(Resale Value)}} = .44758$

15. Proof of Yield on Equity

   Equity Yield Rate: $\underset{\text{(Percent)}}{15}$ Term in Years: $\underset{\text{(Holding Period)}}{10}$

   Present Worth of 1 Per Period: $\underset{\text{(PW 1/P)}}{5.018769}$ Present Worth of 1: $\underset{\text{(PW 1)}}{.247185}$

   Equation of Proof

   Present Worth = $\left(\underset{\text{(Cash Flow)}}{41,487} \times \underset{\text{(PW 1/P)}}{5.018769} \right) + \left(\underset{\text{(Net Reversion)}}{418,466} \times \underset{\text{(PW 1)}}{.247185} \right)$

   $= \underline{\quad 208,214 \quad} + \underline{\quad 103,439 \quad} = \underline{\quad 311,653 \quad}$

Final Check Target Figure = $\underset{\text{(Down Payment, Orig. Equity)}}{311,653}$

$\dfrac{311,653}{\text{Target Figure}} - \dfrac{311,653}{\text{(Present Worth)}} = \dfrac{0}{\text{(Rounding Adjustment)}}$

Interpolation in the OAR Tables:

1. .10214
2. .07744
3. .09821
4. .09101
5. .09951
6. .08357

(Procedure: pages 67-69.)

Extension of the OAR Tables by extrapolation:

1. .095926
2. .116830
3. .105411

(Procedure: pages 69-72.)

Calculation of OAR's from the Compound Interest Tables:

1. OAR, one loan only:
   a. Loan constant: $12 \times .009045 = .10854$ (PR, 9½%, 264 months)
      $.65 \times .10854 = .070551$
   a. $77.281211 \div 12 = 6.440101$ (PW 1/P, 9½%, 120 months
      $.070551 \times 6.440101 = .4543556$
   c. $1.15 - .4543556 = .695644$

d. .070551 × 4.793225 = .3381668   (PW 1/P, 18%, 12 years)
e. .6956444 × .13722 = .0954563   (PW 1, 18%, 12 years)
f. .3381668 − .0954563 = .2427105
g. .35 + .2427105 = .5927105
h. .5927105 ÷ 4.793225 = .123656   (PW 1/P, 18%, 12 years)
(Procedure: pages 72-74.)

2. OAR, multiple financing:
   a. 1st: .70 × .104844 = .0733908   (Supplemental Tables)
      2nd: .20 × .104139 = .0208278   (Supplemental Tables)
   b. 1st: 95.764831 ÷ 12 = 7.9804026   (PW 1/P, 9½%, 180 months)
            .0733908 × 7.9804026 = .585688
      2nd: 80.65447 ÷ 12 = 6.721206   (PW 1/P, 8½%, 120 months)
            .0208278 × 6.721206 = .139988
   c. .585688 + .139988 = .725676
      1.05 − .725676 = .324324
   d. .0733908 + .0208278 = .0942186
      .0942186 × 4.192472 = .3950088   (PW 1/P, 20%, 10 years)
   e. .324324 × .161506 = .0523803   (PW 1, 20%, 10 years)
   f. .3950088 − .0523803 = .3426285
   g. .10 + .3426285 = .4426285
   h. .4426285 ÷ 4.192472 = .105577   (PW 1/P, 20%, 10 years)
   (Procedure: pages 75-76.)

Investment Analysis and Proof of Computations
Fifteen-Point Summary of Calculations

1.	Over-all Rate Selected from OAR Tables or Computed				.105577
2.	Property Value	$132,000 (INCOME)	÷	.105577 (OAR)	= $1,250,272
3.	Original Equity (Down Payment)	.10 (Equity Ratio)	x	$1,250,272 (Value)	= 125,028
4.	Amount of Loan (Original Principal)	1st: .70 / 2nd: .20 (Loan Ratio)	x	1,250,272 / 1,250,272 (Value)	= 875,190 / 250,054 = 1,125,244
5.	Debt Service (Yearly Payments)	1st: .104844 / 2nd: .104139 (Loan Constant)	x	875,190 / 250,054 (Principal)	= 91,758 / 26,040 = 117,798
6.	Cash Flow (Annuity)	132,000 (Net Income)	−	117,798 (Debt Service)	= 14,202
7.	Debt Coverage Ratio	132,000 (Net Income)	÷	117,798 (Debt Service)	= 1.12056

Investment Analysis and Proof of Computations
Fifteen-Point Summary of Calculations
(cont.)

8.	Rate of Current Yield On Equity	14,202 (Cash Flow)	÷	125,028 (Orig. Equity)	= .11359

9.	Loan Balance (End Holding Period)	1st:.836694 2nd:.699938 (% Unpaid)	x x	875,190 250,054 (Principal)	= 732,266 = 175,022 907,288

10.	Resale Value as % of Original Value	100 (Orig. Val. as %)	±	5 (% Appr/Dep)	= 105%

11.	Resale Value as a Dollar Amount	105% (Resale Val. as %)	x	1,250,272 (Original Value)	= 1,312,786

12.	Reversion, Net (Terminal Equity)	1,312,786 (Resale Value)	—	907,288 (Loan Balance)	= 405,498

13.	Deferred Yield (Amount)	405,498 (Reversion Net)	—	125,028 (Down Payment)	= 280,470

14.	Terminal Equity Ratio	405,498 (Reversion Net)	÷	1,312,786 (Resale Value)	= .30888

15. Proof of Yield on Equity

Equity Yield Rate: ___20___ Term in Years: ___10___
(Percent)   (Holding Period)

Present Worth of 1 per period: __4.192472__ Present Worth of 1: __.161506__
(PW 1/P)   (PW 1)

Equation of Proof

Present Worth = (__14,202__ x __4.192472__) + (__405,498__ x __.161506__)
(Cash Flow)   (PW 1/P)   (Net Reversion)   (PW 1)

= __59,541__ + __65,490__ = __125,031__

Final Check Target Figure = __125,028__
(Down Payment, Orig. Equity)

125,028	—	125,031	=	−3
Target Figure		(Present Worth)		(Rounding Adjustment)

3. OAR, holding period exceeding loan term:
   a. Loan constant: 12 × .012241 = .146892   (PR, 10½%, 144 months)
      .80 × .146892 = .1175136
   b. 1.0 + .05 = 1.05
   c. .1175136 × 5.420619 = .63699645   (PW 1/P, 15%, 12 years)
   d. 1.05 × .122894 = .1290387   (PW 1, 15%, 15 years)
   e. .63699645 − .1290387 = .50795775
   f. .20 + .50795775 = .70795775
   g. .70795775 ÷ 5.84737 = .121073   (PW 1/P, 15%, 15 years)
   (Procedure: page 76.)

Note: In the following 15-point analysis, which utilizes the calculated OAR of .121073, Cash Flow (Item 6) is shown as a graduated annuity. Present worth valuation in Item 15 follows *a* through *d* of the procedure outlined on page 56. (*e* is not required in this calculation.)

Investment Analysis and Proof of Computations
Fifteen-Point Summary of Calculations

1.	Over-all Rate Selected from OAR Tables or Computed				.121073
2.	Property Value	$60,000 (INCOME)	÷	.121073 (OAR)	= $495,569
3.	Original Equity (Down Payment)	.20 (Equity Ratio)	x	$495,569 (Value)	= 99,114
4.	Amount of Loan (Original Principal)	.80 (Loan Ratio)	x	495,569 (Value)	= 396,455
5.	Debt Service (Yrs. 1 – 12) (Yearly Payments)	.146892 (Loan Constant)	x	396,455 (Principal)	= 58,236
	Yrs. 1 – 12: 60,000	– 58,236			= 1,764
6.	Cash Flow Yrs. 13 – 15: 60,000 (Annuity)	– 0 (Net Income)		0 (Debt Service)	= 60,000
7.	Debt Coverage (Yrs. 1-12) 60,000 Ratio (Net Income)	÷ 58,236 (Debt Service)			= 1.0303
	Yrs. 1 – 12: 1,764	÷ 99,114			= .0178
8.	Rate of Current Yield 13 – 15: 60,000 On Equity (Cash Flow)	÷ 99,114 (Orig. Equity)			= .60536
9.	Loan Balance (End Holding Period)	0 (% Unpaid)	x	(Principal)	= 0
10.	Resale Value as % of Original Value	100 (Orig. Val. as %)	+	5 (% Appr/Dep)	= 105%
11.	Resale Value as a Dollar Amount	105% (Resale Val. as %)	x	495,569 (Original Value)	= 520,347
12.	Reversion, Net (Terminal Equity)	520,347 (Resale Value)	–	0 (Loan Balance)	= 520,347
13.	Deferred Yield (Amount)	520,347 (Reversion Net)	–	99,114 (Down Payment)	= 421,233
14.	Terminal Equity Ratio	520,347 (Reversion Net)	÷	520,347 (Resale Value)	= 100%

15. Proof of Yield on Equity
   Equity Yield Rate: 15 (Percent)   Term in Years: 15 (Holding Period)
   Present Worth of 1 Per Period: 5.420619 / 5.847370 (PW 1/P)   Present Worth of 1: .122894 (PW 1)

Investment Analysis and Proof of Computations
Fifteen-Point Summary of Calculations
(cont.)

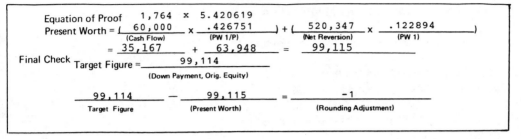

Special Capitalization Rates:

1. OAR, based on current yield requirements:
    1. a. .75 × .111856 = .083892   (Supplemental Tables)
       b. .25 × .10   = .025
       c.   .108892
    2. a. .90 × .100704 = .0906336   (Supplemental Tables)
       b. .10 × .12   = .012
       c.   .1026336
    3. a. .80 × .128953 = .1031624   (Supplemental Tables)
       b. .20 × .09   = .018
       c.   .1211624
   (Procedure: pages 79, 80.)

2. OAR, based on debt coverage ratio requirements:
    1. a. .80 × .115803 = .0926424   (Supplemental Tables)
       b. .0926424 × 1.4 = .129699
    2. a. .70 × .096555 = .0675885   (Supplemental Tables)
       b. .0675885 × 1.3 = .087865
    3. a. .75 × .104844 = .078633   (Supplemental Tables)
       b. .078633 × 1.5 = .1179495
   (Procedure: pages 80, 81.)

Loan Constants (from Compound Interest Tables):

1. 12 × .009382 = .112584   (PR, 10%, 264 months)
2. 12 × .010489 = .125868   (PR, 9%, 168 months)
3. 12 × .011512 = .138144   (PR, 12%, 204 months)
4. 12 × .008461 = .101532   (PR, 9½%, 348 months)

500

5. 12 × .010650 = .127800   (PR, 11%, 216 months)
(Procedure: page 118.)

Note: The loan constant must exceed the interest rate; otherwise, there would be no amortization.

Annual Debt Service (from Supplemental Tables):

1. .096627 × $450,000 = $43,482
2. .088052 × 80,000 = 7,044
3. .128953 × 130,000 = 16,764
4. .132130 × 1,500,000 = 198,195
5. .107967 × 1,500,000 = 161,951

Loan Balances and Debt Reduction (from Supplemental Tables):

	Loan Balance	Debt Reduction
1.	.817706 × $450,000 = $367,968	.182294 × $450,000 = $82,032
2.	.877248 × 80,000 = 70,180	.122752 × 80,000 = 9,820
3.	.505767 × 130,000 = 65,750	.494233 × 130,000 = 64,250
4.	.767463 × 1,500,000 = 1,151,195	.232537 × 1,500,000 = 348,805
5.	.710259 × 1,500,000 = 1,065,389	.289741 × 1,500,000 = 434,611

Principal Balance Unpaid, Percent of (from Compound Interest Tables):

1. .009087 × 100.015633 = .908842   (PR, 10%, 300 months)
          × (PW 1/P, 10%, 216 mos.)
2. .008231 × 98.593409 = .811522   (PR, 9%, 324 months)
          × (PW 1/P, 9%, 180 mos.)
3. .01015 × 54.720488 = .555413   (PR, 9½%, 192 months)
          × (PW 1/P, 9½%, 72 mos.)

(Procedure: page 121.)

Cash Flow (Current Yield:

1. As a percent of value:
  1. a. .7 × .092618 = .064833   (Supplement Tables)
     b. .099869 − .064833 = .035036   (OAR Tables)
  2. a. .75 × .096555 = .0724163
     b. .129034 − .0724163 = .056618
  3. a. .60 × .104139 = .0624834
     b. .085292 − .0624834 = .022809
  4. a. .667 × .155277 = .103570
     b. .007161 − .103570 = −.096409

5. a. .90 × .128953 = .1160577
   b. .128582 − .1160577 = .0125243
(Procedure: page 95.)

Notes:
— Percentages can be converted readily to a dollar amount. For example, Problem 1 shows that cash flow is 3.5036% of property value; and at a value of $100,000, annual cash flow after loan payments would be about $3,500 (.035036 × $100,000).
— In Problem 3 the loan constant *exceeds* the Overall Rate; however, there is a *positive* cash flow because of a relatively low loan ratio. If the *product* of the loan ratio and the loan constant is less than the Overall Rate, there will be a *positive* cash flow.
— Problem 4 indicates a *negative* cash flow of 9.64% of property value (after debt service). Analysis shows that the transaction is definitely one to avoid. The given set of variables shows that if the investor goes into this over-priced investment, the property must appreciate 40% within a 5-year holding period to bail him out with a meager 6% yield to maturity on equity.

2. As a percent of equity:
   1. .035036 ÷ .30 = .1167867
   (Cash flow is 11.678% of equity or down payment. This is the rate of *current yield*.)
   2. .056618 ÷ .25 = .226472
   3. .022809 ÷ .40 = .057023
   4. −.096409 ÷ .333 = −.2895165
   5. .0125243 ÷ .10 = .125243
(Procedure: pages 92-95.)

Processing the Income Stream to an Ordinary Annuity Equivalent

1. Deferred annuity:
   a. .5.650223 − 1.690051 = 3.960172   (PW 1/P, 12%, 10 years − 2 years)
   b. Present worth of the income stream:
      $180,000 × 3.960172 = $712,831
   c. Ordinary annuity equivalent:
      $712,831 × .176984 = $126,160   (PR, 12%, 10 years)
   Proof: $126,160 × 5.650223 = $712,832   (PW 1/P, 12%, 10 years)
   (Adjust $1 for rounding.)
   (Procedure: pages 55-56.)

502

2. Graduated annuity:
   Factor selection:
      PW 1/P, 9%, 5 years: 3.889651
      PW 1/P, 9%, 12 years: 7.160725
      PW 1/P, 9%, 15 years: 8.060688
      PR, 9%, 15 years: .124059
   a. $100,000 × 3.889651 = $388,965   (PW 1/P, 9%, 5 years)
   b. Adjusted factors:
      7.160725 − 3.889651 = 3.271074   (PW 1/P, 9%,
                                     12 years − 5 years)
      8.060688 − 7.160725 = .899963   (PW 1/P, 9%,
                                     15 years − 12 years)
   c. $120,000 × 3.271074 = $392,529
      $130,000 × .899963 = $116,995
   d. Present worth:
      Years 1-5: $388,965
      Years 6-12:   392,529
      Years 13-15:   116,995
                     $898,489
   e. Level ordinary annuity equivalent:
      $898,489 × .124059 = $11,466   (PR, 9%, 15 years)
   Proof: $111,466 × 8.060688 = $898,493 (PW 1/P, 9%, 15 years
   (Adjust $4 for rounding.)
   (Procedure; pages 56-57.)

3. Increasing income:
   a. $5,000 × 7 = $35,000
   b. $70,000 + $35,000 = $105,000
   c. $105,000 × 4.160420 = $436,844   (PW 1/P, 15%, 7 years)
   d. 7 − 4.16042 = 2.83958
   e. 2.83958 × $5,000 = $14,198
   f. $14,198 ÷ .15 = $94,753
   g. $436,844 − $94,653 = $343,191
   h. $342,191 × .240360 = $82,249   (PR, 15%, 7 years)
   Proof: $82,249 × 4.160420 = $342,190 (PW 1/P, 15%, 7 years)
   (Adjust $1 for rounding. Target figure is $342,191, present worth, g.)
   (Procedure: pages 57-59.)
4. Irregular income:
   a. $ 30,000 × .877193 = $ 26,316 (PW 1, 14%, 1 year)
       70,000 × .769468 =   53,863 (PW 1, 14%, 2 years)
      120,000 × .674972 =   80,997 (PW 1, 14%, 3 years)
   b. $161,176

c. $161,176 × .430731 = $69,423   (PR, 14%, 3 years)
Proof: $69,423 × 2.321632 = $161,175   (PW 1/P, 14%, 3 years)
(Adjust $1 for rounding.)
(Procedure: pages 59, 60.)

5. Negative income during build-up period:
   a. ⟨$200,000⟩ × .892857 = ⟨$178,571⟩   (PW 1, 12%, 1 year)
      ⟨$120,000⟩ × .797194 = ⟨   95,663⟩   (PW 1, 12%, 2 years)
                             ⟨$274,234⟩
   b. $300,000 × .635518 = $ 190,655   (PW 1, 12%, 4 years)
      $550,000 × .567427 =   312,085   (PW 1, 12%, 5 years)
      $800,000 × 2.589598 = 2,071,678   (PW 1/P, 12%,
                                             12 years − 5 years)

                            $2,574,418
   c. $2,574,418 − $274,234 = $2,300,184
   d. $2,300,184 × .161437 = $371,335   (PR, 12%, 12 years)
   Proof: $371,335 × 6.194374 = $2,300,188 (PW 1/P, 12%, 12 years)
   (Adjust $4 for rounding.)
   (Procedure: pages 60, 61.)

Nonproducing Properties Purchased For Appreciation

1. Sales price required to return 20% on equity:
   Three-year holding period:
   a. $50,000 ÷ .578704 = $86,400   (PW 1, 20%, 3 years)
   b. Annual interest payments: .09 × $300,000 = $27,000
      Annual property taxes: 4,500
      Total annual holding costs: $31,500
      $31,500 ÷ .274725 = $114,660   (PR − i, 20%, 3 years)
   c. Resale value required: $86,400 + 114,660 + 300,000 = $501,060

   Five-year holding period:
   a. $50,000 ÷ .401878 = $124,416   (PW 1, 20%, 5 years)
   b. $31,500 ÷ .134380 = $234,410   (PR − i, 20%, 5 years)
   c. Resale value required: $124,416 + 234,410 + 300,000 = $658,826

   Eight-year holding period:
   a. $50,000 ÷ .233568 = $214,991   (PW 1, 20%, 8 years)
   b. $31,500 ÷ .060609 = $519,725   (PR − i, 20%, 8 years)
   c. Resale value required: $214,991 + 519,725 + 300,000 = $1,034,716
   (Procedure: pages 145-148.)

Rate of yield on equity, if property is resold for $700,000:

Three-year holding period:
a. Annual holding costs (interest and taxes): $31,500
b. Net reversion (target figure): $700,000 − 300,000 = $400,000
c. Try 75% (use PW 1 and PR factors at 75% for 3 years):
   Future worth = ($50,000 ÷ .186589) + [$31,500 ÷ (.922043 − .75)]
              = $267,969 + ($31,500 ÷ .172043)
              = $267,969 + 183,094
              = $451,063
d. Try 60% (use PW 1 and PR factors at 60% for 3 years):
   Future worth = ($50,000 ÷ .244141 + [$31,500 ÷ (.793798 − .60)]
              = $204,800 + ($31,500 ÷ .193798)
              = $204,800 + 162,540
              = $367,340

"Target figure" from b is the investor's net reversion or terminal equity of $400,000 at the time of resale. This figure has been "bracketed" between $451,063 at 75% yield and $367,340 at 60% yield. Interpolation by simple proportion calculates equity yield rate to be 65.85%, round to 66%.

Five-year holding period:
a. $31,500
b. $400,000
c. Try 25% (use PW 1 and PR factors at 25% for 5 years):
   Future worth = ($50,000 ÷ .32768) + [$31,500 ÷ (.371847 − .25)]
              = $152,588 + ($31,500 ÷ .121847)
              = $152,588 + 258,521
              = $411,109
d. Try 20% (use PW 1 and PR factors at 20% for 5 years):
   Future worth = [$50,000 ÷ .401878) + [$31,500 ÷ (.33438 − .20)]
              = $124,416 + ($31,500 ÷ .13438)
              = $124,416 + 234,410
              = $358,826

"Target figure" is $400,000. Interpolation by simple proportion calculates equity yield to be 23.94%, round to 24%.

Eight-year holding period:
a. $31,500
b. $400,000
c. Try 6½% (use PW 1 and PR factors at 6½% for 8 years):
   Future worth = ($50,000 ÷ .604231) + [$31,500 ÷ (.164237 − .065)]
              = $82,750 + ($31,500 ÷ .099237

$$= \$82,750 + 317,422$$
$$= \$400,172$$

d. Try 6% (use PW 1 and PR factors at 6% for 8 years):

Future worth $= (\$50,000 \div .627412) + [\$31,S00 \div (.161036 - .06)]$
$$= \$79,692 + (\$31,500 \div .101036)$$
$$= \$79,692 + 311,770$$
$$= \$391,462$$

"Target figure" is \$400,000. Interpolation by simple proportion calculates equity yield to be 6.49%, round to 6½%.
(Procedure: pages 141-145.)

Analysis Summary:

Holding Period	Resale Value Required to Produce 20% Yield	Yield Rate if Resale for \$700,000
3 years	\$501,060	66%
5 years	658,826	24%
8 years	1,034,716	6½%

2. Investment value, based on specified equity yield rate:
   Preliminary calculations:

   Annual debt service:

   $\$75,000 \times .136153 = \$10,212$ (PR, 8½%, 12 years)

   Loan balance, end of 4 years:

   $\$10,212 \times 5.639183 = \$57,587$ (PW 1/P, 8½%, 8 years)

   a. Net reversion:

Resale value:	\$140,000
Less cost of clearing lot:	5,000
	\$135,000
Less loan balance:	57,587
	\$77,413

   b. $\$77,413 \times .635518 = \$49,197$ (PW 1, 12%, 4 years)
   c. Net annual holding costs:

Debt service:	\$10,212
Less net annual income:	1,500
	\$8,712

   d. $\$8,712 \times 3.037349 = \$26,461$ (PW 1/P, 12%, 4 years)
   e. $\$49,197 - 26,461 = \$22,736$
   f. $\$75,000 + 22,736 = \$97,736$

Feasible offering price: \$97,750 (rounded), with down payment of \$22,750 (Procedure: pages 136-141. Procedure for "nonproducing

506

properties" is applicable in this problem, since annual holding costs exceed net income.)

Proof:

$22,736 ÷ .635518 = $35,776   (PW 1, 12%, 4 years)
   8,712 ÷ .209234 =   41,638   (PR − i, 12%, 4 years)
                      $77,414

Note: A single investment of $22,736 (the down payment, unrounded would grow to $35,776 in 4 years at a yield rate of 12%. Annual deposits of $8,712 (net annual holding costs) would accumulate a sum of $41,638 in 4 years at 12% yield. Combined, the accumulations total $77,414 (within $1 of the calculated net reversion.)

Valuation and Analysis

1. Analysis of the income stream:
Income for years 2 through 5 is increasing but irregular.
Income for years 6 through 15 constitutes a deferred annuity. (Disregard years 16 through 25.)
Calculation of the ordinary annuity equivalent is made by a combination of two procedures (see pages 59 and 55). To avoid confusion, steps in the following computations will not be identified by letter.
Present worth of the income stream:

$100,000 × .769468 = $ 76,947   (PW 1, 14%, 2 years)
 225,000 × .674972 =   151,869   (PW 1, 14%, 3 years)
 475,000 × .592080 =   281,238   (PW 1, 14%, 4 years)
 700,000 × .519369 =   363,558   (PW 1, 14%, 5 years)
 900,000 × 2.709087 = 2,438,178   (PW 1/P, 14%,
                                    15 years − 5 years)
                      $3,311,790

Ordinary annuity equivalent:
$3,311,790 × .102783 = $539,190 (rounded)   (PR, 14%, 15 years)
Valuation:
OAR: .102783   (OAR Tables)
$539,190 ÷ .102783 = $5,245,906

Investment Analysis and Proof of Computations
Fifteen-Point Summary of Calculations

1.	Over-all Rate Selected from OAR Tables or Computed			.102783
2.	Property Value	$539,190 (INCOME)	÷ .102783 (OAR)	= $5,245,906

Investment Analysis and Proof of Computations
Fifteen-Point Summary of Calculations
(cont.)

3. **Original Equity** (Down Payment)

$$\underset{\text{(Equity Ratio)}}{.25} \times \underset{\text{(Value)}}{5,245,906} = 1,311,477$$

4. **Amount of Loan** (Original Principal)

$$\underset{\text{(Loan Ratio)}}{.75} \times \underset{\text{(Value)}}{5,245,906} = 3,934,429$$

5. **Debt Service** (Yearly Payments)

$$\underset{\text{(Loan Constant)}}{.100903} \times \underset{\text{(Principal)}}{3,934,429} = 396,996$$

6. **Cash Flow** (Annuity)

$$\underset{\text{(Net Income)}}{539,190} - \underset{\text{(Debt Service)}}{396,996} = 142,194$$

7. **Debt Coverage Ratio**

$$\underset{\text{(Net Income)}}{539,190} \div \underset{\text{(Debt Service)}}{396,996} = 1.358175$$

8. **Rate of Current Yield On Equity**

$$\underset{\text{(Cash Flow)}}{142,194} \div \underset{\text{(Orig. Equity)}}{1,311,477} = .108423$$

9. **Loan Balance** (End Holding Period)

$$\underset{\text{(\% Unpaid)}}{.805243} \times \underset{\text{(Principal)}}{3,934,429} = 3,168,171$$

10. **Resale Value as % of Original Value**

$$\underset{\text{(Orig. Val. as \%)}}{100} \overset{+}{-} \underset{\text{(\% Appr/Dep)}}{20} = 120\%$$

11. **Resale Value as a Dollar Amount**

$$\underset{\text{(Resale Val. as \%)}}{120\%} \times \underset{\text{(Original Value)}}{5,245,906} = 6,295,087$$

12. **Reversion, Net** (Terminal Equity)

$$\underset{\text{(Resale Value)}}{6,295,087} - \underset{\text{(Loan Balance)}}{3,168,171} = 3,126,916$$

13. **Deferred Yield** (Amount)

$$\underset{\text{(Reversion Net)}}{3,126,916} - \underset{\text{(Down Payment)}}{1,311,477} = 1,815,439$$

14. **Terminal Equity Ratio**

$$\underset{\text{(Reversion Net)}}{3,126,916} \div \underset{\text{(Resale Value)}}{6,295,087} = .496723$$

15. **Proof of Yield on Equity**

Equity Yield Rate: 14 (Percent) Term in Years: 15 (Holding Period)

Present Worth of 1 Per Period: 6.142168 (PW 1/P) Present Worth of 1: .140096 (PW 1)

Equation of Proof

$$\text{Present Worth} = \left(\underset{\text{(Cash Flow)}}{142,194} \times \underset{\text{(PW 1/P)}}{6.142168} \right) + \left(\underset{\text{(Net Reversion)}}{3,126,916} \times \underset{\text{(PW 1)}}{.140096} \right)$$

$$= 873,379 + 438,068 = 1,311,447$$

Final Check Target Figure = 1,311,477 (Down Payment, Orig. Equity)

$$\underset{\text{Target Figure}}{1,311,477} - \underset{\text{(Present Worth)}}{1,311,447} = \underset{\text{(Rounding Adjustment)}}{30}$$

2. a. Loan constant: .008155 × 12 = .09786   (PR, 7%, 216 months)
    Annual debt service: .09786 × $420,000 = $41,101
    Cash flow: $60,000 − $41,101 = $18,899
  b. Loan balance, end of 10 years:
    .008155 × 73.347569 = .5981494   (PR, 7%, 216 months)
                                × (PW 1/P, 7% 96 months)
    .5981494 × $420,000 = $251,223
  c. $18,899 × 4.833227 = $91,343   (PW 1/P, 16%, 10 years)
  d. $91,343 + $420,000 = $511,343
  e. $251,223 × .226684 = $56,948   (PW 1, 16%, 10 years)
  f. $511,343 − $56,948 = $454,395
  g. 1.15 × .226684 = .2606866   (PW 1, 16%, 10 years)
  h. 1.0 − .2606866 = .7393134
  i. $454,395 ÷ .7393134 = $614,618
(Procedure: pages 100-103.)

Investment Analysis and Proof of Computations
Fifteen-Point Summary of Calculations

1.	Over-all Rate Selected from OAR Tables or Computed				.097622
2.	Property Value	$60,000 (INCOME)	÷	.097622 (OAR)	= $614,618
3.	Original Equity (Down Payment)	.316649 (Equity Ratio)	×	$614,618 (Value)	= 194,618
4.	Amount of Loan (Original Principal)	.683351 (Loan Ratio)	×	614,618 (Value)	= 420,000
5.	Debt Service (Yearly Payments)	.09786 (Loan Constant)	×	420,000 (Principal)	= 41,101
6.	Cash Flow (Annuity)	60,000 (Net Income)	−	41,101 (Debt Service)	= 18,899
7.	Debt Coverage Ratio	60,000 (Net Income)	÷	41,101 (Debt Service)	= 1,45982
8.	Rate of Current Yield On Equity	18,899 (Cash Flow)	÷	194,618 (Orig. Equity)	= .097108
9.	Loan Balance (End Holding Period)	.5981494 (% Unpaid)	×	420,000 (Principal)	= 251,223
10.	Resale Value as % of Original Value	100 (Orig. Val. as %)	+/−	15 (% Appr/Dep)	= 115%

Investment Analysis and Proof of Computations
Fifteen-Point Summary of Calculations
(cont.)

11. Resale Value as a Dollar Amount

$\underline{\quad 115\% \quad}$ x $\underline{\quad 614,618 \quad}$ = $\underline{\quad 706,811 \quad}$
(Resale Val. as %)   (Original Value)

12. Reversion, Net (Terminal Equity)

$\underline{\quad 706,811 \quad}$ − $\underline{\quad 251,223 \quad}$ = $\underline{\quad 455,588 \quad}$
(Resale Value)   (Loan Balance)

13. Deferred Yield (Amount)

$\underline{\quad 455,588 \quad}$ − $\underline{\quad 194,618 \quad}$ = $\underline{\quad 260,970 \quad}$
(Reversion Net)   (Down Payment)

14. Terminal Equity Ratio

$\underline{\quad 455,588 \quad}$ ÷ $\underline{\quad 706,811 \quad}$ = $\underline{\quad .64457 \quad}$
(Reversion Net)   (Resale Value)

15. Proof of Yield on Equity

Equity Yield Rate: $\underline{\quad 16 \quad}$ Term in Years: $\underline{\quad 10 \quad}$
(Percent)   (Holding Period)

Present Worth of 1 Per Period: $\underline{\quad 4.833227 \quad}$ Present Worth of 1: $\underline{\quad .226684 \quad}$
(PW 1/P)   (PW 1)

Equation of Proof

Present Worth = ($\underline{\quad 18,899 \quad}$ x $\underline{\quad 4.833227 \quad}$) + ($\underline{\quad 455,588 \quad}$ x $\underline{\quad .226684 \quad}$)
(Cash Flow)   (PW 1/P)   (Net Reversion)   (PW 1)

= $\underline{\quad 91,343 \quad}$ + $\underline{\quad 103,275 \quad}$ = $\underline{\quad 194,618 \quad}$

Final Check Target Figure = $\underline{\quad 194,618 \quad}$
(Down Payment, Orig. Equity)

$\underline{\quad 194,618 \quad}$ − $\underline{\quad 194,618 \quad}$ = $\underline{\quad 0 \quad}$
Target Figure   (Present Worth)   (Rounding Adjustment)

3.a. $60,000 ÷ $615,000 = .097561
  b. .80 × .109044 = .0872352   (Supplemental Tables)
  c. .097561 − .0872352 = .0103258
  d. .80 × .845613 = .6764904   (Supplemental Tables)
  e. 1.15 − .6764904 = .4735096
  f. "Target figure" is the equity ratio: .20
     Net Annuity (c): .0103258
     Net Reversion (e): .4735096
     Try 13%
          .0103258 × 5.426243 = .0560303   (PW 1/P, 13%, 10 years)
          .4735096 × .294588 = $\underline{.1394902}$ (PW 1, 13%, 10 years)
                                .1955205
     Try 12%:
          .0103258 × 5.650223 = .0583431   (PW 1/P, 12%, 10 years)
          .4735096 × .321973 = $\underline{.1524573}$ (PW 1, 12%, 10 years)
                                .2108004
     By interpolation: About 12.7% yield on equity.
     (Procedure: pages 82-84.)

Index

Index

on amortization analysis, 124-125; reason for limitation, 2; typical length, 2

Income. *See* Net annual income
Income approach, 37
Income Property Valuation, xv
Income stream: segments and pattern of, 2, 9, 37; shapes of, 52-61. *See also* Annuity; Net annual income
Income taxes, 2, 30, 171-176
Inflation, 27-28
Information: sources of, 483
Instant mortgage-equity technique. *See* Mortgage-equity technique
Interest rate, 6, 37
Interpolation by simple proportion, 67-69
Investment analysis:
—after income tax analysis, 171-176
—case studies: Sunset Point Apartments, 153-162; Village Square, 11-14
—multiple financing, 473-476
—negative cash flow, 476-478
—use of uniform forms by MLS, 31
—worksheet form (15 points), 150-151
Investment properties: two types of, ix
Investment value, 19-20, 37
Investors: prime requirements of, 1, 12, 13; types of, 17-18
Inwood coefficient, 37
I-R-V equations, 44-45

Leases, 37
Leased fee, 37
Leasehold interest, 37-38
Leverage, 2, 38
Listing investment properties: steps to follow in sequence, 22-23; testing an asking price, x-xi, 61-64
Loan balance, tables, 209-211
Loan constant, 29, 38, 118
Loan constant: tables, 212
Loan ratio, 38
Loan term, 38

Market value, 19-20
Mini-Math For Appraisers, 34
Mortgage, 38
Mortgage and trust deed calculations, 117-125
Mortgage-equity Overall Rate. *See* Overall Rate (mortgage-equity)
Mortgage-equity technique: basic concepts of, 1-4; building data file, 31; comparison to residual techniques, 14-16; definition of, 5, 38; functions of, 19-26;

procedures utilizing, 43-148; relationship to market, 27, 30-31; types of property to which applicable, 27
"Mortgaging out," 125-129

Negative cash flow, 28-29, 71-72, 95, 476-478
Negative income, 60-61, 134-148
Negotiating a sales price, 25-26
Net annuity, 32
Net annual income, 38, 50: income (operating) statement, reconstructed, 51-52, 478-482; income required to meet equity yield rate demands, 61-64; processing, to ordinary annuity equivalent before capitalization, 52-61. *See also* Annuity; Annuity, types and variations
Net income multiplier, 38-39
Net operating income (NOI). *See* Net annual income
Net reversion, 40
Nonproducing property, purchased for appreciation: investment value, 134-141; rate of yield on equity, 141-145; resale value required, to generate specified yield rate, 145-148

OAR. *See* Overall Rate, Rate, Overall
OAR Tables, 213-465
Objectives of *Selling Real Estate By Mortgage-Equity Analysis*, xii, 22
Offering price: feasible, x-xi, 23-25, 61-64
Overall Rate (mortgage-equity): components of, x, 5-6, 20-22; definition of, 39. *See also* Rate, Overall

Patterned Procedures, 43-148:
—income, 50-64
—miscellaneous, 106-134
—nonproducing properties, 134-148
—rate: overall, 64-81; equity yield, 81-97
—Ready Reference Roster, 47-50
—Value, 97-106
Periodic Repayment (PR): extension of table, 112-113; functions, 39
Pitfalls to avoid, 31
Positive cash flow, 29, 95
Present worth, 39
Present Worth of 1 (PW 1): extension of table, 112; functions, 39
Present Worth of 1 Per Period (PW 1/P): extension of table, 112; functions, 39-40
Presenting the offer to the seller, 25-26
Presenting the property to a client, 23-25
Problems and Suggested Solutions, 485-509
Profile of an Equity, 3

About the Author

Irvin E. Johnson is instructor in Real Estate Investment Analysis at Ventura College, and Pasadena City College, California. A native of California, he received the BA at Pacific Union College and later did graduate work at the University of the Pacific. In 1971 he was awarded the Bernard L. Barnard Award by the International Association of Assessing Officers for an article in the April 1971 *Assessors' Journal* entitled "Compound Interest Tables Made Simple." Subsequent to his development of the simplified method of capitalization, he has been conducting seminars in mortgage-equity valuation and analysis for appraisal and real estate organizations throughout the United States. Author of *The Instant Mortgage-Equity Technique*, (Lexington Books, D.C. Heath and Company, 1972) Mr. Johnson is also active consulting, lecturing, teaching, and conducting seminars in the field of real estate valuation and investment analysis.

Related Lexington Books

Cooper, James R., *Real Estate Investment Analysis*, 400 pp., 1974

Cooper, James R., and Gunterman, Karl L., *Real Estate and Urban Land Analysis*, 768 pp., 1974

Dilmore, Gene, *Real Estate Counseling*, In Press

Downs, Anthony, *Federal Housing Subsidies: How Are They Working?*, 160 pp., 1973

Kinnard, William N., *Effective Business Relocation*, 320 pp., 1970

Johnson, Irvin E., *The Instant Mortgage Equity Technique*, 400 pp., 1972

Kinnard, William N., *Income Property Valuation*, 528 pp., 1971

Kinnard, William N., *Principles and Techniques of Real Property Appraising*, In Press

Mills, Edwin S., and Oates, Wallace E., *Fiscal Zoning and Land Use Controls*, 224 pp., 1975